CLARKSON AND KEATING CRIMINAL LAW:
TEXT AND MATERIALS

CLARKSON AND KEATING CRIMINAL LAW: TEXT AND MATERIALS

ELEVENTH EDITION

By

PROFESSOR SALLY KYD
Professor of Law, University of Leicester

DR DANIEL BANSAL
Associate Professor of Law, University of Leicester

DR TRACEY ELLIOTT
Lecturer in Law, University of Leicester

PROFESSOR MARK AUSTIN WALTERS
Professor of Criminal Law and Criminology, University of Sussex

Sweet & Maxwell

Thomson Reuters™

Published in 2024 by Thomson Reuters trading as Sweet & Maxwell.
Registered in England & Wales, Company No.1679046. Registered Office and address for service: 5 Canada Square, Canary Wharf, London, E14 5AQ.

Typeset by Cheshire Typesetting Ltd, Cuddington, Cheshire.
Printed and bound by CPI Group (UK) Ltd, Croydon, CR0 4YY.

For further information on our products and services, visit
www.sweetandmaxwell.co.uk

FSC
www.fsc.org
MIX
Paper | Supporting responsible forestry
FSC® C013604

A CIP catalogue record of this book
is available from the British Library.

ISBN (print) 978-0-414-11980-2
ISBN (ebook) 978-0-414-11983-3
ISBN (proview) 978-0-414-11984-0

First Edition 1984
Reprinted 1986
Reprinted 1988
Second Edition 1990
Reprinted 1991
Reprinted 1993
Third Edition 1994
Reprinted 1994
Reprinted 1995
Fourth Edition 1998
Reprinted 1999
Reprinted 2000
Reprinted 2001 (twice)
Reprinted 2002
Fifth Edition 2003
Sixth Edition 2007
Seventh Edition 2010
Eighth Edition 2014
Ninth Edition 2017
Tenth Edition 2020
Eleventh Edition 2024

PREFACE

The aim of this book is to examine the main principles and rules of the criminal law and to expose the theoretical bases upon which they are founded.

The criminal law is the backdrop to the operation of the whole criminal justice system. It informs the way in which victims, the public, the police and other law enforcement agencies, the Crown Prosecution Service, judges, and other court personnel react and operate. It is, therefore, inextricably linked to issues of criminal procedure, criminology, moral philosophy and penology. Fletcher stated that "the criminal law should express the way we live". It is a reflection of community values aimed at isolating the blameworthy who are deserving of punishment. Equally, it is a means of social control; it attempts to uphold, as well as reflect, these community values; it sets a standard, albeit at times a minimal one, of necessary compliance. In short, it is a set of moral commandments that are backed up by the legal threat of punishment. It thus follows that whether sanctions are imposed on the basis of retribution or on utilitarian grounds, the rules of the criminal law and the punishment of offenders are the two sides of the same coin. A whole range of substantive issues—such as, whether "recklessness" should include "inadvertence", whether one can justify the existence of offences of "strict liability", how the boundaries of the law of "attempt" and "accessorial" crime should be drawn, and so on—are, in reality, issues relating to the justification of punishment in such cases. A true appreciation of the substantive criminal law must thus involve some understanding of the rationale of punishment and why conduct is criminalised—and it is in this context that we have sought to present the main rules of the law.

Like many other works in this field, this is a book on the actual rules of the criminal law. We have endeavoured to provide a full analysis of these main rules on the topics covered. But, in doing this, we have attempted the more ambitious task of using the law to extract, and develop, some fundamental ideas underlying the law. We explore, in the context of punishment, such issues as: the relationship between blame and harm, the criteria for identifying the blameworthy, the structure of offences in relation to each other and whether such structure fairly represents the differing wrongdoing involved, and the role of the general defences. In short, we have subjected the criminal law to the beginnings of a philosophical analysis that can throw some light on its substantive rules.

The criminal law changes incrementally and this 11th edition reflects the developments that have occurred within the law over the past four years up to April 2024. In particular: *Broughton* [2020] EWCA Crim 1093; Field [2021] EWCA Crim 380; and *Rebelo* [2021] EWCA Crim 306 on causation; the codification of *Brown* [1994] 1 A.C. 212 on consent to bodily harm within s.71 Domestic Abuse Act 2021; the critical analysis of the mens rea element of dishonesty in theft is extensively revised in the light of *R. v Barton (David) and Booth (Rosemary)* [2020] EWCA Crim 575, and developments since that case; various cases on different species of manslaughter which have incrementally developed the law over the last few years, including in relation to joint enterprise liability, are set out; the case of *R. v Keal* [2022] EWCA Crim 341 in relation to cases of irresistible impulse and the defence of insanity is discussed; and the section on coercive and controlling behaviour has been expanded upon to reflect the contemporary relevance of this developing area of law.

However, the main changes for this edition relate to the structure of the book and an attempt to streamline some of the content. As with previous editions, this is neither a straight "textbook", nor a "cases and materials" book. Instead, we have combined what we regard as the best features of both such styles—a book with the flow and coherence of a textbook thus providing the reader with guidance and direction, but one that also enables a substantial amount of original material from a diverse range of sources to be absorbed. Above all, we wanted to improve the accessibility of the book by ensuring only the most relevant and up-to-date materials are included in this new edition. Consequently, we have been more resolute in deciding to jettison out-of-date content than in recent editions, whilst still adding new material where appropriate. We have restructured the order of the chapters to better reflect the sequence in which topics are likely to be taught at undergraduate level (although each chapter remains, to a large extent, independent of the rest of the book, meaning that chapters can be read in any order, with cross-referencing providing guidance). In addition, we have split some of the larger chapters into two in order to make the text more manageable in a way that likely reflects the units of a Criminal Law module. For example, Mens Rea and Actus Reus now have their own chapters, and Sexual Offences have been separated from other Non-Fatal Offences Against the Person. It is also the case that we have moved the topic of Intoxication from the General Defences chapter to the chapter on Mens Rea, given that intoxication is only a "defence" in the sense of being a denial of mens rea for crimes of specific intent.

For this edition, the editorial team has grown once more. We are delighted to welcome Dr Daniel Bansal, colleague of Sally Kyd and Tracey Elliott at the University of Leicester, to the team. Dr Bansal gained his PhD on Causation in criminal law from the University of Birmingham, and is module convenor for Criminal Law at Leicester. He thus complements the existing authorship expertise, and brings a fresh pair of eyes to the 11th edition. All authors are keen, however, to ensure that the voices of the original authors, Professor Chris Clarkson and Professor Heather Keating, remain present in the updated text. This 11th edition marks the 40th anniversary of the publication of the first edition of the book. The world is a different place to what it was 40 years ago (one of the authors was not even born then!), but the legacy of Clarkson and Keating remains an important one, facilitating a new generation of students to develop their own understanding of how the law does, and should, determine the contours of criminal liability.

DEDICATION

Sally Kyd would like to thank her co-authors for all their hard work on this edition, particularly given the degree of changes made. She is also extremely appreciative of the supportive colleagues at the University of Leicester who have allowed her to meet deadlines at a time when her term as Head of School was coming to an end. She extends special thanks to her husband Ragnar and son Ben, who remain ever supportive on the home front.

Daniel Bansal would like to thank Sally, Tracey, and Mark for their generous invitation to join the Clarkson & Keating authorship team. He is extremely grateful for their guidance and support with the writing of this edition. To author a textbook that he used as a student is a real privilege. Daniel would also like to thank his colleagues at the University of Leicester, the students who continue to use this book, and Charlotte for her continued support. This edition is dedicated to his parents, Terry and Alison.

Tracey Elliott would like to thank her co-authors and colleagues at the University of Leicester for their invaluable support. This edition is dedicated to her parents, to her daughters (Naomi, Abigail and Hannah), to Biggles (who is sorely missed) and Mymble, and to Daisy and all young people who are contemplating studying law at university. She would also like to dedicate this edition to the memory of John Harwood-Stevenson, a former colleague at 9-12 Bell Yard and a truly extraordinary and learned character, who sadly died in 2022.

Mark Walters would like to thank his colleagues at Sussex Law School and the students who continue to use this book at both UG and PGT levels. Also, special thanks to Chay Burt, PhD candidate at the University of Sussex, for his very helpful research assistance on this new edition.

S.R. KYD
D. BANSAL
T. ELLIOTT
M.A. WALTERS
June 2024

ACKNOWLEDGMENTS

Grateful acknowledgment is made to the following authors and publishers for permission to quote from their works:

All England Law Reports reprinted by permission of LexisNexis material reproduced with the permission of RELX (UK) Limited, trading as LexisNexis

Andenaes, J.: "General Prevention" (1952) 43 J. Crim. L., C. & P.S. 176. Reprinted by special permission of Northwestern University Pritzker School of Law, Journal of Criminal Law and Criminology

—: "The General Preventive Effects of Punishment" (1966) 114 U. Pa. L. Rev. 949. published by The University of Pennsylvania Law School reproduced with the permission of The Licensor through Copyright Clearance Center

Ashworth, A.: "Change Of Normative Position: Determining the Contours of Culpability in Criminal Law" (2008) 11 New Criminal Law Review 232. Published by University of California Press Journals reproduced with the permission of The Licensor through Copyright Clearance Center

—: "'Manslaughter': Generic or Nominate Offences?" in Clarkson, C.M.V. and Cunningham, S. (eds), Criminal Liability For Non-Aggressive Death (2008). Published by Taylor & Francis Group reproduced with the permission of The Licensor through PLSclear

—: and Horder, J.: Principles of Criminal Law, 7th edn (2013). published by Oxford University Press reproduced with the permission of The Licensor through PLSclear

—: "Belief, Intent and Criminal Liability" in Eekelaar, J. and Bell, J. (eds), Oxford Essays in Jurisprudence (1987). Published by Oxford Publishing Ltd reproduced with the permission of The Licensor through PLSclear

Bansal D. and Elliot D.: "Consent to Bodily Harm and the 'Public Interest'" in Bone M., Child J. and Rogers J. (Eds) Criminal Law Reform Now (Volume ll) 2024, pp 205–206. Published by Hart an Imprint of Bloomsbury Publishing PLC

Bentham, J.: "An Introduction to the Principles of Morals and Legislation" in Bentham and Mill, The Utilitarians (1961). Bloomsbury Publishing

Bottoms, A.E.: "An Introduction to the Coming Crisis'" in Bottoms, A.E. and Preston, R.H., The Coming Penal Crisis (1980). Scottish Academic Press Ltd

—: "Morality, Crime, Compliance and Public Policy" in Bottoms A. and Tonry M., Ideology, Crime and Criminal Justice (2002). Published by Taylor and Francis (Books) Limited UK reproduced with the permission of The Licensor through PLSclear

— and Pettit, P.: Not Just Deserts: A Republican Theory of Criminal Justice (1990). Published by Oxford University Press Academic reproduced with the permission of The Licensor through PLSclear

Clarkson, C.M.V.: "Corporate Manslaughter: Need for a New Offence?" in Clarkson, C.M.V. and Cunningham, S.R. (eds), Criminal Liability for Non-Aggressive Deaths (2008). Published by Taylor & Francis Group reproduced with the permission of The Licensor through PLSclear

—: "Corporate Culpability" (1997) Web Journal of Current Legal Issues

—: "General Endangerment Offences: The Way Forward?" (2005) 32(2) University of Western Australia Law Review 131.

Coles, E.M.: "Scientific support for the legal conception of automatism" (2000) 7 Psychiatry, Psychology and Law 33. Published by Taylor & Francis Group reproduced with the permission of The Licensor through PLSclear

Colvin, E.: "Corporate Personality and Criminal Liability" (1995) 6 Criminal Law Forum 1. Published by Springer-Verlag Dordrecht reproduced with the permission of The Licensor through Copyright Clearance Center

Cross, R. and Ashworth, A.: The English Sentencing System, 3rd edn (1981). Butterworths, a division of LexisNexis Butterworths Tolley

Dennis, I.: "On Necessity as a Defence to Crime: Possibilities, Problems and the Limits of Justification and Excuse" (2009) Criminal Law and Philosophy 29. Published by Springer-Verlag Dordrecht reproduced with the permission of The Licensor through Copyright Clearance Center

Devlin, P.: Morals and the Criminal Law (reprinted in The Enforcement of Morals) (1965). Oxford University Press

Duff, R.A.: Intention, Agency and Criminal Liability: Philosophy of Action and the Criminal Law (1990). Published by John Wiley & Sons Ltd reproduced with the permission of The Licensor through PLS Clear

—:"Peversions and Subversions of Criminal Law", in R.A. Duff et al., The Boundaries of the Criminal Law (2010), pp.89–90. Published by Oxford University Press (Books) reproduced with the permission of The Licensor through PLS Clear

—: "Intentions Legal and Philosophical" (1989) 9 O.J.L.S. 76. Published by Oxford University Press reproduced with the permission of The Licensor through Copyright Clearance Center

—: von Hirsch, A.: "Responsibility, Retribution and the Voluntary': A Response to Williams" [1997] C.L.J. 103. Published by Cambridge University Press

—: "Theories and Policies Underlying Guidelines Systems" (2005) 105 Columbia Law Review 1162. Published by Columbia Law Review Association, Inc reproduced with the permission of The Licensor through Copyright Clearance Center

Elliot, C. and De Than C.: "Prosecuting the Drug Dealer when a Drug User Dies" (2006) 69 M.L.R. 986–995. Published by John Wiley and Sons reproduced with the permission of The Licensor through PLS Clear

Feinberg, J.: The Moral Limits of the Criminal Law: Harm to Others, Vol.1 (1984). Published by Oxford University Press reproduced with the permission of The Licensor through PLSclear

—: The Moral Limits of the Criminal Law: Offense to Others, Vol.2 (1988). Published by Oxford University Press reproduced with the permission of The Licensor through PLSclear

Feldman, D.: Civil Liberties and Human Rights in England and Wales, 2nd edn (2002). Published by Oxford University Press reproduced with the permission of The Licensor through PLSclear

Finnis, J.: "Intention and Side-effects" in Frey, R.G., and Morris, C.W. (eds), Liability and Responsibility (1991). Published by Cambridge University Press reproduced with the permission of The Licensor through PLSclear

Fisse, B. and Braithwaite, J.: "The Allocation of Responsibility for Corporate Crime: Individualism, Collectivism and Accountability" (1988) 11 Sydney Law Review 468. Reprinted by permission of the Sydney Law Review and B. Fisse and J. Braithwaite

Fitz-Gibbon, K.: "Replacing Provocation in England and Wales: Examining the Partial Defence of Loss of Control" (2013) Journal of Law and Society 280. Published by John Wiley and Sons reproduced with the permission of The Licensor through PLSclear

Fletcher, G.P.: Rethinking Criminal Law (1978). Published by Little Brown Book Group Limited reproduced with the permission of The Licensor through PLSclear

Gardner, J: "Justifications and Reasons" in Simester, A.P. and Smith, A.T.H. (eds), Harm and Culpability (1996). Published by Oxford University Press reproduced with the permission of The Licensor through PLSclear

Goldstein, A. and Katz, J.: "Conspiracy to Defraud the United States" (1959) 68 Yale Law Journal 405.

Gross, H.: A Theory of Criminal Justice (1979). Oxford University Press

Hart, H.L.A. and Honoré, A.M.: "Immorality and Treason", 62 The Listener 162–163 (July 30, 1959). Published by Immediate

—: "Negligence, Mens rea and the Elimination of Responsibility" in Punishment and Responsibility (Essays in the Philosophy of Law) (1968). Published by permission of Oxford Publishing Limited (Academic) University reproduced with the permission of The Licensor through PLSclear

—: Punishment and Responsibility, Essays in the Philosophy of Law (1968). Published by Oxford Publishing Limited (Academic) reproduced with the permission of The Licensor through PLSclear

—: "Prolegomenon to the Principles of Punishment" in Punishment and Responsibility, Essays in the Philosophy of Law (1968). Published by Oxford Publishing Limited (Academic) reproduced with the permission of The Licensor through PLSclear

von Hirsch, A.: Doing Justice—The Choice of Punishments (Report of the Committee for the Study of Incarceration). Hill and Wang, a division of Macmillan

—: "Ordinal and Cardinal Desert" in von Hirsch, A. and Ashworth, A. (eds.), Principled Sentencing (1992). Published by Hart an imprint of Bloomsbury Publishing Plc reproduced with the permission of The Licensor through PLSclear

—: Past or Future Crimes: Deservedness and Dangerousness in the Sentencing of Criminals (1985). published by Rutgers University Press reproduced with the permission of The Licensor through PLSclear

—: "Prediction of Criminal Conduct and Preventive Confinement of Convicted Persons" (1972) 21 Buffalo L. Rev. 717

—: and Ashworth, A.: Proportionate Sentencing (2005). Published by Oxford Publishing Limited (Academic) reproduced with the permission of The Licensor through PLSclear

Horder, J.: Ashworth's Principles of Criminal Law, 9th edn (2019). Published by Oxford University Press reproduced with the permission of The Licensor through PLSclear

Hughes, G.: "Criminal Omissions" (1958) 67 Yale Law Journal 590. Published by The Yale Law Journal Company, Inc

Hulley, S., Crewe, B. and Wright, S.: "Making sense of 'joint enterprise' for murder: legal legitimacy or instrumental acquiescence?" (2019) 59 Brit. J. Criminol 1328–1346. Published by Oxford University Press reproduced with the permission of The Licensor through PLSclear

Husak, D.: "The Criminal Law as Last Resort" (2004) 24 O.J.L.S. 207. Published by Oxford University Press reproduced with the permission of The Licensor through Copyright Clearance Center

Lacey, N.: State Punishment: Political Principles and Community Values (1988). Published by Taylor and Francis (Books) Limited UK reproduced with the permission of The Licensor through PLSclear

Leavens, A.: "A Causation Approach to Criminal Omissions" (1988) 76 Cal. L. R. 547 (1988). Published by California Law Review reproduced with the permission of The Licensor through Copyright Clearance Center

Lloyd-Bostock, S.: "The Ordinary Man, and the Psychology of Attributing Causes and Responsibility" (1979) 45 M.L.R. 143. Published by of John Wiley and Sons reproduced with the permission of The Licensor through PLSclear

Mackay, R.D.: Mental Condition Defences in the Criminal Law (1995). Reprinted by permission of Oxford Publishing Limited (Academic) reproduced with the permission of The Licensor through PLSclear

McGregor, J.: Is it Rape? On Acquaintance Rape and Taking Women's Consent Seriously (2005). Published by Taylor & Francis (Books) reproduced with the permission of The Licensor through PLSclear

Mead, G.: "Contracting into Crime: A Theory of Criminal Omissions" (1991) 11 O.J.L.S. 147. Published by permission of Oxford University Press reproduced with the permission of The Licensor through Copyright Clearance Center

Moore, M.S.: Placing Blame: A Theory of the Criminal Law (2010). Reprinted with the permission of Oxford Publishing Limited (Academic) reproduced with the permission of The Licensor through PLSclear

Morris, T. and Blom-Cooper, L.: A Calendar of Murder: Criminal Homicide in England since 1957 (1964) Michael Joseph Publishers Ltd. Dr Terence Morris and Louis Blom-Cooper 1964.

Norrie, A.: "A Critique of Criminal Causation" (1991) 54 M.L.R. 685. Published by John Wiley and Sons reproduced with the permission of The Licensor through PLSclear

—: "Subjectivism, Objectivism and the Limits of Criminal Recklessness" (1992) 12 O.J.L.S. 45. Published by Oxford University Press reproduced with the permission of The Licensor through Copyright Clearance Center

O'Donovan, K.: "Defences for Battered Women Who Kill" (1991) 18 J. Law And Society 219. Published by John Wiley and Sons reproduced with the permission of The Licensor through PLSclear

Ormerod, D. and K. Laird: Smith and Hogan's Criminal Law, 14th edn (2015). Published by Oxford Publishing Limited (Academic) reproduced with the permission of The Licensor through PLSclear

Packer, H.L.: The Limits of the Criminal Sanction (1969). Published by Stanford University Press

Robinson, P.H.: "Criminal Law Defenses: A Systematic Analysis" (1982) 82 Columbia Law Review 199. Published by Columbia Law Review Association, Inc reproduced with the permission of The Licensor through Copyright Clearance Center

—: "Hybrid Principles for the Distribution of Criminal Sanctions" (1988) 82 Northwestern University Law Review 19, 34–36. Used by special permission of Northwestern Pritzker School of Law and the Northwestern University Law Review.

—: and Darley, J.M.: "Does Criminal Law Deter? A Behavioural Science Investigation" (2004) 24 O.J.L.S. 173. Published by Oxford University Press reproduced with the permission of The Licensor through Copyright Clearance Center

Shute, S. and Horder, J.: "Thieving and Deceiving: What is the Difference?" (1993) 56 M.L.R. 548. Published by John Wiley and Sons reproduced with the permission of The Licensor through PLSclear

Simester, A.P.: Appraising Strict Liability (2005). Published by Oxford Pubishing Limited (Academic) reproduced with the permission of The Licensor through PLSclear

Singh, S: Punishing Mothers for Men's Violence: Failure to Protect Legislation and the Criminalisation of Abused Women (2021) 29 Feminist Legal Studies 181–204. Published by Springer-Verlag Dordrecht reproduced with the permission of The Licensor through Copyright Clearance Center

Sorial, S.: "Anger, Provocation and Loss of Self-Control: What Does 'Losing It' Really Mean?" (2019) 13 (2) Criminal Law, Philosophy 13, 247–269. Published by Springer-Verlag Dordrecht reproduced with the permission of The Licensor through Copyright Clearance Center

Stephen, J.F.: A History of the Criminal Law of England (1883). Published by Cambridge University Press reproduced with the permission of The Licensor through PLSclear

Tadros, V.: "Rape without Consent" [2006] 26 O.J.L.S. 515. Published by Oxford University Press reproduced with the permission of The Licensor through Copyright Clearance Center

—: "The Characters of Excuse" (2001) 21 O.J.L.S. 495. Published by Oxford University Press reproduced with the permission of The Licensor through Copyright Clearance Center

Thomas M, and Pegg, S.: "Clarifying the Applicable Test for Dishonesty and Modifying Stare Decisis, but Otherwise a Missed Opportunity (2020) 84 J Crim L 385, P.391

Virgo, G.: "Case Comment: Cheating and dishonesty" (2018) 77(1) Cambridge Law Journal 18. Published by Cambridge University Press

Weekly Law Reports, Queen's Bench Division, Appeal Cases and King's Bench Law Reports are reprinted with permission of The Incorporated Council of Law Reporting for England and Wales

Weihofen, H.: "Retribution is Obsolete," National Probation and Parole Association News, XXXIX (1960) 1

Williams, G.: The Mental Element in Crime (1965). Published by Magnes Press reproduced with permission

Zedner, L.: "Reparation and Retribution: Are They Reconcilable?" (1994) 57 M.L.R. 228. Published by John Wiley and Sons reproduced with the permission of The Licensor through Copyright Clearance Center

While every care has been taken to establish and acknowledge copyright, and contact the copyright owners, the publishers tender their apologies for any accidental infringement. They would be pleased to come to a suitable arrangement with the rightful owners in each case.

CONTENTS

TABLE OF CASES

TABLE OF STATUTES

TABLE OF STATUTORY INSTRUMENTS

Chapter 1

Crime and Punishment

I. Introduction

An attempt to comprehend the rules of criminal law must involve some understanding of the function of those rules. It would, of course, be possible simply to list the rules relating to various offences, e.g. murder, rape, and assault, but such a stark outline would not be particularly illuminating. The student of criminal law must be in a position to evaluate such rules and answer important questions that have profound impacts on individual freedom. Key amongst these questions are, why does the State criminalise certain conduct and how does society ensure that individuals abide by the rules it prescribes? It is only through this critical investigation that the student can answer many of the other questions that will arise during the study of criminal law, such as: why do we regard murder as more serious than manslaughter, when in both cases the victim (V)[1] has been killed? Why do we hold someone liable for attempted murder if no harm has been caused to V, because, say, the gun was defective and could never have injured anyone? Should such a person be held liable? These and numerous other fundamental questions that will be posed in the course of this book cannot be answered, and the present rules and reform proposals cannot be evaluated, without understanding the objective of these rules. 1–001

The function of the criminal law is to lay down a set of rules that prohibit certain acts, omissions or states of affair. The criminal law serves as a framework specifying the parameters of acceptable behaviour. The same is, of course, true of all law and indeed of ethical systems such as morality and religion. What distinguishes the criminal law from other mechanisms of social control, and from other branches of law, is the types of *sanction* that are employed to back up its rules. If you steal property, the law of property (concerned with regulating property rights) might say that the "transaction" is void and you do not become the owner of the property. The criminal law, on the other hand, threatens its own special sanction: if you steal property you are liable to be sent to prison for a maximum of seven years. The convicted thief can be subjected to the shame and censure of public punishment.

1 Throughout this book we refer to the victim as V and the defendant as D.

1-002 In order to make sense of the criminal law and of the substantive rules that make up the whole, it is important to establish a framework. **First, what conduct should be prohibited by the criminal law?** If one accepts that one of the objects of the criminal law is to prevent people unjustifiably being deprived of their property, why should it be theft (a criminal offence) if you take property away from someone, but only breach of contract (generally, not a criminal offence) if you take their property pursuant to a contract without performing your obligations under that contract? If one understands why theft is criminalised, but breach of contract is not, one can begin to understand how theft should be defined so as to distinguish it from breach of contract. The substantive rules can start making sense (or be seen to be in need of reform to the extent they do not make sense).

Second, why do we punish those who break the rules of the criminal law? In the theft example, questions arise regarding the adequacy of property law sanctions, the targets of punishment and the extent of punishment. The structure of criminal law rules is influenced by the chosen perspective on the purposes of punishing the thief. Understanding the rationale underpinning punishment for criminal offences is therefore crucial for comprehending, assessing, critiquing, and proposing reforms to substantive legal rules.

It is these two crucial questions that are the subject of this first chapter.

II. What Conduct Ought to be Criminal?

A. INTRODUCTION

1-003 What conduct should be criminalised? There is no one single answer to this question and, as we will see below, there are myriad and often intersecting justifications for criminalising conduct. It must be conceded at the outset that many decisions to criminalise conduct are often a political response either to highly publicised events, public opinion, public health emergencies, as well as social problems highlighted by pressure groups or to perceived public opinion. This is well illustrated by the COVID-19 pandemic where the perceived risk of contagion resulted in emergency powers to restrict certain acts (e.g. leaving one's home without reasonable excuse and gatherings involving more than two people).[2] Other high profile incidents have resulted in new forms of criminalisation, such as the campaign to criminalise the possession of most handguns—even those held in sports clubs—in the wake of the Dunblane massacre where one man, armed with a handgun, shot and killed 16 children. A combination of factors—an organised campaign by a pressure group comprising parents of the children, a well-orchestrated press crusade and a Government and an opposition party preparing for a general election with both determined to demonstrate a toughness against crime—conspired to ensure the speedy passage of the Firearms (Amendment) Act 1997 through Parliament. The creation of numerous other offences over recent decades

2 Health Protection (Coronavirus, Restrictions) (England) Regulations 2020 (SI 2020/350) regs 6 and 7.

can be accounted for in the same way. In short, there has been a tendency on the part of the Government, in particular, to adopt the view that if there is a problem concerning large parts of the public, an instant panacea is to be found by criminalising the conduct in question. In 2008, reports indicated that the Labour Government, in power since 1997, established 3,605 new criminal offences, averaging almost one per day.[3] Examples include the Hunting Act 2004's prohibition on hunting wild mammals with dogs, while lesser-known offences emerged, like repairing vehicles on a road or falsely posing as a barrister (a caution for undergraduate mooters!).[4] In 2010, the Coalition Government aimed to curb unnecessary criminal offences, introducing a "Criminal Offences Gateway". This requires proposed offences to gain approval from the Secretary of State for Justice, who sanctions them only if deemed necessary.[5] The Ministry of Justice pledged transparency by publishing offence creation figures, revealing 280 new offences in the 12 months ending May 2014.[6] However, critics, such as Chalmers and Leverick, argue that in 2010–2011, 1,760 offences were created, a stark contrast to the Ministry's recorded 174 for that year.[7]

This "frenzied approach to law-making" has led some commentators to assert that it is not possible to find any unifying thread explaining the content of the criminal law.[8] However, occasionally a more principled debate emerges. For instance, in the 1950s, the Wolfenden Committee[9] which investigated offences of homosexuality and prostitution sought to provide a theoretical framework against which the decision to criminalise conduct should be made. More recently, the Law Commission undertook a similar task in examining offences against the person recommending a hierarchy of injury offences.[10] The aim of this section is to explore whether there are any principles that *ought* to inform a debate on whether conduct should be criminalised or decriminalised.

B. CRITERIA FOR CRIMINALISATION

It is common to assert that there are two conditions that need to be satisfied before criminalisation of conduct is justified: **1–004**

- (i) the conduct must be *wrongful*; and
- (ii) it must be *necessary* to employ the *criminal law* to condemn or prevent such conduct.[11]

Since 2000, there has been a third condition:

- (iii) it must be *permissible* to criminalise the activity. Criminalisation of the conduct must not contravene the European Convention on Human Rights brought into force in the UK by the Human Rights Act 1998.

3 *The Independent*, 4 September 2008.
4 Legal Services Act 2007 s.181.
5 Ministry of Justice, *Criminal Offences Gateway Guidance*.
6 Ministry of Justice, *Revision: New Criminal Offences, England and Wales 1 June 2009–31 May 2014: Statistics Bulletin* (2015).
7 Ministry of Justice, *New Criminal Offences England and Wales 1 June 2009–31 May 2011 Statistics Bulletin* (2011).
8 N. Lacey, "Contingency and Criminalisation" in I. Loveland (ed), *The Frontiers of Criminality. Modern Legal Studies* (London: Sweet & Maxwell, 1995).
9 Report of the Committee on Homosexual Offences and Prostitution (1957).
10 The Law Commission Report No.361 *Reform of Offences Against the Person* (2015).
11 H. Packer, *The Limits of the Criminal Sanction* (California: Stanford University Press, 1968).

1. Wrongful conduct

1-005 Conduct should not be prohibited unless it can be regarded as wrongful. There is, however, no agreement as to the criteria for establishing "wrongfulness". Three main theoretical approaches have developed over several hundred years that attempt to answer this question. First, there is the view that conduct is wrongful if it is immoral (legal moralism). Secondly, many assert that conduct is only wrongful if it causes (a risk of) harm or serious offence to others (the harm principle or liberalism). Thirdly, there are those who assert that conduct is wrongful if it causes harm to the actor (paternalism). Each of these competing views will be discussed in turn.

(i) Legal moralism

1-006 Few would deny that the criminal law has a moral content;[12] many actions prohibited by the criminal law, such as theft and violence to the person, are undoubted moral wrongs. It is likely that even in the absence of a prohibitory law, a large majority would still feel that these actions, in most contexts, were morally wrong. Immoral conduct is something that offends against community values and principles. In a secular age, it need have no special religious connotations; indeed immorality is not necessarily the same thing as sin, which has a religious connotation.[13] It is, however, no simple matter to define what it means for something to be "morally wrong". Honoré asserts that morality is:

> ". . . concerned with conduct that has a significant impact on other people, and perhaps also animals, individually or collectively, and with the restraints on behaviour that we should accept because of this. Moral criticism assesses behaviour in the light of its impact on others. It excludes purely self-regarding behaviour. Moreover, since we live in groups and communities, and belong to states and other political entities, the central core of morality is concerned with how to co-exist and co-operate with others. The core of morality is, in a broad sense, political."[14]

One needs to be alert to the difficulties inherent in ascertaining moral opinion, especially within pluralistic societies. Not only does moral opinion change over time but:

> ". . . [t]o assume a common culture or a normative consensus in American society (for example) as in most modern societies, is to ignore the deep and divisive role of class, ethnic, religious, status, and regional culture conflicts which often produce widely opposing definitions of goodness, truth, and moral virtue."[15]

Leaving aside the problem of defining morality, one must still question the nature of the relationship between immorality and the criminal law.

---

12 Some theorists, adopting a conflict view of society, would argue that the criminal law represents nothing more than the vested interests of the powerful, e.g. R. Quinney, *The Social Reality of Crime* (Boston: Little, Brown and Co, 1970).

13 G. Hughes, "Morals and the Criminal Law" (1962) 71 Yale L.J. 662, 666–669.

14 T. Honoré, "The Dependence of Morality on Law" (1993) 13 O.J.L.S. 1, 2.

15 J.R. Gusfield, "On Legislating Morals: The Symbolic Process of Designating Deviance" (1968) 56 Cal. L. Rev. 54, 55–56.

Hyman Gross, A Theory of Criminal Justice (1979), pp.13–15:

"It seems obvious that those crimes of violence, theft and destruction that stand as paradigms of crime and comprise the core of any penal code are also moral wrongs. Everyone has a right to be free of such harm inflicted by others, and when murder, rape, arson, assault or larceny is committed there is also a moral wrong since a moral duty to refrain from doing harm to others has been breached. The right to be free of such harm does not have its origin in law but in a general consensus on the rights enjoyed by any member of society, or even by any person, no matter how he lives. This consensus is a more fundamental element of society even than the law, and for that reason the violation of such a right is a moral wrong and not simply a legal wrong. **1–007**

But beyond the most obvious crimes, legions of others are on the books for the reason that doing what is prohibited (or failing to do what is required) makes life hazardous or unpleasant. Members of the public are entitled to live and to work in safety and to enjoy life in public places without fear, disquiet or embarrassment . . . these rights are also moral rights and not simply legal rights, since entitlement to the security and freedom that they represent is a matter of fundamental social consensus and not a matter simply of legal enactment.

Other crimes that are not common crimes are morally wrong for a different reason. Income tax fraud or draft evasion seem to place an unfair burden on others or deprive others of what is due to them."[16]

Herbert L. Packer, The Limits of the Criminal Sanction (1969), pp.262–264:

"The question remains: whose morality are we talking about? It is easy to slide into the assumption that somewhere in society there is an authoritative body of moral sentiment to which the law should look. That assumption becomes particularly dangerous . . . when it is used to buttress the assertion that the immorality of a given form of conduct is a *sufficient* condition for declaring the conduct to be criminal. But when one is talking about immorality as a *necessary* condition for invocation of the criminal sanction, the inquiry should simply be whether there exists any significant body of dissent from the proposition that the conduct in question is immoral. Is there a social group that will be alienated or offended by making (or keeping) the conduct in question criminal? If there is, then prudence dictates caution in employing the criminal sanction. We can sum up this prudential limitation as follows: the criminal sanction should ordinarily be limited to conduct that is viewed, without significant social dissent, as immoral. The calendar of crimes should not be enlarged beyond that point and, as views about morality shift, should be contracted." **1–008**

We are left with what appears to be a tautological quandary. That is to say, the determination is circular: immoral conduct is conduct that is considered by the vast majority of people to be immoral. **1–009**

16 Gross argues further that committing a crime is necessarily a moral wrong because it involves violating a "solemn promise to live according to the rules" of society. However, we are here concerned with the *content* of these rules and their relationship to morality.

Let us consider the example of sado-masochistic encounters between consenting adults to understand how legal moralism is applied in practice. In *Brown*,[17] the House of Lords was called upon to decide whether consent to sado-masochistic acts could be a defence to charges of assault occasioning actual bodily harm contrary to the Offences Against the Person Act 1861 s.47. By a majority of three to two it was decided that consent was no defence to such charges. Lord Lowry (in the majority) argued that:

> "... [w]hat the appellants are obliged to propose is that the deliberate and painful infliction of physical injury should be exempted from the operation of statutory provisions the object of which is to prevent or punish that very thing, the reason for the proposed exemption being that both those who will inflict and those who will suffer the injury wish to satisfy a perverted and depraved sexual desire. Sado-masochistic homosexual activity cannot be regarded as conducive to the enhancement or enjoyment of family life or conducive to the welfare of society."[18]

Lord Templeman (also in the majority) is more direct with his moral indignation:

> "Society is entitled and bound to protect itself against a cult of violence. Pleasure derived from the infliction of pain is an evil thing. Cruelty is uncivilised."[19]

1–010 Finally, Lord Mustill (in the minority) was of the view:

> "... that whatever the outsider might feel about the subject matter of the prosecutions—perhaps horror, amazement or incomprehension, perhaps sadness—very few could read even a summary of the other activities without disgust."[20]

Even if one accepts that the House of Lords was in tune with public morality, does this mean that one is *bound* to criminalise sado-masochistic conduct? Or must there be additional harms associated with the conduct before it can be lawfully prohibited? In relation to the latter, some commentators have argued in the negative, asserting that it is possible to pinpoint more precisely the relationship between the criminal law and morality. Indeed, they believe that not only is immorality a necessary condition for invocation of the criminal sanction, but that it is a sufficient one. It is not necessary to search for further justification (harm, enforceability, etc) before the criminal law can be brought into action; the fact that the conduct is morally wrong is enough.[21] This view is epitomised by such statements by James Fitzjames Stephen as:

---

17 *R. v Brown (Anthony Joseph)* [1994] 1 A.C. 212; [1993] 2 W.L.R. 556 HL. The facts and an extract from the case are given at 315–318.

18 *Brown* [1994] 1 A.C. 212 at 255.

19 *Brown* [1994] 1 A.C. 212 at 237.

20 *Brown* [1994] 1 A.C. 212 at 256–257.

21 See D. Scoccia, "In Defense of 'Pure' Legal Moralism" (2013) 7 Crim. Law and Philos. 513.

". . . [h]ow can the State or the public be competent to determine any question whatever if it is not competent to decide that gross vice is a bad thing? I do not think the State ought to stand bandying compliments with pimps."[22]

Graphic though this picture is, the view that immorality is a sufficient condition is now likely to be couched in more qualified terms.

Patrick Devlin, Morals and the Criminal Law (reprinted in The Enforcement of Morals) (1965), pp.7–8, 14–17:

"I think it is clear that the criminal law as we know it is based upon moral principle. In a number of crimes its function is simply to enforce a moral principle and nothing else. The law, both criminal and civil, claims to be able to speak about morality and immorality generally. Where does it get its authority to do this and how does it settle the moral principles which it enforces? Undoubtedly, as a matter of history, it derived from Christian teaching. But I think that the strict logician is right when he says that the law can no longer rely on doctrines in which citizens are entitled to disbelieve . . . How are the moral judgments of society to be ascertained? . . . It is surely not enough that they should be reached by the opinion of the majority; it would be too much to require the individual assent of every citizen. English law has evolved and regularly uses a standard which does not depend on the counting of heads. It is that of the reasonable man. He is not to be confused with the rational man. He is not expected to reason about anything and his judgment may be largely a matter of feeling . . . for my purpose I should like to call him the man in the jury box . . . **1–011**

Immorality then, for the purpose of the law, is what every right-minded person is presumed to consider immoral. Any immorality is capable of affecting society injuriously and in effect to a greater or lesser extent it usually does: this is what gives the law *locus standi*. It cannot be shut out. But—and this brings me to the third question—the individual has a *locus standi* too; he cannot be expected to surrender to the judgment of society the whole conduct of his life. It is the old familiar question of striking a balance between the rights and interests of society and those of the individual . . . there must be toleration of the maximum individual freedom that is consistent with the integrity of society. Nothing should be punished by the law that does not lie beyond the limit of tolerance. It is not nearly enough to say that a majority dislike a practice: there must be a real feeling of reprobation . . . I do not think one can ignore disgust if it is deeply felt and not manufactured. Its presence is a good indication that the bounds of toleration are being reached . . .

We should ask ourselves in the first instance whether, looking at it calmly and dispassionately, we regard it as a vice so abominable that its mere presence is an offence. If that is the genuine feeling of the society in which we live, I do not see how society can be denied the right to eradicate it."

22 J. Fitzjames Stephen, *Liberty, Equality, Fraternity* (New York: Holt & Williams, 1873), p.125.

1-012 Criminal sanctions, according to Devlin, should be determined by the deep disgust (dispassionately felt) of the right-minded person or, more accurately, they should depend upon the law-maker's interpretation of the likelihood of the right-minded person being deeply disgusted.

Devlin's criteria are easily applied to many crimes, such as murder and rape. Other crimes such as theft would also undoubtedly be regarded as immoral and generally attract "the real feeling of reprobation", even if not "disgust".

This thesis becomes more difficult when applied to Devlin's own example of homosexuality (he was responding to the Wolfenden Report, which had recommended decriminalising homosexual acts between consenting adult males in private). According to Devlin, speaking in the mid-1960s, although "some people sincerely believe that homosexuality is neither immoral nor unnatural",[23] there is nevertheless a collective judgment against it, and a deep feeling of disgust towards it. In response to this statement, Hughes questioned Devlin's use of "depth of disgust" as an appropriate yardstick and suggested that:

> "It is not beyond the bounds of possibility that proper inquiry might reveal that, while the ordinary man contemplates homosexual behaviour with aversion and distaste, the knowledge of this practice by others does not disgust him so deeply as Lord Devlin suspects."[24]

1-013 Hughes' comment exposes an immediate problem with Devlin's exposition of legal moralism, which is that what one person may find disgusting may not be felt to the same degree, or at all, by the next person. Returning to our previous example of sado-masochism, was it just a coincidence that the activities in *Brown* took place during homosexual encounters? As Bibbings and Alldridge point out, society broadly perceives that "[m]en being whipped by women (and all the other sado-masochist activities) for pleasure is amusing".[25] The implication for some commentators is that, despite all the window-dressing that talk of "harm" provides, *Brown* was really a case about the immorality of certain types of perceivably disgusting *homosexual* encounters.[26]

Whether one accepts such an argument or not, the result of the wide ruling in *Brown* is that most such violent encounters must be regarded as illegal if actual bodily harm results. It is irrelevant whether sexual pleasure is involved as consent is no defence.

---

23 P. Devlin, *Morals and the Criminal Law* (reprinted in *The Enforcement of Morals*) (1965), p.8.

24 G. Hughes, "Morals and the Criminal Law" (1962) 71 Yale L.J. 662, 676–678.

25 L. Bibbings and P. Alldridge accuse their Lordships of being homophobic: "Sexual Expression, Body Alteration, and the Defence of Consent" (1993) J. Law & Soc. 356, 360.

26 Bibbings and Alldridge accuse their Lordships of being homophobic: "Sexual Expression, Body Alteration, and the Defence of Consent" (1993) J. Law & Soc. 356, 358. cf. S. Cowan, "Criminalizing SM: Disavowing the Erotic, Instantiating Violence" in R.A. Duff, *The Structures of the Criminal Law* (Oxford: OUP, 2011), Ch.4. Conversely, some commentators have argued that the development of a contemporary narrative that supports BDSM is now being used to support defence cases where women have been killed during violent sexual encounters. Edwards asserts that "The BDSM narrative is being appropriated by defendants to disguise what is essentially cruel and misogynistic conduct as a strategy to manipulate trial and sentencing outcomes": S. Edwards, "Assault, strangulation and murder—Challenging the sexual libido consent defence narrative" in A. Reed, M. Bohlander, N. Wake and E. Smith, *Consent: Domestic and Comparative Perspectives* (London: Routledge, 2016), p.89.

What can be concluded at this stage is that Lord Devlin's yardstick is not a sound basis upon which to take decisions to criminalise, especially if cloaked behind a mask of public interest. Not only may it be a thin disguise for the criminalisation of immorality simpliciter[27] (as advocated by Stephen more than a century ago) but the criteria employed are too limited. One cannot, as Lord Devlin has done, throw rationality completely to the winds in order to replace it with the reasonable person's disgust—which, as Hart points out, may be based on "ignorance, superstition or misunderstanding".[28] Instead:

> "... the examination of existing law and the debate about proposed laws should be conducted by making as explicit a statement as is possible of the values that the law is designed to protect, by a careful investigation of the harm done to those values by the conduct prohibited or which it is sought to prohibit, and by a careful consideration of the probable efficacy of legal prohibition. In this debate the prevalence of feelings of disgust or revulsion in the community is one factor to be considered and no more than that."[29]

In other words, whilst moral wrongdoing (with all its attendant difficulties of identification) may be a necessary condition for the imposition of the criminal law, it ought *not* to be a *sufficient* one. This has led Duff to call for a "modest legal moralism", where trivial wrongs that can be dealt with more effectively by civil measures should fall outside the purview of the criminal law.[30]

R.A. Duff, "Perversions and Subversions of Criminal Law" in R.A. Duff, The Boundaries of the Criminal Law (2010), pp.89–90, 107–108:

> "To say that the criminal law is concerned with wrongs (with moral wrongs) is to espouse some form of Legal Moralism . . . For the negative Legal Moralist, wrongdoing is a necessary condition of criminal liability and punishment. We should not criminalize conduct that is not in some relevant way morally wrongful, nor impose criminal liability on those who are not morally culpable, but the wrongfulness of the conduct and the culpability of its agent do not give us positive reason to criminalize it: the practice's 'general justifying aim' does not include ensuring the conviction and punishment of the morally guilty. For the positive Legal Moralist, by contrast, the moral wrongfulness of the conduct and its agent's culpability give us positive reason to criminalize it: a central purpose of criminal law as a distinctive mode of legal regulation is to define, and provide for the formal condemnation and punishment of, various kinds of wrongdoing . . . **1-014**

27 For a defence of Lord Devlin, see E.V. Rostow, "The Enforcement of Morals" [1960] C.L.J. 174 where he suggests that Lord Devlin so qualifies his central conditions with cries for tolerance, etc that the gap between him and his critics is very small.

28 H.L.A. Hart, "Immorality and Treason" (1959) 62 *The Listener* 163.

29 Hughes, "Morals and the Criminal Law" (1962) 71 Yale L.J. 662, 682. He points out that this approach will still contain elements of irrationality but that it is better than "throwing the baby out with the bath water" (Hart, "Immorality and Treason" (1959) 62 *The Listener* 163) approach of Devlin.

30 R.A. Duff, "Towards a Modest Legal Moralism" (2014) 8 Crim. Law and Philos. 217; See also R.A. Duff, *Answering for Crime: Responsibility and Liability in the Criminal Law* (Oxford: Hart Publishing, 2007), Chs 4–6; M.S. Moore, *Placing Blame: A Theory of Criminal Law* (Oxford: OUP, 1997). Duff has described himself as a "positive Legal Moralist": R.A. Duff, "Perversions and Subversions of Criminal Law" in R.A. Duff, *The Boundaries of the Criminal Law* (Oxford: OUP, 2010), p.91. cf. M. Thorburn, "Constitutionalism and the Limits of the Criminal Law" in Duff, *The Structures of the Criminal Law* (2011), Ch.5, for a critique of Moore and Duff's approaches to legal moralism.

> A positive Legal Moralist must hold that we have reason to criminalize any public wrong: any such wrong is our collective business; we have reason to call its perpetrator to answer for it and to censure him as a wrongdoer. That is not yet to say, however, that we have conclusive reason to do so: quite apart from the fact that the costs, both material and moral, of enforcing the criminalization of a public wrong might be so great, and the chances of doing it justly and effectively so small, that we should not on balance seek to criminalize it, we might have two other kinds of reason for not criminalizing a public wrong.
>
> First, some public wrongs are too trivial to justify the attention of the criminal law: even if a better system of criminal justice than our own was able to provide appropriately modest, non-oppressive procedures and punishments for minor offences, some wrongs are too minor to warrant even that much formal attention. For just one example, there are kinds of incivility that we may display to each other in public places (barging rudely along a crowded street, for instance) that constitute civic wrongs, and that merit comment from others, but that it would be absurd to think of criminalizing; that is why any sane system of criminal law recognizes a *de minimis* principle.
>
> Second, however, there might be kinds of public wrong that cause or threaten serious harm, but that we should not criminalize because it is more important to ensure that the harm is repaired or paid for, and to allocate the costs of such repair or compensation justly, than to call those who cause it to public, criminal account; and, perhaps, because criminalizing the conduct would hinder the attempt to allocate its costs fairly—if, for instance, those who caused the harm would then be less likely to admit their responsibility for it. In such cases we would see reason to prefer something more like a civil-law than a criminal-law response . . ."

1–015 The negative legal moralist asserts that immorality is not a positive reason for criminalisation but it is a necessary one. In other words, immorality is merely an enabling condition for criminalisation, one that plays a role in limiting the use of criminal law. In choosing to only criminalise conduct that is morally wrongful one might consider that the conduct must be judged as immoral *independent* of whether it is criminalised or not. However, some have argued that it is the actual criminalisation of certain activities that makes the conduct morally wrongful. We distinguish here between the "Strong Wrongness Constraint" which dictates that it is only permissible to criminalise conduct if it can be determined that it is wrong independently of it being criminalised, and the "Weak Wrongness Constraint" which posits that criminalisation is permitted only if the conduct is determined to be wrong either independently of it being criminalised or as a result of it being criminalised.[31] Tadros gives the example of carrying a knife for self-protection, which may not be immoral, but which if criminalised becomes wrongful.[32] The mischief concerning legislators in criminalising the carrying of knives in public spaces is the prevention of serious injury and the protection of society from violence. Criminalising this conduct (with certain exceptions, for example carrying a knife back from a shop to your kitchen) serves to censure the conduct of carrying. The aim is to reduce the number of people carrying knives, thereby reducing knife-based violence, and in turn people will not feel the need to carry a knife to

---

31 R.A. Duff, *The Realm of Criminal Law* (Oxford: OUP, 2018).

32 V. Tadros, "Wrongness and Criminalization" in A. Marmor (ed), *The Routledge Companion to Philosophy of Law* (London: Routledge, 2012).

protect themselves. The need to reduce this type of violence means that the carrying itself becomes wrongful, as well as the injurious activities that are linked with it. However, it remains the case that independent of the law, simply carrying a knife, without intent to injure or damage property, is not an immoral act in and of itself.

Such a position gives rise to further complexity in determining what is and what is not morally wrongful. If acts independent of criminalisation are not immoral but are when they become a criminal offence, the law itself becomes the mechanism from which we ascertain civil morality.

(ii) Liberalism: the harm and offence principle

A basic tenet of liberalism is that respect must be shown to the principle of individual autonomy—the notion that people possess free will and must be allowed, to the maximum extent possible, to make free choices. The liberal contends that although we may view others' behaviour as repugnant, the autonomy of an individual to do as they please must remain paramount. In its purest form, liberalism dictates that the State should therefore only intervene to restrict autonomy when it is necessary to prevent conduct that is more harmful to others than the restriction of liberty is to the individual. **1–016**

Law Commission (Consultation Paper No.139), Consent in the Criminal Law (1995) Appendix C para.C.85:

"The liberal and the moralist disagree fundamentally about the value of autonomy. The liberal can agree with the moralist that the world would be a better place with less of this evil in it, and the liberal might even set about trying to reduce the evil by argument, persuasion, exhortation and/or education of the young. But she will not use the criminal law to this end because she accords primacy to the value of autonomy and the mutually reinforcing ideals of value pluralism and toleration. Given the diversity of human needs, tastes and talents there must be a diversity of eligible life-styles, careers and options to give everybody a fair chance of living a fulfilling, stimulating and enjoyable life. Some of these life-styles will be incompatible or even mutually contradictory, but the liberal will demand that each should extend to the others a degree of tolerance and respect, within the limits set by the harm and offence principles. The liberal asserts that her political theory is the most appropriate for a multicultural and pluralistic society." **1–017**

H.L.A. Hart, "Immorality and Treason" 62 The Listener 162–163 (30 July 1959):

"The Wolfenden Committee on Homosexual Offences and Prostitution recommended by a majority of 12 to 1 that homosexual behaviour between consenting adults in private should no longer be a criminal offence. One of the Committee's principal grounds for this recommendation was expressed in its report in this way: 'There must remain a realm of private morality and immorality which in brief and crude terms is not the law's business.' I shall call this the liberal point of view: for it is a special application of those wider principles of liberal thought which John Stuart Mill formulated **1–018** in his essay on Liberty. Mill's most famous words, less cautious perhaps than the Wolfenden Committee's were:

> 'The only purpose for which power can be rightfully exercised over any member of a civilized community against his will is to prevent harm to others. His own good, either physical or moral, is not a sufficient warrant. He cannot rightfully be compelled to do or forbear . . . because in the opinion of others to do so would be wise or even right.'

[This approach to criminalisation appears on first inspection to be of sound reasoning. It offers a clear and concise basis upon which decisions to restrict individual liberty should be based. However, upon closer scrutiny a number of limitations are exposed] . . .

Mill's formulation of the liberal point of view may well be too simple. The grounds for interfering with human liberty are more various than the single criterion of 'harm to others' suggests: cruelty to animals or organizing prostitution for gain do not, as Mill himself saw, fall easily under the description of harm to others. Conversely, even where there is harm to others in the most literal sense, there may well be other principles limiting the extent to which harmful activities should be repressed by law. So there are multiple criteria, not a single criterion, determining when human liberty may be restricted . . .

No doubt we would all agree that consensus of moral opinion on certain matters is essential if society is to be worth living in. Laws against murder, theft, and much else would be of little use if they were not supported by a widely diffused conviction that what these laws forbid is also immoral. So much is obvious. But it does not follow that everything to which the moral vetoes of accepted morality attach is of equal importance to society; nor is there the slightest reason for thinking of morality as a seamless web: one which will fall to pieces carrying society with it, unless all its emphatic vetoes are enforced by law. Surely even in the face of the moral feeling that is up to concert pitch—the trio of intolerance, indignation, and disgust—we must pause to think . . . First, we must ask whether a practice which offends moral feeling is harmful, independently of its repercussion on the general moral code. Secondly, what about repercussion on the moral code? Is it really true that failure to translate this item of general morality into criminal law will jeopardize the whole fabric of morality and so society?"

(a) Defining harm

1–019 An immediate problem with the harm principle is that one needs a careful definition of the word harm. A trader who sets up a legitimate business in competition with another can severely harm that other person by taking away all their business but, in a capitalist society where business competition is encouraged, should this constitute the sort of harm that ought to be criminalised? If instinctively we decline to criminalise such harms, on what basis do we determine which types of harm ought to be criminal ones?

Liberal perspectives on criminalisation often adopt a narrow approach, focusing mainly on "primary harms" characterised by direct cause-and-effect relationships, often measured in terms of physical or psychological suffering. Laws are established to prevent bodily harm and safeguard the integrity of V's personal safety. However, beyond these evident harms lie numerous discrete acts that can impact individuals, communities and society, making it challenging to identify and measure harms worthy of legal prohibition.

Joel Feinberg's influential work defines harm as the thwarting, setting back or defeating of interests. Interests, according to him, encompass everything in which an individual has "at stake".

JOEL FEINBERG, THE MORAL LIMITS OF THE CRIMINAL LAW: HARM TO OTHERS (1984), PP.33, 34, 36:

"Harm . . . [means] the thwarting, setting back, or defeating of an interest . . . One's interests . . . consist of all those things in which one has a stake . . . Only setbacks of interests that are wrongs, and wrongs that are setbacks to interest, are to count as harms in the appropriate sense . . . **1–020**

This interpretation thus excludes set-back interests produced by justified or excused conduct ('harms' that are not wrongs) . . . A harm in the appropriate sense then will be produced by morally indefensible conduct that not only sets back the victim's interest, but also violates his right . . .

Minor or trivial harms *are* harms despite their minor magnitude and triviality, but below a certain threshold they are not to count as harms for the purposes of the harm principle, for legal interference with trivia is likely to cause more harm than it prevents . . ."

An essential question arises: what interests are at stake for each of us? While Feinberg does not delve into this, Simester and von Hirsch elaborate by asserting that what is "at stake" constitutes a resource with a normative claim, defined as an "asset" or "capability" persisting over time.[33] These resources contribute to a person's quality of life, leading Simester and von Hirsch to argue that the harm principle is fundamentally a principle of "resource protection".[34]

While Simester and von Hirsch's elaboration is helpful in determining what personal interests might include, the measurement of such interests and the question of whether the law should be tailored to protect "resources" remains to an extent uncertain. One essential consideration is whether harmful conduct, even if detrimental to personal interests, is socially desirable or at least tolerable. Numerous activities, unquestionably harmful in certain respects (e.g. physically injurious), may nonetheless be deemed desirable or even necessary in specific circumstances (e.g. surgery). Determining what is harmful and whether that harm is permissible often leads to debate. For instance, certain harms may have a social utility (e.g. contact sports) that, though harmful in a literal sense, are deemed to enhance the welfare of society.[35] However, deciding what conduct is socially desirable is not without disagreement. Consider, for example, whether the criminal law should intervene to prevent conduct perceived by some as endangering societal well-being but that also serves an individual interest, such as activities

33 A.P. Simester and A. von Hirsch, *Crimes, Harms, and Wrongs: On the Principles of Criminalisation* (Oxford: Hart, 2011), p.248.

34 Simester and von Hirsch, *Crimes, Harms, and Wrongs: On the Principles of Criminalisation* (2011).

35 *R. v Barnes (Mark)* [2004] EWCA Crim 3246; [2005] 1 W.L.R. 910.

that involve the risk of physical injury, but which provide some with aesthetic pleasure (e.g. body modification).[36]

(b) Risk of harm

1–021 Beyond the assessment of harms that restrict personal interests are those acts or states of affair that cause no harm at all but instead *risk* differing levels of injury. One of the most sophisticated efforts at defining criteria for such "harms" is that provided by Feinberg.

Joel Feinberg, The Moral Limits of the Criminal Law: Harm to Others (1984), p.217:

1–022 "Where the kind of conduct in question . . . does create a danger to some degree, legislators employing the harm principle must use various rules of thumb as best they can:

a. the greater the *gravity* of a possible harm, the less probable its occurrence need be to justify prohibition of the conduct that threatens to produce it;
b. the greater the *probability* of harm, the less grave the harm need be to justify coercion;
c. the greater the *magnitude of the risk* of harm, itself compounded out of gravity and probability, the less reasonable it is to accept the risk;
d. the more *valuable* (useful) the dangerous conduct, both to the actor and others, the more reasonable it is to take the risk of harmful consequences . . .
e. the more reasonable the risk of harm (the danger), the weaker is the case for prohibiting the conduct that creates it."

There are numerous examples of clear risks that are likely, though not certain, to cause serious injury, such as driving while intoxicated. Beyond assessing whether criminalising such conduct is permissible based on calculations of gravity and probability of harm, is an evaluation of whether criminalisation will decrease the risk of harm eventuating. Questions arise here regarding whether certain acts, though risky in the abstract, can be justified in individual situations where, depending on context, the risk of harm becomes negligible. Take for example the driver who drives in the middle of the night on a completely empty motorway breaching the 70 mph speed limit by 5 mph. Given there are no other road users, and the additional speed is well within the control of the driver, it might be said that there is little to no risk of harming others. Simester and von Hirsch argue that a pre-emptive rule applies in such situations, which dictates that the law must apply to everyone at all times regardless of individual judgements as to risk.[37] The rule is based on the "reciprocal protection" of all road users. The criminalisation of speeding provides a reciprocal benefit to all road users, whereby all drivers have an interest in the efficacy of the rules. Allowing individuals to determine the risk in any given situation threatens the protection that the rules provide for everyone; leading ultimately to a broader failure to adhere to the rules, which in turn increases the risk of harm occurring.

---

36 *R. v BM* [2018] EWCA Crim 560; [2019] Q.B. 1.
37 A.P. Simester and A. von Hirsch, "Remote Harms and Non-constitutive Crimes" (2009) 28(1) Crim. Just Ethics 89.

(c) Other remote harms

A particularly thorny issue for legislatures and the courts are "remote harms" that are difficult to measure, both in terms of the gravity of the harm and the probability of it occurring. **1–023**

These include "accumulative harms" which, like the example above, occur when others join in similar behaviour, thereby creating a compounded harm that is much greater than that carried out by the individual actor. Von Hirsch provides the following example:

> "Dumping household garbage in the river is treated as a health hazard, but the conduct actually endangers health only when numerous other persons do likewise. In such situations, however, the proscribed act is a token of the type of conduct that cumulatively does the harm: the actor cannot draw a moral distinction between his behaviour and that of the others who contribute to the injury."[38]

A second type of remote harm is that which may only occur *if* a third actor involves themself in some sort of injurious behaviour that is indirectly linked to someone else's conduct. The House of Lords' decision in *Brown* again provides us with an example, the court arguing that consensual sado-masochistic sex among adult males should be proscribed, in part, because such conduct might corrupt young boys who are unable to give proper consent. The hypothetical young boys are third party actors who might be harmed by the corrupting conduct of the other men. The criminalisation of conduct that involves the inducing of others to behave badly can be seen in operation more recently in relation to the offence of "extreme pornography" under the Criminal Justice and Immigration Act 2008 s.63. This provision criminalises the possession (not the production or supply) of pornography that is deemed to be "extreme" due to its portrayal of one of a number of acts listed in s.63(7)[39] and which "is grossly offensive, disgusting or otherwise of an obscene character".[40] At first glance this test seems to indicate that the Government, in choosing to create this new offence, did so on the basis of legal moralism.[41] However, McGlynn and Rackley suggest that an offence of possessing extreme pornography could be justified under the harm principle, and identify "cultural harm" as a type of harm that such criminalisation might seek to prevent.[42] "Cultural harm", they assert, is "a concept of harm which moves beyond arguments of immediate cause and effect".[43] Palmer explains further that it is:

---

38 A. von Hirsch, "Extending the Harm Principle: 'Remote' Harms and Fair Imputation" in A.P. Simester and A.T.H. Smith (eds), *Harm and Culpability* (Oxford: Clarendon Press, 1996), p.264.

39 The acts are an act which threatens a person's life; an act which results, or is likely to result, in serious injury to a person's anus, breasts or genitals; an act which involves sexual interference with a human corpse; and a person performing an act of intercourse or oral sex with an animal (whether dead or alive).

40 Criminal Justice and Immigration Act 2008 s.63(6). cf. the offence of possession of prohibited images of children created by the Coroners and Justice Act 2009 s.62, which uses the same terminology.

41 cf. Sexual Offences Act 2003 ss.64 and 65, which criminalise consensual incest between adults. It has been argued that legal moralism lies behind these offences, rather than any clear harm related or public interest justification: T. Hömle, "Consensual Adult Incest: A Sex Offence?" [2014] 76 New Crim. L. Rev. 76; J.R. Spencer, "Incest and Article 8 of the European Convention on Human Rights" (2013) 72 C.L.J. 5. cf. *Stubing v Germany* [2013] 1 F.L.R. 107.

42 C. McGlynn and E. Rackley, "Criminalising Extreme Pornography: A Lost Opportunity" [2009] Crim. L.R. 245.

43 McGlynn and Rackley, "Criminalising Extreme Pornography: A Lost Opportunity" [2009] Crim. L.R. 245, 257.

> ". . . a type of harm which manifests in the normalisation of attitudes and practices deemed negative . . . normalisation in this context [refers] to a process by which attitudes, practices and/or ways of being become accepted as routine, unremarkable or at least understandable aspects of everyday life."[44]

1-024 Ultimately, the harm that allowing the possession of extreme pornography threatens to cause is that it might "contribute to a climate in which sexual violence is not taken seriously".[45] McGlynn and Rackley are of the opinion that the Government's purpose in enacting the legislation:

> ". . . should have been about changing the cultural and social environment in which sexual violence is marginalised, in which rape conviction rates are at an all-time low and in which pornography is becoming (if possible) even more ubiquitous."

Whilst the Government's original consultation paper[46] justified its proposals on this ground, amongst others, following opposition from "arch liberals" the proposals were amended and the Government "[u]ltimately . . . fell back on the easy tradition of the conservative-moralistic and disgust-based arguments which consume the [Obscene Publications Act]".[47]

(d) Causing serious offence

1-025 Harm as it is understood by Feinberg refers to the set back of personal interests and to the violation of individual rights. However, within this conceptualisation of harm Feinberg also speaks of causing "serious offence" to others. For serious offence to come within the harm principle, Feinberg argues that it must be so intense that it would be felt by an "average" or "reasonable" person, and that the offence is caused by witnessing the offensive conduct which is not easily avoidable.

---

44 P. Palmer, "Rape pornography, cultural harm and criminalization" (2018) *Northern Ireland Legal Quarterly* 69, 37.

45 McGlynn and Rackley, "Criminalising Extreme Pornography: A Lost Opportunity" [2009] Crim. L.R. 245, 257. Walters argues the same in relation to criminalising hate crime, which he argues serves to foster a social environment hostile towards certain identity groups, M.A. Walters, *Criminalising Hate: Law as Social Justice Liberalism* (London: Palgrave, 2022).

46 Home Office Consultation Paper: *On the Possession of Extreme Pornographic Material* (2005).

47 McGlynn and Rackley, "Criminalising Extreme Pornography: A Lost Opportunity" [2009] Crim. L.R. 245, 257, 258. See also, E. Rackley and C. McGlynn, "Prosecuting the Possession of Extreme Pornography: A Misunderstood and Mis-Used Law" [2013] Crim. L.R. 400–405. cf. P. Johnson, "Law, Morality and Disgust: The Regulation of 'Extreme Pornography' in England and Wales" (2010) 19 *Social & Legal Studies* 147–163, who argues that: "The morality test in section 63, enables a 'measurement' of harm to be made that is more appropriate to the aims of the legislation. It provides a flexible way to continually pose the crucial question that underpins the justification for the legislation: 'is the private possession of these images harmful to the moral values of society'?", 154–155.

Joel Feinberg, The Moral Limits of the Criminal Law: Offense to Others (1985), pp.1–2, 26:

"It is always a good reason in support of a proposed criminal prohibition that it would probably be an effective way of preventing serious offense (as opposed to injury or harm) to persons other than the actor, and that it is probably a necessary means to that end . . . **1–026**

The offense principle requires that the disliked state of mind . . . be produced wrongfully by another party . . . [It is necessary] to weigh, in each main category and context of offensiveness, the seriousness of the offense caused to unwilling witnesses against the reasonableness of the offender's conduct. The seriousness of the offensiveness would be determined by (1) the intensity and durability of the repugnance produced, and the extent to which repugnance could be anticipated to be the general reaction of strangers to the conduct displayed or represented (conduct offensive only to persons with an abnormal susceptibility to offense would not count as *very* offensive); (2) the ease with which unwilling witnesses can avoid the offensive displays; and (3) whether or not the witnesses have willingly assumed the risk of being offended either through curiosity or the anticipation of pleasure . . .

These factors would be weighed as a group against the reasonableness of the offending party's conduct as determined by (1) its personal importance to the actors themselves and its social utility generally, remembering always the enormous social utility of unhampered expression (in those cases where expression is involved); (2) the availability of alternative times and places where the conduct in question would cause less offense; (3) the extent, if any, to which the offense is caused with spiteful motives. In addition, the legislature would examine the prior established character of various neighbourhoods, and consider establishing licensed zones in areas where the conduct in question is known to be already prevalent, so that people inclined to be offended are not likely to stumble on it to their surprise . . ."

Feinberg argues that the law should not treat offence as if it was as serious as harm and, where possible, should use other modes of regulation such as injunctions or licensing procedures.

It follows that while picking one's nose in public might be an offence to sensibility,[48] it could never, **1–027**
using Feinberg's criteria, amount to *serious* offence. On the other hand, if one were travelling on a bus and the passengers in the seat directly opposite performed oral sex on one another accompanied by sound effects,[49] it could be argued that the test of serious offence is made out.

(e) Combining harm with legal moralism

What this discussion shows is that a determination of harm, including serious offence, is not always **1–028**
clear-cut. Although some direct harms can be easily outlined, other more remote forms of injury can be

48 H. Gross, *A Theory of Criminal Justice* (New York: OUP, 1979), p.120.

49 J. Feinberg, *The Moral Limits of the Criminal Law: Offense to Others* (New York: OUP, 1985), p.12. cf. A.P. Simester and A. von Hirsch, *Crimes, Harms and Wrongs: On the Principles of Criminalization* (Oxford: Hart Publishing, 2011), pp.97–107.

difficult to calculate and may be contingent on the actions of other individuals or on the coincidence of certain situational circumstances. Harm alone, however measured, may be too weak a justification for criminalisation where it is considered in isolation of its moral character. In response to this quandary, more contemporary theorists on criminalisation have advocated a "dual-element" theory, whereby criminalisation can only be justified on the grounds that a particular type of conduct is both harmful and wrongful (immoral).[50] More specifically, the conduct must be injurious in some way to others, whilst being "perpetrated in a manner that makes it wrong".[51] An element of moral wrongfulness in this equation is a necessary (albeit not sufficient) condition for criminalisation of harmful conduct because, amongst other things, criminalisation and its attendant sanctions are intended to convey censure.[52] As we will see further below, censure is a specific response to wrongdoing that is intended to express denunciation for blameworthy behaviour.[53]

Where does this dual-element approach leave us with regards to conduct that is seriously "offensive" but not directly harmful? One example is the use of "insults" or "abusive" language towards another in a public space which may be considered offensive but not necessarily harmful (at least not harmful enough to warrant criminalisation).[54] Simester and von Hirsch assert that offences that are based on causing offence must be attached to a norm of "disrespect or lack of consideration", which in turn is in some way injurious to others.[55] The harmfulness of this type of offensive behaviour, they argue, can be evidenced where the conduct occurs in a public domain and where it risks adversely affecting the utility and attractiveness of the space. In reality many public order offences which involve offensive but non-physical behaviour require evidence that the conduct caused (or was likely to cause) another person to feel harassed, alarmed, or distressed, i.e. that they experienced (or were likely to experience) some level of emotional harm.[56]

(iii) Legal paternalism

1–029 Legal paternalism involves allowing the criminal law to be used to protect a person from harm to themselves. Legal paternalists argue that the law is entitled to interfere with a person's autonomy for their own good and to enhance their welfare. If it were established that consuming certain drugs was harmful to the person concerned, the paternalist would criminalise the sale and possession of such drugs. The legal paternalist is, however, only interested in enhancing the interests that a person actually has and not in protecting interests that they ought to have.

There are, however, a number of problems with a paternalistic approach.

---

50 A. von Hirsch, "Harm and Wrongdoing in Criminalisation Theory" (2014) 8 Crim. Law and Philos. 245. See also Simester and von Hirsch, *Crimes, Harms and Wrongs: On the Principles of Criminalization* (2011).

51 von Hirsch, "Harm and Wrongdoing in Criminalisation Theory" (2014) 8 Crim. Law and Philos. 245, 247.

52 See Duff, *The Realm of Criminal Law* (2018).

53 Simester and von Hirsch, *Crimes, Harms and Wrongs: On the Principles of Criminalization* (2011).

54 See, e.g. Public Order Act 1986 s.4A.

55 Simester and von Hirsch, *Crimes, Harms and Wrongs: On the Principles of Criminalization* (2011), p.100.

56 See, e.g. Public Order Act 1986 s.5.

Law Commission (Consultation Paper No.139), Consent in the Criminal Law (1995), Appendix C para.C.63:

> "[T]he paternalist argues from a philosophical slippery slope and is at constant risk of taking a tumble. The fact is that many of us make life-style choices which do not promote our immediate or long-term interests. Smoking certainly falls into this category of choices: for the paternalist it should be a clear target for criminalisation. But the point goes much further. If (as seems plausible) a balanced, healthy diet and regular exercise would be in every person's interests, the paternalist has a reason for criminalising fatty foods and sedentary life-styles. Risk-taking without good reason would also be ruled out. Sky-diving, mountaineering and most contact sports would have to be criminalised. In principle, the paternalist seems to be committed to using the criminal law to turn us all into super-fit, clean-living 'spartans' whether we like it or not." **1–030**

Despite this,[57] the Law Commission has proposed, in relation to sado-masochistic activities, that the law be based on an approach "redolent of a paternalism that is softened at the edges".[58] Accordingly, while people should be generally entitled to make choices for themselves and consent to injury, even fairly serious injury, they should not be permitted to consent to seriously disabling injury. Because people have interests in their physical health, the normal functioning of their bodies and in avoiding intense pain or grotesque disfigurement, the Law Commission took the view that anybody who consents to seriously disabling injury "has made a mistake and that to be really disabled is against his or her interests".[59] An exception is, however, proposed in relation to activities that are "very widely regarded as beneficial"[60] such as surgery and risky sports. By allowing people to consent to a range of injuries in sado-masochism, the Law Commission clearly regarded its paternalistic view as being softened in favour of liberalism. However, by not allowing people to consent to seriously disabling injuries in the course of sado-masochism while not criminalising the same injuries in the course of, say, boxing, it is possible to assert that in reality the Law Commission has adopted a stance of paternalism hardened at the edges by legal moralism.[61] **1–031**

It is also the case that paternalism is used inconsistently as a justification for the control of certain drugs. One might expect that drugs offences be classed in seriousness according to the harm that they might potentially cause the user and/or any secondary Vs. Studies of the harmfulness of drugs which have shown that this is not in fact how the criminal law operates. The Misuse of Drugs Act 1971 categorises prohibited drugs in three classes A, B and C.[62] Possession and supply of such drugs are prohibited, with the maximum sentence for such offences depending upon the class of drug involved.[63] Examples of those drugs falling within Class A are heroin and cocaine, whilst amphetamines (speed)

---

57 "Appendix C: Consent and the Criminal Law: Philosophical Foundations" was specially commissioned by the Law Commission and written by Paul Roberts. While reproducing his advice, the Law Commission felt itself unable to adopt the approach he favours (para.2.1).

58 "Appendix C: Consent and the Criminal Law: Philosophical Foundations" para.2.15.

59 "Appendix C: Consent and the Criminal Law: Philosophical Foundations" para.2.18.

60 "Appendix C: Consent and the Criminal Law: Philosophical Foundations" para.2.18.

61 The Commission has also noted that immunity for sports like boxing is so embedded in criminal law that it would require special legislation to remove it. Law Commission Consultation Paper No.139, *Consent in the Criminal Law* (1995), paras 12.32–12.38.

62 Misuse of Drugs Act 1971 Sch.2.

63 For offences of possession, Class A drugs attract a maximum sentence of seven years' imprisonment; for Class B drugs the maximum sentence is five years and for Class C drugs it is two years: Misuse of Drugs Act 1971 Sch.4.

are Class B. Cannabis, having been temporarily downgraded to Class C, has again been reclassified as a Class B drug.[64]

House of Commons Science and Technology Committee, Drug Classification: Making a Hash of It? Fifth Report of Session 2005–06 (2006), p.3:

1-032 "With respect to the ABC classification system, we have identified significant anomalies in the classification of individual drugs and a regrettable lack of consistency in the rationale used to make classification decisions. In addition, we have expressed concern at the Government's proclivity for using the classification system as a means of 'sending out signals' to potential users and society at large—it is at odds with the stated objective of classifying drugs on the basis of harm and the Government has not made any attempt to develop an evidence base on which to draw in determining the 'signal' being sent out."

1-033 Evidence provided to the committee suggests, for example, that magic mushrooms, currently classed as a Class A drug, are far less harmful than other drugs in the same category. Official statistics suggest that only one person died from taking such drugs between the years 1993 and 2000; the drugs are thought not to be addictive, and that it is estimated that one would need to consume one's own body weight in magic mushrooms for the dose to be lethal.[65] In comparison, some drugs which are not even prohibited under law may be more harmful; though the production and sale of so-called "legal highs" has now been criminalised.[66] Alcohol and tobacco were ranked by some as being as harmful as the Class A drugs of LSD and ecstasy, and it has been estimated that together alcohol and tobacco cause "approximately 40 times the total number of deaths from all illegal drugs combined".[67] If drugs offences are to be justified in terms of paternalism surely they should bear some relation to the degree of harm they actually cause.

Whilst paternalism has been subjected to much criticism, the harm principle has also been criticised in recent years for failing to curb the expansion of the criminal law,[68] and it may be seen as being both under inclusive, "since it cannot—or cannot without serious distortion—capture kinds of conduct that clearly should be criminalized",[69] and over-inclusive, "in that it renders 'criminalizable' at least in principle, kinds of conduct that should not be criminalized".[70] There is potential for the principle to be used to justify highly

64 Misuse of Drugs Act 1971 (Amendment) Order 2008 (SI 2008/3130) art.2(2)(a) (in force from 26 January 2009).

65 House of Commons Science and Technology Committee, *Drug Classification: Making a Hash of It?*, Fifth Report of Session 2005–06 (2006), p.27. For further discussion of the criminalisation of magic mushrooms, see C. Walsh, "Magic Mushrooms and the Law" [2005] Crim. L.R. 773–783.

66 Psychoactive Substances Act 2016.

67 House of Commons Science and Technology Committee, *Drug Classification: Making a Hash of It?*, Fifth Report of Session 2005–06 (2006), p.47. See P.R. Ferguson, "'Smoke gets in your eyes . . .' the criminalisation of smoking in enclosed public places, the harm principle and the limits of the criminal sanction" (2011) 3 *Legal Studies* 259–278, who argues that the risk of harm to non-smokers from passive smoking is preferable as a justification for this criminalisation to legal paternalism.

68 B.E. Harcourt, "The Collapse of the Harm Principle" (1999) 90 J. Crim. L. & Criminology 109. cf. Thorburn, "Constitutionalism and the Limits of the Criminal Law" in Duff, *The Structures of the Criminal Law* (2011).

69 R.A. Duff, "Introduction: The Boundaries of the Criminal Law" in Duff, *The Boundaries of the Criminal Law* (2010), p.20.

70 Duff, "Introduction: The Boundaries of the Criminal Law" in Duff, *The Boundaries of the Criminal Law* (2010), p.20.

intrusive state intervention into the private life of individuals, for example it might be seen as justifying the criminalisation of parents who cause harm or a risk of harm to their children's health by failing to have them immunised, or smoking at home, or feeding them excessive quantities of calorie-dense food.[71] Feinberg has suggested that, in the case of offensive conduct and speech, there is a particular danger of over-criminalisation because of the tendency of law-makers to overreact to it.[72] Stanton-Ife has also argued that the manner in which the harm principle accounts for crimes in general, in terms of interests, fails adequately to explain the gravity of some particularly horrific crimes, because it "has the effect of shoehorning all crimes into one box",[73] regarding the victims of crime as those whose interests have been violated, when the reality is that the victims of horrific crimes "have been violated themselves".[74]

2. Is it necessary to employ the criminal law?

Whichever of the above views is adopted as the correct basis upon which to justify the determination that conduct is wrongful, most commentators accept that this is merely a minimal or necessary, but not a sufficient, condition for criminalisation. Assuming the conduct in question is adjudged to be wrongful, there is a further condition to be established. It must be *necessary* to use the *criminal law* to condemn and try to prevent the wrongful conduct. In other words, the criminal law should be used as a measure of "last resort". **1–034**

Douglas Husak, "The Criminal Law as Last Resort" (2004) 24 O.J.L.S. 207, 211–212:

"Why not require the state to have a compelling interest for *each* criminal law it enacts? The standards applicable to infringements of fundamental rights (like speech) should be invoked *whenever* persons become subject to punishment. This theory would require the law in question to be *necessary* to achieve a compelling government purpose. In other words, the government's objective must be essential, and the law must be the least restrictive means to attain it. To qualify as the least restrictive means, the law must be *narrowly tailored* to serve the compelling state interest. The requirement of narrow tailoring has two dimensions. First, criminal laws should not be *over inclusive*, proscribing instances of conduct beyond those that serve the compelling state **1–035**

---

71 Nuffield Council on Bioethics, *Public Health: Ethical Issues* (2007), para.5.39; T. Elliott, "Pursued by the 'fat police'? The obesity 'epidemic' and the criminal law" in A.M. Viens, J. Coggon and A. Kessel, *Criminal Law, Philosophy and Public Health Practice* (Cambridge: CUP, 2013), Ch.6.

72 J. Feinberg, *The Moral Limits of the Criminal Law: Offense to Others* (Oxford: OUP, 1985), p.5. See, e.g. the use which has been made of the Malicious Communications Act 1988 s.1 and the Communications Act 2003 s.127, to prosecute "trolls", who send offensive or provocative messages via social media. The CPS, in its Guidelines on Communications Offences at *https://www.cps.gov.uk/legal-guidance/communications-offences*, has indicated that prosecutions under the Malicious Communications Act 1988 s.1 and the Communications Act 2003 s.127 should only be brought where there is sufficient evidence that the communication in question is more than:

> "Offensive, shocking, or disturbing; or
> Satirical, iconoclastic, or rude comment; or
> The expression of unpopular or unfashionable opinion about serious or trivial matters, or banter or humour, even if distasteful to some or painful to those subjected to it; or
> An uninhibited and ill thought-out contribution to a casual conversation where participants expect a certain amount of repartee or 'give and take';

This is with reference to 'contemporary standards . . . the standards of an open and just multi-racial society'".

73 J. Stanton-Ife, "Horrific Crime" in Duff, *The Boundaries of the Criminal Law* (2010), Ch.6 p.162.

74 Stanton-Ife, "Horrific Crime" in Duff, *The Boundaries of the Criminal Law* (2010), Ch.6 p.162.

interest. Next, criminal laws should not be *under inclusive*, and must apply equally to each instance of conduct the state has the same compelling interest to proscribe. The state must treat us as equals in protecting our interest not to be punished; it should not punish some while sparing others if it has the same compelling reason to punish both. Of course, this theory cannot be implemented without criteria to decide which state interests are compelling; attempts to identify these interests are bound to generate enormous dispute. Moreover, since the law must be necessary to achieve the compelling government purpose, the state objective must be more difficult to attain *without* resorting to punishment. This latter requirement, it would seem, expresses the last resort principle. A criminal statute cannot be necessary to accomplish a purpose if other means could do so more easily."[75]

1–036 Husak is building upon the work of others here, in particular that of Packer, who listed the following as conditions to be met before the criminal law can be applied.

Herbert L. Packer, The Limits of the Criminal Sanction (1969), pp.267–272:

1–037 "Remoteness and Triviality:

The conduct proscribed by any criminal code can be ranked in a hierarchy of remoteness from the ultimate harm that the law seeks to prevent. We prohibit the sale of liquor to an intoxicated person to lessen the likelihood that he will drive while drunk (an offense), crash into another car (an offense), injure an occupant of the other car (an offense), or cause the death of someone in the other car (an offense). There we have a spectrum of remoteness ranging from the illegal sale of liquor to manslaughter. Similarly, we make it an offense to possess tools specially adapted for burglary so that we may reduce the incidence of burglary (an offense), and thereby reduce the incidence of further offences, such as larceny, robbery, rape, and even murder, that can ensue from burglary. Mayhem or murder might not be intended by most burglars, but they are nonetheless possible results of the confrontation between burglar and V.

One of the most delicate problems in framing criminal proscriptions is to locate the point farthest removed from the ultimate harm apprehended at which meaningful preventive intervention can take place. If dangerous conduct can be deterred and dangerous persons identified well short of the point at which the danger becomes acute, so much the better. Or so it seems. Actually, increasing the radius of the criminal law in the interest of early intervention is a very risky business. The first question in every case is, or should be: how high is the probability that the preparatory conduct, if not inhibited by the threat of criminal punishment, will result in an ultimate harm of the sort that the law should try to prevent? A related consideration is whether the preparatory conduct is itself socially useful, or at least neutral, so that its proscription or curtailment might unduly inhibit people from doing what they should otherwise be free to do. To put the issue in terms that are familiar in the law, is the risk substantial and is it justifiable? . . .

---

75 See also D. Husak, *Overcriminalization: The Limits of the Criminal Law* (Oxford: OUP, 2008); D. Husak, "Reservations about *Overcriminalization*" (2011) 14 New Crim. L. Rev.97. cf. N. Jareborg, "Criminalisation as a Last Resort (Ultima Ratio)" (2004–2005) 2 Ohio State J. of Crim. Law 521.

Still another consideration relates to the problem of enforcement. By and large, the further removed the conduct in question is from the ultimate harm apprehended, the more difficult it is going to be to detect the occurrence of the conduct and to apprehend people who engage in it. Considerations of maximizing personal freedom and of minimizing the strain on law enforcement combine, then, to suggest considerable caution in the progression towards the remote end of the spectrum.

An example that is amusing because it is so extreme is a recent action of the New York City Council. At the urgent request of the Fire Commissioner, the Council voted to make it a criminal offense, punishable by a hundred-dollar fine, a thirty-day jail term or both, to smoke in bed in a hotel, motel, or other place of public abode. A subsidiary provision required that a notice to that effect be displayed by the proprietor of every place covered by the ban. Now, nobody doubts that a great many serious and sometimes fatal accidents are caused by people's smoking in bed and that it would be a far better thing if people did not smoke in bed. But consider the impossibility of enforcing such a prohibition without the most detailed kind of surveillance. Consider the invasions of privacy that such surveillance would entail. And, enforcement problems aside, consider the effect of announcing that such commonly engaged in conduct has now become criminal. One wonders what was accomplished by the criminal prohibition that would not equally well be accomplished by requiring hotels to display in each room a notice warning about the danger. Alternatively, the solution might have been to make it criminal to cause a fire by smoking in bed, regardless of the amount of harm done. That kind of prohibition would at least have been enforceable, whether or not it was enforced. As it is, given the well-known relationship between intoxication and fires resulting from smoking in bed, I suppose travellers should be grateful that the City Council did not go one step further and make it a crime to go to bed drunk in a New York hotel.

The idea of a criminal conviction no longer inspires the awe that it once did, because of the tendency of legislative bodies (like the New York City Council in this example) to prescribe criminal penalties simply as a means of expressing their disapproval of conduct. This tendency results in two kinds of triviality: triviality of object and triviality of intention. By triviality of object I mean the selection of behaviour for which the regular imposition of criminal punishment is disproportionate. By triviality of intention I mean an attitude of indifference or cynicism on the part of legislators toward the actual enforcement of the proscriptions they vote for. Both forms of triviality should be carefully avoided. A rational legislator should not vote to subject previously legal conduct to criminal proscription unless he is prepared to say, first, that the conduct being proscribed is so threatening to important social interests that he is willing to see people who engage in it subjected to criminal punishment and, second, that he expects law enforcement to devote adequate resources to detecting, apprehending, and convicting violators. The two will tend in most cases to be complementary . . . [Such trivial offences should be decriminalised and made 'civil offences' or 'infractions.'].''

Packer then identifies further conditions that need to be taken into account when making the "ultimate decision" about criminalisation. In addition to what has been said so far, we need to avoid the possibility **1–038** of creating a "crime tariff";[76] by this he means that the demand for the illegalised activity or product may be so inelastic that rather than reducing the incidence of the activity, it merely drives it underground and forces the price up. The provision of illegal abortions and the sale of narcotics are cases in point. The same may well be true of sado-masochistic activities.

1-039 Packer helpfully sets out criteria to assist in final decisions as to whether criminalisation is both practically enforceable and necessary.

HERBERT L. PACKER, THE LIMITS OF THE CRIMINAL SANCTION (1969), P.296:

1-040 "(1) The conduct is prominent in most people's view of socially threatening behaviour, and is not condoned by any significant segment of society.
(2) Subjecting it to the criminal sanction is not inconsistent with the goals of punishment.
(3) Suppressing it will not inhibit socially desirable conduct.
(4) It may be dealt with through even-handed and non-discriminatory enforcement.
(5) Controlling it through the criminal process will not expose that process to severe qualitative or quantitative strains.
(6) There are no reasonable alternatives to the criminal sanction for dealing with it.[77]

These criteria can be used in making up a kind of priority list of conduct for which the legislature might consider invoking the criminal sanction."

1-041 What conclusions are to be drawn about the example of sado-masochism mentioned throughout this section? In *Brown*, the activities all took place with the consent of the passive partners. Was it appropriate to invoke the criminal law? The majority of the House of Lords felt that the public interest took over at the point of actual bodily harm. Consent can thus only operate as a defence to a narrow range of activities involving minimal harm. They largely dealt with the matter as one of violence. But, surely, "violence" presupposes something that is against the will of the recipient. Though couched in terms of public health and individual safety, ultimately the approach of the majority amounted to an exercise of legal moralism. The piercing of genitals for sexual purposes is apparently unlawful. Ear-piercing and cosmetic body piercing is lawful.[78] The infliction of pain for sexual purposes is "uncivilised", yet the aim of punching someone so hard they become unconscious in the sport of boxing is socially desirable. As has been commented: "Eroticism makes a difference".[79] The minority, on the other hand,

76 Packer, *The Limits of the Criminal Sanction* (1968), pp.277–282.

77 Whilst Packer identified the need for criminal law to achieve utilitarian goals as a determinative factor in applying this criterion, Husak notes that there may often be alternatives to the criminal law in *preventing* a particular conduct or harm. However, Husak notes that punishment for crimes additionally has an *expressive* function in stigmatising conduct we wish to censure. It is this latter function which will often determine whether it is necessary to employ the criminal law: D. Husak, "The Criminal Law as Last Resort" (2004) 24 O.J.L.S. 207.

78 Note though that more extreme body modification procedures have been held not to be a legal exception, *R. v BM* [2019] Q.B. 1. See para.9-057.

79 L. Bibbings and P. Alldridge, "Sexual Expression, Body Alteration, and the Defence of Consent" (1993) 20 J. Law & Soc. 356, 362. cf. S. Cowan, "Criminalizing SM: Disavowing the Erotic, Instantiating Violence" in Duff, *The Structures of the Criminal Law* (2011).

dealt with the matter as one of private sexual morality and felt that it was only when grievous bodily harm had been caused that consent should be no defence.

Ultimately, it would seem it is impossible to answer questions such as whether sado-masochism ought to be criminalised without taking a moral stance on the subject, even if one starts out from the position that conduct ought only to be criminalised if it is harmful.

R.A. Duff, Answering for Crime: Responsibility and Liability in the Criminal Law (2007), pp.130–132:

"[A] standard liberal response [to the House of Lords decision in *Brown*] would be to argue that whether or not the physical injuries were inflicted constituted harm, the 'victims' were not wronged. '*Volenti non fit iniuria*': consent might not negate harm, but it negates the wrongfulness that criminalisation requires. A 'bold' liberal would stick to this principle, however serious the physical harm involved: if someone who is rationally competent truly gives informed consent to what another does to him, he is not wronged, and the conduct therefore cannot legitimately be criminalised. However, as one imagines cases involving progressively more serious physical (or psychological) harms, even quite bold liberals tend to become uneasy, and find it harder to insist that consent should always preclude criminalisation. **1–042**

What grounds such unease is not, I suspect, just the degree of seriousness of the physical injuries caused, but a conception of the meaning of the actions that deliberately inflict them: if the point of the action is to inflict extreme pain or serious injury, or to degrade and humiliate others in a ritual of torture, consent surely cannot legitimate it. I might consent to be treated in ways that degrade or deny my humanity; but that does not render the treatment other than wrongful. That is why a more plausible argument for acquitting the *Brown* defendants would appeal not simply to consent (whilst implicitly admitting that the 'victims' were harmed), but to the meaning of the actions in their context: although to the ignorant outsider their activities look like exercises in degradation and humiliation, we should realise that this way of finding sexual gratification is, within that sub-culture, a way in which the participants express their love and respect for each other. But such an argument abandons the Harm Principle, and moves onto the Legal Moralist's ground. For the argument is that the *Brown* defendants' conduct is worthy at least of our moral respect: it is oriented towards morally legitimate ends (mutual sexual pleasure); it is informed by morally admirable values (love and respect); even if the means by which those ends are pursued and those values are expressed are unusual, and to others' eyes shocking, when understood in their particular context they lose their *morally* shocking character. The argument is thus also that their conduct is not harmful: for it fulfils, rather than setting back, the interests of those involved. We need not accept it for ourselves, or approve of it; we may still think it wrong. But we should not see it as meriting public condemnation, since it does not violate the values of mutual respect and concern by which our collective life as a polity is supposedly structured.

A liberal might be tempted to argue that the morality or otherwise of such conduct should not be what is at issue: as consensual sexual activity, it is a matter of 'private' morality which is, 'in brief and crude terms, not the law's business'.[80] The argument just offered was meant to show that this quick liberal response is inadequate. To show that we have no good reason to criminalise such conduct, according to the Harm Principle, we must show either that it is not harmful or that, though harmful, it is not wrongful. To show that it was not harmful we must attend, I have suggested, to its moral significance as an aspect of mutually respectful sexual relationships—which brings to bear a moralised conception of harm. To show that it was not wrongful we cannot, I have suggested, simply appeal to consent, but must look at the substantive character of the conduct, and in particular at whether it must count as degrading or dehumanizing."

1-043 Arguably, Duff's position that conduct should be criminalised only if it is wrongful, and that wrongful conduct includes that which is "degrading or dehumanizing", brings us no closer to finding a workable test which would allow us to determine whether a particular activity ought to be criminalised or not, since it depends on the moral view taken on whether such activity is "dehumanizing" or not. However, his discussion brings us to the almost inevitable conclusion that no single theory can dictate the content of the criminal law:

"Instead of trying to find some single concept or value that will capture *the* essence of crime or *the* essential characteristic in virtue of which crimes are property punished we should opt for a pluralism that recognises a diversity of reasons for criminalisation."[81]

3. Is it permissible to criminalise the conduct?

1-044 Even assuming the above criteria have been met, namely that the conduct is regarded as "wrongful" and it is thought "necessary" to invoke the powers of the criminal law to condemn the activity, there is a final hurdle to be overcome before the conduct should be declared (or remain) criminal. Such criminalisation must not contravene the European Convention on Human Rights which was made directly applicable in English law by the Human Rights Act 1998.

These provisions operate in two ways. First, any new Bill proposing to criminalise conduct must be accompanied by a statement by the Minister responsible that the provisions of the Bill are compatible with the Convention.[82]

Secondly, it is possible that existing criminal offences are structured in such a way as to offend the provisions of the ECHR. Under the Human Rights Act 1998, courts are obliged to interpret all legislation "so far as it is possible to do so" in a manner that is compatible with Convention rights.[83] Firstly, the criminal law must be clear enough that citizens are able to observe the rules which when breached

80 The Committee on Homosexual Offences and Prostitution (Wolfenden Committee), *The Report of the Departmental Committee on Homosexual Offences and Prostitution* (London: HMSO, 1957), para.61.

81 R.A. Duff, *Answering for Crime: Responsibility and Liability in the Criminal Law* (Oxford: Hart, 2007), p.139.

82 Human Rights Act 1998 s.19: this applies to all Bills and not only those creating criminal offences.

83 Human Rights Act 1998 s.3(1).

result in a criminal offence (known as the principle of legality).[84] For example, in *Misra*,[85] the Court of Appeal was faced with the argument that certain aspects of a leading House of Lords' decision, *Adomako*,[86] were incompatible with the Convention. The appellants argued that the charge of gross negligence manslaughter required the jury to determine whether D's conduct should be characterised as gross negligence, meaning that the jury had to define the offence for itself, which meant that the offence, as defined in law, failed to meet the standard of legal certainty. While rejecting this argument on its merits, the Court of Appeal clearly regarded itself as having such a power. A court in Jersey has actually exercised this power in holding that the common law defence of insanity is incompatible with the ECHR.[87]

In addition, criminal offences must not contravene art.8 (respect for private life) or art.14 (non-discrimination). For example, the European Commission found that having different ages of consent for heterosexuals and homosexuals contravened these Convention rights.[88] This led to a change of English law, rendering the age of consent the same for all persons.[89]

While every effort must be made to interpret provisions to ensure compatibility with the ECHR, if this is not possible then, as "a measure of last resort",[90] the High Court and appellate courts may make a declaration of incompatibility. While this does not affect the actual validity of the incompatible legislation, there is an obligation to bring the law into conformity with the Convention since otherwise the UK will not meet its obligations under art.1 of the Convention "to secure to everyone within their jurisdiction the rights and freedoms" set out in the Convention. **1–045**

Similarly, courts are obliged to ensure compatibility between the common law and the Convention even if this involves courts having to override previous authority. While English courts have displayed some reluctance to go down this route, increasingly challenges to established authorities are being mounted.

While the importance of the ECHR cannot be over-estimated, it must be conceded that its impact on the substantive criminal law (as opposed to criminal procedure, evidence and sentencing) has, to date, been somewhat limited. For example, art.8 provides a right to respect for private life. Prima facie, one might think that the decision in *Brown* would be incompatible with this: all the sado-masochistic activities in this case were consensual and in private. If a right to private life is to mean anything, it ought to encompass persons expressing their sexuality in the privacy of their own homes. Indeed, the

---

84 European Convention on Human Rights art.7.

85 *R. v Misra (Amit)* [2004] EWCA Crim 2375; [2005] 1 Cr. App. R. 21.

86 *R. v Adomako (John Asare)* [1995] 1 A.C. 171; [1994] 3 W.L.R. 288 HL. In *R. v Nursing (Ligaya)* [2012] EWCA Crim 2521; [2013] 1 W.L.R. 1031, the Court of Appeal held that the offence of wilful neglect of an adult lacking capacity under the Mental Capacity Act 2005 was sufficiently certain (cf. *R. v Hopkins (Annette)* [2011] EWCA Crim 1513; (2012) 123 B.M.L.R. 1). See more generally, E. Śliwiński, "Principle of proportionality as a threat to criminal-law-related fundamental rights" (2023) 14(3) *New Journal of European Criminal Law*, 327.

87 *Att-Gen v Jason Prior* [2001] *Jersey Law Reports* 146. See Mackay and Gearty [2001] Crim. L.R. 560. This position was doubted by the Court of Appeal in Jersey (*Att-Gen v Prior* [2002] *Jersey Law Reports* 11) and it has not been followed in Guernsey (*R. v Harvey* unreported 3 August 2001). See Mackay [2002] Crim. L.R. 728 and Law Commission, *Insanity and Automatism: Supplementary Material to the Scoping Paper* (2012), paras 5.34–5.35 and C.70–73.

88 *Sutherland v United Kingdom* [1998] E.H.R.L.R. 117.

89 Sexual Offences (Amendment) Act 2000 s.1.

90 *R. v A (No.2)* [2001] UKHL 25; [2002] 1 A.C. 45.

decision in *Brown* was challenged on this basis in the European Court of Human Rights in *Laskey*.[91] However, the European Court, while conceding that there was a violation of the right to respect for private life in art.8(1), nevertheless ruled that criminalisation in cases involving "violence" was justifiable under art.8(2) which permits invasions of privacy if it is "necessary in a democratic society . . . for the protection of health or morals".

1-046 Despite the fact that the Convention applies directly in English law, there is little evidence of English judges adopting a less moralistic/paternalistic stance.[92] The English courts have held, for example, that art.6 is "not concerned with the fairness of provisions of substantive law" and that Contracting States are free "to choose how to define the essential elements of an offence".[93] It is more often the procedural law, rather than substantive criminal law, which is confirmed as falling foul of the Human Rights Act. The example of detention without trial for suspected terrorists is a salient example of the Government introducing laws to satisfy public demand without applying time-honoured principles of justice that existed long before the Human Rights Act was passed. Whilst procedural law is beyond the scope of this book this example does show, at least, that the courts now have a power that they are willing to exercise in making a declaration of incompatibility against laws passed by Parliament.[94]

The precise effect of the Convention and the nature of the various challenges to the substantive criminal law will be explored in the relevant sections of this book, particularly in relation to the structure of the defences to criminal liability which is the area that seems most likely to be affected. For present purposes, it is sufficient to conclude that while the test of permissibility of criminalisation under the ECHR could provide some check on unbridled moralism, the ultimate decision as to whether any particular criminalisation is justifiable will remain to be determined by the other criteria considered above.

III. Punishment

1-047 If the criminal law is to have any real bite it must be underpinned by an effective enforcement mechanism that is backed by a framework of sanctions aimed at compelling compliance. These

91 *Laskey v United Kingdom* (1997) 24 E.H.R.R. 39.

92 Recourse to the European Court of Human Rights is still retained if all domestic remedies have been exhausted (ECHR art.34).

93 *R. v G* [2002] EWCA Crim 1992; [2003] 1 Cr. App. R. 23. See also *R. v G* [2008] UKHL 37; [2009] 1 A.C. 92 (discussed in Ch.3 paras 3-064–3-065), followed in *R. v Brown (Richard)* [2013] UKSC 43; [2013] N.I. 265; *R. v Concannon (John)* [2002] Crim. L.R. 213. J. Arkinstall and C. O'Brien, "Table of Cases under the Human Rights Act" [2002] E.H.R.L.R. 364 provides a comprehensive list of English cases under the Human Rights Act 1998: in only one of the cases cited was there a successful challenge under the Act (*Percy v DPP* [2001] EWHC Admin 1125; (2002) 166 J.P. 93 concerned with the Public Order Act 1986 s.5).

94 The House of Lords, e.g. made a declaration of incompatibility in relation to the Anti-terrorism, Crime and Security Act 2001 s.23 (detention without trial for suspected terrorists) on the basis that it was found to be in breach of the right to liberty provided in the ECHR art.5: *A v Secretary of State for the Home Department* [2004] UKHL 56; [2005] 2 A.C. 68. cf. *Beghal v DPP* [2015] UKSC 49; [2016] A.C. 88: The power to stop, question and detain a person at a port or border under the Terrorism Act 2000 Sch.7, not incompatible with ECHR art.8; See further, A. Ashworth, "A Decade of Human Rights in Criminal Justice" [2014] Crim. L.R. 325–337.

sanctions must be distinguishable from other legal remedies if they are to give criminal law its distinct character, and if they are to help fulfil the key aim of the State to prevent harmful, offensive and/or immoral conduct.

The key distinguishing characteristics of the criminal sanction is that it is *intended* to serve as a form of punishment. There are two main schools of thought that underpin justifications for punishing those who commit criminal offences: (i) retributivist; and (ii) consequentialist.[95] Both retributivist and consequentialist theories of punishment have long histories. Retributivist theories became popular in the 18th century and, although falling out of fashion during the mid-1900s, made a resurgence in the latter part of the 20th century; remaining a cornerstone of the criminal justice system today. "Retribution", as a basis for punishment, is strongly associated with the work of Kant and Hegel, both of whom asserted that criminal offenders are moral agents who are deserving of punishment. "The annulment of the crime is retribution"[96] and is the symbolic restoration of the wrong committed. Retribution is therefore backward looking in that it seeks to punish the wrong doer in order to restore the balance or moral equilibrium that is disturbed by an offence.[97]

Consequentialist theories, on the other hand, are forward looking to the *consequences* of punishment. The theories of "deterrence", "incapacitation", and "rehabilitation" (described more fully below) have been associated with philosophers such as Cesare Beccaria and Jeremy Bentham who have argued that any form of punishment should achieve a "greater good"—namely crime reduction.

In addition to these theories of punishment is a relatively new purpose of sentencing which although not in itself a justification for punishing someone is nonetheless now an important means through which the State can respond to criminal wrongdoing—that of *reparation*. We therefore turn to a discussion of reparation (and more specifically "restorative justice") later in this chapter. **1-048**

A. RETRIBUTION

The word "retribution" is used in several senses. Sometimes it is employed to indicate either vengeance or expiation, but more commonly today it refers to giving offenders their "just deserts" and/or using punishment as a system of censure. **1-049**

---

95 Also referred to as utilitarian theories of punishment. A consequentialist seeks to achieve a consequence at any price; a utilitarian sets a price on the achievement of that goal: in this context, only the minimum amount of punishment thought necessary to achieve the consequence can be justified.

96 G.W.F. Hegel, *Hegel's Philosophy of Right*, T.M. Knox (trans.) (Oxford: OUP, 1967), para.101.

97 For an overview of retributivist rationales, see S. Easton and C. Piper, *Sentencing and Punishment: The Quest for Justice* (Oxford: OUP, 2016).

1. Vengeance

J.F. STEPHEN, A HISTORY OF THE CRIMINAL LAW OF ENGLAND, VOL.II (1883), PP.81–82:

1-050 "[T]he infliction of punishment by law gives definite expression and a solemn ratification and justification to the hatred which is excited by the commission of the offence . . . The criminal law thus proceeds upon the principle that it is morally right to hate criminals, and it confirms and justifies that sentiment by inflicting upon criminals, punishments which express it . . . I am also of opinion that this close alliance between criminal law and moral sentiment is in all ways healthy and advantageous to the community. I think it highly desirable that criminals should be hated, that the punishments inflicted upon them should be so contrived as to give expression to that hatred."

1-051 This desire for vengeance supposedly operates at two levels. First, it is asserted that punishment satisfies V's (or relatives' and friends') desire for vengeance and the State is merely exacting vengeance on their behalf to prevent private retaliation.

Secondly, it is asserted that there is a public need for vengeance. It is argued that there is an instinctive demand which is active in every human being to retaliate. This reaction is not only understandable but desirable as a socially acceptable outlet for our aggressions. If there were no punishment, our aggressions would become repressed to the point when they might break out in an anti-social manner.[98] Such views find little serious support today and have been alleged to "represent the breakdown of human intelligence, as well as good will. It shows perhaps the ugliest phase of our human nature".[99]

2. Expiation

1-052 According to this view, the offender must be made to work off their guilt; they must be purified through suffering. This is regarded as a species of retribution in that the offender is "paying his debt" owed to society and, in so doing, becomes reconciled with that society. The focus is on the past crime; the attempt is to wipe the slate clean. These ideas stem largely from the religious influences on our culture, but some would argue that there is a deeper psychological explanation underlying an offender's need for expiation. From the time we are children, we are conditioned to expect punishment when we have done wrong. Guilt is a state of tension which gives rise to a need for the removal of this tension. We are conditioned to expect this relief through punishment. The most famous illustration of this form of punishment comes from Dostoyevsky's *Crime and Punishment* in which Raskolnikov, after committing a brutal murder, becomes obsessed with feelings of guilt and eventually gives himself up as the only means of coming to terms with himself and achieving peace of mind.

---

98 E.W. Puttkammer, *Administration of Criminal Justice* (Chicago: University of Chicago Press, 1953).
99 M.R. Cohen, "Moral Aspects of the Criminal Law" (1940) 49 Yale L.J. 987, 1025.

While society might offer an offender the opportunity of expiation, it cannot insist or demand it as the will or desire for *true* expiation must proceed from the D himself. One is not necessarily dealing with true expiation of sin. Society simply deems the offender to have purged their guilt by punishment. A modern advocate of this penance theory is Duff.[100]

R.A. Duff, "Theories and Policies Underlying Guidelines Systems" (2005) 105 Columbia L. Rev. 1162, 1182–1183:

"The aim . . . is that the offender should come to understand, and so to repent, that wrong as a wrong both against the individual victim (where there was one) and against the wider political community to which they both belong . . . **1–053**

Central to this richer purpose is an attempt to turn the offender's punishment from a purely one-way process of communication from polity to offender into a two-way process in which there is then a communication back from the offender to the victim and the community: What is to be communicated is a kind of symbolic apology, which is given material and thus more forceful expression by the penal 'hard treatment' that the offender undergoes."

Duff's views have, however, attracted criticism. **1–054**

Andrew von Hirsch and Andrew Ashworth, Proportionate Sentencing (2005), p.94:

"[T]he offender has no choice but to undergo such deprivations; treating the expiatory pains of punishment as a kind of enforced apology thus raises the problem of compulsory attitudinizing—which may be viewed as a form of demeaning treatment . . . [T]here remains the key question of whether this is a proper function of the state. Perhaps an abbot may be entitled to impose penances designed to make erring novices expiate their sins. But why may the *state* do the same to its citizens in a free society?" **1–055**

3. Just deserts

Retribution as justice deserts has become the cornerstone of the criminal justice system.[101] The idea is simple: one who harms must be harmed in return. In other words, the harmer gets their "just deserts". In this way, we are according such persons respect as autonomous and responsible human beings who have chosen to commit a crime and must therefore face the consequences of their decisions. **1–056**

100 R.A. Duff, *Punishment, Communication and Community* (New York: OUP, 2001).
101 Criminal Justice Act 1991 was largely based on this philosophy.

ANDREW VON HIRSCH, DOING JUSTICE—THE CHOICE OF PUNISHMENTS (REPORT OF THE COMMITTEE FOR THE STUDY OF INCARCERATION) (1976), PP.45–49:

1-057 "In everyday thinking about punishment, the idea of desert figures prominently. Ask the person on the street why a wrongdoer should be punished, and he is likely to say that he 'deserves' it . . .

To say someone 'deserves' to be rewarded or punished is to refer to his *past* conduct, and assert that its merit or demerit is reason for according him pleasant or unpleasant treatment. The focus on the past is critical. That a student has written an outstanding paper is grounds for asserting that he deserves an award; but that the award will yield him or others future benefits (however desirable those might be) cannot be grounds for claiming he deserves it. The same holds for punishment: to assert that someone deserves to be punished is to look at his past wrongdoing as reason for having him penalized. This orientation to the past distinguishes desert from the other purported aims of punishment—deterrence, incapacitation, rehabilitation—which seek to justify the criminal sanction by its prospective usefulness in preventing crime."

1-058 There are two main strands to just-deserts thinking.

(i) Just deserts as eliminating an unfair advantage

ANDREW VON HIRSCH, DOING JUSTICE—THE CHOICE OF PUNISHMENTS (REPORT OF THE COMMITTEE FOR THE STUDY OF INCARCERATION) (1976), PP.45–49:

1-059 "A useful place to begin is with Kant's explanation of deserved punishment, which he based on the idea of fair dealing among free individuals. To realise their own freedom, he contended, members of society have the reciprocal obligation to limit their behaviour so as not to interfere with the freedom of others. When someone infringes another's rights, he gains an unfair advantage over all others in the society—since he has failed to constrain his own behaviour while benefitting from other persons' forbearance from interfering with his rights. The punishment—by imposing a counterbalancing disadvantage on the violator—restores the equilibrium: after having undergone the punishment, the violator ceases to be at advantage over his non-violating fellows As Herbert Morris puts it in a recent restatement of the Kantian argument:

> 'A person who violates the rules has something others have—the benefits of the system [of mutual non-interference with others' rights]—but by renouncing what others have assumed, the burdens of self-restraint, he has acquired an unfair advantage. Matters are not even until this advantage is in some way erased Justice—that is punishing such individuals—restores the equilibrium of benefits and burdens'." ("Persons and Punishment" (1968) 52 *The Monist* 475, 478.)

1-060 According to this view, by committing a crime, offenders have gained an unfair advantage over all others who have "toed the line" and restrained themselves from committing crime. They are "free riders" who have failed to observe the moral constraints that others have accepted.[102] Punishment is necessary to take away the benefits gained. Social equilibrium must be restored. Offenders deserve punishment in order to destroy their unfair advantage. Finnis describes the advantage as one of "indulging a (wrongful) self-preference, of permitting himself an excessive freedom in choosing" which, in turn, is punished so that:

> ". . . the criminal has the disadvantage of having his wayward will restricted in its freedom by being subjected to the representative 'will of society' (the 'will' which he disregarded in disregarding the law)."[103]

Hampton, in a variation on this theme, argues that crime involves the infliction of a moral injury; the V is diminished in value. Punishment is necessary "to vindicate the value of the victim".[104] D by committing the crime is asserting an unjustified superiority over the V which must be nullified through punishment.

The concept of just deserts has, however, attracted criticism.

John Braithwaite and Philip Pettit, Not Just Deserts: A Republican Theory of Criminal Justice (1990), pp.158–159:

> "A first objection to this justification for punishment is that law-abiding conduct is not always burdensome and crime is not always advantageous. The rapist might contract syphilis or the burglar break a leg. The conspiracy or the attempted murder might fail. Is the crime to be punished even though no benefits accrued? **1–061**
>
> The benefits and burdens theorist has a reply to this. He can say that it is self-restraint which is the burden, and unrestricted liberty the benefit that criminals gain by eschewing self-restraint. But is the self-restraint of not committing murder really a burden to our law-abiding readers? Even under conditions of unrestricted liberty most of us have no interest in or attraction to committing murder, and so the burden is no actual inconvenience. On the contrary, one influential view is that educating ourselves to adopt a moral character which abhors evil makes us 'better off' . . .
>
> It has been argued that] the burden of self-restraint still does limit options . . . and to have choice is better than not having it . . . Is it a burden in this sense that you are unable to fly to Mars tomorrow? The point we would stress is that some burdens have practical significance for people and some do not. It seems a weak basis for locking people up that they renounced burdens which are not felt to be burdens by most law-abiding citizens."

102 H. Morris, "Persons and Punishment" (1968) 52 *The Monist* 475.

103 J. Finnis, "The Restoration of Retribution" (1971) 32 *Analysis* 131.

104 J. Hampton, "Correcting Harms versus Righting Wrongs: The Goal of Retribution" (1992) 39 U.C.L.A. Law Rev. 1659, 1686.

NICOLA LACEY, STATE PUNISHMENT: POLITICAL PRINCIPLES AND COMMUNITY VALUES (1988), PP.24–26:

1-062 "[Desert theories do not give] very clear practical guidance about the fair measure of punishment in particular cases. What actual punishment would forfeit a set of rights equivalent to those violated by a rapist, a petty thief, a reckless driver? As in the case of the law of the talion and the culpability principle, resort to arguments from conventionally agreed, customary or consequence-based penalty scales seem hard to avoid. Secondly, real difficulties have been raised about the social contract tradition itself; in what sense can a *fictitious* agreement generate obligations for real people? Furthermore, these views are dependent for their force on the existence of a fair set of rules. This is not fatal in itself, but the criteria which dictate that there is indeed a just equilibrium which can be restored are not generated by the forfeiture of rights or unfair advantage principles alone. The views do pre-suppose an independent account of what counts as an unfair advantage and a just equilibrium.

Finally, it seems legitimate to ask whether the metaphorical ideas of restoring relationships of justice or moral equilibria outweigh the obvious disvalues attached to the suffering and other costs of punishment. Do these theories really ignore such costs completely? If not, what weight do they accord to them? In what real sense does punishment 'restore the right'? Do these theories really remove the mystery attaching to the original, simple desert principle, or are they, too, a form of moral alchemy? Or, in trying to avoid the mystery, do they not collapse into versions of utilitarian or other consequentialist justification? Even the more sophisticated versions barely rise above the level of metaphor, and leave us with the suspicion that the idea of desert cannot be distinguished from a principle of vengeance or the unappealing assertion that two wrongs somehow make a right."

1-063 According to these criticisms, it appears that "just deserts" theory struggles to stand up to critical and theoretical scrutiny. Of particular concern to critics is that the harming of wrong doers in order to rebalance the social equilibrium, rather than putting right the wrongs committed, simply increases the amount of harm that is now inflicted on individuals. Perhaps, then, a more cogently formed justification for retribution can be found in the need for public censure and denunciation.

(ii) Just deserts as censure or denunciation

1-064 While some just deserts theorists claim that desert is in itself the only purpose of punishment in that "punishing the guilty achieves something good—namely, justice",[105] others argue that punishment based on desert is necessary to express disapproval and censure of the conduct and the offender.[106]

---

105 M.S. Moore, "The Moral Worth of Retribution" in E. Schoeman (ed), *Responsibility, Character, and the Emotions: New Essays in Moral Philosophy* (Cambridge: CUP, 1987).

106 A. von Hirsch, *Past or Future Crimes: Deservedness and Dangerousness in the Sentencing of Criminals* (Boston: Rutgers University Press, 1985), p.52.

Andrew von Hirsch and Andrew Ashworth, Proportionate Sentencing (2005), pp.17–18:

> "A central reason for such a blaming response concerns penal censure's role as moral communication to the act's perpetrator. The punishment conveys to the actor a certain critical normative message concerning his conduct: for example, that he has culpably harmed or risked harming someone, and is disapproved of for having done so. This message treats him as a moral agent—that is, an agent capable of moral deliberation. He is being confronted with disapproval in virtues of the wrongfulness of his conduct, and not solely in order to produce preventive or other societal benefits that such censure might achieve . . . **1–065**
>
> Penal censure also has the role of addressing third parties—namely, members of the public. Unlike blame in everyday contexts, the criminal sanction announces in advance that specified categories of conduct are punishable. Because the prescribed sanctions are of a kind that express disapprobation, this conveys the message that the conduct is deemed reprehensible."

The role of censure is to ensure that the offender recognises the immorality of his actions. It is hoped that this induces penitence, whereby the offender is now more likely to conform to the law. Denunciation theory can also serve to educate the public by reaffirming social values and reinforcing inhibitions against crime. Von Hirsch and Ashworth argue that any preventive effects of public censure must only be seen as complementing retribution and not as a primary justification for punishment.[107] **1–066**

B. DETERRENCE

Unlike retributive theories, deterrent theories are forward looking in that they are concerned with the consequences of punishment; their aim is to reduce further crime by the threat or example of punishment. Deterrence is commonly thought to operate at three levels.[108] **1–067**

1. Individual deterrence

Deterrent theories seek to discourage crime. In the case of individual deterrence[109] it is hoped that the experience of punishment will be so unpleasant that the offender will not reoffend. The task of the sentencer is to look to the future and select the sentence which is likely to have most impact on the individual. In the case of some offenders, no punishment at all may be necessary as the risk of the convicted person reoffending may be minimal. In other cases, the required sentence may be very severe. **1–068**

---

107 See further under Educative Deterrence.

108 Absolute deterrence may be considered a fourth level. However, as it applies to the criminal justice system in its entirety, as against an individual theory of punishment, it is not discussed in detail in this chapter. We simply note here that absolute deterrence is the theory that by having a body of criminal laws and a justice system which enforces those laws people will be deterred from committing crimes. It is almost impossible to test the plausibility of this theory as it would require the abolition of the criminal justice system of England and Wales, however as Ashworth points out "periods in history when police forces have been on strike or otherwise rendered ineffective . . . were all characterised by increased lawbreaking": A. Ashworth, "The common sense and complications of general deterrent sentencing" [2019] Crim. L.R. 564, 564.

109 Sometimes referred to as "specific deterrence".

It is often said that every time a crime is committed the theory of deterrence is weakened; it is an argument that has some force when applied to the reoffender. One can argue that a reconviction reveals the failure of the previous sentence. However, it is notoriously difficult to measure and assess this.[110] The overall proven reoffending rate was25.2% between July to September 2021.[111] In terms of the deterrent effect of punishment the figures do not read well:

> "... the proven reoffending rates for adults ranged from 6.7% for offenders with no previous offences to 41.4% for offenders with 11 or more previous offences."[112]

This data could be read as suggesting that each time an offender is convicted and punished they are more likely to go on to reoffend. If that were the case, punishment may have the opposite effect to that which is intended. Such a suggestion is supported by a study in the Netherlands of 696 inmates who had been released from prison for approximately six months.[113] The researchers measured the "remembered severity" of imprisonment, controlling for the length of time served. They found that inmates who served longer periods of imprisonment seemed to recall their imprisonment as less aversive than those serving shorter periods. That is to say, the longer the inmates spent in prison the less likely they were to recall their experience as severely negative. The authors conclude that "to the extent that the length of imprisonment effects its recollected aversiveness at all, it does so in the opposite direction than traditional deterrence research presumes".[114]

1-069 Despite the Ministry of Justice's own discouraging statistics and research such as that conducted in the Netherlands, successive governments have remained doggedly committed to increasing punishments as a means of deterring reoffending. They argue that what is needed is an even more severe penalty than that merited by the present offence at an early stage in D's criminal career to have a strong deterrent effect. Indeed, this kind of approach was encapsulated in the much discussed "short, sharp shock" that imposed detention centre orders on young offenders under the Criminal Justice Act 1982.[115] More recently, we have observed a prominent return to the advocation of tough sentences to prevent crime by the Conservative Party. In their 2019 election manifesto, they outlined "tougher sentencing for criminals", including an end to automatic halfway release from prison for serious crimes, life imprisonment without parole for child murderers and doubling the maximum sentence for assaulting workers in emergency services.[116] In an updated plan in 2022 by the Justice Secretary, the Government has committed to creating 20,000 more prison spaces by 2025.[117] Even if research established (and

---

110 N. Walker and N. Padfield, *Sentencing: Theory, Practice and Law*, 2nd edn (Oxford: OUP, 1996), pp.79–95.

111 Ministry of Justice, *Proven reoffending statistics quarterly bulletin, July 2021 to September 2021* (2023).

112 Ministry of Justice, *Proven reoffending statistics quarterly bulletin, July 2021 to September 2021* (2023), p.15.

113 E.A.C. Raaijmakers, J.W. de Keijser, P. Nieuwbeerta and A.J.E. Dirkzwager "Why longer prison terms fail to serve a specific deterrent effect: an empirical assessment on the remembered severity of imprisonment" (2017) 23 *Psychology, Crime & Law* 32.

114 Raaijmakers, de Keijser, Nieuwbeerta and Dirkzwager "Why longer prison terms fail to serve a specific deterrent effect: an empirical assessment on the remembered severity of imprisonment" (2017) 23 *Psychology, Crime & Law* 32, 49. This conclusion is also supported by a recent review of the evidence published by the Sentencing Council which found that "there is evidence that sentence enhancements (i.e. increases in sentence severity) for those with prior records do not appear to produce a deterrent effect in terms of reductions in rates of reoffending". J. Gormley, M. Hamilton and I. Belton, *The Effectiveness of Sentencing Options on Reoffending* (Sentencing Council, 2022), p.26.

115 Abolished by the Criminal Justice Act 1988 s.123.

116 Conservatives, *Get Brexit Done Unleash Britain's Potential: The Conservative and Unionist Party Manifesto 2019* (2019).

117 Brendon Lewis Speech, "Our plan for the justice system and all those who work in it" (2022) Conservative Party Conference 2022.

almost all indications are to the contrary[118]) that such measures were more effective in preventing recidivism, there is the problem of whether it is *just* to impose a more severe punishment than that merited by the offence (discussed further below).

2. General deterrence

Under this theory, it is the threat of punishment that deters people from committing crimes. At the legislative level, Parliament lays down penalties to threaten those who might contemplate crime. At the sentencing level, offenders are punished in order that others will be discouraged from committing crimes; this punishment is held up as an example of what will happen if others engage in similar activities. Jeremy Bentham was a key proponent of general deterrence.[119] Bentham started from the position that all punishment is pain and as such should be avoided. However, punishment should be used where it can produce a greater benefit to society than the pain that such punishment will inflict on the individual offender. This costs benefits analysis is based on the idea of "utility". Utility is understood as the minimisation of pain and suffering and the maximisation of pleasure. Bentham argued that in calculating the costs and benefits of our actions we assess a number of factors including the intensity of pain and pleasure but also the certainty or uncertainty of the benefit/pain occurring. Based upon this, Bentham argued that we can devise social policies which maximise pleasure and minimise pain in society. When this theory is applied to punishment we see punishment is only justified by the good consequences that will be returned to society. Yet to a large extent, the theory of general deterrence simply assumes that people will be deterred from committing crime by the threat of a certain level of punishment. Is this assumption justifiable? **1-070**

J. Andenaes, "The General Preventive Effects of Punishment" (1966) 114 U. Pa. L. Rev. 949, 960–970:

"Reports on conditions of disorganisation following wars, revolution or mutinies provide ample documentation as to how lawlessness may flourish when the probability of detection, apprehension and conviction is low. In these situations, however, many factors work together. The most clear cut examples of the importance of the risk of detection itself are provided by cases in which society functions normally but all policing activity is paralyzed by a police strike or a similar condition. For example, the following official report was made on lawlessness during a 1919 police strike, starting at midnight on July 31st, during which nearly half of the Liverpool policemen were out of service: 'In this district the strike was accompanied by threats, violence and intimidation on the part of lawless persons. Many assaults on the constables who remained on duty were committed. Owing to the sudden nature of the strike the authorities were afforded no opportunity to make adequate provision to cope with the position. Looting of shops commenced about 10pm on August 1st, and continued for some days. In all about 400 shops were looted. Military were requisitioned, special constables sworn in, and police brought from other centers.' (Mannheim, *Social Aspects of Crime in England Between the Wars*, 156–157 (1940).) **1-071**

118 This was the main reason for the abolition of detention centre orders (C. Emmins and G. Scanlan, *The Criminal Justice Act 1988* (New York: Hyperion Books, 1988), p.101).

119 J. Bentham, *An Introduction to the Principles of Morals and Legislation* (London: Pickering, 1823).

A somewhat similar situation occurred in Denmark when the German occupation forces arrested the entire police force in September 1944. During the remainder of the occupation period all policing was performed by an improvised unarmed watch corps, who were ineffective except in those instances when they were able to capture the criminal red handed. The general crime rate rose immediately, but there was a great discrepancy between the various types of crime. The number of cases of robbery increased generally in Copenhagen during the war, rising from ten per year in 1939 to ten per month in 1943. But after the Germans arrested the police in 1944, the figure rose to over a hundred per month and continued to rise. Larcenies reported to the insurance companies quickly increased tenfold or more. The fact that penalties were greatly increased for criminals who were caught and brought before the courts did not offset the fact that most crimes were going undetected. On the other hand, crimes like embezzlement and fraud, where the criminal is usually known if the crime itself is discovered, do not seem to have increased notably.

The involuntary experiments in Liverpool and Copenhagen showed a reduction in law obedience following a reduction of risks. Examples of the opposite are also reported—the number of crimes decreases as the hazards rise. Tarde mentions that the number of cases of poisoning decreased when research in chemistry and toxicology made it possible to discover with greater certainty the causes as well as the perpetrator of this type of crime. (Tarde, *Penal Philosophy* 476 (1912)). A decline in bank robberies and kidnappings in the United States is reported to have followed the enactment of federal legislation which increased the likelihood of punishment (Taft, *Criminology* 322, 361 (rev. ed. 1950))."

1–072 This belief that punishment can deter crime assumes that actors are rational beings who calculate the risks involved in their actions. They can calculate the chances of being apprehended and punished (taking into account the amount of punishment) and can weigh this against the benefits to them in committing the crime. What is important to note here is that punishment in and of itself may not always be enough to deter the rational offender, but rather it is the degree of risk that is attached to being caught, combined with the penalty which is then attached to the crime, which will ultimately determine whether someone chooses to offend. However, as various criminologists have pointed out, many offenders will not think "rationally" before taking such risks.

Paul Robinson and John M. Darley, "Does Criminal Law Deter? A Behavioural Science Investigation" (2004) 24 Oxford J. of Legal Studies 173, 179, 184, 185, 192–3:

1–073 "Available evidence suggests that potential offenders as a group are people who are less inclined to think at all about the consequences of their conduct or to guide their conduct accordingly. They often are risk-seekers, rather than risk-avoiders, and as a group are more impulsive than the average. Further, conduct decisions commonly are altered by alcohol and drug intake. In Anderson's sample, an astounding 66 per cent of those interviewed reported that 'recent drug use' contributed to the commission of the crime.

There are a number of other temporary states of mind that are likely to drive out rational considerations of punishment, such as desires for revenge or retaliation, and suddenly-induced rages or angers, the duration of which can extend from minutes to days. Other states of mind can be in place for longer durations and also can induce flawed reasoning. For instance, paranoia—feelings that others are immediate and overwhelming threats—is known to cycle over the course of months. When it is acute, it is likely that the degree of threat felt will override considerations of the deterrent weight of possible punishments. The grandiose component of manic-depression, which occurs when the manic-depressive cycles into the manic phase, can give the person experiencing it a feeling of incredible brilliance that is likely to cause him to underestimate the likelihood of the not-so-brilliant forces of law ever catching and convicting him.

Consider this picture of the effect of reduced probability of punishment in light of the known rates of arrest and conviction for various crimes. The overall average of conviction for criminal offences committed is 1.3 per cent . . .

We suspect that most citizens would be shocked at how low the punishment rates are, which suggests that the perception of detection rates tends to be higher than the rates actually are. Luckily for deterrence, people tend to overestimate the occurrence of rare events. This error is useful because it is the perceived rate of punishment rather than the actual rate that counts for deterrent effect. Probably the best summary is that the average person's perception of punishment rates is low, but at least higher than the reality.

But, and again, the group of persons who are the most likely offenders—those who have already committed an offence will account for the majority of future crimes—have a greater incentive than other people to learn the actual punishment rates. Thus, the career criminals—just the persons at whom we would wish to aim our deterrent threat of punishment—are the persons most likely to realize how low the punishment rates really are and, therefore, to perceive a lower chance of punishment than non-crime prone people.

. . . The net effect is that most criminals do not think they will be caught and punished. In [one] study when asked about the risk of being caught, it was found that:

> '76 percent of active criminals and 89 percent of the most violent criminals either perceive no risk of apprehension or have no thought about the likely punishments for their crimes.'

[With regard to the amount of punishment affecting deterrence]: Potential offenders may come from social groups in which the threat of stigma for being convicted as a felon may not be as high as it is for other persons. In fact, for many offenders, conviction and imprisonment may lead to very little if any loss of status and respect in the communities within which they function. Similarly, it is likely that potential offenders as a group live a more deprived existence than the average person, and thus the threat of prison, with its provision for meals and shelter, is not so worse an alternative to their current existence as it would be for the more well-to-do person.

Our ultimate conclusion, which we think the evidence strongly supports, is that the threat of punishment amount under current practices is at best unpredictable and at worst unreliable in modulating the threatened amount of punishment."

1-074 Research into the behaviour of criminals supports many of the points made in the preceding extract. For example, Gill's research, based on interviews with commercial robbers, concluded that few of them thought there was a high chance of being caught. The less organised and amateurish robbers did not plan their crimes, acted impulsively and gave no thought to being caught or to the consequences of their actions. On the other hand, the more organised and professional robbers planned to minimise the risks and concluded there was a low chance of apprehension.[120] Wright and Decker's American research into burglary found that most burglars in their sample perceived themselves, when committing the offence, to be "in a situation of immediate need" and "consciously refused to dwell on the possibility of getting caught".[121] Similar English research confirms that most burglars are not rational calculators but act on the spur-of-the-moment.[122]

Research into the effectiveness of "additional" punishment as a deterrent also provides little support to advocates of deterrence theory. A recent review of empirical evidence commissioned by the Sentencing Council found that "the evidence does not suggest that using more severe sentences (particularly sentences of immediate imprisonment over other disposals) has significant deterrent effects on the person sentenced or the general population".[123] Ashworth outlies four major complications affecting marginal deterrence.

A. Ashworth, "The common sense and complications of general deterrent sentencing" [2019] Crim. L.R. 564, 569–573.

1-075 "First, deterrence works through the mind, through the operation of fear of the increased penalty. So it is the potential offender's perceptions that assume importance here. For example, if the penalty for an offence has been increased but the potential offender is unaware of this increase, it follows that that person's decision not to go ahead with the commission of the offence cannot be ascribed to the (marginal) deterrent effect of the increased penalty. This is the first of various subjective elements in the concept of deterrence, elements that vary according to the perceptions, the personal circumstances and the social situation of the potential offender. Thus, in policy terms, increases in sentence levels must be well publicised among those likely to consider committing the offence, if those increases are to have the opportunity to influence the minds of potential offenders. There is evidence that some offenders are typically unaware of, or mistaken as to, the level of probable sentences for the offence . . .

Second, even if the potential offender is aware of the deterrent sentence, the hydraulic relationship ['sentences up, crimes down'] between deterrent sentences and reduced crime rates may be thwarted by a low risk of detection. Once again, it is a question of perception: so, if the potential offender believes that there is a low risk of being caught, he or she may go ahead and commit the crime despite knowing of the enhanced penalty that will be imposed in the (believed to be unlikely) event of conviction. However, if the potential offender believes that there is an enhanced risk of

120 M. Gill, *Commercial Robbery* (London: Blackstone Press, 2000), p.106.
121 P.T. Wright and S.H. Decker, *Burglars on the Job: Streetlife and Residential Break-ins* (Northeastern, 1994), pp.61, 137.
122 T. Bennett and R. Wright, *Burglars on Burglary* (Aldershot: Gower, 1984).
123 Gormley, Hamilton and Belton, *The Effectiveness of Sentencing Options on Reoffending* (2022).

being caught, convicted and sentenced, that increases the probability of desistance. Thus, Durlauf and Nagin found evidence that:

> 'Increasing the visibility of the police by hiring more officers and by allocating existing officers in ways that heighten the perceived risk of apprehension consistently seem to have substantial marginal deterrent effects.'

. . . Third, a deterrent sentencing policy assumes that the potential offenders to whom it is addressed behave rationally . . . giving some thought to benefits and costs. The hydraulic model assumes that marginally greater severity which is not undermined by a perceived low risk of detection will lead to a reduced likelihood of offending, but that assumption is likely to be weaker with some potential offenders than with others. There may be conditions under which the severity of the probable sentence can have a marginal deterrent effect—for example, some (professional) robbers might desist from arming themselves with guns if there was a significant incremental penalty for carrying a firearm. This may be extrapolated to other forms of 'professional' offending and other behaviour that may involve planning, such as corporate offending. However, any such cost/benefit assessment must take account of the problem of thresholds—that some potential offenders may regard the increased penalty as insufficient to turn them away from their planned offending. By way of contrast, offending that is typically impulsive (e.g. many violent offences) or that involves people whose lifestyle includes taking alcohol or drugs will probably be an unpropitious subject for a marginal deterrent strategy . . .

Fourth, even if the probability of the enhanced sentence being imposed is thought to be high, and where this probability is not undermined by a believed lack of promptness in imposing that sentence, the hydraulic relationship may be weakened if the potential offender does not regard the legal penalty as the most important consequence. Correspondingly, the hydraulic relationship may be strengthened where the potential offender fears a loss of respect or social standing if convicted. Thus Nagin has argued that 'individuals who report higher stakes in conventionality are more deterred by perceived risk of exposure for law-breaking', whereas individuals whose informal bonds with non-criminal groups are weaker are likely to be less easily deterred. Similarly, Pratt and collaborators found that 'variables indicating the threat of non-legal sanctions were among the most robust of the deterrence theory predictors.' There may be some potential offenders who do not fear imprisonment, regarding it as a normal part of their lifestyle or even as a kind of badge of honour. . . Put starkly, general deterrence 'functions in relation to those who do not 'need' it. In relation to those who do 'need' it, it does not function'."

Even research into the use of the most severe of punishments—that of the death penalty—has found no reliable evidence that it reduces homicide rates.[124] Moreover, a major Cambridge-based analysis of research asserted that increasing sentence severity could actually have "possible counterproductive effects relating to reduced differential disincentives against the most serious crimes of violence" and **1–076**

124 R. Hood and C. Hoyle, *The Death Penalty: A World Wide Perspective* (Oxford: OUP, 2015).

could cause "destigmatisation of punishment if severe sanctions are very widely employed".[125] Ashworth writing in relation to knife crime concludes that:

> "... if the prevention of offending and re-offending is the goal, altering the sentencing system may be a less promising and less justifiable strategy than tackling knife crime as a social issue."[126]

(i) Moral objections to deterrence theory

1-077 In addition to the empirical objections to the effectiveness of punishment as a deterrent, there is the fundamental moral objection that deterrent sentencing involves using a person as a means to an end. Punishing people to deter others—rather than punishing them for what they have done—is not showing respect for their autonomy. If sentencing for deterrent reasons only, one becomes free to impose any sentence as long as it is felt to be an effective deterrent. In the past, this has led to the imposition of exemplary sentences. For example, exemplary sentences were imposed in the early 1970s to prevent the sudden increase of muggings of elderly people[127] and to contain football hooliganism in the late 1970s.[128] Enhanced sentences were also used for many of those convicted of offences during the 2011 London Riots in an attempt to deter future incidents of social unrest. In supporting the use of such sentences, Lord Judge CJ in *Blackshaw* stated:

> "Those who deliberately participate in disturbances of this magnitude, causing injury and damage and fear to even the most stout-hearted of citizens, and who individually commit further crimes during the course of the riots are committing aggravated crimes. They must be punished accordingly, and sentences should be designed to deter others from similar activity."[129]

However, over the past few decades there has been an increasing acceptance that such sentences are unjust:

> "When you punish a man *in terrorem*, make of him an 'example' to others, you are admittedly using him as a means to an end: someone else's end. This, in itself, would be a very wicked thing to do . . . Why, in Heaven's name, am I to be sacrificed to the good of society in this way?—unless, of course, I deserve it?"[130]

As a consequence of research findings suggesting the ineffectiveness of deterrence and because of these principled objections, in the late 1980s deterrence, as a purpose of punishment, began to fall out of favour. The White Paper preceding the Criminal Justice Act 1991 concluded that:

---

125 A. von Hirsch, *Criminal Deterrence and Sentence Severity* (Oxford: Hart Publishing, 1999), pp.41, 48.
126 A. Ashworth, "The common sense and complications of general deterrent sentencing" [2019] Crim. L.R. 564, 578.
127 e.g. *R. v Storey (Paul Edwin)* [1973] 1 W.L.R. 1045; (1973) 57 Cr. App. R. 840.
128 e.g. *R. v Motley (Gary)* (1978) 66 Cr. App. R. 274.
129 *R. v Blackshaw (Jordan Philip)* [2011] EWCA Crim 2312; [2012] 1 W.L.R. 1126 at [4].
130 C.S. Lewis, "The Humanitarian Theory of Punishment" (1953) *VI Res Judicatae* 224.

> "it is unrealistic to construct sentencing arrangements on the assumption that most offenders will weigh up the possibilities in advance and base their conduct on rational calculation."[131]

The 1991 Act followed this by outlawing exemplary sentences and, subject to exceptions, endorsing the concept of desert. However, since then much legislation,[132] debate and rhetoric[133] about sentencing has been based on deterrence. This culminated in the Criminal Justice Act 2003 s.142 (replaced by the Sentencing Act 2020 s.57) which expressly endorses deterrence as a one of the five purposes of punishment. During the 2000s, the proliferation of knife crime and the theft of lead both led the courts to impose longer sentences for the purposes of deterrence.[134] More recently maximum sentencing for causing death by driving offences have been implemented, increasing the maximum sentence for causing death by dangerous driving and by careless driving whilst under the influence of drink and drugs from 14 years to life imprisonment.[135] The Court of Appeal has previously warned that sentencing judges should refer to statistics to support their view that a particular crime is prevalent, justifying the imposition of a longer sentence in the hope that the trend can be reversed.[136] Whether this is applied in practice remains to be seen. **1–078**

Whatever the "evidence", successive governments have believed (or think the electorate believe) in the effectiveness of punishment as a deterrent. It is unfortunate that such thinking is not informed by the distinction, referred to above, between absolute deterrence (few doubt that punishment in general does have a broad deterrent effect for at least some crimes) and marginal deterrence where evidence that increasing the severity of punishments has an increased deterrent effect is noticeably lacking.

3. Educative deterrence **1–079**

Under the theory of general deterrence, a person who is contemplating committing a crime is deterred by the positive threat that they will suffer the same punishment as others have suffered. However, punishment can have a more profound subconscious effect on society. Over a period of time in the community, punishment of criminals builds up the habit of not breaking the law. It creates unconscious inhibitions against committing crimes and thus serves to educate the public as to the proper distinction between good and bad conduct. Every time someone is punished for theft, the public morality that theft is wrong is strengthened and our habit of not stealing is reinforced. If suddenly nobody were to be punished for theft and this state of affairs were to endure for a considerable period of time, our inhibitions against stealing and our moral view that theft was wrong would start breaking down. The

---

131 *Crime, Justice and Protecting the Public* (1990) Cmnd.965, para.2.8.

132 e.g. the Crime (Sentences) Act 1997 containing minimum sentences for burglars and drug-dealers upon a third conviction (since repealed by the Powers of Criminal Courts (Sentencing) Act 2000).

133 D.M. Kahan, "The Secret Ambition of Deterrence" (1999) 113 Harv. L. Rev. 413 argues that in general "the real value of deterrence—its secret ambition—is to quiet illiberal conflict between contending cultural styles and moral outlooks"; the rhetoric of deterrence is a liberal ploy to defuse or suppress contentious moral issues; it is a cover-up: "the real significance of liberal theory [relating to deterrence] lies not in what it says but in what it stops us from saying", 415–416.

134 *R. v Lanham (Stephen)* [2008] EWCA Crim 2450; [2009] 1 Cr. App. R. (S.) 105; *R. v Povey (Clive Richard)* [2008] EWCA Crim 1261; [2009] 1 Cr. App. R. (S.) 42.

135 Police, Crime, Sentencing and Courts Act 2022 ss.86 and 87. See further analysis, S. Kyd, "Dangerous driving, deterrence, disqualification and a missed opportunity to address destructive behaviour: the new sentencing guidelines for motoring offences" [2024] Crim. L.R. 4.

136 *Povey* [2009] 1 Cr. App. R. (S.) 42.

criminal law, and the punishment that flows from breaking it play an important role in supporting and shaping positive social mores. Take, for example, the banning of smoking in bars and restaurants in 2007 by the Health Act 2006. The ban quickly left smokers literally out in the cold, and within just a few years, the social acceptability of smoking in public plummeted. Platt's longitudinal qualitative review of the impact of the legislation found that "there were shifts in attitudes from initial resentment to acceptance of the changes [to] a growing perception of the personal, health and environmental benefits of smoke free".[137]

The introduction of hate crime offences (examined later in Ch.7) in the latter part of the 20th century can also be said to be an attempt to change attitudes through targeted criminalisation; in this case, challenging pervasive identity-based prejudices that lead to violence and abuse. These new aggravated offences carry enhanced penalties where an offender is motivated, or where they demonstrate, racial or religious hostility during the commission of an offence. Over a period of time, the acceptability of public displays of such hostilities, it is argued, will be reduced as the unacceptability of such behaviours begins to penetrate the public conscience.[138] If this is true, the role of deterrence may in fact prove to be a powerful means of social control.

A.E. Bottoms, "Morality, Crime, Compliance and Public Policy" in A.E. Bottoms and M. Tonry, Ideology, Crime and Criminal Justice (2002), p.25:

1-080 "[I]n a more differentiated society rather than prohibitions arising out of positive morality, they may on occasion not reflect positive morality at all, but rather may be imposed by those in power in the hope of securing obedience through deterrent calculation. Even in such a case, however, sometimes (though not always) the fact of the prohibition, and citizens' evolving response to it, can influence the development of a new strand of positive morality. Something very like this seems to have occurred in relation to drinking and driving: in Britain there is now substantially greater moral disapproval of such behaviour than was the case thirty or so years ago when it was first made a criminal offence."[139]

J. Andenaes, "General Prevention" (1952) 43 J. Crim. L., C. & P.S. 176, 179–181:

1-081 "Later theory puts much stress on the ability of penal law to arouse or strengthen inhibitions of another sort. In Swedish discussion the *moralising*—in other words the *educational*—function has been greatly stressed. The idea is that punishment as a concrete expression of society's disapproval of an act helps to form and to strengthen the public's moral code and thereby creates conscious

---

137 S. Platt, A. Amos, C. Godfrey, C. Martin, D. Ritchie, M. White, K. Hargreaves and G. Highet, *Evaluation of smoke free England: a longitudinal, qualitative study* (2009) Report to the Department of Health. Public Health Research Consortium, p.8.

138 M. Walters, "Conceptualizing 'hostility' for hate crime law: minding 'the minutiae' when interpreting section 28(1)(a) of the Crime and Disorder Act 1998" (2014) 34(1) O.J.L.S 47. Though note that huge spikes in recorded hate crimes are often observed after "trigger events", such as the EU Referendum in June 2016.

139 See, however, the research cited in P. Robinson and J. Darley, "Does Criminal Law Deter? A Behavioural Science Investigation" (2004) 24 O.J.L.S. 177 indicating that the deterrent effect of many drink/driving laws has been temporary (199).

> and unconscious inhibitions against committing crime. Unconscious inhibitions against committing forbidden acts can also be aroused without appealing to the individual's concepts of morality. Purely as a matter of habit, with fear, respect for authority or social imitation as connecting links, it is possible to induce favourable attitudes toward this or that action and unfavourable attitudes toward another action."

Educative deterrence should be contrasted with the retributive theory of denunciation. The theories are similar in that punishment, under both theories, is performing a symbolic, expressive function—but there is an important distinction. The idea of denunciation, as with all retributive theories, is not concerned with the effects of punishment. It is not a forward-looking theory aimed at preventing crime. Rather, it is concerned with the relation of the punishment to the past event, the crime. It is concerned that there be a relationship between the gravity of the offence and the degree of censure or denunciation. The educative theory, on the other hand, is exclusively forward looking, as are all deterrent theories. Punishment is used as a means of preventing crime and maintaining obedience to the law. **1-082**

The educative theory rests upon an important premise, namely, that public morality and inhibitions against committing crimes are created and/or preserved by the regular punishment of others. This is a difficult premise to test although some research suggests a clear link between criminality and moral assessments of behaviour. For instance, Kaufmann asked a group of subjects to evaluate the morality of certain behaviour (failing to rescue a drowning man). Some subjects were told that this behaviour was criminal; others were told that there was no duty to rescue. The former group judged the inaction more harshly than the latter group.[140] Similarly, Walker and Marsh discovered that subjects stated that their disapproval of not wearing a seat-belt would increase when this became an offence.[141] Clearly most laws are designed to have some symbolic or expressive function. The point asserted here is that *punishment* (or at least the real possibility thereof) pursuant to criminal liability is what gives the criminal law its coercive authority.[142]

C. INCAPACITATION

There are two types of incapacitation: collective and selective. Collective incapacitation refers to a strategy of incapacitating large numbers of "would be" offenders in order to decrease crime levels overall. Selective incapacitation aims to identify and incapacitate certain types of offenders who are most likely to re-offend. This approach entails determining which offenders are the most dangerous. This is normally done by looking at a person's past behaviours and predicting whether they are likely to re-offend. In the case of *Sargent*,[143] Lawton LJ acknowledged: **1-083**

---

140 H. Kaufmann, "Legality and Harmfulness of a Bystander's Failure to Intervene as Determinants of Moral Judgment" in J.R. Macaulay and L. Berkowitz (eds), *Altruism and Helping Behaviour: Social Psychological Studies of Some Antecedents and Consequences* (New York: New York Academic Press, 1970).

141 N. Walker and C. Marsh, "Do Sentences Affect Public Disapproval?" (1984) 24 Brit. J. Criminol. 27.

142 Contra Walker and Marsh, "Do Sentences Affect Public Disapproval?" (1984) 24 Brit. J. Criminol. 27 who concluded that public disapproval of conduct was not influenced by *severity* of punishment.

143 *R. v Sargeant (James Henry)* (1974) 60 Cr. App. R. 74; [1975] Crim. L.R. 173 CA.

"... that there are some offenders for whom neither deterrence nor rehabilitation works. They will go on committing crimes as long as they are able to do so. In those cases the only protection which the public has is that such persons should be locked up for a long period."

Protective sentencing aims to render the criminal incapable of committing more crimes. The particular punishment chosen at one stage in our penal history might have been the death penalty, severance of limbs or deportation to a colony. Today it is likely to be imprisonment, although other community measures such as a curfew order or disqualification from driving can also be viewed as incapacitative sentences. In countries such as France, Sweden, Denmark and Poland, and in some states in the US, chemical castration can be used to incapacitate sex offenders, although some of these jurisdictions require the offender to consent to the procedure.[144] The real hallmark of an incapacitative sentence, however, is that it is likely to be longer or more severe than that which would normally be imposed for the offence.

There is much public support for the view that there are cases where society needs protection[145] and that it is permissible to incarcerate dangerous offenders who pose a threat to society for longer than non-dangerous offenders committing the same offence. Furthermore, research has revealed that a significant amount of crime is being committed by relatively few persons, for example those on bail, and so "a policy of selective incapacitation aimed at such 'career criminals' promises a high yield of crime prevention for a low investment of resources".[146]

There are, however, significant objections to incapacitative sentencing. First, such a practice can only be justified (if at all) if predictions of dangerousness are accurate.

Andrew von Hirsch, "Prediction of Criminal Conduct and Preventive Confinement of Convicted Persons" (1972) 21 Buffalo L. Rev. 717, 735–736:

1-084 "What makes violence so particularly difficult to predict is not merely its rarity, but its situational quality. Deterministic models to the contrary notwithstanding, violence generally is not a quality which inheres in certain 'dangerous' individuals: it is an occurrence which may erupt—or may not—in certain crisis situations. Whether it does erupt, whether it is reported, whether the perpetrator is apprehended and punished depends upon a wide variety of fortuitous circumstances, largely beyond the actor's control. Not only the actor's proclivities, but the decisions of other individuals—the victim, the bystanders, the police, the magistrate—may determine whether an act of violence occurs and whether it comes to be included in the criminal statistics."

1-085 The substantial literature that has developed on the subject of prediction is in broad agreement that for every three persons predicted to commit violent offences, only one will do so. It has become common

144 A. Chrisafis, "Killing puts 'castration' on French agenda" *The Guardian*, 3 September 2009.

145 J.M. Walker and N. Hough, *Public Attitudes to Sentencing: Surveys From Five Countries* (Aldershot: Gower, 1988), pp.178–179.

146 R.A. Duff and D. Garland, *A Reader on Punishment* (Oxford: OUP, 1994), p.239.

to refer to those who do not reoffend as "false positives" and for most commentators this is taken to mean that a false prediction of dangerousness was made. However, that view has been challenged by Norval Morris. He argues that if an unexploded bomb were found in the early post-war days in London and then safely defused no-one would talk about it subsequently as if it had not been dangerous simply because it had not caused any damage. He thinks there is no difference in principle between the analogy of the bomb and dangerous people: "In sum, that the person predicted as dangerous does no future injury does not mean that the classification was erroneous."[147]

Most other commentators, however, have greater difficulty justifying the continued incarceration of offenders when predictions are so inaccurate and when many of the most useful predictors are controversial. Beyond the obvious factors of number and type of previous convictions, other considerations might be indicative of future offending. However, to include predictors such as sex, race, age, intelligence, educational attainments, etc would be unacceptable as "factors which are beyond the offender's control and not logically related to culpability".[148] **1–086**

The second central objection to incapacitative sentences is that, even if predictions were accurate, it is wrong in principle to punish someone for what they might do in the future. Such a practice amounts to a radical departure from the constraints of just deserts under which punishment should be proportionate to the seriousness of the current offence committed.

ANDREW VON HIRSCH, PAST OR FUTURE CRIMES (1985), P.11:

"Advocates of the desert model opposed the use of individual prediction in sentencing as a matter of principle, not merely because of such forecasts' tendency to error. Their objection to predictive sentencing was simply that it led to undeserved punishments and would do so even if the false-positive rate could be reduced. The use of predictions, accurate or not, meant that those identified as future recidivists would be treated more severely than those not so identified, not because of differences in the blameworthiness of their past conduct, but because of crimes they supposedly would commit in future. It was felt that punishment, as a blaming institution, was warranted only for past culpable choices and could not justly be levied for future conduct. Unless the person actually made the wrongful choice he was predicted to make, he ought not to be condemned for that choice—and hence should not suffer punishment for it." **1–087**

Most commonly, predictions of dangerousness are based on previous convictions (along, often, with psychiatric reports). The objection to this is that the offender has already been punished for the past crimes and so this amounts to punishing them again for these offences. **1–088**

147 N. Morris, "On 'Dangerousness' in the Judicial Process" (1982) Record of Assn of the Bar of the City of New York 102, 115.

148 M. Tonry, "Prediction and Classification: Legal and Ethical Issues" in D.M. Gottfredson and M. Tonry (eds), *Prediction and Classification: Criminal Justice Decision Making* (Chicago: University of Chicago Press Journals, 1987), p.397.

For some, the need to protect the public outweighs such objections. The Floud Report on Dangerous Offenders[149] took it "as axiomatic that the public is entitled to the protection of a special sentence"[150] against grave harm and recommended a special sentencing framework of sentencing for dangerous offenders. This was done by a utilitarian balancing of risks argument: the harm done to the convicted offender in being punished longer than is deserved is outweighed by the prospect of harm done to the public should the offender be released at an earlier time. In short, where there is a risk of grave harm to potential Vs, the rights of such Vs should prevail over the rights of a convicted offender.

The Sentencing Act 2020 provides specific powers to the courts to sentence for the purpose of "the protection of the public".[151] Sections 306–308 set out the key provisions for sentencing "dangerous offenders". These provisions depend on a risk assessment that the offender is dangerous. The court must be of the opinion that there is a "significant risk to members of the public of serious harm occasioned by the commission by him of further specified offences".[152] In making that assessment, the court must take into account the nature and circumstances of the offence, or any other offence the offender has been convicted of, any pattern of behaviour which these offences form part of, and any other information about the offender which is before the court.[153] In its recent White Paper, *A Smarter Approach to Sentencing,* the Government reiterated its commitment to incapacitating "dangerous offenders" by ensuring that serious sexual and violent offenders spend a longer proportion of their sentence in prison and abolishing the automatic halfway release for certain serious offenders.[154]

1-089 Prior to 2012, the courts could also impose a sentence of imprisonment based on the grounds of public protection (commonly referred to as IPPs).[155] These indeterminate sentences included a set minimum term after which release depended on the Parole Board's judgement that it was safe to release the offender. The indefinite nature of IPPs meant that they were highly controversial instruments of the law and after much resistance from human rights advocates they were subsequently repealed by the Legal Aid, Sentencing and Punishment of Offenders Act 2012.[156] However the Act is not retrospective, meaning that thousands of prisoners already serving IPPs continue to be imprisoned, or released on licence, for an indefinite period of time. In *Roberts,*[157] 13 prisoners appealed to the Court of Appeal on the basis that the court should reconsider the assessments made by sentencing judges (made between 2005–2008) in light of changes to the law and that a term of imprisonment had been reached[158] that was so excessive and disproportionate that it amounted to inhumane treatment under the Convention for the Protection of Human Rights and Fundamental Freedoms art.3, or that it amounted to arbitrary detention under art.5. The Court of Appeal dismissed the appeal noting that rectification of any injustice in the operation of the appellants' sentences was a matter for the Parole Board, and any

149 J. Floud and W. Young, *Dangerousness and Criminal Justice* (London: Heineman, 1981).
150 J. Floud, "Dangerousness and Criminal Justice" (1982) 22 Brit. J. Criminol. 213, 220.
151 Sentencing Act 2020 s.57(2)(d).
152 Sentencing Act 2020 s.308.
153 Sentencing Act 2020 s.308(2).
154 Enacted under the Release of Prisoners (Alteration of Relevant Proportion of Sentence) Order 2020 (SI 2020/158).
155 Previously prescribed under the Criminal Justice Act 2003 s.225(3).
156 Legal Aid, Sentencing and Punishment of Offenders Act 2012 (c.10) Pt 3 (c.5) s.123(a).
157 *R. v Roberts (Mark)* [2016] EWCA Crim 71; [2016] 2 Cr. App. R. (S.) 14.
158 Each applicant had reached the original minimum term that had been set.

further changes to the regime of IPPs to rectify any unfairness (especially in relation to the scope for rehabilitation) was a matter for Parliament to consider.

Some minor reform of the law was recently enacted as part the Police, Crime, Sentencing and Courts Act 2022. In a speech at the Committee Stage of the Bill in the House of Lords, the previous Labour Home Secretary David Blunkett gave his own *mea culpa,* admitting the original intention for the IPPs to provide both safety for the public and rehabilitation of offenders had gone "badly wrong".[159] Former Supreme Court Justice Lord Brown also repeated his description of the IPP sentence as "the greatest single stain on the justice system".[160] The legislation now provides that once a prisoner has served their tariff and released on licence they will automatically be referred to the Parole Board for a decision on termination of the licence upon expiration of the qualifying period. If denied, offenders will be automatically referred every 12 months.[161]

D. REHABILITATION

Punishment with the aim of reforming or rehabilitating the offender has constituted one of the most ambitious developments in penal theory. The aim is to secure conformity, not through threat (which is the more limited object of deterrence) but through some inner positive motivation on the part of the individual. The process has been described as "improving [the offender's] . . . character so that he is less often inclined to commit offences again even when he can do so without fear of the penalty".[162] The source of the change in motivation or improvement in behaviour has been variously described but remains one of the ambiguities of the concept of reform. **1–090**

The origins of the rehabilitative ideal are inextricably linked with the humanitarian movement for prison reform and many who defend the ideal stress the importance of offender welfare. Advocates of rehabilitation asserted that a more humane response to criminality would help to soften strict "law and order" attitudes.[163] The great penal reformers of the 18th century, Beccaria, Bentham, Eden and Romilly, all supported a system of punishment which combined deterrent with rehabilitative features. It was their belief, however, that rehabilitation could come from punishment itself—by, for example, a period of solitude which would induce remorse, repentance and, in turn, reform. Indeed, the first penitentiary in the US was created by the Quakers in Philadelphia in 1793 in order that prisoners could pay "penance" for their sins and thereby become "cleansed".[164] The object was to make offenders "better persons" capable of being reintegrated into society (rather than simply purging their sins and thereby repaying their debt to society, which is the more limited object of expiation). When, towards the end of the 19th century, the aim of rehabilitation became (with deterrence) part of official penal policy in this country, there was more than an element of this thinking present in the measures taken.

---

159 Lord Blunkett, Police, Crime, Sentencing and Courts Bill, Committee Stage, Hansard, HoL, Vol.816 col.29 (15 November 2021).

160 Lord Brown of Eaton-under-Heywood, Police, Crime, Sentencing and Courts Bill, Committee Stage, Hansard, HoL, Vol.816 col.33 (15 November 2021).

161 Police, Crime, Sentencing and Courts Act 2022 s.138.

162 N. Walker, "Punishing, Denouncing or Reducing Crime" in P.R. Glazebrook (ed), *Reshaping the Criminal Law* (London: Stevens, 1978), p.393.

163 See, e.g. F.T. Cullen and K.E. Gilbert, *Reaffirming Rehabilitation* (Cincinnati: Anderson Publishing Co, 1982).

164 See C. Walker, *Crime and Punishment in Great Britain* (Edinburgh: Edinburgh University Press, 1968), pp.134–138; and N. Morris, *The Future of Imprisonment* (Chicago: University of Chicago Press, 1974).

Whilst it soon became clear that, far from making "better individuals", solitude had a severely damaging impact upon offenders, the belief that reform should be a concomitant of punishment continued to hold sway for the first half of the 20th century at least. The moral or religious exhortations to improve were gradually replaced by the behavioural sciences and medicine. In the post-war period, criminality came to be viewed as an illness that was caused by psychiatric, psychological and social conditions. As more was learned about the antecedents of human conduct it was hoped that therapeutic measures could be designed which would reform the offender's behaviour.

H. Weihofen, "Retribution is Obsolete," National Probation and Parole Association News, XXXIX (1960) 1, 4:

1–091 "Half a century ago, Winston Churchill said, in the House of Commons:

> 'The mood and temper of the public with regard to the treatment of crime and criminals is one of the most unfailing tests of the civilisation of any country. A calm, dispassionate recognition of the rights of the accused, and even of the convicted criminal against the State—a constant heart searching by all charged with the duty of punishment—a desire and eagerness to rehabilitate in the world of industry those who have paid their due in the hard coinage of punishment: tireless efforts towards the discovery of curative and regenerative processes: unfailing faith that there is a treasure, if you can only find it, in the heart of every man. These are the symbols which, in the treatment of crime and criminals mark and measure the stored-up strength of a nation.'

Yes; and I would add, these are the sign and proof of its morality."

1–092 Rehabilitative sentencing involves a focus on the individual offender's needs ensuring that the sentence, or programme within a sentence, will help change the offender's behaviour, attitude and responses. A number of non-custodial measures were introduced in the 1960s and 1970s, such as community service orders, about which rehabilitative claims were made—although the introduction of such measures was perhaps more influenced by a desire to reduce the prison population.

However, despite the attractiveness of the idea of rehabilitating offenders so that they would not wish to reoffend, the 1970s saw a major decline in the rehabilitative ideal. As can be seen from the following extracts, criticism has taken many forms. The gist of the case against the rehabilitative ideal is as follows. First, it is highly interventionist and paternalistic, ultimately giving the State the power to try to alter the character and personality of the offender. Apart from raising images of a "Clockwork Orange" society and presenting grave human rights concerns, it also means that judges, who are trained in law and not psychiatry, are not the most appropriate persons to carry out the task of sentencing. This would be best left to "experts" (psychiatrists, etc). Such ideas were condemned as removing the requirement of justice from sentencing.

The second casualty of the rehabilitative ideal is proportionality. Instead of looking to the past—to the offence committed—the sentencer is only concerned with the future needs of the offender. The sentence should be chosen which has the best chance of bringing about the desired change; thus, the principle of treating like cases in a like manner has little part to play. Proportionality links punishment to the seriousness of the offence whereas under the rehabilitative ideal there are few like cases. There ought, in theory at least, to be complete individualisation of sentences—the sentences should depend, not on the offence, but on the offender. This, of course, inevitably leads to widespread sentencing disparity which breaches a fundamental principle of justice that people be accorded equal treatment before the law. It also leads in some cases to excessively long sentences being passed to allow time for rehabilitation.[165]

Finally, research began to question whether rehabilitative programmes actually work. In an influential article in 1974, Martinson concluded that "with few and isolated exceptions, the rehabilitative efforts that have been reported so far have had no appreciable effect on recidivism".[166] Initially such attacks were deflected by the argument that the criminal justice system was not truly committed to rehabilitation; often it was sacrificed completely to other competing ideals (such as deterrence), or that appropriate means had yet to be found to have the desired impact upon D. **1-093**

Whether rehabilitation has been successful is normally measured by studies of recidivism, few of which lent much support to the idea that rehabilitation works for the majority of offenders. However, there were some studies concentrating on treatment strategies for specific categories of offenders which revealed some success and, indeed, Martinson wrote an article in 1979 in which he partially recanted on his earlier views.[167] Nevertheless, the notion that "nothing works" had entered the psyche of penologists and that, coupled with ethical concerns about the treatment model, led to a demand that punishment be more firmly linked to just deserts.

A.E. Bottoms, "An Introduction to 'The Coming Crisis'" in A.E. Bottoms and R.H. Preston, The Coming Penal Crisis (1980), pp.1–3:

"First, and the dominant factor in much current penal consideration, comes *the collapse of the rehabilitative ideal* . . . A succession of negative research reports has—with a few exceptions which do not seriously disturb the conclusion—suggested that different types of treatment make little or no difference to the subsequent reconviction rates of offenders . . . As the Serota Report (ACPS 1977) succinctly put it: **1-094**

> 'A steadily accumulating volume of research has shown that, if reconviction rates are used to measure the success or failure of sentencing policy, there is virtually nothing to choose between different lengths of custodial sentence, different types of institutional regime, and even between custodial and non-custodial treatment; (para.8).'

165 R. Cross, *Punishment, Prison and the Public* (London: Stevens, 1971).

166 R. Martinson, "What Works?" (1974) *Public Interest* 35. Martinson's article has been misquoted as stating that "nothing works". See also, D. Lipton, R. Martinson and J. Wilks, *The Effectiveness of Correctional Treatment* (New York: Praeger, 1975).

167 R. Martinson, "New Findings, New Views: A Note of Caution Regarding Sentencing Reform" (1979) 7 Hofstra L. Rev. 243.

But the objections to the treatment (or rehabilitation) ethic have not been solely based on empirical demonstrations of lack of efficacy. Strong theoretical objections have also been raised, perhaps most influentially in the American Friends Service Committee's (1971) *Struggle for Justice*, which argued that there was:

> 'compelling evidence that the individualised-treatment model, the ideal towards which reformers have been urging us for at least a century, is theoretically faulty, systematically discriminatory in application, and inconsistent with some of our most basic concepts of justice (p.12).'

What lies behind these claims?

(i) *'Theoretically faulty'*—because, it can be claimed, the treatment model implies that criminal behaviour has its roots in the deficiencies of the individual and his upbringing, and that if these are remedied, the crime rate will be cut; but this medical analogy is inappropriate, and crime is far more a result of the overall organization of society than of the deficiencies of the individual.

(ii) *'Systematically discriminatory'*—because the treatment model typically takes more severe coercive action in cases of 'unsatisfactory' home circumstances or 'dubious' moral background; but these judgments are made by middle-class workers who unwittingly but systematically discriminate against the poor and the disadvantaged, and in favour of the 'good' homes of the privileged.

(iii) *'Inconsistent with justice'*—because judgments involving the liberty of the individual are made (in the name of 'casework' or whatever) on the basis of extremely impressionistic evidence which is usually not revealed to the offender, and which he cannot therefore challenge; and the result may be, for example, that some will serve long sentences for trivial crimes because their 'attitudes have not improved,' while others convicted of serious crime but who have allegedly 'responded' are let out.

Underneath criticisms like these, it will be noted, lies a fundamental conviction by the critics as to the essentially *coercive* nature of the rehabilitative ideal . . . Many adherents of the ideal blinded themselves as to this coerciveness, in the false belief that benevolent intentions preclude a coercive result."

1–095 Von Hirsch has suggested that much of the true appeal of rehabilitative ideology lies in the fact that its advocates were able both to have their cake and eat it:

> "[I]t offered both therapy and restraint. One did not have to assume that all criminals were redeemable but could merely hope that some might be. Therapy could be tried on apparently amenable defendants, but always with a fail-safe: the offender who seemed unsuitable for, or unresponsive to, treatment could be separated from the community."[168]

168 A. von Hirsch, *Past or Future Crimes* (Manchester: Manchester University Press, 1987), p.5.

Despite these concerns, the rehabilitative ideal underwent something of a revival during the 1990s and 2000s with the catchphrase "what works" replacing the gloom of "nothing works" that had dominated the 1970s and 1980s.[169] Various programmes have been introduced for offenders who have received both custodial and non-custodial sentences. Apart from drug and alcohol programmes, there has been a growing implementation of cognitive-behavioural programmes: these focus on training offenders in decision-making and problem-solving, management of emotions (such as anger-management), negotiation skills and critical reasoning with offenders being encouraged to reflect on the consequences of their actions. Programmes also include various educational and life-skills courses, such as ones aimed at improving literacy and numeracy, designed to improve offenders' chances of employment. New statistical techniques of meta-analysis (aggregating findings from a number of smaller studies) have been employed and are revealing some success for these programmes particularly in relation to certain types of offenders.[170] For example, in the US, a number of different programmes of varying effectiveness are used in dealing with drug offenders.[171]

In the UK, since the 2000s, there has been a greater commitment to evidence-based initiatives and research. In 2001, the Halliday Report strongly endorsed the "What Works" strategies and programmes and estimated that they could lead to a reduction in the overall reconviction rate of 5 to 15% on the basis that "some things can work for some people, provided the right programmes are selected and implemented properly".[172] In July 2019, the Justice Secretary called for an "evidence-led, rehabilitative and humane agenda" to reducing reoffending, noting that new research by the Ministry of Justice had revealed statistics that estimated that if all current custodial sentences of less than six months were replaced with community alternatives there would be approximately 32,000 fewer offences committed per year.[173] **1–096**

The Sentencing Act 2020 expressly provides judges with powers to sentence offenders for the purpose of "reform and rehabilitation".[174] When a community sentence is passed, a range of "requirements" may be made as a community order: for example an unpaid work requirement, a drug rehabilitation requirement or a supervision requirement.[175] Such requirements must be tailored to ensure they are the "most suitable for the offender".[176] However, such rehabilitative sentences may only be imposed within the confines of the just deserts principle of proportionality on the basis that the offence is "serious enough to warrant such a sentence".[177] As such, it is incredibly difficult to determine what rehabilitative measures are most impactful in terms of increasing desistance and enhancing reintegration of offenders. Isolating good practice can be complicated when there are multiple social

169 See, generally, M. Tonry, "Obsolescence and Immanence in Penal Theory and Policy" (2005) 105 Col. L.R. 1233.

170 J. McGuire (ed), *What Works: Reducing Reoffending* (Chichester: John Wiley, 1995); P. Raynor, "Community Penalties, Probation, and Offender Management" in M. Maguire, R. Morgan and R. Reiner (eds), *The Oxford Handbook of Criminology*, 5th edn (Oxford: OUP, 2012); Parliamentary All-Party Penal Affairs Group, *Changing Offending Behaviour—Some Things Work* (1999).

171 See e.g. P.H. Robinson, *Distributive Principles of Criminal Law: Who Should be Punished and How Much?* (Oxford University Press, 2008).

172 Halliday Report (2001), paras 1.49, 1.50.

173 G. Eaton, and A. Mews, *The impact of short custodial sentences, community orders and suspended sentence orders on reoffending* (2019), Ministry of Justice.

174 Sentencing Act 2020 s.57(2)(c).

175 Sentencing Act 2020 s.201.

176 Sentencing Act 2020 s.208(3). Some of the requirements that can be imposed are not rehabilitative in their aim: for example, a prohibited activity requirement or a curfew requirement.

177 Sentencing Act 2020 s.204(2).

and justice factors affecting individual outcomes. In a recent review by the Sentencing Council of the impact of rehabilitative measures on offenders, they note that:

> "positive outcomes (such as desistance or reintegration) may be due to a combination of the rehabilitative effects (or despite criminogenic effects) of a sentence and other factors unrelated to the sentence. Unpacking these factors, which can interact in complex ways, to establish a causal connection is one of the key challenges for the sentencing evidence base."[178]

E. REPARATION

1–097 Though not strictly a theory of punishment, reparation is now of significant importance to any discussion about crime and punishment. This is because the use of reparation as a sentencing purpose, and more generally as a means of responding to offending, has proliferated within England and Wales over the past 20 years. Its growth is a reflection of a movement towards including Vs more centrally within the criminal justice process. Critics of conventional methods of criminal justice have argued that the system fails to respond adequately to the needs of Vs, offenders and local communities. Traditionally, the commission of an offence has been viewed as a violation against the State which, as representative of society, must punish the offender. Vs and other community members are often involved in the criminal process merely as sources of evidence, such as prosecution witnesses. Nils Christie has argued that the State has, in effect, appropriated conflict from those which are most affected by it.[179] Rather than those directly impacted by an offence helping to resolve the harms it causes, legal professionals are tasked with prosecuting offenders and administering what they consider to be "deserved" punishment.

Reparation, on the other hand, is concerned with the restoration of harms caused by crime. It is intrinsically linked to what is now commonly referred to as "restorative justice" (RJ), a contemporary theory and practice of justice which developed within Western jurisdictions from the late 1970s.[180] There is no single definition of RJ, but many advocates assert that it is based on the premise that crime is a wound to human relations which requires convalescence. This is best achieved by those most affected by the offence, including the V, the offender and other community members. Howard Zehr explains that:

> "Crime is a violation of people and relationships. It creates obligations to make things right. Justice involves the victim, the offence, and the community in a search for solutions which promote repair, reconciliation, and reassurance."[181]

---

178 Gormley, Hamilton and Belton, *The Effectiveness of Sentencing Options on Reoffending* (2022), p.15.

179 N. Christie, "Conflicts as Property" (1977) 17 Brit. J. Criminol. 1.

180 Christie, "Conflicts as Property" (1977) 17 Brit. J. Criminol. 1. Though it is often claimed that the RJ is rooted to ancient and/or indigenous practices of justice, see G. Maxwell and A. Morris, *Families, Victims and Culture: Youth Justice in New Zealand* (Wellington, Institute of Criminology, Victoria University of Wellington and Social Policy Agency, 1993).

181 H. Zehr, *Changing Lenses: A New Focus for Crime and Justice* (Scottdale, PA: Herald Press, 1990), p.181.

In order to restore harm the offender must first take responsibility for their actions. Part of the restorative process is the facilitation of inclusive dialogue which involves the (reintegrative) shaming of the offender. In some ways, this shaming process is similar to aims of retributive justice where the offender is personally censured for their conduct. However, unlike censure as stigmatic shaming, restorative justice aims to shame the behaviour as harmful and not the individual as a bad person. Braithwaite asserts:

> "Because shaming is a participatory form of social control, compared with formal sanctioning which is more professionalized than participatory, shaming builds consciences through citizens being instruments as well as targets of social control. Participation in expressions of abhorrence toward the criminal acts of others is part of what makes crime an abhorrent choice for us ourselves to make."[182]

Social condemnation is expressed both via the offender's active participation in a restorative intervention **1–098**
and through the disapproval of harmful conduct which is conveyed by the community participants in restorative meetings. The "stakeholders" of an offence (i.e. the V, offender and their community supporters) help the offender to understand the hurt and suffering that they have caused. Maxwell and Morris explain that such a process is likely to induce feelings of remorse which are the result of "empathy or understanding the effects on victims".[183] In turn it is argued that the offender is less likely to reoffend because they will have seen first-hand the direct impacts of their actions.

The use of restorative justice practices by other police services has quickly proliferated, with the vast majority of the 43 police services across England and Wales now using some form of restorative justice.[184] Restorative interventions are also used within the Youth Justice System[185] as well as for adults by probation services and within some prisons.[186] A popular measure used by practitioners within these parts of the justice system is the family group conference (conferencing). Conferencing involves the participation of Vs, offenders and their community supporters in a direct meeting that aims to find restoration for all involved. Conferences, like VOM, are facilitated by restorative practitioners who create safe spaces for participants to talk about their experiences of victimisation. The stakeholders decide together how the offender should repair any harms caused. Meetings often end with the parties signing a "reparation agreement" which outlines the undertakings which have been agreed.

The growing body of empirical evidence for RJ has provided positive findings on its effectiveness, **1–099**
particularly in relation to procedural justice. Studies conducted in Australia, England and the US, many of which have used control groups comparing restorative conferencing with the court process, have found higher satisfaction levels, perceptions of fairness and respectfulness, amongst Vs when

---

182 J. Braithwaite, *Crime, Shame and Reintegration* (Cambridge: CUP, 1989), p.80.

183 G. Maxwell and A. Morris, "The Role of Shame, Guilt, and Remorse in Restorative Justice Processes for Young People" in E. Weitekamp and H. Kerner (eds), *Restorative Justice: Theoretical Foundations* (Cullompton, Devon: Willan Publishing, 2002) pp.280–281.

184 Criminal Justice Joint Inspection (CJJI), *Facing Up to Offending: Use of Restorative Justice in the Criminal Justice System* (London: HMIC, HMI Probation, HMI Prisons and the HMCPSI, 2012), p.15.

185 e.g. Referral Orders, see the Powers of the Criminal Courts (Sentencing) Act 2000 ss.16–32 and Sch.1.

186 Referral Orders; see the Powers of the Criminal Courts (Sentencing) Act 2000 ss.16–32 and Sch.1.

compared to court.[187] Furthermore, the emotional traumas caused by crime, such as fear, anger and anxiety, have also been shown to reduce more significantly post RJ. Yet while these findings are encouraging, studies that have examined the effect of RJ on reoffending rates have produced findings that are far from unequivocal. For example, although some studies have shown reductions in reoffending rates for certain violent offences, other studies have found little to no difference in reoffending levels between court processes and RJ; with some research suggesting that RJ may even increase recidivism.[188]

The increased emphasis that is now placed on restoring harm (as against punishing offenders) has resulted in "reparation" becoming one of the five prescribed sentencing purposes as set out in the Sentencing Act 2020. This means that sentencers can consider the purpose of restoring harm when determining an appropriate penalty for every D that comes before them. In 2012, the Government outlined a vision that RJ should become accessible for Vs at "all stages of the criminal justice system".[189] Indeed, the Code of Practice for Victims of Crime now states that Vs are entitled to receive information on Restorative Justice from the police, including how they can take part.[190] Judges also have the power to defer sentence for a restorative meeting to take place between the V and offender before sentencing.[191]

It is yet unknown to what extent the use of RJ between conviction and sentencing will affect the sentencer's use of other theories of punishment. Indeed, many criminologists have questioned whether RJ can ever be used in conjunction with theories of punishment which focus on harming offenders as a means of resolving crime—it being considered antithetical to the restorative ideal. Others have, however, suggested that RJ can be reconciled with the current system of retribution. In particular, the act of repairing can in itself be conceived as a form of punishment due to the fact that it requires the offender to make amends while restricting their freedom to do as they please.

L. Zedner, "Reparation and Retribution: Are They Reconcilable?" (1994) 57 M.L.R. 228, 248–249 and 250:

1–100 "[I]t might be argued that both reparation and retribution derive their 'authority' from the offence itself and impose penalties according to the seriousness of the particular crime. Unlike the utilitarian aims of general deterrence or rehabilitation which import wider notions of societal good, both retribution and reparation exclude (or nearly exclude) consideration of factors beyond the particular offence. The offender's personal history, the social or economic causes of crime or the need to prevent future offending (all of which extend the limits of intrusion by the state under deterrent or rehabilitative theories) are here deemed irrelevant. As such, both retributive and reparative justice, it is said, impose strict constraints on the intrusion of the state into the lives of offenders. This apparent congruity is not, however, as close as it first seems. The seriousness of the

187 A. M. Nascimento, J. Andrade and A. de Castro Rodrigues, "The Psychological Impact of Restorative Justice Practices on Victims of Crimes—a Systematic Review" (2023) 24(3) Trauma, Violence & Abuse. 1929.

188 L. Iham, J. Blais, T. Rugge and E.A Schultheis, "The effectiveness of restorative justice programs: A meta-analysis of recidivism and other relevant outcomes" (2023) Criminology & Criminal Justice 0(0).

189 Ministry of Justice, *Restorative Justice Action Plan for the Criminal Justice System* (2012), p.5.

190 Ministry of Justice, *Code of Practice for Victims of Crime* (10th June, 2024).

191 Sentencing Act 2020 s.7.

> offence is set according to two different sets of criteria. Retribution demands punishment proportional primarily to the intent of the offender, whereas reparative justice derives its 'proportionality' from the harm inflicted on the victim. Whilst intent is generally focused on outcomes, and intent and harm may thus coincide, the two may point to very different levels of gravity. If reparation and retribution were to be wholly reconciled, then it would be necessary to devise a measure which integrated intent and harm in setting offence seriousness. A greater difficulty still is that, if reparative justice is to be more than a criminal analogue to civil damages, then it should go beyond the offence itself to enquire about its wider social costs and the means to making them good . . .
>
> The danger, however, is that the attempt to accommodate reparative justice to the rationale of punishment so perverts its underlying rationale as to strip it of much of its original appeal, not least its commitment to repairing ruptured social bonds. We are accustomed to seeing criminal justice as the repressive arm of the state, but might it not better be conceived as one end of a continuum of practices by which social order is maintained? Punishment has a very limited ability to control crime and, to the extent that it is disintegrative, it inflicts further damage on society. Given that the high profile 'law and order policies' . . . have done little to stem spiralling crime figures, perhaps it is time to explore the integrative potential of reparative justice on its own terms."

Whether RJ will become a main focus within criminal justice or simply a practice which operates at the periphery of the system may well depend on whether society accepts the use of reparation on its own merits. However, there are a number of difficulties that the theory and practice of RJ is yet to get to grips with which may limit its application as a mainstream response to criminality. One concern relates to the legitimacy of Vs and community members determining how an offender will repair the harms of crime. For instance, Ashworth questions whether the expansion of RJ practices will encroach upon the right of the offender to be sentenced by an independent and impartial tribunal.[192] This issue is yet to be resolved and it is therefore far from clear to what extent RJ will shape the future of criminal justice in England and Wales. **1–101**

F. COMBINING THE THEORIES

It is difficult to make any sense of the above competing "theories" until one knows precisely what question they are trying to answer. Building on the work of Hart[193] one can distinguish four separate questions: **1–102**

1. What is the purpose of punishment?
2. Who may be punished?
3. How much punishment should be imposed?
4. What type of punishment should be imposed?

---

192 A. Ashworth, "Responsibilities, Rights and Restorative Justice" (2002) 42 Brit. J. Criminol. 578.

193 "Prolegomenon to the Principles of Punishment" in H.L.A. Hart, *Punishment and Responsibility* (Oxford: Clarendon Press, 1969), p.1.

Many commentators have attempted to combine both retributive and utilitarian considerations in answering these questions. One approach, exemplified by Hart, is that a distinction needs to be drawn between two issues. First, one needs to ascertain what the purpose of the whole institution of punishment is; Hart called this "the general justifying aim" and the justification for this was to be found in utilitarian considerations. In short, the reason why we have an institution of punishment is because we want to reduce crime. However, there is a second separate issue of "distribution": this relates to the second two questions above, namely, who to punish and how much punishment? According to Hart, the question of distribution should be answered in retributive terms. Only persons who have committed criminal offences deserve punishment and the amount of punishment should be proportionate to the seriousness of the crime. According to this approach, one could say that the aim of the institution of punishment was, for example, deterrence but one would not be justified in punishing innocent people (say, the children of the offender) purely because this might be an effective deterrent. Punishment can only be justified in a particular case on the retributive basis that it is deserved.

George P. Fletcher, Rethinking Criminal Law (1978), p.419:

1–103 "The analogy that comes to mind is the distinction between justifying the income tax as a whole and justifying the imposition of burdens on particular taxpayers. The justification of the system as a whole is raising revenue for the government; the justification of burdens on particular taxpayers is (roughly) the taxpayer's relative ability to pay. It would obviously be improper to interweave these two levels of justification and justify the denial of claim for a charitable deduction on the ground of the claimant's relative ability to pay. Similarly, if the justification for the criminal law as a whole is the isolation of dangerous offenders, it is improper to decide particular cases by appealing to the alleged offender's relative dangerousness."

1–104 One could advocate such a "dualist"[194] approach but, instead of accepting Hart's views, it can be argued, for instance, that the aim of the institution of punishment is desert but that one needs utilitarian justifications to punish in individual cases.[195] Much of this chapter has been devoted to answering the first question: what is the purpose of punishment? Nothing further need be added here. The focus of the remainder of this section is on whether a dualist approach is justifiable and, if so, how matters of distribution of punishment should be determined. In assessing this it is helpful to examine the above three distributive questions separately.

194 D. Wood, "Retribution, Crime Reduction and the Justification of Punishment" (2002) 22 O.J.L.S. 301.

195 A.H. Goldman, "The Paradox of Punishment" (1979) 9 *Philosophy and Public Affairs* 42.

1. Who may be punished?

H.L.A. Hart, "Prolegomenon to the Principles of Punishment", in Punishment and Responsibility (1968), pp.11–13, 21–24:

"The root question to be considered is, however, why we attach the moral importance which we do to retribution in Distribution . . . **1–105**

The standard example used by philosophers to bring out the importance of retribution in Distribution is that of a wholly innocent person who has not even unintentionally done anything which the law punishes if done intentionally. It is supposed that in order to avert some social catastrophe officials of the system fabricate evidence on which he is charged, tried, convicted and sent to prison or death. Or it is supposed that without resort to any fraud more persons may be deterred from crime if wives and children of offenders were punished vicariously for their crimes. In some forms, this kind of thing may be ruled out by a consistent sufficiently comprehensive utilitarianism. Certainly expedients involving fraud or faked charges might be very difficult to justify on utilitarian grounds . . . [Such an approach] would awaken such apprehension and insecurity that any gain from the exercise of these powers would by any utilitarian calculation be offset by the misery caused by their existence. But official resort to this kind of fraud on a particular occasion in breach of the rules and the subsequent indemnification of the officials responsible might save many lives and so be thought to yield a clear surplus of value. Certainly vicarious punishment of an offender's family might do so and legal systems have occasionally resorted to this . . . In extreme cases many might still think it right to resort to these expedients but we should do so with the sense of sacrificing an important principle. We should be conscious of choosing the lesser of two evils, and this would be inexplicable if the principle sacrificed to utility were itself only a requirement of utility . . .

It is clear that like all principles of Justice it (punishment) is concerned with the adjustment of claims between a multiplicity of persons. It incorporates the idea that each individual person is to be protected against the claim of the rest for the highest possible measure of security, happiness or welfare which could be got at his expense by condemning him for a breach of the rules and punishing him. For this a moral licence is required in the form of proof that the person punished broke the law by an action which was the outcome of his free choice, and the recognition of excuses is the most we can do to ensure that the terms of the licence are observed. Here perhaps, the elucidation of this restrictive principle should stop. Perhaps we (or I) ought simply to say that it is a requirement of Justice, and Justice simply consists of principles to be observed in adjusting the competing claims of human beings which (i) treat all alike as persons by attaching special significance to human voluntary action and (ii) forbid the use of one human being for the benefit of others except in return for his voluntary actions against them . . .

We may look upon the principle that punishment must be reserved for voluntary offences from two different points of view. The first is that of the rest of society considered as *harmed* by the offence (either because one of its members has been injured or because the authority of the law essential to its existence has been challenged or both). The principle then appears as one securing that the suffering involved in punishment falls upon those who have voluntarily harmed others: this is valued, not as the Aim of punishment, but as the only fair terms on which the General Aim (protection of society, maintenance of respect for law, etc) may be pursued.

The second point of view is that of society concerned not as harmed by the crime but as *offering* individuals including the criminal the protection of the laws on terms which are fair, because they not only consist of a framework of reciprocal rights and duties, but because within this framework each individual is given a *fair* opportunity to choose between keeping the law required for society's protection or paying the penalty. From the first point of view the actual punishment of a criminal appears not merely as something useful to society (General Aim) but as justly extracted from the criminal who has voluntarily done harm; from the second it appears as a price justly extracted because the criminal had a fair opportunity beforehand to avoid liability to pay."

1–106 This dualist approach has been criticised on the basis that confining retribution to the issue of distribution of punishment amounts to a downgrading of its importance.[196] It has been further suggested that the whole dualist enterprise is flawed.

Nicola Lacey, State Punishment: Political Principles and Community Values (1988), pp.51–52:

1–107 "All these hybrid theories proceed on the assumption that there are genuinely separate questions to be answered: . . . It seems to be true . . . that rules themselves contain their own conditions of application. No sensible system has rules and then fails to apply them: prima facie, the reasons for having the rules generate the reasons for applying them in individual cases. This seems to indicate that the principle of distribution, if one is (as it seems to be) needed, must come in at the first stage: *a* principle of distribution is inevitably contained within or at least envisaged by the general justifying aim of the rules. And if the general justifying aim is straightforwardly utilitarian, the project of grafting on a separate distributive principle, begins to look deeply problematic, for utilitarianism does *not*, as its critics sometimes claim, lack such a principle. It rather embodies criteria of distribution which are vulnerable to serious objection. It is necessary, then, to identify an alternative general justifying aim which incorporates or is consistent with an acceptable distributive principle, rather than to separate different questions and give different answers to them. Conversely, I think it can be argued that a justification for institutions of punishment must include a justification for their actual use in individual cases, and that the individual question is in some ways primary: can any single infliction of punishment ever be justified? The mere fact that such an infliction is according to rules does not seem to generate any additional justification in itself. In justifying a system of rules, we generally assume that those rules will be applied: therefore the justification which we seek must also justify the application of the rules. For these reasons it is my belief that the . . . Hartian distinction does not really withstand close analysis."[197]

---

196 Wood, "Retribution, Crime Reduction and the Justification of Punishment" (2002) 22 O.J.L.S. 301, 307.

197 For a similar argument, see J. Braithwaite and P. Pettit, *Not Just Deserts: A Republican Theory of Criminal Justice* (New York: OUP, 1992), p.167.

Lacey's approach is, however, dependent on the "general justifying aim" itself embodying *effective* criteria of "distribution". To assess this, let us briefly consider the utilitarian response to the problem of punishing the innocent. Why not punish an innocent person if, say, it would be an effective deterrent? The answer here is that such punishment could never in fact be an effective deterrent as punishment would become a lottery and there would be no special disincentive to would-be offenders. Punishing the innocent would cause suffering to the V, general insecurity, disrespect for the law and could encourage the guilty person to reoffend. In short, such punishment would cause more evil than it prevented and thus could not be justifiable. **1–108**

Furthermore, even if the "general justifying aim" did embody criteria of distribution, *why would they be any better* than those yielded by the concept of just deserts, which, as demonstrated in the Hart extract above, provides fair, consistent and just results?

2. How severely do we punish?

The amount of punishment imposed again depends on the rationale for the imposition of that punishment. Let us start with the utilitarian view of punishment. How would a utilitarian determine the amount of punishment to be imposed for a particular offence? If it were thought necessary, for example, for reasons of deterrence, could extreme sentences be imposed that bore no relationship to the seriousness of the crime? Could one give life sentences for parking on double yellow lines if this were thought to be an effective deterrent? Could one give life sentences to persons who repeatedly stole milk bottles from doorsteps if this would prevent the recurrence of the crime? **1–109**

The classic answer to this question is still that provided by Jeremy Bentham, that all punishment is evil and ought only to be imposed to achieve some greater good—and, accordingly, one should only impose the minimum punishment necessary to achieve that objective.

Jeremy Bentham, "An Introduction to the Principles of Morals and Legislation", Ch.13, in Bentham and Mill, The Utilitarians (1961), pp.162, 166:

"The general object which all laws have, or ought to have, in common, is to augment the total happiness of the community; and therefore, in the first place, to exclude, as far as may be, every thing that tends to subtract from that happiness: in other words, to exclude mischief. **1–110**

But all punishment is mischief: all punishment in itself is evil. Upon the principle of utility, if it ought at all to be admitted, it ought only to be admitted in as far as it promises to exclude some greater evil.

It is plain, therefore, that in the following cases punishment ought not to be inflicted.

1. Where it is *groundless*: where there is no mischief for it to prevent, the act not being mischievous upon the whole.
2. Where it must be *inefficacious*: where it cannot act so as to prevent the mischief.
3. Where it is *unprofitable*; or too *expensive*: where the mischief it would produce would be greater than what it prevented.

> 4. Where it is *needless*: where the mischief may be prevented, or cease of itself, without it: that is, at a cheaper rate . . .
>
> Now the evil of the punishment divides itself into four branches, by which so many different sets of persons are affected. 1. The evil of *coercion* or *restraint*: or the pain which it gives a man not to be able to do the act, whatever it be, which by the apprehension of the punishment he is deterred from doing. This is felt by those by whom the law is *observed*. 2. The evil of *apprehension*: or the pain which a man, who has exposed himself to punishment, feels at the thought of undergoing it. This is felt by those by whom the law has been *broken*, and so feel themselves in *danger* of its being executed upon them. 3. The evil of *sufferance*: or the pain which a man feels, in virtue of the punishment itself, from the time when he begins to undergo it. This is felt by those by whom the law is broken, and upon whom it comes actually to be executed. 4. The pain of sympathy, and the other *derivative* evils resulting to the persons who are in *connection* with the several classes of original sufferers just mentioned."

1–111 Accordingly, the utilitarian reason why we do not punish parking on a double yellow line with life imprisonment is that it is thought that the aim of deterrence can be effectively achieved at a lower cost—and crime must be prevented as economically in terms of the suffering of the offender as possible. Furthermore, such an extreme sentence would undoubtedly attract public sympathy for the offender and thus:

> ". . . instead of reaffirming the law and intensifying men's consciousness that the kind of act punished is wrong, will have the opposite effect of casting discredit on the law and making the action of the law-breaker appear excusable or even almost heroic."[198]

The problem with this approach is that while it might explain why preposterous sentences cannot be imposed for minor crimes, it does not necessarily prohibit exemplary sentences whereby one person is given *a longer sentence than is deserved*. Desert theory is emphatic here: the crime itself provides the necessary guidance as to the amount of punishment necessary. The punishment must be proportionate to the crime; it must "fit" the crime. Desert theorists, such as von Hirsch, argue that punishment must be proportionate to the seriousness of the crime in order to reflect an *appropriate degree of censure*.

Andrew von Hirsch, Past or Future Crimes (1985), pp.35–36:

1–112 "The requirement of proportionate punishment is derived directly from the censuring implications of the criminal sanction. Once one has created an institution with the condemnatory connotations that punishment has, then it is a requirement of justice, not merely of efficient law enforcement, to punish offenders according to the degree of reprehensibleness of their conduct. Disproportionate punishments are unjust not because they are ineffectual or possibly counterproductive, but because the state purports to condemn the actor for his conduct and yet visits more or less censure on him than the gravity of that conduct warrants."

198 A.C. Ewing, "A Study of Punishment II: Punishment as Viewed by the Philosopher" (1943) 21 Can. B. Rev. 102, 116.

3. How does one determine what level of punishment is proportionate to the seriousness of the crime?

ANDREW VON HIRSCH, "ORDINAL AND CARDINAL DESERT", IN A. VON HIRSCH AND A. ASHWORTH (EDS), PRINCIPLED SENTENCING (1992), PP.209–210:

"One must distinguish between *ordinal* and *cardinal* magnitudes of punishment: That is, between (1) the question of how defendants should be punished relative to each other, and (2) the question of what absolute severity levels should be chosen to anchor the penalty scale . . . **1–113**

For modern desert theory, this distinction is critical. Advocates of desert-oriented sentencing such as myself do not assert that desert is determinative for all purposes. Rather, our claim is a more restricted one, to wit: desert is a determinative principle in deciding ordinal magnitudes, but only a limiting principle in deciding cardinal magnitudes. To see what this means in practice, consider the crime of burglary. The issues of ordinal magnitude deal with how a particular burglary should be penalized compared to other burglaries and to other more or less serious crimes. When desert theorists assert that desert is a determining principle here, they mean that the ordering of penalties must meet the following two requirements. The first is the requirement of *parity*: criminal conduct of equal seriousness should be punished equally, with deviations from such equality permitted only where special circumstances alter the harm or culpability—that is, the degree of blameworthiness—of the defendant's conduct. The other is that of *rank ordering*: penalties should be ranked and spaced to reflect the ranking and spacing in degree of seriousness among crimes. What desert theorists object to is deciding these questions of *comparative* punishments on grounds other than the blameworthiness of the defendant's conduct: for example, to punish a particular burglar more severely than other burglars not because his particular crime is any worse but because he is a worse risk or because giving him a higher-than-usual punishment would make him an example to others.

To espouse this view does not, however, require one to hold that desert is determinative in deciding cardinal magnitudes. Here, rather, most modern desert theorists—certainly I—would admit that desert is a limiting principle only. I do not claim to know precisely how tough or lenient a sentencing scale should be, but only that punishments beyond certain levels of harshness or leniency are *undeserved*."

A fundamental flaw is revealed in von Hirsch's final paragraph, that being that he does not claim to know how tough or lenient a sentencing scale should be for it to be proportionate. Indeed, how is this be calculated in any precise way? The answer seems to be: not consistently. Nicola Lacey and Hannah Pickard lament that proportionality is a "chimera", based on abstract theory that has not translated well into praxis; as evidenced by the vastly diverging penalties that are applied under the principle both historically and in recent times.[199] They conclude that "what has been thought of as proportionality is **1–114**

199 N. Lacey and H. Pickard, "The Chimera of Proportionality: Institutionalising Limits on Punishment in Contemporary Social and Political Systems" (2015) M.L.R. 78, 216. See also, J. Bronsther, "Vague comparisons and proportional sentencing" (2019) L.T. 25, 26.

not a naturally existing relationship, but a product of political and social construction, cultural meaning-making, and institution-building".[200]

A final, but critical, issue remains. *Must* one punish to the exact extent dictated by the seriousness of the crime, or does the concept of just deserts merely provide a ceiling beyond which punishment is undeserved?

The strict Kantian response is that the offender must be punished to that extent, *no more and no less*, which is necessary to destroy the unfair advantage gained from committing the crime. A failure to punish the offender, either at all, or to the extent necessary to eliminate the advantage gained, would not restore social equilibrium and would amount to society endorsing the criminal's acts and thus becoming participants in it. It would further involve failing to treat the criminal as a responsible human being who deserves the consequences of their actions.

1–115 On the other hand, drawing on the approach advocated by Hart earlier in this section, it could be that the concept of just deserts should only specify the maximum possible penalty beyond which punishment is undeserved.[201] Within a permissible range, punishment is deserved—one is justified in punishing—but one has a choice as to the severity of the punishment, that choice being informed by all the circumstances of the offence and perhaps even by utilitarian considerations. In short, within a range set by desert principles, the precise allocation of punishment could be determined on a utilitarian basis. This approach, sometimes called limited or *negative retributivism*, was endorsed by the Halliday Report[202] which proposed that desert should provide a "punitive envelope"[203] indicating a permissible range of sentence. No sentence outside that range would be permissible. However, once the "envelope was opened", the actual sentence imposed, within the defined limits, would depend on utilitarian considerations. Within the range the sentencer would select the punishment that would most closely serve the purpose of crime reduction (and reparation) in the individual case. This would involve an assessment of the likelihood of reoffending and the measures most likely to reduce that risk.[204]

Nicola Lacey, State Punishment: Political Principles and Community Values (1988), pp.54–55:

1–116 "The idea that desert furnishes the state with a non-conclusive reason to punish raises the question of what types of extra reasons must be adduced in order to produce a justification of particular acts of punishment. On some accounts, apparently non-utilitarian factors are appealed to—factors such as fairness and justice. But it is clear that the most obvious candidates are utilitarian reasons such as prevention, deterrence, avoidance of private vengeance and so on. It is important to note that on most weak retributivist views desert operates not only as the central justification but also

200 Lacey and Pickard, "The Chimera of Proportionality: Institutionalising Limits on Punishment in Contemporary Social and Political Systems" (2015) M.L.R. 78, 216.
201 N. Morris, *Punishment, Desert and Rehabilitation* (Washington DC: US Government Printing Office, 1976).
202 Halliday Report (2001).
203 Halliday Report (2001), para.2.39.
204 Halliday Report (2001), para.2.31. See E. Baker and C.M.V. Clarkson, "Making Punishments Work? An Evaluation of the Halliday Report on Sentencing in England and Wales" [2002] Crim. L.R. 81.

> as a limit on the amount of punishment: the only function of the consequentialist considerations is to add an element which provides the sufficient reason for some punitive action. On this view, consequentialism cannot tell us whom to punish or how much to punish; it merely defeats the argument from the pointlessness of purely retributive punishment. The difficulty here is that these utilitarian arguments do purport to provide not just an explanation of when we may exercise our right or power of punishment, but actually to make it right for us to punish. According to utilitarianism, it is right to punish wherever such an action maximises the aggregate of pleasure over pain. It is thus hard to see how it is that the weak retributive principle fails to become redundant. In addition, it is not clear whether the desert argument is intended to apply to the design of institutions and the utilitarian one to individual acts of punishment . . . If this were so, we would be invited to endorse the unattractive vision of a legal system based on a principle of desert, in which individual acts of punishment were left to judicial discretion which should be exercised on the basis of consequentialist reasoning, or else of a system in which the legislator made utilitarian generalisations in framing the rules which were nevertheless primarily based on considerations of desert."

As Lacey makes clear, sentencing cannot be left to unfettered judicial discretion. Justice demands that like cases be treated alike. There needs to be an organising principle to structure and control such discretion. The Halliday Report made some effort in this direction—but was ultimately flawed for two reasons. First, the limits of permissible punishment based on desert were overly influenced by the existence of previous convictions.[205] This leaves too broad a band within which punishment is "deserved". Secondly, once the envelope has been opened, utilitarianism takes complete control and there is insufficient guidance as to the relationship between the various utilitarian considerations. Halliday's recommendations were not adopted in their entirety, but instead a potential problem with the ensuing Criminal Justice Act 2003 (now Sentencing Act 2020) lists multiple purposes of sentencing. **1–117**

SENTENCING ACT 2020 S.57(2):

> *"Purposes of sentencing* **1–118**
>
> The court must have regard to the following purposes of sentencing—
>
> (a) the punishment of offenders,
> (b) the reduction of crime (including its reduction by deterrence),
> (c) the reform and rehabilitation of offenders,
> (d) the protection of the public, and
> (e) the making of reparation by offenders to persons affected by their offences."

No relative weighting or ranking of these purposes is provided, creating the danger that different sentencers might pick and choose and prioritise different sentencing purposes, in turn creating the **1–119**

205 Halliday Report (2001), pp.39–40.

potential for sentencing disparity. Von Hirsch and Roberts have criticised what they see as a return to the "'smorgasbord' approach to sentencing aims".[206]

Andrew von Hirsch and Julian V. Roberts, "Legislating Sentencing Principles: The Provisions of the Criminal Justice Act 2003 Relating to Sentencing Purposes and the Role of Previous Convictions" [2004] Crim. L.R. 639, 642:

1–120 "Section 142 [now s.57 Sentencing Act 2020] lists punishment, deterrence, incapacitation, rehabilitation, and reparation to victims as aims which the judge must consider in each sentencing case. It does not indicate what priority should be observed among these various aims.

The recent penological literature does not support this new emphasis on crime-preventive aims in sentencing; indeed, the leading English authorities on sentencing continue to endorse an emphasis on proportionality in imposing criminal sentences. The initiative has come, instead, from the Home Office. Developing measures to prevent crime and reduce re-offending has for years been part of the Government's criminal justice policy strategy. It is not surprising therefore that these ideas have permeated the area of sentencing and finally reached the statute book. Starting with claims made by Mr Jack Straw while shadow Home Secretary, senior Home Office officials have asserted their increasing impatience with a proportionality standard for sentencing, and recommended that greater weight be given in sentencing to crime prevention concerns. In part, such officials' stated reasons reflect concern with assuaging public opinion."

1–121 The extent to which public opinion ought to play a role in informing what sentence purposes should be used in practice is not without controversy. What is clear is that a perceived hardening of public opinion on sentencing has influenced sentencing policy and the law, with a plethora of new legislation increasing sentences for a range of offences since the early 2000s.[207] Although public opinion should not affect individual sentencing decisions of the courts, there is some evidence to suggest that it does just that.

Andrew Ashworth and Mike Hough, "Sentencing and the Climate of Opinion" [1996] Crim. L.R. 776, 783.

1–122 "Did the 'moral panic' evident during 1993 [in the aftermath of the killing of William Bulger] have any effect on judges and magistrates? Sentencers have rarely admitted this, but it would be hard to account for the increasing use of custody by reference to changes in the law . . . or by reference to a sudden and exponential increase in the seriousness of the offences with

206 A. von Hirsch and J.V. Roberts, "Legislating Sentencing Principles: The Provisions of the Criminal Justice Act 2003 Relating to Sentencing Purposes and the Role of Previous Convictions" [2004] Crim. L.R. 639, 642.

207 House of Commons Justice Committee, *Public opinion and understanding of sentencing* (2023) Tenth Report of Session 2022–23.

which the courts were having to deal. The most straightforward explanation is that judges and magistrates believed that the climate of opinion was changing, and attempted to reflect it to some degree. A more sophisticated version of the same argument is that they were in part responding to a shift in the climate of opinion."

4. What type of punishment?

Once a determination is made about how much punishment is warranted, the courts must then decide what method of punishment ought to be employed. This is yet another complex decision that sentencers must make. **1–123**

Paul H. Robinson, "Hybrid Principles for the Distribution of Criminal Sanctions" (1988) 82 Northwestern University L. Rev. 19, 34–36:

"The [next] issue, concerning the method of sanction, is distinguishable from the distribution of amount. Two offenders may merit the same *amount* of sanction yet different *methods* of sanctioning may be suitable for imposing that amount. These two issues—how much for whom and what method—are not only functionally distinguishable but also may properly be subject to different distributive principles. **1–124**

. . . The desert requirement of a proper ordinal ranking of offenders by overall blameworthiness, for example, concerns the ranking of *amounts* of sanction. As long as the ordinal ranking is correct, the *method* by which each amount is imposed is not relevant to desert. If one month in the state prison is the punitive equivalent to five months of weekends in the local jail, then desert is satisfied even if the more blameworthy offender gets probation, with a condition of seven months of weekends in jail, while the less blameworthy offender goes to prison for one month. It is critical, of course, that the sanction equivalencies be properly set. Some empirical research has been done on perceptions of relative seriousness of sanctions, but the work is still in its infancy.

With an estimate of equivalencies, one can construct a sentencing system that allows independent determination of the amount and method issues. The principles governing the 'amount' issue can generate total 'sanction units' for each offender, which can then be allocated to a particular sanctioning method or combination of methods according to a different set of 'method' principles. As long as the issues can be effectively segregated in practice, one can develop a hybrid distributive principle for governing the amount of sanction that is different from the principle used to determine the method of sanction. One could, for example, emphasize desert in determining the amount of sanction, but ignore it in determining the method. The selection of method could be made to maximize pure utilitarian concerns without infringing desert interests—a precious no-loss, all-win opportunity.

The separation of amount and method issues has other important collateral advantages. For example, unwarranted disparity in sentencing primarily concerns disparity in amount, rather than disparity in method. Thus, one might significantly reduce judicial sentencing discretion on the amount issue, in order to reduce disparity among judges, yet maintain broad judicial discretion on the method issue. As long as the total 'sanction units' for an offender are satisfied and the sanction equivalencies are properly set, it does not matter what method or methods an individual judge selects; the punitive 'bite' will be the same."

1-125 According to this analysis, within a desert framework, decisions as to the type of punishment can be based on utilitarian considerations. For instance, when imposing a (deserved) community sentence involving a community order the court should normally obtain a pre-sentence report and then decide which requirements to impose and should indicate the purposes to be achieved thereby. For example, a court could impose a supervision requirement or an alcohol treatment requirement aimed at the rehabilitation of the offender. Alternatively, a curfew requirement, an exclusion requirement or a prohibited activity request could be imposed aimed at protecting the public.

G. SENTENCING GUIDELINES

1-126 Until the rise of the just deserts movement, sentencers were generally free to impose whatever sentence they deemed appropriate—up to the maximum permitted. Such broad discretionary powers meant several things could occur. Different judges could impose different sentences for different reasons without having to give any explanation in open court. For example, some judges could impose a sentence for deterrent reasons but other judges in similar cases could sentence offenders in order to rehabilitate them. Even the same judge was not always consistent in sentencing. There was no agreement among judges as to what criteria ought to be taken into account in the sentencing decision and what weight ought to be given to factors such as previous convictions, age, good family, perceived future dangerousness, whether the accused pleaded guilty and other such matters. Criticism of this lack of consistency was speedily met with the response that sentences were individualised; they were tailored to meet the needs of D and therefore consistency in punishments for similar crimes was not to be expected. The result was widespread sentencing disparity with similar cases being treated differently.

Another consequence of judges sentencing for a mixture of reasons, many of them utilitarian, was that excessively long sentences were being imposed in some cases. In particular, the rationale of exemplary sentencing resulted in some persons receiving sentences in excess of those imposed on others committing similar crimes. This provided fertile soil for the growth of the just deserts movement. The agenda was set: judicial discretion had to be controlled; sentencing disparity had to be eliminated: this would necessarily involve eliminating disproportionately long sentences; there needed to be "truth in sentencing": equal sentences imposed in open court had to mean the same thing for different offenders. The concept of just deserts with its liberal emphasis on justice involving like cases being treated alike was the obvious facilitator. However, it was clearly not enough simply to embrace the concept of just deserts and reduce the importance of utilitarian considerations. Different judges could have different conceptions of what sentence was deserved in any particular case. What was needed was a mechanism for ensuring that judicial discretion was controlled by forcing judges to sentence in accordance with agreed and objective standards of desert.

There have been significant responses in England and Wales to sentencing disparity. First, since 1989. the Attorney-General has been able to refer an unduly lenient sentence, imposed by the Crown Court, to the Court of Appeal which has the power to increase that sentence.[208] A disparate sentence can be an unduly light one as well as an unduly heavy one and so this right of appeal does go some way towards the elimination of unwarranted disparity. However, it is only Crown Court sentences (and not ones from magistrates' courts), and only sentences imposed for "indictable only" offences, that are referable. **1–127**

However, the right to appeal had only a limiting impact on reducing disparity in sentencing. In an attempt to create greater consistency, the Sentencing Advisory Panel was established in 1999.[209] Its function was to give advice to the Court of Appeal which was obliged to have regard to these views and, if practicable or at the next appropriate opportunity, include guidelines in its judgment. Several years later the Criminal Justice Act 2003 set up the Sentencing Guidelines Council, which was empowered to issue "definitive guidelines" based on advice provided by the Sentencing Advisory Panel. In 2009, the Sentencing Guidelines Council and the Sentencing Advisory Panel merged into a single body called the Sentencing Council.[210] The Council is made up of eight "judicial" and six "non-judicial" members, selected by the Lord Chief Justice and Lord Chancellor, respectively.[211] The Council is entrusted with preparing draft guidelines with the requirement to consult with the Lord Chief Justice and House of Commons Justice Select Committee before producing definitive guidelines. The Council's guidelines may be general in nature or limited to a particular category of offence or offender.[212] In passing any sentence, the courts "must . . . follow any sentencing guideline . . . unless the court is satisfied that it would be contrary to the interests of justice to do so".[213] The Council has issued definitive guidelines, on multiple offence types including, for example, robbery, sexual offences, motoring offences, theft and burglary offences. In 2022–23, the Council produced a number of revised and new guidelines including sentencing of the offence of sexual communication with a child and sentencing retailers who fail to ensure that adequate safeguards are in place to prevent the sale of knives to under 18s either in-store or online.[214] The Sentencing Act 2020 s.59 states that the courts "must . . . follow any sentencing guidelines . . .".

The Sentencing Council also publishes definitive guidelines for sentencing in magistrates' courts,[215] having taken over responsibility for such guidelines from the Magistrates' Association. The duty on judges to have regard to sentencing guidelines now applies equally to magistrates. It should be noted that magistrates deal with around 97% of all criminal cases, and although one often thinks of imprisonment as the "normal" punishment for criminal offences, in magistrates' courts, the penalty applied in around 75% of cases is a fine.[216]

---

208 Criminal Justice Act 1988 s.36.

209 Crime and Disorder Act 1998 ss.80–81.

210 Established under the Coroners and Justice Act 2009 s.118.

211 Coroners and Justice Act 2009 Sch.15.

212 Coroners and Justice Act 2009 s.120(2).

213 Coroners and Justice Act 2009 s.125(1).

214 Sentencing Council, *Sentencing Council Annual Report 2022/23* (2023), Sentencing Council.

215 Sentencing Council, *Sentencing Guidelines for use in Magistrates' Court* at *https://www.sentencingcouncil.org.uk/the-magistrates-court-sentencing-guidelines*.

216 J. Raine and E. Dunstan, "How Well do Sentencing Guidelines Work?: Equity, Proportionality and Consistency in the Determination of Fine Levels in the Magistrates' Courts of England and Wales" (2009) 48 *The Howard Journal* 13, 15.

1–128 There will always be tension between the need to ensure that sentencers can do justice without their discretion becoming unduly fettered and the desire to discourage disparity in sentencing. These reforms constitute a major step towards ensuring consistency in sentencing. The Sentencing Council has taken a "narrative" approach in producing its guidelines for indictable offences, tending to consist of a first part discussing the features of the offence and factors that might increase or decrease its seriousness, and a second part which is set out in the form of a table, assigning a sentencing range to different levels of offence seriousness.[217] The approach to be taken by sentencers has been carefully set out in the guidelines, explaining the factors to be taken into account in a step-by-step methodology. Sentencers should start with looking at offence seriousness, the starting point for sentencing under the Sentencing Act 2020, by assessing culpability of the offender and harm caused or threatened by the offence. This should lead the sentencer to identify a "starting point" for the sentence. Consideration should then be given to any mitigating or aggravating factors, to either move up or down the sentencing "range" from the starting point.

Although the range is set to try to encourage consistency in sentencing, it is possible for a sentence to be passed outside the range laid down in the guidelines. Once a provisional sentence has been arrived at, sentencers should then look at whether that sentence should be reduced due to offender mitigation (e.g. whether the offender has shown remorse) or a guilty plea. The Sentencing Council notes that previous convictions may take a sentence beyond the sentencing range provided.[218]

Until recently, there was a lack of data to show whether the Sentencing Council's work had improved previous issues relating to consistency and transparency in sentencing. In 2021, the Council conducted its own survey of over 1,000 judges. Their analysis found that "of those sentencers who had begun sentencing before 2011, the vast majority thought transparency and consistency had improved and fewer, though still a majority, thought fairness had improved".[219] While encouraging, further independent quantitative and qualitative research is required to analyse sentence disparities, and their potential causes.

1–129 It is a major theme of this book that all offences should be structured and labelled to reflect a hierarchy of seriousness. The extent to which seriousness should be reflected in the substantive law or left to the sentencing stage (being regulated by sentencing guidelines) is a crucial matter. It is to these issues of substantive law—and the relationship between that law and sentencing—that the remainder of this book is devoted.

---

217 A. Ashworth, "Techniques for Reducing Sentencing Disparity" in A. von Hirsch, A. Ashworth and J. Roberts (eds), *Principled Sentencing*, 3rd edn (Oxford: OUP, 2009).

218 Research has found that in a significant number of cases (46% of 222 offences of assault, sexual assault and robbery), sentencers imposed a sentence outside the guideline ranges for the levels of offence seriousness described: Sentencing Commission Working Group, *Crown Court Sentencing Survey*, July 2008.

219 Sentencing Council, *Investigating the Sentencing Council's impact in three key areas* (Sentencing Council, 2021).

Chapter 2

The General Principles of Criminal Liability: Actus Reus

I. Introduction

The criminal law is an institution of blame and punishment. Blame is attached to D's conduct, and if that conduct violates the law, provided they have the requisite fault, they are punished for it. However, in what circumstances are we to blame someone for their conduct and blame them to a degree sufficient to justify the imposition of punishment? And in what circumstances can someone's actions be said to have violated the law? **2-001**

Generally, the law is concerned with punishing harmful actions that are committed in circumstances or in conditions in which we can fairly blame the perpetrator of the actions. This is, of course, only a general proposition. Not all acts that are criminal cause an obvious harm. With the crime of attempt, for instance, no actual harm has been caused. Similarly, criminal liability is often imposed in circumstances where many feel that no blame can be attached to the actor. Thus, in crimes of strict liability, a person who has acted to the best of their ability can be punished if, albeit inadvertently, they violate a statute making certain conduct criminal. The question of whether such conduct, which either involves no obvious harm or is generally perceived to involve no blameworthiness, should be punishable will be considered later in this book.

Let us return to the general proposition, which can be broken down into two limbs:

1. **Harmful conduct:** Sometimes "conduct" can in itself be proscribed on the basis that it constitutes or threatens harm. Alternatively, it is conduct that causes a harmful result that is proscribed by the criminal law. The word "conduct" is here used in its broadest sense to encompass an act, omission and state of affairs. The law has developed a short-hand term, actus reus, to describe this.
2. **Committed in conditions in which we can fairly blame the actor:** The problem here is to determine the indicators of blame. It is widely accepted that two such indicators exist:

(a) *Mens rea*. Some would only blame those who acted with a subjective fault element (for example, an intention to kill). Others would blame those whose actions objectively failed to conform to a set standard. Either way, the law has developed a short-hand term, mens rea, to describe this.[1]

(b) *Absence of defence*. D might have committed the actus reus with the requisite fault (mens rea), but because of the circumstances, we might not wish to hold them liable or punish them. D might have a valid supervening defence in that D acted (say) in self-defence or under duress.

One way of interpreting this is that the constituent ingredients of a criminal offence are three-fold: actus reus, mens rea and the absence of a valid defence.[2]

2-002 There are, however, other modes of analysing the constituent elements of an offence. Glanville Williams, for instance, argued that all elements of a crime are divisible into either actus reus or mens rea and that the actus reus requirement incorporates an "absence of defence".[3] Others argue that mens rea means blameworthiness in the sense of mental fault incorporating an "absence of defence".[4]

This lack of academic agreement illustrates the important point that the terms "actus reus" and "mens rea" are no more than tools that are useful in the exposition of the criminal law. Dividing an offence into its constituent elements in this way is no more than a matter of analytical convenience.[5] Whether D is to be convicted of an offence should depend on important principles aimed at deciding whether their conduct deserves condemnation as criminal; such questions should not be answered by reference only to definitions of actus reus and mens rea. Questions of policy should not be determined by reference to definitions and terminology.[6]

2-003 In *Miller*, Lord Diplock disapproved of such terminology:

> "My Lords, it would I think be conducive to clarity of analysis of the ingredients of a crime that is created by statute, as are the greater majority of criminal offences today, if we were to avoid bad Latin and instead to think and speak about the conduct of the accused and his state of mind at the time of that conduct, instead of speaking of actus reus and mens rea."[7]

---

1 Whether an objective failure to conform to a set standard of behaviour (negligence) is accurately described as a species of mens rea is a controversial matter. See paras 3-011-3-013, where a distinction is drawn between cognitive mens rea (involving a subjective mental element) and normative mens rea (involving an assessment of culpability taking account of all the circumstances, including a failure to conform to set standards).

2 D. Lanham, "Larsonneur Revisited" [1976] Crim. L.R. 276.

3 G. Williams, *Criminal Law: The General Part* (London: Stevens & Sons Ltd, 1961), p.20; G. Williams, "Statutory Exceptions to Liability and the Burden of Proof" (1976) 126 New L.J. 1032, 1034; see also *R. v Williams (Gladstone)* (1984) 78 Cr. App. R. 276; [1984] Crim. L.R. 163 CA.

4 S.H. Kadish, "The Decline of Innocence" (1968) 26 C.L.J. 273, 273–275.

5 There have been judicial decisions that have lost sight of the mere analytical convenience of dividing an offence into these elements, and made criminal liability dependent upon a particular mode of analysing the constituent elements of a crime. See R.H.S Tur, "Subjectivism and Objectivism: Towards Synthesis" in Shute, Gardener and Horder, Action and Value in Criminal Law (1993), p.213, pp.217–222 for a view that this process of reclassifying defence elements as definitional elements has been largely a matter of "dry legal technique" flowing from a commitment to subjectivism with the consequence that pressing moral and public concerns have been overlooked.

6 A.T.H. Smith, "On *Actus reus* and *Mens rea*" in P.R. Glazebrook (ed), *Reshaping the Criminal Law: Essays in Honour of Glanville Williams* (London: Stevens, 1978), pp.95, 96, 102.

7 *R. v Miller (James)* [1983] 2 A.C. 161; [1983] 2 W.L.R. 539 HL at 175. See also P.H. Robinson, "Should the Criminal Law Abandon the *Actus Reus* and *Mens Rea* Distinction?" in S. Shute, J. Gardner and J. Horder (eds), *Action and Value in Criminal Law* (Oxford: OUP, 1993) who argues that these phrases are misleading and obscure understanding.

In this textbook, we have chosen to disregard Lord Diplock's command. We shall analyse offences in terms of actus reus, mens rea and absence of defence. We do this for the simple reason that as long as one appreciates that these terms are no more than tools, they are tools that *can* usefully aid the clear exposition of the rules of criminal law. Furthermore, they have been so much part of the criminal law vocabulary for hundreds of years, and still are, that many of the cases to be discussed in this book would be highly confusing, if not totally meaningless, without some understanding of the orthodox meaning of these terms.

The focus of this chapter is on the principal constituent element of criminal liability: actus reus. Before analysing this element, it is worthwhile explaining why all criminal offences have actus reus elements and why they cannot be defined solely in terms of mens rea.

To many people, evil thoughts, desires and intentions are as morally reprehensible as evil deeds, and if we had the means to detect such criminal propensities, we would be justified in punishing such persons. The law, however, is not concerned with punishing people for thinking evil thoughts or having evil intentions.[8] The law will not interfere unless there has been some conduct, some physical manifestation of the evil intention.[9] Some offences only require the slightest manifestation: in conspiracy, for example, all that is needed is an agreement to commit a crime. However, minimal as it might be, this agreement is nevertheless a physical manifestation of the evil intention; it is conduct and can form the basis of an actus reus.

Why does the law insist upon an actus reus as a prerequisite of criminal liability? One obvious reason is the desire to avoid punishment of thoughts alone:

> "[t]here can hardly be anyone who has never thought evil. When a desire is inhibited it may find expression in fantasy; but it would be absurd to condemn this natural psychological mechanism as illegal."[10]

Furthermore, in addition to it being morally inappropriate to punish mere intentions, there is doubt as to whether people have sufficient control over their thoughts to be held responsible for them.[11]

A. Goldstein, "Conspiracy to Defraud the United States" (1959) 68 Yale L.J. 405, 405–406:

> "[The notion of not punishing evil intentions alone] expresses today, as it did three centuries ago, the feeling that the individual thinking evil thoughts must be protected from a state which may **2–004**

8 For a view that it could be justifiable to punish evil intentions alone, see D. Husak, "Does Criminal Liability Require an Act?" in A. Duff (ed), *Philosophy and the Criminal Law* (Cambridge: CUP, 1998). See, generally, R.A. Duff, *Answering for Crime: Responsibility and Liability in the Criminal Law* (Oxford: Hart, 2007), pp.102–105.

9 Duff, *Answering for Crime: Responsibility and Liability in the Criminal Law* (2007), pp.95–101.

10 Williams, *Criminal Law: The General Part* (1961), p.2.

11 Robinson, "Should the Criminal Law Abandon the *Actus Reus* and *Mens Rea* Distinction?" in Shute, Gardner and Horder (eds), *Action and Value in Criminal Law* (1993), p.191.

> class him as a threat to its security. Rooted in scepticism about the ability either to know what passes through the minds of men or to predict whether antisocial behaviour will follow from antisocial thoughts, the act requirement serves a number of closely-related objectives: it seeks to assure that the evil intent of the man branded a criminal has been *expressed in a manner signifying harm to society*; that there is no longer any substantial likelihood that he will be deterred by the threat of sanction; and that there has been an identifiable occurrence so that multiple prosecution and punishment may be minimized."

2-005 As seen above, a mere agreement to commit a crime is regarded as a sufficient manifestation of evil intentions to constitute the actus reus of conspiracy; similarly, mere words of instruction or encouragement are, inter alia, sufficient to render one liable for assisting or encouraging a criminal offence. Whether these ought to be regarded as a sufficient manifestation of evil intentions to justify the imposition of criminal liability is a question to be considered later.

II. Constituent elements of actus reus

2-006 The term "actus reus" refers to the external elements of criminal offences—the objective requirement(s) necessary to constitute the offence. These elements extend beyond D's "guilty act" (conduct) and, depending on the offence, also include the legally relevant circumstances in which the offence must have been completed, as well as the prohibited result that must be caused by D's conduct. The actus reus of every crime is to be determined from its offence definition. For example, the actus reus of theft is the "appropriation of property belonging to another",[12] and the actus reus of rape is the "penetration of the vagina, anus or mouth of another person who does not consent to the penetration ".[13]

Generally, offences can be divided into two categories, and the essential elements of the actus reus depend on which of these two species of crime one is dealing with. First, there are conduct crimes, where the only external elements required are that the prohibited conduct occurred in legally relevant circumstances. Thus, the actus reus of the offence of dangerous driving is simply driving a mechanically propelled vehicle on a road or other public place.[14] No consequence of that dangerous driving need be established.[15] Secondly, there are result crimes, which also require proof that the conduct caused a prohibited result. Thus, the actus reus of the offence of causing death by dangerous driving is causing the "death of another person by driving a mechanically propelled vehicle dangerously on a road or

---

12 Theft Act 1968 s.1.

13 Sexual Offences Act 2003 s.1(1).

14 Road Traffic Act 1988 s.2.

15 Beyond the creation of a *danger* of injury to others or serious damage to property: the Road Traffic Act 1988 s.2A(3).

other public place".[16] Here it is necessary to establish that the dangerous driving caused the prohibited result specified in the actus reus, namely, the death of another person.

Consequently, conduct and result offences have two elements in common: (1) both require an "act" or conduct; and (2) both require that the act be carried out in defined *legally relevant circumstances.* For example, the actus reus of theft is only completed if the appropriated property "belongs to another". In the absence of this circumstance, if the property is owned by the would-be thief, the actus reus of the offence is not made out. Just as mens rea may or may not be required for the act and for the consequences in result crimes, liability may similarly depend upon whether the accused has the required mental state in relation to the legally relevant circumstances. So, in theft, if D honestly believes that they are the owner of the property, there would be no mens rea in relation to an essential element of the actus reus.[17]

For result crimes, it is necessary to establish an additional third element, namely, that D's conduct *caused* the prohibited result. For example, for homicide offences, that D's conduct *caused* the death of another person. If D puts poison into V's drink with the intention to kill, if V subsequently dies with the drink found beside them, liability for murder cannot exist unless it was the poison that *caused* the death. If V died of an unrelated heart attack, the only possible charge would be attempted murder.[18] **2-007**

Putting these elements together, it is common to find an actus reus described as:

(1) an "act";
(2) committed in legally relevant circumstances; and
(3) (for result crimes) causing the prohibited result.

One final point needs to be made by way of introduction. While many offences are so defined that D may be convicted on the basis of the actus reus alone, without the need for proof of *mens rea* (crimes of so-called strict liability), the converse is not true. There must always be an actus reus for liability to be at issue at all. If, for example, in an alleged case of theft, the property already belongs to the person taking it, then despite any intention to steal, the actions cannot amount to the crime of theft. Similarly, where D persuades another to purchase their car by representing that it is free from encumbrances, believing they are lying, D cannot be found guilty of fraud if it turns out that it was, in fact, free from encumbrances.[19] D has unwittingly told the truth; the car was theirs to sell, and their dishonest state of mind counts for nothing. The fact that D *believes* they have committed an actus reus is not enough. The actus reus must be proved objectively to exist. We are now in a position to examine in greater detail the requirements of an actus reus.

---

16 Road Traffic Act 1988 s.1.

17 Theft Act 1968 s.2(1)(a).

18 *R. v White (John)* [1910] 2 K.B. 124; (1910) 4 Cr. App. R. 257. See also *Re Hensler* (1870) 11 Cox C.C. 570.

19 *R. v Deller (Charles Avon)* (1952) 36 Cr. App. R. 184; (1952) 102 L.J. 679. This case is commonly discussed in relation to *The Queen v George Dadson* 169 E.R. 407; (1850) 2 Den. 35.

A. AN "ACT"

1. The act must be voluntary

2-008 The distinction between an act and any accompanying mental element required by the law for the imposition of liability has already been drawn. Thus, if we define murder as killing when there is an intention to kill or cause serious harm, we can readily accept the acquittal of someone whose claim that it was all a dreadful accident is accepted by the courts. But the circumstances of the accident might lead us to very different conclusions about the basis of the acquittal. If D claims that the "accident" lay in thinking the weapon was an imitation one rather than a real one, then this translates into a denial of mens rea; D did not have the necessary intention to kill or cause serious harm. However, if D claims to have shot V as a result of stumbling down some icy steps, the "accident" here appears to be of a more fundamental kind; the act itself seems defective. Punishment seems inappropriate—even if we were dealing with an offence where no mental element extends beyond the voluntary movement or to the result or circumstances (referred to as strict liability). The difficulty lies in trying to pinpoint the defect. The law has generally shied away from identifying why it is inappropriate to punish in such circumstances beyond affirming that acts must be "voluntary". Instead, it has been left to academic lawyers and philosophers to explore what this means.

John Austin, Lectures on Jurisprudence (5th edn) (XVIII–XIX) Vol.I 411–415:

2-009 "Certain movements of our bodies follow invariably and immediately our wishes and desires for those same movements. Provided, that is, that the bodily organ be sane, and the desired movement be not prevented by any outward obstacle . . . These antecedent wishes and these consequent movements, are human volitions and acts (strictly and properly so-called) . . . And as these are the only volitions, so are the bodily movements by which they are immediately followed the only acts or actions (properly so-called). It will be admitted on the mere statement, that the only objects which can be called acts are consequences of volitions. A voluntary movement of my body, or a movement which follows a volition, is an act. The *in*voluntary movements which (for example) are the consequences of certain diseases, are *not* acts."

2-010 We are asked, therefore, to divide the human act into two elements: the desire for the muscular movement and the movement itself. In the case of D who kills another as a result of falling down some steps, there would be no accountability for the harm done because of the absence of a willed or desired muscular movement. However, this breakdown of human behaviour has been fiercely criticised. Hart points out that, described in these terms, it cannot apply to omissions (where to speak of the necessity for a willed failure to move one's muscles is not only clumsy but an inaccurate reflection of the law).[20] Furthermore, such an analysis does not reflect the reality of our movements.

---

20 H.L.A. Hart, *Punishment and Responsibility* (Oxford: OUP, 1968), p.100: "It is surely absurd even to attempt to fit omissions into such a picture of voluntary or involuntary conduct . . . [because] in the case of omissions no muscular movement or contraction need occur . . . [Such a theory] would have very unwelcome consequences for legal responsibility: for the only omissions which would then be culpable would be deliberate omissions. We could then only punish those who failed to stop at traffic lights if they deliberately shot the lights."

H.L.A. Hart, Punishment and Responsibility (1968), pp.101–102:

"[A] desire to contract our muscles is a very rare occurrence: there are no doubt *some* special occasions when it would be quite right to say that what we are doing is contracting our muscles, and that we have a desire to do this. An example of this is what we may do under instruction in a gymnasium. The instructor says 'lift your right hand and contract the muscles of the upper arm'. If we succeed in doing this (and it is not so easy) it would be quite appropriate to say we desired to and did contract our muscles . . . [But] when we shut a door, or when we hit someone, or when we fire a gun at a bird, these things are done without any previous thought of the muscular movements involved and without any desire to contract the muscles . . . The simple but important truth is that when we deliberate and think about actions, we do so not in terms of muscular movements but in the ordinary terminology of actions." **2–011**

Glanville Williams, The Mental Element in Crime (1965), pp.17–18:

"[O]ne cannot by introspection, identify a conscious exercise of will previous to movement. Indeed, one cannot always find an exercise of will at all. Many acts are performed unthinkingly; not only a reflex like dropping a hot poker but much of the routine of life, such as shaving, eating, walking. We seem to switch on an 'automatic pilot' for many of the familiar tasks we perform; yet we are undoubtedly acting. Even when we make a conscious decision and act to carry it out, the act is something different from the preceding deliberation." **2–012**

In this statement, Williams, in accordance with many commentators, tacitly upholds the distinction drawn in English law between mens rea and actus reus. But other critics of the willed movement principle do not. Welzel,[21] a German philosopher, argued that the causal theory upon which this principle, and much of the criminal law rests, is misconceived. He does not accept that there is a set of desires which *cause* the movements to occur. Instead, he favours a view of acting that looks to the actor's goal. The distinction between a bodily movement and an "act" lies not in any preceding will but in the purpose of the actor—what they were seeking to achieve. According to this philosophical stance, not only is it wrong to divide up the act, as Austin and his supporters do, but to divide any mental state from its act would be equally invalid. The two, he would claim, are inextricably linked and are incapable of separate analysis. **2–013**

More representative of the standard approach is the view of Williams that:

"Notwithstanding these difficulties of definition everyone understands the proposition that an act is something more than bodily movement—for bodily movement might occur in tripping and falling, which would not be described as an act."[22]

---

21 For a discussion of Welzel's view, see G.P. Fletcher, *Rethinking Criminal Law* (Boston: Little Brown, 1978), pp.434–439.

22 G. Williams, *The Mental Element in Crime* (Jerusalem: Magnes Press, 1965), p.18.

Broad consensus does seem to exist that it would be unjust to punish in these situations, despite the harm done. Those who feel that the willed movement analysis is unhelpful argue that what is missing is an ability to control one's actions. In no real sense are the actions "D's"[23] and, therefore, criminal liability is inappropriate. At this point, however, the consensus breaks down. Some commentators argue that involuntariness:

> ". . . is best analysed as representing a spectrum or continuum of potentially excusing conditions running from total incapacitation or involuntariness, as in sleep-walking or muscular spasm, to cases say of (concussion-induced) confusion. These conditions are all reducible to an absence of fault and therefore, . . . share the same underlying rationale of other excusing conditions such as duress, provocation and diminished responsibility."[24]

In short, a person whose actions are classified as involuntary can be afforded a type of defence called an *excuse* and can be exempted from criminal liability. The essence of an excuse is that the actor is blameless. If it were the actor's own fault that the involuntary conduct occurred, the law will not excuse that conduct. If the reason that the person fell down the stairs was that she was extremely drunk, we are entitled to say that carrying a loaded gun in that state of intoxication is culpable conduct and, accordingly, the resultant death or injury ought not to be excused.

2–014 Other commentators, however, argue that in cases of involuntary conduct, the absence of "the ordinary link between mind and behaviour",[25] is more fundamental than that involved when, for example, duress is pleaded. D, who shoots another because there is a gun pointed at their partner's head, accepts that they have done it but pleads that they lacked any real opportunity to do otherwise. Conversely, D, who is jostled in a crowd and pushed into V, causing V to lose their balance and fall, denies authorship. In the latter example, there is a complete denial of basic responsibility, and D is afforded an *exemption*; a denial of proof.[26] D has done no wrong; there is nothing to excuse.[27]

Whatever the theoretical basis of the exemption from liability, the law has tended to describe these cases of involuntariness as involving a defence of *automatism*. The precise nature and effect of this defence depend on a variety of circumstances surrounding the involuntary conduct. Accordingly, detailed consideration of this exemption from liability based on involuntariness is best left to Ch.9 where defences are considered.

---

23 This is not, as Packer says, to "be read as plunging into the deep waters of free will vs determinism . . . The law is not affirming that some conduct is the product of the free exercise of conscious volition; it is excluding, in a crude kind of way, conduct that in any view is not" (*The Limits of the Criminal Sanction* (California: Stanford University Press, 1969), p.76).

24 K.J.M. Smith and W. Wilson, "Impaired Voluntariness and Criminal Responsibility: Reworking Hart's Theory of Excuses—The English Judicial Response" (1993) 13 O.J.L.S. 69, 74.

25 A. Ashworth and J. Horder, *Principles of Criminal Law*, 9th edn (Oxford: OUP, 2019), p.100.

26 J. Gardner, "The Gist of Excuses" [1998] 1 Buff. Crim. L.R. 575.

27 For a discussion of the importance of the distinction between exemptions and excuses, see C.M.V. Clarkson, *Understanding Criminal Law*, 4th edn (London: Sweet & Maxwell, 2005), pp.81–82 where it is suggested that it might be helpful to regard the former as "status excuses" and the latter as "non-status excuses".

2. Status offences

The requirement that there must be an act and that this involves voluntary human conduct has caused problems in the context of "status offences". An offence can be defined in such a manner that no conduct is required, but the offence is committed when a certain state of affairs exists, or D is in a certain condition or is of a particular status. The following is a classic example of this. **2–015**

R. v Larsonneur (1933) 24 Cr. App. R. 74 (Court of Criminal Appeal):

"D (a French national) was permitted to land in the UK subject to certain conditions endorsed on her passport. These conditions were subsequently varied by a condition requiring her to depart from the UK not later than a certain date. On that date, she went to the then Irish Free State (Ireland). An order for D's deportation from the Irish Free State was made by the executive authorities of that country, and she was subsequently brought back to Holyhead in the custody of the Irish Free State police, who then handed her over to the police of the UK, by whom she was detained. D was convicted on a charge that she "being an alien to whom leave to land in the United Kingdom has been refused was found in the United Kingdom", contrary to the Aliens Order 1920 arts 1(3)(g) and 18(1)(b). D appealed against her conviction. **2–016**

HEWART, LCJ:

'[T]he appellant is an alien. She has a French passport, which bears [a] statement . . . [requiring] "departure from the United Kingdom not later than March 22, 1933" . . . In fact, the appellant went to the Irish Free State and afterwards, in circumstances which are perfectly immaterial, so far as this appeal is concerned, came back to Holyhead. She was at Holyhead on April 21, 1933, a date after the day limited by the condition on her passport.

In these circumstances, it seems to be quite clear that art.1(4) of the Aliens Order, 1920 . . . applies. The article is in the following terms:

> ". . . An alien who fails to comply with any conditions so attached or varied, and an alien who is found in the United Kingdom at any time after the expiration of the period limited by any such conditions, shall for the purposes of this Order be deemed to be an alien to whom leave to land has been refused."

The appellant was, therefore, on April 21, 1933, in the position in which she would have been if she had been prohibited from landing by the Secretary of State and, that being so, there is no reason to interfere with the finding of the jury. She was found here and was, therefore, deemed to be in the class of persons whose landing had been prohibited by the Secretary of State, by reason of the fact that she had violated the condition on her passport. The appeal, therefore, is dismissed and the recommendation for deportation remains."

Appeal dismissed

2-017 What is objectionable about convictions for status offences, such as in *Larsonneur,* is that D's actions are involuntary. There is nothing objectionable about the offence per se in *Larsonneur*, and had Larsonneur brought herself voluntarily into the UK, her conviction would have aroused no comment. It was the involuntary nature of her forced entry that provoked the controversy. In short, status offences are not objectionable if D has control over the status. It would be wrong to have an offence of having a common cold, but, as Husak argues, it could be justifiable to have an offence of having a beard as this is a process over which one has control.[28]

Under the Terrorism Act 2000 s.11(1), it is a criminal offence to belong to a proscribed organisation such as ISIS. This provision is not aimed merely at prohibiting the "act" of joining the proscribed organisation; it applies equally to those who joined before the date of commencement of the statute. This looks as though it is punishing persons for the mere status of being members of ISIS. However, s.11(2) provides a defence if one became a member before the organisation was proscribed and if one has not taken part in any of its activities while the organisation is proscribed. Thus, what is being punished in reality is a status over which there is control—evidenced by action (i.e. either joining the proscribed organisation after the date of commencement of the statute or, if one joined before then, taking part in its activities).[29]

Following this reasoning, status offences are only unjustifiable if the person had no control over their status. However, as seen earlier when examining involuntary conduct, the general requirement of voluntariness can be dispensed with if it was D's own fault that their actions were involuntary (prior fault). For example, if D chose to get very drunk. So, too, liability for a status offence becomes justifiable if it was D's own fault they got into that status or were in that situation. It has even been argued that the decision in *Larsonneur* was justifiable because it was D's fault that she was in the situation of being an illegal immigrant and the "author of her own fortune", having fled to Ireland after being caught attempting to enter into a marriage of convenience.[30]

However, it is difficult to see that this justifies the decision in *Larsonneur*. What is meant by D being "at fault"? Surely the fault must be related in some way to the offence charged. To illustrate this, consider the facts of *Winzar v Chief Constable of Kent*.[31] D was taken to hospital on a stretcher but was found to be drunk and told to leave. While slumped on a seat in the corridor, the police were called, who took him to their police car parked in the highway outside the hospital. He was then arrested and subsequently convicted of being "found drunk" in the highway. Here, D's prior fault in becoming voluntarily intoxicated was related to the offence charged. Conversely, trying to go through a marriage of convenience (not an unlawful act) is not connected in the same way to the offence committed by Larsonneur.

It has been argued that status offences could be regarded as contrary to the European Convention of Human Rights (ECHR) art.6(1).[32] The best approach to rebut this would be to focus on the voluntariness

---

28 D. Husak, *Philosophy of Criminal Law* (Oxford: OUP, 1987), p.102. Similarly, while it would be contrary to principle to make it an offence to be HIV positive, it could be permissible to make it an offence to have sexual intercourse while HIV positive.

29 Husak, "Does Criminal Liability Require An Act" in Duff (ed), *Philosophy and the Criminal Law* (1998), p.75.

30 Lanham, "Larsonneur Revisited" [1976] Crim. L.R. 276, 278.

31 *Winzar v Chief Constable of Kent* (1983) *The Times*, 28 March 1983.

32 G.R. Sullivan, "Strict Liability for Criminal Offences in England and Wales Following Incorporation into English Law of the European Convention on Human Rights" in A.P. Simester (ed), *Appraising Strict Liability* (New York: OUP, 2005), p.208.

of D's conduct. On this basis, the question is simply whether Larsonneur had control over her status or, even if she did not, whether it was her own fault that she allowed herself to get into that status. It is only this approach that is likely to be regarded as compatible with the ECHR. In *Robinson-Pierre*,[33] the Court of Appeal held that Parliament is at liberty to create a status offence in such a way as to make D liable irrespective of their control, or lack thereof, over the situation. However, on principled grounds, unless the statutory provision creating such an offence is clearly worded to that effect, liability for a status offence requires proof that D's conduct, with or without fault, caused or permitted the state of affairs to come about. Consequently, status offences are strict but not absolute.

3. Omissions

Most offences are committed by positive action. However, in certain circumstances, a failure to act may constitute the requisite "act" to satisfy the actus reus. A failure to act may result in the imposition of criminal liability in two situations. **2–018**

1. In conduct crimes, the failure to act may itself, without more, constitute the offence. This usually occurs in statutory offences, which are specifically defined in terms of an omission to act. For example, failing to provide for a child in one's care[34] or failing to provide a specimen of breath under road traffic legislation.[35]
2. In result crimes, the failure to act may contribute towards the harm specified in the offence and may thus, in certain circumstances, be deemed the requisite "act" for the purposes of the offence. This will only be so if the actor is under a duty to act. For example, a parent would be under a duty to rescue their child drowning in a shallow pool; their failure to act would constitute the requisite "act" of the crime of homicide. However, a stranger could, with impunity, watch the same child drowning. There is no general duty to act in English law. As Lord Diplock stated in *Miller*:

> "The conduct of the parabolical priest and Levite on the road to Jericho may have been indeed deplorable, but English law has not so far developed to the stage of treating it as criminal."[36]

Thus, criminal liability in these cases is dependent upon the existence of a duty to act. It is to this, and other related problems, that we now turn.

(i) Duty to act

Whether there is a duty to act is a question of law. The trial judge must direct the jury that if they find certain facts established, there will or will not be a duty to act. For example, in *Evans* (below), V was supplied with heroin by D (her half-sister), which she self-injected and died of heroin poisoning. It was **2–019**

33 *R. v Robinson-Pierre (Symieon)* [2013] EWCA Crim 2396; [2014] 1 W.L.R. 2638.
34 Children and Young Persons Act 1933 s.1(2)(a).
35 Road Traffic Act 1988 s.6(4).
36 *R. v Miller (James)* [1983] 2 A.C. 161 at 175.

a matter of fact for the jury whether it was D who supplied the drugs. If the jury were satisfied that D did supply the drugs, then, as a matter of law, she was under a duty to act.

R. v EVANS [2009] 2 CR. APP. R. 10 (COURT OF APPEAL, CRIMINAL DIVISION)

2-020 Lord Judge CJ:

"45. In some cases, such as those arising from a doctor/patient relationship where the existence of the duty is not in dispute, the judge may well direct the jury that a duty of care exists. Such a direction would be proper. But if, for example, the doctor were on holiday at the material time, and the deceased asked a casual question over a drink, it may well be that the question whether a doctor/patient relationship existed, and accordingly whether a duty of care arose, would be in dispute. In any cases where the issue is in dispute, and therefore in more complex cases, and assuming that the judge has found that it would be open to the jury to find that there was a duty of care, or a duty to act, the jury should be directed that if facts a + b and/or c or d are established, then in law a duty will arise, but if facts x or y or z were present, the duty would be negatived."

Unfortunately, there is a lack of doctrinal certainty as to when a duty to act will arise.[37] The following situations generally give rise to a duty to act; however, as will be seen, their parameters are not clearly defined.

(a) Special relationship

2-021 This special relationship may be professional or familial. A doctor owes a duty to their patients. There may also be a duty to act where there is a close familial relationship. Parents are under a duty to aid their small children; married couples are under a duty to aid each other.[38]

In *Downes*,[39] D (a parent), being a member of a religious sect called the Peculiar People, who believed in prayer rather than in medicine, failed to call a doctor for his sick child who died. D was convicted of manslaughter.[40] Outside of these core examples, it is not entirely certain which relationships possess the "features of familial duty or responsibility" to fall within the remit of this category.[41] Does this

37 The first draft of the Criminal Code Bill specified the circumstances in which one would be under a duty to act (cl.20(2)). These detailed proposals were dropped from the revised Draft Criminal Code; they were regarded as matters that should remain for the development of the common law (Law Com. No.77 Vol.2 para.7.12). The Draft Criminal Law Bill 1993 cl.19, follows this latter approach (Law Com. No.218, *Legislating the Criminal Code: Offences against the Person and General Principles* (1993) Cmnd.2370).

38 *R. v Smith* [1979] Crim. L.R. 251 CC; *R. v Hood (Kenneth)* [2003] EWCA Crim 2772; [2004] 1 Cr. App. R.(S.) 73.

39 *R. v Downes* (1875) 13 Cox C.C. 111.

40 In this case and in *R. v Shepherd* (1862) 9 Cox C.C. 123, it was indicated that the duty was imposed by statute (Poor Law Amendment Act 1868 s.37). In *Downes* (1875) 13 Cox C.C. 111, Coleridge CJ deliberately left open the question of whether there would be a duty to act in the absence of such a statutory duty. While many of the earlier cases were decided on this basis, it is now generally accepted that there is a *common law* duty to act in such cases but there is little express authority on this point.

41 *R. v Evans (Gemma)* [2009] EWCA Crim 650; [2009] 2 Cr. App. R. 10 at [20].

category extend to siblings? While there was some indication of this in *Stone and Dobinson*,[42] this has not been extended to half-siblings.[43]

It used to be asserted that the reason for the imposition of a duty of act in such cases was that the blood or marriage relationship was so strong as to generate a legal duty to preserve life. In the US decision of *People v Beardsley*,[44] for instance, it was held that D owes no duty to his "weekend mistress", as distinguished from his wife. However, such a rationale can no longer be accepted. The true reason for the existence of a duty in such cases must be the interdependence that springs from shared family life or close communal living.[45] In such a situation, one comes to rely on the other members of the family, and it is this reliance and expectation of assistance, if necessary, that generates the duty to act rather than any blood or marriage tie.

Unfortunately, the uncertainty does not cease there. Once a relationship is deemed sufficiently "special" to fall within the remit of this category, it is unclear how long and in what circumstances D remains duty-bound. In *Shepherd*,[46] the court held that no duty to act is owed by a parent to their "entirely emancipated" child over the age of 18. Accordingly, it is suggested that separated spouses owe no duty to each other. With regards to others, such as relatives, it is not a question of blood or marriage relationship but a question of dependence. However, with this comes the added layer of complexity in determining degrees of dependence; an issue that has not yet been explicitly deliberated by the appellate courts.

(b) Assumption of responsibility

If D voluntarily assumes responsibility towards another, they become under a legal duty to act, irrespective of the formal relationship between the parties. This arises where D's promise of care is explicit, as in *Nicholls*,[47] and where it is implicit, as in *Instan*. **2–022**

R. v Instan [1893] 1 Q.B. 450 (Court for Crown Cases Reserved)

D lived with V, her 73-year-old aunt. V, who had been healthy until shortly before her death, developed gangrene in her leg. During the last 12 days of her life, she could not fend for herself, move about or summon help. Only D knew of her state; she gave V no food and did not seek medical assistance. D was charged with manslaughter and was convicted. **2–023**

---

42 *R. v Stone (John Edward)* [1977] Q.B. 354; [1977] 2 W.L.R. 169 CA. While Lane LJ alluded to the fact that V was D's "blood-relation", it is clear that the true basis of the duty stemmed from the fact that D had assumed responsibility for V. Ashworth describes Lord Lane's judgment as "notoriously unsatisfactory", given that it is uncertain whether all three of the duty-supporting reasons he lists (blood relative; assumption of duty by allowing V to stay; assumption of duty by making efforts to wash and feed V were essential: A. Ashworth, "Manslaughter by omission and the rule of law" [2015] Crim. L.R. 563–577, 566.

43 *Evans* [2009] 2 Cr. App. R. 10 at [20] at [34].

44 *People v Beardsley* 150 Mich. 206; 113 N.W. 1128; 13 L.R.A. (N.S.) 1020; 121 Am. St. Rep. 617; 13 Ann. Cas. 39 (1907). This case was cited with approval in England in *Sinclair* [1998] EWCA Crim 2590.

45 Fletcher, *Rethinking Criminal Law* (1978), p.613.

46 *Shepherd* (1862) 9 Cox C.C. 123.

47 *R. v Nicholls* (1874) 13 Cox C.C. 75.

LORD COLERIDGE CJ:

"We are all of the opinion that this conviction must be affirmed. It would not be correct to say that every moral obligation involves a legal duty; but every legal duty is founded on a moral obligation. A legal common law duty is nothing else than the enforcing by law of that which is a moral obligation without legal enforcement. There can be no question in this case that it was the clear duty of the prisoner to impart to the deceased so much as was necessary to sustain life of the food which she from time to time took in, and which was paid for by the deceased's own money for the purpose of the maintenance of herself and the prisoner; it was only through the instrumentality of the prisoner that the deceased could get the food. There was, therefore, a common law duty imposed upon the prisoner which she did not discharge.

Nor can there be any question that the failure of the prisoner to discharge her legal duty at least accelerated the death of the deceased, if it did not actually cause it. There is no case directly in point; but it would be a slur upon and a discredit to the administration of justice in this country if there were any doubt as to the legal principle, or as to the present case being within it. The prisoner was under a moral obligation to the deceased from which arose a legal duty towards her; that legal duty the prisoner has wilfully and deliberately left unperformed, with the consequence that there has been an acceleration of the death of the deceased owing to the non-performance of that legal duty."

Conviction affirmed

2–024 These cases seem accurate and impose responsibility in just circumstances. However, it is unclear how much D must do for V for this duty to arise. The case law suggests that D will become duty-bound after minor or ineffectual acts of care are provided to V. For example, in *Stone and Dobinson*,[48] D1 and D2 took V (D1's anorexic and infirm sister) into their home. V failed to care for herself properly and eventually died. D1 was described by the court as being of low intelligence and D2 as somewhat inadequate, and their ineffectual care of V gave rise to a voluntary assumption of responsibility. Both were convicted of gross negligence manslaughter.

R. v Sinclair [1998] EWCA Crim 2590 (Court of Appeal, Criminal Division)

2–025 D (Sinclair) and his friend (V) visited a flat owned by a third party, Johnson (J), to buy methadone from another man there. Needles and syringes were available in the flat. D and V each injected themselves with the methadone at 2.30pm, and V soon became unconscious. D remained with V from mid-afternoon until the next morning and only then called an ambulance. Before the ambulance was called, D and J took limited and ineffectual remedial action to care for V; D poured water over V, and J administered a saline solution. V was certified dead on arrival at the hospital. Both were convicted of manslaughter and appealed.

48 *R. v Stone (John Edward)* [1977] Q.B. 354.

ROSE LJ:

"[Counsel for D] referred to a decision of the New South Wales Supreme Court in *Tak* 1988 NSWLR 226 which emphasised, as a pre-condition for a legal duty of care to arise, the need for the disabled person to be secluded by the defendant to prevent others from affording aid . . .

So far as Johnson is concerned, there is no English authority in which a duty of care has been held to arise, over a period of hours, on the part of a medically unqualified stranger. *Beardsley* and *Tak Tak* are both persuasive authorities pointing away from the existence of any such duty, although we do not accept in the light of *Stone* and *Dobinson*, that the concept of seclusion is, in English law, a necessary prerequisite to the existence of a legal duty of care. But Johnson did not know the deceased. His only connection with him was that he had come to his house and there taken methadone and remained until he died. Others were coming and going in the meantime. The fact that Johnson had prepared and administered to the deceased saline solutions does not, as it seems to us, demonstrate on his part a voluntary assumption of a legal duty of care rather than a desultory attempt to be of assistance. In our judgment, the facts in relation to Johnson were not capable of giving rise to a legal duty of care . . .

Sinclair was in a different position. The evidence was that he was a close friend of the deceased for many years and the two had lived together almost as brothers. It was Sinclair who paid for and supplied the deceased with the first dose of methadone and helped him to obtain the second dose. He knew that the deceased was not an addict. He remained with the deceased throughout the period of his unconsciousness and, for a substantial period, was the only person with him. In the light of this evidence, there was in our judgment material on which the jury properly directed, could have found that Sinclair owed the deceased a legal duty of care.

[The appeal was, however, allowed on the ground that a fuller direction on causation should have been given: as to whether acceleration of the moment of death was other than minimal.]"

Appeal allowed

Sinclair was cited with approval in *Ruffell*.[49] V self-injected heroin in D's home and became unwell. D made some attempts to revive V that night, but early in the morning, V was still unwell. D put him outside the house and left him there while he went back inside the house and fell asleep. V died from hypothermia and opiate intoxication. The Court of Appeal approved the trial judge's reasoning that there was a sufficient nexus between the parties to give rise to a duty to act because: **2–026**

". . . the deceased was a guest of the appellant in the appellant's family home and he was a friend . . . that had taken upon himself the duty of trying to revive him."

49 *R. v Ruffell (Stephen David)* [2003] EWCA Crim 122; [2003] 2 Cr. App. R. (S.) 53.

The rationale for holding D to be duty-bound in *Ruffell* is complicated by the fact that the court emphasised D's ineffectual assistance *and* the long-standing close relationship between him and V. Therefore, this could be seen as a mixing of two categories of duty. In *Evans* (where V died of heroin poisoning), it was held that merely placing V in a recovery position, putting her to bed and taking turns to check if she was alright would not be sufficient to amount to an assumption of responsibility.[50] However, it was added that in certain circumstances, there could be a voluntary assumption of responsibility where D does acts which "led the victim, or others, to become dependent on him to act".[51]

Geoffrey Mead, "Contracting into Crime: A Theory of Criminal Omissions" (1991) 11 O.J.L.S. 147, 168:

2–027 "The presence of an undertaking often gives rise to other reasons for the presence of a duty . . . If D has given an undertaking he may be in the best position to avert the harm. I shall refer to this as the 'Best Position' argument. This may be for one or more of the following reasons. First, he is more likely to be aware that a person may be in a position of peril and in need of assistance. He will know of the vulnerability of the victim in a way that others may not. Second, he may be more capable of carrying out the required task than will a third party. We might assume that, in most cases where D undertakes to do a particular thing, he feels he has the ability to do it, whereas a third party, who has not given such an undertaking will not necessarily possess the required skills to do what is needed in order to avert danger to V. The third point is that if other people are aware of the undertaking they might feel it unproductive for them to get involved as well. They might reasonably think that they would simply get in the way and hinder the proper completion of the task in question."

2–028 The real problem in these cases is one of determining the circumstances in which an individual can be said to have undertaken a duty towards another. A ship captain would be liable for failing to pick up a seaman or passenger who had fallen overboard.[52] Depending on the circumstances of employment, an employer could be liable for failing to aid her endangered employee. And as LaFave and Scott assert:

> "If two mountain climbers, climbing together, are off by themselves on a mountainside, and one falls into a crevasse, it would seem that the nature of their joint enterprise, involving a relationship of mutual reliance, ought to impose a duty upon the one mountaineer to extricate his imperilled colleague. So also if two people, though not closely related, live together under one roof, one may have a duty to act to aid the other who becomes helpless."[53]

---

50 *Evans* [2009] 2 Cr. App. R. 10 at [34], [35].

51 *Evans* [2009] 2 Cr. App. R. 10 at [36].

52 *US v Knowles* 26 Fed. Cas. 800 (N.D. Cal. 1864).

53 W.R. LaFave and A.W. Scott, *Criminal Law*, 2nd edn (Eagan: West Group, 1986), p.204.

Thus, it ought to be a question of whether, because of the relationship or the circumstances or both together, the parties rely on assistance from each other. *Sinclair* is explicable on this basis: while J was effectively in as good a position as S to render aid (following Mead's Best Position argument), it was the closeness of the relationship between S and V and their embarking on the enterprise of procuring drugs together that would have led V to rely on assistance from S. Although V was at J's house, J was a stranger. There would not have been the same reliance on and expectation of assistance from him.

(c) Contractual duty

D may owe another person a duty to act arising from contractual obligations. Such a duty might arise where D is a carer or healthcare professional, where they are contracted to protect another's property, or in the course of employment. A lifeguard employed at a swimming pool to ensure the safety of swimmers cannot sit idly by while a swimmer is drowning. **2–029**

In *Pittwood,*[54] D (a railway gatekeeper) was employed to keep a gate shut whenever a train was passing. He opened the gate to let a cart cross the lines and then went to lunch, forgetting to close it again. As a result, a subsequent cart collided with a train, killing the train driver. D was charged with manslaughter based on his omission.

Again, the basis of the duty in these cases is not so much the contract itself, but rather the fact that the contract is evidence of an assumption of responsibility creating an expectation in the mind of others that D will act. The public expects lifeguards to rescue drowning swimmers. It is their reliance on this fact that creates the duty to act. The fact that the railway gatekeeper has been contracted to perform these duties is merely strong evidence that he has assumed these responsibilities. It is submitted that the position would be no different if, during a strike, a volunteer offered (without any contract) to perform these duties. The fact that he has undertaken this responsibility would cause the public to rely upon him to perform these tasks. On this basis, this whole category (along with the first category above) simply becomes a species of the second category, namely the voluntary assumption of responsibility.

(d) Statutory duty

A failure to act may itself, without more, constitute a criminal offence. Failing to provide for a child in one's care is a criminal offence contrary to the Children and Young Persons Act 1933 s.1(1), even if this failure to act causes no further harm. Similarly, the Health and Safety at Work, etc. Act 1974 ss.2–7 imposes duties on employers to operate a safe working environment. A specific penalty is provided for breach of this duty irrespective of whether any other harm results. **2–030**

54 *R. v Pittwood (Philip)* (1902) 19 T.L.R. 37.

In recent years, the number of specific statutory offences has increased, with Ashworth identifying three types of a new generation of omissions offences in statutes: failure to report,[55] failure to prevent,[56] and failure to protect.[57]

Andrew Ashworth, "A New Generation of Omissions Offences?" [2018] Crim. L.R. 354–364, 359

2-031 "The three types of omissions offence described above—failure to report, failure to prevent, and failure to protect—have been created against the background of what is claimed to be a common law presumption against omissions liability. The offences create criminals where there were none before, by adding another layer of responsibility related to the basic wrong—a basic wrong that may be connected, as we have seen, with misconduct as diverse as money-laundering, terrorism, bribery, and female genital mutilation or other forms of serious familial abuse. All these forms of misconduct are offences that are already surrounded at common law with the usual doctrines of complicity, the inchoate offences and encouragement and assistance under the Serious Crime Act 2007, but the new generation of omissions offences imposes criminal liability going beyond the standard doctrines. However, unlike those standard doctrines, the new omissions offences have no general application. They apply selectively, reflecting the particular concerns of government and the legislature at given points in history: they do not proceed from a broad examination of whether there are good arguments for a general offence of failure to report a crime, or of failure to prevent an offence from taking place, or of 'consent or connivance' to a corporate offence."

2-032 Ashworth questions whether it is appropriate to invoke the criminal law to try to change corporate culture by providing an incentive to put preventive procedures in place. He also questions whether the wrong in failing to carry out the duty placed on individuals is serious enough to opt for criminalisation over a regulatory response in many of these cases. His main criticism is that these statutory offences of omission create a new layer of criminal law, and we ought to think carefully before expanding the law in this way.

However, unlike breaches of common law duties, a breach of a statutory duty will not always constitute the necessary "act" for the purpose of an ulterior offence if further harm results from the breach of duty. In *Lowe*,[58] D neglected his nine-week-old daughter by failing to call for a doctor when she became ill. He was charged with neglecting the child contrary to the Children and Young Persons Act 1933 s.1(1) and with manslaughter. One way in which manslaughter can be committed is by committing an

---

55 Ashworth provides the examples of failure by certain professionals to report suspected money-laundering (Proceeds of Crime Act 2002 ss.330–331), failure by certain employees to report financial offences related to terrorism (Terrorism Act 2000 ss.19 and 21A), and failure by any person to report information about acts of terrorism (Terrorism Act 2000 s.38B): A. Ashworth, "A new generation of omissions offences?" [2018] Crim. L.R. 354–364, 358.

56 Failure to prevent bribery by an employee, agent or subsidiary intended to benefit that organisation (Bribery Act 2010 s.7), failure to prevent the facilitation of a UK tax evasion offence (Criminal Finances Act 2017 s.45), failure to prevent the facilitation of a foreign tax evasion offence (Criminal Finances Act 2017 s.46): Ashworth, "A new generation of omissions offences?" [2018] Crim. L.R. 354–364, 358.

57 e.g. the offence under the Female Genital Mutilation Act 2003 s.3A, under which a person who is responsible for a girl under 16 fails unreasonably to take sufficient steps to protect her from genital mutilation, and the offence of allowing the death or serious injury of a child or vulnerable adult under the Domestic Violence, Crime and Victims Act 2004 s.5 (see Ch.9): Ashworth, "A new generation of omissions offences?" [2018] Crim. L.R. 354–364, 358.

58 *R. v Lowe (Robert)* [1973] Q.B. 702; [1973] 2 W.L.R. 481 CA.

unlawful act that is dangerous and causes death (constructive manslaughter). It was held that the requirement of an unlawful act was not satisfied by an omission. Phillimore LJ stated:

> "We think there is a clear distinction between an act of omission and an act of commission likely to cause harm. Whatever may be the position in regard to the latter it does not follow that the same is true of the former. In other words if I strike a child in a manner likely to cause harm it is right that if the child dies I may be charged with manslaughter. If, however, I omit to do something with the result that it suffers injury to health which results in its death, we think that a charge of manslaughter should not be an inevitable consequence, even if the omission is deliberate."

This case provides an interesting illustration of the reluctance of the English courts to impose criminal liability for omissions. Phillimore LJ is suggesting that there needs to be greater culpability for offences committed through omission than for offences where there has been a positive act of commission, and so an omission will not suffice for constructive manslaughter because this species of manslaughter[59] only requires a relatively low degree of culpability. Similarly, if a worker were to die as a result of an employer's breach of statutory duty, the employer would not be liable for constructive manslaughter because, as the Law Commission has noted, Parliament, in creating this duty, has provided a specific and limited punishment for its breach.[60] This approach is only justifiable if positive acts are regarded as "worse" than omissions.[61]

(e) Creation of a dangerous situation

A duty to act will arise where D's previous conduct has created, or contributed to, the creation of a dangerous situation. In such circumstances, D is under an obligation to try to prevent harm to others from occurring because of the dangerous situation. **2–033**

R. v Miller [1983] 2 A.C. 161 (House of Lords)

One night, while squatting in someone else's house, D lit a cigarette and then lay down on a mattress in one of the rooms. He fell asleep before he had finished smoking the cigarette and it dropped onto the mattress. Later he woke up and saw that the mattress was smouldering. He did nothing about it; he merely moved to another room and went to sleep again. The house caught fire. D was rescued and subsequently charged with arson, contrary to the Criminal Damage Act 1971 s.1(1) and (3). At this trial, he submitted that there was no case to go to the jury because his omission to put out the fire, which he had started inadvertently, could not amount to a sufficient actus reus. The judge ruled that once he had discovered the mattress was smouldering, D was under a duty to act. D was convicted, and the Court of Appeal upheld his conviction on the ground **2–034**

59 However, the species of gross negligence manslaughter might be the more appropriate charge in such cases.

60 Law Commission Consultation Paper No.122, *Legislating the Criminal Code: Offences against the Person and General Principles* (1992), para.6.19.

61 See paras 2–048 and 2–052.

that his whole course of conduct constituted a continuous actus reus. On appeal to the House of Lords:

LORD DIPLOCK:

> "I see no rational ground for excluding from conduct capable of giving rise to criminal liability, conduct which consists of failing to take measures that lie within one's power to counteract a danger that one has oneself created, if at the time of such conduct one's state of mind is such as constitutes a necessary ingredient of the offence . . .
>
> I cannot see any good reason why, so far as liability under criminal law is concerned, it should matter at what point of time before the resultant damage is complete a person becomes aware that he has done a physical act which, whether or not he appreciated that it would at the time when he did it, does in fact create a risk that property of another will be damaged; provided that, at the moment of awareness, it lies within his power to take steps, either himself or by calling for the assistance of the fire brigade if this be necessary, to prevent or minimise the damage to the property at risk.
>
> Let me take first the case of the person who has thrown away a lighted cigarette expecting it to go out harmlessly, but later becomes aware that, although he did not intend it to do so, it has, in the event, caused some inflammable material to smolder and that unless the smoldering is extinguished promptly, an act that the person who dropped the cigarette could perform without danger to himself or difficulty, the inflammable material will be likely to burst into flames and damage some other person's property. The person who dropped the cigarette deliberately refrains from doing anything to extinguish the smoldering. His reason for so refraining is that he intends that the risk which his own act had originally created, though it was only subsequently that he became aware of this, should fructify in actual damage to that other person's property; and what he so intends, in fact occurs. There can be no sensible reason why he should not be guilty of arson. If he would be guilty of arson, having appreciated the risk of damage at the very moment of dropping the lighted cigarette, it would be quite irrational that he should *not* be guilty if he first appreciated the risk at some later point in time but when it was still possible for him to take steps to prevent or minimise the damage . . .
>
> The recorder, in his lucid summing up to the jury . . . told them that the accused having by his own act started a fire in the mattress which, when he became aware of its existence, presented an obvious risk of damaging the house, became under a duty to take some action to put it out. The Court of Appeal upheld the conviction, but its ratio decidendi appears to be somewhat different from that of the recorder. As I understand the judgment, in effect it treats the whole course of conduct of the accused, from the moment at which he fell asleep and dropped the cigarette on to the mattress until the time the damage to the house by fire was complete, as a continuous act of the accused, and holds that it is sufficient to constitute the statutory offence of arson if at any stage in that course of conduct the state of mind of the accused, when he fails to try to prevent or minimise the damage which will result from his initial act, although it lies within his power to do so, is that of being reckless whether property belonging to another would be damaged.

> My Lords, these alternative ways of analysing the legal theory that justifies [the] decision . . . provoked academic controversy. Each theory has distinguished support. Professor J. C. Smith espouses the 'duty theory' (see [1982] Crim.L.R.526 at 528); Professor Glanville Williams . . . now prefers that of the continuous act (see [1982] Crim.L.R.773). When applied to cases where a person has unknowingly done an act which sets in train events that, when he becomes aware of them, present an obvious risk that property belonging to another will be damaged, both theories lead to an identical result; and since what your Lordships are concerned with is to give guidance to trial judges in their task of summing up to juries, I would for this purpose adopt the duty theory as being the easier to explain to a jury; though I would commend the use of the word 'responsibility,' rather than 'duty' which is more appropriate to civil than to criminal law, since it suggests an obligation owed to another person, i.e. the person to whom the endangered property belongs, whereas a criminal statute defines combinations of conduct and state of mind which render a person liable to punishment by the state itself . . .
>
> [A] suitable direction to the jury would be: that the accused is guilty of the offence under s.1(1) of the Criminal Damage Act 1971 if, when he does become aware that the events in question have happened as a result of his own act, he does not try to prevent or reduce the risk of damage by his own efforts or if necessary by sending for help from the fire brigade, and [if he has the appropriate *mens rea* at the time of failing to act]."
>
> *Appeal dismissed*

Lord Diplock's reasoning is to be welcomed. We all bear responsibility for our actions, even if those actions are unintentional. They are *our* actions. Where others are placed in danger from these actions, they expect us to "do something". They would rely on us to provide reasonable assistance, even if that only amounts to summoning help. Furthermore, "the person who creates a danger may be more aware than others of the existence of the danger, and ought not feel a reluctance to intervene that may be felt by others".[62] Accordingly, we should be under a duty to act when we become aware of the danger. On this basis, it is irrelevant whether D's initial actions involved any fault. Thus if, as in *Fagan v MPC*,[63] D inadvertently parks his car with a wheel resting on a policeman's foot, we would surely be justified in saying that D had assumed a responsibility (to get off the foot); his initial action would raise an expectation on the part of the police officer that he would act. He is under a duty to act. **2–035**

It is, however, difficult to determine the precise circumstances in which a duty can be said to arise because of the creation of a "dangerous situation". In *DPP v Santana-Bermudez*,[64] D stated that he had no needles on him and was then searched by a police officer. The police officer put her fingers in D's pocket and was pierced by a hypodermic needle. On a charge of assault occasioning actual bodily harm, it was stated by the Court of Appeal that D had created a dangerous situation by having the

---

62 G. Meade, "Contracting into Crime: A Theory of Criminal Omissions" (1991) 11 O.J.L.S. 147, 171.

63 *Fagan v Commissioner of Police of the Metropolis* [1969] 1 Q.B. 439; [1968] 3 W.L.R. 1120 Div Ct. The actual reasoning adopted in this case was somewhat different to the proposal here: see para.3–127.

64 *DPP v Santa-Bermudez* [2003] EWHC 2908 (Admin); [2004] Crim. L.R. 471.

needles in his pocket and not telling the police officer they were there. This provided an evidential basis that he was under a duty and had breached that duty.

R. v Evans [2009] 2 Cr. App. R. 10 (Court of Appeal, Criminal Division)

2–036 D supplied V (her half-sister, Carly) with drugs. V became very ill. D, knowing this, took ineffectual steps to care for her. V died from heroin poisoning. D was convicted of manslaughter by gross negligence and appealed.

LORD JUDGE:

"20 The question in this appeal is not whether the appellant may be guilty of manslaughter for having been concerned in the supply of the heroin which caused the deceased's death. It is whether, notwithstanding that their relationship lacked the features of familial duty or responsibility which marked her mother's relationship with the deceased, she was under a duty to take reasonable steps for the safety of the deceased once she appreciated that the heroin she procured for her was having a potentially fatal impact on her health.

21 When omission or failure to act are in issue two aspects of manslaughter are engaged . . . The second arises when the defendant has created a dangerous situation and when, notwithstanding his appreciation of the consequent risks, he fails to take any reasonable preventative steps . . . [His Lordship then discussed *Miller* and other authorities, including the drug supply cases of *Khan* and *Sinclair*.]

31 . . . The duty necessary to found gross negligence manslaughter is plainly not confined to cases of a familial or professional relationship between the defendant and the deceased. In our judgment, . . . for the purposes of gross negligence manslaughter, when a person has created or contributed to the creation of a state of affairs which he knows, or ought reasonably to know, has become life threatening, a consequent duty on him to act by taking reasonable steps to save the other's life will normally arise . . .

34 The judge . . . directed the jury that they had heard that the appellant

> 'did perform some acts to assist Carly during the evening of 2nd May, in particular she and her mother placed Carly in the recovery position and they took turns to look to see if she was alright. However, I direct you that as a matter of law there is nothing in that course of conduct which is capable of amounting to an acceptance or an assumption by Gemma Evans of responsibility for Carly so as to give rise to a duty of care. In the present case, the only matter which in law is capable of giving rise to a duty of care owed by Gemma Evans to Carly Townsend would be if Gemma Evans did, on this occasion, as the prosecution allege, act as an intermediary, giving the drugs to Carly . . .'

35 In relation to the circumstances in which a duty of care might arise in this case, these observations must be seen in their context, which is that the only issue of fact which the jury

had to decide was the supply issue. Unless the jury was sure of this fact, the remaining undisputed areas of appellant's involvement . . . would, on the judge's directions, have been insufficient for the purposes of gross negligence manslaughter. Without her involvement in the supply of heroin, the jury was directed that there was no duty on the appellant to act even after she became aware of the serious adverse effect of the drug taking on Carly. If on the other hand she was so involved, that fact, taken with the other undisputed facts would, and on our analysis of the relevant principles did give rise to a duty on the appellant to act. In law the judge's directions about the ingredients of gross negligence manslaughter, as applied to this case, were correct.

36 We would merely record that the judge's direction that a duty to act did not arise from a voluntary assumption of risk by the appellant may have been appropriate in this case, but it would not be of universal application where, for example, a voluntary assumption of risk by the defendant had led the victim, or others, to become dependent on him to act."

Appeal dismissed

When precisely does the duty to act arise in these cases where a dangerous situation has been created? One view is that it arises from the initial creation of the dangerous situation. This would mean that the duty arose in *Miller* when the fire was inadvertently started[65] and in *Evans* when the drugs were supplied. However, this view is no longer tenable because, as will be seen later in this chapter when causation is discussed, V's self-injection of the drugs breaks the causal chain.[66] Accordingly, as is clear from the dicta above in both *Miller* and *Evans*, the duty only arises when D realises that their acts have created a dangerous situation. In *Miller,* Lord Diplock refers to the duty arising when D "becomes aware that the events in question have happened as a result of his own act". This is echoed in *Evans* when it is stated that the duty arises "once she appreciated that the heroin she procured for her was having a potentially fatal impact on her health".[67] On this basis, if a drug supplier sells drugs to a client and then leaves the scene before the client self-injects, the supplier will not be under any duty to act. As Rogers points out: **2–037**

"Professional drug suppliers . . . now have every incentive not even to associate with their clients after supplying the drug . . . So the burden of the duty of care in *Evans* will fall more typically upon those close friends or family members who supply the drug and then stay with the victim . . . Any policy based reasoning which accepts that the dealer, who knowingly supplies potentially lethal drugs for profit, should not be guilty of any form of manslaughter when a client dies—but which tolerates the punishment of anyone else who was involved with the victim—is seriously flawed."[68]

---

65 J.J. Child, A.P. Simester, J.R. Spencer, F. Stark and G.J. Virgo, *Simester and Sullivan's Criminal Law: Theory and Doctrine*, 8th edn (Oxford: Hart, 2022), p.81.

66 *R. v Kennedy (Simon)* [2008] 1 A.C. 269; G. Williams, "Gross Negligence Manslaughter and Duty of Care in 'Drugs' Cases: *R. v Evans*" [2009] Crim. L.R. 631, 638.

67 *Evans* [2009] 2 Cr. App. R. 10 at [20].

68 "Death, Drugs and Duties" [2009] *Archbold News* 6, 6–9.

In *Evans*, it was added that the duty arises when D "knows, *or ought reasonably to know*" that the state of affairs has become life-threatening. The words in emphasis are obiter as the D in *Evans* was well aware that her sister's life was in danger. For many offences, such as arson in *Miller*, D, who did not himself appreciate the danger, would lack mens rea and so not be liable in any event. But for offences that can be committed negligently or through gross negligence as was the case in *Evans*, the italicised words become important. It can be argued that it would be inappropriate to impose a duty to act on a person who was completely unaware of the fact that she had created a dangerous situation. The opposing view is that if the dangers are obvious, D should not escape liability simply because she did not appreciate that fact. If negligence (or gross negligence) suffices for the offence, then negligence should also suffice in determining whether a duty to act has arisen.

(ii) Performance of duty

2-038 If D is duty-bound to act, one must ask how much danger, inconvenience, or expense D must undergo in order to fulfil that duty and avoid criminal liability. The current position is that D must take reasonable steps to discharge their duty to act.

Vehicle Inspectorate v Nuttall [1999] 1 W.L.R. 629

2-039 D, an owner of a coach business, did not examine charts produced by tachographs installed in his vehicles and was convicted of permitting his drivers to contravene various requirements of the Transport Act 1968 s.96(11A).

LORD HOBHOUSE OF WOODBOROUGH:

> "This offence of permitting is a crime of omission which arises from the duty to act and involves the failure to perform that duty. What actual conduct will amount to the offence of permitting will be a question of fact depending on the circumstances of the particular case. For example, an employer whose employees are always, to his knowledge, back in the yard within the required time need not carry out the same checks as one whose employees are sent out on longer journeys which will necessitate the taking of breaks if the Regulations are not to be infringed. Such an employer must certainly carry out some checks . . . The test of reasonableness must be applied objectively having regard to the relevant circumstances which will vary from case to case. But it is not a question of the employer doing what he thinks is reasonable. He must do whatever is involved in taking the reasonable steps to prevent breaches. It is an objective not a subjective criterion. If he does not perform his duty, he has committed the *actus reus* of the offence . . .
>
> The employer is under a positive duty to take the steps which an employer can reasonably take to detect and prevent breaches. He is not required to do the impossible; but he is not at liberty to omit to take those reasonable steps."

In *Hood*,[69] D delayed for three weeks in summoning medical assistance for his wife, who had accidentally fallen and broken several bones, which ultimately led to her death. The fact that the wife did not want to go to the hospital and could herself have called for assistance did not affect the fact that the husband had breached his duty, although these factors were relevant to sentencing. **2–040**

(iii) Distinguishing positive acts from omissions

The distinction between positive acts and omissions is crucial, as criminal liability will only be imposed for the latter if a duty to act can be established. However, whether one is dealing with an act or omission is not always clear. Suppose a road worker digs a deep hole in the road and then forgets to place a cover over it, with the result that a child falls in the hole and is killed: has the death been caused by the positive act of digging the hole or the omission to cover the hole? **2–041**

Katz has suggested that we can distinguish between acts and omissions by asking: "if the defendant did not exist, would the harmful outcome in question still have occurred in the way it did?".[70] On this analysis, the road worker is acting as their existence is critical to the causing of death. On the other hand, there is an omission where the stranger fails to rescue the drowning child because the child would still have died even if the stranger had not existed.

(iv) Omissions and causation

If the offence that D has been charged with is capable of being completed through an omission, D was under a duty to act, which they failed to reasonably discharge, D's omission will satisfy the conduct element of the actus reus. However, as identified above, for result crimes, it is also necessary to prove that D's conduct caused the resulting harm. When a mother fails to rescue her drowning child, how can her inactivity be said to *cause* the death of the child? Hogan has written: **2–042**

> "[T]here is no way you can cause an event by doing nothing . . . to prevent it. If grandma's skirts are ignited by her careless proximity to the gas oven, the delinquent grandson cannot be said to have killed her by his failure to dowse her . . . To say to the child, 'You have killed your grandmother' would simply be untrue."[71]

This view is untenable. When we examine causation later, we shall see that many causal contributions could be classed as "causes" of the resulting harm. When the child drowns in the pool with the mother watching and doing nothing, we could say that the causes of the child's death were the following: that the child was in the park and was taken near the pool, that the child fell in the pool, that there was sufficient water in the pool for him to drown, that he could not swim, that his lungs filled with water, or that his mother did not rescue him when she could easily have done so. Hart and Honoré, in their

---

69 *Hood* [2004] 1 Cr. App. R. (S.) 73.

70 L. Katz, *Bad Acts and Guilty Minds: Conundrums of the Criminal Law* (Chicago: University of Chicago Press, 1987), p.143. For further discussion of the distinction between acts and omissions, see A.P. Simester, "Why Omissions are Special" (1995) 1 *Legal Theory* 311.

71 B. Hogan, "Omissions and the Duty Myth" in P. Smith (ed), *Criminal Law: Essays in Honour of J.C. Smith* (London: Butterworths, 1986), pp.85–86.

seminal work on causation, argue that in selecting a cause (as opposed to a condition) from a list such as this, one will count as causes those things or events that are a deviation from 'normal' behaviour.[72] There are two abnormal occurrences in our list: the child fell in the pool and the mother failed to rescue him. Both are deviations from what might be expected and can thus be held to be concurrent causes of the resulting harm (death).

Arthur Leavens, "A Causation Approach to Criminal Omissions" (1988) 76 Cal. L. Rev. 547, 572–575:

2–043 "[I]t seems at first inappropriate to apply commonsense causation analysis to an individual's failure to engage in particular conduct. If one focuses solely on the circumstances of an omission at the time directly preceding the harm, the omission often appears not to have affected the at rest state of affairs. For example, a person sitting in the park while a nearby flower dies from lack of water is usually not considered to have caused the plant's demise, even if a full watercan sits nearby . . .

The difficulty in conceptualizing an omission as a causal force is that omissions do not seem to fit within the parameters of the physical cause and effect model. In the physical paradigm, there is a direct and identifiable chain of events through which the actor can readily be seen as intervening and changing what existed before. In cases of omission, however, the actor does not physically alter the status quo, but rather appears simply to permit the preexisting state of affairs to continue. Without direct physical involvement in the causal process leading to a particular result, an omitter seems no more causally responsible for the result than anyone else . . .

Such a view of causation is flawed because its inquiry is too limited. It depends on a definition of the status quo as the existing physical state of affairs at the precise time of the omission, much as if we took a picture of the scene at the moment before the omission and then compared it to a similar picture taken immediately thereafter, searching for a change in circumstances physically attributable to the omissive conduct. Our everyday notions of causation, however, are not so limited because we understand that the status quo encompasses more than the physical state of affairs at a given time. Indeed, in everyday usage the status quo is taken to include expected patterns of conduct, including actions designed to avert certain unwanted results. When, for example, a driver parks a car on a steep hill, it is normal to set the parking brake and put the car in gear. If the driver forgets to do so and the car subsequently rolls down the hill, smashing into another car, we would say that the failure to park properly was a departure from the status quo. This failure, not the visibly steep hill or the predicate act of pulling the car to the curb, was the cause of the collision.

Once we realize that a particular undesirable state of affairs can be avoided by taking certain precautions, we usually incorporate these precautions into what we see as the normal or at rest state of affairs. A failure to engage in the preventive conduct in these cases can thus be seen as an intervention that disturbs the status quo. When such a failure to act is a necessary condition

72 H.L.A. Hart and T. Honoré, *Causation in the Law*, 2nd edn (Oxford: OUP, 1985), p.37.

(a 'but for' cause) of a particular harm, then that failure fairly can be said to cause that harm. In the above example, the driver's failure to park the car in a proper manner caused the accident as surely as if he had actually driven his car into the other . . .

[W]e do expect certain persons to engage in particular types of preventive conduct as a matter of routine. Because of this expectation, we perceive any failure of those persons to take prescribed actions as a departure from normality. While we do not see the bystander's failure to water the flower as the cause of its withering away, we take a different view of such a failure by the park's gardener. We expect that the gardener will take reasonable steps to prevent the flower's demise, that is, his preventive conduct represents normality. A departure from that status quo—his failure to water—is thus more than a necessary condition of the flower's death: it causes that result every bit as much as the act of an intruder pulling the plant from its soil.

Of course, society's expectation of particular preventive conduct could be described as merely another formulation of 'duty.'

A 'duty' sufficient to support criminal sanctions must be founded on both an empirically valid expectation that persons in similar circumstances will act to prevent a harm—the probability aspect of normality—and also a deeply ingrained common understanding that society relies on that individual to prevent the harm—the normative aspect of normality. Thus parents have a 'duty' to prevent harm to their children because empirically, almost all parents act this way, and normatively, our society would consider it reprehensible if they did not. It is this combination of deviance—departing from a pattern of regular performance—and reprehensibility—being blameworthy—that makes us conclude that failure to act caused the harm."

Following this reasoning, according to the rules examined above, only those who are under a duty to act can be said to cause a result through their failure to act. This conclusion has important implications in the next section, where we consider whether there should be a general duty to act. **2–044**

To prove causation in circumstances where D has failed to act while duty-bound to do so, the prosecution must show that D's intervention *would* have made a difference.[73] It is insufficient to prove that D's intervention *might* have made a difference; a point explicitly endorsed by the Court of Appeal in *Broughton*.[74] In that case, while at a music festival, D supplied V (his girlfriend) with a Class A drug, 2-CP, that had been "bumped" with ecstasy or ketamine, which she voluntarily consumed. V became increasingly unwell and, a few hours after consuming the drugs, was at obvious and serious risk of dying. D failed to seek medical attention, despite the medical tent being 400 metres away, because he was fearful of the legal consequences of supplying drugs. Despite owing V a duty of care,[75] the Court

73 *R. v Morby* (1882) 8 Q.B.D. 571.

74 *R. v Broughton (Ceon)* [2020] EWCA Crim 1093; [2021] 1 W.L.R. 543.

75 Throughout the judgment, there is an undefended assumption that D was duty-bound to assist V. Unfortunately, there is no discussion in Lord Burnett's judgment as to *why* D owed V a duty of care. Presumably, this could have been on the basis that D voluntarily assumed responsibility for V (*R. v Stone (John Edward)* [1977] Q.B. 354; [1977] 2 W.L.R. 169) or that D had contributed to the creation of a dangerous situation (*Evans*), but it would have been beneficial for this to have been explicitly addressed.

of Appeal quashed D's conviction for gross negligence manslaughter on the grounds that there was only a 90% chance that, had D sought medical attention, V's life would have been saved. Thus, since D's intervention only *might* have made a difference, the jury should not have been invited to consider whether D's omission caused V's death.[76]

(v) A general duty to act?

2–045 It is sometimes asserted that liability for omissions ought not to be restricted to those cases where there is a recognised legal duty to act. If D sees V (a stranger child) drowning in a shallow pool of water and fails to rescue them when D could have easily done so with no danger to themselves, then D has killed V as surely as if she had held V's head under the water, and ought to be punished to the same extent. If one of the objects of the criminal law is to stimulate socially approved conduct, then the imposition of criminal liability in such cases would encourage people to act in situations such as these.

Andrew Ashworth, "The Scope of Liability for Omissions" (1989) 105 L.Q.R. 424, 430–432:

2–046 "Individuals tend to place a high value on interpersonal contacts, relationships, mutual support and the fulfilment of obligations, and a society which values collective goals and collective goods may therefore provide a wider range of worthwhile opportunities for individual development . . . The counter-argument to the conventional view is thus that a duty to co-operate with or to assist others should not be ruled out *ab initio* by an asocial and falsely restricted view of individual autonomy . . .

Individuals need others, or the actions of others, for a wide variety of tasks which assist each one of us to maximise the pursuit of our personal goals. A community or society may be regarded as a network of relationships which support one another by direct and indirect means . . .

. . . It follows that there is a good case for encouraging co-operation at the minimal level of the duty to assist persons in peril, so long as the assistance does not endanger the person rendering it . . .

. . . The foundation of the argument is that a level of social co-operation and social responsibility is both good and necessary for the realisation of individual autonomy . . . Each member of society is valued intrinsically, and the value of one citizen's life is generally greater than the value of another citizen's temporary freedom. Thus it is the element of emergency which heightens the social responsibility in 'rescue' cases, and which focusses other people's vital interests into a 'deliberative priority,' and it is immediacy to *me* that generates *my* obligation. The concepts of immediacy and the opportunity of help (usually because of physical nearness) can thus be used to generate, and to limit the scope of, the duty of assistance to those in peril."

---

76 cf. *R. v Misra (Amit)* [2004] EWCA Crim 2375; [2005] 1 Cr. App. R. 21, where D's conviction for gross negligence manslaughter was affirmed despite evidence that if D had intervened, V would have had a 95% chance of survival. See paras 7–055–7–057.

Graham Hughes, "Criminal Omissions" (1958) 67 Yale L.J. 590, 626, 634:

"But a view of moral responsibility is surely outmoded which imposes liability on the father who does not warn his child of the precipice before him, but not on a stranger who neglects to warn the child . . . The law often lags a half century or so behind public mores, but the spectacle cannot be lightly entertained in a field of this importance. The duty to take active steps to save others, and a liability for homicide in the absence of such action, could well be based on the defendant's clear recognition of the victim's peril plus his failure to take steps which might reasonably be taken without risk to himself to warn or protect the victim . . . **2–047**

Conventional criticisms of the imposition of a duty to rescue are usually based on objections to compelling one man to serve another, to creating a fear of prosecution which might cause citizens to interfere officiously in the affairs of others, and to the feasibility of imposing liability on a crowd of spectators all of whom had knowledge of the peril but were too selfish to intervene. These objections, however, do not seem to have much merit. To the first, the reply may be made that the evil of interfering with individual liberty by compelling assistance is much outweighed by the good of preserving human life. The second is a speculation which would be difficult to support. The third point appears to pose a real difficulty, but it is no different from a situation which commonly occurs in offenses of commission. In a riot, for example, it is difficult if not impossible to bring all the participants to book, but this has never been considered an obstacle to trial and punishment of those who can be reached. If a crowd of spectators stands by and watches a child drown in shallow water, nothing seems objectionable in trying and punishing all who can be tracked down and cannot show a reasonable excuse. To think that such an example of selfish group inertia could exist in our society is distressing, but, if it did, there would be every reason for invoking the criminal law against it."

There are many arguments as to why English law should not introduce a general duty to act. The central argument relates to individual liberty and autonomy.[77] Our freedom should only be restricted insofar as it is necessary to prevent persons from causing harm to others. Furthermore: **2–048**

". . . the criminal law should recognise an individual's choices rather than allowing liability to be governed by chance, and the obligation to assist someone in peril may be thrust upon a chance passer-by, who may well prefer not to become involved at all."[78]

It is further argued that the imperilled stranger has no *right* to be rescued, and therefore, D is under no *duty* to rescue.[79] These arguments are fortified by the claim that it is basic to our morality that it is

---

77 Simester, "Why Omissions are Special" (1995) 1 *Legal Theory* 311.

78 A. Ashworth, "The Scope of Criminal Liability for Omissions" (1989) 105 L.Q.R. 424, 425–426.

79 J. Murphy, "Blackmail: A Preliminary Inquiry" *The Monist* 63 No.2 (1980), fn.6; L.K. Stell, "Dueling and the Right to Life" (1979) 90 *Ethics* 7, 12 cites John Stuart Mill's distinction between perfect and imperfect obligations: "Duties of perfect obligation are those duties in virtue of which a correlative right resides in some person or persons; duties of imperfect obligation are those moral obligations which do not give birth to any right" (*Utilitarianism* (1957), p.61).

worse for D to (say) shoot or drown V than merely to look the other way while they are drowning. As Fletcher puts it:

> "The difference between killing and letting die, between creating a risk, and tolerating a risk, is one of the principles that sets the framework for assessing moral responsibility."[80]

This point is underlined by Moore: "Drowning [a child] makes the world a worse place, whereas not preventing its drowning only fails to improve the world."[81] Husak suggests the reason why it is worse to kill than to let die is that D has more control in the former than in the latter:

> ". . . persons generally exercise far less control over what happens as a result of their omission than as a result of their positive actions. Control over a consequence is typically exercised by positive action."[82]

English law has endorsed this view: in *Airedale NHS Trust v Bland,* the House of Lords ruled that in certain circumstances, it was lawful for doctors to let a patient die, but it was unlawful to bring a patient's life to an end:

> "So to act is to cross the Rubicon which runs between on the one hand the care of the living patient and on the other hand euthanasia—actively causing his death to avoid or to end his suffering. Euthanasia is not lawful at common law."[83]

2-049 Additionally, there are many objections of a more practical nature to any idea of introducing a general duty to act. If a large crowd watches someone drown, would they all be liable? How much help needs be given? After dragging a drowning person from the sea, would one be under a duty to provide mouth-to-mouth resuscitation (irrespective of the risk of disease) and then drive the rescued person to the nearest hospital if necessary? How much danger would the rescuer be expected to risk? What if the rescuer's efforts exacerbated the situation and worsened the plight of the imperilled person? Might such a law not be counterproductive in that fear of being forced to intervene might keep people away from places where they might be called upon to help?

A final objection to any attempt to introduce a general duty to act is that it will not usually be possible to establish causation in situations other than those where there is a duty to act. To explore this, recall *Stone and Dobinson* (discussed above). In that case, D1 (Stone) and D2 (Dobinson) failed to care for V properly, leading to her death. In that case, two other individuals also provided *some* care to V; one washed V and the other (a local landlady) encouraged D1 and D2 to call for medical

---

80 Fletcher, *Rethinking Criminal Law* (1978), p.601.

81 M. Moore, *Act and Crime: The Philosophy of Action and Its Implications for Criminal Law* (Oxford: Clarendon Press, 1993), p.59.

82 Husak, *Philosophy of Criminal Law* (1987), p.100. Husak advocates replacing the actus reus requirement in criminal law generally with a "control principle".

83 *Airedale NHS Trust v Bland* [1993] A.C. 789; [1993] 2 W.L.R. 316 HL at 865.

assistance. If there were a general duty to act in English law, could either of the third parties have been charged with manslaughter? If they had summoned medical assistance, V would have likely survived.

The answer here must be in the negative. It is possible to hold that D1 and D2 caused V's death because it was their deviation from an expected norm that stands out as abnormal among the other causal conditions. The inactions of the third parties do not stand out as abnormal. V was dependent and reasonably relied upon D1 and D2. This reliance generates a duty on their part to take care of her, and it is the breach of this duty that stands out as a "deviation" and thus a cause. On the other hand, V did not rely on either of the third parties any more than she would have relied on a passing milkman who happened to become aware of her situation, meaning that they had not voluntarily assumed responsibility for her, and thus did not cause her death.

Does this thesis apply in all cases? It will be recalled that Leavens, in the above extract,[84] used the example of a person sitting on a park bench watching a flower die from lack of water even though a full watering can was nearby. We would not say that that person caused the death of the flower. As they were under no duty to water the flower, their failure to act was "normal". But we would say that the park's gardener caused the death of the flower if they failed to water it. Because of their duty (by contract), the failure becomes significant; it represents a marked alteration of the status quo and can count as a cause. **2–050**

Thus, to summarise, it would be futile to impose a general duty to act as the only people who could be held responsible in terms of causation would be those who owed duties to their victims under one of the recognised heads. It is only *because of* the special relationship, the voluntary assumption of duty, etc, that causation is established. Without this pre-existing duty, the causative link between the inactivity and the ensuring consequence would be too remote.[85]

In discussing whether there ought to be a general duty to act, we have, until now, assumed that the purpose of such a general duty is that a breach thereof constitutes the requisite "act" for the purposes of some ulterior offence—for example, a failure to rescue becomes the requisite act for the purposes of manslaughter. It is, however, not necessary to go as far as this. The law could still issue its moral directive that people must assist others but avoid all problems of causation and mens rea by creating separate offences imposing strict liability for a failure to act. A failure to act would render one liable for this separate offence.[86] **2–051**

If such a provision were part of English law, then the Ds in *Stone and Dobinson* could have been charged with this offence instead of manslaughter. Some might argue that this would have been preferable: in

84 See para.2–043.

85 This point was recognised in *Miller* [1983] 2 A.C. 161, when Lord Diplock indicated that a "passive bystander" could not be said to have caused a fire, or presumably any injuries sustained in the fire.

86 In other countries, such as France and Spain, there is a duty to rescue others. In France, D is criminally liable for failing to assist a person in danger under the French Penal Code arts 223–226. For critical commentary on this provision, see A. Ashworth and E. Steiner 'Criminal Omissions and Public Duties: The French Experience' (1990) 10 L.S. 153. Similarly, in Spain, D is criminally liable for failing to assist a person who is unprotected or in serious, manifest danger, when able to do so without risk to himself or third parties under the Spanish Criminal Code art.195.

moral terms, one can condemn D1 and D2 for neglecting V, but can we really condemn them morally for *killing* V?[87] Of course, if such a provision were introduced in England, without more, the Ds in *Stone and Dobinson* would have been guilty of both this offence *and* manslaughter, their duty to act being now statutory in addition to the other grounds giving rise to their duty. It would need to be made clear whether such a new provision *replaced* the possibility of any criminal liability for an ulterior offence or not. Where there is a duty under one of the already established heads, there is a strong case for continuing to impose criminal liability for the ulterior offence. The mother who watches her young child drown in the shallow pool *ought* arguably to be liable for manslaughter (at least) and not merely liable for a lesser offence of failing to act. This would, of course, leave unresolved the problem of whether the Ds like those in *Stone and Dobinson* should simply be charged with the new statutory offence or whether they should be charged with manslaughter on the basis that they have breached one of the existing categories of duty.

As noted above, the legislature has in recent decades created a new generation of specific statutory offences based on omissions, including that of causing or allowing the death of a child or vulnerable adult in one's household.[88] Ashworth suggests that many people may be unaware of the existence of this offence and of the duty that arises, leading to rule-of-law concerns.[89] If the law is to be effective in enforcing moral duties that arise, the existence of such offences needs to be effectively communicated to members of the public. That becomes a particular issue where the legislature chooses to create a large number of offences criminalising omissions. Ashworth reports that 42 (26%) of the offences created by primary legislation in 2005 are offences of omission.[90]

(vi) Punishment of omissions

2-052 Under English law, once liability for an offence has been established, one is liable to any punishment up to the maximum, regardless of whether one's "act" consisted of positive action or an omission to act. This approach can be defended: the harm is the same in both cases, and sometimes it is difficult to distinguish between acts of commission and omissions to act. On the other hand, it can be argued that omissions ought, in principle, to be punished less severely than positive acts and that this lesser level of punishment should be clearly articulated. One of the views considered earlier was that it was worse to "kill" than to "let die". If this were accepted, it should be reflected at the punishment level.

B. LEGALLY RELEVANT CIRCUMSTANCES

2-053 It was seen earlier in this chapter that the traditional definition of an actus reus involves: (1) an act; (2) committed in legally relevant circumstances; and (3) that (for result crimes) causes the prohibited consequence. An example is the offence of causing death by dangerous driving, which requires that D caused the death by dangerously driving a mechanically propelled vehicle on a road or other public

87 See, e.g. Ashworth, "Manslaughter by omission and the rule of law" [2015] Crim. L.R. 563–577, 576.
88 Domestic Violence, Crime and Victims Act 2004 s.5. This offence carries a penalty of a maximum of 14 years' imprisonment.
89 A. Ashworth, "Ignorance of the Criminal Law, and Duties to Avoid it" (2011) 74(1) M.L.R. 1, 18.
90 Ashworth, "Ignorance of the Criminal Law, and Duties to Avoid it" (2011) 74(1) M.L.R. 1, 13.

place. The act of dangerous driving must be committed in the legally relevant circumstance that it was on a road or other public place, and it must have caused death.

All offences require core circumstances: D is a person over the age of criminal responsibility (10 yrs old), but these can be presumed unless there is evidence to the contrary. Beyond these, the circumstance elements of the actus reus are crucial in classifying an otherwise everyday act as serious wrongdoing. Having sexual intercourse can be seen as a very positive activity, with the benefit of expressing love and affection or obtaining sexual pleasure. However, the act of a person inserting their penis into the vagina, anus or mouth of another person will only be seen in this positive light *if* it is an act done in circumstances in which the other person consents. If the surrounding circumstances are that the other person does not consent, the serious offence of rape is committed.

It is important to distinguish between the actus reus components because they will commonly have specific mens rea requirements. For example, attempted aggravated criminal damage under s.1(2) requires D to attempt to commit criminal damage being reckless as to whether life would be endangered.[91] As will be seen in Ch.5, for attempts, D must intend the consequence but be reckless as to surrounding circumstances. Whether the offence element of "whether the life of another would be thereby endangered" is a legally relevant circumstance or a consequence becomes a critical issue.[92]

C. CAUSATION

1. Introduction

For result crimes, it is always necessary to prove that D's conduct *caused* the resulting harm. If D's conduct does not cause the result specified by the offence, there can be no liability for that offence. Often, establishing causation is straightforward. In most cases, we can trace a series of physical chain reactions from D's conduct to the resulting harm without any issues, much like a forensic scientist or pathologist might track when investigating a person's cause of death. For example, if D pulls the trigger of a gun, firing a projectile into V's chest, and V dies from the resultant blood loss, it would be uncontroversial to find that D caused V's death. However, not all causal inquiries will be this simple. For example, what if D thought the gun a prop that was unable to fire live rounds, or V has a medical condition meaning they are unusually vulnerable to injury (e.g. haemophilia), or if another party fired at V at exactly the same time or a split second later? In these cases, whether or not D's conduct caused the resulting harm (death) is likely to be contested at trial. They also invoke interesting theoretical questions about the nature and role of causation in criminal law. **2-054**

In straightforward cases, the trial judge will direct the jury to use their "common sense" to determine whether D caused the resulting harm. However, in more complicated cases, the common law has

91 Criminal Damage Act 1971 s.1(2).

92 See para.10-038 where this point and the case in which it arose (*Att-Gen's Reference (No.3 of 1992)* [1994] 1 W.L.R. 409 CA; (1994) 98 Cr. App. R. 383) are discussed.

developed numerous legal principles to assist with the attribution of causal responsibility. This is applied through a two-stage test: factual and legal causation. In order to establish causation, it is necessary for the prosecution to prove *both* factual and legal causation.

2. Factual causation

2–055 Factual causation provides us with the starting point and asks whether D's conduct is a *sine qua non* (or "but for" cause) of the result: *but for* D's conduct, would the resulting harm have occurred? If the answer to this question is "no", D is a factual cause. One example where factual causation was not proven is *White*.[93] D laced his mother's (V's) drink with cyanide with the intention of killing her. Although it is unclear whether she consumed any of the poisoned drink, medical evidence presented at trial demonstrated that she died of an unrelated heart attack shortly afterwards. Consequently, D was not a factual cause of her death and was not liable for her murder.[94]

Factual causation encompasses an extremely wide range of causal contributors. This is for two primary reasons. First, it is unable to discriminate between multiple causes. If D1 and D2 independently contribute to the resulting harm, D1 will not be availed of responsibility simply because D2 is also a factual cause. This was confirmed in *Benge*,[95] where the court held that D need not be the sole or main cause; the contribution of others does not undermine D's causal contribution. Secondly, D's conduct is a factual cause of the resulting harm even if they only accelerated the result.[96] Indeed, in the case of homicide, D only accelerates the inevitability of death. For these reasons, we must supplement factual causation with additional legal rules.

3. Legal causation

2–056 Once it has been established that D is a factual cause of the result, we move to legal causation. The purpose of legal causation is to determine whether D should, in law, be held causally responsible for the result. In performing this function, it seeks to narrow the remit of the objective test of factual causation to find those actors that ought to be morally and legally answerable for bringing about the resulting harm. Or, in other terms, legal causation helps to narrow down from those factual causes those that can be labelled as a *legal* cause for the purposes of the criminal law.

It is not possible to provide a definitive or formulaic account of causation in criminal law here. This is because although causation will often involve a mechanical or scientific evaluation of D's conduct in relation to the resulting harm, ascribing causal responsibility often involves the evaluation of socio-economic, political and moral considerations. However, a number of guiding principles and legal rules can be offered.

---

93 *White* [1910] 2 K.B. 124.
94 Instead, D was convicted of attempted murder.
95 *Benge* (1846) 2 Car. & Kir. 230.
96 *R. v Dyson (AE)* [1908] 2 K.B. 454; (1909) 1 Cr. App. R. 13.

The first requirement is that D's conduct must have made a "significant" contribution to the occurrence of the actus reus.[97] However, this is not to be interpreted as requiring D's conduct to be the main, sole, or substantial cause;[98] D's contribution must only be more than insignificant or de minimis.[99]

The second requirement is that D's conduct must also be an "operative" cause of the resulting harm.[100] This means that D's conduct must be significant at the time the result occurs. For example, suppose that D is driving at a speed that is in excess of the speed limit. Before arriving at the junction, D slows to the correct speed, exits the junction and collides with another vehicle. Here, D's speeding is inoperative at the time of the collision and, therefore, insignificant to the occurrence of the resulting harm. Although D's speeding is a factual cause of the result, insofar as they would have arrived at the junction at a later time if driving at the speed limit, thus avoiding the other vehicle, D's conduct in driving at excess speed is not a legal cause of the resulting harm.

The final guiding requirement is that D's conduct in bringing about the resulting harm must be **2–057** "blameworthy".[101] This principle is more controversial and tends to be more visible and do more "work" when ascribing causal responsibility for crimes of strict liability. To illustrate this, consider the facts of *Hughes*: D, who was driving in a faultless manner, rounded a corner and was hit head-on by V's car, which was travelling on the wrong side of the road. D was unable to avoid the collision, in which V died. D was charged with causing death by driving at a time when uninsured; a strict liability offence.[102] The Supreme Court quashed D's conviction on the grounds that his conduct in causing death was not open to criticism; "being involved in a fatal collision" is not the same thing as "*causing* death by driving". Therefore, the basic point is that for strict liability offences that have a result element within the actus reus, it is insufficient to simply establish a "but for" cause (*sine qua non*) between D's conduct and the resulting harm; it is necessary for D's conduct to be blameworthy in causing the result. However, this principle will do little/no work for those offences that have a mens rea requirement for the resulting harm.

The requirement that D's conduct be significant, operative, and blameworthy in bringing about the resulting harm provides us with a causal baseline. All of the subsequent legal rules and principles serve to inform whether this baseline is established. For example, if, after D's conduct, a third party (T) intervenes and "breaks the chain" of causation, T's intervention will render D's causal contribution insignificant, inoperative and blameless. Such interventions are known as *novus actus interveniens* and often pose problems for the appellate courts. Indeed, in *Empress Car*, Lord Hoffmann held that ". . . it is of course the causal significance of acts of third parties (as in this case) or natural forces that gives rise to almost all the problems about the notion of 'causing' and drives judges to take refuge in metaphor or Latin".[103] It is to these "breaks" that we now turn.

---

97 *R. v Cato (Ronald Philip)* [1976] 1 W.L.R. 110; [1976] 1 All E.R. 260 at 265–6; *R. v Kennedy (Simon)* [2007] UKHL 38; [2008] 1 A.C. 269; *R. v Wallace (Berlinah)* [2018] EWCA Crim 690 at [64]; [2018] 2 Cr. App. R. 22.

98 *R. v Hennigan (James)* (1971) 55 Cr. App. R. 262 CA.

99 *R. v Cato (Ronald Philip)* [1976] 1 W.L.R. 110; *R. v Notman* [1994] Crim. L.R. 518 CA.

100 *R. v Malcherek (Richard Tadeusz)* [1981] 1 W.L.R. 690; (1981) 73 Cr. App. R. 173 CA.

101 *R. v Hughes (Michael)* [2013] UKSC 56; [2013] 1 W.L.R. 2461. The approach in *Hughes* was reaffirmed by a seven-member Supreme Court in *R. v Taylor (Jack)* [2016] UKSC 5; [2016] 1 W.L.R. 500.

102 Contrary to the Road Traffic Act 1998 s.3ZB. For a critical discussion of *Hughes* [2013] 1 W.L.R. 2461 and *Taylor* [2016] 1 W.L.R. 500, see S. Kyd and G. Turton, "Causing controversy: interpreting the requirements of causation in criminal law and tort law" (2019) 70(4) N.I.L.Q. 425.

103 *Environment Agency (formerly National Rivers Authority) v Empress Car Co (Abertillery) Ltd* [1999] 2 A.C. 22; [1998] 2 W.L.R. 350 HL.

4. Novus actus interveniens

2–058 After D's unlawful conduct, some subsequent act by another person or coincidental event could occur that is the more "immediate" or "proximate" cause of the resulting harm. This subsequent contribution might be sufficient to displace D's causal responsibility, rendering D's contribution to the resulting harm *in*significant and *in*operative. This can be a natural event, the act of a third party, or an act of the V. In these cases, the problem is determining whether this intervening event is sufficient to displace D's causal responsibility for the resulting harm.

Two general principles can be stated at the outset. First, a voluntary ("free, deliberate and informed") act by a third party will normally break the chain of causation. Secondly, particularly with regard to responses by V and natural events, only those acts or events that are not reasonably foreseeable will break the chain of causation. These principles, and whether they are reconcilable, can now be examined in more depth.

(i) Natural events

2–059 What is the position if D attacks V and leaves them unconscious in a field where they are struck by lightning and killed? The rule here is that if the supervening natural event (being struck by lightning) is unforeseen by D and unforeseeable to the reasonable person, it will break the chain of causation. As Hart and Honoré describe, such an event is a "coincidence".[104]

On the other hand, if the supervening natural event is reasonably foreseeable, the causal chain will not be broken. In *Hart*,[105] D attacked V and left her unconscious on a beach below the high-water mark. V subsequently drowned by the incoming tide. Such an event was reasonably foreseeable, and D's conduct (assault) was held to have caused the result (death). However, if D attacks V and leaves them in a seemingly safe environment, but V is subsequently killed by an unforeseen and unforeseeable event (e.g. a falling tree), the natural event will break the chain of causation. The natural event is described as being "extraordinary". In such circumstances, D's criminal liability is limited to the harm from the initial attack.

(ii) Human intervention

2–060 The picture is more complicated when there is a subsequent human intervention. It is useful here to distinguish between the actions of third parties and the V.

(a) Acts of third party

2–061 Where a third party (T) makes a "free, deliberate, and informed" (FDI) intervention, which causes the resulting harm, this will typically amount to a novus actus and render D's conduct insignificant and inoperative. For T's conduct to amount to a novus actus, T must knowingly intervene to bring about the resulting harm. If T is induced or constrained by the circumstances created by D, T's intervention will

104 H.L.A. Hart and T. Honoré, *Causation in the Law*, 2nd edn (Oxford: OUP, 1985), pp.77–81.
105 *Hart* [1986] N.Z.L.R. 48.

not be FDI. For example, if D stabs V, leaving them lying in the street dying, and another (T) shoots V killing them instantly, T's conduct breaks the chain of causation. However, if T merely kicks V, accelerating death by a matter of seconds, T's FDI conduct will not break the causal chain. The issue is one of determining the circumstances in which the conduct of the third party will be so significant as to break the causal chain.

R. v Rafferty [2007] EWCA Crim 1846:

D and two others seriously assaulted and robbed V on a beach. D took V's debit card and went to try to draw money from a cashpoint machine. While he was away, the others dragged V into the sea, where he drowned. D was convicted of manslaughter and appealed. **2–062**

HOOPER LJ:

"[40] . . . Hart and Honore . . . [wrote]:

> 'The free deliberate and informed intervention of a second person, who intends to exploit the situation created by the first, but is not acting in concert with him, is normally held to relieve the first actor of criminal responsibility.' . . .

[43] . . . [T]he judge gave the following direction on *novus actus interveniens* [that the jury had to be sure]:

'that the drowning of [the victim] by [the others] was not such a new and intervening act in the chain of events, which was so completely different from the injuries for which Rafferty was responsible, that it overwhelmed those injuries and destroyed any causal connection between them and the death of [the victim].'

[44] We have reached the conclusion that no jury could properly conclude that the drowning of [the victim] by [the others] was other than a new and intervening act in the chain of events."

Appeal allowed

That an FDI intervention of a third party breaks the causal chain was not applied in the following much-criticised House of Lords' decision. **2–063**

Environment Agency v Empress Car Co (Abertillery) Ltd [1999] 2 A.C. 22 (House of Lords):

D (a company) maintained a diesel oil tank on its premises. An outlet from the tank was governed by a tap which had no lock. An unknown person (probably a vandal) opened the tap causing the oil to run into a river. D was convicted of causing polluting matter to enter controlled waters contrary to the Water Resources Act 1991 s.85(1). **2–064**

LORD HOFFMANN:

"[O]ne cannot give a common sense answer to a question of causation for the purpose of attributing responsibility under some rule without knowing the purpose and scope of the rule . . .

What, therefore, is the nature of the duty imposed by s.85(1)? . . . It is immediately clear that the liability imposed is strict: it does not require mens rea in the sense of intention or negligence. Strict liability is imposed in the interests of protecting controlled waters from pollution . . .

. . . [T]o frame the question as 'who or what caused the result under consideration' is wrong and distracting, because it may have more than one right answer. The question is whether the defendant caused the pollution. How is foreseeability a relevant factor to consider in answering this question? . . . [T]he question is not whether the consequences ought to have been foreseen; it is whether the defendant caused the pollution. And foreseeability is not the criterion for deciding whether a person caused something or not. People often cause things which they could not have foreseen.

The true common sense distinction is, in my view, between acts and events which, although not necessarily foreseeable in the particular case, are in the generality a normal and familiar fact of life, and facts or events which are abnormal and extraordinary . . . There is nothing unusual about people putting unlawful substances into the sewage system and the same, regrettably, is true about ordinary vandalism. So when these things happen, one does not say: that was an extraordinary coincidence, which negatived the causal connection between the original act of accumulating the polluting substance and its escape . . . On the other hand, the example I gave of the terrorist attack would be something so unusual that one would not regard the defendant's conduct as having caused the escape at all . . .

I shall try to summarise the effect of this discussion . . .

(2) The prosecution need not prove that the defendant did something which was the *immediate* cause of the pollution: maintaining tanks, lagoons or sewage systems full of noxious liquid is doing something, even if the immediate cause of the pollution was lack of maintenance, a natural event or the act of a third party.

(3) When the prosecution has identified something which the defendant did, the justices must decide whether it caused the pollution. They should not be diverted by questions like 'What was the cause of the pollution?' or 'Did something else cause the pollution?' Because to say that something else caused the pollution (like brambles clogging the pumps or vandalism by third parties) is not inconsistent with the defendant having caused it as well.

(4) If the defendant did something which produced a situation in which the polluting matter could escape but a necessary condition of the actual escape which happened was also the act of a third party or a natural event, the justices should consider whether the act or event

should be regarded as a normal fact of life or something extraordinary. If it was in the general run of things a matter of ordinary occurrence, it will not negative the causal effect of the defendant's acts, even if it was not foreseeable that it would happen to that particular defendant or take that particular form. If it can be regarded as something extraordinary, it will be open to the justices to hold that the defendant did not cause the pollution.

(5) The distinction between ordinary and extraordinary is one of fact."

Appeal dismissed

This decision received a hostile reception on the basis that while the test laid down in this case (ordinary v extraordinary events) is the correct test for natural events (such as brambles clogging the pumps), it is not the appropriate test for the FDI actions of third parties: the acts of the vandal should have been held to have caused the pollution to the river. **2-065**

However, the decision is perhaps understandable in policy terms. The offence here was one of strict liability. Many offences are deliberately made ones of strict liability to ensure that persons and companies take every precaution to prevent the harm occurring. Such persons are under a legal duty to guard against the harm that is caused, albeit by another; this includes taking steps to prevent deliberate interventions by third parties.

Lord Hoffmann has since stated, extra-judicially, that the FDI rule *should* be applied to crimes where fault is required; it is only where liability is strict that the wider rule endorsed in *Empress* is appropriate.[106] Such a limitation has now been introduced by the House of Lords' decision of *Kennedy (No.2)* (extracted and discussed below), which strongly reaffirms the FDI rule and arguably restricts *Empress* to offences of strict liability or, even more narrowly, to "cases of pollution and environmental crimes".[107]

Whether the subsequent conduct of a third party (T) breaks the chain of causation requires an evaluation of whether T's conduct is, in fact, "free, deliberate and informed".

R. v Pagett (1983) 76 Cr. App. R. 279 (Court of Appeal, Criminal Division):

D shot at police officers who were attempting to arrest him for various serious offences. He had V (a 16-year-old girl) with him, who was pregnant by him and held hostage, and against her will, D used her body to shield himself from any retaliation by the officers. The officers returned D's fire; three of their bullets hit the girl and she died from her injuries. D was convicted of manslaughter and appealed to the Court of Appeal. **2-066**

---

106 Hoffmann, "Causation" (2005) 30 L.Q.R. 121.

107 D. Ormerod, "Commentary to *Kennedy (No.2)*" [2008] Crim. L.R. 224; *R.v Hughes* [2013] UKSC 56.

GOFF LJ:

"[One of the] specific points raised on behalf of the appellant . . . [was that] the learned judge . . . ought to have held that the appellant had not in the circumstances of this case caused the death of the deceased. The learned judge, in directing himself upon the law, ought to have held that where the act which immediately resulted in a fatal injury was the act of another party, albeit in legitimate self-defence, then the ensuing death was too remote or indirect to be imputed to the original aggressor . . .

[I]t was pressed upon us by [counsel for the appellant] that there either was, or should be, a . . . rule of English law, whereby, as a matter of policy, no man should be convicted of homicide (or, we imagine, any crime of violence to another person) unless he himself, or another person acting in concert with him, fired the shot (or, we imagine, struck the blow) which was the immediate cause of the victim's death (or injury).

No English authority was cited to us in support of any such proposition, and we know of none. So far as we are aware, there is no such rule in English law; and . . . we can see no basis in principle for any such rule in English law . . .

In our judgment, the question whether an accused person can be held guilty of homicide, either murder or manslaughter, of a victim the immediate cause of whose death is the act of another person must be determined on the ordinary principles of causation . . .

In cases of homicide, it is rarely necessary to give the jury any direction on causation as such . . . Even where it is necessary to direct the jury's minds to the question of causation, it is usually enough to direct them simply that in law the accused's act need not be the sole cause, or even the main cause, of the victim's death, it being enough that his act contributed significantly to that result. Occasionally, however, a specific issue of causation may arise. One such case is where although an act of the accused constitutes a *causa sine qua non* of (or necessary condition for) the death of the victim, nevertheless the intervention of a third person may be regarded as the sole cause of the victim's death, thereby relieving the accused of criminal responsibility. Such intervention, if it has such an effect, has often been described by lawyers as a *novus actus interveniens* . . .

Professors Hart and Honoré, *Causation in the Law* . . . consider the circumstances in which the intervention of a third person, not acting in concert with the accused, may have the effect of relieving the accused of criminal responsibility. The criterion which they suggest should be applied in such circumstances is whether the intervention is voluntary, *i.e.* whether it is 'free, deliberate and informed'. We resist the temptation of expressing the judicial opinion whether we find ourselves in complete agreement with that definition; though we certainly consider it to be broadly correct and supported by authority. Among the examples which the authors give of non-voluntary conduct, which is not effective to relieve the accused of responsibility, are two which are germane to the present case, *viz.* a reasonable act performed for the purpose of self-preservation, and an act done in performance of a legal duty.

> There can, we consider, be no doubt that a reasonable act performed for the purpose of self-preservation, being of course itself an act caused by the accused's own act, does not operate as a *novus actus interveniens* . . . Now one form of self-preservation is self-defence; for present purposes, we can see no distinction in principle between an attempt to escape the consequences of the accused's act, and a response which takes the form of self-defence. Furthermore, in our judgment, if a reasonable act of self-defence, against the act of the accused causes the death of a third party we can see no reason in principle why the act of self-defence, being an involuntary act caused by the act of the accused, should relieve the accused from criminal responsibility for the death of the third party . . .
>
> The principles which we have stated are principles of law . . . It follows that where, in any particular case, there is an issue concerned with what we have for convenience called *novus actus interveniens*, it will be appropriate for the judge to direct the jury in accordance with these principles.
>
> . . . [I]t is for the judge to direct the jury with reference to the relevant principles of law relating to causation, and then to leave it to the jury to decide, in the light of those principles, whether or not the relevant causal link has been established."
>
> *Appeal dismissed*

In this case, the self-defensive actions of the police were regarded as "involuntary" and so did not constitute FDI intervention and, accordingly, did not break the causal chain. The fact that they were acting negligently was not relevant.[108] That the police officer's response to D's conduct was involuntary does not seem right; it was reactive to the moment but nevertheless a voluntary action. It would have been preferable for the court to have argued on the principled basis that the response was reasonably foreseeable. **2–067**

What, though, of a case in which two gunmen engaged in a shoot-out cause the death of an innocent member of the public who happens to be passing by? Could it be said that not only the first gunman, from whose weapon the fatal shot was fired, but also his adversary at whom he was shooting, caused the death? According to the dissenting judgment of Lord Kerr in *Gnango*, the answer is no: by returning fire the second gunman does not "cause" the first gunman to fire again; the first gunman's act of firing another shot is a FDI act breaking the chain of causation between the second gunman's—engagement in the shoot-out, and the passer-by's death.[109] As will be seen later, the second gunman was, however, found liable for murder in this case.[110]

In several of the leading cases it has been the conduct of medical professionals, often acting negligently, that has been alleged to be a novus actus.

---

108 Some 10 years later the deceased girl's mother was awarded damages against the police for their negligent handling of the siege (*The Guardian*, 4 and 5 December 1990).

109 *R. v Gnango (Armel)* [2011] UKSC 59; [2012] 1 A.C. 827 at [131]–[132].

110 See para.3–138 and Ch.11, paras 11–055–11–057.

R. v Jordan (1956) 40 Cr. App. R. 152 (Court of Appeal, Criminal Division):

2–068 D stabbed V. At hospital, when V's injuries were nearly healed, T (a doctor) administered a large quantity of terramycin, an antibiotic to which V had shown he was intolerant. V subsequently died. D was convicted of murder at trial, but appealed on the grounds that it was T's "palpably wrong" treatment that caused V's death, not his stabbing of V.

HALLET J:

"There were two things other than the wound which were stated by these two medical witnesses to have brought about death. The stab wound had penetrated the intestine in two places, but it was mainly healed at the time of death. With a view to preventing infection it was thought right to administer an antibiotic, terramycin.

It was agreed by the two additional witnesses that that was the proper course to take, and a proper dose was administered. Some people, however, are intolerant to terramycin, and Beaumont was one of those people. After the initial doses he developed diarrhoea, which was only properly attributable, in the opinion of those doctors, to the fact that the patient was intolerant to terramycin. Thereupon the administration of terramycin was stopped, but unfortunately the very next day the resumption of such administration was ordered by another doctor and it was recommenced the following day. The two doctors both take the same view about it. Dr Simpson said that to introduce a poisonous substance after the intolerance of the patient was shown was palpably wrong. Mr Blackburn agreed.

Other steps were taken which were also regarded by the doctors as wrong—namely, the intravenous introduction of wholly abnormal quantities of liquid far exceeding the output. As a result the lungs became waterlogged and pulmonary oedema was discovered. Mr Blackburn said that he was not surprised to see that condition after the introduction of so much liquid, and that pulmonary oedema leads to broncho-pneumonia as an inevitable sequel, and it was from broncho-pneumonia that Beaumont died.

We are disposed to accept it as the law that death resulting from any normal treatment employed to deal with a felonious injury may be regarded as caused by the felonious injury . . . It is sufficient to point out here that this was not normal treatment. Not only one feature, but two separate and independent features, of treatment were, in the opinion of the doctors, palpably wrong and these produced the symptoms discovered at the post-mortem examination which were the direct and immediate cause of death, namely, the pneumonia resulting from the condition of oedema which was found . . .

We feel no uncertainty at all that, whatever direction had been given to the jury and however correct it had been, the jury would have felt precluded from saying that they were satisfied that death was caused by the stab wound."

Conviction quashed

R. v Smith [1959] 2 Q.B. 35 (Courts Martial Appeal Court):

During a fight in a barracks, D twice stabbed V, Private Creed, with a bayonet. D appealed against his conviction for murder on the ground, inter alia, that the summing up by the judge-advocate on the question of causation was defective. **2-069**

LORD PARKER CJ:

"The second ground concerns a question of causation. The deceased man in fact received two bayonet wounds, one in the arm and one in the back. The one in the back, unknown to anybody, had pierced the lung and caused haemorrhage. There followed a series of unfortunate occurrences. A fellow-member of his company tried to carry him to the medical reception station. On the way he tripped over a wire and dropped the deceased man. He picked him up again, went a little further, and fell apparently a second time, causing the deceased man to be dropped on to the ground. Thereafter he did not try a third time but went for help, and ultimately the deceased man was brought into the reception station. There, the medical officer, Captain Millward, and his orderly were trying to cope with a number of other cases . . . and it is clear that they did not appreciate the seriousness of the deceased man's condition or exactly what had happened. A transfusion of saline solution was attempted and failed. When his breathing seemed impaired, he was given oxygen and artificial respiration was applied, and, in fact, he died after he had been in the station about an hour, which was about two hours after the original stabbing. It is now known that, having regard to the injuries which the man had in fact suffered, his lung being pierced, the treatment that he was given was thoroughly bad and might well have affected his chances of recovery . . . There was evidence that, if he had received immediate and different treatment, he might not have died. Indeed, had facilities for blood transfusion been available and been administered, Dr Camps, who gave evidence for the defence, said that his chances of recovery were as high as 75 per cent.

In these circumstances Mr Bowen [counsel for the appellant] urges that not only was a careful summing-up required but that a correct direction to the court would have been that they must be satisfied that the death of Private Creed was a natural consequence and the sole consequence of the wound sustained by him and flowed directly from it. If there was, says Mr Bowen, any other cause, whether resulting from negligence or not, if, as he contends here, something happened which impeded the chance of the deceased recovering, then the death did not result from the wound. The court is quite unable to accept that contention. It seems to the court that if at the time of death the original wound is still an operating cause and a substantial cause, then the death can properly be said to be the result of the wound, albeit that some other cause of death is also operating. Only if it can be said that the original wounding is merely the setting in which another cause operates can it be said that the death does not result from the wound. Putting it in another way, only if the second cause is so overwhelming as to make the original wound merely part of the history can it be said that the death does not flow from the wound . . .

Mr Bowen placed great reliance on . . . *Jordan* . . . The court is satisfied that *Jordan's* case was a very particular case depending on its exact facts . . .

In the present case . . . a man is stabbed in the back, his lung is pierced and haemorrhage results; two hours later he dies of haemorrhage from that wound; in the interval there is no time for a careful examination, and the treatment given turns out in the light of subsequent knowledge to have been inappropriate and, indeed, harmful. In those circumstances no reasonable jury or court could, properly directed, in our view possibly come to any other conclusion than that the death resulted from the original wound."

Appeal dismissed

R. v CHESHIRE (1991) 93 CR. APP. R. 251 (COURT OF APPEAL, CRIMINAL DIVISION):

2–070 D shot the deceased (V) in the leg and stomach. As part of his treatment in the hospital, a tracheotomy tube was placed in his windpipe. Some two months later, at a time when his wounds were no longer threatening his life, his windpipe became obstructed, and he died. This was due to a narrowing of the windpipe where the tracheotomy had been performed—a rare but not unknown complication. At D's trial for murder, evidence was given that the medical treatment had been negligent. The trial judge directed the jury that only recklessness, not negligence, could break the causal chain. He was convicted of murder and appealed.

BELDAM LJ:

"[Causation] is a question of fact for the jury, but it is a question of fact to be decided in accordance with legal principles explained to the jury by the judge . . .

In the criminal law the jury . . . will we think derive little assistance from figures of speech more appropriate for conveying degrees of fault or blame in questions of apportionment . . . [W]e think such figures of speech are to be avoided in giving guidance to a jury on the question of causation . . .

[W]hen the victim of a criminal attack is treated for wounds or injuries by doctors or other medical staff attempting to repair the harm done, it will only be in the most extraordinary and unusual case that such treatment can be said to be so independent of the acts of the accused that it could be regarded in law as the cause of the victim's death to the exclusion of the accused's acts . . .

[T]he accused's acts need not be the sole cause or even the main cause of death it being sufficient that his acts contributed significantly to that result. Even though negligence in the treatment of the victim was the immediate cause of his death, the jury should not regard it as excluding the responsibility of the accused unless the negligent treatment was so independent of his acts, and in itself so potent in causing death, that they regard the contribution made by his acts as insignificant.

It is not the function of the jury to evaluate competing causes or to choose which is dominant provided they are satisfied that the accused's acts can fairly be said to have made a significant contribution to the victim's death. We think the word 'significant' conveys the necessary substance of a contribution made to the death which is more than negligible . . .

[W]e think that the judge erred when he invited the jury to consider the degree of fault in the medical treatment rather than its consequences, [but] we consider that no miscarriage of justice has actually occurred. Even if more experienced doctors than those who attended the deceased would have recognised the rare complication in time to have prevented the deceased's death, that complication was a direct consequence of the appellant's acts, which remained a significant cause of his death."

Appeal dismissed

The effect of these decisions is that the actions of medical professionals will rarely break the causal chain. It will require a "most extraordinary and unusual case" (*Cheshire*) for this to occur; it is not necessarily enough that the treatment received was negligent or even reckless. Therefore, where D harms V, and V receives normal treatment from T, from which they then die, *both* D and T's conduct can be said to have caused V's death.[111] There must be "abnormal" treatment for T's conduct to amount to a novus actus. Perhaps *Jordan* was such a case; the original wound had almost healed, and V can properly be said to have been killed by the administration of a drug by T, to which he was known to be allergic. **2–071**

In *Smith,* V's treatment was described as being "thoroughly bad", and V had a 75% chance of recovery had he received proper medical treatment. Despite this poor treatment, the court held that D's conduct remained significant and operative at the time of V's death; it was not "merely part of the history". The medical treatment and D's conduct were concurrent causes of death.

Cheshire is more complicated than *Jordan* and *Smith*. Recall that in *Cheshire*, despite V's wounds being nearly healed at the point of T's negligent intervention, T's conduct did not break the chain of causation. *Cheshire* is materially different to *Smith* in the sense that V did not die from the injuries caused by D; he died because T inserted a tracheotomy tube in his windpipe, which was properly done, but was then negligent in their subsequent treatment (through a failure to prevent a rare side-effect of the procedure). T's conduct did not amount to a novus actus. Why, then, was T's conduct in *Jordan* an abnormal contingency, but it was not in *Cheshire*? The answer is that in *Cheshire*, the "intervention" was an omission, which cannot break the causal chain, whereas in *Jordan*, the intervention was a grossly negligent action by the medical professionals.

Cheshire clarified that T's negligent treatment would only relieve D of causal responsibility for the resulting harm if T's conduct was "so independent of [D's] acts, and in itself so potent in causing death, that the [initial injuries] regard the contribution made by [D's] acts as insignificant". Should T's conduct

---

111 If the criteria established in *R. v Adomako (John Asare)* [1995] 1 A.C. 171; [1994] 3 W.L.R. 288 HL are satisfied, T be liable for V's manslaughter by gross negligence. See paras 7–043–7–048.

reach this threshold, T's conduct becomes an 'abnormal contingency', to appropriate Hart and Honoré's terminology, and breaks the chain of causation.

The picture that starts to emerge is that Hart and Honoré's "abnormal contingency", and indeed other causal concepts such as "potency", could be criticised as being hollow, to be interpreted as the courts see fit. One could take the view that all these "principled tests" provide no more than a veil under which decisions are ultimately based on other considerations, such as policy. With a National Health Service hard pressed for funds, the courts are not going to exempt violent assailants from liability because V did not receive the best treatment—except in what can be regarded as the most exceptional cases, such as *Jordan*.

Additionally, are these cases consistent with the now dominant principle that an FDI intervention by a subsequent actor will break the causal chain? One view is that medical professionals are not acting voluntarily, thus not encapsulated within the scope of the FDI rule. Ashworth argued otherwise: "doctors work under pressure, occasionally having to make rapid decisions, but they are trained and trusted to exercise clinical judgment in these circumstances. Doctors are under a duty to treat patients, but they surely do so voluntarily".[112]

2–072 The better view is that the medical professionals, in most of these cases, were simply performing their duty to their patients, and so their actions cannot count as FDI interventions, thus breaking the causal chain (although it is hard to see why this did not apply to the doctors in *Jordan*). "Voluntariness", as determined by the FDI rule, here does not mean literal voluntariness. In Pagett, the court accepted the examples given by Hart and Honoré of non-voluntary conduct, which included "a reasonable act . . . done in performance of a legal duty". The actions of medical professionals can be brought within this: they owe a legal duty to their patients. Whether their actions constitute a "reasonable act" in the discharge of that duty is obviously a context-sensitive issue in which the pressures of hard-worked doctors operating in an under-funded National Health Service must be considered.

(b) Acts of victim

2–073 Much like the actions of a third party can break the chain of causation, so too can the actions of the V. The general rule is that the consequences of V's intervention, after D's unlawful conduct, remain attributable to D provided that: (a) V's intervention was not voluntary (FDI); and (b) V's conduct was a reasonably foreseeable possibility.

The cases involving V interventions can be divided into three categories: V response, V escape and suicide cases and V vulnerability cases. We will review each in turn.

(i) Victim responses

2–074 What is the position if V responds to D's unlawful conduct and makes things worse rather than better for themselves? The courts have authoritatively stated that where V's response is voluntary (FDI), such

112 J. Horder, *Ashworth's Principles of Criminal Law*, 10th edn (Oxford: OUP, 2022), p.134.

an intervention will amount to a novus actus, relieving D of causal responsibility for the resulting harm. This principle has developed from the drug-supply manslaughter case law.

For many years, the courts deliberated whether D's supply of a controlled substance, which is fatally consumed or administered by V, is a legal cause of V's death. Early cases on this held that D is a cause of death in such cases. In *Kennedy (No.1)*,[113] the court held that the supplier (D) could be regarded as having caused the death of the person (V) self-injecting the drugs. The Court of Appeal briefly moved away from this position in *Dias*,[114] where it was held that V has a *choice* whether to inject, and so this can break the causal chain. However, causation was found in these cases once again in *Finlay*.[115] The court held that causation could be established on such facts as D was a "joint principal in V's act". In this case, the *Empress* principles were applied: only if the acts of the injector were "extraordinary" would the causal chain be broken. However, *Kennedy (No.1)* and *Finlay* have now been overruled by the following decision.

R. v Kennedy (No.2) [2008] 1 A.C. 269 (House of Lords):

D prepared a "hit" of heroin for V and gave him the syringe ready for injection. V injected himself and returned the syringe to D, who left the room. The injection resulted in V's death. D was convicted of manslaughter and appealed. **2–075**

LORD BINGHAM OF CORNHILL:

"2 The question certified by the Court of Appeal (Criminal Division) for the opinion of the House neatly encapsulates the question raised by this appeal:

'When is it appropriate to find someone guilty of manslaughter where that person has been involved in the supply of a class A controlled drug, which is then freely and voluntarily self-administered by the person to whom it was supplied, and the administration of the drug then causes his death?' . . .

14 The criminal law generally assumes the existence of free will. The law recognises certain exceptions, in the case of the young, those who for any reason are not fully responsible for their actions, and the vulnerable, and it acknowledges situations of duress and necessity, as also of deception and mistake. But, generally speaking, informed adults of sound mind are treated as autonomous beings able to make their own decisions how they will act, and none of the exceptions is relied on as possibly applicable in this case. Thus D is not to be treated as causing V to act in a certain way if V makes a voluntary and informed decision to act in that way rather than another. There are many classic statements to this effect. In his article 'Finis for Novus Actus?' [1989] CLJ 391, 392, Professor Glanville Williams wrote:

113 *R. v Kennedy (Simon)* [1999] Crim. L.R. 65.

114 *R. v Dias* [2001] 2 Cr. App. R. 96.

115 *R. v Finlay (Paul Anthony)* [2003] EWCA Crim 3868.

> 'I may suggest reasons to you for doing something; I may urge you to do it, tell you it will pay you to do it, tell you it is your duty to do it. My efforts may perhaps make it very much more likely that you will do it. But they do not cause you to do it, in the sense in which one causes a kettle of water to boil by putting it on the stove. Your volitional act is regarded (within the doctrine of responsibility) as setting a new "chain of causation" going, irrespective of what has happened before.'

In chapter XII of *Causation in the Law*, 2nd ed (1985), p 326, Hart & Honoré wrote:

> 'The free, deliberate, and informed intervention of a second person, who intends to exploit the situation created by the first, but is not acting in concert with him, is normally held to relieve the first actor of criminal responsibility.'

This statement was cited by the House with approval in *R v Latif* [1996] 1 WLR 104, 115. The principle is fundamental and not controversial.

15 Questions of causation frequently arise in many areas of the law, but causation is not a single, unvarying concept to be mechanically applied without regard to the context in which the question arises. That was the point which Lord Hoffmann, with the express concurrence of three other members of the House, was at pains to make in *Environment Agency (formerly National Rivers Authority) v Empress Car Co (Abertillery) Ltd* [1999] 2 A.C. 22. The House was not in that decision purporting to lay down general rules governing causation in criminal law. It was construing, with reference to the facts of the case before it, a statutory provision imposing strict criminal liability on those who cause pollution of controlled waters. Lord Hoffmann made clear that common sense answers to questions of causation will differ according to the purpose for which the question is asked; that one cannot give a common sense answer to a question of causation for the purpose of attributing responsibility under some rule without knowing the purpose and scope of the rule; that strict liability was imposed in the interests of protecting controlled waters; and that in the situation under consideration the act of the defendant could properly be held to have caused the pollution even though an ordinary act of a third party was the immediate cause of the diesel oil flowing into the river. It is worth underlining that the relevant question was the cause of the pollution, not the cause of the third party's act.

16 The committee would not wish to throw any doubt on the correctness of the *Empress Car* case. But the reasoning in that case cannot be applied to the wholly different context of causing a noxious thing to be administered to or taken by another person contrary to section 23 of the 1861 Act . . .

18 . . . If the conduct of the deceased was not criminal he was not a principal offender, and it of course follows that the appellant cannot be liable as a secondary party. It also follows that there is no meaningful legal sense in which the appellant can be said to have been a principal jointly with the deceased, or to have been acting in concert. The finding that the deceased freely and voluntarily administered the injection to himself, knowing what it was, is fatal to any contention that the appellant caused the heroin to be administered to the deceased or taken by him . . .

20 [Counsel for the appellant] relied on *R v Rogers* [2003] 1 WLR 1374 . . . The relevant finding was that the defendant physically assisted the deceased by holding his belt round the deceased's arm as a tourniquet, so as to raise a vein in which the deceased could insert a syringe, while the deceased injected himself. It was argued in support of his appeal to the Court of Appeal that the defendant had committed no unlawful act for purposes of either count. This contention was rejected. The court held that it was unreal and artificial to separate the tourniquet from the injection. By applying and holding the tourniquet the defendant had played a part in the mechanics of the injection which had caused the death. There is, clearly, a difficult borderline between contributory acts which may properly be regarded as administering a noxious thing and acts which may not. But the crucial question is not whether the defendant facilitated or contributed to administration of the noxious thing but whether he went further and administered it. What matters, in a case such as *R v Rogers* and the present, is whether the injection itself was the result of a voluntary and informed decision by the person injecting himself. In *R v Rogers*, as in the present case, it was. That case was, therefore, wrongly decided . . .

24 It is possible to imagine factual scenarios in which two people could properly be regarded as acting together to administer an injection. But nothing of the kind was the case here. As in *R v Dalby* [1982] 1 WLR 425 and *R v Dias* [2002] 2 Cr App R 96 the appellant supplied the drug to the deceased, who then had a choice, knowing the facts, whether to inject himself or not. The heroin was, as the certified question correctly recognises, self-administered, not jointly administered. The appellant did not administer the drug. Nor, for reasons already given, did the appellant cause the drug to be administered to or taken by the deceased.

25 The answer to the certified question is: 'In the case of a fully-informed and responsible adult, never.'"

Appeal allowed

The restriction of *Empress* to its context (strict liability offences of pollution) was welcomed. Furthermore, as a result of this judgment, the general rule that a FDI intervention will amount to a novus actus need not be defended further.[116] Moreover, the approach taken by the House of Lords is consistent with the policy and fair-labelling arguments that drug suppliers ought generally to be labelled and punished as drug suppliers and not as manslaughterers. In cases with facts such as *Kennedy (No.2)*, the general rule should be that V "has a choice". This is not an instance of non-voluntary conduct coming within the examples given by Hart and Honoré and approved in *Pagett*. Ultimately, it should be for the jury, applying the FDI rule, to determine whether V's self-injection or consumption of a controlled substance is a novus actus. V's intervention will typically be regarded as FDI unless **2–076**

116 The approach adopted in *R. v Kennedy (Simon)* [2008] 1 A.C. 269 has since been rejected in Scotland: *MacAngus and Kane v HM Advocate* [2009] H.C.J.A.C. 8.

considerations such as age, mental condition,[117] improper pressure or influence can rebut such an inference.[118] For example, in *Khan*,[119] V, a 15-year-old prostitute, took heroin for probably the first time:

> "... there must be some doubt ... [whether her actions] should have been regarded as truly capable of consenting to the risks inherent in heroin use; her assumption of risk ... 'seems at the borderline of voluntariness'."[120]

It has been suggested that *Kennedy (No.2)* is inconsistent with the V escape cases (discussed below) where, if V's actions are reasonably foreseeable, they will not break the causal chain. In most drug-supply cases, it is reasonably foreseeable that the drugs will be taken. That is why they are supplied.[121] However, the reasonable foreseeability of V's actions is only relevant once it has been established that they were not voluntary. For liability to be found in these circumstances post-*Kennedy (No 2)*, it would have to be shown that either (a) V's intervention was not FDI; (b) that D and V were "acting in concert";[122] or (c) to focus on D's behaviour *after* V's self-administration.[123] Unfortunately, in recent years, the Court of Appeal has failed properly to employ both principles relevant to legal causation in victim response cases.

2-077 In *Field*,[124] D pretended to enter a loving relationship with a vulnerable older man (V). D had been (allegedly) covertly drugging V (with Dalmane and other drugs) and gaslighting him. D seduced V and convinced him to amend his will in D's favour. Once the will had been amended, D set bringing about V's death in a manner that would seem self-inflicted. One evening, D encouraged V to drink a bottle of whisky by pouring out the glasses and handing them to V. V died overnight from acute alcohol poisoning. The Court of Appeal upheld D's conviction for murder on the basis that V's decision to drink the whisky was not sufficiently voluntary. This was on the grounds that although V consumed the whisky, he was not *informed* of D's motivation (to kill V).

Regrettably, there are several issues with this case. First, there is ambiguity as to the cause of V's death. The initial pathology report stipulated the cause of death as "acute alcohol toxicity", but the second report stipulated the cause of death as "acute alcohol toxicity *and* Dalmane use". This difference has significant implications for the application of the FDI rule. If the first report is accurate, the Court of Appeal's judgment cannot be reconciled with *Kennedy (No.2)*. Recall in that case, V's self-injection of heroin was held to be FDI; the question was not whether V was informed as to whether the self-injection would be fatal. Therefore, in *Field*, because V freely chose to drink the whisky, knowing its strength and the effect of alcohol, D's conduct cannot be said to have caused V's death. However, *if* V's death is attributable to *both* V's consumption of whisky (FDI) *and* Dalmane, as indicated in the second pathologist report, and it can be proven that D covertly caused V to consume it (not FDI), then it is D's

117 *R. v Rebelo (Bernard)* [2021] EWCA Crim 306; [2021] 4 W.L.R. 52.
118 R. Heaton, "Principals? No Principles" [2004] Crim. L.R. 463, 464.
119 *R. v Khan (Rungzabe)* [1998] Crim. L.R. 830 CA.
120 *MacAngus and Kane v HM Advocate* [2009] H.C.J.A.C. 8, citing Jones, "Causation, Homicide and the Supply of Drugs" (2006) 26 L.S. 139.
121 L. Cherkassky, "Kennedy and Unlawful Act Manslaughter: An Unorthodox Application of the Doctrine of Causation" (2008) 72 Jo.C.L. 387.
122 T.H. Jones, "Causation, Homicide and the Supply of Drugs" (2006) 26 L.S. 139, 149.
123 *R. v Evans* [2009] 2 Cr. App. R. 10.
124 *R. v Field (Benjamin Luke)* [2021] EWCA Crim 380; [2021] 1 W.L.R. 3543.

covert drugging of V that can be said to be a significant cause of D's death. Secondly, and related to the first, the jury was directed to convict D if they were satisfied that D intended to kill V and that D did one or more of the alleged acts (giving V whisky, and/or Dalmane, and/or suffocating him), which was/were a more than minimal cause of V's death. However, the Court of Appeal passed no comment on the correctness of these being separate and sufficient grounds for establishing liability—an oversight given the inconclusive evidence for two of the alleged acts (administration of Dalmane and suffocation). Finally, although the Court of Appeal recognised that D's supplying of whisky to V was the crucial element in the case, they erroneously agreed with the trial judge that D's murderous intent made his supply of whisky to V a cause of death. As we have seen above, without more (i.e. the covert administration of Dalmane), this is in direct contradiction to *Kennedy (No.2)*.[125]

Similarly, in *Rebelo*,[126] D advertised for sale online a "food supplement" which claimed to promote weight loss. The supplement was actually a dangerous chemical (DNP). V, a young woman with a complex mental health history, purchased the supplements online and became addicted to them. She was warned by her GP, social worker and friends of the potentially fatal consequences of taking DNP. However, despite these warnings, she died following an excessive intake of the drugs. The Court of Appeal upheld D's conviction for gross negligence manslaughter. The court held that although V's consumption of DNP was deliberate, it was not sufficiently free or informed; her capacity to assess the risk and understand the consequences of taking the drug was impacted by her mental illness. However, that V's consumption of DNP was not FDI is not enough to prove causation alone, her consumption must have also been reasonably foreseeable. This point was missed completely by the trial judge's direction to the jury and the Court of Appeal's evaluation of the suitability of those directions.[127]

(ii) Victim escape and suicide

There are also cases where V, while escaping from or responding to D's unlawful conduct, contributes to the resulting harm. **2–078**

R. v ROBERTS (1972) 56 CR. APP. R. 95 (COURT OF APPEAL, CRIMINAL DIVISION):

V, a passenger in D's car, injured herself by jumping out of the car while it was in motion. Her explanation was that D had made sexual advances to her and was trying to pull her coat off. D was convicted of an assault occasioning actual bodily harm. He appealed on the ground, inter alia, that causation had not been established. **2–079**

STEPHENSON LJ:

> "The test is: Was it the natural result of what the alleged assailant said and did, in the sense that it was something that could reasonably have been foreseen as the consequence of what he was saying or doing? As it was put in one of the old cases, it had got to be shown to be his

125 For a critical discussion of this case, see G.R. Sullivan and A.P. Simester, "Deadly whisky" (2022) 138 L.Q.R. 11.

126 *R. v Rebelo* [2021] EWCA Crim 306.

127 *R. v Rebelo* [2021] EWCA Crim 306 at [31], quoting [34] of the trial judge's direction to the jury.

act, and if of course the victim does something so 'daft', in the words of the appellant in this case, or so unexpected, not that this particular assailant did not actually foresee it but that no reasonable man could be expected to foresee it, then it is only in a very remote and unreal sense a consequence of his assault, it is really occasioned by a voluntary act on the part of the victim which could not reasonably be foreseen and which breaks the chain of causation between the assault and the harm or injury."

Appeal dismissed

R. v Williams and Davis (1992) 95 Cr. App. R. 1 (Court of Appeal, Criminal Division):

2–080 D1 and D2 gave a lift to V (a hitchhiker) and allegedly tried to rob him. V jumped from the moving car (travelling about 30 mph) and died from head injuries caused by falling into the road. Both were convicted of manslaughter and appealed.

STUART-SMITH LJ:

"There must be some proportionality between the gravity of the threat and the action of the deceased in seeking to escape from it . . . [T]he deceased's conduct . . . [must] be something that a reasonable and responsible man in the assailant's shoes would have foreseen . . . [T]he nature of the threat is of importance in considering both the foreseeability of harm to the victim from the threat and the question whether the deceased's conduct was proportionate to the threat, that is to say that it was within the ambit of reasonableness and not so daft as to make it his own voluntary act which amounted to a *novus actus interveniens* and consequently broke the chain of causation. It should of course be borne in mind that a victim may in the agony of the moment do the wrong thing . . .

The jury should consider two questions: first, whether it was reasonably foreseeable that some harm, albeit not serious harm, was likely to result from the threat itself; and, secondly, whether the deceased's reaction in jumping from the moving car was within the range of responses which might be expected from a victim placed in the situation which he was. The jury should bear in mind any particular characteristic of the victim and the fact that in the agony of the moment he may act without thought and deliberation . . .

In our judgment the failure of the judge to give any direction on causation was a misdirection and the conviction on this count must be quashed."

Appeals allowed

In *Corbett*,[128] D assaulted a drunk, intellectually disabled man (V) who, while fleeing from D, fell into a gutter where he was struck by a passing car and killed. The Court of Appeal approved the trial judge's direction that the issue was whether V's reaction was within the foreseeable range and, in assessing this, they had to decide whether this was something that might be expected as a reaction of somebody in that state. While the foreseeability test accounts for V's situation and characteristics, this is not true of D's. In *Marjoram*,[129] it was stated that the test of reasonable foresight is purely objective, and so no account could be taken of the age or sex or any other characteristics of D—otherwise, where D1 and D2 with different characteristics acted together, D1 might be held to have caused the result but not D2. **2-081**

The test does not require V's act to be an immediate response to D's threat. In *Tarasov*,[130] even where there was a gap in time between D's threat and V's response (in this case of jumping out of a bathroom window 90 minutes after the initial assault), D could be found to have caused V's death, provided that V acted as a result of fear of being hurt in a further attack.

Are these cases consistent with the rule that the FDI intervention of a third party will break the chain of causation? One view is that this rule does not apply to the actions of victims as they are not "third parties". However, such an argument seems implausible and inconsistent with the House of Lords decision in *Kennedy (No.2)*. The better view is that these cases are consistent with the FDI rule; V's fear in these cases was such that they had no real *choice* but to do as they did. It will be recalled that one of Hart and Honoré's examples of non-voluntary conduct, approved in *Pagett*, was a "reasonable act performed for the purpose of self-preservation", such as an act by V escaping from D's violence.

There are also cases where V, in a state of anguish or fear as a result of D's unlawful conduct, have died of suicide.

R. v Dear [1996] Crim. L.R. 595 (Court of Appeal, Criminal Division) (Lexis Transcript, 14 March 1996):

D slashed V repeatedly with a Stanley knife. V died two days later. The defence was that V died by suicide either by reopening his wounds or, the wounds having reopened themselves, by failing to take steps to stop the bleeding. The trial judge directed the jury that causation was established if V did what he did because of the wounds and would not have done so unless he had been wounded. The chain of causation would only be broken if V acted only for some reason unconnected to the attack on him, for example, shame at his own prior conduct (it was alleged that V had sexually interfered with D's daughter). D was convicted of murder and appealed. **2-082**

128 *R. v Corbett (Christopher)* [1996] Crim. L.R. 594 CA.
129 *R. v M (Richard) (A Juvenile)* [2000] Crim. L.R. 372 CA.
130 *R. v Tarasov (Valodia)* [2016] EWCA Crim 2278 CA.

ROSE LJ:

"[Counsel for the appellant argues that] 'voluntary' suicide . . . is a *novus actus interveniens*. A suicide where the deceased can be taken to know and understand the nature of his act, and thus exercise a choice, is a *novus actus*, even if it follows upon an attack upon the victim . . .

[E]ven assuming that there was evidence of suicide, through shame or some other reason unrelated to the defendant's conduct . . . this did not . . . render inaccurate . . . the direction which the judge gave on causation . . .

The correct approach in the criminal law is . . .: were the injuries inflicted by the defendant an operating and significant cause of death? That question, in our judgment, is necessarily answered, not by philosophical analysis, but by common sense according to all the circumstances of the particular case.

In the present case the cause of the deceased's death was bleeding from the artery which the defendant had severed. Whether or not the resumption or continuation of that bleeding was deliberately caused by the deceased, the jury were entitled to find that the defendant's conduct made an operative and significant contribution to the death."

Appeal dismissed

2–083 Smith commented on this case that if:

> ". . . the wounds were effectively healed when D took the Stanley knife to himself, it is not so clear that the wounds were an operating and substantial cause of death. Arguably, it was then the same as if he had cut his throat or blown his brains out."[131]

In *Dhaliwal*,[132] a woman who had been subjected to various forms of abuse committed suicide. In the Court of Appeal, it was stated obiter that "at least arguably" D's violence could be regarded as the cause of her death.

Jeremy Horder and Laura McGowan, "Manslaughter by Causing Another's Suicide" [2006] Crim. L.R. 1035, 1042–3:

2–084 "When a relationship is characterised by persistent domestic abuse (especially in the kind of cultural and religious context to be found in *Dhaliwal*), the experience of living with the abuse is liable to affect the victim's decision-making processes, and to influence the range and character of actions she regards as legitimate, inevitable or natural . . .

131 *R. v Dear (Patrick)* [1996] Crim. L.R. 595 CA.
132 *R. v D* [2006] EWCA Crim 1139; [2006] 2 Cr. App. R. 24.

> There has been strong support for an approach to causation in which the destructive effect domestic abuse has on the victim's autonomy can be regarded as rendering the defendant criminally responsible for the victim's suicide . . .
>
> It might be that a decision on the part of a victim of abuse to commit suicide is best explained, in straightforward causal terms, by a depressive condition induced by the abuse . . . [H]is abuse triggered the operation of a special vulnerability of the victim. On our account, however, the causal link between the abuse and the suicide can be (lack of) freedom-based, and need not be based on a victim's special vulnerability. An abuse-based controlling influence can, in this context, make a decision to commit suicide something that the victim was not truly free to avoid, because other avoiding actions were in practical terms ruled out by the effect of that influence."

The question of whether D can be liable for causing the death of V, who dies because of the circumstances created by D, was more recently addressed by the Court of Appeal in the following case. However, in this case, V died by voluntary euthanasia and not by their own hand. The case was one involving a single serious act of physical abuse on the part of D rather than persistent domestic abuse, and its facts are both tragic and unusual. **2–085**

R. v Wallace (Berlinah) [2018] EWCA Crim 690 (Court of Appeal):

> The events that gave rise to this prosecution arose after the relationship between D and V (Mr van Dongen) had broken down. D and V remained living together. On the evening of 22 September 2015, D returned home and poured sulphuric acid over V while he was asleep in bed, saying, "If I can't have you, no-one else will'. V, almost naked when the attack occurred, sustained burns to two-thirds of his face and a large percentage of his upper chest, arms and thighs. V suffered permanent and life-changing injuries of the most extreme and appalling nature, causing him permanent and unbearable physical and psychological pain. He lost sight in his left eye and most of his sight in his right eye. His lower left leg had to be amputated. He was diagnosed with depression, sometimes saying that he wanted to live and at other times that he wanted to die. **2–086**
>
> One year later, and with the help of his father, V travelled to Belgium. On 1 December 2016, V made an application for voluntary euthanasia. Euthanasia is legal in Belgium, and the legal requirements of the Belgian law were satisfied. On 2 January 2017, a doctor (T) ended V's life by inserting drugs via a catheter into his heart, bringing about his immediate death. D was charged with murder and applying a corrosive liquid with intent.[133] At trial, the judge withdrew the charge of murder from the jury on the basis that T's intervention was a novus actus. On an interlocutory appeal, the Crown appealed to the Court of Appeal against this ruling.

---

133 Contrary to the Offences Against the Person Act 1861 s.29.

SHARP LJ:

"51. The argument for the defence in summary is that the defendant did not kill Mr van Dongen, the doctors in Belgium did. Their free, voluntary and informed act was designed to end life rather than to save it, would be charged as murder in this jurisdiction, and was properly to be regarded as the immediate cause of death, relegating the actions and responsibility of the defendant to no more than the factual context. This was not a case of suicide, where the victim ended his own life; thus Mr van Dongen's conduct did not fall to be looked at in isolation. It was instead inextricably linked with the conduct of the doctors. In any event, Mr van Dongen, unaffected by any psychiatric condition, had a free choice, and his choice of an act, carried out by his doctors and prohibited in this jurisdiction, broke the chain of causation. The prosecution contends however, as it did to the judge, that where causation is in issue in homicide cases, it is a question for the jury whether the injuries caused by a defendant are a substantial and operating cause of death, or whether an act or acts since then has relegated those injuries to history, so that they are no more than the setting in which the subsequent acts occur.

60. The intervening acts of Mr van Dongen and the doctors were not, on these facts, random extraneous events, or acts unconnected with the fault element of the defendant's conduct. They were very closely, indeed inextricably, bound up with it. Equally, the injuries and their sequelae were not a random result of the defendant's conduct: on the evidence of Mr van Dongen, the defendant planned to inflict permanent and horrific injuries on him and succeeded ('If I can't have you, no-one else will').

61. Looked at in this way, Mr van Dongen's death, his request to the doctors, and the act of euthanasia itself carried out in accordance with his wishes, were not discrete acts or events independent of the defendant's conduct, nor were they voluntary, if by this is meant they were the product of the sort of free and unfettered volition presupposed by the *novus actus* rule. Instead they were a direct response to the inflicted injuries and to the circumstances created by them for which the defendant was responsible. If the question is then asked whether, on a common sense view, the defendant's conduct merely set the stage for Mr van Dongen's death, or was instrumental in bringing it about, we consider the jury could properly answer that question in the prosecution's favour.

75. It is undoubtedly the case that, generally speaking, informed adults of sound mind are treated by the law as autonomous beings able to make their own decisions about how they would act, and that a defendant may not be held responsible for the deliberate act of such a person. See for example *R v Latif R v Shahzad* [1996] 2 Cr. App. R. 92 and *R v Kennedy (No 2)* [2007] UKHL 38, [2008] 1 AC 269 . . .

76. However, it could be said that the position of the drug addict was not truly analogous to that of Mr van Dongen, any more than it would have been to that of the victims in Dear, Roberts and Williams or to that of the third party doctors in Cheshire and Smith. Kennedy was not concerned, as some of those cases were, and the jury could conclude this one is, with a response by a victim to (extreme) circumstances created by a defendant's

unlawful act, which were persisting, and which had put the victim into a position where he made a 'choice' that he would never otherwise have had to make or would have made (not therefore, as we have already said, the sort of free and unfettered volition presupposed by the *novus actus* rule). In the circumstances, in our view the fact that the Belgian doctors considered Mr van Dongen's decision/request to be 'voluntary' for the purposes of the Belgian law on euthanasia does not determine whether his decision was voluntary for the purposes of the different legal issues arising here . . . [T]here was nothing that could decently be described as voluntary either in the suffering or in the decision by Mr van Dongen to end his life, given the truly terrible situation he was in.

81. As can be seen the Court of Appeal held in *Pagett* that an act done in the execution of a legal duty (being an act caused by the act of the accused) does not operate as a *novus actus interveniens* because as a matter of principle such an act cannot be regarded as a voluntary act, independent of the wrongful act of the accused. However *Pagett* described acts that were not to be treated as constituting a voluntary intervening act; the court was not defining the outer limits or boundaries of what must be treated as a *novus actus interveniens* in all circumstances. We think it is going too far therefore to say that the fact that the doctors in Belgium were not obliged to carry out Mr van Dongen's wishes, because of the existence of what amounted to a conscience clause in Article 14, precludes a finding by the jury that legal causation is established in this case. On the evidence, the doctors were doing no more than lawfully carrying out Mr van Dongen's wishes. They were acting in accordance with the law. In those circumstances, it seems to us there is little that is meaningful—on the duty issue at least—in the distinction between their conduct and that of the officers in *Pagett* who were surely not obliged to fire at the accused in that case, even if on the facts their conduct in doing so was lawful."

Appeal allowed; retrial ordered

Unfortunately, there are several issues with this judgment. First, the court sought to provide guidance on the meaning to be given to the term "voluntary". However, in doing so, the court moved away from the language of the well-established FDI rule to that of "free and unfettered volition". This additional lexicon is both unhelpful and unnecessary. Secondly, the court erroneously focused on whether V's conduct amounted to a novus actus. This would have been the relevant question had V died by suicide, but he did not; he died by lethal injection administered by a third party (T). Finally, Sharp LJ ruled that the question of whether D caused V's death should be left to the jury, which should be asked to consider, inter alia, whether V's request for euthanasia was a reasonably foreseeable consequence of D's unlawful conduct: **2–087**

"Are you sure that at the time of the acid attack it was reasonably foreseeable that the defendant would commit suicide as a result of his injuries? In answering this question consider all the circumstances, including the nature of the attack, what the defendant did and said at the time and whether or not Mr van Dongen's decision to undergo voluntary euthanasia fell within the range of responses which might have been expected from a victim in his situation. If your answer is yes, your verdict on count 1 will be guilty. If your answer is no, your verdict on count 1 will be not guilty."[134]

---

134 *R. v Wallace (Berlinah)* [2018] EWCA Crim 690; [2018] 2 Cr. App. R. 22 at [86].

2–088 However, as stated above, this would only be applicable had V died by suicide, and he did not. V's death only resulted because of the administration of a lethal injection by T. As such, the jury should have been directed to consider whether *T's intervention* was both FDI and reasonably foreseeable. This analysis would have ensured full compliance with the leading authority of *Kennedy (No.2)*.

On retrial in 2018, the jury acquitted D of murder and manslaughter.[135] The jury did not find that it was reasonably foreseeable at the time that D threw sulphuric acid on V that he would go on to undergo voluntary euthanasia. It is questionable, though, whether it is right that the *way* in which death eventually occurred must be reasonably foreseeable at the time that the unlawful act was committed. It was reasonably foreseeable that V might die immediately from his injuries, and it was lucky that he did not do so. There was evidence that D herself was aware of this risk, given her internet search history. The thought process of a jury, in order to convict, would have to be that although it was reasonably foreseeable that D would die immediately, it was also reasonably foreseeable that he would survive but suffer catastrophic injuries and, as a result, that it was reasonably foreseeable that he would want to end his life, and that he might undergo voluntary euthanasia, rather than live a limited one with such injuries. That is a difficult question for any jury to have to answer. The role of luck in determining D's liability in this case was, to some extent, mitigated by the fact that she was sentenced to life imprisonment for an offence related to the throwing of the acid.[136]

(iii) Victim vulnerabilities

2–089 There are several cases where V's vulnerabilities contributed to the occurrence of the resulting harm. In such cases, there is a long-established principle of criminal law that D must "take his victim as he finds him". This is often referred to as the "thin skull" rule. The operation of this principle is most visible where V has a pre-existing physical vulnerability, making them more susceptible to injury. For example, in *McKechnie*,[137] D (and two others) entered V's home late at night. D violently attacked V and caused him severe brain damage. V was taken to the hospital unconscious. At hospital, it was discovered that he was suffering from a (pre-existing) duodenal ulcer, which required surgery. However, it was concluded that, because of his serious head injuries, to administer anaesthesia to enable surgery could be fatal; for this reason, they did not operate on the ulcer. One month later, while still unconscious from the head injuries caused by D's attack, V's ulcer burst, from which V died. The court held that V's pre-existing medical condition (duodenal ulcer), which hastened death following D's assault, did not alleviate D of causal responsibility for the resulting harm (death). It is no defence to say that a healthy V might not have died.[138] This principle has been advanced to explain the decision in *Blaue*.

135 S. Morris, "Berlinah Wallace jailed for life for 'sadistic' acid attack on Mark van Dongen" (2018) *The Guardian, 23 May 2018, https://www.theguardian.com/uk-news/2018/may/23/berlinah-wallace-jailed-years-sadistic-acid-attack-mark-van-dongen*.

136 Contrary to the Offences Against the Person Act 1861 s.29.

137 *R. v McKechnie (Roy Maurer)* (1992) 94 Cr. App. R. 51; [1992] Crim. L.R. 194.

138 Additionally, see *R. v Hayward* [1908] 21 Cox C.C. 692. In this case, D chased V (his wife) into the street whilst shouting threats. Unknown to both of them, V had an undiagnosed medical condition (rare thyroid condition). Due to the condition, V collapsed from fright and exhaustion, from which she died. The court held that D's unlawful conduct was a significant and operative cause of V's death; her pre-existing physical vulnerability did not alleviate D of causal responsibility for death.

R. v Blaue (1975) 61 Cr. App. R. 271 (Court of Appeal, Criminal Division):

D stabbed V after she refused to have sex with him, piercing her lung. At hospital, she refused to have a blood transfusion as it was contrary to her religious beliefs as a Jehovah's Witness. The surgeon advised her that without the transfusion, she would die. Medical evidence established that with the transfusion, she would have survived. She died, and D was convicted of manslaughter (on the grounds of diminished responsibility). He appealed on the ground that causation was not established. **2–090**

LAWTON LJ:

"Maule J's direction to the jury reflected the common law's answer to the problem. He who inflicted an injury which resulted in death could not excuse himself by pleading that his victim could have avoided death by taking greater care of himself. See Hale, *Pleas of the Crown* (1800 edn) pp.426–428. The common law in Sir Matthew Hale's time probably was in line with contemporary concepts of ethics. A man who did a wrongful act was deemed *morally* responsible for the natural and probable consequences of that act. [Counsel for the appellant] . . . asked us to remember that since Sir Matthew Hale's day the rigour of the law relating to homicide has been eased in favour of the accused. It has been—but this has come about through the development of the concept of intent, not by reason of a different view of causation . . .

The physical cause of death in this case was the bleeding into the pleural cavity arising from the penetration of the lung. This had not been brought about by any decision made by the deceased girl but by the stab wound.

[Counsel for the appellant] . . . tried to overcome this line of reasoning by submitting that the jury should have been directed that, if they thought the girl's decision not to have a blood transfusion was an unreasonable one, then the chain of causation would have been broken. At once the question arises—reasonable by whose standards? Those of Jehovah's Witnesses? Humanists? Roman Catholics? Protestants of Anglo-Saxon descent? The man on the Clapham omnibus? But he might well be an admirer of Eleazar who suffered death rather than eat the flesh of swine . . . or of Sir Thomas More who, unlike nearly all his contemporaries, was unwilling to accept Henry VIII as Head of the Church in England. Those brought up in the Hebraic and Christian traditions would probably be reluctant to accept that these martyrs caused their own deaths.

As was pointed out to . . . [counsel for the appellant] in the course of argument, two cases, each raising the same issue of reasonableness because of religious beliefs, could produce different verdicts depending on where the cases were tried . . . It has long been the policy of the law that those who use violence on other people must take their victims as they find them. This in our judgment means the whole man, not just the physical man. It does not lie in the mouth of the assailant to say that his victim's religious beliefs which inhibited him from accepting certain kinds of treatment were unreasonable. The question for decision is what caused her death. The answer is the stab wound. The fact that the victim refused to stop this end coming about did not break the causal connection between the act and death."[139]

Appeal dismissed

2-091 In terms of causation, two contributions undoubtedly caused V's death in *Blaue*: (1) D's act of stabbing V; and (2) the refusal of medical treatment. However, since legal causation only requires that D's conduct made *a* significant and operative contribution to the resulting harm, it is difficult to envisage D's conduct as not satisfying this threshold. Notwithstanding this, counsel for D sought to argue that V's refusal of medical treatment was unreasonable. Consequently, the question in *Blaue* (misguidedly) became whether the refusal of medical treatment could constitute a novus actus, rendering D's contribution *in*significant and *in*operative. In responding to this, the court erroneously relied on the application of the thin skull rule to reject the submission that V's refusal amounted to a novus actus. The effect of this meant that V's religious beliefs (much like a pre-existing physical vulnerability) form part of the causal baseline and D could not repudiate causal responsibility because of how those beliefs influenced V's response to the harm inflicted.

As such, the decision in *Blaue* is often taken to mean that V's refusal of treatment for their injuries, owing to pre-existing psychological vulnerabilities, has the potential to amount to a novus actus, thus relieving D of causal responsibility for resulting harm. If this were true, it would require very difficult decisions to be made about which characteristics are to be encapsulated by this extended "thin skull" rule: a fear of hospitals or needles, racism towards medical professionals, religious fanaticism, or even a malicious refusal of treatment to increase D's liability? Fortunately, such decisions need not be made. That V's refusal of treatment on religious grounds could amount to a novus actus is an erroneous interpretation of *Blaue* and the "thin skull" rule. While it is true that V's omission (refusal of treatment) was *a* cause of death, it is only a concurrent cause along with D's contribution. If one enquires, "of what did V die", the answer will always be blood loss resulting from D's stabbing of V; V's omission does nothing to affect this.[140] The principle that an omission cannot alter the causal path is overtly visible in the medical negligence case of *Smith*, discussed above, where the court held that T's omission (failure to properly treat V) did not relieve D of causal responsibility.

Consequently, the thin skull rule, properly construed, only applies to pre-existing physical vulnerabilities; V's subsequent omission or positive intervention falls outside the scope of this rule. Regrettably, the court in *Blaue* was also mistaken in their statement that we are unable to question the reasonableness of V's response because of their physical or psychological vulnerabilities. A string of cases confirm that V's response will not amount to a novus actus where it was voluntary (FDI) and reasonably foreseeable. Thus, D does not need to take V's *positive* responses "as he finds them", only those that are non-voluntary and reasonably foreseeable.

---

139 See also *Holland* (1841) 2 Mood. & R. 351, where V, who could have recovered, ignored medical advice and died two weeks later; D was held to have caused the death.

140 A. Simester, "Causation in (Criminal) law" (2017) 133 L.Q.R. 416, 439.

(iii) Approaches to causation

In the sections above, the guiding principles of causation in criminal law have been outlined and critiqued. It is evident from this analysis that causal principles are often applied and interpreted both differently and inconsistently. This is because they serve the function of assisting in the attribution of causal responsibility. This enquiry is often, but not always, normatively loaded. As such, the motivation for employing certain rules over others depends on the nature and purpose of the enquiry. There have been numerous attempts to provide a coherent theory of causation in criminal law. In this section, we outline three approaches that can be adopted in relation to the problem of causation. **2–092**

(a) Common sense approach

The most influential theoretical account of causation in criminal law is HLA Hart and Tony Honoré's "common sense" approach. The claim is that judges, when using causal principles, might be relying on the same principles that are used by "ordinary people" in their causal judgements *outside the law*. In their treatise, they sought to identify common sense principles of causal reasoning through an analysis of how causation is used in ordinary language, and then they sought to determine whether the same principles explained judicial decisions on legal causation by examining legal judgments. **2–093**

Events do not have single "causes", but only occur when there is a combination of counterfactually necessary conditions (*but for* causes). We might identify the dropping of a lighted cigarette in a waste-paper basket as the cause of a fire; but, in reality, this leads to a fire only if certain other conditions are satisfied: there must be oxygen in the air, there must be combustible material in the waste-paper basket, and so on. Each of these conditions is equally necessary if a fire is to be started. How are we to distinguish between "mere conditions" and "the cause"?

Hart and Honoré identified two main common sense principles to answer this question. The first is that the ordinary person, when picking "the cause" from a range of *but for* causes, do so based on whether it was a departure from the norm; the abnormality principle. Second, they contrast between voluntary (FDI) actions and all other conditions.

H.L.A. Hart and T. Honoré, Causation in the Law, 2nd edn (1985), pp.29, 33–34, 42, 77–80, 326, 340–341:

"Human action in the simple cases, where we produce some desired effect by the manipulation of an object in our environment, is an interference in the natural course of events which *makes a difference* in the way these develop . . . Common experience teaches us that, left to themselves, the things we manipulate, since they have a 'nature' or characteristic way of behaving, would persist in states or exhibit changes different from those which we have learnt to bring about in them by our manipulation. The notion that a cause is essentially something which interferes with or intervenes in the course of events which would normally take place, is central to our commonsense concept of cause . . . **2–094**

[I]n distinguishing between causes and conditions two contrasts are of prime importance. These are the contrasts between what is abnormal and what is normal in relation to any given thing or subject-matter, and between a free deliberate human action and all other conditions . . .

(a) Abnormal and normal conditions

. . . In the case of a building destroyed by fire 'mere conditions' will be factors such as the oxygen in the air, the presence of combustible material or the dryness of the building . . . These factors are, of course, just those which are present alike both in the case where such accidents occur and in the normal cases where they do not; and it is this consideration that leads us to reject them as the cause of the accident, even though it is true that without them the accident would not have occurred . . . such factors do not 'make the difference' between disaster and normal functioning, as . . . the dropping of a lighted cigarette [does] . . .

(b) Voluntary action

. . . [A] voluntary human action intended to bring about what in fact happens, and in the manner in which it happens, has a special place in causal inquiries; not so much because this, if present among a set of conditions required for the production of the effect, is often treated as the cause (though this is true), but because, when the question is how far back a cause shall be traced through a number of intervening causes, such a voluntary action very often is regarded both as a limit and also as still the cause even though other later abnormal occurrences are recognized as causes . . .

[However in certain cases even when an actor intends to achieve a result (and that result occurs), the chain of causation between the actor's conduct and the result might be broken.]

Tracing consequences

. . . A hits B who falls to the ground stunned and bruised by the blow; at that moment a tree crashes to the ground and kills B. A has certainly caused B's bruises but not his death . . .

The connection between A's action and B's death . . . would naturally be described in the language of *coincidence*. 'It was a coincidence: it just happened that, at the very moment when A knocked B down, a tree crashed at the very place where he fell and killed him.' . . . We speak of a coincidence whenever the conjunction of two or more events in certain spatial or temporal relations (1) is very unlikely by ordinary standards and (2) is for some reason significant or important, provided (3) that they occur without human contrivance and (4) are independent of each other . . .

In the present case the fall of the tree just as B was struck down within its range satisfies the four criteria for a coincidence which we have enumerated. First, though neither event was of a very rare or exceptional kind, their conjunction would be rated very unlikely judged by the standards of ordinary experience. Secondly, this conjunction was causally significant for it was a necessary part of the process terminating in B's death. Thirdly, this conjunction was not consciously designed by

A; had he known of the impending fall of the tree and hit B with the intention that he should fall within its range B's death would not have been the result of any coincidence. A would certainly have caused it. The common-sense principle that a contrived conjunction cannot be a coincidence is the element of truth in the legal maxim (too broadly stated even for legal purposes) that an intended consequence cannot be too 'remote'. Fourthly, each member of the conjunction in this case was independent of the other; whereas if B had fallen against the tree with an impact sufficient to bring it down on him, this sequence of physical events, though freakish in its way, would not be a coincidence and in most contexts of ordinary life, as in the law, the course of events would be summarized by saying that in this case, unlike that of the coincidence, A's act was the cause of B's death, since each stage is the effect of the preceding stage. Thus, the blow forced the victim against the tree, the effect of this was to make the tree fall and the fall of the tree killed the victim.

One further criterion in addition to these four must be satisfied if a conjunction of events is to rank as a coincidence and as a limit when the consequences of the action are traced . . . An abnormal *condition* existing at the time of a human intervention is distinguished both by ordinary thought and, with a striking consistency, by most legal systems from an abnormal event or conjunction of events subsequent to that intervention; the former, unlike the latter, are not ranked as coincidences or 'extraneous' causes when the consequences of the intervention come to be traced. Thus A innocently gives B a tap over the head of a normally quite harmless character, but because B is then suffering from some rare disease the tap has, as we say, 'fatal results'. In this case A has caused B's death though unintentionally. The scope of the principle which thus distinguishes contemporaneous abnormal conditions from subsequent events is unclear; but at least where a human being initiates some physical change in a thing, animal, or person, abnormal physical states of the object affected, existing at the time, are ranked as part of the circumstances in which the cause 'operates'. In the familiar controlling imagery these are part of 'the stage already set' before the 'intervention'.

. . . Just how unlikely must a conjunction be to rank as a coincidence, and in the light of what knowledge is likelihood to be assessed? The only answer is: 'very unlikely in the light of the knowledge available to ordinary men.'

. . . [S]o in criminal law courts have often limited responsibility by appealing to the causal distinctions embedded in ordinary thought, with their emphasis on voluntary interventions and abnormal or coincidental events as factors negativing responsibility.

Voluntary conduct

The free, deliberate, and informed intervention of a second person, not acting in concert with the first, and intending to bring about the harm which in fact occurs or recklessly courting it, is normally held to relieve the first actor of criminal responsibility. One must distinguish, however, the situation where the first actor's conduct was sufficient in the existing circumstances to bring about the harm (. . . the case for holding the first actor responsible despite the voluntary intervention of the

> second is naturally much stronger) . . . from that where it was not sufficient without the intervention of the second actor (. . . here most decisions relieve the first actor of responsibility) . . .
>
> ***Abnormality***
>
> The basic principle here is that a physical state or event, even if subsequent to the act of the defendant, does not negative causal connection if it is normal or usual in the context. In criminal as in civil law a conjunction of events amounting to a coincidence is held to negative causal connection."

2–095 There have been several House of Lords decisions that have explicitly endorsed this "common sense" approach. In *Stapley v Gypsum Mines*, Lord Reid held that:

> To determine what caused an accident from the point of view of legal liability is a most difficult task. If there is any valid logical or scientific theory of causation it is quite irrelevant in this connection . . . The question must be determined by applying common sense to the facts of each particular case. "[141]

Indeed, more recently, Lord Hughes and Lord Toulson, in *Hughes*, held that "there is a well-recognised distinction between conduct which sets the stage for an occurrence and conduct which *on a common sense view* is regarded as instrumental in bringing about the occurrence".[142] However, a central problem with this analysis is that much depends on one's definition of "normal", "abnormal" and "voluntary". As Norrie writes:

> "Thus, individuals are held to be causes until something abnormal intervenes, but what is abnormal depends upon social perception, and therefore upon a socio-political label being stuck upon it. Similarly, causation stretches as far as the new voluntary act of a third party, but what is meant by voluntary can be as narrow or as broad as one likes, depending upon how much one is prepared to recognise the social character of the lives of individuals."[143]

(b) "Policy" approach

2–096 Those that subscribe to this approach argue that there are no underlying general *principles* of causation. Instead, judges simply resort to considerations of "policy" to determine whether D caused the resulting harm.

---

141 *Stapley v Gypsum Mines Ltd* [1953] A.C. 663; [1953] 3 W.L.R. 279 HL at 781.
142 *Hughes* [2013] UKSC 56 at [23].
143 A. Norrie, "A Critique of Criminal Causation" (1991) 54 M.L.R. 685, 692.

Alan Norrie, "A Critique of Criminal Causation" (1991) 54(5) M.L.R. 685, 693:

> "My argument is that it is the limited, abstract individualist character of the law's causation analysis that makes it rely on 'policy' to draw the lines for it. The causation analysis is both genuine and operative in legal decision-making and fundamentally flawed by its focus on individuals in abstraction from social relations. . . . Hart and Honoré's analysis is a paradigmatic, if late, expression of Enlightenment thought. Rooted in the philosophy of Hume and Mill, it rests upon the analysis of the individual, engaging with other individuals and with nature as a self-contained monad, capable of producing effects in the world as a cause in him/herself. This is the law's approach too, but what is missing from both is any recognition of the way in which individual agency is fundamentally constructed and constituted within pre-existing social relations. It is the gap between the individual and the social that hounds the case law on causation." **2–097**

Norrie argues that any "principles" that might exist require "constant supplementation by policy considerations to reach decisions in individual cases" because causation can only be explained by taking into account the social context within which people act.[144] **2–098**

In deciding who to prosecute, are prosecutors to be guided by the same considerations of "policy"? Is such an ad hoc approach acceptable? It must be remembered that, apart from crimes of strict liability, criminal liability does not necessarily follow from a finding that causation is established. Some mens rea or culpability must also be found to exist. If policy considerations are to affect legal decisions, should they not be reserved for the mens rea assessment, or is it unrealistic to divorce policy considerations from any one aspect of a crime?

(c) Mens rea approach

There are two strands to the argument here. The first is that causation will generally be established if D has mens rea regarding the resulting harm. It is often stated (for example, in the Hart and Honoré extract above) that an intended consequence can never be too remote. The alternative analysis (theoretically quite different, but similar in effect) is that because of the doctrine of mens rea and the test of responsibility, principles of causation are unnecessary in the criminal law. Any factual cause can be held to be the legal cause because actual liability will be limited to those who have mens rea: **2–099**

> "Under the modern conception of mens rea no hardship can result from any finely drawn investigation of causes, since the more remote the cause the greater the difficulty of proving that the accused person intended or realised what the effect of it would be."[145]

---

144 Norrie, "A Critique of Criminal Causation" (1991) 54 M.L.R. 685, 701.

145 C.S. Kenny and J.W.C. Turner, *Kenny's Outlines of Criminal Law*, 19th edn (Cambridge: CUP, 1966), pp.20–21. See *Royall v The Queen* (1991) 65 A.L.J.R. 451 per McHugh J, discussed in S. Shute, "Causation: Foreseeability *v* Natural Consequences" (1992) 55 M.L.R. 584.

On these views, all the "real work" is done by the doctrine of mens rea. Either the rules on causation are shaped by the existence of mens rea, or, alternatively, no rules on causation are necessary. All that is needed, in either case, is a simple proposition that D's act must have been *a* cause in the sense that without it the ultimate harm would not have occurred (known as the *sine qua non* rule or "but for" causation).

There are problems with these approaches. How can they be adopted when dealing with crimes of strict liability? Clearly, the first view that causation is only established if there is a "blameable" cause[146] is problematic. Particularly when dealing with strict liability offences, the courts have tended to emphasise that whether causation is established is a question of fact and not law.[147] It has been argued that this amounts to an invitation to juries and magistrates only to find causation established if the defendant was blameworthy:

> "By delegating the question of causation to the finders of fact, the courts are able to avoid the rigours of strict liability. The device allows both courts and Parliament to bury their heads in the sand, and to avoid any reassessment of the role of strict liability in criminal law. The courts undermine the rigidity of the strict liability rules by allowing juries to introduce a judgmental or culpability element into their decision-making on causation."[148]

2–100 However, in *Empress*,[149] it was expressly stated that causation may be established even though D did not intend the harm and was not even negligent; any other approach would defeat the object of strict liability legislation. Under the second view, causation would be established on a simple "but for" basis in all cases regardless of how far removed the act was from the result. Such an approach would be unacceptable and does not represent the law. While it is arguable that causation is more easily established in cases of strict liability, it is nevertheless clear that legal rules of causation do exist. As stated in *Empress*:

> ". . . while liability is strict . . . it is not an absolute liability in the sense that all that has to be shown is that the polluting matter escaped from the defendant's land."[150]

In *Alphacell v Woodward*,[151] it was indicated that causation depended on a "proper attribution of responsibility". While "responsibility" in this context should not be confused with culpability, it is clear that more than "but for" causation needs to be established. This was most recently confirmed by the Supreme Court in the case of *Hughes*.[152]

---

146 G. Williams, *Textbook of Criminal Law*, 2nd edn (London: Stevens, 1983), p.381.

147 *National Rivers Authority v Yorkshire Water Services Ltd* [1994] Env. L.R. 177; [1994] Crim. L.R. 451 QBD; *Alphacell v Woodward* [1972] A.C. 824; [1972] 2 W.L.R. 1320 HL.

148 N. Padfield, "Clean Water and Muddy Causation: Is Causation a Question of Law or Fact, or Just a Way of Allocating Blame?" [1995] Crim. L.R. 683, 692–693.

149 *Empress Car Co (Abertillery) Ltd* [1999] 2 A.C. 22. See also *Southern Water Authority v Pegrum and Pegrum* [1989] Crim. L.R. 442.

150 *Empress Car Co (Abertillery) Ltd* [1999] 2 A.C. 22 at 33.

151 *Alphacell v Woodward* [1972] A.C. 854.

152 *Hughes* [2014] 1 Cr. App. R. 6 at [29].

Even in cases where mens rea is established, there are problems with these approaches to causation.[153] Is it right that *all* liability should turn on such a nebulous and elusive concept as mens rea? It might well be thought better to clarify and strengthen the rules on causation which could lead to a diminution of the importance of the doctrine of mens rea.[154]

III. Conclusion

It is interesting that, leaving aside the medical and strict liability judgments, many of the problem cases discussed above involved constructive manslaughter,[155] which is a species of crime where no mens rea is required regarding the resulting harm. *Hughes* similarly involved a constructive homicide offence.[156] Another leading case, *Roberts*, involved the Offences Against the Person Act 1861 s.47 which, as another constructive crime, also does not require mens rea as to the result. This tends to lend some credence to the view that principles of causation are subservient to those of mens rea. Where there is clear mens rea as to the result, problems of causation will not be allowed to intrude. But, where one is dealing with constructive crime, the job cannot be left to mens rea and it is in this area that "principles", such as they are, have started emerging. However, even in these, and certainly in the other cases, it would be a mistake to ignore the role of policy: for example, the policy of not allowing medical treatment to break the chain of causation. **2-101**

It must be remembered that most of the Ds in the above cases could have been charged with, or found guilty of, lesser offences. *Pagett* was convicted of possession of a firearm, kidnapping, and attempted murder. *Kennedy* was convicted of supplying a Class A drug to another. *McKechnie* was charged, in the alternative, with causing grievous bodily harm with intent. *Blaue* could have been convicted of attempted murder, *Hayward* of assault, *Hughes* of driving whilst uninsured and unlicensed, and so on. Policy considerations dictated that they all be blamed and punished for something, but the question is: what were the policy considerations that dictated they be found liable for homicide offences, as opposed to these lesser offences? It is interesting how much importance has been attached to the resulting harm as opposed to the more immediate "wrongdoing" of the D. However, whether this approach is justifiable remains disputed and subject to academic debate.

153 V. Tadros, *Criminal Responsibility* (Oxford: OUP, 2005), pp.175–181.

154 One way to do this might be to introduce a "harm within the wrong" test, akin to the "harm within the risk" test used in establishing causation in the tort of negligence. See G. Turton and S. Kyd, "Causing controversy: interpreting the requirements of causation in criminal law and tort law" (2019) 70(4) *Northern Ireland Legal Quarterly* 425–444.

155 The defendant was convicted of murder in *R. v Dear* [1996] Crim. L.R. 596. In *R. v Blaue (Robert Konrad)* [1975] 1 W.L.R. 1411; (1975) 61 Cr. App. R. 271 CA, the conviction was for manslaughter by diminished responsibility.

156 The approach in *Hughes* [2014] 1 Cr. App. R. 6 was affirmed by the Supreme Court in another case of constructive liability involving road death. In *Taylor* [2016] UKSC 5, the certified question to be addressed was whether the offence of aggravated vehicle taking under the Theft Act 1968 s.12A is committed when, following the basic offence (of taking a vehicle without the owner's consent) and before recovery of the vehicle, the defendant drove the vehicle, and without fault in the manner of his driving the vehicle was involved in an accident which caused injury (or death) to a person. The Supreme Court answered the question in the negative, taking the same approach as in *Hughes* and requiring that some fault in D's driving must be found before he can be said to have caused V's death.

In this chapter, we have focused on the external elements of criminal offences, critically evaluating the constituent elements within actus reus. However, to establish criminal liability, there is often (but not always) a corresponding mens rea requirement that must also be proven. For example, to establish liability for murder, it is insufficient to prove that D caused V's death, it must also be proven that D *intended* to kill or cause serious bodily harm to V. Similarly, to establish liability for criminal damage, it is insufficient to prove that D damaged property belonging to another, it must also be proven that D *intended* or was *reckless* as to causing damage to another's property. These requirements focus on the "internal" elements of criminal offences: D's state of mind or fault. In the next chapter, we move to consider the meaning of terms such as "intention", "recklessness", and "negligence" in English criminal law.

Chapter 3

The General Principles of Criminal Liability: Mens Rea

I. Introduction

Having established the need for actus reus in the sense of an act (or omission where a duty to act applies) carried out in defined *legally relevant circumstances* which, for a result crime, *causes* a specified harm, we must now turn our attention to the question of what is required in terms of mens rea. As a reminder, mens rea is used simply as a short hand term to describe the mental element of a crime. **3–001**

A. BLAME AND RESPONSIBILITY

The normal consequence of a criminal conviction is punishment. The offender is subjected to censure and blame. Blame and censure are only appropriate if the offender was morally responsible for their behaviour. We do not blame animals, small children and the insane that have caused a harm because we do not hold them responsible. In a liberal society where political freedom is valued, people must be free from criminal liability and punishment unless they "voluntarily" break the law[1] in the sense of doing something that they can properly acknowledge as wrongdoing.[2] A morally responsible agent is one who understands the social norms to which they are subject[3] and can understand and accept responsibility for wrongdoing (whether or not this is associated with feelings of guilt). Such an agent can understand the "communicative enterprise of punishment"[4] in a way that young children and the insane cannot. The state may use its coercive powers against citizens who lack responsibility (for example, imposing tax on the purchase of goods[5]), but the use of its censuring powers of punishment **3–002**

1 B. Williams, "Moral Responsibility and Political Freedom" [1997] C.L.J. 96.

2 R.A. Duff and A. von Hirsch, "Responsibility, Retribution and the 'Voluntary': A Response to Williams" [1997] C.L.J. 103, 109.

3 F.G. Jacobs, *Criminal Responsibility* (London: Orion Publishing Group, 1971), p.13.

4 Duff and von Hirsch "Responsibility, Retribution and the 'Voluntary': A Response to Williams" [1997] C.L.J. 103, 109.

5 Duff and von Hirsch "Responsibility, Retribution and the 'Voluntary': A Response to Williams" [1997] C.L.J. 103, 104.

in such cases would not be consistent with the demands of political freedom. There would be no freedom in a state that chose to punish persons with green eyes. In short, the link between responsibility and criminal liability is one of the hallmarks of a free society.

How is responsibility assessed? There are two main theories: the capacity theory and the character theory.[6]

Under the capacity theory, the necessary attributes are knowledge, reason and control (which include the capacity to make choices).[7]

H.L.A. Hart, Punishment and Responsibility: Essays in the Philosophy of Law (1968), p.152:

3-003 "What is crucial is that those whom we punish should have had, when they acted, the normal capacities, physical and mental, for doing what the law requires and abstaining from what it forbids, and a fair opportunity to exercise these capacities. Where these capacities and opportunities are absent, as they are in different ways in the varied cases of accident, mistake, paralysis, reflex action, coercion, insanity etc., the moral protest is that it is morally wrong to punish because 'he could not have helped it' or 'he could not have done otherwise' or 'he had no real choice'."

3-004 According to this traditional view, because D could choose to do otherwise we are entitled to hold them morally blameworthy and to punish them. Because it is difficult to say that the mentally disordered D could have done otherwise they are exonerated from blame and punishment.[8]

This capacity theory can be applied to crimes of recklessness and negligence.

Antony Duff and Andrew von Hirsch, "Responsibility, Retribution and the 'Voluntary': A Response to Williams" [1997] C.L.J. 103, 109–110:

3-005 "We might do better to focus on the notion of rational agency. By this, we mean not action that is in fact guided by good reasons; but action which is in principle susceptible to being guided by reasons, done by an agent who would be capable of recognising whether such reasons are good ones . . . [I]t seems to us to be the best way to try to capture the idea of moral responsibility which is appropriate to ascriptions of criminal liability: what we condemn the agent for is a failure to recognise, to accept, or to be adequately motivated by, reasons for action (those offered by the law) which were within his grasp."

---

6 See generally, N. Lacey, *State Punishment: Political Principles and Community Values* (London: Routledge, 1988), pp.62–68; J. Horder, "Criminal Culpability: The Possibility of a General Theory" (1993) 12 *Law and Philosophy* 193; N. Lacey, "In Search of the Responsible Subject: History, Philosophy and Social Sciences in Criminal Law Theory" (2001) 64 M.L.R. 350; Tadros, *Criminal Responsibility* (Oxford: OUP, 2005), Ch.2.

7 Arenella would insist that an actor also be capable of some form of moral evaluation and be able to incorporate these moral beliefs and values into practical judgements about how to act ("Convicting the Morally Blameless: Reassessing the Relationship between Legal and Moral Accountability" (1992) 39 U.C.L.A. Law Rev. 1511). This approach is not accepted by present English law.

8 Because of the danger of repetition of harm in such circumstances, it might be necessary to retain control over the defendant.

There have been many challenges to this notion that people are free or autonomous agents capable of rational action and free choice. The argument here is that this conception of individuals as autonomous, self-determined beings ignores the social context within which people operate. As Norrie puts it: **3–006**

> ". . . while we feel in control of what we say or do, we sometimes appear only to speak the parts bequeathed to us by history and context."[9]

An extension of this argument is known as determinism. According to this view, all human action is the result of preceding events and conditions (environmental, biological or even chemical). All actions are "determined" and freedom of will is a myth. Under this view, a person cannot be held responsible for something that they were inevitably going to do.

GEORGE P. FLETCHER, RETHINKING CRIMINAL LAW (1978), PP.801–802:

> "It is difficult to resolve [the issue of determinism and responsibility] except by noting that we all blame and criticise others, and in turn subject ourselves to blame and criticism, on the assumption of responsibility for our conduct. In order to defend the criminal law against the determinist critique, we need not introduce freighted terms like 'freedom of the will.' Nor need we 'posit' freedom as though we were developing a geometric system on the basis of axioms. The point is simply that the criminal law should express the way we live. Our culture is built on the assumption that, absent valid claims of excuse, we are accountable for what we do. If that cultural presupposition should someday prove to be empirically false, there will be far more radical changes in our way of life than those expressed in the criminal law." **3–007**

The alternative conception of responsibility is one based upon the character of D: **3–008**

> "Actions for which we hold a person fully responsible are those in which her usual character is centrally expressed. The finding of a mental element such as intention or recklessness on the character model provides an important piece of evidence from which the existence of character responsibility may be inferred, given that single acts do not always indicate settled dispositions."[10]

Thus, we would hold responsible a person who makes unreasonable mistakes because such behaviour manifests an undesirable character trait of practical indifference to others. On the other hand, a person who acts under duress is not expressing their usual character. As they have been forced to act in a particular way, we are unable to draw an inference to a flawed character. This approach does have certain attractions; not least it accords with our tendency to regard as significant the fact that someone acts "out of character" and may be more in keeping with the function of the criminal law as a form of

9 A. Norrie, "The Limits of Justice: Finding Fault in the Criminal Law" (1996) 59 M.L.R. 540, 552.

10 Lacey, *State Punishment: Political Principles and Community Values* (1988), p.66.

social control. However, it is this intuitive appeal that reveals a central weakness of this character theory. The infliction of a serious harm could be regarded as non-culpable if the agent acted "out of character".[11] But how would we know if any action were uncharacteristic of the agent? This theory is unlikely to replace the capacity conception of responsibility because it looks too much like punishing people for what they are rather than for what they do. Such a person:

> ". . . remains a moral cripple, a flawed person in his own eyes, a person who understands that he committed a crime because of 'the kind of person he is' . . . [This amounts to an] enormous and sadistic cruelty."[12]

B. BLAME AND MENS REA

3–009 The fact that one is a responsible agent does not necessarily mean that criminal liability is justifiable when a harm is caused or a wrong committed. Duff puts it that:

> ". . . responsibility is a necessary but not a sufficient condition of liability. I am liable to conviction or blame for *X* only if I am responsible for *X*; but I can be responsible for *X* without being thus liable."[13]

The question is thus: in what circumstances should the actions of a responsible actor be held criminal? The answer is when they are sufficiently blameworthy in causing the harm or committing the wrong. The mechanisms for establishing this appropriate degree of blame are the subject of the ensuing sections. But it should be emphasised at the outset that the indicators of blame are largely fashioned according to which of the above competing conceptions of responsibility we adopt. For example, if we adopted the "character conception" of responsibility, we might need to evaluate an actor's motivations because a laudable motive would not reveal a flawed character. The law, however, has been fearful of adopting such a course as it might necessitate exempting from blame those who rob the rich to give to the poor or those who, as in *Chandler v DPP*,[14] commit offences to express their opposition to nuclear weapons. Accordingly, the law adopts the stance that motive is generally irrelevant to the assessment and has instead preferred the "capacity conception" of responsibility. We blame those who have control over their actions and have chosen to commit a crime. The process of choosing to commit a crime is a mental process involving *cognition* (knowing or realising that a consequence could occur or that a circumstance could exist). This mental state became known as mens rea. (We shall see, however, that the term mens rea has been expanded to encompass more than pure mental states.)

But what does "mens rea" mean?

---

11 M.S. Moore, "Choice, Character and Excuse" (1990) 7 *Social Philosophy and Policy* 29; Horder, "Criminal Culpability: The Possibility of a General Theory" (1993) *Law and Philosophy* 193, 207.

12 J.R. Lindgren, "Criminal Responsibility Reconsidered" (1987) 6 *Law and Philosophy* 89, 94. This criticism of the character theory is rejected by Tadros, *Criminal Responsibility* (2005), pp.49–51.

13 Duff, *Answering for Crime: Responsibility and Liability in the Criminal Law* (2007), p.20.

14 *Chandler v DPP* [1964] A.C. 763; [1962] 3 W.L.R. 694 HL.

J.F. Stephen, History of the Criminal Law of England, Vol.II (1883), pp.94–95:

"The maxim, *'Actus non facit reum nisi mens sit rea'*, is sometimes said to be the fundamental maxim of the whole criminal law . . . 3–010

It is frequently though ignorantly supposed to mean that there cannot be such a thing as legal guilt where there is no moral guilt, which is obviously untrue, as there is always a possibility of a conflict between law and morals.

It also suggests the notion that there is some state of mind called a *'mens rea'*, the absence of which, on any particular occasion, deprives what would otherwise be a crime of its criminal character. This also is untrue. There is no one such state of mind, as any one may convince himself by considering the definitions of dissimilar crimes. A pointsman falls asleep, and thereby causes a railway accident and the death of a passenger; he is guilty of manslaughter. He deliberately and by elaborate devices produces the same result: he is guilty of murder. If in each case there is a *mens rea*, as the maxim seems to imply, *mens rea* must be a name for two states of mind, not merely differing from but opposed to each other, for what two states of mind can resemble each other less than indolence and an active desire to kill?

The truth is that the maxim about *mens rea* means no more than that the definition of all or nearly all crimes contains not only an outward and visible element, but a mental element, varying according to the different nature of different crimes. Thus, in reference to murder, the *mens rea* is any state of mind which comes within the description of malice aforethought. In reference to theft the *mens rea* is an intention to deprive the owner of his property permanently, . . . Hence the only means of arriving at a full comprehension of the expression *mens rea* is by a detailed examination of the definitions of particular crimes, and therefore the expression itself is unmeaning."

Mens rea is the term generally used to indicate the mental element required by the definition of the crime. Older law and statutes used evaluative terms such as "malice aforethought" and "maliciously". For the past century, and particularly the last half-century, more cognitive terms such as knowledge and belief in relation to circumstances, and intention and recklessness in relation to consequences, have become prevalent. The courts have embraced these new concepts and have reinterpreted the older terms in the light of them. For example, "maliciously" in the Offences Against the Person Act 1861 s.20 has been construed as meaning "recklessly". Other forms of affective (as opposed to cognitive) mens rea also exist. For example, theft requires "dishonesty": this is a state of mind relating to the wrongfulness of actions. 3–011

However, the term mens rea has also been used to describe other forms of culpability that do not necessarily involve a "state of mind" in its cognitive sense of intending or being subjectively aware that a consequence could occur. For example, in the 1980s the law adopted an "objective" test of recklessness that involved a failure to foresee an obvious risk (an interpretation abandoned in 2003). Also, it has long been established that the mens rea for one species of manslaughter is satisfied by proof of gross negligence. In *Misra*, it was stated that:

> ". . . the term *'mens rea'* is also used to describe the ingredient of fault or culpability before criminal liability for the defendant's actions may be established . . . The requirement for gross negligence provides the necessary element of culpability."[15]

The Sentencing Advisory Panel (now known as the Sentencing Council) stated that there are four levels of culpability: intention, recklessness, knowledge and negligence.[16] Indeed, there is an increasing number of crimes for which only negligence is required. A prime example of this is the crime of rape.[17] It would be churlish to describe rape as a crime not involving mens rea.

One approach to this issue would be to conclude that there are two species of mens rea. First, there is "cognitive mens rea" which involves intention or foresight on the part of D. Secondly, there is "normative mens rea" under which an assessment of culpability involves an evaluation of the D's actions, taking into account all the circumstances including D's state of mind.[18]

Kumaralingham Amirthalingam, "Caldwell Recklessness is Dead, Long Live Mens rea's Fecklessness" (2004) 67 M.L.R. 491, 492:

3–012 "The doctrine of mens rea itself needs to be restored to its normative roots of attributing blameworthiness . . .

Briefly, blameworthiness goes beyond mere conduct responsibility; it is a normative enquiry as to whether the person deserves to be labelled and punished as a criminal. The blameworthiness of an accused is not determined merely by enquiring whether there existed a 'subjective' mens rea; it requires an additional crucial step of asking whether the 'mens was rea'. This inquiry involves an 'objective' element and includes inadvertence within mens rea."[19]

3–013 This approach, which is more consistent with the "character conception" of responsibility, has the advantage that it focuses attention on the central issue whether D is blameworthy.[20] In many cases, cognitive mens rea is a prime indicator of blameworthiness but an assessment of blame can be based on other non-cognitive factors. For example, a D can be blamed for causing a harm when, even though there was no awareness of the possibility of the harm occurring at the time of acting, it was D's prior own fault for getting themselves into a situation or condition (for example, intoxicated) whereby they were deprived of the capacity for awareness. Also, the fact that a D has cognitive mens rea does not

15 *R. v Misra (Amit)* [2004] EWCA Crim 2375; [2005] 1 Cr. App. R. 21 at [57].

16 *Overarching Principles: Seriousness* (2004), p.4.

17 Whilst it is true that under the Sexual Offences Act 2003 s.1, D must intend to penetrate V's vagina, anus or mouth with his penis, there is no cognitive mens rea requirement regarding the surrounding circumstances of the actus reus – i.e. whether V is consenting. Only a lack of reasonable belief in consent is needed. See paras 6–036–6–040 below.

18 C.M.V. Clarkson, *Understanding Criminal Law*, 4th edn (London: Sweet and Maxwell, 2005), pp.19–20, 56.

19 K. Amirthalingam, "Caldwell Recklessness is Dead, Long Live Mens rea's Fecklessness" (2004) 67 M.L.R. 491. Amirthalingam suggests that mens rea could be construed as follows: the "mens" should refer to the state of mind of D and the "rea" should involve a normative evaluation of that mental state in all the circumstances. The better view is that this evaluation should include—but not be limited to—D's mental state.

20 This approach was rejected in *R. v Kingston (Barry)* [1995] 2 A.C. 355; [1994] 3 W.L.R. 519 HL.

conclusively establish that they are blameworthy. They might intentionally bring about a prohibited harm but be exempt from blame because of a recognised excuse or justification (for example, duress or self-defence).

Accordingly, it must be borne in mind throughout this book that the term "mens rea" is no more than a tool in the identification of culpability. The construction of the various mens rea terms, such as recklessness, should be governed by the central quest of identifying blameworthiness. For example, in assessing whether "recklessness" should be interpreted as including a failure to consider obvious risks, the central issue is whether such a failure can be regarded as sufficiently culpable to justify the imposition of criminal liability.

C. PROOF OF COGNITIVE MENS REA

Most of the mens rea concepts mentioned above require proof of a person's state of mind. Did the actual defendant intend the consequence or foresee the risk of it occurring? This is commonly described as being a "subjective" test. Such a subjective test assumes that a person's state of mind is ascertainable. However, is it possible to inquire into a person's mind to ascertain what their intentions were when they committed the crime (maybe many months or even years previously)? As Ackner J said in his summing-up to the jury in *Hyam*: **3–014**

> "There is no scientific measurement or yardstick for gauging a person's intention. Unfortunately, there is no form of meter which one can fix to an accused person, like an amp meter or something of that kind, in order to ascertain what the intention is, no X-ray machine which will produce a useful picture."[21]

Despite the scientific impossibility of ascertaining what a person's state of mind was at the time of the alleged crime, cognitive mens rea requires courts to try to establish these subjective states of mind. How is this done?

Without direct evidence of a person's state of mind, such as a confession (although even this might not be reliable), mens rea has to be established by drawing inferences from facts; the jury must consider all the circumstantial evidence—the conduct of D before, during and after the crime, motive, statements by D, type of weapon used, etc—and from that infer what D must have intended. The jury can only perform this task by trying to ascertain what any normal or reasonable person would have intended or foreseen in those circumstances. From this developed the important maxim that a person must be taken to intend the natural and probable consequences of their actions. This maxim, which of course went a long way towards destroying any subjective notion of mens rea, was interpreted rigidly by the House of Lords in the following decision.

---

21 *Hyam* No.6530 C.72, Warwick Crown Court; tried 22–24 November 1972.

DIRECTOR OF PUBLIC PROSECUTIONS V SMITH [1961] A.C. 290 (HOUSE OF LORDS):

3-015 The respondent was driving a car in which there was stolen property. He was stopped by a police officer who told him to draw into the near side. The respondent began to do so and the constable walked beside the car. Then the respondent suddenly accelerated down an adjoining road. The constable succeeded in hanging on to the car which pursued an erratic course until he was thrown off in the path of a vehicle which ran over him, killing him.

At his trial for murder, the respondent maintained that he had no intention of killing or causing serious injury to the constable. Donovan J directed the jury:

> "if you are satisfied that he must, as a reasonable man, have contemplated that grievous bodily harm was likely to result to that officer and that such harm did happen and the officer died in consequence, then the accused is guilty of capital murder."

The jury returned a verdict of guilty. The Court of Criminal Appeal quashed his conviction on the ground of misdirection. The Crown appealed to the House of Lords.

VISCOUNT KILMUIR:

> "The unlawful and voluntary act must clearly be aimed at someone in order to eliminate cases of negligence or of careless or dangerous driving. Once, however, the jury are satisfied as to that, it matters not what the accused in fact contemplated as the probable result or whether he ever contemplated at all, provided he was in law responsible and accountable for his actions, that is, was a man capable of forming an intent, not insane within the M'Naghten Rules and not suffering from diminished responsibility. On the assumption that he is so accountable for his actions, the sole question is whether the unlawful and voluntary act was of such a kind that grievous bodily harm was the natural and probable result. The only test available for this is what the ordinary responsible man would, in all the circumstances of the case, have contemplated as the natural and probable result. That, indeed, has always been the law . . .
>
> Another criticism of the summing-up and one which found favour in the Court of Criminal Appeal concerned the manner in which the trial judge dealt with the presumption that a man intends the natural and probable consequences of his acts. The real question is whether the jury should have been told that it was rebuttable. In truth, however, as I see it, this is merely another way of applying the test of the reasonable man. Provided that the presumption is applied, once the accused's knowledge of the circumstances and the nature of his acts have been ascertained, the only thing that could rebut the presumption would be proof of incapacity to form an intent, insanity or diminished responsibility. In the present case, therefore, there was no need to explain to the jury that the presumption was rebuttable."

Appeal allowed

This decision was greeted with howls of derision by most English commentators.[22] The exact effect of the decision was never settled: did it lay down an irrebuttable evidential presumption that intention was to be ascertained objectively for all crimes? Or did it lay down a new mens rea for murder—a completely objective test where it was only necessary to establish that death or grievous bodily harm was objectively foreseeable? Either way, its effect was profound. Murder (and possibly all crimes) had been transformed into a crime of negligence: if the reasonable man would have foreseen the harm, D was liable. **3-016**

Intense criticism of this decision[23] led to the passing of the Criminal Justice Act 1967 s.8:

> "A court or jury, in determining whether a person has committed an offence—
>
> (a) shall not be bound in law to infer that he intended or foresaw a result of his actions by reason only of its being a natural and probable consequence of these actions; but
> (b) shall decide whether he did intend or foresee that result by reference to all the evidence, drawing such inferences from the evidence as appear proper in the circumstances."

The legislature has thus clearly endorsed the idea that intention is to be subjectively ascertained—as must foresight.[24] Of course, one way to establish a person's state of mind is by obtaining a confession. There is evidence that historically this led to the police exerting more pressure to get confessions from Ds to strengthen the case for the prosecution.[25] The results were seen in a number of successful appeals against convictions.

Section 8 does not actually solve the practical problem of proving mens rea at all; it merely states what ought to be done in theory. It is true that if there is clear evidence that D did not intend a result, the jury can so find. But in what circumstances would a jury conclude that while a reasonable person would have foreseen a result, D did not? Surely this would generally only occur where there was clear evidence that D's state of mind was in some material way different from that of the reasonable person—say, because they were a schizophrenic. But Viscount Kilmuir in *DPP v Smith* was careful to exclude those persons not capable of conforming to the standards of the reasonable person.

In other cases, however, it is doubtful if juries can do otherwise than draw inferences from conduct and apply their own standards, the standards of ordinary people: "If I had been in that situation, what would I have foreseen?" Perhaps this is what was meant by the startling extract from a training manual for magistrates which stated: **3-017**

---

22 Fletcher regards the reaction to this case as "even more unfortunate" than the decision itself in that English judges and commentators have "gone to the opposite extreme" in eschewing "any reliance on the projected behaviour of a reasonable person" (*Rethinking Criminal Law* (1978), p.704).

23 e.g. Law Commission, *Imputed Criminal Intent (Director of Public Prosecutions v Smith)* (1965).

24 See also *Frankland (Graham Ralph) v The Queen* [1987] A.C. 576; [1987] 2 W.L.R. 1251, where the Privy Council reiterated the point that the test is a subjective one.

25 A. Sanders, "Some Dangers of Policy Oriented Research—The Case of Prosecutions" in I. Dennis (ed), *Criminal Law and Justice* (London: Sweet & Maxwell, 1987), p.208.

> "It is sometimes said on the defendant's behalf that he did not intend to inflict the particular injury which the victim suffered. This is always a weak point because any sane person who commits an act of violence must expect injury to result. The fact that it happens to be greater than anticipated provides no excuse whatsoever."[26]

We are now in a position to examine some of the core mens rea concepts, in particular, intention, recklessness and negligence. Other mens rea concepts, such as dishonesty and knowledge, are discussed later in the book in relation to the offences to which they apply. Which of these mens rea concepts is applicable depends on the definition of the offence on question. For some offences, this is specified by statute. For example, the Theft Act 1968 s.1 defines theft as requiring proof of dishonesty. For other offences, case law has established the type of mens rea required. For example, for an assault proof of recklessness suffices.[27]

II. Intention

A. INTRODUCTION

3–018 For many crimes it is unnecessary to distinguish intention from recklessness because proof of either will suffice. For example, the Criminal Damage Act 1971 s.1(1) provides that it is an offence to destroy or damage any property belonging to another "intending to destroy or damage any such property or being reckless as to whether any such property would be destroyed or damaged". However, there are some crimes that can only be committed intentionally: for example, the Offences Against the Person Act 1861 s.18 makes it an offence to wound or cause grievous bodily harm "with intent to cause grievous bodily harm". For these crimes, it is essential to define intention with some precision in order to distinguish it from recklessness.

B. THE LAW

3–019 As seen above, the Criminal Justice Act 1967 s.8 lays down an evidential rule as to *how* intention is to be proved and makes it clear that intention is a subjective state of mind. What matters is whether D intended the result, not whether the reasonable man would have intended it. In trying to ascertain what D did intend, the court or jury must draw inferences from all the relevant evidence.

26 R. Bartle, *Crime and the New Magistrate* (London: B. Rose, 1985), quoted from D. Nelken, "Criminal Law and Criminal Justice" in Dennis (ed), *Criminal Law and Justice* (1987), p.149.

27 *R. v Venna (Henson George)* [1976] Q.B. 421; [1975] 3 W.L.R. 737 CA.

However, while this is clear as to the process for ascertaining intention, there is no statutory definition of intention in English law. Indeed, over the past few decades there has been much controversy over the actual meaning of the concept "intention". Two views have dominated this debate:

(1) a consequence is intended when it is the aim or the objective of the actor. This is called "direct" intention;
(2) a consequence is intended when it is the aim or objective of the actor, or is foreseen as a virtual, practical or moral certainty. If this second state of mind is classed as intention, it is usually called "oblique" intention.

The courts used to adopt an even broader view in holding that a consequence was intended when it was foreseen as a probable or likely result D's actions.[28] In *Hyam*,[29] for instance, Mrs Hyam poured petrol through the letterbox of the house of her lover's new mistress and then ignited it knowing people were asleep in the house. She claimed that she had not meant to kill but had foreseen death or grievous bodily harm as a highly probable result of her actions. Her conviction for murder was upheld with the House of Lords arguably ruling that her state of mind amounted to an *intention* to kill or cause grievous bodily harm.

However, since then there has been a retreat from this position and it is now clear that foresight of a consequence as probable, likely or even highly probable does not amount to intention. The precise status and meaning of oblique intention have greatly troubled the courts.

R. v Moloney [1985] A.C. 905 (House of Lords):

The appellant and his stepfather, both of whom had been drinking heavily, engaged in a contest to ascertain who was quicker on the draw with a shotgun. The appellant shot and killed his stepfather but claimed he had not realised the gun was pointing at him. He was convicted of murder and his appeal was dismissed by the Court of Appeal. He appealed to the House of Lords. **3-020**

LORD BRIDGE OF HARWICH:

"[L]ooking on their facts at the decided cases where a crime of specific intent was under consideration, they suggest to me that the probability of the consequence taken to have been foreseen must be little short of overwhelming before it will suffice to establish the necessary intent. The golden rule should be that, when directing a jury on the mental element necessary in a crime of specific intent, the judge should avoid any elaboration or paraphrase of what is meant by intent, and leave it to the jury's good sense to decide whether the accused acted with the necessary intent, unless the judge is convinced that, on the facts and having regard to the way the case has been presented to the jury in evidence and argument, some further explanation

28 This was the view (obiter) of the House of Lords in *R. v Lemon (Denis)* [1979] A.C. 617; [1979] 2 W.L.R. 281 HL and was arguably the view adopted in *Hyam v DPP* [1975] A.C. 55; [1974] 2 W.L.R. 607 HL. The alternative interpretation of *Hyam* is that the House of Lords was there defining "malice aforethought", the mens rea of murder—and not defining "intention". See generally, J. Buzzard, "Intent" [1978] Crim. L.R. 5 and J.C. Smith, "'Intent': A Reply" [1978] Crim. L.R. 14.

29 *Hyam* [1975] A.C. 55.

or elaboration is strictly necessary to avoid misunderstanding. In trials for murder or wounding with intent, I find it very difficult to visualise a case where any such explanation or elaboration could be required, if the offence consisted of a direct attack on the victim with a weapon . . . Even where the death results indirectly from the act of the accused, I believe the cases that will call for a direction by reference to foresight of consequences will be of extremely rare occurrence . . .

I do not, of course, by what I have said in the foregoing paragraph, mean to question the necessity, which frequently arises, to explain to a jury that intention is something quite distinct from motive or desire. But this can normally be quite simply explained by reference to the case before the court or, if necessary, by some homely example. A man who, at London Airport, boards a plane which he knows to be bound for Manchester, clearly intends to travel to Manchester, even though Manchester is the last place he wants to be and his motive for boarding the plane is simply to escape pursuit. The possibility that the plane may have engine trouble and be diverted to Luton does not affect the matter. By boarding the Manchester plane, the man conclusively demonstrates his intention to go there, because it is a moral certainty that that is where he will arrive . . .

Starting from the proposition . . . that the mental element in murder requires proof of an intention to kill or cause really serious injury, the first fundamental question to be answered is whether there is any rule of substantive law that foresight by the accused of one of those eventualities as a probable consequence of his voluntary act, where the probability can be defined as exceeding a certain degree, is equivalent or alternative to the necessary intention. I would answer this question in the negative . . .

The irrationality of any such rule of substantive law stems from the fact that it is impossible to define degrees of probability, in any of the infinite variety of situations arising in human affairs, in precise or scientific terms . . .

I am firmly of opinion that foresight of consequences, as an element bearing on the issue of intention in murder, or indeed any other crime of specific intent, belongs, not to the substantive law, but to the law of evidence . . .

In the rare cases in which it is necessary to direct a jury by reference to foresight of consequences, I do not believe it is necessary for the judge to do more than invite the jury to consider two questions. First, was death or really serious injury in a murder case (or whatever relevant consequence must be proved to have been intended in any other case) a natural consequence of the defendant's voluntary act? Secondly, did the defendant foresee that consequence as being a natural consequence of his act? The jury should then be told that if they answer yes to both questions it is a proper inference for them to draw that he intended that consequence."

Appeal allowed

R. v HANCOCK AND SHANKLAND [1986] A.C. 455 (HOUSE OF LORDS):

The defendants, two striking miners, pushed a large lump of concrete from a bridge on to a convoy of cars below carrying a miner to work. The concrete struck a taxi's windscreen and killed the driver. The defendants claimed they had not meant to kill or cause serious injury. Their plan was to drop the concrete in the middle lane of the carriageway while the convoy was in the nearside lane. Their aim was to frighten the miner or block the road in order to prevent him from getting to work. The defendants were convicted of murder. The Court of Appeal allowed their appeals and substituted verdicts of manslaughter. The Crown appealed to the House of Lords. **3-021**

LORD SCARMAN:

"The question for the House is . . ., whether the *Moloney* guidelines are sound . . .

[Lord Bridge of Harwich in *Moloney*] omitted any reference in his guidelines to probability. I agree with the Court of Appeal that the probability of a consequence is a factor of sufficient importance to be drawn specifically to the attention of the jury and to be explained. In a murder case where it is necessary to direct a jury on the issue of intent by reference to foresight of consequences the probability of death or serious injury resulting from the act done may be critically important. Its importance will depend on the degree of probability: if the likelihood that death or serious injury will result is high, the probability of that result may be seen as overwhelming evidence of the existence of the intent to kill or injure. Failure to explain the relevance of probability may, therefore, mislead a jury into thinking that it is of little or no importance . . . In my judgment, therefore, the *Moloney* guidelines as they stand are unsafe and misleading. They require a reference to probability. They also require an explanation that the greater the probability of a consequence the more likely it is that the consequence was foreseen and that if that consequence was foreseen the greater the probability is that that consequence was also intended. But juries also require to be reminded that the decision is theirs to be reached upon a consideration of all the evidence . . .

In a case where foresight of a consequence is part of the evidence supporting a prosecution submission that the accused intended the consequence, the judge, if he thinks some general observations would help the jury, could well, having in mind section 8 of the Criminal Justice Act 1967, emphasise that the probability, however high, of a consequence is only a factor, though it may in some cases be a very significant factor, to be considered with all the other evidence in determining whether the accused intended to bring it about. The distinction between the offence and the evidence relied on to prove it is vital . . .

For these reasons I would hold that the *Moloney* guidelines are defective and should not be used as they stand without further explanation."

Appeal dismissed

R. v Nedrick [1986] 1 W.L.R. 1025 (Court of Appeal, Criminal Division):

3–022 The appellant poured paraffin through the letterbox of a house and set light to it. The house caught fire and a child died. The appellant claimed that he did not want anyone to die. He was convicted of murder and appealed.

LORD LANE CJ:

> "What then does a jury have to decide so far as the mental element in murder is concerned? It simply has to decide whether the defendant intended to kill or do serious bodily harm. In order to reach that decision the jury must pay regard to all the relevant circumstances, including what the defendant himself said and did.
>
> In the great majority of cases a direction to that effect will be enough, particularly where the defendant's actions amounted to a direct attack upon his victim, because in such cases the evidence relating to the defendant's desire or motive will be clear and his intent will have been the same as his desire or motive. But in some cases, of which this is one, the defendant does an act which is manifestly dangerous and as a result someone dies. The primary desire or motive of the defendant may not have been to harm that person, or indeed anyone. In that situation what further directions should a jury be given as to the mental state which they must find to exist in the defendant if murder is to be proved?
>
> We have endeavoured to crystallise the effect of their Lordships' speeches in *R. v Moloney* and *R. v Hancock* in a way which we hope may be helpful to judges who have to handle this type of case.
>
> It may be advisable first of all to explain to the jury that a man may intend to achieve a certain result whilst at the same time not desiring it to come about . . .
>
> When determining whether the defendant had the necessary intent, it may therefore be helpful for a jury to ask themselves two questions. (1) How probable was the consequence which resulted from the defendant's voluntary act? (2) Did he foresee that consequence?
>
> If he did not appreciate that death or serious harm was likely to result from his act, he cannot have intended to bring it about. If he did, but thought that the risk to which he was exposing the person killed was only slight, then it may be easy for the jury to conclude that he did not intend to bring about that result. On the other hand, if the jury are satisfied that at the material time the defendant recognised that death or serious harm would be virtually certain (barring some unforeseen intervention) to result from his voluntary act, then that is a fact from which they may find it easy to infer that he intended to kill or do serious bodily harm, even though he may not have had any desire to achieve that result . . .
>
> *Where the charge is murder and in the rare cases where the simple direction is not enough, the jury should be directed that they are not entitled to infer the necessary intention, unless they*

> *feel sure that death or serious bodily harm was a virtual certainty (barring some unforeseen intervention) as a result of the defendant's actions and that the defendant appreciated that such was the case.*[30]
>
> Where a man realises that it is for all practical purposes inevitable that his actions will result in death or serious harm, the inference may be irresistible that he intended that result, however little he may have desired or wished it to happen. The decision is one for the jury to be reached upon a consideration of all the evidence."
>
> *Appeal allowed*
> *Conviction of manslaughter substituted*

R. v Woollin [1999] 1 A.C. 82 (House of Lords):

The appellant lost his temper with his three-month-old son and threw him with great force causing the child to hit his head on something hard and die. In an interview, the appellant admitted that he had realised there was a risk of serious injury. The trial judge directed the jury that they might infer intention if they were satisfied that the appellant appreciated that there was a substantial risk that he would cause serious harm. The appellant was convicted of murder and appealed on the ground that the judge should not have used the phrase "substantial risk", which is a test of recklessness, but should have used the phrase "virtual certainty". **3–023**

LORD STEYN:

> "The Crown did not contend that the appellant desired to kill his son or to cause him serious injury. The issue was whether the appellant nevertheless had the intention to cause serious harm . . .
>
> I approach the issues arising on this appeal on the basis that it does not follow that 'intent' necessarily has precisely the same meaning in every context in the criminal law. The focus of the present appeal is the crime of murder.
>
> . . .
>
> The Crown did not argue that as a matter of policy foresight of a virtual certainty is too narrow a test in murder . . . Moreover, over a period of 12 years since *Nedrick* the test of foresight of virtual certainty has apparently caused no practical difficulties. It is simple and clear. It is true that it may exclude a conviction of murder in the often cited terrorist example where a member of the bomb disposal team is killed. In such a case it may realistically be said that the terrorist did not foresee the killing of a member of the bomb disposal team as a virtual certainty. That

30 This section was emphasised by Lord Steyn in *R. v Woollin (Stephen Leslie)* [1999] 1 A.C. 82; [1998] 3 W.L.R. 382 HL when he cited this passage with approval.

may be a consequence of not framing the principle in terms of risk-taking. Such cases ought to cause no substantial difficulty since immediately below murder there is available a verdict of manslaughter which may attract in the discretion of the court a life sentence . . . I am satisfied that the *Nedrick* test, which was squarely based on the decision of the House in *Moloney*, is pitched at the right level of foresight . . .

It may be appropriate to give a direction in accordance with *Nedrick* in any case in which the defendant may not have desired the result of his act. But I accept the trial judge is best placed to decide what direction is required by the circumstances of the case . . .

It follows that the judge should not have departed from the *Nedrick* direction. By using the phrase 'substantial risk' the judge blurred the line between intention and recklessness, and hence between murder and manslaughter. The misdirection enlarged the scope of the mental element required for murder. It was a material misdirection . . . The conviction of murder must be quashed.

The status of Nedrick

In my view Lord Lane CJ's judgment in *Nedrick* provided valuable assistance to trial judges . . . [His Lordship then repeated part of Lord Lane's judgment]:

> '. . . (B) Where the charge is murder and in the rare cases where the simple direction is not enough, the jury should be directed that they are not entitled to infer the necessary intention, unless they feel sure that death or serious bodily harm was a virtual certainty (barring some unforeseen intervention) as a result of the defendant's actions and that the defendant appreciated that such was the case. (C) Where a man realises that it is for all practical purposes inevitable that his actions will result in death or serious harm, the inference may be irresistible that he intended that result, however little he may have desired or wished it to happen. The decision is one for the jury to be reached upon a consideration of all the evidence.' (Lettering added)
>
> . . . [It has been observed] that the use of the words 'to infer' in (B) may detract from the clarity of the model direction. I agree. I would substitute the words 'to find'. Thirdly, the first sentence of (C) does not form part of the model direction. But it would always be right for the judge to say, as Lord Lane CJ put it, that the decision is for the jury upon a consideration of all the evidence in the case."

Appeal allowed

The following conclusions can be drawn from these cases. 3-024

1. Wanting result

A defendant who wants a result to happen or is prepared to do acts to achieve a consequence even if not (emotionally) desired[31]—when it is the aim or objective (direct intention)—clearly intends that result. 3-025

R.A. DUFF, INTENTION, AGENCY AND CRIMINAL LIABILITY: PHILOSOPHY OF ACTION AND THE CRIMINAL LAW (1990), PP.47–48:

"To say that she intended to bring about a particular result is to say that that result formed at least part of her reason for acting as she did . . . What Mrs Hyam did fitted both the description 'setting fire to the house' and the description 'making work for the fire brigade': what makes the former description, but not the latter, appropriate as a description of her intended action is its relation to her reasons for action." 3-026

Duff goes on to suggest that direct intention can be measured by employing a "test of failure": would D count her actions as a failure if the result did not ensue?[32] Employing this test, Mrs Hyam did not directly intend to kill or cause injury because she would not have regarded her actions as a failure had no one been killed or injured. 3-027

Such wanted results are intended even if the chances of the result occurring are slim: if D shoots at V half a mile away knowing that they could easily miss, they still intend to kill because that is what they are trying to do. Lord Reid has expressed this point in terms of a golfing analogy:

"If I say I intend to reach the green, people will believe me although we all know that the odds are ten to one against my succeeding."[33]

However, no matter how much one may want to achieve a result, one can only be said to intend it if one recognises that there is a chance of achieving it. If one does not believe that the consequence is a possible result of one's actions one can hardly be said to be trying to achieve it.[34]

---

31 In *R. v Hales (Ricky)* [2005] EWCA Crim 1118 it was held that it was enough that the defendant was "prepared to kill" in order to escape police custody (at [28]).

32 R.A. Duff, *Intention, Agency and Criminal Liability: Philosophy of Action and the Criminal Law* (London: Blackwell, 1990), p.61. See also R.A. Duff, "Intention, Mens Rea and the Law Commission Report" [1980] Crim. L.R. 147, 150–151.

33 *Gollins v Gollins* [1964] A.C. 644 at 664; [1963] 3 W.L.R. 176 HL.

34 R.A. Duff, "The Obscure Intentions of the House of Lords" [1986] Crim. L.R. 771, 779; Duff, *Intention, Agency and Criminal Liability: Philosophy of Action and the Criminal Law* (1990), p.58.

2. Question of fact for jury

3–028 In the normal case, the term "intention" should not be given a legal definition. Judges should refrain from giving juries guidance as to what it means. This is particularly true in common cases where there has been a direct attack upon V.[35] Whether a D intended a result is a question of fact which only the jury, applying their common sense to an ordinary English word, can answer. It is thus impossible to define intention or to know precisely what it means. It could well mean different things to different juries. Presumably, although one is only guessing, most juries will opt for the ordinary, common-sense meaning, namely, "as 'a decision to bring about a certain consequence' or as the aim".[36]

3. "Exceptional" cases: oblique intention

3–029 However, there may be other cases where a D has a purpose other than causing the prohibited harm—but where that result is an inevitable or likely consequence. For example, D's main aim in *Nedrick* was to burn down the house in order to frighten its occupant but, in so doing, causing death was a likely result. In *Woollin*, it was again emphasised that a direction was only necessary in cases where D does not desire the consequence that has occurred. In *Moloney*, Lord Bridge thought such guidance would only be necessary in "rare" and "exceptional" cases.[37] However, Lord Scarman in *Hancock* stated that such cases would not be at all rare or exceptional—and, accordingly, guidance to the jury will be necessary in most cases where D has a primary aim in acting other than causing the prohibited harm.[38] Despite this, more recent cases have stressed that a *Woollin* direction will only be required in "rare circumstances".[39] Furthermore, giving a *Woollin* direction when it is not appropriate can amount to a misdirection providing grounds for quashing a conviction because it can lead to the trial judge analysing the evidence differently from how it should be analysed in the normal cases of direct intention.[40]

So, in rare cases it is permissible to give juries some guidance. However, it is far from clear precisely what intention does mean in such cases. The central problem is that there are two possible interpretations of *Woollin*.

(i) *Definitional interpretation*: a new extended *definition* of intention was laid down. If a consequence is foreseen as virtually certain the jury may be told that this amounts to intention. This view is supported by two passages in *Woollin*. First, Lord Steyn cited with approval from *Moloney* that "if a person foresees the probability of a consequence as little short of overwhelming, this will suffice *to establish* the necessary intent" (Lord Steyn's emphasis). Secondly, after citing the italicised passage from *Nedrick* (p.152), Lord Steyn added: "The effect of the critical direction is that a result foreseen as virtually certain *is* an intended result" (emphasis added). This interpretation is strengthened by the fact that in *Woollin* the Crown

---

35 *Gregory and Mott* [1995] Crim. L.R. 507; *R. v Fallon* [1994] Crim. L.R. 519 CA.

36 *R. v Mohan (John Patrick)* [1976] Q.B. 1; [1975] 2 W.L.R. 859 CA.

37 See also *Gilmour* [2000] Cr. App. R. 407.

38 In *R. v Walker (John Charles)* (1990) 90 Cr. App. R. 226; [1990] Crim. L.R. 44 CA, it was held that a mere request from a jury for a further direction did not make the case a rare and exceptional one requiring a direction on foresight.

39 *R. v MD* [2004] EWCA Crim 1391 at [29]. See also *R. v Allen (Tony John)* [2005] EWCA Crim 1344 at [63] and *Hales* [2005] EWCA Crim 1118 at [27].

40 *MD* [2004] EWCA Crim 1391 at [36].

did not contend that D desired to kill or seriously injure his son. The case proceeded on the basis that there could be another species of intention apart from direct intention.

(ii) *Evidential interpretation*: there is still no definition of intention. Where a consequence is foreseen as virtually certain this is evidence entitling a court or jury to find intention. Lord Steyn emphasised his approval of the critical direction in *Nedrick* (the passage in emphasis on p.217). While he substituted "find" in place of "infer",[41] he endorsed the *Nedrick* view that the jury was:

> ". . . not entitled to [find] the necessary intention unless they feel sure that death or serious bodily harm was a virtual certainty . . . and the defendant appreciated that such was the case."

While endorsing the virtual certainty test as evidence from which the jury is entitled to find intention, Lord Steyn immediately went on to rule that the *Nedrick* proposition (first sentence of (C) cited in *Woollin*) that the inference may be irresistible, does not form part of the model direction. This seems to confirm that there is no test of intention. While foresight of a virtual certainty is a prerequisite to a finding of intention, the jury may (is "entitled to") find intention in such cases, but equally they may not. This evidential interpretation was adopted in the following case.

R. v MATTHEWS AND ALLEYNE [2003] 2 CR. APP. R. 30 (COURT OF APPEAL, CRIMINAL DIVISION):

The defendants deliberately threw a non-swimmer into a deep, wide river where he drowned. They were convicted of murder and appealed on the ground that the trial judge had misdirected the jury that if they were satisfied the defendants foresaw death as virtually certain they had to convict (i.e. that the trial judge adopted the definitional interpretation). 3–030

RIX LJ:

> "Mr Coker for the Crown on this appeal submits that in *Woollin* the House of Lords has finally moved away from a rule of evidence to a rule of substantive law. In this connection he drew attention to a sentence in Lord Steyn's speech where he says . . . that—
>
> > 'The effect of the critical direction is that a result foreseen as virtually certain is an intended result.' . . .
>
> In our judgment, however, the law has not yet reached a *definition* of intent in murder in terms of appreciation of a virtual certainty . . . [W]e do not regard *Woollin* as yet reaching or laying down a substantive rule of law. On the contrary, it is clear from the discussion in *Woollin* as a whole that *Nedrick* was derived from the existing law, at that time ending in *Moloney* and

---

41 Some commentators have suggested that the substitution of "find" for "infer" "seems a clear indication that the connection between virtual certainty and intention is not merely evidential" (A. Simester, "Murder, Mens Rea and the House of Lords—Again" (1999) 115 L.Q.R. 17). However, the jury is only *entitled* to find intention suggesting that this is still an evidential proposition.

Hancock, and that the critical direction in *Nedrick* was approved, subject to the change of one word.

In these circumstances we think that the judge did go further than the law as it stands at present permitted him to go . . .

Having said that, however, we think that, once what is required is an appreciation of virtual certainty of death, and not some lesser foresight of merely probable consequences, there is very little to choose between a rule of evidence and one of substantive law. It is probably this thought that led Lord Steyn to say that a result foreseen as virtually certain is an intended result . . .

We also think that on the particular facts of this case, reflected in the judge's directions, the question of the appellants' intentions to save Jonathan from drowning highlight the irresistible nature of the inference or finding of intent to kill, once the jury were sure both that the defendants appreciated the virtual certainty of death '(barring some attempt to save him)' and that at the time of throwing Jonathan from the bridge they then 'had no intentions of saving him'. If the jury were sure that the appellants appreciated the virtual certainty of Jonathan's death when they threw him from the bridge and also that they then had no intention of saving him from such death, it is impossible to see how the jury could not have found that the appellants intended Jonathan to die."

Appeal dismissed

3–031 In an ambiguous judgment in *Stringer*,[42] Toulson LJ seemed to accept that if a consequence was foreseen as virtually certain, a finding of intention "was bound to follow". Despite this, the evidential interpretation endorsed in *Matthews and Alleyne* appears to represent the current law. Nevertheless, the question still remains: which of these interpretations is preferable? The definitional interpretation has the advantage of being more simple and more workable. There are two separate species of intent: direct intent (aim/purpose) and oblique intent (foresight of virtual certainty). Each is clearly defined and proof of either will suffice (for murder, at any rate: see below). It avoids the absurdity of having to infer one state of mind (intention) from another state of mind (foresight of virtual certainty).

The problem with the evidential interpretation is that if one is inferring (or finding) intention from foresight of a virtual certainty, one must know what intention means. If intention (A) may be found from foresight of a virtual certainty (B), (A) and (B) must logically mean different things. But what does intention (A) mean? It is not foresight of a virtual certainty (B) because that is merely an evidential pre-condition.[43] It should not mean direct intention[44] because juries should only be given a *Nedrick/Woollin* direction in cases where D does not aim to achieve the consequence. It is a logical nonsense to tell the

42 *R. v Stringer (Matthew)* [2008] EWCA Crim 1222.

43 W. Wilson, "Doctrinal Rationality after *Woollin*" (1999) 62 M.L.R. 448, 155.

44 Norrie has argued that one can only infer intention from foresight where intention connotes direct intention plus foresight of a moral certainty (oblique intention) because one cannot infer a mental state (A) from the facts (b) where A and b are qualitatively different (A. Norrie, "Oblique Intention and Legal Politics" [1989] Crim. L.R. 793, 803). However, as Duff has effectively responded: "intention is inferable from foresight

jury that because D does not want the result they are going to be given the special direction but that if they are satisfied that D foresaw the consequence as a virtual certainty, they may conclude that D did want it after all.

The result is that intention can only mean something mysterious: "some ineffable, indefinable notion of intent, locked in the breasts of the jurors".[45] Where there is such a "logical gap"[46] between foresight of a virtual certainty and this mysterious, undefined concept of intention, it becomes difficult to predict when and in what circumstances the finding of intent will or will not be made. Such an approach allows the jury maximum flexibility to make moral assessments of D's actions and to do justice as they perceive it.[47]

On the other hand, the definitional interpretation places the jury in a moral straight-jacket. If D foresees a consequence as virtually certain the jury is bound (in theory) to conclude that the test of oblique intention is satisfied.

Alan Norrie, "After Woollin" [1999] Criminal L. Rev. 532, 538:

> "[There] are cases where there is a 'moral threshold' such that even though the accused could foresee a result as virtually certain, it is so at odds with his moral conception of what he was doing that it could not be conceived as a result that he intended . . . [T]here is a good argument for saying that a person does not intend indirectly those results which may be foreseen as virtually certain where they are at serious moral odds with what he intended to do . . . [Judges] and juries would be 'entitled' to find, in terms of *principle* and without strain, that the moral threshold between what the accused intended and what she foresaw as virtually certain was sufficiently large to avoid attribution of fault." **3-032**

In most cases (certainly murder cases) what D foresees is not going to be "at serious moral odds with what he intended to do". Such defendants are usually engaged in reprehensible conduct such as that in *Matthews and Alleyne* where it was stated that *on the facts* the inference was "irresistible" and that if D appreciated the virtual certainty of death, it would be "impossible" for the jury not to find the requisite intention to kill. **3-033**

However, as argued by Norrie, the advantage of the evidential interpretation is that in other cases where their sympathy is aroused the jury is given a "get out clause"[48] in that while they are entitled to find intention, equally they are entitled not to find intention. This approach gives juries "moral elbow-room"[49] to acquit in such cases without having to resort to perverse verdicts. As Wilson puts it: by not

only if they are distinct"; if they are the same thing, no further inference is needed ("The Politics of Intention: A Response to Norrie" [1990] Crim. L.R. 637, 639).

45 J. Smith "Commentary to *Woollin*" [1998] Crim. L.R. 891.

46 Duff, "The Obscure Intentions of the House of Lords" [1986] Crim. L.R. 771.

47 This approach is criticised in Clarkson, *Understanding Criminal Law*, 4th edn (2005), p.213. Norrie says it "permits the law to have its principled cake of subjectivism, and to eat it" ("Oblique Intention and Legal Politics" [1989] Crim. L.R. 79, 806).

48 Wilson, "Doctrinal Rationality after *Woollin*" (1999) 62 M.L.R. 448, 456.

49 J. Horder, "Intention in the Criminal Law—A Rejoinder" (1995) 58 M.L.R. 678, 687.

having a strict definition of intention the judge or jury have a "flexible friend, which, in appropriate circumstances can allow good intentions to take doctrinal precedence over knowledge".[50]

R. v Steane [1947] K.B. 997 (Court of Criminal Appeal):

3-034 The appellant, a British film actor, was resident and working in Germany before World War II. When war broke out, he was arrested. As a result of threats to place his wife and children in a concentration camp and physical threats to himself, the appellant reluctantly agreed to broadcast on the radio for the Germans. For four months he read the news three times a day. After the war, he was convicted of doing acts likely to assist the enemy, with intent to assist the enemy, contrary to of the Defence (General) Regulations 1939 reg.2A and was sentenced to three years' imprisonment. He appealed against the conviction.

GODDARD LCJ:

"The appellant also asserted . . . that he never had the slightest idea or intention of assisting the enemy and what he did was done to save his wife and children . . .

The . . . difficult question that arises, however, is in connection with the direction to the jury with regard to whether these acts were done with the intention of assisting the enemy . . . While no doubt the motive of a man's act and his intention of doing the act are in law different things, it is nonetheless true that in many offences a specific intention is a necessary ingredient, and the jury have to be satisfied that a particular act was done with that specific intent . . .

British soldiers who were set to work on the Burma Road, or if invasion had unhappily taken place, British subjects who might have been set to work by the enemy digging trenches would undoubtedly be doing acts likely to assist the enemy. It would be unnecessary surely in their cases to consider any of the niceties of the law relating to duress because no jury would find that merely doing this work they were intending to assist the enemy . . . The proper direction to the jury in this case would have been that it was for the prosecution to prove the criminal intent, and that while the jury would be entitled to presume that intent if they thought that the act was done as the result of the free uncontrolled action of the accused, they would not be entitled to presume it if the circumstances showed that the act was done in subjection to the power of the enemy or was as equally consistent with an innocent intent as with a criminal intent, for example, a desire to save his wife and children from a concentration camp. They should only convict if satisfied by the evidence that the act complained of was in fact done to assist the enemy and if there was doubt about the matter the prisoner was entitled to be acquitted."

Conviction quashed

50 Wilson, "Murder and the Structure of Homicide" in A. Ashworth and B. Mitchell (eds), *Rethinking English Homicide Law* (Oxford: OUP, 2000), p.48.

This case was, of course, decided many years before the current law on intention had been settled. If it were decided today under the definitional interpretation of *Woollin*, the jury would be forced (short of a perverse verdict) to conclude that Steane intended to assist the enemy: he would certainly have foreseen that consequence as a virtual certainty. However, under the evidential interpretation, the jury would have the moral elbow-room to conclude that, despite such foresight, the result was not intended. **3–035**

This approach also provides flexibility in medical cases where doctors administer drugs or other treatment with lawful motives (for example, to relieve pain) but knowing the treatment will kill the patient.

RE A (CONJOINED TWINS: SURGICAL SEPARATION) [2000] 4 ALL E.R. 961 (COURT OF APPEAL, CIVIL DIVISION):

The issue in this case was whether a declaration should be made that it would be lawful for doctors to separate conjoined twins even though such a procedure would certainly result in the death of the weaker twin. One of the matters canvassed was whether the doctors would have the mens rea of murder, namely, an intention to kill or cause grievous bodily harm. **3–036**

WARD LJ:

"I have to ask myself whether I am satisfied that the doctors recognise that death or serious harm will be virtually certain (barring some unforeseen intervention) to result from carrying out this operation. If so, the doctors intend to kill or do that serious harm even though they may not have any desire to achieve that result. It is common ground that they appreciate that death to Mary would result from the severance of the common aorta. Unpalatable though it may be . . . to stigmatise the doctors with 'murderous intent', that is what in law they will have if they perform the operation and Mary dies as a result.

The doctrine of double effect . . . teaches that an act which produces a bad effect is nevertheless morally permissible if the action is good in itself, the intention is solely to produce the good effect, the good effect is not produced through the bad effect and there is sufficient reason to permit the bad effect. It may be difficult to reconcile with *R. v Woollin* . . . I can readily see how the doctrine works when doctors are treating one patient administering pain-killing drugs for the sole good purpose of relieving pain, yet appreciating the bad side-effect that it will hasten the patient's death. I simply fail to see how it can apply here where the side-effect to the good cure for Jodie is another patient's, Mary's, death, and when the treatment cannot have been undertaken to effect any benefit for Mary."

BROOKE LJ:

"[A]n English court would inevitably find that the surgeons intended to kill Mary, however little they desired that end, because her death would be the virtual certain consequence of their acts, and they would realize that for all practical purposes her death would inevitably follow . . ."

ROBERT WALKER LJ:

"However the stark facts of *R. v Woollin* and the speeches in the House of Lords in that case say nothing at all about the situation in which an individual acts for a good purpose which cannot be achieved without also having bad consequences (which may be merely possible, or very probable, or virtually certain). This is the doctrine (or dilemma) of double effect. In one class of case the good purpose and the foreseen but undesired consequence (what Bentham called 'oblique intention') are both directed at the same individual. This can be illustrated by a doctor's duty to his patient . . . [H]e may in order to palliate severe pain, administer large doses of analgesics even though he knows that the likely consequence will be to shorten the patient's life . . . In these cases the doctrine of double effect prevents the doctor's foresight of accelerated death from counting as a guilty intention. This type of double effect cannot be relevant to conduct directed towards Mary . . .

There is another class of case in which a person may be faced with the dilemma of whether to save himself or others at the cost of harm or even death to a third person. The dilemma generally arises as the result of an emergency . . . [such as] disasters at sea. If a person, faced with such a dilemma, acts with the intention of saving his own life (or the lives of others) it may be said that that leaves no room for a guilty intention to harm or even kill the third person. Equally, it may be said that although he must (on *R. v Woollin* principles) be taken to have intended the death which he foresaw as virtually certain, he has a defence of necessity. That is the way the submission was put by Miss Davies . . .

In *Gillick v West Norfolk and Wisbech Area Health Authority* [1986] 1 A.C. 112 at 190, Lord Scarman . . . said . . .:

> 'The bona fide exercise by a doctor of his clinical judgment must be a complete negation of the guilty mind which is an essential ingredient of the criminal offence . . .'

Here the court is concerned with the possibility of the commission of a much more serious criminal offence, that is murder. But in the wholly exceptional case of these conjoined twins I consider that the same principles apply . . . Mary's death would be foreseen as an inevitable consequence of an operation which is intended, and is necessary, to save Jodie's life. But Mary's death would not be the purpose or intention of the surgery."

3–037 This case is significant in two respects. First, it demonstrates the difference between the two interpretations of intention. Ward LJ and Brooke LJ, in effect, followed the definitional interpretation. The doctors would foresee death as a virtual certainty and therefore they *would* intend death.[51] However, Robert Walker LJ (implicitly) allowed himself moral elbow-room in holding that the doctors would not intend to kill the weaker twin because that was not "the purpose or intention of the surgery".

---

51 A similar approach was approved (obiter) in *R. (on the application of Burke) v General Medical Council* [2005] EWCA Civ 1003; [2006] Q.B. 273.

Secondly, this divergence of approach brings to the fore a central dilemma here. Is intention a psychological state of mind or a moral conclusion?[52] While Robert Walker LJ clearly adopted the latter view that there was no intention because the doctors would not be morally responsible for the death, the other two members of the Court of Appeal proceeded on the basis that intention is a psychological state. The issue was quite simply whether the doctors would, as a matter of fact, foresee death as a virtual certainty.

A conclusion that D is criminally liable must, of course, involve a judgement of moral responsibility but the issue is ascertaining where such moral assessments should be located: ought they to be part of the question whether D intended a result or should they affect the issue of whether a defence is available? For example, Ward LJ and Brooke LJ were clear that the doctors would not be guilty of murder but they achieved this result by holding that, while they would intend death, they would be afforded a defence of medical necessity. Similarly, *Steane* could have been decided on the basis that he did intend to assist the enemy but had a defence of duress because he was forced to broadcast.

The argument in favour of the view that intention should be a moral conclusion is that actions must pass a "threshold of responsibility" before there can be intention. For example, the teacher who gives a student a (deserved) bad mark knowing it will upset the pupil does not intend such upset because of a moral assessment that the teacher is only performing her duty to grade properly.[53] On this basis, Norrie argues that: **3–038**

> ". . . there is a *moral* objection in common sense to saying [that Steane obliquely intended to assist the enemy], which stems from the duress under which Steane operated. The threats to his family represented the basis of a moral excuse for saying that he did not possess the oblique intention to assist the enemy, but only intended to save his family."[54]

C. EVALUATION

From the above discussion, it should be clear that in the wake of *Woollin* foresight of a virtual certainty is an alternative species of intention or, at least, an evidential precondition to a finding of intention.[55] The implications of these two interpretations have been assessed. However, a final question remains. *Should* foresight of a virtual certainty suffice for intention? Is such an approach too narrow in that intention should perhaps be found to exist in a wider range of cases such as where a consequence is foreseen as probable or likely? Or, is the foresight of a virtual certainty approach too broad in that intention should be restricted to its core meaning of direct intention (aim/purpose)? It is suggested **3–039**

---

52 A.P. Simester and S. Shute, *Letter to the Editor* [2000] Crim. L.R. 204.

53 Duff, "Intention, Mens Rea and the Law Commission Report" [1980] Crim. L.R. 147, 152–154.

54 Norrie, "Oblique Intention and Legal Politics" [1989] Crim. L.R. 793, 797.

55 Although it seems beyond question that the test for oblique intention is now settled and requires foresight of the result as a virtual certainty, the courts have been seen to cast the slightest element of doubt on this. In troubling dicta in the case of *R. v Thacker (Edward)* [2021] EWCA Crim 97; [2021] Q.B. 644, Lord Burnett of Maldon CJ suggested "there remains some debate as to whether foresight of 'virtual certainty' as opposed to 'a very high degree of probability' is required", although he concluded by stating that virtual certainty "probably" represents the law (at [86]).

that an appropriate meaning can only be ascribed to "intention" after the following four matters have been considered.

1. Semantic precision

3-040 There ought to be some semantic precision about the law's use of the word "intention" so that it correlates with the layman's perceptions of the word. Intention is an ordinary word in everyday usage. The criminal law ought to reflect the values of society and, thus, if the word "intention" is to have any useful function, it ought to bear this ordinary meaning. As Duff states:

> "[T]he 'appeal to ordinary language' should not be despised: not just because it may cause confusion if the law uses terms whose legal and extra-legal meanings differ radically; but because the term's ordinary usage reflects our moral understanding of its relevance to ascriptions of responsibility, and of those distinctions which we regard as morally significant. Thus if it is any part of the law's purpose to assign legal liability in accordance with moral responsibility, there must be a presumption in favour of preserving the ordinary meanings of the concepts through which responsibility is assigned."[56]

Furthermore, the task of the jury is made easier when legal terms are given their ordinary meanings. It was this reasoning that led Lord Bridge in *Moloney* to his view that generally juries needed no guidance as to the meaning of "intention". It was a matter of fact to be decided by them according to the ordinary usage of the word.

On the other hand, as Lacey has suggested:

> "if ordinary usage is as consistent and reliable as [the House of Lords] presumably think it is given the importance they accord to it, guidelines would be irrelevant."[57]

3-041 In short, it is not always easy to ascertain the "ordinary, everyday" meaning of words. This difficulty in assigning an "ordinary" meaning to intention is illustrated by the fact that while most commentators agree with the Oxford English Dictionary definition of "intend" as aim or design, Lord Cross in the now discredited House of Lords' decision of *Hyam* considered that the "ordinary man" would equate foresight of injury with intentionally causing injury. It may well be that Lord Cross was falling into the common trap of confusing the issue of how ordinary people would describe the concept of intention with the issue of whom ordinary people would want to hold responsible for their actions. However, despite this potential problem, it seems tolerably clear that to most people the term "intend" means "aiming at" or "meaning to achieve". The consequence must be one's purpose, objective or goal. Even the Law Commission in an earlier draft Bill accepts that it is attributing an artificial meaning to the word intention when it defined its "standard test of intention" as being "either [to] intend or have no

56 Duff, "Intention, Mens Rea and the Law Commission Report" [1980] Crim. L.R. 147, 148.
57 N. Lacey, "A Clear Concept of Intention: Elusive or Illusory?" (1993) M.L.R. 621, 634.

substantial doubt"[58] that a result will occur. Having no substantial doubt is clearly accepted as being something different from intention. As has been stated:

> "Oblique intention is not really any kind of intention at all. It is a label for a different sort of mental state altogether, namely foresight or, in Model Penal Code terminology, knowledge. Calling it a species of intention is pure obfuscation."[59]

Should intention be defined or simply left to the jury? It is becoming increasingly common in criminal law to leave crucial issues such as this to the jury. For instance, one of the critical concepts in theft, "dishonesty", is largely left to jury determination. However, a concept such as "dishonesty" involves the application of standards; ethical stances have to be taken. In short, a judgment has to be made as to the morality of D's actions. The jury, as the mouthpiece of community values, is probably the most appropriate body to express such judgements. It has been argued that this is no less true of the concept "intention" and that judicial reliance on "the haven of 'ordinary language'"[60] allows judges to let in through the back door ethical questions concerning the appropriateness of criminal liability "under the guise of supplementing conceptual analysis in a value-neutral way".[61] As already seen, however, many commentators argue that the meaning to be attributed to "intention" should involve moral judgements but these are less various, and perhaps more capable of reduction to a single formula, than the never-ending range of factors affecting ethical judgements as to the meaning of a concept such as dishonesty.[62] Accordingly, it would be preferable for "intention" to be given a legal definition, and that definition should largely reflect the ordinary meaning of the word.

2. Distinction from recklessness

One of the main problems with the old *Hyam* formulation that foresight of a probable or highly probable consequence amounted to intention was that no principle could be discerned to establish the cut-off point between recklessness and intention. Foreseeing a consequence as probable or likely was intention but foreseeing it as less than probable was recklessness. Such a test involved having to define "probable" and "likely".[63] While these problems are perhaps reduced after *Woollin*, they have not been eradicated. The boundary between intention and recklessness has simply shifted. If a consequence is foreseen as extremely likely this will presumably still amount to recklessness whereas if it is foreseen as virtually certain it can count as intention (or intention can be found). No principled basis for distinguishing between these two states of mind exists because, in both situations, the consequence is not the objective of the action. In both, it is simply a by-product of the actor's actions that is foreseen as having varying chances of occurring. The only clear basis for drawing the distinction would be to limit intention to direct intention. **3-042**

---

58 Law Commission Paper No.89, *Report on the Mental Element of Crime* (1978), p.56.

59 C. Finkelstein, "No Harm No Foul? Objectivism and the Law of Attempts" (1999) 18 *Law and Philosophy* 69, 75.

60 Lacey, "A Clear Concept of Intention: Elusive or Illusory?" (1993) M.L.R. 621, 633. Lacey has argued that the appeal to "ordinary usage" implies that the criminal law "operates on the basis of widely shared meanings and widely endorsed judgments. It hence suppresses the idea that criminal law is hierarchical, an exercise of power, based on meanings which are imposed" (p.636).

61 Horder, "Intention in the Criminal Law—a Rejoinder" (1995) 58 M.L.R. 678, 679, summarising Lacey's views.

62 C.M.V. Clarkson and H.M. Keating, "Codification: Offences against the Person under the Draft Criminal Code" (1986) 50 J. Crim. L. 405, 410.

63 For a discussion of these issues, see the 4th edn of this book at p.147.

3. Moral content

3-043 The final factor to be taken into account in ascribing a meaning to the concept of intention is the most important, but also the most elusive. Is there a moral difference between foreseeing a consequence as likely, foreseeing it as virtually certain, and aiming at it? If so, where should this "moral line" be drawn?

The prevailing view, both judicial and extra-judicial, is that intention should extend beyond its core meaning to include foresight of a consequence as a virtual, practical or moral certainty ("oblique intent").

Glanville Williams, Textbook of Criminal Law, 2nd edn (1983), pp.84–85:

3-044 "Clearly, a person can be taken to intend a consequence that follows under his nose from what he continues to do, and the law should be the same where he is aware that a consequence in the future is the certain or practically certain result of what he does. As Lord Hailsham said in *Hyam*, 'intention' includes 'the means as well as the end and the inseparable consequences of the end as well as the means.' (What he evidently meant was the consequences known to the defendant to be inseparable) . . .

To take a hypothetical case: suppose that a villain of the deepest dye sends an insured parcel on an aircraft, and includes in it a time-bomb by which he intends to bring down the plane and consequently to destroy the parcel. His immediate intention is merely to collect on the insurance. He does not care whether the people on board live or die, but he knows that success in his scheme will inevitably involve their deaths as a side-effect. On the theoretical point, common sense suggests that the notion of intention should be extended to this situation; it should not merely be regarded as a case of recklessness. A consequence should normally be taken as intended although it was not desired, if it was foreseen by the actor as the *virtually certain* accompaniment of what he intended. This is not the same as saying that any consequence foreseen as *probable* is intended . . .

Clearly, one cannot confine the notion of foresight of certainty to certainty in the most absolute sense. It is a question of human certainty, or virtual certainty, or practical certainty. This is still not the same as speaking in terms of probability."

In 2005, the Law Commission published a Consultation Paper on homicide seeking views as to whether the law should adopt a definition of intention as a matter of law (the definitional approach) or whether it should set preconditions which must be satisfied before the jury may find that a person acted intentionally (the evidential approach).[64] After consultation, the Law Commission concluded that the latter approach should be adopted.

64 Law Commission Consultation Paper No.177, *A New Homicide Act for England and Wales?* (2005), paras 4.3, 4.4.

LAW COMMISSION NO.304, MURDER, MANSLAUGHTER AND INFANTICIDE (2006), PARA.3.27:

"We recommend that the existing law governing the meaning of intention is codified as follows: 3–045

(1) A person should be taken to intend a result if he or she acts in order to bring it about.
(2) In cases where the judge believes that justice may not be done unless an expanded understanding of intention is given, the jury should be directed as follows: an intention to bring about a result may be found if it is shown that the defendant thought that the result was a virtually certain consequence of his or her action."

There are, however, contrary views that intention should not be expanded so as to include oblique intention. The argument here is that there are strong moral justifications for distinguishing between an actor who foresees a result as virtually certain and one who tries to achieve that result. A person's objectives or aims influence our perceptions of their character as a moral agent. Actions become more reprehensible if they are deliberate and purposeful. A boy, throwing a ball dangerously near a window and realising that it is virtually certain that in the course of his game he could break the window, will instinctively cry out: "I didn't mean to break it", when the window is duly shattered. Our characterisation of the boy as a moral agent would be different if he had deliberately taken aim and thrown the ball, trying to break the window. As Duff says: 3–046

"To do what I believe will help the enemy, or cause injury, may be counted criminal even when I do it for reasons which have nothing to do with helping the enemy or causing injury: but to act with the intention of helping the enemy, or causing injury, gives a quite different moral character to the action, which we may wish to mark by making only that an offence, or by making it a more serious offence."[65]

JOHN FINNIS, "INTENTION AND SIDE-EFFECTS" IN R.G. FREY AND CHRISTOPHER W. MORRIS, LIABILITY AND RESPONSIBILITY (1991), P.46:

"[I]t is well to recall how foreign to the commonsense concept of intention is the academics' notion that what is foreseen as certain is intended. 3–047

One who hangs curtains knowing that the sunlight will make them fade does not thereby intend that they shall fade. Those who wear shoes don't intend them to wear out. Those who fly the Atlantic foreseeing certain jetlag don't do so with the intention to get jetlag; those who drink too heavily rarely intend the hangover they know is certain . . . Indeed, we might call the academics' extended notion of intent the Pseudo-Masochist Theory of Intention—for it holds that those who foresee that their actions will have painful effects upon themselves *intend* those effects."

65 Duff, "Intention, Mens Rea and The Law Commission Report" [1980] Crim. L.R. 147, 159.

R.A. Duff, Intention, Agency and Criminal Liability: Philosophy of Action and the Criminal Law (1990), pp.111–113:

3–048 "[A] non-consequentialist view . . . finds an intrinsic moral difference in intended action; a significance which depends not on its expected consequences, but on the intentions which structure it . . . One who tries to kill me . . . *attacks* my life and my most basic rights; and the harm which I suffer in being murdered (or in being the victim of an attempted murder) essentially involves this wrongful attack on me. The point is not that a murder victim suffers the same (consequential) harm of death as a victim of natural causes, and also suffers the *separate* harm of being attacked: it is that she suffers the distinctive harm of being killed by one who attacks her life. The 'harm' at which the law of murder is aimed is thus not just the consequential harm of death, but the harm which is *intrinsic* to an attack on another's life . . . [A] n attack is an action which is *intended* to do harm . . . It is through the intentions with which I act that I engage in the world as an agent, and relate myself most closely to the actual and potential effects of my actions; and the central or fundamental kind of wrong-doing is to *direct* my actions towards evil—to *intend* and to *try* to do what is evil."[66]

3–049 This is the approach recommended in the US by the American Law Institute's Model Penal Code and which has been widely adopted in state code revisions throughout the US. The Code does not adopt the view of intention favoured by the Law Commission and leading commentators in England. It adopts the narrower view that a person acts intentionally "when it is his conscious object to engage in conduct of that nature or to cause such a result".[67] What of foresight of a virtual certainty? The Model Penal Code does not assimilate this with intention, nor does it relegate it to the realms of recklessness. Instead, it has created a special category of mens rea between intention and recklessness, namely, knowledge. Section 202(2)(b) defines "knowingly" in the following terms:

> "A person acts knowingly with respect to a material element of an offense when: . . . (ii) if the element involves a result of his conduct, he is aware that it is practically certain that his conduct will cause such a result."

The commentary to this sub-section recognises that the distinction drawn is a narrow one and is "no doubt inconsequential for most purposes of liability". But apart from being conceptually necessary and helping to promote clarity of definition, the distinction does have some practical utility as:

> ". . . there are areas where the discrimination is required . . . This is true in treason, for example, in so far as a purpose to aid the enemy is an ingredient of the offense . . . and in attempts and conspiracy, where a true purpose to effect the criminal result is requisite for liability . . . The distinction also has utility in differentiating among grades of an offense for purposes of sentence, e.g. in the case of homicide."[68]

---

66 Duff does, however, argue that such direct intention should only be required in exceptional cases (see para.3–040). Duff, "Intention, Mens Rea and The Law Commission Report" [1980] Crim. L.R. 147, 148.

67 American Law Institute, Model Penal Code s.2.02(2)(a) prefers the term "purposely". However, most code revisions have used this same definition for the term "intention".

68 American Law Institute, Model Penal Code, Tent. Draft No.4 (1955) art.2, pp.124 and 125.

Thus, according to this view, there is a moral, as well as a linguistic, justification for drawing this fine distinction. Indeed, there are some states in the US that have employed this Model Penal Code terminology and have felt the distinction to be sufficiently material to warrant using it as the basis for a grading of homicide offences. Alaska provides that it is murder in the first degree to kill "with intent to cause the death of another person", but only murder in the second degree to kill "knowing that the conduct is substantially certain to cause death".[69] New Hampshire provides that it is first degree murder to kill "purposely" and second-degree murder to kill "knowingly".[70]

One final question remains. How should one classify cases where a consequence is foreseen as *certain*, as opposed to virtually certain? In these situations, the consequence is foreseen as something that *must* happen; it is a condition precedent to the occurrence of the actor's primary aim.[71] To take the classic example where I intend to shoot you; you are standing behind a glass window that cannot open. Do I intend to break the window? In this case, I foresee it as certain that I will break the glass; I cannot shoot you without doing so. This means that breaking the glass is my aim or objective, albeit only a secondary aim or objective to my main one of killing you. It is a necessary and "wanted" means to my end. I intend to break the window. Lord Hailsham in *Hyam* endorsed this when he spoke of: **3–050**

> "intention, which embraces, in addition to the end, all the necessary consequences of an action including the means to the end and any consequences intended along with the end."[72]

However, where an undesired consequence is only foreseen as "virtually certain" or "morally certain" it ceases to be an inescapable consequence or a necessary means to an end. It thus ceases to be a secondary aim and should no longer be described as intention. In the celebrated example where I blow up an aircraft in flight in order to obtain the insurance money and the passengers are killed, I would foresee the death of these passengers as virtually certain. But, if it is not my object to kill them, the fact that there is a chance (albeit one in a million) that they could parachute to safety, means that their death is not a necessary means to an end and cannot be described as intention. Using Duff's "test of failure",[73] blowing up the aeroplane without killing the occupants would not mark the failure of the enterprise but would represent the ultimate in success. Similarly, flying across the Atlantic and not suffering jetlag would be a cause for celebration. On the other hand, failing to break the window represents a failure of the agent's action because this necessarily involves not killing the person behind it. The line of demarcation is a thin one and would only apply in the most exceptional cases.[74] Nevertheless, it is a conceptually clear distinction and provides a principled basis for distinguishing intention from recklessness. There is no intention to kill the passengers on the aeroplane, but there is an intention to break the glass.

---

69 Alaska Stat. tit. 11 ss.11.41.100, 110.

70 N.H. Rev. Stat. Ann. ss.630: 1-a, b.

71 This need not be scientific certainty, but the consequence must be inseparable in terms of the agent's conception of the world as he understands it (A.P. Simester, "Moral Certainty and the Boundaries of Intention" (1996) 16 O.J.L.S. 445, 459).

72 *Hyam* [1975] A.C. 55 at 73.

73 See para.3–027.

74 A. Norrie, "Oblique Intention and Legal Politics" [1989] Crim. L.R. 793, 801, denies the possibility of drawing such a distinction on the basis that virtual certainty "denote[s] the only kind of certainty that it is ever possible to have in any practical intervention in the natural or social world". This ignores the fact that one is dealing with a subjective concept. It is D's aims and foresight that matter. To most Ds firing at the person standing behind the window, it is only possible to shoot V by breaking the glass. The fact that it might actually be possible to achieve the result without breaking the window (an earthquake might break the glass at the critical moment) does not alter the fact that D is trying to break the window.

III. Recklessness

A. INTRODUCTION

3–051 Some crimes, such as attempted offences, can only be committed intentionally and so it is crucial to be able to distinguish intention from recklessness. This line of demarcation depends, as we have just seen, on how broadly one chooses to define "intention". Any degree of foresight less than that specified in the definition of intention will constitute recklessness. But a large number of crimes can be committed "intentionally or recklessly". For all these crimes, the distinction between intention and recklessness is unimportant; what matters, instead, is the distinction between recklessness and negligence or other forms of conduct not regarded as equally blameworthy. This demarcation is vital as it has been the general policy of English law to punish reckless wrongdoing, but, with notable exceptions, to exempt negligent wrongdoing from criminal liability.

B. LAW PRIOR TO G: TWO SPECIES OF RECKLESSNESS

3–052 The concept of "recklessness" has had a chequered and uncertain history with judges vacillating as to whether it meant "gross negligence"[75] (an objective major deviation from the standards of the reasonable person) or whether it meant simply failing to foresee an obvious risk or whether it should be limited to cases where D subjectively realised that there was a possibility of the consequence occurring (or the circumstance existing) but carried on regardless. Between the early 1980's and the landmark decision of *G*,[76] however, there were two distinct species of recklessness.

1. *Cunningham* recklessness

3–053 By the late 1970s, following the leading decision of *Cunningham*,[77] a subjective meaning of recklessness had been approved. Recklessness entailed the conscious running of an unjustifiable risk. The following case illustrates this approach.

R. v STEPHENSON [1979] Q.B. 695 (COURT OF APPEAL, CRIMINAL DIVISION):

3–054 The appellant, who had crept into a hollow in the side of a large straw stack to sleep, felt cold and lit a fire of twigs and straw inside the hollow. The stack caught fire and was damaged. He was charged with arson contrary to the Criminal Damage Act 1971 (the 1971 Act) s.1(1). Evidence on his behalf was given by a consultant psychiatrist that the appellant suffered from schizophrenia that could have the effect of depriving him of the ability of a normal person to foresee or

75 *Andrews v DPP* [1937] A.C. 576; (1938) 26 Cr. App. R. 34 HL.

76 *R. v G* [2003] UKHL 50; [2004] 1 A.C. 1034.

77 *R. v Cunningham (Roy)* [1957] 2 Q.B. 396; [1957] 3 W.L.R. 76 CA. See also *R. v Briggs (Basil Ian)* [1977] 1 W.L.R. 605; (1976) 63 Cr. App. R. 215 CA; *R. v Parker (Daryl Clive)* [1977] 1 W.L.R. 600; (1976) 63 Cr. App. R. 211 CA; Law Commission Paper No.89, *Report on the Mental Element in Crime* (1978), paras 20–21.

appreciate the risk of damage from the act of lighting the fire. The judge directed the jury that a person was "reckless as to whether any such property would be destroyed or damaged", within s.1(1) of the 1971 Act, if he closed his mind to the obvious fact of risk from his act, and that schizophrenia might be a reason which made a person close his mind to the obvious fact of risk. The jury returned a verdict of guilty and the appellant was convicted. He appealed against the conviction on the ground, inter alia, of a misdirection by the judge on what constituted recklessness.

GEOFFREY LANE LJ:

> "Does the word 'reckless' require that the defendant must be proved actually to have foreseen the risk of some damage resulting from his actions and nevertheless to have run the risk (the subjective test), or is it sufficient to prove that the risk of damage resulting would have been obvious to any reasonable person in the defendant's position (the objective test)? In our view it is the subjective test which is correct.
>
> . . . A man is reckless when he carries out the deliberate act appreciating that there is a risk that damage to property may result from his act. It is however not the taking of every risk which could properly be classed as reckless. The risk must be one which it is in all the circumstances unreasonable for him to take.
>
> Proof of the requisite knowledge in the mind of the defendant will in most cases present little difficulty. The fact that the risk of some damage would have been obvious to anyone in his right mind in the position of the defendant is not conclusive proof of the defendant's knowledge, but it may well be and in many cases doubtless will be a matter which will drive the jury to the conclusion that the defendant himself must have appreciated the risk. The fact that he may have been in a temper at the time would not normally deprive him of knowledge or foresight of the risk. If he had the necessary knowledge or foresight and his bad temper merely caused him to disregard it or put it to the back of his mind not caring whether the risk materialised, or if it merely deprived him of the self-control necessary to prevent him from taking the risk of which he was aware, then his bad temper will not avail him. This was the concept which the court in *R. v Parker (Daryl)* [1977] 1 W.L.R. 600 at 604 was trying to express when it used the words 'or closing his mind to the obvious fact that there is some risk of damage resulting from that act.' . . . We wish to make it clear that the test remains subjective, that the knowledge or appreciation of risk of some damage must have entered the defendant's mind even though he may have suppressed it or driven it out . . .
>
> How do these pronouncements affect the present appeal? The appellant, through no fault of his own, was in a mental condition which might have prevented him from appreciating the risk which would have been obvious to any normal person. When the judge said to the jury 'there may be . . . all kinds of reasons which make a man close his mind to the obvious fact—among them may be schizophrenia'—we think he was guilty of a misapprehension, albeit possibly an

understandable misapprehension. The schizophrenia was on the evidence something which might have prevented the idea of danger entering the appellant's mind at all. If that was the truth of the matter, then the appellant was entitled to be acquitted. That was something which was never left clearly to the jury to decide."

Appeal allowed

3-055 Under this "subjective" approach, the definition of recklessness, both as to consequences and circumstances,[78] imposes a double test:

(1) whether D foresaw the possibility of the consequence occurring; and
(2) whether it was unjustifiable or unreasonable to take the risk.

Whether a risk is justifiable or not depends on the social importance of the acts and on the chances of the forbidden consequence occurring. As the Law Commission has stated:

"The operation of public transport, for example, is inevitably accompanied by risks of accident beyond the control of the operator, yet it is socially necessary that these risks be taken. Dangerous surgical operations must be carried out in the interests of the life and health of the patient, yet the taking of these risks is socially justifiable."[79]

Thus, if there is perceived to be a one in a thousand chance of high-speed trains being involved in an accident, the social value of high-speed public transport is such as to render the taking of such a remote risk justifiable, but if it is realised that there is a one in 20 chance of these trains being involved in an accident, then the chances of an accident occurring outweighs the social importance of the activity and it becomes unjustifiable to take such a risk. On the other hand, if there is the same (subjectively perceived) one in a thousand chance of killing a friend while playing Russian roulette, the complete absence of any social value attached to the activity renders the taking of the risk unjustifiable. Thus, the test involves a subtle balancing operation between the following questions: how socially useful is the activity? What are the perceived chances of the harm occurring? How serious is the harm that could occur? For example, in *Vehicle Inspectorate v Nuttall*,[80] it was stated that if one was dealing with conduct that could imperil the safety of the public, foresight of the slightest possibility (of a breach of contraventions) would suffice.

Whether a risk is justifiable or unreasonable is an objective issue and does not depend on D's view of the matter. For example, in *Dodman*,[81] it was stated that it was irrelevant that D did not know his conduct was wrongful. Of course, the question whether there is any social utility in an activity is a highly evaluative one which has led some writers to argue that the concept of recklessness is an inherently

78 For the sake of simplicity, the remainder of this section will refer only to consequences, but this should be taken to include circumstances.
79 Law Commission Paper No.31, *Working Paper on the Mental Element in Crime*, p.53.
80 *Vehicle Inspectorate v Nuttall* [1999] 1 W.L.R. 629; [1999] R.T.R. 264 HL.
81 *R. v Dodman (Darryl Philip)* [1998] 2 Cr. App. R. 338 CA.

political one.[82] This is true inasmuch as a value judgement is involved, a point that can always be made when employing a value-ridden concept such as "reasonableness".[83] The advantage, however, of employing such a concept and leaving it to members of the jury is that they can reflect the ever-shifting notions of social utility.

2. *Caldwell/Lawrence* recklessness

In 1981, there was a radical change of direction when the House of Lords handed down two judgments on the same day, both concerned with the meaning of recklessness. It should be stressed that this change only affected the first limb of the test cited above, namely, whether D must foresee the possibility of harm occurring. It did not affect the second requirement that it must be unjustifiable to take the risk. **3–056**

R. v Caldwell [1982] A.C. 341 (House of Lords):

The respondent had done some work for the owner of a hotel as the result of which he had a quarrel with the owner, got drunk and set fire to the hotel in revenge. The fire was discovered and put out before any serious damage was caused and none of the ten guests in the hotel at the time was injured. The respondent was indicted on two counts of arson under the Criminal Damage Act 1971 s.1(1) and (2). At his trial, he pleaded not guilty to the more serious charge under s.1(2) of damaging property with intent to endanger life or being reckless whether life would be endangered. He claimed that he was so drunk at the time that the thought that he might be endangering the lives of the people in the hotel had never crossed his mind. The trial judge directed the jury that drunkenness was not a defence to a charge under s.1(2) and he was convicted. **3–057**

The Court of Appeal allowed his appeal. The Crown appealed to the House of Lords, where in order to decide whether drunkenness was a defence to a charge under s.1(2), the House ruled that it was necessary to decide upon the precise meaning of the term recklessness as employed in s.1(2).

LORD DIPLOCK (with whom Lord Keith and Lord Roskill concurred; Lord Edmund-Davies and Lord Wilberforce dissented):

> "'Reckless' as used in the new statutory definition of the *mens rea* of these offences is an ordinary English word. It had not by 1971 become a term of legal art with some more limited esoteric meaning than that which it bore in ordinary speech—a meaning which surely includes not only deciding to ignore a risk of harmful consequences resulting from one's acts that one has recognised as existing, but also failing to give any thought to whether or not there is any such risk in circumstances where, if any thought were given to the matter it would be obvious that there was.

82 A. Norrie, "Subjectivism, Objectivism and the Limits of Criminal Recklessness" (1992) 12 O.J.L.S. 45.
83 J.A.G. Griffiths, *The Politics of the Judiciary*, 4th edn (London: Fontana Press, 1991).

If one is attaching labels, the latter state of mind is neither more nor less 'subjective' than the first. But the label solves nothing. It is a statement of the obvious; *mens rea* is by definition, a state of mind of the accused himself at the time he did the physical act that constitutes the *actus reus* of the offence; it cannot be the mental state of some non-existent, hypothetical person.

Nevertheless, to decide whether someone has been 'reckless' as to whether harmful consequences of a particular kind will result from his act, as distinguished from his actually intending such harmful consequences to follow, does call for some consideration of how the mind of the ordinary prudent individual would have reacted to a similar situation. If there were nothing in the circumstances that ought to have drawn the attention of an ordinary prudent individual to the possibility of that kind of harmful consequence, the accused would not be described as 'reckless' in the natural meaning of that word for failing to address his mind to the possibility; nor, if the risk of the harmful consequences was so slight that the ordinary prudent individual upon due consideration of the risk would not be deterred from treating it as negligible, could the accused be described as 'reckless' in its ordinary sense if, having considered the risk, he decided to ignore it. (In this connection the gravity of the possible harmful consequences would be an important factor. To endanger life must be one of the most grave.) So to this extent, even if one ascribes to 'reckless' only the restricted meaning, adopted by the Court of Appeal in *R. v Stephenson* of foreseeing that a particular kind of harm might happen and yet going on to take the risk of it, it involves a test that would be described in part as 'objective' in current legal jargon. Questions of criminal liability are seldom solved by simply asking whether the test is subjective or objective.

In my opinion, a person charged with an offence under section 1(1) of the Criminal Damage Act 1971 is 'reckless as to whether any such property would be destroyed or damaged' if (1) he does an act which in fact creates an obvious risk that property will be destroyed or damaged and (2) when he does the act he either has not given any thought to the possibility of there being any such risk or has recognised that there was some risk involved and has nonetheless gone on to do it. That would be a proper direction to the jury; cases in the Court of Appeal which held otherwise should be regarded as overruled. [His Lordship then went on to consider the defence of drunkenness.]"

Appeal dismissed

R. v LAWRENCE [1982] A.C. 510 (HOUSE OF LORDS):

3–058 The appellant was riding his motorcycle at an excessive speed along an urban road and ran into and killed a pedestrian who was crossing the road. The appellant was convicted of causing death by reckless driving, contrary to the Road Traffic Act 1972 s.1 and appealed against his conviction.

LORD DIPLOCK (with whom Lord Fraser, Lord Roskill and Lord Bridge agreed):

"I turn now to the *mens rea* . . . Recklessness on the part of the doer of an act does presuppose that there is something in the circumstances that would have drawn the attention of an ordinary prudent individual to the possibility that his act was capable of causing the kind of serious harmful consequences that the section which creates the offence was intended to prevent, and that the risk of those harmful consequences occurring was not so slight that an ordinary prudent individual would feel justified in treating them as negligible. It is only when this is so that the doer of the act is acting 'recklessly' if before doing the act, he either fails to give any thought to the possibility of there being any such risk or, having recognised that there was such risk, he nevertheless goes on to do it.

In my view, an appropriate instruction to the jury on what is meant by driving recklessly would be that they must be satisfied of two things:

> *First*, that the defendant was in fact driving the vehicle in such a manner as to create an obvious and serious risk of causing physical injury to some other person who might happen to be using the road or of doing substantial damage to property; and
>
> *Second*, that in driving in that manner the defendant did so without having given any thought to the possibility of there being any such risk or, having recognised that there was some risk involved, had nonetheless gone on to take it . . .
>
> If satisfied that an obvious and serious risk was created by the manner of the defendant's driving, the jury are entitled to infer that he was in one or other of the states of mind required to constitute the offence and will probably do so; but regard must be given to any explanation he gives as to his state of mind which may displace the inference."

Appeal dismissed

(i) Implications of Caldwell/Lawrence recklessness

These decisions had a profound effect on English criminal law. What was the precise meaning of the test of recklessness developed by these cases? **3–059**

Lord Diplock stated that recklessness involved the doing of an act "which in fact creates an obvious risk" of the relevant harm occurring. What was meant by the phrase "creates an obvious risk"? Obvious to whom? To the reasonable person? Or, to D? There was a strong argument that the risk must have been obvious to D themselves had they bothered to think about the matter.[84] Indeed, there are dicta in *Caldwell* that recklessness "presupposes that, if thought were given to the matter by the doer before the act was done, it would have been apparent to *him*"[85] that there were risks involved. However, there

84 Williams, "Recklessness Redefined" [1981] C.L.J. 252; Williams, "Divergent Interpretations of Recklessness" (1982) 132 N.L.J. 289, 313, 336 at 289–290; G. Syrota, "A Radical Change in the Law of Recklessness" [1982] Crim. L.R. 97.

85 *R. v Caldwell* [1982] A.C. 341 at 351.

are numerous other passages in both *Caldwell* and *Lawrence*, fortified by the model direction in *Caldwell*, that the risk must have been obvious to the "ordinary prudent individual". This was the view endorsed by later decisions.

Elliott v C (A Minor) (1983) 77 Cr. App. R. 103 (Queen's Bench Divisional Court):

3-060 The defendant was a 14-year-old schoolgirl, with learning difficulties. After staying out all night without sleep she poured white spirit on the carpet of a garden shed and then threw two lighted matches on the spirit. The shed was destroyed by fire. She was charged with criminal damage contrary to the Criminal Damage Act 1971 s.1(1), it being alleged that she had been reckless as to whether the shed be destroyed. The justices concluded that because of her age, lack of understanding, lack of experience and exhaustion, the risk of destroying the shed would not have been obvious to her if she had given any thought to the matter. Accordingly, they found she was not reckless and dismissed the information. The prosecutor appealed by way of case stated.

GLIDEWELL J:

> "Mr Moses [counsel for the prosecution] submits that the phrase 'creates an obvious risk' means that the risk is one which must have been obvious to a reasonably prudent man, not necessarily to the particular defendant if he or she had given thought to it. It follows, says Mr Moses, that if the risk is one which would have been obvious to a reasonably prudent person, once it has also been proved that the particular defendant gave no thought to the possibility of there being such a risk, it is not a defence that because of limited intelligence or exhaustion she would not have appreciated the risk even if she had thought about it . . .
>
> In the light of [the authorities, viz. *Caldwell, Lawrence* and *Miller*], we are in my judgment bound to hold that the word 'reckless' in section 1 of the Criminal Damage Act 1971 has the meaning ascribed to it by Mr Moses."

Appeal allowed

3-061 This approach was unfortunate. It is only possible to defend the *Caldwell/Lawrence* test of recklessness if one is dealing with an actor who is *capable* of improving their behaviour. We have seen that the notion of responsibility, upon which the doctrine of mens rea is premised, is based on choice. We can blame a D for making the wrong choice. How can we realistically blame the schizophrenic in *Stephenson* or the young girl in *Elliott v C*? They were not able to assume the responsibility we expect most people to shoulder. They "chose" to act as they did only in the most meaningless sense of the word "choice". And, crucially, their actions did not demonstrate lack of concern; they were simply the inevitable product of their inadequacy. No civilised society should blame people for inadequacies or immaturity over which they have no control (as opposed to self-induced inadequacies such as the drunkenness in *Caldwell*).

(ii) A variable meaning

The concept of recklessness is employed in both statutory and common law offences. During the period that the law employed two tests of recklessness, a critical issue was whether recklessness bore its *Cunningham* or its *Caldwell/Lawrence* meaning. **3-062**

In *Seymour,*[86] the House of Lords indicated that recklessness should bear its *Caldwell/Lawrence* meaning throughout the criminal law, whether the offence was a statutory or a common law one. However, in *Reid* it was made clear that recklessness could be interpreted differently for different offences. Lord Goff said of recklessness that "as used in our law, it has more than one meaning". Lord Browne-Wilkinson said that he did "not accept that the constituent elements of recklessness must be the same in all statutes. In particular [various] factors may lead to the word being given different meanings in different statutes".[87]

The unfortunate result was that for some offences recklessness bore its *Caldwell/Lawrence* meaning but for other offences it bore its *Cunningham* meaning. The result was confusion and unpredictability. The stage was thus set for the courts and/or Parliament to make a choice between the two tests.

C. PRESENT LAW

As will be seen later, both tests had supporters but one thing was agreed upon: with the exception of some of the (now repealed) driving offences requiring recklessness, the two tests of recklessness should not be allowed to co-exist. The matter was brought to a head and largely resolved by the following leading House of Lords' decision. While the ratio of this decision is limited to criminal damage, it has been interpreted, as we shall see, as applying to other offences as well, resulting in the effective demise of *Caldwell/Lawrence* recklessness. **3-063**

R. v G [2004] 1 A.C. 1034 (House of Lords):

Two boys, aged 11 and 12, respectively, set fire to newspapers and threw them under a wheelie-bin. The bin was set alight and adjoining buildings caught fire causing some £1 million damage. They claimed they thought the lit newspapers would burn themselves out on the concrete floor and that it never crossed their minds that there was a risk of the fire spreading. They were convicted of arson with the trial judge ruling that whether there was an obvious risk of the property being damaged was to be assessed by reference to the reasonable man and not a person endowed with the characteristics of the defendants: "the ordinary reasonable bystander is an adult". The defendants were convicted. Their appeal to the Court of Appeal was dismissed and they appealed to the House of Lords. **3-064**

86 *R. v Seymour (Edward John)* [1983] 2 A.C. 493; [1983] 3 W.L.R. 349 HL.
87 *Seymour* [1983] 2 A.C. 493 at 412. Lord Ackner endorsed this view (at 402).

LORD BINGHAM OF CORNHILL:

"The task confronting the House in this appeal is, first of all, one of statutory construction: what did Parliament mean when it used the word 'reckless' in section 1(1) and (2) of the 1971 Act? In so expressing the question I mean to make it as plain as I can that I am not addressing the meaning of 'reckless' in any other statutory or common law context. In particular, but perhaps needlessly since 'recklessly' has now been banished from the lexicon of driving offences, I would wish to throw no doubt on the decisions of the House in *R. v Lawrence* and *R. v Reid* . . .

[Lord Bingham, along with the other two Law Lords extracted below, engaged in a detailed historical analysis and concluded that Parliament, in enacting the Criminal Damage Act 1971, intended to give effect to the Law Commission's proposals that 'reckless' bear its subjective *Cunningham* meaning. *Caldwell* was based on a 'misinterpretation' of that Act. Additionally, he put forward three other reasons to justify departing from *Caldwell*.]

First, it is a salutary principle that conviction of serious crime should depend on proof not simply that the defendant caused (by act or omission) an injurious result to another but that his state of mind when so acting was culpable . . . The most obviously culpable state of mind is no doubt an intention to cause the injurious result, but knowing disregard of an appreciated and unacceptable risk of causing an injurious result or a deliberate closing of the mind to such risk would be readily accepted as culpable also. It is clearly blameworthy to take an obvious and significant risk of causing injury to another. But it is not clearly blameworthy to do something involving a risk of injury to another if (for reasons other than self-induced intoxication: *R. v Majewski* [1977] AC 443) one genuinely does not perceive the risk. Such a person may fairly be accused of stupidity or lack of imagination, but neither of those failings should expose him to conviction of serious crime or the risk of punishment.

Secondly, the present case shows, more clearly than any other reported case since *R. v Caldwell*, that the model direction formulated by Lord Diplock is capable of leading to obvious unfairness . . . [T]he trial judge regretted the direction he (quite rightly) felt compelled to give, and it is evident that this direction offended the jury's sense of fairness. The sense of fairness of 12 representative citizens sitting as a jury (or of a smaller group of lay justices sitting as a bench of magistrates) is the bedrock on which the administration of criminal justice in this country is built. A law which runs counter to that sense must cause concern . . . It is neither moral nor just to convict a defendant (least of all a child) on the strength of what someone else would have apprehended if the defendant himself had no such apprehension . . .

Thirdly, I do not think the criticism of *R. v Caldwell* expressed by academics, judges and practitioners should be ignored . . .

It is perhaps unfortunate that the question at issue in [*Caldwell*] fell to be answered in a case of self-induced intoxication. For one instinctively recoils from the notion that a defendant can escape the criminal consequences of his injurious conduct by drinking himself into a state

> where he is blind to the risk he is causing to others. In *R. v Caldwell* it seems to have been assumed that the risk would have been obvious to the defendant had he been sober. Further, the context did not require the House to give close consideration to the liability of those (such as the very young and the mentally handicapped) who were not normal reasonable adults. The overruling by the majority of *R. v Stephenson* does however make it questionable whether such consideration would have led to a different result.
>
> In the course of argument before the House it was suggested that the rule in *R. v Caldwell* might be modified, in cases involving children, by requiring comparison not with normal reasonable adults but with normal reasonable children of the same age. This is a suggestion with some attractions but it is open to four compelling objections. First, even this modification would offend the principle that conviction should depend on proving the state of mind of the individual defendant to be culpable. Second, if the rule were modified in relation to children on grounds of their immaturity it would be anomalous if it were not also modified in relation to the mentally handicapped on grounds of their limited understanding. Third, any modification along these lines would open the door to difficult and contentious argument concerning the qualities and characteristics to be taken into account for purposes of the comparison. Fourth, to adopt this modification would be to substitute one misinterpretation of section 1 for another. There is no warrant in the Act or in the travaux préparatoires which preceded it for such an interpretation.
>
> A further refinement, advanced by Professor Glanville Williams in his article 'Recklessness Redefined' [1981] CLJ 252, 270–271 . . . is that a defendant should only be regarded as having acted recklessly by virtue of his failure to give any thought to an obvious risk that property would be destroyed or damaged, where such risk would have been obvious to him if he had given any thought to the matter. This refinement also has attractions, although it does not meet the objection of principle and does not represent a correct interpretation of the section. It is, in my opinion, open to the further objection of over-complicating the task of the jury (or bench of justices). It is one thing to decide whether a defendant can be believed when he says that the thought of a given risk never crossed his mind. It is another, and much more speculative, task to decide whether the risk would have been obvious to him if the thought had crossed his mind. The simpler the jury's task, the more likely is its verdict to be reliable."
>
> *Appeal allowed*

This unanimous decision by the House of Lords adopts the *Cunningham* view that recklessness involves foresight of the possibility of an unjustified risk. **3–065**

Three further points emerge from the judgments. First, Lord Steyn, added that "if a defendant closes his mind to a risk he must realise that there is a risk" and so will be reckless. In *Booth v CPS*,[88] D ran across a road without checking whether it was safe to cross; he collided with a car, denting it. It was held that:

---

88 *Booth v Crown Prosecution Service* [2006] EWHC 192 (Admin); (2006) 170 J.P. 305.

> "... aware of those risks (risk of collision and damage to property), he then deliberately put them out of his mind ... The magistrates have found that the appellant was aware of the risk and closed his mind to it ... [Accordingly], they had applied the correct test [of recklessness as laid down in G]."

Secondly, the law on self-induced intoxication (which was the context in which *Caldwell* was decided) is unaffected. Lord Bingham exempted self-induced intoxication stating that "one instinctively recoils from the notion that a D can escape the criminal consequences of his injurious conduct by drinking himself into a state where he is blind to the risk he is causing to others". The law on self-induced intoxication is discussed in Ch.4.

3-066 Thirdly, and very importantly, Lord Bingham (with whom all their Lordships agreed) restricted his judgment to the meaning of recklessness in the Criminal Damage Act 1971:

> "I mean to make it as plain as I can that I am not addressing the meaning of 'recklessness' in any other statute or common law context."

In particular, he approved the *Lawrence* meaning of recklessness adopted for offences involving reckless driving. Lord Rodger also stated that *Caldwell* "may be better suited to some offences than to others. For example, in the context of reckless driving".

However, all offences involving reckless driving have been abolished and replaced by offences requiring dangerous driving. Prior to *G*, *Caldwell* had become largely restricted to the offence of criminal damage and, as regards that offence at least, it has been overruled. As was stated in *Brady*,[89] "many of their Lordships observations [in G] have much wider application" and apply to crimes other than criminal damage. In *Att-Gen's Reference (No.3 of 2003)* the Court of Appeal stated that in *G* "general principles were laid down".[90]

D. EVALUATION

3-067 English law has progressed to the point where there is now only one test of recklessness. *Cunningham* recklessness has prevailed over *Caldwell/Lawrence* recklessness. However, while certainty and simplicity in this area of the law is to be welcomed, it is less clear that the House of Lords in *G* did in fact adopt the better test in terms of policy and principle. Most of the decision is devoted to a technical, historical examination as to the meaning intended by Parliament when it enacted the Criminal Damage Act 1971

89 *Brady* [2006] EWCA Crim 2413.

90 *Att-Gen's Reference (No.3 of 2003)* [2004] Cr. App. R. 367 at 371. See also *R. v C* [2007] EWCA Crim 1068. It is, of course, possible for Parliament expressly to provide an objective definition of recklessness in a specific statute: see, e.g. Uranium Enrichment Technology (Prohibition of Disclosure) Regulations 2004 (SI 2004/1818) (made under the Anti-terrorism Crime and Security Act 2001 s.80(7)) reg.2(2) of which defines recklessness as including being "indifferent" as to whether a risk is created and "fail[ing] to give any thought to the possibility" of creating a risk.

and to judicial decisions relating to the interpretation of that Act. The only discussion of matters of policy and principle are extracted above. It is to these issues that we now turn.

The argument over the merits or otherwise of *Caldwell/Lawrence* is a dispute as to whether blameworthiness is dependent on cognition. Are we justified in blaming only those who realise that their actions could cause the prohibited harm? This was described earlier as "cognitive mens rea". Or, should the law adopt what was earlier described as "normative mens rea" under which an assessment of culpability involves an evaluation of the D's actions, taking into account all the circumstances including, but not limited to, D's state of mind?

Many of the arguments over which of these two approaches should be adopted have focused on whether negligence is an appropriate basis for the imposition of criminal liability and reference should be made to the next section where this issue is addressed. However, *Caldwell/Lawrence* recklessness was not synonymous with pure negligence. In particular, as the House of Lords in *Reid* emphasised, *Caldwell/Lawrence* recklessness still involved looking at the D's attitude, motive, emotional state and capacities.[91] Not all cases of inadvertence are regarded as involving blameworthiness. Where the inadvertence arose from drink, rage, an attitude of indifference or wilful blindness D could be adjudged blameworthy and therefore reckless. But where the lack of foresight arose from some other factor over which D had no control such as "some condition not involving fault on his part" (Lord Keith in *Reid*) there is no blame and no recklessness. Accordingly, the remainder of this section focuses on whether the House of Lords in *G* was right to jettison the *Caldwell/Lawrence* test of recklessness.

Lord Diplock's reasoning in *Caldwell* and *Lawrence* has been described as "pathetically inadequate",[92] **3–068**
"slap-happy", and "profoundly regrettable".[93] The case for cognitive mens rea is that recklessness is a species of mens rea, and mens rea should be based on the notion of responsibility which involves ideas of choice. D has chosen to act in a certain way and that choice only becomes blameworthy if there was knowledge that the actions could cause the prohibited harm. For example, in the infamous case of *Lamb*,[94] D pointed a revolver at his best friend in jest and pulled the trigger. His friend was similarly treating the incident as a joke. The revolver had a five-chambered cylinder which, unknown to D, rotated clockwise each time the trigger was pulled. There were two bullets in the chambers but, before firing, neither was in the chamber opposite the barrel. The pulling of the trigger caused the cylinder to rotate, placing a bullet opposite the barrel so that it was struck by the striking pin. The bullet was discharged killing his friend. Lamb's defence was that he was unaware that the pulling of the trigger would bring one bullet into the firing position opposite the barrel and thus the killing was an accident. Lamb was convicted of manslaughter and sentenced to three years' imprisonment. On appeal, this conviction was quashed because of a misdirection on the law of manslaughter. However, the Court of Appeal stated that with a proper direction, Lamb would have been convicted and no criticism was made of the sentence originally imposed. Glanville Williams has written of this:

91 J. Stannard, "Subjectivism, Objectivism, and the Draft Criminal Code" (1985) 101 L.Q.R. 540, 543.
92 J. Smith [1981] Crim. L.R. 393, 394.
93 Williams, "Recklessness Redefined" [1981] C.L.J. 252.
94 *R. v Lamb (Terence Walter)* [1967] 2 Q.B. 981; [1967] 3 W.L.R. 888 CA.

> "I do not hesitate to say that I regard the sentence as outrageous, a wholly mistaken exercise of judicial discretion. Lamb was a fool, but there is no need to punish fools to that degree. There is no need to punish Lamb at all. He had killed his friend, and that was punishment enough."[95]

According to this view, because there was no advertence to the possibility of the consequence occurring, blame becomes inappropriate.

However, there are opposing views supporting a broader normative approach to mens rea under which the decisions in *Caldwell/Lawrence* could be supported. There are two central arguments here. The first relates to the immense difficulty in proving a person's state of mind. As seen earlier, in most cases where there is no confession, juries, in drawing inferences from conduct, can do little other than apply their own standards as being the standards of ordinary people. If, in the circumstances, they think they would have foreseen a result, then, unless there is an explanation that D is in some way materially different from them, for example suffering from a mental illness, they will conclude that D did foresee the result.

R.A. Duff, Intention, Agency and Criminal Liability (1990), pp.120–121:

3-069 "Our inferences from another's behaviour to his mental states cannot be based on correlations which we have observed between the behaviour of others and their mental states: for we can never directly observe the mental states of others. The only case in which we can observe correlations between external behaviour and inner mental states is our own. I am directly aware of my own mental states, and can observe correlations between them and my external behaviour and situation; these observed correlations must provide the basis of my inferences from the behaviour of others to their mental states.

This is the Argument from Analogy. I see bodies around me, which resemble mine and behave in ways similar to mine. I know that my body is connected to a mind. So I infer, by analogy with my own case, that these other bodies are also connected to minds [and have similar responses to mine to stimuli]."

3-070 The difficulties in proving a person's state of mind were an important reason behind Lord Diplock's conclusion in *Caldwell* that recklessness should be given a more objective meaning. He described the distinction between consciously running a risk and failing to appreciate a risk as "not being a practicable distinction for use in a trial by jury". He stated that:

> ". . . [t]he only person who knows what the accused's mental processes were, is the accused himself, and probably not even he can recall them accurately when the rage or excitement under which he acted has passed."

95 G. Williams, "Recklessness Redefined" [1981] C.L.J. 252, 281–282.

He was not prepared to perpetuate such "fine and impracticable distinctions". This, taken to its logical conclusion, is the argument that, because it is unrealistic to believe that one can reliably determine the state of a person's mind, the criminal law should not attempt to make criminal liability turn on states of mind.

The second strand to the arguments supporting the objectively-based test in *Caldwell/Lawrence* relates to the central question of how culpability *should* be established.

R.A. Duff, "Recklessness" [1980] Crim.L.R.282, 289–292:

"[There is a] view that inadvertence, however negligent, cannot constitute *mens rea* since we cannot blame a man for what he does not know. That view has been convincingly demolished: whether I notice some aspect of my action or its context may depend on the attention I pay to what I am doing, and be thus within my control; failures of attention may be as 'voluntary' and culpable as other omissions . . . **3-071**

Some failures of attention or realisation may manifest, not mere stupidity or 'thoughtlessness,' but the same indifference or disregard which characterises the conscious risk-taker as reckless. If I intend to injure someone seriously, I may not realise that this might kill them: not because I am mistaken about the likely effect of my assault, but because it 'just doesn't occur to me'—I am blind to that aspect of my action. But such blindness to such an essential and integral aspect of a serious assault, though possible, itself manifests a 'reckless disregard' for my victim's life no different from that of an assailant who knows he is endangering life . . .

[M]y failure to realise this aspect of my action expresses a certain attitude to it. I do not realise it because I regard it as unimportant; my failure expresses my complete lack of concern about it. In general, the extent to which I notice or realise the various aspects of my action, its context, and its results, is a function as much of my attitudes and values as of my powers of observation and attention: to say that I forgot or did not realise something is to admit that I thought it unimportant, and thus to convict myself of a serious lack of concern for it (which is why a bridegroom would hardly mitigate his offence of missing his wedding by the plea that he forgot it). If, as I have suggested, an agent is reckless to the extent that his actions manifest a serious kind of 'practical indifference,' a 'willingness' to bring about some harm, then such recklessness, indifference, and willingness can be exhibited as much in his failure to notice obvious and important aspects of his action as in his conscious risk-taking. A man may be reckless even though, and even partly because, he does not realise the risk which is in fact an essential and significant aspect of his action."

R.A. Duff, Intention, Agency and Criminal Liability: Philosophy of Action and the Criminal Law (1990), p.172:

"[A]n appropriate general test of recklessness would be—did the agent's conduct (including any conscious risk-taking, any failure to notice an obvious risk created by her action, and any unreasonable belief on which she acted) display a seriously culpable practical indifference to the interests which her action in fact threatened?" **3-072**

3-073 Duff stresses that this is still a subjective test. What matters is the D's "practical indifference"; it is subjective to them. Recklessness is not just failing to conform to an objective standard:

> ". . . for what matters is not just that, but why, the agent fails to notice an obvious risk; she is reckless only if she fails to notice it because she does not care about it."[96]

On this basis, he rejects the conclusion in *Caldwell*: it cannot be established that because Caldwell failed to notice the risk to life from his actions that he was displaying reckless indifference thereto. On the other hand, D in *Lawrence* was driving recklessly: no-one could drive in the manner in which he did unless they were utterly indifferent to the safety of others.

This approach presents an immediate problem. On what basis are we to decide that Lawrence displayed this practical indifference but that Caldwell did not?

Alan Norrie, "Subjectivism, Objectivism and the Limits of Criminal Recklessness" (1992) 12 O.J.L.S. 45, 50–52:

3-074 "This then raises the broader question of how one could tell the callous from the stupid, the negligent or the thoughtless. Is it not likely that one person's callousness will be another person's stupidity, negligence or thoughtlessness? [What matters] on Duff's analysis is the attitude of the interpretive audience to the conduct on display. It is the inference which 'we,' the observers of the events, or the jury, draw from the facts of the case which is relevant . . . [Norrie then gives the rape example of a man who makes an unreasonable mistake as to the woman's consent to sexual intercourse. While Duff would describe this as utter practical indifference to the woman's interests and therefore recklessness, there might be others in our 'society characterised by male chauvinism' who might have different views 'about how willing women are to be forcibly seduced.']

This is not a matter of social consensus in a sexist society. The world ought to be as Duff wants it to be but it is not. So the 'we' who judge callous indifference to consent to be unreasonable cannot claim that our judgment is apolitical because universal. And the attribution of responsibility on the basis of a conception of practical indifference therefore relies here upon an interpretation of behaviour and attitude that may have nothing to do with the way in which the defendant himself would explain them. It requires the reading onto, the imposition of an interpretation of, an attitude on behaviour from 'outside.' It is practical indifference as interpreted objectively by an audience, and having no necessary subjective link with the accused. The accused does not necessarily share Duff's worldview, and hence interpretation of attitudes, yet may be adjudged subjectively guilty on Duff's account. It may be right to argue politically that the law ought to promote Duff's enlightened values through the requirement of a particular moral attitude, but it should not be presented as a form of subjectivism."

---

96 Duff, *Intention, Agency and Criminal Liability* (1990), pp.165–166. Similarly, Horder argues that rather than basing culpability on cognition, we should adopt "a moral theory whose focus is the evaluation of actions stemming from the desires associated with emotions" ("Cognition, Emotion, and Criminal Culpability" (1990) 106 L.Q.R. 469, 476).

There is much to be said for Norrie's criticisms. Nevertheless, Duff's test of "practical indifference" does offer the distinct advantage that it enables one to escape from some of the rigours of the more formally objective test as laid down in *Caldwell* and then subsequently applied in *Elliott v C (a Minor)* without having to return to a full-blooded test based on cognition. Indeed, one might not really ascertain what D's true attitude was, but equally under the cognitive tests one never really establishes what D foresaw. One simply draws inferences from facts and then tries to deduce what that state of mind must have been. The *Caldwell/Lawrence* test of recklessness (assuming the dicta in *Reid*, qualifying it, had been built upon) is at least asking the right questions: who can we adjudge to be reckless in the sense that they are blameworthy and deserving of punishment? Those who advert to the risks involved in their actions might[97] well be blameworthy but there is no reason why the inquiry should stop there. **3–075**

IV. Negligence

A. INTRODUCTION

When people cause harm accidentally, in circumstances where they are acting impeccably, they will not be blamed; indeed, they will probably have our sympathy. However, the "accident" may have been one which, with some simple care and precautions, could have been avoided. In this latter situation, our tendency is now to blame the actor: "You should have been more careful". The question is whether this moral blame should be translated into criminal liability. **3–076**

The legal concept of negligence has developed to reflect this responsibility that is attributed in everyday life. The following is a classic definition of negligence:

> "A person is negligent if he fails to exercise such care, skill or foresight as a reasonable man in his situation would exercise."[98]

B. NEGLIGENCE AS A BASIS OF LIABILITY

For much of the last century, the law was strongly committed to subjectivism in the form of cognitive mens rea. Negligence was regarded as imposing an objective test which could not be accommodated within such an approach and, accordingly, particularly at common law, negligence was not widely utilised in the criminal law. **3–077**

97 It is interesting that Duff concludes that advertent risk-taking necessarily exhibits practical indifference whereas inadvertent risk-taking has to pass the "lack of concern" test thereby demonstrating indifference. This is criticised by J. Gardner and H. Jung, "Making Sense of Mens Rea: Anthony Duff's Account" (1991) 11 O.J.L.S. 559.

98 Law Commission, Working Paper No.31, p.57.

There were, however, notable exceptions at common law. First, there has long been a crime of careless driving (now driving without due care and attention or without reasonable consideration for other persons contrary to the Road Traffic Act 1988 s.3). Secondly, in extreme cases where death results, the law has been prepared to depart from its traditional insistence on advertence and allow liability for negligence, provided D had shown such lack of care that the conduct could be regarded as grossly negligent. The law thus developed the idea that there can be degrees of negligence and that a person can be liable for manslaughter if there is gross negligence. Thirdly, for much of the last century there was a trend that mistakes in relation to certain defences had to be reasonable. For example, if a person claimed that they were acting in self-defence but in reality they were mistaken in their belief that they were under attack, the defence would only be available if the mistake were reasonable. As we shall see shortly, the courts over the past 30 years have largely abandoned this approach to mistaken beliefs in defences.

However, over the past half-century, the law has tended to expand these exceptions and has started to adopt a normative theory of mens rea under which D's actions in the circumstances are subjected to a broader moral assessment. From this perspective, it is legitimate to regard negligence as a species of mens rea. As seen earlier, the Sentencing Advisory Panel (the precursor to the Sentencing Council) regarded negligence as one means (along with intention, recklessness and knowledge) of establishing culpability.[99] With the proliferation of statutory offences regulating commercial and other aspects of daily life these views have been gaining ground and have led to the creation of many new offences based on negligence: for example, insider dealing,[100] harassment[101] and selling firearms or ammunition to "another person whom he knows or has reasonable cause for believing to be drunk or of unsound mind".[102] Furthermore, as we shall see, many prima facie strict liability offences allow "due diligence" defences.[103] If D can establish that they were not negligent they will escape liability. For example, the Food Safety Act 1990 s.21 provides a defence to any person who "took all reasonable precautions and exercised all due diligence to avoid the commission of the offence".

3–078 Additionally, negligence as to an aspect of the actus reus has been employed for some serious criminal offences. Prior to the Sexual Offences Act 2003 (SOA), rape and other sexual offences required subjective mens rea. For example, if a man honestly believed the other was consenting to intercourse, he would not be guilty of rape, no matter how unreasonable that belief.[104] The SOA abandoned this subjectivist stance and substituted negligence as a new basis of liability; under the Act D is liable unless he *reasonably* believed that the other was consenting. The Domestic Violence, Crime and Victims Act 2004 s.5 introduced the offence of causing or allowing the death of a child or vulnerable adult. This offence can be committed negligently, the test being whether D was, *or ought to have been*, aware of a significant risk of serious physical harm being caused to V. The Criminal Justice and Courts Act 2015 s.20 has created an offence of ill-treatment or wilful neglect applicable to care-workers punishable by a maximum of five years' imprisonment when tried at the Crown Court. No definition of "ill-treatment or wilful neglect" is provided, although presumably no further mens rea is required beyond an objective

99 *Overarching Principles: Seriousness* (2004), p.4.
100 Criminal Justice Act 1993 s.52.
101 Protection from Harassment Act 1997 ss.1(1), 2(1).
102 Firearms Act 1968 s.25.
103 See paras 4–019–4–020.
104 *DPP v Morgan* [1976] A.C. 182; [1975] 2 W.L.R. 913 HL.

test of negligence. It is perhaps strange that the statutory provision should provide a definition of most of the terms in the offence (e.g. care worker; health care), without defining the wrongdoing that it seeks to punish.

C. NEGLIGENCE AND CAPACITY

Negligence was earlier defined as failing to exercise such care, skill or foresight as a reasonable person *in that situation* would exercise. Rape requires that D have no reasonable belief in the other's consent and the SOA 2003 s.1(2) provides that "whether a belief is reasonable is to be determined *having regard to all the circumstances*". What is meant by "in that situation" and "having regard to all the circumstances"? Does this mean that D's characteristics or capacities must be taken into account?[105] **3–079**

In the following classic exposition of negligence, Hart suggested that the characteristics and capacities of D should be taken into account.

H.L.A. Hart, "Negligence, Mens Rea and the Elimination of Responsibility" in Punishment and Responsibility (Essays in the Philosophy of Law) (1968), pp.152–157:

"What is crucial is that those whom we punish should have had, when they acted, the normal capacities, physical and mental, for doing what the law requires and abstaining from what it forbids, and a fair opportunity to exercise these capacities. Where these capacities and opportunities are absent, as they are in different ways in the varied cases of accident, mistake, paralysis, reflex action, coercion, insanity, etc., the moral protest is that it is morally wrong to punish because 'he could not have helped it' or 'he could not have done otherwise' or 'he had no real choice'. But . . . there is no reason (unless we are to reject the whole business of responsibility and punishment) *always* to make this protest when someone who 'just didn't think' is punished for carelessness. For in some cases at least we may say 'he could have thought about what he was doing' with just as much rational confidence as one can say of any intentional wrong-doing 'he could have done otherwise'. **3–080**

Of course, the law compromises with competing values over this matter of the subjective element in responsibility . . .

The most important compromise which legal systems make over the subjective element consists in its adoption of what has been unhappily termed the 'objective standard'. This may lead to an individual being treated for the purposes of conviction and punishment as if he possessed

105 This question will be addressed in more detail below in Ch.6. The Court of Appeal has considered the question of whether account can or cannot be taken of D's mental condition in deciding whether he held a reasonable belief in consent. It was held that a D's delusional belief in consent owing to his schizophrenia cannot in law render reasonable a belief that his partner was consenting when she was not. Beliefs in consent arising from conditions such as delusional psychotic illness or personality disorders must be judged by objective standards of reasonableness and not by taking into account a mental disorder which induced a belief which could not reasonably arise without it: *R. v B* [2013] EWCA Crim 3; [2013] 1 Cr. App. R. 36.

capacities for control of his conduct which he did not possess, but which an ordinary or reasonable man possesses and would have exercised. The expression 'objective' and its partner 'subjective' are unhappy because, as far as negligence is concerned, they obscure the real issue. We may be tempted to say with Dr Turner that just because the negligent man does not have 'the thought of harm in his mind,' to hold him responsible for negligence is *necessarily* to adopt an objective standard and to abandon the 'subjective' element in responsibility. It then becomes vital to distinguish this (mistaken) thesis from the position brought about by the use of objective standards in the application of laws which make negligence criminally punishable. For, when negligence is made criminally punishable, this itself leaves open the question: whether, before we punish, both or only the first of the following two questions must be answered affirmatively.

(i) Did the accused fail to take those precautions which any reasonable man with normal capacities would in the circumstances have taken?

(ii) Could the accused, given his mental and physical capacities, have taken those precautions? . . . If our conditions of liability are invariant and not flexible, *i.e.* if they are not adjusted to the capacities of the accused, then some individuals will be held liable for negligence though they could not have helped their failure to comply with the standard. In *such* cases, indeed, criminal responsibility will be made independent of any 'subjective element', since the accused could not have conformed to the required standard. But this result is nothing to do with negligence being taken as a basis for criminal liability; precisely the same result will be reached if, in considering whether a person acted intentionally, we were to attribute to him foresight of consequences which a reasonable man would have foreseen but which he did not. 'Absolute liability' results, not from the admission of the principle that one who has been grossly negligent is criminally responsible for the consequent harm even if 'he had no idea in his mind of harm to anyone,' but from the refusal in the application of this principle to consider the capacities of an individual who has fallen below the standard of care."

3–081 This approach is to be welcomed. If such an approach had been adopted in the recklessness case of *Elliott v C*, it could well have lessened the criticism levelled at the *Caldwell/Lawrence* test. The Law Commission has similarly endorsed this approach in relation to gross negligence for the purposes of manslaughter stressing that it is important that:

". . . the grossness of negligence be made relative to someone's individual capacity to appreciate the nature and degree of risks, which may be affected by youth or disability."[106]

However, the degree to which individual characteristics or qualities should be taken into account is brought into question in relation to regulatory offences, where an individual is expected to live up to a particular standard of care as a condition of engaging in a particular risky activity. The obvious example

106 Law Commission Consultation Paper No.177, *A New Homicide Act for England and Wales?* (2005), para.3.185.

of offences of negligence forming part of a regulatory regime is that of driving offences such as careless and dangerous driving. Both are offences of negligence, but of different degrees: careless driving requires that D drove below the standard of driving expected of a competent and careful driver;[107] dangerous driving that D's driving fell far below that standard and that it would have been obvious to a competent and careful driver that such driving was dangerous.[108] All those who take control of a potentially lethal weapon such as a car are expected to live up to the standard of a competent and careful driver, whether they are on their first driving lesson or have 30 years of experience of driving.

D. SHOULD NEGLIGENCE BE A BASIS FOR THE ATTRIBUTION OF CRIMINAL RESPONSIBILITY?

Some have argued that none of the goals of punishment (retribution, deterrence, rehabilitation or incapacitation) are furthered by punishing negligent conduct.[109] The opposing view is that "punishment supplies men with an additional motive to take care before acting, to use their faculties and to draw upon their experience".[110] As Brett puts it: **3–082**

> "It is common knowledge that as soon as traffic police appear on the roads drivers begin to pay greater attention to what they are doing, and the standard of driving rises sharply."[111]

Furthermore, perhaps those who fail to consider the obvious consequences of their actions reveal their dangerousness and need incapacitation (say, having their driving licence removed) and rehabilitation.

However, many of the arguments in favour of negligence as a basis for the imposition of criminal liability have not concentrated on such utilitarian considerations, but have stressed that judgements of blameworthiness should not be limited to cases where D realises that harm could occur. Even accepting the premise of responsibility involving the notion of choice, we can blame those who make choices of which we disapprove. We can blame Lamb[112] for acting as he did in total disregard of an obvious and serious risk. In the context of recklessness, Lord Diplock in *Caldwell* regarded non-advertence as no less blameworthy than advertence. Lord Goff in *Reid* went further and said that:

> ". . . it can be argued with force that, in many cases of failing to think, the degree of blameworthiness to be attached to the driver can be greater than that to be attached in some cases to the driver who recognized the risk and decided to disregard it."[113]

107 Road Traffic Act 1988 s.3ZA.
108 Road Traffic Act 1988 s.2A.
109 See, e.g. R.P. Fine and G.M. Cohen, "Is Criminal Negligence a Defensible Basis for Penal Liability" (1967) 16 Buffalo L. Rev. 749, 750–752.
110 Model Penal Code, *Tentative Draft No.4*, pp.126–127.
111 P. Brett, *An Inquiry into Criminal Guilt* (Sydney: Law Book Company of Australasia, 1963), p.98.
112 See para.3–068.
113 *Reid* (1992) 95 Cr. App. R. 393 at 406.

V. Intoxication

A. BACKGROUND

3–083 A significant proportion of criminal offences are committed by persons who are under the influence of alcohol and/or drugs. In the year ending March 2023, the V believed the D to be under the influence of alcohol in 38% of all violent incidents.[114] Although this proportion looks high, it is a reduction from 52% 10 years earlier.[115] This data are not necessarily claiming that the consumption of alcohol *caused* the criminal acts, but that there is a strong association between the two. The problem for the criminal law is one of determining what importance should be attached to the intoxication (whether by drink or drugs or both) of Ds who might claim either that they would never have committed the crime but for their drunkenness which loosened their inhibitions, or, alternatively, that they were so drunk that they did not know what they were doing and thus lacked mens rea. An example of the latter claim can be seen from *Lipman*[116] where D, a drug addict, while on an LSD "trip" had the illusion of descending to the centre of the earth and being attacked by snakes. In his attempt to fight off these reptiles, he struck V (also a drug addict on an LSD "trip") two blows on the head causing haemorrhage of the brain and crammed some eight inches of bed sheet into her mouth causing her to die of asphyxia. He claimed to have had "no knowledge of what he was doing and no intention to harm her". A similar example can be found in the Scottish case of *Brennan v HM Advocate,*[117] where D consumed between 20 and 25 pints of beer, a glass of sherry and a quantity of the drug LSD. He then stabbed his father to death with a knife. In both these cases, D claimed that because of drunkenness he was unable to foresee the consequences of his actions and so lacked mens rea.

The law here is faced with a dilemma. On the one hand, strict principle suggests that Ds such as Lipman and Brennan lack mens rea, or perhaps did not even "act" and, accordingly, should escape criminal liability. On the other hand, particularly given the statistics on the correlation between crime and alcohol, the law is concerned with protecting the public (and deterrence) and cannot allow drunken persons to escape criminal liability and punishment. In short, there is a clash between a "strictly logical, subjective approach" and an "absolutist" policy-led approach, "which would focus solely on D's conduct and its effects, but which would disregard D's state of mind where affected by voluntary intoxication".[118] The law has tried to achieve some sort of compromise between the two approaches. It is also, as a matter of principle, informed by what is known as the "doctrine of prior fault":

---

114 Office for National Statistics, *Nature of crime: Violence, https://www.ons.gov.uk/peoplepopulationandcommunity/crimeandjustice/datasets/natureofcrimetablesviolence*, table 9a.

115 Office for National Statistics, *Nature of crime: Violence, https://www.ons.gov.uk/peoplepopulationandcommunity/crimeandjustice/datasets/natureofcrimetablesviolence*, table 9a.

116 *R. v Lipman (Robert)* [1970] 1 Q.B. 152; [1969] 3 W.L.R. 819 CA.

117 *Brennan (Ian) v HM Advocate* 1977 J.C. 38; (1977) S.L.T. 151.

118 Law Commission No.314, *Intoxication and Criminal Liability* (Cmnd. 75262009), para.1.56.

ANDREW ASHWORTH, *PRINCIPLES OF CRIMINAL LAW*, 6TH EDN (2009), P.81

> "Even though the defendant did not have the required fault when performing the prohibited conduct, the doctrine of prior fault may be invoked to hold him liable—by fastening on to the defendant's fault at an earlier stage, which then led to an absence of fault at the time when the prohibited conduct took place. The title of Paul Robinson's seminal article, 'Causing the Conditions of One's Own Defence', explains the rationale of the doctrine. A person should not be allowed to rely on an exculpatory condition (e.g. lack of fault through automatism or intoxication) if he or she had deliberately or even negligently brought about that condition (e.g. by failing to take proper medication or by drinking alcohol to excess). Thus the doctrine operates by way of exception to—or, some would say, it conflicts with—the principle of contemporaneity." **3–084**

It should come as no surprise that in *Lipman*, D did not escape all liability for a homicide offence. He was not liable for murder, as he did not have the necessary mens rea of intention to kill or cause GBH, but he was liable for manslaughter. Despite arguing that he did not know what he was doing at the time he killed, the doctrine of prior fault allowed him to be held liable for manslaughter. How the law determines liability in such case is explained under the heading on Law of Voluntary Intoxication, below.

B. DRUNKEN INTENT

The law is *not* concerned with a D who has several (or many) drinks that merely "loosen them up" and remove their inhibitions. If at the time of the crime they know what they are doing, it is irrelevant that they would not have committed the crime, but for the drinks they have consumed. It was stressed in *Sheehan and Moore* that "a **drunken intent is nevertheless an intent**".[119] **3–085**

Equally, the law is not concerned with persons who claim that they would not have committed the crime had they not been intoxicated. The loss of self-control was D's fault. At the time of the crime, they knew what they were doing and so must be held fully responsible.

Accordingly, the only cases in which the criminal law might consider intoxication to be an issue relevant to blameworthiness and liability are those where D is so intoxicated as to lack mens rea or to be in a state of automatism. It is not a matter of whether D was *capable* of forming mens rea. It is a question of whether mens rea was, in fact, formed.[120]

---

119 *R. v Sheehan (Michael); Moore (George Allen)* [1975] 1 W.L.R. 739 (emphasis added); (1974) 60 Cr. App. R. 308 CA; see further, *R. v Stubbs (Kevin John)* (1989) 88 Cr. App. R. 53; (1988) 10 Cr. App. R. (S.) 97 CA; *R. v Mohamadi (Hamid)* [2020] EWCA Crim 327; [2020] Crim. L.R. 1077.

120 *R. v Pordage* [1975] Crim. L.R. 575; *Cole* [1993] Crim. L.R. 300; *R. v Hayes (Dennis Francis)* [2002] EWCA Crim 1945; [2003] Crim. L.R. 48.

C. INTOXICATION AS A "DEFENCE"

3–086 Even in cases where D does lack mens rea, the law is unwilling to allow drunken persons to escape criminal liability and draws a distinction between voluntary and involuntary intoxication, the general rule being that drunkenness is only an answer to a charge in the latter situation.

Being voluntarily intoxicated is usually no answer to a criminal charge. However, this rule is subject to a significant exception. Quite how this exception should be classified, however, has always been a matter of difficulty. Judges and texts commonly refer to voluntary intoxication, in these exceptional circumstances, as providing a partial excuse or defence for D. Certainly, in terms of its effect upon the liability of an intoxicated D, charged, say, with murder, and eventually convicted of manslaughter, this is how it appears to operate. But as the Law Commission has emphasised:

> ". . . [t]here is no common law or statutory 'defence' of intoxication. That is to say, the simple fact that D was voluntarily intoxicated at the time he or she allegedly committed the offence charged does not provide D with a 'defence'."[121]

So how does intoxication have an impact upon D's liability?

A.P. Simester, "Intoxication is Never a Defence" [2009] Crim. L.R. 3, 4–5:

3–087 "The criminal law does contain an intoxication doctrine, but it is a doctrine of *inculpation*, not exculpation. Whether the intoxication doctrine is evidential or substantive is uncertain . . . Either way, however, it operates for the benefit of the prosecution, not the defence. Wherever the doctrine applies, its function—its sole function—is to treat the defendant as if he acted with mens rea, when in fact, he did not.

The intoxication doctrine is a supplementary device that assists the prosecution to 'prove' mens rea where that does not actually exist . . .

Suppose . . . that D lacked mens rea at the time when he perpetrated the actus reus of the offence charged. Ordinarily, he is then entitled to an acquittal. Yet before we acquit, we need to consider *why* mens rea was missing. If D lacked mens rea because intoxicated (i.e. where D would have foreseen the risk of perpetrating the actus reus had he been sober), the intoxication doctrine then comes into operation. The doctrine holds that, where D lacks mens rea because intoxicated and certain additional criteria are satisfied, D is to be *treated as if* he had mens rea."

121 Law Com. No.314 (2009), para.1.15.

This is a persuasive analysis of the approach taken by the law. In effect, as will be seen, it reverses the standard account and, arguably, intoxication becomes a form of constructive liability.[122] But before examining this further, the concept of voluntary intoxication requires elaboration. **3–088**

D. MEANING OF VOLUNTARY INTOXICATION

Where an accused knows that they are drinking alcohol, they will not be able to claim that they are involuntarily intoxicated merely because they were unaware of the strength of the alcoholic drink, or of its effect on them. In *Allen*,[123] D claimed that he had not realised that the wine he had drunk had a high alcohol content. It was held that this was a clear case of voluntary Intoxication: where an accused knows they are drinking alcohol, it is irrelevant whether they know the precise nature or strength of the alcohol. Involuntary intoxication is narrowly defined. **3–089**

R. v Hardie (1985) 80 Cr. App. R. 157 (Court of Appeal, Criminal Division):

PARKER LJ: **3–090**

> "The problem is whether . . . [the taking of] valium . . . should properly be regarded as self-induced intoxication . . .
>
> There can be no doubt that the same rule applies both to self-intoxication by alcohol and intoxication by hallucinatory drugs, but this is because the effects of both are well-known and there is therefore an element of recklessness in the self-administration of the drug . . .
>
> In the present instance the defence was that the valium was taken for the purpose of calming the nerves only, that it was old stock and that the appellant was told it would do him no harm. There was no evidence that it was known to the appellant or even generally known that the taking of valium in the quantity taken would be liable to render a person aggressive or incapable of appreciating risks to others or have other side effects such that its self-administration would itself have an element of recklessness. It is true that valium is a drug and it is true that it was taken deliberately and not taken on medical prescription, but the drug is, in our view, wholly different in kind from drugs which are liable to cause unpredictability or aggressiveness. It may well be that the taking of a sedative or soporific drug will, in certain circumstances, be no answer, for example in a case of reckless driving, but if the effect of a drug is merely soporific or sedative the taking of it, even in some excessive quantity, cannot in the ordinary way raise a *conclusive* presumption against the admission of proof of intoxication for the purpose of disproving *mens rea* in ordinary crimes, such as would be the case with alcoholic intoxication or incapacity or automatism resulting from the self-administration of dangerous drugs."

---

122 In the light of this there is an argument for removing the discussion of intoxication from a chapter on defences. However, given that it has long been referred to as a "defence" and pending enactment of the Law Commission's proposals, it is to be retained in this chapter.

123 *R. v Allen (Kevin)* [1988] Crim. L.R. 698 CA.

3-091 Thus, the fact that the court thought that the drug was non-dangerous was highly significant. It can be argued that the current position, that the courts should have to determine whether or not a drug is dangerous on a case-by-case basis, is unsatisfactory.[124]

E. INVOLUNTARY INTOXICATION

3-092 Where a D is reduced to a state of intoxication through no fault of their own (because, for example, their drinks were "laced"), they cannot be "blamed" for their actions and will accordingly have a defence to any criminal charge. However, this protection extends only to the D who is so intoxicated that they do not form mens rea.

R. v KINGSTON [1995] 2 A.C. 355 (HOUSE OF LORDS):

3-093 The appellant, his drink having been laced with drugs, indecently assaulted a 15-year-old boy. He was convicted after the judge directed the jury that they should acquit if they found that he was so affected by the drugs that he lacked intent, but to convict if he had intent. The defendant appealed, claiming that he would not have committed the offence but for the drugs. The Court of Appeal upheld his appeal on the basis that the "operative fault" was not his. The Crown appealed to the House of Lords.

LORD MUSTILL:

> "[T]he general nature of the case is clear enough. In ordinary circumstances the respondent's paedophiliac tendencies would have been kept under control, even in the presence of the sleeping or unconscious boy on the bed. The ingestion of the drug (whatever it was) brought about a temporary change in the mentality or personality of the respondent which lowered his ability to resist temptation so far that his desires overrode his ability to control them. Thus we are concerned with a case of disinhibition . . .
>
> On these facts there are three grounds on which the respondent might be held free from criminal responsibility. First, that his immunity flows from general principles of the criminal law. Secondly, that this immunity is already established by a solid line of authority. Finally, that the court should, when faced with a new problem acknowledge the justice of the case and boldly create a new common law defence.
>
> It is clear . . . that the Court of Appeal adopted the first approach. The decision was explicitly founded on general principle . . .:
>
>> 'the law recognises that, exceptionally, an accused person may be entitled to be acquitted if there is a possibility that although his act was intentional, the intent itself arose out of circumstances for which he bears no blame.'

---

124 Law Com. No.229, *Legislating the Criminal Code: Intoxication and Criminal Liability* (1995), para.5.42. See also, Law Com. No.314 (2009), paras 1.25, 2.85–2.86.

My Lords, with every respect I must suggest that no such principle exists or, until the present case, had ever in modern times been thought to exist. Every offence consists of a prohibited act or omission coupled with whatever state of mind is called for by the statute or rule of the common law which creates the offence. In those offences which are not absolute the state of mind which the prosecution must prove to have underlain the act or omission—the 'mental element'—will in the majority of cases be such as to attract disapproval. The mental element will then be the mark of what may properly be called a 'guilty mind' . . . [His Lordship then surveyed cases both here and in other jurisdictions and concluded that there was no basis] for holding that the defence relied upon is already established by the common law, any more than it can be derived from general principles. Accordingly I agree with the analysis of Professor Griew, *Archbold News*, May 28 1993, pp.4–5:

'What has happened is that the Court of Appeal has recognised a new *defence* to criminal charges in the nature of an exculpatory excuse. It is precisely because the defendant acted in a prohibited way with the intent (the *mens rea*) required by the definition of the offence that he needs this defence.'

To recognise a new defence of this type would be a bold step . . . I can only say that the defence runs into difficulties at every turn. In point of theory, it would be necessary to reconcile a defence of irresistible impulse derived from a combination of innate drives and external disinhibition with the rule that irresistible impulse of a solely internal origin (not necessarily any more the fault of the offender) does not in itself excuse although it may be a symptom of disease of the mind . . . Equally, the state of mind which founds the defence superficially resembles a state of diminished responsibility . . . On the practical side there are serious problems . . .

My Lords, the fact that a new doctrine may require adjustment of existing principles to accommodate it . . . is not of course a ground for refusing to adopt it, if that is what the interests of justice require. Here, however, justice makes no such demands, for the interplay between the wrong done to the victim, the individual characteristics and frailties of the defendant, and the pharmacological effects of whatever drug may be potentially involved can be far better recognised by a tailored choice from the continuum of sentences available to the judge than by the application of a single yea-or-nay jury decision.

. . . I consider that both the ruling and the direction of the judge were correct."

Appeal allowed

Many commentators condemned the Court of Appeal decision in *Kingston* as surprising, dangerous and contrary to principle,[125] and favoured the narrower view of blame adopted by the House of Lords. However, others have argued that a new exculpatory defence should be developed for circumstances such as those in *Kingston*. Many persons might have secret urges to commit criminal acts, but blame **3–094**

125 e.g. J.C. Smith [1993] Crim. L.R. 784; E. Griew, *Archbold News*, 28 May 1993.

is inappropriate if they exercise control and restraint. If the only reason their inhibitions are removed is because someone else has secretly laced their drink, they are no longer able to evaluate their actions[126] and should not be blamed. It has been suggested that such a defence, if it were to be afforded, should depend upon an assessment whether the conduct was "out of character".[127] This would involve comparing D's "settled" character with D's intoxicated character. If the involuntary intoxication "destabilises" their character so that they commit an offence they should have an excuse.[128] Such an approach, however, is perceived by others to be blaming persons for what they are rather than what they have done. Apart from difficulties of proof (for example, establishing whether or not Kingston had abused children on previous occasions), the fact is that the evidence established on this occasion that Kingston only gave way to his desires because of the unforeseen actions of a third party. The real blame should be directed at that third party. Where a person commits a crime because of threats by another, we blame that other person and allow D a defence of duress. We do not enquire whether the actions were "out of character". The same approach should be adopted to those whose inhibitions are removed by the secret acts of others.

Criminal liability should generally only be imposed upon blameworthy actors who cause prohibited harms. It was seen above that mens rea has increasingly been given a normative meaning, equating it with blameworthiness or culpability—rather than bearing its cognitive meaning as involving intention or foresight. Following this, it is appropriate to blame actors who voluntarily become intoxicated—even though they might lack cognitive mens rea. On this basis, however, we ought not to blame people such as Kingston. As the Court of Appeal put it, "the law should exculpate him because the operative fault is not his".[129] Judicial developments to date, however, suggest that while courts are prepared to expand the concept of mens rea to inculpate blameworthy actors, they are unwilling to restrict mens rea to exculpate non-blameworthy actors such as Kingston. Accordingly, an alternative might be to reflect the lack of fault on the part of an actor like Kingston through the creation of a new defence. Lacey, for example, has argued for the creation of a new defence of "blocked evaluation" which, rather than operating on the basis of lapse of character, could be thought of in:

> ". . . terms of temporary lapses of normal conditions of agency, given that the lapse is of the kind which removes or seriously undermines the normal reasoning process."[130]

Such a defence might not only be available to those Ds (with mens rea) pleading involuntary intoxication.[131] The House of Lords, has, however, rejected any such approach and, clinging to orthodoxy, proclaimed that Kingston must be liable as he acted with mens rea and no established defence was

126 Horder, "Pleading Involuntary Lack of Capacity" (1993) 52 C.L.J. 298. See also, R. Smith and L. Clements, "Involuntary Intoxication, the Threshold of Inhibition and the Instigation of Crime" [1995] 46 N.I.L.Q. 210. cf. T. Brooks, "Involuntary Intoxication: a new six-step procedure" (2015) J. Crim. L. 138.

127 See G.R. Sullivan, "Involuntary Intoxication and Beyond" [1994] Crim. L.R. 272 and W. Wilson, "Involuntary Intoxication: Excusing the Inexcusable" [1995] 1 *Res Publica* 25.

128 Sullivan, "Making Excuses" in Simester and Smith (eds), *Harm and Culpability* (Oxford: Clarendon Press, 1996), p.131. See also Tadros, *Criminal Responsibility* (Oxford: OUP, 2005), pp.502–506.

129 *R. v Kingston (Barry)* [1994] Q.B. 81; (1993) 97 Cr. App. R. 401 CA.

130 Lacey, "Partial Defences to Homicide" in Ashworth and Mitchell (eds), *Rethinking Homicide Law* (New York: OUP, 2000), p.107 at 120.

131 Lacey discusses whether it could be used in situations of mercy-killing, e.g. where the extreme distress or despair edges out the normal processes of reasoning: Lacey, "Partial Defences to Homicide" in Ashworth and Mitchell (eds), *Rethinking Homicide Law* (2000), pp.123–125.

applicable. It must be seriously doubted whether this severing of the link between moral fault and blame can be justified.

Despite these concerns, the Law Commission has endorsed the rule in *Kingston*, agreeing with their Lordships' reasoning and approach.[132] It believes that the common law position should be retained and "that there should be no defence of reduced inhibitions or blurred perception of morality where D's condition was caused by involuntary intoxication".[133]

In relation to involuntary intoxication more generally, the Law Commission's proposals also restate the common law but do provide a non-exhaustive list of situations which would count as involuntary intoxication, such as where intoxication results from the administration of an intoxicant under duress, or where intoxication results from taking an intoxicant for a proper medical purpose.[134] **3–095**

F. LAW ON VOLUNTARY INTOXICATION

1. Specific and basic intent

We are now in a position to examine further the impact voluntary intoxication has upon a D's liability for offences. In the leading case of *Majewski*,[135] the House of Lords confirmed a long line of authority[136] that drunkenness was an answer to charges involving crimes of "specific intent" and not to crimes of "basic intent".[137] Whilst being so drunk that D did not form the mens rea of a crime of specific intent would mean that D avoided liability for that offence,[138] if the crime committed was one of basic intent, D's drunkenness does not allow them to avoid liability by arguing that they were so drunk that they did not form the necessary mens rea. Essentially, for basic intent crimes, D's voluntary intoxication *constitutes* their culpability. **3–096**

This distinction between crimes of specific and basic intent caused little problem at first. A rough list was drawn up by judges: for example, murder and the Offences Against the Person Act 1861 s.18 were deemed to be crimes of specific intent while manslaughter and the Offences Against the Person Act 1861 s.20 were held to be crimes of basic intent. This distinction was a functional one aimed at achieving a "compromise between the rigours of denying the relevance of intoxication and allowing it to undercut

132 Law Com. No.314 (2009), para.4.25.
133 Law Com. No.314 (2009), para.4.8.
134 Law Com. No.314 (2009), paras 3.121–3.136.
135 *DPP v Majewski* [1977] A.C. 443; [1976] 2 W.L.R. 623 HL.
136 *DPP v Beard* [1920] A.C. 479; (1920) 14 Cr. App. R. 159; *Att-Gen of Northern Ireland v Gallagher (Patrick)* [1963] A.C. 349; [1961] 3 W.L.R. 619 HL; *Bratty v Att-Gen of Northern Ireland* [1963] A.C. 386; [1961] 3 W.L.R. 965.
137 For crimes requiring specific intent, intoxication will be part of all the evidence that the jury must consider in determining whether the prosecution has established that D had the necessary mens rea (earlier dicta in *DPP v Beard* [1920] A.C. 479; (1920) 14 Cr. App. R. 159 HL that the onus of proof is on D cannot now be relied upon). If the issue of intoxication emerges as a material factor at the trial, the judge should direct the jury on it, even if D does not raise the issue themselves: *Bennett* [1995] Crim. L.R. 877; *Groark* [1999] Crim. L.R. 669; *Hayes* [2002] EWCA Crim 1945. However, the key decision as to whether it is "material" rests with the judge and there is some indication that the threshold is being raised: see *R. v Porceddu (Stefano)* [2004] EWCA Crim 1043; and Ormerod and Laird, *Smith, Hogan and Ormerod's Criminal Law*, 16th edn (2021), p.330.
138 But if mens rea is formed, then D's drunkenness has no effect on liability because, as noted above, drunken intent is still intent according to *R. v Sheehan (Michael)* [1975] 1 W.L.R. 739; (1974) 60 Cr. App. R. 308 CA, drunken intent is still intent.

all liability".[139] Drunken Ds charged with murder and s.18 could instead be convicted of manslaughter and s.20, respectively.

Intoxication could be seen, in effect, to be acting as a mitigating factor and hence operated in a defence-like way. However, Simester has pointed out that this apparent similarity with partial defences is very limited; indeed, he argues that this thinking needs to be abandoned.

A.P. Simester, "Intoxication is Never a Defence" [2009] Crim. L.R. 3, 13:

3–097 "Unlike partial exculpations, intoxication is a doctrine of (partial) inculpation. Structurally speaking, they work in opposite directions.

True partial defences, such as provocation [now loss of control], operate to excuse a defendant's *deliberate choice* to harm the victim. Provocation does not deny that D has the mens rea for murder. Quite the reverse: it explains why he did. It prevents conviction of an offence for which the necessary inculpatory elements are satisfied . . . Disregard provocation, and the case is a culpable murder.

For intoxication, by contrast, it is not the drunkenness that is supplying the exception. It is the lack of mens rea. Indeed, strictly speaking exculpation is not required. The core inculpatory element is missing. This is why, in a specific intent offence, intoxication informs no substantive defence known to the criminal law (and why the defendant bears no burden to establish it). The defendant's submission is like the 'defence' of alibi: that the prosecution has not proved the elements, the actus reus and mens rea, of the offence. Of course, courtroom lawyers frequently call such denials a defence, but we should not confuse this usage with the corresponding substantive-law term. The prosecution bears the burden of proving actus reus and mens rea, it has simply failed to do so.

When we come to basic intent offences, on the other hand, now intoxication becomes relevant as a matter of substantive law. The prosecution acquires a supplementary way to establish culpability. It need not, though it may, prove mens rea. Or it may prove that D would have had mens rea but for his voluntary intoxication. Where it succeeds in the latter, this is not to conclude that D somehow had mens rea in fact, but rather that he evinced the level of culpability that the mens rea requirement is designed to track."

3–098 As a result of the rule in *Majewski,* the terms "specific" and "basic" intent are crucially important and need to be explained. However, initially they were concepts without substance. They meant nothing. They were like elephants—the courts knew them when they saw them (i.e. they knew when a D's liability could be reduced without escaping all punishment)—but they could not be defined. Difficulties started arising when judges began trying to define these concepts. Attempting to identify a coherent rationale for a practice born out of a compromise between principle and policy considerations was always going to be problematic.

139 G.P. Fletcher, *Rethinking Criminal Law* (Boston: Little, Brown, 1978), p.849.

Several views started emerging. For example, Lord Simon in *Majewski* equated specific intent with "direct" intent (i.e. aim or purpose): "the prosecution must in general prove that the purpose for the commission of the act extends to the intent expressed or implied in the definition of the crime."[140] This view, however, never won judicial support and instead the "ulterior intent test" was the first to gain broad acceptance. Under this view, crimes of specific intent are crimes where the mens rea of the offence extends beyond the actus reus, while in crimes of basic intent the mens rea goes no further than extending to the elements of the actus reus itself. An example will illustrate this distinction. Assault is a crime of basic intent: the actus reus is causing apprehension of immediate force; the mens rea is an intention (or recklessness) to cause such apprehension; no mens rea extending beyond the actus reus is required. But assault with intent to resist arrest[141] is a crime of specific intent: the actus reus is the same as that of common assault, namely, causing apprehension of immediate force; the mens rea is two-fold—there must be the mens rea of the assault *and in addition* there must be an intent to resist arrest. This additional intention does not relate to anything in the actus reus of the crime; it extends beyond the actus reus; the crime is thus one of specific intent.

However, an alternative view was also expressed in *Majewski*,[142] and endorsed in the subsequent House of Lords' decision of *Caldwell*, namely, the "recklessness test". According to this, drunkenness can only be relevant to crimes that require proof of intention (such as murder and s.18) and is no answer to crimes that can be committed recklessly (such as manslaughter and s.20). In short, a crime of "specific intent" is one that cannot be committed recklessly. Whilst such a simple test is an extremely and easy one to apply, doubt was cast as to its reliability.

R. v Heard [2008] Q.B. 43 (Court of Appeal, Criminal Division):

The defendant was charged with sexual assault, contrary to the Sexual Offences Act 2003 s.3. The defendant, who had been drinking heavily, claimed he could not remember the sexual assault upon a policeman. He was convicted and appealed on the ground that s.3 created an offence of specific intent and that the jury should have been directed to consider whether the drink he had taken meant he did not have an intention to touch as required under s.3. **3–099**

HUGHES LJ:

> "The first thing to say is that it should not be supposed that every offence can be categorised simply as either one of specific intent or basic intent. So to categorise an offence may conceal the truth that different elements of it may require proof of different states of mind . . . The current legislative practice of itemising separately different elements of offences created by statute, which is much exhibited in the Sexual Offences Act 2003, may occasionally have the potential to complicate matters for a jury, but it demonstrates the impossibility of fitting an offence into a single pigeon-hole, whether it be labelled 'basic intent' or specific intent'.

---

140 *Majewski* [1977] A.C. 443 at 479.
141 Offences Against the Person Act 1861 s.38.
142 *Majewski* [1977] A.C. 443 at 475 (Lord Elwyn-Jones).

The offence of sexual assault, with which this case is concerned, is an example . . . [I]t is only the touching which must be intentional, whilst the sexual character of the touching is unless equivocal, to be judged objectively, and a belief in consent must be objectively reasonable . . .

In the present case, what the appellant did and said at the time . . . made it perfectly clear that this was a case of drunken intentional touching. Although the Judge directed the jury that drunkenness was no defence, he also directed the jury that it must be sure that the touching was deliberate. That amounted to a direction that for conviction the appellant's mind (drunken or otherwise) had to have gone with his physical act of touching . . .

[W]e agree that the Judge's direction that the touching must be deliberate was correct . . .

The remaining question is whether the Judge was also correct to direct the jury that drunkenness was not a defence.

We do not agree with [counsel's] submission for the appellant that the fact that reckless touching will not suffice means that voluntary intoxication can be relied upon as defeating intentional touching. We do not read the cases, including *DPP v Majewski*, as establishing any such rule . . . The Judge was accordingly correct, not only to direct the jury that the touching must be deliberate, but also to direct it that the defence that voluntary drunkenness rendered him unable to form the intent to touch was not open to him . . .

[Counsel for the appellant's] proposition that *Majewski* decides that it is only where recklessness suffices that voluntary intoxication cannot be relied upon derives from a part of the speech by Lord Elwyn-Jones LC in *Majewski*, and some observations, obiter of Lord Diplock in the subsequent case of *Caldwell* . . .

3–100 There are a number of difficulties about extracting [counsel's] proposition from the [two cases] . . .

(i) Lord Elwyn-Jones was addressing the submission made on behalf of the appellant in *Majewski* that it was unprincipled or unethical to distinguish between the effect of drink upon the mind in some crimes and its effect upon the mind in others. In rejecting that submission, and upholding the distinction between crimes of basic and specific intent, he was drawing attention to the fact that a man who has got himself into a state of voluntary intoxication is not, by ordinary standards, blameless. Both the Lord Chancellor and others of their Lordships made clear their view that to get oneself into such a state is, viewed broadly, as culpable as in any sober defendant convicted of a crime of basic intent, whether because he has the basic intent or because he is reckless as to the relevant consequence or circumstance. Throughout *Majewski* it is clear that their Lordships regarded those two latter states of mind as equivalent to one another for these purposes. It therefore does not follow from the references to recklessness that the same rule (that voluntary intoxication cannot be relied upon) does not apply also to basic intent; on the contrary, it seems to us clear that their Lordships were treating the two as the same.

(ii) The new analysis of recklessness in *Caldwell* may have led readily to the proposition that voluntary intoxication is broadly equivalent to recklessness, thus defined. But that analysis and definition of recklessness have now been reversed by the House of Lords in *R. v G* [2004] 1 A.C. 1034. As now understood, recklessness requires actual foresight of the risk.

(iii) Since the majority in *Caldwell* held that it was enough for recklessness that the risk was obvious objectively (thus, to the sober man) no question of drink providing a defence could arise; it follows that the explanation of *Majewski* which was advanced was plainly obiter.

(iv) Lord Diplock's proposition in *Caldwell* attracted a vigorous dissent from Lord Edmund-Davies . . . [He] dissented not only from the new definition of recklessness, but also from the analysis of *Majewski* . . .

(v) There were, moreover, many difficulties in the proposition that voluntary intoxication actually supplies the *mens rea*, whether on the basis of recklessness as re-defined in *Caldwell* or on the basis of recklessness as now understood; if that were so the drunken man might be guilty simply by becoming drunk and whether or not the risk would be obvious to a sober person, himself or anyone else. That reinforces our opinion that the proposition being advanced was one of broadly equivalent culpability, rather than of drink by itself supplying the *mens rea*.

It is necessary to go back to *Majewski* in order to see the basis for the distinction there upheld between crimes of basic and of specific intent. It is to be found most clearly in the speech of Lord Simon . . . [and] was that crimes of specific intent are those where the offence requires proof of purpose or consequence, which are not confined to, but amongst which are included, those where the purpose goes beyond the *actus reus* (sometimes referred to as cases of 'ulterior intent') . . .

That explanation of the difference is consistent with the view of Lord Edmund-Davies that an offence contrary to s.1(2)(b) Criminal Damage Act is one of specific intent in this sense, even though it involves no more than recklessness as to the endangering of life; the offence requires proof of a state of mind addressing something beyond the prohibited act itself, namely its consequences. We regard this as the best explanation of the sometimes elusive distinction between specific and basic intent in the sense used in *Majewski*, and it seems to us that this is the distinction which the Judge in the present case was applying when he referred to the concept of a 'bolted-on' intention . . .

[O]ur view is that the Judge's directions were substantially correct."

Appeal dismissed

Everything said in this decision about the distinction between specific and basic intent was technically obiter.[143] It was clear that D had a drunken intent and this has never been a defence. Despite being obiter, the Court of Appeal has, here, disapproved the recklessness test and expressed a strong preference for the "purposive intent" approach and for the ulterior intent test. In doing this, however, **3–101**

143 D. Ormerod and K. Laird, *Smith, Hogan and Ormerod's Criminal Law*, 16th edn (2021), p.333.

the judgment is riddled with ambiguity. It is stated that specific intent *includes* ulterior intent but is "not confined to" such cases. It is far from clear when an offence, which is not one of ulterior intent, would nevertheless be one of specific intent. There are significant problems with this approach. There is abundant precedent that murder and s.18 are crimes of specific intent yet neither of these is generally[144] a crime of ulterior intent. Equally, neither of these crimes requires direct, "purposive" intent; oblique intent suffices. It is unfortunate that the simple "recklessness test" has been disapproved by the Court of Appeal (on some rather selective reading of the House of Lords' decisions) and cannot be regarded as resolved. It is submitted that the better view is that drunkenness should be an answer to crimes that can only be committed intentionally. This would not necessarily lead to unmeritorious acquittals. In the above case, for example, there was ample evidence of an intention to touch the policeman.

In *Heard*, it is stated that offences cannot be rigidly categorised as being of specific or basic intent. However, there are clear precedents and judicial pronouncements concerning the specific/basic intent distinction. On the basis of these it would appear that the following are crimes of specific intent.

(i) Murder

3-102 There is no doubt that intoxication leads to an acquittal for the crime of murder where D lacks the necessary intent; D will instead be found guilty of the lesser included offence of manslaughter.[145] This rule can be reconciled with the "recklessness test" as it is clear that murder is a crime of intention; it cannot be committed recklessly. In murder cases, there is always the possibility of a manslaughter conviction operating as a safety-net. Drunken Ds do not escape liability completely so it is "safe" to deem murder to be a crime of specific intent. This has the further advantage that it enables the judge to avoid the imposition of the mandatory sentence for murder.[146] Drunken killers are blameworthy and deserve punishment, but they are, perhaps, not always as blameworthy as deliberate murderers. Conviction for manslaughter allows the judge flexibility to assess the degree of blameworthiness and punish appropriately.

(ii) Section 18

3-103 The crime of wounding or causing grievous bodily harm with intent to cause grievous bodily harm or with intent to resist apprehension is a crime that cannot be committed recklessly. Drunkenness can lead to D escaping liability for s.18 but D will then be convicted of the lesser basic intent offence of s.20, an offence that can be committed recklessly.[147] However, there is a problem here. While wounding with intent to cause grievous bodily harm, and wounding or causing grievous bodily harm with intent to resist apprehension, are clearly crimes of ulterior intent, the same cannot be said of causing grievous bodily harm with intent to cause grievous bodily harm. Thus, if ulterior intent were required, drunkenness would be no answer to such a charge. This view, however, is not consistent with the better "recklessness test" and is not supported by authority which suggests that s.18 is *always* a specific intent offence.[148]

---

144 See paras 3-102–3-103.

145 *Beard* [1920] A.C. 479; *Att-Gen of Northern Ireland v Gallagher* [1963] A.C. 349; *Majewski* [1977] A.C. 443.

146 J. Sellers, "Mens Rea and the Judicial Approach to 'Bad Excuses' in the Criminal Law" (1978) 41 M.L.R. 245, 261.

147 *Pordage* [1975] Crim. L.R. 575; *Majewski* [1977] A.C. 443; *R. v Bailey (John Graham)* [1983] 1 W.L.R. 760; (1983) 77 Cr. App. R. 76 CA; *R. v Davies* [1991] Crim. L.R. 469 CA.

148 It is conceded that in none of these cases was the charge causing grievous bodily harm with intent to cause grievous bodily harm.

(iii) Theft[149]

This is a crime of intention; recklessness does not suffice; it is also a crime of ulterior intent. **3–104**

(iv) Robbery[150]

Again, recklessness will not suffice here and it is a crime of ulterior intent. **3–105**

(v) Burglary

While recklessness as to whether entry to a building as a trespasser will suffice, such entry must be accompanied by an intention (only) to commit a listed offence.[151] It would thus appear to be a crime of specific intent, passing the "recklessness test". It is also a crime of ulterior intent. **3–106**

(vi) Handling stolen goods

In *Durante*,[152] it was accepted that this was an offence of specific intent. This is not an offence of intention at all. The mens rea stipulated by the Theft Act 1968 s.22 is that D must act dishonestly and must know or believe that the goods are stolen. If one adopts the "recklessness" test it is difficult to see why this should be regarded as a crime of specific intent. **3–107**

(vii) Attempt

Only intention suffices; furthermore, any attempted crime is a crime of ulterior intent.[153] **3–108**

(viii) Assault with intent to resist arrest

As with burglary, while one of the elements, the assault, may be committed recklessly, there must be a further intention to resist arrest. **3–109**

It must be emphasised that this list does not purport to be exhaustive.

Most other offences are crimes of basic intent. The most prominent on this list are the following: manslaughter, s.20, s.47 and common assault. Occasionally, a statute specifically provides that intoxication cannot be a defence: the Public Order Act 1986 is an example of this.[154] It is also widely accepted that rape was, under the law prior to the Sexual Offences Act 2003, and continues to be, a

149 Theft Act 1968 s.1; *Ruse v Read* [1949] 1 K.B. 377; Lord Salmon in *Majewski* [1977] A.C. 443 at 482.
150 Theft Act 1968 s.8.
151 Theft Act 1968 s.9.
152 *R. v Durante (Reginald William)* [1972] 1 W.L.R. 1612; (1972) 56 Cr. App. R. 708 CA.
153 In *Durante* [1972] 1 W.L.R. 1612, endeavouring to obtain money on a forged instrument was accepted as a crime of specific intent; this is analogous to an *attempt* to commit a crime.
154 Public Order Act 1986 s.6(5).

crime of basic intent. *Heard* was followed in *Grewal*,[155] where D had been convicted of sexual assault,[156] with the Court of Appeal observing that: "following the decision of this court in *R v Heard* . . . intoxication cannot negative intention in relation to an assault of this nature." It may therefore be presumed that rape, assault by penetration,[157] sexual assault and causing a person to engage in sexual activity,[158] are all crimes of basic intent, since the mens rea element of these offences is cast in very similar terms.[159]

What is the rationale of this "recklessness test"? In *Majewski*, Lord Elwyn-Jones LC said:

> "If a man of his own volition takes a substance which causes him to cast off the restraints of reason and conscience, no wrong is done to him by holding him answerable criminally for any injury he may do while in that condition. His course of conduct in reducing himself by drugs and drink to that condition in my view supplies the evidence of *mens rea*, of guilty mind certainly sufficient for crimes of basic intent. It is a reckless course of conduct and recklessness is enough to constitute the necessary *mens rea* in assault cases . . . The drunkenness is itself an intrinsic, an integral part of the crime, the other part being the evidence of the unlawful use of force against the victim. Together they add up to criminal recklessness."[160]

3–110 Essentially, D is thought to be blameworthy due to their "prior fault" in allowing them to get in such a state that they become violent.[161] There were two problems with this approach. Suppose a D starts drinking at 8pm and by 10pm is no longer aware of their actions. At 11pm, they commit the actus reus of the crime. The mens rea of the crime (getting so drunk which is a reckless thing to do) precedes the actus reus. There is no coincidence of actus reus and mens rea.[162] The second problem with Lord Elwyn-Jones' approach is that recklessness does not exist in the abstract. One has to be reckless as to a particular consequence. Thus, under the subjective test of recklessness it should have been necessary to establish that when D was getting drunk (the recklessness) they foresaw the possibility of committing the crime.

It is quite clear that the courts were less concerned with fine arguments such as these than with ensuring that a fair and just solution (in terms of balancing the competing interests of protection of society and the rights of D) was achieved. As Lord Simon said:

> "One of the prime purposes of the criminal law, with its penal sanctions, is the protection from certain proscribed conduct of persons who are pursuing their lawful lives. Unprovoked violence has, from time immemorial, been a significant part of such proscribed violence. To accede to the

155 *R. v Grewal (Amanpreet Singh)* [2010] EWCA Crim 2448 at [29].
156 Sexual Offences Act 2003 s.3.
157 Sexual Offences Act 2003 s.2.
158 Sexual Offences Act 2003 s.4.
159 See Ch.6.
160 *Majewski* [1977] A.C. 443 at 474–475. In *Kingston* [1995] 2 A.C. 355 at 369, Lord Mustill stated that he was not required to decide how this rationalisation (or that of D being estopped from relying on his self-induced incapacity) stood up to attack.
161 For a more in-depth analysis, see J. Child, H. Crombag and R. Fortson, "Understanding the 'fault' in prior-fault intoxication: insights from behavioural neuroscience" in A. Reed and M. Bohlander (eds), *Fault in criminal law: A research companion*, (Oxford: Routledge, 2022).
162 On the general need for coincidence of actus reus with mens rea, see paras 3–121–3–132.

> argument on behalf of the appellant would leave the citizen legally unprotected from unprovoked violence where such violence was the consequence of drink or drugs having obliterated the capacity of the perpetrator to know what he was doing or what were its consequences."[163]

In *Caldwell*, Lord Diplock was able to avoid these problems by re-casting recklessness in an objective mould. If the risks would have been obvious to an ordinary person at the time of drinking, then D *was* reckless *as to the particular consequence*; it was irrelevant whether D, because of intoxication, foresaw the risk himself. However, despite the fact that the *Caldwell*-recklessness test was, in this respect, a more principled approach to the issue of intoxication, it has been jettisoned from English law.[164] The clash between principle and policy is marked. When subjective mens rea correlates with ordinary people's notions of fault or blameworthiness (say, cases of sober mistakes or accidents) it can be employed. When it does not (as in cases of drunken violence), the concept of subjective mens rea has to be abandoned. The true basis of mens rea is the attribution of blame, which might, or might not, coincide with a D's state of mind. Blame is attributed to persons who render themselves insensible through drink or drugs and then commit a crime. As Lord Russell in *Majewski* said: **3–111**

> "*Mens rea* has many aspects. If asked to define it in such a case as the present I would say that *the element of guilt or moral turpitude* is supplied by the act of self-intoxication reckless of possible consequences."[165]

Such views were endorsed by Lord Simon in *Majewski*:

> "*Mens rea* is therefore on ultimate analysis the state of mind stigmatised as wrongful by the criminal law which, when compounded with the relevant prohibited conduct, constitutes a particular offence. There is no juristic reason why mental incapacity brought about by self-induced intoxication, to realise what one is doing or its probable consequences should not be such a state of mind stigmatised as wrongful by the criminal law."[166]

In *Heard*, the Court of Appeal recognised the fallacy (particularly since *G*) in the reasoning that getting drunk is a reckless thing to do and that this can constitute the mens rea of an offence. Instead, it suggested that the issue was one of "broadly equivalent culpability" rather than the drink by itself supplying the mens rea. Quite what the culpability relates to was left unclear although an answer has since been supplied by the Law Commission: **3–112**

---

163 *Majewski* [1977] A.C. 443 at 476. See also Hughes LJ in *R. v Coley (Scott)* [2013] EWCA Crim 223; [2013] M.H.L.R. 17 at [82]; *R. v Taj (Simon)* [2018] EWCA Crim 1743; [2019] Q.B. 655 at [54]–[55].

164 *R. v G* [2004] 1 A.C. 1034. cf. P.H. Robinson, "A brief summary and critique of criminal liability rules for Intoxicated conduct" (2018) 82 J. Crim. L. 381.

165 *Majewski* [1977] A.C. 443 at 498 (emphasis added).

166 *Majewski* [1977] A.C. 443 at 478.

> "[G]iven the culpability associated with knowingly and voluntarily becoming intoxicated, and the associated increase in the known risk of aggressive behaviour . . . the advertent recklessness in voluntarily choosing to become intoxicated, and becoming a greater danger to society, may be equated, morally, with the subjective (advertent) recklessness required for liability."[167]

This is probably the closest we are likely to get to a satisfactory answer. It lends support to Simester's analysis of the intoxication doctrine as a form of constructive liability: "becoming voluntarily drunk supplies a gateway to liability, without further mens rea, for basic intent offences."[168]

Whilst the courts and reform bodies have endeavoured to distinguish specific and basic intent, those applying the law suggest that it has caused little difficulty in practice. The Law Commission has acknowledged the importance of this perspective but has stated that the lack of general agreement on the test:

> ". . . must inevitably lead to uncertainty, wasted court time and the unnecessary incurring of legal costs when a new offence is introduced, since, until the matter is decided by the courts, it will not be possible to ascertain into which category it falls."[169]

Its latest proposals are based upon the belief that the distinction between offences of specific and basic intent is "ambiguous, misleading and confusing, and that it should be abandoned".[170] These proposals were made over a decade ago, with no indication that there is the political appetite to adopt them.

2. A partial "defence"?

3–113 Thus, the compromise has developed so that intoxication is an answer to those crimes of intention where there is a lesser included offence for which D can be convicted. One way of looking at this is that intoxication has the practical effect of a partial defence reducing murder to manslaughter[171] and of reducing s.18 to s.20. However, it is clear that intoxication can sometimes, at least in theory, lead to a complete acquittal under English law. As Lord Russell stated in *Majewski*:

> "[S]pecial intent cases are not restricted to those crimes in which the absence of a special intent leaves available a lesser crime embodying no special intent, but embraces all cases of special intent even though no alternative lesser criminal charge is available."[172]

---

167 Law Com. No.314 (2009), paras 1.55, 1.61.

168 Simester, "Intoxication is never a defence" [2009] Crim. L.R. 3, 7.

169 Law Com. No.229 (1995), para.3.27. e.g. in *DPP v Kellett* (1994) 158 J.P. 1138; [1994] Crim. L.R. 916 QBD the court had to decide whether the Dangerous Dogs Act 1991 s.1(7) created an offence of basic or specific intent. It was held to be the former.

170 Law Com. No.314 (2009), para.1.28.

171 See C.M.V. Clarkson, "Drunkenness, Constructive Manslaughter and Specific Intent" (1978) 41 M.L.R. 478.

172 *Majewski* [1977] A.C. 443 at 499.

The crime of theft is just such a case. Intoxication is an answer to a charge of theft where D lacks the intention permanently to deprive, although there is no lesser included offence of which D can be convicted. This sudden reassertion of principle is somewhat anomalous and, while there are dicta supporting this approach, it is unlikely that the courts actually will take this step and allow a complete defence in such circumstances.[173]

3. "Dutch courage" intoxication

Where persons deliberately reduce themselves to a state of intoxication to give themselves "Dutch courage" to commit a crime, their intoxication will not be a defence even to crimes that can only be committed with a specific intention. They are to be "blamed" to the same extent as the person who intentionally commits a crime. As Lord Denning stated in *Gallagher*: **3–114**

> "If a man, whilst sane and sober, forms an intention to kill . . . and then gets himself drunk so as to give himself Dutch courage to do the killing . . . he cannot rely on his self-induced drunkenness as a defence to a charge of murder, nor even as reducing it to manslaughter . . . the wickedness of his mind before he got drunk is enough to condemn him, coupled with the act which he intended to do and did do."

G. REFORM OF THE LAW ON INTOXICATION

The law on intoxication has long been considered to be in need of reform. Over the past few decades, English law reform bodies have vacillated between proposals to modify *Majewski* and the more radical proposal of abolishing *Majewski* and replacing it with a separate offence. **3–115**

In 1980, a majority of the Criminal Law Revision Committee rejected the proposal for a special intoxication offence and instead recommended a codification of the law, endorsing a "recklessness test", namely, that intoxication should never be a defence to crimes that can be committed recklessly; it could at most negative the mental element of intention required for the commission of an offence.[174] This proposal was reproduced by the Draft Criminal Code Bill 1989 cl.22[175] and in the Law Commission's proposals in 1995.

LAW COMMISSION (LAW COM. NO.229), LEGISLATING THE CRIMINAL CODE, INTOXICATION AND CRIMINAL LIABILITY (1995), PARAS 6.6–6.7:

> "6.6 We . . . have concluded that the best way of codifying the present law, whilst avoiding the problems inherent in the present distinction between offences of specific and basic intent, is to confine the *Majewski* principle, broadly speaking, to offences for which proof of recklessness (or awareness of risk) is sufficient . . . **3–116**

173 A common circumstance is that of "stealing" a vehicle whilst drunk. Even if D was drunk enough to be acquitted of a charge of theft, he would still be liable for the offence of taking and driving away, contrary to the Theft Act 1968 s.12.

174 Criminal Law Revision Committee, 14th Report, *Offences Against the Person* (Cmnd.7844, 1980), paras 259–264.

175 Law Com. No.177 (1989).

6.7 This policy *may* represent the present law, although it is difficult to state this with any certainty . . . [I]t has the advantages of simplicity and clarity, both matters of great importance in any system of criminal law. Finally, this change in the law will have a negligible practical effect in relation to crimes already judicially categorised as being of basic or specific intent, since most crimes designated as being of basic intent are capable of reckless commission."

3–117 This recommendation (which was substantially adopted in the subsequent Government proposals[176]) was criticised by Horder for being "designed to fend off public criticism rather than to provide a principled basis on which the law can operate".[177] Almost 15 years later, Horder, as Law Commissioner, was in a position to try to identify the principles underlying the common law and to base new proposals upon them. The Law Commission then accepted that its earlier proposals might have been too complex[178] and "returned to the subject with a stripped down approach".[179] As noted earlier, it believes that the rationale of the law is and ought to be that the subjective recklessness involved in becoming intoxicated (and thus more dangerous to society) is the moral equivalent of the subjective recklessness usually required for liability. It takes the view now that the concepts of specific and basic intent are "ambiguous, confusing and misleading" and proposes to abandon them.[180] However, the substance of the distinction is retained.

LAW COMMISSION (LAW COM. NO.314), INTOXICATION AND CRIMINAL LIABILITY (CMND.7526, 2009), PARAS 3.35–3.48:

3–118 *"Recommendation 1: the Majewski rule*

3.35 There should be a general rule that:

(1) if D is charged with having committed an offence as a perpetrator;
(2) the fault element of the offence is not an integral fault element (for example, because it merely requires proof of recklessness); and
(3) D was voluntarily intoxicated at the material time;

then, in determining whether or not D is liable for the offence, D should be treated as having been aware of anything which D would have been aware of but for the intoxication.

3.36 The approach we recommend would apply regardless of the degree to which D was intoxicated and regardless of whether D's state of intoxication was caused by alcohol or some other drug or substance (such as a solvent) or any combination of intoxicants.

176 Draft Offences Against the Person Bill 1998 cl.19.
177 J. Horder, "Sobering Up? The Law Commission on Criminal Intoxication" [1995] 58 M.L.R. 534, 536.
178 Law Com. No.314 (2009), para.1.67.
179 I. Dennis, "Editorial: Intoxication and Criminal Liability" [2009] Crim. L.R. 133.
180 Law Com. No.314 (2009), para.1.28.

3.37 We include recklessness within the scope of this general rule as an 'example', but the practical effect of the rule . . . would be to limit the application of the rule to allegations of recklessness . . .

3.38 If the allegation is one of subjective recklessness, D would be treated as having been aware of any risk or circumstance D would have been aware of but for his or her self-induced state of intoxication . . .

Recommendation 2: the rule for integral fault elements

3.42 If the subjective fault element in the definition of the offence, as alleged, is one to which the justification for the *Majewski* rule does not apply, then the prosecution should have to prove that D acted with that relevant state of mind.

3.43 . . . For such fault elements, evidence of D's voluntary intoxication should be taken into consideration by the court when determining whether the prosecution has proved that D acted (or failed to act) with the required state of mind. We list the integral fault elements below under our next recommendation.

3.44 Importantly, it would be *the particular state of mind* alleged by the prosecution, not the offence itself, which would determine whether the general rule applies. Our recommendation would abandon the courts' unhelpful categorisation which distinguishes between *offences* of 'specific intent' and *offence* of 'basic intent' . . .

3.45 If recklessness is alleged then, as explained above, the general rule would apply. But if the prosecution alleges that D acted with an integral fault element, it would be necessary to prove that D had that required state of mind at the relevant time; and the jury would be directed that D's intoxication should be taken into account in determining whether the allegation has been proved.

Recommendation 3: the integral fault elements

3.46 The following subjective fault elements should be excluded from the application of the general rule and should, therefore, always be proved:

(1) intention as to a consequence [but not intention as to conduct];
(2) knowledge as to something;
(3) belief as to something (where the belief is equivalent to knowledge as to something);
(4) fraud; and
(5) dishonesty.

3.47 Two other states of mind we recommend for inclusion . . . [relate to specific recommendations for those who assist or encourage crime].

3.48 The list of integral fault elements we recommend would be exhaustive."

3–119 The term "integral fault element" is not perhaps the most felicitous of expressions but otherwise the recommendations bring greater clarity to the underlying rationale of intoxication (very much like the analysis adopted by Simester discussed earlier) and to the law. The Government rejected these proposals.[181]

VI. Relationship of Mens Rea to Actus Reus

A. INTRODUCTION

3–120 A general rule of the criminal law is that mens rea must exist in relation to the actus reus. Bearing in mind that an actus reus can consist of:

(1) an act;
(2) committed in certain specified circumstances; and
(3) leading to the prohibited consequence.

Mens rea should exist in relation to each of these separate elements. However, it does not necessarily follow that the same degree of mens rea is required in relation to each. Thus, the crime of attempt, for example, could require (1) an intentional act; (2) recklessness as to surrounding circumstances; and (3) an intention to bring about the forbidden consequences. But whatever the level of mens rea, it must exist "in relation to" the actus reus, or, to put it another way, the actus reus must be attributable to the mens rea. In order to understand this rule, it is necessary to investigate two "principles" that are well established in criminal law, and to consider the problem of mistake.

B. COINCIDENCE OF ACTUS REUS AND MENS REA

3–121 In the Rhodesian case of *Shorty*,[182] D violently assaulted V with intent to kill him. D, genuinely believing V to be dead, attempted to dispose of the "body" by putting it down a sewer. V was in fact still alive at the time but died of drowning in the sewer. The court ruled that these actions must be divided into:

(1) the assault which did not cause death—this was accompanied by an intent to kill; and
(2) the actus reus of murder (placing the "body" in a sewer with resultant drowning)—but this was not accompanied by mens rea at this stage.

181 Law Commission, "Current project status" at *http://www.lawcom.gov.uk/project/intoxication-and-criminal-liability-2009*.
182 *Shorty* (1950) S.R. 280.

Because the actus reus of murder did not coincide with the mens rea thereof, D could not be convicted of murder. He was convicted only of attempted murder (stage 1), the actus reus of which did coincide with the requisite mens rea.

Is such a result realistic? D intended to kill V; he did kill him. Should his mistake as to the method and time of death affect his liability?

THABO MELI V R. [1954] 1 ALL E.R. 373 (PRIVY COUNCIL):

The appellants, in accordance with a pre-arranged plan, took a man to a hut, gave him beer so that he was partially intoxicated and then struck him over the head. Believing him to be dead, they took his body and rolled it over a low cliff, making the scene look like an accident. In fact, the man was not dead, but died of exposure when unconscious at the foot of the cliff. **3–122**

LORD REID:

> "The point of law which was raised in this case can be simply stated. It is said that two acts were done:—first, the attack in the hut; and, secondly, the placing of the body outside afterwards—and that they were separate acts. It is said that, while the first act was accompanied by *mens rea*, it was not the cause of death; but that the second act, while it was the cause of death, was not accompanied by *mens rea*; and on that ground, it is said that the accused are not guilty of murder, though they may have been guilty of culpable homicide. It is said that the *mens rea* necessary to establish murder is an intention to kill, and that there could be no intention to kill when the accused thought that the man was already dead, so their original intention to kill had ceased before they did the act which caused the man's death. It appears to their Lordships impossible to divide up what was really one series of acts in this way. There is no doubt that the accused set out to do all these acts in order to achieve their plan, and as parts of their plan; and it is much too refined a ground of judgment to say that, because they were under a misapprehension at one stage and thought that their guilty purpose had been achieved before, in fact, it was achieved, therefore they are to escape the penalties of the law . . . Their crime is not reduced from murder to a lesser crime merely because the accused were under some misapprehension for a time during the completion of their criminal plot."

Appeal dismissed

Dealing with a similar situation (except there was no preconceived plan) in *Church*,[183] it was stated that the jury should have been told they could convict of murder: **3–123**

> ". . . if they regarded the appellant's behaviour from the moment he first struck her to the moment when he threw her into the river as a series of acts designed to cause death or grievous bodily harm."[184]

---

183 *R. v Church (Cyril David)* [1966] 1 Q.B. 59; (1965) 49 Cr. App. R. 206 CA.

184 See also *R. v Moore and Dorn* [1975] Crim. L.R. 229. In *Att-Gen's Reference (No.4 of 1980)* [1981] 1 W.L.R. 705; (1981) 73 Cr. App. R. 40 CA the Court of Appeal left open the question whether this "series of acts" test was a correct extension of the *Thabo Meli* principle (*Meli v Queen, The* [1954] 1 W.L.R. 228; (1954) 98 S.J. 77 PC).

R. v Le Brun (1992) 94 Cr. App. R. 101 (Court of Appeal, Criminal Division):

3–124 The defendant hit his wife on the chin knocking her unconscious. While trying to drag her body away (probably to avoid detection) he dropped her causing her to fracture her skull and die. He was convicted of manslaughter and appealed.

LORD LANE CJ:

"[After citing *Church* with approval his Lordship continued]

It seems to us that where the unlawful application of force and the eventual act causing death are parts of the same sequence of events, the same transaction, the fact that there is an appreciable interval of time between the two does not serve to exonerate the defendant from liability. That is certainly so where the appellant's subsequent actions which caused death, after the initial unlawful blow, are designed to conceal his commission of the original unlawful assault.

It would be possible to express the problem as one of causation. The original unlawful blow to the chin was a *causa sine qua* of the later *actus reus*. It was the opening event in a series which was to culminate in death: the first link in the chain of causation, to use another metaphor. It cannot be said that the actions of the appellant in dragging the victim away with the intention of evading liability broke the chain which linked the initial blow with the death.

In short, in circumstances such as the present . . . the act which causes death and the necessary mental state to constitute manslaughter need not coincide in point of time . . .

[The trial judge had drawn a correct distinction] between actions by the appellant which were designed to help his wife and actions which were not so designed: on the one hand that would be a way in which the prosecution could establish the connection if he was not trying to assist his wife; on the other hand if he was trying to assist his wife, the chain of causation would have been broken and the *nexus* between the two halves of the prosecution case would not exist."

Appeal dismissed

3–125 Ashworth argues that these decisions "take a rather elastic view of the contemporaneity principle, and seem to be motivated by considerations akin to constructive liability".[185] However, in all the above cases the so-called problem of a "coincidence of actus reus and mens rea" is illusory. In each case, D's actions caused the ultimate death (that is, the chain of causation was not broken); D was held liable for either murder or manslaughter[186] depending on the mens rea present at the time of the original assault.

185 Ashworth and Horder, *Principles of Criminal Law*, 7th edn (2013), p.159.

186 This solution was not adopted in *Shorty* (1950) S.R. 280. It is submitted that under English causation principles, *Shorty* would be regarded as wrong.

This approach was confirmed by the House of Lords in *Att-Gen's Reference (No.3 of 1994)* where Lord Mustill stated:

> "The existence of an interval of time between the doing of an act by the defendant with the necessary wrongful intent and its impact on the victim in a manner which leads to death does not in itself prevent the intent, the act and the death from together amounting to murder, so long as there is an unbroken causal connection between the act and the death."[187]

Lord Hope added that:

> ". . . the act which caused the death and the mental state which is needed to constitute manslaughter need not coincide in point of time . . . [as long as] the original unlawful and dangerous act, to which the required mental state is related, and the eventual death of the victim are both part of the same sequence of events."[188]

It has been suggested that this causation analysis will not apply and that the "continuing actus reus" doctrine will still be necessary in cases where the second event is the overwhelming cause of death and breaks the chain of causation[189]—for example, if the wife in *Le Brun* had been dropped by a Good Samaritan trying to take her to hospital.[190] The short answer to this is that if the second event is so overwhelming as to break the causal chain, it would not be regarded as part of the same "series of acts" (*Church*) or "same sequence of events" (*Le Brun*). The continuing actus reus principle would not apply.

In such cases where there are two separate incidents which cannot be conflated into a continuous act or the "same sequence of events", the jury must be unanimous as to which of the acts forms the basis of the D's liability.[191] In *Boreman,*[192] D seriously assaulted V (with the mens rea of murder) and later (perhaps accidentally) started a fire at V's flat. V died but the medical evidence was divided as to the cause of death. It was held that: **3-126**

> ". . . where the two possible means by which the killing is effected comprise completely different acts, happening at different times, it can properly be said that the jury ought to be unanimous on which act leads them to the decision to convict."

187 *Att-Gen's Reference (No.3 of 1994)* [1997] 3 All E.R. 936 at 942.

188 *Att-Gen's Reference (No.3 of 1994)* [1997] 3 All E.R. 936 at 956–957.

189 J.J. Child, A.P. Simester, J.R. Spencer, F. Stark and G.J. Virgo, *Simester and Sullivan's Criminal Law: Theory and Doctrine*, 8th edn (Oxford: Hart Publishing, 2022), p.195.

190 D. Ormerod and K. Laird, *Smith and Hogan: Criminal Law*, 16th edn (Oxford: OUP, 2021), p.130.

191 *Brown* (1983) 79 Cr. App. R. 115.

192 *R. v Boreman (Victor)* [2000] 2 Cr. App. R. 17; [2000] Crim. L.R. 409 CA.

However, the appeal was dismissed on the ground that the jury must have been satisfied that the injuries were an operating cause of death.

There are other "coincidence cases" where the initial act is not accompanied by mens rea but D forms mens rea at a later stage in the sequence of events.

Fagan v Metropolitan Police Commissioner [1969] 1 Q.B. 439 (Queen's Bench Divisional Court):

3–127 The appellant was told by a police officer to park his car in an exact position against the kerb. He drove the vehicle forward and stopped with its front off-side wheel on the constable's left foot. When told to reverse off, the appellant replied, "Fuck you, you can wait", and turned off the ignition. After several further requests, the appellant reversed the vehicle off the constable's foot. He was convicted of assaulting a police officer in the execution of his duty. On appeal, he claimed that the initial driving on to the foot was unintentional and therefore not an assault, and that his refusal to drive off was not an "act" capable of amounting to an assault.

JAMES J:

> "We think that the crucial question is whether, in this case, the act of the appellant can be said to be complete and spent at the moment of time when the car wheel came to rest on the foot, or whether his act is to be regarded as a continuing act operating until the wheel was removed. In our judgment, a distinction is to be drawn between acts which are complete—though results may continue to flow—and those acts which are continuing . . . For an assault to be committed, both the elements of *actus reus* and *mens rea* must be present at the same time . . . It is not necessary that *mens rea* should be present at the inception of the *actus reus*, it can be superimposed on an existing act. On the other hand, the subsequent inception of *mens rea* cannot convert an act which has been completed without *mens rea* into an assault . . .
>
> There was an act constituting a battery which at its inception was not criminal because there was no element of intention, but which became criminal from the moment the intention was formed to produce the apprehension which was flowing from the continuing act. The fallacy of the appellant's argument is that it seeks to equate the facts of this case with such a case as where a motorist has accidentally run over a person and, that action having been completed, fails to assist the victim with the intent that the victim should suffer."

Appeal dismissed

3–128 In *Miller*,[193] D fell asleep holding a lit cigarette which started a fire. When he awoke, he failed to do anything about the fire but simply moved to another room. The House of Lords adopted the "duty theory" that by creating the dangerous situation (starting the fire) D became under a duty to act and

193 *Miller* [1983] A.C. 161. A fuller extract from this case is provided at para.2–034.

so could be held responsible for the omission to act. Lord Diplock, however, conceded that the "continuous act" theory would provide an alternative route to liability.

R. v Miller [1983] A.C. 161 (House of Lords):

LORD DIPLOCK: 3–129

"[T]he conduct of the accused, throughout the period from immediately before the moment of ignition to the completion of the damage to the property by the fire, is relevant; so is his state of mind throughout that period . . .

[The *ratio decidendi* of the Court of Appeal] treats the whole course of conduct of the accused, from the moment at which he fell asleep and dropped the cigarette on to the mattress until the time the damage to the house by fire was complete, as a continuous act of the accused, and holds that it is sufficient to constitute the statutory offence of arson if at any stage in that course of conduct the state of mind of the accused, when he fails to try to prevent or minimise the damage which will result from his initial act, although it lies within his power to do so, is that of being reckless as to whether property belonging to another would be damaged."

In 1998, the Government published a Consultation Document containing a Draft Bill which would deal with the problem in *Miller* in the following manner. 3–130

Home Office, Violence: Reforming the Offences Against the Person Act 1861, Draft Offences Against the Person Bill 1998 cl.16:

"(1) Where it is an offence under this Act to be at fault in causing a result by an act and a person lacks the fault required when he does an act that may cause or does cause the result, he nevertheless commits the offence if— 3–131

(a) being aware that he has done the act and that the result may occur or (as the case may be) has occurred and may continue, and
(b) with the fault required, he fails to take reasonable steps to prevent the result occurring or continuing and it does occur or continue."

This is, as indicated in *Miller*, a better way of resolving the problem. Rather than resorting to fictions concerning a "continuing actus reus", D is effectively treated as having created a dangerous situation. This generates a duty to take reasonable steps to prevent harm resulting from that danger. 3–132

C. TRANSFERRED MALICE

3–133 There are two well-established and accepted rules of criminal law.

(a) If D causes the actus reus by a different method than they intended they are nevertheless liable. Thus, if D intended to kill V by stabbing them but after the first stab V fell and struck their head on a kerb, the blow killing them, D is clearly guilty of murder and cannot claim that the death is accidental. They intended to kill V; by their actions they have killed V; they have mens rea in relation to the actus reus; they are liable.

(b) If D is mistaken as to the identity of V, they are nevertheless liable. Thus if D shoots at V thinking they are Smith but in fact they are Jones and Jones dies, D is clearly guilty of murder. Again, D has committed the actus reus of murder; they had the requisite mens rea; they are liable.

However, what of the following scenarios?

(a) What if D fires their gun at Smith, but misses and hits a passing stranger, Jones, and kills them? If D was unaware of the existence of Jones, can they nevertheless be liable for murder?

(b) What if D throws a brick at Smith, but misses and breaks a window near Smith? If D was unaware of the existence of the window, can they be liable for criminal damage?

The response of English law to these two situations is clear.

(a) D will be liable for murder. They intended to cause the actus reus of murder; they did cause the actus reus of murder. Their malice against Smith is transferred to Jones. The actus reus of murder is killing a human being. This they have done, intentionally; the identity of the victim is irrelevant. The leading illustration of this principle is *Latimer*[194] where D swung his belt at a man with whom he was quarrelling but the belt hit the face of a woman to whom he was talking. Lord Coleridge CJ held:

> ". . . if a person has a malicious intent towards one person, and in carrying into effect that malicious intent he injures another man, he is guilty of what the law considers malice against the person so injured."

(b) D will *not* be liable for criminal damage because the doctrine of transferred malice does not apply where the actus reus (criminal damage) is different from the mens rea (of an offence against the person). Only if the actus reus intended and the actus reus caused are the same can the malice be transferred from the one to the other. In *Pembliton*,[195] where the facts were similar to the hypothetical example, D was acquitted (on appeal) of malicious damage to a window.

---

194 *Latimer* (1886) 17 Q.B.D. 369. For a more recent illustration of transferred malice (and where the doctrine was expressly approved), see *Mitchell* (1983) 75 Cr. App. R. 293. In *Jones (Peter)* [1987] Crim. L.R. 701, the doctrine was applied in a provocation case.

195 *Pembliton* (1874) 12 Cox 607.

The rationale of, and limits to, the doctrine of transferred malice were explored in the following case. In order to understand the decision, it is necessary to appreciate two rules to be explored in Ch.8. First, a foetus cannot be the victim of a crime of violence. If the foetus dies in utero, it cannot be murder or manslaughter. If, however, the child is born alive but later dies from violence aimed at it while in utero, the assailant may be liable for manslaughter. Secondly, the mens rea of murder is satisfied by either an intention to kill or an intention to cause grievous bodily harm. **3–134**

ATT-GEN'S REFERENCE (NO.3 OF 1994) [1998] A.C. 245 (HOUSE OF LORDS):

The appellant stabbed a pregnant woman intending to cause her grievous bodily harm. As a result, her child was born prematurely and 121 days later died because of the prematurity of the birth. The trial judge directed the jury to acquit the appellant of both murder and manslaughter because the foetus, at the time of the attack, was not a live person. The doctrine of transferred malice was not applicable because "the intent to stab the mother (a live person) could not be transferred to the foetus (not a live person)". On a reference by the Attorney General, the Court of Appeal allowed the appeal on the ground that the foetus is part of the mother so that an intention to cause grievous bodily harm to the mother is equivalent to the same intent directed towards the foetus. The appellant appealed to the House of Lords. **3–135**

LORD MUSTILL:

> "[His Lordship rejected the Court of Appeal's views on the ground that] the mother and the foetus were two distinct organisms living symbiotically, not a single organism with two aspects. The mother's leg was part of the mother; the foetus was not . . .
>
> I turn to . . . 'transferred malice' . . . One explanation [of this rule is that it is] founded on the notion of risk. The person who committed a crime took the chance that the outcome would be worse than he expected . . . but as a foundation of a modern doctrine of transferred malice broad enough to encompass the present case it seems to me quite unsupportable . . .
>
> [T]here was [also] the idea of 'general malice', of an evil disposition existing in the general and manifesting itself in the particular, uniting the aim of the offender and the result which his deeds actually produced. According to this theory, there was no need to 'transfer' the wrongful intent from the intended to the actual victim; for since the offender was . . . 'an enemy to all mankind in general', the actual victim was the direct object of the offender's enmity. Plainly, this will no longer do, for the last vestiges of the idea disappeared with the abolition of the murder/felony doctrine.
>
> What explanation is left: for explanation there must be, since the 'transferred malice' concept is agreed on both sides to be sound law today? . . . [His Lordship then discussed *Pembliton* and *Latimer*.] I find it hard to base a modern law of murder on these two cases . . . [although the answers they gave] would be the same today. But the harking back to a concept of general malice, which amounts to no more than this, that a wrongful act displays a malevolence which can be attached to any adverse consequence, has long been out of date. And to speak of a

particular malice which is 'transferred' simply disguises the problem by idiomatic language. The defendant's malice is directed at one objective, and when after the event the court treats it as directed at another object it is not recognising a 'transfer' but creating a new malice which never existed before. As Dr Glanville Williams pointed out . . . the doctrine is 'rather an arbitrary exception to general principles'. Like many of its kind this is useful enough to yield rough justice . . .

My Lords, the purpose of this enquiry has been to see whether the existing rules are based on principles sound enough to justify their extension to a case where the defendant acts without an intent to injure either the foetus or the child which it will become. In my opinion they are not. To give an affirmative answer requires a double 'transfer' of intent: first from the mother to the foetus and then from the foetus to the child as yet unborn . . . For me, this is too much . . . I am willing to follow old laws until they are overturned, but not to make a new law on a basis for which there is no principle.

Moreover, even on a narrower approach the argument breaks down. The effect of transferred malice, as I understand it, is that the intended victim and the actual victim are treated as if they were one, so that what was intended to happen to the first person (but did not happen) is added to what actually did happen to the second person (but was not intended to happen), with the result that what was intended and what happened are married to make a notionally intended and actually consummated crime. The cases are treated as if the actual victim had been the intended victim from the start. To make any sense of this process there must, as it seems to me, be some compatibility between the original intention and the actual occurrence, and this is, indeed, what one finds in the cases. There is no such compatibility here. The defendant intended to commit and did commit an immediate crime of violence to the mother. He committed no relevant violence to the foetus, which was not a person, either at the time or in the future, and intended no harm to the foetus or to the human person which it would become . . . I would not overstrain the idea of transferred malice by trying to make it fit the present case.

Accordingly, . . . the judge was right to direct an acquittal on the count of murder.

[His Lordship then went on to hold that the appellant could have been guilty of manslaughter for which recourse to transferred malice was not necessary.]"

Appeal allowed

3–136 This decision can be supported because what was intended (grievous bodily harm to the mother) was qualitatively different to what occurred (death of the child who, at the time of the attack, was not legally a person). As Lord Mustill put it, for the doctrine of transferred malice to apply, there must be "some compatibility between the original intention and the actual occurrence".

Jeremy Horder, Transferred Malice and the Remoteness of Unexpected Outcomes from Intentions" [2006] Crim. L.R. 383, 388, 385, 386, 388–389:

"In my terms, 'compatibility' can be maintained by asking the jury to consider whether the way in which the death of an unanticipated victim resulted was too remote from the death that the defendant intended or anticipated, for a conviction for murder . . . to constitute a representative label . . . **3–137**

Example 1: D fires a gun at V1 intending to kill V1. D misses, but the noise of the gun being fired startles a bystander, V2, who consequently dies of a heart attack.

. . . What should matter in these examples is not only that the actual victims were unintended victims, but also that they died in an unanticipated way. This double element of deviation from D's plan is what, in principle, may make the deaths too 'remote' from what D intended for murder to be a representative label . . .

[T]he remoteness principle comes into play only when (a) the victim was not the intended victim; and (b) the victim was not killed in the way intended. These two conditions were met in *Attorney General's Reference (No.3 of 1994)*. Although they are necessary conditions, they should not, however, be treated as sufficient conditions for the purposes of the remoteness principle. Crucial in this regard is the evidence that *B deliberately stabbed M in the abdomen, knowing that she was pregnant*. If D is aware that something might go awry, and *a fortiori* of how it may go awry, when they try to put their intention into effect, that awareness is highly relevant to the question of how far, morally speaking, D can distance himself from the unintended outcome. Morally speaking, it makes the outcome less 'remote' from what B intended, and more compatible with it."

Horder's suggested approach is somewhat impractical. It involves leaving too much to the jury who have to decide whether the death is too remote from what was intended or anticipated for murder to constitute a representative label. This is effectively telling the jury that "if it looks like murder, if it feels like murder, then it is murder". **3–138**

Real life has provided a complex scenario in which to consider the boundaries of the doctrine of transferred malice, albeit not quite as complex as Horder's fictional one. In the case of *Gnango*,[196] two gunmen were engaged in a shoot-out in a car-park when a passer-by got caught in the crossfire and was killed. The gunman who fired the fatal shot was, for unknown reasons, not prosecuted, and the question for the court was whether the doctrine of transferred malice could be used, in conjunction with the doctrine of joint enterprise liability,[197] to convict the second gunman of the murder of the passer-by. The Supreme Court held that D was indeed guilty of murder on the basis that he had aided and abetted the other gunman in the attempted murder of himself, and his malice towards himself could therefore be transferred to the passer-by. This is surely stretching the doctrine too far.[198]

---

196 *Gnango* [2011] UKSC 59.

197 See Ch.11.

198 See R. Buxton, "Being an accessory to one's own murder" [2012] Crim. L.R. 275–281.

D. PRINCIPLE OF CORRESPONDENCE

3–139 The previous paragraphs in this section have set out how the law currently manages the relationship between mens rea and actus reus by following specific rules that have been developed through the case law. Before ending the chapter, however, it is useful to pause to identify one particular principle developed from a more theoretical standpoint, which can be used to critically analyse the current substantive law relating to specific offences. We will we see when we come to particular chapters later in the book, particularly Ch.5 on Non-fatal Offences Against the Person,[199] and Ch.7 on Homicide,[200] that existing law falls fowl of what the eminent commentator on criminal law, Professor Andrew Ashworth KC, has defined as the principle of correspondence:

ANDREW ASHWORTH, *PRINCIPLES OF CRIMINAL LAW*, 6TH EDN (2009), PP.76–77

3–140 "[An] implication of the principle of individual autonomy (with its emphasis on choice and control) and the 'rule of law' ideal (with its emphasis on the ability of individuals to plan) is the principle of correspondence. Not only should it be established that the defendant had the required fault, in terms of mens rea or belief; it should also be established that the defendant's intention, knowledge, or recklessness related to the proscribed harm. Thus, if the conduct element of a crime is 'causing serious injury', the principle of correspondence demands that the fault element should be intention or recklessness as to causing serious injury, and not intention or recklessness as to some lesser harm such as a mere assault. Another example, as we shall see, is the law of murder: in English law a person may be convicted of murder if he either intended to kill or intended to cause grievous bodily harm. However, the latter species of fault breaches the principle of correspondence: the fault element does not correspond with the conduct element (which is, causing death), and so a person is liable to conviction for a higher crime than contemplated. In effect, murder and other crimes that breach the correspondence principle are constructive crimes. They reduce 'rule of law' protections and respect for autonomy by rendering D liable to conviction for a more serious offence than intended or knowingly risked; and, to that extent, the offence of conviction turns on the chance element of whether or not the more serious (unintended and unforeseen) harm results."

3–141 The extent to which an individual commentator values the principle of correspondence might depend upon the extent to which they subscribe to the capacity conception of criminal responsibility, discussed above. The principle is no more than a useful tool to bear in mind when thinking about whether the current law is successful in framing responsibility in a way which is fair and balanced, and whether reforms could be proposed to improve the current position.

199 See paras 5–080–5–086.
200 See paras 7–063–7–066.

Chapter 4

Strict Liability and Corporate Culpability

I. Strict Liability

A. INTRODUCTION

It was explained in Ch.2 that to be convicted of an offence, this typically requires proof that D completed the actus reus with the requisite mens rea, in circumstances where there was no valid defence. For the most serious criminal offences, this is usually true. However, there are some offences which lack a mens rea requirement regarding one (or more) of the actus reus elements. These offences impose strict liability.[1] 4–001

These offences are often regulatory in nature and, subject to a few isolated exceptions, statutory in origin. For instance, in the first "modern" case of strict liability,[2] D (a tobacconist) was held guilty of possessing adulterated tobacco. An excise officer seized D's tobacco, having found it adulterated with sugar, molasses and other saccharine matter. D was held liable even though he had no grounds for suspecting that the tobacco was adulterated. However, this does not mean the offence requires no mens rea element. It still had to be shown that D intended to sell the tobacco, but no mens rea was required with regard to the adulteration of the tobacco. Similarly, in the much later case of *Alphacell v Woodward*,[3] the D company was held liable for causing polluted water to enter a river. The fact that D did not know the pollution was taking place and that they mistakenly thought their filtering system was operating effectively was irrelevant.

The majority of strict liability offences exist within schemes of regulation where the emphasis is on the maintenance of standards such as safety. Regulatory schemes that make extensive use of strict liability cover areas such as food, consumer protection, the environment, agriculture, the countryside,

---

1 In 2000, it was estimated that more than half the (then) roughly 8,000 crimes in English law were ones involving strict liability (A. Ashworth, "Is the Criminal Law a Lost Cause?" (2000) 116 L.Q.R. 225).

2 *Woodrow* (1846) 153 E.R. 907 (Exch).

3 *Alphacell Ltd v Woodward* [1972] A.C. 824; [1972] 2 W.L.R. 1320 HL.

construction, and fire. These areas focus on securing compliance with the law, and administrative remedies such as improvement notices are used extensively. However, as a last resort, a criminal prosecution can be brought, often where there are sustained breaches of regulations. While much of the literature and debate in this area has revolved around these "regulatory offences", it must be emphasised that there are countless other strict liability offences that do not exist within regulatory schemes.

B. THE LAW

4-002 How are the courts to determine whether an offence is one of strict liability? At first sight, the issue resolves itself into a problem of statutory interpretation. When the legislature has done its job efficiently, there is no difficulty. It may indicate, by the inclusion of terms such as "knowingly" or "recklessly", that the offence being created is one requiring mens rea. It may, alternatively, make it clear that an offence of strict liability is being created.[4] All too often, however, legislation is silent regarding the mens rea elements(s) for each element of the actus reus, meaning that it is for the courts to either imply mens rea requirements or to find the offence as one of strict liability. The absence of mens rea requirement(s) is not determinative of liability being strict. On the contrary, there is an:

> ". . . established common law presumption that a mental element, traditionally labelled mens rea, is an essential ingredient unless Parliament has indicated a contrary intention either expressly or by necessary implication."[5]

1. The presumption of mens rea

4-003 The initial presumption from which one starts is that mens rea is required for every actus reus element.

SWEET V PARSLEY [1970] A.C. 132 (HOUSE OF LORDS):

4-004 D (a teacher) sublet rooms to students in a farmhouse in which she did not reside, although she occasionally stayed overnight. She exercised no control over the students beyond collecting rent from them and occasionally shouting at them to be quiet if, on her visits, there was excessive noise late at night.

D was convicted of being concerned in the management of premises which were used for the purpose of smoking cannabis contrary to the Dangerous Drugs Act 1965 s.5(b), when such substances were found during a police search. The Divisional Court upheld her conviction on the basis that she was not only in a position of being able to choose her tenants but could have made

4 See, e.g. the offence of causing the death of another person by driving a vehicle while uninsured (Road Traffic Act s.3ZB). The injustice of making this serious offence one of strict liability has been lessened by the Supreme Court in *R. v Hughes (Michael)* [2013] UKSC 56; [2014] 1 Cr. App. R. 6 (see para.2–046).

5 *B (A Child) v DPP* [2000] 2 A.C. 428 at 460 per Lord Nicholls; [2000] 2 W.L.R. 452 HL.

it a term of the letting that the smoking of cannabis was prohibited.[6] D appealed to the House of Lords.

LORD REID:

"How has it come about that the Divisional Court has felt bound to reach such an obviously unjust result? It has in effect held that it was carrying out the will of Parliament because Parliament has chosen to make this an absolute offence. And, of course, if Parliament has so chosen the courts must carry out its will, and they cannot be blamed for any unjust consequences. But has Parliament so chosen? Our first duty is to consider the words of the Act: if they show a clear intention to create an absolute offence that is an end of the matter. But such cases are very rare. Sometimes the words of the section which creates a particular offence make it clear that *mens rea* is required in one form or another. Such cases are quite frequent. But in a very large number of cases there is no clear indication either way. In such cases there has for centuries been a presumption that Parliament did not intend to make criminals of persons who were in no way blameworthy in what they did. That means that whenever a section is silent as to *mens rea* there is a presumption that, in order to give effect to the will of Parliament, we must read in words appropriate to require *mens rea*.

In the absence of a clear indication in the Act that an offence is intended to be an absolute offence, it is necessary to go outside the Act and examine all relevant circumstances in order to establish that this must have been the intention of Parliament. I say 'must have been' because it is a universal principle that if a penal provision is reasonably capable of two interpretations, that interpretation which is most favourable to the accused must be adopted."

LORD PEARCE:

"My Lords, the prosecution contend that any person who is concerned in the management of premises where cannabis is in fact smoked even once, is liable, though he had no knowledge and no guilty mind. This is, they argue, a practical act intended to prevent a practical evil. Only by convicting some innocents along with the guilty can sufficient pressure be put upon those who make their living by being concerned in the management of premises. Only thus can they be made alert to prevent cannabis being smoked there. And if the prosecution have to prove knowledge or *mens rea*, many prosecutions will fail and many of the guilty will escape. I find that argument wholly unacceptable.

The notion that some guilty mind is a constituent part of crime and punishment goes back far beyond our common law. And at common law *mens rea* is a necessary element in a crime . . . Before the court will dispense with the necessity for *mens rea* it has to be satisfied that Parliament so intended. The mere absence of the word 'knowingly' is not enough. But the nature of the crime, the punishment, the absence of social obloquy, the particular mischief

6 J.C. Smith [1968] Crim. L.R. 328 points out that such a term in the letting agreement would not have absolved the defendant from liability if the crime were one of strict liability.

and the field of activity in which it occurs, and the wording of the particular section and its context, may show that Parliament intended that the act should be prevented by punishment regardless of intent or knowledge."

Appeal allowed

4–005 The strength of this presumption of mens rea has been strongly affirmed. It has been described by the appellate courts as being both "well-established"[7] and a matter of "great importance".[8]

B (A Child) v DPP [2000] 2 A.C. 428 (House of Lords):

4–006 During a bus journey, D (a 15-year-old boy) persistently invited a 13-year-old girl to perform oral sex on him. D was charged with the (now-repealed) offence of inciting a girl under the age of 14 to commit an act of gross indecency.[9] D honestly believed she was over 14 years of age. The Youth Court ruled that the offence was one of strict liability regarding the complainant's age. As such, D's fault concerning her age was irrelevant. D appealed to the House of Lords on the grounds that since the Act did not specify a mens rea element, the presumption that a mens rea requirement was necessary should apply.

LORD NICHOLLS OF BIRKENHEAD:

"The starting point for a court is the established common law presumption that a mental element, traditionally labelled *mens rea*, is an essential ingredient unless Parliament has indicated a contrary intention either expressly or by necessary implication . . .

In section 1(1) of the Indecency with Children Act 1960 Parliament has not expressly negatived the need for a mental element in respect of the age element of the offence. The question, therefore, is whether, although not expressly negatived, the need for a mental element is negatived by necessary implication. 'Necessary implication' connotes an implication which is compellingly clear. Such an implication may be found in the language used, the nature of the offence, the mischief sought to be prevented and any other circumstances which may assist in determining what intention is properly to be attributed to Parliament when creating the offence.

I venture to think that, leaving aside the statutory context of section 1, there is no great difficulty in this case. The section created an entirely new criminal offence, in simple unadorned language. The offence so created is a serious offence. The more serious the offence, the greater is the weight to be attached to the presumption, because the more severe is the punishment and the graver the stigma which accompany a conviction. Under section 1 conviction originally attracted a punishment of up to two years' imprisonment. This has since

---

7 *R. v Lane (Sally)* [2018] UKSC 36; [2018] 1 W.L.R. 3647 at [8].

8 *Att-Gen's Reference (No.1 of 2020)* [2020] EWCA Crim 1665; [2021] Q.B. 441 at [42].

9 Contrary to the Indecency with Children Act 1960 s.1(1).

been increased to a maximum of ten years' imprisonment. The notification requirements under Part I of the Sex Offenders Act 1997 now apply, no matter what the age of the offender: see Schedule 1, paragraph 1(1) (b). Further, in addition to being a serious offence, the offence is drawn broadly ('an act of gross indecency'). It can embrace conduct ranging from predatory approaches by a much older paedophile to consensual sexual experimentation between precocious teenagers of whom the offender may be the younger of the two. The conduct may be depraved by any acceptable standard, or it may be relatively innocuous behaviour in private between two young people. These factors reinforce, rather than negative, the application of the presumption in this case.

Similarly, it is far from clear that strict liability regarding the age ingredient of the offence would further the purpose of section 1 more effectively than would be the case if a mental element were read into this ingredient. There is no general agreement that strict liability is necessary to the enforcement of the law protecting children in sexual matters."

LORD HUTTON:

"It would be reasonable to infer that it was the intention of Parliament that liability under section 1(1) of the Act of 1960 should be strict so that an honest belief as to the age of the child would not be a defence. But the test is not whether it is a reasonable implication that the statute rules out *mens rea* as a constituent part of the crime—the test is whether it is a *necessary* implication. Applying this test, I am of the opinion that there are considerations which point to the conclusion that it is not a necessary implication."

Appeal allowed

In these cases where the presumption is applied, the courts must specify the precise form of mens rea implied. This is generally taken to mean intention or subjective recklessness or knowledge or belief.[10] Negligence has not traditionally been regarded as sufficiently blameworthy for this purpose. Perhaps, despite the strength of the presumption emphasised in the above cases, this "all or nothing" approach (subjective mens rea or strict liability) has resulted in the presumption being displaced so often. The presumption might have been applied in a broader range of situations if the courts had been prepared to utilise negligence as an appropriate fault requirement. **4–007**

Taylor[11] does hint at a potential shift in approach. In relation to the offence of aggravated vehicle taking under the Theft Act 1968 s.12A, which had previously been interpreted as requiring no fault element,[12] the Supreme Court followed the approach in *Hughes*[13] in requiring that some fault in D's driving must be found before D could be punished for the fatal outcome of such driving. Despite showing that the Supreme Court is prepared to utilise negligence as an appropriate fault element instead of displacing

10 This was the approach adopted in the House of Lords' decisions of *B (A Child) v DPP* [2000] 2 A.C. 428, *R. v K (Age of Consent: Reasonable Belief)* [2001] UKHL 41; [2002] 1 A.C. 462 and *DPP v Collins* [2006] UKHL 40; [2006] 1 W.L.R. 2223.

11 *R. v Taylor (Jack)* [2016] UKSC 5; [2016] 1 W.L.R. 500.

12 *R. v Marsh (William)* [1997] 1 Cr. App. R. 67; (1996) 160 J.P. 721 CA.

13 *Hughes* [2013] UKSC 56.

the presumption in favour of mens rea, this does not necessarily indicate a general change in approach. It is more likely to have been prompted by the particular constructive offence under examination. Indeed, the court appears to have conflated two separate issues here: whether D had caused V's death and whether the offence was one of strict liability or not.

2. Displacing the presumption

4–008 The common-law presumption of mens rea will only be displaced if, according to the House of Lords in *B*,[14] there is a *necessary* implication that Parliament intended the offence to be strict.[15] If legislation is silent on one of the mens rea requirement(s) and the courts have not previously settled the issue, the court will have to make a fresh decision.[16] In such circumstances, the presumption of mens rea is simply a point of departure that can be outweighed by other factors.[17] The "*Gammon* principles" provide guidance on this matter and have been regularly applied as the appropriate test to determine whether the offence is one of strict liability.[18]

GAMMON LTD V ATT-GEN OF HONG KONG [1985] 1 A.C. 1 (PRIVY COUNCIL):

4–009 LORD SCARMAN:

"In their Lordships' opinion, the law may be stated in the following propositions: (1) there is a presumption of law that *mens rea* is required before a person can be held guilty of a criminal offence; (2) the presumption is particularly strong where the offence is 'truly criminal' in character; (3) the presumption applies to statutory offences, and can be displaced only if this is clearly or by necessary implication the effect of the statute; (4) the only situation in which the presumption can be displaced is where the statute is concerned with an issue of social concern, and public safety is such an issue; (5) even where a statute is concerned with such an issue, the presumption of *mens rea* stands unless it can also be shown that the creation of strict liability will be effective to promote the objects of the statute by encouraging greater vigilance to prevent the commission of the prohibited act."

4–010 Although these principles are clear and authoritative, their application to determine whether mens rea is required with regard to an actus reus element is often far from straightforward. In making this assessment, the courts have emphasised the importance of the following factors.

---

14 *B (A Child) v DPP* [2000] 2 A.C. 428.

15 *Nurse v Trinidad and Tobago* [2019] UKPC 43 at [2] (Lady Arden); [2021] A.C. 1.

16 In *Pwr v DPP* [2022] UKSC 2; [2022] 1 W.L.R. 789, the Supreme Court held that the Terrorism Act 2000 s.13(1), which makes it a criminal offence for D to "wear, carry or display an article in a public place, in such a way or in such circumstances as to arouse reasonable suspicion that he is a member or supporter or a proscribed organisation". This is a strict liability offence. There was no extra mental element required over and above the knowledge required for the wearing or carrying or displaying of the article to be deliberate. The court held that the strong presumption as to mens rea was rebutted by necessary implication, which was compellingly clear having regard to the words used, the context and the purpose of the provision. See F. Lee, "Terrorism Act 2000: strict liability: *Pwr v DPP*" (2024) 4 Crim. L.R. 277.

17 *Lane* [2018] UKSC 36; [2018] 1 W.L.R. 3647 at [9].

18 *R. v Bezzina (Anthony)* [1994] 1 W.L.R. 1057; (1994) 99 Cr. App. R. 356 CA; *R. v Brockley (Frank)* [1994] B.C.C. 131; (1994) 99 Cr. App. R. 385 CA; *R. v Blake (Albert Philip)* [1997] 1 W.L.R. 1167; [1997] 1 Cr. App. R. 209; *R. v Paine (Nicholas)* [1998] 1 Cr. App. R. 36 CA; *R. v Ezeemo (Godwin Chukwnaenya)* [2012] EWCA Crim 2064; [2014] P.T.S.R. 284.

(i) Type of offence

The most important consideration in determining whether the presumption should be displaced is whether the offence in question is a "serious" offence or is a "regulatory", "public welfare", or "quasi-criminal" offence. These latter offences are typically imposed for social regulation and public welfare, carry little to no stigma or public condemnation, and carry a light punishment (e.g. a fine). It is, however, not always clear what a "public welfare" offence is. "The connection between 'public welfare'/'quasi' crime and strict liability is self-fulfilling at both a legislative and an interpretive level."[19] An offence can be held to be one of strict liability because it is only "quasi-criminal", and then because it is an offence of strict liability, it can be labelled a "public welfare" offence. Similarly, it is unclear whether an offence is sufficiently "serious" to warrant a mens rea requirement for each actus reus element. **4–011**

R. v Muhamad [2003] 2 W.L.R. 1050 (Court of Appeal, Criminal Division):

D was convicted of materially contributing to the extent of his insolvency by gambling contrary to the Insolvency Act 1986 s.362(1)(a) and appealed. **4–012**

DYSON LJ:

"It is not clear to us whether an offence under section 362(1) (a) would have been classified by Lord Reid as 'quasi-criminal', or 'truly criminal'. A maximum penalty of two years' imprisonment is by no means insignificant, although it is towards the lower end of the scale of maximum custodial sentences. On the other hand, it is open to doubt whether, at any rate in 2002, such an offence would be regarded as 'truly criminal' . . .

The question whether the presumption of law that *mens rea* is required applies, and, if so, whether it has been displaced can be approached in two ways. One approach is to ask whether the act is truly criminal, on the basis that, if it is not, then the presumption does not apply at all. The other approach is to recognise that any offence in respect of which a person may be punished in a criminal court is, *prima facie*, sufficiently 'criminal' for the presumption to apply. But the more serious the offence, the greater the weight to be attached to the presumption, and conversely, the less serious the offence, the less weight to be attached. It is now clear that it is this latter approach which, according to our domestic law, must be applied.

The starting point, therefore, is to determine how serious an offence is created by section 362(1) (a), and accordingly how much weight, if any, should be attached to the presumption. Some weight must undoubtedly be given to the presumption, but in our judgment it can be readily displaced. As we have said, the maximum sentence indicates that Parliament considered this to be an offence of some significance, but not one of the utmost seriousness. This is not surprising. We do not believe that great stigma attaches to a conviction of this offence. In our view, this is not, and never has been, a particularly serious offence . . .

---

19 C. Wells, *Corporations and Criminal Responsibility* (Oxford: OUP, 1993), p.8.

> It is self-evident that section 362(1) (a) is aimed at an issue of social concern. [A]n offence of strict liability may have a more chilling effect on gambling that may materially contribute to insolvency than an offence which requires a mental element. We are satisfied that strict liability will encourage greater vigilance to prevent gambling which will or may materially contribute to insolvency . . .
>
> We conclude, therefore, that the offence created by section 362(1) (a) of the 1986 Act is one of strict liability."
>
> *Appeal dismissed*

4–013 The approach towards offence seriousness is by no means universally applied. There are glaring examples of cases where strict liability has been imposed where the crime has the stamp of traditional criminality. For example, the possession of dangerous drugs[20] and possessing an indecent photograph of a child[21] are both strict liability offences. In *Barnfather*, it was held that the strict liability offence committed by a parent whose child failed regularly to attend school involved:

> ". . . a real stigma (being) attached . . . It suggests either an indifference to one's children, or incompetence at parenting, which in the case of the blameless parent will be unwarranted."[22]

As seen in *Muhamad*, it is often stated that the level of punishment attached to a crime is essential in assessing whether the offence is one of strict liability. In the US, the Model Penal Code proposes that the possibility of imprisonment should conclusively indicate that the offence is not one of strict liability.[23] However, this is again only a guiding principle. In *Jackson*,[24] it was held that strict liability was not precluded merely because the offence imposed the sanction of imprisonment. In many cases, offences carrying reasonably severe penalties have been held to be crimes of strict liability. In *Hussain*,[25] D was convicted of unlawful possession of a firearm[26] even though he believed it was a toy used by his son. Despite the offence carrying a maximum penalty of three years' imprisonment, it was held to be one of strict liability.

One of the most serious offences created by the Sexual Offences Act 2003 is that of the crime of rape of a child under 13, which carries a maximum penalty of life imprisonment. Yet this is an offence of strict liability: it is irrelevant that D believes the child is over 13.[27] Whether strict liability for an offence as serious as this can be justified is a matter to which we shall return.

---

20 *R. v Warner* [1969] A.C. 256; Contrary to the Drugs (Prevention of Misuse) Act 1964 s.1.

21 *R. v Land (Michael)* [1999] Q.B. 65; [1998] 3 W.L.R. 322 CA and *R. v Lemon (Denis)* [1979] A.C. 617; [1979] 2 W.L.R. 281 HL; Contrary to the Protection of Children Act 1978 s.1(1)(c).

22 *Barnfather v Islington Education Authority* [2003] EWHC 418 (Admin); [2003] 1 W.L.R. 2318 at [57]. See J. Horder, "Whose Values Should Determine When Liability is Strict?" in A.P. Simester (ed), *Appraising Strict Liability* (Oxford: OUP, 2005).

23 US Model Penal Code art.6.02(4).

24 *R. v Jackson (Robert Valentine)* [2006] EWCA Crim 2380; [2007] 1 Cr. App. R. 28.

25 *R. v Hussain* (1981) 47 Cr. App. R. 143.

26 Contrary to the Firearms Act 1968 s.1.

27 *R. v G* [2008] UKHL 37; [2009] 1 A.C. 92.

(ii) Statutory context

It has been repeatedly stated that the common-law presumption of mens rea will only be displaced if there is a *necessary* implication that Parliament intended the offence to be strict. If the Act is silent as to the mens rea requirement(s), the legislature's intention to (not) impose a mens rea requirement can be implied from the scheme or context of the provision in question. **4-014**

PHARMACEUTICAL SOCIETY OF GREAT BRITAIN V STORKWAIN LTD (1986) 83 CR. APP. R. 359 (HOUSE OF LORDS):

D (a pharmacist) supplied prescription-only drugs in accordance with a forged prescription. D was charged with an offence contrary to the Medicines Act 1968 s.58(2)(a), which provides that: **4-015**

> "... no person shall sell by retail, or supply in circumstances corresponding to retail sale, a medical product of a description, or falling within a class, specified in an order under this section except in accordance with a prescription by an appropriate practitioner."

It had to be determined whether this was an offence of strict liability.

LORD GOFF OF CHIEVELEY:

> "It is, in my opinion, clear from the Act of 1968 that Parliament must have intended that the presumption of *mens rea* should be inapplicable to s.58(2) (a). First of all, it appears from the Act of 1968 that, where Parliament wished to recognize that *mens rea* should be an ingredient of an offence created by the Act, it has expressly so provided. Thus, taking first of all offences created under provisions of Part II of the Act of 1968, express requirements of *mens rea* are to be found in both s.45(2) and in s.46(1), (2) and (3) of the Act. More particularly, in relation to offences created in Part III and Parts V and VI of the Act of 1968, section 121 makes detailed provision for a requirement of *mens rea* in respect of certain specified sections of the Act, including ss.63 to 65 (which are contained in Part III), but significantly not s.58 . . . It is very difficult to avoid the conclusion that, by omitting s.58 from those sections to which s.121 is expressly made applicable, Parliament intended that there should be no implication of a requirement of *mens rea* in s.58(2) (a)."[28]

If Parliament intends to impose a mens rea requirement, it might do so by including a verb within part of the actus reus requirements; for example, "possession"[29] and "permitting"[30] have been held to imply fault in some instances. If, however, several sections of a statute allow due diligence defences (see below), but the provision under consideration omits such a defence, it will be easier to infer strict liability.[31]

---

28 See also *Sherras v De Rutzen* [1895] 1 Q.B. 918; *Neville v Mavroghenis* [1984] Crim. L.R. 42 CA; and *R. v Bradish (Liam Christopher)* [1990] 1 Q.B. 981; [1990] Crim. L.R. 723 CA.

29 *R. v Johnson (Wayne)* [2017] EWCA Crim 189; [2018] 1 W.L.R. 19.

30 *James & Son Ltd v Smee* [1955] 1 Q.B. 78 at 91; [1954] 3 W.L.R. 631.

31 K. Reid, "Strict Liability: Some Principles for Parliament" (2008) Statute L. Rev. 173, 174; see also *R. v Deyemi (Danny)* [2007] EWCA Crim 2060 at [21]; [2008] 1 Cr. App. R. 25.

(iii) Effectiveness in promoting the objectives of the statute

Lim Chin Aik v The Queen [1963] A.C. 160 (Privy Council):

4–016 D was convicted of contravening an immigration ordinance by remaining in Singapore after he had been declared a prohibited immigrant. There was no evidence that the prohibition order had been brought to his attention or that any effort had been made to do so. D appealed against conviction.

LORD EVERSHED:

> "But it is not enough in their Lordships' opinion merely to label the statute as one dealing with a grave social evil and from that to infer that strict liability was intended. It is pertinent also to inquire whether putting the defendant under strict liability will assist in the enforcement of the regulations. That means there must be something he can do, directly or indirectly, by supervision or inspection, by improvement of his business methods or by exhorting those whom he may be expected to influence or control, which will promote the observance of the regulations. Unless this is so, there is no reason in penalising him, and it cannot be inferred that the legislature imposed strict liability merely in order to find a luckless victim. Their Lordships prefer [this] to the alternative view that strict liability follows simply from the nature of the subject matter and that persons whose conduct is beyond any sort of criticism can be dealt with by the imposition of a nominal penalty.[32]
>
> Where it can be shown that the imposition of strict liability would result in the prosecution and conviction of a class of persons whose conduct could not in any way affect the observance of the law, their Lordships consider that, even where the statute is dealing with a grave social evil, strict liability is not likely to be intended. The subject-matter, the control of immigration, is not one in which the presumption of strict liability has generally been made. Nevertheless, if the courts of Singapore were of the view that unrestricted immigration is a social evil which it is the object of the Ordinance to control most rigorously, their Lordships would hesitate to disagree. That is a matter peculiarly within the cognisance of the local courts. But [counsel for the respondent] was unable to point to anything that the appellant could possibly have done so as to ensure that he complied with the regulations. It was not, for example, suggested that it would be practicable for him to make continuous inquiry to see whether an order had been made against him. Clearly one of the objects of the Ordinance is the expulsion of prohibited persons from Singapore, but there is nothing that a man can do about it if, before the commission of the offence, there is no practical or sensible way in which he can ascertain whether he is a prohibited person or not."

Appeal allowed

32 As happened in the case of *Hussain* (1981) 47 Cr. App. R. 143 where the defendant was only fined £100.

R. v MATUDI [2003] EWCA CRIM 697 (COURT OF APPEAL, CRIMINAL DIVISION):

D was convicted of importing animal products (meat from Africa) contrary to the Products of Animal Origin (Import and Export) Regulations 1996[33] regs 21 and 37. D received a consignment which he believed contained leaves and herbs; he had no idea that it contained any meat. D appealed on the ground that the offence ought to require mens rea. **4–017**

SCOTT BAKER LJ:

> "[The issue] is whether strict liability will be effective to promote the objects of the legislation. There will obviously be a temptation with some importers to by-pass the notice provisions and thus save the delay and expense involved in the consignment being diverted to a border inspection post. It seems to us that strict liability is inevitably going to make the regulation more effective . . .
>
> [T]he mischief sought to be prevented . . . is likely to be better achieved if the offence is one of strict liability."

Appeal dismissed

3. Defences to strict liability

(i) General defences

It has been explained that strict liability offences are where mens rea is not required concerning one or more elements of the actus reus. Liability is thus strict and not absolute, although courts often misleadingly use this latter term. The importance of this point is only fully realised when considering the defences available to an individual charged with a strict liability offence. If the offence were "absolute", then no defences would save D from the consequences of their actions. But, given that this is not the case, one has to consider whether D may plead (say) duress, self-defence, or automatism in answer to a charge. **4–018**

There is appellate authority that duress, by threats and circumstances, is available as a defence to a strict liability offence. This has predominantly arisen in cases involving driving offences,[34] but other jurisdictions, such as Canada, support the availability of the defence as a general proposition.[35] On this basis, self-defence would also seem to be available. Non-insane automatism is similarly available; here, the "defence" is the denial of the "voluntary act" requirement, meaning that the actus reus elements are not satisfied.[36] More controversial is the availability of insanity to a charge of a strict liability offence. In *DPP v Harper*,[37] the court held that insanity could only be a defence to crimes

---

33 Products of Animal Origin (Import and Export) Regulations 1996 (SI 1996/3124).

34 *R. v Martin (Colin)* (1989) 88 Cr. App. R. 343; (1989) 153 J.P. 231 CA and *DPP v Mullally* [2006] EWHC 3448 (Admin).

35 *Cancoil Thermal Corp v Parkinson* (1986) 27 C.C.C. (3d) 295 at 301–2.

36 *Hill v Baxter* [1958] 1 Q.B. 277; [1958] 2 W.L.R. 76.

37 *DPP v Harper* [1997] 1 W.L.R. 1406; (1997) 161 J.P. 697 QBD.

requiring mens rea and, accordingly, was not a defence to the strict liability offence of driving with excess alcohol. However, this was a misstep. Insanity is not a denial of mens rea but rather a denial of moral responsibility for the actus reus. Fortunately, this has now been rectified by the Divisional Court in *Loake v CPS*,[38] enabling insanity to be raised in response to a strict liability offence. However, as we shall see, whether strict liability offences are *ever* justifiable is a controversial matter. Recognising that all established defences are available to such offences goes a long way towards "sweetening the bitter pill" of their (perhaps necessary) existence.

(ii) Due diligence defences

4–019 In addition to general defences, there is the possibility that the offence may contain within it a specific defence. This will be based upon showing an absence of fault; these are often called "due diligence" defences. An example of such a defence is found in the Food Safety Act 1990. This statute creates several offences relating to the preparation and sale of food not complying with food safety requirements and selling food not of the nature, substance, or quality demanded. Section 21(1) creates a due diligence defence:

> "[I]t shall be a defence for the person charged to prove that he took all reasonable precautions and exercised all due diligence to avoid the commission of the offence by himself or by a person under his control."

A research study into 41 statutory instruments concerning food found that 34 of them included due diligence defences.[39] This research revealed extensive use of due diligence defences in the other main areas of regulatory crime: environmental health, trading and consumer laws and construction.

However, placing the burden on D to establish due diligence does present problems. In *Woolmington v DPP*,[40] the House of Lords declared that it was for the prosecution to establish D's liability. It was not D's responsibility to establish their innocence. The European Convention on Human Rights (ECHR) art.6(2) provides that "everyone charged with a criminal offence shall be presumed innocent until proven guilty according to law". This raises the issue of whether due diligence defences are compatible with art.6(2).

4–020 Broadly speaking, the courts have tackled this issue in the following manner. Suppose a provision imposes a legal burden of proof on D (where they must prove on the balance of probabilities that, in this context, they have exercised due diligence or reasonable care). In that case, it will be incompatible with the presumption of innocence unless the provision serves a legitimate aim and is a proportionate and justifiable response. For example, in *Matthews*,[41] D was charged with possession of a knife contrary to the Criminal Justice Act 1988 s.139 and claimed a due diligence defence under s.139(4). He claimed

---

38 *Loake v Crown Prosecution Service* [2017] EWHC 2855 (Admin); [2018] Q.B. 998.

39 A.P. Simester and P. Roberts, "Strict Liability in UK Regulation" in R. Macrory, *Regulatory Justice: Sanctioning in a Post-Hampton World* (2006), Annex E, E17.

40 *Woolmington v DPP* [1935] A.C. 462; (1935) 51 T.L.R. 446 HL.

41 *R. v Matthews (Mark Anthony)* [2003] EWCA Crim 813; [2003] 2 Cr. App. R. 19.

he had a good reason for having the article with him in a public place: to cut Lino. It was held that this reverse burden of legal proof was not incompatible with the ECHR art.6(2) because it was a justifiable and proportionate response. The reason for having a knife in a public place was something peculiarly within the knowledge of the accused; the reverse onus provision struck a fair balance between the interests of the community and the individual and went:

> ". . . no further than is necessary to accomplish Parliament's objective in protecting the public from the menace posed by persons having bladed articles in public places without good reason."[42]

However, suppose a reverse burden of proof is not regarded as a reasonable and proportionate response. In that case, the court can "read down" the provision as only placing an *evidential burden* on the defence. An evidential burden requires D to raise sufficient evidence to show that the defence could apply, but the burden remains on the prosecution to establish beyond reasonable doubt that the defence does not apply. For example, in *Lambert,*[43] D was charged with possession of a controlled drug with intent to supply, contrary to the Misuse of Drugs Act 1971 s.5(3). D raised the due diligence defence available in s.28(2) and (3) that he did not know or suspect that he was possessing controlled drugs. The House of Lords declared, obiter, that placing a legal burden on D would be incompatible with art.6(2) as being a disproportionate measure for such a serious offence. However, the majority stated that s.28(2) and (3) should be "read down" so that only an evidential burden was placed on D, and this would not be incompatible with the presumption of innocence established in art.6(2).[44] Such a "reading down" will almost always be possible,[45] but, if the provision cannot be "read down", then as a last resort under the Human Rights Act 1998 s.4, the court should declare the reverse burden incompatible with art.6(2).

The result of this approach is inevitable uncertainty. It is difficult to see why "a strong public interest in bladed articles not being carried in public" makes a due diligence defence a proportionate response. In contrast, a similar defence to possession of drugs is a disproportionate response. We shall see in the next section that, since the coming into force of the Human Rights Act 1998, the English courts have considered the status of some strict liability offences and have held that they are not, per se, incompatible with the ECHR. If such (admittedly lesser) offences without due diligence defences represent a proportionate response to a problem, it would be odd to hold that affording a due diligence defence with a reverse burden of legal proof (admittedly for more serious offences) could be incompatible with the ECHR. We shall shortly examine the many objections to offences of strict liability. As a response to these problems, courts in some Commonwealth countries, such as Canada, have declared that all strict liability offences should presumptively be construed as incorporating due diligence defences.[46] The Law Commission of England and Wales has also consulted on whether courts

42 A similar approach was adopted in *R. v Johnstone (Robert Alexander)* [2003] UKHL 28; [2003] 2 Cr. App. R. 33.

43 *R. v Lambert* [2001] 2 Cr. App. R. 511.

44 A similar approach was approved in *R. v DPP Ex p. Kebeline* [2000] 2 A.C. 326; [2000] 1 Cr. App. R. 275 HL and applied in *Sheldrake v DPP* [2004] UKHL 43; [2005] 1 A.C. 264.

45 I. Dennis, "Reverse Onuses and the Presumption of Innocence: In Search of Principle" [2005] Crim. L.R. 901.

46 *R. v City of Sault Ste Marie* (1978) 85 D.L.R. (3d) 161.

should be given the power to apply a due diligence defence to any statutory offence not requiring fault.[47]

4. Strict liability and the European Convention on Human Rights (ECHR)

4-021 As seen above, in certain circumstances, strict liability offences with reverse burdens of proof could be incompatible with the ECHR art.6(2). There is, however, a further argument that some strict liability offences could, in dispensing with any fault element, contravene other articles of the ECHR. The English courts have not adopted this approach.[48]

R. v Muhamad [2003] 2 W.L.R. 1050 (Court of Appeal, Criminal Division):

4-022 D was convicted of materially contributing to the extent of his insolvency by gambling, contrary to the Insolvency Act 1986 s.362(1)(a).

DYSON LJ:

"[It is argued that Article 7 of the ECHR] requires the criminal law to be sufficiently accessible and precise to enable an individual to know in advance whether his conduct is criminal. No gambler can necessarily know, when he places his bet, whether he runs a real risk of prosecution if he loses. The only way to avoid running this risk is not to gamble at all, or to gamble for low stakes. Without *mens rea* the offence is objectionably uncertain. Furthermore, a construction of strict liability is neither necessary in a democratic society, nor proportional to any legitimate aim . . .

[T]he narrow question that arises is whether the fact that the offence is one of strict liability is disproportionate so as to render it in breach of Article 7. We accept that a strict liability offence is easier to prove than one requiring a mental element, and that, if section 362(1)(a) is interpreted as creating an offence of strict liability, it may deter persons from gambling who, if the offence required a mental element, might not be so deterred. We do not consider that either of these consequences indicates that it is disproportionate to hold that the section creates an offence of strict liability. [I]f strict liability does have a chilling effect on gambling, we are not convinced that the imposition of strict liability is a disproportionate response to the need, in the public interest, to deter persons from gambling in such a way as to cause loss to their creditors.

We should add that, so far as concerns the ECHR, there is nothing objectionable in principle with strict liability offences. In *Salabiaku v France* 13 E.H.R.R. 379 at [27] the ECtHR said:

---

47 Law Commission Consultation Paper No.195, *Criminal Liability in Regulatory Contexts* (2010), para.1.68. The paper considers whether the test of due diligence should be less strict than is currently formulated (paras 1.78–1.79).

48 See generally, G.R. Sullivan, "Strict Liability for Criminal Offences in England and Wales Following Incorporation into English Law of the European Convention on Human Rights" in Simester (ed), *Appraising Strict Liability* (2005).

'27. As the Government and the Commission have pointed out, in principle the Contracting States remain free to apply the criminal law to an act where it is not carried out in the normal exercise of one of the rights protected under the Convention and, accordingly, to define the constituent elements of the resulting offence. In particular, and again in principle, the Contracting States may, *under certain conditions*, penalise a simple or objective fact as such, irrespective of whether it results from criminal intent or from negligence. Examples of such offences may be found in the laws of the Contracting States.'

In our judgment, therefore, there is nothing in the ECHR and in particular in Article 7 which requires us to reach a different conclusion from that which we expressed earlier on the basis of an application of domestic law principles. Upon its true construction, section 362(1)(a) creates an offence of strict liability." (Emphasis added)

In *Barnfather,* it was held that these "certain conditions" (emphasised above) related to procedural matters (such as reverse burdens of proof) and did not apply to the substantive elements of an offence. It was held that art.6(2) does not impose any restrictions on the right of Parliament to create strict liability offences.[49] In *G*, Lord Hope stated that these "certain conditions" simply referred to the fact that a strict liability offence *could* be incompatible with other articles of the Convention.[50] The ironic result (conceded in *Barnfather*) is that: **4–023**

". . . a state's laws are subject to fuller review when they include a defence which places a burden on the defence than they are when no defence at all is conferred."[51]

In *G*, it was held that the strict liability offence of rape of a child under 13[52] was not incompatible with art.6.2 (presumption of innocence) or with art.8 (right to respect for privacy and family life) of the ECHR.

R. v G [2009] 1 A.C. 92 (House of Lords):

D, aged 15, had consensual sexual intercourse with a 12-year-old girl. He believed she was 15. He was convicted of rape of a child under 13 contrary to the Sexual Offences Act 2003 s.5 and appealed. **4–024**

LORD HOFFMANN:

"[3] . . . [T]he offence is one of strict liability and it is no defence that the accused believed the other person to be 13 or over.

49 *Barnfather* [2003] 1 W.L.R. 2318.

50 *R. v G* [2009] 1 A.C. 92 at [28]. Lord Hoffmann recommended that *Salabiaku v France (A/141-A)* (1991) 13 E.H.R.R. 379 should in future be "ignored" (at [6]).

51 *Barnfather* [2003] 1 W.L.R. 2318 at [45].

52 Contrary to the Sexual Offences Act 2003 s.5.

> [4] Article 6(1) guarantees fair procedure but not that either the civil or criminal law will have any particular substantive content . . . Likewise, article 6(2) requires him to be presumed innocent of the offence but does not say anything about what the mental or other elements of the offence should be. In *R. v G* [2003] 1 Cr App R 343, para 33 Dyson LJ said:
>
> > 'The position is quite clear. So far as article 6 is concerned, the fairness of the provisions of the substantive law of the contracting states is not a matter for investigation. The content and interpretation of domestic substantive law is not engaged by article 6.'
>
> [7] The other ground of appeal is that the conviction violated the defendant's right of privacy under article 8 . . .
>
> [10] Prosecutorial policy and sentencing do not fall under article 8. If the offence in question is a justifiable interference with private life, that is an end of the matter. If the prosecution has been unduly heavy handed, that may be unfair and unjust, but not an infringement of human rights."
>
> BARONESS HALE:
>
> "[54] In effect, therefore, the real complaint is that the defendant has been convicted of an offence bearing the label 'rape'. Parliament has very recently decided that this is the correct label to apply to this activity. In my view this does not engage the article 8 rights of the defendant at all, but if it does, it is entirely justified. The concept of private life 'covers the physical and moral integrity of the person, including his or her sexual life': *X and Y v The Netherlands* 8 EHRR 235, para 22. This does not mean that every sexual relationship, however brief or unsymmetrical, is worthy of respect, nor is every sexual act which a person wishes to perform. It does mean that the physical and moral integrity of the complainant, vulnerable by reason of her age if nothing else, was worthy of respect."
>
> *Appeal dismissed*[53]

4–025 The one area where the ECHR can have an impact is in relation to sentencing for strict liability offences. In *International Transport Roth GmbH*,[54] it was stated that to be compatible with art.6(1), there needed to be an investigation into D's culpability at the sentencing stage to ensure that a punitive response is proportionate to the offending. In *G*, D had been sentenced to a 12-month detention and training order. The Court of Appeal reduced this to a conditional discharge for 12 months; he had already spent five months in custody. Baroness Hale and Lord Mance stated that this final sentence was rational and

---

53 An application by G to the ECtHR was declared inadmissible on similar reasoning to that of the House of Lords: *G v United Kingdom (Admissibility)* (37334/08) [2012] Crim. L.R. 46; (2011) 53 E.H.R.R. SE25. See A. Ashworth, "Human Rights: Presumption of Innocence, art.6(2)" [2012] Crim L.R. 47. For a recent application of *G* see *R. v Brown (Richard)* [2013] UKSC 43; [2013] N.I. 265.

54 *International Transport Roth GmbH v Secretary of State for the Home Department* [2002] EWCA Civ 158; [2002] 3 W.L.R. 344.

proportional, impliedly suggesting that the original sentence imposed might have been incompatible with the Convention.

5. Are strict liability offences justifiable?

The Law Commission has stated: **4–026**

> "The criminal law should only be employed to deal with wrongdoers who deserve the stigma associated with criminal conviction because they have engaged in seriously reprehensible conduct. It should not be used as the primary means of promoting regulatory objectives."[55]

Given this strong statement of principle, possible justifications for the imposition of strict liability require close scrutiny, starting with the general purposes of punishment.

Herbert L. Packer, "Mens Rea and the Supreme Court" (1962) Sup. Ct. Rev. 107, 109:

> "To punish conduct without reference to the actor's state of mind is both inefficacious and unjust. It is inefficacious because conduct unaccompanied by an awareness of the factors making it criminal does not mark the actor as one who needs to be subjected to punishment in order to deter him or others from behaving similarly in the future, nor does it single him out as a socially dangerous individual who needs to be incapacitated or reformed. It is unjust because the actor is subjected to the stigma of a criminal conviction without being morally blameworthy." **4–027**

From this, two major questions emerge. **4–028**

(i) Can strict liability be justified on utilitarian or instrumental grounds?
(ii) Is strict liability a morally justifiable doctrine?

(i) The utilitarian and instrumental arguments

In favour of strict liability, it is claimed that the interests of the public require that the highest possible standards of care be exercised by people engaged in certain forms of conduct and that "strict liability can reduce the risks of harm to private and public interests".[56] Expressed in utilitarian terms, the greater good to be achieved by occasionally convicting someone who may have taken all reasonable care to abide by the law could not be achieved to the same extent if, for example, the defence of reasonable mistake were available. **4–029**

---

55 Law Commission Consultation Paper No.195, *Criminal Liability in Regulatory Contexts* (2010), para.1.28.
56 G. Lamond, "What is a Crime?" (2007) 27 O.J.L.S. 609, 630.

R. Macrory, Regulatory Justice: Sanctioning in a Post-Hampton World (2006), paras D4–D8:

4-030 "D4 A core argument in favour of the use of strict liability offences is that it improves deterrence . . . This is likely to be especially important where the non-compliance involves technical and managerial complexities of which only the regulated body, rather than the regulator, has full knowledge.

D5 Prosecution of legitimate businesses should generally be a matter of last resort after other sanctioning tools have failed or where the offence is serious enough to warrant a prosecution in the first instance. However, without the existence of criminal offences which are reasonably easy to prove, the regulator's power to advise and warn regulated business would be seriously jeopardised: 'Routine enforcement is conducted against a background of the criminal law and the implied threat of invocation . . .'

D6 Strict liability offences are also an important tool in securing convictions of corporate entities . . .

D7 Strict liability for regulatory offences can also be justified on the grounds that business operating in regulatory areas can be said to implicitly accept the risk of criminal liability even where no intention or recklessness is involved . . . Strict liability encourages companies not just to do what they can reasonably be capable of, but to do everything possible to comply. Further, it may be consistent with a public view that regulatory breaches causing serious damage (such as a major pollution incident, or death or serious injury in the workplace or elsewhere) are truly criminal in their own right, whatever the state of mind of the perpetrator.

D8 Finally, in practice, any perceived injustices from strict criminal liability is tempered by the fact that 'fault creeps back in during the various stages of the enforcement process'. Prosecution bodies have discretion whether or not to prosecute in a particular case, and are more likely to prosecute where in their view there is some element of fault. Courts have discretion in the sentence they impose, and lack of intention or recklessness can be presented by the offender in mitigation."

4-031 Opponents of strict liability have argued that there is no evidence that a higher standard of care results from the imposition of strict liability. Those engaged in activities will only do what is *reasonable* to prevent harm. Indeed, some have argued that strict liability may operate as a disincentive to do even this. If operators know that prosecution could follow irrespective of their precautions, they may be tempted to take none whatsoever. In other words, D may as well be "hanged for a sheep as for a lamb".[57] Such an attitude scarcely increases respect for the law. There may be further harmful effects: the innocent may be made to feel insecure not only in general psychological terms but to the extent that they may be deterred from entering into socially beneficial enterprises governed by strict liability.[58]

---

57 P. Brett, *An Inquiry into Criminal Guilt* (Sydney: Law Book Co of Australia, 1963), p.8.
58 R.B. Brandt, *Ethical Theory* (Englewood Cliffs: Prentice-Hall, 1959), p.493.

James B. Brady, "Strict Liability Offences: A Justification" (1972) 8 Crim. L. Bulletin 217, 224:

"There are two replies to this argument. First, there is little evidence to show that the effect of strict liability offences has been to make these socially beneficial enterprises less attractive. The second, and more important point is that a person who does not have the capacity to run (for example) a dairy in such a manner as to prevent the adulteration of milk is not to be protected on the sole ground that he is engaged in a 'socially beneficial' enterprise. An incompetent carrying on an enterprise in which there is the danger of widespread harm actually is not engaged in a 'socially beneficial' enterprise. There can be no objection, therefore, to his choosing not to enter the business." **4–032**

In addition to the arguments above, a further instrumental argument may be adduced. Owing to the sheer volume of criminal offences, particularly those of a regulatory nature, it is argued that requiring the prosecution to prove a mental element would be too time-consuming. **4–033**

A.P. Simester, "Is Strict Liability Always Wrong?" in A.P. Simester (ed), Appraising Strict Liability (2005), p.26:

"From an administrative perspective, the costs involved before and during trial are likely to be considerably decreased if [the activity] is made a criminal offence, since the number of elements required to be proved at trial, and the number of potential issues, is reduced. This consideration matters because criminal justice is very expensive. It is plausible that, if every one of a nation's offences required proof of *mens rea* with respect to all elements of the *actus reus*, administration of the criminal law would not be merely cumbersome but unaffordable . . . If it is impossible fully to protect victims from harm while maintaining a Rolls-Royce system of criminal justice, the conflicting interests of defendants and victims may be mediated, in part, by simplifying the *mens rea* elements of certain offences . . . The state should consider *which* offences to 'skimp' on. If the choice is either cutting corners or abandoning the prohibition altogether, a pared-down regulation (say, with reduced sanctions attached) may well be preferable." **4–034**

Supporters of the expediency argument sometimes temper their support by claiming that prosecutorial discretion will prevent the obviously blameless being charged. There are, however, significant challenges with this approach. Prosecutorial discretion is notoriously unreliable; there is no guidance on how extreme the case must be to justify a prosecution. Most importantly, it amounts to a negation of strict liability. To some extent, at least, liability is being made to depend upon fault. We shall return to this point later. **4–035**

(ii) Is strict liability morally justifiable?

It has already been noted that the concept of mens rea is deeply embedded in the development of the **4–036**
criminal law. For many commentators, its importance is so great that utilitarian considerations cannot

trump it. According to this view, the criminal law should only be invoked when D has done something *deserving* of blame. Somebody who has taken all reasonable precautions is not blameworthy (negligent) and does not deserve to be punished. Labelling a blameless person as a criminal "amounts to systematic moral defamation by the state".[59]

The classic response to this argument is that while these views might be true of stigmatic crimes, most offences of strict liability are not "real" crimes but are "quasi-criminal" offences.[60] Simester has argued that sometimes "strict liability may be legitimate in non-stigmatic offences".[61] In *Wings Ltd v Ellis,* Lord Scarman referred to the Trade Descriptions Act 1968, which creates consumer protection offences, as being "not a truly criminal statute. Its purpose is not the enforcement of the criminal law but the maintenance of trading standards".[62]

The distinction drawn between "real" and "quasi-criminal" crimes or between stigmatic and non-stigmatic crimes (sometimes known as crimes *mala in se* and *mala prohibita*) is, however, problematic. How can one determine whether a crime is stigmatic or not? Is it based on whether the convicted person feels stigmatised (psychological stigma) or on whether such a person ought to feel stigmatised (normative stigma)?[63] Referring to the offence under the Insolvency Act 1986 in *Muhamad*, extracted above, Stanton-Ife asks:

> "How is it that stigma gets attached to criminal convictions on his Lordship's view? Does he mean the population at large or the business community or some other group does not *believe* this behaviour to be stigmatic or that it is not *deserving* of stigma, whatever any group of people may think about the matter?" (emphasis in original)[64]

4–037 Baroness Wootton argued that the distinction between *mala in se* and *mala prohibita* does not rest on any inherent characteristics of the former category other than the antiquity of such crimes.[65] Particularly once one steps beyond offences that are part of a regulatory scheme, it becomes far from obvious that a clear line can be drawn between truly criminal and quasi-criminal offences. Even with regulatory offences, there are problems with making them offences of strict liability because this "marginalises" such offences; nobody, least of all the perpetrator, has to take them seriously because, after all, they are not really criminal.

6. Enforcement and sentencing

4–038 One of the classic arguments against strict liability is that it results in the prosecution and conviction of people who were not at fault and who might even have done everything they possibly could to avoid

59 A.P. Simester, "Is Strict Liability Always Wrong?" in Simester (ed), *Appraising Strict Liability* (2005), p.34.

60 For a more nuanced argument that strict liability may be legitimate in the grading of offences, see, K.W. Simons, "Is Strict Liability in the Grading of Offences Consistent With Retributive Desert?" (2012) 32 O.J.L.S. 445.

61 Simester, "Is Strict Liability Always Wrong?" in Simester (ed), *Appraising Strict Liability* (2005), p.21.

62 *Wings v Ellis* [1985] A.C. 272; [1984] 3 All E.R. 577 at 587 HL.

63 J. Stanton-Ife, "Strict Liability: Stigma and Regret" (2007) 27 O.J.L.S 151.

64 Stanton-Ife, "Strict Liability: Stigma and Regret" (2007) 27 O.J.L.S 151, 158.

65 B. Wootton, *Crime and the Criminal Law*, 2nd edn (London: Stevens and Son, 1981), pp.42–44.

bringing about the harm. However, empirical studies of the enforcement of many strict liability offences do not always support this conclusion.

Storkwain[66] provides an interesting case study. In this case, the D company were found guilty of the strict liability offence of supplying prescription-only drugs without a valid prescription; it had been forged. At first sight, it seems that D could not be blamed for what had happened. How, in a busy chemist, could checks be made on the validity of every prescription? Yet closer examination of the case reveals that the Pharmaceutical Society (the regulatory body) believed the pharmacist's conduct fell short of normal good practice (amounting to negligence). The prescription was a blatant forgery. Moreover, because the prescription was for controlled drugs, it was expected that the pharmacist would telephone for confirmation. D did so, but rather than checking in the directory, he called the number given on the prescription. Unsurprisingly, an accomplice confirmed the forgery. The pharmacist was prosecuted because he was at fault; even a due diligence defence, had one existed, would not have saved him.[67]

Empirical studies of many strict liability offences also point to highly selective enforcement practices amongst different enforcement agencies.[68] Fault appears to play an important role in the decision to prosecute (although the magnitude of the harm is also significant). However, compliance is typically secured through cooperation rather than coercion, and the inspectors' self-image is that of educators and advisers rather than police; advice, repeat visits, warnings, improvement notices, and the like are more likely to secure compliance. In 2022/23, the Health and Safety Executive commenced 216 prosecutions, yet, in contrast, issued over 8,000 enforcement notices.[69] The emphasis is on administrative procedures, with the criminal law being a remedy of last resort.[70]

Sentences for strict liability offences (particularly white-collar crimes) are generally light. This may be because D is regarded as less blameworthy than for "real" crimes or may even be seen as blameless. On the other hand, there may be a number of other factors having little to do with blame or the amount of harm caused that influence such sentencing practices. The fact that D has lost their job or business may be seen as punishment enough. The level of fine may be affected by the sentencer's perception of D's ability to pay.[71] D's previous good character may be persuasive but likely to figure is, once again, the judgement that such offences are not really criminal. The result is that the fines imposed may be no more than "pin-pricks" to an organisation which may be able to write them off as a minor business expense.[72]

The Sentencing Council has sought to enhance uniformity in sentencing and, as with other offences, has taken a methodical approach in determining sentence ranges dependent on a combination of

66 *Pharmaceutical Society of Great Britain v Storkwain Ltd* [1986] 1 W.L.R. 903; (1986) 83 Cr. App. R. 359 HL. See para.4–015.

67 B.S. Jackson, "Storkwain: A Case Study in Strict Liability and Self-Regulation" [1991] Crim. L.R. 892.

68 I. Paulus, *The Search for Pure Food: A Sociology of Legislation in Britain* (Littleton: Fred B. Rothman & Co, 1974); W.F. Carson, "White-Collar Crime and the Enforcement of Factory Legislation" (1970) 10 Brit. J. Criminol. 383.

69 HSE, *Health and Safety Executive: Annual Report and Accounts 2022/23* (HC 1599), *https://www.gov.uk/government/publications/the-health-and-safety-executive-annual-report-and-accounts-2022-to-2023*.

70 See generally, K. Hawkins, *Law as Last Resort* (New York: OUP, 2002).

71 N. Padfield, "Clean Water and Muddy Causation: Is Causation a Question of Law or Fact, or Just a Way of Allocating Blame?" [1995] Crim. L.R. 683, 693.

72 H. Croall, *White Collar Crime* (Berkshire: McGraw-Hill Education, 1992), pp.112–125.

culpability and harm. In relation to environmental offences, for example, culpability is measured in four bands: deliberate, reckless, negligent, and no or low culpability. "Deliberate", however, does not include only deliberate pollution, but also, "flagrant disregard" of the law.[73]

7. Conclusion

4-039 Despite the weight of the arguments against strict liability offences, it would be naïve to imagine that they can all be transformed into offences requiring full mens rea or that they could all be decriminalised. It seems clear that there is a cogent argument in favour of strict liability for the most minor of offences. However, for the rest, several possibilities exist.

First, it is open to the courts to extend the presumption in favour of mens rea.[74] One important enhancement, copied from Canada, would be to state that if the penalty for the offence involves imprisonment, then strict liability is precluded.[75]

Secondly, again following the lead set elsewhere,[76] and as recommended in the Law Commission's consultation paper,[77] existing offences of strict liability could be converted into what would amount to offences of negligence by the general, rather than selective, use of due diligence defences. This would not have the effect of making the prosecutor's task too difficult because the onus would be on D to show that they were not negligent. However, as seen, it is possible that such a general shifting of the burden of proof could be incompatible with the ECHR.

Thirdly, increased use of administrative procedures and civil sanctions could be made to secure compliance. In 2006, the Government commissioned the *Macrory Report* to examine regulatory sanctions.[78] This Report proposed that much regulatory non-compliance should be dealt with by administrative remedies outside of the criminal justice system. These recommendations have been given effect by the Regulatory Enforcement and Sanctions Act 2008, permitting Ministers to introduce statutory instruments providing civil sanctions to a wide range of strict liability offences contained in a long list of statutes: for example, the Control of Pollution Act 1974, the Dangerous Dogs Act 1991, the Fireworks Act 2003, the Food Safety Act 1990 and the Medicines Act 1968.[79]

In these cases, where a Regulator (e.g. the Environment Agency, the Food Standards Agency, the Health and Safety Executive, the Financial Conduct Authority[80]) is satisfied beyond reasonable doubt

---

73 See, e.g. the sentencing guidelines for the offence under the Environment Protection Act 1990 s.33, *https://www.sentencingcouncil.org.uk/offences/magistrates-court/item/individuals-unauthorised-or-harmful-deposit-treatment-or-disposal-etc-of-waste-illegal-discharges-to-air-land-and-water.*

74 Under the Draft Criminal Code cl.20, there is a presumption in favour of mens rea "unless otherwise provided" (Law Commission Paper No.177, *A Criminal Code for England and Wales* (1989)).

75 See A. Ashworth, "Editorial: Trumping Strict Liability" [1987] Crim. L.R. 721, 721–723.

76 e.g. see the American Law Institute, Model Penal Code, Tent. Draft No.4, 1985 s.2.05 and comment at p.140.

77 Law Commission Consultation Paper No.195, *Criminal Liability in Regulatory Contexts* (2010), para.1.68.

78 *Regulatory Justice: Making Sanctions Effective* (Final Report, 2006) (Macrory Report). See also, Law Commission Consultation Paper No.195, *Criminal Liability in Regulatory Contexts* (2010), paras 3.21–3.51.

79 In all, 135 statutes are listed. These civil sanctions can also be applied to a further 44 statutes under which Ministers have power by statutory instrument to create criminal offences. See Regulatory Enforcement and Sanctions Act 2008 s.62, Sch.6 and Sch.7.

80 Regulatory Enforcement and Sanctions Act 2008 Sch.5 lists 26 designated regulators.

that a person has committed one of the specified offences, instead of a criminal prosecution, the Regulator may impose one of the following civil sanctions:

(1) fixed monetary penalty[81]: usually capped at £5,000[82];
(2) discretionary requirements.[83] The Regulator may impose one or more of the following:
    - a variable monetary penalty;
    - a compliance notice; and
    - a restoration notice.
(3) stop notices[84] (preventing a person from carrying on an activity until specified steps have been taken);
(4) enforcement undertakings[85] (an undertaking to take specified corrective action).

In all these cases, there is a right of appeal to a tribunal, but not a court of law.[86] Provision may be made for the Regulator to recover monetary penalties either as a civil debt or, on a court order, as if payable under a court order.[87]

Under these provisions, the criminal process and criminal courts will be bypassed, although a breach of any of the orders could ultimately result in judicial sanctions. These provisions do not involve any decriminalisation of existing offences. A criminal prosecution remains an option. As we have seen, those enforcement agencies already involved in such procedures rely upon the stick of the criminal sanction as their last resort.

The increase of civil sanctions can have twin benefits. It can close the "compliance gap, where some regulators lack the appropriate enforcement tools to address regulatory non-compliance".[88] Also, bypassing the criminal process, civil sanctions will not carry the same stigma as a criminal conviction. This might lessen the objections to such strict liability offences. However, some caution is necessary here as this bypassing of the criminal process could result in a loss of the protection offered by the criminal justice system, for example, in relation to the burden of proof. **4–040**

Many of the provisions in the Regulatory Enforcement and Sanctions Act 2008 are aimed at corporate non-compliance with regulatory laws (but are not limited to such cases). Perhaps this differentiation between individual and corporate responsibility should be extended. Many, if not most, strict liability offences govern the operations not of individuals but of businesses. Those who object to strict liability when applied to individuals might be prepared to support its use for corporations, especially if a broader range of sentencing options were introduced. It is to this and related matters that we now turn.

---

81 Regulatory Enforcement and Sanctions Act 2008 s.39.
82 Ministry of Justice, *Guidance on Creating New Regulatory Penalties and Offences* (2009), para.11.
83 Regulatory Enforcement and Sanctions Act 2008 s.42.
84 Regulatory Enforcement and Sanctions Act 2008 s.46.
85 Regulatory Enforcement and Sanctions Act 2008 s.50.
86 Regulatory Enforcement and Sanctions Act 2008 s.54.
87 Regulatory Enforcement and Sanctions Act 2008 s.52(2).
88 Ministry of Justice, *Guidance on Creating New Regulatory Penalties and Offences* (2009), para.3.

II. Corporate Criminal Liability

A. INTRODUCTION

4-041 The criminal law has developed principally as a mechanism for responding to *individual* wrongdoing. Individuals are regarded as autonomous; they are free to control their actions, to think and make decisions, including the choice to do wrong. Accordingly, such persons can be held responsible for those choices and can be praised or blamed and punished for them. This individualistic notion of responsibility does not naturally encompass artificial organisations such as companies.

Much of our lives today is affected by companies and other organisations: we work for them (in conditions that might be dangerous); we purchase their products (that might explode or poison us); we travel in their ferries and trains (that might be unsafe); we drink the water they provide (which might be unclean); and we breathe the air (into which they might have emitted their fumes). In short, companies can destroy our environment or kill or injure us, but can they be held criminally responsible?

A company is a legal entity. It has a legal personality. It can sue and be sued in its own name, and, as seen in the previous section on strict liability where there are many D companies, it can be held criminally liable.[89] In principle, there is no reason why a company should not be capable of committing any criminal offence, subject to two exceptions. First, it is unlikely that a company could commit crimes that necessarily involve human action, such as sexual offences.[90] Secondly, as the only criminal penalty that can be imposed on a company in English law is a fine (apart from remedial orders and publicity orders), a company cannot be convicted of murder as this carries a mandatory sentence of life imprisonment.

4-042 Companies have long been held liable for a wide array of offences, such as pollution and financial irregularity offences, and cases where company activity has led to the death or injury of workers or members of the public have led to a change in approach in corporate liability. Two sets of developments heightened the interest in this subject. First, there were a series of highly publicised "disasters" in which large numbers of persons were killed. In 1988, there was the Piper Alpha oil rig explosion in which 167 people were killed. The inquiry which followed identified "unsafe practices", "grave shortcomings" and "significant flaws" in the management's approach to safety as causes of the

---

89 A partnership can be criminally liable as a separate entity from the partners if there are partnership assets available to meet any penalty imposed: *R. v W Stevenson & Sons (A Partnership)* [2008] EWCA Crim 273; [2008] Bus. L.R. 1200.

90 *R. v P&O European Ferries (Dover) Ltd* (1991) 93 Cr. App. R. 72 at 73; [1991] Crim. L.R. 695. In *Richmond upon Thames LBC v Pinn & Wheeler Ltd, The Times,* 14 February 1989, it was held that a company could not be convicted of an offence of driving a lorry without a permit. The act of driving was a physical act which could only be performed by a natural person. In *R. v Robert Millar (Contractors) Ltd* [1970] 2 Q.B. 54; [1970] 2 W.L.R. 541 CA, a company was convicted of causing death by dangerous driving. This was, however, on the basis that the company had counselled and procured the offence. In *Kosar v Bank of Scotland Plc (t/a Halifax)* [2011] EWHC 1050 (Admin); [2011] B.C.C. 500, it was held that it would be possible for a corporation to commit the offence of harassment. In a private prosecution, a bank was accused of committing the offence of harassment under the Protection from Harassment Act 1997 s.2. The District Judge ordered the case to be dropped, on the basis that the offence could only be committed by a person who is an individual. Section 7(5) of the Act states: "references to a person, in the context of the harassment of a person, are references to a person who is an individual." The appellant argued this applied only to *victims* not to perpetrators. The High Court agreed, interpreting Parliament's intention as being that the body corporate could be a perpetrator but not a victim of this offence.

explosion and subsequent deaths.[91] In 1987, there was the King's Cross fire in which 31 people died and 60 people injured; the cause was the failure of the various groups and individuals within the overall corporate structure to identify their respective areas of responsibility.[92] And, most infamously, in 1987, there was the Zeebrugge "disaster" in which the ferry, *Herald of Free Enterprise*, capsized, killing 192 people. The official inquiry found that:

> "... from top to bottom the body corporate was infected with the disease of sloppiness ... The failure on the part of the shore management to give proper and clear directions was a contributory cause of the disaster."[93]

Furthermore, there was a series of high-profile train crashes (Southall: seven killed and 151 injured; Paddington: 31 killed and over 400 injured; Hatfield: four killed and 102 injured) accompanied by mounting accusations of incompetence and complacency and poor safety management by the rail companies concerned.[94] There has been strong condemnation of deaths caused in hospitals: in 2006, it was revealed that 33 people had died from *C Difficile* bacterium over the previous two years at Stoke Mandeville Hospital. Over the same period, this bacterium directly caused the deaths of 90 people and contributed to the deaths of a further 345 people at two Kent hospitals. In both cases, a Healthcare Commission Report revealed "serious failings" by senior managers.[95]

Secondly, there has been an increased awareness of the number of persons annually being killed and seriously injured in their places of work. In 2022/23, 135 people were killed at work. Over the same year, an estimated 0.6 million workers self-reported as having sustained injuries, whilst employers only reported 60,645 non-fatal injuries to employees.[96] **4–043**

Many of these incidents will have been the result of corporate fault. The Health and Safety Executive (HSE) itself has publicly stated in the past that 90% of deaths could have been prevented and that "in 70 per cent of cases positive action by management could have saved lives".[97]

Publicity of these "disasters" and other work-related fatality cases has had a profound effect on "transmitting messages about risk to the wider population".[98] The result of these two developments

---

91 Department of Energy, *The Public Inquiry into the Piper Alpha Disaster* (The Cullen Report) (1990) Cmnd.1310, paras 11.4, 11.14, 14.52.

92 *Investigation into the Kings Cross Underground Fire* (1988) (Fennell Report).

93 Department of Transport, *The Merchant Shipping Act 1894, MV Herald of Free Enterprise*, Report of Court No.8074 (Sheen Report), para.14.1.

94 e.g. the Cullen Report on the Paddington (Ladbroke Grove) train crash accused Railtrack of complacency and "underlying deficiencies in the management of safety" (*Ladbroke Grove Rail Enquiry* (Cullen Report), 2001). Other "disasters" that have contributed to the growing clamour for corporate accountability have included the Clapham Junction rail disaster in 1988 where faulty signalling caused the death of 35 people, the Purley train crash in 1989 where five people were killed and there were strong claims that British Rail management shortcomings had contributed to the crash.

95 Healthcare Commission, *Investigation into Outbreaks of Clostridium Difficile at Stoke Mandeville Hospital, Buckinghamshire Hospitals NHS Trust* (2006); Healthcare Commission, *Investigation into Outbreak of Clostridium Difficile at Maidstone and Tunbridge Wells NHS Trust* (2007).

96 Health and Safety Executive, *Health and Safety at Work: summary statistics for Great Britain 2022/23, https://www.hse.gov.uk/statistics/overview.htm.*

97 Health and Safety Executive, *Blackspot Construction* (1988), p.4. See also, Health and Safety Executive, *The Role of Managerial Leadership in Determining Workplace Safety Outcomes* (2003).

98 P. Almond, "Regulating Crisis: Evaluating the Potential Legitimizing Effects of 'Corporate Manslaughter' Cases" (2007) 29 *Law and Policy* 285, 291–293.

was mounting pressure for the introduction of laws to make it easier to hold corporations accountable in such cases. This pressure led to the enactment of the Corporate Manslaughter and Corporate Homicide Act 2007 for cases where people have been killed through corporate gross negligence. This statute will be considered towards the end of this section, but first, more general issues concerning corporate criminal liability and its application to other offences must be considered.

B. CORPORATE OR PERSONAL CRIMINAL LIABILITY

4–044 A central question is whether the criminal law should hold *corporations* accountable or seek to punish the culpable *individuals* within the company. The argument in favour of only prosecuting individuals is that it is they who are blameworthy and deserve punishment. In some cases, an individual manager, to secure promotion, for example, might implement a policy with short-term rewards that are contrary to the company's long-term interests. In such cases, the company does not deserve blame and punishment. Furthermore, it is argued that individuals within a company are the ones most amenable to deterrence. To deter the company itself, fines would need to be significant. A company is only likely to be deterred if its expected costs exceed its expected gains. Suppose a company anticipates making £10 million from a criminal act, and the risk of apprehension is 20%. In that case, it has been argued that the fine would need to be at least £50 million to be an effective deterrent.[99] There is a further problem here with the "deterrence trap": this is where the risk of apprehension is so low that no penalty will operate as a deterrent.[100] In terms of incapacitation and rehabilitation, it could be said that it is culpable individuals who should be removed from office, disciplined, or made to improve their work practices.

Finally, it is argued that punishing a company with a fine amounts to punishing innocent shareholders, creditors, employees who might be made redundant, or the public, who will ultimately have to bear the burden of the fine. In short, the ones who will suffer will be those the law aims to protect. On the other hand, the case in favour of corporate criminal liability is formidable.

Brent Fisse and John Braithwaite, "The Allocation of Responsibility for Corporate Crime: Individualism, Collectivism and Accountability" (1988) 11 Sydney L. Rev. 468, 479–508:

4–045 "In the case of organisations, individuals may be the most important parts, but there are other parts, as is evident from factories with manifest routines which operate to some extent independently of the biological agents who flick the switches. Organisations are systems . . . not just aggregations of individuals . . . Indeed, the entire personnel of an organisation may change without reshaping the corporate culture; this may be so even if the new incumbents have personalities quite different from those of the old . . . The fact is that organisations are blamed in

99 J.C. Coffee, "'No Soul to Damn: No Body to Kick': An Unscandalised Inquiry into the Problem of Corporate Punishment" (1981) 79 Mich. L. Rev. 386, 389 drawing on the work of R.A. Posner, *Economic Analysis of Law*, 2nd edn (Boston: Little, Brown, 1977), p.167.

100 Coffee, "'No Soul to Damn: No Body to Kick': An Unscandalised Inquiry into the Problem of Corporate Punishment" (1981) 79 Mich. L. Rev. 386, 390.

their capacity as organisations for causing harm or taking risks in circumstances where they could have acted otherwise. We often react to corporate offenders not merely as impersonal harm-producing forces but as responsible, blameworthy entities. When people blame corporations they . . . [are not] pointing the finger at individuals behind the corporate mantle. They are condemning the fact that the organisation either implemented a policy of non-compliance or failed to exercise its collective capacity to avoid the offence for which blame attaches . . . We routinely hold organisations responsible for a decision when and because that decision instantiates an organisational policy and instantiates an organisational decision-making process which the organisation has chosen for itself . . .

Punishment directed at a corporate entity typically seeks to deter a wide range of individual associates from engaging in conduct directly or indirectly connected with the commission of an offence. Individual persons who are directly implicated in offences may be difficult or impossible to prosecute successfully, and those who influence the commission of offences indirectly may fall outside the scope of liability for complicity or other ancillary heads of criminal liability . . . Companies value a good reputation for its own sake, just as do universities, sporting clubs and government agencies. Individuals who take on positions of power within such organisations, even if they as individuals do not personally feel any deterrent effects of shaming directed at their organisation, may find that they confront role expectations to protect and enhance the repute of the organisation . . . Another factor which tends to limit the deterrent efficacy of individual criminal liability for corporate crime is the expendability of individuals within organizations . . . [T]he corporation 'marches on its elephantine way almost indifferent to its succession of riders.' The risk thus arises of rogue corporations exploiting their capacity to toss off a succession of individual riders and, if necessary, to indemnify them in some way . . . Consider also the extreme tactic adopted by some companies of setting up internal lines of accountability so as to have a 'vice-president responsible for going to jail.' By offering an attractive sacrifice the hope is that prosecutors will feel sufficiently satisfied with their efforts to refrain from pressing charges against the corporation or members of its managerial elite . . .

[I]n some respects corporations may be better endowed than individuals to be the subject of responsibility. Corporations, it may be argued, have a number of advantages when it comes to rational decision-making, including access to a pool of intelligence and the resources to acquire a superior knowledge of legal and other obligations. The conclusion is thus invited that although corporations do not have a 'soul to be damned' they can deserve to be blamed . . .

[With regard to the argument that punishing companies amounts to punishment of innocent shareholders etc] [f]irst, cost-bearing associates are not themselves subject to the stigma of conviction and criminal punishment—they are not convicts but corporate distributees. Secondly, employees and stockholders accede to a distributional scheme in which profits and losses from corporate activities are distributed on the basis of position in the company or type of investment rather than degree of deserved praise or blame . . . Thirdly, and above all, not to punish an enterprise at fault would be to allow corporations to accumulate and distribute to associates a pool of resources which does not reflect the social cost of production. Justice as fairness requires, as a minimum, that the cost of corporate offences be internalised by the enterprise."

4–046 Many large corporations have complex structures, making it difficult for outsiders to ascertain who is responsible for a particular decision. Punishing the company can trigger the most appropriate institutional response because it is in the best position to identify and discipline its employees. In many cases, prosecution of individuals might be inappropriate as it ignores the pressures the corporate structure might have placed upon them; these pressures will often remain even after the individual has been sacrificed. Only by punishing the company itself can one hope for a corporate response to the wrongdoing by implementing the appropriate safety procedures.

Modern companies now often promote themselves as distinct, identifiable entities. Such advertising:

> "... designed to 'humanise' the company in the interests of image-building, has reinforced the anthropomorphic perception of the company in the public mind, which in turn has led to a public demand to apportion blame and to criminalise and punish companies for serious transgressions."[101]

The concept of fair-labelling applies not just to offences themselves but to whom we choose to blame for the offences committed. After the capsize of the *Herald of Free Enterprise*, a manslaughter prosecution was brought against the company involved (P&O) and seven of its employees. For reasons to be explored shortly, the judge directed acquittals against P&O and the five most senior employees. It is a telling fact that the relatives of the Vs who died on the *Herald of Free Enterprise* were primarily interested in the prosecution of P&O and not of the individuals. Even the prosecution seemed of a similar mind when it dropped the charges against the two most immediate "causers" of the sinking as soon as the judge had directed acquittals against P&O and its senior executives. Perhaps there was a realisation that junior employees should never have been left in a position where the entire safety of the ferry and its passengers depended on them without adequate checks or controls. The true fault lay with the company.

4–047 However, a final and critical point must be stressed here. The above argument is that companies *should* be capable of being held criminally liable. However, this does *not* mean that individuals within the company should be exempt from liability. In appropriate cases, where an individual has committed the actus reus with the mens rea of the offence, they should also be liable. Indeed, in the case of small companies, particularly "one-person companies", imposing criminal liability on the company and the individual is somewhat pointless. Even with larger companies, individual criminal liability should be imposed in addition to corporate criminal liability. The central case for this is based on deterrence. People are more amenable to deterrence than corporations. The evidence suggests that employer groups are most vocal in their opposition to new laws when there is a risk that company directors or senior managers might go to prison under those laws.[102]

Indeed, for many statutory offences, there is a specific provision for holding individuals liable when a company commits an offence. A standard form employed in many statutes, such as the Health and Safety at Work etc. Act 1974 s.37(1), is as follows:

---

101 L. Dunford and A. Ridley, "No Soul to be Damned, No Body to be Kicked: Responsibility, Blame and Corporate Punishment" (1996) 24 Int. J. Soc. L. 1, 7.

102 C.M.V. Clarkson, "Corporate Manslaughter: Need for a Special Offence?" in C.M.V. Clarkson and S. Cunningham (eds), *Criminal Liability for Non-Aggressive Deaths* (Aldershot: Ashgate, 2008), p.88.

"Where an offence under any of the relevant statutory provisions committed by a body corporate is proved to have been committed with the consent or connivance of, or to have been attributable to any neglect on the part of, any director, manager, secretary or other similar officer of the body corporate or a person who was purporting to act in any such capacity, he as well as the body corporate shall be guilty of that offence and shall be liable to be proceeded against and punished accordingly."

Liability under such a provision is broader and easier to establish than the complex common law rules on accessorial liability. The extent to which this provision is utilised in the controversial cases of death at work is considered later in this section.

C. THE LAW

There are two ways a company can be criminally liable: vicarious and direct liability. **4–048**

1. Vicarious liability

With many offences of strict liability and negligence, a company can be vicariously liable for the acts of its employees in the course of their duties. **4–049**

NATIONAL RIVERS AUTHORITY V ALFRED MCALPINE HOMES EAST LTD [1994] 4 ALL E.R. 286 (QUEEN'S BENCH DIVISIONAL COURT):

The D company was charged with causing pollution (wet cement) to enter controlled waters contrary to the Water Resources Act 1991 s.85(1). Two company employees accepted responsibility for the pollution. At their trial in the magistrates' court, the company was acquitted on the ground that a company can only be criminally liable if senior persons within the company commit the criminal acts. The prosecution appealed by way of the case stated. **4–050**

SIMON BROWN LJ:

"I for my part see *Alphacell* as an illustration of vicarious liability . . . [A]n employer is liable for pollution resulting from its own operations carried out under its essential control, save only where some third party acts in such a way as to interrupt the chain of causation . . . It is sufficient that those immediately responsible on site (those who in the event acknowledged what had occurred) were employees of the company and acting apparently within the course and scope of that employment."

MORLAND LJ:

"The object of the relevant words of s.85(1) and the crime created thereby is the keeping of streams free from pollution for the benefit of mankind generally and the world's flora and

> fauna. Most significantly deleterious acts of pollution will arise out of industrial, agricultural or commercial activities . . . In almost all cases the act or omission will be that of a person such as a workman, fitter or plant operative in a fairly low position in the hierarchy of the industrial, agricultural or commercial concern.
>
> In my judgment, to make the offence an effective weapon in the defence of environmental protection, a company must by necessary implication be criminally liable for the acts or omissions of its servants or agents during activities being done for the company."
>
> *Appeal allowed*
> *Case remitted for rehearing*

4–051 The doctrine of vicarious liability is well established in English law in relation to strict liability offences dealing with matters such as pollution, food and drugs, and trading standards.[103] It has also been applied to hybrid offences; those strict liability offences that permit a due diligence defence.[104] However, it is clear that vicarious liability will not necessarily apply to all offences of strict liability. In *Seaboard Offshore Ltd,*[105] the House of Lords held that the doctrine of vicarious liability did not apply to the offence before it,[106] irrespective of whether the offence was one of strict liability. Whether vicarious liability applies or not is a matter of statutory interpretation, considering the law's policy and whether vicarious liability will assist enforcement.[107] For example, in *McAlpine,* the law could only be made effective by holding the company vicariously liable. In *Seaboard,* it was concluded that the statute was aimed at the company's safety policies rather than the actions of menial employees. The result is that, at present, it is rather difficult to predict whether an offence will be held to be one to which the doctrine of vicarious liability will be applicable.

Is the doctrine of vicarious liability justifiable? The doctrine can be defended on pragmatic grounds. It is easy to apply. As long as someone (anyone) acting in their employment has committed an offence, the company can be held liable. It prevents companies from shielding themselves from criminal liability by delegating potentially illegal operations to employees. Companies delegate powers to act to all their employees in their respective spheres and should be held responsible for their criminal acts accordingly. It is also argued that optimum deterrence is achieved through the imposition of vicarious liability in that companies will "know where they stand".[108] These arguments are, of course, compelling when applied to strict liability offences. If no fault is required on the part of the individual committing the crime, there seems little point in requiring fault on the part of the company to be established. There are, however, strong arguments against the doctrine.

---

103 *R. v British Steel Plc* [1995] 1 W.L.R. 1356; [1995] I.C.R. 586 CA.

104 *Tesco Supermarkets Plc v Brent LBC* [1993] 1 W.L.R. 1037; (1994) 158 J.P. 121.

105 *Seaboard Offshore Ltd v Secretary of State for Transport* [1994] 1 W.L.R. 541; [1994] 1 Lloyd's Rep. 589.

106 Merchant Shipping Act 1988 s.31: failing to take reasonable steps to ensure that a vessel is operated in a safe manner.

107 See, e.g. *R. v Gateway Foodmarkets Ltd* [1997] 2 Cr. App. R. 40; [1997] I.C.R. 382 CA.

108 G.R. Sullivan, "The Attribution of Culpability to Limited Companies" [1996] C.L.J. 515, 541.

Eric Colvin, "Corporate Personality and Criminal Liability" (1995) 6 Criminal Law Forum 1, 8:

"Vicarious corporate liability has been criticized for being both underinclusive and overinclusive. It is underinclusive because it is activated only through the criminal liability of some individual. Where offenses require some form of fault, that fault must be present at the individual level. If it is not present at this level, there is no corporate liability regardless of the measure of corporate fault. Yet vicarious liability is also overinclusive because, if there is individual liability, corporate liability follows even in the absence of corporate fault. The general objection to vicarious liability in criminal law—that it divorces the determination of liability from an inquiry into culpability—applies to corporations as it does to other defendants. The special characteristics of corporations do not insulate them from the stigmatizing and penal consequences of a criminal conviction." **4-052**

An example of the doctrine's over-inclusiveness is that a company could be liable for an offence despite having adopted clear policies and issued express instructions to avert the wrongdoing. It hardly seems justifiable to hold a company liable for the actions of a menial employee who breaches company rules and commits a crime. A possible compromise would be to make companies prima facie vicariously liable for all offences committed by employees during their employment (whether a particular individual could be identified or not) but to afford a due diligence defence. **4-053**

2. Direct liability: the identification doctrine

When it comes to crimes of mens rea, the commitment to individualistic notions of responsibility meant that English criminal law was reluctant to hold companies criminally liable. However, as company law developed the fiction of corporate personality—the idea that a company was a legal "person" that could sue and be sued in its own name—the criminal law did not take long to lift this fiction and superimpose it on its individualist conception of criminal liability. The courts started "lifting the veil" of companies to see if an individual had committed the actus reus of a crime with the appropriate mens rea. This individual had to be sufficiently senior in the corporate structure for their acts to be identified with the company itself; in such circumstances, the company could be criminally liable (as well as the individual). This is known as the identification doctrine. **4-054**

Tesco Supermarkets Ltd v Nattrass [1972] A.C. 153 (House of Lords):

Tesco were prosecuted under the Trade Descriptions Act 1968 s.11(2) for advertising outside their shop that they were selling goods for less than they were being offered for sale inside the shop. The fault for the incorrect advertisement lay with the local manager, whose system of daily checks had broken down. Tesco claimed a defence under s.24 of the same Act that the "failure was due to the default of another person". The question then arose as to whether the local manager was "another person" or whether he was to be identified with the company. **4-055**

LORD REID:

"I must start by considering the nature of the personality which by a fiction the law attributes to a corporation. A living person has a mind which can have knowledge or intention or be negligent and he has hands to carry out his intentions. A corporation has none of these: it must act through living persons, though not always one or the same person. Then the person who acts is not speaking or acting for the company. He is acting as the company and his mind which directs his acts is the mind of the company. There is no question of the company being vicariously liable. He is not acting as a servant, representative, agent or delegate. He is an embodiment of the company or, one could say, he hears and speaks through the persona of the company, within his appropriate sphere, and his mind is the mind of the company. If it is a guilty mind then that guilt is the guilt of the company. It must be a question of law whether . . . a person . . . is to be regarded as the company or merely as the company's servant or agent . . .

Reference is frequently made to the judgment of Denning LJ in *HL Bolton (Engineering) Co Ltd v TJ Graham & Sons Ltd* [1957] 1 Q.B. 159. He said, at p.172:

> 'A company may in many ways be likened to a human body. It has a brain and nerve centre which controls what it does. It also has hands which hold the tools and act in accordance with directions from the centre. Some of the people in the company are mere servants and agents who are nothing more than hands to do the work and cannot be said to represent the mind or will. Others are directors and managers who represent the directing mind and will of the company, and control what it does. The state of mind of these managers is the state of mind of the company and is treated by the law as such.'

In that case the directors of the company only met once a year: they left the management of the business to others, and it was the intention of those managers which was imputed to the company. I think that was right. There have been attempts to apply Lord Denning's words to all servants of a company whose work is brain work, or who exercise some managerial discretion under the direction of superior officers of the company. I do not think that Lord Denning intended to refer to them. He only referred to those who 'represent the directing mind and will of the company, and control what it does.'

[The local manager was not to be identified with the company. He was, therefore, 'another person'.]"

Appeal allowed

4–056 There were significant objections to this strict interpretation of the identification doctrine, particularly with larger companies where it is most unlikely that a senior manager would commit the actus reus of an offence with the accompanying mens rea. Arguably, the Privy Council adopted a more flexible approach in the following case.

Meridian Global Funds Management Asia Ltd v Securities Commission [1995] 2 A.C. 500 (Privy Council):

The Chief Investment Officer (CIO) and senior portfolio manager of *Meridian*, unknown to the board of directors and managing director, invested in another company without making disclosures to the stock exchange as required by the New Zealand Securities Amendment Act 1988 s.20(3). The company was convicted of failing to comply with s.20. The New Zealand Court of Appeal upheld the conviction on the basis that the CIO was the directing mind and will of the company, and so his knowledge was attributable to the company. The company appealed to the Judicial Committee of the Privy Council. **4–057**

LORD HOFFMANN:

"Any proposition about a company necessarily involves a reference to a set of rules. A company exists because there is a rule (usually in a statute) which says that a *persona ficta* shall be deemed to exist and to have certain of the powers, rights and duties of a natural person . . . It is . . . a necessary part of corporate personality that there should be rules by which acts are attributed to the company. These may be called 'the rules of attribution' . . .

Judges sometimes say that a company 'as such' cannot do anything; it must act by servants or agents . . . [A] reference to a company 'as such' might suggest that there is something out there called the company of which one can meaningfully say that it can or cannot do something. There is in fact no such thing as the company as such, no ding an sich, only the applicable rules. To say that a company cannot do something means only that there is no one whose doing of that act would, under the applicable rules of attribution, count as the act of the company.

. . . [T]he criminal law . . . ordinarily impose[s] liability only for the *actus reus* and *mens rea* of the defendant himself. How is such a rule to be applied to a company?

. . . In such a case, the court must fashion a special rule of attribution for the particular substantive rule. This is always a matter of interpretation: given that it was intended to apply to a company, how was it intended to apply? Whose act (or knowledge, or state of mind) was *for this purpose* intended to count as the act etc of the company? One finds the answer to this question by applying the usual canons of interpretation, taking into account the language of the rule (if it is a statute) and its content and policy.

. . . The policy of section 20 of the Securities Amendment Act 1988 is to compel, in fast-moving markets, the immediate disclosure of the identity of persons who become substantial security holders in public issuers. Notice must be given as soon as that person knows that he has become a substantial security holder. In the case of a corporate security holder, what rule should be implied as to the person whose knowledge for this purpose is to count as the knowledge of the company? Surely the person who, with the authority of the company, acquired the relevant interest. Otherwise the policy of the Act would be defeated. Companies

> would be able to allow employees to acquire interests on their behalf which made them substantial security holders but would not have to report them until the board or someone else in senior management got to know about it. This would put a premium on the board paying as little attention as possible to what its investment managers were doing. Their Lordships would therefore hold that upon the true construction of section 20(4) (e), the company knows that it has become a substantial security holder when that is known to the person who had authority to do the deal . . .
>
> It was therefore not necessary in this case to inquire whether [the CIO] could have been described in some more general sense as the 'directing mind and will' of the company. But their Lordships would wish to guard themselves against being understood to mean that whenever a servant of a company has authority to do an act on its behalf, knowledge of that act will for all purposes be attributed to the company. It is a question of construction in each case as to whether the particular rule requires that the knowledge that an act has been done, or the state of mind with which it was done, should be attributed to the company . . . [T]he fact that a company's employee is authorised to drive a lorry does not in itself lead to the conclusion that if he kills someone by reckless driving, the company will be guilty of manslaughter. There is no inconsistency. Each is an example of an attribution rule for a particular purpose, tailored as it always must be to the terms and policies of the substantive rule."
>
> *Appeal dismissed*

4–058 This decision is unfortunately ambiguous and could lead to uncertainty. Lord Hoffmann states, "the court must fashion a special rule of attribution for the particular substantive rule". On the facts of *Meridian,* this was easy. The issue was whether the company knew it had invested in another company without making the required disclosures. The person who had the "authority to do the deal" was the CIO; his knowledge was attributed to the company. But what was the "special rule of attribution" that enabled this sensible result to be achieved? Is Lord Hoffmann saying that, depending on the statute, one has a choice between utilising the identification doctrine or imposing vicarious liability—and that the company here was vicariously liable for the acts of its CIO? Or does it mean that, again, depending on the statute, one can broaden the identification doctrine so that a company can be directly liable for the acts of someone not traditionally associated with the "controlling mind" of the company, which in this case was the CIO? Perhaps the answer to these questions is not important. After all, the identification doctrine can be viewed, in substance, as being very close to vicarious liability;[109] companies can only be held "vicariously" liable for the acts of persons representing the 'controlling mind' of the company. Whichever route is adopted, the effect of *Meridian* is the same. Companies can be liable for crimes of mens rea based on acts by persons not traditionally regarded as sufficiently senior to satisfy the identification doctrine.

How can this approach be applied to statutes dealing with non-regulatory areas and creating stigmatic offences, such as the Offences Against the Person Act 1861 or to cases where there is no statute to be construed? If the acts and knowledge of an investment manager can be attributed to a company for investment offences, logic would dictate that the acts and knowledge of a health and safety manager

109 J.J. Child, A.P. Simester, J.R. Spencer, F. Stark and G.J. Virgo, *Criminal Law: Theory and Doctrine*, 8th edn (Oxford: Hart, 2022), p.306.

should be attributed to a company for all health and safety purposes, which would include cases where a worker sustained serious injuries. In *Odyssey v OIC Run-Off Ltd*,[110] it was stated that the *Meridian* principle was of general application and could be applied to "a substantive rule of judge-made law" (whether the finality of a judgment could be displaced by the perjury of a party). In this case, a company was identified through the acts of a former director because, at the trial where the perjury took place, he was "part of a team which was helping to row [the company] to victory". However, Brooke LJ was careful to emphasise that this was a civil case where the approach to corporate liability was "fundamentally different". In a strong dissent, Buxton LJ stated that the same rules of attribution should be applied in criminal and civil cases. His view was that *Meridian* is "at best an imperfect guide to the correct approach to the rule for attribution of a crime" and that he was "bound by *Tesco v Nattrass* to apply the 'directing mind and will' formulation, or something very near to it".[111]

Indeed, the following criminal decision confirmed that any flexibility introduced by *Meridian* regarding statutory offences had no application to the common law offence of manslaughter.

Att-Gen's Reference (No.2 of 1999) [2000] 2 Cr. App. R. 207 (Court of Appeal, Criminal Division):

Following a train collision at Southall, seven passengers died and 151 were injured. Great Western Trains was prosecuted for manslaughter but was acquitted, as there was no human being with whom the company could be identified. On reference by the Attorney General: **4–059**

ROSE LJ:

> "There is, as it seems to us, no sound basis for suggesting that, by their recent decisions, the courts have started a process of moving from identification to personal liability as a basis for corporate liability for manslaughter . . . [T]he identification principle is in our judgment just as relevant to the *actus reus* as to *mens rea* . . .
>
> In our judgment, unless an identified individual's conduct, characterisable as gross criminal negligence, can be attributed to the company the company is not, in the present state of the common law, liable for manslaughter. Civil negligence rules . . . are not apt to confer criminal liability on a company.
>
> None of the authorities relied on by [counsel] as pointing to personal liability for manslaughter by a company supports that contention. In each, the decision was dependent on the purposive construction that the particular statute imposed . . . In each case there was an identified

110 *Odyssey v OIC Run-Off Ltd, The Times,* 17 March 2000.

111 In the Scottish case of *Transco Plc v HM Advocate (No.1)* 2004 J.C. 29; 2004 S.L.T. 41, the English civil case of *El-Ajou v Dollar Land Holdings Plc (No.1)* [1994] B.C.C. 143; [1994] 1 B.C.L.C. 464 was discussed. In this latter case, it was held that the directing mind and will of the company need not be the person with general management of the company; the directing mind of a company can be found in different persons for different activities. In *Transco*, Lord Hamilton described both *El-Anjou* and *Meridian Global Funds Management Asia Ltd v Securities Commission* [1995] 2 A.C. 500; [1995] 3 W.L.R. 413 PC as being of "no assistance" in a case dealing with corporate homicide (the Scottish equivalent of corporate manslaughter).

> employee whose conduct was held to be that of the company. In each case it was held that the concept of directing mind and will had no application when construing the statute. But it was not suggested or implied that the concept of identification is dead or moribund in relation to common law offences . . . Indeed, Lord Hoffmann's speech in the *Meridian* case, in fashioning an additional special rule of attribution geared to the purpose of the statute, proceeded on the basis that the primary 'directing mind and will' rule still applies although it is not determinative in all cases. In other words, he was not departing from the identification theory but re-affirming its existence . . .
>
> [T]he identification principle remains the only basis in common law for corporate liability for gross negligence manslaughter."
>
> *Opinion accordingly*

4–060 The ratio of this decision only extends to the common law offence of corporate manslaughter (which, as we shall see, has now been abolished) and would probably apply to other common law offences. While the point has not been settled, it likely applies to statutes creating stigmatic offences, such as the Offences Against the Person Act 1861 (the OAPA). So, if a prosecution had been brought under the OAPA concerning the 151 people seriously injured (probably under s.20), it would seem that the company would only have been liable if a person representing the controlling mind of the company had actually committed the offence. This is intolerably narrow. Managing directors do not drive trains, and it would be extraordinarily difficult, if not impossible, to establish that their gross negligence in the boardroom *caused* the death of workers or members of the public.

The extent of *Meridian* has even been brought into question in relation to regulatory offences. In *St Regis Paper Co Ltd*,[112] the trial judge relied on Lord Hoffmann's observations to conclude that the D company could be identified as having committed an offence of intentionally making a false entry in a record required to be kept under the condition of a permit (Pollution Prevention and Control Regulations 2000[113] reg.32) through the acts and state of mind of the technical manager of the smallest of five paper mills owned by the company. The offence involved the manager making a false entry about the number of solids the company was discharging into a river. The Court of Appeal quashed the conviction, holding that to attribute an employee's act to the company, the individual must be seen as the directing mind and will of the company, and such persons would typically be on the board of directors, a managing director, or some other superior officer of the company who carried out the functions of management and spoke and acted as the company. That was the case even though the offence fell within a regulatory regime. If Parliament had intended vicarious liability to be possible, it would not have imposed mens rea requirements. The lesson to be learned from *Meridian*, noted Moses LJ, is the importance of construing the statute, which creates the statutory offence, in order to determine the rules of attribution applicable to the statutory offence in question.[114]

---

112 *R. v St Regis Paper Co Ltd* [2011] EWCA Crim 2527; [2012] 1 Cr. App. R. 14.

113 Pollution Prevention and Control Regulations 2000 (SI 2000/1973).

114 This is in agreement with the Law Commission, which proposes that in the absence of specific legislative provisions setting out the basis upon which companies are to be found liable, the courts should treat the question of how corporate fault may be established as a matter of statutory interpretation. The Law Commission, however, would "encourage the courts not to presume that the identification doctrine applies

That the question revolves around statutory interpretation concerning offences designed explicitly as part of a regulatory regime may not be particularly enlightening in determining the rules of attribution about a statutory offence, such as one under the OAPA, which was not drafted with the liability of corporations in mind. However, even if the more flexible *Meridian* approach were adopted, the identification doctrine would still have significant problems. It still requires an individual to be identified within the company whose acts and knowledge can be attributed to the company. In many cases, the wrong might have occurred because no person within the company was responsible for (say) health and safety. Alternatively, the company's structures may be so complex and impenetrable, with decision-making buried at many different departmental levels, that it becomes impossible to pinpoint any individual responsible for a particular area of activity. For these and other reasons, explored below, there has been a call for the complete abandonment of the identification doctrine in English law.

D. RESTRUCTURING CORPORATE CRIMINAL LIABILITY

The identification doctrine is inadequate to deal with the reality of decision-making in many modern companies. Accordingly, several alternative methods for establishing corporate culpability have been suggested. Some such methods have been considered most recently by the Law Commission in its project on Corporate Criminal Liability for which the Government tasked the Law Commission with answering six questions, including: "whether the 'identification doctrine' is fit for purpose when applied to organisations of differing sizes and scales of operation", and "whether an alternative approach to corporate liability for crimes could be provided for in legislation".[115] The Law Commission concluded that "we are in no doubt that the identification doctrine is an obstacle to holding large companies criminally responsible for offences committed in their interests by their employees".[116] No concrete recommendations for reform were made, but the Law Commission presented a number of options having reviewed alternative ways in which liability *could* be reformed. What follows is not a full analysis of the Law Commission's Options Paper, and it should be noted that whilst the Law Commission's focus was on reforming the law of corporate criminal liability to address particular issues of corporate corruption in the context of economic crime;[117] we do not necessarily share that focus here. **4–061**

when interpreting the scope of criminal offences applicable to companies": Law Commission Consultation Paper 195, *Criminal Liability in Regulatory Contexts* (2010), Proposal 13. Pinto and Evans argue that Moses LJ in *St Regis Paper Co* [2012] 1 Cr. App. R. 14 misinterpreted the statute, and that the particular provision of reg.32(1), rather than pointing away from liability for the company, invited the opposite conclusion. They suggest that for the purpose of the regulation it is the person who produced the daily environmental reports whose acts should be attributable to the company, and that would have been the technical manager. Despite the court acknowledging that the purpose of the statute was to protect the environment, the effect of the decision, they argue, is that a company can immunise itself against the risk of liability under the regulation by assigning the duty of keeping the record to a sufficiently lowly employee, which will not discourage environmental pollution: A. Pinto QC and M. Evans, *Corporate Criminal Liability*, 3rd edn (London: Sweet & Maxwell, 2013), pp.60–61.

115 Law Commission's *Terms of Reference* for the Corporate Criminal Liability project, para.1.5, *https://s3-eu-west-2.amazonaws.com/cloud-platform-e218f50a4812967ba1215eaecede923f/uploads/sites/30/2020/11/CCL-ToR-FINAL.pdf.*

116 Law Commission, *Corporate Criminal Liability: an options paper* (2022), para.3.91, *https://s3-eu-west-2.amazonaws.com/cloud-platform-e218f50a4812967ba1215eaecede923f/uploads/sites/30/2022/06/Corporate-Criminal-Liability-Options-Paper_LC.pdf.*

117 This followed the particular difficulties encountered in *R. v Barclays* [2020] Lloyd's Rep. F.C. 325 CC in which Barclays was charged with conspiring to commit fraud by false representation, with the prosecution failing to reach trial. For discussion of how this precipitated the Law Commission to be tasked with its project, see R. Lööf, "The Law Commission Options Paper: doubtful progress on reforming criminal corporate liability" [2022] Crim. L.R. 814–836.

1. Aggregation doctrine

4-062 In *HM Coroner for East Kent Ex p. Spooner*,[118] the aggregation doctrine was considered and rejected.[119] Under this doctrine, one aggregates all the acts and mental elements of the various relevant persons within the company to ascertain whether collectively they would amount to an offence if they had all been committed by one person. This doctrine recognises that isolating a single individual who has committed the crime with mens rea is often impossible. This doctrine can deter companies from burying responsibility deep within the corporate structure.

However, this doctrine perpetuates the myth of the personification of companies. Instead of finding one person with whom the company can be identified (as required by the identification doctrine), one finds several people. The doctrine ignores the reality that the real essence of the wrongdoing might not be what each individual did but the fact that the company had no organisational structure or policy to prevent each individual from doing what they did in a way that cumulatively amounts to a criminal offence. Indeed, in the *Herald of Free Enterprise* case, it is doubtful whether the aggregation of the acts and omissions of the various personnel would have amounted to a corporate offence. The real fault in that case lay with the lack of policy and responsibility for safety within the company.

This was in fact recognised by the Law Commission, in its Options Paper, which concluded that although the aggregation doctrine does not satisfactorily address the issue of finding liability in offences requiring fault, a form of aggregation could be useful in relation to offences of negligence. Drawing on examples taken from Canada (Canadian Criminal Code s.22.1) and Australia (Australian Criminal Code s.12.4) it concluded that:

> "For offences of negligence, . . . it should be possible to convict a corporation on the basis of collective negligence even if it is not possible to identify an individual whose conduct was personally negligent. A corporation might be collectively negligent, precisely because there was no individual with the necessary responsibility."[120]

2. Reactive corporate fault

4-063 Fisse and Braithwaite have proposed a different approach to corporate criminal liability. As many company structures are impenetrable to outsiders, they propose that companies "activate and monitor [their own] private justice systems of corporate defendants".

---

118 *R. v HM Coroner for East Kent Ex p. Spooner* (1987) 3 B.C.C. 636; (1989) 88 Cr. App. R. 10.

119 This rejection was confirmed in *Att-Gen's Reference (No.2 of 1999)* [2000] Q.B. 796; [2000] 2 Cr. App. R. 207 CA.

120 Law Commission, *Corporate Criminal Liability: an options paper* (2022), para.7.30, *https://s3-eu-west-2.amazonaws.com/cloud-platform-e218f50a4812967ba1215eaecede923f/uploads/sites/30/2022/06/Corporate-Criminal-Liability-Options-Paper_LC.pdf*.

Brent Fisse and John Braithwaite, "The Allocation of Responsibility for Corporate Crime: Individualism, Collectivism and Accountability" (1988) 11 Sydney L. Rev. 468, 511–512:

"One possible approach would be to restructure the imposition of corporate liability so as to enforce internal accountability. Where the *actus reus* of an offence is proven to have been committed by or on behalf of a corporation, the court, if equipped with a suitable statutory injunctive power, could require the company (a) to conduct its own enquiry as to who was responsible within the organisation, (b) to take internal disciplinary measures against those responsible, and (c) to return a report detailing the action taken. If the corporate defendant returned a report demonstrating that due steps had been taken to discipline those responsible then corporate criminal liability would not be imposed. If the reaction of the company was inexcusably deficient then both the company and its top managers would be criminally liable for their failure to comply with the order of the court. The range of punishments for corporate defendants would include court-ordered adverse publicity, community service, and punitive injunctive sentences."[121] **4–064**

There are, however, many problems with this reactive fault doctrine. What corrective measures and disciplinary actions will suffice to avoid liability? Would a formal reprimand of an employee coupled with the circulation of an internal memorandum advising staff that specific actions need to be taken in future suffice?[122] If a company fails to take sufficient steps, what offence would be committed? If the company were liable for established offences such as theft or fraud, there would be a severe danger of "false labelling"[123] in that the established prerequisites of the crime, in terms of actus reus and mens rea, would not be made out. On the other hand, if new special offences relating to reactive fault were created, there is the danger that the crimes committed by such companies will continue to be perceived as "poor cousins" to the "real criminal offences". Convicting companies of a failure to comply with a court order conveys the same message as a conviction under the Health and Safety legislation. What is needed is a more direct public shaming of the company itself for the actual harm that the company's culpable acts have caused. **4–065**

Nevertheless, such proposals could be useful for lesser regulatory offences, and English law has adopted this approach to a certain extent. In these situations, statutory notices can be imposed requiring a company to do or refrain from certain behaviour, with failure to comply being a specific criminal offence. For example, it is common in environmental and health and safety law for such an approach to be adopted.[124] The Regulatory Enforcement and Sanctions Act 2008, discussed earlier,[125] enables Regulators to serve "stop notices" on corporations prohibiting them from carrying on specified activities until specific steps have been taken.[126] Furthermore, Regulators can accept enforcement undertakings

121 For a statutory model based on this proposal, see B. Fisse, "The Attribution of Criminal Liability to Corporations: A Statutory Model" (1991) 13 Sydney L. Rev. 277.

122 Clarkson, "Corporate Culpability" [1998] 2 Web J.C.L.I.

123 Sullivan, "The Attribution of Culpability to Limited Companies" [1996] C.L.J. 515, 526.

124 See generally, Macrory Consultation Document, *Regulatory Justice: Sanctioning in a post-Hampton World* (2006), Annex F.

125 At paras 4–039–4–040.

126 Regulatory Enforcement and Sanctions Act 2008 s.46.

from corporations that they will take specified action to ensure that the offence does not continue or recur.[127] As will be seen at the end of this chapter, something similar has been introduced in relation to corporate liability for economic crime in the form of Deferred Prosecution Agreements (DPAs).

3. Corporate culture doctrine

4-066 What is needed is a recognition that corporate policies and behaviour often depend on the organisational structure and lines of authority within the corporation, which is responsible for standard procedures, such as those relating to safety, being spread throughout the company. Corporate acts and policies are not simply an aggregation of individual choices but are often the acts and policies of the company itself. A company might have "no soul to be damned, and no body to be kicked",[128] but it can be likened to "an intelligent machine".[129] Much of the modern literature on corporate culpability has rejected the individualistic conceptions underlying the identification doctrine and favours an organisational model in which companies are seen as more than the sum of their total numbers: "they are discrete and unique moral entities which can be criminally culpable in their own right."[130] The focus should be on corporate structures and systems, practices and policies, and whether the corporation has allowed a "corporate culture" to develop which facilitated the commission of the crime. From such a corporate culture of non-compliance with the law, it becomes possible to infer corporate mens rea by the corporation itself.

C.M.V. Clarkson, "Corporate Culpability" [1998] 2 Web Journal of Current Legal Issues:

4-067 "While it is perhaps easy to grasp the notion of a company being grossly negligent in that no subjective mental element is required, it is important to stress that both recklessness or intention can also be found in a company's policies, operational procedures and lack of precautions. If the corporate culture permitted or encouraged the wrongdoing, it may be easy to infer that the corporate body itself must have foreseen the possibility of the harm occurring (*Cunningham* recklessness) . . . or that the consequence was virtually certain to occur from which intention may be inferred (*Moloney/Hancock* intention). The important point about this approach is that it is not whether any individual within the company would have realised or foreseen the harm occurring but whether in a properly structured and organised careful company the risks would have been obvious . . . Possibly the only avenue of escape would be for a company to assert that while the risks looked objectively obvious, they had special expertise enabling them to rule out the risk (which would negate both . . . recklessness and intention). In the unlikely event of this claim being believed (bearing in mind that the risk clearly did materialise), the company would (rightly) escape liability.

---

127 Regulatory Enforcement and Sanctions Act 2008 s.50.

128 Coffee, "'No Soul to Damn: No Body to Kick': an Unscandalised Inquiry into the Problem of Corporate Punishment" (1981) 79 Mich. L. Rev. 386.

129 M. Dan-Cohen, *Rights, Persons, and Organisations: A Legal Theory for Bureaucratic Society* (Berkeley: University of California Press, 1986), p.49. For an argument that a company can be a culpability-bearing agent, see C.M.V. Clarkson, "Kicking Corporate Bodies and Damning Their Souls" (1996) 59 M.L.R. 557. See also, Wells, *Corporations and Criminal Responsibility*, 2nd edn (Oxford: OUP, 2001).

130 T. Woolf, "The Criminal Code Act 1995 (Cth)—Towards a Realist Vision of Corporate Criminal Liability" (1997) 21 Crim. L.J. 257.

The major objection to the corporate *mens rea* doctrine is the difficulty of determining whether the policies and practices of a company are sufficiently defective to be adjudged blameworthy to the requisite degree. In *Herald of Free Enterprise* this could easily have been done. The company had no proper safety procedures, no director responsible for safety and had received and ignored prior warnings of open-door sailings. In other cases, however, particularly where there is no pattern of wrongdoing, it could be more difficult to identify the policies and practices as amounting to *mens rea*. One method of addressing this problem in the United States would be to inquire whether a company had a Corporate Compliance Programme (a formal system or programme designed to ensure that all employees know the relevant laws affecting the company's operations and seeking to ensure corporate compliance with the law) which has been enforced in good faith."

In 2001, Australia enacted the Criminal Code Pt 2.5,[131] permitting corporations that do not have a culture of compliance to be held liable for any offence with a fault element.[132] In addition to this, in 2004, the Australian Capital Territory (ACT) introduced a new criminal offence (industrial manslaughter),[133] expressly endorsing this approach whereby mens rea can be inferred from a corporate culture. Recklessness is needed for the offence and is attributed to the company itself if it "expressly, tacitly or impliedly authorised or permitted the commission of the offence".[134] Corporate culture is defined to mean: **4–068**

". . . an attitude, policy, rule, course of conduct or practice existing within the corporation generally or in that part of the corporation where the relevant conduct happens."[135]

In assessing whether a relevant corporate culture exists, it is relevant to consider whether the employee etc, who committed the offence reasonably believed that senior managers of the corporation would have authorised or permitted the commission of the offence. The Law Commission considered the Australian experience as part of its recent project, but consultees responded that "in practice, this option is not viable" on the basis that the concept of "corporate culture" is "too nebulous" and there have been few prosecutions in Australia.[136] **4–069**

E. CORPORATE HOMICIDE

The issues discussed above apply to all criminal offences that can be committed by corporations. However, it was the application of these rules in cases where workers or others had been killed or **4–070**

131 Criminal Code Act 1995. The Criminal Code applies in the states of the Australian Capital Territory, the Northern Territory, Queensland, Tasmania and Western Australia. See S. Quo, "Corporate Culture and Corporate Criminal Responsibility in Australia" (2016) 37(12) Comp. Law. 389–393.

132 To date there have been no prosecutions based on the Criminal Code Pt 2.5. See Quo, "Corporate Culture and Corporate Criminal Responsibility in Australia" (2016) 37(12) Comp. Law. 389–393.

133 Crimes (Industrial Manslaughter) Amendment Act 2003, amending the Crimes Act 1900 (ACT).

134 ACT s.51(2)(c) and (d).

135 ACT s.51(6).

136 Law Commission, *Corporate Criminal Liability: an options paper* (2022), para.6.14, *https://s3-eu-west-2.amazonaws.com/cloud-platform-e218f50a4812967ba1215eaecede923f/uploads/sites/30/2022/06/Corporate-Criminal-Liability-Options-Paper_LC.pdf.*

injured at work or through other corporate operations (such as transport) that proved most controversial. The result was a sustained and vigorous campaign for law reform, culminating in the Corporate Manslaughter and Corporate Homicide Act 2007 (CMCHA).

1. Corporate manslaughter

4–071 The inadequacy of the law, particularly in relation to securing a manslaughter conviction against larger companies, led to a sustained campaign for reform of the law, resulting in the enacting of the Corporate Manslaughter and Corporate Homicide Act 2007 (CMCHA). This statute abolished the common law of manslaughter by gross negligence in its application to corporations and other organisations, and replaced it with the offence of corporate manslaughter.[137] The offence is essentially gross negligence manslaughter without the need to rely on the identification doctrine. The liability for this offence focuses on the corporation itself. As such, an individual cannot be an accessory to corporate manslaughter.[138]

A corporation will be liable for corporate manslaughter if the way that its activities are managed or organised causes a person's death and amounts to a gross breach of a relevant duty owed by that corporation to the deceased.[139]

Corporate Manslaughter and Corporate Homicide Act 2007 s.1:

4–072 "The offence

(1) An organisation to which this section applies is guilty of an offence if the way in which its activities are managed or organised—

(a) causes a person's death, and
(b) amounts to a gross breach of a relevant duty of care owed by the organisation to the deceased . . .
(3) An organisation is guilty of an offence under this section only if the way in which its activities are managed or organised by its senior management is a substantial element in the breach referred to in subsection (1)."

4–073 From this somewhat cumbersome offence definition, it can be seen that the following core ingredients need to be established:

- organisation;
- relevant duty of care;
- senior management failure;
- gross breach of duty; and
- causing death.

137 The offence is termed corporate homicide in Scotland.
138 Corporate Manslaughter and Corporate Homicide Act 2007 s.18(1).
139 Corporate Manslaughter and Corporate Homicide Act 2007 s.1(1).

Each of these ingredients will be examined in turn.

(i) Organisation

Despite the nomenclature of "corporate" manslaughter, the offence can be committed by any of the "organisations" listed in the CMCHA s.1(2), which includes a variety of organisations, including corporations, partnerships, trade unions, police forces, and various government departments. **4-074**

The CMCHA Sch.1 lists various government departments and other public bodies, such as the Department of Transport, the Department of Health and His Majesty's Revenue and Customs. This list may be amended by statutory instrument.[140] Crown immunity for all such bodies is removed by s.11. While this extension of the law to these other bodies is significant, we shall see in the next section that ss.3–7 provides that public authorities do not owe a relevant duty of care in a wide range of circumstances meaning that the lifting of Crown immunity is essentially a matter of "symbolism".[141]

(ii) Relevant duty of care

As with the current law of manslaughter by gross negligence, the organisation must owe a relevant duty of care to the deceased, per the CMCHA s.2. This is a duty owed under the civil law of negligence; whether a duty of care is owed is a question of law. **4-075**

This requirement is drawn from *Adomako;*[142] the test for gross negligence manslaughter, under which D must owe a duty of care to the deceased. However, under this common law test, the civil law concept of duty of care has not been fully employed by the criminal law. In *Wacker,*[143] it was stated that tort law and criminal law have different objectives, so concepts such as duty of care need to be adapted to the areas of law in which they are being applied.[144] Accordingly, in this case, it was held that the tortious doctrine of *ex turpi causa non oritur* action did not apply in a case where a lorry driver smuggled 58 illegal immigrants (who died) into the country. To preserve the effect of this decision and to ensure that the civil law rules on *volenti non fit injuria* do not apply, the CMCHA s.2(6) specifically provides that neither doctrine applies to corporate manslaughter. Thus, a corporate D in a *Wacker*-type case will be regarded as being under a duty of care. Similarly, the fact that a worker has accepted a risk of harm will not prevent the employer company from being under a duty of care.

The extent to which public authorities owe a duty of care, the military, police and law enforcement agencies, emergency services, child-protection and probation agencies are severely limited by the CMCHA ss.3–7, which provides various exemptions from liability. Some of these exemptions are "comprehensive".[145] Public authorities do not owe a relevant duty of care "in respect of a decision as to matters of public policy (including in particular the allocation of public resources or the weighing of **4-076**

---

140 Corporate Manslaughter and Corporate Homicide Act 2007 s.22. Amendments have been made several times, in order to reflect restructuring of government departments, the most recent being in November 2016.

141 D. Ormerod and R.D. Taylor, "The Corporate Manslaughter and Corporate Homicide Act 2007" [2008] Crim. L.R. 589, 597.

142 *R. v Adomako (John Asare)* [1995] 1 A.C. 171; [1994] 3 W.L.R. 288 HL.

143 *R. v Wacker (Perry)* [2002] EWCA Crim 1944; [2003] 1 Cr. App. R. 22.

144 This point was endorsed in *R. v Willoughby (Keith Calverley)* [2004] EWCA Crim 3365; [2005] 1 W.L.R. 1880.

145 Ministry of Justice, *Understanding the Corporate Manslaughter and Corporate Homicide Act 2007* (2007), p.9.

competing public interests)".[146] Thus, if the Department of Health decides not to allocate public resources to, for example, the purchase of certain drugs, there will be no duty of care owed to any patients who might die because of the unavailability of the drug.

Other exemptions are "partial". For example, for policing and law enforcement activities, the emergency response of fire authorities, and other emergency response organisations, there is, in essence,[147] no duty of care concerning their operational activities. There is only a duty of care where the death relates to the organisation's responsibility as an employer or as occupier of premises.[148] So, for example, if a fire authority acts negligently while rescuing people from a fire, there will be no liability. However, if the fire authority negligently fails to maintain its fleet of fire engines with the result that a death is caused, the fire authority can be liable for the new offence. The exemption that applies in relation to military operations is broadly accepted, but the exemption of a duty of care owed by the military with respect to the training of a hazardous nature or carried out in a hazardous way has recently come under attack. The House of Commons Select Committee recommended that the CMCHA ought to be amended to allow for appropriate prosecutions in relation to deaths arising from training exercises.[149]

(iii) Senior management failure

4–077 The corporation will only be liable for corporate manslaughter if the way its activities are organised by its *senior management* is a substantial element in the breach of duty.[150]

Corporate Manslaughter and Corporate Homicide Act 2007 s.1:

4–078 "(3) An organisation is guilty of an offence under this section only if the way in which its activities are managed or organised by its senior management is a substantial element in the breach referred to in subsection (1) . . .,

(4)(c) 'senior management', in relation to an organisation, means the persons who play significant roles in—

(i) the making of decisions about how the whole or a substantial part of its activities are to be managed or organised, or
(ii) the actual managing or organising of the whole or a substantial part of those activities."

---

146 Corporate Manslaughter and Corporate Homicide Act 2007 s.3(1).

147 Detail of these provisions is beyond the scope of this book. See Ormerod and Taylor, "The Corporate Manslaughter and Corporate Homicide Act 2007" [2008] Crim. L.R. 589, 605–9.

148 e.g. Corporate Manslaughter and Corporate Homicide Act 2007 s.5(3).

149 House of Commons Defence Committee, *Beyond Endurance? Military exercises and the duty of care*, Third Report of Session 2015–16, HC 598, [150], *http://www.publications.parliament.uk/pa/cm201516/cmselect/cmdfence/598/598.pdf*.

150 Corporate Manslaughter and Corporate Homicide Act 2007 s.1.

MINISTRY OF JUSTICE, UNDERSTANDING THE CORPORATE MANSLAUGHTER AND CORPORATE HOMICIDE ACT 2007 (2007), PP.12–14:

"The offence is concerned with the way in which activities were managed or organised. This represents a new approach to establishing corporate liability for manslaughter . . . and does not require the prosecution to establish failure on the part of particular individuals or managers. It is instead concerned with how an activity was being managed and the adequacy of those arrangements. **4–079**

- This approach is not confined to a particular level of management within an organisation: the test considers how an activity was managed within the organisation as a whole. However, it will not be possible to convict an organisation unless a substantial part of the organisation's failure lay at a senior management level . . .
- Exactly who is a member of an organisation's senior management will depend on the nature and scale of an organisation's activities. Apart from directors and similar senior management positions, roles likely to be under consideration include regional managers in national organisations and the managers of different operational divisions . . .

Can the offence be avoided by senior management delegating responsibility for health and safety?

- No. The Act is concerned with the way an activity was being managed or organised and will consider how responsibility was being discharged at different levels of the organisation. Failures by senior managers to manage health and safety adequately, including through inappropriate delegation of health and safety matters, will therefore leave organisations vulnerable to corporate manslaughter . . . charges."

The above provisions focus on the way in which the organisation's activities are managed and organised by the senior management. This is to ensure "that the new offence is targeted at failings in the strategic management of an organisation's activities, rather than failings at relatively junior levels".[151] The insistence on fault by senior management is a response to critics of earlier proposals who argued that because companies are purely creatures of law, crimes can only be committed by people and not companies, and so the real issue is one of determining when the acts of these people should be attributed to a company.[152] **4–080**

DAVID ORMEROD AND RICHARD TAYLOR, "THE CORPORATE MANSLAUGHTER AND CORPORATE HOMICIDE ACT 2007" [2008] CRIM. L.R. 589, 593–594:

"This test returns the focus, at least to some extent, to the evaluation of the relative contribution of groups of individuals. It can thus be described as implementing a 'qualified aggregation principle' **4–081**

151 Home Office, *Corporate Manslaughter: The Government's Draft Bill for Reform* (2005), para.28.

152 Sullivan, "The Attribution of Culpability to Limited Companies" (1996) 55 C.L.J. 515; P.R. Glazebrook, "A Better Way of Convicting Businesses of Avoidable Deaths and Injuries" (2002) 61 L.Q.R. 405.

in two respects: (1) because it adds together the failings of a number of individuals or groups of individuals, not in creating an artificial level of fault of an appropriate degree than can be anthropomorphically attributed to the company but rather, in characterising the company's management failure as the aggregate of those (groups of) individuals' failures; and (2) because whilst the failures might be found in and aggregated from a variety of places within the company, there is a proviso or qualification that failures must include to an appropriate (substantial) extent, failure or failures by 'senior management'."

4-082 Once the decision had been made to abandon the identification doctrine (and not to adopt the aggregation doctrine)[153] and instead to focus "responsibility on the working practices of the organisation",[154] this insistence on identifying the "senior management" seems unduly restrictive and threatens to open the door to endless argument in court as to whether certain persons do or do not qualify as part of the "senior management". A further obvious problem with this approach is that it replicates one of the main problems of the previous law: it could apply inequitably to small and large organisations. It will be easier to identify senior management failings in small companies.[155] In essence, this senior management test is little more than a broadening of the identification doctrine. Ormerod and Taylor suggest that this is an endorsement of a version of the aggregation doctrine where, instead of identifying one senior directing mind, one aggregates the actions and culpability of several senior persons. It is unfortunate that the Law Commission approach was not adopted whereby the definition of a management failure removed the need to identify persons representing the senior management and placed emphasis on the *activities* of the company: "the way in which its activities are managed or organised".[156] This placed the focus where it should be: on the activities and organisational practices of the company.

(iv) Gross breach of duty

4-083 Once a duty of care has been established, it is necessary to show that there is a gross breach of the relevant duty of care in how the senior managers manage the organisation's activities.[157] This follows the contours of gross negligence manslaughter laid down in *Adomako*.[158] There must be a *gross* breach of the relevant duty of care in how the senior managers manage the organisation's activities, with the breach falling far below what can be reasonably expected of the organisation In the circumstances.

It is for the jury to determine whether a breach of duty is *gross*. One of the main criticisms of *Adomako* is that this requirement is too vague; the jury must assess the broad, open issue of whether the conduct was "so bad" that it deserves to be labelled as manslaughter. In response to this and similar criticisms

153 A point made explicitly in Home Office, *Corporate Manslaughter: The Government's Draft Bill for Reform* (2005), para.27.
154 Home Office, *Corporate Manslaughter: The Government's Draft Bill for Reform* (2005), para.26.
155 Of the first five companies to be successfully prosecuted under the Act, the largest is Lion Steel Equipment Ltd which had 142 employees: *R. v Lion Steel Equipment Ltd* unreported, 20 July 2012.
156 Law Commission Paper No.237, Legislating the Criminal Code: Involuntary Manslaughter (1996).
157 Corporate Manslaughter and Corporate Homicide Act 2007 s.1(4)(b).
158 *R. v Adomako (John Asare)* [1995] 1 A.C. 171. See paras 7-044-7-046.

that the Law Commission's proposals were too vague in this respect, the CMCHA provides a range of criteria for the jury to assess whether there was a gross breach.[159] These are (a) failure to comply with health and safety legislation; (b) the corporate culture; and (c) any other relevant matters.

(a) Failure to comply with health and safety legislation

In deciding whether there has been a *gross* breach, the jury must consider whether the organisation failed to comply with any health and safety legislation that relates to the alleged breach, and if so, (a) how serious that failure was; and (b) how much of a risk of death it posed. **4–084**

Four points should be made about this provision. First, the jury *must* consider the issues specified in s.8(2). This is to be welcomed. Companies are expected to comply with the health and safety legislation. Their failure to do so raises at least a prima facie case of a gross breach. Secondly, it is only compliance with health and safety *legislation* that must be considered. Whether there has been compliance with health and safety *guidance* is a matter to which the jury *may* have regard.[160] Thirdly, the jury must consider whether the *organisation* (as a whole) failed to comply with the health and safety legislation. While it has been stated that this "further supports the argument that the activities of non-senior managers are relevant in determining whether there has been a management failure",[161] the fact remains that the failure to comply with the health and safety legislation by the organisation must be substantially attributable to how its senior management organises their activities. Fourthly, it is right that not every (perhaps trivial) breach of health and safety laws should give rise to liability for this offence. The jury must go on to assess *how serious* the failure was and how much of a *risk of death* it posed.

Of course, there is an inevitable circularity in asking whether conduct falls far below a standard and then measuring this by "how serious" the failure is to comply with the law. However, making these decisions regarding something tangible (the breach of health and safety laws) is a helpful step compared to the position under *Adomako,* where no guidance is specified. The approach is not without practical problems, though. As highlighted by Dobson,[162] proving breaches of health and safety legislation involves a reverse burden of proof, allowing a company to escape liability if it can show that it did what was practicable.[163] It is unclear whether such a reverse burden would apply when the jury assesses whether a breach of health and safety legislation has occurred for s.8.[164] Given that a company may well be facing charges of breach of health and safety legislation alongside a corporate manslaughter charge (see below), such procedural issues could become confusing for the jury.

---

159 Corporate Manslaughter and Corporate Homicide Act 2007 s.8.

160 Corporate Manslaughter and Corporate Homicide Act 2007 s.8(3)(b).

161 Ormerod and Taylor, "The Corporate Manslaughter and Corporate Homicide Act 2007" [2008] Crim. L.R. 589, 603.

162 A. Dobson, "Shifting Sands: Multiple Counts in Prosecutions for Corporate Manslaughter" [2012] Crim. L.R. 200.

163 Health and Safety at Work etc. Act 1974 s.40.

164 Dobson notes that in *R. v Cotswold Geotechnical Holdings Ltd* [2011] EWCA Crim 1337; [2012] 1 Cr. App. R. (S.) 26, Field J held that the Health and Safety at Work etc. Act 1974 s.40 did not apply when analysing the Corporate Manslaughter and Corporate Homicide Act 2007 s.8: Dobson, "Shifting Sands: Multiple Counts in Prosecutions for Corporate Manslaughter" [2012] Crim. L.R. 200, 207.

(b) Corporate culture

4-085 As a result of the Parliamentary Subcommittees' Report on the 2005 Bill, the CMCHA introduced an additional test for the jury to determine whether the breach was gross. The jury *may* also "consider the extent to which the evidence shows that there were attitudes, policies, systems or accepted practices within the organisation that were likely to have encouraged" the failure to comply with health and safety laws or to have produced tolerance of such a failure.

This draws upon the corporate culture test applied in the Australian Capital Territory.[165] This approach has tried to escape from the notion that corporate acts must be linked to individual human beings' choices and actions. It has adopted an organisational model focusing on corporate structures and systems, practices and policies, and whether the corporation has allowed a "corporate culture" to develop, which has facilitated the commission of the crime. In such cases, it seems right to criminalise the actions of a corporate which can be traced to a permissive attitude.

It should be noted that the UK Parliamentary Subcommittees' Report proposed this corporate culture test as a substitute for the senior management test. The CMCHA has, however, utilised the corporate culture test as an additional mechanism to determine whether there has been the required senior management failure. While the Australian test has been criticised as too vague,[166] the provision in the CMCHA s.8(3) is less amenable to attack because it is an *additional* test to the breach of health and safety laws. Only when there has been a breach of health and safety laws can the jury consider the corporate culture within the corporation; the provision specifically relates to how the corporate culture encouraged the failure to comply with the health and safety laws.

(c) Any other relevant matters

4-086 Neither of the above two provisions prevents the jury from having regard to "any other matters they consider relevant". As such, it is difficult to see that this provision will be much utilised. It is unthinkable that a jury could conclude that there had been no breach of health and safety laws, yet because of "other matters", there was a gross breach of duty. So, the relevance of this provision must relate to the issue of "how serious" the failure was to comply with the health and safety laws. Such matters would normally fall to be determined by the corporate culture test.

(v) Causing death

4-087 In many cases, when a death occurs at work, the most immediate cause of the death will be the act of a particular individual. To prevent arguments that this could constitute a free, deliberate, and informed (FDI) act breaking the chain of causation, the Law Commission Report recommended that liability could not be avoided because the most immediate cause of death was the act or omission of "an individual".[167] The Government rejected this approach.

---

165 See para.4-068.

166 J. Clough and C. Mulhern, *The Prosecution of Corporations* (Oxford: OUP, 2002), pp.140-147.

167 Law Commission Paper No.237, *Legislating the Criminal Code: Involuntary Manslaughter* (1996), para.8.39.

Home Office, Corporate Manslaughter: The Government's Draft Bill for Reform, Cmnd.6497 (2005), para.51:

> "The case law in this area has, however, developed since the Law Commission reported and we are satisfied that no separate provision is now needed. An intervening act will only break the chain of causation if it is extraordinary—and we do not consider that corporate liability should arise where an individual has intervened in the chain of events in an extraordinary fashion causing death, or the death was otherwise immediately caused by an extraordinary and unforeseeable event." **4-088**

Accordingly, the CMCHA s.1(1)(a) specifies that how the organisation managed or organised its activities must "cause a person's death". The normal rules of causation apply. This Home Office view was based on the then-leading decision in *Empress*.[168] However, since then, the House of Lords has reaffirmed the supremacy of the rule that a FDI intervention will break the chain of causation.[169] This has opened the door to arguments that the action of an individual employee, who is the most immediate cause of the death, will be regarded as FDI and break the chain of causation. It is unfortunate that the Law Commission's proposal was not included in the legislation. If, however, the death was caused by something independent of the breach, an acquittal for corporate manslaughter should follow.[170] **4-089**

Having outlined the main ingredients of the new offence, the following matters deserve consideration.

(vi) Relationship to health and safety legislation

An organisation may be charged with both corporate manslaughter and a health and safety offence, and the jury may return a verdict on only the lesser charge.[171] Under the CMCHA s.17, the consent of the Director of Public Prosecutions is required for a corporate manslaughter prosecution.[172] The CMCHA does not change the position that the CPS (and not the HSE) is responsible for prosecuting the offence.[173] **4-090**

Sentencing Guidelines Council, Corporate Manslaughter and Health and Safety Offences Causing Death: Definitive Guideline (2010), para.4:

> "There are considerable differences between these two offences: **4-091**
>
> (a) because corporate manslaughter involves both a *gross* breach of duty of care and senior management failings as a substantial element in that breach, those cases will generally

168 *Environmental Agency (formerly National Rivers Authority) v Empress Car Co (Abertillery) Ltd* [1999] 2 A.C. 22; [1998] 2 W.L.R. 350 HL. See para.2-064.

169 *R. v Kennedy (Simon)* [2007] UKHL 38; [2008] 1 A.C. 269. See para.2-075.

170 *R. v Wood Treatment Ltd* [2021] EWCA Crim 618; [2021] Crim. L.R. 872.

171 CMCHA s.19.

172 See *R. (on the application of Canham) v DPP* [2021] EWHC 3361 (Admin); [2022] Inquest L.R. 100, where the decision of the DPP not to prosecute a UAE diplomat and his wife for offences relating to modern slavery was reviewed.

173 See generally, Almond, "An Inspector's Eye View: The Prospective Enforcement of Work-Related Fatality Cases" (2006) 46 Brit. J. Criminol. 893, 896.

> involve systemic failures; by contrast the HSWA offences are committed whenever the defendant cannot show that it was not reasonably practicable to avoid a risk of injury or lack of safety; that may mean that the failing is at an operational rather than systemic level and can mean in some cases that there has been only a very limited falling below the standard of reasonable practicability;
>
> (b) in corporate manslaughter the burden of proof remains on the prosecution throughout; in particular this will ordinarily involve the prosecution identifying the acts or omissions which it relies upon as constituting the breach, and then proving them; by contrast, in a HSWA prosecution the prosecutor need only prove that there has been a failure to ensure safety or absence of risk, which it may often be able to do simply by pointing to the injury; once it has done so the burden of proof shifts to the defendant; the prosecution need not identify the precautions which it says ought to have been taken, nor need it prove how the accident happened (*R. v Chargot* [2008] UKHL 73, *Electric Gate Services Ltd* [2009] EWCA Crim 1942); usually however it will do so.
>
> (c) in corporate manslaughter the prosecution must prove that the breach was *a* (but not necessarily *the only*) substantial cause of death; by contrast the HSWA offences can be proved without demonstrating that any injury was caused by the failure to ensure safety . . ."[174]

(vii) No individual liability

4–092 One of the most controversial aspects of corporate manslaughter under CMCHA is the exemption from accessorial liability for individuals, such as directors or managers.[175] Such persons can still be liable to prosecution under the health and safety legislation (Health and Safety at Work etc. Act 1974 s.37) or for the common law offence of gross negligence manslaughter.[176] However, the reality is that few company directors (mostly of small companies) are personally convicted under health and safety legislation, and even fewer have been convicted of manslaughter.[177] With the introduction of the new corporate manslaughter offence, it was feared that even fewer prosecutions would be brought against individuals as prosecutors could view companies as easier targets.[178]

However, what appears to be emerging is a tendency to use prosecutions of both companies and their directors to open the door to plea bargains. In *Lion Steel*, for example, a guilty plea to corporate manslaughter was offered and accepted once the charges against individual directors were dropped.[179] Woodley worries that this is cause for concern:

---

174 The 2010 guidelines have now been superseded by the *Health and Safety Offences, Corporate Manslaughter and Food Safety and Hygiene Offences Definitive Guideline* (2015), effective from February 2016, which contains less discussion and explication than the 2010 version. There is nothing to suggest that these points apply any less now than they did when the previous guidelines were published and, indeed, the fact that offences under the HSW Act s.33 are endangerment offences penalising the creation of a *risk* of harm is emphasised on p.5 of the new guidelines.

175 Corporate Manslaughter and Corporate Homicide Act 2007 s.18.

176 See *R. v Lievers (Gillian Valerie)* [2023] EWCA Crim 1469.

177 For full statistics, see Clarkson, "Corporate Manslaughter: Yet More Government Proposals" [2005] Crim. L.R. 677, 687.

178 Clough and Mulhern, *The Prosecution of Companies* (2002), p.9.

179 *R. v Lion Steel Equipment Ltd*, unreported, 20 July 2012.

> "Will plea bargains be offered as a matter of course in the hope that directors facing individual prosecution will instruct their company's solicitors to plead guilty? Or will the initiative come from those same directors to offer a corporate guilty plea in the hope or knowledge that any individual liability will be dropped with the added 'bonus' of a reduction in any subsequent fine on the company?"[180]

Antrobus concludes that in cases combining gross negligence manslaughter charges against individual directors and a corporate manslaughter charge against their company, where the prosecution seeks to persuade the jury that the:

> ". . . corporate entity is little more than the vehicle of those directors, then the risk is run that the company's liability will stand or fall with the liability of those individuals. It is therefore tempting to conclude that in many respects the liability of corporations and their directors is little different from the situation prior to the CMCHA 2007 coming into force."[181]

(viii) Need for a special offence

The inadequacies of the old law were primarily due to failings of the identification doctrine in the context of disasters where it was felt that corporate greed was the primary culprit for causing loss of life in disasters. The identification doctrine made a conviction for homicide extremely difficult, as illustrated in *HM Coroner for East Kent Ex p. Spooner*,[182] regarding the *Herald of Free Enterprise* case. Here, the applicants sought judicial review of the coroner's decision that a company could not be indicted for manslaughter and that the acts or omissions of the company personnel could not be aggregated to render the company liable. At the inquest, the jury ignored the coroner's instruction that there were no grounds for a verdict of corporate manslaughter and returned verdicts of unlawful death. Eventually, prosecutions for manslaughter were instituted against P&O and seven employees of the company. At a preliminary hearing, it was finally established that a company could be liable for manslaughter.[183] At the end of the prosecution case, the trial judge, Turner J, directed acquittals against P&O and the five most senior employees.[184] This indicates that there was a case to be answered by the two most junior employees. However, the prosecution immediately dropped all charges against these two on the grounds that it was not in the public interest to proceed against them alone. The reason for directing an acquittal against P&O and the senior managers was that it could not be proved that the risks of open-door sailing were obvious to any of them. **4-093**

The collapse of this prosecution is not surprising. There was no one individual sufficiently senior in the hierarchy of P&O who could be said to have committed the actus reus and mens rea of manslaughter. For similar reasons, the failure to secure a manslaughter conviction in the *Great Western Trains* case, **4-094**

---

180 M. Woodley, "Bargaining over Corporate Manslaughter—What Price a Life?" (2013) 77(1) J. of Crim. Law 33–40.
181 S. Antrobus, "The Criminal Liability of Directors for Health and Safety Breaches and Manslaughter" [2013] Crim. L.R. 309, 322.
182 *R. v HM Coroner for East Kent Ex p. Spooner* (1987) 3 B.C.C. 636; (1989) 88 Cr. App. R. 10 QBD.
183 *DPP v P&O European Ferries (Dover) Ltd* (1991) 93 Cr. App. R. 73.
184 *R. v Alcindor*, unreported, 19 October 1990, Central Criminal Court. See D. Bergman, "Recklessness in the Boardroom" (1990) 140 N.L.J. 1496.

discussed above,[185] was predictable. In short, this whole approach of "humanising" companies will generally only be appropriate for small owner-managed companies where it will not be too difficult to pinpoint a senior individual with whom the company can be identified. However, with larger companies, it will be challenging to find a corporate officer who committed an offence that can be attributed to the company. The identification doctrine ignores the reality of modern corporate decision-making, which is often the product of corporate policies and procedures rather than individual decisions.

It became clear that reform of the law was essential. However, was it necessary to introduce an entirely new offence? Two views can be adopted here.

The first view is that there was no need for the introduction of a new special offence. All unlawful killings should be prosecuted under the general law of homicide (in these situations, manslaughter). Whether someone is killed by an attack, by a car, by a negligent doctor or as a result of corporate activities should make no difference. As long as the identification doctrine were abolished or reformed, "corporate killings" could have been dealt with in the same way as other unlawful killings. Separate treatment through the introduction of a new offence could lead to a marginalisation of the seriousness of such killings. The offence will not be regarded as serious as "real" manslaughter and much of the law's censuring and symbolic role will be defeated. Furthermore, while the introduction of this new offence could greatly facilitate prosecutions in cases where death has been caused, the identification doctrine still continues to apply to all other cases, in particular, those where serious injury has been caused and with the high-profile problem of corporate killings being catered for, pressure for reform of the identification doctrine has been significantly reduced.

The alternative view is that the new offence can be supported.

C.M.V. Clarkson, "Corporate Manslaughter: Need for a New Offence?" in C.M.V. Clarkson and S. R. Cunningham (eds), Criminal Liability for Non-Aggressive Deaths (2008), pp.84–86:

4–095 "Special homicide offences are perhaps needed when there is something distinctive about the context in which the killing occurred that justifies labelling the offence as something different from manslaughter . . .

Where a death has been caused in the context of corporate activities, the killing is far removed from the paradigmatic manslaughter. Duff ('Criminalising Endangerment' in R. A. Duff and S. Green (eds), *Defining Crimes* (2005)) distinguishes attacks from endangerments and argues that there is a significant moral difference between them. Attacks manifest 'practical hostility' towards people and their interests. An attack involves being guided by the wrong reasons: I attack you because I want to harm you; this is not a reason by which I should be guided. Endangerment involves not being guided by the right reasons.

185 *Att-Gen's Reference (No.2 of 1999)* [2000] 2 Cr. App. R. 207.

> Corporate activities do not involve attacks on the interests of others. Harming people is not the object of corporate enterprises. Such activities are widely regarded as acceptable and beneficial . . . But if a company allows dangerous machinery or operations it is not being guided by all the reasons against allowing danger at work. These different actions reveal different wrongs (compared to attacks) and show the company's character in different lights . . . [D]eath is still the product of a lack of health and safety measures. It is very far-removed from manslaughter and so should be marked by the existence of a special offence. To underwrite this difference, it can be strongly argued that the label 'corporate killing' would have been more appropriate than 'corporate manslaughter'."

(ix) Punishment for corporate manslaughter

(a) Fines

Traditionally, the penalty imposed on corporations for these offences has been a fine. This continues to be the main penalty under the CMCHA. Fines imposed on companies under the health and safety legislation have traditionally been low and (arguably) little more than a "public morality tax".[186] This is one of the reasons contributing to the marginalisation of such offences. However, the last 25 years have seen a change of attitude. In *F Howe & Sons (Engineers) Ltd*,[187] it was stated that: **4–096**

> "Generally where death is the consequence of a criminal act it is regarded as an aggravating feature of the offence. The penalty should reflect public disquiet at the unnecessary loss of life . . . The objective of prosecutions for health and safety offences in the work place is to achieve a safe environment for those who work there and for other members of the public who may be affected. A fine needs to be large enough to bring that message home where the defendant is a company not only to those who manage it but also to its shareholders. [It was argued] that the fine should not be so large as to imperil the earnings of employees or create a risk of bankruptcy. Whilst in general we accept that submission . . . there may be cases where the offences are so serious that the defendant ought not to be in business."

The average fine following a death at work increased steadily between the 20th and 21st centuries, and in a few high-profile cases, the fines have been significant. In the *Great Western Trains* case, a fine of £1.5 million was imposed following the Southall train crash. In 2005, the two biggest fines ever for breach of health and safety laws were imposed on Balfour Beatty (£10 million) and Network Rail (£3.5 million) following the Hatfield derailment, where four people were killed and 70 injured.[188] However, while this new attitude to the level of fines is to be welcomed, it should be pointed out that the fine in the *Great Western Trains* case represented only 5.6% of the company's profit for the preceding year.[189] Under the **4–097**

---

186 Coffee, "'No Soul to Damn: No Body to Kick': an Unscandalised Inquiry into the Problem of Corporate Punishment" (1981) 79 Mich. L. Rev. 386, 407.

187 *R. v F Howe & Son (Engineers) Ltd* [1999] 2 Cr. App. R. (S.) 37; (1999) 163 J.P. 359 CA.

188 The fine on Balfour Beatty was reduced on appeal to £7.5 million (*R. v Balfour Beatty Rail Infrastructure Services Ltd* [2006] EWCA Crim 1586; [2007] Bus. L.R. 77).

189 S. Trotter, "Corporate Manslaughter" (2000) N.L.J. 454.

Criminal Justice Act 2003 s.164(3), the court must inquire into the financial circumstances of the offender before fixing the amount of a fine. Equality in sentencing means equality of impact. If large corporations with vast profits were to be fined according to their means (say a percentage thereof), a new attitude toward corporate violence and other crimes might start emerging.

Since the CMCHA, sentencing guidelines have been issued and revised for both corporate manslaughter and for breaches of health and safety legislation causing death. These provide clearer guidance on the level of fine to be imposed, applying the now standard sentencing approach of using harm and culpability to assess offence seriousness whilst also taking account of the size of the company (large, medium, small, or micro-organisation).[190] This evaluation enables the court to ascertain the appropriate starting point for a fine within a category range.[191] Having established a starting point, the court must consider a list of aggravating and mitigating circumstances to result in an upward or downward movement from the starting point. Once this has been done, the court must take a "step back" to review and, if necessary, adjust the initial fine based on turnover to ensure that it fulfils the objectives of sentencing for these offences. The main objective is emphasised as being that:

> ". . . the fine must be sufficiently substantial to have a real economic impact which will bring home to management and shareholders the need to achieve a safe environment for workers and members of the public affected by their activities."[192]

This more punitive stance is to be welcomed. It demonstrates that the courts should be taking death caused by corporations seriously, and it is encouraging to see the objective being expressed as one which addresses safety culture rather than solely providing retribution for the bereaved. It appears that this change in the guidelines has translated into sentencing practice, with the average fine rising from £328,820 in the first 10 years of the offence, to £528,571 between 2016 and 2018, although Field suggests this does not constitute a "substantial shift in sentencing outcomes".[193] The highest fine imposed on a company is that of £1.2 million against Martinisation (London) Ltd in 2017, in relation to the deaths of two employees who died after falling from a first-floor balcony.[194] Field notes that sentences for the manslaughter offence are not particularly severe when comparing them to offences under the Health and Safety at Work Act, with four companies prosecuted in relation to deaths at work under the HSWA in 2017, all receiving considerable fines.[195] Given the far higher threshold for proving corporate manslaughter compared to the endangerment offences under health and safety legislation,

---

190 Sentencing Council, *Health and Safety Offences, Corporate Manslaughter and Food Safety and Hygiene Offences, Definitive Guideline* (2015), *https://www.sentencingcouncil.org.uk/wp-content/uploads/Health-and-Safety-Corporate-Manslaughter-Food-Safety-and-Hygiene-definitive-guideline-Web.pdf.*

191 Sentencing Council, *Health and Safety Offences, Corporate Manslaughter and Food Safety and Hygiene Offences, Definitive Guidance* (2015), pp.22–24.

192 Sentencing Council, *Health and Safety Offences, Corporate Manslaughter and Food Safety and Hygiene Offences, Definitive Guideline* (2015), p.25.

193 S. Field, "Ten Years On: The Corporate Manslaughter and Corporate Homicide Act 2007: plus ca change?" (2018) 29(8) *International Company and Commercial Law Review* 511–521, 518.

194 V. Roper, "The Corporate Homicide and Corporate Manslaughter Act 2007—A 10 Year Review" (2018) 82(1) *Journal of Criminal Law* 48–75, 69.

195 Field, "Ten Years On: The Corporate Manslaughter and Corporate Homicide Act 2007: plus ça change?" (2018) 29(8) *International Company and Commercial Law Review* 511–521, 518.

it may not be surprising that the CPS prefers to opt for offences under the latter even in relation to fatal incidents, given the sentencing powers available.

(b) Penalties other than fines

The CMCHA permits other penalties to be imposed, including remedial and publicity orders.[196] These penalties are to be welcomed, although it must be recognised that there is a risk that with the sanction for failing to comply with the order being a monetary penalty, a corporation could deliberately refuse to comply with the order, thus converting the remedial order into a fine.[197] **4–098**

Remedial orders are also available for HSWA offences.[198] Such orders are rarely imposed as, by the time an organisation is sentenced for an offence, the offender should have remedied any specific failings involved in the offence and if it has not, will be deprived of significant mitigation.[199] The Sentencing Council states that publicity orders "should ordinarily be imposed in cases of corporate manslaughter", the object of it being deterrence and punishment.[200] Moreover, the Law Commission has recently expressed the view that publicity orders are particularly valuable in circumstances where the offender is a public body or charity and where imposition of a large fine would have a detrimental impact on public services or beneficiaries.[201] However, in *Lion Steel,* the judge failed to make full use of the available sentencing options, choosing not to make a publicity order, instead commenting that such an order would "achieve nothing which will not be achieved by the reporting of these sentencing remarks".[202] Although publicity orders have been imposed in a handful of cases,[203] it has been argued that because corporate manslaughter media reporting has sometimes been inaccurate, publicity orders should be routinely imposed to ensure the information is balanced, correct, and not misleading.[204]

F. CORPORATE LIABILITY FOR NON-FATAL INJURIES AND OTHER HARMS

Early in the process that led to the CMCHA, it was suggested that the statute should be extended to cover cases where serious injuries had been caused by corporate gross negligence. As was seen earlier, the number of people seriously injured at work grossly exceeds the number killed (135 people killed; 60,645 injured in 2022/23). It was argued that it was illogical that a company could be liable for the **4–099**

---

196 Corporate Manslaughter and Corporate Homicide Act 2007 ss.9–10.

197 Gobert, "Controlling Corporate Criminality: Penal Sanctions and Beyond" [1998] Web J.C.L.I.

198 Health and Safety at Work etc. Act 1974 s.42.

199 Sentencing Council, Health and Safety Offences, Corporate Manslaughter and Food Safety and Hygiene Offences, Definitive Guideline (2015), p.12. See *R. v Lion Steel Equipment Ltd*, unreported, 20 July 2012.

200 Sentencing Council, Health and Safety Offences, Corporate Manslaughter and Food Safety and Hygiene Offences, Definitive Guideline (2015), p.27.

201 Law Commission, *Corporate Criminal Liability: an options paper* (2022), para.10.56, *https://s3-eu-west-2.amazonaws.com/cloud-platform-e218f50a4812967ba1215eaecede923f/uploads/sites/30/2022/06/Corporate-Criminal-Liability-Options-Paper_LC.pdf.*

202 *R. v Lion Steel Equipment Ltd*, unreported, 20 July 2012 at [48].

203 Publicity orders have been ordered following the conviction of Mobile Sweepers (2014), Peter Mawson Ltd (2015), Cheshire Gates Ltd (2015) and Linley Developments (2015). The publicity orders required them to publicise their conviction in the local newspaper, their website, and trade publications. See Law Commission, Corporate Criminal Liability: an options paper (2022), para.10.51 fn.316, *https://s3-eu-west-2.amazonaws.com/cloud-platform-e218f50a4812967ba1215eaecede923f/uploads/sites/30/2022/06/Corporate-Criminal-Liability-Options-Paper_LC.pdf.*

204 V. Roper, "The Corporate Manslaughter and Corporate Homicide Act 2007—A Ten Year Review" (2018) 82(1) J. Crim. Law 48, 71.

death of a worker but not for the serious injury to another worker when both might have been involved in the same incident and the second worker's life might only have been saved by the quick actions of the emergency services or by sheer luck.[205]

However, such a proposal was not pursued. The view that prevailed was that while it was acceptable to criminalise corporate manslaughter on the basis of gross negligence as such culpability has always sufficed for manslaughter, it would be anomalous and a major extension of the law to criminalise serious injury caused negligently as subjective mens rea has traditionally been required for non-fatal offences against the person. It was also felt that it could "lead to dilution of the corporate killing offence and could potentially over-stretch investigation and enforcement resources".[206] However, the most important reason for the limitation of the offence to killings was because of political expedience:

> ". . . it might lose its current clear focus on manslaughter, and the ensuing controversy and drafting difficulties might further delay the introduction of the actual Bill."[207]

Accordingly, for serious, stigmatic offences—such as non-fatal offences against the person (where vicarious liability cannot be applied)—the common law, with its notorious identification doctrine, continues to apply and will continue to hamper the prosecution of companies in cases where serious injury is caused at work. The most realistic charge will be for inflicting grievous bodily harm contrary to s.20 of the OAPA. However, for such a charge to succeed, it will be necessary to prove that the senior person representing the directing mind and will of the company *inflicted* the grievous bodily harm and did so *foreseeing the risk of some harm*.[208] It will only be in the most extraordinary circumstances that this could be proved—which is why there have been no reported convictions to date for such a corporate offence. Such cases continue to be prosecuted under the Health and Safety legislation. At the time the CMCHA was passed, the Government was urged to consider the possibility of using the CMCHA as a template for introducing further criminal offences, such as an offence of corporate grievous bodily harm, in due course.[209] This suggestion can be further bolstered by the fact that such an offence would no longer be an anomaly, thanks to the introduction of various causing serious injury offences.[210]

4–100 In the meantime, health and safety offences remain the main avenue for pursuing justice in the case of non-fatal injuries at work. The sentencing guidelines on health and safety offences are even more complex than those for corporate manslaughter, given that they must cater for a full range of harms, including risks that materialised in some kind of injury falling short of death, as well as those that did

205 House of Commons, Home Affairs and Work and Pensions Committee, *Draft Corporate Manslaughter Bill: First Report of Session 2005–06, Vol.I: Report*, para.77.

206 House of Commons, Home Affairs and Work and Pensions Committee, *Draft Corporate Manslaughter Bill: First Report of Session 2005–06, Vol.I: Report*, para.80.

207 House of Commons, Home Affairs and Work and Pensions Committee, *Draft Corporate Manslaughter Bill: First Report of Session 2005–06, Vol.I: Report*, para.81.

208 See paras 7–044–7–057.

209 House of Commons, Home Affairs and Work and Pensions Committees, *Draft Corporate Manslaughter Bill: First Report of Session 2005–06, Vol.I: Report*, para.81.

210 e.g. there are now three offences of causing serious injury by driving (dangerous (s.1A), careless (s.2C) and disqualified (s.3ZD) contrary to the Road Traffic Act 1998) and an offence of causing or allowing a child to suffer serious physical harm contrary to the Domestic Violence, Crime, and Victims Act 2004 s.5.

not give rise to any physical harm. As a result, the starting point for a medium-sized company ranges from £3,000 to £1,600,000.[211] The case of *Merlin Attractions Operations*[212] represents how the change in the guidelines may signal a change in approach to sentencing, representing as it does the highest fine imposed under the new guidelines as of 2020. The company that runs Alton Towers theme park was fined £5 million for failures that resulted in a collision of two trains on a rollercoaster at the park. A total of 16 people were injured in the incident, several seriously. Merlin Attractions pleaded guilty to a breach of the Health and Safety at Work Act s.3(1) in that the conduct of its undertaking had exposed persons other than its employees at its theme park (i.e. visitors) to risks to their safety. In sentencing, Judge Chambers emphasised that the:

> "... offence is concerned primarily with punishing the criminality for the exposure to a material risk; the fact that actual injuries were in fact caused is simply a manifestation of that risk and an aggravating feature."[213]

Although no general offence of corporate grievous bodily harm has yet been created, the CMHCA has been used as a template for creating an additional specific offence resulting in corporate liability. One such example of this is the offence of ill-treatment or wilful neglect by care providers.[214] The offence imports the same concept of a breach of a relevant duty of care and applies to corporations and individuals. The penalties include a fine, remedial order and publicity order.[215] Unlike corporate manslaughter, this is not a result crime but a conduct crime; it does not require a resulting harm to have been caused by the ill-treatment or wilful neglect. However, it is up to the courts to decide how this provision should be interpreted.[216]

In this chapter, we have by no means explored the full extent of corporate criminal liability. While we have concentrated on ways in which corporations may be held responsible for the causing of injury and other physical harms, further harms can also be caused by corporations, and offences exist specifically to deal with such harms. For example, in recent years, Parliament has introduced a number of "failure to prevent" offences in respect of bribery,[217] the facilitation of tax evasion[218] and fraud.[219] Unfortunately, for reasons of space, we are unable to cover these offences here.

---

211 Sentencing Council, *Health and Safety Offences, Corporate Manslaughter and Food Safety and Hygiene Offences, Definitive Guideline* (2015), p.7.

212 *R. v Merlin Attractions Operations Ltd* [2012] EWCA Crim 2670; [2013] 2 Cr. App. R. (S.) 36. See H. Fidderman, "Merlin Failed to Manage Ride's Human-technology Interface" (2016) 454 H.S.B. 10.

213 Fidderman, "Merlin Failed to Manage Ride's Human-technology Interface" (2016) 454 H.S.B. 10.

214 Criminal Justice and Courts Act 2015 s.21.

215 Criminal Justice and Courts Act 2015 s.23.

216 This offence has yet to be prosecuted. It should be noted that the Law Commission has taken the view that the degree of fault required for this offence to be proven is "surprisingly high", and has suggested that it could be replaced with a "failure to prevent" ill-treatment or neglect offence with a reverse burden of proof: Law Commission, *Corporate Criminal Liability: an options paper* (2022), paras 8/134–8.136, *https://s3-eu-west-2.amazonaws.com/cloud-platform-e218f50a4812967ba1215eaecede923f/uploads/sites/30/2022/06/Corporate-Criminal-Liability-Options-Paper_LC.pdf.*

217 Bribery Act 2010 s.7. See C. Wells, "Bribery: Corporate Liability under the Draft Bill 2009" [2009] Crim. L.R. 479 and C. Wells, "Corporate Criminal Liability: A Ten Year Review" [2014] Crim L.R. 849, 862–876.

218 Criminal Finances Act 2017 ss.45–46.

219 Economic Crime and Corporate Transparency Act 2023 s.119.

4–101 As an alternative to the trial and conviction of companies in relation to certain financial crimes, the Crime and Courts Act 2013 introduced Deferred Prosecution Agreements (DPA). These target economic crime in the form of theft, fraud, forgery, bribery, money laundering etc.[220] Essentially, the DPA is a type of conditional caution for companies, which permits the prosecution to achieve the objectives of punishment without the cost of a trial. The prosecution commences proceedings against the company for one of the offences listed, after which such proceedings are automatically suspended once the prosecution and defendant company have negotiated the content of the DPA. So long as the terms of the DPA are met, the company will avoid the prosecution resuming.

The Ministry of Justice, in proposing the creation of DPAs, suggested that they were designed to overcome particular obstacles to successfully prosecuting a company for economic crime. Such obstacles stem from the law of corporate criminal liability, the increasingly sophisticated criminal behaviour in the area of economic crime, the size of commercial organisations, the difficulties of identifying criminal activity, and of prosecution at national level for what can often be wrongdoing across a number of jurisdictions.[221] What is not clear is how DPAs circumvent the need for the Crown Prosecution Service to have collected sufficient evidence against a company for the relevant offences in order to be able to bring charges to begin with before a DPA can be negotiated.[222] Campbell suggests that DPAs raise issues of consistency, proportionality and fairness, and act to supplement as well as dilute corporate criminal liability.[223]

While DPAs are not relevant to corporate wrongdoing involving corporate violence, the point is that there is a range of sentencing options that could be employed to tackle corporate wrongdoing generally. As already stressed, nothing in this chapter should be taken as suggesting that corporate criminal liability should, in all cases, replace individual liability. In many cases where an individual has "gone out on a limb", that individual should be prosecuted. In many cases, both the company and individuals should be prosecuted.[224] Indeed, culpable persons should never be allowed to hide behind the corporate facade. Equally, however, in many cases, the real fault lies with the company and not with any individual. In such cases, there should be a real possibility of prosecution and conviction, with appropriate, meaningful punishment being available to reflect the true fault of the company. It has been argued that the Grenfell Tower tragedy, in which 72 people died in a fire in June 2017, will provide

---

220 Regulatory Enforcement and Sanctions Act 2008 Sch.17 Pt 2 sets out the offences to which DPAs can be applied. Some of these offences are also the subject of a sentencing guideline applying to corporate offenders, *https://www.sentencingcouncil.org.uk/publications/item/fraud-bribery-and-money-laundering-offences-definitive-guideline*.

221 MoJ CP 9/2012, *Consultation on a new enforcement tool to deal with economic crime committed by commercial organisations: Deferred Prosecution Agreements* (May 2012).

222 K. Laird, "Deferred prosecution agreements: the latest developments" (2021) 4 Crim. L.R. 283.

223 L. Campbell, "Trying corporations: why not prosecute?" [2019] 31(2) *Current Issues in Criminal Justice* 269–291.

224 The most recent sentencing guidelines for health and safety offences provide guidance on sentencing individuals separately to sentencing companies: Sentencing Council: *Health and Safety Offences, Corporate Manslaughter and Food Safety and Hygiene Offences, Definitive Guideline* (2015).

the CMCHA with its most significant test to date.[225] However, it is by far from clear that the CMCHA will be successful in bringing those responsible for the deaths to justice.[226] As of April 2024, the number of corporate manslaughter convictions remains relatively small, with a total of 36 convictions since the CMCHA was first introduced in 2007.[227]

225 Roper, "The Corporate Homicide and Corporate Manslaughter Act 2007—A 10 Year Review" (2018) 82(1) *Journal of Criminal Law* 48–75, 75.

226 R. Booth, "Grenfell fire: focus shifts to possible criminal convictions as inquiry ends" *The Guardian*, 10 November 2022, *https://www.theguardian.com/uk-news/2022/nov/10/grenfell-fire-focus-shifts-to-possible-criminal-convictions-as-inquiry-ends*.

227 Roper has argued that case numbers and convictions are a crude way to measure the CMCHA's "success", or lack thereof. She argues that although the number of convictions is relatively low, expectations ought to be adjusted to account for the period of transition from common law to statutory prosecutions, the decline of work-related deaths since the CMCHA came into force, and that only eight convictions were ever achieved using the identification doctrine. Consequently, she argues that the CMCHA is a clear improvement on the common law position, and the 'low' number of convictions is attributable to the offence's complex enforcement environment. See V. Roper, "The Corporate Manslaughter and Corporate Homicide Act 2007: a re-evaluation 10 years on from the first case" (2022) 4 Crim. L.R. 290.

Chapter 5

Non-Fatal Offences Against the Person

I. Introduction

It is often stated that society is becoming more violent, a perception that is frequently portrayed through certain media outlets,[1] but there is little empirical evidence to show that this is true. In fact, the Crime Survey for England and Wales has documented a two-thirds decrease in violent crime since 1995; the level being lower now than when the crime survey began in 1982.[2] This means that statistics on actual violent crimes (as compared to recorded figures) suggest that we are now living in a less violent society than the generation before us. Such statistics do not mean, however, that violence is becoming a thing of the past. It is therefore important that the criminal law remains responsive to the differing forms of violence that continue to pervade our ever-expanding society. **5–001**

There are many offences involving personal violence, ranging from "mainstream" offences such as causing grievous bodily harm, through kidnapping and administering poison to those such as assaulting a clergyman in the execution of his duties. The main offences, which are mostly statutory, will be considered as these represent an ideal forum for considering how the law deals with the various configurations of degrees of harm and levels of mens rea. The offences are ranked in some sort of hierarchy of seriousness: the extent to which this ordering is based on principle will emerge as the offences are examined. As we shall see, they range from "the merest touching of another in anger",[3] to injuries which fall only just short of death. As several of the offences contain the basic element of assault, and as it constitutes the lowest rung in the hierarchy of seriousness, this will be examined first.

1 Y. Jewkes, *Media and Crime*, 3rd edn (London: Sage, 2015).

2 Office for National Statistics, *Crime in England and Wales: year ending March 2023* (2023), Table 1.

3 *Cole v Turner* 87 E.R. 907; (1704) 6 Mod. 149.

A. ASSAULT AND BATTERY

5–002 The terms "assault", "common assault" and "battery" are often used interchangeably by laypeople and even lawyers. This terminological confusion which causes "angels [to] prepare to dance on needles and legal pedants [to] sharpen their quill pens"[4] is compounded by statute. The Criminal Justice Act 1988 s.39 refers to "common assault and battery" as two separate offences while s.40(3) refers only to a "common assault". In *Lynsey*,[5] it was held that this latter phrase includes a battery and in *Ireland; Burstow*,[6] it was held that the term "assault" includes both a common assault and battery.

To avoid confusion in this book, the term "assault" is used in its broad generic sense as encompassing either of these specific crimes and the two specific offences will be referred to as "technical assault" (common assault) and "battery". In its most basic form, a technical assault can be defined as putting someone in fear of immediate "force",[7] whereas a battery is the actual infliction of violence on a person.[8]

Both these offences are only triable summarily (in the magistrates' court) and subject to a maximum penalty of six months' imprisonment. These offences can be used in many cases where injury has resulted and a more serious charge could have been brought. The CPS *Charging Standards* state that:

> ". . . the appropriate charge will usually be contrary to section 39 where injuries amount to no more than the following: grazes; scratches; abrasions; minor bruising; swellings; reddening of the skin; superficial cuts."[9]

Where there is serious injury and the likely sentence is clearly more than six months' imprisonment a more serious charge should be brought. There are significant advantages to trial in the magistrates' court instead of the Crown Court; the CPS perceives this as being quicker and cheaper, more likely to result in conviction and, particularly in the context of domestic violence, involving a less onerous task for the V/witness.[10] Under the Criminal Law Act 1967 s.6, common assault is an alternative verdict to more serious charges of aggravated assault even if the count has not been included in the indictment.

1. Technical assault

5–003 This offence is committed when D intentionally or recklessly causes V to apprehend imminent force.

4 *R. v Lynsey (Jonathan Simon)* [1995] 2 Cr. App. R. 667 at 671; (1995) 159 J.P. 437 CA.
5 *Lynsey* [1995] 2 Cr. App. R. 667 at 671.
6 *R. v Ireland; R. v Burstow* [1998] A.C. 147 at 161; [1997] 3 W.L.R. 534 HL. See also *DPP v Taylor (Keith Richard)* [1992] Q.B. 645; (1992) 95 Cr. App. R. 28 QBD.
7 *DPP v Ahmed* [2021] EWHC 2122 (Admin); [2022] 1 W.L.R. 314.
8 Readers may wish to note that in practice a technical assault will be charged as "common assault", while an assault involving the infliction of violence (i.e. a battery) will be charged as "assault by beating"; *DPP v Taylor (Keith Richard)* [1992] Q.B. 645; [1992] 2 W.L.R. 460.
9 CPS, *Offences Against the Person, Incorporating the Charging Standard, https://www.cps.gov.uk/legal-guidance/offences-against-person-incorporating-charging-standard*.
10 A. Cretney and G. Davis, "Prosecuting Domestic Assault: Victims Failing Courts, or Courts Failing Victims" (1997) 36 *Howard Journal of Criminal Justice* 146.

(i) Actus reus

D must do something to make V apprehend imminent force. It is often stated that V must fear an immediate attack. This latter formulation, while descriptive of most situations of technical assault, is deceptive for two reasons. First, V need not be placed in "fear" in the sense of being frightened; they might be confident of their ability to repel the attack. They are nevertheless assaulted as they are made to apprehend the force. Secondly, they need not apprehend an "attack" in the sense of a severe measure of aggressive or destructive force; they need only apprehend any degree of force, which, as we shall see, in some circumstances need amount to little more than an unlawful touching. **5–004**

(a) Can mere words amount to a technical assault?

While it has always been clear that physical gestures such as shaking a fist or pointing a gun at V would suffice, there used to be doubt as to whether words could constitute an assault. This issue has been resolved in the following decision. **5–005**

R. v Ireland; R. v Burstow [1998] A.C. 147 (House of Lords):

In the first appeal, D made repeated silent telephone calls, mostly at night, to three women. Sometimes, he resorted to heavy breathing. As a result, the women suffered psychiatric illness. He was charged with assault occasioning actual bodily harm, contrary to the Offences against the Person Act 1861 s.47. One of the issues on appeal was whether such conduct could amount to an assault. **5–006**

LORD STEYN:

> "The proposition that a gesture may amount to an assault, but that words can never suffice, is unrealistic and indefensible. A thing said is also a thing done. There is no reason why something said should be incapable of causing an apprehension of immediate personal violence, *e.g.* a man accosting a woman in a dark alley saying 'come with me or I will stab you'. I would, therefore, reject the proposition that an assault can never be committed by words."

LORD HOPE OF CRAIGHEAD:

> "[I]t is not true to say that mere words or gestures can never constitute an assault. It all depends on the circumstances . . . The words or gestures must be seen in their whole context."

Appeals dismissed

Another rule has long been beyond doubt: words may negate an assault. In *Tuberville v Savage*,[11] D placed his hand on his sword hilt and exclaimed to V: "If it were not assize-time, I would not take such language **5–007**

11 *Tuberville v Savage* 86 E.R. 684; (1669) 1 Mod. Rep. 3.

from you." This was held not to be an assault. The words accompanying the action (of placing the hand on the sword) clearly demonstrated that because the assize judge was in town, D was *not* going to use his sword. There could thus be no apprehension of immediate force.

(b) Conditional and empty threats

5–008 The situation in *Tuberville v Savage* must be carefully distinguished from cases involving a conditional threat, such as *Read v Coker*[12] where it was held to be an assault to threaten to break V's neck *if* he did not leave the premises. In such a case, there is a threat to use immediate force; V *does* apprehend immediate force and the onus is on him to do something to avert that force. If the rule were otherwise it would mean there could be no assault where a robber says "your money or your life"; such a position would be intolerable.

Another point to be considered is the stance that the law takes in relation to empty threats. For example, V might be threatened with a toy gun or an unloaded gun. In *Bentham*, D placed his hand inside his jacket causing a bulge to give the impression he had a gun and threatened to shoot unless V handed over money and jewellery.[13] Understandably, the law regards this fact as immaterial as long as V is made to fear an attack;[14] after all, V cannot be expected to know whether the threat is real or not.

(c) Immediacy of the threat

5–009 V must apprehend the "imminent" use of force. It is a serious gap in the law that it is no offence whatsoever to tell someone that you intend to break both their legs the next day rather than there and then.[15] The Law Commission's 2015 report on Offences Against the Person[16] proposes an amendment to the law, referring to the Draft Offences against the Person Bill 1998 cl.10 which extends threatening to kill to include non-immediate threats to cause serious injury.[17] One of the consequences of this present gap, has been the development by the courts of a broad interpretation of "imminence" or "immediacy". In *Smith*,[18] it was held that a woman had been assaulted when she saw a man looking through her closed bedsit room window at night. Although he was outside her room and would have had to break or force open her window and climb in before he could have actually inflicted violence upon her, it was held that she had apprehended a sufficiently immediate application of force. In *Siadatan*, it was stated that "immediate" (for purposes of the Public Order Act 1986 s.4[19]):

12 *Read v Coker* 138 E.R. 1437; (1853) 13 C.B. 850. See also *Ansell v Thomas* [1974] Crim. L.R. 31 CA.

13 *R. v Bentham (Peter)* [2005] UKHL 18; [2005] 2 Cr. App. R. 11. In this case, the charge was robbery and possession of an imitation firearm contrary to the Firearms Act 1968 s.17(2). The House of Lords held there could be no liability for the latter offence as one could not possess one's hand or fingers. On these facts, there would clearly have been an assault.

14 *Logdon v DPP* [1976] Crim. L.R. 121 Div Ct; *R. v St George* 173 E.R. 921; (1840) 9 Car. & P. 483.

15 See, generally, P. Alldridge, "Threats Offences—A Case for Reform" [1994] Crim. L.R. 176.

16 Law Commission Paper No.361, *Reform of Offences against the Person* (2015).

17 Home Office, *Violence: Reforming the Offences Against the Person Act 1861* (1998), cl.10.

18 *Smith v Chief Superintendent, Woking Police Station* (1983) 76 Cr. App. R. 234; [1983] Crim. L.R. 323 QBD.

19 This is a public order offence very similar to common assault. It involves a person using threatening, abusive or insulting words or behaviour with intent to cause that person to believe that immediate unlawful violence will be used against them.

"... connotes proximity in time and proximity in causation; that it is likely that violence will result within a reasonably short period of time and without any other intervening occurrence."[20]

This problem of imminence or immediacy was of particular importance in cases in the latter part of the 20th century where Ds made silent or verbally threatening telephone calls.

R. v Ireland; R. v Burstow [1998] A.C. 147 (House of Lords):

LORD STEYN: **5–010**

"That brings me to the critical question whether a silent caller may be guilty of an assault. The answer to this question seems to me to be 'Yes, depending on the facts'. It involves questions of fact within the province of the jury. After all, there is no reason why a telephone caller who says to a woman in a menacing way 'I will be at your door in a minute or two' may not be guilty of an assault if he causes his victim to apprehend immediate personal violence. Take now the case of the silent caller. He intends by his silence to cause fear and is so understood. The victim is assailed by uncertainty about his intentions. Fear may dominate her emotions, and it may be the fear that the caller's arrival at her door may be imminent. She may fear the *possibility* of immediate personal violence. As a matter of law the caller may be guilty of an assault: whether he is or not will depend on the circumstance and in particular on the impact of the caller's potentially menacing call or calls on the victim."

Appeals dismissed

This decision is best understood in the context of events leading up to the appeal. For at least two years prior to the House of Lords' judgment the media had been conducting a high-profile campaign against stalking. **5–011**

(d) The development of separate harassment and stalking offences

Home Office, Stalking—The Solutions: A Consultation Paper (1996):

"1.2 Stalking ... can be broadly described as a series of acts which are intended to, or in fact, cause harassment to another person ... **5–012**

1.6 The methods employed by stalkers can take many forms ... [such as] making obscene telephone calls, using abusive and threatening language, or committing acts of violence ... However, frequently stalkers do not overtly threaten their victims but use behaviour which is ostensibly routine and harmless and therefore not caught by existing laws. But even apparently

20 *R. v Horseferry Road Magistrates' Court Ex p. Siadatan* [1991] 1 Q.B. 260; (1991) 92 Cr. App. R. 257 at 262.

> innocuous behaviour, such as following someone down the street, or sending them flowers, can be intimidating if it is persistently inflicted on a victim against their will. This is one of the defining characteristics of stalking: irrespective of the nature of its component acts, stalking can be distressing and threatening to a victim because of its sheer, oppressive persistence . . ."

5–013 Responding to the media clamour for more effective criminal laws against stalking, the Government enacted the Protection from Harassment Act 1997 which introduced two criminal offences of harassment. Section 2 creates the offence of harassment which is committed where a person pursues a course of conduct (in breach of s.1(1) or 1(A)) on at least two occasions which amounts to harassment of another and which D knows or ought to know amounts to harassment. This offence carries a maximum penalty of six months' imprisonment. The emphasis in this crime is upon D's conduct and pursuit of V, even if V initiates contact,[21] and not upon an impending attack on V. The two or more acts in question must be connected in type and context. The fewer the incidents and the longer the period between them, the more necessary it will be to consider whether separate incidents can be properly described as a "course of conduct".[22]

The Act does not specifically define harassment. In *Tuppen*,[23] Douglas Brown J held that as the Act does not define "harassment" it was legitimate for the court to have recourse to Parliamentary records on the matter. Such records made it clear that the behaviour sought to be controlled was conduct such as stalking, antisocial behaviour by neighbours and racial harassment. In *Dowson*,[24] Simon J held, after an extensive review of the relevant authorities, that for conduct to constitute harassment within the Act:

> "A line is to be drawn between conduct which is unattractive and unreasonable, and conduct which has been described in various ways: 'torment' of the victim, 'of an order which would sustain criminal liability'. . ."

Such conduct must also be "objectively judged to be oppressive and unacceptable".[25] What is deemed to be oppressive and unacceptable may "depend on the social or working context in which the conduct occurs".[26]

Section 4(1) of the Act also creates the more serious offence of pursuing a course of conduct (on at least two occasions) which causes another to fear, on at least two occasions, that violence *will* be used

---

21 *James v Crown Prosecution Service* [2009] EWHC 2925 (Admin); [2010] Crim. L.R. 580.

22 *R. v Patel (Niton)* [2004] EWCA Crim 3284; [2005] 1 Cr. App. R. 27.

23 *Tuppen v Microsoft Corp Ltd, The Times,* 15 November 2000 (QB).

24 *Dowson v Chief Constable of Northumbria* [2010] EWHC 2612 (QB).

25 Reiterated in *R. v N* [2016] EWCA Crim 92; [2016] 2 Cr. App. R. 10 CA where the court held that conduct causing alarm and distress may not necessarily amount to harassment, the conduct must also be "oppressive".

26 *Dowson* [2010] EWHC 2612 (QB) at [142].

against them. D will be liable if they know or ought to know that their course of conduct will cause the other so to fear on each of those occasions. The maximum penalty is five years' imprisonment.[27]

The Act was amended in 2012[28] to include the new offence of stalking, largely the result of a Stalking Law Reform Campaign that was launched in July 2011.[29] Under s.2A of the Act, a person is guilty of an offence if they pursue a course of conduct in breach of s.1(1) *and* the course of conduct amounts to stalking. This offence carries a maximum sentence of 51 weeks' imprisonment.[30] The section does not define "stalking" but does provide a list of examples of acts and omissions which are associated with it, including: following a person; contacting, or attempting to contact, a person by any means; publishing any statement or other material relating or purporting to relate to a person, or purporting to originate from a person; monitoring the use by a person of the internet, email or any other form of electronic communication; loitering in any place (whether public or private); interfering with any property in the possession of a person; and watching or spying on a person.[31] **5–014**

Section 4A also creates a more serious offence of "stalking involving fear of violence or serious alarm or distress". D's course of conduct must amount to stalking, and either cause another to fear, on at least two occasions, that violence will be used against another,[32] or causes another serious alarm or distress which has a substantial adverse effect on their usual day-to-day activities. D will only be guilty of such an offence if they know or ought to know that their course of conduct will cause V to fear violence on each of those occasions, or, as the case may be, that their actions will cause alarm or distress.[33] D ought to know their conduct will cause fear or alarm or distress if a reasonable person in possession of the same information would think the course of conduct would cause V fear, or alarm or distress which has a substantial adverse effect on V's usual day-to-day activities.[34] This offence carries a maximum sentence of 10 years' imprisonment.

It is likely that offenders such as *Ireland* would now be pursued either under the harassment or stalking offences. However, the Protection from Harassment Act 1997 was not in force at the time of the *Ireland* prosecution and, in any event, Lord Steyn described the original harassment offences as "not ideally suited" to deal with the case before him where V only feared that violence *might* be used against her. Under s.4 of the Act there has to be fear that violence *will* be used.[35] It was against this background that the appeal in *Ireland* was heard. Lord Steyn commenced his judgment by outlining the "significant

---

27 Discussion of these provisions is beyond the scope of this book. See, generally, D. Ormerod, *Smith and Hogan: Criminal Law*, 13th edn (Oxford: OUP, 2011), pp.695–705.

28 Added by the Protection of Freedoms Act 2012 s.111(1).

29 See Home Office, *Consultation on Stalking* (2011). For an overview of the new offences, see J. Gowland, "Protection from Harassment Act 1997: The 'New' Stalking Offences" (2013) 77 J. Crim. L. 387.

30 The Stalking Protection Act 2019 created stalking protection orders that can include specific prohibitions and requirements as set out by the court. It is an offence to breach an order; the maximum sentence is five years' imprisonment.

31 Harassment Act 1997 s.2A(3).

32 In *R. v Qosja (Robert)* [2016] EWCA Crim 1543; [2017] 1 W.L.R. 311, the court had to consider what degree of immediacy and/or specificity was required in relation to the fear of violence for the purpose of s.4A. The court found that, based on a plain and natural reading of the wording of the section, fear of violence included incidents in the future as well as those arising directly out of the incident in question. The court went on to hold that there was no "requirement for the fear to be of violence on a particular date or time in the future, or at a particular place or in a particular manner, or for there to be a specific threat of violence": [318]–[319].

33 Harassment Act 1997 s.4A(1).

34 Harassment Act 1997 s.4A(2) and (3).

35 As noted above, this is not the case under the newer s.4A where an offence will be committed where D has pursued a course of conduct that has caused V "serious alarm or distress which has a substantial adverse effect on the victim's usual day-to-day activities".

social problem" of harassment of women by repeated silent telephone calls and immediately pronounced that it was "self-evident" that the criminal law had to be capable of dealing with the problem. His stance was clear. If the law of assault had to be stretched beyond all previously recognised limits, then so be it. Ireland's appeal was doomed from the start. However, as shall be explained, the law has not been radically altered and securing a conviction of similar telephone callers is still no simple matter.

(e) Stalking as technical assault

5–015 As seen in the *Ireland* extract above, Lord Steyn accepted the basic definition of an assault involving the apprehension of imminent personal violence—with "violence" meaning physical violence. The only extension of the law was his ruling that V need only fear the *possibility* of immediate personal violence. They need only fear that "the caller's arrival at her door may be imminent". On the facts of the particular appeal, the House of Lords was able to sidestep the problem of immediacy on the basis that Ireland had pleaded guilty at his trial.[36] In other cases, however, this problem will not be easily overcome. If V has received hundreds of phone calls and none of them has been followed by "the caller's arrival at her door", it will be extremely difficult to establish that V genuinely feared the possibility of immediate personal violence. In *Ramos*,[37] it was held that it was "the state of mind of Vs which is crucial rather than the statistical risk of violence actively occurring within a short space of time". Nevertheless, the more incidents that have not been followed up by violence, the less plausible the claimed apprehension becomes. Furthermore, even in extreme cases where the seriousness of the threats increases, such as *Cox*[38] where after "hundreds of incidents" the caller told V that before she went on holiday, she was "going to her death", it is going to be no less difficult to establish that she feared *there and then* the possibility of immediate personal violence—as opposed to fearing violence at some time and at some place in the future. These difficulties were conceded by Lord Steyn when he concluded:

> "I nevertheless accept that the concept of an assault involving immediate personal violence as an ingredient of the section 47 offence is a considerable complicating factor in bringing prosecutions under it in respect of silent telephone callers and stalkers. That the least serious of the ladder of offences is difficult to apply in such cases is unfortunate."

A similar unduly broad approach was adopted by the Court of Appeal in *Constanza*[39] (a case decided a few months before, and not referred to in, *Ireland*). This case involved a stalker who made repeated silent telephone calls and sent 800 letters culminating in two further letters which V interpreted as clear threats. It was held that the assault was committed when V read these latter letters as there was a "fear of violence at some time *not excluding the immediate future*". This is similar to Lord Steyn's test that V need only fear the *possibility* of immediate personal violence. This is surely going too far. While the recipient of a telephone call might well fear that the call is from a mobile phone and that the caller

36 *R. v Ireland (Robert Matthew)* [1997] Q.B. 114; [1996] 3 W.L.R. 650 CA. See Lord Steyn at 163 and Lord Hope at 167.
37 *DPP v Ramos* [2000] Crim. L.R. 768; [2000] C.O.D. 287 Div Ct.
38 *R. v Cox (Paul Andrew)* [1998] Crim. L.R. 810 CA.
39 *R. v Constanza (Gaetano)* [1997] 2 Cr. App. R. 492; [1997] Crim. L.R. 576 CA.

will be at her door "in a minute or two",[40] it seems inconceivable that she would apprehend such *immediate* violence upon receipt of a letter.

Many recipients of silent or menacing telephone calls will probably not be afraid that the caller will arrive soon at the front door to inflict violence upon them. The fear is more likely to be one of future physical violence, future harassment and similar future calls increasing tension and anxiety. The relentless pressure combined with fear of the unknown is likely to cause Vs significant psychological trauma. The Court of Appeal in *Ireland*[41] recognised this by reformulating an assault as the apprehension of immediate violence with "violence" including psychological damage. In the Court of Appeal, Swinton Thomas LJ stated:

> "[W]hen a telephone call is made by the appellant and the victim lifts the telephone and then knows that the man is telephoning them yet again, they will be apprehensive of suffering the very psychological damage from which they did suffer, namely palpitations, difficulty in breathing, cold sweats, anxiety, inability to sleep, dizziness, stress and the like . . . [T]he fact that the violence is inflicted indirectly, causing psychological harm, does not render the act to be any less an act of violence."

Although Lord Hope rejected this view in the House of Lords, it does not mean such phone calls will fall outside the offence of assault. He notes:

> "In my opinion silent telephone calls of this nature are . . . capable . . . of causing an apprehension of immediate and unlawful violence . . . Whether this requirement, and in particular that of immediacy, is in fact satisfied will depend on the circumstances. This will need in each case, if it is disputed, to be explored in evidence."[42]

(ii) Mens rea

The mens rea for technical assault involves D intentionally or recklessly cause their V to apprehend the infliction of immediate force.[43] Thus if they intend to alarm their V, or are reckless thereto, the mens rea requirement is satisfied, even if they never intended to carry out the threat. **5–016**

What is meant by recklessness here? In *DPP v K*,[44] it was held that the *Caldwell* meaning applied. However, this was disapproved in *Spratt*[45] where it was held that the subjective *Cunningham* test of recklessness applied, i.e. did D foresee putting V in apprehension of imminent force and continue

---

40 *Ireland* [1998] A.C. 147 at 162.
41 *Ireland* [1997] Q.B. 114 at 122.
42 *Ireland* [1998] A.C. 147 at 166–167.
43 *R. v Venna (Henson George)* [1976] Q.B. 421; [1975] 3 W.L.R. 737 CA.
44 *DPP v K (A Minor)* [1990] 1 W.L.R. 1067; (1990) 91 Cr. App. R. 23 QBD. The Court of Appeal in *R. v Savage (Susan)* [1992] 1 A.C. 714 (Note); [1991] 2 W.L.R. 418 CA adopted a similar view.
45 *R. v Spratt (Robert Michael)* [1990] 1 W.L.R. 1073; (1990) 91 Cr. App. R. 362 CA. This same view was adopted in *R. v Nash (Lee)* (1991) 155 J.P. 709; [1991] Crim. L.R. 768 CA and by the Court of Appeal in *Parmenter* [1991] 2 All E.R. 225.

regardless of this risk? The House of Lords, in the leading case of *Savage; Parmenter*,[46] did not deal with this issue, possibly indicating an acceptance that the *Spratt* line of cases represents the law and that *Cunningham* recklessness is required.[47] Although the leading House of Lords' decision in *G*[48] restricts itself to criminal damage, it is widely accepted that the subjective meaning of recklessness there endorsed will be applicable throughout the criminal law.[49]

2. Battery

5–017 A battery is the intentional or reckless infliction of unlawful personal force by one person upon another. While a technical assault is the *threatening* of such force, a battery is the actual *infliction* of the force.

(i) Actus reus

5–018 D must inflict unlawful personal force. It is often assumed that the force inflicted must be injurious for the offence to be completed. The courts have made it clear that this need not necessarily be the case.

(a) The meaning of "force"

WILSON V PRINGLE [1986] 2 ALL E.R. 440 (COURT OF APPEAL, CIVIL DIVISION):

5–019 CROOM-JOHNSON LJ:

"In our view the authorities lead to the conclusion that in a battery there must be an intentional touching or contact in one form or another of the plaintiff by the defendant. That touching must be proved to be a hostile touching. That still leaves unanswered the question, when is a touching to be called hostile? Hostility cannot be equated with ill-will or malevolence. It cannot be governed by the obvious intention shown in acts like punching, stabbing or shooting. It cannot be solely governed by an expressed intention, although that may be strong evidence. But the element of hostility, in the sense in which it is now to be considered, must be a question of fact for the tribunal of fact . . .

Although we are all entitled to protection from physical molestation, we live in a crowded world in which people must be considered as taking on themselves some risk of injury (where it occurs) from the acts of others which are not in themselves unlawful."

---

46 *Savage* [1991] 2 W.L.R. 418; *Parmenter* [1992] 1 A.C. 699.

47 This point was conceded on appeal in *Haystead v Chief Constable of Derbyshire* [2000] 2 Cr. App. R. 339; (2000) 164 J.P. 396 Div Ct.

48 *R. v G* [2003] UKHL 50; [2004] 1 A.C. 1034.

49 *R. v Brady (Philip)* [2006] EWCA Crim 2413; [2007] Crim. L.R. 564: "many of their Lordships observations [in *G*] have a much wider application" than merely to criminal damage.

This was approved by the House of Lords in *Brown*.[50] Lord Jauncey, however, unhelpfully added that if D's actions are unlawful they are necessarily hostile. Thus, because it is unlawful to cause injuries in the course of sado-masochistic activities, the element of hostility is satisfied. Such circular reasoning defies explanation. To say that injuries are inflicted with hostility when they have been consented to is to deprive the word "hostility" of any literal meaning. A better approach was adopted by Lord Mustill, dissenting in *Brown*, who stated that hostility was not a crucial matter in determining guilt or innocence, "although its presence or absence may be relevant when the court has to decide as a matter of policy how to react to a new situation".[51] **5–020**

Several further matters need consideration. Firstly, while many of the cases speak of "force" or "violence", it is clear that any unlawful touching suffices. So, taking a person's arm firmly to escort them out of a dinner reception is capable of amounting to a battery.[52] Secondly, in the "crowded world" (*Wilson v Pringle*) of today where there is much pushing or jostling in queues, etc there is a "general exception embracing all physical contact which is generally acceptable in the ordinary conduct of daily life".[53] Thirdly, a battery involves the application of physical force upon V. Actual touching body to body is not necessary. For example, in *Lynsey*,[54] there was a battery when D spat in the face of a police officer. However, the force must be physical. In *Ireland; Burstow* it was held that silent telephone calls resulting in psychiatric injury could not constitute a battery.[55] Fourthly, it used to be thought that a battery could not be committed by omission.[56] However, in *Santana-Bermudez*, D was held liable when he failed to warn a police officer searching him that he had hypodermic needles in his pockets and her finger was pierced by a needle. Maurice Kay J was critical of the "undesirable complexity [that] has bedevilled our criminal law as a result of quasi-theological distinctions between acts and omissions" and simply ruled that:

> "[W]here someone (by act or word or by a combination of the two) creates a danger and thereby exposes another to a reasonably foreseeable risk of injury which materialises, there is an evidential basis for the *actus reus* of an assault occasioning actual bodily harm . . ."[57]

However, it is unclear from this whether liability was based on his omission (with him being under a duty to tell her about the needles because he had created a dangerous situation) or on the fiction of a continuing act (putting the needles in his pocket was an act which continued until the police officer injured herself). The rather limited ratio of the case seems to suggest that there will be no liability for

---

50 *R. v Brown (Anthony Joseph)* [1994] 1 A.C. 212; [1993] 2 W.L.R. 556 HL. See also *Faulkner v Talbot* [1981] 1 W.L.R. 1528; (1982) 74 Cr. App. R. 1 Div Ct. On the issue of the amount of everyday contact to which we are deemed to consent, see *R. v Sutton (Terence)* [1977] 1 W.L.R. 1086; (1978) 66 Cr. App. R. 21.

51 *Brown* [1994] 1 A.C. 212 at 261.

52 *McMillan v Crown Prosecution Service* [2008] EWHC 1457 (Admin); (2008) 172 J.P. 485. See also *Marland v DPP* [2023] EWHC 1046 (Admin); [2023] 2 Cr. App. R. 5 where the court held that a magistrates' court had been entitled to convict a man for assault where he had grabbed his partner's shoulders in order to guide her to his car due to the fact he was concerned she was intoxicated whilst walking down a busy road late in the evening. Because she had not consented to the grabbing and had resisted, implied consent did not apply.

53 *Collins v Willcock* [1984] 1 W.L.R. 1172; (1984) 79 Cr. App. R. 229 Div Ct.

54 *R. v Lynsey (Jonathan Simon)* [1995] 2 Cr. App. R. 667; (1995) 159 J.P. 437 CA. See also *Pursell v Horn* 112 E.R. 966; (1838) 8 Ad. & El. 602 where D threw boiling water scalding V. The majority of the court accepted that a battery was not limited to body-to-body contact.

55 *Ireland; Burstow* [1998] A.C. 147 at 161.

56 M. Hirst, "Assault, Battery and Indirect Violence" [1999] Crim. L.R. 577.

57 *DPP v Santa-Bermudez* [2003] EWHC 2908 (Admin) at [10]; (2004) 168 J.P. 373.

an omission in other situations where there is a duty to act: for example, where a mother (who did not create the dangerous situation) fails to rescue her child who suffers actual bodily harm as a consequence.

(b) Indirect force

5–021 A final issue is whether the force need be applied directly. Is it necessary, for example, that D physically come into contact with V with his fist, spittle or some weapon? Older authorities[58] suggest that this was indeed the case (although "direct" was interpreted with a certain amount of flexibility). However, the case of *Martin*[59] can be read as dispensing with the requirement of direct force. In this case, D barred the exit to a theatre with an iron bar, turned off the lights and shouted "fire". Some people subsequently were injured when they were crushed against the exit in the panic to escape. D was convicted under the Offences against the Person Act 1861 s.20 of inflicting grievous bodily harm (an offence then thought to require proof of an assault).

The decision of *Wilson*,[60] however, interpreted *Martin* somewhat differently as supporting the view that "to inflict" grievous bodily harm under s.20 does not necessitate an assault taking place. On the issue of whether an assault itself necessitates direct force, Lord Roskill in *Wilson* approved a passage from the Australian decision of *Salisbury*[61] where a distinction was drawn between "directly and violently" inflicting a harm (an assault) and inflicting harm that was "not itself a direct application of force to the body of the victim, [but] does directly result in force being applied violently to the body of the victim" (not an assault). The House of Lords in *Savage; Parmenter*, albeit obiter, endorsed this approach in holding that there would be no assault in cases like *Martin* or where D had interfered with the breaking mechanism of a car thereby causing a crash and injuries to the driver. Furthermore, in *Ireland; Burstow*[62] Lord Hope stated that a battery could not be committed over the telephone because there was no physical contact between D and V.

On the other hand, the following case clearly suggests that a battery can be committed even if the force is applied indirectly.[63]

DPP v K (A MINOR) (1990) 91 CR. APP. R. 23 (QUEEN'S BENCH DIVISIONAL COURT):

5–022 D, a 15-year-old schoolboy, was carrying out an experiment using concentrated sulphuric acid in a chemistry class at school when he splashed some of the acid on his hand. He was given permission to go to the toilet to wash it off and without his teacher's knowledge, took a test-tube of the acid with him to test its reaction on some toilet paper. While he was in the toilet he heard footsteps in the corridor and in a panic poured the acid into a hot air drier to conceal it. He returned to his class intending to return later to remove it and wash out the drier. Before he could do so another pupil used the drier. Acid squirted onto his face causing a permanent scar. D was charged with assault

58 See, e.g. *Scott v Shepherd* 96 E.R. 525; (1772) 2 Wm. Bl. 892.
59 *R. v Martin* (1881) 8 Q.B.D. 54.
60 *R. v Wilson (Clarence George)* [1984] A.C. 242; [1983] 3 W.L.R. 686 HL.
61 *Salisbury* [1976] V.R. 452 at 461.
62 *Ireland; Burstow* [1998] A.C. 147 at 165.
63 For a view that this case was decided per incuriam and that a battery does require a direct physical attack, see Hirst, "Assault, Battery and Indirect Violence" [1999] Crim. L.R. 557.

occasioning actual bodily harm but was acquitted because he had not intended to harm anyone. The prosecution appealed by way of case stated.

PARKER LJ:

> "[I]n my judgment there can be no doubt that if a defendant places acid into a machine with the intent that it shall, when the next user switches the machine on, be ejected onto him and do him harm there is an assault when the harm is done. The position was correctly and simply stated by Stephen J in *R. v Clarence* (1888) 22 Q.B.D. 23 at 45, where he said:
>
> > 'If a man laid a trap for another into which he fell after an interval, the man who laid it would during the interval be guilty of an attempt to assault, and of an actual assault as soon as the man fell in.'
>
> This illustration was also referred to by Wills J in the same case in relation to s.20 of the 1861 Act. Wills J there also referred to *R. v Martin* (1881) 8 Q.B.D. 54, saying:
>
> > 'The prisoner in that case did what was certain to make people crush one another, perhaps to death, and the grievous bodily harm was as truly inflicted by him as if he had hurled a stone at somebody's head.'
>
> In the same way a defendant who pours a dangerous substance into a machine just as truly assaults the next user of the machine as if he had himself switched the machine on."

Appeal allowed

The actions of a person who leaves acid in a hot air drier (which will inevitably be used by someone) seem morally indistinguishable from those of a person who throws acid directly at another. **5–023**

In *Haystead*, D punched a woman who was holding a child. The child fell from her arms and hit his head on the floor. The main argument on appeal was whether there could be a battery when force was indirectly applied. In a highly ambiguous judgment it was indicated that this "may well be" so, but it was unnecessary to decide as, on the facts, there was a direct application of force even though there was no physical contact with the child:

> ". . . [dropping] the child was entirely and immediately the result of the appellant's action in punching her. There is no difference in logic or good sense between the facts of this case and one where the defendant might have used a weapon to fell the child to the floor."[64]

64 *Haystead v Chief Constable of Derbyshire* [2000] 2 Cr. App. R. 339 at 346; (2000) 164 J.P. 396 Div Ct.

(ii) Mens rea

5–024 D must intentionally or recklessly inflict force upon V.

R. v VENNA [1976] Q.B. 421 (COURT OF APPEAL, CRIMINAL DIVISION):

5–025 JAMES LJ:

"In our view the element of mens rea in the offence of battery is satisfied by proof that the defendant intentionally or recklessly applied force to the person of another . . .

We see no reason in logic or in law why a person who recklessly applies physical force to the person of another should be outside the criminal law of assault. In many cases the dividing line between intention and recklessness is barely distinguishable."

5–026 The same arguments considered in relation to technical assault apply here with the prevailing consensus being that recklessness bears its "subjective" *Cunningham* meaning. In *D v DPP*,[65] it was stated that recklessness involves foresight of the risk of unlawful force and the taking of that risk.

(iii) Punishment

5–027 A common assault is punishable upon summary conviction by a fine of up to (currently) £5,000 and/or six months' imprisonment. The offence is no longer triable upon indictment.[66] The Magistrates' Courts Sentencing Guidelines provide that the starting point where there is lesser culpability and lesser harm is a fine (Category 3). The maximum sentence for high culpability and high level harm (Category 1) is 26 weeks' custody.[67]

B. AGGRAVATED ASSAULTS

5–028 The more serious offences of violence are commonly termed "aggravated assaults" although, as we shall see, for some of these offences it is not necessary to prove the existence of an assault. Some assaults are aggravated because of the circumstances in which they are committed, for example, assault with intent to resist arrest[68] or because of the identity of V, for example, assault on a police

65 *D v DPP* [2005] EWHC 967 (Admin); [2005] Crim. L.R. 962.

66 Criminal Justice Act 1988 s.39(1). Exceptionally, common assault can still be tried on indictment if it is founded on the same facts as an indictable offence which is charged, or if it forms part of a series of offences of a similar character to an indictable offence charged (Criminal Justice Act 1988 s.40).

67 Sentencing Council, Common assault/Racially or religiously aggravated common assault/ Battery/ Common assault on emergency worker, *https://www.sentencingcouncil.org.uk/offences/magistrates-court/item/common-assault-racially-or-religiously-aggravated-common-assault-common-assault-on-emergency-worker/*.

68 Offences Against the Person Act 1861 s.38.

constable in the execution of his duty[69] or assault on an immigration officer.[70] The following three sections deal with the core aggravated assaults which can be committed in any circumstances and against any V; the chapter then examines the law dealing with "racially or religiously aggravated" assaults and finally the causing of serious injury by dangerous driving.

1. Assault occasioning actual bodily harm

Offences against the Person Act 1861 s.47:

"Whosoever shall be convicted on indictment of any assault occasioning actual bodily harm shall be liable . . . to be imprisoned for any term not exceeding five years." 5–029

(i) Actus reus

Two conditions need to be satisfied here. First, there must be an "assault". This means there must be either a technical assault or a battery.[71] Second, this assault must "occasion" or *cause* actual bodily harm. For example, in *Roberts*,[72] D tried to pull a girl's coat off in a moving car. She jumped out of the car and was injured. Here there was an assault and she had suffered actual bodily harm. The sole issue in this case was whether causation had been established.[73] Where it is alleged that the actual bodily harm has been caused by a technical assault (as opposed to a battery) it must be established that it was the apprehension of imminent force—as opposed to general fear and upset—that caused the actual bodily harm.[74] 5–030

(a) What is actual bodily harm?

Actual bodily harm includes "any hurt or injury calculated to interfere with health or comfort".[75] In *Chan-Fook*, it was held that the words "actual bodily harm" were ordinary words generally requiring no elaboration: 5–031

> "The word 'harm' is a synonym for injury. The word 'actual' indicates that the injury (although there is no need for it to be permanent) should not be so trivial as to be wholly insignificant."[76]

---

69 Police Act 1996 s.89.

70 UK Borders Act 2007 s.22. Assaults against emergency workers is also an aggravating factor at sentencing, Assaults on Emergency Workers (Offences) Act 2018 s.2.

71 *Ireland; Burstow* [1998] A.C. 147 at 161.

72 *R. v Roberts (Kenneth Joseph)* (1972) 56 Cr. App. R. 95; [1972] Crim. L.R. 27 CA.

73 See para.2–079.

74 J.C. Smith, "Commentary to *Cox*" [1998] Crim. L.R. 810.

75 *R. v Miller (Peter)* [1954] 2 Q.B. 282; [1954] 2 W.L.R. 138.

76 *R. v Chan-Fook (Mike)* [1994] 1 W.L.R. 689 at 694; (1994) 99 Cr. App. R. 147 CA.

Accordingly, as long as it is not "wholly insignificant", almost any injury will suffice and indeed may simply be inferred from the facts of the case as in *R. v Ward*[77] where the court held that "bodily harm meant some bodily injury, even if that injury is slight, and that bruises would suffice". The evidence established in this case was that V had sustained strangulation marks and mild bruising to both her arms.

Questions have arisen as to whether less typical injuries, that do not directly reveal observable bodily injuries, are included within the ambit of actual bodily harm. For instance, in *R. (on the application of T) v DPP*,[78] it was held that a momentary loss of consciousness could amount to actual bodily harm as it involved an injurious impairment to V's sensory functions. Other types of "injury" have been more contestable in nature.

DPP v Smith [2006] 2 Cr. App. R. 1 (Queen's Bench Divisional Court):

5–032 D cut off a girl's pony tail without her consent. The justices accepted that this could not amount to actual bodily harm. The prosecution appealed by way of case stated.

SIR IGOR JUDGE P:

> "16 . . . In ordinary language, 'harm' is not limited to 'injury', and according to the Concise Oxford English Dictionary extends to 'hurt' or 'damage'. According to the same dictionary, 'bodily', whether used as an adjective or an adverb, is 'concerned with the body'. 'Actual', as defined in the authorities, means that the bodily harm should not be so trivial or trifling as to be effectively without significance.
>
> 17. Recent authority shows that evidence of external bodily injury, or a break in or bruise to the surface of the skin, is not required . . . It follows that physical pain consequent on an assault is not a necessary ingredient of this offence.
>
> 18. In my judgment, whether it is alive beneath the surface of the skin or dead tissue above the surface of the skin, the hair is an attribute and part of the human body. It is intrinsic to each individual and to the identity of each individual. Although it is not essential to my decision, I note that an individual's hair is relevant to his or her autonomy. Some regard it as their crowning glory. Admirers may so regard it in the object of their affections. Even if, medically and scientifically speaking, the hair above the surface of the scalp is no more than dead tissue, it remains part of the body and is attached to it. While it is so attached, in my judgment it falls within the meaning of 'bodily' in the phrase 'actual bodily harm'."

Appeal allowed

---

77 *R. v Ward (Harry John)* [2023] EWCA Crim 1310. See also, *Taylor v Granville* [1978] Crim. L.R. 482 Div Ct. cf. R. v *Reigate Justices Ex p. Counsell* (1984) 148 J.P. 193 Div Ct.

78 *T v DPP* [2003] EWHC 266 (Admin); [2003] Crim. L.R. 622.

While there is much to be said for the court's reasoning in this case, it is extraordinary that the charge here was for s.47 rather than for common assault. This case demonstrates the ease with which a common assault (punishable by a maximum of six months' imprisonment) can be transformed into an offence punishable by up to five years' imprisonment. This case also gives rise to a slightly bizarre anomaly. As noted above a V can only consent to harm (which is more than merely trivial and trifling) that has occurred in the course of an activity that has been accepted by the case law as providing a lawful excuse for the injury or risk of injury. Examples provided in *Brown* include sport, horseplay, tattooing and surgery. Extensive case searches did not reveal any case law on hairdressing. **5–033**

(b) Psychiatric harm

What is the position where D's conduct causes psychiatric illness? Previously the test of "any hurt or injury calculated to interfere with health or comfort" was thought to include hysterical and nervous conditions and shock. This position has now been qualified. **5–034**

R. v IRELAND; R. v BURSTOW [1998] A.C. 147 (HOUSE OF LORDS):

In *Ireland*, Vs of repeated silent telephone calls suffered psychiatric illness. D was charged with an assault occasioning actual bodily harm under s.47. In *Burstow*, V of an eight-month stalking campaign suffered from a severe depressive illness. D was charged with unlawfully and maliciously inflicting grievous bodily harm contrary to the Offences against the Person Act 1861 s.20. Both were convicted and appealed. **5–035**

LORD STEYN:

> "The appeals under consideration do not involve structural injuries to the brain such as might require the intervention of a neurologist. One is also not considering either psychotic illness or personality disorders . . . The case was that they developed mental disturbances of a lesser order, namely neurotic disorders. For present purposes the relevant forms of neurosis are anxiety disorders and depressive disorders. Neuroses must be distinguished from simple states of fear, or problems in coping with everyday life. Where the line is to be drawn must be a matter of psychiatric judgment. But for present purposes it is important to note that modern psychiatry treats neuroses as recognisable psychiatric illnesses . . . [N]eurotic illnesses affect the central nervous system of the body, because emotions such as fear and anxiety are brain functions . . .
>
> [I]n *Chan-Fook* the Court of Appeal squarely addressed the question whether psychiatric injury may amount to bodily harm under section 47 of the 1861 Act . . . Hobhouse LJ stated:
>
>> 'The first question . . . is whether the inclusion of the word "bodily" in the phrase "actual bodily harm" limits harm to harm to the skin, flesh and bones of the victim . . . The body of the victim includes all parts of the body, including his organs, his nervous system and his brain. Bodily injury therefore may include injury to any of those parts of his body responsible for his mental and other faculties.'

In concluding that 'actual bodily harm' is capable of including psychiatric injury Hobhouse LJ emphasised that:

> 'it does not include mere emotions such as fear or distress or panic nor does it include, as such, states of mind that are not themselves evidence of some identifiable clinical condition.'

He observed that in the absence of psychiatric evidence a question whether or not an assault occasioned psychiatric injury should not be left to the jury . . .

In my view the ruling in [*Chan-Fook*] was based on principled and cogent reasoning and it marked a sound and essential clarification of the law. I would hold that 'bodily harm' in ss.18, 20 and 47 must be interpreted so as to include recognisable psychiatric illness."

5–036 In *Morris*,[79] the conviction of a stalker, who had allegedly caused V to suffer pains, sleeplessness, tension and fear of being alone, was quashed because the trial judge had allowed the issue of whether the assault had occasioned psychiatric injury to be left to the jury without expert evidence. Even with respect to her physical pains, psychiatric evidence should have been adduced to testify that they were the result of D's non-physical attack.[80]

In *Dhaliwal*,[81] a clear distinction was drawn between psychological injury (for example, palpitations, breathing difficulties, cold sweats, anxiety, inability to sleep and so on) and recognisable psychiatric illness. Only the latter can constitute bodily harm. It was stated that any blurring of this distinction would introduce uncertainty into the law.

(ii) Mens rea

5–037 Section 47 makes no express reference to any mens rea requirement, but it is settled that liability is established if D has the mens rea of common assault.

R. v Savage; DPP v Parmenter [1992] 1 A.C. 699 (House of Lords):

5–038 In the first appeal, the appellant, Mrs Savage, threw a pint glass full of beer over Miss Beal. The glass slipped out of her hand, broke, and a piece of it cut Miss Beal's wrist. Savage was convicted of unlawful wounding contrary to the Offences against the Person Act 1861 s.20. The Court of Appeal partially allowed her appeal substituting a verdict of assault occasioning actual bodily harm contrary to s.47 of the Act. She appealed to the House of Lords.

---

79 *R. v Morris (Clarence Barrington)* [1998] 1 Cr. App. R. 386; (1997) 94(43) L.S.G. 29 CA.

80 Critics have argued that limiting non-physical harm solely to acknowledged and diagnosed psychiatric injuries can be overly narrow. Rather, the emphasis should be on evaluating the symptoms experienced by V, with the jury tasked to decide if a V's symptoms amount to more than trivial harm, thereby qualifying as actual bodily harm. E Finch, "Psychological injury: Where's the Harm in it?" [2022] Crim. L.R. 358.

81 *R. v D* [2006] EWCA Crim 1139; [2006] 2 Cr. App. R. 24.

LORD ACKNER:

"[Mrs Savage assaulted Miss Beal when she threw beer over her. Her actions also caused actual bodily harm: the cut wrist.] Was the offence thus established or is there a further mental state that has to be established in relation to the bodily harm element of the offence? Clearly the section, by its terms, expressly imposes no such requirement. Does it do so by necessary implication? It uses neither the word 'intentionally' or 'maliciously'. The words 'occasioning actual bodily harm' are descriptive of the word 'assault', by reference to a particular kind of consequence . . .

[His Lordship then discussed *Roberts* (*above*, 117) where it was held that] once the assault was established, the only remaining question was whether the victim's conduct was the natural consequence of that assault. The word 'occasioning' raised solely a question of causation, an objective question which does not involve inquiring into the accused's state of mind. In *R. v Spratt* [1990] 1 W.L.R. 1073 McCowan LJ said, at 1082:

> 'However, the history of the interpretation of the Act of 1861 shows that, whether or not the word 'maliciously' appears in the section in question, the courts have consistently held that the mens rea of every type of offence against the person covers both actual intent and recklessness, in the sense of taking the risk of harm ensuing with foresight that it might happen.'

McCowan LJ then quotes a number of authorities for that proposition . . . [However] none of the cases cited were concerned with the mental element required in s.47 cases. Nevertheless, the Court of Appeal in *R. v Parmenter* [1991] 2 W.L.R. 408 [approved] the decision in *R. v Spratt* [1990] 1 W.L.R. 1073 . . .

My Lords, in my respectful view, the Court of Appeal in *Parmenter* were wrong in approving the decision in *Spratt's* case. The decision in *Roberts's* case was correct. The verdict of assault occasioning actual bodily harm may be returned upon proof of an assault together with proof of the fact that actual bodily harm was occasioned by the assault. The prosecution are not obliged to prove that the defendant intended to cause some actual bodily harm or was reckless as to whether such harm would be caused."

Appeal in R. v Savage dismissed

There is thus no requirement that D foresees actual bodily harm. All that is required is that they have **5–039** the mens rea of the assault, namely, intention or recklessness to cause force or apprehension of force. Recklessness here bears the same meaning as in assault. The result is that the degree of moral culpability required for s.47 and for assault is the same despite the maximum penalties for the two offences being five years' and six months' imprisonment, respectively.

The effect is that s.47 is a constructive crime of "half mens rea" where the mens rea requirement does not correspond with the actus reus. Whether constructive liability is justified is a controversial matter.[82] What is unfortunate is that the House of Lords should simply reach this decision with no reasoning at all. Surely, we are entitled to expect their Lordships to have explicated why *Roberts* was correct but *Spratt* and *Parmenter* (Court of Appeal) were wrong.

(iii) Punishment

5–040 The maximum punishment is five years' imprisonment. The offence is triable either way. If D is tried on indictment in the Crown Court, the jury can return an alternative verdict of guilty of assault even if such a charge was not included in the indictment. As seen earlier, many offences that could have been charged under s.47 are in fact charged as common assault, ensuring trial in the magistrates' court. The Magistrates' Courts Sentencing Guidelines and the Sentencing Guidelines for the Crown Court provide that the starting point for assault occasioning actual bodily harm that has been categorised as lesser harm and lower culpability is a medium level community order with a sentencing range of a Band A fine—High level community order.[83] For Crown Courts only, the Sentencing Guidelines state that if the assault is pre-meditated and causes serious injury (greater harm and higher culpability) the starting point is two years and six months' custody, with a sentencing range of one year six months to four years' custody.[84]

2. Malicious wounding and inflicting grievous bodily harm

Offences against the Person Act 1861 s.20:

5–041 "Whosoever shall unlawfully and maliciously wound or inflict any grievous bodily harm upon any other person, either with or without any weapon or instrument, shall be guilty of [an offence punishable up to a term not exceeding five years' imprisonment]."

(i) Actus reus

5–042 There must be a wounding or infliction of grievous bodily harm.

(a) Wounding

5–043 A *wound* necessitates a breakage in the continuity of the whole of the outer skin, or the inner skin within the cheek or lip.[85] It does not include the rupturing of internal blood vessels.[86] Given medical advances

82 F. Stark, "Deconstructing Constructive Liability" [2023] Crim. L.R. 118. This issue is also discussed further below. The arguments are also considered at paras 7–061–7–069 in relation to constructive manslaughter.

83 Sentencing Council, *Assault occasioning actual bodily harm/Racially or religiously aggravated ABH, https://www.sentencingcouncil.org.uk/offences/magistrates-court/item/assault-occasioning-actual-bodily-harm-racially-or-religiously-aggravated-abh/*.

84 Sentencing Council, *Assault occasioning actual bodily harm/Racially or religiously aggravated ABH, https://www.sentencingcouncil.org.uk/offences/magistrates-court/item/assault-occasioning-actual-bodily-harm-racially-or-religiously-aggravated-abh/*.

85 Both the dermis and the epidermis must be broken (*Moriarty v Brooks* 172 E.R. 1419; (1834) 6 Car. & P. 684). Thus, a scratch or break to the outer skin is not sufficient if the inner skin remains intact (*R. v M'Loughlin* 173 E.R. 651; (1838) 8 Car. & P. 635).

86 *JJC (A Minor) v Eisenhower* (1984) 78 Cr. App. R. 48; [1984] Q.B. 331.

it is highly questionable whether minor wounds, for example, a slight cut, should be capable of forming the basis for so serious a charge. The CPS *Charging Standard* states that this offence should only be charged when the wounding is considered to be "really serious". However, it will be appropriate to charge a D with a s.20 offence where the wound was caused by a knife or other weapon, even if the wound itself is not considered "serious".[87]

(b) Grievous bodily harm

Grievous bodily harm means nothing more technical than "really serious bodily harm".[88] What amounts to grievous bodily harm is, to a large extent, open to interpretation. We must therefore turn to case examples to glean what types of injury will likely fall into this category. For example, the courts have made it clear that internal injuries and infecting a person with a virus such as HIV can also amount to grievous bodily harm.[89] While many forms of really serious bodily harm will amount to permanent injuries, it is not necessary that the harm should be either permanent or dangerous,[90] nor that V require medical treatment.[91] Indeed, whether an injury amounts to really serious bodily harm can depend on the "context" in which it is inflicted, including the vulnerability of V. In *Bollom*,[92] it was held that bruising and abrasions could amount to grievous bodily harm for an infant, an elderly or unwell person even if they would not be so regarded for a fit adult.[93] **5–044**

Ultimately, whether any particular injury amounts to grievous bodily harm is a question of fact to be determined by the jury.

(c) Really serious harm must be "inflicted"

The grievous bodily harm has to be "inflicted". Until 1983, the word "inflict" was generally interpreted[94] to mean that it was necessary to prove that there had been an assault (a technical assault or a battery). Section 20 was truly an "aggravated assault". For example, in *Clarence*,[95] D, knowing he was suffering from venereal disease, had sexual intercourse with his wife and transmitted the disease to her. It was held that because of the wife's consent there had been no battery and, accordingly, he could not be liable under s.20. However, the House of Lords in *Wilson*,[96] held that while most cases of inflicting grievous bodily harm would involve an assault, this was not a prerequisite. There could be an infliction **5–045**

87 CPS, *Offences against the Person, Incorporating the Charging Standard, https://www.cps.gov.uk/legal-guidance/offences-against-person-incorporating-charging-standard*.

88 *DPP v Smith* [1961] A.C. 290; [1960] 3 W.L.R. 546 HL. It has been held that it is not necessary to include the word "really" in the summing up to the jury (*R. v Saunders (Ian)* [1985] Crim. L.R. 230; (1985) 82 L.S.G. 1005 CA; *R. v Janjua (Nadeem Ahmed)* [1999] 1 Cr. App. R. 91; [1998] Crim. L.R. 675 CA).

89 *R. v Dica (Mohammed)* [2004] EWCA Crim 1103; [2004] Q.B. 1257.

90 *R. v Golding (David)* [2014] EWCA Crim 889; [2014] Crim. L.R. 686.

91 *R. v Bollom (Stephen Clayton)* [2003] EWCA Crim 2846; [2004] 2 Cr. App. R. 6 at [53].

92 *Bollom* [2004] 2 Cr. App. R. 6.

93 Note the Domestic Violence, Crime and Victims Act 2004 s.5(1) creates the offence of causing or allowing a child or vulnerable adult to die or suffer serious physical harm. A person ("D") is guilty of an offence if—(a) a child or vulnerable adult ("V") dies or suffers serious physical harm as a result of the unlawful act of a person who—(i) was a member of the same household as V; and (ii) had frequent contact with him; (c) at that time there was a significant risk of serious physical harm being caused to V by the unlawful act of such a person.

94 *R. v Clarence (Charles James)* (1888) 22 Q.B.D. 23; *R. v Halliday* (1889) 61 L.T. 701 QBD; *R. v Lewis* [1970] Crim. L.R. 647 CA; and *Cartledge v Allen* [1973] Crim. L.R. 530 QBD.

95 *Clarence* (1888) 22 Q.B.D. 23.

96 *Wilson* [1984] A.C. 242; [1983] 3 W.L.R. 686 HL.

of grievous bodily harm contrary to s.20 without an assault being committed. This same reasoning was applied in *Savage; Parmenter* to cases of unlawful wounding where, although it would require "quite extraordinary facts", one can have an unlawful wounding for the purposes of s.20 without the necessity of proving an assault. It was, however, implicit in *Wilson* that one could only "inflict" grievous bodily harm if there were a direct or indirect application of force to V's body. With regard to psychiatric injuries, this view has now been rejected.

R. v Ireland; R. v Burstow [1998] A.C. 147 (House of Lords):

5–046 [The facts are given at para.5–006.]

LORD STEYN:

"Counsel argued that the difference in wording [between 'causing' in s.18 and 'inflicting' in s.20] reveals a difference in legislative intent: inflict is a narrower concept than cause. This argument loses sight of the genesis of ss.18 and 20 [as the various sections in the 1861 Act were taken from different Acts passed at different times] . . . The difference in language is therefore not a significant factor . . .

[C]ounsel . . . submitted that it is inherent in the word 'inflict' that there must be a direct or indirect application of force to the body . . . [I]n *Mandair* [1995] 1 A.C. 208 at 215 Lord Mackay of Clashfern L.C. observed . . .: 'In my opinion . . . the word "cause" is wider or at least not narrower than the word "inflict".' . . . I regard this observation as making clear that in the context of the 1861 Act there is no radical divergence between the meaning of the two words.

The problem is one of construction. The question is whether as a matter of current usage the contextual interpretation of 'inflict' can embrace the idea of one person inflicting psychiatric injury on another. One can without straining the language in any way answer that question in the affirmative. I am not saying that the words cause and inflict are exactly synonymous. They are not. What I am saying is that in the context of the 1861 Act one can nowadays quite naturally speak of inflicting psychiatric injury. Moreover, there is internal contextual support in the statute for this view. It would be absurd to differentiate between ss.18 and 20 in the way argued . . . The interpretation and approach should so far as possible be adopted which treats the ladder of offences as a coherent body of law."

LORD HOPE OF CRAIGHEAD:

"[*R. v Wilson*, referring with approval to *R. v Salisbury*, does] not wholly resolve the issue which arises in this case, in the context of grievous bodily harm which consists only of psychiatric injury.

The question is whether there is any difference, in this context, between the word 'cause' and the word 'inflict' . . . [F]or all practical purposes there is, in my opinion, no difference between these two words . . . But I would add that there is this difference, that the word 'inflict' implies that the consequence of the act is something which the victim is likely to find unpleasant or harmful. The relationship between cause and effect, when the word 'cause' is used, is neutral. It may embrace pleasure as well as pain. The relationship when the word 'inflict' is used is more precise, because it invariably implies detriment to the victim of some kind.

In the context of a criminal act therefore the words 'cause' and 'inflict' may be taken to be interchangeable. As the Supreme Court of Victoria held in *R. v Salisbury*, it is not a necessary ingredient of the word 'inflict' that whatever causes the harm must be applied directly to the victim. It may be applied indirectly, so long as the result is that the harm is caused by what has been done. In my opinion it is entirely consistent with the ordinary use of the word 'inflict' in the English language to say that the appellant's actions 'inflicted' the psychiatric harm from which the victim has admittedly suffered."

Appeals dismissed

This reasoning has been extended to the causing of physical injuries. **5–047**

R. v Dica [2004] 2 Cr. App. R. 28 (Court of Appeal, Criminal Division):

D, who was HIV positive, had unprotected sexual intercourse with two women as a result of which they contracted HIV. D was convicted of inflicting grievous bodily harm on them contrary to s.20. **5–048**

JUDGE LJ:

"Such differences as may be discerned in the language used by Lord Steyn and Lord Hope respectively do not obscure the fact that this decision confirmed that even when no physical violence has been applied, directly or indirectly to the victim's body, an offence under s.20 may be committed. Putting it another way, if the remaining ingredients of s.20 are established, the charge is not answered simply because the grievous bodily harm suffered by the victim did not result from direct or indirect physical violence. Whether the consequences suffered by the victim are physical injuries or psychiatric injuries, or a combination of the two, the ingredients of the offence prescribed by s.20 are identical. If psychiatric injury can be inflicted without direct or indirect violence, or an assault, for the purposes of s.20 physical injury may be similarly inflicted."

In *Brady*,[97] the D was perched on a balcony railing and either lost his balance (his version of events) or jumped deliberately and landed on a woman below causing her serious injuries. The Court of Appeal affirmed that, as a result of *Ireland; Burstow*, "even when no physical force has been applied, directly or **5–049**

97 *Brady* [2006] EWCA Crim 2413.

indirectly to V's body, an offence under s.20 may be committed". The defence further argued that (on D's account) the injuries had not been "inflicted" because there had not been "deliberate, non-accidental conduct" by D (i.e. he had accidentally fallen). The court was "reluctant to come to a concluded view" on this but, on the facts, stated that the deliberate and precarious perching on the railing was a deliberate act. This defence argument seems misplaced. Any act suffices for the actus reus of s.20 provided it causes the result and was not the product of automatism, as would have been the case if he had been pushed off the balcony. Of course, in most cases where the act was accidental, no mens rea will be established. However, if mens rea is present, there should be no requirement of "deliberate, non-accidental conduct".

In *Stranney*,[98] D was convicted of inflicting grievous bodily harm when, as a result of very bad dangerous driving, two of the passengers in his car sustained grievous bodily harm. There was no assault in this case and the force was, at most, indirectly applied.

(d) The difference between "inflict" and "causes"?

5–050 It is clear from all these cases that both psychiatric injury and physical injury may be inflicted without an assault and without direct or indirect force. What, then, is the difference between "inflict" in s.20 and "cause" in s.18?

Lord Steyn in *Ireland; Burstow* was careful to state that he was "not saying that the words cause and inflict are exactly synonymous. They are not". The only hint as to what the difference might be is provided by Lord Hope when he stated that the word "inflict" implies that "the consequence of the act is something which V is likely to find unpleasant or harmful". This is extraordinary. The word "harmful" here must refer to V subjectively interpreting the injury as harmful because objectively there must, of course, be grievous bodily harm; the word thus adds nothing to the word "unpleasant". Taken literally, this seems to suggest that sado-masochistic activities such as those in *Brown*[99] cannot be prosecuted under s.20 because Vs do not find their injuries unpleasant and do not suffer "detriment". On the contrary, they find the pain and injury pleasant and to their benefit as an expression of their sexuality. While, for rather different reasons,[100] such an approach could be welcomed, these dicta can hardly be taken to cast doubt on the well-established principles laid down in *Brown*. Some clarification on this matter can be found in the law on sexual assault. Under the Domestic Abuse Act 2021 s.71, a D cannot rely on the defence that the V consented to the "infliction" of the serious harm for the purposes of obtaining sexual gratification. While this relates to the offence of sexual assault, it infers that "infliction" need not be "unpleasant" as suggested by Lord Hope of Craighead.

Nevertheless, the broader implications of the decision in *Ireland; Burstow* remain disconcerting. The fact that a psychiatric injury can constitute grievous bodily harm in non-sexual contexts combined with the fact that no assault, nor any direct or indirect application of force, is required for s.20 raises the potential for liability in situations far removed from those traditionally associated with s.20.

98 *R. v Stranney (Andrew Paul)* [2007] EWCA Crim 2847; [2008] 1 Cr. App. R. (S.) 104.
99 *Brown* [1994] 1 A.C. 212.
100 See paras 1-044–1-046; 9-045–9-050.

For example, if I fail a student's essay with the result that he suffers a psychiatric illness, I have committed the actus reus of s.20, and if I know of his mental instability and foresee him sustaining some psychiatric injury, I have mens rea and could be liable. This is removing s.20 too far from its paradigm. While one can understand that the seriousness of psychiatric illnesses can be such that it is justifiable to conclude that they are the equivalent of serious bodily harm, liability for s.20 should be limited to cases where there has been an assault or the application of some force. This, however, is not the law since *Ireland; Burstow* and *Dica*.

Where D has been charged with a s.20 offence, it has long been possible for a jury, where they were not satisfied that all the elements of s.20 have been proven, to return a verdict of guilty of s.47 as this was a lesser included offence,[101] that is, all the elements of the lesser offence, s.47 (an assault causing actual bodily harm), were included in the greater offence, s.20 (an assault causing grievous bodily harm). However, if the greater offence, s.20, no longer requires proof of an assault, how could the jury convict of s.47 which does require an assault? Lord Roskill in *Wilson* answered this by stating that while it was not necessarily so, most s.20 cases would involve an assault. "Inflicting" therefore impliedly *includes* "inflicting by assault" and therefore s.47 could be a lesser included offence. This was endorsed in *Savage; Parmenter*. Such an approach is not surprising. Without the power to convict of lesser offences many Ds would escape liability altogether. However, the result is that in some cases D can be convicted of an offence (s.47) when one of the elements of that offence (an assault) has not been proved to exist. Given the broad interpretation of assault in *Ireland* this is unlikely to be a common occurrence. However, as the appeal in *Burstow* itself demonstrates, there can be cases, particularly concerning stalking, when grievous bodily harm is inflicted without an assault. Such situations demonstrate that it is not always appropriate to stretch the present offences against the person to cover inappropriate cases. In cases of stalking, utilisation of the Protection from Harassment Act 1997 will generally be more appropriate. **5–051**

(ii) Mens rea

The mens rea element of s.20 is supplied by the inclusion of the word "maliciously" within the section. It has long been accepted that the terms "maliciously" and "recklessly" are synonymous. In *Savage; Parmenter* (below), the House of Lords endorsed the view of Professor Kenny[102] that "malice" includes: **5–052**

> ". . . recklessness as to whether such harm should occur or not (i.e. the accused has—foreseen that the particular kind of harm might be done and yet has gone on to take the risk of it)."[103]

---

101 Criminal Law Act 1967 s.6(3). Of course, s.47 is not actually a lesser offence as it carries the same maximum penalty as s.20. It is nevertheless treated as a lesser offence in sentencing practice.

102 C.S. Kenny and J.W.C. Turner, *Outlines of Criminal Law*, 1st edn (Cambridge: CUP, 1902).

103 *Savage* [1992] 1 A.C. 699 at 705.

What is it that must be foreseen? In the case of *Cunningham*,[104] where the charge concerned the malicious administration of a noxious thing under s.23 of the Act, the Court of Criminal Appeal interpreted "maliciously" to mean that D had to foresee the particular kind of harm that might be done and that he nevertheless went on to take the risk of it occurring. It was held that D had to foresee that V might inhale gas which D knew was, or might be, noxious. In other words, the crime was one of "full *mens rea*", where the mens rea "matched" or corresponded with the actus reus.

Since then, however, this principle has been considerably whittled away. In *Mowatt*,[105] it was held that it was unnecessary for D to foresee a wound or grievous bodily harm. It was enough that *some* physical harm, albeit of a minor character, was foreseen. This approach has been endorsed by the House of Lords.

R. v Savage; DPP v Parmenter [1992] 1 A.C. 699 (House of Lords):

5–053 LORD ACKNER:

"4. . . . It is convenient to set out once again the relevant part of the judgment of Diplock LJ in *R. v Mowatt* . . .:

> 'It is quite unnecessary that the accused should have foreseen that his unlawful act might cause physical harm of the gravity described in the section, i.e. a wound or serious physical injury. It is enough that he should have foreseen that some physical harm to some person, albeit of a minor character, might result.'

Mr Sedley submits that this statement of the law is wrong. He contends that properly construed, the section requires foresight of a wounding or grievous bodily harm . . .

The contention is apparently based on the proposition that as the actus reus of a section 20 offence is the wounding or the infliction of grievous bodily harm, the mens rea must consist of foreseeing such wounding or grievous bodily harm. But there is no such hard and fast principle. To take but two examples, the actus reus of murder is the killing of the victim, but foresight of grievous bodily harm is sufficient and indeed, such bodily harm, need not be such as to be dangerous to life. Again, in the case of manslaughter, death is frequently the unforeseen consequence of the violence used.

The argument that as section 20 and section 47 have both the same penalty, this somehow supports the proposition that the foreseen consequences must coincide with the harm actually done, overlooks the oft repeated statement that this is the irrational result of this piece-meal legislation. The Act 'is a rag-bag of offences brought together from a wide variety of sources with no attempt, as the draftsman frankly acknowledged, to introduce consistency

104 *R. v Cunningham (Roy)* [1957] 2 Q.B. 396; [1957] 3 W.L.R. 76 CA.
105 *R. v Mowatt (Sidney Linton)* [1968] 1 Q.B. 421; [1967] 3 W.L.R. 1192 CA.

> as to substance or as to form': Professor Smith in his commentary on *R. v Parmenter* [1991] Crim.L.R.43.
>
> If section 20 was to be limited to cases where the accused does not desire but does foresee wounding or grievous bodily harm, it would have a very limited scope . . .
>
> My Lords, I am satisfied that the decision in *Mowatt* was correct and that it is quite unnecessary that the accused should either have intended or have foreseen that his unlawful act might cause physical harm of the gravity described in section 20, i.e. a wound or serious physical injury. It is enough that he should have foreseen that some physical harm to some person, albeit of a minor character, might result."

Was the House of Lords justified in holding that D need only foresee *some harm*? If D only foresees some harm resulting, but is then convicted and punished for ensuing serious harm, does this impute an element of luck into criminal liability for a serious offence? Horder argues that one should distinguish between "pure" luck and making one's own luck and in the latter situation: **5–054**

> "[B]y doing something intended to harm V, D changes her own normative position, making the bad luck of V's serious injury her (D's) own. There is nothing inappropriate in holding D criminally liable for the serious injury actually inflicted, if there was any risk of such injury resulting from D's intended conduct."[106]

Issues such as these, however, were not considered by the House of Lords. No serious attempt to justify its position was made. Simply pointing out that anomalies also exist in other areas of law is not a justification, nor is it enough for them metaphorically to shrug their shoulders by stating that the 1861 Act is simply "a rag-bag of offences" with no consistency. Such platitudes reinforce the need for statutory intervention—a matter to be dealt with shortly.

(iii) Punishment

The maximum penalty is five years' imprisonment, the same penalty as s.47. While this seemingly distorts any firm structure of offences based on seriousness, in practice it is treated as a more serious offence with longer prison sentences (on average) being imposed for s.20 compared with s.47. The Sentencing Council guidelines provide that where there is a lower level of harm and culpability (such as where the act was not premeditated and no weapon was used) the starting point is 26 weeks' custody.[107] **5–055**

---

106 J. Horder, "A Critique of the Correspondence Principle" [1995] Crim. L.R. 759, 765. See also J. Gardner, "Rationality and the Rule of Law in Offences against the Person" [1994] C.L.J. 502, 508–509. This approach is criticised in A. Ashworth, "A Change of Normative Position: Determining the Contours of Culpability in Criminal Law" (2008) 11 New Criminal L. Rev. 232.

107 Sentencing Council *Inflicting grievous bodily harm/Unlawful wounding/Racially or religiously aggravated GBH/Unlawful wounding, https://www.sentencingcouncil.org.uk/offences/magistrates-court/item/inflicting-grievous-bodily-harm-unlawful-wounding-racially-or-religiously-aggravated-gbh-unlawful-wounding/.*

However, if the offence is categorised as high-level harm and high-level culpability, a starting point of four years is given, with a sentencing range of three years and four years and six months' custody.

3. Wounding and causing grievous bodily harm with intent

OFFENCES AGAINST THE PERSON ACT 1861 s.18:

5–056 "Whosoever shall unlawfully and maliciously by any means whatsoever wound or cause any grievous bodily harm to any person, with intent . . . to do some grievous bodily harm to any person, or with intent to resist or prevent the lawful apprehension or detainer of any person, shall be guilty of [an offence and shall be liable . . . to imprisonment for life]."

(i) Actus reus

5–057 The terms "wound" and "grievous bodily harm" bear the same meaning as in s.20. "Cause", however, has never been held to imply that the injury need be the result of an assault. Until the decision of *Wilson*[108] it was, therefore, true to say that "cause" was wider than "inflict" with the paradoxical result that it was easier to prove the actus reus of the more serious offence, s.18, than that of s.20. In *Mandair*,[109] the House of Lords held that "causing" was "wider or at least not narrower than the word 'inflict'". This statement was approved in *Ireland; Burstow* where it was added that there was "no radical divergence between the meaning of the two words".

(ii) Mens rea

5–058 Two mens rea elements are contained within s.18; the offence must be committed "maliciously" and "with intent".

(a) Maliciously

5–059 In order to appreciate the significance of this term in s.18, it is necessary to dismantle the section to find the possible charges contained within it. If one is charged with maliciously causing grievous bodily harm with intent to cause grievous bodily harm, then *Mowatt*[110] is right in suggesting that the word "maliciously" adds nothing that is not already present in the requirement of intent.

On the other hand, if D is charged with maliciously causing grievous bodily harm with intent to resist or prevent arrest, the inclusion of the term "malicious" may be crucial. If, for example, D intends only to resist arrest and has no state of mind at all in relation to the possibility of harm, they cannot be convicted because they are not malicious.[111] They must, at least, foresee the possibility of some harm.[112]

---

108 *Wilson* [1984] A.C. 242.
109 *R. v Mandair (Singh Mandair)* [1995] 1 A.C. 208; [1994] 2 W.L.R. 700 HL.
110 *Mowatt* [1967] 1 Q.B. 421.
111 See also, *R. v Butt (Mohammed Fike)* [2022] EWCA Crim 155.
112 *R. v Morrison (Lawrence Andrew)* (1989) 89 Cr. App. R. 17 CA.

(b) With intent

D must either intend grievous bodily harm or intend to resist arrest. **5–060**

It has been held that "intent" here bears the same meaning as in *Nedrick*.[113] Whether the House of Lords' decision in *Woollin* apples to crimes other than murder is a moot point discussed elsewhere.[114] The better view is that *Woollin* (to the extent that it may have modified *Nedrick*) should apply to s.18. It would be unfortunate if intention in "intention to cause grievous bodily harm" bore different meanings for s.18 and for murder. It is perhaps because of the difficulty of establishing this requisite intention that so few of those indicted under s.18 are actually convicted of the offence. The cases in which offenders are finally convicted under s.18 tend to be those where there is some objective evidence of premeditation, such as when a weapon has been taken to the scene of the crime.[115]

The CPS *Charging Standard* states that the following factors may indicate a specific intent, "repeated or planned attack, deliberate selection of a weapon or adaptation of an article to cause injury, such as breaking a glass before an attack, making prior threats or using an offensive weapon against, or kicking, V's head".[116]

(iii) Punishment

Section 18 carries a maximum sentence of life imprisonment. The sentences imposed under the guidelines depend on the seriousness of the injury, whether the offence was premeditated and whether a weapon was used. When the injury is life-threatening or particularly grave and was pre-meditated or involved the use of a weapon, the starting point is 12 years' custody, with a sentencing range of 10–16 years' custody. Where V's injuries are considered to be less serious in the context of the offence, the starting point is three years' custody with a sentencing range of two to four years' custody.[117] **5–061**

4. Racially and religiously aggravated assaults

In 1998, the then New Labour Government introduced the first set of so-called "hate crime" offences under the Crime and Disorder Act 1998. The Act when first enacted covered only "racially aggravated" versions of the basic offences of assault, assault occasioning actual bodily harm, s.20 grievous bodily harm, and harassment.[118] Three years later, the Act was amended to include "religiously aggravated" versions of these offences.[119] **5–062**

---

113 *R. v Purcell (Frank)* (1986) 83 Cr. App. R. 45; [1986] Crim. L.R. 466 CA.

114 See para.3–029.

115 E. Genders, "Reform of the Offences against the Person Act: Lessons from the Law in Action" [1999] Crim. L.R. 689.

116 CPS, *Offences against the Person, Incorporating the Charging Standard, https://www.cps.gov.uk/legal-guidance/offences-against-person-incorporating-charging-standard*.

117 Sentencing Council, *Causing grievous bodily harm with intent to do grievous bodily harm/Wounding with intent to do GBH, https://www.sentencingcouncil.org.uk/offences/crown-court/item/causing-grievous-bodily-harm-with-intent-to-do-grievous-bodily-harm-wounding-with-intent-to-do-gbh-2/*.

118 Crime and Disorder Act 1998 s.29. Note that assaults aggravated by hostilities demonstrated towards V's sexual orientation, disability and/or transgender identity are dealt with at sentencing; Sentencing Act 2020 s.66. The Law Commission has recommended that these characteristics be included under the Crime and Disorder Act 1998, Law Commission Report No.402, *Hate Crime Laws* (2021).

119 Amended by the Anti-terrorism, Crime and Security Act 2001 s.39.

The main purpose of these offences is to significantly increase the penalty for racist and anti-religious violence in order to recognise the enhanced levels of harm that such crimes are likely to cause; not only to individual Vs, but to entire minority ethnic and religious communities.[120]

R. v ROGERS [2007] 2 A.C. 62 (HOUSE OF LORDS):

5–063 BARONESS HALE:

"The mischiefs attacked by the aggravated versions of these offences are racism and xenophobia. Their essence is the denial of equal respect and dignity to people who are seen as somehow other. This is more deeply hurtful, damaging and disrespectful to the victims than the simple version of these offences. It is also more damaging to the community as a whole, by denying acceptance to members of certain groups not for their own sake but for the sake of something they can do nothing about."

(i) Meaning of "racially or religiously aggravated"

CRIME AND DISORDER ACT 1998 S.28:

5–064 "(1) An offence is racially or religiously aggravated for the purposes of sections 29 to 32 below if—

(a) at the time of committing the offence, or immediately before or after doing so, the offender demonstrates towards the victim of the offence hostility based on the victim's membership (or presumed membership) of a racial or religious group; or
(b) the offence is motivated (wholly or partly) by hostility towards members of a racial or religious group based on their membership of that group."

5–065 For an assault to be aggravated by either racial or religious hostility D must first commit the basic offence of assault, assault occasioning actual bodily harm or s.20 grievous bodily harm. In addition, the prosecution must then prove either that D "demonstrated" hostility (s.28(1)(a)) or that they were (partly) motivated by it (s.28(1)(b)). The difference between (1)(a) and (1)(b) has caused some confusion within the lower courts which have frequently failed to differentiate between the two subsections.[121] Such confusion led Baroness Hale in *Rogers* to clarify the distinction by stating that s.28(1)(a) is concerned with the "outward manifestation . . . of racial hostility" (a largely objective test), while s.28(1)(b) is concerned with the "inner motivation of the offender" (a subjective test). The distinction will often be reduced to whether D has used certain racist or anti-religious slurs during the commission of the

120 As evidenced by a number of empirical studies: see review in M. Walters, *Criminalising Hate: Law as Social Justice Liberalism* (London: Palgrave, 2022), Ch.3.

121 See M.A. Walters, "Conceptualizing 'Hostility' for Hate Crime Law: Minding 'the Minutiae' when Interpreting Section 28(1)(a) of the Crime and Disorder Act 1998" (2014) 34 Oxford J. Legal Studies 47.

assault (an objective demonstration of hostility) or whether there is evidence of premeditation based on their antipathy of V's ethnic or religious identity (motivation).[122]

(ii) Meaning of "hostility"

The legislation does not define "hostility" and thus whether D demonstrates, or is motivated by it, is a question of fact for the magistrate or jury to determine. Even where D has admitted to using racial expletives during the commission of an assault, uncertainty has arisen as to whether D's words must be *intended* by him to demonstrate racial or religious hostility or whether his words objectively express hostility in the eyes of the jury; regardless of whether D actually meant his actions to express racial or religious hostility or not. **5–066**

DPP v Woods [2002] EWHC 85 (Admin) (Queen's Bench Division, Administrative Court):

In this case, D assaulted a doorman at a nightclub out of frustration when his friend was refused entry. During the assault, D called the doorman a "black bastard". **5–067**

MAURICE KAY J:

"The conclusions of the [trial] Justices are set out in these paragraphs from the case stated:

'. . . We found the Respondent's hostility to be borne out of his frustration and annoyance as a result of his companion being denied entry to the premises, and whilst he may have intended to cause offence by the words, this was not 'hostility based on the victim's membership (or presumed membership) of a racial group'. We believed that the Respondent's frame of mind was such that he would have abused any person standing in [D's] shoes by reference to an obvious physical characteristic had that individual happened to possess one . . .'

The case stated poses the single question: 'Did we err in law in concluding that, in all the circumstances of this case, the words 'you black bastard' uttered a few moments before the assault were not such to prove that the Respondent had demonstrated hostility towards the victim based upon his membership of a racial group?' . . .

Section 28(1)(a) was not intended to apply only to those cases in which the offender is motivated solely, or even mainly, by racial malevolence. It is designed to extend to cases which may have a racially neutral gravamen but in the course of which there is demonstrated towards the victim hostility based on the victim's membership of a racial group. Any contrary construction would emasculate section 28(1)(a)."

Remitted to the Justices with a direction to convict

122 M.A. Walters, A. Owusu-Bempah and S. Wiedlitzka, "Hate crime and the 'justice gap': the case for law reform" [2018] Crim. L.R. 12. Note the offender need not be solely motivated by racial hostility; see s.28(3) and *DPP v Green* [2004] EWHC 1225 (QB).

5–068 The result of *Woods* is that even where D demonstrates hostility unthinkingly in the "heat of the moment", it matters not that D felt no genuine hostility towards V's racial or religious group, only that they demonstrated hostility (objectively) towards V during the commission of the offence, or immediately before or after.[123] Some have questioned whether this is a fair outcome, especially if we consider that the offender will be labelled as a "racist" and be subject to a more severe punishment.[124] There is also the concern that D may be convicted of a racially aggravated assault where they "objectively" demonstrate hostility but where they lacks awareness that their expression could be interpreted as racial.[125] Such a scenario occurred in one case where D had used the term "black bastard" towards a police officer, later claiming that this was an old derogatory term used towards the police that referred to the colour of their uniform, but where the officer in question perceived this to be a racial slur.[126]

(iii) The meaning of "racial or religious group"

Crime and Disorder Act 1998 s.28

5–069 "(4) In this section 'racial group' means a group of persons defined by reference to race, colour, nationality (including citizenship) or ethnic or national origins.

(5) In this section 'religious group' means a group of persons defined by reference to religious belief or lack of religious belief."

5–070 The demonstration of hostility must be towards a V's (presumed) membership of a racial or religious group. But what if the offender's demonstration does not refer explicitly to a specific racial, ethnic or national group? In the case of *Pal*,[127] D, a young Asian male was ejected from a community centre by the caretaker, who was described as of "Asian appearance". In response, D called the caretaker a "White man's arse licker" and a "brown Englishman" and later physically attacked him. D was charged with racially aggravated common assault under the Crime and Disorder Act 1998 s.29(1)(c). On appeal, the Divisional Court held that the offence was not racially aggravated because his remarks were motivated by his anger at being ejected from the building and referred not to V's racial group but to his relationship with white people. Interestingly, the court was not convinced of the applicability of s.28(2) of the Act which states that "'membership', in relation to a racial or religious group, includes association with members of that group". The court noting instead that "it is quite unreal to suggest on the basis of the

---

123 In *Green* [2004] EWHC 1225 (QB), Rafferty J similarly held that "Section 28(1)(a), as distinct from (b), creates a racially aggravated offence without the requirement to prove racist motive. Disposition at the time is irrelevant" (at [16]).

124 A. Owusu-Bempah, M.A. Walters and S. Wiedlitzka, "Racially and religiously aggravated offences: 'God's gift to defence'?" [2019] Crim. L.R. 6, 463.

125 Walters argues that there ought to at least be some correspondence between the demonstration of hostility (part of the conduct element of the offence) and the mens rea of the offence, asserting that D must be "aware that his expression is likely to be perceived by other right-minded individuals as being one of racial or religious hostility". M.A. Walters, "Conceptualizing 'Hostility' for Hate Crime Law: Minding 'the Minutiae' when Interpreting Section 28(1)(a) of the Crime and Disorder Act 1998" (2014) 34 Oxford J. Legal Studies 47, 67.

126 The unreported case example is taken from a recent study on hate crime laws, Owusu-Bempah, Walters and Wiedlitzka, "Racially and religiously aggravated offences: 'God's gift to defence'?" [2019] Crim. L.R. 6, 463 and 482.

127 *DPP v Pal* [2000] EWHC 1575 (QB); [2000] Crim. L.R. 756.

facts found that the Respondent is anti-white men". The facts being that D had been with a group including white youths.[128]

In *Rogers*,[129] D shouted at a group of three Spanish women walking along a street in an aggressive manner, calling them "bloody foreigners" as well as telling them to "go back to your own country". The appellant, who had been convicted of a racially aggravated public order offence, appealed on the basis that his comments had not been directed at a specific racial group. The House of Lords held that it did not matter that the phrase used did not refer to a specific race or nationality as it was necessary to take a "flexible, non-technical approach" when interpreting s.28(4).[130] As such, language that refers to V being from some *other* race or nationality should fall within the meaning of "racial group" under the Act.[131] As is the case with determining the presence of "hostility", decisions about whether words spoken by D fall within the meaning of s.28(4) are questions of fact for the jury to determine.[132]

(iv) Immediately before or after the commission of the offence

Most racially and religiously aggravated assaults are committed where D exclaims racist or anti-religious words *during* the commission of the offence. However, s.28(1)(a) also states the demonstration of hostility can be "immediately" before or after the commission of the offence. This has led to questions on how contemporaneous the hostility has to be with the basic offence. In *Parry*,[133] D referred to his Vs as "Irish c*nts" to the police some 20 minutes after the basic offence was committed. The Crown Court held that this amounted to a demonstration of racial hostility immediately after the offence was committed. On appeal the Divisional Court held that the words immediately before or after had to be given: **5–071**

> "[T]heir plain and ordinary meaning and consequently their effect was to make the subsection strike at words uttered or acts done in the immediate context of the substantive offence."[134]

The court found that the offence could not be racially aggravated given that D had left the scene and had been sitting in his own home when he expressed racial hostility.

A very different decision was given in the case of *Babbs*,[135] where D had been verbally abusive towards V and his companion calling them "fucking foreigners" whilst they were queuing in a fast food restaurant. This resulted in a scuffle and an argument which was quelled by the staff manager.

---

128 *Pal* [2000] Crim. L.R. 756 has since been said to be heavily dependent upon its facts and it is likely that such demonstrations of hostility would fall within s.28(1) of the Act: *DPP v McFarlane* [2002] EWHC 485 (Admin); *R. v Rogers (Philip)* [2007] UKHL 8; [2007] 2 A.C. 62.

129 *Rogers* [2007] 2 A.C. 62.

130 *Rogers* [2007] 2 A.C. 62 at [12].

131 Other ambiguous phrases which have fallen within the meaning of "racial group" have included "immigrant doctor", central to the case of *Att-Gen's Reference (No.4 of 2004)* [2005] EWCA Crim 889; [2005] Crim. L.R. 799 CA and "a monkey" *R. v SH* [2010] EWCA Crim 1931; [2011] 1 Cr. App. R. 14.

132 Note that an offender can commit a racially aggravated offence against someone of the (presumed) same racial group: *R. v White (Anthony Delroy)* [2001] EWCA Crim 216; [2001] 1 W.L.R. 1352; *Cain v DPP* [2022] EWHC 1466 (Admin); [2022] 2 Cr. App. R. 15. Ds from minority ethnic backgrounds can also commit racially aggravated offences against Vs from the majority white population, see *Johnson v DPP* [2008] EWHC 509 (Admin); (2008) 105(10) L.S.G. 27.

133 *Parry v DPP* [2004] EWHC 3112 (Admin); [2005] A.C.D. 64.

134 *Parry v DPP* [2005] A.C.D. 64 at [13].

135 *R. v Babbs (Richard John)* [2007] EWCA Crim 2737.

Between 5 and 15 minutes passed when D gestured to V that they should leave the restaurant in order to fight, V then responded by calling D "white trash", immediately after which D headbutted V. Lord Latham held that the judge had been entitled to leave the matter of whether the hostility was demonstrated immediately before the assault to the jury. This was because the words used by D at the initial confrontation "were capable of colouring the behaviour of the defendant throughout the subsequent events".

5–072 It appears then that where hostility is demonstrated some 15 minutes before an assault it may be considered as part of a continuum of violence depending on the context of the altercation. Whereas if the hostility is demonstrated 20 minutes after the offence and it falls outside the original context of the altercation the hostility will become detached from the assault. As with almost all aspects of racially and religiously aggravated offences, context is everything.

(v) Punishment

5–073 If a common assault is "racially or religiously aggravated", the maximum sentence is two years' imprisonment—four times higher than the maximum for a non-aggravated assault. If an assault occasioning actual bodily harm is "racially or religiously aggravated" the maximum penalty is increased from five years' to seven years' imprisonment.[136] "Racially or religiously aggravated" s.20 grievous bodily harm is also increased to seven years' imprisonment.[137] Note that s.18 grievous bodily harm is not covered by the Crime and Disorder Act 1998. With the maximum penalty for this offence already set at life imprisonment it was reasoned that there is no justifiable purpose to aggravate the offence in law.

5. Controlling or coercive behaviour in an intimate or family relationship

5–074 Throughout this chapter, we have highlighted how offences against the person are not always acts of physical violence, but that different types of conduct can still cause severe emotional and psychological trauma. As per the offences of stalking and harassment, domestic abuse between intimate partners and other family members can occur continuously over protracted periods of time.[138] Behaviour is often intended to undermine V's autonomy through the regulation of their everyday routine activities. When viewed in isolation, much of this abuse can seem unserious or even trivial. However, the cumulative effects of ongoing controlling conduct can be severe, resulting in many cases in the suicide of Vs or the killing of the perpetrator.[139] In response to the pervasive forms of physical and nonphysical violence experienced by, mostly, women in the home, the Government enacted the new offence of controlling or coercive behaviour in an intimate or family relationship.

---

136 Crime and Disorder Act 1998 s.29, as amended by the Anti-Terrorism, Crime and Security Act 2001 s.39.

137 Crime and Disorder Act 1998 s.29.

138 Note in recognition of this the Police, Crime, Sentencing and Courts Act 2022 s.49 extended the time limit for prosecution of common assault or battery in domestic abuse cases—amending Criminal Justice Act 1988 s.39.

139 V. Bettinson, "Aligning Partial Defences to Murder with the Offence of Coercive or Controlling Behaviour" (2019) J. Crim. L. 71.

SERIOUS CRIME ACT 2015 S.76

"(1) A person (A) commits an offence if— **5–075**

(a) A repeatedly or continuously engages in behaviour towards another person (B) that is controlling or coercive,
(b) at the time of the behaviour, A and B are personally connected,
(c) the behaviour has a serious effect on B, and
(d) A knows or ought to know that the behaviour will have a serious effect on B."

(i) Actus reus

The conduct element of the offences falls into four parts. First, a person commits an offence if they repeatedly or continuously engage in behaviour towards another person, and second that behaviour is controlling or coercive. What behaviour amounts to "controlling or coercive"? The Act does not define these two words. As with the offences of harassment and stalking, the behaviour will need to be viewed in context. In *F v M*, the Family Court noted that "understanding and evaluating coercive and controlling behaviour requires isolating what may sometimes seem to be relatively innocuous incidents and locating them in a context which illuminates their greater significance".[140] Examples of these types of behaviour have been provided by the CPS, including: isolating a person from their friends and family; monitoring their time; monitoring a person via online communication tools or using spyware; taking control over aspects of their everyday life, such as where they can go, who they can see, what to wear and when they can sleep; repeatedly putting them down, such as telling them they are worthless; enforcing rules and activity which humiliate, degrade or dehumanise V; controlling the ability to go to school or place of study; threats to reveal or publish private information; threats to hurt or physically harming a family pet; preventing a person from having access to transport or from working; and limiting access to family, friends and finances.[141] **5–076**

Though helpful in elucidating the types of behaviour that can amount to "controlling or coercive", Weiner notes that it is not clear whether actual acts of physical violence, as against conduct that causes a V to fear it, are part of the offence—or whether these will be charged separately.[142] In the case of *Barratt*,[143] the Court of Appeal observed that a sentence of 30 months imprisonment was not manifestly excessive given that the offence involved a prolonged period of violence and aggression; thereby supporting the assertion that the offence can include physical as well as non-physical forms of violence. However, in *Conlon*, the Court of Appeal noted that "[t]he new offence targets psychological abuse in which one partner to a relationship coerces or controls the life of the other without necessarily or

140 *F v M* [2021] EWFC 4.
141 CPS, *Controlling or Coercive Behaviour in an Intimate or Family Relationship, https://www.cps.gov.uk/legal-guidance/controlling-or-coercive-behaviour-intimate-or-family-relationship#:~:text=Section%2076%20Serious%20Crime%20Act,penalty%20of%20five%20years%27%20imprisonment*. Further examples are provided in this guide.
142 Weiner, *Coercive Control and the Criminal Law* (2022).
143 *R. v Barratt (Leon)* [2017] EWCA Crim 1631, cited in Weiner, *Coercive Control and the Criminal Law* (2022).

frequently using threats or violence",[144] suggesting here that the main purpose of the offence is to capture non-physical violent behaviour.

5–077 The third element of the offence is that D and V must be "personally connected". Previously the Act stated that these connections included intimate partners; former partners who still lived together; or family members who lived together.[145] These definitions were criticised as being too narrow, since it implied that s.76 might not always offer protection to a V attempting to separate from an abusive partner or to individuals who had terminated their relationship and no longer reside with the perpetrator.[146] This led to an amendment to the Act redefining "personally connected" as individuals who: are, or have been, married or civil partnered; have agreed to marry or enter into a civil partnership; are, or have been, in an intimate personal relationship; have, or there has been a time when they each have had, a parental relationship in relation to the same child; or are relatives.[147]

Fourth, the behaviour must be shown to have had a serious effect on V. A serious effect includes behaviour that causes fear of violence on two occasions or that which causes serious alarm or distress which has a substantial adverse effect on V's day-to-day activities.[148] This mirrors the wording of the stalking offence under the Protection from Harassment Act 1997 s.4A, discussed above. This result element of the offence has been questioned by some critics who have noted that the particularly resilient survivor who continues to maintain family life, friendships and still excels in the workplace may find it difficult to evidence the often hidden torment of being subjected to a controlling and coercive relationship.[149]

(ii) Mens rea

5–078 D must know or ought to know that the behaviour will have a serious effect on V, again mirroring the mens rea element of harassment and stalking offences.[150] D "ought to know" that which a reasonable person in possession of the same information would know. This objective test means it is not necessary to show that D knew his behaviour was either controlling or coercive.[151]

(iii) Punishment

5–079 Section 76 carries a maximum sentence of five years' imprisonment. The Sentencing Guideline provides a starting point of Medium Level Community Order for lower level harm and culpability and a starting point of two years six months' custody for offences in the higher ranges of harm and

144 *R. v Conlon (Robert Joseph)* [2017] EWCA Crim 2450 at [26], cited in Weiner, *Coercive Control and the Criminal Law* (2022).
145 Serious Crime Act 2015 s.76(2).
146 Weiner, *Coercive Control and the Criminal Law* (2022).
147 Serious Crime Act 2015 s.76(6) as amended by Domestic Abuse Act 2021 s.68.
148 Serious Crime Act 2015 s.76(4).
149 Weiner, *Coercive Control and the Criminal Law* (2022).
150 Serious Crime Act 2015 s.76(1)(d).
151 A defence to controlling or coercive behaviour is available where D was acting in the best interests of D (s.76(8)(a)) or his behaviour is considered to be reasonable in the circumstances (s.76(8)(b)). The defence is not available to D who causes V to believe that physical violence will be used against them (s.76(10)).

culpability.[152] Factors indicating high culpability include: conduct intended to maximise fear or distress; persistent action over a prolonged period; use of multiple methods of controlling or coercive behaviour; sophisticated offence; conduct intended to humiliate and degrade V. Factors indicating high level of harm include: fear of violence on many occasions; very serious alarm or distress which has a substantial adverse effect on V and significant psychological harm.

II. Evaluation

The present structure of non-fatal offences against the person, both in terms of substance and penalty structure, is little short of chaotic.[153] There are many problems with the law (most of which are discussed above), we summarise some of the key issues again here. **5–080**

- The language contained in the Offences against the Person Act is archaic with words such as "maliciously" and "grievous" sitting ill at ease with contemporary vernacular.
- It is not always clear what the terms assault and common assault specifically refer to (especially in relation to statute) as sometimes they are described as stand-alone offences while in other cases they are seemingly combined with battery.
- Given the large difference in penalty, it is highly anomalous that the same mens rea suffices for both common assault/battery and s.47, often meaning that the mens rea does not correspond with the harm occasioned.
- The difference in harm caused in cases of common assault/battery and assault occasioning actual bodily need only be slight.[154]
- Section 20 is supposed to be a far more serious offence than s.47,[155] yet both carry the same maximum penalty (although, in practice, heavier sentences are imposed for s.20).
- Both s.18 and s.20 cover the same harm—grievous bodily harm; can the difference in their maximum penalties (life imprisonment and five years' imprisonment respectively) be justified exclusively in terms of their differing mens rea requirements?

It is clear that both the substance of these offences and their scale of punishments should be restructured so as to represent a true hierarchy of seriousness. Failure to do this "might either confuse moral judgments or bring the law into disrepute, or both".[156] Furthermore, "principles of justice or **5–081**

---

152 Sentencing Council, *Controlling or coercive behaviour in an intimate or family relationship, https://www.sentencingcouncil.org.uk/offences/magistrates-court/item/controlling-or-coercive-behaviour-in-an-intimate-or-family-relationship/*.

153 Note we have covered some of the main offences that full under the OAPA 1861. Many other offences involving violence are covered by newer legislation, e.g. causing serious injury by dangerous driving, Road Traffic Act 1988 s.1A.

154 This situation has been exacerbated by the decision in *Brown* [1994] 1 A.C. 212 where it was held that consent could be a defence to common assault but not to assault occasioning actual bodily harm.

155 M. Cavadino and P. Wiles, "Seriousness of Offences: The Perceptions of Practitioners" [1994] Crim. L.R. 489.

156 H.L.A. Hart, *Law, Liberty and Morality* (Palo Alto: Stanford University Press, 1963), p.36.

fairness between different offenders require morally distinguishable offences to be treated differently and morally similar offences to be treated alike".[157]

How should this relative seriousness of the offences be determined? The present unhappy distinction between offences rests mostly on a confused conjunction of mens rea and harm done. Since 1980, there have been seven attempts at law reform in this area. These efforts have been mainly aimed at achieving a more rational combination of these two elements. The most recent attempt by the Law Commission draws on the previous 1998 Home Office Draft Bill, combined with some new amendments.[158]

Home Office, Violence: Reforming the Offences against the Person Act 1861, Draft Offences against the Person Bill 1998:

5–082 "1(1) A person is guilty of an offence if he intentionally causes serious injury to another. (Max: life imprisonment)

2(1) A person is guilty of an offence if he recklessly causes serious injury to another. (Max: seven years' imprisonment)

3(1) A person is guilty of an offence if he intentionally or recklessly causes injury to another. (Max: five years' imprisonment) . . .

4(1) A person is guilty of an offence if—

(a) he intentionally or recklessly applies force to or causes an impact on the body of another, or
(b) he intentionally or recklessly causes the other to believe that any such force or impact is imminent.

(2) No such offence is committed if the force or impact, not being intended or likely to cause injury, is in the circumstances such as is generally acceptable in the ordinary conduct of daily life and the defendant does not know or believe that it is in fact unacceptable to the other person. (Max: six months' imprisonment) . . .

10(1) A person is guilty of an offence if he makes to another a threat to cause the death of, or serious injury to, that other or a third person, intending that other to believe that it will be carried out. (Max: ten years' imprisonment) . . .

15(1) In this Act 'injury' means—

(a) physical injury, or
(b) mental injury.

157 Hart, *Law, Liberty and Morality* (1963), p.37.
158 Law Commission Paper No.361, *Reform of Offences against the Person* (2015).

(2) Physical injury does not include anything caused by disease but (subject to that) it includes pain, unconsciousness and any other impairment of a person's physical condition.

(3) Mental injury does not include anything caused by disease but (subject to that) it includes any impairment of a person's mental health.

(4) In its application to section 1 this section applies without the exceptions relating to things caused by disease.

[The Bill contains a definition of both intention (cl.14(1)) and recklessness (cl.14(2)), the latter being defined in terms of subjective awareness (*Cunningham* recklessness).]"

The Law Commission report makes several minor modifications to the original Bill:[159] **5–083**

- "physical assault"—where a person intentionally or recklessly applies force to or causes an impact on the body of another, without the consent of that other;[160]
- "threatened assault"—where a person intentionally or recklessly causes another to think that any such force or impact is or may be imminent, and that other does not consent to the conduct in question.

Sitting between cl.3 and the assaults is a new offence that would be triable in the magistrates' court only:

- "aggravated assault"—any physical or threatened assault that has the effect of causing injury (12 months).[161]

The retention of the words "serious injury" and "injury" in the Bill is particularly noteworthy. No distinction is made between wounding and bodily harm. It is assumed that a wounding (i.e. breakage of the skin) would only fall under either of cl.1 or cl.2 where the injury is deemed to be serious. Hence a minor cut would not amount to a serious injury. The Commission also states that physical injury would include sexually transmitted diseases,[162] while mental injuries would include only recognised psychiatric conditions; both replicating the current common law position.

The Bill's restructuring of the law into a clearer hierarchy of offences represents an improvement on the law. Underpinning much (but not all) of the proposed changes is the correspondence principle, which asserts that "the fault element of an offence should relate to the same facts or results as those specified in the external elements of that offence".[163] This approach is aligned with the notion of cognitive mens **5–084**

159 Law Commission Paper No.361, *Reform of Offences against the Person* (2015).
160 Note: should not be used for cases of low-level injury, as these may be charged as aggravated assault.
161 Note: includes every physical or threatened assault which in fact causes injury, whether or not D intended or was reckless about injury.
162 Though the Commission also recommends further formal consultation on this issue is required.
163 Law Commission Paper No.361, *Reform of Offences against the Person* (2015), p.208. See also, S. Demetriou, "Not giving up the fight: a review of the Law Commission's scoping report on non-fatal offences against the person" (2016) J. Crim. L. 188, 193–196. See further Ch.3 paras 3-139–3-141.

rea, which dictates that D must have intended or foreseen a particular result before they are held responsible for the consequences of his actions. The corresponding of mens rea and consequence limits the normative standards currently imposed by the criminal law that often imputes an element of (bad) luck when imposing criminal liability for offences against the person.

The reform proposals do, however, raise several important questions.[164] First, the distinction between intention and recklessness is thought to be so significant as to justify a maximum of life imprisonment for intentionally causing serious injury as opposed to seven years' imprisonment for recklessly causing serious injury. This is because there is "a definite moral and psychological difference between the two offences which it is appropriate for the criminal law to reflect".[165] However, when it comes to causing lesser injuries, these concerns have evaporated into thin air and no distinction is drawn between intention and recklessness. It seems odd that the difference in moral blame between intention and recklessness should be regarded as sufficiently significant to warrant such a huge difference in sentencing maxima for serious injury and yet simply be dismissed as inconsequential for lesser injuries.

5–085 Secondly, there is the problem of defining injury. "Injury" is divided into serious and non-serious harms, yet there is little to no guidance as to the distinction between these two. This leaves juries to determine when an injury is considered serious without any statutory guidance. There is likely to be significant disparities between juries as to when an offence will fall within cl.1 or cl.2 or not. Some further guidance as to the word serious may therefore be helpful in ensuring greater levels of consistency and certainty within this area of law. In the US, the Model Penal Code has defined "serious injury" as:

> ". . . bodily injury which creates a substantial risk of death or which causes serious, permanent disfigurement, or protracted loss or impairment of the function of any bodily member or organ."[166]

The difference between serious injury which is of a temporary nature (such as a broken limb) and injuries which are permanently disfiguring or leave V in a permanent vegetative state[167] can be so fundamental that it should be reflected at the substantive, rather than at the sentencing stage. As such, there is a cogent argument in favour of creating a more structured division of injury; for example, minor injury (trivial and transient harms), serious injury (harms that have a substantial impact on the physicality and mental health of V) and really serious injury (permanent or life threatening injuries).

5–086 Thirdly, although the creation of "aggravated assault" may bring about a useful distinction between batteries where no injury is inflicted and those where some harm (albeit of a minor nature) is caused,[168] there are two main issues with adding this new offence to the ladder. The first relates to the fact that unlike all of the other new offences, aggravated assault would allow for constructive liability where minor injury is caused but not foreseen. This clearly subverts the Commission's own commitment to the

164 See M. Gibson, "Getting their 'act' together? Implementing statutory reform of offences against the person" [2016] Crim. L.R. 597; Demetriou, "Not giving up the fight: a review of the Law Commission's scoping report on non-fatal offences against the person" (2016) J. Crim. L. 188.

165 Law Commission Paper No.218, *Offences against the Person* (1980), para.152.

166 Proposed Official Draft s.210.0(3).

167 As in *R. v Cross (Adam Stuart)* [2008] EWCA Crim 1194; [2009] 1 Cr. App. R. (S.) 34 where it was stated of V that "in practical terms . . . his life was really ended".

168 Gibson, "Getting their 'act' together? Implementing statutory reform of offences against the person" [2016] Crim. L.R. 597.

correspondence principle, as supported by the majority of consultees to the reform proposals. The Commission defends this by noting that the assault would remain as the central feature of the offence, with the injury simply serving as an aggravating factor.[169] However there is no escaping the fact that a different offence with a harsher penalty can be applied to a consequence not foreseen by D. A second issue with the new offence is that it is not clear what level of injury or harm will suffice for the offence to be elevated from aggravated assault to the cl.3 causing injury offence. This again leaves the hierarchy of offences somewhat uncertain.

A final question needs to be asked: must the restructuring of these offences be based *entirely* on new combinations of mens rea and harm? Could other factors not also be utilised in informing our moral assessments (to be translated into legal judgments) of the relative seriousness of offences? For instance, Gardner[170] rejects the Law Commission's view that the structure of these offences should be restricted to variations in the configuration of mens rea and resulting harm as this "does not capture all that is interesting, or rationally significant, about the wrong".[171] What matters is the *wrong* involved and not just the harm caused and "the wrong is that of bringing the harm about in that way. In morality, as in law, it matters how one brings things about".[172] Gardner argues that ss.20 and 47 are neither more serious nor less serious than each other, but rather each belongs to its "own family of offences":[173] s.20 is a crime of violence; s.47 is a crime of assault which is "not a crime of violence. Its essential quality lies in the invasion by one person of another's body space".[174] Drawing an analogy with the Theft Acts where theft, obtaining by deception (now replaced by fraud), false accounting, making off without payment, etc are differentiated, not by the harm done (the same property might have been lost), but by the different mode of wrongdoing, he points to lesser known provisions of the Offences against the Person Act 1861 where distinctions are drawn between different modes of violence. For example:

> "Section 21 deals with choking, suffocating, or strangling; section 22 deals with the use of stupefacients and overpowering substances, sections 23 and 24 with poisoning, section 26 with starving and exposing to the elements; sections 28 to 30 deal with burning, maiming, disfiguring and disabling by use of explosives . . ."

Such offences, he claims "are notable for the moral clarity with which they are differentiated".[175] In much the same vein, Horder argues that in terms of fair labelling the Law Commission's recommendations amount to "a slide into the vice of moral vacuity".[176] There are "important qualitative moral distinctions" between deliberately punching someone hard and breaking his nose and castrating a person; these distinctions should be marked in the offence committed.[177]

---

169 Law Commission, *Reform of Offences against the Person* (2015), [5.52]. It would also ensure that assaults which cause some harm albeit of a minor nature remain in the Magistrates' Court, thereby reducing the number of Ds electing for the more costly trials in the Crown Court.

170 Gardner, "Rationality and the Rule of Law in Offences against the Person" [1994] C.L.J. 502.

171 Gardner, "Rationality and the Rule of Law in Offences against the Person" [1994] C.L.J. 502, 511.

172 Gardner, "Rationality and the Rule of Law in Offences against the Person" [1994] C.L.J. 502, 505.

173 Gardner, "Rationality and the Rule of Law in Offences against the Person" [1994] C.L.J. 502, 507.

174 Gardner, "Rationality and the Rule of Law in Offences against the Person" [1994] C.L.J. 502, 507–508.

175 Gardner, "Rationality and the Rule of Law in Offences against the Person" [1994] C.L.J. 502, 515. For a recent example see, Domestic Abuse Act 2021 s.70 which inserts into Serious Crime Act 2015 s.75A a new offence of non-fatal strangulation or suffocation.

176 J. Horder, "Rethinking Non-Fatal Offences against the Person" (1994) 14 O.J.L.S. 335, 340.

177 Horder, "Rethinking Non-Fatal Offences against the Person" (1994) 14 O.J.L.S. 335, 342.

5–087 One could go even further and argue that other factors such as the identity of V or D or the motive underlying the crime could significantly mark out the wrong involved. Examples of such an approach under the current law include the racially or religiously aggravated assaults under the Crime and Disorder Act 1998. The distinctive wrong of these aggravated offences is that the assault is not simply against an individual but also expresses hatred or contempt of an entire group of people. V and other community members who share a similar characteristic are also likely to be impacted to a greater degree.[178] The normal assault-prevention mechanisms commonly employed (looking away; doing nothing to precipitate the assault) are worthless if one is attacked simply because of one's race or religious beliefs. This distinctive wrong needs to be marked out by a separate offence with a different sentencing maximum.[179] It is difficult to explain, however, why only racial and religious aggravated offences are specifically proscribed under the criminal law, while offences aggravated by sexual orientation, disability and transgender identity hostility remain within sentencing provisions only.[180]

M.A. Walters, A. Owusu-Bempah and S. Wiedlitzka, "Hate Crime And The 'Justice Gap': The Case For Law Reform" [2018] Crim. L.R. 12, 961, 973

5–088 "The failure to treat all recognised strands of hate crime the same in law sends the message that some types of hate are more serious than others, and/or that certain victim groups are more deserving of protection under the law than others . . . By creating parity of protection, new hate crime laws could serve a strong symbolic function, not only expressing that all hate crimes will be treated seriously by the CJS, but that all strands of hostility are equally morally reprehensible. The criminal law plays a fundamental role in furnishing the boundaries of (un)acceptable conduct. The additional criminalisation of certain identity-based hostilities is a form of social control that simultaneously supports positive norms (i.e. the acceptance of 'difference') while condemning the proscribed harmful conduct (i.e. demonstrations of prejudice)."[181]

5–089 A major problem with an approach to criminalising offences against the person that is dictated by level of injury, modus operandi, and identity of V is that it can lead to over-specificity. One could be left with a bewildering array of offences—the vice of "particularism"[182]—each marking a separate wrong but with a failure to distinguish the offences *in terms of seriousness.*[183] Fair labelling should involve not only capturing the essential wrong involved but also communicating the relative seriousness of that

178 J.L. Paterson, R. Brown and M.A. Walters, "The short and longer term impacts of hate crimes experienced directly, indirectly and through the media" (2019) *Personality and Social Psychology Bulletin* 45, 994.

179 See M.A. Walters, *Criminalising Hate: Law as Social Justice Liberalism* (Oxford: Palgrave, 2022).

180 See Walters, Owusu-Bempah and Wiedlitzka, "Hate crime and the 'justice gap': the case for law reform" [2018] Crim. L.R. 12, 961. The Law Commission is currently consulting on hate crime law reform.

181 The Law Commission is currently consulting on hate crime law reform.

182 Horder, "Rethinking Non-Fatal Offences against the Person" (1994) 14 O.J.L.S. 335, 340 at 338.

183 Such is the case with an array of new offences which specify particular types of physical harm, for e.g. the Domestic Violence, Crime and Victims Act 2004 s.5(1) sets out the offence of causing or allowing a child or vulnerable adult to die or suffer serious physical harm.

wrongdoing.[184] One response to this is that all these various factors should be dealt with at the sentencing stage rather than through the creation of specific offences. Indeed, the current Sentencing Guidelines list a wide range of general aggravating factors, including the use of a weapon, a significant degree of premeditation, and whether D demonstrated hostility against V's identity characteristic.

If and when a decision is made by Parliament to restructure the various offences of violence, the issues raised in this section may require further consideration. In implementing such reforms, it is important to remember that individual criminal offences should communicate the essence of the wrongdoing involved. It is also important that the relative seriousness of such offences be communicated and that the criminal law as a whole conveys a morally-informative set of messages.

184 Gardner does not accept that fair labelling is concerned with marking relative seriousness between offences. See, further, C.M.V. Clarkson, *Understanding Criminal Law*, 4th edn (London: Sweet & Maxwell, 2005), p.191; G. Betts, "Robbery and the principle of fair labelling" (2019) J. Crim. L. 83, 205.

Chapter 6

Sexual Offences

I. Introduction

There is a large and increasing number of offences that proscribe certain forms of sexual behaviour. They vary widely in the type of conduct encompassed, from non-consensual penile penetration of someone's vagina, anus or mouth, to the exposing of genitalia in a public place. Prior to 2003, the law was condemned as "archaic, incoherent and discriminatory".[1] The Sexual Offences Act 2003 resulted from a process of consultation that lasted over three years and had as its objectives the need to modernise the law to reflect "changes in society and social attitudes"[2]; to clarify the law, in particular in relation to core concepts such as consent; to improve protection for vulnerable groups, such as children; to ensure that the penalties available were commensurate with the gravity of the offence; and to improve the conviction rate for the offence of rape. It constituted a fundamental reform of the law relating to sexual offences. Many of the changes made were very welcome but concern has remained that the criminalisation of some behaviour is unwarranted and that there is a good deal of complexity in and overlap between the numerous offences contained within the Act. This chapter will focus on the crime of rape but it will also consider assault by penetration, sexual assault, causing someone to engage in sexual activity and offences against children to illustrate both the strengths and weaknesses of the law. **6-001**

A. WHAT IS RAPE?

Before outlining the law on rape it is helpful to try to identify the "essence" of the offence and other sexual crimes, such as assault by penetration or sexual assault.[3] For some, sexual offences are essentially crimes of physical violence. One effect of this could be that the offence of rape should be **6-002**

---

1 *Protecting the Public, Strengthening Protection against Sexual Offenders and Reforming the Law on Sexual Offences* (Cmnd.5668, 2002), para.8.

2 *Protecting the Public, Strengthening Protection against Sexual Offenders and Reforming the Law on Sexual Offences* (Cmnd.5668, 2002), para.4.

3 For a review of the literature see, J. Conaghan, "The Essence of Rape" (2019) 39 O.J.L.S. 151. Conaghan argues that a single essence is not realisable due to the flaws that can be exposed in different accounts.

defined so that it only occurs where V has shown physical resistance.[4] Rape also involves specific harms that are distinct from other offences against the person. Research shows that rapes cause significant psychological trauma,[5] in addition there is the risk of specific physical injuries, as well as the risk of unwanted pregnancy and sexually transmitted infections.[6]

More commonly, rape has been conceptualised by reference to its violation of bodily autonomy.[7] Under this construction, not all "rapes" are accompanied by physical violence or harm, but instead pivot on the non-consent of V.[8] There are difficulties with both approaches of violence and autonomy.

VICTOR TADROS, "RAPE WITHOUT CONSENT" [2006] 26 O.J.L.S. 515, 515–516:

6–003 "In some jurisdictions, for example, Canada, Michigan and New South Wales, the focus is primarily on force. The will of the complainant plays a subsidiary role or no role at all. Reforms of this kind were motivated by three feminist concerns. First, rape is to be considered a crime of violence. That ought to be reflected in the definition of the offence. Second, defining rape around the will of the victim tends to encourage criminal trials to focus problematically on the conduct and sexual history of the complainant rather than the conduct of the accused. Third, sexual offences ought to be defined with precision to prevent them being manipulated by defence counsel or subject to problematic interpretation in the light of the prejudices of participants in the criminal process, and in particular judges and juries . . .

In other jurisdictions, the focus is primarily on the will, or rather consent, of the victim, relegating force to a subsidiary role. This is true of England and Wales . . . Such [laws] reflect a fourth feminist concern: undermining the sexual autonomy of the victim need not involve violence or the threat of violence . . .

Meeting the fourth concern . . . appears to involve failing properly to reflect the first three."

6–004 Perceiving rape as a crime of physical violence makes for a relatively straightforward offence but ignores the dynamics of sexual relationships and enables some husbands, partners and "date-rapists" to deny that what they do is rape. However, making consent the pivotal concept "does not mark out the offence as a crime of violence even where there has been violence".[9] Nevertheless, whether violence, as physical force, has been inflicted or not, for some commentators the essence of the conduct is in its distinct moral wrongfulness.[10] For instance, Gardner and Shute provide a hypothetical scenario in

---

4 In the US, many states used to require a woman to show utmost resistance; even now rape may be defined as non-consensual and forced sexual intercourse. See R. West, "A Comment on Consent, Sex and Rape" (1996) 2 *Legal Theory* 232.

5 J. Temkin, *Rape and the Legal Process*, 2nd edn (Oxford: OUP, 2002).

6 A.P. Simester and G.R. Sullivan, *Criminal Law: Theory and Doctrine*, 3rd edn (Oxford: OUP, 2007), p.467.

7 N. Lacey, "Unspeakable Subjects, Impossible Rights: Sexuality, Integrity and Criminal Law" (1998) 11 C.J.L.J. 47.

8 See Temkin, *Rape and the Legal Process*, 2nd edn (2002), pp.167–168.

9 V. Tadros, "Rape Without Consent" [2006] 26 O.J.L.S. 515, 517.

10 For an argument that sexual penetration is itself a prima facie wrong, see M.M. Dempsey and J. Herring, "Why Sexual Penetration Requires Justification" (2007) 27 O.J.L.S. 467 and J. Wall, "Sexual Offences and General Reasons Not to Have Sex" (2015) 35 O.J.L.S. 777.

which V is unconscious, physically unharmed and never learns that sexual intercourse (with a condom) has taken place. They assert that it is still right to state that V has been raped:

> "Rape, in the pure case, is the sheer use of a person . . . Rape is humiliating even when unaccompanied by further affronts because the sheer use of a person, and in that sense the objectification of a person, is a denial of their personhood. It is literally dehumanizing."[11]

If one views rape as the sheer use of a person as an object[12] there is no case for its being subdivided into more or less serious offences depending upon whether a relationship or acquaintance existed between V and the offender. As well as denying the autonomy of V it has been further argued that the rape of a woman amounts to a distinct moral harm, not only against V, but also against women as a group.

Joan McGregor, Is it Rape? (2005), pp.230–232:

> "Rapes express very clearly the inferiority of women. The rapist, whether the violent rapist or the subtler 'date rapist', sends the message that this woman is for his enjoyment, an object to be used for his pleasure. His actions express her inferiority to him since he does not feel the need to bother to investigate whether she was really consenting even in the face of evidence that she was not or may not be. Her physical and verbal rejections are not worth investigating as to whether they were 'real' since her interests do not really matter. For him, her wishes and desires are irrelevant. He is superior to her, his desires matter and hers do not, making her an object rather than an equal person. Sending this message is the expressive moral injury of rape. The message of inferiority is received by all women, not merely the woman who experiences the rape. Not wanting to diminish the real physical and psychological harms to rape victims, I am not claiming that all women experience those harms, which are very real and serious. But there is something peculiar to rape and the response that women have to other women being raped . . . **6–005**
>
> The meaning of rape involves the victim's worth and the wrongdoer's worth and we can 'read off' the expression of the offender's superiority. In the case of rape, the diminishment in the victim's worth is tied to group membership. Women are the target of rape in society and women get the message that the rapist sends. In this sense, the moral injury of rape is shared by women as a group."

11 "The Wrongness of Rape" in J. Horder (ed), *Oxford Essays in Jurisprudence* (Oxford: OUP, 2000), p.205.

12 See also, J. Herring, "Mistaken Sex" [2005] Crim. L. R. 511, 515–617.

II. The Law

A. CONSENT

6–006 The issue of consent is fundamental to many of the sexual offences contained within the Sexual Offences Act 2003. It has also proved to be a highly problematic concept to define and one of the key objectives of the reform was to clarify the meaning of consent. Indeed, as the majority of Vs know their assailant, the issue of consent is, in many trials, the pivotal issue.

But how does one know whether they have the consent to perform or receive a sexual act? Does one require a verbal communication of agreement, or can consent be given using just context and social cues?[13] Some commentators have even argued that consent may be valid even where there is no communication or miscommunication between individuals.[14] Before exploring this contested concept, one matter can be settled: what is required in *law* is a lack of consent and not positive dissent.[15] English law does not define rape as sexual intercourse by force. It absolves V from having to make a show of resistance. Thus, in theory, responsibility rests with the instigator to secure consent. That said, it is clear that in the absence of marks or injuries V's claim not to have consented may not be believed.[16] Moreover, although changes to legislation mean judges are no longer obliged to warn the jury of the dangers of accepting V's uncorroborated story, they have discretion still to do so.[17] One further related question is relevant at this point. The defence in seeking to show that V did, in fact, consent to sexual intercourse may wish to adduce evidence, for example, of prior relationships with D or with other men. Should evidence of this type be introduced at the trial?

CLARE MCGLYNN, "RAPE TRIALS AND SEXUAL HISTORY EVIDENCE: REFORMING THE LAW ON THIRD-PARTY EVIDENCE" (2017) 81 J. CRIM. L. 367, 369–370:

6–007 "Sexual history evidence is most controversially introduced to support inferences of consent and/or to challenge credibility. In relation to consent, adducing sexual history evidence relies on an assumption that previous consent is indicative of consent on the occasion in question. Such a rationale profoundly challenges the notion of consent being person and situation specific. Specifically in relation to sexual activity with the accused, it assumes that consent can be inferred from prior consent. This position was articulated by Lord Steyn in *R v A* where he stated that:

13 See T. Dougherty, "Yes means yes: consent as communication" (2015) 43(3) Phil. & Pub.Aff. 225.

14 L. Alexander, H. Hurd and P. Westen, "Consent does not require communication: a reply to Dougherty" (2016) 35(6) Law & Phil. 655.

15 *Lang* (1975) 62 Cr. App. R. 50; *Olugboja* (1981) 73 Cr. App. R. 344; *Malone* [1998] 2 Cr. App. R. 454.

16 There are higher conviction rates where violence is established: Harris and Grace, *A Question of Evidence? Investigating and Prosecuting Rape in the 1990s* (1999); T.P. Cross, M. Alderden, A. Wagner, L. Sampson, B. Peters, M. Spencer and K. Lounsbury, *Forensic evidence and criminal justice outcomes in a statewide sample of sexual assault cases* (Washington DC: US Department of Justice, Office of Justice Programs, National Institute of Justice, 2014).

17 Criminal Justice and Public Order Act 1994 s.32.

> As a matter of common sense, a prior sexual relationship between the complainant and the accused may, depending on the circumstances, be relevant to the issue of consent. It is a species of prospectant evidence which may throw light on the complainant's state of mind . . .
>
> While this is a commonly held position . . . it is based on one of the "twin myths'. In particular, such an approach does not sufficiently recognise that consent is given afresh on each occasion. Also, in assuming consent to be more likely, it does not sufficiently recognise the variety of contexts of sexual relationships, including coercive or abusive relationships. Further, it neglects to consider the possibility that, in fact, having once engaged in sexual activity with the accused, he may become the person to which the complainant is least likely to consent in future. Indeed, assuming that someone is more likely to consent to sexual activity if they have done so in the past, is not so far away from the once-held assumption, and legal position, of implied consent during marriage."[18]

As a result of such reasoning, the law was changed to give the trial judge complete discretion as to whether general or specific past history and reputation of V might be introduced.[19] However, studies subsequently concluded that courts were far too ready to allow evidence to be admitted[20] and the report *Speaking up for Justice* concluded that there was "overwhelming evidence that the . . . practice in the courts [was] unsatisfactory and that the existing law [was] not achieving its purpose".[21] As a consequence, a much tighter scheme governing sexual history evidence was introduced by the Youth Justice and Criminal Evidence Act 1999.[22] Under s.41 of the Act no such evidence can be adduced unless certain statutory criteria are satisfied: for example, that the issue is one of consent and the sexual behaviour of the complainant to which the evidence relates is alleged to have taken place at about the same time as the event which is the subject matter of the charge. **6–008**

18 Historically, the offence of rape contained the phrase "unlawful". This was taken to refer to intercourse outside marriage. This meant that, in law, a husband could not "rape" his wife. The law was not changed until the case of *R. v R* [1992] 1 A.C. 599; [1991] 3 W.L.R. 767 HL, where Lord Keith of Kinkel held ". . . it is clearly unlawful to have sexual intercourse with any woman without her consent, and that the use of the word [unlawful] adds nothing . . . [T]here are no rational grounds for putting the suggested gloss on the word, and it should be treated as mere surplusage in this enactment" at 622–623. This was supported later via legislative change removing the exception under Criminal Justice and Public Order Act 1994 s.142.

19 Sexual Offences (Amendment) Act 1976 s.2.

20 J. Temkin, "Sexual History Evidence—the Ravishment of Section 2" [1993] Crim. L.R. 3. See also, A. McColgan, "Common Law and the Relevance of Sexual History Evidence" [1996] 15 O.J.L.S. 275 and G. Durston, "Cross-examination of Rape Complainants: Ongoing Tensions between Conflicting Priorities of the Criminal Justice System" (1998) 62 Jo.C.L. 91.

21 Home Office, *Speaking Up for Justice: Report of the Interdepartmental Working Group on the Treatment of Vulnerable and Intimidated Witnesses in the Criminal Justice System* (1998), para.9.64.

22 Youth Justice and Criminal Evidence Act 1999 ss.41–43. In addition, the Criminal Justice Act 2003 s.100 requires D to obtain leave from the judge when they wish to introduce evidence that amounts to an attack upon V's character. See further, C. Withey, "Female Rape—an Ongoing Concern: Strategies for Improving Reporting and Conviction Levels" [2007] 74 Jo. C.L. 54.

R. v A (Complainant's Sexual History) [2002] 1 A.C. 45 (Court of Appeal, Criminal Division):

6–009 LORD STEYN:

"... sometimes logically relevant sexual experiences between a complainant and an accused may be admitted under section 41(3)(c) ... It is of supreme importance that the effect of the speeches today should be clear to trial judges who have to deal with problems of the admissibility of questioning and evidence on alleged prior sexual experience between an accused and a complainant. The effect of the decision today is that under section 41(3)(c) of the 1999 Act, construed where necessary by applying the interpretive obligation under section 3 of the Human Rights Act 1998, and due regard always being paid to the importance of seeking to protect the complainant from indignity and from humiliating questions, the test of admissibility is whether the evidence (and questioning in relation to it) is nevertheless so relevant to the issue of consent that to exclude it would endanger the fairness of the trial under article 6 of the Convention. If this test is satisfied the evidence should not be excluded."

Appeal dismissed

6–010 Case law has since reiterated that there must be relevant similarity between the alleged conduct and previous conduct which necessitates an exploration of the circumstances in order to avoid unfairness to D.[23] In addition, there has to be a sufficient chronological nexus between the events to render the previous behaviour probative.[24] The court must also believe that a failure to admit the evidence would render the conviction unsafe.[25] Finally, it should be noted that courts should not allow cross examination of sexual history which is tantamount to asserting that the complainant is a person who engages in casual sex, thereby inferring that she is likely to have engaged in casual sex with D.[26]

One basis for admitting evidence or permitting cross-examination about sexual history might be where the complainant is biased against D or has a motive for fabricating the evidence.[27] In such a case, an application to introduce evidence should be made in advance of the trial.[28] New sexual history evidence has also been admitted on appeal. In the very high profile case of *Evans*,[29] sexual history evidence was allowed to be admitted on appeal in order to show that the complainant had used similar words during sex with previous partners which could not be explained by mere coincidence, and was therefore evidence that could have supported D's defence of consent. The appeal was successful and a retrial ordered. The fact that sexual history evidence is still being used to support the defence of consent in

---

23 Relevant similarity does not necessarily mean there must be a striking similarity, *R. v M (M)* [2011] EWCA Crim 129 at [48].

24 *R. v G (Germaine)* [2016] EWCA Crim 1633; [2016] 4 W.L.R. 185; [2017] 1 Cr. App. R. 27.

25 For illustrations of where leave was denied see, e.g. *R. v Beedall (Lee James)* [2007] EWCA Crim 23; [2007] Crim. L.R. 910 (defence wished to ask V if he was homosexual) and *R. v Winter (Robert Michael)* [2008] EWCA Crim 3; [2008] Crim. L.R. 971 (defence wished to ask V—who was in a long-term relationship with one man—about her relationship with another man).

26 *R. v Harris (Wayne Lee)* [2009] EWCA Crim 434 at [17]; [2010] Crim. L.R. 54.

27 *R. v A (Complainant's Sexual History)* [2001] UKHL 25; [2002] 1 A.C. 45 at [79] per Lord Hope.

28 However, research has shown that this safeguard is not observed in the vast majority of cases: L. Kelly, J. Temkin and S. Griffiths, *Section 41: An Evaluation of New Legislation Regarding Sexual History Evidence in Rape Trials* (2006) (Home Office Online Report 20/06).

29 *R. v Evans (Chedwyn)* [2016] EWCA Crim 452; [2016] 4 W.L.R. 169.

such cases has attracted much scholarly criticism, with many agreeing with Lord Woolf in *Mokrecovas*[30] who foresaw that s.41(3)(a) would be used to "ride a coach and horses" through the desirable policy reflected in s.41(4).[31] As such, some commentators have argued that only a complete ban on such history will solve the problem.[32]

Against this background, we can now consider what it means to say that someone has consented to sex. There have been numerous attempts to answer these questions, both philosophically and legally.[33] For the first time, however, the Sexual Offences Act 2003 provides a statutory definition which, as we shall see, is supplemented by presumptions as to the absence of consent.

SEXUAL OFFENCES ACT 2003 SS.74, 75 AND 76:

"**74. 'Consent'** **6–011**

For the purposes of this Part, a person consents if he agrees by choice, and has the freedom and capacity to make that choice.

75. Evidential Presumptions about consent

(1) If in proceedings for an offence to which this section applies it is proved—

(a) that the defendant did the relevant act,
(b) that any of the circumstances specified in subsection 2 existed, and
(c) that the defendant knew that those circumstances existed—

the complainant is to be taken not to have consented to the relevant act unless sufficient evidence is adduced to raise an issue as to whether he consented and the defendant is to be taken not to have reasonably believed that the complainant consented unless sufficient evidence is adduced to raise an issue as to whether he reasonably believed it.

(2) The circumstances are that—

(a) any person was, at the time of the relevant act or immediately before it began, using violence against the complainant or causing the complainant to fear that immediate violence would be used against him;

---

30 *R. v. Mokrecovas (Andrius)* [2001] EWCA Crim 1644; [2002] 1 Cr. App. R. 20.

31 See, e.g. J. McEwan, "The Rape Shield Askew? *R. v A*" [2001] 5 International J. of Evidence and Proof 267. Indeed, trial judges who have failed to consider admissions of sexual history evidence that is later deemed to be potentially relevant and similar on appeal have been sufficient grounds to render a conviction unsafe, see, e.g. *R. v Andrade* [2015] EWCA Crim 1722; [2016] Crim. L.R. 424 CA.

32 See C. McGlynn, "Rape trials and sexual history evidence: reforming the law on third-party evidence" (2017) 81 J. Crim. L. 367; C. McGlynn, "Challenging the law on sexual history evidence: a response to Dent and Paul" [2018] Crim. L.R. 216. Others have defended the current use of s.41 (see N. Dent and S. Paul, "In defence of section 41" [2017] Crim. L.R. 613), while some have commented that the provisions are so tightly drawn as to prevent the court hearing evidence which is relevant (see e.g. D.J. Birch, "A Fairer Deal for Vulnerable Witnesses" [2000] Crim. L.R. 223).

33 See, e.g. L. Alexander, "The Moral Magic of Consent" (1996) 2 *Legal Theory* 165; S. Estrich, *Real Rape* (Cambridge, MA: Harvard University Press, 1987); D.A. Dripps, "Beyond Rape: An Essay on the Difference Between the Presence of Force and the Absence of Consent" (1992) 92 Colum. L.R. 1780; A. Wertheimer, *Consent to Sexual Relations* (Cambridge: CUP, 2003).

> (b) any person was, at the time of the relevant act or immediately before it began, causing the victim to fear that violence was being used, or that immediate violence would be used, against another person;
> (c) the complainant was, and the defendant was not, unlawfully detained at the time of the relevant act;
> (d) the complainant was asleep or otherwise unconscious at the time of the relevant act;
> (e) because of the complainant's physical disability, the complainant would not have been able at the time of the relevant act to communicate to the defendant whether the complainant consented.
> (f) any person had administered to or caused to be taken by the complainant, without the complainant's consent, a substance which, having regard to when it was administered or taken was capable of causing or enabling the complainant to be stupefied or overpowered at the time of the relevant act.
>
> **76. Conclusive Presumptions about consent**
>
> (1) If in proceedings for an offence to which this section applies it is proved that the defendant did the relevant act, that any of the circumstances specified in subsection (2) existed, it is to be conclusively presumed—
>
> that the complainant did not consent to the relevant act, and that the defendant did not believe that the complainant consented to the relevant act.
>
> (2) The circumstances are that—
>
> (a) the defendant intentionally deceived the complainant as to the nature or purpose of the relevant act;
> (b) the defendant intentionally induced the complainant to consent to the relevant act by impersonating a person known personally to the complainant."

1. The general definition

6–012 There are two fundamental constituent parts to the definition of consent under s.74:

(1) freedom to choose to agree; and
(2) the capacity to choose to agree.

We explore each of these concepts in turn.

(i) Freedom

6–013 Basing consent upon freedom might, at first sight, appear to be an obvious good. Sexual intercourse ought to occur when, borne of their own free will, both parties make their choice to consent. That is to say, both (or all) participants have it as their purpose to engage in sexual activity. Freedom to choose will often align with conduct that is welcomed and where either party might have initiated the encounter.[34] Yet the notion of "freedom" is far from uncontroversial. MacKinnon has argued that any attempt to distinguish rape from sexual intercourse on the basis of free choice, and thus consent, is naïve.[35] That is because women must make their "free" choices to consent in a society where they are socialised to passive receptivity and where sex is something men *do* to them. In a gendered world where women are still treated unequally, it is not always (if ever) clear when a woman has consented independently of external pressures, and when she has consented subject to the social constraints of male dominion.

Even if one eschews the more far-reaching critique of the use of the concept of freedom within the context of consent, it is obvious that not all sexual choices are completely freely made and yet a form of consent may well have been given. Palmer reflects that "[b]etween [the] two poles of totalizing patriarchal dominance and almost unfettered free choice, lies the reality of sexual agency".[36] An individual's free choice may be constrained for all sorts of reasons: it may be a desire to avoid the row that will follow if sex is not forthcoming; a need for cash; a need to keep one's job; a fear of being beaten or even killed. If a person says "yes" in any of these scenarios—or if they permit intercourse after persuading the assailant to wear a condom[37]—is this consent real? The difficult task for the law has been to determine when such constraints operate to nullify consent. If rape is viewed predominantly as a crime of violence the answer is relatively unproblematic. Traditionally, only threats of death or serious harm would vitiate an apparent consent. However, as rape is now perceived as an offence against sexual autonomy, the more open-ended have become the types of constraints which may nullify consent.[38]

In *Olugboja*,[39] a case decided under the old law, V had intercourse with D after his companion had raped her and her friend. D claimed that these circumstances did not nullify her consent since only a threat of death or serious harm would suffice. The Court of Appeal held that, using the "ordinary meaning" of the word consent, V could not be said to have consented to sexual intercourse. The court held that there was a difference between the state of mind of real consent[40] and that of mere submission. The difference between the two was a matter of degree and it was for the jury to decide which side of the line a particular sequence of events falls. For example, a jury would almost inevitably decide that a wife who "reluctantly acquiesced" to intercourse to avoid a sulking husband, though submitting, would nevertheless have consented.

34 M. Chamallas, "Consent, Equality and the Legal Control of Sexual Conduct" (1988) 61 Southern Calif. L. Rev. 777.

35 C. McKinnon, *Towards a Feminist Theory of the State* (Cambridge: Harvard University Press, 1989).

36 T. Palmer, "Distinguishing Sex from Sexual Violation: Consent, Negotiation and Freedom to Negotiate" in A. Reed, M. Bohlander, N. Wake and E. Smith (eds), *Consent: domestic and comparative perspectives. Substantive issues in criminal law* (Oxford: Routledge, 2017).

37 In 1992, in Texas, a grand jury refused to indict a man who had broken into a house at night, held a knife to a woman's throat and then had intercourse with her on the ground that, because she had begged him to put on a condom, she had consented: *The Washington Post,* 31 October 1992.

38 J. Gardner, "Appreciating Olugboja" [1996] 16 *Legal Studies* 275, 277–282.

39 *R. v Olugboja (Stephen)* [1982] Q.B. 320; [1981] 3 W.L.R. 585 CA.

40 In *R. v C* [2012] EWCA Crim 2034; [2013] Crim. L.R. 358, the Court of Appeal held that there is a distinction to be drawn between "apparent" consent and "real" consent. D was charged with 18 sexual offences perpetrated against his step-daughter from when she was five years old until she was 25. The court held that the jury were entitled to find that her *apparent* consent when she was an adult was not, in fact, real given the abusive and controlling conduct of D since V's childhood.

6-014 However, there were difficulties with *Olugboja*. Although the flexibility of its approach had its merits, the distinction between mere submission and real consent was not able to bear close scrutiny.[41] It was rejected as the way forward for reform because it had "led to confusion and [risked] very different conclusions being drawn on similar facts in different cases".[42] Instead, in an attempt to be clear and unambiguous,[43] a statutory definition of consent was preferred. However, the issues discussed above have not been swept away by the definition. It is necessarily vague—but this means that a jury's preconceptions about sexual behaviour and consent may well still affect their interpretation of whether a "free choice" has been made.

(ii) Capacity

6-015 The statutory definition also refers to the capacity of V to choose. Capacity is undefined in the Act but must relate to awareness, knowledge and understanding. A person may be incapable of giving consent, because, say, they have been knocked unconscious or because they are suffering from a mental disorder that precludes understanding.[44] However, it is in the context of intoxication that the issue of capacity to consent has become a matter of concern and it is here that societal attitudes towards rape and drinking have the very real potential to influence the outcome of proceedings. Previous research showed the existence of a double standard whereby "intoxicated defendants tend to be held *less* responsible than their sober counterparts while intoxicated complainants tend to be held *more* responsible".[45] However, a recent public survey conducted by the CPS and Equally Ours found that only 8% of respondents agreed that if a man has been drinking or taking drugs, he is less responsible if he rapes someone; indicating that fewer people now agree that intoxication reduces an offender's culpability for rape. In contrast, 18% of respondents thought the victim should take some responsibility if they were intoxicated when raped.[46] As research reveals that alcohol has been ingested by a significant proportion of Vs, this remains of great concern.[47]

---

41 In *McAllister* [1997] Crim. L.R. 233, the jury, e.g. asked for an explanation of the difference between the two phrases.

42 Home Office, *Setting the Boundaries: Reforming the Law on Sexual Offences* (2000), para.2.2.3. See also *R. v PK* [2008] EWCA Crim 434, at paras 7-125–7-126.

43 *Protecting the Public, Strengthening Protection against Sexual Offenders and Reforming the Law on Sexual Offences* (Cmnd.5668, 2002), para.30.

44 Sexual Offences Act 2003 creates a number of offences specifically to protect people suffering from mental disorder: ss.30–41. In *R. v C* [2009] UKHL 42; [2009] 1 W.L.R. 1786, the House of Lords considered the issue of capacity in relation to the offence of sexual activity with a person with a mental disorder under s.30. Baroness Hale concluded that in order to have capacity a person must be able to understand the information relevant to making a decision and must also be able to weigh that information to arrive at a choice. A mentally disordered person might be able to appreciate that the act was sexual but not be able to weigh it in order to arrive at a choice [24]. Whilst, strictly, this decision relates to s.30 only, there will be situations involving mentally disordered Vs when charges under ss.1–4 could be brought and, it is submitted, this explanation of capacity should be adopted. For a discussion on how the notion of consent to sexual activity for persons with mental disabilities is interpreted by health professionals and lawyers, see S. Doyle, "The Notion of Consent to Sexual Activity for Persons With Mental Disabilities" (2010) 31 Liverpool L.R. 111.

45 E. Finch and V. Munro, "The Demon Drink and the Demonised Woman: Socio-sexual Stereotypes and Responsibility Attribution in Rape Trials involving Intoxicants" (2007) 16 *Social and Legal Studies* 591, 591. Recent research in the US indicates high levels of acceptance of the belief "he didn't mean to" when intoxicated, especially amongst survivors of sexual violence. M. E. PettyJohn, K. M. Cary and H. L. McCauley, "Rape Myth Acceptance in a Community Sample of Adult Women in the Post #MeToo Era" (2023) 38 *Journal of Interpersonal Violence* 8211.

46 CPS and Equally Ours, *Rape and serious sexual offences: public understanding and attitudes* (2024), p.60.

47 See further, Advisory Council on the Misuse of Drugs, *Drug Facilitated Sexual Assault* (2007). The concept of DAR (drug assisted rape) includes both alcohol and drugs such as Rohypnol. The evidence suggests that alcohol is the most common weapon in DAR while the incidence of drug facilitated sexual assault is unclear (paras 5.2–5.3).

In 2005, a case involving an alleged rape upon a female student who was drunk but conscious at the time of the offence collapsed.[48] Had she been unconscious at the time of the intercourse, the evidential presumption in s.75(2)(d) would have been invoked.[49] The judge directed the jury to return a verdict of "not guilty" when the prosecution revealed that they were unable to proceed further because they could not prove that the complainant had not given consent because of her level of intoxication. It has been argued that the judge could have put the matter to the jury to consider in terms of the complainant's capacity to consent.[50] This issue arose for reconsideration in the following decision.

R. v Bree [2007] 3 W.L.R. 600 (Court of Appeal, Criminal Division):

D and M spent the evening together, drinking heavily before returning to D's flat where they had sexual intercourse. Initially, the prosecution alleged that M was unconscious throughout most of the activity and thus lacked capacity to consent. Following evidence by M at the trial, the prosecution changed its stance and alleged that M's ability to resist had been hampered by the effects of alcohol but that she had had the capacity to consent. M accepted that her memory of the evening was very patchy; however, she maintained that she had made it clear, in so far as she could, that she did not consent. D claimed that M had been conscious throughout and that he reasonably believed she was consenting. D was convicted of rape and appealed. **6–016**

SIR IGOR JUDGE P:

"[26] In cases which are said to arise after voluntary consumption of alcohol the question is not whether the alcohol made either or both less inhibited than they would have been if sober, nor whether either or both might afterwards have regretted what had happened, and indeed wished that it had not. If the Complainant consents, her consent cannot be revoked. Moreover it is not a question whether either or both may have had very poor recollection of precisely what had happened. That may be relevant to the reliability of their evidence. Finally, and certainly, it is not a question whether either or both was behaving irresponsibly. As they were both autonomous adults, the essential question for decision is, as it always is, whether the evidence proved that the Appellant had sexual intercourse with the Complainant without her consent . . .

[34] In our judgment, the proper construction of s 74 of the 2003 Act, as applied to the problem now under discussion, leads to clear conclusions. If, through drink (or for any other reason) the Complainant has temporarily lost her capacity to choose whether to have intercourse on

---

48 *R. v Dougal* unreported, Swansea Crown Court. See C Gammell, "Judge 'dreadfully wrong' over rape ruling" *The Independent*, 24 November 2005.

49 The original proposals in the Home Office's consultation paper, *Setting the Boundaries: Reforming the Law on Sexual Offences* (2000), specifically included a presumption about consent that covered cases where "a person is asleep, unconscious or too affected by alcohol or drugs to give consent". This recommendation was dropped in *Protecting the Public, Strengthening Protection against Sexual Offenders and Reforming the Law on Sexual Offences* (Cmnd.5668, 2002). See further, Finch and Munro, "The Sexual Offences Act 2003: Intoxicated Consent and Drug Assisted Rape Revisited" [2004] Crim. L.R. 789, 793.

50 Centre for Law, Gender and Sexuality, *Response to the Office for Criminal Justice Reform's Consultation Paper: Convicting Rapists and Protecting Victims of Rape—Justice for Victims of Rape* (2006), p.13. In *R. v Tambedou (Seedy)* [2014] EWCA Crim 954, the court held that a rape V's evidence that she had little memory of the events was not sufficient for the judge to remove the case from the jury. The jury had been entitled to consider the issue of the absence of consent and to distinguish it from the absence of memory.

the relevant occasion, she is not consenting, and subject to questions about the Defendant's state of mind, if intercourse takes place, this would be rape. However, where the Complainant has voluntarily consumed even substantial quantities of alcohol, but nevertheless remains capable of choosing whether or not to have intercourse, and in drink agrees to do so, this would not be rape. We should perhaps underline that, as a matter of practical reality, capacity to consent may evaporate well before a Complainant becomes unconscious. Whether this is so or not, however, is fact specific, or more accurately, depends on the actual state of mind of the individuals involved on the particular occasion.

[35] Considerations like these underline the fact that it would be unrealistic to endeavour to create some kind of grid system which would enable the answer to these questions to be related to some prescribed level of alcohol consumption. Experience shows that different individuals have a greater or lesser capacity to cope with alcohol than others, and indeed the ability of a single individual to do so may vary from day to day. The practical reality is that there are some areas of human behaviour which are inapt for detailed legislative structures. In this context, provisions intended to protect women from sexual assaults might very well be conflated into a system which would provide patronising interference with the right of autonomous adults to make personal decisions for themselves.

[36] For these reasons, notwithstanding criticisms of the statutory provisions, in our view the 2003 Act provides a clear definition of 'consent' for the purposes of the law of rape, and by defining it with reference to 'capacity to make that choice', sufficiently addresses the issue of consent in the context of voluntary consumption of alcohol by the Complainant. The problems do not arise from the legal principles. They lie with infinite circumstances of human behaviour, usually taking place in private without independent evidence, and the consequent difficulties of proving this very serious offence . . .

[39] In this case the jury should have been given some assistance with the meaning of 'capacity' in circumstances where the Complainant was affected by her own voluntarily induced intoxication, and also whether, and to what extent they could take that into account in deciding whether she had consented . . .[51]

[43] . . . In a trial in which the issues of consent and voluntary intoxication were fundamental to the outcome, the jury were given no or no sufficient directions to enable the verdict which they reached to be regarded as safe.[52] Accordingly the conviction is quashed."

Appeal allowed

---

51 In *R. v Kamki (Gael Tameu)* [2013] EWCA Crim 2335, D had been convicted of raping V who at the time had been heavily intoxicated. D appealed arguing that the important point that a sexual encounter that was drunken and regretted did not make it non-consensual was not addressed by the trial judge. The Court of Appeal held that where the elements of capacity to consent had been fully dealt with, it was not necessary for the judge to state in every case the simple words that a drunken consent remained a consent.

52 In *R. v Kamki (Gael Tameu)* [2013] EWCA Crim 2335, D had been convicted of raping V who at the time had been heavily intoxicated. D appealed arguing that the important point that a sexual encounter that was drunken and regretted did not make it non-consensual was not addressed by the trial judge. The Court of Appeal held that where the elements of capacity to consent had been fully dealt with, it was not necessary for the judge to state in every case the simple words that a drunken consent remained a consent.

The Government (which had been consulting on ways to remove the barriers to successful prosecutions) subsequently commented that this decision provided vital guidance and that there was, therefore, no need for capacity to be defined for the purposes of the Sexual Offences Act.[53] Both the decision in *Bree* and the Government's response has divided opinion. While it is true that attempting to determine capacity using a grid system based on blood-alcohol levels would be unhelpful for the reasons given by the Court of Appeal, the idea that there need be no further attempts to clarify capacity in the context of intoxication is open to challenge: **6–017**

> ". . . what appears to be part of a liberal non-interventionist approach to regulating private sexual behaviour, in reality can also be seen as a means by which some men's disregard for the sexual autonomy of women is maintained."[54]

Such arguments have led some to call for the inclusion of "extreme drunkenness" as a rebuttal presumption of non-consent.[55] This, it has been argued, would cover situations where it is considered that the complainant was too intoxicated to be able to give free consent. Alternatively, Clough asserts that it might also:

> ". . . be advantageous to have a non-exhaustive list of precursors that might be used as evidence of incapacity to consent. This could include physical manifestations of heavy intoxication such as vomiting, inability to stand and walk, having to be undressed and a wish to lay down."[56]

2. The presumptions

The new law distinguishes between two types of presumptions of non-consent: those that are conclusive and those that raise an evidential presumption that consent was absent.[57] Both types of presumptions apply not only to the issue of consent as an element of the actus reus but also apply to the question of whether D had mens rea. **6–018**

(i) The conclusive presumptions

In the case of the two conclusive presumptions, once it is proved that D did the relevant act and that either of the circumstances existed, then both consent and lack of belief in consent are conclusively **6–019**

---

53 Centre for Law, Gender and Sexuality, *Response to the Office for Criminal Justice Reform's Consultation Paper: Convicting Rapists and Protecting Victims of Rape—Justice for Victims of Rape* (2006), pp.10–11. The Government did state that it would keep the issue under review and invite the Judicial Studies Board to consider whether a specimen direction on capacity and consent would assist judges. However, no such direction was issued. In *R. v H* [2007] EWCA Crim 2056, the Court of Appeal stressed that the issue of capacity to consent should normally be left to the jury to determine.

54 P.N.S. Rumney and R.A. Fenton, "Intoxicated Consent in Rape: *Bree* and Juror Decision-making" (2008) 71 M.L.R. 279, 289. See also, A. Ashworth, "Rape: Consent—Intoxication" [2007] Crim. L.R. 901 and J. Elvin, "The Concept of Consent under the Sexual Offences Act 2003" (2008) 72 J. Crim. L. 519.

55 Rumney and Fenton, "Intoxicated Consent in Rape: *Bree* and Juror Decision-making" (2008) 71 M.L.R. 279; B. Simpson, "Why has the Concept of Consent Proven So Difficult to Clarify?" (2016) 80(2) J. Crim. L. 97.

56 A. Clough, "Sober regrets and shared risk taking: navigating intoxicated consent and rape in the courtroom" (2018) 82 J. Crim. L. 482.

57 The presumptions apply to offences under ss.1 (rape), 2 (assault by penetration), 3 (sexual assault) and 4 (causing a person to engage in sexual activity without consent).

established.[58] Both build upon previous law. In *Clarence*,[59] Stephen J identified two such kinds of fundamental circumstances, the first relates to the identity of the actor and the second goes to the nature of the act, either of which negated the apparent consent of V if induced by the deceit of D. Each of these are examined below.

(a) Impersonation

6-020 The old law only protected Vs where the person impersonated was V's husband although the Court of Appeal in *Elbekkay*[60] extended this to cover boyfriends as well. The new conclusive presumption applies to the impersonation of anyone known personally to V.[61] While this is broader than the old law, it would not, of course, come into operation if D claimed to be, say, Tom Holland who was only known to the complainant through his films.

Recent case law has also made it clear that deceptions relating to identity pertaining to profession do not fall within the conclusive presumptions.[62] In the case of *Monica*,[63] the CPS declined to pursue a prosecution of a police officer who had worked undercover for a number of years as an environmental activist, during which he had formed a sexual relationship with the claimant. The claimant asserted that his deception as to identity had vitiated her consent and sought judicial review of the CPS' decision. The Divisional Court accepted that the claimant would not have had sex with the officer had she known of his background and that the officer's deception had gone to every aspect of his identity *except* for his body. However, this did not mean that her consent, in law, had been vitiated. In reviewing the current case law, the court noted that the concept of deception vitiating consent did not apply to deceptions which were "not closely connected with the performance of the sexual act", or intrinsically so fundamental owing to that connection that they could be treated as cases of impersonation.[64] To extend the interpretation of consent to include the facts of this case would inevitably result in the criminalisation of much conduct which, hitherto, had fallen outside the purview of the criminal law. Only the legislature could make such a change to the law.

(b) Deception as to nature or purpose of the act

6-021 The second conclusive presumption of non-consent refers to the nature or purpose of the act. These deceptions frequently relate to medical or health procedures that are carried out for a sexual purpose by D. In *Flattery*,[65] D induced a woman to submit to intercourse by maintaining the deception that he was performing a surgical operation. He was convicted of rape. This was followed in the not dissimilar

---

58 This has led McEwan to conclude that they are not presumptions at all but introduce a substantive rule of law. She also notes that in the US conclusive presumptions have been declared unconstitutional as derogating from the presumption of innocence: McEwan, "Proving Consent in Sexual Cases: Legislative Change and Cultural Evolution" [2005] *International J. of Evidence and Proof* 1.

59 *R. v Clarence (Charles James)* (1888) 22 Q.B.D. 23.

60 *Elbekkay* [1995] Crim. L.R. 163.

61 Note that the impersonation must have induced the complainant to consent; J. Temkin and A. Ashworth, "The Sexual Offences Act: (1) Rape, Sexual Assaults and the Problems of Consent" [2004] Crim. L.R. 328, 334–335.

62 *R. (on the application of Monica) v DPP* [2018] EWHC 3508 (Admin); [2019] Q.B. 1019.

63 *Monica* [2019] Q.B. 1019.

64 *Monica* [2019] Q.B. 1019 at [80].

65 *R. v Flattery (John)* (1877) 2 Q.B.D. 410; (1887) 13 Cox C.C. 388.

case of *Williams*[66] where D, who was a singing-master, had intercourse with one of his pupils aged 16. She made no resistance as she believed his claim that he was merely improving her breathing. He too was convicted. The principle upon which both cases were decided was that there had been no consent to sexual intercourse; what had been consented to was a surgical operation or health-related procedure.

Prior to the 2003 Act, the courts had generally declined to extend the ambit of the law of rape to cases other than those involving the two types of fundamental deception outlined above. In *Linekar*, for example, D deceived a sex worker into having intercourse with him by claiming (falsely) that he would pay her. Although she would not have had intercourse with him had she known the truth this was held not to be a deception as to the nature of the act.[67] The court reasoned that this was because the complainant knew who D was and that the nature of the act was to have sex. However, the narrowness of this approach was put in doubt by the decision of *Tabassum*.[68] In this case, concerning the former offence of indecent assault but raising the issue of consent, the court took the view that the Vs, who had consented to breast examinations for what they thought was medical research, would never have done so had they known that D was not medically qualified. It was held that they had consented to the nature of the act but not to its "quality"—and that accordingly there was no real consent. This is a controversial distinction yet it is one that is replicated by the language of the conclusive presumption in s.76(2)(a) which refers to both the nature and the *purpose* of the act.

(c) Deceptions that have fallen outside of s.76 but within s.74: "Active" deceptions

R. v Jheeta [2007] 2 Cr. App. R. 34 (Court of Appeal, Criminal Division):

By a series of bizarre and unpleasant lies, including texts from D which purported to come from the police telling her that if she did not sleep with him she would be liable to a fine, D induced V to continue to have sexual intercourse with him. When the truth came to light, V claimed that she had only had intercourse with D because of the texts and that she had not truly consented. D pleaded guilty to rape having been advised that his behaviour fell within s.76(2)(a). He then appealed. **6–022**

JUDGE P:

> "[24] In our judgment the ambit of section 76 is limited to the 'act' to which it is said to apply. In rape cases the 'act' is vaginal, anal or oral intercourse. Provided this consideration is constantly borne in mind, it will be seen that section 76 (2)(a) is relevant only to the comparatively rare cases where the defendant deliberately deceives the complainant about the *nature or purpose* of one or other form of intercourse. No conclusive presumptions arise merely because the complainant was deceived in some way or other by disingenuous blandishments of or common or garden lies by the defendant. These may well be deceptive and persuasive, but they will rarely go to the nature or purpose of intercourse. Beyond this

66 *R. v Williams (Owen Richard)* [1923] 1 K.B. 340; (1924) 17 Cr. App. R. 56 CA.

67 *R. v Linekar (Gareth)* [1995] Q.B. 250; [1995] 2 Cr. App. R. 49 CA.

68 *R. v Tabassum (Naveed)* [2000] 2 Cr. App. R. 328; [2000] Crim. L.R. 686 CA. See also *R. v Green (Peter Donovan)* [2002] EWCA Crim 1501.

> limited type of case, and assuming that, as here, section 75 has no application, the issue of consent must be addressed in the context of section 74 . . .
>
> [28] With these considerations in mind, we must return to the present case. On the written basis of plea the appellant undoubtedly deceived the complainant. He created a bizarre and fictitious fantasy which, because it was real enough to her, pressurised her to have intercourse with him more frequently than she otherwise would have done. She was not deceived as to the nature or purpose of intercourse, but deceived as to the situation in which she found herself. In our judgment the conclusive presumption in section 76 (2)(a) had no application, and counsel for the appellant below were wrong to advise on the basis that it did. However that is not an end of the matter . . . the persuasion took the form of the pressures imposed on her by the complicated and unpleasant scheme which he had fabricated. This was not a free choice, or consent for the purposes of the Act. In these circumstances we entertain no reservations that on some occasions at least the complainant was not consenting to intercourse for the purposes of section 74, and that the appellant was perfectly well aware of it. His guilty plea reflected these undisputed facts."
>
> *Appeal dismissed*

6–023 This was the first case to examine the meaning of s.76(2)(a) and it is thus of some importance. The approach taken before the Act and highlighted by *Tabassum* has been confirmed. Mere "disingenuous blandishments" or "common or garden lies" will "rarely go to the nature or purpose of the act". However, this does not mean that it will be straightforward to determine whether there has been a material deception as to "purpose" in future cases. Purpose is capable of being interpreted in a limited way, as in *Jheeta*, or more broadly.[69] Some support (albeit limited) for the latter approach comes from the case of *Devonald*. The male D posed as a woman over the internet to entice V (who had broken off a relationship with D's teenage daughter) to masturbate in front of a webcam with a view to publishing the pictures so as to embarrass the boy and teach him a lesson. The Court of Appeal held that D had deceived V as to the purpose of the act.[70] Oddly, this is an instance of the deception in reverse: the *victim* thought that the act was for sexual purposes. While V clearly would not have acted as he did had he known the truth the same would also have been true of V in *Linekar* and, given that the judgment is both unreserved and brief, it would probably be unwise to place too much reliance on *Devonald*.[71]

Is it appropriate to take a narrow approach to s.76(2)(a) as in *Jheeta* or should a broader approach be adopted? Answering this question requires one to weigh two competing considerations. First, it may

---

69 See *R. v Piper (Geoffrey Kenneth)* [2007] EWCA Crim 2151; [2008] 1 Cr. App. R. (S.) 91, where D's conviction for sexual assault was upheld on the basis that he had deceived Vs into thinking that they were being measured for bikinis to determine their potential to model when it was for his sexual gratification. See also D. Selfe, "The Meaning of Consent Within the Sexual Offences Act 2003" (2008) *Criminal Lawyer* 174.

70 *R. v Devonald (Stephen)* [2008] EWCA Crim 527. The relevant offence was causing activity without consent under the Sexual Offences Act 2003 s.4. The prosecution had sought to rely on s.76(2)(b) as well but the Court of Appeal restricted its judgment to s.76(2)(a).

71 Indeed, in *R. v B* [2013] EWCA Crim 823; [2013] 2 Cr. App. R. 29, a case involving an elaborate online deception to pressure V to perform sexual acts over the internet, the court held that there had to be a deception as to the nature or purpose of the sexual acts for s.76 to apply. Doubting *Devonald* [2008] EWCA Crim 527 and following *R. v Jheeta (Harvinder Singh)* [2007] EWCA Crim 1699; [2007] 2 Cr. App. R. 34, the court found that the complainant was not deceived as to the purpose of her acts online and thus s.76 was not applicable, instead the prosecution need look no further than s.74.

absolutely be the case that V would not have consented had the truth been told. In other words, the deception has operated to remove the possibility of real consent. On the other hand, does D in such cases deserve to be labelled a rapist? When V has knowingly consented to D's penetration will they suffer the same degree of emotional and psychological trauma as in other rape cases? Many commentators would argue that such admittedly limited, conditional, and, possibly, naïve consent is still valid and that sexual intercourse in such circumstances is not, therefore, rape.[72] However, it can be argued that consent should be understood in a "richer" sense: as full and truthful understanding of what is involved that is free from all pressures.[73]

R. v McNally [2014] 2 W.L.R. 200 (Court of Appeal, Criminal Division):

In this case, D, "who was female", contacted V (Y) over a social networking website and had claimed to be a young male.[74] Over a period of three-and-a-half years, M and Y developed a romantic relationship. Y considered D, who "presented as a boy", to be her boyfriend. M visited Y on four occasions when M was aged 17 and Y 16. During those visits, there were numerous occasions of oral and digital penetration of Y. Y later discovered that M was not in fact "biologically male". M was subsequently convicted of assault by penetration. The case for the prosecution was that Y's consent was obtained by fraudulent deception that D was a male and that had she known this she would not have consented to acts of vaginal penetration. **6–024**

LEVESON LJ:

"[25] In reality, some deceptions (such as, for example, in relation to wealth) will obviously not be sufficient to vitiate consent. In our judgment, Lord Judge CJ's observation that 'the evidence relating to 'choice' and the 'freedom' to make any particular choice must be approached in a broad commonsense way' identifies the route through the dilemma.

[26] Thus while, in a physical sense, the acts of assault by penetration of the vagina are the same whether perpetrated by a male or a female, the sexual nature of the acts is, on any common sense view, different where the complainant is deliberately deceived by a defendant into believing that the latter is a male. Assuming the facts to be proved as alleged, M chose to have sexual encounters with a boy and her preference (her freedom to choose whether or not to have a sexual encounter with a girl) was removed by the defendant's deception.

[27] It follows from the foregoing analysis that we conclude that, depending on the circumstances, deception as to gender can vitiate consent . . ."

Appeal against conviction dismissed

---

72 H. Gross, "Rape, Moralism and Human Rights" [2007] Crim. L.R. 220 and McEwan, "The Rape Shield Askew? *R. v A*" [2001] 5 International J. of Evidence and Proof 267.

73 See further, Herring, "Mistaken Sex" [2005] Crim. L. R. 511, 515–617, and J.W. Herring, "Human Rights and Rape: A Reply to Hyman Gross" [2007] Crim. L.R. 228.

74 *R. v McNally (Justine)* [2013] EWCA Crim 1051; [2014] 2 W.L.R. 200.

6-025 The Court of Appeal in *McNally* did not interpret whether D's deceit fell within the ambit of s.76(2)(a), as it was never suggested that the conclusive presumptions applied, therefore, the relevance of the deception was restricted to the impact it had on the construction of s.74. It was clear that the court was persuaded by previous authority that included situations of "active deception", as against cases involving Ds who fail to correct an assumption.[75] This approach is similar to that taken in *Jheeta* in that the courts appear to be willing to utilise the breadth of s.74 in cases involving active deceptions where a narrow interpretation of s.76 is applied, or as in this case where s.76 is not raised at all. However, we are to some extent left unsure whether deceit as to gender will ever fall under s.76(2)(a), or alternatively whether this is a question of fact that must be left to the jury to determine with reference only to the meaning of freedom of choice under s.74.

Whether such a deceit should conclusively vitiate consent is highly questionable, especially if we consider the fact that the nature and purpose of the act, i.e. to penetrate the vagina for sexual pleasure, remains the same regardless of the gender of D.[76] Lord Leveson's statement that common sense tells us that the nature of the sexual act changes where there is a deception as to gender may not be as commonsensical as he suggests. Can the nature of an act change retrospectively when *both* parties previously understood that act to be *sexual* penetration of one person by another? Lord Leveson's reasoning seems to assume that the nature is changed, not simply because D was of a different gender to that portrayed to the complainant, but also because the assumed sexual orientation of the complainant was heterosexual, inferring the sexual contact must have been unwanted. It is less than clear whether the crucial element in the court's decision in *McNally* was that the deception was "active" or whether the change in nature of the act was simply contingent on the sexual orientation of the complainant. There may well be implications for each of these questions to the notions of "free choice" and "agreement", such that V was denied a free choice to make an informed agreement about the sexual act, but it is considered to be disingenuous to conclude that deception as to gender retrospectively modifies the sexual quality of the act in such a situation. Sexual acts do not become non-sexual just because they are carried out between people of the same gender. Indeed, Sharpe argues that non-disclosure of one's gender identity is neither deceptive nor particularly harmful, and that the "common sense" belief that non-disclosure is either of these things is the result of transphobic and homophobic attitudes, which the courts should not accept as the norm.[77]

One problem with the reasoning provided in *McNally* is that it may lead to a situation where transgender individuals must reveal the sex they are assigned at birth to prospective sexual partners or risk being prosecuted and labelled as rapists/sexual offenders. This will surely give rise to potential breaches of the European Convention on Human Rights art.8, which guarantees the right to respect for a private

---

75 e.g. where the D fails to disclose a material fact, such as their HIV status; see *R. v B* [2006] EWCA Crim 2945; [2007] 1 W.L.R. 1567.

76 Unlike the example of the doctor who purports that they need to provide a medical examination of V's vagina, but instead penetrates V for their own sexual gratification. In such a situation, the nature and purpose of the act is clearly different between the two parties; for one it is medical, for the other it is sexual.

77 A. Sharpe, "Criminalising Sexual Intimacy: Transgender Defendants and the Legal Construction of Non-consent" [2014] Crim. L.R. 207. See also, V. Brooks and J.C. Thompson, "Dude looks like a lady: gender deception, consent and ethics" (2019) 83 J. Crim. L. 258; M. Travis, "The vulnerability of heterosexuality: consent, gender deception and embodiment" (2019) 28 S. & L.S. 2019, 303.

life.[78] By analogy, and if taken literally, Lord Leveson's assertion could also mean that a heterosexual person will have potentially been raped by a homosexual person, where the homosexual person actively makes the representation that they are in fact straight. If after a sexual act the former finds out that the homosexual person was not in fact heterosexual but was instead "experimenting", the question arises: does the sexual nature of the act change rendering the homosexual partner a rapist? Such an outcome would certainly not be commonsensical.

Whether the case of *McNally* is an example of the courts extending the grounds for vitiating consent via s.74 is debatable. Interestingly, the court in *Monica*[79] stated that to broaden the interpretation of impersonation under s.76(1)(b), where a police officer pretended to be a member of an environmental protest group, would be to extend too far the reach of the criminal law, and that inclusion of further deceptions was a job for Parliament. Yet simultaneously they approved the judgment in *McNally*, concluding that this decision, and other cases discussed below, are examples of the courts "developing" the law rather than creating new grounds of deception. To a large extent, it remains unclear which types of active deceptions will fall within the meaning of s.74 and which should be excluded as extending the reach of the law too far.[80] **6–026**

(d) Deceptions that have fallen outside of s.76 but within s.74: Deceptions involving preconditions

There have been a number of other situations where deceptions involve an expressed precondition. That is to say, A agrees to sexual intercourse with B but only where a certain condition is met first. Such was the case in *Assange*[81] where the Divisional Court was concerned with the question of whether sexual intercourse without a condom, where it had been made clear that consent was conditional on the use of a condom, would vitiate consent. Taking a narrow approach to interpreting s.76(2)(a), Sir John Thomas P held that the conclusive presumption did not apply in such a situation but that s.74 could and should be used to determine whether the deliberate removal of the condom restricted the complainant's capacity to make a free choice.[82] **6–027**

In *R. (F)*,[83] a complainant agreed to sexual intercourse on the basis that D would not ejaculate into her vagina. D agreed to this knowing that he would in fact ejaculate. The court held that:

> ". . . if before penetration began the intervener had made up his mind that he would penetrate and ejaculate within the claimant's vagina, or . . . he decided that he would not withdraw at all, just because he deemed the claimant subservient to his control, she was deprived of choice relating to the crucial feature on which her original consent to sexual intercourse was based. Accordingly her

---

78 One might also wish to consider whether the courts were therefore justified in *McNally* [2014] 2 W.L.R. 200 in sentencing a young trans man struggling to come to terms with his transgender identity to three years' custody and to lifetime registration on the Sex Offenders' Register.

79 *Monica* [2019] Q.B. 1019.

80 See further, R. Clement, "Deception and Consent to Sex" (2019) 78 *The Cambridge Law Journal* 264; T. Alencar, "Conditional consent and sexual crime: time for reform?" 85 (2021) *Journal of Criminal Law* 455.

81 *Assange v Sweden* [2011] EWHC 2849 (Admin); (2011) 108(44) L.S.G. 17.

82 For a discussion on deception and consent see, K. Laird, "Rapist or rogue? Deception, consent and the Sexual Offences Act 2003" [2014] Crim. L.R. 492; C. Sjolin, "Ten years on: consent under the Sexual Offences Act 2003" (2015) J. Crim. L. 20.

83 *R. (on the application of F) v DPP* [2013] EWHC 945 (Admin); [2014] 2 W.L.R. 190.

> consent was negated. Contrary to her wishes, and knowing that she would not have consented, and did not consent to penetration or the continuation of penetration if she had any inkling of his intention, he deliberately ejaculated within her vagina. In law, this combination of circumstances falls within the statutory definition of rape."[84]

A similar precondition arose in the case of *Lawrance,*[85] but with a very different outcome. D told a sexual partner online that he had had a vasectomy. Upon meeting, D reconfirmed that he had undergone a vasectomy and on this basis she agreed to unprotected sexual intercourse. D texted her the next day and told her he had lied about the vasectomy. The complainant later discovered that she was pregnant and underwent a termination. At trial, the judge ruled that a deceit about fertility was capable of negating consent, and D was found guilty of rape. However, on appeal, the Court of Appeal concluded that a lie about fertility was different from one about whether a condom was being worn (*Assange*), whether withdrawal would take place during sex (*R. (F)*), or a misrepresentation about gender (*McNally*). This, they reasoned, was because the complainant was not deceived as to nature and quality of the sexual act, but instead had been deceived about the nature or quality of the ejaculate. In other words, consent related not to the act of penetration but to the risks or possible consequences of intercourse.[86] D's lie was therefore "not capable in law of negating consent", and his convictions were found to be unsafe and were quashed.[87]

The outcome of this case has been criticised by a number of legal scholars who have argued that it runs contrary to the expansive approach to interpreting consent prior to *Lawrance*, which had given a greater role for sexual autonomy by focusing on the boundaries of free choice of the complainant.[88] Indeed it requires some interpretative gymnastics to conclude that a precondition to wear a condom before sex can vitiate consent, but a that a precondition that someone has had a vasectomy does not.

(e) Deceptions that have fallen outside of s.76 but within s.74: Failure to disclose information

6–028 Beyond active deceptions and situations involving preconditions are those cases where someone fails to reveal a fact that will affect someone's freedom of choice to consent. Such a situation may arise where D fails to inform their sexual partner that they are HIV positive. The courts have taken a more restrictive approach in these cases, holding that consent to sexual intercourse is valid.[89] Instead, the failure to inform the complainant will negate consent for the purposes of, for example, the Offences against the Person Act

---

84 *R. (on the application of F) v DPP* [2014] 2 W.L.R. 190 at [26].

85 *R. v Lawrance (Jason)* [2020] 1 W.L.R. 5025; [2020] EWCA Crim 971.

86 The court notes that this was analogous to *R. v B* [2006] EWCA Crim 2945, where transmission of HIV was not part of the performance of intercourse but a consequence of it.

87 *Lawrance* [2020] 1 W.L.R. 5025 at [43].

88 See e.g. K. Murray and T. Beattie "Conditional Consent and Sexual Offences: Revisiting the Sexual Offences Act 2003 after Lawrance" [2021] Crim LR 556.

89 *R. v B* [2006] EWCA Crim 2945. Note that in *McNally* [2014] 2 W.L.R. 200, Lord Leveson distinguished *R. v B* stating that this was not a case of deception but a failure to disclosure [19].

1861 ss.18 or 20 if that person were to become infected with HIV.[90] However, it should be noted that Lord Leveson in *McNally* suggested that the court in *B* did not decide that deception as to HIV status could never vitiate consent. Rather, the court had left it open as to whether consent would be negated, if for example D was asked about their HIV status and actively deceived the complainant. This again leaves open the possibility that deception as to one's sexual health may in some circumstances lead to the vitiation of consent.[91]

(ii) The evidential presumptions

As well as the conclusive presumptions, s.75 creates six evidential presumptions. This is an exhaustive list; thus, additions may only be made to it by Parliament.[92] The content of s.75 changed significantly during the reform process. Threats of harm (other than immediate violence) or other serious detriment to V or others and cases where the consent of V had only been indicated by a third party were dropped from the list and s.75(2)(f) was added.[93] If the prosecution can prove that D did the relevant act in any of the six circumstances and that they knew of the circumstance, it will be presumed that there was no consent and that they lacked a reasonable belief in consent. The defence will then be under an evidential burden to introduce sufficient evidence to raise the issue of consent or reasonable belief in consent.[94] It might be, for example, that D claims that the couple were engaging in consensual sado-masochistic sexual intercourse. If sufficient evidence is raised, the prosecution will have to prove lack of consent or reasonable belief beyond reasonable doubt.[95] As the Judicial Studies Board has noted, the Act does not specify whether it is for the judge or the jury to decide whether the evidential burden is discharged, but the Board's direction assumes that it is a matter for the judge and that "although each case will turn on its facts, it is thought that in many cases a section 75 direction will not be appropriate".[96] In circumstances when it is necessary to give a direction, the Court of Appeal has urged trial judges to take care so as to avoid the risk of elevating the presumptions to the level of the conclusive presumptions.[97] **6-029**

---

90 *R. v Dica (Mohammed)* [2004] EWCA Crim 1103; [2004] Q.B. 1257; *Konzani* [2005] 2 Cr. App. R. 98. See paras 9-062–9-063.

91 One way to address the issue of deception in cases such as *Assange* (2011) 108(44) L.S.G. 17, *R. (on the application of F) v DPP* [2014] 2 W.L.R. 190 and *McNally* [2014] 2 W.L.R. 200 is to consider a separate offence of procuring sexual activity by deception, see J.R. Spencer, "Sex by Deception" [2013] 9 Arch. Rev. 6.

92 Temkin and Ashworth, "The Sexual Offences Act: (1) Rape, Sexual Assaults and the Problems of Consent" [2004] Crim. L.R. 328, 338. Home Office, *Setting the Boundaries: Reforming the Law on Sexual Offences* (2000) had conceived of the list as a starting point, with further circumstances being added as the case law developed (para.2.10.7).

93 See further, Temkin and Ashworth, "The Sexual Offences Act: (1) Rape, Sexual Assaults and the Problems of Consent" [2004] Crim. L.R. 328, 338–340.

94 In *R. v Ciccarelli (Yuri)* [2011] EWCA Crim 2665; [2012] 1 Cr. App. R. 15, it was held that before the question of D's reasonable belief in the complainant's consent could be left to the jury, some evidence beyond the fanciful or speculative had to be adduced to support the reasonableness of a belief. D's mere assertion of his belief in her consent was insufficient.

95 On issues of proof, see Temkin and Ashworth, "The Sexual Offences Act: (1) Rape, Sexual Assaults and the Problems of Consent" [2004] Crim. L.R. 328, 342–344.

96 Judicial Studies Board, *Specimen Directions: 16a* (2007).

97 *R. v Zhang (Shanjil)* [2007] EWCA Crim 2018.

3. The relationship between the presumptions and the general definition

Jennifer Temkin and Andrew Ashworth, "The Sexual Offences Act 2003: (1) Rape, Sexual Assaults and the Problems of Consent" [2004] Crim. L.R. 328, 336–337:

6–030 By introducing a three-track approach to matters of consent and belief in consent—irrebuttable presumptions, rebuttable presumptions, and a general definition of consent—the Act raised a number of questions. Are the three categories intended to reflect some kind of moral hierarchy, so that the most serious cases on non-consent give rise to irrebuttable presumptions and the next serious cases of non-consent to rebuttable presumptions with the remainder falling within the general definition? Or is the organising principle one of clarity and certainty, so that it is the clearest cases (not necessarily the worst) that give rise to irrebuttable presumptions and the next clearest to rebuttable presumptions, with the remainder falling within the general definition? Or is it a mixture of the two, with an added element of common law history? One would have thought that consideration ought to be given to marking out the worst cases of non-consent by means of irrebuttable presumptions, but that appears not to have happened."

6–031 It is by no means certain that all the right circumstances have been included in the list of evidential presumptions and it is certainly questionable whether the conclusive presumptions are necessarily the "worst".[98] There is a compelling argument, for example, that the fact that V was unconscious at the time of the act should have been included as a conclusive presumption rather than an evidential presumption. Had the presumptions only applied to rape and assault by penetration then this might well have been easier to achieve. As it is, it is appropriate that a conclusive presumption should not be applied to a D who sexually touches their sleeping partner, as is their habit, during the course of a night.[99]

What does seem clear is that juries are directed to the presumptions first, but only, of course, if applicable to the facts of the case. In practice, it seems that cases falling under s.75 are rare and so it is uncommon for the presumptions to be introduced. The general definition applies in the many cases where the presumptions do not, such as, for example, where there are threats of non-immediate violence or threats of other kinds. It is in such situations that juries will continue to experience difficulties in coming to a conclusion from all the evidence as to the presence or absence of consent. The fact that we now have a definition of consent may focus the jury's attention on the right questions.[100] However, given a definition of consent that "positively sprouts uncertainties"[101] it will not make the answers any easier. Indeed, it seems that judges, in trying to guide juries, are tempted to continue to employ the distinction drawn in *Olugboja* between mere submission and real consent even though, as we have seen, the Government rejected it.[102]

---

98 See also Sjolin, "Ten years on: consent under the Sexual Offences Act 2003" (2015) J. Crim. L. 20.

99 Temkin and Ashworth, "The Sexual Offences Act: (1) Rape, Sexual Assaults and the Problems of Consent" [2004] Crim. L.R. 328, 338–339.

100 Although this is contested: see Tadros, "Rape Without Consent" [2006] 26 O.J.L.S. 515, 518–532.

101 Temkin and Ashworth, "The Sexual Offences Act: (1) Rape, Sexual Assaults and the Problems of Consent" [2004] Crim. L.R. 328, 338. See also, C.S. Elliot and C. de Than, "The Case for a Rational Reconstruction of Consent in Criminal Law" (2007) 70 M.L.R. 225, 236–249.

102 See *W* [2015] EWCA Crim 559 where the court held that "[i]t is possible for a person to submit to a demand which he or she feels unable to resist, but without lacking capacity or freedom to make a choice. This is an example of reluctant consent" (at [34]). However, see also *R. v Ali*

B. RAPE

SEXUAL OFFENCES ACT 2003 s.1

"(1) A person (A) commits an offence if— 6–032

(1) he intentionally penetrates the vagina, anus or mouth of another person (B) with his penis,
(2) B does not consent to the penetration, and
(3) A does not reasonably believe that B consents.

(2) Whether a belief is reasonable is to be determined having regard to all the circumstances, including any steps A has taken to ascertain whether B consents."

Rape is punishable by a maximum of life imprisonment.[103] **6–033**

1. Actus reus

The Sexual Offences Act 2003 extended the old definition of rape to include penetration of the mouth by the penis, as well as penile penetration of the vagina or anus. Penetration of the mouth has been recognised as "horrible, [and] as demeaning and as traumatising as other forms of penile penetration".[104] It is clear that full sexual intercourse need not take place for rape to occur; the slightest degree of penetration of the vagina, anus or the mouth with the penis suffices.[105] Furthermore, penetration is a continuing act from entry to withdrawal.[106] Thus, if a sexual partner revokes consent during penetration and the other, aware of this, does not withdraw within a reasonable time, this will be rape.[107] Of particular concern is that a poll by YouGov found that a third of men believed that a woman cannot change her mind after sex has started.[108] **6–034**

Penetration of the vagina, anus or mouth with other parts of the body or inanimate objects is not rape but instead falls within the new offence under s.2 of assault by penetration.[109] To this extent, rape continues to be a gender-specific offence whilst assault by penetration is not. As well as establishing penetration, it must be proved, as discussed above, that V did not consent to penetration.

(Yasir Ifran) [2015] EWCA Crim 1279; [2015] 2 Cr. App. R. 33 where the court held that in cases of grooming the groomer's actions may subvert V's capacity to make free decisions, resulting in V being confused as to the "distinction between acquiescence and genuine agreement . . ." (at [58]).

103 Sexual Offences Act 2003 s.1(4).

104 *Setting the Boundaries: Reforming the Law on Sexual Offences* (2000), para.2.8.4; *Protecting the Public, Strengthening Protection against Sexual Offenders and Reforming the Law on Sexual Offences* (Cmnd.5668, 2002), para.40. No distinction is drawn between the forms of penetration for sentencing purposes: *R. v Ismail (Abokar Ahmed)* [2005] EWCA Crim 397; [2005] Crim. L.R. 491.

105 *R. v Hughes* 173 E.R. 1038; (1841) 9 Car. & P. 752. Vaginal penetration occurs as soon as the vulva has been entered: Sexual Offences Act 2003 s.79(9).

106 Sexual Offences Act 2003 s.79(2).

107 See the pre-Act case of *Kaitamaki v The Queen* [1985] A.C. 147; [1984] 3 W.L.R. 137 PC. The issue of what amounts to a reasonable amount of time is left to the jury.

108 YouGov, *Attitudes to Sexual Consent* (2018).

109 See para.6–041.

2. Mens rea

6–035 Section 1 provides that the defendant will be liable for rape if:

(1) the penetration is intentional; and
(2) he does not reasonably believe that the victim consents.

It is, by the very nature of the acts involved, unlikely that difficulties will occur in establishing that the penetration was intentional.

However, the issue of D's state of mind in relation to V's consent is highly problematic. Under the old law, as well as intending to have sexual intercourse D also had to *know* that the person was not consenting, or be *reckless* as to whether they were consenting.[110] In the House of Lords' decision in *Morgan*, it was held that where a D honestly believed the woman was consenting he could not be said to have the required mens rea for rape.[111] It is important to remember that *Morgan* was decided, and the Sexual Offences (Amendment) Act 1976 enacted,[112] at a time when recklessness bore only its "subjective" meaning: D had actually to be aware that there was a risk the woman was not consenting. This meant that where D asserted that he was genuinely unaware that there was a risk the woman was not consenting, the prosecution would then have to prove beyond reasonable doubt that he was in fact aware of such a risk. This was without doubt a difficult burden to surpass.

Subsequently, the House of Lords in *Caldwell* and *Lawrence* redefined the concept of recklessness so as to encompass a failure to consider an obvious risk and initially it seemed as if this interpretation would be applied to the mens rea of rape.[113] However, shortly afterwards, mirroring developments elsewhere in the criminal law, the *Caldwell/Lawrence* definition of recklessness was rejected in *R. v S.*[114] As a result, for almost 20 years, the mens rea requirement was expressed as whether D was reckless in the sense that they "couldn't care less" whether V had consented or not in situations where the claim was not that a genuine mistake had been made. That is to say, if the jury concluded that D could not care less whether V wanted to have sexual intercourse or not, but continued regardless, then they would have been reckless and guilty of rape.

The controversy surrounding the decision in *Morgan* did not, however, subside during this time. While some agreed that its conclusions were a matter of "inexorable logic"[115] others believed that, as far as an offence such as rape was concerned, it still left women unacceptably vulnerable.

---

110 Sexual Offences Act 1956 s.1(2)(b) as amended by Sexual Offences (Amendment) Act 1976 s.6A. In deciding whether D believed V was consenting, the jury should have regard to the presence or absence of reasonable grounds for such a belief (s.1(2)).

111 *DPP v Morgan* [1976] A.C. 182; [1975] 2 W.L.R. 913 HL.

112 Which statutorily endorsed the decision in *Morgan* [1976] A.C. 182.

113 *R. v Pigg (Stephen)* [1982] 1 W.L.R. 762; (1982) 74 Cr. App. R. 352 CA.

114 *R. v S (Satnam)* (1984) 78 Cr. App. R. 149; [1985] Crim. L.R. 236 CA.

115 per Lord Hailsham in *Morgan* [1976] A.C. 182 at 214 and echoed by Smith [1975] Crim. L.R. 717, 719.

(i) Reasonable belief in consent

The Sexual Offences Act 2003 removed subjective recklessness from the mens rea element of sexual offences, replacing it with a question of whether D "reasonably" believed that V consented.[116] If the factual circumstances of the case fall within either ss.75 or 76 then the presumptions will operate.[117] **6–036**

However, when considering whether D reasonably believed in consent, s.1(2) states:

> "Whether a belief is reasonable is to be determined having regard to all the circumstances, including any steps A has taken to ascertain whether B consents."

Some scholars have criticised this additional provision as potentially reintroducing a subjective element into the mens rea of sexual offences.

Jennifer Temkin and Andrew Ashworth, "The Sexual Offences Act 2003: (1) Rape, Sexual Assaults and the Problems of Consent" [2004] Crim. L.R. 328, 341–242:

> "This wording discards the 'reasonable person' in favour of a general test of what is reasonable in the circumstances. The Home Affairs Committee applauded the change as avoiding the 'potential injustice' of a test that would operate regardless of individual characteristics: 'by focusing on the individual defendant's belief, the new test will allow the jury to look at characteristics such as learning disability or mental disorder—and take them into account' . . . **6–037**
>
> Has Parliament replaced the 'couldn't care less' test with one that is more demanding on the prosecution and more favourable to the defence? Much depends on how the phrase 'all the circumstances' comes to be interpreted. The Government's view was that 'it is for the jury to decide whether any of the attributes of the defendant are relevant to their deliberations, subject to directions from the judge where necessary'. Beverly Hughes [Government Minister] expressed the matter slightly differently, stating that it would be for the judge 'to decide whether it was necessary to introduce consideration of the defendant's characteristics and which characteristics . . . The judge and jury can take into account all or any characteristics and circumstances that they wish to, and it is best that we leave that decision to the judge and jury for each case.' By what standards is it to be decided which characteristics are 'relevant'? Much will depend upon the Specimen Directions and the Court of Appeal . . .
>
> The broad reference to 'all the circumstances' is an invitation to the jury to scrutinise the complainant's behaviour to determine whether there was anything about it which could have

---

116 In *R. v Taran (Farid)* [2006] EWCA Crim 1498, the court concluded that a direction as to reasonable belief was only required in cases where the jury might conclude that there had been some misunderstanding. It was not necessary to give the jury "an abstract lesson on the law" by giving the complicated direction in cases where it was unnecessary.

117 See paras 6–018–6–031.

induced a reasonable belief in consent. In this respect the Act contains no challenge to society's norms and stereotypes about either the relationship between men and women or other sexual situations, and leaves open the possibility that these stereotypes will determine assessments of reasonableness."

6–038 So what "circumstances" are the courts likely to decide are relevant? It might well be that youth, learning disabilities, or an autistic spectrum condition would be deemed to be relevant in determining whether D's belief in consent was reasonable. In *TS*,[118] for example, when fresh evidence was introduced concerning the diagnosis of D with Asperger's syndrome, the Court of Appeal quashed his conviction and ordered a retrial as his condition could have affected his ability to understand V's intentions. Given many judges' strong adherence to subjectivism in the past, taking into account the characteristics of the individual D might well be seen to be a "means of ameliorating what they might perceive to be the harshness involved in the objective test".[119] However, it is submitted that the courts must exercise the utmost caution. For instance, what if D has been brought up with the complete conviction that a woman's consent is worthless? Are these attributes that the jury can consider when determining whether D's belief is a reasonable one? Such an issue was raised in the case of *R. v MA* where at sentencing it was asserted by defence counsel that D (who originated from outside the UK) should have been treated:

"... slightly differently from a man who had been brought up in the United Kingdom ... to reflect that his offending was based on his belief that he had a right to rape his wife."[120]

This submission received short shrift from Mr Griffith Williams J who held that:

"We reject that submission out of hand. No man, whatever his background, whatever his race, whatever his creed, has the right to rape his wife."[121]

Taking such characteristics and circumstances into account would largely subvert the objective test enshrined in the Sexual Offences Act 2003. Although the decision in *R. v MA* relates to sentencing matters, it suggests that the courts will be reluctant to entertain evidence pertaining to D's cultural background which gives rise to a belief that would otherwise be seen "objectively" as unreasonable. Similarly in *Ivor*,[122] the Ds were aware that V's partner, who derived sexual gratification from observing her engage in sexual activities with other men, had imposed coercive dominance over her. Additionally, they knew that she felt compelled to consume drugs and alcohol prior to engaging in sexual acts with them. Despite their assertion that they genuinely believed the V had consented to having sex with them, their belief was deemed not to be "reasonable".

---

118 *R. v TS* [2008] EWCA Crim 6.
119 Clarkson, *Understanding Criminal Law*, 4th edn (2005), p.201.
120 *R. v MA* [2012] EWCA Crim 1646 at [20].
121 *MA* [2012] EWCA Crim 1646 at [21].
122 *R. v Ivor* [2021] EWCA Crim 923; CLW/21/30/4.

What, though, if the D's belief is based on a delusion caused by a psychiatric condition? Should such a circumstance be considered when determining whether D's belief is reasonable?

R. v B [2013] 1 Cr. App. R. 36 (Court of Appeal, Criminal Division):

D was convicted, inter alia, of the rape of his partner. A medical expert submitted that at the time of the offences D had likely to have been suffering from paranoid schizophrenia which had resulted in a number of delusional beliefs. The expert submitted that the acts of sexual intercourse might have been motivated by D's delusional beliefs that he had sexual healing powers. However, any such delusions had not affected his ability to understand whether the complainant was consenting. **6–039**

HUGHES LJ:

"[24] The [trial] judge was invited to direct the jury that if and when it came to considering the reasonableness of any belief by the defendant that the complainant was consenting, it was entitled to take into account his mental condition at the time. After argument and careful consideration, he declined to do so. He gave the jury an admirably clear and untechnical direction that the mental condition was not to be taken into account. He said:

> 'If you are satisfied so that you are sure that she was not consenting on the occasion you are considering, you then go on to consider this issue of reasonable belief. This is where you are focusing on what is in the defendant's mind. You have considered her position as to whether she was consenting. Now let us look at him and what he was or might have been believing . . .
>
> As a matter of public policy the law does not permit defendants suffering from mental illness to avoid the consequences of their crimes by relying upon the explanation: "I only did it because I was mentally ill". That may sound harsh but you can see the sense behind it, because if mental illness did operate as an excuse for criminal conduct it would be *carte blanche*. The law is not a total ass, because mental illness may well have a role to play in influencing sentence . . .
>
> If . . . you find that he did have a belief or might have had a belief that she was consenting to the particular act of intercourse, then you have to go on and consider the reasonableness of that belief.
>
> Given the facts in this case it is important to understand that a delusional belief in consent or a belief in consent which is the result of his mental illness cannot be a reasonable belief . . .
>
> Ask yourselves what society would reasonably expect of a person not suffering from mental illness, who found themselves in the circumstances that pertained on each of the occasions . . .

> To try to explain it in simple terms, if you put the mental illness out of the question, were all the signs and signals such that someone who had been in a relationship with her all those years would have picked up on the signals and realised that she was not consenting, or were the signals such that someone would have, or might have, thought "Yes, she is consenting" and have carried on?' . . .
>
> [35] . . . we take the clear view that such delusional beliefs cannot in law render reasonable a belief that his partner was consenting when in fact she was not . . . A delusional belief in consent, if entertained, would be, by definition, irrational and thus unreasonable, not reasonable. If such delusional beliefs were capable of being described as reasonable, then the more irrational the belief of the defendant the better would be its prospects of being held reasonable . . .
>
> [40] We conclude that unless and until the state of mind amounts to insanity in law, then under the rule enacted in the Sexual Offences Act 2003 beliefs in consent arising from conditions such as delusional psychotic illness or personality disorders must be judged by objective standards of reasonableness and not by taking into account a mental disorder which induced a belief which could not reasonably arise without it . . .
>
> [41] It does not follow that there will not be cases in which the personality or abilities of the defendant may be relevant to whether his positive belief in consent was reasonable. It may be that cases could arise in which the reasonableness of such belief depends on the reading by the defendant of subtle social signals, and in which his impaired ability to do so is relevant to the reasonableness of his belief. We do not attempt exhaustively to foresee the circumstances which might arise in which a belief might be held which is not in any sense irrational, even though most people would not have held it. Whether (for example) a particular defendant of less than ordinary intelligence or with demonstrated inability to recognise behavioural cues might be such a case, or whether his belief ought properly to be characterised as unreasonable, must await a decision on specific facts. It is possible, we think, that beliefs generated by such factors may not properly be described as irrational and might be judged by a jury not to be unreasonable on their particular facts. But once a belief could be judged reasonable only by a process which labelled a plainly irrational belief as reasonable, it is clear that it cannot be open to the jury so to determine without stepping outside the Act."
>
> *Appeal dismissed*

6–040 Following this decision, it seems clear that psychological disorders which give rise to a delusional belief in consent cannot be considered as part of "all the circumstances" when determining whether the D's belief was reasonable. The reasoning for this is twofold. First, is that a delusion is considered to be irrational and as such by its very definition cannot be considered to be reasonable; thereby falling outside the ambit of the section. Secondly, it is a matter of public policy that Ds who are mentally ill are not to be provided with a carte blanche excuse for raping others. The decision is also interesting in that it leaves open the possibility for those who miss certain social cues, or who are of low intelligence, to raise such factors when a determination is made about the reasonableness of their belief in consent.[123] What this could mean in practice is that those with learning disabilities may raise their disability during such considerations, while those whose belief is "irrational" based on a psychological disorder will be excluded from doing so. Whether it is fair to treat someone with a psychological disorder as culpable for their acts while potentially exonerating those who miss social cues, is far from incontestable. It remains to be seen what other circumstances of D will be considered.

C. OTHER NON-CONSENSUAL SEXUAL OFFENCES

1. Assault by penetration

SEXUAL OFFENCES ACT 2003 S.2:

"(1) A person (A) commits an offence if— **6-041**

(a) he intentionally penetrates the vagina or anus of another person (B) with a part of his body or anything else,
(b) the penetration is sexual,
(c) B does not consent to the penetration, and
(d) A does not reasonably believe that B consents."

Assault by penetration is punishable by a maximum of life imprisonment.[124] **6-042**

This offence, together with sexual assault under s.3, broadly replaces the old law of indecent assault which carried a maximum of 10 years' imprisonment.[125] The offence of assault by penetration is an overdue recognition that penetration by objects other than the penis may be every bit as traumatising and harmful as rape.[126] Thus, non-consensual, sexual penetration of the vagina or anus by, for example, a finger or a bottle or other object carries the same maximum as the offence of rape. This is a broad offence. It might be feared that routine internal medical examinations might fall foul of its provisions. However, two factors preclude this. First, in such cases the doctor or nurse obtains the consent of the patient to conduct the examination. Secondly, the penetration is not "sexual". This term is present in a number of offences in the Act and is considered below in relation to sexual assault where it may be more problematic than in relation to assault by penetration.

The mens rea for assault by penetration is that D intends to penetrate and does not reasonably believe that V consents.[127]

---

123 Such factors not being considered to be irrational.

124 Sexual Offences Act 2003 s.2(4).

125 Sexual Offences Act 1956 ss.14 and 15. Some actions, such as oral penetration of the mouth by the penis, formerly charged as indecent assault would now be charged as rape.

126 See Home Office, *Setting the Boundaries: Reforming the Law on Sexual Offences* (2000), paras 2.3.1, 2.91; *Protecting the Public, Strengthening Protection against Sexual Offenders and Reforming the Law on Sexual Offences* (Cmnd.5668, 2002), para.44.

127 The same provisions apply as to rape, discussed immediately above.

2. Sexual assault

SEXUAL OFFENCES ACT 2003 s.3:

6-043 "(1) A person (A) commits an offence if—

(a) he intentionally touches another person (B),
(b) the touching is sexual,
(c) B does not consent to the touching, and
(d) A does not reasonably believe that B consents."

6-044 Sexual assault is punishable by a maximum of 10 years' imprisonment.[128]

This offence replaces the repealed offence of indecent assault.[129] In *Protecting the Public*, the view taken was that "some non-penetrative sexual assaults amount to extremely serious offending and can cause high levels of fear, degradation and trauma".[130] Thus, this offence carries a high maximum penalty but it is also recognised that this is a very broad offence and that less serious instances will receive lower sentences.[131] In addition to establishing that V does not consent, there are two key elements to be considered in the actus reus. First, there must be touching (a term used in other offences in the Act as well). Section 79(8) states that this "includes touching (a) with any part of the body, (b) with anything else, (c) through anything and in particular includes touching amounting to penetration". In *H*,[132] D approached a woman who was walking her dog and asked her: "Do you fancy a shag?" He then grabbed her tracksuit bottom and pulled her towards him. She was able to break free and run to safety. His conviction under s.3 was upheld by the Court of Appeal: "Where a person is wearing clothing we consider that touching of the clothing constitutes touching for the purpose of section 3."[133]

(i) The meaning of sexual

6-045 The other matter that has to be established under s.3 is that the touching is "sexual", a term used in many offences of the Act. In many instances, it will be very clear that the touching is sexual. If there is doubt, however, guidance can be given to the jury in accordance with the following provision.

---

128 Sexual Offences Act 2003 s.3(4). The offence is triable either way.

129 In one sense, the new offence is narrower than the old law: the new offence requires a touching to occur; the old offence occurred when V was made to apprehend an (indecent) assault. See further, D. Ormerod, "Sexual Assault: Whether Touching of Complainant's Clothing Without Bringing Pressure Against Complainant's Body 'Touching' for Purposes of Sexual Assault" [2005] Crim. L.R. 734, 736.

130 *Protecting the Public, Strengthening Protection against Sexual Offenders and Reforming the Law on Sexual Offences* (Cmnd.5668, 2002), para.45.

131 See para.6-058.

132 *R. v H (Karl Anthony)* [2005] EWCA Crim 732; [2005] 2 Cr. App. R. 9.

133 per Woolf CJ in *H* [2005] 2 Cr. App. R. 9 at [24]. D had argued it could not amount to touching because he had not touched V's body through the clothing.

SEXUAL OFFENCES ACT 2003 S.78:

"[P]enetration, touching or any other activity is sexual if a reasonable person would consider that— 6–046

(a) whatever its circumstances or any person's purpose in relation to it, it is because of its nature sexual, or
(b) because of its nature it may be sexual and because of its circumstances or the purpose of any person in relation to it (or both) it is sexual."[134]

Under (a) the focus is upon the nature of the act itself, rather than surrounding circumstances: would a reasonable person consider that the act is inherently sexual?[135] Paragraph (b), however, is much broader. If a reasonable person would conclude that the behaviour *might be* sexual, whether it *is* sexual is then decided by looking at D's motive and the surrounding circumstances. In *H* (above), the Court of Appeal had doubts as to whether the removal of shoes by a fetishist[136] satisfied the first part of (b) (that the touching "may be sexual"). If this view was taken by a jury, in theory it would not go on to consider D's purpose or the surrounding circumstances at all. This seems a little unrealistic. First, a jury might well decide that the removal of shoes was by itself capable of being sexual. Secondly, even though (b) requires a jury to separate the two questions, it seems more likely that it would look at the facts holistically in deciding whether what happened was "sexual". There are dangers in leaving such an important concept as "sexual" to be decided by the jury and as the court comments in *H*, it is perhaps over-optimistic to hope that recourse to s.78(b) will be limited to unusual circumstances.[137] 6–047

The mens rea of sexual assault is that D touches intentionally and does not reasonably believe that V consents.[138]

3. Intentionally causing someone to engage in sexual activity

SEXUAL OFFENCES ACT 2003 S.4:

"(1) A person (A) commits an offence if— 6–048

(a) he intentionally causes another person (B) to engage in an activity,
(b) the activity is sexual,
(c) B does not consent to engaging in the activity, and
(d) A does not reasonably believe that B consents.

---

134 As approved by the court in *H* [2005] 2 Cr. App. R. 9, this "cannot be said to provide a definition of the term, rather it sets out an approach for determining whether the activity in question is sexual where this may be in doubt" (331).

135 In *Att-Gen's Reference (No.1 of 2020)* [2020] EWCA Crim 1665; [2021] Q.B. 441, the court stated that "[i]t was not necessary for the prosecution to prove, as an element of the offence of sexual assault, . . . that the offender. . . intended his touching of that person to be sexual" at [47].

136 *H* [2005] 2 Cr. App. R. 9 at [11], referring to the pre-2003 Act decision in *R. v George* [1956] Crim. L.R. 52.

137 *H* [2005] 2 Cr. App. R. 9 at [4]. On the meaning of "sexual" see further, R. Morgan, "What Makes an Attack Sexual?" (2021) 38 *J Appl Philosophy* 518.

138 As with the offences under ss.1 and 2, the question of whether D reasonably believed V consented is determined by reference to all the circumstances, including any steps taken by D to ascertain whether V consented (s.3(2)). See further, I. Bantekas, "Can Touching Always be Sexual When There is No Sexual Intent?" (2008) 73 Jo. C.L. 251.

> (2) Whether a belief is reasonable is to be determined having regard to all the circumstances, including any steps A has taken to ascertain whether B consents."

6–049 Where the offence involves penetration of the vagina or anus or mouth (in the latter case by D's penis), the maximum sentence is that of life imprisonment.[139] In other situations, the maximum sentence is 10 years' imprisonment.[140] The indictment must specify whether the basic or aggravated offence is being charged.

This is a very broad offence that, like s.3, encompasses behaviour that previously would have been prosecuted as indecent assault. The offence consists of causing another person to engage in sexual activity without consent. Thus, for example, women who force men to penetrate them can be prosecuted under this provision. Furthermore, as *Devonald* demonstrates, a D who forces V to masturbate falls within this offence irrespective of whether he is present at the time.[141]

D. CHILD SEXUAL OFFENCES

6–050 It is beyond the scope of this book to explore in detail the very large number of offences which have been created to protect children. In addition to the non-consensual offences discussed above, there are three further types of offences involving children: unlawful sexual activity with a child under 13 or under 16; familial offences; and abuse of position of trust offences. The Act has made significant improvements to the old law. It has, for example, removed the discriminatory provisions that distinguished indecent assault upon a girl from that upon a boy[142] in a move towards gender-neutral laws. It has also created new offences, such as meeting following grooming,[143] while other legislation has introduced the new offence of sexual communication with a child[144] to protect children from new dangers. However, in determining the question of whether the law:

> ". . . strikes an appropriate balance between sexual abuse and exploitation, on the one hand, and permitting the sexual expression of young persons as they proceed through to adulthood, on the other . . ."[145]

a number of commentators have expressed grave reservations.

139 Sexual Offences Act 2003 s.4(4).

140 Sexual Offences Act 2003 s.4(5). This form of the offence can be tried summarily, in which case the maximum penalty is six months' imprisonment.

141 See para.6–023.

142 Sexual Offences Act 1956 ss.5, 6, 14 and 15.

143 Sexual Offences Act 2003 s.15. See further, S. Ost, "Getting to Grips with Sexual Grooming? The New Offence under the Sexual Offences Act 2003" (2004) 26 J. of Social Welfare and Family Law 147; A.A. Gillespie, "Indecent Images, Grooming and the Law" [2006] Crim. L.R. 412.

144 Sexual Offences Act 2003 s.15A.

145 A. Khan, "Comment: Sexual Offences Act 2003" [2004] 68 Jo. C.L. 220, 220.

J.R. Spencer, "The Sexual Offences Act 2003: (2) Child and Family Offences" [2004] Crim. L.R. 347, 347–352:

"The new offences are too many, and there is needless overlap between them; they are badly drafted in a style that combines an excess of detail on minor matters with a failure to deal with certain major ones; and, most seriously, the new law is exceptionally heavy-handed. It ratchets culpability requirements down, building grave stigmatic offences on negligence or even strict liability. And more fundamentally, it renders theoretically punishable with severe penalties (2, 5, 10 and 14 years, and even life) a range of behaviour for which it is inconceivable that anyone will in practice be prosecuted—and for which it would be scandalous if they were . . ."[146] **6–051**

The following is a list of the main offences designed to protect children: **6–052**

- rape of a child under 13;[147]
- assault of a child under 13 by penetration;[148]
- sexual assault of a child under 13;[149]
- causing or inciting a child under 13 to engage in a sexual activity;[150]
- sexual activity with a child;[151]
- causing or inciting a child to engage in sexual activity;[152]
- engaging in sexual activity in the presence of a child;[153]
- causing a child to watch a sexual activity;[154]
- child sex offences committed by children or young persons;[155]
- arranging or facilitating commission of a child sex offence;[156]
- meeting a child following sexual grooming;[157] and
- sexual communication with a child.[158]

The first four offences mirror the core sexual offences (the first three of which were discussed above) but are designed to protect children under the age of 13. In pursuit of this aim, the purported consent of a child under the age of 13 is irrelevant. Furthermore, there is no need to prove mens rea on the part

---

146 See also H. Keating, "'When the Kissing Has to Stop': Children, Sexual Behaviour and the Criminal Law", in M. Freeman (ed), *Law and Childhood Studies* (Oxford: OUP, 2012); T. Palmer, "State control of consensual sexual behaviour through the Sexual Offences Act 2003" in C. Ashford, A. Reed and N. Wake (eds), *Legal perspectives on state power: consent and control* (Newcastle-Upon-Tyne: Cambridge Scholars Publishing, 2016).

147 Sexual Offences Act 2003 s.5 (maximum life imprisonment).

148 Sexual Offences Act 2003 s.6 (maximum life imprisonment).

149 Sexual Offences Act 2003 s.7 (maximum 14 years' imprisonment).

150 Sexual Offences Act 2003 s.8 (maximum 14 years' imprisonment).

151 Sexual Offences Act 2003 s.9 (maximum 14 years' imprisonment).

152 Sexual Offences Act 2003 s.10 (maximum 14 years' imprisonment).

153 Sexual Offences Act 2003 s.11 (maximum 10 years' imprisonment).

154 Sexual Offences Act 2003 s.12 (maximum 10 years' imprisonment).

155 Sexual Offences Act 2003 s.13, makes punishable by a maximum of five years anything done by a person under 18 which would have been an offence under ss.9–12 had that person been over 18. This provision, creating a lower maximum penalty, is a very limited recognition of the reality of children and young people's sexual behaviour.

156 Sexual Offences Act 2003 s.14 (maximum aligns with offence facilitated under ss.5–13).

157 Sexual Offences Act 2003 s.15 (maximum 10 years' imprisonment).

158 Sexual Offences Act 2003 s.15A (maximum of two years' imprisonment). This list does not include ss.16–19 dealing with abuse of trust provisions, nor ss.25–26 dealing with familial offences.

of D in relation to the child's age. These offences are thus ones of strict liability. While these provisions were intended to and do catch the adult predator, they also catch much younger persons who engage in sexual activity with the (irrelevant) consent of the child under 13. It is entirely possible from the wording of the offences that a boy of 13 could find himself convicted of causing a child to engage in sexual activity under s.8 for kissing and fondling a girl of 12 with her consent—even if he believed she was aged 13 or over. Research reveals that the average age of first sexual experience is 14 for girls and 13 for boys.[159] We may wish this were not true and we may point to the harmful effects early sexual experience may have, but it can hardly be a proportionate response to hold a 13 year old liable for an offence that carries a maximum of 14 years' imprisonment for such behaviour. Also, if the young couple engage in consensual sexual intercourse, it is absurd—and manifest false labelling—to hold the boy to be a rapist.

The Government's response to such concerns is that prosecutorial discretion will prevent such cases occurring.[160] However, as the following case demonstrates there is a danger of disproportionate responses.

R. v G [2009] 1 A.C. 92 (House of Lords):

6–053 D, a boy of 15, pleaded guilty to rape of a child under 13 (she was 12). The girl initially alleged that she had not consented to sexual intercourse and it was on this basis that the most serious charge was proceeded with. The boy argued that the girl had consented and told him she was 15, but pleaded guilty when told that neither her consent nor his reasonable belief as to her age was relevant. He was sentenced to a 12-month detention and training order and to the sexual offender notification requirements under the 2003 Act. The Court of Appeal dismissed his appeal against conviction but allowed his appeal against sentence (imposing instead a conditional discharge).

LORD HOFFMANN:

> "[2] [The Court of Appeal certified two questions as being of general public importance: '(1) May a criminal offence of strict liability violate article 6(1) and/or 6(2) [ECHR] . . .? (2) Is it compatible with a child's rights under article 8 . . . to convict him of rape contrary to section 5 . . . in circumstances where the agreed basis of plea establishes that his offence fell properly within the ambit of s 13 . . .?'
>
> [3] The mental element of the offence under s 5, as the language and structure of the section makes clear, is that penetration must be intentional but there is no requirement that the accused must have known that the other person was under 13. The policy of the legislation is to protect children. If you have sex with someone who is on any view a child or young person,

159 K. Wellings, J. Field, A. Johnson and J. Wadsworth, *Sexual Behaviour in Britain: the National Survey of Attitudes and Lifestyles* (London: Penguin Publishing, 1994), p.40; K. Wellings, "Sexual Behaviour in Britain: Early Heterosexual Experience" (2001) 358 *The Lancet* 1843.

160 See, e.g. *Hansard* 646, paras 1176/77, 1 April 2003. See further, J. Spencer, "The Sexual Offences Act 2003: (2) Child and Family Offences" [2004] Crim. L.R. 347, 354–355.

you take your chance on exactly how old they are. To that extent the offence is one of strict liability and it is no defence that the accused believed the other person to be 13 or over . . .

[7] The other ground of appeal is that the conviction violated the Appellant's right of privacy under art 8.

[8] [Counsel] for the Appellant . . . says that, as he was only 15 at the time of the offence, the Crown acted unduly harshly by prosecuting him under s 5 rather than under s 13, which deals with sexual offences committed by persons under 18 and carries a maximum penalty of imprisonment for five years.

[9] Assuming this to be right, the case has in my opinion nothing to do with art 8 or human rights . . .

[10] Prosecutorial policy and sentencing do not fall under art 8. If the offence in question is a justifiable interference with private life, that is an end of the matter. If the prosecution has been unduly heavy handed, that may be unfair and unjust, but not an infringement of human rights. It is a matter for the ordinary system of criminal justice . . .

[12] In my opinion, therefore, the answers to the certified questions are no and yes respectively. That leaves only the question of whether in the particular circumstances of this case, it was an abuse of process for the Crown to prosecute under s 5. That is not a question which has been certified. For what it is worth, I agree with the Court of Appeal that the Crown was not obliged to withdraw the charge under s 5 when they found themselves having to accept the Appellant's version of events. 'Rape of a child under 13' still accurately described what the Appellant had done. Parliament decided to use this description because children under 13 cannot validly or even meaningfully consent to sexual intercourse. So far as the basis of plea provided mitigation, they were entitled to leave the judge to take it into account. I would dismiss the appeal."

LORD HOPE OF CRAIGHEAD (DISSENTING): **6–054**

"[13] Section 5 of the Sexual Offences Act 2003, which makes sexual intercourse with a child under 13 a crime of strict liability irrespective of the age of the Defendant and calls it rape, has given rise to some important and difficult questions . . . Section 13 of the same Act, read with s 9(1)(c)(ii), makes it an offence for a person under 18 to have sexual intercourse with a child under 13. Unlike s 5, it does not attach the label of rape to this offence. What behaviour then should the criminal law prohibit, and what should it not? To what extent is it reasonable to leave it to the police and other authorities to decide when to prosecute and, where there is a choice, for which offence? These questions have been brought out into the real world by this case.

[14] . . . the creation of an unqualified offence of this kind carries with it the risk of stigmatising as rapists children who engage in a single act of mutual sexual activity. A heavy responsibility has been placed on the prosecuting authorities, where both parties are of a similar young age, to discriminate between cases where the proscribed activity was truly mutual on the one hand

and those where the Complainant was subjected to an element of exploitation or undue pressure on the other. In the former case more harm than good may be done by prosecuting. In the latter case the threshold will have been crossed and prosecution is likely to be inevitable. But if in the former case it is decided to prosecute, a decision still has to be made about the section under which the perpetrator is to be prosecuted . . .

[34] Article 8(1) guarantees to everyone the right to respect for his private life, and a teenager has as much to respect for his private life as any other individual. It is unlawful for a prosecutor to act in a way which is inconsistent with a Convention right. So I cannot accept Lord Hoffmann's proposition that the Convention rights have nothing to do with prosecutorial policy . . . The questions then are whether the Appellant's continued prosecution for rape under s 5 was necessary in a democratic society for the protection of any of the interests referred to in art 8(2), and whether it was proportionate. Account must be taken in this assessment of the alternative courses that were open to the prosecutor, including proceeding under s 13 instead of s 5, as well as the sentencing options that are available to the court in the event of a conviction under either alternative and the labels which each of them would attract . . .

[38] . . . There are grounds for thinking that the sanctions that can be imposed under s 13 for mutual sexual activity by a person under 18 with a child under 13 provide all that is needed by way of punishment that is proportionate to the offence. The message that this is an offence can be conveyed to children as well as adults very effectively by the use of these sanctions . . .

[39] Section 5, the rape of a child under 13, on the other hand is designed for a different and much more serious situation . . . The description of the offence as rape, and all the consequences that go with that description, are entirely appropriate where the act has been committed upon a child under 13 by a person over the age of 18. It may also be appropriate where the person who committed it was under that age. But the lower the age, the less appropriate it will be. The question in such a case, given the choice that is available, must be whether in all the circumstances to proceed under s 5 would be proportionate . . .

[40] I would hold that it was unlawful for the prosecutor to continue to prosecute the Appellant under s 5 in view of his acceptance of the basis of the Appellant's plea which was that the Complainant consented to intercourse. This was incompatible with his art 8 Convention right, as the offence fell properly within the ambit of s 13 and not s 5 . . . I would allow the appeal and quash the conviction."

Appeal dismissed

6–055 In her speech, Baroness Hale (in the majority) drew attention to the positive obligation of the state under art.8 which might "require the criminal law to provide effective protection for those who cannot protect themselves from the sexual attentions of others". This protection is needed:

"... whether they like it or not ... [A]nyone who has practiced in the family courts is only too well aware of the long term and serious harm both physical and psychological, which premature sexual activity can do. And the harm which may be done by premature sexual penetration is not necessarily lessened by the age of the person penetrating."[161]

This stance was recently reiterated in *Gribby* where the court held that:

"... 'consent' by the underage victim, even if it of itself is of some relevance, does not cause the offence to be considered as in some way exceptional. The underlying statutory rationale ... is that children under the age of 13 require protection for their own benefit. They need, as it were, to be protected from themselves. Their emotional immaturity precludes, as has frequently decided and as Parliament has confirmed, the notion of any informed consent."[162]

As Horder has commented: **6–056**

"The approach of the Sexual Offences Act 2003 to cases involving children or young people close in age is woefully inadequate and potentially unjust, as G demonstrates. Reliance on prosecutorial discretion is unsatisfactory in principle, and is unpersuasive in European human rights law. Greater efforts should have been made to ensure clarity in the law: if an age difference of up to two years is acceptable so long as no coercion (howsoever defined) is present, then that should be used as a model for legislation, as in other jurisdictions. Faced with the inadequacy of the legislation in this respect, the majority of the House of Lords in G should have followed human rights (and children's rights) reasoning more faithfully by focusing on the fairness of convicting this defendant on these assumed facts of this serious offence carrying life imprisonment."[163]

This case illustrates the very real difficulties that the offences create. Moreover, the problems are not confined to the offences concerning Vs under 13. The other offences are very broad and overlap. For example, s.9 creates two offences of sexual activity with a child; one of sexual touching and an aggravated offence of sexual activity by penetration. Both carry the same maximum sentence. The offence distinguishes between Vs over and under 13: if V is over 13 but under 16 it is open to D to show that they had a reasonable belief that V was over 16. That possibility is not open to D if the

---

161 *R. v G* [2008] UKHL 37; [2009] 1 A.C. 92 at [41] and [49]. Baroness Hale further stated that it could not be wrong to apply the label of rape given that the law disabled a child under 13 giving consent (at [55]).

162 *R v Gribby (Brendan Clifford)* [2016] EWCA Crim 1847 at [26]; [2017] 1 Cr. App. R. (S.) 18. This is the position of the law regardless of whether a child under the age of 13 is seemingly an enthusiastic participant (*Att-Gen's Reference (No.142 of 2015) (R. v Brown)* [2016] EWCA Crim 80; [2016] 1 Cr.App.R.(S.) 68), nor does the fact that D is under the age of 18 matter (*Att-Gen's Reference (No.105 of 2014) (Harrak)* [2014] EWCA Crim 2751; [2015] 1 Cr.App.R.(S.) 45). See also, comparatively, *Sutherland v HM Advocate for Scotland (Scotland)* [2020] UKSC 32; [2021] A.C. 427.

163 J. Horder, *Ashworth's Principles of Criminal Law*, 10th edn (Oxford: OUP, 2009), p.406. Note that the applicant later complained to the European Court of Human Rights that his conviction was not compatible with the presumption of innocence (art.6) and that the criminal proceedings amounted to a disproportionate interference with his right to respect for private life (art.8). The court found that the criminal proceedings did interfere with his art.8 rights but the interference pursued the legitimate aims of the prevention of crime and the protection of the rights and freedoms of others; *G v United Kingdom (Admissibility) (37334/08)* [2012] Crim. L.R. 46; (2011) 53 E.H.R.R. SE25.

child is under 13.[164] Yet, if the child is less than 13 years old, ss.5–8 (that specifically relate to children younger than 13) could also be charged. This duplication makes the selection of an appropriate charge problematic. More controversial, however, is the fact that all consensual sexual touching between young people under 16 is unlawful. Lord Millett has argued that:

> "... the age of consent has long ceased to reflect ordinary life, and in this respect Parliament has signally failed to discharge its responsibility for keeping the criminal law in touch with the needs of society."[165]

While setting the age of consent at 16 has much to commend it, as Spencer has commented, the offences "are so far out of line with the sexual behaviour of the young ... they will eventually make indictable offenders of the whole population".[166] If the offences are not prosecuted, as one would hope would be the case with consensual sexual exploration between young people, children may come to perceive them as empty threats. If offences are prosecuted, not only may individual injustices result, but also other children may be deterred from seeking medical advice or treatment. In the light of *G*, the CPS has issued detailed guidelines for prosecutors and it is to be hoped that this will help to ensure that prosecutions are brought in appropriate circumstances and for the appropriate offence.[167]

E. OTHER SEXUAL OFFENCES

6–057 The SOA 2003 and other legislation create various other sexual offences, a full exploration of which are outside the scope of this book. Below is a list of some of the main offences:

- "revenge porn" (disclosing private sexual photographs and films with intent to cause distress) (Criminal Justice and Courts Act 2015 s.33);
- making indecent photographs of persons aged 16 or 17 (Sexual Offences Act 2003 s.45);[168]
- paying for sexual services of a prostitute subjected to force etc (Sexual Offences Act 2003 s.53A);
- exposure (Sexual Offences Act 2003 s.66);
- voyeurism (Sexual Offences Act 2003 ss.67–68);
- "upskirting" (voyeurism: additional offences) (Sexual Offences Act 2003 s.67A);
- intercourse with an animal (Sexual Offences Act 2003 s.69);
- sexual penetration of a corpse (Sexual Offences Act 2003 s.70); and
- sexual activity in a public lavatory (Sexual Offences Act 2003 s.71).

---

164 Sexual Offences Act 2003 s.9 is, thus, also an offence of strict liability if V is under 13.

165 *R. v K (Age of Consent: Reasonable Belief)* [2001] UKHL 41; [2002] 1 A.C. 462 at [44].

166 Spencer, "The Sexual Offences Act 2003: (2) Child and Family Offences" [2004] Crim. L.R. 347, 354, and Keating, "'When the Kissing Has to Stop': Children, Sexual Behaviour and the Criminal Law" in Freeman (ed), *Law and Childhood Studies* (Oxford: OUP, 2012).

167 CPS, *Rape and Sexual Offences—Chapter 13: Sexual Offences and Youths, https://www.cps.gov.uk/legal-guidance/rape-and-sexual-offences-chapter-13-sexual-offences-and-youths*.

168 The Law Commission has undertaken a recent review of offences involving sharing of intimate images, see law Commission Report No.417, *Intimate image abuse: a final report* (2022).

III. Sentencing

Rape is punishable by a maximum sentence of life imprisonment as is the offence of assault by penetration. It is now almost axiomatic that if Ds are convicted, they will serve a period of immediate imprisonment. The Sentencing Council guideline for rape states that five years' imprisonment should be the starting point for adult rape where there are no aggravating features (category 3), either in terms of severity of harm or level of culpability.[169] However, for most cases the term of imprisonment is likely to be much higher. For instance, the Court of Appeal has stated that aggravating features, such as a "campaign of rape" or a "terrible breach of trust" will mean that a sentence of 20 years' imprisonment is not regarded as excessive.[170] In *Att-Gen's Reference (No.86 of 2006)*, the Court of Appeal confirmed that the fact that rape occurred within a domestic context did not justify a reduction in sentence.[171] In considering the extended definition of rape, the Court of Appeal has also stated: **6–058**

> "[I]n approaching the question of sentencing no distinction should be made because of the category of rape. One form could be more offensive than another to the victim. It was very much a subjective matter."[172]

Assault by penetration under s.2 is punishable by a maximum of life imprisonment. The Sentencing Council guideline states that in the case of an adult V (category 3/B) the starting point should be two years' imprisonment. Where the offence falls into category 1/A (for example, where there is severe psychological or physical harm and previous violence has been used against V) the starting point is 15 years' imprisonment.[173]

The offence of sexual assault under s.3 is punishable by a maximum of ten years or 14 years if V is under the age of 13 (s.7). As we have seen, this is an offence that ranges from the very serious to the more minor and the sentencing guideline reflects this.[174]

---

169 The Sentencing Council, *Rape*, *https://www.sentencingcouncil.org.uk/offences/crown-court/item/rape/*. In the case of a rape of a child under 13 where there are no aggravating factors, the starting point is eight years, Sentencing Council, *Rape of a Child Under 13*, *https://www.sentencingcouncil.org.uk/offences/crown-court/item/rape-of-a-child-under-13/*.

170 *R. v O* [2008] EWCA Crim 738; (2008) 105(13) L.S.G. 30. See also, *R. v AF* [2009] EWCA Crim 1428.

171 *Att-Gen's Reference (No.86 of 2006)* [2006] EWCA Crim 3077; (2006) 103(44) L.S.G. 29.

172 *R. v Ismail (Abokar Ahmed)* [2005] EWCA Crim 397; [2005] 2 Cr. App. R. (S.) 88.

173 The Sentencing Council, *Sexual Offences: Definitive Guideline (2017).Assault by penetration*, *https://www.sentencingcouncil.org.uk/offences/crown-court/item/assault-by-penetration/*.

174 The Sentencing Council, *Sexual Assault*, *https://www.sentencingcouncil.org.uk/offences/magistrates-court/item/sexual-assault/*.

IV. Evaluation

6-059 The law of sexual offences often evokes much controversy and there is still much cause for concern in the (lack of) response of the criminal justice system. Conviction rates for sexual offences remain low, with prosecution numbers and the overall conviction rate declining over recent years.[175] Where cases do proceed to trial, complainants are frequently exposed to humiliating cross-examinations by defence barristers and, in some cases, by Ds themselves.[176] The statutory provisions to prevent previous sexual history is in need of further reform if we are to protect complainants from harrowing experiences of re-victimisation during the criminal process. At least in relation to sentencing, the stereotypical image of what is rape, which has in the past led to lenient sentencing, appears to be retreating.

In so far as the substantive law is concerned, there have been very considerable improvements as a result of the Sexual Offences Act 2003. Reform to child sex offences, which had been the subject of piecemeal development over many years, was long overdue. However, the enforcement of strict liability rape for children who have sex with other children remains highly controversial. In relation to the offence of rape, it is absolutely right that no truck has been given to the idea that there should be different levels of rape depending upon whether there was or had been a relationship between the complainant and D. Any such view, based upon the paradigm of the stranger/violent rape, is built upon a false premise. Not only are most Vs likely to know their assailant, but also strangers do not have exclusive dominion over the use of violence. With or without violence, relationship or acquaintance rape may destroy the possibility of future relationships. If the wrong in rape is the objectification of a person, then those who are made to have sexual intercourse without consent by people they know, are raped.

The extension of the actus reus of rape to include penile penetration of the mouth reflected modern understandings about the nature of sexual violence. In addition, the recognition of the gravity of other forms of penetrative sexual assault by the offence of assault by penetration, punishable by a maximum of life imprisonment, was also welcomed. There can be no doubt, hearing evidence from Vs, that the trauma and harm involved in these assaults can be as bad as that involved in rape. Whether such penetrative assaults should be included within a broadened definition of rape, as has been done in some other jurisdictions, may well be the next step in reforming sexual offences. On the one hand, there is the view that if the wrong is the violation of a person's bodily autonomy, one should not distinguish between penetration by the penis and penetration by an inanimate object. On the other hand, there is the argument that rape is a form of gendered violence where the penis has been used as a weapon against, mostly, women.[177]

---

175 Office for National Statistics data revealed that just 5% of recorded rape offences were assigned a summons or charge, Office for National Statistics, *Sexual offending: victimization and the path through the criminal justice system* (2018).

176 See also, A. Carline and C. Gunby, "Rape Politics, Policies and Practice: Exploring the Tensions and Unanticipated Consequences of Well-Intended Victim-Focused Measures" (2017) 56 *Howard Journal of Criminal Justice* 34, whose qualitative interviews with barristers suggested that some measures that focus on supporting complainants by placing them at the heart of the system can frequently sit in tension with the objective of improving conviction rates.

177 For further argument on this point, see Clarkson, *Understanding Criminal Law*, 4th edn (2005), p.206 and D. Warbuton, "The Rape of a Label—Why it Would be Wrong to Follow Canada in Having a Single Offence of Unlawful Sexual Assault" [2004] 68 Jo. C.L. 533.

With regard to the mens rea of rape, the rule that D need only make an honest mistake about V's consent has been rightly consigned to history. Whether the revised law, which requires a reasonable belief in V's consent, has directly helped to increase conviction ratios[178] in rape trials is difficult to assess empirically. The number of prosecutions for rape has increased over recent years, from 2102 completed cases in the year ending 2020 to 2655 cases in the year ending 2023. However, the percentage of convictions has dropped from 68.5% to 63.5% during this same period.[179] It is also noteworthy to mention that, despite recent increases in prosecutions, the overall number of cases prosecuted by the CPS has dropped by almost 50% since 2017.[180] A potential contributory factor resulting in fewer cases going to court has been the contested use of electronic communication data from Vs' mobile phone devices as becoming more frequently essential during prosecution decision-making.[181] Another factor causal to the drop in prosecution rates is likely to be the significant cuts in resources that have brought the criminal justice system to "breaking point".[182] Without adequate reinvestment, the successful prosecution of complex cases involving sexual offences will continue to be disproportionately affected. **6–060**

It may be that further consideration needs to be given to difficult questions about the burden of proof in relation to the rebuttable and conclusive presumptions. Some commentators have argued for the abolition of the presumptions, replacing them with a "mandatory judicial direction to assist juries with the application of the broad terms of s.74 and pass on Parliament's views about situations where consent is unlikely".[183] Although there are problems with the consistent use of such directions, and evidence of their effects on juries, Sjolin argues that they remain the most direct way of communicating important information to a jury. Whether this approach would improve the way in which jurors understand both consent and the applicability of elements of the law in any given case is far from certain.

It may also be that alternative justice mechanisms operating outside, and in tandem with the law, should be more fully utilised, such as restorative justice practices, which a growing body of practitioners and academics have argued provide for a more effective means of addressing the harms caused by sexual violence.[184] The main limitation with such an approach is that Vs will need to voluntarily agree to participate, while perpetrators will need also to have admitted guilt prior to any dialogical process. Other approaches could be to encourage Vs to pursue civil claims against rapists (where the status is one of complainant rather than V)—although this should be as well as, rather than instead of, resorting to the criminal law.[185]

---

178 Calculated as the number of convictions as a proportion of the number of completed proceedings in the Crown Court.

179 CPS, *Rape Annual Data Tables Year Ending March 2020* and CPS, *Rape Annual Data Tables Year Ending March 2023*, *https://www.cps.gov.uk/publication/cps-quarterly-data-summaries*.

180 CPS, *Rape Annual Data Tables Year Ending March 2023*, *https://www.cps.gov.uk/publication/cps-quarterly-data-summaries* combined with HM Crown Prosecution Service Inspectorate, *2019 rape inspection. A thematic review of rape cases by HM Crown Prosecution Service Inspectorate* (2019), p.8.

181 See P. Rumney and D. McPhee, "The Evidential Value of Electronic Communications Data in Rape and Sexual Offences Cases" [2021] Crim L.R. 20.

182 HM Crown Prosecution Service Inspectorate, *2019 rape inspection. A thematic review of rape cases by HM Crown Prosecution Service Inspectorate* (2019), p.8.

183 Sjolin, "Ten years on: consent under the Sexual Offences Act 2003" (2015) J. Crim. L. 20, 29.

184 See, e.g. C. McGlynn, N. Westmarland and N. Godden, "'I just wanted him to hear me': sexual violence and the possibilities of restorative justice" (2012) 39(2) J. L. Soc'y 213.

185 J. Conaghan, "Extending the Reach of Human Rights to Encompass Victims of Rape" (2005) 13 *Feminist Legal Studies* 145.

6-061 Other commentators have argued that we need to completely rethink the legal framework for sexual offences. Conaghan remarks:

> "Rape is a maelstrom of conceptual and normative contestation, a 'category in crisis'. The term is apparently so devoid of shared social and cultural meaning as to question its fitness for purpose. Has the time come to eschew rape as a term, to look afresh at questions of sexual wrongdoing unencumbered by the ideological baggage it imports?"[186]

A key issue is that of "consent" as central to defining rape, with liberal and feminist scholars differing both in their views as to the meaning of consent and its role in defining sexual offences.[187] This has led some academics to argue that the law of rape ought to jettison the concept of consent from the definition (and use force instead) since in an unequal society no woman is in a position to consent freely.[188] This position asserts that "consent is no more than a notion men conveniently employ to characterise women's submission as the product of free choice".[189] Indeed, if views such as "[n]o can mean yes if I persist long enough" linger in the minds of Ds and even some judges, a woman's consent (or lack of it) is meaningless anyway.

6-062 Others have similarly argued that consent is a legal construct that pays little attention to the reality of sexual interactions between individuals. For instance, MacKinnon reflects that " [c]onsenting is not what women do when they want to be having sex. Sex women want is never described by them or anyone else as consensual. No one says, 'We had a great hot night, she (or I or we) consented'."[190] In this same vein, Palmer notes that:

> "while consent is clearly absent from the worst sexual encounters it will also be absent in the most positive encounters jointly instigated by mutually active partners, because both partners are in a state beyond consent, a state of active involvement rather than reaction or submission."[191]

Palmer proposes an alternative concept called "freedom to negotiate", whereby evidence of consent and reasonable belief in it is removed and instead emphasis is given to the context in which sexual activity takes place. This, she asserts, requires that, at a minimum, individuals participating in sexual activity have the freedom to negotiate both the fact and nature of their participation, from start to finishing the activity. At a practical level, this would require "questions about the behaviour of the

---

186 Conaghan, "The Essence of Rape" (2019) 39 O.J.L.S. 151, 156.

187 Dripps, "Beyond Rape" (1992) 92 Colum. L. Rev. 1780; R. West, "Legitimating the Illegitimate: A Comment on Beyond Rape" (1993) 93 Colum. L. Rev. 1442; D.A. Dripps, "More on Distinguishing Sex, Sexual Assault: A Reply to Professor West" (1993) 93 Colum. L. Rev. 1460. In addition, there is the unsettled issue of the timing of consent, and in particular whether consent can be given in advance of an act, such as where a partner sexually touches their partner who is asleep and who reasonably believes that consent was given to such touching, even though the consent to such conduct was given years before. See P. Jarvis, "The timing of consent" [2019] Crim. L.R. 394.

188 For a proposal that rejects consent in favour of a differentiated offence of rape (one offence that could be committed in different ways: by force, fraud, intoxication etc), see Tadros, "Rape Without Consent" [2006] 26 O.J.L.S. 515, 536–543.

189 This position is referenced by E. Sherwin, "Infelicitous Sex" (1996) 2 *Legal Theory* 209, 214.

190 C.A. MacKinnon, "Rape Redefined" (2016) 10 *Harvard Law & Policy Review* 431, 450.

191 Palmer, "Distinguishing Sex from Sexual Violation: Consent, Negotiation and Freedom to Negotiate" in Reed, Bohlander, Wake and Smith (eds), *Consent: domestic and comparative perspectives. Substantive issues in criminal law* (2017), p.13.

defendant: did they do anything to restrict the complainant's freedom? Did they make the complainant feel like their wishes would not be respected? Did they ignore the complainant's words or body language?".[192]

Whether replacing consent with alternative concepts such as freedom to negotiate would assist in challenging harmful stereotypes about sexual conduct and improve criminal justice responses to it is unknown. Any redefinition of sexual offences could bring their own, potentially greater, dangers.[193]

192 Palmer, "Distinguishing Sex from Sexual Violation: Consent, Negotiation and Freedom to Negotiate" in Reed, Bohlander, Wake and Smith (eds), *Consent: domestic and comparative perspectives. Substantive issues in criminal law* (2017), p.16.

193 See K. Chadha, "Sexual Consent and Having Sex Together" (2020) 40 *Oxford Journal of Legal Studies* 619.

Chapter 7

Homicide

I. Introduction

Homicide is a catch-all term that covers all killings of one human being by another. What is it that makes a person resort to such extremes of violence that they end up killing another human? There is no single criminological explanation of why and how people kill. One thing is clear, however: homicides are rarely the result of the pathological killer who plans to take the life of others. Some writers have explored the interaction between victim and offender: **7–001**

> "Murder and assault are not one-sided, mechanical activities, with offenders simply acting out aggressive dispositions and victims serving as mere instigators or passive foils. Rather, they are products of a dynamic interchange. The opponents establish and escalate conflict, reject peaceful or mildly aggressive means for resolving it, and turn to massive force as an effective, perhaps mutually agreed-upon method."[1]

Thus, to think of homicide as an entirely separate phenomenon to other offences of violence would be a mistake. Rather, homicide tends to be an extension of offences against the person often resulting from an escalation in the degree of force used. That said, homicide is regarded as the most serious offence category. Our revulsion against it is embedded deep within us and our reactions to certain killings may be extreme. The following extract attempts to explain the underlying significance of homicide.

---

1 D. F. Luckenbill, "Murder and Assault" in R. F. Meier, *Major Forms of Crime* (Beverly Hills: Sage Publications, 1984), p.32.

George P. Fletcher, Rethinking Criminal Law (1978), pp.235–236, 341:

7–002 "What makes homicide unique is, among other things, the uniqueness of causing death. While all personal injuries and destruction of property are irreversible harms, causing death is a harm of a different order. Killing another human being is not only a worldly deprivation; in the Western conception of homicide, killing is an assault on the sacred, natural order. In the Biblical view, the person who slays another was thought to acquire control over the blood—the life force—of the victim . . .

Though we are inclined today to think of homicide as merely the deprivation of a secular interest, the historical background of desecration is essential to an adequate understanding . . . of the current survival of many historic assumptions. For example, consent is not a defense to homicide, as it is in cases of battery and destruction of property. The reason is that the religious conception of human life still prevails against the modern view that life is an interest that the bearer can dispose of at will . . .

There are three prominent starting places for thinking about criminal liability. In the pattern of manifest criminality, the point of departure is an act that threatens the peace and order of community life. In the theory of subjective criminality, the starting place is the actor's intent to violate a protected legal interest. In the law of homicide, the focal point is neither the act nor the intent, but the fact of death. This overpowering fact is the point at which the law begins to draw the radius of liability. From this central point, the perspective is: who can be held accountable, and in what way, for the desecration of the human and divine realms? The question is never where to place the point of the legal compass, but how far the arc should sweep in bringing in persons to stand responsible for the death that has already occurred."

7–003 The task of this chapter is to determine who should be swept within the arc of liability for homicide and to assess the bases upon which we grade the liability of such persons. In England, there are three official categories of homicide: murder, manslaughter (of which there are several species, including corporate manslaughter) and infanticide. Although not classified as homicide by the official statistics, there are further similar offences of "vehicular homicide" and causing or allowing the death of a child or vulnerable adult, which will also be briefly explored in this chapter. We shall examine each in turn before exploring whether the current structure of offences could be improved.

II. Actus Reus of Murder and Manslaughter

Both these forms of homicide share a common actus reus. Historically, the actus reus of homicide was defined as "unlawfully killing a reasonable person who is in being and under the King's Peace, the death following within a year and a day".[2] **7–004**

The last requirement of this test, the year and a day rule, developed at a time when medical science was primitive, and was abolished by the Law Reform (Year and a Day Rule) Act 1996 s.1. However, because of concerns about prosecutions being brought many years after the infliction of injury, s.2 requires the consent of the Attorney General to proceedings against a person for a fatal offence if the injury alleged to have caused the death was sustained more than three years before the death occurred.[3] Where there has been a delay between the original attack and death, and the attacker has already been convicted of a non-fatal offence such as wounding with intent prior to the death of the deceased, it has been held that a subsequent prosecution for murder following the death of the victim from their injuries is possible and does not breach the European Convention on Human Rights (ECHR) Protocol 7 art.4 (double-jeopardy rule).[4]

The remaining elements of the actus reus remain the same: **7–005**

(1) *"unlawfully"*: some killings, such as those in self-defence, may be justified and therefore lawful;
(2) *"killing"*: the act (or omission) of D must have killed V; it must have been the legal cause of the death of V;
(3) *"a reasonable person who is in being"*: V must be a human being who was alive at the time of D's actions. This raises problems outside the scope of this book as to the precise moment when life begins and ends. In view of developments with heart transplant operations and life-support machines, the problem of determining the exact moment of death has assumed some importance in recent times. According to English law, a foetus is not a human being for the purposes of the law of homicide. However, it is possible for a charge of manslaughter to be brought against a defendant who causes injury to a mother carrying a child in utero if that child is born alive and then subsequently dies from the injuries.[5] If a miscarriage is intentionally procured, and is not a lawful abortion within the terms of the Abortion Act 1967 s.1, the procurer will be guilty of the offence of criminal abortion.[6] There is also a separate offence of child destruction covering cases of destroying a foetus that is capable of being born alive.[7]

---

2 Coke, 3 Inst. 47.

3 This term is defined in s.2(3) as murder, manslaughter, infanticide or any other offence of which one of the elements is causing a person's death, or the offence of encouraging or assisting a person's suicide, or the offence under the Domestic Violence, Crime and Victims Act 2004 s.5 of causing or allowing the death of a child or vulnerable adult.

4 *R. v Young (Kerry Rena)* [2005] EWCA Crim 2963.

5 In *Att-Gen's Reference (No.3 of 1994)* [1998] A.C. 245; [1997] 3 W.L.R. 421 HL, the House of Lords held it was not possible for D to be guilty of murder where the injury was caused to the mother whilst the child was in utero. Their Lordships did not accept the idea that a foetus could be treated as part of the mother's body in the same way as, e.g. an arm. As far as unlawful act manslaughter was concerned, however, liability is not negated by the fact that the death of the child is caused as a consequence of injury to the mother rather than as a consequence of direct injury to the foetus. See para.3–135.

6 Offences against the Person Act 1861 s.58.

7 Infant Life (Preservation) Act 1929 s.1.

A pregnancy that has lasted 24 weeks provides prima facie proof that the foetus is capable of being born alive.[8] Both these offences—criminal abortion and child destruction—carry the same maximum penalty as manslaughter, namely, life imprisonment; and

(4) *"under the King's Peace"*: all human beings are under the "King's" peace except an alien enemy "in the heat of war, and in the actual exercise thereof".[9]

III. Murder

A. THE LAW OF MURDER

7–006 Murder is committed when D commits the actus reus of homicide with *malice aforethought*. Murder is the most serious form of homicide carrying the severest penalty in English law—mandatory life imprisonment. The law reserves this category of homicide for those who kill with the most blameworthy state of mind, known technically as "malice aforethought".[10] Defining the parameters of murder is thus primarily[11] a task of defining malice aforethought, the mens rea of murder.

The mens rea of murder can now be simply stated. D must either:

(1) intend to cause death; or
(2) intend to cause grievous bodily harm.

The term "malice aforethought" originally[12] bore its literal meaning and it would only be murder if D had thought out, planned or premeditated the killing. In the 15th and 16th centuries, an intentional homicide "on the sudden" was not murder but manslaughter. However, it became clear that this was too narrow a definition for murder. Other types of homicide were just as reprehensible and deserving of the ultimate penalty. Accordingly, the judges started expanding the concept "malice aforethought" and dispensing with the requirement of a premeditated intent, until by the mid-17th century it was clear that malice aforethought could be established in one of two ways.

---

8 Human Fertilisation and Embryology Act 1990 s.37(1)(a).

9 Hale, 1 P.C. 433. Hirst, however, argues that the relevance of "under the Queen/King's peace" is not to do with whether the killing was in time of war, but rather that the offence of murder must have been committed either in England and Wales or abroad in circumstances where by statute the English law of murder now has extraterritorial application. This, he argues, is fundamental, as it determines to whom the English law of murder applies: M. Hirst, "Murder Under the Queen's Peace" [2008] Crim. L.R. 541.

10 This phrase was described in *R. v Moloney (Alistair Baden)* [1985] A.C. 905 at 920; [1985] 2 W.L.R. 648 HL as "anachronistic and now wholly inappropriate".

11 In certain cases, such as where there is loss of control, a killing can be committed with malice aforethought but, because of the circumstances of the killing, the crime is reduced to voluntary manslaughter. See para.7–070.

12 For a full discussion of the earliest development of the term "malice aforethought," and of the separation of murder from manslaughter in the late 15th century, see E.B. Sayre, "Mens Rea" (1932) 45 Harv. L. Rev. 974; R. Moreland, *The Law of Homicide* (Indianapolis: Bobbs-Merrill, 1952), pp.1–16 (and references cited therein); and J. Horder, "Two Histories and Four Hidden Principles of *Mens Rea*" (1997) 113 L.Q.R. 95, 100–109.

First, it became clear that malice aforethought was present whenever there was an intent to kill.[13] This is sometimes known as "express malice". Second, it has long been established that intent to cause grievous bodily harm (GBH) is a form of malice aforethought. This species of malice aforethought is often called "implied malice".

In *Vickers,*[14] the Court of Appeal confirmed that this second form of malice, often known as the "GBH rule", was an independent species of malice aforethought and not merely a particular example of the felony-murder rule and so had survived the abolition of the felony murder rule. [15] The validity of the GBH rule would appear to be beyond doubt as a result of the House of Lord's decision of *Cunningham.*[16] Despite the decision in *Vickers,* the minority in *Hyam*[17] supported the view that the GBH rule was abolished alongside the felony-murder rule, but this view was rejected in *Cunningham*. It had further been argued in *Hyam* that the reason for the GBH rule was that in the last century, because of the poor state of medical knowledge and experience, persons sustaining such injuries were likely to die; such a rationale was unacceptable in modern times with the advances in medical knowledge. If transplanting the GBH rule into modern times it would need qualifying so that only GBH which endangered life should come within the mens rea of murder. This argument was similarly rejected. **7-007**

R. v Cunningham [1982] A.C. 566 (House of Lords):

LORD EDMUND-DAVIES: **7-008**

"[T]he view I presently favour is . . . that there should be no conviction for murder unless an intent to kill is established, the wide range of punishment for manslaughter being fully adequate to deal with all less heinous forms of homicide. I find it passing strange that a person can be convicted of murder if death results from, say, his intentional breaking of another's arm, an action which, while undoubtedly involving the infliction of 'really serious harm' and, as such, calling for severe punishment, would in most cases be unlikely to kill. And yet, for the lesser offence of attempted murder, nothing less than intent to kill will suffice. But I recognise the force of the contrary view that the outcome of intentionally inflicting serious harm can be so unpredictable that anyone prepared to act so wickedly has little ground for complaint if, where death results, he is convicted and punished as severely as one who intended to kill.

So there are forceful arguments both ways . . . Resolution of that conflict cannot, in my judgment, be a matter for your Lordships' House alone. It is a task for none other than Parliament."

---

13 Moreland, *The Law of Homicide* (1952), Ch.1; R. Perkins, "A Re-examination of Malice Aforethought" (1934) 43 Yale L.J. 537.

14 *R. v Vickers (John Willson)* [1957] 2 Q.B. 664; [1957] 3 W.L.R. 326 CA.

15 Under the felony murder rule, the commission of a felony (such as intentionally causing GBH) that resulted in death would be murder. This rule was abolished by the Homicide Act 1957.

16 *R. v Cunningham (Anthony Barry)* [1982] A.C. 566; [1981] 3 W.L.R. 223 HL.

17 *Hyam v DPP* [1975] A.C. 55; [1974] 2 W.L.R. 607 HL.

7-009 An example of how medical treatment can prolong life when serious harm is caused can be found in the case of *Clift*.[18] Here D attacked V in 2000, plunging a screwdriver into V's brain and causing a catastrophic brain injury. V survived the attack for a number of years, reliant on carers and being fed through a tube. In 2002, D was convicted of causing GBH with intent, and sentenced to 10 years' imprisonment, and was released in 2007. In 2009, V died after complications developed following a medical procedure to reinsert the feeding tube. D was convicted of murder; the post mortem having concluded that the original attack and the death were connected. The Court of Appeal confirmed that D's conviction for the offence under the Offences against the Person Act 1861 s.18 could be adduced as evidence that D intended to cause GBH, providing him with the necessary mens rea for murder.

It is clear that a form of intention is required for malice aforethought, either intention to kill or to cause GBH. This does not, however, solve the central problem of determining the meaning of intention. The leading decisions on intention are *Nedrick* and *Woollin*, which are extracted and discussed in Ch.2 and to which reference should be made. Whether these cases lay down an appropriate test is discussed later, as is the question of whether the GBH rule should be retained.

B. PENALTY FOR MURDER

7-010 The Murder (Abolition of the Death Penalty) Act 1965 abolished capital punishment for murder and substituted a sentence of mandatory life imprisonment. The judge has no discretion as to sentence. A convicted murderer must be sentenced to imprisonment for life.[19]

However, convicted murderers seldom remain in prison for the duration of their lives. They can be released from prison on "licence". This means that the offender does not regain absolute liberty. The licence is subject to conditions: for example, requiring supervision by a probation officer. All such persons released on licence are liable to be recalled to prison at any time during the rest of their lives should there be a breach of the conditions of licence or should their conduct indicate that there is a risk of a serious offence being committed.

The minimum term that a murderer must spend in prison before being released on licence is set by the judge, in accordance with the Sentencing Act 2020, Sch.21. This provides starting points according to criteria related to seriousness. These starting points may be increased or decreased after taking into account aggravating and mitigating factors.[20] The starting points fall into one of four categories of seriousness: "exceptionally high", "particularly high", knife crime murders and all others.

18 *R. v Clift (Leigh George)* [2012] EWCA Crim 2750; [2013] 1 Cr. App. R. 15.

19 Sentencing Act 2020 s.275. Such a sentence is not incompatible with either art.3 or art.5 of the ECHR (*R. v Lichniak (Daniella Helen)* [2002] UKHL 47; [2003] 1 A.C. 903).

20 Sentencing Act 2020 Sch.21 paras 7–10.

The starting point for a case falling in the "exceptionally high" category is a whole life order,[21] with examples of such cases being given as including the murder of two or more persons involving a substantial degree of premeditation or planning, the abduction of the victim, or sexual or sadistic conduct. A single murder might also result in a whole life order if it involves the murder of a police officer or prison officer in the course of their duty, a murder committed for the purpose of advancing a political, religious, racial or ideological cause, the murder of a child involving a substantial degree of premeditation or planning, or involving abduction of the child and sexual or sadistic motivation or a murder committed by an offender previously convicted of murder.[22] The starting point for a murder falling in the "particularly high" category is 30 years.[23] These include, inter alia, a murder involving the use of a firearm or explosive, a murder committed in the course of a robbery or burglary or in the expectation of gain or a murder intended to obstruct the course of justice.[24] If the offender took a knife or other weapon to the scene intending to either commit any offence, or have it available to use as a weapon, the starting point is 25 years.[25] The starting point for all other murders is 15 years, if D is an adult.[26]

The lists in paras 9 and 10 of Sch.21 provide mere examples of aggravating and mitigating circumstances, and are not exhaustive.[27] The cases demonstrate that the courts are able to manoeuvre around the provisions to do justice in a particular case. In *Inglis*,[28] for example, D killed her son by injecting him with heroin in what was described as the first "mercy killing" to reach the Court of Appeal since the Sch.21 guidance came into force.[29] This was a carefully planned murder, D having failed on the first attempt, motivated by D's wish to put her son, who had suffered severe brain injuries and was reliant on medical care, out of his misery. The Court of Appeal held that the factors listed under para.9 of: a significant degree of planning or premeditation; the fact that V was particularly vulnerable because of disability; and the abuse of a position of trust, should not operate as aggravating factors in a case such as this, and reduced the minimum term from nine to five years. **7-011**

The setting of minimum terms means that the sentencing of murderers is not dissimilar to the sentencing of other offenders,[30] and the statutory, more transparent scheme may lead to murderers

---

21 Sentencing Act 2020 Sch.21 para.2(1).

22 Sentencing Act 2020 Sch.21 para.2(2).

23 Sentencing Act 2020 Sch.21 para.3(1).

24 Sentencing Act 2020 Sch.21 para.3(2).

25 Sentencing Act 2020 Sch.21 para.4(1).

26 Sentencing Act 2020 Sch.21 para.5.

27 *R. v Last (Emma)* [2005] EWCA Crim 106; [2005] Crim. L.R. 407; *R. v Peters (Benjamin)* [2005] EWCA Crim 605; [2005] Crim. L.R. 492. It should be noted that Sch.21 has been added to several times since it first came into force. At the time of writing, Parliament was considering whether to add to the list of aggravating factors by inserting para.9(bb) into Sch.21, to specify that if the murder is connected to the break-up of a relationship, this will amount to an aggravating factor (Criminal Justice Bill (Bill 155, 2023–24), cl.31). The paragraph had only recently amended through secondary legislation, with the Sentencing Act (Amendment of Schedule 21) Regulations 2024 (SI 2024/137) having inserted para.9(ba) to create an aggravating factor of D having engaged in coercive and controlling behaviour of V.

28 *R. v Inglis (Frances)* [2010] EWCA Crim 2637; [2011] 2 Cr. App. R. (S.) 13.

29 Originally under the Criminal Justice Act 2003.

30 Roberts and Saunders argue, however, that as the drafting of Sch.21 did not undergo a comprehensive analysis of the type the Sentencing Council conducts when consulting on guidelines, the guidance has compromised rather than promoted proportional sentencing for murder. They suggest that Sch.21 should be repealed and the Sentencing Council tasked with drafting the guidance, as for other offences: Julian V. Roberts and Sir John Saunders, "Sentencing for murder: the adverse and unintended effects of Schedule 21 to the Criminal Justice Act 2003" [2020] Crim. L.R. 900–911.

being encouraged to plead guilty in the hope of securing a discount on the minimum term[31] where, previously, they would have felt there was nothing to lose by pleading not guilty.[32] However, there are important differences in sentencing murderers. First, the length of the minimum term is set in "real-time" to be served. Whilst an offender sentenced to a determinate sentence for some other offence may be released on licence having served a half to two-thirds of the term, depending on the offence,[33] a murderer will not be released before they have served the actual number of years of the minimum term. Secondly, there is never a right to release on parole. Once the murderer has served their minimum term the Parole Board must judge whether it is safe to release them. Thirdly, the released murderer is always on licence and liable to recall to prison. The mandatory life sentence has been criticised with suggestions that it should be abolished on the basis that, as murder is not a homogenous offence but a crime of considerable variety, the judge should be given discretion to pass a fixed term of imprisonment:

> "It ranges from deliberate cold-blooded killing in pursuit of purely selfish ends to what is commonly referred to as 'mercy killing'. Instead of automatically applying a single sentence to such an offence, . . . sentences for murder should reflect this variety with correspondingly variable terms of imprisonment . . ."[34]

C. EVALUATION OF MURDER

7–012 With a rigid sentencing regime in place it is arguably more important than ever that the mandatory life sentence be reserved for the most heinous of killings and that the definition of murder be clear and include only the most culpable of killings. Apart from criticism of the mandatory penalty of life imprisonment for murder, there are two further criticisms of the present law:

(1) criticism of the grievous bodily harm rule;
(2) criticism of the *Woollin* test of intention.

1. The grievous bodily harm rule

7–013 There are arguments in favour of the retention of the GBH rule as a species of malice aforethought. If D intends *really* serious bodily harm to another there is always a probability that death may result from such injuries. Most Ds would know this. Thus, people who intend to cause GBH have chosen to run a

---

31 According to guidelines issued by the Sentencing Guidelines Council, a guilty plea in a murder case should lead to a discount of up to one-sixth of the minimum term or five years, whichever is the lesser. Where the court determines that there should be a whole life term, a reduction will not be given for a guilty plea. Guilty pleas can generally lead to a discount of up to one third in cases other than murder, but the Council is of the view that the differences in the sentencing scheme for murder, and the unique seriousness of the offence, warrant a special approach: Sentencing Council, *Reduction in sentence for a guilty plea: Definitive Guideline* (2017), p.8.

32 D. Thomas, "Sentencing Murderers" [2004] 3 *Archbold News* 7.

33 See the Criminal Justice Act 2003 s.244ZA and Sch.15.

34 Report of the Advisory Council on the Penal System, *Sentences of Imprisonment (A Review of Maximum Penalties)* (1978), para.244. See also House of Lords Select Committee on Murder and Life Imprisonment (Session 1988–89, H.L. Paper 78). Note, however, that these proposals were made before the sentencing regime was introduced under Sch.21.

risk of endangering life. They are as dangerous and as blameworthy as those who actually intend to kill. Their excessive risk-taking as to the death should render them liable for murder.

Criminal Law Revision Committee, Working Paper on Offences against the Person, 1976, para.29:

"It is argued that a person who inflicts serious injury on another intentionally must know that by so doing there is a real chance that his victim will die and if death results it is right that he should be convicted of murder. There is force also in the argument that a person who is minded to use violence in achieving an unlawful purpose may take more care to refrain from inflicting serious injury if he knows that he may be convicted of murder if his victim dies. A few of our members are in favour of an intent to cause serious injury, simpliciter, remaining a sufficient intent in murder." **7–014**

Notwithstanding the approval of the GBH rule in *Hyam* and *Cunningham*, it has been the subject of severe judicial criticism. **7–015**

Attorney General's Reference (No.3 of 1994) [1998] A.C. 245 (House of Lords):

LORD MUSTILL: **7–016**

"Murder is widely thought to be the gravest of crimes. One could expect a developed system to embody a law of murder clear enough to yield an unequivocal result on a given set of facts, a result which conforms with apparent justice and has a sound intellectual base. This is not so in England, where the law of homicide is permeated by anomaly, fiction, misnomer and obsolete reasoning. One conspicuous anomaly is the rule which identifies the 'malice aforethought' (a doubly misleading expression) required for the crime of murder not only with a conscious intention to kill but also with an intention to cause grievous bodily harm . . . Many would doubt the justice of this rule, which is not the popular conception of murder and . . . no longer rests on any intellectual foundation . . . [I]t is, I think, right to recognise that the grievous bodily harm rule is an outcropping of old law from which the surrounding strata of rationalisations have weathered away."

Despite this criticism, Lord Mustill recognised that there was no ground upon which the House of Lords could abolish such an established rule. However, the Law Commission has also rejected the GBH rule in its present form. **7–017**

The Law Commission, Imputed Criminal Intent (Director of Public Prosecutions v Smith), 1965, paras 15, 18:

7-018 "15. The main arguments for changing the present law, which prescribes intent to inflict grievous bodily harm as an alternative to the intent to kill in murder, are as follows:

(a) Murder is commonly understood to mean the intentional killing of another human being; and, unless there are strong reasons which justify a contrary course, it is generally desirable that legal terms should correspond with their popular meaning.

(b) To limit intent in murder to the intent to kill is not to disregard the very serious nature of causing death by the infliction of grievous bodily harm, but, since the suspension of the death sentence, if such an offence were to be treated as manslaughter only, it could nevertheless be punished by a maximum penalty as severe as the penalty prescribed for murder, namely, imprisonment for life . . .

(c) Furthermore, a man should not be regarded as a murderer if he does not *know* that the bodily harm which he intends to inflict is likely to kill . . . If there is any special deterrent effect in the label 'murder' as distinguished from manslaughter, it should be attached to an act done with intent to inflict bodily harm which the accused knows is likely to kill . . . "

7-019 The Law Commission's Draft Criminal Code recommended modification of the GBH rule so that it would only be murder in such cases when D acts "intending to cause serious personal harm and being aware that he may cause death".[35] The Law Commission has more recently proposed dividing murder into two degrees and has adopted a similar test for its proposed offence of first degree murder, which would be committed where D killed either intending to kill or intending "to do serious injury where the killer was aware that his or her conduct involved a serious risk of causing death".[36] Where D intended to cause serious injury without the awareness that it might cause death this would, under the Law Commission's recommendations, amount to second degree murder.[37] Included in the recommendations was the suggestion that the word "harm" be replaced by "injury" in order to clarify that it ought not to be stretched to include severe or persisting emotional states that do not amount to a recognised psychiatric illness or injury.[38]

35 Law Commission Paper No.177, *Draft Criminal Code Bill* 1989 cl.54(1). This proposal was endorsed by the House of Lords Select Committee on Murder and Life Imprisonment (Session 1988–89, HL Paper 78) (1989), para.71.

36 Law Commission Paper No.304, *Murder, Manslaughter and Infanticide* (2006), para.2.50.

37 Law Commission Paper No.304, *Murder, Manslaughter and Infanticide* (2006), para.2.70. It would also be second degree murder if there was an intention to cause injury or fear or risk of injury while aware of a serious risk of causing death.

38 Law Commission Paper No.304, *Murder, Manslaughter and Infanticide* (2006), para.2.84. Under current law "bodily harm" for the purposes of non-fatal offences has been interpreted to include recognised psychiatric conditions (*R. v Chan-Fook (Mike)* [1994] 1 W.L.R. 689; (1994) 99 Cr. App. R. 147 CA), but not to include a severely depressed state that does not amount to a recognised psychiatric illness (*R. v Dhaliwal* [2006] EWCA Crim 1139; [2006] 2 Cr. App. R. 236).

Whilst current English law continues to classify someone who kills intending to cause GBH as a murderer,[39] such a state of mind is at least recognised as a possible mitigating factor for courts in setting the minimum term as part of the mandatory life sentence.[40] Should the law go further? Is a defendant who takes such a clear risk as to death so much less culpable or blameworthy as to deserve liability for manslaughter only? Perhaps this question cannot be fully answered until the *Woollin* test of intention has been considered.

2. Woollin test of intention

Following *Woollin*, the generally accepted position is that intention remains undefined but the jury is entitled to find intention only where there is foresight that death or GBH was a virtual certainty.[41] While they are "entitled" to find such intention, equally they are entitled to find that D did not intend death or GBH. Under this interpretation, where intention is not defined and the jury is allowed "moral elbow-room" to decide whether D deserves to be labelled a murderer, the hypocrisy of the past century is continued. Murder is a "crime of intention", but maximum flexibility is retained by not defining the concept. **7–020**

We saw in Ch.3 that this moral elbow room allows the jury to do justice in a particular case by finding someone not guilty of murder where the facts give rise to sympathy for D, despite having foreseen death or GBH as a virtual certainty, Norrie has extended this argument to suggest that those responsible for the deaths resulting from the Grenfell Tower fire[42] might be prosecuted for murder, on the basis that the "moral elbow-room" argument ought to cut both ways.

Alan Norrie, "Legal and Social Murder: What's the Difference?" [2018] Crim. L.R. 531–542:

"The nature of the morally negative motive that might be identified in Grenfell is somewhat different from these existing examples. But if it were to be found there had been a reckless disregard for human life leading to the Grenfell fire; if a flagrant danger was found to have been set loose in the world through decision-making that was judged callous as to the value of human life; **7–021**

39 In *R. v Sidhu (Ryandeep Singh)* [2019] EWCA Crim 1034; [2019] 2 Cr. App. R. (S.) 34, the Court of Appeal heard an appeal against sentence for manslaughter on the ground that the judge had sentenced D with reference to his intention to "cause serious injury". It was argued that if the jury had thought D had such an intent, they would have convicted him of murder rather than manslaughter. The appeal was dismissed on the basis that there are multiple degrees of seriousness and intent, leading up to the threshold of intent required for murder. Whilst judges may have expressed the necessary intent for murder as "intention to cause injury" or "intention to cause serious injury", these were shorthand terms for intention to cause serious harm "sufficient to amount in law to murder". It was clear that, given the Sentencing Council made reference in its recent guideline for manslaughter to defendants who intended serious injury, some defendants will be convicted of manslaughter rather than murder whilst displaying an intention to cause serious injury falling short of the threshold for murder. The judge's use of the term "serious" was descriptive of the middle ground below murder. This may be true, but neither the Court of Appeal nor the Sentencing Council are contributing to clarity of the law by making such statements. It would be helpful if judges used more accurate language when describing the mens rea for murder.

40 In *R. v Wilby (Christopher Keith)* [2007] EWCA Crim 2823; [2008] 1 Cr. App. R. (S.) 98, the Court of Appeal held, correspondingly, that intent to kill was not an aggravating factor in sentencing for murder.

41 See Ch.3 above, para.3–023.

42 In June 2017, a fire broke out in a 23-storey block of flats in West London, known as Grenfell Tower. It spread quickly, it seems caused by the polyethylene material used in the cladding on the outside of the building, and killed 72 people: "Grenfell: What Happened" *BBC News*, 29 October 2019, *https://www.bbc.co.uk/news/uk-40301289*.

if a meretricious motive of putting costcutting above lives was considered to have been at play; and if all this were put together with the analysis of system risk discussed above, then there could be a question as to whether the law of murder ought to reflect deaths that occur in such conditions. There is, as we have seen, a certain openness of the law as to how it finds the mens rea of murder, and into that opening may emerge ideas of wicked recklessness, indiscriminate malice or moral callousness as interpretive ancillaries to finding intention for murder. The law remains to a degree formally open: it is a matter of a rule of evidence and an 'entitlement to find' rather than a clearly stated law, leaving a gap for negative moral judgment in the legal form. If juries may respond to good motives by refusing to apply the virtual certainty rule in such cases, might they not also do so in the way they respond to callous, wickedly reckless, indiscriminately malicious forms of behaviour that produce injury and lead to death? Might they then find it possible to call these murder? I repeat that these are questions for a jury and here, where the law is vague, this is particularly so."

7-022 Such an approach is, however, a recipe for unpredictability and opens the door to irrelevant factors being taken into consideration. Fair labelling requires an open acknowledgment of what forms of killing are murder. An alternative approach is that we should in fact narrow the required mens rea for murder to single out the worst examples of killing. This presents the question: should not the crime of murder be restricted to those who *directly* intend to kill (or cause GBH)?

The argument for limiting the mens rea of murder to a *direct* intention is a two-fold one. Murder is the most serious crime under English law and carries the most severe penalty. It should be reserved for the worst cases which are directly intended killings. In such cases, D has acted with a degree of control and deliberation that enhances their responsibility for the outcome of their actions and affects our judgement of them as a moral agent. They are not simply showing indifference to the value of human life; they are actually taking positive and purposeful steps towards the ending of the life of another. This evil aim marks them out as more blameworthy. Also, a person who is trying to achieve a result is usually more likely to succeed than someone who merely foresees that result as a by-product of their actions, and can thus perhaps be regarded as more blameworthy than one who engages in conduct with a lesser chance of harm.

Secondly, such an approach avoids all problems of having to draw fine lines on the continuum of risk taking—for example, distinguishing between foresight of the virtually certain (murder) and foresight of the extremely probable (manslaughter).

7-023 The argument against such a strict limitation is that it would unduly restrict the crime of murder and that many persons, such as the bomber on the aeroplane wanting the insurance money,[43] deserve to be brought within the category of murder. This raises the question as to whether there is a moral distinction between one who wants death to result and one who foresees death as virtually certain—or one who merely foresees death as likely. In short, should murder be expanded beyond intent (as

---

43 See Ch.3, para.3-050 where this example is used to illustrate further argument on this point.

currently understood) to kill (or cause GBH)? Should cases of gross recklessness be included within the crime of murder?

In the context of proposing the creation of two degrees of murder, the Law Commission has recommended that second degree murder should require a test of "killings intended to cause injury or fear or risk of injury where the killer was aware that his or her conduct involved a serious risk of causing death".[44] This was recommended as an alternative mens rea requirement for second degree murder, in addition to killings intended to cause serious injury. Arguably the Law Commission has had to resort to recommending the creation of a second degree of murder in order to circumvent the problems of drawing a rigid line between murder, conviction for which must lead to a mandatory life sentence, and manslaughter, providing discretion in sentencing. As will be seen towards the end of this chapter, creating a middle offence carrying a label of murder, but avoiding the mandatory life sentence, would allow the law to temper criticisms of the GBH rule whilst equating that level of blameworthiness with a high degree of recklessness.[45] In this way there would no longer be a need to have one clear line distinguishing the "worst" types of killing (murder) from all others (manslaughter).

IV. Manslaughter

The crime of manslaughter is committed when a D commits the actus reus of homicide but the killing is not sufficiently blameworthy to warrant liability for murder. This will be so in two situations: **7–024**

(1) where D does not have the necessary mens rea for murder, but can nevertheless be regarded as blameworthy to some extent (involuntary manslaughter); or
(2) where D does possess the necessary mens rea for murder, but has killed under certain specific circumstances which the law regards as mitigating the seriousness of the offence (voluntary manslaughter).

The lesser blameworthiness is reflected by an avoidance of both the label and stigma of murder and the mandatory penalty of life imprisonment imposed for murder. The maximum penalty for the crime of manslaughter is life imprisonment, enabling the judge to impose any sentence up to that maximum to reflect the appropriate degree of culpability of D.[46]

---

44 Law Commission No.304 (2006), para.2.70.

45 It has been argued that there is no need for the GBH rule to be maintained in addition to a test of recklessness, since it is likely that all those who intend to cause serious harm would also be caught by an appropriately defined test for reckless: V. Tadros, "The Homicide Ladder" (2006) 69 M.L.R. 601.

46 Offences against the Person Act 1861 s.5.

A. INVOLUNTARY MANSLAUGHTER

7–025 "[O]f all crimes manslaughter appears to afford most difficulties of definition, for it concerns homicide in so many and so varying conditions."[47]

This is because manslaughters range from killings just short of murder to killings only just above the accidental.[48] This can be represented diagrammatically:[49]

<table>
<tr><td></td><td colspan="2">A</td><td colspan="2">B</td><td></td></tr>
<tr><td colspan="2"></td><td colspan="2"></td><td colspan="2"></td></tr>
<tr><td colspan="2">MURDER</td><td colspan="2">MANSLAUGHTER</td><td colspan="2">ACCIDENTAL KILLINGS</td></tr>
<tr><td colspan="2"></td><td colspan="2"></td><td colspan="2"></td></tr>
</table>

In assessing the parameters of the crime of manslaughter, attention must be focused on two questions.

(a) How is manslaughter distinguished from murder (A)? Despite the minimal discussion of manslaughter in *Woollin* and the other leading cases, the House of Lords, in defining the parameters of the crime of murder was, in essence, focusing on the distinction between murder and manslaughter. The point at which this line was drawn was considered above.

(b) How is manslaughter distinguished from accidental or non-culpable killings (B)? What factors make a killing sufficiently blameworthy to justify liability for manslaughter as opposed to liability for some lesser offence or no liability at all?

It is this question that requires close consideration in this section. It might be useful to note at the outset, however, that many cases of manslaughter start out as cases of murder, only to be reduced to manslaughter either due to acceptance of a guilty plea to that offence, or following trial. In a survey of cases resulting in convictions for involuntary manslaughter, Mitchell and Mackay found that only 13 of the 152 Ds had been indicted for manslaughter (six of those 13 having originally been charged with murder); the majority had been indicted for murder.[50] It seems that in most cases of homicide arising out of violence, the prosecution will chance its arm on a murder charge, and it is not clear what factors influence the decision to charge only manslaughter from the outset.

7–026 During the final decades of the 20th century, the law of involuntary manslaughter was the subject of very considerable change. It is now common to assert that it takes three forms:

(1) (subjective) reckless manslaughter;
(2) constructive or unlawful act manslaughter; and
(3) gross negligence manslaughter.

---

47 *Andrews v DPP* [1937] A.C. 576; (1938) 26 Cr. App. R. 34 HL per Lord Atkin.

48 For a flavour of the variations in culpability exhibited by those convicted of involuntary manslaughter, see B. Mitchell and R. Mackay, "Investigating Involuntary Manslaughter: An Empirical Study of 127 Cases" (2011) 31 O.J.L.S. 165–191.

49 Justifiable killings have not been included in this diagram.

50 Mitchell and Mackay, "Investigating Involuntary Manslaughter: An Empirical Study of 127 Cases" (2011) 31 O.J.L.S. 165–191, 178.

It should be stressed at the outset that these are not three separate crimes. Indeed, there is no discreet crime of "involuntary manslaughter" in the sense that one is charged with or convicted of the offence. The term "involuntary manslaughter" is simply a convenient label to describe those residual unlawful killings not otherwise specifically catered for by the law and the culpability necessary for the offence can be established in one of the above three ways.

1. (Subjective) reckless manslaughter

Where D subjectively foresees a risk of death or serious injury (but the degree of foresight fails to come within the *Woollin* test of intention required for murder), there will be liability for manslaughter.[51] As the law of murder has been progressively narrowed with tighter tests of intention, so this category of manslaughter has been correspondingly broadened to occupy the "area vacated by murder".[52] There is little specific authority on this species of manslaughter because, in practice, such cases are usually dealt with as constructive manslaughter.[53] Stark has doubted its existence as a separate form of manslaughter, arguing that proof of subjective recklessness is actually simply a factor for consideration in proving a case of unlawful act or gross negligence manslaughter.[54] Despite reaching this conclusion, he is in favour of its existence, and argues that it fills a gap and ought to be recognised in legislation. If Stark is correct that reckless manslaughter does not currently exist as a separate form of the offence, there is certainly force in his argument that it ought to be created, particularly for reasons of fair labelling. If it does not do so already, this category ought to cover cases where D is charged with murder but the jury convict of manslaughter,[55] or the appellate courts substitute a verdict of manslaughter,[56] or where D pleads guilty to manslaughter having a plea of not guilty to murder accepted.[57] At present, such cases are simply labelled as manslaughter, without labelling the killer as someone who has adverted to a risk of death or serious harm, or as someone who has committed an unlawful and dangerous act, or has breached a duty of care in a way which amounts to gross negligence. Given the different blame demonstrated in these various forms of manslaughter, there Is reason to agree that legislation should be passed to acknowledge such differences. **7–027**

2. Constructive or unlawful act manslaughter

As a corollary of the felony-murder rule, the law developed a misdemeanour-manslaughter rule whereby it was manslaughter to kill in the course of committing a misdemeanour. The obvious rigours of such a rule were soon mitigated, and this species of manslaughter survived the abolition of the **7–028**

51 Law Commission Paper No.237, *Legislating the Criminal Code: Involuntary Manslaughter* (1996), para.5.15. The Law Commission's more recent Consultation Paper on homicide does, however, suggest that what is needed is knowledge of a risk of killing (rather than foresight of death *or* serious injury): Law Commission Consultation Paper No.177, *A New Homicide Act for England and Wales?* (2005), para.1.10. The existence of this category of manslaughter was confirmed in *Lidar,* LTL, 12 November 1999.

52 J.C. Smith, Commentary to *Adomako* [1994] Crim. L.R. 758, 759.

53 Law Commission Paper No.237 (1996), para.2.27.

54 F. Stark, "Reckless manslaughter" [2017] Crim. L.R. 763–784.

55 See, e.g. *R. v Kime (Darren John)* [1999] 2 Cr. App. R. (S.) 3 CA. In *R. v Coutts (Graham James)* [2006] UKHL 39; [2006] 1 W.L.R. 2154, the House of Lords held that, as a matter of principle, a trial judge in a murder case should always leave an alternative count of manslaughter to the jury, even if the defence case is to rely on a complete defence (such as accident) which, if successful, would lead to complete acquittal.

56 See, e.g. *R. v Woollin (Stephen Leslie)* [1999] 1 A.C. 82; [1999] 1 Cr. App. R. 8 HL.

57 See, e.g. *R. v Jackson (Leslie Joseph)* [1999] 2 Cr. App. R. (S.) 77 CA.

felony-murder rule and abolition of the distinction between felonies and misdemeanours. The present law may be stated in the following terms:

(1) D must commit an unlawful act; and
(2) the unlawful act must be dangerous, namely, it must expose the victim to the risk of some bodily harm resulting therefrom.

(i) The unlawful act

7–029 Not all unlawful acts will suffice for constructive manslaughter. Three limitations upon the earlier rule have been developed:

(1) the unlawful act must constitute a crime. A tort or other civil wrong will not suffice. In *Franklin*,[58] Field J ruled that:

> "... the mere fact of a civil wrong committed by one person against another ought not to be used as an incident which is a necessary step in a criminal case. I have a great abhorrence of constructive crime."

Furthermore, if D would have a defence (say, self-defence) to the unlawful act, then there is no "crime" for the purposes of constructive manslaughter.[59]

(2) The act must be criminal for some other reason than that it has been negligently performed. For example, driving a car is a lawful act; driving that car negligently is a criminal offence. Such a crime will not suffice for constructive manslaughter. In *Andrews v DPP* Lord Atkin held:

> "There is an obvious difference in the law of manslaughter between doing an unlawful act and doing a lawful act with a degree of carelessness which the legislature makes criminal. If it were otherwise a man who killed another while driving without due care and attention would *ex necessitate* commit manslaughter."[60]

(3) It is doubtful whether an omission will suffice for constructive manslaughter. In *Lowe*,[61] it was held that the mere fact that a parent was guilty of the statutory offence of wilful neglect of a child, did not make that parent liable for unlawful act manslaughter if the child died in consequence of the neglect (as we will see below, they could instead by liable for gross negligence manslaughter).

---

58 *R. v Franklin* (1883) 15 Cox C.C. 163.
59 *R. v Scarlett (John)* (1994) 98 Cr. App. R. 290; [1994] Crim. L.R. 288 CA.
60 *Andrews v DPP* [1937] A.C. 576 at 585; (1938) 26 Cr. App. R. 34 HL.
61 *R. v Lowe (Robert)* [1973] Q.B. 702; [1973] 2 W.L.R. 481 CA.

Apart from these three limitations it would appear that any unlawful act will suffice. It is irrelevant whether that act previously constituted a felony or a misdemeanour. In practice, however, the majority of constructive manslaughter cases are based on some form of assault as the unlawful act. In a survey of 110 cases of unlawful act manslaughter, all but one was found to involve some sort of assault against the deceased (although assault was not the main unlawful act in nine of the cases; where a burglary, robbery or arson occurred, assault was committed as part of that unlawful act).[62] However, it is important to establish that each of the elements of the underlying unlawful act can be proved. **7-030**

R. v Lamb [1967] 2 Q.B. 981 (Court of Appeal, Criminal Division):

Lamb, in jest, with no intention of doing any harm, pointed a revolver at his best friend who was similarly treating the incident as a joke. He knew there were two bullets in the chambers but as neither bullet was in the chamber opposite the barrel he did not foresee any danger. He pulled the trigger; this rotated the cylinder and placed a bullet opposite the barrel so that it was struck by the striking pin. The bullet was fired and the friend killed. Three experts agreed that Lamb's mistake was natural for somebody unfamiliar with the way the revolver mechanism worked. Lamb was convicted of manslaughter and appealed. **7-031**

SACHS J:

> "The trial judge took the view that the pointing of the revolver and pulling of the trigger was something which could of itself be unlawful even if there was no attempt to alarm or intent to injure.
>
> It was no doubt on that basis that he had before commencing his summing-up stated that he was not going to 'involve the jury in any consideration of the niceties of the question whether or not the' action of the 'accused did constitute or did not constitute an assault': and thus he did not refer to the defence of accident or the need for the prosecution to disprove accident before coming to a conclusion that the act was unlawful.
>
> Mr Mathew, [counsel for the Crown] however, had at all times put forward the correct view that for the act to be unlawful it must constitute at least what he then termed 'a technical assault.' In this court moreover he rightly conceded that there was no evidence to go to the jury of any assault of any kind. Nor did he feel able to submit that the acts of the defendant were on any other ground unlawful in the criminal sense of that word. Indeed no such submission could in law be made: if, for instance, the pulling of the trigger had had no effect because the striking mechanism or the ammunition had been defective no offence would have been committed by the defendant.

62 Mitchell and Mackay, "Investigating Involuntary Manslaughter: An Empirical Study of 127 Cases" (2011) 31 O.J.L.S. 165–191, 186.

Another way of putting it is that *mens rea*, being now an essential ingredient in manslaughter (compare *Andrews v Director of Public Prosecutions* and *R. v Church*) that could not in the present case be established in relation to the first ground except by proving that element of intent without which there can be no assault."

(Sachs J went on to rule that, while an appropriately directed jury could have convicted Lamb of manslaughter by gross negligence, the jury had not been so directed and so the verdict could not stand.)

Appeal allowed

7-032 This case can be contrasted with that of *Larkin*[63] where D brandished a razor at a man in order to terrify him. His mistress fell against the razor, cut her throat and died. Larkin's conviction for manslaughter was upheld. In this case, unlike *Lamb*, there was clearly an unlawful act, namely, an assault by intentionally terrifying the man.[64]

Where an unlawful act has been committed which can easily be proved, the prosecution will usually rely on this species of manslaughter rather than attempting to prove either reckless manslaughter or gross negligence manslaughter. One exception to this was the case of *Willoughby*[65] in which D was convicted of manslaughter and arson[66] after the person whom he had recruited to help him set fire to his pub in order to collect on the insurance was killed in the resulting explosion. What is surprising about this case is that the prosecution based their case on gross negligence, arguing that D owed the deceased a duty of care and breached that duty in failing to ensure that he was safe during the enterprise of destroying the pub, thereby causing his death. Whilst the issue for the Court of Appeal was whether or not a duty of care was owed to V by D,[67] the court expressed some dismay in relation to the prosecution's tactics:

"... [i]t would have been preferable and much simpler if this case had been left to the jury on the basis of death caused by an unlawful and dangerous act."[68]

7-033 The converse of this prosecutorial mistake can be seen in the case of *Meeking*,[69] where D was prosecuted for constructive manslaughter where gross negligence manslaughter would have been more appropriate. Here, D was a passenger in her husband's car, and the pair had been arguing. Without

---

63 *R. v Larkin (Henry)* [1943] K.B. 174; (1944) 29 Cr. App. R. 18 CA.

64 cf. *R. v Arobieke* [1988] Crim. L.R. 314 CA where a conviction for manslaughter was quashed on the basis of lack of an unlawful act. The victim, terrified of D, had run away and electrocuted himself. D had, however, done no more than look for V which was insufficient to amount to an assault.

65 *R. v Willoughby (Keith Calverley)* [2004] EWCA Crim 3365; [2005] 1 W.L.R. 1880 CA.

66 Contrary to the Criminal Damage Act 1971 ss.1(2) and (3).

67 It was held that D did owe V a duty of care. However, this was not because he owned the property in which V died, but because he engaged V to participate in spreading petrol with a view to setting fire to the premises for the D's benefit.

68 *Willoughby* [2004] EWCA Crim 3365 at [24].

69 *R. v Meeking (Caroline)* [2012] EWCA Crim 641; [2013] R.T.R. 4.

warning, she pulled on the handbrake whilst the car was travelling at 60mph, causing the car to spin out of control and collide with an oncoming vehicle. D's husband was killed in the collision, and she was prosecuted for manslaughter on the basis of committing the unlawful act of interfering with a motor vehicle so as to endanger road users, contrary to the Road Traffic Act 1988 s.22A(1)(b). The Court of Appeal upheld her conviction,[70] but noted that:

> "[i]t was perhaps an unnecessary complication for the prosecution to have relied on unlawful act manslaughter in this case, rather than taking what might have seemed the more natural approach of presenting the case as one of gross negligence manslaughter, but on the facts of this case we find it impossible to conclude that the jury could have come to any other verdict than guilty if the case had been prosecuted as one of gross negligence manslaughter."[71]

It was held in *Jennings*[72] that it is necessary to identify the unlawful act upon which a prosecution for constructive manslaughter is based. In this case, the Crown had relied on the offence of carrying an offensive weapon, contrary to the Prevention of Crimes Act 1953 s.1, but, as it had not been proved that the knife was an offensive weapon, there was no unlawful act for the purposes of constructive manslaughter. Consequently, in *Grey,* D's conviction for manslaughter was quashed by the Court of Appeal in the absence of the prosecution having proved the presence of an unlawful act.[73] In this case, D had objected to V's presence on a bicycle on a shared-use footpath, and had waved her arms and shouted at V. V had wobbled on her bike and fallen off it, into the path of a car on the adjacent road. The Court of Appeal noted that the only unlawful act ("base offence") that could have been applicable was common assault. However, the jury had not been directed to consider whether the elements of common assault were present, resulting in a finding that the conviction was unsafe.

In the earlier case of *Cato,*[74] D injected his friend, at the friend's request, with a mixture of heroin and water. The friend died. The unlawful act here was administering a noxious thing contrary to the Offences against the Person Act 1861 s.23. Since then, there followed a string of similar cases where the courts struggled to establish that an unlawful act upon which liability for manslaughter can be constructed has been committed. Whilst it is clear that the Offences against the Person Act 1861 s.23 can be relied upon where D is the one to actually inject the syringe into the victim,[75] the principles of causation will usually prevent the supplier of a drug who does not themselves inject the deceased from being held liable for the death of the drug-taker.[76] This was confirmed by the House of Lords in *Kennedy (No.2),*[77] clarifying the law and holding that facilitating or contributing to the administration was not sufficient **7–034**

70 It is not at all clear that it was right to do so. As noted by Ashworth, the unlawful act on which the manslaughter was based is primarily one of negligence, and the case should not have been allowed to go ahead on the basis of unlawful act manslaughter, on the authority of *Andrews v DPP* [1937] A.C. 576; (1938) 26 Cr. App. R. 34 HL: Ashworth, Commentary to *R. v Meeking (Caroline)* [2013] Crim. L.R. 333.

71 *Meeking* [2013] R.T.R. 4 at [14].

72 *R. v Jennings* [1990] Crim. L.R. 588 CA.

73 *R. v Grey (Auriol)* [2024] EWCA Crim 487.

74 *R. v Cato (Ronald Philip)* [1976] 1 W.L.R. 110; (1976) 62 Cr. App. R. 41 CA.

75 It would appear that V's consent to be injected will not provide a defence. Where the drug injected is not unlawful but a prescription drug under the Medicines Act 1968, it is an offence to administer such a drug under s.67 of that statute unless the person doing so is an appropriate practitioner. It has been held that consent to injection (in this case of insulin) by a non-practitioner is, as a matter of policy, no defence to a charge of manslaughter: *R. v Andrews (Christopher Kenneth)* [2002] EWCA Crim 3021; [2003] Crim. L.R. 477.

76 See Ch.2 above, paras 2–074–2–075.

77 *R. v Kennedy (Simon)* [2007] UKHL 38; [2008] 1 A.C. 269.

to amount to "administering" of "causing another to administer" the drug. In this case, D had prepared a syringe of heroin and handed it to V, who injected themselves and returned the syringe to the D, who then left the room. As seen in Ch.2 where this case is extracted, the House of Lords reversed the decision of the Court of Appeal, which had managed to uphold the conviction on the basis that both D and V had acted together in administering the drugs, and quashed the conviction. Lord Bingham conceded that:

> "It is possible to imagine factual scenarios in which two people could properly be regarded as acting together to administer an injection. But nothing of the kind was the case here."

7-035 As noted by Ormerod, it is difficult to imagine a scenario that Lord Bingham had in mind, aside from where D injects the deceased.[78] Whilst *Burgess; Byram*[79] provides the potential for such a factual scenario (where D had not only prepared the syringe of heroin but also helped V locate a vein), the Court of Appeal did not have the opportunity to provide any authority on that issue, and merely quashed D's conviction for the reason that his guilty plea was offered on the basis of a point of law decided erroneously (before the House of Lords' judgment in *Kennedy (No.2)*).[80] What *Kennedy (No.2)* does make clear, however, is that the answer to the question of whether a D who supplies drugs to V to self-inject can ever be guilty of manslaughter is "never", so long as V is a fully informed adult making a voluntary (FDI) decision to self-inject.[81]

Given that *Kennedy (No.2)* confirms that in situations where D has assisted in some way in the taking of drugs, but has not injected V, there is, in reality, no suitable unlawful act to form the basis of a manslaughter prosecution without intractable problems of causation being presented, perhaps a more radical approach is necessary.

Catherine Elliott and Claire de Than, "Prosecuting the Drug Dealer When a Drug User Dies" (2006) 69 M.L.R. 986–995, 992:

7-036 "There is a persuasive case for the creation of a new statutory offence for deaths caused by the supply of drugs. The difficulties the courts have had fitting such cases within the current confines of manslaughter, culminating in the case of *Kennedy (No.2)*, would be avoided. Any new statutory

---

78 D. Ormerod, Commentary to *Kennedy (No.2)* [2008] 3 Crim. L.R. 222, 225.

79 *R. v Burgess (Lee)* [2008] EWCA Crim 516.

80 There are a number of convictions for manslaughter that have been quashed on this basis since the House of Lords' decision in *Kennedy (No.2)* [2007] UKHL 38; [2008] 1 A.C. 269: e.g. *R. v Glover (Peter)* [2008] EWCA Crim 1782; *R. v Keen (Lisa Marie)* [2008] EWCA Crim 1000.

81 Although it is not possible for such a supplier to be liable under the heading of constructive manslaughter they might, depending on the circumstances, be liable for gross negligence manslaughter. If they were present when the drugs were taken and assumed responsibility for V by taking action to help them, e.g. by giving mouth to mouth resuscitation or administering adrenalin, but failed to take further action such as calling for an ambulance when the V's condition failed to improve, they might be liable for gross negligence manslaughter. These are the circumstances in which the defendant in *R. v Phillips (Ben)* [2013] EWCA Crim 358; [2013] 2 Cr. App. R. (S.) 67 pleaded guilty to gross negligence manslaughter. See also *R. v Evans (Gemma)* [2009] EWCA Crim 650; [2009] 2 Cr. App. R. 10, where the defendant drug supplier was liable for manslaughter, having created a dangerous situation. Additionally, it might be possible, particularly following *R. v Rebelo (Bernard)* [2021] EWCA Crim 306; [2021] 4 W.L.R. 52 (see para.7-056 below) for a drug supplier to be guilty of gross negligence manslaughter where it is argued that the supply of the drug itself represented a breach of a duty of care, and that this breach caused death where V's act of taking the drugs was not "free, deliberate and informed" due to V's addiction and/or other mental health problems.

offence will be controversial and raises complex issues. Defining its parameters raises difficult questions, but such an offence could be defined in the following terms:

1 (a) A person is liable for an offence if he or she knowingly and unlawfully supplies to the victim a Category A controlled drug, or is an accessory to the supply of the controlled drug or is part of a conspiracy to supply the controlled drug, and the person's conduct causes the death of the victim.

(b) A person will be held to have caused the death of the victim when:

(i) he or she does an act which makes a more than merely negligible contribution to its occurrence or
(ii) he or she omits to do an act which might have prevented its occurrence.

(c) A person does not cause a result where, after he or she does such an act or makes such an omission, an act or event occurs

(i) which is the immediate and sufficient cause of the result;
(ii) which he or she did not foresee, and
(iii) which could not in the circumstances reasonably have been foreseen.

(d) A defence to this offence will apply where the defendant has attempted to seek medical assistance for the victim within a reasonable time. [E.]

The main benefits of this statutory offence over and above the existing common law offences are that it would satisfy the requirements of fair labelling, while at the same time allowing for an extended concept of causation; limit the problems with mens rea and establish a statutory defence.

For the purposes of fair labelling, it would be an inadequate response for the law to simply impose liability for the supply of drugs without acknowledging that a death has occurred. By having this homicide offence, a moral message is being conveyed that the accused deserves to be associated with the victim's death and to suffer condemnation and punishment for it."

(ii) The unlawful act must be dangerous

It is clear that constructive manslaughter requires more than simply an unlawful act which causes death. The unlawful act must be a dangerous one, in the sense that it must expose the victim to the risk of some bodily harm resulting therefrom. The fact that an act is unlawful does not necessarily mean that it is dangerous. The requirement of dangerousness is a separate matter requiring proof.[82] **7–037**

82 *Scarlett* (1994) 98 Cr. App. R. 290.

R. v CHURCH [1966] 1 Q.B. 59 (COURT OF CRIMINAL APPEAL):

7–038 The appellant knocked a woman unconscious. On failing to revive her he threw her into a river where she drowned. He appealed against his conviction for manslaughter on the ground of a misdirection by the trial judge.

EDMUND-DAVIES LJ:

"In the judgment of this court [the trial judge's direction on unlawful act manslaughter] . . . was a misdirection. It amounted to telling the jury that, whenever any unlawful act is committed in relation to a human being which resulted in death there must be, at least, a conviction for manslaughter. This might at one time have been regarded as good law: . . . But it appears to this court that the passage of years has achieved a transformation in this branch of the law and, even in relation to manslaughter, a degree of *mens rea* has become recognised as essential . . . [T]he conclusion of this court is that an unlawful act causing the death of another cannot, simply because it is an unlawful act, render a manslaughter verdict inevitable. For such a verdict inexorably to follow, the unlawful act must be such as all sober and reasonable people would inevitably recognise must subject the other person to, at least, the risk of some harm resulting therefrom, albeit not serious harm . . .

[However the trial judge's direction was not sufficiently defective to warrant quashing the conviction; further, the defendant might have been convicted on grounds of criminal negligence.]"

Appeal dismissed

DPP v NEWBURY [1977] A.C. 500 (HOUSE OF LORDS):

7–039 The appellants, two boys aged 15, pushed part of a paving stone off the parapet of a railway bridge. The stone struck an oncoming train, went through the glass window of the driver's cab and killed a guard who was sitting next to the driver. The boys were convicted of manslaughter. The Court of Appeal dismissed their appeal but certified the following point of law:

"Can a defendant be properly convicted of manslaughter, when his mind is not affected by drink or drugs, if he did not foresee that his act might cause harm to another?"

LORD SALMON:

"In *R. v Larkin*, Humphreys J said:

'Where the act which a person is engaged in performing is unlawful, then if at the same time it is a dangerous act, that is, an act which is likely to injure another person, and quite inadvertently the doer of the act causes the death of that other person by that act, then he is guilty of manslaughter.'

> I agree entirely . . . that that is an admirably clear statement of the law which has been applied many times. It makes it plain (a) that an accused is guilty of manslaughter if it is proved that he intentionally did an act which was unlawful and dangerous and that that act inadvertently caused death and (b) that it is unnecessary to prove that the accused knew that the act was unlawful or dangerous. This is one of the reasons why cases of manslaughter vary so infinitely in their gravity. They may amount to little more than pure inadvertence and sometimes to little less than murder . . .
>
> The test is still the objective test. In judging whether the act was dangerous the test is not did the accused recognise that it was dangerous but would all sober and reasonable people recognise its danger."
>
> *Appeal dismissed*

These authorities make it clear that whether the act was dangerous is an objective test, and does not require D to be aware that their act might cause any degree of harm. How, though, is the reasonable bystander test applied? In *Watson*,[83] it was held that the "sober and reasonable" bystander was to be endowed with whatever knowledge D possessed. In this case, D and another burgled an elderly man's house and verbally abused him. The victim was suffering from a serious heart condition and died an hour-and-a-half later. It was held that the unlawful act, the burglary, lasted throughout the time D was on the premises and during that time D must have become aware of the victim's frailty and age. The question then was whether a sober and reasonable bystander, armed with this knowledge, would have recognised that the burglary was likely to expose that elderly man to the risk of some harm. In *Ball*,[84] however, it was emphasised that the sober and reasonable bystander could *not* be endowed with any mistaken belief held by D. In this case, D fired at V thinking his gun contained blanks (he kept live and blank cartridges together and had grabbed a handful when picking up his gun). Such an act was unquestionably dangerous from the required objective point of view. In *Dawson*,[85] it was held that the unlawful act must expose V to the risk of some physical harm. Shock or pure emotional disturbance produced by terror would not suffice. However, there could be liability for manslaughter if it was likely that the shock would cause a physical injury, for example, cause a heart attack.[86] Furthermore, in *R. v M*[87] it was made clear that the sober and reasonable bystander does not have to foresee the specific sort of physical harm caused. In that case, a seemingly fit doorman died after suffering from an aneurysm following his dealings with an affray committed by the Ds. It was held by the Court of Appeal that the judge was wrong to rule that a jury could not reasonably conclude that any sober and reasonable person, having knowledge that the Ds had during the incident, would realise there was a risk of V suffering an aneurysm rather than some other injury from a fall or blow. The test, as set out in *Church*, was only whether "some harm" was foreseeable.[88] **7-040**

---

83 *R. v Watson (Clarence Archibald)* [1989] 1 W.L.R. 684; (1989) 89 Cr. App. R. 211 CA.

84 *R. v Ball* [1989] Crim. L.R. 730 CA.

85 *R. v Dawson (Brian)* (1985) 81 Cr. App. R. 150; (1985) 149 J.P. 513 CA.

86 *R. v Williams (Barry Anthony)* [1992] 1 W.L.R. 380; [1992] 2 All E.R. 183 at 191.

87 *R. v M* [2012] EWCA Crim 2293; [2013] 1 Cr. App. R. 10.

88 In *Rebelo* [2021] EWCA Crim 306, the second of two appeals against convictions for manslaughter on different grounds, the Court of Appeal explained that the initial conviction for unlawful act manslaughter was quashed on the basis that placing unsafe food on the market (in this case by selling the diet drug DNP on the internet) was not a dangerous act.

It is important to note that the question is not whether the offence on which the manslaughter charge is based is dangerous generally, but whether it was dangerous in the particular circumstances of the case. In *Bristow*,[89] the Ds burgled a vehicle-repair business located down a private track on a farm, the plan being to steal a number of vehicles. The owner of the business disturbed the Ds and was killed as the Ds escaped in their own vehicle and a stolen vehicle, running him over. In the Court of Appeal, Treacy LJ noted that:

> "This is not a case like *Dawson* or *Watson* where the circumstances demonstrating the risk of harm to the occupier of property did not arise until a point during the burglary or at all. Whilst burglary of itself is not a dangerous crime, a particular burglary may be dangerous because of the circumstances surrounding its commission."[90]

The relevant circumstances of the case were that the only means of escape from the scene of the crime involved a single track road, passing the victim's home and another property. It was clear that the burglary involved a risk of being interrupted and, if that happened, the means of escape (driving at speed down a single track road) created the risk of harm to any person intervening.

(iii) The unlawful act must cause the death of the victim

7–041 This last point can again be illustrated by contrasting the decision in two cases involving the unlawful act of affray: *R. v M*, above, and *Carey*. In *Carey*,[91] it was stressed that the dangerousness of the act must correspond with its unlawfulness. In this case, one group of young people attacked another at a local beauty spot. The deceased was punched in the face and suffered only minor bruises, but in running away from the scene she suffered a heart attack from which she died. It was found that she suffered from a severely diseased heart and the doctors were of the view that the precipitating factor which led to her death was her running away from the incident. At trial, the Ds were convicted of affray and manslaughter. The unlawful act upon which manslaughter was based was that of affray. On appeal, although the convictions for affray were upheld, the convictions for manslaughter were quashed. The court took the view that the only unlawful and *dangerous* act upon which the Ds could have been convicted was that of assault. However, in this case, although it could be said that the act of assault was dangerous, it was not the cause of death. The conviction for manslaughter could not be based on the unlawful act of affray, which was not dangerous "in the relevant sense" on the facts of the case. However, the affray in *R. v M* was seen to be dangerous in the relevant sense. In his commentary on *Carey*,[92] Ormerod argues that it seems entirely possible that a conviction for manslaughter could have been founded upon an unlawful and dangerous act of assault (rather than affray) on the basis that D caused the victim to die by triggering a previously undiagnosed medical condition, since D must take V as they find them.[93]

---

89 *R. v Bristow (Terrence)* [2013] EWCA Crim 1540; [2014] Crim. L.R. 457.
90 *Bristow* [2013] EWCA Crim 1540 at [34].
91 *R. v Carey (Claire Anne)* [2006] EWCA Crim 17; [2006] Crim. L.R. 842.
92 *Carey* [2006] Crim. L.R. 842.
93 Ormerod cites *Hayward* (1908) 21 Cox C.C. 692 in support of this argument.

However, the approach taken in *Carey* was replicated by the Court of Appeal in the case of *R. v DJ*.[94] In this case, a group of young boys shouted abuse and spat at an elderly man who was playing cricket with his son. They also threw stones, one of which hit the man. The man, who had suffered from coronary heart disease, had a heart attack and died. The unlawful and dangerous act relied on was the throwing of stones (a battery) rather than the abuse, given that, as noted by Gage LJ: "insults and spittle can hardly be described as dangerous acts".[95] The difficulty for the prosecution at this point, however, was that it was not clear what the factual cause of the heart attack was. From the expert evidence, although it was possible that it was the incident as a whole, including the battery, which caused the heart attack, "it was impossible . . . for the jury to exclude the insults and spitting as the sole cause of . . . death".[96] Since it was impossible to establish that the battery, as the unlawful and dangerous act, was a cause of death, D's conviction for manslaughter was quashed.

Other rules of causation may also be relevant here. As seen elsewhere, V's own voluntary act, for example of self-injection of drugs, may break the causal chain between D's unlawful and dangerous act (e.g. of supplying drugs) and V's death.[97] However, once factual and legal causation can be proved, linking the unlawful and dangerous act to V's death, no further link in terms of *mens rea* need be proven. This explains the House of Lords' decision In *Att-Gen's Reference (No.3 of 1994)*,[98] in which D was not liable for the murder of his intended victim's baby, since the mens rea towards the mother could not be transferred to the foetus and then to the baby, but he was liable for manslaughter because all the elements of unlawful act manslaughter were satisfied, and D had caused the baby's death. **7–042**

Thus, when considering the elements of constructive manslaughter, each of the elements above come under the heading of actus reus (unlawful act; dangerous act; act caused death). The only mens rea requirement of constructive manslaughter is that D committed the underlying unlawful act with the necessary mens rea of that offence.[99] Accordingly, if the charge is based on an unlawful act of arson, for example, D must have intended or been subjectively reckless as to causing damage to property belonging to another by fire.[100]

3. Gross negligence manslaughter

Most manslaughter cases involve the commission of an unlawful act, usually an assault,[101] and so constructive manslaughter is easier to establish. Accordingly, gross negligence manslaughter is usually **7–043**

94 *R. v DJ* [2007] EWCA Crim 3133.

95 *DJ* [2007] EWCA Crim 3133 at [33].

96 *DJ* [2007] EWCA Crim 3133 at [53].

97 *Kennedy* [2008] 1 A.C. 269.

98 *Att-Gen's Reference (No.3 of 1994)* [1998] A.C. 245. See para.3–135.

99 See *DPP v Newbury (Neil)* [1977] A.C. 500; [1976] 2 W.L.R. 918 HL.

100 The approach in *R. v Church (Cyril David)* [1966] 1 Q.B. 59; [1965] 2 W.L.R. 1220 and *Newbury* [1977] A.C. 500 was again confirmed in the case of *R. v JF* [2015] EWCA Crim 351; [2015] 2 Cr. App. R. 5, in which convictions for manslaughter were upheld on proof of mens rea of simple arson (criminal damage), where the Ds had at the same time been acquitted of arson, being reckless as to whether life was endangered. The Ds were found by the jury to have had foresight of the risk of damage to the building by fire, and it was not necessary for them to have foreseen a risk of endangering life in order to be convicted of manslaughter. However, they had foreseen some harm and so even if the *Church* test had been modified so as to be a subjective test, they would still have been liable.

101 In a sample of 127 cases of involuntary manslaughter only one case was identified as having been a clear case of gross negligence manslaughter: Mitchell and Mackay, "Investigating Involuntary Manslaughter: An Empirical Study of 127 Cases" (2011) 31 O.J.L.S. 165–191, 171.

utilised where D is engaged in a prima facie lawful activity, such as treating a patient or taking care of an aged aunt, from which death results.[102] Mere negligence does not suffice for manslaughter: gross negligence must be established. The classic statement on gross negligence is that of Lord Hewitt CJ in *Bateman* that:

> ". . . in order to establish criminal liability the facts must be such that, in the opinion of the jury, the negligence of the accused went beyond a mere matter of compensation between the subjects and showed such disregard for the life and safety of others as to amount to a crime against the state and conduct deserving of punishment."[103]

For a period, it was thought that this basis of manslaughter had been subsumed into *Lawrence* recklessness manslaughter.[104] However, in the following case, the House of Lords jettisoned *Lawrence* in the context of manslaughter and reverted to the test of gross negligence.

R. v Adomako [1995] 1 A.C. 171 (House of Lords):

7–044 The defendant was an anaesthetist in an eye operation which involved paralysing the patient. During the operation, a tube became disconnected from the ventilator. The defendant became aware that something was wrong four-and-a-half minutes after the disconnection when an alarm sounded. However, the checks he carried out failed to reveal the disconnection. The patient suffered a cardiac arrest and died. The defendant was convicted of manslaughter and appealed.

LORD MACKAY OF CLASHFERN LC:

> "For the prosecution it was alleged that the appellant was guilty of gross negligence in failing to notice or respond appropriately to obvious signs that a disconnection had occurred and that the patient had ceased to breathe. In particular the prosecution alleged that the appellant had failed to notice at various stages during the period after disconnection and before the arrest either occurred or became inevitable that the patient's chest was not moving, the dials on the mechanical ventilating machine were not operating, the disconnection in the endotracheal tube, that the alarm on the ventilator was not switched on and that the patient was becoming progressively blue. Further the prosecution alleged that the appellant had noticed but failed to understand the significance of the fact that during this period the patient's pulse had dropped and the patient's blood pressure had dropped.
>
> Two expert witnesses gave evidence for the prosecution. Professor Payne described the standard of care as 'abysmal' while Professor Adams stated that in his view a competent

---

102 But see *Willoughby* [2005] 1 Cr. App. R. 29 where, despite the possibility of proving manslaughter via the unlawful act route, the prosecution chose instead to argue their case based on gross negligence.

103 *R. v Bateman (Percy)* (1925) 19 Cr. App. R. 8 CCA.

104 *R. v Seymour (Edward John)* [1983] 2 A.C. 493; [1983] 3 W.L.R. 349 HL.

anaesthetist should have recognised the signs of disconnection within 15 seconds and that the appellant's conduct amounted to 'a gross dereliction of care'.

On behalf of the appellant it was conceded at his trial that he had been negligent. The issue was therefore whether his conduct was criminal . . .

The jury convicted the appellant of manslaughter . . . The Court of Appeal (Criminal Division) dismissed the appellant's appeal against conviction but certified that a point of law of general public importance was involved in the decision to dismiss the appeal, namely: 'in cases of manslaughter by criminal negligence not involving driving but involving a breach of duty is it a sufficient direction to the jury to adopt the gross negligence test . . . [as in *Bateman*] without reference to the test of recklessness as defined in *R. v Lawrence (Stephen)*?' . . .

[Counsel for the appellant] criticised the concept of gross negligence which was the basis of the judgment of the Court of Appeal submitting that its formulation involved circularity, the jury being told in effect to convict of a crime if they thought a crime had been committed and that accordingly using gross negligence as the conceptual basis for the crime of involuntary manslaughter was unsatisfactory . . .

[Lord Mackay begins with reference to *R v Bateman]* . . .

Next I turn to *Andrews v Director of Public Prosecutions* [1937] A.C. 576 which was a case of manslaughter through the dangerous driving of a motor car . . . Lord Atkin said: **7–045**

> '. . . Simple lack of care such as will constitute civil liability is not enough: for purposes of the criminal law there are degrees of negligence: and a very high degree of negligence is required to be proved before the felony is established. Probably of all the epithets that can be applied 'reckless' most nearly covers the case. It is difficult to visualise a case of death caused by reckless driving in the connotation of that term in ordinary speech which would not justify a conviction for manslaughter: but it is probably not all-embracing, for 'reckless' suggests an indifference to risk whereas the accused may have appreciated the risk and intended to avoid it and yet shown such a high degree of negligence in the means adopted to avoid the risk as would justify a conviction. If the principle of *Bateman's* case is observed it will appear that the law of manslaughter has not changed by the introduction of motor vehicles on the road. Death caused by their negligent driving, though unhappily much more frequent, is to be treated in law as death caused by any other form of negligence: and juries should be directed accordingly.'

In my opinion the law as stated in these two authorities is satisfactory as providing a proper basis for describing the crime of involuntary manslaughter. Since the decision in *Andrews* was a decision of your Lordships' House, it remains the most authoritative statement of the present law which I have been able to find . . . On this basis in my opinion **the ordinary principles of the law of negligence apply to ascertain whether or not the defendant has been in breach of**

> **a duty of care towards the victim who has died. If such breach of duty is established the next question is whether that breach of duty caused the death of the victim. If so, the jury must go on to consider whether that breach of duty should be characterised as gross negligence and therefore as a crime. This will depend on the seriousness of the breach of duty committed by the defendant in all the circumstances in which the defendant was placed when it occurred. The jury will have to consider whether the extent to which the defendant's conduct departed from the proper standard of care incumbent upon him, involving as it must have done a risk of death to the patient, was such that it should be judged criminal.** [Emphasis added]
>
> 7–046 It is true that to a certain extent this involves an element of circularity, but in this branch of the law I do not believe that is fatal to its being correct as a test of how far conduct must depart from accepted standards to be characterised as criminal. This is necessarily a question of degree and an attempt to specify that degree more closely is I think likely to achieve only a spurious precision. The essence of the matter which is supremely a jury question is whether having regard to the risk of death involved, the conduct of the defendant was so bad in all the circumstances as to amount in their judgment to a criminal act or omission . . .
>
> I consider it perfectly appropriate that the word 'reckless' should be used in cases of involuntary manslaughter, but as Lord Atkin put it 'in the ordinary connotation of that word'. Examples in which this was done, to my mind, with complete accuracy are *R. v Stone [and Dobinson]* [1977] Q.B. 354 and *R. v West London Coroner Ex p. Gray* [1988] Q.B. 467.
>
> In my opinion it is quite unnecessary in the context of gross negligence to give the detailed directions with regard to the meaning of the word 'reckless' associated with *R. v Lawrence* . . .
>
> For these reasons I am of the opinion that this appeal should be dismissed and that the certified question should be answered by saying:
>
>> 'In cases of manslaughter by criminal negligence involving a breach of duty, it is a sufficient direction to the jury to adopt the gross negligence test set out by the Court of Appeal in the present case following *Rex v Bateman* and *Andrews v Director of Public Prosecutions* and that it is not necessary to refer to the definition of recklessness in *R. v Lawrence*, although it is perfectly open to the trial judge to use the word 'reckless' in its ordinary meaning as part of his exposition of the law if he deems it appropriate in the circumstances of the particular case.'"
>
> *Appeal dismissed*

7–047 Following this, the courts have further developed the law to the extent that it is now established that there are five conditions to be satisfied for this type of manslaughter:

(1) D must owe a duty of care to V;
(2) D must breach that duty;

(3) the breach of duty gave rise to an obvious and serious risk of death;
(4) the breach of duty caused death; and
(5) the breach must amount to gross negligence.[105]

(i) Duty of care

The first requirement that there be a "duty of care" has the potential to cause confusion. It is simply not helpful to import civil concepts into this area of the criminal law without discrimination. The following decision states that concepts such as "duty of care" and "breach" do not bear the same meaning in the criminal law as under the law of tort. **7–048**

R. v WACKER [2003] 1 CR. APP. R. 22 (COURT OF APPEAL, CRIMINAL DIVISION):

The appellant attempted to smuggle illegal Chinese immigrants into the country in a lorry. On arrival at Dover, one of the containers was found to contain the dead bodies of most of the immigrants. The appellant was convicted of 58 offences of manslaughter and appealed. **7–049**

KAY LJ:

"[Counsel for the appellant] submitted that the first question to be decided was whether applying 'the ordinary principles of the law of negligence', the appellant owed to those in the container a duty of care. He submitted that one of the general principles of the law of negligence, known by the Latin maxim of *ex turpi causa non oritur actio*, was that the law of negligence did not recognise the relationship between those involved in a criminal enterprise as giving rise to a duty of care owed by one participant to another . . .

We venture to suggest that all right minded people would be astonished if the propositions being advanced on behalf of the appellant correctly represented the law of the land. The concept that one person could be responsible for the death of another in circumstances such as these without the criminal law being able to hold him to account for that death even if he had shown not the slightest regard for the welfare and life of the other is one that would be unacceptable in civilised society . . .

[I]t is clear that the criminal law adopts a different approach to the civil law in this regard [because] . . . the very same public policy that causes the civil courts to refuse the claim points in a quite different direction in considering a criminal offence. The criminal law has as its function the protection of citizens and gives effect to the state's duty to try those who have deprived citizens of their rights of life, limb or property. It may very well step in at the precise moment when civil courts withdraw because of this very different function. The withdrawal of a civil remedy has nothing to do with whether as a matter of public policy

105 Conditions 1, 2, 4 and 5 are set out in Lord Mackay's judgment in *R. v Adomako (John Asare)* [1995] 1 A.C. 171; [1994] 3 W.L.R. 288 HL, reproduced in bold above. Condition 3 has since been added by further cases, as explained below. These five requirements are set out in *R. v Rose* [2017] EWCA Crim 1168 at [77]; [2018] Q.B. 328.

the criminal law applies. The criminal law should not be disapplied just because the civil law is disapplied. It has its own public policy aim which may require a different approach to the involvement of the law.

Further, the criminal law will not hesitate to act to prevent serious injury or death even when the persons subjected to such injury or death may have consented to or willingly accepted the risk of actual injury or death. By way of illustration, the criminal law makes the assisting another to commit suicide a criminal offence and denies a defence of consent where significant injury is deliberately caused to another in a sexual context (*Brown* [1994] 1 A.C. 212). The state in such circumstances has an overriding duty to act to prevent such consequences . . .

[W]e can see no justification for concluding that the criminal law should decline to hold a person as criminally responsible for the death of another simply because the two were engaged in some joint unlawful activity at the time or, indeed, because there may have been an element of acceptance of a degree of risk by the victim in order to further the joint unlawful enterprise. Public policy, in our judgment, manifestly points in totally the opposite direction."

Appeal dismissed

7–050 Although this case rejects the criminal law's use of the civil law defence of *ex turpi causa,* Herring and Palser argue that, in other regards, whether a duty of care existed was decided on the same basis as a tort case would have been.[106] However, they recognise that there are disadvantages in the criminal law determining whether a duty of care exists on the same basis as the civil law. They note that in the law of tort, if a victim is partly to blame for the resulting harm, this can be recognised in one of three ways: damages can be reduced due to contributory negligence; the principle of *volenti non fit injuria* is applied; or D is given the defence of *ex turpi causa*. In the criminal law, on the other hand, V's role is irrelevant:

> "Criminal proceedings are not about balancing the responsibility between the defendant and the victim, but in determining whether the activity engaged in by the defendant is sufficiently harmful and blameworthy in the eyes of the state to justify a criminal conviction."[107]

Despite this recognition, however, they conclude that:

> "Though there may be calls for the criminal law to develop its own understanding of the duty of care, distinct from that in tort, we would suggest that use is made of the development of the concept of a duty of care in the law of tort as the normal meaning of 'duty of care' in gross negligence manslaughter but recognising that there may be rare cases where the judge can direct that the tortious duty will not be relied upon. These will be in cases where the blameworthiness of the

106 J. Herring and E. Palser, "The Duty of Care in Gross Negligence Manslaughter" [2007] Crim. L.R. 24, 33.
107 Herring and Palser, "The Duty of Care in Gross Negligence Manslaughter" [2007] Crim. L.R. 24, 37.

> victim leads to there being no duty of care in tort when it may still be appropriate to impose a criminal liability (e.g. the *ex turpi causa* doctrine) and cases involving omissions, where the court will need to find not only a duty of care, but also a duty to act."[108]

There is something to be said for this suggestion. If the civil law is not to be employed here, it is difficult to see what the *Adomako* requirement of "duty of care" actually means. Possibly the requirement has most significance for the law relating to manslaughter by omission. Herring and Palser list circumstances in which a duty of care arises in tort cases for omissions, showing that generally there is overlap between the criminal law and civil law.[109] As in the criminal law, a duty of care arises in tort where there is a voluntary assumption of responsibility; a special relationship of vulnerability or control between parties; and where D creates a source of danger. An additional source of duty of care in tort is where D's position as occupier gives rise to a duty in respect of the safety of lawful visitors. There is clearly no such duty to act under the criminal law.[110] This raises the question of whether there is a difference between a duty to act (omissions) and a duty of care (manslaughter). In *Evans*,[111] these two terms were used interchangeably but, as the example of the occupier demonstrates, there can be cases where there is a duty of care in civil law but no duty to act in criminal law. Furthermore, the application of these principles may differ in tort law. **7–051**

A separate question is that of who it is that decides in a particular case whether a duty of care arose. In *Willoughby*, the Court of Appeal has stressed that "whether a duty of care exists is a matter for the jury once the judge has decided that there is evidence capable of establishing a duty".[112] However, the more recent case of *Evans*[113] clarified the law on this point. As noted in Ch.2, this case confirmed that a duty of care arises in omissions leading to death where D has created a dangerous situation. It also clearly stated that whether D owes a duty of care is a question of law. The jury should be directed on what the law is, for example whether a duty exists if they find certain facts to be established, and it is for them to decide the facts.

(ii) Breach of duty

Whether D breached the duty of care owed to V is a question of fact for the jury. The question is whether D has departed from the standards of a reasonably competent and careful person in D's position, which will often involve the jury listening to expert evidence about what might be expected of someone with the same qualifications in cases of those who breach a duty in a professional context. The same will be true when considering whether the breach was bad enough to amount to gross negligence (the fifth requirement, below). **7–052**

---

108 Herring and Palser, "The Duty of Care in Gross Negligence Manslaughter" [2007] Crim. L.R. 24, 39–40.
109 Herring and Palser, "The Duty of Care in Gross Negligence Manslaughter" [2007] Crim. L.R. 24, 32.
110 Herring and Palser, "The Duty of Care in Gross Negligence Manslaughter" [2007] Crim. L.R. 24, 37. *Willoughby* [2004] EWCA Crim 3365 can be seen as a rejection of this principle in the criminal law.
111 *Evans* [2009] 2 Cr. App. R. 10.
112 *Willoughby* [2004] EWCA Crim 3365. Whether a duty of care exists under the Corporate Manslaughter and Corporate Homicide Act 2007 s.2(5) is a question of law. This is discussed in Ch.3.
113 *Evans* [2009] 2 Cr. App. R. 10.

(iii) Obvious and serious risk of death

7-053 The argument that an actual awareness of a risk of death is required for manslaughter in order to bring the law in line with the subjective test applied in *G*[114] was rejected in the case of *Mark*,[115] in which the Court of Appeal made it clear that the case of *G* had no bearing on the test for gross negligence manslaughter. The test is an objective one. Although Lord Mackay in *Adomako* was keen to move away from the language of objective (*Lawrence*) recklessness, more recent cases have resurrected some of that language by requiring that it was reasonably foreseeable that D's breach of duty give rise to an *obvious and serious* risk of death. The Court of Appeal discussed this on two occasions in the context of examining what would be obvious to a medical practitioner, given the information available to them. In both *Rose*[116] and *Rudling*[117] the practitioners involved failed to carry out examinations that would have uncovered an obvious risk of death to their patient. The question for the court was whether the knowledge that the Ds *would* have had, if they had carried out such examinations, should be taken into account by the jury in deciding whether there was an obvious and serious risk of death. In *Rose*, an optometrist who failed to carry out a routine eye test that would have identified that V was suffering from a life-threatening condition, was convicted of manslaughter. However, the conviction was quashed on appeal on the basis that, in assessing the reasonable foreseeability of a serious and obvious risk of death, it is not appropriate to take into account what D *would have* known but for her breach of duty. Laird has criticised the approach taken by the Court of Appeal in these cases:

> "There is no principled distinction between the case of the optometrist who conducts an internal investigation negligently and the optometrist who is so negligent that he or she does not even attempt an internal investigation. If anything, the latter seems more culpable than the former. For this reason, it is irrational that he or she is at less risk of being held criminally liable. The most worrying aspect of the Court of Appeal's judgment [in *Rose*], however, is that in endowing the reasonably competent GP/optometrist/surgeon, etc. with D's shortcomings, it has undermined the objective nature of the test set out in *Adomako*."[118]

Stark, on the other hand, welcomes the Court of Appeal's approach in *Rose*, arguing that it accords better with a belief-based approach to culpability:[119]

---

114 *R. v G* [2003] UKHL 50; [2004] 1 A.C. 1034.

115 *R. v Mark (Alan James)* [2004] EWCA Crim 2490. See also *R. v Misra (Amit)* [2004] EWCA Crim 2375; [2005] 1 Cr. App. R. 21.

116 *Rose* [2017] EWCA Crim 1168.

117 *Rudling* [2016] EWCA Crim 741; (2016) 151 B.M.L.R. 79. *Rudling* was a case in which a GP failed to make a home visit to examine a young patient whose mother had telephoned with concerns about V's symptoms on a Friday evening, telling the mother to "phone again after the weekend". Unbeknown to the GP, the boy was suffering from a rare auto-immune disease and did not survive the weekend. The Court of Appeal upheld the judge's ruling of no case to answer, on the basis that there was insufficient evidence to show that a reasonably competent GP should have recognised an obvious and serious risk to life as a result of the information provided by the mother.

118 K. Laird, Case comment on *R. v Rose* [2018] Crim. L.R. 76–81, 81.

119 See also Greenberg, who supports the approach in *Rose* [2017] EWCA Crim 1168 as an example of an "evidence-relative" conception of criminal negligence: A. Greenberg, "Why Criminal Responsibility for Negligence Cannot be Indirect" (2021) 80(3) *Cambridge Law Journal* 489–514.

> "*Rose* captures something crucial about when the controversial concept of negligence can legitimately be recognised as part of the criminal law's culpability arsenal. It does so by bringing gross negligence closer to more familiar and less controversial fault elements by focussing on the defendant's beliefs and what conclusions about risks she could reasonably be expected to draw from them."[120]

Whether one agrees with Laird or Stark as to whether the test of gross negligence should be more objective or more subjective, they both agree that the courts' inconsistent approach is a problem in practice. In *Winterton*,[121] a construction site manager was convicted of the manslaughter of a labourer who was killed when a trench collapsed on him. The Court of Appeal distinguished the facts from those in *Rose* to make it clear that where all the information showing that there was an obvious and serious risk of death was available to D at the time of the breach, D would not avoid liability on the basis that he had failed to take notice of the information available to him. The appeal against conviction was dismissed. In *Kuddus*,[122] on the other hand, a restaurant owner/chef who had not been made aware of a note warning of an allergy to nuts on a takeaway order he was preparing, had his conviction for manslaughter quashed on the basis that he was not "armed with the notice" of the facts giving rise to an obvious and serious risk of death.[123] **7–054**

(iv) Breach caused death

The jury must also find that the breach caused the death of V, applying the rules on causation discussed in Ch.2. **7–055**

It is worth mentioning a recent case where the application of pre-existing rules, as discussed in Ch.2, led to what could be seen to be a surprising outcome. In *Broughton*,[124] D supplied his girlfriend, V, with a cocktail of Class A drugs (including 2CP) at a music festival. The couple had left the well-populated area and gone into local woodland at around 4.30pm, where V took the drugs. D filmed V with his phone, with her consent. The videos show V becoming more and more agitated. An hour and a quarter later, D phoned V's mother and the mother could hear V in the background sounding distressed, and D trying to calm her down. Throughout the evening V's family tried to keep in contact with D and encouraged him to take V to the medical tent. However, D stayed where he was until around 11.45pm, when he said he would try to carry her to get help, but did not want to leave her. A short time later, D emerged from the wood and told security guards his girlfriend had taken an overdose. Her body was found at around 1am.

The issue at trial for gross negligence manslaughter was whether it could be proved that timely medical intervention would have saved V's life. The prosecution argued that by failing to obtain medical help in

---

120 F. Stark, "In Praise of Rose" (2019) 8 Arch. Rev. 7–10.

121 *R. v Winterton (Andrew)* [2018] EWCA Crim 2435; [2019] 2 Cr. App. R. 12.

122 *R. v Kuddus (Mohammed Abdul)* [2019] EWCA Crim 837; [2019] 1 W.L.R. 5199.

123 The restaurant manager who was aware of the warning, however, was convicted for manslaughter and did not appeal his conviction. This accords with the earlier decision of *R. v Zamman (Mohammed Khalique)* [2017] EWCA Crim 1783; [2018] 1 Cr. App. R. (S.) 26, in which a restaurant owner admitted that he knew that customers with peanut allergies were at risk of fatal consequences if they ingested peanut.

124 *R. v Broughton (Ceon)* [2020] EWCA Crim 1093; [2021] 1 W.L.R. 543.

time, D had breached his duty and that breach made a substantial contribution to the cause of death. The defence case was that by the time there was any breach of duty, it was already too late, and that getting help would have made no difference; the omission was not a substantial contribution to the cause of death. One of the expert witnesses stated "[i]n view of the lack of previously documented deaths from 2CP, the combined effect of three stimulant drugs and the unknown mechanism that resulted in Louella's death, it is not possible to state beyond reasonable doubt that earlier medical intervention would have been able to save Louella's life once she had ingested the 2CP".[125]

The Court of Appeal stated that in cases such as this there needs to be a clear focus on when the condition of V reached the threshold of serious and obvious risk of death, what the accused should have done then and the prospects of survival at that point. The court was of the view that the expert evidence was all that the jury had to assist them with the question of causation. The expert's opinion that at 9.10pm there was a 90% chance of survival, with medical help, left a realistic possibility that she could have died even if help had been sought. Thus, the evidence was not capable of establishing causation to the criminal standard and the case should have been withdrawn from the jury, and the appeal against conviction was allowed. This case perhaps highlights the particular problems of proving causation in cases of omission.[126]

7–056 It might, then, be more straight forward to prove a causal link between a positive act and death. In *Rebelo*,[127] D had supplied the diet drug Dinitrophenol (DNP) via the internet to V, a 21-year-old student with a history of poor mental health and self-harm who suffered from bulimia nervosa and had developed a psychological addiction to DNP. After taking eight of the capsules in quick succession, she died. D had originally been convicted of unlawful and dangerous act manslaughter as well as gross negligence manslaughter, but his convictions were quashed[128] on the basis that D's unlawful act of placing unsafe food on the market[129] was not dangerous in the relevant sense (on application of the *Church* test) and the judge had not given sufficient direction on the issue of causation in relation to gross negligence manslaughter. The case was sent back to the Crown Court for a second trial, at which the Crown argued their case based on gross negligence manslaughter alone and D was again convicted. On appeal against this second conviction, D sought to argue that the judge's direction relating to causation, addressing as it did the issue of whether V's act of taking the pills was a free, deliberate and informed act, which broke the chain of causation according to the House of Lords decision in *Kennedy (No.2)*,[130] was again a misdirection. The Court of Appeal rejected this argument, finding that the judge had provided a clear direction to the jury which allowed them to make a decision as to whether V's decision to take the pills was "fully free", bearing in mind her mental health issues.

---

125 *Broughton* [2020] EWCA Crim 1093 at [62].

126 It also appears to be at odds with *Misra* [2004] EWCA Crim 2375, where D's conviction for gross negligence manslaughter was affirmed despite evidence that if D had intervened, V would have had a 95% chance of survival.

127 *Rebelo* [2021] EWCA Crim 306.

128 *Rebelo* [2019] EWCA Crim 633.

129 D had committed the offence of placing an unsafe food on the market contrary to Regulation 19 of the Food and Hygiene (England) Regulations 2017.

130 *Kennedy (No.2)* [2007] UKHL 38.

(v) The breach must amount to gross negligence

It is clear that the critical requirement for this type of manslaughter is that there has been gross negligence, which forms the normative mens rea requirement for the offence. The test is simply one of determining how far the standard of behaviour of D departs from accepted standards and this is "supremely a jury question".[131] The jury must assess whether, having regard to the risk of death, the conduct was so bad in all the circumstances as to be criminal. **7-057**

There are substantial problems with the decision of the House of Lords in *Adomako*. The main criticism is that the test to be employed by juries is circular. They should find D's actions criminal (manslaughter) if they think the conduct falls so far below proper standards of care that it should be judged criminal. This arguably amounts to leaving questions of law to the jury as it is for them to decide whether the conduct amounts to a crime. Furthermore, no guidance is given as to how far below accepted standards of behaviour D's conduct must fall other than that the conduct must be "so bad" in all the circumstances as to warrant criminalisation as manslaughter. This absence of any legally defined criteria renders the law highly uncertain and increases the chances of inconsistency of verdicts.

However, the Court of Appeal has endeavoured to rebuff such criticisms.

R. v Misra and Srivastava [2005] 1 Cr. App. R. 21 (Court of Appeal, Criminal Division):

Two Senior House Officers failed to diagnose and treat a case of toxic shock syndrome in a patient following an operation on his knee. The patient died. On appeal against conviction for manslaughter the appellants argued that the circular test of gross negligence in *Adomako* breached arts 6 (right to a fair trial) and 7 (no punishment without law) of the ECHR because it leads to lack of certainty.[132] **7-058**

JUDGE LJ:

> "[62] On proper analysis [of the test in *Adomako*] . . . the jury is not deciding whether the particular defendant ought to be convicted on some unprincipled basis. The question for the jury is not whether the defendant's negligence was gross, and whether *additionally*, it was a crime, but whether his behaviour was grossly negligent and *consequently* criminal. This is not a question of law, but one of fact, for decision in the individual case.
>
> [63] On examination, this represents one example, amongst many, of problems which juries are expected to address on a daily basis . . .

131 per Lord Mackay in *Adomako* [1995] 1 A.C. 171.

132 Article 7 provides that "no-one shall be held guilty of any criminal offence on account of any act or omission which did not constitute a criminal offence under national or international law at the time when it was committed nor shall a heavier penalty be imposed than the one that was applicable at the time the criminal offence was committed".

> [64] In our judgment the law is clear. The ingredients of the offence have been clearly defined, and the principles decided in the House of Lords in *Adomako*. They involve no uncertainty."
>
> *Appeal dismissed*

7-059 Thus, once the jury has agreed that it was reasonably foreseeable that D's breach of duty created an obvious and serious risk of death, whether D is liable for manslaughter (assuming that causation is not in issue) is dependent on their interpretation of whether what D did, in breaching their duty in such circumstances, was bad enough to amount to a crime. The danger is not only that juries are left to decide for themselves what gross negligence means, with little guidance on whether or not an individual is liable, but also that there will be variations in prosecution practice. Quick found that there was a greater propensity to prosecute cases of medical negligence (where death has resulted) in some geographical regions than others, largely depending on the ability of prosecutors to find medical experts willing to give evidence for the prosecution, who "effectively *decide* on the vague legal question of whether the conduct is grossly negligent".[133] Griffiths and Sanders have found that the CPS only decides to bring a prosecution in 5% of cases of medical manslaughter referred to it by the police.[134] In 95% of cases, then, a prosecution is not brought. In 27% of cases this was because no breach of duty of care was found in relation to the individuals investigated. In 44% of cases the CPS concluded that they could not prove causation.[135] In 17% of cases the CPS were of the opinion that the negligence displayed failed to reach the "gross" threshold, although on Griffiths and Sanders' assessment there was clear evidence of gross negligence in around half of the cases.[136]

4. Sentencing involuntary manslaughter

7-060 Involuntary manslaughter of any species carries a maximum life sentence, leaving the sentencing judge with a wide-ranging discretion to do justice in a particular case. Because of the gap between the blameworthiness of D and the outcome of their act, discussed in the next section, cases of constructive manslaughter lead to difficult sentencing decisions for judges. Some assistance in this difficult task has been available since 2018, when the Sentencing Council published its much needed definitive guideline for sentencing manslaughter cases.[137] This is divided into sections to deal separately with unlawful act manslaughter and gross negligence manslaughter, followed by sections for voluntary manslaughter (discussed below). It follows the format of all recent sentencing guidelines in setting out step one to establish the offence category, determined by culpability (since the harm is constant throughout), followed by step two to identify the starting point and category range, determined by a non-exhaustive list of mitigating and aggravating factors. For unlawful act manslaughter, the most

133 O. Quick, "Prosecuting 'Gross' Medical Negligence: Manslaughter, Discretion, and the Crown Prosecution Service" (2006) 33 J. Law and Society 421, 448.

134 D. Griffiths and A. Sanders, "The Road to the Dock: Prosecution Decision-Making in Medical Manslaughter Cases" in Griffiths and Sanders, *Bioethics, Medicine and the Criminal Law, Vol.2, Medicine, Crime and Society* (Cambridge: CUP, 2013), p.136.

135 Griffiths and Sanders, "The Road to the Dock: Prosecution Decision-Making in Medical Manslaughter Cases" in Griffiths and Sanders, *Bioethics, Medicine and the Criminal Law, Vol.2, Medicine, Crime and Society* (2013), p.140.

136 Griffiths and Sanders, "The Road to the Dock: Prosecution Decision-Making in Medical Manslaughter Cases" in Griffiths and Sanders, *Bioethics, Medicine and the Criminal Law, Vol.2, Medicine, Crime and Society* (2013), p.143.

137 Sentencing Council, *Manslaughter: Definitive Guideline* (2018).

serious cases involving very high culpability may result in a determinate sentence of up to 24 years' imprisonment. Examples of manslaughter at the bottom end of the culpability scale, for example where there was no intention to cause any harm and no obvious risk of anything more than minor harm, are likely to result in only one to four years' custody. The offence range for gross negligence manslaughter is shorter, spanning from one to 18 years' imprisonment. In relation to medical manslaughter cases, mitigating factors acknowledge the external pressures which may have contributed to a breach of a duty of care when working in an underfunded National Health Service, as arguably occurred in the case of *Bawa-Garba*:[138] These mitigating factors are that:

"• for reasons beyond the offender's control, the offender lacked the necessary expertise, equipment, support or training which contributed to the negligent conduct;
- for reasons beyond the offender's control, the offender was subject to stress or pressure (including from competing or complex demands) which related to and contributed to the negligent conduct;
- for reasons beyond the offender's control, the negligent conduct occurred in circumstances where there was reduced scope for exercising usual care and competence;
- the negligent conduct was compounded by the actions or omissions of others beyond the offender's control."[139]

5. Evaluation of involuntary manslaughter

In cases where a charge of manslaughter is brought, the law here raises, yet again, the fundamental question of what importance should be attached to the actual harm done. If D has acted with gross negligence, or has committed an unlawful act, why should they not simply be punished for that gross negligence or for that unlawful act? Why should they be punished for the more serious crime of manslaughter merely because their actions cause death—if that death was not within their range of contemplation? **7-061**

Criminal Law Revision Committee, 14th Report, Offences Against the Person, 1980, Cmnd.7844, paras 120–121, 124:

"120 . . . Suppose that A strikes B and gives him a bleeding nose; B, unknown to A, is a haemophiliac and bleeds to death. Or, A strikes B who falls and unluckily hits his head against a sharp projection and dies. Or A chases B with the object of chastising him; B runs away, trips and falls into a river in which he drowns. In each of these cases, although A is at fault and is guilty of an assault or of causing injury, his fault does not extend to the causing of death or to the causing of serious injury which he did not foresee and in some cases could not reasonably have foreseen. In our opinion, they should not be **7-062**

---

138 *R. v Bawa-Garba (Hadiza)* [2016] EWCA Crim 1841; [2016] Inquest L.R. 320. In this case, a six-year-old child died after being admitted to hospital. His death was attributed to Dr Bawa-Garba's failure to call the consultant, given the patient's continued deterioration, but it was also accepted that there were "multiple systemic failures" beyond the control of Dr Bawa-Garba. Despite this, she was convicted of gross negligence manslaughter and her conviction was upheld on appeal. It has been argued that the merits of restorative justice should be explored as an appropriate outcome in such cases: A.-M. Farrell, A. Alghrani and M. Kazarian, "Gross Negligence Manslaughter in Healthcare: Time for a Restorative Justice Approach?" (2020) 28(3) *Medical Law Review* 526–548.

139 Sentencing Council, *Manslaughter: Definitive Guideline* (2018), p.13.

treated as manslaughter because the offender's fault falls too far short of the unlucky result. So serious an offence as manslaughter should not be a lottery . . . [T]here seems to be no reason for calling it manslaughter. Indeed, the name is positively objectionable for several reasons, among which are the fact that it gives a false idea of the gravity of the defendant's moral offence and that there is always the possibility that it may receive a punishment going beyond that appropriate to the assault."

7-063 Is it right that someone who commits what might be a fairly minor assault, or act of criminal damage, should be liable for causing death where circumstances combine to result in a fatal outcome? As with the GBH rule for murder, there is a clear lack of correspondence between the required mens rea for unlawful act manslaughter and the actus reus of causing death. For gross negligence manslaughter, there is no requirement that D advert to the risk of death, despite that being also part of the actus reus. If an anesthetist, such as the defendant in *Adomako*, were to breach their duty resulting in lack of oxygen to the brain which, due to circumstances outside D's control, resulted in severe brain damage rather than death, D would not be liable for any criminal offence (although he would be liable under civil law). Whether it is right that criminal liability should be dependent on outcome luck has been a hotly debated issue over the last few decades.[140]

Jeremy Horder: "A Critique of the Correspondence Principle in Criminal Law" [1995] Crim. L.R. 759–770, 764

7-064 "Suppose I am unlawfully cleaning my gun in the garden, and it goes off. My neighbour, V, given a severe shock by the noise, consequently dies of a heart attack. Despite my unlawful act, this is probably not manslaughter, as the risk of some harm to V was not obvious. This conclusion might be the same even if the unsuspecting V dies of shock after I deliberately discharged the gun close to him, in order to frighten him. Paying scant regard to the nature of the unlawful act, the law makes a conviction hang principally on whether the risk of resulting harm was obvious. This gets things the wrong way around. In the second case, the fact that I deliberately wrong V arguably changes my normative position vis à vis the risk of adverse consequences of that wrongdoing to V, whether or not foreseen or reasonably foreseeable. Subject to any questions about causation, I should be criminally responsible in the second case, but not in the first. In the first case, my unlawful conduct is not directed at V, so (if my liability is not to depend crudely on causation and the unlawfulness of my actions) its relevance should be merely evidential: can it be inferred that I foresaw harm, or should obviously have foreseen it? Yet if, as in the second case, my unlawful act is meant to wrong V, its relevance is normative, and not merely evidential. Its deliberateness changes my relationship with the risk of adverse consequences stemming therefrom, for which I may now be blamed and held criminally responsible, irrespective of their reasonable foreseeability.

. . . Where I deliberately fire the gun close to the unsuspecting V, I have made my own bad luck (or, rather, made V's bad luck my own) when V is killed by the shock, by directing my efforts towards harming V. This is not so in the case where V is killed when the gun goes off while being cleaned.

140 In relation to non-fatal offences against the person, see above para.5-054.

Such cases are cases of "pure" (bad) luck. None the less, the more foreseeable the outcome the more tainted the purity of D's 'pure' bad luck in producing it; hence the possibility of a manslaughter conviction, even in cases of 'pure' bad luck, where the purity of D's 'pure' bad luck is entirely corrupted by the grossness of his negligence."

The significance of a D changing their "normative position" towards their victim has come under question by Ashworth in the following extract. Ashworth points out that it is assumed that a change in normative position should make a D who engaged in a violent attack liable for a more serious offence than they foresaw, but we are not told why this is. **7–065**

Andrew Ashworth, "Change of Normative Position: Determining the Contours of Culpability in Criminal Law" (2008) 11 New Criminal L. Rev. 232–256, 250–252:

"To illustrate some of the issues we may take the case of *Williams* [1996] 2 Crim. App. (S) 72, where D pushed V and slapped her once, with the result that she fell backwards and cracked her head on a heater, which severed an artery and caused her death. Accepting D's plea of guilty to manslaughter, the judge commented that V's death 'was fortuitous and, in a sense, accidental.' There is, in principle, a whole range of possible fault elements in such a case. To take four, D could have been (i) walking past V when he tripped over, pushing her against the heater; (ii) leaving the house after burgling it when he encountered V and in his surprise tripped over, pushing her against the heater; (iii) assaulting V by pushing and slapping her once, as in *Williams* itself; or (iv) attacking her with punches and kicking her in the abdomen, causing her to fall against the heater. In which of these scenarios does D change his normative position, or cross a moral threshold, sufficiently for liability for manslaughter? Of course there is a labelling issue here, and we should assume that the crime of manslaughter is understood to be a lower grade of homicide than murder, requiring a lesser degree of fault. Case (i) can be eliminated swiftly, on the ground that D did not intend to assault V or indeed to commit any wrong against V. Perhaps, in order to retain our focus, we can also deal swiftly with case (iv): kicking V in the abdomen suggests an intention to cause at least moderate injury, if not serious injury, and might therefore be regarded as a sufficient fault element for a crime of manslaughter. But what about cases (ii) and (iii)? Is it satisfactory to say that case (iii) ought to be sufficient for manslaughter because D has intentionally assaulted V, thereby changing his normative position in relation to harms that might result to V (including death)? . . . [W]hen Gardner considered the distinction between the offenses of common assault and assault occasioning bodily harm, he argued that committing an assault was a sufficient change of normative position to justify holding D liable for any actual bodily harm that might result, and that the law puts people on notice about that. Can that argument be extended to manslaughter, even if, to adopt Gardner's imagery, one asks the question by travelling 'downhill' from D's responsibility for causing V's death? **7–066**

In relation to case (ii), can one say that D has sufficiently changed his normative position by intentionally committing a crime against V (burglary), so that it is fair to hold him criminally liable for any resulting harms? One obvious difference between cases (ii) and (iii) is that the crimes of burglary and assault form part of different families of offences. That is a restrictive consideration that points away from the unlawful act approach, which allows the intentional commission of *any* crime to constitute a sufficient change of normative position or crossing of a moral threshold, and we [can see] that Horder's formulation of the malice principle restricts it to conduct wrongfully directed at a particular type of interest. So, if we return to case (iii), the key question is how the moral connection between a death caused by D and D's intentional assault on V is to be established. If D intended nothing more than a common assault, and if the possibility of causing death was statistically very low (as it must be if a simple assault is intended), is it merely a question of putting D on notice of the risk of a manslaughter conviction if death should by mischance ensue? If notice alone were sufficient, that would raise the question whether due notice could convert case (ii) into a morally satisfactory foundation for a manslaughter conviction."

7–067 The Law Commission, following a number of failed attempts to reform the law of homicide, most recently recommended that two versions of manslaughter be recognised in statute:

Law Commission No.304, Murder, Manslaughter and Infanticide (2006), para.2.163:

7–068 "We recommend that manslaughter should encompass:

(1) killing another person through gross negligence ('gross negligence manslaughter'); or
(2) killing another person

  (a) through the commission of a criminal act intended by the defendant to cause injury, or
  (b) through the commission of a criminal act that the defendant was aware involved a serious risk of causing some injury ('criminal act manslaughter')."

7–069 Gross negligence manslaughter under these recommendations would follow the contours of the current law, and accords with the principle of correspondence to the extent that it requires gross negligence as to the risk of *death* (an objective, rather than subjective link).[141] The recommended replacement for the current law of unlawful and dangerous act/constructive manslaughter, however, perpetuates a version of manslaughter where D can be liable in the absence of either foresight of death (subjective mens rea), or a foreseeable obvious risk of death (normative mens rea). Interestingly, Stark has recently suggested that:

141 Although subjectivists would argue that the correspondence principle requires D to have foreseen the particular harm caused, Tadros argues that the correspondence principle can be "refined" in line with objectivist reasoning to require not that D foresaw the harm, but that D *ought* to have foreseen the particular harm with which the offence is concerned: V. Tadros, *Criminal Responsibility* (Oxford: OUP, 2007), p.95.

> "unlawful and dangerous act manslaughter should at the very least be reformed to require at minimum reasonable foreseeability of death, or simply collapsed into gross negligence manslaughter."[142]

His suggestion that gross negligence manslaughter could cater for both of the current forms of manslaughter results from his reasoning that if death is a reasonably foreseeable consequence of engaging in a particular wrongful and unlawful activity, and death results from that activity, then negligence becomes an appropriate basis on which to hold D responsible. This has the attraction of moving away from having to explain liability for manslaughter on the basis of "change of normative position" and is in many senses far simpler. It allows the principle of correspondence to be respected through the requirement of a reasonably foreseeable risk of death, and thus arguably limits the role that luck plays in determining criminal responsibility. Stark further opines that examples of "one punch" manslaughter (such as, arguably, *Williams*) should be a case of battery, not manslaughter.[143] However, his suggestion would involve considerable further amendment to the Law Commission's recommendations, and some might argue that fair labelling requires that we keep the two forms of manslaughter distinct from one another in order to communicate the difference in the context and culpability of someone who kills after engaging in unlawful, rather than otherwise lawful, activity.

B. VOLUNTARY MANSLAUGHTER

A D who possesses malice aforethought may, when charged with murder, be convicted of the lesser crime of manslaughter if they satisfy one of three mitigating criteria. At common law, there was only one such mitigating criterion: killing under provocation. Two further partial defences were added by statute: diminished responsibility[144] and killing in pursuance of a suicide pact.[145] The main reason for the existence of these partial defences is the mandatory life sentence for murder and the need to provide the judge with discretion in sentencing in cases where the killer's blameworthiness is reduced due to some factor personal to them or the surrounding circumstances of the killing. The term voluntary manslaughter is nothing more than a convenient label for these forms of killing. Most recently, the defence of "provocation" has been abolished and replaced with a statutory partial defence of "loss of control".[146] **7-070**

142 F. Stark, "Deconstructing constructive liability" [2023] Crim. L.R. 118–135, 127.

143 Stark, "Deconstructing constructive liability" [2023] Crim. L.R. 118–135, 127.

144 Homicide Act 1957 s.2.

145 Homicide Act 1957 s.4.

146 Coroners and Justice Act 2009 s.56.

1. Loss of control

(i) Introduction

7-071 In *Duffy*,[147] a young woman killed her husband after having been savagely beaten by him; in *Camplin*,[148] a 15-year-old boy who had been buggered[149] killed his assailant; in *Bedder*,[150] a man, who knew himself to be impotent, stabbed to death a prostitute who had jeered at him and kicked him in the groin after he had unsuccessfully tried to have intercourse with her. All claimed that they had been provoked into losing their self-control and killing their victims.

To what extent should we blame such persons for their actions and hold them criminally responsible? If we can envisage situations in which violence of this sort would be a natural response to their suffering, how is our understanding of their plight to be reflected in the law? By no punishment? By less punishment?

Provocation, now replaced by loss of control, has allowed murder to be reduced to manslaughter[151] because it has been felt unjust to subject D to the full rigour of a conviction for murder; in other words, the courts have wished to avoid the mandatory life sentence. A conviction for manslaughter, on the other hand, gives the courts the necessary flexibility to impose whatever sentence is deemed appropriate. Loss of control, or its predecessor provocation, is not a defence to any other crime as no other serious offence in England carries a fixed penalty. For other crimes, loss of control can be taken into account as a mitigating factor, lessening the severity of the sentence.

7-072 Under the common law of provocation, a D to a charge of murder was provided with a partial defence if the killing could be attributed to D's angry response to some act of provocation from V or from a third party. The test for the jury in such cases was elaborated on in the Homicide Act 1957 s.3, since repealed.

The defence was traditionally divided into two tests: (i) a subjective test that D must have lost their self-control; and (ii) an objective test that D must have responded in a way that the reasonable man would have responded. The law proved troublesome and controversial in respect to both of these tests, and led to a great deal of instability in the case law. Some called for complete abolition of the defence, whilst others argued for reform. The Law Commission sought to widen the ambit of the provocation defence by allowing emotions other than anger, namely fear, to form the basis of the defence, whilst at the same time attempting to narrow the defence in other ways.[152] The view it took was that so long as the Government resists calls for the abolition of the mandatory life sentence for murder, it is pointless to consider the arguments for and against complete abolition of the partial defence.[153]

---

147 *R. v Duffy* [1949] 1 All E.R. 932 CA.

148 *R. v Camplin (Paul)* [1978] A.C. 705; [1978] 2 W.L.R. 679 HL.

149 This was an offence at the time of *Camplin* [1978] A.C. 705. It means anally raped.

150 *Bedder v DPP* [1954] 1 W.L.R. 1119; (1954) 38 Cr. App. R.133 HL.

151 In *Marks* [1998] Crim. L.R. 676, the Court of Appeal accepted that the defence of provocation was available to an accomplice to murder.

152 Law Commission Paper No.290, *Partial Defences to Murder* (2004).

153 Law Commission Paper No.290, *Partial Defences to Murder* (2004), para.3.35.

(ii) Rationale of the law

In reviewing the law of provocation and making recommendations for its reform, the Law Commission naturally attempted to identify the rationale of the law's response, so that it could identify the aims of the law, all the better to develop improvements. However, the Law Commission described the rationale underlying the defence as "elusive".[154] One possible rationale of the law's response historically is that in weighing the competing interests of the eventual victim against those of D it decides that the victim, by participating in the chain of events, is to *some* extent responsible for their own demise. V, therefore, loses some of their claim to be protected by the law. Viewed in this light one could regard provocation as a partial justification for D's actions and an historical analysis of the defence affords considerable support for this. The common-law defence of provocation was of ancient origin but: **7-073**

> "it emerged in recognisably modern form in the late seventeenth and early eighteenth centuries. It comes from a world of Restoration gallantry in which gentlemen . . . acted in accordance with a code of honour which required insult to be personally avenged by instant angry retaliation . . . To show anger 'in hot blood' for a proper reason by an appropriate response was not only permissible but the badge of a man of honour. The human frailty to which the defence of provocation made allowance was the possibility that the man of honour might overreact and kill when a lesser retaliation would have been appropriate. Provided that he did not grossly overreact in the extent or manner of his retaliation, the offence would be manslaughter."[155]

However, while it may well be that for at least some of its history the defence of provocation was a partial justification,[156] the law, by the 19th century had already begun to shift in emphasis. Rather than focusing upon the rightfulness of anger, judges "preferred to look upon provocation as something which temporarily deprived the accused of his reason"[157] and were concerned with whether there had been a loss of control. However, this loss of control had to manifest itself in a particular way: extreme anger. This trend continued and the law seems to have regarded the defence as a "partial excuse". The law ceased to be solely concerned with the victim-offender relationship. Provocation could be pleaded even if V was not the provoking agent[158] (in other words, was entirely innocent in the affair). V need not have committed an "unlawful act";[159] indeed, V may have been far too young to appreciate the quality of their actions at all.[160] In short, the thrust of the inquiry shifted from V (and their provocative acts) to D (and their loss of self-control)[161] and the rationale of the defence became "compassion for human

154 Law Commission Paper No.290, *Partial Defences to Murder* (2004), para.3.21.

155 *R. v Smith (Morgan James)* [2001] 1 A.C. 146 at [159]–[160] per Lord Hoffmann; [2000] 3 W.L.R. 654, drawing upon the work of J. Horder, *Provocation and Responsibility* (Oxford: OUP, 1992).

156 See A. Ashworth, "The Doctrine of Provocation" [1976] C.L.J. 292; P. Alldridge, "The Coherence of Defences" [1983] Crim. L.R. 665.

157 *Smith* [2001] 1 A.C. 146 per Lord Hoffmann at [160].

158 e.g. *R. v Davies (Peter John Brinley)* [1975] Q.B. 691; [1975] 2 W.L.R. 586 CA. The requirement in s.3 that the provocation resulted from "things done or said" does, however, suggest that human activity must have been involved: D could not plead, e.g. that they were provoked by bad weather.

159 See Alldridge, "The Coherence of Defences" [1983] Crim. L.R. 665.

160 As in *R. v Doughty (Stephen Clifford)* (1986) 83 Cr. App. R. 319; [1986] Crim. L.R. 625 CA.

161 See, generally, on this transmutation of provocation from a partial justification to a partial excuse, Alldridge, "The Coherence of Defences" [1983] Crim. L.R. 665, 669–672.

infirmity".[162] As in cases of diminished responsibility and duress, the law recognised that people are not in perfect control of their emotions and actions, particularly when subject to great pressure.

7-074 It may be that the underlying rationale of the replacement defence of loss of control still contains elements of both excuse and justification. The current law requires that D lost control and this can be categorised as an excusatory element. Furthermore, it also insists that they did so in circumstances in which a person with a normal degree of tolerance and self-restraint might well have done the same. This latter requirement mirrors the objective test developed under the common law of provocation, in relation to which it has been suggested that it retains an element of justification in the defence.[163] The law also recognises, however, that it is sometimes natural to react to a threat of serious violence through the use of excessive, pre-emptive violence, brought on by a state of fear.

(iii) The law

Coroners and Justice Act 2009 s.54: Partial defence to murder: loss of control:

7-075 "(1) Where a person ('D') kills or is a party to the killing of another ('V'), D is not to be convicted of murder if—

- (a) D's acts and omissions in doing or being a party to the killing resulted from D's loss of self-control,
- (b) the loss of self-control had a qualifying trigger, and
- (c) a person of D's sex and age, with a normal degree of tolerance and self-restraint and in the circumstances of D, might have reacted in the same or in a similar way to D.

(2) For the purposes of subsection (1)(a), it does not matter whether or not the loss of control was sudden.
(3) In subsection (1)(c) the reference to "the circumstances of D" is a reference to all of D's circumstances other than those whose only relevance to D's conduct is that they bear on D's general capacity for tolerance or self-restraint.
(4) Subsection (1) does not apply if, in doing or being a party to the killing, D acted in a considered desire for revenge.
(5) On a charge of murder, if sufficient evidence is adduced to raise an issue with respect to the defence under subsection (1), the jury must assume that the defence is satisfied unless the prosecution proves beyond reasonable doubt that it is not.
(6) For the purposes of subsection (5), sufficient evidence is adduced to raise an issue with respect to the defence if evidence is adduced on which, in the opinion of the trial judge, a jury, properly directed, could reasonably conclude that the defence might apply.

---

162 *Hayward* (1908) 21 Cox C.C. 692 at 694 per Lord Tindal CJ.

163 See further, Ashworth, "The Doctrine of Provocation" [1976] C.L.J. 292; J. Horder, "Autonomy, Provocation and Duress" [1992] Crim. L.R. 706, 707–711; Horder, *Provocation and Responsibility* (1992).

(7) A person who, but for this section, would be liable to be convicted of murder is liable instead to be convicted of manslaughter.
(8) The fact that one party to a killing is by virtue of this section not liable to be convicted of murder does not affect the question whether the killing amounted to murder in the case of any other party to it."

The common law defence of provocation was abolished by s.56 of the 2009 Act. As under the pre-existing common law, the burden of proof is on the prosecution to prove that the defence is not satisfied (s.54(5)) once the judge is satisfied that there is sufficient evidence that would enable a jury to decide that the defence might apply (s.54(6)).[164] **7–076**

In comparison to the Homicide Act 1957 s.3, the new provision provides far more detail, and the elements of the defence are further clarified in s.55, as discussed below. The three main requirements to be addressed are essentially:

a) loss of self-control (subjective test);
b) the loss of self-control was attributable to a qualifying trigger (subjective and objective element);
c) whether someone of D's sex and age with a normal degree of tolerance and self-restraint and in might have reacted in the same or similar way in such circumstances (objective test).

(a) Loss of self-control

This first requirement mirrors that under the common law defence of provocation, which was meant to exclude from the ambit of the defence planned or revenge killings. No matter how severe the provocation, if D was in control at the time of the killing, there was no evidence upon which the defence could be based.[165] Although the new law now explicitly excludes pure revenge killings through s.54(4), the loss of control requirement is retained, since it is the law's desire to make concessions to "human frailty" which provides a great deal of rationale for the defence. This is despite the Law Commission having recommended that a reformed version of provocation jettison the need for a loss of control.[166] The question that remains, however, is what is meant by "loss of self-control"? It is clearly a subjective test: the issue is whether D lost their self-control, causing them to kill. **7–077**

Under the common law, in the majority of cases where a sudden killing followed on from a highly provocative incident, it was more or less assumed that D had lost control. However, in some cases it

---

164 In *R. v Dawes (Carlos)* [2013] EWCA Crim 322; [2013] 2 Cr. App. R. 3, the Court of Appeal emphasised the need for there to be sufficient evidence of all three elements of the defence (loss of self-control, qualifying trigger and reaction of a person of normal tolerance and self-restraint) before the judge is required to leave the defence to the jury. Furthermore, in *R. v Gurpinar (Mustafa)* [2015] EWCA Crim 178; [2015] 1 W.L.R. 3442, the Court of Appeal stated that: "A much more rigorous evaluation of the evidence had to be undertaken before the defence was left to the jury than was required under the law of provocation".

165 As in *R. v Cocker* [1989] Crim. L.R. 740 CA, where the undeniably provocative behaviour of his terminally-ill wife did *not* cause D to lose control (as it could have done) but led him *calmly* to accede to her requests to die.

166 For a discussion of the Law Commission's reasoning, and arguments that the Government was mistaken to reject it, see Horder, *Homicide and the Politics of Law Reform* (2012), Ch.8.

was more problematic and the case law was disappointing in explaining what "loss of self-control" meant. Cases referred to D not being "master of his own understanding",[167] although beyond using phrases such as "snapping", or "exploding into anger", little further attention was generally paid to this element.[168] The meaning of the term under the present law is no clearer.[169] In *Jewell*, the Court of Appeal accepted the description given in the 13th edition of *Smith and Hogan's Criminal Law*, that it is considered to mean "a loss of the ability to act in accordance with considered judgment or a loss of normal powers of reasoning".[170] Ashworth has commented that:

> "... what amounts to the loss of self-control required by s.54(1)(a) of the Coroners and Justice Act 2009 remains clouded ... One can say that a mere loss of temper is not enough, but that does not greatly advance the explanation."[171]

A fundamental change in the law has been introduced by s.54(2) which states that "it does not matter whether or not the loss of control was sudden". Under the old common law, in the case of *Duffy*,[172] it was established that the loss of self-control suffered by D had to be of a "sudden and temporary" nature. Thus, loss of self-control was equated with anger and not with fear or despair or other strong emotions. The person who killed through terror of what might happen to them was traditionally excluded from the ambit of the provocation defence if this terror did not express itself in anger.

7–078 It is worth considering how the old case law dealt with this issue, in order to understand the challenges the Law Commission faced in seeking to address such issues by removing the sudden and temporary requirement. When it existed prior to the 2009 Act, the sudden and temporary requirement had posed particular problems for abused women who had killed their abuser in circumstances where, rather than reacting immediately to a bout of abusive behaviour, they had waited until they were less likely to come under renewed attack, such as when their abuser was asleep. The courts stated that the more time "to cool down", the less likely it was that D could be regarded as acting in anger, and the more likely it was that it would be seen as "planned" or "revenge".[173] However, in re-examining the requirement that there be a sudden and temporary loss of control in cases of cumulative provocation, the courts relaxed the requirement somewhat. In *Ahluwalia*,[174] the Court of Appeal was faced with deciding what

---

167 per Tindal CJ in *Hayward* (1833) 6 C. & P. 157 at 159, repeated in *R. v Ahluwalia (Kiranjit)* (1993) 96 Cr. App. R. 133 at 138 by Taylor LCJ.

168 Horder, *Provocation and Responsibility* (Oxford: OUP, 1992), p.109; A. Ashworth, *Principles of Criminal Law*, 5th edn (Oxford: OUP, 2006), pp.265–266.

169 In *R. v Goodwin (Anthony Gerard)* [2018] EWCA Crim 2287; [2018] 4 W.L.R. 165, D killed his neighbour with a hammer. He claimed that V had attacked him with the hammer and that he had retaliated, acting in self-defence. The jury rejected the claim that he was acting in self-defence and the judge refused to leave the defence of loss of control to the jury, on the basis that D failed the third, objective, test. The Court of Appeal upheld this decision, but also questioned whether there was in fact a loss of control in this case. The fact that D himself had not claimed during his trial to have lost his self-control "will not necessarily be decisive of the issue ... But on any view, it is a very powerful point against the issue arising in such a case" (at [43]).

170 *R. v Jewell (Darren)* [2014] EWCA Crim 414 at [23].

171 A. Ashworth, Commentary to *Dawes* [2013] Crim. L.R. 770, 772.

172 *Duffy* [1949] 1 All E.R. 932.

173 The issue could be withdrawn from the jury if the delay was considerable. See, e.g. *R. v Ibrams (James David)* (1982) 74 Cr. App. R. 154 CA in which the Court of Appeal upheld the withdrawal of the defence from the jury in the case of two appellants who had delayed several days before retaliating.

174 *Ahluwalia* (1993) 96 Cr. App. R. 133.

the requirement was in the context of a D who had endured 10 years of violence and humiliation from her husband and threw petrol in his bedroom and set it alight. He sustained severe burns and died six days later and she was convicted of murder. On appeal, it was argued that the direction that there be a sudden and temporary loss of control was wrong, with counsel for the appellant suggesting that women who have been subjected frequently over a period to violent treatment may react to the final act or words by a "slow-burn" reaction rather than by immediate loss of self-control. Without accepting this argument in full, the Court of Appeal conceded that a delayed reaction would not necessarily rule out that there was a "sudden and temporary" loss of self-control.[175]

The appellant in *Ahluwalia* failed in her defence of provocation but was afforded the partial defence of diminished responsibility, based on depression caused by her being a victim of domestic violence. Thus, whilst the stringency of the requirement of "sudden and temporary" loss of self-control was lessened somewhat by the courts, it still remained an obstacle to certain classes of D successfully pleading provocation. The Government saw the abandonment of the sudden and temporary requirement under the Coroners and Justice Act as "a fresh approach which builds on the common law" and "allows for situations where D's reaction has been delayed or builds gradually."[176] The removal of the "sudden and temporary" requirement means that Ds suffering from domestic violence such as Ahluwalia might now be more likely to plead "loss of control" successfully. This is a matter to which we return below.

(b) Qualifying trigger

Under the old common law defence of provocation, D was required to have lost their self-control due to things said or done. Although, as has been discussed, the defence developed historically on the basis that V, having provoked D, lost some of their claim to be protected by the law, the modern (but no longer applicable) law of provocation did not require that V was to blame for D's loss of control, nor that they were even the cause of it. The extent to which the law rejected this rationale of the defence can be seen in the case of *Doughty*[177] where D killed his 17-day-old son in circumstances where D had had to look after both his wife and the baby since their return from the hospital. The baby was extremely restless and cried persistently, leading to D finally trying to stop the crying by placing a cushion over the baby's head and then kneeling on it. The trial judge ruled that the perfectly natural episodes of crying or restlessness by a young baby could not constitute evidence of provocation. D appealed against the conviction and the Court of Appeal held that the judge was wrong not to have left the defence of provocation to the jury on the basis that D had lost control because of things said or done. The issue for the jury would then have been, in applying the objective test, whether it was reasonable for D to have done so. **7–079**

The replacement law, however, attempts to avoid such controversies by setting out in more detail what it is that must have caused D to lose their self-control.

175 *Ahluwalia* (1993) 96 Cr. App. R. 133 at 139.
176 Ministry of Justice, *Murder, Manslaughter and Infanticide: Proposals for Reform of the Law*, CP 19/08, 2008, para.37.
177 *Doughty* (1986) 83 Cr. App. R. 319.

CORONERS AND JUSTICE ACT 2009 S.55: MEANING OF "QUALIFYING TRIGGER":

7-080 "(1) This section applies for the purposes of section 54.
(2) A loss of self-control had a qualifying trigger if subsection (3), (4) or (5) applies.
(3) This subsection applies if D's loss of self-control was attributable to D's fear of serious violence from V against D or another identified person.
(4) This subsection applies if D's loss of self-control was attributable to a thing or things done or said (or both) which—

(a) constituted circumstances of an extremely grave character, and
(b) caused D to have a justifiable sense of being seriously wronged.

(5) This subsection applies if D's loss of self-control was attributable to a combination of the matters mentioned in subsections (3) and (4).
(6) In determining whether a loss of self-control had a qualifying trigger—

(a) D's fear of serious violence is to be disregarded to the extent that it was caused by a thing which D incited to be done or said for the purpose of providing an excuse to use violence;
(b) a sense of being seriously wronged by a thing done or said is not justifiable if D incited the thing to be done or said for the purpose of providing an excuse to use violence;
(c) the fact that a thing done or said constituted sexual infidelity is to be disregarded.

(7) In this section references to 'D' and 'V' are to be construed in accordance with section 54."

7-081 Essentially, the loss of self-control must be attributable to one of two specified "qualifying triggers":

1. fear of serious violence; or
2. something done or said in the circumstances specified in s.55(4)(a) and (b).

Section 55(6) provides for exclusions in particular cases, which will be discussed below.

(1) Fear of serious violence

7-082 This was an entirely new basis of a partial defence to murder when the Act was passed. It allows for Ds who are likely to fail in a plea of self-defence because they have reacted disproportionately to a threat from the deceased to avoid a murder conviction and be convicted of the lesser offence of manslaughter. The Law Commission, in recommending this addition, was of the view that: "D should not be prejudiced because he or she over-reacted in fear or panic, instead of overreacting due to an angry loss of self-control."[178]

178 Law Commission *Murder, Manslaughter and Infanticide* (LC 304) (2006), para.5.54.

The Government envisaged that loss of control as a response to fear of serious violence would cover two scenarios: (i) where a victim of sustained abuse kills their abuser in order to thwart an attack which is anticipated but not immediately imminent; and (ii) where someone overreacts to what they perceive as an imminent threat.[179] This approach can be supported. It is right that emotions other than anger should allow for mitigation in homicide cases, where warranted, as a concession to human frailty. Just because one can trace the law back to much earlier notions of outraged honour does not mean that anger should continue to be a privileged emotion. Put simply, why should someone who kills out of (uncontrolled) anger be regarded today as morally more excusable than someone who kills through fear or despair of what has happened or may happen to them?

Victims of domestic violence had for a long time fallen between a number of stools, unable to plead provocation due to the requirement of a "sudden" loss of self-control and also unable to plead self-defence because that defence requires that D respond to an imminent threat of violence. Accordingly, all they were left with was the unpalatable option of admitting an "abnormality of mind" and pleading diminished responsibility. Not only does this hamper the law in doing justice in a particular case, but it is also one of the sources of "the sexual asymmetry in the matter of who kills whom and who pleads passion/provocation".[180] The case of *Duffy*, the very case which established the modern (but no longer applicable) test for provocation, with its requirement for a "sudden and temporary" loss of self-control,[181] was in fact a case of a victim of domestic abuse who killed her sleeping (or resting) husband after a long history of domestic abuse. She failed in her defence of provocation, but was "more desperate and fearful than angry".[182] Allowing for fear as well as anger to trigger the loss of control defence might go some way to rebalancing the law against such "sexual asymmetry", although Edwards remains unconvinced of this, arguing that "the law continues by lending legitimacy to some conduct to sustain a gendered normative universe".[183]

There remains a problem with this s.55(3) provision. The mere fear of serious violence is not sufficient to trigger the new defence. The fear of serious violence must cause a loss of self-control. While it is plausible that some victims of domestic abuse, such as *Ahluwalia*, might be continuously in such fear that they do lose self-control, this is implausible in many cases of excessive self-defence where D overreacts.[184] As seen in Ch.9 there have been calls for the introduction of a partial defence of excessive self-defence to cover Ds such as those in *Martin* and *Clegg*.[185] The defence of loss of control will not cover either of the Ds in those cases, both of whom, calmly and rationally, used more force than was necessary. The loss of control defence is only available to those who are so fearful of serious violence that they panic and lose self-control. **7–083**

179 Ministry of Justice, CP 19/08, para.28.

180 A. Howe, "Mastering Emotions or Still Losing Control? Seeking Public Engagement with 'Sexual Infidelity' Homicide" (2013) 21 Fem. Leg. Stud. 141–161, 146.

181 *Duffy* (1949) 1 All E.R. 932.

182 S. Edwards, "Justice Devlin's Legacy: Duffy—A Battered Woman 'Caught' in Time" [2009] Crim. L.R. 851–869, 869.

183 S. Edwards, "Loss of Self-Control: When His Anger is Worth More than Her Fear" in Reed and Bohlander, *Loss of Control and Diminished Responsibility: Domestic, Comparative and International Perspectives* (Aldershot: Ashgate, 2011), p.79.

184 On this point, see also B. Mitchell, "Loss of Self-control under the Coroners and Justice Act 2009: Oh No!" in Reed and Bohlander, *Loss of Control and Diminished Responsibility: Domestic, Comparative and International Perspectives* (2011). See also comments by respondents in the form of policy stakeholders to interview questions in Fitz-Gibbon, "Replacing Provocation in England and Wales: Examining the Partial Defence of Loss of Control" (2013) 40 Journal of Law and Soc. 280–305, 291.

185 See paras 9–101–9–103. Whilst such a partial defence has not been created, the Criminal Justice and Immigration Act 2008 s.76(5A) now allows householders, at least, to use force which may be seen to be disproportionate, so long as it is not *grossly* disproportionate.

The fear must be one of "serious" violence. This is not defined. Although responses to the Government's consultation paper provided suggestions for greater clarity of the distinction between serious and non-serious violence, the Government did not feel it was desirable to be more specific in the statute, since this might depend on the circumstances of the victim and the perpetrator, and concluded that it is a question for the jury to decide based on the individual facts of a case.[186] This is the kind of question that juries are often given the task of determining, and it is right that the Act avoids the thorny issue of defining further what exactly is required.

(2) Circumstances of an extremely grave character causing the defendant to have a justifiable sense of being seriously wronged

7–084 It must be established that the loss of control was attributable to a thing/things done or said (or both) which:

(1) constituted circumstances of an extremely grave character, and
(2) caused D to have a justifiable sense of being seriously wronged.

7–085 *(i) Circumstances of an extremely grave character*

This is an objective test, rather than a question of whether D regards the circumstances as being of an extremely grave character. Lord Judge CJ in *Dawes* suggested that this trigger is:

> "... much more limited than the equivalent provisions in the former provocation defence. The result is that some of the more absurd trivia which nevertheless required the judge to leave the provocation defence to the jury will no longer fall within the ambit of the qualifying triggers defined in the new defence."[187]

The intended effect of this provision is to exclude unmeritorious cases such as parents killing their young babies to shut them up (as in *Doughty*). This intention can be seen in the Government's statement that:

> "... this formulation should ensure that the defence is only available in a very narrow set of circumstances in which a killing in response to things said or done should rightly be classified as manslaughter rather than murder."

However, if the formulation had been truly effective, there would be no need for the statutory exclusions, discussed below.

186 Ministry of Justice, *Murder, Manslaughter and Infanticide: Proposals for Reform of the Law: Summary of Responses and Government Position*, CP(R) 19/08 (2009), para.28.
187 *Dawes* [2013] EWCA Crim 322 at [60].

(ii) Caused a justifiable sense of being seriously wronged **7–086**

These circumstances of an extremely grave character must cause D to have a justifiable sense of being seriously wronged. This term was adopted from the Law Commission's proposals, and was believed by the Government to be so obviously objective in nature that the statute need not confirm this.[188] Clearly, whether D has a sense of being seriously wronged is a subjective matter. The word "justifiable" imports an objective quality to the test, implying that if called upon to justify their sense of being seriously wronged to a group of their peers, D would be capable of doing so. If it were otherwise, an extremely sensitive person who was insulted and who regarded the insult as extremely grave (even though reasonable people would not) might be able to rely on the defence. This was the approach taken by Lord Judge CJ in *Dawes*, where he stated that "the presence, or otherwise, of a qualifying trigger is not defined or decided by the defendant", and emphasised the word *justifiable*.[189] It is not for D to be able to say "the circumstances were extremely grave to me and caused me to have what I believed to be a justifiable sense that I had been seriously wronged". In *Hatter*, a case heard alongside *Dawes*, the Court of Appeal was of the opinion that the fact of the break-up of a relationship, of itself, will not normally constitute such circumstances.[190] In *Bowyer*, in the same case, D was a burglar who attacked the occupier on his return home. The Court of Appeal said it was absurd to suggest that:

> ". . . the entirely understandable response of the deceased to finding a burglar in his home provided the appellant with the remotest beginnings of a basis for suggesting that he had any justifiable sense of being wronged, let alone seriously wronged."[191]

These are examples of what do not constitute the trigger, so what *would* amount to circumstances of an extremely grave nature giving a justifiable sense of being seriously wronged? In recommending the test, the Law Commission gave the following example as one which ought to fall within such a defence:

> "An Asian woman returned home to find two white men attempting to rape her 15-year-old daughter. She got a knife from the kitchen. The men shouted racist abuse at her and started to run away. She chased after them and stabbed one of them several times in the back, killing him."[192]

Such a scenario is one that would no doubt attract much sympathy for the killer, and perhaps provides the prime example of conduct warranting an escape from the label of murder and the mandatory life sentence.

---

188 Ministry of Justice, CP(R) 19/08, para.45.

189 *Dawes* [2013] EWCA Crim 322 at [61].

190 *Dawes* [2013] EWCA Crim 322 at [65].

191 *Dawes* [2013] EWCA Crim 322 at [66].

192 This example was used in a public opinion survey conducted by Barry Mitchell for the Law Commission: Law Com. No.290, *Partial Defences to Murder* App.C.

7-087 Beyond this extreme example, the "justifiable sense of feeling seriously wronged" clause can be seen as yet another in the package designed to provide abused women with more scope for employing the partial defence to murder. Herring has argued that domestic abuse is typically a serious wrong to the woman and that such serious wrong includes, in addition to physical abuse, four elements: "the coercive effect of domestic abuse; the breach of trust involved; the impact of children; and its contribution to patriarchy".[193]

(3) Qualifying trigger: exclusions

7-088 Section 55(6) provides three exceptions to cases which would otherwise amount to a qualifying trigger. The first and second of these find their origins in the Law Commission's recommendations, which sought to provide a bar to the defence where "the provocation was itself incited by D for the purpose of providing an excuse to use violence". The exclusion is worded as follows:

> (a) D's fear of serious violence is to be disregarded to the extent that it was caused by a thing which D incited to be done or said for the purpose of providing an excuse to use violence;
> (b) a sense of being seriously wronged by a thing done or said is not justifiable if D incited the thing to be done or said for the purpose of providing an excuse to use violence.

The Court of Appeal had the opportunity to consider the contours of this exclusion in the case of *Dawes*. Lord Judge CJ noted that:

> ". . . as a matter of statutory construction, the mere fact that in some general way the defendant was behaving badly and looking for and provoking trouble does not of itself lead to the disapplication of the qualifying triggers based on s.55(3), (4) and (5) unless his actions were intended to provide him with the excuse or opportunity to use violence."[194]

The third exclusion, under s.55(6)(c), that "the fact that a thing done or said constituted sexual infidelity it is to be disregarded", did not appear in the Law Commission's recommendations but was added by the Government, surviving a challenge to it by the House of Lords during the parliamentary process.[195] Although historically, sexual infidelity has been a typical example providing a D with something "said or done" giving rise to provocation, the Government was clear that times have changed:

> "It is quite unacceptable for a defendant who has killed an unfaithful partner to seek to blame the victim for what occurred. We want to make it absolutely clear that sexual infidelity on the part of the victim can never justify reducing a murder charge to manslaughter. This should be the case even if sexual infidelity is present in combination with a range of other trivial and commonplace factors."[196]

---

193 J. Herring, "The Serious Wrong of Domestic Abuse and the Loss of Control Defence" in Reed and Bohlander, *Loss of Control and Diminished Responsibility: Domestic, Comparative and International Perspectives* (2011), p.78.

194 *Dawes* [2013] 2 Cr. App. R. 3 at [58].

195 *Hansard*, House of Lords, 11 November 2009, col.836.

196 Ministry of Justice, CP 19/08, para.32.

The exclusion has been controversial, however.[197] In interviews with policy stakeholders, barristers and judges, Fitz-Gibbon reported that: **7–089**

> ". . . rather than welcoming the exclusion of such cases from the new partial defence, respondents across all samples interviewed were overwhelmingly critical of this provision in the formulation of the new defence. Legal counsel respondents described the exclusion as 'incredibly convoluted' (UKCounselE) and 'barmy' (UKCounselQ), while one judicial respondent posed that it was 'ill-advised' and 'bad law' (UKJudgeB). Similarly, policy respondents described the sexual infidelity provision as 'very problematic' (UKPolicyA), 'dire' (UKPolicyB), and 'really unnecessary' (UKPolicyC). These criticisms were often based upon respondents' belief that the exclusion of a particular situation was not conducive to good law-making and that it would lead to significant questions surrounding the situations in which the new partial defence would and would not apply."[198]

Reed and Wake also predicted that the exclusion would create interpretational difficulties, and would be "up for debate in terms of disentanglement of 'infidelity' from other circumstances of taunts regarding inadequacy and disaffection".[199] It was not long until the Court of Appeal were given the opportunity to consider these matters.

R. v Clinton [2013] Q.B. 1:

The defendant killed his wife by beating her about the head with a wooden baton, strangling her with a belt, and then tightening a piece of rope around her neck with the aid of the baton. She had admitted to him that she had been having an affair and the defendant claimed that, just prior to the killing, his wife had taunted him about a range of matters including her sexual infidelity to him, that he did not have the courage to kill himself and that she did not care about their children. The trial judge withdrew the defence of loss of self-control from the jury for three reasons: the taunts as to fidelity were excluded as a trigger because they fell into the category of things said or done which "constituted sexual infidelity" within the meaning of the Coroners and Justice Act 2009 s.55(4); the other matters could not constitute circumstances of an extremely grave character; and they could not have caused the defendant to have a justifiable sense of being seriously wronged. The defendant appealed against his conviction for murder. **7–090**

LORD JUDGE CJ:

> "34 We must now address the full extent of the prohibition against 'sexual infidelity' as a qualifying trigger for the purposes of the loss of control defence. The question is whether or not sexual infidelity is wholly excluded from consideration in the context of features of the

197 A. Howe, "'Red Mist' Homicide: Sexual Infidelity and the English Law of Murder (glossing *Titus Andronicus*)" (2013) 33 *Legal Studies* 407–430.

198 K. Fitz-Gibbon, "Replacing Provocation in England and Wales: Examining the Partial Defence of Loss of Control" (2013) 40 J. of Law and Society 280–305, 293.

199 A. Reed and N. Wake, "Sexual Infidelity Killings: Contemporary Standardisations and Comparative Stereotypes" in Reed and Bohlander, *Loss of Control and Diminished Responsibility: Domestic, Comparative and International Perspectives* (2011), p.133.

individual case which constitute a permissible qualifying trigger or triggers within section 55(3)(4).

35 We have examined the legislative structure as a whole. The legislation was designed to prohibit the misuse of sexual infidelity as a potential trigger for loss of control in circumstances in which it was thought to have been misused in the former defence of provocation. Where there is no other potential trigger, the prohibition must, notwithstanding the difficulties identified earlier in the judgment, be applied.

36 The starting point is that it has been recognised for centuries that sexual infidelity may produce a loss of control in men, and, more recently, in women as well as men, who are confronted with sexual infidelity. The exclusion created by section 55(6) cannot and does not eradicate the fact that on occasions sexual infidelity and loss of control are linked, often with the one followed immediately by the other. Indeed on one view if it did not recognise the existence of this link, the policy decision expressly to exclude sexual infidelity as a qualifying trigger would be unnecessary.

37 In section 54(1)(c)(3) the legislation further acknowledges the impact of sexual infidelity as a potential ingredient of the third component of the defence, when all the defendant's circumstances fall for consideration, and when, although express provision is made for the exclusion of some features of the defendant's situation, the fact that he/she has been sexually betrayed is not. In short, sexual infidelity is not subject to a blanket exclusion when the loss of control defence is under consideration. Evidence of these matters may be deployed by the defendant and therefore the legislation proceeds on the basis that sexual infidelity is a permissible feature of the loss of control defence.

38 The ambit of section 55(3)(4)—the second component, the qualifying triggers—is clearly defined. Any qualifying trigger is subject to clear statutory criteria. Dealing with it broadly, to qualify as a trigger for the defendant's loss of control, the circumstances must be extremely grave and the defendant must be subject to a justifiable sense of having been seriously wronged. These are fact specific questions requiring careful assessment, not least to ensure that the loss of control defence does not have the effect of minimising the seriousness of the infliction of fatal injury. Objective evaluation is required and a judgment must be made about the gravity of the circumstances and the extent to which the defendant was seriously wronged, and whether he had a justifiable sense that he had been seriously wronged.

39 Our approach has . . . been influenced by the simple reality that in relation to the day to day working of the criminal justice system events cannot be isolated from their context. We have provided a number of examples in the judgment. Perhaps expressed most simply, the man who admits, 'I killed him accidentally', is never to be treated as if he had said 'I killed him'. That would be absurd. It may not be unduly burdensome to compartmentalise sexual infidelity where it is the only element relied on in support of a qualifying trigger, and, having compartmentalised it in this way, to disregard it. Whether this is so or not, the legislation imposes that exclusionary obligation on the court. However, to seek to compartmentalise

sexual infidelity and exclude it when it is integral to the facts as a whole is not only much more difficult, but is unrealistic and carries with it the potential for injustice. In the examples we have given . . ., we do not see how any sensible evaluation of the gravity of the circumstances or their impact on the defendant could be made if the jury, having, in accordance with the legislation, heard the evidence, were then to be directed to excise from their evaluation of the qualifying trigger the matters said to constitute sexual infidelity, and to put them into distinct compartments to be disregarded. In our judgment, where sexual infidelity is integral to and forms an essential part of the context in which to make a just evaluation whether a qualifying trigger properly falls within the ambit of subsections 55(3) and 55(4), the prohibition in section 55(6)(c) does not operate to exclude it."

Appeal allowed

The result of this case is that sexual infidelity may be taken into account as part of the background of a case (i.e. when assessing other triggers), but cannot itself constitute a trigger.[200] The irony of the case, though, is that having had his conviction for murder quashed and won a retrial at which loss of control should, according to the Court of Appeal, be put to the jury, D went on to plead guilty to murder and discarded his opportunity to be found guilty of manslaughter instead.[201] **7–091**

Why might that be? Could it be an appreciation that even if a jury were to be directed to take into account sexual infidelity in considering the defence of loss of control they were still likely to have convicted of murder in any case (which does raise the question of why launch an appeal in the first place)? If social mores have changed to the extent that sexual infidelity is no longer accepted as an excuse for loss of self-control, one assumes that the jury would not accept that D had experienced a *justifiable* sense of feeling seriously wronged. Furthermore, and again assuming this change in social mores, it would be unlikely that the "objective test", discussed below, would be satisfied in such cases.

Should the law be used to enforce a particular response to male-perpetrated intimate homicide? It was suggested at the time that the law was reformed that there might be other triggers which ought to be similarly excluded. If the statute were to go so far as to list one trigger that under no circumstances would provide a partial defence to murder, why not add others,[202] such as honour killings? The response was that an additional exclusion was not required because cases of honour killings will not satisfy the requirements that the circumstances were of an extremely grave character and caused a justifiable sense of being seriously wronged, and are also likely to fall within the exemption for cases where there is a "considered desire for revenge" under s.54(4).[203] **7–092**

---

200 A. Ashworth, Commentary to *Clinton* [2012] Crim. L.R. 539, 544.

201 "Jon-Jaques Clinton makes U-turn at retrial for wife's murder" *BBC News,* 3 September 2012, *http://www.bbc.co.uk/news/uk-england-berkshire-19469372*.

202 Horder gives the example of disqualifying as provocation anything said or done by a child in order to explicitly overrule *Doughty*: Horder, *Homicide and the Politics of Law Reform* (2012), p.211.

203 Ministry of Justice, CP(R) 19/08, para.56.

(c) The objective test

7-093 It is not sufficient simply to show that D lost control. There is also, by virtue of s.54(1)(c), the question of whether:

> ". . . a person of D's sex and age, with a normal degree of tolerance and self-restraint and in the circumstances of D, might have reacted in the same or in a similar way to D."

This test has been designed to accord with the Privy Council's most recent interpretation of the "reasonable man" test under s the Homicide Act 1957 s.3,[204] as outlined below.

The central question which this test seeks to answer, is whether D is as culpable as a murderer, or whether D's conduct can be understood as an instance of human frailty, leading to lesser culpability. Prior to the Coroners and Justice Act 2009, the courts had evaded the moral question of whether D could be expected to control the impulse to kill, by constructing the reasonable man test, which has been used in provocation cases since the 19th century.[205] The courts struggled, however, to firmly establish which characteristics of D should be attributed to the reasonable man, recognising that certain characteristics ought to be taken into account, but not being clear as to where to draw the line. Following a long line of judgments from the House of Lords and Privy Council starting with *DPP v Camplin*,[206] and including *Morhall*,[207] *Luc Thiet Thuan*,[208] and *Smith*,[209] the case of *Att-Gen for Jersey v Holley*[210] supplied the final instalment, providing an interpretation of the reasonable man test from which the Law Commission took inspiration in drafting the test adopted by the Government in passing the new law. It is worth exploring the controversies surrounding this issue in order to understand the weakness that the reform is designed to strengthen.

The question with which the courts grappled was what, if any, characteristics of the accused ought to be attributed to the reasonable person in applying the objective test? Although *Holley* was the most recent authority on the question prior to the enactment of the Coroners and Justice Act, *Camplin* remained the source of the law's interpretation of the test within the Homicide Act s.3.

---

204 *Att-Gen for Jersey v Holley* [2005] UKPC 23; [2005] 2 A.C. 580.

205 From the dicta of Keating J in *R. v Welsh* (1869) 11 Cox C.C. 336 at 339 who stated that provocation would be sufficient if it was "something which might naturally cause an ordinary and reasonably minded man to lose his self-control and commit such an act".

206 *Camplin* [1978] A.C. 705.

207 *R. v Morhall (Alan Paul)* [1996] A.C. 90; [1995] 3 W.L.R. 330 HL.

208 *Luc Thiet Thuan v The Queen* [1997] A.C. 131; [1996] 3 W.L.R. 45 PC.

209 *R. v Smith (Morgan James) [2001] 1 A.C. 146;* [2000] 3 W.L.R. 654 HL.

210 *Holley* [2005] 2 A.C. 580.

DPP v Campin [1978] A.C. 705 (House of Lords):

[The facts appear from the judgment of Lord Diplock.] 7–094

LORD DIPLOCK:

"The respondent, Camplin, who was 15 years of age, killed a middle-aged Pakistani, Mohammed Lal Khan, by splitting his skull with a chapati pan, a heavy kitchen utensil like a rimless frying pan. At the time the two of them were alone together in Khan's flat. At Camplin's trial for murder before Boreham J his only defence was that of provocation so as to reduce the offence to manslaughter. According to the story that he told in the witness box but which differed materially from that which he had told to the police, Khan had buggered him in spite of his resistance and had then laughed at him. Whereupon Camplin had lost his self-control and attacked Khan fatally with the chapati pan . . .

The point of law of general public importance involved in the case has been certified as being:

> 'Whether, on the prosecution for murder of a boy of 15, where the issue of provocation arises, the jury should be directed to consider the question, under s. 3 of the Homicide Act 1957 whether the provocation was enough to make a reasonable man do as he did by reference to a "reasonable adult" or by reference to a "reasonable boy of 15."' . . .

[F]or the purposes of the law of provocation the 'reasonable man' has never been confined to the adult male. It means an ordinary person of either sex, not exceptionally excitable or pugnacious, but possessed of such powers of self-control as everyone is entitled to expect that his fellow citizens will exercise in society as it is today. A crucial factor in the defence of provocation from earliest times has been the relationship between the gravity of provocation and the way in which the accused retaliated, both being judged by the social standards of the day . . . [N]ow that the law has been changed so as to permit of words being treated as provocation, even though unaccompanied by any other acts, the gravity of verbal provocation may well depend on the particular characteristics or circumstances of the person to whom a taunt or insult is addressed. To taunt a person because of his race, his physical infirmities or some shameful incident in his past may well be considered by the jury to be more offensive to the person addressed, however equable his temperament, if the facts on which the taunt is founded are true than it would be if they were not. It would stultify much of the mitigation of the previous harshness of the common law in ruling out verbal provocation as capable of reducing murder to manslaughter if the jury could not take into consideration all those factors which in their opinion would affect the gravity of taunts and insults when applied to the person to whom they are addressed . . .

In my opinion a proper direction to a jury on the question left to their exclusive determination by s.3 of the Act of 1957 would be on the following lines. The judge should state what the question is using the very terms of the section. He should then explain to them that the reasonable man

> referred to in the question is a person having the power of self-control to be expected of an ordinary person of the sex and age of the accused, but in other respects sharing such of the accused's characteristics as they think would affect the gravity of the provocation to him; and that the question is not merely whether such a person would in like circumstances be provoked to lose his self-control but also whether he would react to the provocation as the accused did."
>
> *Appeal dismissed*

7-095 What Lord Diplock made clear in *Camplin* was that not all characteristics of D had to be taken into account by the court. Two characteristics are deemed to be relevant to the standard of self-control which may be expected of a D: age and sex. Age is included because "to require old heads on young shoulders is inconsistent with law's compassion of human infirmity". The reason why this concession was also extended to sex has never been made clear. In fact, the Law Commission's recommendation for the objective test contained reference to D's age alone, and omitted any reference to gender.[211] "Sex" was added to the draft provision by the Government without comment and, although responses to the public consultation raised the question of whether it should be omitted, on the grounds that it might reinforce sexism,[212] the Government was not persuaded by these.[213] Whilst some commentators have welcomed the retention of sex as a relevant factor, as a way of addressing gender bias,[214] others have argued that the law would more effectively tackle gender stereotypes by leaving sex as something that should be taken account of as part of the wider circumstances of D.[215]

Beyond the need to include sex and age in applying the reasonable man test, the cases applying the test in relation to provocation wavered between allowing other aspects of D which affected their ability to exercise control to be taken into account, and excluding such factors. A particular focus of such cases was the question of whether mental abnormalities such as clinical depression should be taken into account. The majority in the case of *Smith*[216] permitted such characteristic to be attributed to the reasonable man. That decision was swiftly brought into question by the Privy Council in *Holley*,[217] where a chronic alcoholic murdered his girlfriend whilst under the influence of drink.

7-096 The effect of *Holley* was to exclude characteristics which might impact D's ability to control himself unless they were taunted about that particular characteristic. The Coroners and Justice Act 2009 was designed to ensure that the objective test as confirmed in *Holley* remained applicable to the new defence of loss of control. The Law Commission, in deciding on the wording of the new provision, identified the mischief that it sought to avoid.

---

211 Law Commission Paper No.304, para.5.11.

212 Ministry of Justice, CP(R) 19/08, para.77.

213 Ministry of Justice, CP(R) 19/08, para.78.

214 See, e.g. S. Edwards, "Anger and Fear as Justifiable Preludes for Loss of Self-Control" (2010) 74 J. of Criminal Law 223 and A. Carline, "Reforming Provocation: Perspectives from the Law Commission and the Government" [2009] 2 Web J. of Current Legal Issues.

215 N. Cobb and A. Gausden, "Feminism, 'Typical' Women, and Losing Control" in Reed and Bohlander, *Loss of Control and Diminished Responsibility: Domestic, Comparative and International Perspectives* (2011).

216 *Smith* [2001] 1 A.C. 146.

217 *Holley* [2005] 2 A.C. 580.

Law Commission No.304, Murder, Manslaughter and Infanticide (2006):

"5.38 . . . In our view, the function of the reasonable person requirement is to test D's own reaction against the standards of someone of his or her age possessed of an ordinary temperament: someone who is neither intolerant nor lacking in a reasonable measure of self-restraint when facing provocation. Unless the jury concludes that D's reaction might have been that of such a person, the defence ought to fail, even if D only killed as a result of a provoked and momentary loss of temper. 7–097

5.39 We are reluctant to speculate on how the courts would interpret the provisions [proposed] above. Still less would we wish to insist that they interpret them in a given way. None the less, the following examples may provide some guidance on the kinds of distinctions we think that it would be helpful to draw.

5.40 Our provisions impose a duty on the judge to instruct the jury to ignore factors that affect D's general capacity to exercise self-control. Alcoholism, for example, or another mental deficiency or disorder that is liable to affect temper and tolerance are obvious examples. A person who has killed because his or her capacity for self-control was reduced by such a characteristic must look to the defence of diminished responsibility for a partial defence, because such characteristics constitute an abnormality of mental functioning, unlike, for example, D's age.

5.41 Abnormal states of mind, such as intoxication or irritability, should also be left out, as should other factors that affect a general capacity to exercise adequate self-control, like a claim that D is 'more jealous or obsessive than most'. This approach to the general capacity to exercise adequate self-control will produce some hard cases. Examples might be ones in which, at the time of the provoked killing, D's general capacity for self-control was temporarily impaired by the effect of taking prescribed medicine, by having suffered a stroke, by involuntary intoxication, by an allergic reaction of some kind or by a bang on the head . . .

5.43 By way of contrast, a low IQ could be taken into account as part of the circumstances of D . . . if it meant, for example, that D misinterpreted a provocation, thinking it to be more grave than a person of higher intelligence might have done. To give a different example, the fact that D was dumb and thus unable to respond verbally, is a factor that might legitimately be taken into account when considering D's reaction to a particular provocation given on a particular occasion. In each example, the characteristic is not being used as evidence that the D lacked a general capacity to exercise adequate self-control . . .

5.45 In many instances, the circumstances liable quite properly to influence the jury in D's favour will bear on how 'gross' the provocation was, or on how justifiable it was for D to feel seriously wronged . . . An example is the cumulative effect of repeated provocations given, quite possibly over many years, in circumstances where it may also have been impossible for D to escape the provocation's effects. There is usually no theoretical difficulty about taking such background factors into account because they do not necessarily suggest that D is someone with a reduced general capacity to exercise self-control. A classic example would be the intimidated spouse who has been subject to abuse, the cumulative effect of which has become intolerable over the years."

7-098 Section 54(1)(c) specifies that the issue is whether a person of D's sex and age, with a normal degree of tolerance and self-restraint *and in the circumstances of D*, might have reacted in the same or in a similar way to D. Section 54 (3) explains what "the circumstances of D" means.

> "[T]the reference to 'the circumstances of D' is a reference to all of D's circumstances other than those whose only relevance to D's conduct is that they bear on D's general capacity for tolerance or self-restraint."

in *Rejmanski*,[218] the Court of Appeal had opportunity to interpret this requirement. In that case, involving a D with PTSD and a D with a personality disorder, the court emphasised that a D was to be judged against the standard of a person with a normal degree of tolerance and self-restraint. The Ds had their convictions for murder upheld because there was no evidence that the mental disorders from which they were each suffering were relevant in any way other than to explain why they lost their self-control more readily than a "normal" person. The court made it clear that it remains the case that a characteristic about which D is taunted will be relevant to the "objective" test, but beyond this, it is unclear how much wider the loss of control defence is compared to provocation. It is rather disappointing the way in which the court concluded their consideration of this point:

> "We do not exclude the possibility of other circumstances where a disorder might be relevant to the third component, but none has been put before us. This suggests the question is of academic interest only."[219]

However, what is clear is that being intoxicated will not, of itself, be a relevant characteristic, as specified in para.5.41 of the Law Commission's Report above. This was confirmed in the case of *Asmelash*.[220] Here, D had been drunk at the time that he stabbed the victim, and said that he had lost self-control and did not really know what had happened, but (somewhat inexplicably) was not so drunk that he did not know what he was doing. The judge directed the jury that they should consider whether a person unaffected by drink would have reacted in a similar way. The Court of Appeal held that the judge was right to direct the jury as he had done, and dismissed the appeal against conviction for murder.

7-099 It is only right that a D's intoxication should be ignored when applying s.54(1)(c) and s.54(3) of the 2009 Act. However, it would seem that this provision has (perhaps unintentionally) opened the door to a wide variety of characteristics being taken into account—as long as their *only* relevance is not that they bear on D's general capacity for tolerance or self-restraint. So, while s.54(1)(c) only specifies the characteristics of sex and age, under s.54(3) there is no reason why D's impotence, pregnancy, physical disability, sensitivity or even mental disability cannot be taken into account—unless the only relevance of these characteristics is that they affect D's capacity for tolerance or self-restraint. As can be seen

---

218 *R. v Rejmanski (Bartosz)* [2017] EWCA Crim 2061; [2018] 1 W.L.R. 2721.

219 *R. v Rejmanski* [2017] EWCA Crim 2061 at [28].

220 *R. v Asmelash (Dawit)* [2013] EWCA Crim 157; [2014] Q.B. 103.

from the case of *Clinton*, above, sexual infidelity on the part of V may be seen as a relevant factor in assessing D's reaction to a qualifying trigger.

2. Diminished responsibility

Where D is suffering from "diminished responsibility" they will have a partial defence to murder and will instead be convicted of manslaughter—again giving the court the necessary flexibility as to sentence. The defence is important not only to allow such a D to avoid the mandatory penalty for murder, but it has also been recognised by some that it is necessary and desirable for labelling purposes, in avoiding the label of "murderer",[221] particularly given the narrowness of the M'Naghten rules in pleading insanity.[222] **7–100**

(i) Introduction

ROYAL COMMISSION ON CAPITAL PUNISHMENT, CMND.8932 (1949–1953), PARA.411:

> "It must be accepted that there is no sharp dividing line between sanity and insanity, but that the two extremes of 'sanity' and 'insanity' shade into one another by imperceptible gradations. The degree of individual responsibility varies equally widely; no clear boundary can be drawn between responsibility and irresponsibility. The existence of degrees of responsibility has been recognised in . . . [other] legal systems . . . The acceptance of the doctrine of diminished responsibility would undoubtedly bring the law into closer harmony with the facts." **7–101**

The doubts that have led many to argue for the abolition of the insanity defence[223] have here been used to justify a halfway house for those who kill while suffering from mental disorder; some device, it was felt, was needed to reflect the view that where there was less responsibility there ought to be less punishment. Such acceptance of partial responsibility allows the courts to avoid the fixed penalty for murder by convicting the killer of manslaughter instead. For all other crimes which do not carry a fixed penalty, a partial defence was unnecessary. The lesser degree of responsibility could be reflected at the sentencing stage by "less punishment". **7–102**

---

221 This was the view of several consultees to the Law Commission's review of partial defences to murder: Law Commission Paper No.290, para.5.18.

222 See Ch.9 below, paras 9–188–9–207.

223 See Ch.9 below, para.9–214.

(ii) The law

HOMICIDE ACT 1957 S.2 (AS AMENDED BY THE CORONERS AND JUSTICE ACT 2009 S.52):

7–103 "(1) A person ('D') who kills or is a party to the killing of another is not to be convicted of murder if D was suffering from an abnormality of mental functioning which—

(a) arose from a recognised medical condition,
(b) substantially impaired D's ability to do one or more of the things mentioned in subsection (1A), and
(c) provides an explanation for D's acts and omissions in doing or being a party to the killing.

(1A) Those things are—

(a) to understand the nature of D's conduct;
(b) to form a rational judgment;
(c) to exercise self-control.

(1B) For the purposes of subsection (1)(c), an abnormality of mental functioning provides an explanation for D's conduct if it causes, or is a significant contributory factor in causing, D to carry out that conduct

. . .

(3) A person who but for this section would be liable, whether as principal or accessory, to be convicted of murder shall be liable instead to be convicted of manslaughter."[224]

7–104 The plea is raised by the defence on whom, as with insanity, the burden rests. Attempts to argue that this contravened the ECHR art.6(2) which guarantees the presumption of innocence were rejected outright by the Court of Appeal in *Lambert*.[225] This was confirmed in *Foye*,[226] where it was stated that the fundamental reason why a reverse burden of proof applies is that because the defence depends on the inner workings of the D's mind, it would be a practical impossibility for the Crown to disprove an assertion that D suffered from diminished responsibility, since D might refuse to submit to or cooperate with a medical examination.

---

224 *R. v Antoine (Pierre Harrison)* [2001] 1 A.C. 340; [2000] 2 W.L.R. 703 HL decided that once a D has been found unfit to plead they cannot go on to plead diminished responsibility (to avoid indefinite mandatory commitment) because the trial terminates. Since D is no longer liable to be convicted of murder the defence in s.2 cannot arise.

225 *R. v Lambert (Steven)* [2002] Q.B. 1112; [2001] 1 Cr. App. R. 14 CA. The subsequent appeal to the House of Lords did not deal with diminished responsibility. The prosecution may raise the plea if D is pleading insanity: *R. v Campbell (Colin Frederick)* (1987) 84 Cr. App. R. 255; [1987] Crim. L.R. 257 CA.

226 *R. v Foye (Lee Robert)* [2013] EWCA Crim 475; [2013] Crim. L.R. 839. That art.6 is not breached by the amended version of s.2 was further confirmed in *R. v Wilcocks (Callum Paul)* [2016] EWCA Crim 2043; [2017] 4 W.L.R. 39.

Before the amendments to s.2 were made by the Coroners and Justice Act 2009, the provision required that D suffered an "abnormality of mind" arising from one of a number of "bracketed causes" (arrested or retarded development of mind or any inherent causes or induced by disease or injury). "Abnormality of mind" was extremely vague; the concept was only slightly clarified by the case of *Byrne*.[227] The appellant strangled and then mutilated a girl. It was alleged that he suffered from violent perverted sexual desires which he found difficult or impossible to control. He was, in fact, described as a sexual psychopath. In the course of his judgment (allowing the appeal), Lord Parker CJ defined "abnormality of mind" thus:

> ". . . [it is] a state of mind so different from that of ordinary human beings that the reasonable man . . . would term it abnormal. It appears to us wide enough to cover the mind's activities in all its aspects, not only the perception of physical acts and matters, and the ability to form a rational judgment as to whether the act was right or wrong, but also the ability to exercise will-power to control physical acts in accordance with that rational judgment."

This interpretation still left the meaning of "abnormality of mind" somewhat imprecise. It was a quasi-legal, quasi-medical formula that could satisfy no-one.

In recommending reform of the law, the Law Commission saw the need to consider the needs and practices of medical practitioners, and drew inspiration from a definition of the defence adopted in New South Wales in 1997, to replace the requirement of an "abnormality of mind" with an abnormality of mental functioning arising either from a medically recognised condition or, in defendants under the age of 18, developmental immaturity.[228] The developmental immaturity limb was abandoned by the Government in drafting the new provision. **7–105**

One might assume that the "abnormality of mental functioning" requirement adds little, and that a defence of diminished responsibility will succeed providing that D was suffering from a recognised medical condition and that there is expert evidence that this substantially impaired their ability to do one of the things specified in s.2(1A). What is clear is that the new law is intended to be a lot more user-friendly for psychiatrists who are asked to provide evidence for the prosecution and defence in such cases. The abnormality of mental functioning must have arisen from a "recognised medical condition", meaning that the law can now keep pace with developments in diagnostic practice. For a medical condition to be recognised, it would seem that it would have to be listed in one of the accepted classificatory systems such as the World Health Organisation's *International Classification of Diseases* or the American Psychiatric Association's *Diagnostic and Statistical Manual of Mental Disorders*.[229]

---

227 *R. v Byrne (Patrick Joseph)* [1960] 2 Q.B. 396; (1960) 44 Cr. App. R. 246 CA.

228 Law Commission Paper No.304, para.5.112.

229 Ministry of Justice, CP 19/08, para.49. See also R. Mackay, "The Coroners and Justice Act 2009—partial defences to murder (2) the new diminished responsibility plea" [2010] Crim. L.R. 290–302, 294. However, the fact that a condition is listed in such a guide does not in itself, it appears, make it an abnormality of mental functioning for the purposes of s.2(1). See *R. v Dowds (Stephen Andrew)* [2012] EWCA Crim 281; [2012] 1 Cr. App. R. 34.

7-106 The abnormality of mental functioning must substantially impair D's ability to either understand the nature of their conduct; to form a rational judgement; or to exercise self-control. Of the three abilities that may be impaired the first is, as noted by Mackay, reminiscent of the M'Naghten rules. He notes that not a single case in his empirical study was based on this ability being impaired.[230] In relation to an impairment to form a rational judgment, Mackay notes that when this ability is discussed "sometimes no distinction is being made between the terms 'judgment' and 'decision'".[231] Mackay notes that the final ability, to exercise self-control, uses the same terminology as the other partial defence of loss of control, and emphasises the common practice as part of a defence strategy to plead both defences together.[232]

Under the original drafting of the Homicide Act s.2, the question of whether D's responsibility was substantially impaired was a moral question for the jury on which expert psychiatrists should not have given their own views.[233] Under the amended law, the question of "substantial" impairment remains one for the jury.[234] However, under the amended law, the jury no longer have to address the impossible issue of whether "responsibility" was substantially impaired and psychiatrists will no longer go through the charade of testifying about such a non-medical concept. Instead, juries have to assess whether D's recognised psychiatric condition substantially impaired their ability to do one of the specified things. In doing this, they are undoubtedly to be guided by psychiatric evidence[235] but now, psychiatrists will be testifying about matters within their medical expertise (for example, whether a D could form a rational judgement) rather than matters beyond their competence (issues of responsibility). Mackay and Mitchell, in examining reports submitted by experts, found that such experts expressed a positive view that 's ability to do one of the three things under s.2(1A) was substantially impaired in 72.7% of reports, with experts declining to comment on this in 8.2% of reports.[236]

However, the cases in Mackay and Mitchell's sample were determined before the Court of Appeal and Supreme Court decisions in the case of *Golds*. The Supreme Court was tasked with clarifying which of two interpretations of "substantial impairment" was correct.

R. v GOLDS [2016] UKSC 61 (SUPREME COURT):

7-107 The appellant had attacked his partner with a knife at their home in front of her young children after a running argument which had taken place on and off throughout much of the day. He had inflicted 22 knife wounds together with blunt impact internal injuries. Two consultant forensic psychiatrists gave evidence that there was an abnormality of mental functioning arising from a

230 R. Mackay, "What's happening with the reformed diminished responsibility plea?" (2021) 72(2) *Northern Ireland Legal Quarterly* 224–244, 235.

231 Mackay, "What's happening with the reformed diminished responsibility plea?" (2021) 72(2) *Northern Ireland Legal Quarterly* 224–244, 236. Mackay points to the case of *R. v Conroy (Jason John)* [2017] EWCA Crim 81; [2017] 2 Cr. App. R. 26.

232 Mackay, "What's happening with the reformed diminished responsibility plea?" (2021) 72(2) *Northern Ireland Legal Quarterly* 224–244, 239.

233 It was found, however, that whilst a minority of psychiatrists tended to restrict themselves to the first part of the test in s.2 in giving evidence at trials, almost 70% of them expressed an opinion in relation to whether D's responsibility was substantially impaired: Law Commission Paper No.290 (2004), para.5.51.

234 Law Commission Paper No.304 (2006), para.5.118.

235 Judicial College, Crown Court Compendium: Part 1: Jury and Trial Management and Summing Up (May 2016) 19-1 [9].

236 R. Mackay and B. Mitchell, "The new diminished responsibility plea in operation: some initial findings" [2017] Crim. L.R. 18–35, 33.

recognised medical condition, although they disagreed what that condition was. There was no contradictory psychiatric evidence. On the issue of substantial impairment, the judge told the jury that "substantial" was an everyday word not requiring further elucidation. The appellant was convicted of murder and appealed to the Court of Appeal, contending (a) that the judge had been wrong not to direct the jury as to what "substantially impaired" meant; and (b) that the jury might in the absence of such direction have applied a more stringent test than it ought to have done. It was contended on his behalf that so long as the impairment was more than merely trivial, the test of "substantially impaired" was met. The Court of Appeal dismissed the appellant's appeal[237] but certified in relation to this ground that the following two questions of law of general public importance were involved:

1. Where a defendant, being tried for murder, seeks to establish that he is not guilty of murder by reason of diminished responsibility, is the court required to direct the jury as to the definition of the word "substantial" as in the phrase "substantially impaired" found in the Homicide Act 1957 s.2(1)(b) as amended by the Coroners and Justice Act 2009 s.52?
2. If the answer to the first question is in the affirmative, or if for some other reason the judge chooses to direct the jury on the meaning of the word "substantial", is it to be defined as "something more than merely trivial", or alternatively in a way that connotes more than this, such as "something whilst short of total impairment that is nevertheless significant and appreciable"?

LORD HUGHES: **7–108**

[Lord Hughes sets out the law before and after the amendment by the 2009 Act.]

"[7] It follows that the expression 'substantially impaired' has been carried forward from the old Act into its new form. But whereas previously it governed a single question of 'mental responsibility', now it governs the ability to do one or more of three specific things, to understand the nature of one's acts, to form a rational judgment and to exercise self-control. Those abilities were frequently the focus of trials before the re-formulation of the law. But previously, the question for the jury as to 'mental responsibility' was a global one, partly a matter of capacity and partly a matter of moral culpability, both including, additionally, consideration of the extent of any causal link between the condition and the killing. Now, although there is a single verdict, the process is more explicitly structured. The jury needs to address successive specific questions about (1) impairment of particular abilities and (2) cause of behaviour in killing. Both are of course relevant to moral culpability, but the jury is not left the same general 'mental responsibility' question that previously it was. The word used to describe the level of impairment is, however, the same . . .

[13] [In] *R. v Simcox The Times* 25 February 1964; [1964] Crim. L.R. 402 . . . [t]he judge left the question [of substantial Impairment] to the jury in the terms of the section, adding only that they should ask:

---

237 *R. v Golds (Mark Richard)* [2014] EWCA Crim 748; [2015] 1 W.L.R. 1030.

> 'do we think, looking at it broadly as commonsense people, there was a substantial impairment of his mental responsibility in what he did? If the answer to that is "yes" then you find him not guilty of murder but guilty of manslaughter. If the answer to that is "no, there may be some impairment but we do not think it was substantial. We do not think it was something which really made any great difference although it may have made it harder to control himself to refrain from crime", then you would find him guilty as charged.'

The Court of Appeal, whilst observing that the final sentence needed the previous focus on the word 'substantial' in order that it should not be thought that the absence of self-control had to be total, approved this direction . . .

[14] Three years later the Court of Criminal Appeal considered the case of *R. v Lloyd* [1967] 1 Q.B. 175, which would appear to be the indirect origin of the submission made in the present case that 'substantially impaired' means any impairment greater than the merely trivial . . . At trial, Ashworth J had directed the jury in the terms of the statute, but he had then added:

> 'Fourthly, this word "substantial", members of the jury. I am not going to try to find a parallel for the word "substantial". You are the judges, but your own common sense will tell you what it means . . . . Substantial does not mean total, that is to say, the mental responsibility need not be totally impaired, so to speak destroyed altogether. At the other end of the scale substantial does not mean trivial or minimal. It is something in between and Parliament has left it to you and other juries to say on the evidence, was the mental responsibility impaired, and, if so, was it substantially impaired?' (178)

. . .

[Lord Hughes continues to discuss subsequent cases, including *Ramchurn* [2010] 2 Cr. App. R. 3, followed by the case law in Scotland and the Law Commission's recommendations for reform.]

[35] It follows that there is nothing in the change of the formulation of the test for diminished responsibility to cause a different view to be taken now of the sense in which the word 'substantially' is used in conjunction with 'impairment'.

[36] This use of the expression accords with principle. Diminished responsibility effects a radical alteration in the offence of which a defendant is convicted. The context is a homicide. By definition, before any question of diminished responsibility can arise, the homicide must have been done with murderous intent, . . . Whilst it is true that at one end of the scale of responsibility the sentence in a case of diminished responsibility may be severe, or indeed an indefinite life sentence owing to the risk which the defendant presents to the public, the difference between a conviction for murder and a conviction for manslaughter is of considerable

importance both for the public and for those connected with the deceased. It is just that where a substantial impairment is demonstrated, the defendant is convicted of the lesser offence and not of murder. But it is appropriate, as it always has been, for the reduction to the lesser offence to be occasioned where there is a weighty reason for it and not merely a reason which just passes the trivial

. . .

[38] . . . Although it is for the jury, and not for the doctors, to determine whether the partial defence is made out, and this important difference of function is well recognised by responsible forensic psychiatrists, it is inevitable that they may express an opinion as to whether the impairment was or was not substantial, and if they do not do so in their reports, as commonly many do, they may be asked about it in oral evidence. It is therefore important that if they use the expression, they do so in the sense in which it is used by the courts. If there is doubt about the sense in which they have used it, their reports may be misunderstood and decisions made upon them falsified, and much time at trials is likely to be taken up unnecessarily by cross examination on the semantic question . . . **7–109**

[39] The sense in which 'substantially impaired' is used in relation to diminished responsibility is, for the reasons set out above, the second of the two senses. It is not synonymous with 'anything more than merely trivial impairment' . . .

[43] It follows that the questions certified by the Court of Appeal should be answered as follows:

(1) Ordinarily in a murder trial where diminished responsibility is in issue the judge need not direct the jury beyond the terms of the statute and should not attempt to define the meaning of 'substantially'. Experience has shown that the issue of its correct interpretation is unlikely to arise in many cases. The jury should normally be given to understand that the expression is an ordinary English word, that it imports a question of degree, and that whether in the case before it the impairment can properly be described as substantial is for it to resolve.

(2) If, however, the jury has been introduced to the question of whether *any* impairment beyond the merely trivial will suffice, or if it has been introduced to the concept of a spectrum between the greater than trivial and the total, the judge should explain that whilst the impairment must indeed pass the merely trivial before it need be considered, it is not the law that *any* impairment beyond the trivial will suffice. The judge should likewise make this clear if a risk arises that the jury might misunderstand the import of the expression; whether this risk arises or not is a judgment to be arrived at by the trial judge who is charged with overseeing the dynamics of the trial. Diminished responsibility involves an impairment of one or more of the abilities listed in the statute to an extent which the jury judges to be substantial, and which it is satisfied significantly contributed to his committing the offence. Illustrative expressions of the sense of the word may be employed so long as the jury is given clearly to understand that no single synonym is to be substituted for the statutory word . . . "

Appeal dismissed

7–110 The result of the Supreme Court's decision to confirm the approach taken in the Court of Appeal is that the degree of impairment to be present is greater than psychiatrists had perhaps previously interpreted the requirement to be.[238] The consequence of this may be that the number of successful pleas of diminished responsibility will continue to fall (see below).

The final requirement of s.2 is that the recognised medical condition must have caused D's involvement in the killing. The Law Commission noted that it was never clear under the pre-existing law whether the abnormality of mind had to in some sense "cause" D to kill.[239] The new s.2(1)(c) requires that the abnormality of mental functioning provides an explanation for D's acts and omissions in doing or being a party to the killing, and s.2(1B) further states that the abnormality of mental functioning provides an explanation for D's conduct if it causes or is a significant contributory factor in causing D to carry out that conduct. The inclusion of an apparent causal requirement has been criticised by Mackay, who notes that there is no real support for such a requirement and other jurisdictions, such as New South Wales (Australia), have not seen the need to include one.[240] The law now makes it clear that there must be a connection between the abnormality of mental functioning and the killing, although there is some disagreement amongst commentators as to whether subs.(1B) requires a strict causal link.[241] This means that where the jury think that the abnormality of mental functioning made no difference to D's behaviour, they will not succeed in their plea of diminished responsibility.[242]

7–111 As confirmed in *Bunch*,[243] expert evidence is necessary for the defence to be successfully raised. The amended s.2 leaves much to be determined by psychiatrists in supporting or otherwise a plea of diminished responsibility. In cases where such experts are in agreement, and evidence of diminished responsibility is unchallenged, the Court of Appeal has held in *Brennan*[244] that the judge should withdraw the murder charge from the jury.[245] Since the 2009 Act came into force there has, however, been an increase in the number of contested cases of diminished responsibility in which the experts are not in agreement. Mackay and Mitchell found that 43.3% of the cases in their post-2009 Act sample were decided by a jury trial, compared to 22.9% in Mackay's earlier sample for the Law Commission.[246] In addition to this, the number of pleas of diminished responsibility failing at trial had increased, with the number of murder convictions rising from 61.1% in the pre-2009 Act sample to 79.5% in the post-2009 Act sample. Furthermore, Mackay argues that the causal requirement under s.2(1B) presents particular challenges to the psychiatric experts, with 60% of the reports in his sample

---

238 Mackay and Mitchell, "The new diminished responsibility plea in operation: some initial findings" [2017] Crim. L.R. 18–35, 33.

239 Law Commission Paper No.304, para.5.122.

240 Mackay, "The Coroners and Justice Act 2009—partial defences to murder (2) the new diminished responsibility plea" [2010] Crim. L.R. 290–302, 300. For a recent comparison of the law of England and Wales with that of New South Wales, see T. Crofts and N. Wake, "Diminished responsibility determinations In England and Wales and New South Wales: whose role is it anyway?" (2021) 72(2) *Northern Ireland Legal Quarterly* 324–362.

241 Mackay and Hughes note that Smith, Hogan and Ormerod have argued that s.2(1B) provides just one example of how the killing might be explained, whilst Simester and Sullivan are of the view that it is essential to prove a causal link: R. Mackay and D. Hughes, "Explaining the 'explanation' requirement in the new diminished responsibility plea" [2032] *Criminal Law Review* 461–477, 467-468, citing D. Ormerod and K. Laird, *Smith, Hogan and Ormerod's Criminal Law*, 15th edn (Oxford; OUP, 2018), p.560 and A. Simester, *Simester and Sullivan's Criminal Law: Theory and Doctrine* (2019), p.789.

242 Ministry of Justice, 19/08(R), para.95.

243 *R. v Bunch (Martin John)* [2013] EWCA Crim 2498; [2014] M.H.L.R. 331.

244 *R. v Brennan (Michael James)* [2014] EWCA Crim 2387; [2015] 1 Cr. App. R. 14.

245 The approach in *Brennan* [2014] EWCA Crim 2387 was endorsed by the Supreme Court in *Golds* [2016] UKSC 61 at [51].

246 Mitchell and Mackay, "The new diminished responsibility plea in operation: some initial findings" [2017] Crim. L.R. 18–35, 26.

being silent on the issue, and the remaining reports suggesting some confusion over what is required.[247]

This reduction in the number of Ds being able successfully to rely on diminished responsibility to reduce liability from murder to manslaughter may partially be explained by, and give weight to, concerns over the types of cases that the new law is likely to cover. Under the pre-existing s.2, the woolliness of the language enabled psychiatrists, as expert witnesses (with the collusion of judges and juries) to simply stretch the interpretation of the provision to cover cases where a conviction of murder was thought to be inappropriate. Persons suffering from reactive depressions and alcoholism, as well as mercy-killers, have been brought within the ambit of the defence. Indeed, the Law Commission noted that long-term carers of terminally ill spouses who kill with their spouse's consent "are already quite commonly dealt with under s.2 of the Act as persons suffering from diminished responsibility. It is the prosecution that normally accepts the plea".[248] Following the Supreme Court's decision in *Golds,* Mackay is concerned that the lack of flexibility in the court's interpretation of "substantially impaired" will lead to deserving cases, including mercy killers, falling outside the defence of diminished responsibility.[249] Mackay and Mitchell found that the primary diagnoses in more recent cases were the same as those found by Mackay's research prior to the reform of s.2:[250] schizophrenia (37.8%), depression (14.4%), personality disorder (16.7%) and psychosis (16.7%).[251] What is clear is that, despite the fact that the defence has become more "medicalised", the question of whether it succeeds or not remains a question of fact for the jury, who have discretion to reject the defence even in cases where the expert evidence is unanimous and uncontradicted.[252]

One of the most difficult types of cases the courts have had to deal with in respect of diminished responsibility is perhaps the case of the alcoholic.[253] It was held in *Tandy* that alcoholism may amount to an "injury",[254] one of the bracketed causes required of an abnormality of mind under the previous incarnation of the defence, if the first drink of the day was "involuntary". It has been confirmed under the new version of the law that expert evidence will be required to prove that D was suffering from alcohol dependency syndrome.[255] However, for policy reasons the courts have consistently upheld the distinction between alcoholism and mere intoxication. In *Dietschmann*,[256] the House of Lords held that where a D pleads diminished responsibility resulting from the combination of mental abnormality and intoxication the jury should be satisfied that, despite the drink, D's mental abnormality substantially **7–112**

247 Mackay and Hughes, "Explaining the 'explanation' requirement in the new diminished responsibility plea" [2032] Criminal Law Review 461–477, 475.

248 Law Commission Consultation Paper No.177, *A New Homicide Act for England and Wales?* (2005), para.8.84.

249 R. Mackay, "Case Comment: *R. v Golds*" [2017] Arch. Rev. 1, 4–5. Gibson, on the other hand, argues that diminished responsibility remains "a pragmatic ally" for defendants in mercy killer cases, on the basis that "the interpretation of substantial will, as ever, depend on the sympathetic whim of experts and—where a trial is contested—juries. In any event, juries may apply a *less* strenuous definition of 'substantial' given that *Golds* only requires a trial judge to give a direction on that definition *if* a jury requires it": M. Gibson, "Pragmatism Preserved? The Challenges of Accommodating Mercy Killers in the Reformed Diminished Responsibility Plea" (2017) 81(3) J. Crim. L. 177–200.

250 R. Mackay, "The Diminished Responsibility Plea in Operation—An Empirical Study", App.B to Law Com. No.290 (2004), table 15b.

251 Mackay and Mitchell, "The new diminished responsibility plea in operation: some initial findings" [2017] Crim. L.R. 18–35, 29.

252 See, e.g. *v Hussain (Imran)* [2019] EWCA Crim 666; [2019] Crim. L.R. 877.

253 For a discussion of intoxication and diminished responsibility, see M. Gibson "Intoxicants and Diminished Responsibility" [2011] Crim. L.R. 909–924.

254 *R. v Tandy (Linda Mary)* [1989] 1 W.L.R. 350; [1988] Crim. L.R. 308 CA.

255 *Bunch* [2013] EWCA Crim 2498.

256 *R. v Dietschmann (Anthony)* [2003] UKHL 10; [2003] 1 A.C. 1209.

impaired his mental responsibility for his fatal acts. In *Kay and Joyce*,[257] decided in relation to the reformed version of s.2, it was held that a D suffering from schizophrenia who killed while intoxicated could rely on diminished responsibility if their condition was of such severity that, even without intoxication, it would have impaired their responsibility. However, the court found that in this case there was no medical evidence that D's underlying illness was of such a degree that, independent of drug or alcohol abuse, it substantially impaired his responsibility, and his conviction for murder was upheld. Most recently in *Foy*[258] D appealed against his conviction for murder by attempting to adduce fresh evidence of a second defence expert psychiatrist where previously both the prosecution expert and the expert initially engaged by defence counsel had concluded that there was insufficient evidence to support a plea of diminished responsibility. D had a history of poor mental health, having suffered from depression, anxiety and paranoia. On the day that he stabbed a French tourist in public in London, he had consumed a large quantity of alcohol and cocaine. The original defence expert had concluded that although D might have been suffering from an abnormality of mental functioning that arose from a recognised medical condition in the form of paranoid psychosis, which impaired his ability to form a rational judgment or exercise self-control, his view was that without the ingestion of alcohol and cocaine it would not have *substantially* impaired his responsibility for the killing. The second defence expert formed the opinion that despite being intoxicated, D was suffering from an acute transient psychotic episode which substantially impaired his mental responsibility for the killing. In rejecting the appeal against conviction and application to adduce the fresh evidence from the second expert, the Court of Appeal warned against "expert shopping" to attempt to appeal against conviction, and concluded that if the involvement of voluntarily ingested alcohol and cocaine was excluded, as it should be according to the case law, "there is simply no solid basis for asserting an abnormality of mental functioning arising from a recognised medical condition which *substantially* impaired the appellant's ability in the relevant respects and which provided an *explanation* . . . for his acts".[259] As noted by Simpson, the problem highlighted by this case is that "[t]he revised plea of diminished responsibility is heavily medicalised, thereby inviting greater input from psychiatric experts who are increasingly likely to hold differing opinions".[260]

7–113 In *Dowds*,[261] a slightly different issue pertaining to the effects of intoxication was addressed. D was drunk at the time that he stabbed his partner 60 times, killing her, but there was no suggestion that he was suffering from alcohol dependency syndrome. Instead, he tried to argue diminished responsibility on the basis that "acute intoxication" is listed in the WHO ICD-10 and should therefore amount to a recognised medical condition for the purposes of pleading diminished responsibility. The Court of Appeal rejected this argument on the basis that the Law Commission explicitly did *not* include writing the terms of ICD-10 and/or DSM-IV[262] into the legislation, for which purpose those terms are "demonstrably unsuited". Pleading diminished responsibility successfully is not as simple as relying on

---

257 *R. v Joyce (Trevor)* [2017] EWCA Crim 647; [2017] 4 W.L.R. 121.

258 *R. v Foy (Nicholas John)* [2020] EWCA Crim 270; [2020] Crim. L.R. 840.

259 *Foy* [2020] EWCA Crim 270 at [95].

260 B. Simpson, "*R. v Foy (Nicholas)*: voluntary intoxication, mental health and the case for diminished responsibility" (2021) 72(2) *Northern Ireland Legal Quarterly* 397–405, 404.

261 *R. v Dowds (Stephen Andrew)* [2012] EWCA Crim 281; [2012] 1 Cr. App. R. 34.

262 This has now been updated to the DSM-V. The fact that conditions listed in the DSM do not remain static from edition to edition might in itself prove problematic.

the presence of a particular condition on any such diagnostic list. Being on the list is a necessary but not sufficient condition for diminished responsibility to apply.

3. Killing in pursuance of a suicide pact

Homicide Act 1957 s.4:

"(1) It shall be manslaughter, and shall not be murder, for a person acting in pursuance of a suicide pact between him and another to kill the other or be a party to the other being killed by a third person . . . 7–114

(3) For the purposes of this section 'suicide pact' means a common agreement between two or more persons having for its object the death of all of them, whether or not each is to take his own life, but nothing done by a person who enters into a suicide pact shall be treated as done by him in pursuance of the pact unless it is done while he has the settled intention of dying in pursuance of the pact."

The law acts with some clemency towards a D who survives a suicide pact when they had intended to die themselves. Such clemency does not, however, extend to other situations. If the agreement to "kill and then die" is merely a front for murder where D has no intention of killing themselves, then they will be convicted of murder. This will be the case even if V consented to die and even if, furthermore, it can be described as a mercy killing. It is, therefore, thought to be more blameworthy to kill in such situations than where a suicide pact exists. The basis of this distinction in blameworthiness must lie in the "settled intention" of D to die themselves. Perhaps it is felt that the person killed would not have consented had they not been aware of the intention of the other; more probably, however, the consent of the "victim" is still irrelevant and the partial defence represents "a concession to human frailty". It recognises with compassion the state of despair of one who would kill and then die themselves.[263] 7–115

Killing in pursuance of a suicide pact is distinguished from the separate crime of encouraging or assisting suicide.

4. Sentencing Voluntary Manslaughter

Manslaughter by provocation was the only species of manslaughter to already benefit from sentencing guidelines prior to the introduction of the Sentencing Council's manslaughter guideline in 2018.[264] The Sentencing Council has now had the opportunity to consider how changes to the substantive law brought about by the Coroners and Justice Act 2009 should be reflected in the sentencing guidelines, as well as considering these within the context of sentences for unlawful killing as a whole. 7–116

263 In *Dunbar v Plant* [1998] Ch. 412; [1997] 3 W.L.R. 1261 CA, it was stated that the public interest does not generally call for the survivor of a suicide pact to be prosecuted.

264 Sentencing Guidelines Council, *Manslaughter by Reason of Provocation* (2005).

In comparison to the guidelines for involuntary manslaughter, the guideline for murder by reason of loss of control is narrower, in the sense that there are three rather than four levels of culpability for the judge to select from, with the starting point for Culpability level A being 14 years' imprisonment, and the starting point for Culpability level C being five years imprisonment. This guideline has come under attack from both Wasik[265] and Wake[266] for the way in which they fail properly to take account of factors relevant to culpability in cases where a victim of domestic abuse has killed his or her abuser.

Sentencing for diminished responsibility manslaughter, on the other hand, requires additional factors to be considered. The maximum penalty is the same as other forms of manslaughter—life imprisonment—but where D continues to suffer from a mental disorder, the judge should consider whether a hospital order is appropriate under the Mental Health Act 1983 s.37. The rationale here is that an offender who has killed because of their mental disorder is in need of treatment in the hope that any dangerous tendencies resulting from the disorder can be reduced, and D is not necessarily deserving of punishment if their behaviour was caused by illness. Whilst hospital orders are common, the use of imprisonment has seen an increase, although life sentences are fairly rare.[267]

7–117 In cases where the judge determines that imprisonment is appropriate, the starting points are higher than for other forms of manslaughter. As with the other offences, the judge should begin by determining the culpability level of the offender, but here that is measured by assessing the degree of responsibility retained. This recognises that D's responsibility is necessarily diminished but not extinguished by an abnormality of mental functioning. In assessing whether D's responsibility falls within the high, medium or lower category, the judge may consider the degree to which the offender's actions contributed to the seriousness of their mental disorder. The highest culpability has a starting point of 24 years' custody; twice that of gross negligence manslaughter.

Although a life sentence might be thought necessary in cases of offenders whose dangerous behaviour is prone to recur, judges should ensure that they correctly apply the alternative disposals under the Mental Health Act 1983. In the case of *Fisher*,[268] D suffered from a psychotic illness and stabbed his mother once in the chest, pleading guilty to manslaughter by diminished responsibility. His sentencing hearing occurred on the day that the new guidelines came into force. The Court of Appeal held that the judge erred in passing a life sentence, and instead should have made a hospital order under s.37 with a s.41 restriction order.[269] This was on the basis that D's responsibility fell into the lowest category, and that the minimum term of two years' imprisonment set by the judge as the punitive element of the sentence was far shorter than the period during which they would in fact be required to be treated in a

265 Wasik, "Reflections on the manslaughter sentencing guidelines" [2019] Crim. L.R. 315–332.

266 N. Wake, "Manslaughter by Loss of Control: Sentencing Primary Victims Who Kill" [2019] Crim L.R. 291–314.

267 In his study of 126 convictions for diminished responsibility manslaughter over the years 1997–2001, Mackay found that a discretionary life sentence was imposed in 10 cases. In his more recent study with Mitchell, the proportion of such convictions resulting in a life sentence was higher: Mitchell and Mackay, "The new diminished responsibility plea in operation: some initial findings" [2017] Crim. L.R. 18–35, 27–28.

268 *R. v Fisher (Thomas)* [2019] EWCA Crim 1066; [2020] M.H.L.R. 103.

269 Conversely, in *R. v Lall (Gurjeet)* [2021] EWCA Crim 404; [2021] M.H.L.R. 346, the Court of Appeal rejected a submission by the Attorney General that a life sentence was justified and should be substituted for the hospital order and a restriction, without limit of time, that the judge had imposed under the Mental Health Act 1983 ss.37 and 41. It was agreed that the offender was highly dangerous, and the unanimous view of the three psychiatrists who had given evidence was that the public protection could best be achieved by an indeterminate hospital order.

secure hospital, meaning that the life sentence did not enhance the protection of the public, and D could be more effectively rehabilitated with a restricted hospital order.

The Sentencing Guideline lists aggravating and mitigating factors, many of which are common to the other species of manslaughter elsewhere in the guideline. One mitigating factor which is specific to manslaughter by diminished responsibility, however, is that of "belief by the offender that the killing was an act of mercy".[270] An example of such a case before the guidelines existed can be seen in the case of *Webb*,[271] where D, having been requested on many occasions by his wife to help end her life, smothered her after the overdose she had taken seemed not to have been effective and she had told him not to let her wake up. His sentence of two years' imprisonment was reduced to a suspended 12-month sentence of imprisonment. Cases such as this raise the question of whether those that kill out of compassion should have to rely on the defence of diminished responsibility to avoid the label of murder and a mandatory life sentence. It has been seen that where a killing is motivated by the emotion of fear or anger, the killer may be able to rely on the partial defence of loss of control to reduce a murder conviction to one of manslaughter. Keating and Bridgeman have noted that compassion, like fear and anger, is an emotion, but unlike those emotions it is an altruistic emotion and reflects well on the person who experiences it and acts upon it.[272] Should we not, then, afford a defence of compassionate killing to those such as the D in *Webb* who act to end another's suffering?

5. Evaluation of Voluntary Manslaughter

Have the reforms of the partial defences to murder introduced by the Coroners and Justice Act 2009 improved the law as desired? There is considerable strength of opinion that they have not: **7–118**

> "The Coroners and Justice Act 2009, sections 52–56 were prescribed as a legislative response to cure ills in extant law(s) over the ambit and parameters of partial defences to murder. Unfortunately, rather than a panacea, the statutory reforms have opened a new Pandora's Box in terms of the opaque and uncertain operation of loss of control and diminished responsibility defences."[273]

In relation to diminished responsibility we have seen that, despite the Law Commission's aim to improve the law and bring it in line with expert diagnostic practice, the defence has become more difficult to establish. Fortson echoes Mackay's arguments above by attributing the reduction in successful pleas to a number of factors related to the interpretation of the new law, including the difficulty of proving a "substantial" impairment of D's ability, and the inclusion of a causation requirement, and concludes that further reforms are warranted.[274]

270 Sentencing Council, *Manslaughter: Definitive Guideline* (2018), p.25.

271 *R. v Webb (George Hugh)*[2011] EWCA Crim 152; [2011] 2 Cr. App. R. (S.) 61.

272 H. Keating and J. Bridgeman, "Compassionate Killings: The Case for a Partial Defence" (2012) 75 M.L.R. 697–721.

273 A. Reed, N. Wake and B. Simpson, "Domestic and comparative perspectives on loss of control and diminished responsibility as partial defences to murder: a 10-yaer review of the Coroners and Justice Act 2009 reform framework" (2021) 72(2) *Northern Ireland Legal Quarterly* 161–170, 170.

274 R. Fortson, "Partial defences to murder: changed landscape and nomenclature" (2021) 72(2) *Northern Ireland Legal Quarterly* 171–199.

The issue that has attracted most academic criticism in relation to the reformed partial defences is, however, their application to victims of domestic abuse who kill their abusive partners. The Law Commission had assumed that in the worst cases of domestic violence, the victim of that violence would be able to rely on diminished responsibility as a partial defence.[275] In the past, a woman's ability to do so, whilst recognised in law, has not necessarily been seen to be desirable. Such women have had to fall back on diminished responsibility when both self-defence and provocation have been unlikely to succeed. In *Ahluwalia*,[276] for example, D was beaten and threatened with death for over 10 years before she poured petrol over her husband whilst he was asleep and then set light to him. At her trial, she pleaded provocation (or alternatively lack of mens rea) but was found guilty of murder. The Court of Appeal, however, very exceptionally, permitted medical evidence that was not brought before the court at the trial to be admitted at the appeal stage. On the basis of the evidence of her depressive condition, her conviction was quashed; at the re-trial, a plea of manslaughter on the basis of diminished responsibility was accepted and she was sentenced to 40 months' imprisonment (exactly the amount she had already served).[277] Forcing such Ds to resort to diminished responsibility has been severely criticised, however, on the basis that it labels them as "abnormal" or "crazy".[278]

7–119 The case law and the literature show that victims of intimate partner violence who resort to killing their partners continue to fall between the two partial defences in trying to avoid the mandatory life sentence for murder. A high profile case of an alleged primary victim who killed her abuser is that of Sally Challen, although it should be noted that the older law of provocation applied in this case, before the amendments that came into force in 2010.[279] Challen was convicted of murder in 2011, having killed her husband and been portrayed at her trial as a jealous woman taking revenge on him for his infidelity. Challen's appeal against conviction eight years later relied on evidence that she was the victim of coercive and controlling behaviour, the abuse being psychological rather than necessarily physical. Whilst the Court of Appeal's decision to quash Challen's murder conviction and order a retrial was welcomed by many as a victory for victims of coercive control, it is far from clear that a D in her situation would succeed in pleading loss of control. The court merely accepted that there was fresh evidence of a psychiatric condition that could have impacted on her ability to exercise self-control or her responsibility for her actions. The court did not, however, comment on whether such evidence was sufficient to successfully rely on loss of control or diminished responsibility as a defence. Others have commented that it might be difficult to persuade the jury to accept that the provocation was of an extremely grave character, giving her a justifiable sense of being seriously wronged, and that a person with a normal degree of tolerance and self-restraint might have reacted as she did.[280] As evidenced by Challen's decision to plead guilty to manslaughter on the grounds of diminished responsibility when facing her retrial for murder, the fate of primary victims who kill has arguably not progressed very far

---

275 Law Commission Paper No.304, para.5.100.

276 *Ahluwalia* (1993) 96 Cr. App. R. 133.

277 See also *R. v Hobson (Kathleen)* [1998] 1 Cr. App. R. 31; | (1998) 43 B.M.L.R. 181 CA where the Court of Appeal ordered a retrial on the basis that the issue of "Battered Women's Syndrome" (added to the British Classification of Mental Diseases after her trial but prior to the appeal) should have been put to the jury.

278 See, e.g. K. O'Donovan, "Defences for Battered Women Who Kill" (1991) 18 J.L. and Soc. 219.

279 *R. v Challen (Georgina Sarah)* [2019] EWCA Crim 916; [2020] M.H.L.R. 260.

280 K. Laird, Commentary to *Challen* [2019] Crim. L.R. 980–982; T. Storey, "*Case Note (Challen)*: Coercive Control: An Offence But not a Defence" (2019) 8.(6) J. Crim. L. 513–515. This theory is supported by the jury's decision in the case of *R. v Jackson (Penelope)* [2023] EWCA Crim 735.

since the case of *Ahluwalia*. Both women received acknowledgement from the Court of Appeal that they should perhaps be able to attract liability for manslaughter rather than murder, but both resorted to relying on mental abnormalities brought on by their husbands' abuse to plead diminished responsibility in order to achieve such a conclusion.[281]

Edwards has conducted research that suggests that the s.55(3) "fear of serious violence" trigger is scarcely used by women who kill their abusive partners.[282] There may be two reasons for this: first, such killings may take place in circumstances in which the killer has not lost their control, and so fall at the first hurdle. Secondly, the form of abuse that they fear may not be of "serious violence" in the traditional sense, since the abuse they have suffered may take the form of coercive control, as in *Challen*. Clough argues that the requirement of a fear of serious violence under s.55(3) forces abused women to plead loss of control under the alternative "anger" trigger, claiming that the emotional, financial or sexual abuse they have experienced amount to circumstances of an extremely grave character giving her a justifiable sense of being seriously wronged.[283] The legal challenges faced by women who kill abusive and violent intimate partners are by no means unique to this jurisdiction. Edwards notes that similar problems in Canada have particular impacts on marginalised women, adding further complexity to the picture.[284] Some have argued that the householder defence under the Criminal Justice and Immigration Act 2008 s s.76(5A) should be extended to cover domestic abuse victims.[285] Others have argued that a discrete partial defence for victims of domestic violence,[286] and/or those suffering from coercive control,[287] ought to be further considered. Perhaps what is needed is a more fundamental reconsideration of the former partial defence of provocation to ensure that it is inclusive of those who deserve to avoid the mandatory life sentence for murder, whilst moving away from a patriarchal view of who is so deserving.

Sarah Sorial, "Anger, Provocation and Loss of Self-Control: What Does 'Losing It' Really Mean?" (2019) 13(2) Criminal Law and Philosophy 247–269, 265–269

"[W]hile we may have no control over feeling emotions, we have significant control over how we express them. Moreover, expressing anger using violence is only one way among many other ways we can express anger, suggesting that we cannot explain violence by reference to the loss of **7–120**

281 The more recent case of *R. v Martin (Farieissia Surayah)* [2020] EWCA Crim 1798, can perhaps be added to the list. In *Martin*, the court accepted that the fresh evidence, including diagnoses of PTSD and dissociative behaviour, provided a proper basis for the defence of diminished responsibility, but also provided support for a defence of loss of control. Following the quashing of the conviction for murder, the Crown accepted a plea to manslaughter and D was sentenced to 10 years' imprisonment. It is not clear form the press reports whether this was on the basis of diminished responsibility or loss of control.

282 S.S.M. Edwards, "Women who kill abusive partners: reviewing the impact of section 55(3) 'fear of serious violence' manslaughter—some empirical findings" (2021) 72(2) *Northern Ireland Legal Quarterly* 245–270.

283 A. Clough, "Coercive Control: Transforming Partial Defences to Murder in England and Wales" (2023) 87(2) *Journal of Criminal Law* 110–121, 111–112.

284 S.S.M. Edwards, "Woman Who Kill Abusive Men: The Limitations of Loss of Control, Provocation and Self-Defence in England and Wales and Canada" 87(2) (2023) *Journal of Criminal Law* 76–96.

285 See, e.g. S.K. Howes, K.S. Williams and H. Wistrich, "Women who kill: why self-defence rarely works for women who kill their abuser" [2021] Crim. L.R. 945–957; V. Bettinson and N. Wake, "A New Self-Defence Framework for Domestic Abuse Survivors Who Use Violent Resistance in Response" (2024) 87(1) M.L.R. 141–171.

286 A. Carline and P. Eastel, *Shades of Grey—Domestic and Sexual Violence Against Women* (London: Routledge, 2014).

287 V. Bettinson, "Aligning partial defences to murder with the offence of coercive or controlling behaviour" (2019) 83(1) J. Crim.L. 71–86.

self-control. The fact that we have some choice in how we express emotions suggests that using violence is also a choice, based on assessment of the situation and on one's chances of success. It is therefore misleading to claim that the provoked, angry defendant lost his self-control, causing him to kill his victim.

Similarly, it is also misleading to suggest that the abused woman, because of fear, lost her self-control, and this is what caused her to kill her abusive partner. Given what we know about domestic violence and its effects on victims, it is likely that the woman feels several conflicting and intense emotions, including fear of further violence against her or her children, anger and resentment at her abuser, desperation at her inability to leave the relationship, feelings of entrapment, and a desire to protect her children. These reasons are all rational ones, given the circumstances and suggest, as Susan Edwards puts it:

> '[the battered woman's] state of mind and manifestation of behaviour at the time of the killing are not a loss of self-control in the traditionally masculinist sense at all. Nor is she in the period before the killing in a state of anger. She is in a state of fearful contemplation.'

To explain these killings as ones motivated by an irrational loss of self-control not only mischaracterises what occurs in these cases, but also fails to capture the complexity of various emotions and the cumulative effect they may have on an agent's state of mind and her reasons for acting.

To summarise: because we have some control over how we express our emotions, claims about loss of self-control are not really cases of loss of self-control. They are simply cases where people acted for various reasons: because they felt a sense of entitlement, or simply because they thought they would get away with it. Alternatively, a person might kill because she sees no other way out of a situation or to protect herself and/or her children from further violence. Moreover, these reasons for acting are assessable and may be found justifiable or not.

. . .

In assessing a defendant's reasons for acting, we would need to scrutinise the initial wrongdoing or provoking conduct, and whether it constituted a violation of a person's rights, in order to determine whether the response was justified . . . Women and children who have been subjected to abuse fall into this category, whereas men whose partners have left them do not. A 'justifiable sense of being seriously wronged' can thus be restricted to those cases where the defendant's rights were being violated, or where a person's autonomy was been undermined.

. . .

The offender's conduct is thus mitigated, and the sentence reduced only in those cases when the reasons for being frightened, angry, and resentful are good reasons, and are proportionate to the circumstances. For example, culpability would not be mitigated had the offender killed her husband on the basis of a one-off argument because this would not qualify as a good enough reason. It does not interfere or violate her rights or her autonomy and so would not qualify as a moral harm. Focusing on the reasons for action thus shifts the emphasis from an offender's alleged loss of self-control to whether her reasons for acting qualify as good reasons given the circumstances. It also gives judges a sound theoretical framework for making decisions in those cases where 'loss of self-control' does not follow the traditional narrative."

V. Statutory Homicide Offences

In addition to the common law offences of murder and manslaughter, a number of statutory homicide offences exist, having been created by Parliament to deal with specific contexts in which death may result and it is felt that a separate offence is needed. **7–121**

A. ENCOURAGING OR ASSISTING SUICIDE

SUICIDE ACT 1961 S.2 (AS AMENDED BY THE CORONERS AND JUSTICE ACT 2009 S.59):

"(1) A person ('D') commits an offence if— **7–122**

(a) D does an act capable of encouraging or assisting the suicide or attempted suicide of another person, and
(b) D's act was intended to encourage or assist suicide or an attempt at suicide.

(1A) The person referred to in subsection (1)(a) need not be a specific person (or class of persons) known to, or identified by, D.

(1B) D may commit an offence under this section whether or not a suicide, or an attempt at suicide, occurs.

(1C) An offence under this section is triable on indictment and a person convicted of such an offence is liable to imprisonment for a term not exceeding 14 years."

Prior to the amendments made by the Coroners and Justice Act 2009, the provision was couched in the same terms as those used in the Accessories and Abettors Act 1861, requiring that D aid, abet, counsel or procure the suicide or attempted suicide of another. The new provisions were intended solely to **7–123** modernise the language used and bring it in line with the law under the Serious Crime Act 2007;[288] the change is not intended to extend the law or alter the kinds of cases in which a prosecution will be brought.[289] Hirst notes, however, that the key change is the substitution of a conduct crime for a result crime.[290] Now that it is a purely inchoate offence the chances are that it could bring within its ambit more cases than it did previously, given that it can be charged in cases where the would-be "victim" has not got as far as attempting to commit suicide, as required under the old law.

It has been pointed out that:

> ". . . [t]he distinction between . . . [complicity in suicide and manslaughter by suicide pact] . . . may be very fine. If D and V agree to gas themselves with car exhaust fumes and D alone survives, it appears that he will be liable under the Homicide Act if he turned on the engine and possibly under the Suicide Act if V did."[291]

The distinction is of importance in terms of punishment. Killing in pursuance of a suicide pact is punishable as manslaughter by a maximum of life imprisonment, while encouraging or assisting suicide is punishable by a maximum of 14 years' imprisonment. The Law Commission's Draft Criminal Code recognised the strength of this point and proposed to make both offences subject to a seven-year maximum sentence.[292] The Law Commission proposed repealing the Homicide Act s.4 on the basis that its proposed reformulation of the definition of the partial defence of diminished responsibility would cater adequately for the deserving cases.[293] However, following consultation, the Law Commission retracted this proposal and recommended that the Homicide Act s.4 be retained pending the outcome of a further consultation on the question of whether a separate partial defence of mercy killing ought to be created.[294]

7–124 The consent of the DPP is required before a prosecution may be brought under the Suicide Act 1961.[295] In *Pretty*,[296] it was held that the DPP is unable to give an undertaking to people that they will not be prosecuted if they assist their spouse to commit suicide—even if that spouse, by virtue of their incurable condition, is unable to carry out their wishes themselves.[297] The House of Lords in *Purdy*[298] again had occasion to consider the issue of how prosecutorial discretion should be controlled in such cases. The facts were similar to those of *Pretty*, with the claimant arguing that, if the DPP could not give an

288 See Ch.10.

289 This was confirmed by the then DPP, Keir Starmer QC, in evidence to the House of Commons Public Bill Committee on the Coroners and Justice Bill at its fourth sitting on 5 February 2009, *https://www.publications.parliament.uk/pa/cm200809/cmpublic/coroners/090205/pm/90205s01.htm*.

290 M. Hirst, "Assisted Suicide after Purdy: The Unresolved Issue" [2009] Crim. L.R. 870, 875.

291 D. Ormerod and K. Laird, *Smith and Hogan: Criminal Law*, 14th edn (Oxford: OUP, 2015), p.678.

292 Law Commission Paper No.177 (1989), cl.63.

293 Law Commission Consultation Paper No.177 (2005), para.10.32.

294 Law Commission Paper No.304 (2006), para.7.50.

295 Suicide Act 1961 s.2(4).

296 *R. (on the application of Pretty) v DPP* [2001] UKHL 61; [2002] 1 A.C. 800.

297 Mrs Pretty brought her case under a number of the articles of the ECHR: arts 2, 3, 8, 9 and 14. It was decided that the Suicide Act 1961 s.2 was not incompatible with the ECHR and thus did not breach the Human Rights Act 1998. See generally, M.D.A. Freeman, "Death, Dying and the Human Rights Act 1998" (1999) 52 C.L.P. 218.

298 *R. (on the application of Purdy) v DPP* [2009] UKHL 45; [2010] 1 Cr. App. R. 1.

undertaking not to prosecute, they should at least be obliged to provide clear guidance as to what factors would be taken into account when deciding whether to prosecute. The House of Lords allowed the appeal, finding that the right to respect for private life under the ECHR art.8 was engaged and that if the law was to interfere with that right, there should be accessible and precise guidance to enable an individual to foresee the consequences of their actions so that they could regulate their conduct without breaking the law. The DPP would be required to issue offence-specific policy.

In response, following a consultation process, the DPP issued a policy in February 2010 providing a list of factors for and against prosecution in the public interest in cases of assisted suicide.[299] Such guidance should assure those suffering from a terminal illness, a severe and incurable physical disability or severe degenerative condition, such as the claimants in *Pretty* and *Purdy*, that if they seek to take their own lives, assisted by their loved ones, that said loved ones will not be prosecuted if they can be said to be truly motivated by compassion. However, where the suspect was acting in their capacity as a medical doctor, nurse, other healthcare professional, a professional carer or as a person in authority, such as a prison officer, and V was in their care, this will act as a factor in favour of prosecution. The Supreme Court in *Nicklinson*,[300] in addition to finding that s.2 does not impose what would be regarded under the ECHR as a "blanket ban" on assisted suicide, meaning that the UK is acting within the margin of appreciation and not in breach of the Convention,[301] also declined to order the DPP to amend the prosecution policy in response to arguments that it was insufficiently clear. This raises general questions not only about the degree of discretion that should be afforded to the CPS in prosecuting cases, and how that discretion ought to be controlled but, more fundamentally, about whether the criminal law ought to criminalise conduct it does not seek to punish, and whether the law on assisted suicide, mercy killings and euthanasia needs amending. Leaving such issues to the discretion of Crown prosecutors is less desirable than legislating clearly on what is or is not a criminal offence.

The maximum penalty is 14 years' imprisonment. Prosecutions are rare, making the sentencing task for the judge quite difficult. In *Howe*,[302] the first case prosecuted after *Purdy* was decided and the guidance was issued by the DPP, a 12-year custodial sentence was reduced to one of 10 years. D, who was 19, walked to a petrol station to fill a petrol can with petrol and buy a lighter which he returned to his 30-year-old friend. The friend, who was of a vulnerable character, had mental health problems and had on a number of occasions threatened to kill himself, poured petrol over himself and lit himself on fire. Miraculously he survived, albeit suffering 95% burns. The Court of Appeal, in reducing the sentence, considered that it was wrong of the trial judge to make reference to the sentencing guidelines in

---

299 This was updated in 2014. See *https://www.cps.gov.uk/legal-guidance/suicide-policy-prosecutors-respect-cases-encouraging-or-assisting-suicide*. It should be noted, however, that there is recently updated separate guidance on prosecuting "mercy killings" and how the Public Interest test applies in such cases under the more general legal guidance on prosecuting homicide, published in October 2023, *https://www.cps.gov.uk/legal-guidance/homicide-murder-manslaughter-infanticide-and-causing-or-allowing-death-or-serious*.

300 *R. (on the application of Nicklinson) v Ministry of Justice* [2014] UKSC 38; [2015] A.C. 657. For more on this case see Ch.4.

301 The Court of Appeal again agreed this in *R. (on the application of Conway) v Secretary of State for Justice* [2018] EWCA Civ 1431; [2020] Q.B. 1. Mr Conway, who suffered from motor neurone disease, had claimed that s.2 breached ECHR art.8, and proposed an alternative statutory regime for those in his position who wished to choose when to die. The Court dismissed these arguments and agreed with the conclusion of the Divisional Court that "section 2 of the 1961 Act achieves a fair balance between the interests of the wider community and the interests of people in the position of Mr Conway" (at [206]).

302 *R. v Howe (Kevin James)* [2014] EWCA Crim 114; [2014] 2 Cr. App. R. (S.) 38.

relation to Offences against the Person Act s.18 and provided guidance as to relevant factors for a court to consider in dealing with the offence.

B. INFANTICIDE

INFANTICIDE ACT 1938 S.1:

7-125 "(1) Where a woman by any wilful act or omission causes the death of her child being a child under the age of twelve months, but at the time of the act or omission the balance of her mind was disturbed by reason of her not having fully recovered from the effect of giving birth to the child or by reason of the effect of lactation consequent upon the birth of the child, then, if[303] the circumstances were such that but for this Act the offence would have amounted to murder or manslaughter,[304] she shall be guilty of . . . infanticide, and may for such offence be dealt with and punished as if she had been guilty of the offence of manslaughter of the child.

(2) Where upon the trial of a woman for the murder of her child, being a child under the age of twelve months, the jury are of opinion that she by any wilful act or omission caused its death, but that at the time of the act or omission the balance of her mind was disturbed by reason of her not having fully recovered from the effect of giving birth to the child or by reason of the effect of lactation consequent upon the birth of the child, then the jury may, if the circumstances were such that but for the provisions of this Act they might have returned a verdict of murder or manslaughter, return in lieu thereof a verdict of infanticide."

7-126 This offence/defence can only be committed by a very specific group of defendants (women who have given birth), within a particular period of time (12 months from giving birth), against a specific victim (D's child). Infanticide is similar to voluntary manslaughter in that it can effectively operate as a partial defence to murder.[305] It has especially close links with the partial defence of diminished responsibility and, indeed, there is some question as to whether infanticide is redundant given the existence of this wider defence.[306] The Court of Appeal has expressed clear discontent with the current law in the case of *Kai-Whitewind*, describing it as "unsatisfactory and outdated".[307] While the existence of the offence/ defence is useful in giving effect to both a judicial and societal desire to express understanding for and

303 The word "if" was substituted for "notwithstanding that" by the Coroners and Justice Act 2009 s.57.

304 The words "or manslaughter" were added by the Coroners and Justice Act 2009 s.57.

305 In R. v *Gore (Lisa Therese) (Deceased)* [2007] EWCA Crim 2789; [2008] Crim. L.R. 388, the Court of Appeal noted that infanticide is an offence under the Infanticide Act 1938 s.1(1), but a partial defence to murder is provided under the Infanticide Act 1938 s.1(2). Mackay has found that, in practice, infanticide is charged as an offence rather than being raised as a partial defence at a murder trial. However, of 49 cases prosecuted between 1990 and 2003, 37 were initially charged as murder, with the charge being altered to infanticide following pre-trial negotiations. There was no jury trial in all but two of these 49 cases: R. Mackay, "Infanticide and Related Diminished Responsibility Manslaughters: An Empirical Study", App.D to Law Commission Paper No.304, *Murder, Manslaughter and Infanticide* (2006), paras D17–D.18. It is therefore usually up to the defence to raise the issue, leading the prosecution to alter the charges.

306 Mason argues that a young mother who keeps her pregnancy secret and kills the baby shortly after birth may be able to show she suffered from a recognised medical condition in the form of a dissociative disorder: J. Mason, "The Myth of Madness: Murderous Mothers and Maternal Infanticide" (2021) 85 *Journal of Criminal Law* 442–454.

307 *R. v Kai-Whitewind (Chaha'oh Niyol)* [2005] EWCA Crim 1092; [2005] 2 Cr. App. R. 31 at [140].

sympathy with D's plight, the medical basis upon which infanticide has rested since the 20th century[308] has never been beyond doubt. It is estimated that 20% of women suffer mental health problems during the perinatal period (pregnancy and the first year after childbirth).[309] The most severe forms of psychiatric illnesses of postpartum psychosis and psychotic depression are thought to be much less common but do exist. The case of *Tunstill*[310] clarified that childbirth need not be the only cause of a mental instability in order for infanticide to be successfully pleaded. Medically, therefore, it can be argued that there is a case for a special defence (although no one is suggesting that all these women are likely to kill their children).[311] However, the most serious cases would probably fall within the defence of diminished responsibility.[312] Moreover, there are clear problems with both the terminology employed in the Infanticide Act and its use in practice, with Mason arguing that it "constructs filicidal women as 'mad' in circumstances where they are not—it maintains a myth of madness".[313] There have been only eight convictions for infanticide in the last 10 years.[314]

C. CAUSING OR ALLOWING THE DEATH OF A CHILD OR VULNERABLE ADULT

Domestic Violence, Crime and Victims Act 2004 s.5:

"(1) A person ('D') is guilty of an offence if— **7–127**

(a) a child or vulnerable adult ('V') dies [or suffers serious physical harm][315] as a result of the unlawful act of a person who—

(i) was a member of the same household as V, and
(ii) had frequent contact with him,

(b) D was such a person at the time of that act,
(c) at that time there was a significant risk of serious physical harm being caused to V by the unlawful act of such a person, and
(d) either D was the person whose act caused V's death [or serious physical harm] or—

308 It was not until 1922 that infanticide was framed with reference to the medical effects of childbirth; previously it had been more concerned with social conditions and moral values. Originally, e.g. infanticide applied only to the killing of illegitimate children and was more concerned with the concealment of death (which acted as a presumption of guilt to murder) rather than the death itself (21 Jac. 1, c.27, 1623). See A. Loughnan, "The 'Strange' Case of the Infanticide Doctrine" (2012) 32 O.J.L.S. 685–711.

309 A. Bayer, M. Parsonage, M. Knapp, V. Iemmi and B. Adelaja, *The costs of perinatal health problems*, LSE and the Centre for Mental Health (2015), *https://eprints.lse.ac.uk/59885/1/__lse.ac.uk_storage_LIBRARY_Secondary_libfile_shared_repository_Content_Bauer%2C%20M_Bauer_Costs_perinatal_%20mental_2014_Bauer_Costs_perinatal_mental_2014_author.pdf.*

310 *R. v Tunstill (Rachel Julie)* [2018] EWCA Crim 1696; [2019] 1 W.L.R. 416.

311 D. Maier-Katkin and R. Ogle, "A Rationale for Infanticide Laws" [1993] Crim. L.R. 90,t 906–909.

312 For a discussion of empirical research on the subject, see R. Mackay, App.D to Law Commission Paper No.304 (2006).

313 J. Mason, "The Myth of Madness: Murderous Mothers and Maternal Infanticide" (2021) 85 *Journal of Criminal Law* 442–45, 4544.

314 Office for National Statistics (ONS), *Homicide in England and Wales: year ending March 2022* (2023), Appendix Table 23.

315 Words inserted by the Justice Act (Northern Ireland) 2015. This amendment broadens the application of this offence beyond homicide. There are therefore two alternative versions of the actus reus: either causing or allowing death or causing or allowing serious harm. The offence construction is unusual in that the different harms constitute one offence rather than two separate offences, although not unique (see the offence of aggravated vehicle taking under the Theft Act 1968 s.12A).

> (i) D was, or ought to have been, aware of the risk mentioned in paragraph (c),
> (ii) D failed to take such steps as he could reasonably have been expected to take to protect V from the risk, and
> (iii) the act occurred in circumstances of the kind that D foresaw or ought to have foreseen . . .
>
> (7) A person guilty of an offence [of causing or allowing a person's death] is liable
> (a) on conviction on indictment in England and Wales, to imprisonment for life[316] or to a fine, or to both."

7–128 Such an offence was deemed to be necessary for practical reasons. Essentially, the problem it aimed to solve was the situation where:

> "A child is cared for by two people (both parents, or a parent and another person). The child dies and medical evidence suggests that the death occurred as a result of ill-treatment. It is not clear which of the two carers is directly responsible for the ill-treatment which caused death. It is clear that at least one of the carers is guilty of a very serious criminal offence but it is possible that the ill-treatment occurred while one carer was asleep, or out of the room."[317]

The offence provides that any parent or carer has a duty not only to refrain from abusing the child, but to prevent anyone else within the household from doing so. However, this duty is not new; the offence of child neglect or cruelty under the Children and Young Persons Act 1933 s.1 would apply in such a case, with a maximum penalty of 10 years' imprisonment.[318] The question is, should someone who has failed to prevent the abuse of their child which has ended in that child's death be liable for a more serious offence because of their failure to prevent that death?

7–129 It should be remembered that, in *Lowe*,[319] it was held that an offence of child neglect, as an omission, cannot amount to the unlawful act on which a conviction for constructive manslaughter can be based. It might be possible, however, that a parent or carer could be liable under the species of gross negligence manslaughter. Whilst there have been reported cases of neglect of vulnerable family members resulting in manslaughter convictions,[320] such cases are rare. Parents will satisfy the requirement of owing a duty of care to their child, in accordance with *Adomako*.[321] The question is whether they breached that duty either by abusing the child themselves or by allowing someone else to do so. If this is established, the issue then becomes whether the breach caused the death of the child. This is where the difficulty arises in relation to manslaughter. If one parent omitted to prevent another parent harming their child, can that first parent be said to have caused the child's death?

---

316 Raised from 14 years by Police, Crime, Sentencing and Courts Act 2022.

317 Law Commission No.282, *Children: Their Non-Accidental Death or Serious Injury* (Criminal Trials) (2003), para.1.1.

318 This is also the penalty for the version of the offence under s.5 of causing or allowing serious physical harm.

319 *Lowe* [1973] Q.B. 702. See para.8–046.

320 e.g. *R. v Stone (John Edward)* [1977] Q.B. 354; [1977] 2 W.L.R. 169 CA; *R. v Barrass (John Morris)* [2011] EWCA Crim 2629; [2012] 1 Cr. App. R. (S.) 80.

321 *Adomako* [1995] 1 A.C. 171.

The statutory offence makes provision for an alternative of *allowing* the child's death to avoid this problem. As an alternative to D causing death themselves, they may be liable under subs.(1)(d) on the basis that they knew of, or should have known of, the significant risk of serious physical harm and failed to take reasonable steps to protect V.[322]

Are parents who fail to prevent abuse directed at their children sufficiently culpable to warrant punishment for an offence of homicide (particularly given that they will probably be suffering tremendously from the loss of that child)? The mens rea requirement can be said to amount to mere negligence.[323] The Court of Appeal has, however, been unhelpful in its interpretation of the mens rea requirement. In *Khan,* it stated that in relation to the requirement that D either was, or ought to have been, aware of the risk of serious physical harm:

> "The objective therefore is to bring within the ambit of the offence, not only those who are actually aware of the risk and foresaw the unlawful act, but those who chose to close their eyes to a risk of which they ought to have been aware, and which they ought to have foreseen."[324]

As noted by Ormerod, however, this confuses wilful blindness, where D has some awareness of the risk, with negligence, where D need not have any awareness provided that the reasonable person would.[325] This is misleading, given that s.5(1)(d)(i) does not require any awareness of the risk.

Much of the terminology used in s.5 is rather woolly. Herring identifies as many as 11 ambiguities within **7–130** the definition of the offence.[326] The question of what amounts to a "significant risk" of serious physical harm was addressed by the Court of Appeal in *Stephens; Mujuru*.[327] Whilst it was clear to the court that the trial judge had set the bar too low by interpreting "significant risk" to mean "more than minimal", the court went no further in giving its own interpretation other than stating that it should be given its ordinary meaning by the jury. In *Khan,* the Court of Appeal addressed a number of other issues of definition within s.5 in the context of the death of a vulnerable adult, rather than a child. First, in relation to the requirement that D was a member of the same household as V, it noted that this was a question of fact and that any adult living in the household was a member of it, but that visitors to the house, including carers, were not members of the household for the purposes of the provision. The judgment appears to have narrowed the offence somewhat in stating that even if D lived in the same house as V, s.5 would not apply unless D came into frequent contact with V.[328] Only if the jury was sure that a particular D had frequent contact with V should they go on to consider the question of mens

322 Freer argues that the way in which s.5 is drafted is unsatisfactory, in that it does not allow for the basis upon which the defendant has been convicted to be known. The defendant is convicted of "causing or allowing" V's death; even where the jury is clear that D has caused V's death this cannot be reflected in their verdict and, as a result, the judge must sentence D without knowing the basis of the conviction: E. Freer, "'Causing or allowing the death of a child': challenges to working out 'which of you did it'?" [2016] Crim. L.R. 618–626.

323 J. Herring, "Mum's Not the Word: An Analysis of Section 5" in C.M.V. Clarkson and S. Cunningham (eds), *Criminal Liability for Non-Aggressive Death* (Oxford: Routledge, 2008), p.135.

324 *R. v Khan (Uzma)* [2009] EWCA Crim 2; [2009] 1 Cr. App. R. 28 at [32].

325 Commentary to *Khan* [2009] Crim. L.R. 348, 352.

326 J. Herring, "Mum's Not the Word: An Analysis of Section 5" in Clarkson and Cunningham (eds), *Criminal Liability for Non-Aggressive Death* (2008), pp.129–137.

327 *R. v Stephens (Jerry)* [2007] EWCA Crim 1249; [2007] 2 Cr. App. R. 26.

328 *Khan* [2009] 1 Cr. App. R. 28 at [28].

rea in s.5(1)(d). Secondly, in relation to the requirement that V's death occur in circumstances of the kind that D foresaw or ought to have foreseen, it was noted that this does not mean that the circumstances of which D ought to have been aware need be *identical* to those that occurred, only that they are of the same kind.[329]

In some cases of child abuse, the parent is arguably just as blameworthy in standing by and watching their partner abuse the child as if they had abused the child themselves. The kind of case for which the offence was designed is the infamous case of Baby P, or Peter as his name was later revealed to be, in which a toddler died after 10 months of abuse and was the victim of broken ribs and a broken spinal cord.[330] Three adults were convicted of causing or allowing his death under s.5: his mother, her boyfriend and her boyfriend's brother, Jason Owen. In Jason Owen's appeal against sentence, Hughes LJ noted that after the nine-week trial:

> "It was impossible at the end for the jury to resolve the question of who had inflicted those injuries which had been maliciously done, as some of them clearly must have been. No defendant as a result was convicted of either murder or manslaughter."[331]

Jason Owen had had his charge of murder withdrawn from the jury by the judge when the evidence showed that it was either Peter's mother or her boyfriend who had inflicted the violence upon him.

7-131 But what of the abused woman who is too afraid to intervene when her husband is chastising their child for fear that he could turn on her and do worse? Some may argue that a mother should sacrifice herself for her child, but it is difficult to see that if she fails to do so she should be charged with having caused or allowed the child's death. Herring argues that the problem with s.5 is that it deflects attention away from the main problems faced by society in such cases and makes criminals out of mothers who are themselves victims of domestic violence.[332] Singh's research results support this suggestion.

S. Singh, "Punishing Mothers for Men's Violence: Failure to Protect Legislation and the Criminalisation of Abused Women" (2021) 29 Feminist Legal Studies 181–204, 199:

7-132 > ["W]hen women are charged under section 5, prosecutors commonly seize upon a history of domestic abuse in order to prove that the defendant knew harm was foreseeable. My analysis of unreported case law confirms that the foreseeability of harm can more readily be established in the case of mothers due to conventional expectations of them that do not apply to fathers. This crime of omission is all too easily proven in a culture where mothers are expected to be omnipresent and are assumed to be responsible for every aspect of childcare and child safety. Moreover, I have shown how prosecutors rely upon archaic maternal ideals when trying to

329 *Khan* [2009] 1 Cr. App. R. 28 at [39].

330 See S. Laville, "Baby P Case: The final chapter in a story of appalling cruelty and deprivation" *The Guardian*, 22 May 2009.

331 *R. v Owen (Jason)* [2009] EWCA Crim 2259.

332 J. Herring, "Mum's Not the Word: An Analysis of Section 5" in Clarkson and Cunningham (eds), *Criminal Liability for Non-Aggressive Death* (2008).

convince the jury that the defendant failed to take reasonable steps to prevent harm. The 'reasonable steps' expected of mothers demonstrate little understanding of the realities of domestic abuse; the prosecutorial inference that the only way an abused woman may protect her children is by leaving the relationship fails to acknowledge that the dissolution of the relationship is the most dangerous time for women and children."[333]

She urges Parliament to reconsider the offence to ensure it does not apply to women who have suffered abuse and did not actively harm their child.[334] Ashworth is of the opinion that there was a good reason for creating some such offence as that under s.5, but that the offence as drafted is much wider than necessary to cover such cases, and raises questions about how many people at which it might be aimed are unaware of its existence.[335] The offence, however, does have its supporters, such as Morrison, who argues that "[t]he current framework is the fairest and most appropriate way of determining the liability of defendants who have been victims of domestic violence",[336] since she interprets *Khan* as applying a test of "qualified objective" reasonableness, meaning that D's abuse can be taken into account when judging whether she did what could have been reasonably expected of her. However, Singh's research indicates that such a reading of the case amounts to false optimism. **7–133**

D. VEHICULAR HOMICIDE (CAUSING DEATH BY DRIVING)

There are five statutory offences of vehicular homicide in English law: causing death by dangerous driving; causing death by careless driving; causing death by careless driving while under the influence of drink or drugs; causing death by unlicensed or uninsured driving; and causing death by disqualified driving.[337] In *Government of US v Jennings*,[338] it was held that that "motor manslaughter" had not been impliedly repealed by the Road Traffic Act 1956 and that causing death by reckless driving (the predecessor of causing death by dangerous driving) co-existed alongside the common law offence. In cases where persons are killed by motor vehicles the prosecution has a choice,[339] it can either charge D with one of these statutory offences, it can charge with manslaughter, or it can, in theory at least, charge both.[340] Gross negligence manslaughter may be relevant where the test in *Adomako* is satisfied. It is, of course, also possible for a driver to be convicted of manslaughter on the basis of an unlawful and dangerous act if they use their car as a weapon of assault (by driving directly at V in order to cause **7–134**

333 S. Singh, "Punishing Mothers for Men's Violence: Failure to Protect Legislation and the Criminalisation of Abused Women" (2021) 29 *Feminist Legal Studies* 181–204, 199.

334 Singh, "Punishing Mothers for Men's Violence: Failure to Protect Legislation and the Criminalisation of Abused Women" (2021) 29 *Feminist Legal Studies* 181–204, 198.

335 A. Ashworth, "Ignorance of the Criminal Law, and Duties to Avoid it" (2011) 74(1) M.L.R. 1, 18.

336 S. Morrison, "Should there be a Domestic Violence Defence to the Offence of Familial Homicide?" [2013] Crim. L.R. 826–838, 838.

337 In addition to these, there is also the offence of aggravated vehicle taking under Theft Act 1968 s.21A, which carries a maximum sentence of 14 years' imprisonment where death is caused.

338 *R. v Governor of Holloway Prison Ex p. Jennings* [1983] 1 A.C. 624; [1982] 3 W.L.R. 450 HL.

339 It is, of course, possible for murder to be the relevant charge where D has chosen to use a motor vehicle to attack V and the necessary intention to cause death or GBH is present. Such was the case for the principal offender (Mohammed Khan) in the case of *R. v Grant (Tony Lee)* [2021] EWCA Crim 1243; [2022] Q.B. 857.

340 The statutory causing death by driving offences are lesser included offences of manslaughter in cases involving mechanically propelled vehicles, by virtue of the Road Traffic Offenders Act 1988 s.24, amended by the Road Safety Act 2006.

fear) and in doing so kill.[341] Guidance issued by the CPS makes it clear that manslaughter will be the appropriate charge in cases where a motor vehicle has been used as an instrument of attack, but also recognises that there may be some cases in which manslaughter ought to be charged based on gross negligence. Despite the maximum penalty for the most serious death by driving offences now being the equivalent of that for manslaughter (i.e. life imprisonment), the CPS advises that "[h]omicide offences should be considered for all fatal driving incidents".[342]

1. Causing Death by Dangerous Driving

7–135 The Road Traffic Act 1988 s.1, as amended by the Road Traffic Act 1991, provides as follows:

> "A person who causes the death of another person by driving a mechanically propelled vehicle dangerously on a road or other public place is guilty of an offence."

The offence is triable only on indictment and is punishable by a maximum penalty of life imprisonment.[343]

Before 1977, the offence covered causing death by reckless or dangerous driving. In 1977, it was narrowed to causing death by reckless driving.[344] The *Lawrence* test of recklessness, as qualified in *Reid*, applied. In 1991, this was abolished and replaced by the new offence of causing death by dangerous driving. In order to understand the requirements of the constructive offence under s.1, one must look to the definition of dangerous driving under s.2A on which it is built.

Road Traffic Act 1988 (as amended by the Road Traffic Act 1991) s.2A:

7–136

> "2A. Meaning of dangerous driving.
>
> (1) For the purposes of sections 1 and 2 above a person is to be regarded as driving dangerously if (and, subject to subsection (2) below, only if)—
>
> (a) the way he drives falls far below what would be expected of a competent and careful driver, and
> (b) it would be obvious to a competent and careful driver that driving in that way would be dangerous.

---

341 See, e.g. *R. v Ripley (Samuel)* [1997] 1 Cr. App. R. (S.) 19; *Att-Gen's Reference (No.64 of 2001) (David Little)* [2001] EWCA Crim 2028; [2002] 1 Cr. App. R. (S.) 94; *R. v Wright* [2004] 1 Cr. App. R.(S.) 4; *R. v Franks (Jamie John)* [2004] EWCA Crim 1241; [2005] 1 Cr. App. R. (S.) 13; *R. v Clarke (John Amos)* [2005] EWCA Crim 3047; [2006] 1 Cr. App. R. (S.) 132; *R. v Dudley (Leayon Davi)* [2006] EWCA Crim 387; [2006] 2 Cr. App. R. (S.) 77; *R. v Kwaik (Abid Abu)* [2013] EWCA Crim 2397; [2014] Crim. L.R. 454; *R. v Williams (Clayton Ronald)* [2017] EWCA Crim 305; [2017] 4 W.L.R. 78; *R. v Parry (Benjamin Richards)* [2023] EWCA Crim 421; [2023] 2 Cr. App. R. (S.) 35. Constructive manslaughter has also been successful in a case of driving causing death where the unlawful act on which the charge was based was burglary (*Bristow* [2013] EWCA Crim 1540) and, potentially, theft (*R. v Long (Henry)* [2020] EWCA Crim 1729; [2021] 4 W.L.R. 5, where the defendants had committed theft of a quad bike and in the process caused the death of a police officer).

342 See *https://www.cps.gov.uk/legal-guidance/road-traffic-charging*.

343 The penalty was raised from 14 years' imprisonment by the Police, Crime, Sentencing and Courts Act 2022.

344 Criminal Law Act 1977 s.50(1).

(2) A person is also to be regarded as driving dangerously for the purposes of sections 1 and 2 above if it would be obvious to a competent and careful driver that driving the vehicle in its current state would be dangerous.

(3) In subsections (1) and (2) above 'dangerous' refers to danger either of injury to any person or of serious damage to property; and in determining for the purposes of those subsections what would be expected of, or obvious to, a competent and careful driver in a particular case, regard shall be had not only to the circumstances of which he could be expected to be aware but also to any circumstances shown to have been within the knowledge of the accused.

(4) In determining for the purposes of subsection (2) above the state of a vehicle, regard may be had to anything attached to or carried on or in it and to the manner in which it is attached or carried."

The emphasis is on the objective nature of the driving rather than on D's state of mind.[345] What is the difference between this test of dangerous driving and that required for gross negligence manslaughter as laid down in *Adomako* (apart from the fact that causing death by dangerous driving can only be committed on a road or other public place whereas manslaughter can be committed anywhere)? The most important distinction is that for manslaughter the driving must have involved a *risk of death*: it must be "not only dangerous but inherently life-threatening".[346] However, given the potential danger of all motor vehicles, "measuring the risk to determine whether it was one of death or one of mere physical injury is surely a near impossible task, given that death did in fact occur".[347] **7–137**

Why is it necessary to have a special offence, particularly given that the maximum penalty for s.1 is now the same as for manslaughter? Why are such persons not simply charged with manslaughter? Is it different to kill another with a motor vehicle than with some other instrument?

Sir Brian MacKenna, "Causing Death by Reckless or Dangerous Driving: A Suggestion" [1970] Crim. L.R. 67:

"By 1955–56 it was clear to all that prosecutions for motor manslaughter were a failure: juries just would not convict. Different reasons were assigned for their perversity . . . 'The very word "manslaughter" is ugly and is associated in the minds of most people with brawls and sordid **7–138**

345 In *Milton v Crown Prosecution Service* [2007] EWHC 532 (Admin); [2007] R.T.R. 43, the High Court used the rule in s.2A(3) to argue that it should be possible to take into account the fact that a driver has special skills when deciding the issue of dangerousness. A police officer's conviction for dangerous driving was quashed on the basis that the fact that he was a police-trained advanced driver should have been taken into account when deciding whether driving at speeds of up to 148 mph was dangerous. *Milton* was, however, overruled by the Court of Appeal in *R. v Bannister (Craig)* [2009] EWCA Crim 1571; [2010] R.T.R. 4. In this case, involving another police driver, the Court of Appeal noted that to take account of the special skill of a police driver would be to substitute the test of the competent and careful driver in the statute and to re-write the test Parliament had laid down.

346 I.D. Brownlee and M. Seneviratne, "Killing with Cars after Adomako: Time for Some Alternatives" [1995] Crim. L.R. 389.

347 S. Cunningham, "The Reality of Vehicular Homicide: Convictions for Murder, Manslaughter and Causing Death by Dangerous Driving" [2001] Crim. L.R. 679.

offences of various kinds. A jury is therefore reluctant to convict of this offence a person who is obviously very decent, and about whom the jury may think "there but for the grace of God, go I"'(Mr. Molson, *Hansard*, HC Vol.534 cols 782–783). For those who favoured this diagnosis the remedy seemed obvious: a new offence of causing death by reckless driving . . ."

Sally Lloyd-Bostock, "The Ordinary Man, and the Psychology of Attributing Causes and Responsibility" (1979) 42 M.L.R. 143, 156–157:

7–139 "[It has been pointed out] that the more relevant a particular type of accident becomes to the perceiver, the more he is forced to find ways of avoiding acknowledging that he could be blamed for, as distinct from just injured in, such an accident. He may therefore be expected to attribute less blame in accidents which are situationally relevant to himself. For example, a motorist may be more lenient in his judgment about someone involved in a road accident. As well as situational relevance, a misfortune may be personally relevant, *i.e.* the actor or victim may be similar to the perceiver. Similarity to oneself has often been found to relate to empathy and liking and to a tendency to judge another's actions more leniently . . . [Another possibility is that where] the judger can identify with an actor and his act, he is more likely to perceive the situation as if he were himself the actor and hence assign less personal responsibility."

7–140 This attitude to drivers who kill appears to be changing, assisted in part by changes to the language used: "accidents" tend to be referred to as "collisions" in recognition that in most cases someone will be at fault; they are not random occurrences. Road safety charities and victims' groups such as Brake and RoadPeace have been calling for drivers to be charged with manslaughter, with recent developments showing that such campaigns have developed considerable traction Others have, in the past at least, argued that the special offence is in fact not needed: prosecutions should simply be brought under the Road Traffic Act 1988 s.2 for dangerous driving, punishable by a maximum of two years' imprisonment. Manslaughter could be charged in the very worst cases.

Criminal Law Revision Committee, 14th Report, Offences against the Person, Cmnd.7844 (1980), para.142:

7–141 "We consider that the fact that death occurs in motoring cases should not enable a graver charge than reckless driving to be preferred unless the facts are that the full mental element appropriate to manslaughter can be proved. The real mischief where that mental element cannot be proved is the very bad driving, and the fact that it causes death should be treated as no more than an aggravating factor of that road traffic offence for sentencing purposes in appropriate cases."

This is the simple view that it is the bad driving that is reprehensible and D should be blamed for that. The fact that death has been caused is "chance" and should be irrelevant in terms of substantive criminal liability.[348] This approach was not adopted by the Government.[349] **7–142**

2. Other causing death by driving offences

In addition to causing death by dangerous driving, there are now an additional four death by driving offences under the Road Traffic Act (RTA) 1988, as amended by subsequent legislation: **7–143**

Offence	*Statutory provision*	*Underlying offence*	*Maximum penalty*
Causing death by careless driving when under the influence of drink or drugs	RTA 1988 s.3A (inserted by the Road Traffic Act 1991)	Driving without due care and attention AND driving while unfit through drink or drugs (RTA 1988 s.4)/driving with drink/drug concentration above the specified limit (RTA 1988 s.5/5A)/failing to provide a specimen for analysis, or permission to test such a specimen (RTA 1988 s.7/7A).	Life imprisonment (indictable only)
Causing death by careless driving	RTA 1988 s.2B (inserted by the Road Safety Act 2006)	Driving without due care and attention/reasonable consideration (RTA 1988 s.3, as defined under s.3ZA).	Five years' imprisonment (triable either way)
Causing death by driving: unlicensed and uninsured drivers	RTA 1988 s.3ZB (inserted by the Road Safety Act 2006)	Driving other than in accordance with a licence (RTA 1988 s.87) OR driving while uninsured (RTA 1988 s.143).	Two years' imprisonment (triable either way)
Causing death by driving: disqualified drivers	RTA1988 s.3ZC (inserted by the Criminal Justice and Courts Act 2015).	Driving while disqualified (RTA 1988 s.103).	10 years' imprisonment (indictable only)

348 Such an approach was adopted in *R. v Krawec (Ihor)* (1984) 6 Cr. App. R. (S.) 367; [1985] 149 J.P. 709 CA but disapproved in *R. v Simmonds (Derek)* [1999] 2 Cr. App. R. 18; [1999] 2 Cr. App. R. (S.) 218. See further, C.M.V. Clarkson, *Understanding Criminal Law*, 4th edn (London: Sweet & Maxwell, 2005), pp.163–168.

349 Department of Transport and Home Office, Road Traffic Law Review Report (The North Report) (1988).

7-144 As was seen in Ch.2,[350] the introduction of serious constructive crimes such as those under s.3ZB (and now s.3ZC) has caused some controversy, with the courts seeing the need to temper the impact of the blunt legislation through statutory interpretation and the meaning of "causing death" as applied by the Supreme Court in the case of *Hughes*.[351] The facts of *Hughes* involved a D whose driving could not be faulted, who was involved in a collision when the deceased, who was fatigued and under the influence of drugs, swerved across the carriageway. The Supreme Court held that while D's acts were a "but for" cause of death (in that if he had not been driving, the deceased would not have collided with his car and died), his actions could not be the legal cause of death. The offence required that there must be "something which he did or omitted to do by way of driving [the car] which contributed in a more than minimal way to the death[352] "and that there needs to be "something properly to be criticised in the driving of the defendant".[353]

Quite what is needed in terms of the quality of driving to prove the offence has not been further defined. The court noted that the driving does not need to be as severe as careless or inconsiderate driving (which requires that D fell below the standard of a competent and careful driver), but there has to be an action or omission that amounts to more than mere presence at the scene.[354] If the driving were to be as bad as careless driving, then arguably D ought to be charged under the Road Traffic Act 1988 s.2B. However, in relation to causing death by disqualified driving, which attracts double the maximum penalty compared to causing death by careless driving, charging practice is likely to be different. The perverse outcome is that a driver whose driving does not fall below the standard of a competent and careful driver may receive a higher sentence than one whose driving is clearly careless.

E. CORPORATE MANSLAUGHTER

7-145 The Corporate Manslaughter and Corporate Homicide Act 2007 introduced a separate homicide offence of corporate manslaughter. This offence is considered in Ch.4 where the criminal liability of corporations for all offences is discussed.[355]

---

350 At para.2-057.

351 *R. v Hughes (Michael)* [2013] UKSC 56; [2014] 1 Cr. App. R. 6.

352 *Hughes* [2014] 1 Cr. App. R. 6 at [28].

353 *Hughes* [2014] 1 Cr. App. R. 6 at [32].

354 This has been considered further in *R. v Wilson (James Samuel)* [2018] EWCA Crim 1184; [2019] 1 W.L.R. 3916. The court emphasised that the causal link in question is between the driving and the death rather than the driving and the collision. The defendant had been driving at 10mph above the speed limit when he hit a pedestrian. Expert evidence showed that this significantly and materially increased the likelihood of death, even though a collision may have been unavoidable, D was therefore liable on the basis that his driving had contributed in some more than minimal way to death.

355 See paras 4-071-4-098.

VI. Reform of Homicide Offences

In England and Wales, there are several categories of homicide. The main distinction is between murder and involuntary manslaughter, a distinction resting on the presence or absence of a mental element, malice-aforethought. However, murder is also distinguished from voluntary manslaughter, this distinction being based either on the mental condition of D (diminished responsibility), or on the circumstances of the killing (the "loss of control" defence and suicide pacts). As we have seen, there are four further species of homicide:[356] infanticide, which refers specifically to the death of a particular type of victim (child under one year of age); the offence under the Domestic Violence, Crime and Victims Act 2004 s.5, which is also defined with reference to the victim (children or vulnerable adults); corporate manslaughter (which can only be committed by organisations); and the various offences of vehicular homicide, which refer to death being caused in a particular manner. **7–146**

The multitude of discreet homicide offences raises the following questions.

(1) Why do we distinguish between different categories of homicide?
(2) Do we distinguish between these categories with sufficient particularity?
(3) On what basis ought such distinctions to be made?

A. SENTENCING AND FAIR LABELLING IN HOMICIDE

Homicides range from cold-blooded, malicious killings to killings not far removed from accidents or killings where there are severe mitigating circumstances, such as fear of serious violence triggering a loss of control. It is necessary to differentiate between these homicides in terms of their perceived seriousness. This differentiation is useful for two purposes. **7–147**

(1) Different penalties can be attached for the different categories of homicide. Thus, the fact that murder is perceived as being far more serious than manslaughter is clearly reflected in the sentence: capital punishment before 1965 and mandatory life imprisonment since then, as opposed to a *maximum* of life imprisonment for manslaughter. That said, this grading of offences determined by sentence with murder at its pinnacle has been eroded in recent years, as noted by Norrie:

> "the 2003 Act[357] has in symbolic terms chipped away at the notion of one, uniquely serious, crime possessing one, uniquely serious, penalty."[358]

More recently, the increase in the maximum penalty from 14 years to life imprisonment applying to both causing death by dangerous driving and causing or allowing the death of a child or vulnerable

356 It should be noted that "homicide" within the official statistics refers only to murder, manslaughter and infanticide.
357 Referring to the Criminal Justice Act 2003 s.269.
358 A. Norrie, "Between Orthodox Subjectivism and Moral Contextualism: Intention and the Consultation Paper" [2006] Crim. L.R. 489–501, 489.

adult, bringing them in line with same sentence as manslaughter, represents a further example of this erosion.

(2) Differentiating between homicide offences emphasises the different stigma attached to each and enables us to differentiate between different kinds of moral wrong. For example, the label "murder" emphasises the special stigma attached to that crime. One of the main purposes of the criminal law and punishment is its symbolic value in communicating messages to the public as to what is permissible or not. Different labels are used for different crimes to communicate the degree of rejection of the specific crime. The label "murder" is used to emphasise the "dreadfulness"[359] and the "uniquely horrible [nature of the] crime".[360] Also, it may have a significant deterrent value.[361] Abolishing the label "may appear to have the effect of lessening the seriousness of taking life".[362] Similar arguments may be put forward to explain why we retain the label "manslaughter" and treat separately the offences of infanticide and vehicular homicide.

T. Morris and L. Blom-Cooper, A Calendar of Murder (Criminal Homicide in England since 1957) (1964), pp.271–272:

7–148 "Murder produces a sense of profound social shock—heightened in our own society by dissemination of the details through modern mass media. It can normally be relieved only by some highly dramatic act on the part of the community towards the offender. In days gone by this act was the public imposition of capital punishment; latterly . . . the criminal trial and the dramatisation of its preliminaries may be gradually taking its place . . . Clearly, it is the special character of murder, the attendant sensationalism of the re-enactment of the killing with its actual risk of imitation, which wide advertisement brings in its trial, that gives murder its quintessential quality—a crime apart."

7–149 Given the above views, another question presents itself. Does English law distinguish with sufficient precision between different homicides? Many would assert that it does not. Murder and manslaughter, in particular, are far too broad, each encompassing too many different types of conduct, circumstances and offenders—in short, too many different degrees of "heinousness". Murders, for example, vary widely: they cover planned, cold-blooded killings, deliberate killings with torture all the way down to killings only marginally qualifying as intentional under *Woollin*. They cover people who coldly kill for no reason, down through all the different motivations and explanations to mercy killings, where an anguished D kills a loved one to end their suffering. Manslaughters, too, cover a vast field: they range from conduct just short of murder to just above the non-criminal category of justifiable or accidental death. Is not each crime, each label, covering too vast a field?

---

359 *La Fontaine* 11 A.L.R. 507 at 535 per Jacobs J.
360 Cross, "Penal Reform in 1965" [1966] Crim. L.R. 184, 189.
361 CLRC, *Working Paper on Offences against the Person* (1976), para.7.
362 CLRC, *Working Paper on Offences against the Person* (1976), para.7.

At the other end of the spectrum from murder, we have seen that more specificity is being added to the law of homicide. Whilst manslaughter exists as a common law "dustbin" crime, new homicide offences have been created in recent decades in the form of causing or allowing the death of a child or vulnerable adult and various offences of causing death by driving. In addition, corporate manslaughter has been created to punish deaths caused by corporate gross negligence. What all of these statutory offences have in common is that they cater for killings that take place outside the context of a violent attack where D has chosen to engage in violence against another person.[363] Further specific offences could be added to this category, however. Medical negligence leading to death might warrant a separate offence.[364] As noted above, drug supply causing death is an offence in some jurisdictions, and could form the basis of a new offence here.[365] However, Wilson's arguments against such a move are forceful.[366] A further suggestion has been for a separate homicide offence of "liability for suicide".[367] This would be targeted at those who are guilty of domestic abuse, and whose partners, such as V in the case of *Dhaliwal*,[368] are driven to suicide. Such offenders are not caught by the scope of the law on encouraging suicide since they would not have the necessary mens rea for that offence. They might be guilty of constructive manslaughter, if it could be proved that they committed an unlawful and dangerous act which caused death. In *Dhaliwal*, it was suggested that such a charge would be possible in cases where V was suffering from a recognised psychiatric illness which was caused by the abuse suffered at the hands of her partner, and which in turn caused her to commit suicide. However, in many cases it will be difficult to show that this was the case, and yet arguably V's partner can be blamed for her death.[369] If we were to entertain the idea of creating such a specific offence, however, where would such specificity end?

Andrew Ashworth, "'Manslaughter': Generic or Nominate Offences?" in C.M.V. Clarkson and S. Cunningham (eds), *Criminal Liability for Non-Aggressive Death* (2008), pp.243, 246–247:

"[W]e must now confront the question whether the law should be structured around generic homicide offences or nominate offences. Three arguments in favour of nominalism stand out—that it is much more communicative, thereby emphasising the special duties of citizens in certain roles or positions; that the circumstances of some types of case are so unlike others that a separate category is a more accurate label; and that, if there were not a nominate offence for certain conduct, the law might be misapplied by juries. One argument against nominate offences is that their creation may convey the impression, however wrongly, that they are regarded as less serious than manslaughter because they are labelled separately and differently. Another counter-argument 7–150

363 See generally, Clarkson and Cunningham (eds), *Criminal Liability for Non-Aggressive Death* (2008).

364 Quick, "Medical Killing, Need for a Special Offence?" in Clarkson and Cunningham (eds), *Criminal Liability for Non-Aggressive Death* (2008).

365 For arguments in favour of such a move, see Elliott and de Than, "Prosecuting the Drug Dealer When a Drug User Dies: *R. v Kennedy (No.2)*" (2006) M.L.R. 986; and Elliott and de Than, "Restructuring the Homicide Offences to Tackle Violence, Discrimination and Drugs in a Modern Society" (2009) 20 K.L.J. 69.

366 Wilson, "Dealing with Drug-induced Homicide" in Clarkson and Cunningham (eds), *Criminal Liability for Non-Aggressive Death* (2008).

367 *The Independent*, 17 November 2009, p.12.

368 *R. v D* [2006] EWCA Crim 1139; [2006] 2 Cr. App. R. 24. See paras 2–083 and 7–019.

369 Elliott and de Than argue that liability could arise in such cases under either constructive manslaughter or gross negligence manslaughter but that, given the practical difficulties in proving such cases, a new statutory offence with a maximum term of 10 years' imprisonment ought to be introduced: Elliott and de Than, "Restructuring the Homicide Offences to Tackle Violence, Discrimination and Drugs in a Modern Society" (2009) 20 K.L.J. 69, 84.

raises questions about the deliberate mis-labelling of certain homicides in order to avoid controversy . . .

One general argument against nominate offences is that they may amount to a down-grading of the offence. Classifying the offences as manslaughter or culpable homicide would be an appropriate signification of the degree of wrongdoing, but a nominate offence (perhaps using the less censuring term, 'causing death by . . .') may not be a proper valuation. In order to grapple with this we need to separate the label from the essence. Applying a separate label to an offence (causing death by dangerous driving, infanticide) may lead people to believe—and this would be an empirical question—that certain forms of wrongdoing are being taken less seriously. But then there is the further and arguably more important question of whether that amounts to a real under-valuation, i.e. whether the 'valuation' consists not merely of the label attached but also of the level of sentence imposed. That, too, would be an empirical question. As intimated above, this question is rendered complex by the increasing levels of sentencing for causing death by dangerous driving in recent years, sentences that are often higher than those for manslaughter by gross negligence and unlawful act manslaughter, and sometimes higher than for manslaughter upon provocation (where the considerations are, of course, very different).

A further argument against nominalism, though limited in its scope, draws our attention back to the political context in which proposals for homicide law have to be assessed. Any proposal explicitly to reduce the censuring of homicides resulting from assisted suicide, suicide pacts and mercy killing tends to stir up formidable political opposition. Fears about the effects of such opposition led the Law Commission to leave these cases out of its final report in 2006. Some will decry this as cowardice, but the pragmatic truth is that recommendations that were viewed as relaxations of the law in those areas might well undermine all the other proposals in a package of reforms, so strong is the feeling among some religious groups and others. The tendency is therefore to leave these difficult cases aside, consigning them to a twilight world in which other doctrines (notably diminished responsibility) are stretched to accommodate such cases but only if sympathetic medical witnesses can be found. This is an unusual face of nominalism: there seems to be less controversy and greater public acceptance to be gained through mislabelling these cases, often as manslaughter by reason of diminished responsibility, than through using a clear and representative label that draws attention to the circumstances."

B. REFORM PROPOSALS

7–151 Given the problem of the breadth of the existing murder and manslaughter offences, the Law Commission in England and Wales has proposed a new hierarchy of homicide offences incorporating two distinct degrees of murder.

Law Commission No.304, Murder, Manslaughter and Infanticide (2006):

"1.64 In structuring the general homicide offences we have been guided by a key principle: the 'ladder' principle. Individual offences of homicide should exist within a graduated system or hierarchy of offences. This system or hierarchy should reflect the offence's degree of seriousness, without too much overlap between individual offences . . . 7–152

1.65 The 'ladder' principle also applies to sentencing. The mandatory life sentence should be confined to the most serious kinds of killing. A discretionary life sentence should be available for less serious (but still highly blameworthy) killings.

1.66 Partial defences currently only affect the verdict of murder. This is because a verdict of murder carries a mandatory sentence. That sentence is not appropriate where there are exceptional mitigating circumstances of the kind involved in the partial defences. These mitigating circumstances necessitate a greater degree of judicial discretion in sentencing. The law creates this discretion by means of the partial defences which reduce what would otherwise be a verdict of murder, which carries a mandatory sentence, to manslaughter, which does not. Therefore, our recommended scheme does not extend the application of the partial defences to second degree murder or manslaughter. These offences would permit the trial judge discretion in sentencing and they therefore lack the primary justification for having partial defences.

The structure of offences

1.67 We believe that the following structure would make the law of homicide more coherent and comprehensible, whilst respecting the principles just set out above:

(1) **First degree murder** (mandatory life penalty)

- (a) Killing intentionally.
- (b) Killing where there was an intention to do serious injury, coupled with an awareness of a serious risk of causing death.

(2) **Second degree murder** (discretionary life maximum penalty)

- (a) Killing where the offender intended to do serious injury.
- (b) Killing where the offender intended to cause some injury or a fear or risk of injury, and was aware of a serious risk of causing death.
- (c) Killing in which there is a partial defence to what would otherwise be first degree murder.

(3) **Manslaughter** (discretionary life maximum penalty)

- (a) Killing through gross negligence as to a risk of causing death.
- (b) Killing through a criminal act:
    - (i) intended to cause injury; or
    - (ii) where there was an awareness that the act involved a serious risk of causing injury."

7–153 There is much to recommend these proposals.[370] The "ladder" principle attempts to facilitate a logical approach being taken to the question of distinguishing between different offences and appears to succeed. The proposals shed the areas of homicide law which are often seen as most objectionable at present, namely the GBH rule for murder and the offence of constructive manslaughter. Yet they do so without sacrificing the underlying principles which some might say justify the current position. Those who intend to cause GBH and kill are blameworthy, since whether their victim will die or not is beyond their control. The proposals place this level of blameworthiness on the same rung of the ladder as foresight of a risk of death whilst intending to cause injury. Similarly, those who would fall under the current law of constructive manslaughter through assault resulting in death remain liable for manslaughter, but only where they foresee that injury could result. One issue with the final recommendations from the Law Commission is, however, that unlike its original proposals, it recommends that manslaughter would attract a discretionary life maximum penalty as it does under the current law. Rogers suggests that this "would seem to undermine the integrity of the whole new structure of homicide offences", given that there would be nothing in the sentence to differentiate manslaughter from second degree murder.[371] Arguably, the situation is now aggravated by the fact that, with the increase in maximum sentence for causing death by dangerous driving, if the Law Commission's recommendations were made law without further amendment, we would have multiple homicide offences all with the same penalty. It seems undesirable for second degree murder, manslaughter and causing death by dangerous driving to all with the same penalty.

We have already seen that deciding where to draw the line between murder and manslaughter through the use of mens rea is a much debated topic. The Law Commission has sought to blur the line between the offences by inserting between them the offence of second degree murder to incorporate what would, under the current law, fall within the lower ranks of murder and the upper reaches of manslaughter. Questions remain, however, over where on the ladder certain levels of blameworthiness should be placed. In its provisional proposals, the Law Commission singled out killing with intention to kill as the most serious form of homicide and proposed that this be the only way of committing first degree murder.[372] Following consultation, the Law Commission was persuaded that intention to kill is not always more blameworthy than other forms of mens rea. In the Report, an alternative form of mens rea for first degree murder was added: killing with intention to cause serious injury whilst aware of a serious risk of death. Norrie, in commenting on the Law Commission's Consultation Paper,[373] provides some arguments in favour of the view that an extreme form of recklessness might actually be sufficient for first degree murder, and that it would equate in terms of blameworthiness with an intention to kill. His view is that there is something, in addition to intentionality, that determines how serious a killing is.[374] This can be referred to as D's "attitudinal state". Norrie's view is that if we take account of the attitude of killers who display "reckless indifference" we might find that they are just as blameworthy as those who intend to kill:

---

370 For a critique of the recommendations, see A. Ashworth, "Principles, Pragmatism and the Law Commission's Recommendations on Homicide Law Reform" [2007] Crim. L.R. 333.

371 J. Rogers, "The New Homicide Ladder" (2007) 157 N.L.J. 48.

372 Law Commission Consultation Paper No.177, *A New Homicide Act for England and Wales?* (2005).

373 Law Commission Consultation Paper No.177, *A New Homicide Act for England and Wales?* (2005).

374 Norrie, "Between Orthodox Subjectivism and Moral Contextualism: Intention and the Consultation Paper" [2006] Crim. L.R. 486–513.

> ". . . [d]oing harm so serious as to endanger life can be regarded *substantively* as of the same order of culpability [as intention to kill]. It exhibits a practical indifference that is as bad as intending to kill."[375]

The other area of concern surrounding the ladder of offences is how the partial defences would operate. A preliminary point is that mercy killing, except in cases in which D can show diminished responsibility, would amount to first degree murder with no partial defence to accommodate the lesser blameworthiness that many would argue such killers demonstrate. The main reason for this, the Law Commission states, is that euthanasia was outside the terms of its reference.[376] **7–154**

The defences are, however, extended beyond the current law by the proposal to allow duress to act as a full defence to first degree murder, second degree murder and attempted murder.[377] This is in addition to the two partial defences of provocation (now replaced by loss of control) and diminished responsibility which would operate only in relation to first degree murder, reducing the offence to second degree murder rather than to manslaughter. The reasoning behind this is that the existing partial defences were created in order to avoid the mandatory life penalty for murder; with the mandatory sentence being confined to first degree murder and judges enjoying discretion in sentencing for second degree murder there would be no need to reduce the liability of such killers to that of manslaughter. That ignores, however, the need to group killers together in a way that labels them fairly.[378]

As discussed above, the partial defences to murder, as designed by the Law Commission as part of their ladder of offences, are not operating in practice as might have been hoped when these reforms were recommended. That does raise the question of whether a different approach is needed. Sullivan *et al.* have recently suggested that the problems with the defence of loss of control could best be resolved through the abolition of the mandatory life sentence for murder and subsequent abolition of the partial defences.[379] They are, as they acknowledge, by no means the first to suggest this "obvious" solution,[380] but also accept that it is not a particularly "realistic" option. There is very little political appetite to interfere with the common law homicide offences generally, let alone the idea that we as a society might become so "soft" on murderers as to do away with the mandatory life sentence. This suggestion similarly does not assist us with being able to communicate variations in culpability through offence labelling, since such differences would be reflected only in the sentence passed by a judge. That said, it is one of the options that the Government has recently been encouraged to consider following horrific killings in Nottingham on 13 June 2023, in relation to which Valdo Calocane was **7–155**

375 Norrie, "Between Orthodox Subjectivism and Moral Contextualism: Intention and the Consultation Paper" [2006] Crim. L.R. 486–513, 494.

376 Law Commission Consultation Paper No.177 (2005), para.8.3.

377 Law Commission Paper No.304 (2006), para.6.212. At present, duress is not a defence to murder or attempted murder. Some have in the past argued that there are compelling reasons for adding duress to the current group of partial defences: see, e.g. Lacey, "Partial Defences to Homicide: Questions of Power and Principle in Imperfect and Less Imperfect Worlds" in Ashworth and Mitchell (eds), *Rethinking English Homicide Law* (Oxford: OUP, 2000), p.107.

378 O. Quick and C. Wells, "Getting Tough with Defences" [2006] Crim. L.R. 514.

379 G.R. Sullivan, H.S Crombag and J.J. Child, "Loss of control in the appeal courts" 72(2) *Northern Ireland Legal Quarterly* 200–223.

380 Report of the Advisory Council on the Penal System: Sentences of Imprisonment (1978); House of Lords Select Committee on Murder and Life Imprisonment (Session 1988-1989), HL Paper 78.

convicted of manslaughter after pleas were accepted on the basis of diminished responsibility.[381] Calocane carried out two separate knife attacks in the early hours of the morning in the street, killing three people. Calocane had mental health problems, having previously been detained under the Mental Health Act 1983 s.2, and was diagnosed with schizophrenia. The public controversy caused by this case, and concerns expressed by the bereaved families, gave rise to a review by His Majesty's Crown Prosecution Service Inspectorate (HMCPSI) of the way in which the case was handled. HMPCPSI concluded that the decision to accept the pleas of not guilty to murder but guilty to manslaughter by reason of insanity were correct.[382] However, it also concluded that "[d]espite our findings that the CPS has complied with the law and their obligations, the families' concerns and the public disquiet about this case highlights aspects where further consideration is needed" and that the Government needs to consider whether either the Law Commission's recommendations on creating three tiers of homicide (first and second degree murder, and manslaughter) ought to be enacted or, alternatively, whether the mandatory life sentence should remain.[383]

---

381 Calocane was sentenced to a hospital and restrictions order, pursuant to the Mental Health Act 1983 ss.37 and 41. This was challenged by the Solicitor General as being unduly lenient, but that challenge was rejected by the Court of Appeal, which refused leave to appeal against sentence: *R. v Calocane (Valdo)* [2024] EWCA Crim 490.

382 HM Crown Prosecution Service Inspectorate, *An inspection of Crown Prosecution Service actions in the Valdo Calocane case* (2024), *https://www.justiceinspectorates.gov.uk/hmcpsi/inspections/an-inspection-of-crown-prosecution-service-actions-in-the-valdo-calocane-case/*, para.1.6.

383 HM Crown Prosecution Service Inspectorate, *An inspection of Crown Prosecution Service actions in the Valdo Calocane case* (2024), *https://www.justiceinspectorates.gov.uk/hmcpsi/inspections/an-inspection-of-crown-prosecution-service-actions-in-the-valdo-calocane-case/*, para.1.15.

Chapter 8

Property Offences

I. Introduction

There are a wide variety of offences against property in English law, for example, theft, fraud, robbery, burglary, taking a motor vehicle or other conveyance without authority, abstracting electricity, blackmail, handling stolen goods, forgery, criminal damage—and many more. Property offences encompass a wide variety of harms, from damage that endangers life, through robbery and "professional" theft and fraud, to small scale acts of dishonesty and damage to property, and behaviour that lies at the very fringes of criminality. The type of offender also varies widely: whilst large-scale professional crimes such as the Hatton Garden jewellery burglary capture the news headlines and cinematic interest,[1] there is a vast army of occasional criminals: the opportunist burglar or mobile phone-snatcher, the shoplifter, the teenage joyrider and the "respectable" employee who takes advantage of his employer's trust to embezzle funds or steal stationery. **8–001**

A. THE LEGAL BACKGROUND

The structure of property offences is very different from the offences against the person already covered. With the latter, the seriousness of the injury was critical in the structuring of offences and concomitant levels of punishment: for example, causing death is more serious than causing grievous harm, which in turn is worse than causing actual bodily harm—and so on. Offences against property, however, are not structured in such a clear manner. It is not possible to follow the same pattern in structuring liability because of the difficulty in measuring the "harm" done. One possible method here is by assessing the value of the property involved. English law, however, has not followed such an approach at a substantive level (although this is an important factor at the sentencing stage) and instead has chosen to distinguish property offences by the method of taking or dealing with the property. According to this approach, telling lies in order to deceive someone into agreeing to part with their property (fraud)) is treated differently from coercing someone with threats into parting with property (blackmail). Whether each **8–002**

1 "Hatton Garden jewellery heist: final three guilty over £14M burglary" *BBC News online*, 16 January 2016.

grouping is sufficiently precise and/or meaningful will be considered after an examination of the offences themselves.

Another distinctive feature of the offences against property is that they are mainly statutory and largely found in modern statutes, in particular, the Theft Act 1968, the Theft Act 1978, the Fraud Act 2006 and the Criminal Damage Act 1971. These statutes are somewhat distinctive in that they are similar to a code. Most English statutes consolidate, amend or add to the pre-existing law. The approach here is different. For example, the Theft Act 1968 swept away the previous law on the subject, creating entirely new law dealing with most forms of dishonest dealings with property.

Before examining the property offences themselves two important preliminary points must be made. First, the Criminal Law Revision Committee, in putting forward proposals[2] which largely became the Theft Act 1968, wished to avoid the technicality and complexity of the previous law under the Larceny Acts and deliberately tried to frame as much of the legislation as possible in ordinary "simple" language capable of being easily understood by the layperson. Accordingly, many key concepts (for example, "dishonesty") were inserted into the legislation without being defined. The courts could have developed their own legal definitions of such concepts but have instead preferred to leave the meaning of such words to the jury, as questions of fact. The jury are ordinary people; they know what ordinary words mean—and do not need judges to explain their meaning to them. This approach, leading to a lack of fixed standards and inconsistency, has proved highly controversial, as will be seen in this chapter.

8–003 The second preliminary issue in some ways completely contradicts the above point. Crimes such as theft deal with interference with other persons' rights or interests in property. One is free to do as one likes with one's own property. It is therefore always necessary to ascertain that there is some other person who has some right or interest in the property. For instance, in *Corcoran v Whent*,[3] D ate a meal in a hotel restaurant and left without paying. In order to determine his liability for theft, it became necessary to determine whether at the time he decided not to pay (after he had eaten the food), the food (in his stomach) belonged to anyone else! If it belonged to him he could commit no crime as he would not be interfering with anyone else's rights or interests in property.[4]

However, how is one to determine whether anyone else has such a proprietary right or interest in the property? There is a whole body of law—the law of property, contract and quasi-contract—devoted to answering such questions. The Theft Act 1968, for example, uses many technical legal terms such as "trespasser",[5] "proprietary right or interest",[6] "trust"[7] etc. As these terms are undefined in the Act it would appear reasonable that they be assigned their established civil law meaning. Such an approach would, however, fly in the face of the philosophy that words in such legislation be assigned their ordinary meaning by ordinary people, the jury. There is some force in such an approach. Civil law meanings of words need adaptation to the purposes of the criminal law, for instance, to accommodate

---

2 Criminal Law Revision Committee, Eighth Report, *Theft and Related Offences*, Cmnd.2977 (1966).

3 *Corcoran v Whent* [1977] Crim. L.R. 52 Div Ct.

4 D's conviction for theft was quashed. Once he had eaten the food he could not "deal with it" and it was no longer property "belonging to another". This would now be dealt with as making off without payment under the Theft Act 1978 s.3.

5 Theft Act 1968 s.9.

6 Theft Act 1968 s.5(1).

7 Theft Act 1968 s.5(2).

the normal requirement of mens rea. Furthermore, the criminal law ought to reflect everyday values and "the way we live". Who better to reflect such values than those "everyday folk", the jury? In *Morris*,[8] one of the leading House of Lords' decisions on theft, Lord Roskill was highly critical of the approach that relied on the civil law meaning of concepts. For instance, whether a contract was void or voidable, was "so far as possible" not a relevant question in relation to the law of theft.[9] Yet in some cases, for example, where an issue arises as to whether property "belongs to another" for the purposes of the Theft Act 1968 s.5, it may still be necessary to refer to civil law concepts. The courts are not always prepared to jettison established legal meanings and replace them with "ordinary meanings". What is the ordinary meaning of those ordinary words, "trust" or "equitable interest"? A thorough consideration of all property offences is not possible, even in a book of this size. Accordingly, the enquiry will be limited to those offences that tell us most about the purposes and structures of this area of law. The main offences to be considered will be theft and fraud. Briefer consideration will also be given to the offences of obtaining services dishonestly, robbery, burglary, handling stolen goods and criminal damage.

II. Theft

Theft Act 1968 s.1(1)

"A person is guilty of theft if he dishonestly appropriates property belonging to another with the intention of permanently depriving the other of it; and 'thief' and 'steal' shall be construed accordingly." **8-004**

The maximum penalty for this offence is seven years' imprisonment.[10] This definition involves five elements,[11] all of which must be proved to coincide before liability can be imposed. Each of these elements is defined, wholly or partially, in the Theft Act 1968 as follows: **8-005**

- s.2: dishonesty;
- s.3: appropriation;
- s.4: property;
- s.5: belonging to another; and
- s.6: intention of permanent deprivation.

8 *R. v Morris (David Alan)* [1984] A.C. 320; [1983] 3 W.L.R. 697 HL.

9 *Morris* [1984] A.C. 320 at 334.

10 Theft Act 1968 s.7. The Sentencing Council has produced sentencing guidelines for the offences of theft (2016) and theft from a shop or stall (2016).

11 *Lawrence v Commissioner of Police of the Metropolis* [1972] A.C. 626; [1971] 3 W.L.R. 225 HL.

A. ACTUS REUS

8-006 We shall deal first with the actus reus elements, namely, appropriation of property belonging to another—before turning to the mens rea elements, dishonesty and intention of permanent deprivation.

1. Appropriation

THEFT ACT 1968 S.3:

8-007 "(1) Any assumption by a person of the rights of an owner amounts to an appropriation, and this includes, where he has come by the property (innocently or not) without stealing it, any later assumption of a right to it by keeping or dealing with it as owner.

(2) Where property or a right or interest in property is or purports to be transferred for value to a person acting in good faith, no later assumption by him of rights which he believed himself to be acquiring shall, by reason of any defect in the transferor's title, amount to theft of the property."

8-008 An appropriation is an *assumption of the rights of an owner*. But what are the rights of an owner?

An owner has the right to "use, enjoy and abuse" their property as they see fit.[12] They may keep it, sell it, give it away or destroy it. *Assuming* the rights of an owner is laying claim to be in such a position. The method of acquiring the property is not important. There does not have to be a taking or removal, although this is what occurs in the paradigmatic theft. The second part of s.3(1) makes this clear. If the owner accidentally leaves a book in D's room there can be an appropriation the moment D decides to keep the book. At this point, they will be assuming a right to the book by keeping or dealing with it as owner, despite the fact that they originally came by the property quite innocently.

The interpretation of s.3 has not been unproblematic, and the term "appropriation" has been considered by the House of Lords on four separate occasions.[13]

(i) Appropriation of "all" or "any" of the rights of an owner?

8-009 Section 3(1) might be interpreted as requiring that *all* of the rights of the owner need to be assumed for there to be an appropriation. However, in *Morris*,[14] Lord Roskill held that it was sufficient if the prosecution proved the assumption by D of *any* of the rights of the owner of the property in question.

---

12 This is subject, of course, to numerous restrictions aimed at protecting the interests of others.

13 *Lawrence* [1972] A.C. 626 HL; *R. v Morris, Anderton and Burnside* [1984] A.C. 320 HL; *DPP v Gomez (Edwin)* [1993] A.C. 442; [1992] 3 W.L.R. 1067 HL; *R. v Hinks (Karen Maria)* [2001] 2 A.C. 241; [2000] 3 W.L.R. 1590 HL.

14 *Morris, Anderton and Burnside* [1984] A.C. 320 HL.

R. v MORRIS, ANDERTON v BURNSIDE [1984] A.C. 320 (HOUSE OF LORDS) AT 331:

Two Ds took goods from a shelf in a supermarket, removed the proper price labels, and replaced them with labels from cheaper goods. The goods, bearing their incorrect price labels were presented at the checkout counter. One D was arrested before, and the other after, paying for the goods. The appeals were heard together. **8–010**

LORD ROSKILL:

"Mr Denison [counsel for the defendants] submitted that the phrase in section 3(1) 'any assumption by a person of *the rights*' (emphasis added) 'of an owner amounts to an appropriation' must mean any assumption of '*all* the rights of an owner.' Since neither respondent had at the time of the removal of the goods from the shelves and of the label switching assumed *all* the rights of the owner, there was no appropriation and therefore no theft. Mr Jeffreys for the prosecution, on the other hand, contended that *the* rights in this context only meant *any* of the rights. An owner of goods has many rights—they have been described as 'a bundle or package of rights'. Mr Jeffreys contended that on a fair reading of the subsection it cannot have been the intention that every one of an owner's rights had to be assumed by the alleged thief before an appropriation was proved and that essential ingredient of the offence of theft established.

My Lords, if one reads the words 'the rights' at the opening of section 3(1) literally and in isolation from the rest of the section, Mr Denison's submission undoubtedly has force. But the later words 'any later assumption of a right' in subsection (1) and the words in subsection (2) 'no later assumption by him of rights' seem to me to militate strongly against the correctness of the submission. Moreover the provisions of section 2(1)(a) also seem to point in the same direction. It follows therefore that it is enough for the prosecution if they have proved in these cases the assumption by the respondents of *any* of the rights of the owner of the goods in question . . ."

This approach was approved by the House of Lords in *Gomez*.[15] It is clear, therefore, that an appropriation involves the assumption of *any* of the rights of the owner. There need not be an assumption of all of the rights of the owner. **8–011**

(ii) Is there an appropriation where D assumes rights over property with the consent of the owner?

Section 3 does not specify whether, to amount to an appropriation, any assumption of the rights of the owner must be unauthorised. **8–012**

15 *Gomez* [1993] A.C. 442, Lord Keith at 489.

In *Morris*, although the House of Lords dismissed the appeals (on the basis that the removal of the goods from the shelves and switching of the price labels amounted to an appropriation), it was held that D must have done something objectively wrong for there to be an appropriation.

R. v Morris, Anderton v Burnside [1984] A.C. 320 (House of Lords):

8–013 LORD ROSKILL

"My Lords, Mr Jeffreys sought to argue that any removal from the shelves of the supermarket, even if unaccompanied by label switching, was without more an appropriation. In one passage in his judgment in Morris's case, the learned Lord Chief Justice appears to have accepted the submission, for he said [1983] Q.B. 587, 596:

'it seems to us that in taking the article from the shelf the customer is indeed assuming one of the rights of the owner—the right to move the article from its position on the shelf to carry it to the check-out.'

With the utmost respect, I cannot accept this statement as correct. If one postulates an honest customer taking goods from a shelf to put in his or her trolley to take to the checkpoint there to pay the proper price, I am unable to see that any of these actions involves any assumption by the shopper of the rights of the supermarket. In the context of section 3(1), the concept of appropriation in my view involves not an act expressly or impliedly authorised by the owner but an act by way of adverse interference with or usurpation of those rights. When the honest shopper acts as I have just described, he or she is acting with the implied authority of the owner of the supermarket to take the goods from the shelf, put them in the trolley, take them to the checkpoint and there pay the correct price, at which moment the property in the goods will pass to the shopper for the first time . . .

If, as I understand all your Lordships to agree, the concept of appropriation in section 3(1) involves an element of adverse interference with or usurpation of some right of the owner, it is necessary next to consider whether that requirement is satisfied in either of these cases. As I have already said, in my view mere removal from the shelves without more is not an appropriation. Further, if a shopper with some perverted sense of humour, intending only to create confusion and nothing more both for the supermarket and for other shoppers, switches labels, I do not think that that act of label switching alone is without more an appropriation, though it is not difficult to envisage some cases of dishonest label-switching which could be. In cases such as the present, it is in truth a combination of these actions, the removal from the shelf and the switching of the labels, which evidences adverse interference with or usurpation of the right of the owner. Those acts, therefore, amount to an appropriation and if they are accompanied by proof of the other three elements to which I have referred, the offence of theft is established. Further, if they are accompanied by other acts such as putting the goods so removed and re-labelled into a receptacle, whether a trolley or the shopper's own bag or basket, proof of appropriation within section 3(1) becomes overwhelming . . ."

This requirement that D must do acts objectively inconsistent with the rights of the owner is consistent with what Fletcher calls the "theory of manifest criminality". Fletcher states that "manifestly criminal" activities must exhibit at least the following essential features. First, the criminal act must manifest, on its face, the actor's criminal purpose. And secondly, the conduct should be "of a type that is unnerving and disturbing to the community as a whole".[16] **8–014**

The approach adopted in *Morris* can be seen as being consistent with the "harm principle": conduct should only be criminalised to prevent the causing of harm, albeit of a "second-order" nature,[17] to others. D, by doing something manifestly observable as wrong, for example, switching price labels, is doing something that is a threat to the security of the store; the interests of the store have been violated and they have sustained a "second-order harm". This approach stands in sharp contrast to "protectionalist criminology"[18] sustained by the utilitarian philosophies of punishment. Where the main interest is the protection of the property of others, then whatever measures are necessary to effect such protection become acceptable, even if this means imposing liability at an early stage when a D has done nothing observably wrong. If an individual has a blameworthy state of mind, then for deterrent, incapacitative and rehabilitative reasons they need punishment.

Lord Roskill's comments in *Morris* in relation to the requirement for there to be an act which adversely Interferes with or usurps the rights of the owner were obiter, because the switching of the price labels by the appellants was clearly not authorised by the shop. They were also inconsistent with the earlier decision of the House of Lords in *Lawrence v Metropolitan Police Commissioner*.[19] In that case, Occhi, an Italian student who spoke little English, arrived in England at Victoria Station and asked the D, Lawrence, a taxi driver, to take him to an address in Ladbroke Grove. Lawrence informed Occhi that it was a long way and would be expensive. In reality, the correct fare would have been about 10s. 6d. [52½p]. Occhi got into the taxi and offered a £1 note. Lawrence said that this was not enough and, with Occhi holding out his wallet for him, helped himself to a further £6 from the wallet. He then drove Occhi to his destination. The D was convicted of the theft of the approximate sum of £6 and the House of Lords upheld the conviction, holding that Occhi's consent to the taking of the money was irrelevant.

LAWRENCE V MPC [1972] A.C. 626 (HOUSE OF LORDS):

VISCOUNT DILHORNE: **8–015**

> "Prior to the passage of the Theft Act 1968, which made radical changes in and greatly simplified the law relating to theft and some other offences, it was necessary to prove that the property alleged to have been stolen was taken 'without the consent of the owner' (Larceny Act 1916, section 1 (1)).
>
> These words are not included in section 1 (1) of the Theft Act . . .

---

16 G.P. Fletcher, *Rethinking Criminal Law* (Boston, Little Brown, 1978), pp.82–89.

17 See paras 1–022–1–027.

18 Fletcher, *Rethinking Criminal Law* (1978), p.101.

19 *Lawrence* [1972] A.C. 626.

I see no ground for concluding that the omission of the words "without the consent of the owner" was inadvertent and not deliberate, and to read the subsection as if they were included is, in my opinion, wholly unwarranted. Parliament by the omission of these words has relieved the prosecution of the burden of establishing that the taking was without the owner's consent. That is no longer an ingredient of the offence . . .

That there was an appropriation in this case is clear. Section 3(1) states that any assumption by a person of the rights of an owner amounts to an appropriation. Here there was clearly such an assumption . . ."

8-016 In *Gomez*,[20] the House of Lords resolved this conflict between *Morris* and *Lawrence*, affirming the approach adopted in *Lawrence*.

R. v Gomez [1993] A.C. 442 (House of Lords):

8-017 D, an assistant manager of an electrical goods shop, lied to the manager of the store that two cheques were valid, with the result that £16,000 worth of goods were supplied to a rogue. D and the rogue were convicted of theft. Their appeal was allowed by the Court of Appeal (Criminal Division). The Crown appealed to the House of Lords.

LORD KEITH OF KINKEL (WITH WHOM LORD JAUNCEY OF TULLICHETTLE AND LORD SLYNN OF HADLEY AGREED):

"On the facts of [Morris] . . . it was unnecessary to decide whether . . . the mere taking of the article from the shelf and putting it in a trolley or other receptacle amounted to the assumption of one of the rights of the owner, and hence an appropriation. There was much to be said in favour of the view that it did, in respect that doing so gave the shopper control of the article and the capacity to exclude any other shopper from taking it. However, Lord Roskill expressed the opinion that it did not, on the ground that the concept of appropriation in the context of section 3(1) 'involves not an act expressly or impliedly authorised by the owner but an act by way of adverse interference with or usurpation of those rights'.

While it is correct to say that appropriation for purposes of section 3(1) includes the latter sort of act, it does not necessarily follow that no other act can amount to an appropriation and in particular that no act expressly or impliedly authorised by the owner can in any circumstances do so. Indeed, *R. v Lawrence* is a clear decision to the contrary since it laid down unequivocally that an act may be an appropriation notwithstanding that it is done with the consent of the owner. It does not appear to me that any sensible distinction can be made in this context between consent and authorisation . . .

20 *Gomez* [1993] A.C. 442, Lord Keith at 460–464. In doing so, the HL extensively relied on the civil case of *Dobson v General Accident Fire & Life Assurance Corp LLP* [1990] 1 Q.B. 274, Parker LJ at 281; [1989] 3 W.L.R. 1066 CA.

The actual decision in *Morris* was correct, but it was erroneous, in addition to being unnecessary for the decision, to indicate that an act expressly or impliedly authorised by the owner could never amount to an appropriation. There is no material distinction between the facts in *Dobson* and those in the present case. In each case the owner of the goods was induced by fraud to part with them to the rogue. *Lawrence* makes it clear that consent to or authorisation by the owner of the taking by the rogue is irrelevant. The taking amounted to an appropriation within the meaning of section 1(1) of the Act of 1968. *Lawrence* also makes it clear that it is no less irrelevant that what happened may also have constituted the offence of obtaining property by deception under section 15(1) of the Act . . .

The decision in *Lawrence* was a clear decision . . . which had stood for 12 years when doubt was thrown upon it by obiter dicta in *Morris*. *Lawrence* must be regarded as authoritative and correct, and there is no question of it now being right to depart from it . . ."

LORD BROWNE-WILKINSON:

"The fact that Parliament used that composite phrase—'dishonest appropriation'—in my judgment casts light on what is meant by the word 'appropriation'. The views expressed (obiter) by this House in *Morris* that 'appropriation' involves an act by way of adverse interference with or usurpation of the rights of the owner treats the word appropriation as being tantamount to 'misappropriation'. The concept of adverse interference with or usurpation of rights introduces into the word appropriation the mental state of both the owner and the accused. So far as concerns the mental state of the owner (did he consent?), the Act of 1968 expressly refers to such consent when it is a material factor: see section 2(1)(b), 11(1), 12(1) and 13. So far as concerns the mental state of the accused, the composite phrase in section 1(1) itself indicates that the requirement is dishonesty.

For myself, therefore, I regard the word 'appropriation' in isolation as being an objective description of the act done irrespective of the mental state of either the owner or the accused. It is impossible to reconcile the decision in *Lawrence* (that the question of consent is irrelevant in considering whether there has been an appropriation) with the views expressed in *Morris*, which latter views in my judgment were incorrect."

LORD LOWRY (DISSENTING):

"The ordinary and natural meaning of 'appropriate' is to take for oneself, or to treat as one's own, property which belongs to someone else. The primary dictionary meaning is 'to take possession of, take to oneself, especially without authority', and that is in my opinion the meaning which the word bears in section 1(1). The act of appropriating property is a one-sided act, done without the consent or authority of the owner. And, if the owner consents to transfer property to the offender or to a third party, the offender does not appropriate the property, even if the owner's consent has been obtained by fraud . . . Coming now to section 3, the *primary* meaning of 'assumption' is 'taking to oneself', again a unilateral act, and this meaning is consistent with subsections (1) and (2). To use the word in its secondary, neutral sense would neutralise the word 'appropriation', to which assumption is here equated, and would lead to a number of strange results. Incidentally . . . 'the rights' may mean '*all* the rights', which would be the normal grammatical meaning, or (less probably, in my opinion) 'any rights' see *R. v Morris* . . .

I would respectfully agree with [Lord Roskill's description in *Morris*] . . . in relation to dishonest actions, of appropriation as involving an act by way of adverse interference with or usurpation of the owner's rights, but I believe that the less aggressive definition of appropriation which I have put forward fits the word as used in an honest sense in section 2(1) as well as elsewhere in the Act . . . [He then expressly declined to discuss whether *Morris* itself was really an example of theft.]

It is true that *Morris* contains no disapproval or qualification of *Lawrence*, but, in my view, the main statements of principle in these cases cannot possibly be reconciled and the later case therefore must not be regarded as providing any support for the earlier . . .

[In the Court of Appeal in the present case] Lord Lane CJ said:

> '. . . We therefore conclude that there was a de facto, albeit voidable, contract between the owners and Ballay [one of Gomez's associates]; that it was by virtue of that contract that Ballay took possession of the goods; that accordingly the transfer of the goods to him was with the consent and express authority of the owner and that accordingly there was no lack of authorisation and no appropriation . . .'

I respectfully agree . . . [and] would dismiss the Crown's appeal."

Appeal allowed

8–018 Following *Gomez*, where the D obtains property by deception there is an appropriation: it is irrelevant that the owner of the property "consents" to the transfer. This considerably expanded the scope of the offence of theft and meant that there was an almost[21] complete overlap between theft and the former offence of obtaining property by deception contrary to the Theft Act 1968 s.15 (now abolished by the Fraud Act 2006). In any case where D deceived V into parting with property the prosecution had the choice of charging either offence.[22]

---

21 Certain categories of land, wild flowers and wild animals cannot be stolen (s.4(2)–(4)) but could be obtained by deception as these subsections did not apply to s.15 (s.34(1)). Furthermore, R. Heaton ("Deceiving without Thieving" [2001] Crim. L.R. 712) has argued that there could have been cases where, as a result of D's deception, ownership passed to D prior to any appropriation so while property had been obtained by deception, there was no theft because D was not appropriating property belonging to another.

22 In *R. v Briggs (Linda Joan)* [2003] EWCA Crim 3662; [2004] 1 Cr. App. R. 34, a narrow interpretation of appropriation was adopted in order to avoid too great an overlap between theft and obtaining by deception. This approach is not consistent with the leading House of Lords' decisions. See para.8–028.

The offence of theft will be complete when there is a dishonest appropriation of property with intention permanently to deprive. As V's consent is irrelevant, it is unnecessary for D to do anything involving "adverse interference with or usurpation of" the owner's rights. For example, in *Atakpu*,[23] the Ds, using false passports and licences, deceived a car-rental firm in Germany into parting with cars to them. They brought the cars to England with a view to selling them here. It was held that the theft had been committed in Germany and therefore there could be no theft in England. The Ds who rented the cars in Germany did nothing beyond what they were permitted to do but were nevertheless held to have stolen the cars in Germany because that was where the appropriation had taken place.

The House of Lords in *Gomez* overruled a number of earlier cases in which appellate courts had allowed appeals on the basis that the appellants had done nothing inconsistent with the rights of the owner. In *Skipp*,[24] D, posing as a genuine haulage contractor, obtained instructions and collected two loads of oranges and onions to be delivered from London to Leicester. He had the intention of stealing the goods from the outset but only made off with them after loading them. The Court of Appeal held that he did not appropriate the goods when he loaded them because at that stage, he was not doing anything inconsistent with the owner's rights, and the appropriation had only occurred when the goods were "diverted from their true destination". In *Fritschy*,[25] D, acting under the instructions of the owner, collected a quantity of krugerrands (South African gold coins) in London to deliver them to Switzerland. All along he had a secret intention to steal the coins, which he did in Switzerland. The Court of Appeal held that there was no appropriation in England because D had acted with the owner's authority at that stage. The coins were only appropriated in Switzerland where the defendant committed the acts that amounted to an adverse interference with the owner's rights. The House of Lords in *Gomez* expressly overruled both of these cases.[26] The position post-*Gomez* is that in *Fritschy* the goods were appropriated and stolen when he took possession of them in England, and in *Skipp*, there were three appropriations (and therefore three thefts), each of which took place when a load was collected.

(iii) Can there be an appropriation when the owner transfers all of his rights in the property to D?

The decision of the majority of the House of Lords in *Gomez* may have resolved the conflict between **8–019**
Lawrence and *Morris*, but in *Gomez*, the D had induced the shop manager to part with possession of the electrical equipment by means of a fraudulent deception. This meant that, at common law, D only obtained a voidable title to the goods, and the shop manager had the right to rescind the contract.[27] It might therefore be argued that *Gomez* could be distinguished and was not applicable in a case where the original owner of the property parted with all of his rights in the property and the D acquired full, indefeasible title. However, this point was firmly resolved in the case of *Hinks*.

---

23 *R. v Atakpu (Austin)* [1994] Q.B. 69; [1993] 3 W.L.R. 812 CA.

24 *R. v Skipp* [1975] Crim. L.R. 114 CA.

25 *R. v Fritschy* [1985] Crim. L.R. 745 CA.

26 *Gomez* [1993] A.C. 442, Lord Keith at 464–465.

27 H. Beale (ed), *Chitty on Contracts*, 35th edn (London: Sweet & Maxwell, 2023), Vol.I para.10-056.

R. v Hinks [2001] 2 A.C. 241 (House of Lords):

8–020 D made friends with a man of limited intelligence. She regularly accompanied him to his building society where he made withdrawals from his account amounting to a total of about £60,000 which was deposited into D's account. A consultant psychiatrist gave evidence that the man was naïve and trusting and had no idea of the value of his assets or the ability to calculate their value, and that, although he was capable of making the decision to divest himself of money, it was unlikely he could make that decision alone. D was convicted of theft of the money withdrawn from his account. The Court of Appeal dismissed her appeal. She appealed to the House of Lords.

LORD STEYN:

"The certified question before the House is as follows: 'Whether the acquisition of an indefeasible title to property is capable of amounting to an appropriation of property belonging to another for the purposes of section 1(1) of the Theft Act 1968.' In other words, the question is whether a person can 'appropriate' property belonging to another where the other person makes him an indefeasible gift of property, retaining no proprietary interest or any right to resume or recover any proprietary interest in the property . . .

[I]t is immaterial whether the act was done with the owner's consent or authority. It is true of course that the certified question in *Gomez* referred to the situation where consent had been obtained by fraud. But the majority judgments do not differentiate between cases of consent induced by fraud and consent given in any other circumstances. The ratio involves a proposition of general application. *Gomez* therefore gives effect to section 3(1) of the Act by treating 'appropriation' as a neutral word comprehending 'any assumption by a person of the rights of an owner'. If the law is as held in *Gomez*, it destroys the argument advanced on the present appeal, namely that an indefeasible gift of property cannot amount to an appropriation.

Counsel for the appellant submitted in the first place that the law as expounded in *Gomez* and *Lawrence* must be qualified to say that there can be no appropriation unless the other party (the owner) retains some proprietary interest, or the right to resume or recover some proprietary interest, in the property. Alternatively, counsel argued that 'appropriates' should be interpreted as if the word 'unlawfully' preceded it. Counsel said that the effect of the decisions in *Lawrence* and *Gomez* is to reduce the *actus reus* of theft to 'vanishing point'. He argued that the result is to bring the criminal law 'into conflict' with the civil law. Moreover, he argued that the decisions in *Lawrence* and *Gomez* may produce absurd and grotesque results. He argued that the mental requirements of dishonesty and intention of permanently depriving the owner of property are insufficient to filter out some cases of conduct which should not sensibly be regarded as theft . . .

[I]n such cases a prosecution is hardly likely and if mounted, is likely to founder on the basis that the jury will not be persuaded that there was dishonesty in the required sense. And one must retain a sense of perspective . . . If the law is restated by adopting a narrower definition of appropriation, the outcome is likely to place beyond the reach of the criminal law dishonest persons who should be found guilty of theft . . .

Counsel for the appellant further pointed out that the law as stated in *Lawrence* and *Gomez* creates a tension between the civil and the criminal law. In other words, conduct which is not wrongful in a civil law sense may constitute the crime of theft. Undoubtedly, this is so. The question whether the civil claim to title by a convicted thief, who committed no civil wrong, may be defeated by the principle that nobody may benefit from his own civil *or* criminal wrong does not arise for decision. Nevertheless, there is a more general point, namely that the interaction between criminal law and civil law can cause problems . . . The purposes of the civil law and the criminal law are somewhat different. In theory the two systems should be in perfect harmony. In a practical world there will sometimes be some disharmony between the two systems. In any event, it would be wrong to assume on *a priori* grounds that the criminal law rather than the civil law is defective . . . The tension between the civil and the criminal law is therefore not in my view a factor which justifies a departure from the law as stated in *Lawrence* and *Gomez*. Moreover, these decisions of the House have a marked beneficial consequence. While in some contexts of the law of theft a judge cannot avoid explaining civil law concepts to a jury (*e.g.* in respect of section 2(1)(a)), the decisions of the House of Lords eliminate the need for such explanations in respect of appropriation. That is a great advantage in an overly complex corner of the law.

My Lords, if it had been demonstrated that in practice *Lawrence* and *Gomez* were calculated to produce injustice that would have been a compelling reason to revisit the merits of the holdings in those decisions. That is, however, not the case. In practice, the mental requirements of theft are an adequate protection against injustice. In these circumstances I would not be willing to depart from the clear decisions of the House in *Lawrence* and *Gomez*. This brings me back to counsel's principal submission, namely that a person does not appropriate property unless the other (the owner) retains, beyond the instant of the alleged theft, some proprietary interest or the right to resume or recover some proprietary interest. This submission is directly contrary to the holdings in *Lawrence* and *Gomez*. It must be rejected. The alternative submission is that the word 'appropriates' should be interpreted as if the word 'unlawfully' preceded it so that only an act which is unlawful under the general law can be an appropriation. This submission is an invitation to interpolate a word in the carefully crafted language of the 1968 Act. It runs counter to the decisions in *Lawrence* and *Gomez* and must also be rejected. It follows that the certified question must be answered in the affirmative . . . *I would dismiss the appeal to the House*."

LORD HOBHOUSE (DISSENTING): **8–021**

"The reasoning of the Court of Appeal therefore depends upon the disturbing acceptance that a criminal conviction and the imposition of custodial sanctions may be based upon conduct which involves no inherent illegality and may only be capable of being criticised on grounds of lack of morality. This approach itself raises fundamental questions. An essential function of the criminal law is to define the boundary between what conduct is criminal and what merely immoral. Both are the subject of the disapprobation of ordinary right-thinking citizens and the distinction is liable to be arbitrary or at least strongly influenced by considerations subjective to the individual members of the tribunal. To treat otherwise lawful conduct as criminal merely because it is open to such disapprobation would be contrary to principle and open to the objection that it fails to achieve the objective and transparent certainty required of the criminal law by the principles basic to human rights . . .

If one treats the 'acceptance' of the gift as an appropriation, and this was the approach of the judge and is implicit in the judgment of the Court of Appeal (despite their choice of words), there are immediate difficulties with section 2(1)(a). The defendant did have the right to deprive the donor of the property. The donor did consent to the appropriation; indeed, he intended it. There are also difficulties with section 6 as she was not acting regardless of the donor's rights; the donor has already surrendered his rights. The only way that these conclusions can be displaced is by showing that the gift was not valid. There are even difficulties with section 3 itself. The donee is not 'assuming the rights of an owner': she has them already . . .

Section 3 does not use any qualitative expression such as '*mis*appropriates' nor does it repeat the Larceny Act expression 'without the consent of the owner'. It has thus been read by some as if 'appropriates' was a wholly colourless expression. This reading declines to draw any guidance from the context in which the word is used in the definition in section 1(1) and the scheme of sections 2 to 6. It also declines to attach any significance to the use of the word 'assumption'. This led some curious submissions being made to your Lordships.

It was for example suggested that the garage repair mechanic employed to change the oil of a car would have appropriated the car. The reasoning is that only the owner has the right to do this or tell someone to do it therefore to do it is to assume the rights of the owner. This is an absurdity even when one takes into account that some of the absurd results can be avoided by other parts of the definition of theft. The mechanic is not assuming any right; he is merely carrying out the instructions of the owner. The person who accepts a valid gift is simply conforming to the wishes of the owner. The words 'appropriate' (property belonging to another) and 'assume' (the rights of that other) have a useful breadth of meaning but each of them in its natural meaning includes an element of doing something which displaces the rights of that other person. The rights of that other (the owner) include the right to authorise another (the defendant) to do things which would otherwise be an infringement of the rights of the owner . . .

My Lords, the relevant law is contained in sections 1 to 6 of the Act. They should be construed as a whole and applied in a manner which presents a consistent scheme both internally and with the remainder of the Act. The phrase 'dishonestly appropriates' should be construed as a composite phrase. It does not include acts done in relation to the relevant property which are done in accordance with the actual wishes or actual authority of the person to whom the property belongs. This is because such acts do not involve any assumption of the rights of that person within section 3(1) or because, by necessary implication from section 2(1), they are not to be regarded as dishonest appropriations of property belonging to another.

> Actual authority, wishes, consent (or similar words) mean, both as a matter of language and on the authority of the three House of Lords cases, authorisation not obtained by fraud or misrepresentation. The definition of theft therefore embraces cases where the property has come to the defendant by the mistake of the person to whom it belongs and there would be an obligation to restore it—section 5(4)—or property in which the other still has an equitable proprietary interest—section 5(1). This would also embrace property obtained by undue influence or other cases coming within the classes of invalid transfer . . .
>
> In cases of alleged gift, the criteria to be applied are the same. But additional care may need to be taken to see that the transaction is properly explained to the jury. It is unlikely that a charge of theft will be brought where there is not clear evidence of at least some conduct of the defendant which includes an element of fraud or overt dishonesty or some undue influence or knowledge of the deficient capacity of the alleged donor. This was the basis upon which the prosecution of the appellant was originally brought in the present case. On this basis there is no difficulty in explaining to the jury the relevant parts of section 5 and section 2(1) and the effect of the phrase 'assumption of the rights of an owner' . . .
>
> I would answer the certified question in the negative. But, in any event, I would allow the appeal and quash the conviction because the summing up failed to direct the jury adequately upon the other essential elements of theft, not just appropriation."
>
> *Appeal dismissed*

The combined effect of *Gomez* and *Hinks* in relation to the meaning of "appropriation" is that it is irrelevant that the person receiving the property acquires an indefeasible title to the property. On the facts of *Hinks* itself, the woman might only in fact have acquired a voidable title in civil law if there had been undue influence. It was emphasised, however, that the validity of the gift was irrelevant.[28] **8–022**

The approach adopted by the House of Lords in *Lawrence, Gomez* and, particularly, *Hinks* is most unfortunate. First, it is lamentable that the majority judgments in *Gomez* and *Hinks* do not specify the precise actions that constitute the appropriation. This leads to a failure to consider whether *at the time of the appropriation* the property still belongs to another. For instance, it is arguable that if the appropriation in *Gomez* occurred when the goods were physically collected by the rogue, ownership had already passed to him and so there was no appropriation of property belonging to another.[29]

The concept of appropriation has become "wholly colourless" (Lord Hobhouse in *Hinks*); it has been stripped of any practical meaning and has become no more than a minimal triggering condition for theft with the entire emphasis transferred to whether the conduct was dishonest or not. The absurdity of this approach is revealed in the following examples, considered obiter in *Gallasso*, a case decided prior to *Hinks*:

28 cf. *R. v Barton (David) and Booth (Rosemary)* [2020] EWCA Crim 575 at [137]–[140]; [2021] Q.B. 685.

29 Heaton, "Deceiving without Thieving" [2001] Crim. L.R. 712.

> "... for example, the shopper carelessly knocks an article off the shelf; if he bends down and replaces it on the shelf nobody could regard that as an act of appropriation. Or suppose a lady drops her purse in the street. If a passer-by picks it up and hands it back there is no appropriation even though the passer-by is in temporary control."[30]

8–023 As a result of *Hinks*, these actions, along with those of Lord Hobhouse's motor mechanic, all now amount to an appropriation. An appropriation has become a neutral, value-free act with the mental element of the D being irrelevant. This purely objective description ignores the definition of appropriation in s.3(1) that it must involve an "*assumption* by a person of the rights of the owner". But, "assumption" is not a value-free word. It suggests that one is laying claim to rights one does not have over property. There must be an assertion of dominion over the property; it involves a positive decision to treat the property as one's own.[31] It has been argued that there should be an element of "proprietary subjectivity" by D towards the property: "a mental connection of the person with the thing, the sense of dominion ... he behaves as if the property were *his*."[32] It is absurd to assert that picking up a dropped purse to hand it back to the owner is assuming the rights of the owner.

For similar reasons, it is objectionable that persons who have done nothing wrong yet, but have secret dishonest intentions, should be liable for theft. As seen above, the D in *Eddy v Niman* took goods from a shelf in a store and, intending not to pay for them, placed them in a trolley. Following *Gomez* and *Hinks* this would now be an appropriation and, because of their dishonest intent, theft. Again, it is difficult to accept that this is *assuming* the rights of an owner. One can surely only lay claim to, or assert, the rights of an owner if there is an open representation that one is assuming such a right. In the supermarket situation, as long as the goods are in the trolley D is recognising and respecting the rights of the owner by doing exactly what he is expected to do. If, on the other hand, D slips the goods into their own pocket, they are laying claim to the goods and treating themselves as owner without any recognition of the rights of another. Using Fletcher's test of "manifest criminality" discussed earlier, the reasonable observer would recognise the theftuous criminality of the D's actions.[33] However, following *Hinks*, such considerations are irrelevant. This marks an alarming return to "protectionist criminology" whereby liability is imposed primarily on the basis of the D's blameworthy state of mind—even if they have done nothing observably wrong.

8–024 A further objection to the ruling in *Hinks* is that persons can be liable for theft despite committing no civil wrong thus creating a conflict between the civil law and the criminal law: "It is surely intolerable

---

30 *R. v Gallasso (Lesley Caroline)* (1994) 98 Cr. App. R. 284 at 289; [1993] Crim. L.R. 459 CA. The appeal in *Gallasso* was heard on the same day that the House of Lords judgment was handed down in *Gomez* [1993] A.C. 442. In the light of *Gomez*, *Gallasso* should be regarded as being wrongly decided.

31 A.T.H. Smith, *Property Offences* (London: Sweet & Maxwell, 1994), p.163.

32 E. Melissaris, "The Concept of Appropriation and the Offence of Theft" [2007] 70 M.L.R. 581, 590–591.

33 See also M. Giles and S. Uglow, "Appropriation and Manifest Criminality in Theft" (1992) 56 Jo. C.L. 179. Melissaris, "The Concept of Appropriation and the Offence of Theft" [2007] 70 M.L.R. 581 argues that "it is necessary the act [should] be manifested and sensibly identifiable" (596). Obviously, one could not expressly employ a test of manifest criminality as this would involve asking the jury vague questions such as, does this conduct look like theft to you? What is suggested is that in developing a suitable test of appropriation the courts should have been, and hopefully Parliament will be, *guided* by this test.

that the performance of a perfectly valid contract should be a crime."[34] It has been argued, however, that congruence between these two areas of law is not possible: criminal courts are not well placed to determine whether a valid title has been acquired; civil courts are unable to determine liability for theft which depends on the establishment of dishonesty (a question of fact for a jury or magistrate). Nor is harmony necessary because the relevant rules of civil and criminal law are not aimed at the same thing: for example, the civil law has an interest, inter alia, in protecting the rights of third parties who subsequently acquire property.[35] The problem with these views is that criminal courts do have to decide questions of civil law[36] and civil courts do have to decide questions of dishonesty.[37] More significantly, this argument misses the central point that the law of theft is there to protect persons' interests in property. These interests can only exist at civil law: "remove dependence on the law of property, and property offences have no rationale."[38] A different argument in favour of the *Hinks* position is that it is legitimate to criminalise conduct that does not breach civil law proprietary rights because such conduct:

> ". . . may nonetheless have a *tendency* to undermine property rights, either directly by attacking the interests that they protect, or indirectly by weakening an established system of property rights and so threatening the public good that that system represents."[39]

Of course, it is legitimate to criminalise conduct that threatens security interests—but that is the function of the law of attempt and the other inchoate and endangerment offences. Attempted theft, for example, involves criminalising conduct that threatens the interests protected by the law of theft. The substantive law of theft should, however, be aimed at protecting existing property rights which can only be established by reference to the civil law.

A final objection to the decisions of *Lawrence, Gomez* and *Hinks* is that it was quite wrong to have collapsed the distinction between theft and the former offence of obtaining property by deception (now abolished by the Fraud Act 2006). The effect of *Gomez* and *Hinks* is that theft became a very broad offence of dishonesty. The general offence of fraud created by the Fraud Act 2006, which replaced the deception offences, is also a very broad offence of dishonesty,[40] which means that there is considerable overlap between the offences of theft and fraud.[41]

---

34 J.C. Smith [2001] Crim. L.R. 163, 165.

35 S. Gardner, "Property and Theft" [1998] Crim. L.R. 35. See also A.L. Bogg and J. Stanton-Ife, "Protecting the Vulnerable: Legality, Harm and Theft" (2003) 23 *Legal Studies* 402.

36 e.g. in relation to "belonging to another" under s.5.

37 See *Ivey v Genting Casinos UK Ltd (t/a Crockfords Club)* [2017] UKSC 67; [2018] A.C. 391 discussed at paras 8–079–8–094.

38 J. Beatson and A.P. Simester, "Stealing One's Own Property" (1999) 115 L.Q.R. 372, 374. cf. A.P. Simester and G.R. Sullivan, "On the Nature and Rationale of Property Offences" in R.A. Duff and S. Green (eds), *Defining Crimes: Essays on the Criminal Law's Special Part* (Oxford: OUP, 2005), pp.170–181. cf. S. Green, "Theft and Conversion—Tangibly Different?" (2012) 128 L.Q.R. 564.

39 S. Shute, "Appropriation and the Law of Theft" [2002] Crim. L.R. 445, 455.

40 See paras 8–117–8–156.

41 This is recognised by the Crown Prosecution Service in their charging guidance: CPS, *The Fraud Act 2006: Legal Guidance, Fraud and economic crime* (2024). The guidance recommends that "Prosecutors must decide which offence properly reflects the criminality concerned, p.3.

Stephen Shute and Jeremy Horder, "Thieving and Deceiving: What is the Difference?" (1993) 56 M.L.R. 548, 549–553:

8–025 "It has long been recognised that there is some common sense distinction between theft and obtaining property by deception . . . The criminal law seeks to find appropriate labels for different kinds of wrongdoers, as part of its 'representative labelling' function. The label 'thief' does not carry the same moral import as the label 'conman' . . .

There is in our society a general social practice of uncoerced voluntary transfers ('givings'), even when they are the product of another's advice, influence or persuasion . . . [which] serve[s] to enhance the transferor's autonomy . . . [T]he nature of the wrongdoing in theft has a separate moral foundation from that of obtaining by deception. The wrongful conduct in obtaining by deception is internal to the practice of voluntary transfer. Its wrongfulness centres on the abuse of what should have been an autonomy enhancing transaction. The fraudster abuses the control that he or she has over the information on which victims make their decisions about an admittedly voluntary transfer: the victim's chances of making an authentic choice are deliberately or recklessly undermined by the fraudster. The wrongful act in theft, however, is external to the legitimate social practice of voluntary transfers of property. Its wrongfulness centres on the fact that the thief bypasses the entire social practice at the victim's expense. Putting it metaphorically, whereas the thief makes war on a social practice from the outside, the deceiver is the traitor within."

8–026 Offences should be structured, labelled and punished to reflect the extent of wrongdoing and harm involved. Crimes are generally described in terms of their paradigms. The paradigmatic theft involves a surreptitious or forcible taking while deception offences involved a confrontation and a participation by the victim in the loss of the property.[42] With theft, the owner is generally helpless against such a taking. If interrupted there is a risk of violence.

As shall be seen later, the Fraud Act 2006 has abolished all the deception offences and replaced them with two offences: fraud (which can be committed in one of three ways) and obtaining services dishonestly. One of the three ways in which fraud can be committed is through the making of a false representation with a dishonest intention to make a gain or cause a loss. This offence thus differs significantly from the previous offence of obtaining property by deception. First, there need be no deception. It does not have to be established that V believed the false representation and that that caused them to part with property. Secondly, no property need actually be obtained. The offence of fraud adopts an inchoate model. What is criminal is making the false representation with the requisite intent. It can, however, be anticipated that prosecutions will mostly be brought in cases where property has actually been obtained and V has sustained a loss. In such cases, there will still be considerable overlap between fraud and theft and the above criticisms of the over-broad interpretation of appropriation still apply. However, the overlap is no longer nearly so complete. In cases where no property has been obtained there will very seldom be an appropriation and so fraud will be the only

---

42 C.M.V. Clarkson, "Theft and Fair Labelling" (1993) 56 M.L.R. 554.

available charge. The next section, however, demonstrates that even in such cases there will sometimes be an appropriation.

(iv) Appropriation and control

Another problem that has arisen is whether there can be an appropriation by a D who is not in a position to exercise power or control over the property. Can a D sitting in a pub in Leicester appropriate the Crown Jewels (situated in the Tower of London) by "selling" them to a gullible foreign tourist? In *Pitham and Hehl*,[43] a man called Millman, knowing that his friend was in prison, decided to take advantage of his incarceration by stealing his furniture and selling it. He took the appellants to the friend's address, showed them the property and invited them to buy what they wanted. The Court of Appeal held that, at the moment he did this, he was "assuming the rights of the owner" and the appropriation was complete.[44] **8–027**

It has been argued that there can be no assumption of a right of an owner in such a case because an owner has no general right that others shall not contract to sell or purport to pass ownership in their property: "He does not need such a right, because other people, generally, can do him no harm by offering to sell his goods, and cannot pass ownership without his authority."[45] Furthermore, the fact that the owner suffers no harm because ownership cannot be passed is irrelevant. It is only in rare cases that theft deprives the owner of their ownership (as opposed to possession) of the goods[46] and causing loss of ownership is simply not a prerequisite of the law of theft.

However, while an offer to sell another's property can probably amount to an appropriation,[47] this should only be so where the actor is in a position to threaten the owner's rights.[48] Sitting in a pub offering to sell the Crown Jewels poses no threat whatsoever and therefore does not amount to an assumption of a right of an owner. Indeed, viewed from another perspective, it would not even amount to an attempted theft as the acts would still be preparatory. On the other hand, the rogue Millman in *Pitham* was in a position to threaten his friend's rights. His was an act of adverse interference with the rights of owner and was an assumption of the rights of owner.

(v) Limits on appropriation: *Briggs* and *Darroux*

In *Briggs*,[49] D, who had been acting on behalf of her great uncle and aunt in respect of the sale of their house and the purchase of a property known as Welwynd Lodge, arranged for the title in Welwynd **8–028**

---

43 *R. v Pitham and Hehl* (1977) 65 Cr. App. R. 45; [1977] Crim. L.R. 285 CACD.

44 *Pitham and Hehl* (1976) 65 Cr. App. R. 45, 49. Pitham and Hehl were acquitted of burglary, but convicted of the offence of handling stolen goods on the basis that they had received the goods 'otherwise than in the course of the stealing' (s.22 Theft Act 1968). See paras 8–189–8–195.

45 Smith, *Property Offences* (1994), p.160.

46 cf. D. Ormerod and K. Laird, *Smith, Hogan and Ormerod's Criminal Law*, 16th edn (Oxford: OUP, 2021), p.876.

47 On its particular facts, *Pitham and Hehl* (1976) 65 Cr. App. R. 45 is probably wrong. As all the parties concerned knew that Millman had no authority to sell the property, Millman was not "assuming the rights of owner"; it was a proposal for a joint theft (Ormerod and Laird, *Smith and Hogan: Criminal Law*, 16th edn (2021), p.877).

48 Melissaris, "The Concept of Appropriation and the Offence of Theft" [2007] 70 M.L.R. 581, states that under present English law: "The greater the proximity, the greater the risk to the owner's rights" (588).

49 *Briggs* [2003] EWCA Crim 3662; [2004] 1 Cr. App. R. 34.

Lodge to be transferred to and registered into the names of herself and her father. There was evidence that the great uncle and aunt's consent to the transfer of money used to purchase Welwynd Lodge was induced by fraud, since they believed that property would by conveyed to them, but the prosecution charged Briggs with theft in respect of this transaction. On appeal, the Court of Appeal held that, "where a victim causes a payment to be made in reliance on deceptive conduct by the defendant, there is no 'appropriation' by the defendant",[50] suggesting that the word "appropriation" was "a word which connotes a physical act rather than a more remote action triggering the payment which gives rise to the charge".[51] The court did not refer to the cases of *Gomez* or *Hinks*, so it may be regarded as having been decided *without due regard for the law or facts*.[52] In *Darroux*,[53] the court noted that *Gomez* and *Hinks* had not been discussed in *Briggs*, and expressed "considerable reservations" about the accuracy of some of Silber LJ's reasoning on the issue of appropriation: "it is well established that appropriation, within the meaning of section 3(1), does not necessarily require there to be a 'physical' act".[54] However, the Court of Appeal was still prepared to follow *Briggs* in holding that Darroux, a manager of a housing association residential care home who had submitted false overtime claims, leading to her being overpaid by electronic transfer, had not appropriated property belonging to the housing association:

> "[61] In submitting the monthly time forms and holiday forms the appellant was not, in our judgment, assuming any rights of an owner with regard to the bank account . . . Rather, the appellant was doing, albeit in some instances dishonestly, what she was employed to do as part of her employment—viz. submitting to PCS the monthly forms for payroll preparation purposes. She had no contact with the bank at all and no control of the bank account What she did, we consider, was too far removed to be an act of appropriation with regard to the bank account . . . conduct which ultimately is causally operative in reducing a bank balance does not necessarily become an assumption of rights of the owner with regard to the bank balance simply and solely because it is causally operative . . ."

The problems which arose in *Darroux* could have been avoided if D had been charged with fraud. Indeed, the Court of Appeal clearly thought that Darroux had been wrongly charged: "This was, on the facts, a clear potential case of fraud by misrepresentation. But that was not charged."[55]

---

50 *Briggs* [2003] EWCA Crim 3662; [2004] 1 Cr. App. R. 34 per Silber LJ at [12].

51 *Briggs* [2003] EWCA Crim 3662; [2004] 1 Cr. App. R. 34 per Silber LJ at [13]. Nor was there any reference to the case of *R. v Williams (Roy)* [2001] 1 Cr. App. R. 23; [2001] Crim. L.R. 253 CA in which the Court of Appeal had held that there was an appropriation where a dishonest builder, who grossly overcharged vulnerable elderly customers presented their cheques to the bank.

52 *Gomez* [1993] A.C. 442 was apparently referred to in skeleton arguments before the court: [2004] 1 Cr. App. R. 34, H8. cf. J.J. Child, A.P. Simester, F. Stark, J.R. Spencer and G.J. Virgo, *Simester and Sullivan's Criminal Law: Theory and Doctrine*, 8th edn (Oxford: Hart Publishing, 2022), p.629.

53 *R. v Darroux (Pamela)* [2018] EWCA Crim 1009; [2019] Q.B. 33. For discussion of this case, see: J.R. Spencer, "Two cases on the law of theft: a concertina movement?" [2018] *Archbold Review* 4; K. Laird, "Fraud: *R. v Darroux (Pamela)* (Case Comment)" (2018) *Criminal Law Review* 1006. The court distinguished the case of *Williams* [2001] 1 Cr. App. R. 23 (at [61]) on the basis the forms submitted by the D were not to be equated with cheques.

54 *Darroux* [2018] EWCA Crim 1009; [2019] Q.B. 33 at [55].

55 *Darroux* [2018] EWCA Crim 1009; [2019] Q.B. 33 per Davis LJ at [63].

(vii) Continuing appropriation

Is an appropriation complete as soon as there is an assumption of a right of an owner or does it continue for as long as the owner continues to assume that right? This can be important. For example, there can only be liability for handling stolen goods if the handling is "otherwise than in the course of stealing".[56] **8–029**

R. v Atakpu [1994] Q.B. 69 (Court of Appeal, Criminal Division):

The Ds hired cars in Germany and Belgium dishonestly intending to sell them in England. **8–030**

WARD J:

"It would seem that (1) theft can occur in an instant by a single appropriation but it can also involve a course of dealing with property lasting longer and involving several appropriations before the transaction is complete; (2) theft is a finite act—it has a beginning and it has an end; (3) at what point the transaction is complete is a matter for the jury to decide upon the facts of each case; . . . In our judgment, if goods have once been stolen, even if stolen abroad, they cannot be stolen again by the same thief exercising the same or other rights of ownership over the property.

We find it more difficult to answer . . . whether or not theft is a continuous offence. On a strict reading of *Reg. v. Gomez* any dishonest assumption of the rights of the owner made with the necessary intention constitutes theft and that leaves little room for a continuous course of action.

We would not wish that to be the law. Such restriction and rigidity may lead to technical anomalies and injustice. We would prefer to leave it for the common sense of the jury to decide that the appropriation can continue for so long as the thief can sensibly be regarded as in the act of stealing or, in more understandable words, so long as he is 'on the job'. [However], since the matter is not strictly necessary for our decision we will leave it open for further argument. It is not necessary for us to decide because no jury properly directed could reasonably arrive at a conclusion that the theft of these motor cars was still continuing days after the appellants had first taken them. If the jury had been asked when and where these motor cars were stolen they could only have answered that they were stolen in Frankfurt or Brussels. The theft was complete abroad and the thieves could not steal again in England."

Appeals allowed

Inevitably, such a fluid test of whether the D is "on the job" raises problems. If a burglar steals valuable goods from a house and hands them to a "fence" in a car parked outside on the street, is he still "on the job"? The liability of the "fence" for theft or handling will depend upon such a determination. **8–031**

---

56 Theft Act 1968 s.22(1), see paras 8–189–8–195.

(viii) No need for loss

8–032 As long as there is an appropriation, accompanied by an intention to permanently deprive someone of property, there is no need for that person actually to sustain any loss. In *Wheatley*,[57] the case involved a corrupt public official, who awarded a lucrative construction contract to the second appellant, in whose companies he had a public interest. The magistrate had dismissed theft charges against the appellants on the basis that the government had not been adversely affected by their acts, since the construction work had been carried out. The Court of Appeal of the British Virgin Islands entered convictions on these charges of theft, on the basis that consideration of whether there had been loss or gain was irrelevant to the question of whether there had been an "appropriation". The Privy Council concluded that this approach was correct:

> "It is certainly true that in most cases of theft there will be an original owner of money or goods who will be poorer because of the defendant's conduct. But in one of the two cases in *R. v Morris* . . . the defendant was arrested before paying the reduced price for the goods, so that the supermarket suffered no loss, and in *R. (A) v Crown Court at Snaresbrook*[58] . . . it was accepted that the alleged theft was carried out for a purpose which could financially benefit the company."[59]

In *Chan Man-sin*,[60] presenting a forged cheque was held to be an appropriation even though D's actions were legally ineffective as the transaction was a nullity and the bank would have had to repay the money. These decisions reveal the almost inchoate nature of the crime of theft following *Gomez* and *Hinks*.

(ix) Bona fide purchasers

8–033 Section 3(2) provides a special exemption for the bona fide purchaser for value of stolen goods. If a person bought goods at a reasonable price not knowing they were stolen and then later discovered they were, but decided to keep them, this would (without s.3(2)) come within the latter half of s.3(1), namely, they would have come by the property innocently without stealing it but would be appropriating it when they decided to keep it. The Criminal Law Revision Committee specifically proposed this exception on the ground that while there was a case for the imposition of criminal liability in such cases, "on the whole it seems to us that, whatever view is taken of the buyer's moral duty, the law would be too strict if it made him guilty of theft".[61] In *Wheeler*, D innocently purchased some stolen military antiques. He was later informed by the police that the goods were stolen but, nevertheless, sold one of the items. It was held that he could not be guilty of theft if he kept the goods for himself or sold them to another.[62] It is, however, possible that in selling such goods the D could be liable for the offence of

---

57 *Wheatley v Commissioner of Police of the British Virgin Islands* [2006] UKPC 24; [2006] 2 Cr. App. R. 21.

58 *Re (A) v Snaresbrook Crown Court* [2001] EWHC Admin 456 at [25].

59 *Re (A) v Snaresbrook Crown Court* [2001] EWHC Admin 456 at [11].

60 *Chan Man-sin v Att-Gen of Hong Kong* [1988] 1 W.L.R. 196; (1988) 86 Cr. App. R. 303 at 306 PC.

61 CLRC, 8th Report, *Theft and Related Offences* (1966), Cmnd.2977, para.37.

62 *R. v Wheeler (Stephen Godfrey)* (1991) 92 Cr. App. R. 279 at 283 CA.

fraud (if they represented that they had good title) or of aiding and abetting the offence of handling stolen goods by the purchaser (if both knew the goods were stolen).[63]

2. Property

Theft Act 1968 s.4:

"(1) 'Property' includes money and all other property, real or personal, including things in action and other intangible property. 8–034

(2) A person cannot steal land, or things forming part of land and severed from it by him or by his directions, except in the following cases, that is to say—

- (a) when he is a trustee or personal representative, or is authorised by power of attorney, or as liquidator of a company, or otherwise, to sell or dispose of land belonging to another, and he appropriates the land or anything forming part of it by dealing with it in breach of the confidence reposed in him; or
- (b) when he is not in possession of the land and appropriates anything forming part of the land by severing it or causing it to be severed or after it has been severed; or
- (c) when, being in possession of the land under a tenancy, he appropriates the whole or part of any fixture or structure let to be used with the land.

For purposes of this subsection 'land' does not include incorporeal hereditaments; 'tenancy' means a tenancy for years or any less period and includes an agreement for such a tenancy, but a person who after the end of a tenancy remains in possession as statutory tenant or otherwise is to be treated as having possession under the tenancy, and 'let' shall be construed accordingly.

(3) A person who picks mushrooms growing wild on any land, or who picks flowers, fruit or foliage from a plant growing wild on any land does not (although not in possession of the land) steal what he picks, unless he does it for reward or for sale or other commercial purpose.

For purposes of this subsection 'mushroom' includes any fungus, and 'plant' includes any shrub or tree.

(4) Wild creatures, tamed or untamed, shall be regarded as property; but a person cannot steal a wild creature not tamed nor ordinarily kept in captivity, or the carcass of any such creature, unless either it has been reduced into possession by or on behalf of another person and possession of it has not since been lost or abandoned, or another person is in course of reducing it into possession."

---

63 *R. v Bloxham (Albert John)* [1983] 1 A.C. 109 at 114; [1982] 2 W.L.R. 392 HL, approved in *Wheeler* (1991) 92 Cr. App. R. 279 at 284.

8-035 Theft is an offence against property and inevitably the question arises as to the meaning of "property". Section 4(1) provides an extremely wide definition of property that includes:

1. *Money*: This refers to current coins and bank notes, including foreign ones. Obsolete coins and notes would constitute other personal property. It does not cover money placed in a bank account, which then constitutes a debt owed by the bank to the account holder and is a thing in action (see below).
2. *All real property*: i.e. land and things attached to the land such as houses. However, the breadth of this provision is greatly limited by ss.4(2), (3) and (4).
   Section 4(2) isolates the only circumstances in which land and the things attached to the land may be stolen. Where D dishonestly tries to dispose of an interest in another's land, a charge of fraud under the Fraud Act 2006 s.1 is likely to be the most appropriate charge.[64] By virtue of s.4(2)(a), a trustee authorised to sell or dispose of trust land, or an attorney appointed to deal with a house belonging to an incapacitated person under a Lasting Power of Attorney, would commit theft if they dishonestly made an unauthorised disposal of the property. Reference must be made to the civil law to determine whether the defendant is authorised to deal with land for the purposes of s.4(2). In *Gimbert*,[65] D was charged (inter alia) with the theft of a house. The prosecution alleged that s.4(2) applied because D had taken dishonest advantage of his role as a purported attorney for an incapacitated relative under an Enduring Power of Attorney (EPA). However, the EPA had never been legally valid because the relative lacked capacity to make it and because it had not been registered.[66] The Court of Appeal was not prepared to extend s.4(2) to cover a case where, although not actually legally authorised to deal with another's property, a D was purporting to act as if they were. As the EPA was not legally valid, D was not authorised by a power of attorney when the house was transferred and therefore s.4(2) did not apply.
   Section 4(2)(b) deals with the appropriation by persons not in possession of the land: for example, it is not theft where D moves the fence to their garden so as to annex part of their neighbour's lawn into their own garden. Nor do squatters steal the land that they "squat" on.[67] However, a person not in possession of land can steal anything forming part of the land by severing it from the land or appropriating it after severance, so it would be theft if D were to remove trees or shrubs planted in his neighbour's garden.[68] Under s.4(2)(c), a tenant may be guilty of theft where they appropriate any fixture or structure let to be used with the land, e.g. removing a bath. This subsection does not require that the thing actually be severed from

---

64 cf. *R v. Gimbert (John David)* [2018] EWCA Crim 2190; [2019] Q.B. 590 at [2].

65 *Gimbert* [2018] EWCA Crim 2190; [2019] Q.B. 590. For discussion of this case, see: Laird, "Theft: *R. v Gimbert (John David)* (Case Comment)" [2019] *Crim. L.R.* 358.

66 Enduring Powers of Attorney Act 1985 ss.4–6. The Mental Capacity Act 2005 replaced the EPA scheme with a new Lasting Power of Attorney system: ss.9–14.

67 Specific offences have been created to criminalise certain squatters: Criminal Law Act 1977 ss.6–7; Legal Aid, Sentencing and Punishment of Offenders Act 2012 s.144. See N. Cobb, "Property's Outlaws: Squatting, Land Use and Criminal Trespass" [2012] Crim. L.R. 114–127; Crown Prosecution Service, *Trespass and Nuisance on Land* (2019).

68 Whether an item "forms part of the land" is a question of land law, depending on the degree of annexation and the purpose of annexation. For guidance re this, see *Elitestone Ltd v Morris* [1997] 1 W.L.R. 687; (1998) 30 H.L.R. 266 HL (wooden bungalow on concrete stand which could only be removed by demolishing it held to be part of the land); S. Bridge, E. Cooke and M. Dixon, *Megarry and Wade, The Law of Real Property*, 9th edn (London: Sweet & Maxwell, 2019), paras 22-005–22-010. cf. *Borwick Development Solutions Ltd v Clear Water Fisheries Ltd* [2019] EWHC 2272 (Ch); [2020] 1 W.L.R. 559: solar panels attached to the land were fixtures and formed part of the land (this issue was not pursued on appeal); *Mew v Tristmire Ltd* [2011] EWCA Civ 912; [2012] 1 W.L.R. 852: houseboats on wooden platforms not part of the land.

the land, merely that the fixture be wholly or partly appropriated. So "if the tenant contracted to sell the unsevered fireplace in the house leased by him, he would be guilty of theft".[69]

Section 4(3) deals with the circumstances in which things growing wild on land may be stolen. A person is not guilty of theft if they pick wild mushrooms, or "flowers, fruit or foliage from a plant growing wild on any land", unless the picking is done "for reward or sale or other commercial purpose". This exemption would not apply to cultivated flowers or crops, or if the whole plant were taken (except in the case of mushrooms), or if part of the plant was removed by an act which cannot be regarded as "picking" for example, taking cuttings with a knife, cutting grass with a lawnmower or strimmer, or sawing off branches.[70] **8–036**

Section 4(4) deals with wild animals. All tame creatures may be stolen. Wild creatures cannot be stolen,[71] except where (i) the creature has been tamed or is ordinarily kept in captivity (so animals in a circus or the zoo could be stolen); or (ii) the creature either has been reduced into the possession of another person, or is in the course of being reduced into the possession of another person. If, for example, V shoots a grouse on their farm, and before their dog can retrieve the carcass, a dishonest walker bags the bird for themself, the walker will commit theft. In *Borwick Development Solutions Ltd v Clear Water Fisheries Ltd,* it was held that fish reared and/or introduced into a closed commercial fishery were wild animals for the purposes of the law of property.[72]

3. *All personal property*: i.e. all property that is not real property. Nothing in the Theft Act:

> ". . . suggests that what would otherwise constitute or be regarded as 'property' for the purposes of the Theft Act 1968 ceases to be so because its possession or control is, for whatever reason, unlawful or illegal or prohibited."[73]

Personal property includes:

4. *Things in action*: a thing in action is non-physical property; one's rights in it can only be enforced by a legal action. The best example of such a "thing in action" is a debt. A bank owns the money in an account but owes a debt to the account holder.[74] This debt is a thing in action; it is property and can be stolen.[75] For example, in *Williams,*[76] D dishonestly overcharged elderly householders for building work; by cashing their cheques he was causing a diminution of their

---

69 D. Ormerod and D.H. Williams, *Smith's Law of Theft*, 9th edn (Oxford: OUP, 2007), para.2.139.

70 The Wildlife and Countryside Act 1981 makes it an offence intentionally to pick, uproot or destroy certain wild plants: s.13 and Sch.8. See M. Welstead, "Seasons of Mist and Mellow Fruitfulness" (1995) 145 N.L.J. 1499; J. Johnson, "Police hunt thief who stole rare 'dementia-easing' mushroom" *The Telegraph*, 22 November 2018. Some local authorities have also passed byelaws to prohibit foraging in parks and green spaces: S. Usborne, "No fungi! Why we're cracking down on mushroom pickers" *The Guardian*, 27 April 2016. In 2006, a businesswoman was prosecuted for picking chanterelle mushrooms to sell to top London hotels and restaurants. The case was halted by the judge, who commented that it was "wholly Inappropriate for public money to be spent on criminal proceedings such as these": C. Milmo, "Mushroom-picker wins court battle of the chanterelles" *The Independent*, 17 May 2006, p.17.

71 cf. *Cresswell v DPP* [2006] EWHC 3379 (Admin); (2007) 171 J.P. 233. There are, however, a number of statutory provisions which criminalise the poaching of various animals: see D. Ormerod and D. Perry (eds) *Blackstone's Criminal Practice* (Oxford, OUP, 2024), B13.106.

72 *Borwick Development Solutions Ltd v Clear Water Fisheries Ltd* [2020] EWCA Civ 578; [2021] Ch. 153.

73 *R. v Smith (Michael Andrew)* [2011] EWCA Crim 66; [2011] 1 Cr. App. R. 30 at [7] (Ds guilty of robbery when they attacked a drug dealer and stole his heroin). A.T.H. Smith, "Can proscribed drugs be the subject of theft?" (2011) 70(2) C.L.J. 289–291.

74 *R. v Davenport (Laurence Henry Christopher)* [1954] 1 W.L.R. 569 per Lord Goddard CJ at 576; (1954) 38 Cr. App. R. 37.

75 *R. v Kohn (David James)* (1979) 69 Cr. App. R. 395; [1979] Crim. L.R. 675 CA; *R. v Hilton (Peter Arnold)* [1997] 2 Cr. App. R. 445; (1997) 161 J.P. 459 CA.

76 *R. v Williams (Roy)* [2001] 1 Cr. App. R. 362.

credit balances and so was appropriating their thing in action, namely part of the debt owed to them.

8–037 Problems have arisen with regard to whether cheques can be stolen in the situation where the D induces a V to draw a cheque in their favour. Following dicta in *Preddy*,[77] it has been held in *Graham*[78] and *Clark*[79] that cheques cannot be stolen in such cases. This is because the moment the cheque is written, the thing in action belongs to the D. It does not belong to the V because they cannot sue themself. However, the better view is that the requisite property here is not the thing in action, but the cheque itself which is a valuable security ("any document . . . authorising the payment of money"[80]); it is a piece of paper with special qualities like a key to a safe[81] and is, therefore, capable of being stolen. Other examples of things in action are a copyright, a trademark and shares in a company.[82]

5. *Other intangible property*: this is also non-physical property in which one can have a legal interest: for example, statute has declared that a patent is intangible property but not a thing in action.[83] In *Nai Keung*,[84] it was held that export quotas were "other intangible property" and capable of being stolen.
6. The issue of whether cryptoassets, including cryptocurrencies such as Bitcoin and Ether,[85] and non-fungible tokens (NFTs) such as digital artworks,[86] may be regarded as property for the purposes of the Theft Act 1968 has not yet been specifically considered by the criminal courts. As cryptoassets have no physical existence, and are purely "virtual" balances kept in a public ledger in the "cloud", they are not a "thing in possession" and cannot be the subject of an action in conversion.[87] However, the UK jurisdiction Network's *Legal statement on cryptoassets and smart contracts* concluded that cryptoassets were to be regarded as intangible property,[88]

---

77 *R. v Preddy (John Crawford)* [1996] A.C. 815; [1996] 3 W.L.R. 255 HL.

78 *R. v Graham (Hemamali Krishna)* [1997] 1 Cr. App. R. 302; [1997] Crim. L.R. 340 CA.

79 *R. v Clark (Brian James)* [2001] EWCA Crim 884; [2002] 1 Cr. App. R. 14. This case concerned obtaining property by deception. The same principles, with regard to the meaning of property, apply to theft.

80 Theft Act 1968 s.20(3).

81 J.C. Smith, "Obtaining Cheques by Deception or Theft" [1997] Crim. L.R. 39,t 400.

82 If D presents, or intends to present the cheque, problems also arise in relation to the issue of whether he intends to permanently deprive the owner of the cheque: see *Preddy* [1996] A.C. 815 at 836-837; *Graham* [1997] 1 Cr. App. R, 302; *Clark* [2001] EWCA Crim 884.

83 Patents Act 1977 s.30.

84 *Att-Gen of Hong Kong v Nai Keung (Daniel Chan)* [1987] 1 W.L.R. 1339; (1987) 3 B.C.C. 403 PC. For further analysis, see S.P. Green, *13 Ways to Steal a Bicycle: Theft law In the Information Age* (Cambridge, MA: Harvard University Press, 2012), pp.234–269; S.P. Green, "Property Offenses" in M.D. Dubber and T. Hörnle (eds), *The Oxford Handbook of Criminal Law* (Oxford: OUP, 2014), pp.779–781. cf. the civil cases of *Swift v Dairywise Farms Ltd (No.1)* [2000] 1 W.L.R. 1177; [2000] B.C.C. 642 and *Armstrong DLW GmbH v Winnington Networks Ltd* [2012] EWHC 10 (Ch); [2013] Ch. 156 where, respectively, EU milk quotas and carbon emission allowances were treated as intangible property.

85 Bitcoin (B) was the first cryptocurrency, created in 2009, see S. Nakamoto, *Bitcoin: A Peer-to-Peer Electronic Cash System* (2008). Ether (ETH) is the cryptocurrency of the Etherium network. Both Bitcoin and Ether are digital currencies, which can be traded via online exchanges, making use of public and private cryptographic "keys" to access the cryptocurrency. See House of Commons Treasury Committee, *Crypto Assets*, 22nd Report of 2017–2019 session, HC910 (2018). Cryptocurrencies are 'fungible' assets: each token is identical, has the same properties and can be traded or exchanged for one another.

86 NFTs are digital assets that are individually unique, and which are tokenised via a blockchain. Because each has a unique digital signature, they have different properties and are provably scares, so are non-fungible and cannot be exchanged for or equal to each other. The use of NFTs to buy and sell digital artwork has become increasingly popular in recent years and in 2021 the work by Beeple, entitled "Everydays: The First 5000 Days" sold at Christie's for a record-breaking $69.3 million: S. Hufnagel and C. King, "Non-fungible tokens: art and crime in a virtual world" (2023) 5 Crim. L.R. 338.

87 The LawTech Delivery Panel, *Legal statement on cryptoassets and smart contracts: UK Jurisdiction Taskforce* (2019); *OBG Ltd v Allen* [2007] UKHL 21; [2008] 1 A.C. 1; *Your Response Ltd v Datateam Business Media Ltd* [2014] EWCA Civ 281; [2015] Q.B. 41.

88 The LawTech Delivery Panel, *Legal statement on cryptoassets and smart contracts: UK Jurisdiction Taskforce* (2019), pp.21–22. The Panel concluded that a cryptocurrency private key was not to be treated as property because it is information (p.22): see para.8–039.

and in *AA v Persons Unknown*,[89] this approach was approved as accurately reflecting the position in English law. More recently, in *Osbourne v Persons Unknown*,[90] Lavender J held that it was arguable that NFTs were to be treated as property as a matter of English Law. Should the question arise in the context of a criminal; prosecution, it is suggested that a court would be likely to follow the approach of the civil courts and find that cryptocurrencies are "other intangible property" for the purposes of the Theft Act 1968.

Three areas are of particular interest and deserve consideration.

(i) Electricity

In *Lowe v Blease*,[91] it was held that electricity is not property for the purposes of theft. The Theft Act s.13 creates a special offence of abstracting electricity, carrying a maximum of five years' imprisonment. The s.13 offence has been used to prosecute those who dishonestly bypass the electricity meter to avoid paying for electricity.[92] Gas, however, is property that can be stolen.[93] **8–038**

(ii) Confidential information

In *Oxford v Moss*,[94] a university student acquired a proof of one of his examination papers. He read the questions but did not intend to deprive the university of the piece of paper on which the questions were printed. He was charged with theft of intangible property, namely, the confidential information contained in the examination questions. On appeal, it was held that this was not intangible property within the meaning of s.4. Following this, in *Absolom*,[95] it was held that a person who obtained valuable trade secrets relating to oil exploration, worth between £50,000 and £100,000, and tried to sell them to a rival oil company could not be guilty of theft as such information did not amount to property. While there are other offences of infringing rights in intellectual property, counterfeiting registered trade marks,[96] and gaining unauthorised access to data held on a computer,[97] it is arguable that it is "absurd and disgraceful that we should still be making do without any legislation specifically designed to discourage this modern form of commercial piracy".[98] **8–039**

---

89 *AA v Persons Unknown* [2019] EWHC 3556 (Comm) per Bryan J at [61] and [63]; [2020] 4 W.L.R. 35 (Bitcoins constituted property for the purposes of a proprietary injunction). This approach was followed in *Ion Science Ltd v Persons Unknown*, unreported, 21 December 2020 at [13]; *Fetch.AI Ltd v Persons Unknown* [2021] EWHC 2254 (Comm) at [9] and *DPP v Briedis (Jurijs)* [2021] EWHC 3155 (Admin) at [10]; [2022] A.C.D. 19, a case involving proceedings under the Proceeds of Crime Act 2002. cf. *B2C 2 Ltd v Quoin Pte Ltd* [2019] S.G.H.C.(I.) 03 (Singapore International Commercial Court). For further discussion, see D. Fox and S. Green, *Crytpocurrencies in Public and Private Law* (Oxford: OUP, 2019), Ch.6; *Ruscoe and Moore v Cryptopia Ltd (In Liquidation)* [2020] NZHC 728; A. Taylor and M. Ó Flynn, "Bitcoin burglaries and the Theft Act 1968" [2021] Crim L.R. 163.

90 *Osbourne v Persons Unknown* [2023] EWHC 39 (KB) at [18], following *Osbourne v Persons Unknown* [2022] EWHC 1021 (Comm) at [13].

91 *Low v Blease* [1975] Crim. L.R. 513; (1975) 119 S.J. 695 Div Ct.

92 e.g. in order to provide power for the cultivation of cannabis. See e.g. *R. v Herber (Peter)* [2014] EWCA Crim 519. It is not necessary to prove that the meter has been tampered with to prove the s.13 offence: *R. v McCreadie (Malcolm)* (1993) 96 Cr. App. R. 143; (1993) 157 J.P. 541 CA.

93 *Firth* (1865–1872) L.R.1 C.C.R. 172; *R. v Hughes (Colin David)* [2000] 2 Cr. App. R. (S.) 399 CA.

94 *Oxford v Moss* (1979) 68 Cr. App. R. 183; [1979] Crim. L.R. 119 QBD.

95 *Absolom, The Times*, 14 September 1983. In *Your Response Ltd v Datateam Business Media Ltd* [2014] EWCA Civ 281; [2015] Q.B. 41 it was held that information contained in an electronic client database was not intangible property of a kind that was capable of being the subject matter of a possessory lien. cf. *Ruscoe and Moore v Cryptopia Ltd (In Liquidation)* [2020] NZHC 728 at [126]–[128].

96 Copyright, Designs and Patents Act 1988 ss.107 and 198.

97 Computer Misuse Act 1990 s.1.

98 G. Williams, *Textbook of Criminal Law*, 2nd edn (London: Stevens & Sons, 1983), p.739. cf. C.R. Davies, "Protection of Intellectual Property—A Myth?" (2004) J.C.L. 398.

The Law Commission investigated the law relating to the misuse of trade secrets and provisionally concluded that confidential information is not "property" and that it "would be a mistake for the criminal law to pretend that it is".[99] However, because "there is no distinction in principle between the harm caused by such misuse and the harm caused by theft",[100] the Commission proposed a new offence covering the use or disclosure of another's trade secret where the "owner does not consent to its use or disclosure".[101]

The deliberate copying of a registered design in the course of a business is criminalised by the Registered Designs Act 1949 s.35ZA,[102] but the Government was not prepared to extend this protection to unregistered design rights because they feared that the uncertainties surrounding unregistered designs might make it difficult for third parties to know if they were infringing a right and that it might inhibit design innovation.[103]

(iii) The human body and its parts

8-040 Can one steal a human body or any parts thereof? It has been stated that "nobody owns my body, not even me".[104] However, in relation to the criminal law, the answer may not be that simple and to answer the question, some distinctions need to be drawn.

First, for most practical purposes it seems unlikely that parts of the human body, while still a part of a live person, can be property for purposes of theft. In *Bentham*,[105] the House of Lords held that one does not possess one's hand or any part of the body that is not separate and distinct from oneself.

However, once a limb, organ or sample has been removed from the body and stored in, say, a sperm or blood bank, it possesses all the attributes of personal property and should fall within s.4(1). In *Yearworth*,[106] it was held that semen stored in a hospital's fertility storage unit was property owned by the men who had provided the samples. Indeed, it has been held that blood[107] and urine[108] are property capable of being stolen. In the US, it has been held that a university hospital owned a patient's spleen

---

99 Law Commission Consultation Paper No.150, *Legislating the Criminal Code: Misuse of Trade Secrets* (1997), para.3.26. See J. Hull, "Stealing Secrets: A Review of the Law Commission's Consultation Paper on the Misuse of Trade Secrets" [1998] Crim. L.R. 246.

100 Law Commission Consultation Paper No.150, *Legislating the Criminal Code: Misuse of Trade Secrets* (1997), para.3.60.

101 Law Commission Consultation Paper No.150, *Legislating the Criminal Code: Misuse of Trade Secrets* (1997), para.1.30.

102 Inserted by Intellectual Property Act 2014 s.13.

103 Viscount Younger of Leckie, Grand Committee, Intellectual Property Bill, *Hansard*, 13 June 2013, col.GC 393.

104 J.W. Harris, "Who Owns My Body?" (1996) 16 O.J.L.S. 55. See, generally, A.T.H. Smith, "Stealing the Body and its Parts" [1976] Crim. L.R. 622; J. Herring and P.L. Chau, "My Body, Your Bodies, Our Bodies" (2007) 15 Med. L. Rev. 34.

105 *R. v Bentham (Peter)* [2005] UKHL 18; [2005] 2 Cr. App. R. 11. cf. A.C. Singh, "The Body as Me and Mine: The Case for Property Rights in Attached Body Parts" (2021) 66 McGill L.J. 565.

106 *Yearworth v North Bristol NHS Trust* [2009] EWCA Civ 37; [2010] Q.B. 1. cf. *Holdich v Lothian Health Board* [2013] CSOH 197; 2014 S.L.T. 495; *Cresswell, Re* [2018] QSC 142.

107 *R. v Rothery (Henry Michael)* (1976) 63 Cr. App. R. 231; [1976] R.T.R. 550 CA. The defendant was charged with theft of the capsule containing the blood, not the actual blood itself. The appellant did not appeal the conviction for theft, but it may be argued that the Court of Appeal (albeit obiter) suggested that blood was property capable of being stolen: P. Matthews, "Whose Body? People as Property" (1983) C.L.P. 193, 224.

108 *R. v Welsh* [1974] R.T.R. 478 CA. In *Herbert* (1961) 25 Jo. C.L. 163, a defendant was convicted of larceny and common assault by magistrates for cutting a girl's hair without consent and "taking and carrying away" the hair once it had been cut. No point appears to have been taken as to whether "hair" could amount to "property", and the case was not appealed. cf. *DPP v Smith* [2006] EWHC 94 (Admin); [2006] 1 W.L.R. 1571, above para.5-032.

and other body substances after they had been removed.[109] Such organs and tissue can be extremely valuable and while, for policy reasons, it might be appropriate to ban the purchase or sale of, say, organs for transplantation,[110] that should not alter the basic proposition that such organs, once removed, can be property capable of being stolen.[111]

Secondly, in relation to corpses, there was a commonly accepted view that a corpse was not property and nobody could have a proprietary right or interest in it.[112] For the purposes of the criminal law, this is clearly outmoded. Take, for instance, a cadaver "owned" by a university medical faculty. If the university does not "own" the cadaver under property law, it does have a bailment of the corpse,[113] or, at least, "possession or control" over it. However, although there might be a "proprietary right or interest" or "possession or control" over a corpse as required by s.5, that does not conclusively establish that the corpse is "property" under s.4. The traditional rule that a corpse, or part of a corpse, is not property was confirmed in *Kelly*,[114] but it was added that parts of a corpse can become property for the purpose of s.4 if they have "acquired different attributes by virtue of the application of skill, such as dissection or preservation techniques, for exhibition or teaching purposes". In this case, D was held liable for the theft of some 40 body parts (heads, a part of a brain and an assortment of arms, legs and feet) from the Royal College of Surgeons. These parts were used for the training of surgeons. Rose J added that in future body parts might be held to be property: **8–041**

> "... even without the acquisition of different attributes, if they have a use or significance beyond their mere existence . . . if, for example, they are intended for use in an organ transplant operation, for the extraction of DNA, or . . . as an exhibit in a trial."

3. Belonging to another

Theft is an interference with the proprietary rights of another. One of the central problems here has been identifying who has sufficient "rights" in property to be afforded protection by the criminal law. The owner clearly needs protection, but ownership is only one form of proprietary right and others, particularly those with possession of property, need similar protection. Accordingly, the Theft Act 1968 s.5 identifies the situations in which property is regarded as "belonging to another". In some of these situations, the property does not *really* (under the civil law) belong to anyone else, but someone else **8–042**

109 *Moore v Regents of the University of California* [1990] 271 Cal. Rptr 146. In *Washington University v Catalona* (2006) 437 F. Supp. 2d 985, a US District Court held that the university owned samples provided by participants enrolled in cancer research conducted by one of their employees. This was subsequently affirmed on appeal: (2007) 490 F. 3d 667 (8th Circuit Court of Appeals).

110 Human Tissue Act 2004 s.32. The prohibition on commercial dealings does not apply to "material which is the subject of property because of an application of human skill": s.32(9)(c).

111 In 2005, Christopher Ibbotson, a laboratory manager, used his position to steal bones from a bone bank at Sheffield Hospital and to sell them to private clinics. He was charged with stealing the bones and with obtaining money by deception. The judge directed the jury to acquit him of the theft charges after Ibbotson pleaded guilty to 10 counts of obtaining money by deception and asked for 34 offences to be taken into consideration: *The Guardian*, 20 January 2005; *The Independent*, 23 December 2005.

112 *Dr Handyside's Case* (1749) 3 East P.C. 652; *R. v Sharpe (George Brereton)* 169 E.R. 959; [1857] Dears & B. 160; *Williams v Williams* (1852) 20 Ch.D. 657.

113 D. Brahams, "Bailment and Donation of Parts of the Human Body" (1989) 139 N.L.J. 803. cf. *Yearworth v North Bristol NHS Trust* [2010] Q.B. 1.

114 *R. v Kelly (Anthony Noel)* [1999] Q.B. 621; [1999] 2 W.L.R. 384 CA. In *In the Matter of X* [2003] J.C.A. 050, the Jersey Court of Appeal held that an aborted human foetus was incapable of forming the subject of a true property interest. This was confirmed in *Yearworth v North Bristol NHS Trust* [2010] QB 1, [45].

has an interest thought to be worth protecting and, therefore, the property is *deemed* to belong to that person. Section 5 lays down five situations where property "belongs to another". There is substantial overlap between some of these situations but they are "essentially intended to be cumulative in effect".[115] It is convenient to deal with each of them separately.

(i) Possession or control; proprietary right or interest

THEFT ACT 1968 S.5(1):

8–043 "Property shall be regarded as belonging to any person having possession or control of it, or having in it any proprietary right or interest (not being an equitable interest arising only from an agreement to transfer or grant an interest)."

(a) Possession or control

8–044 "Possession" is a complex legal concept which involves both physical control and an intention to possess. "Control," on the other hand, signifies no more than its literal meaning, namely, physical control—and, therefore, covers many of the cases that could be described as possession, making it unnecessary to draw any distinction between the two concepts. Thus, a customer in a shop examining a book has control of the book; a diner in a restaurant has control over the cutlery with which they are eating; a golf club has either possession or control (it does not matter which) over balls lost on its golf course;[116] and a person has possession or control over any articles in their house or on their land even if they have forgotten or do not know they are there.[117] Property that has been intentionally abandoned does not belong to anyone and cannot be stolen, but where this issue has arisen in criminal cases, the courts have been reluctant to decide that property has been abandoned. So, for example, it has been decided that a householder who puts rubbish in the dustbin, or leaves bags of clothing outside their home for collection by a charity, does not abandon the property,[118] and that property is not abandoned merely because it has been lost by the owner.[119]

Theft by owner: The law of theft is designed to protect a variety of interests in property. The result is that theft can be committed by a person with an interest in the property against another with an interest

115 *R. v Arnold (Lydon Ewart)* [1997] 4 All E.R. 1 at 9; [1997] Crim. L.R. 833 CA.

116 *Hibbert v McKiernan* [1948] 2 K.B. 142; 64 T.L.R. 256; *R. v Rostron (Terry)* [2003] EWCA Crim 2206.

117 *R. v Woodman (George Eli)* [1974] Q.B. 754; [1974] 2 W.L.R. 821 CA.

118 *Williams v Phillips* (1957) 41 Cr. App. R. 5; (1957) 121 J.P. 163 Div Ct. Under the Environmental Protection Act 1990 s.60, it is an offence to interfere with waste sites and receptacles for waste. For a discussion of the legal issues in relation to "freegans", who take and make use of discarded items, see S. Thomas, "Do Freegans Commit Theft?" [2010] 30 L.S. 98–125. cf. *R. (on the application of Ricketts) v Basildon Magistrates' Court* [2010] EWHC 2358 (Admin); [2011] P.T.S.R. 180: it was open to magistrates to find that bags of donated items left outside a charity shop had not been abandoned. The donors had not intended to abandon the property, but to gift it to the charity. In *R. v Toleikis (Donald)* [2013] EWCA Crim 600, it was held that clothing placed into a charity's marked bags outside householders' homes for the charity to collect had been gifted to the property and were therefore "property belonging to another". Peñalver and Katyal suggest that doctrine of abandonment plays an important role in property law, since it helps to return property into circulation and reduces waste and need: E.M. Peñalver and S.K. Katyal, *Property Outlaws: How Squatters, Pirates, and Protestors Improve the Law of Ownership* (New Haven: Yale University Press, 2010), pp.202.

119 *Hibbert v McKiernan* [1948] 2 K.B. 142; 64 T.L.R. 256; *Rostron* [2003] EWCA Crim 2206.

(even a lesser interest) in the same property. In particular, this means that the real owner may be guilty of stealing their own property from another who has possession or control of that property. For instance, if D pawns their watch as security for a loan and then surreptitiously takes the watch back, they would be appropriating property (the watch) belonging to another (the pawnbroker who, at a minimum, has possession or control over the watch).

R. v Turner (No.2) [1971] 1 W.L.R. 901 (Court of Appeal, Criminal Division):

D took his car to a garage to be repaired. The repairs were almost completed and the car parked outside in the road. The defendant, without telling the garage or offering to pay for the repairs, drove his car away. He was convicted of theft and appealed against his conviction. **8-045**

LORD PARKER CJ:

> "[T]he judge directed the jury that they were not concerned in any way with lien and the sole question was whether Mr Brown [the garage proprietor] had possession or control. This court is quite satisfied that there is no ground whatever for qualifying the words 'possession or control' in any way. It is sufficient if it is found that the person from whom the property is taken . . . was at the time in fact in possession or control. At the trial there was a long argument whether that possession or control must be lawful, it being said that by reason of the fact that this car was subject to a hire-purchase agreement, Mr Brown could never even as against the appellant obtain lawful possession or control . . . As I have said, this court is quite satisfied that the judge was quite correct in telling the jury that they need not bother about lien, and that they need not bother about hire-purchase agreements. The only question was: was Mr Brown in fact in possession or control?"

Appeal dismissed

Glanville Williams described this case as "one of the most extraordinary cases decided under the Theft Act" and stated that "it is hard to believe that the decision represents the law".[120] The gist of his argument is that, if one ignores the lien,[121] which the jury were instructed to do, D had a right to repossess his car whenever he liked and one should not be held guilty of theft for doing what one has a right to do. In similar vein, it has been argued that, if a D takes back their television set from a thief who has stolen it (but who now has possession), there should be no liability because the thief has "no property right in the television maintainable against D. *Vis-à-vis* D, the television set belongs to no-one else".[122] **8-046**

It is submitted that this criticism is misplaced. The Theft Act has chosen to protect a wide range of proprietary interests, including possession and control—irrespective of the rights or interests of the

120 Williams, *Textbook of Criminal Law*, 2nd edn (1983), pp.749 and 750. See also the criticisms expressed at Child, Simester, Spencer, Stark and Virgo, *Simester and Sullivan's Criminal Law: Theory and Doctrine*, 8th edn (2022), p.597, and J. Horder, *Ashworth's Principles of Criminal Law*, 10th edn (2022), p.428.

121 A lien is a legal right to keep possession of property belonging to another person until a debt owed by that person is paid.

122 Child, Simester, Spencer, Stark and Virgo, *Simester and Sullivan's Criminal Law: Theory and Doctrine*, 8th edn (2022), p.596.

defendant. In *Turner (No.2)*, there can be little doubt that the D appropriated property belonging to another (Mr Brown, by virtue of his possession or control). In most cases, Ds with greater property rights than their Vs, such as rights to repossession of their property, will not be acting dishonestly. Generally, the owner who takes back their own property would not be condemned by ordinary community standards as dishonest and would thus not be convicted of theft. The owner retrieving the stolen television set would argue that they believed that they had a legal right to take the property and so was not dishonest under the Theft Act 1968 s.2(1)(a). But the D in *Turner (No.2)* surreptitiously removed his car without paying for the repairs and without the garage proprietor knowing his name or address so as to be able to send him his bill. In such a case, a conviction for theft, based on the ordinary meaning of the words "possession or control", does seem more appropriate than an acquittal based on a technical analysis of the position at civil law The short point is that whatever else he might have had at civil law, Mr Brown clearly had possession or control of the car and D acted dishonestly and satisfied the remaining elements of the offence of theft. A conviction was inevitable.[123]

(b) Proprietary right or interest

8–047 The most obvious instance of a proprietary right or interest is that of ownership. Ownership is a proprietary right and thus property belongs to an owner. With co-owners of property, each owner has a proprietary right and therefore one co-owner can steal from another.[124]

Particular problems have arisen here with regard to the "passing of property". This phrase is used to signify ownership passing from one person to another. When goods are bought and paid for in a shop "property passes" from the shop to the purchaser. The basic rule at civil law is that property passes when the parties intend it to pass. For example, in a supermarket parties are deemed normally to intend that property should pass only on payment for the goods.

In some cases, however, the transaction might be defective because one of the parties has made a mistake. Such a mistake might prevent property passing. The basic rule here is that if one of the parties has made a *fundamental mistake*,[125] the transaction is rendered *void* and property does not pass pursuant to a void transaction. On the other hand, a lesser or *non-fundamental mistake* can render a contract merely *voidable* and property *does* pass pursuant to a voidable transaction.[126]

8–048 The requirement that at the time of the appropriation the property must "belong to another" used to mean that the imposition of criminal liability and punishment could depend entirely on whether property passed pursuant to a transaction. For example, in *Kaur v Chief Constable of Hampshire*,[127] D chose a pair of shoes from a rack of shoes marked £6.99 per pair. One shoe was marked at £6.99 and

123 cf. *R. v Meredith* [1973] Crim. L.R. 253 CC where a D who had had his car towed away to a police yard took his car back without paying any fee. It was held that a charge of theft was improper as "the police had no right, as against the owner to retain it". This Crown Court decision cannot be accepted. The police had possession or control of the car; it therefore "belonged" to them for the purposes of theft. The only proper route to an acquittal on these facts should have been lack of dishonesty.

124 *R. v Bonner (George Andrew)* [1970] 1 W.L.R. 838; (1970) 54 Cr. App. R. 257 CA.

125 A mistake is fundamental "if and only if its existence makes it reasonable to say that there is in fact no consent (intention, agreement) on the part of the transferor to transfer *this* property to *this* person", G. Williams, "Mistake in the Law of Theft" (1977) 36 C.L.J. 63, 64.

126 Child, Simester, Spencer, Stark and Virgo, *Simester and Sullivan's Criminal Law: Theory and Doctrine*, 8th edn (2022), pp.598–603.

127 *Kaur v Chief Constable of Hampshire* [1981] 1 W.L.R. 578; (1981) 72 Cr. App. R. 359 Div Ct.

the other at £4.99. The cashier charged her £4.99. On appeal against a conviction for theft, it was held that the appropriation occurred when, having paid, she put the shoes in her bag. The issue was whether property had passed to her when she paid for the goods. If the cashier had made a fundamental mistake, the contract would have been void. As ownership would not then have passed she would have been appropriating property belonging to another. It was held, however, that the cashier had made a mere mistake as to quality, rendering the contract, at most, voidable. Accordingly, the ownership had passed to D and she was not liable as she had not appropriated property belonging to another.

Following *Gomez* and *Hinks, Kaur would now be decided differently,* because the appropriation would be held to have taken place at the earlier stage when she took the shoes from the rack. At that point, they still belonged to the store. The same would be true of the infamous case of *Gilks,*[128] where a punter at the races was mistakenly paid out £106 even though his horse came nowhere. It was held that the bookmaker, in paying out the money in the mistaken belief that a certain horse had won, was making a fundamental mistake. Accordingly, property did not pass and so when the punter decided to keep the money he was appropriating property that did still belong to another. Again, after *Gomez* and *Hinks* the appropriation would be held to occur as the money was handed over and, at that moment (or, at any rate, the split second before) the money would still have belonged to the bookmaker.[129]

With regard to equitable interests it is important to note that there have been significant changes in the civil law relating to constructive trusts since the coming into force of the Theft Act 1968. For example, it is now possible that even though property has passed, the person who made a mistake in delivering the goods retains an equitable interest in them[130] and so the property "belongs" to them by virtue of s.5(1).[131] Whether these developments in the civil law of constructive trusts should be reflected by a corresponding broadening of the law of theft is considered below.

However, s.5(1) specifically excludes "equitable interests arising only from an agreement to transfer or grant an interest". With some contracts, for example, contracts to buy land or shares, the person contracting to purchase acquires an equitable interest, while the other party retains legal ownership. If that legal owner then sells to a third party they do not commit theft as the original contracting party only has an "equitable interest arising from an agreement" which is not sufficient for the property to be regarded as belonging to them. **8–049**

It is with regard to this ascertainment of whether a person has a "proprietary right or interest" that we see the sharpest tensions between the criminal law and the civil law because the criminal law, with its traditional emphasis on blame and harm, is having to define part of the harm component in terms of the civil law. On the one hand, there is the view that criminal liability should only be imposed on blameworthy actors who cause harm and that this determination should be divorced from technical

---

128 *R. v Gilks (Donald)* [1972] 1 W.L.R. 1341; (1972) 56 Cr. App. R. 734 CA.

129 In *R. v Goodwin (Phillip)* [1996] Crim. L.R. 262 CA, where D inserted foreign money (of less value than the required coin) into a gaming machine, it was held that ownership in any coins paid out would not have passed. Such a ruling was unnecessary. The appropriation would occur as the defendant received each coin. At that moment, the property still belonged to the owner of the machine.

130 *Chase Manhattan Bank NA v Israel British Bank (London) Ltd* [1981] Ch. 105; [1980] 2 W.L.R. 202.

131 For fuller discussion, see: Child, Simester, Spencer, Stark and Virgo, *Simester and Sullivan's Criminal Law: Theory and Doctrine*, 8th edn (2022), pp.608–611.

analyses of the civil law. This view tends to maintain that words in the Theft Acts be given their "ordinary meanings" by ordinary people, the jury. This approach was supported by the House of Lords in *Morris*, where dissatisfaction was expressed at allowing criminal liability to turn on fine points of civil law.

R. v Morris, Anderton v Burnside [1984] A.C. 320 (House of Lords):

8–050 LORD ROSKILL:

"I respectfully suggest that it is on any view wrong to introduce into this branch of the criminal law questions whether particular contracts are void or voidable on the ground of mistake or fraud or whether any mistake is sufficiently fundamental to vitiate a contract. These difficult questions should so far as possible be confined to those fields of law to which they are immediately relevant and I do not regard them as relevant questions under the Theft Act 1968."

8–051 Reliance on civil law concepts, particularly whether there is a constructive trust or not, can present extremely complicated questions of civil law and generate uncertainty. For example, in *Powell v MacRae*,[132] D, a turnstile operator at Wembley Stadium, accepted a bribe and allowed a member of the public to enter the ground without a ticket. On a charge of theft, the justices ruled that as the money had been received in the course of employment it belonged to the employer. On appeal, this view was rejected: there was no constructive trust and so the employer had no fiduciary interest in the property. In *Att-Gen's Reference (No.1 of 1985)*,[133] D was the salaried manager of a "tied" public house. In breach of the terms of his agreement with the brewery, he bought beer from a wholesaler, intending to make a secret profit by selling the beer in his public house. The Court of Appeal held that a person in a fiduciary position[134] who uses that position to make a secret profit for which he will be held accountable was not a trustee, and that even if he was, this was not a trust that fell within the terms of s.5(1). The longstanding authority which supported the approach taken in these cases was the case of *Lister & Co v Stubbs*,[135] in which Stubbs, a foreman employed by the plaintiffs, took substantial sums by way of bribes from a firm which supplied large quantities of goods to the plaintiff company. The Court of Appeal held that the monies paid to Stubbs by way of bribes did not belong to the plaintiffs and were not held by Stubbs as a trustee for the company: the relationship between the foreman and the plaintiffs was one of debtor and creditor, not one of trustee and beneficial owner.

However, in *FHR European Ventures v Cedar Capital Partners LLC*,[136] the Supreme Court overruled *Lister v Stubbs* and subsequent decisions relying on that case (including *Att-Gen's Reference (No.1 of 1985)*),

---

132 *Powell v MacRae* [1977] Crim. L.R. 571; 141 J.P. Jo. 432 Div Ct.

133 *Att-Gen's Reference (No.1 of 1985)* [1986] Q.B. 491; [1986] 2 W.L.R. 733 CA.

134 Company directors, agents and partners are in a fiduciary position. Employees may be in a fiduciary position, depending on their position and role within their employer's organisation. For further discussion, see J. Fisher, A. Milne, J. Bewsey and A. Herd, *Arlidge and Parry on Fraud*, 6th edn (London: Sweet & Maxwell, 2020), paras 6–016–6–029; and Child, Simester, Spencer, Stark and Virgo, *Simester and Sullivan's Criminal Law: Theory and Doctrine*, 8th edn (2022), p.609. See A.T.H. Smith, "Constructive Trusts in the Law of Theft" [1977] Crim. L.R. 395, 398, re: the argument in favour of there being a fiduciary relationship between employers and employees.

135 *Lister & Co v Stubbs* (1890) 45 Ch.D. 1 CA.

136 *FHR European Ventures LLP v Cedar Capital Partners LLC* [2014] UKSC 45; [2015] A.C. 250.

holding that a bribe or secret commission accepted by an agent is held on trust for the principal and that the principal has a proprietary claim to it. The position is therefore now clear: where an employee in a fiduciary position enriches himself by taking a bribe or a secret profit, the amount of the bribe or payment is treated as the property of the employer and it is caught by s.5(1). Following this, an employer on facts similar to those in *Powell v MacRae* would have a proprietary interest in the bribe.[137]

It must be questionable whether criminal liability for theft should depend on changes in the law relating to constructive trusts, particularly as the purposes of the law of constructive trusts are very different to those of the criminal law.[138] Furthermore, holding such persons liable for theft raises the risk of false labelling. The essence of the D's wrongdoing in *Powell v MacRae* was that he took a bribe. A D in such circumstances should be found liable for that,[139] rather than for the subsequent theft of the proceeds.

The fact remains that theft is an offence involving interference with the property rights of another and **8–052**
such property rights can only exist at civil law (whether the law of property, contract or quasi-contract). It is not justifiable to convict a defendant of theft if nobody else has any interest in the property because, as seen, an owner is generally free to use, enjoy and abuse their own property as they see fit. Equally, while other charges might be more appropriate, it is not justifiable to acquit a defendant of theft on the ground that the property does not belong to another when, by civil law, it plainly does. If the existence of property rights is not to be ascertained by reference to the civil law, then how are they to be ascertained? As was stressed in *Dobson v General Accident, Fire and Life Insurance Corp Plc*,[140] the issue of whether goods belong to another "is a question to which the criminal law offers no answer and which can only be answered by reference to civil law principles".
The CPS has advised that:

> "The criminal law is not a suitable vehicle to regulate such disputes [over ownership of property]. Before a criminal charge can proceed the ownership of any property must be absolutely clear. If that ownership is in real dispute the criminal law should not be invoked until ownership has been established in the civil courts."[141]

(ii) Trusts

THEFT ACT 1968 S.5(2):

> "Where property is subject to a trust, the persons to whom it belongs shall be regarded as including any person having a right to enforce the trust, and an intention to defeat the trust shall be regarded accordingly as an intention to deprive of the property any person having that right." **8–053**

137 *FHR European Ventures LLP v Cedar Capital Partners LLC* [2014] UKSC 45; [2015] A.C. 250.

138 Smith, "Constructive Trusts in the Law of Theft" [1977] Crim. L.R. 395.

139 Bribery Act 2010 s.2. See Child, Simester, Spencer, Stark and Virgo, *Simester and Sullivan's Criminal Law: Theory and Doctrine*, 8th edn (2022), pp.610–611. An employee receiving a secret commission or bribe might also be charged with fraud by abuse of position (Fraud Act 2006 ss.1, 4): *R. v Knowles (Ross)* [2013] EWCA Crim 646 at [14].

140 *Dobson v General Accident Fire and Life Insurance Corp Plc* [1990] 1 Q.B. 274; [1989] 3 All E.R. 927 at 937 CA.

141 CPS, *The Fraud Act 2006: Legal Guidance, Fraud and economic crime* (2024).

8-054 With most trusts the beneficiary already has a "proprietary right or interest", making s.5(2) unnecessary.[142] However, with charitable trusts there are no specified beneficiaries having beneficial interests in the trust property. Such trusts are enforced by the Attorney-General[143] and under s.5(2) the trust property is deemed to belong to the Attorney-General.[144]

(iii) Obligation to deal with property in particular way

THEFT ACT 1968 S.5(3):

8-055 "Where a person receives property from or on account of another, and is under an obligation to the other to retain and deal with that property or its proceeds in a particular way, the property or proceeds shall be regarded (as against him) as belonging to the other."

8-056 If a person receives property and ownership passes to them then they are generally free to do as they like with the property. Sometimes, however, even if the recipient has become the "true owner" of the property,[145] they may be obliged to deal with it in a particular way. For instance, a person collecting for charity is obliged to hand over the money to the appropriate charity. When the donor places their coin in the tin can this is the clear understanding between donor and collector. Accordingly, s.5(3) deems that money still belongs to the donor and if the collector makes off with the money they are appropriating money "belonging to" the donor.

In many cases, where s.5(3) could apply, the person to whom the obligation is owed will have a legal or equitable interest in the property and so the property will still belong to that person under s.5(1). Under s.5(3), however, it is not necessary for courts to engage with the intricacies of establishing that a trust has been created and that the person supplying the property retains an equitable interest in it.[146] As said in *Klineberg*,[147] s.5(3):

> ". . . is essentially a deeming provision by which property or its proceeds 'shall be regarded' as belonging to another, even though, on a strict civil law analysis, it does not."

For s.5(3) to apply, there are several conditions that need to be satisfied:

(a) The property must have been received from or on account of another to whom the obligation is owed

8-057 Two alternative situations are covered here. First, as with the charity-collector above, the property is received from the person to whom the obligation is owed. Secondly, it can be received from one person

---

142 *R. v Arnold (Lydon Ewart)* [1997] 4 All E.R. 1 at 9; [1997] Crim. L.R. 833 CA.
143 cf. Charities Act 2011 s.115; *Halsbury's Law of England* Vol.8, *Charities* (2019), para.514.
144 This point was overlooked in *R. v Dyke (Ian James) and Munro (Deborah Betty)* [2001] EWCA Crim 2184; [2002] 1 Cr. App. R. 30.
145 *Arnold* [1997] 4 All E.R. 1.
146 *R. v Klineberg (Jonathan Simon)* [1999] 1 Cr. App. R. 427; [1999] Crim. L.R. 417 CA; *Floyd v DPP* [2000] Crim. L.R. 411 QBD.
147 *Klineberg* [1999] 1 Cr. App. R. 427; *Floyd* [2000] Crim. L.R. 411.

on account of another; in this situation, the obligation must be owed to that other person. On this basis, the charity-collector could also be said to have received the property on account of the charity. The operation of these two principles can be seen in *Floyd v DPP*[148] where the D collected money weekly from work colleagues who had ordered goods from Home Farm Hampers Ltd but failed to pay the money to the company. On these facts, it would be possible to invoke either of the above bases. First, she received money from her colleagues; being under an obligation to pay the money to the company, the money would be regarded as belonging to her colleagues. Secondly, and this was the basis of the actual decision, she received money on account of the company and therefore owed them an obligation to hand over the money,[149] so the property was regarded as belonging to the company.

(b) There has to be an obligation to deal with that property or its proceeds in a particular way

Under s.5(3) there has to be a legal obligation to deal with *the property handed over* or *its proceeds* in a particular way. If I give my decorator £100 in order to buy paint, an obligation to use that money or its proceeds is imposed. If I give him £100 as a down-payment, no such obligation is imposed. This simple distinction (in theory) has caused problems in practice, particularly in cases where deposits have been paid. For example, in *Hall*,[150] D was a travel agent who accepted deposits for air trips to US. The flights never materialised and the deposits, which had been paid into the firm's general trading account, were never returned. The Court of Appeal quashed Hall's conviction for theft on the basis that, as he was not under an obligation to deal with the deposit money in a particular way, he was not guilty of theft, even though he had been found to have acted dishonestly in dealing with the deposit money. **8–058**

In *Klinesberg and Marsden*,[151] the Ds sold timeshare apartments in Lanzarote. The purchasers paid money, to be held by a trust company until the apartments were ready to be occupied, but almost none of this money was in fact transmitted to the trust company. In the circumstances, the Ds were found to be under an obligation to pay the monies paid by timeshare purchasers into a trust company:

> "The intending purchasers in each case, and prior to the handing over of any money, were made aware by documents and in at least some cases by oral representations that, if they were to enter into an agreement, they would have the security of knowing that any money they handed over would be held in independent trusteeship until the apartment in question was ready for occupation . . . One of the pivotal features of the whole scheme was that their money would be safeguarded by trusteeship pending completion. In such circumstances there must have been, at the very least, an implied obligation in favour of each intending purchaser to transfer his money into the appropriate trusteeship without undue delay."[152]

148 *Floyd* [2000] Crim. L.R. 411.

149 As there was no evidence of any contract between the defendant and the Home Farm, it is far from clear that she did in fact owe them any obligation. See J. Smith, "Commentary to *Floyd v DPP*" [2000] Crim. L.R. 412.

150 *R. v Hall (Geoffrey)* [1973] Q.B. 126; [1972] 3 W.L.R. 381 CA.

151 *Klineberg* [1999] 1 Cr. App. R. 427.

152 *Klineberg* [1999] 1 Cr. App. R. 427 per Kay LJ at 433.

Similarly, in *Re Kumar*,[153] a travel agent was held to be under an obligation to use money paid to secure flight tickets because there was an agreed trustee relationship for such money to be transferred into specific bank accounts. In *McHugh*,[154] it was stressed that both the D and the client must "clearly understand" that the client's money is to be kept separate from the D's business money. In other cases, whether one is under an obligation to keep a separate fund in existence depends entirely on the facts of each case.[155]

8–059 Section 5(3) has been applied in cases involving charity sponsorship money. In *Wain*,[156] D had raised money for a charity "telethon" held by Yorkshire Television. He paid the money raised into a separate bank account and then, with Yorkshire Television's permission, paid the money into his own bank account and spent it. The Court of Appeal held that Wain was under an obligation to retain at least the proceeds of the charity money collected.

> "[I]t seems to us that by virtue of section 5(3), the appellant was plainly under an obligation to retain, if not the actual notes and coins, at least their proceeds, that is to say the money credited in the bank account which he opened for the trust with the actual property. When he took the money credited to that account and moved it over to his own bank account, it was still the proceeds of the notes and coins donated which he proceeded to use for his own purposes, thereby appropriating them."[157]

(c) The defendant must have direct knowledge of the obligation

8–060 In *Wills*,[158] the D and two assistants operated a business as financial consultants advising clients on investments and loans. The assistants each received money from different clients with instructions to invest the money with an insurance company. Those monies were used for the general purposes of the business and not invested in accordance with the clients' instructions. D was not present when either transaction took place, and there was no evidence that he personally knew of the obligation. D was convicted of theft (as were the assistants). On appeal, it was held that, for s.5(3) to apply, the prosecution must prove that the D has knowledge of the nature and extent of the obligation to deal with the property in a particular way. It is not enough merely to show that the property was not dealt with in a manner that conformed with the obligation.

---

153 *Germany v Kumar (No.1)* [2000] Crim. L.R. 504 QBD.

154 *R. v McHugh (Christopher John)* (1993) 97 Cr. App. R. 335 CA.

155 cf. *Davidge v Bunnett* [1984] Crim. L.R. 297 QBD; *DPP v Huskinson* (1988) 152 J.P. 582; [1988] Crim. L.R. 620 QBD.

156 *R. v Wain (Peter)* [1995] 2 Cr. App. R. 660 CA. *Lewis v Lethbridge* [1987] Crim. L.R. 59 Div Ct, in which it was held that D was not guilty of stealing sponsorship money, on the basis that there was no obligation to keep a separate fund in existence equivalent to the amount of money he had received and therefore the money did not "belong to another" under s.5(3), was disapproved in *Wain*.

157 *Wain* [1995] 2 Cr. App. R. 660 at 665–666.

158 *R. v Wills (Graham George)* (1991) 92 Cr. App. R. 297 CA.

In *Wain*, it was stated that whether the D:

> ". . . is a trustee to be judged on an objective basis. It is an obligation on him by law. It is not essential that he should have realised that he was a trustee, but of course the question remains as to whether he was acting honestly or dishonestly."[159]

Thus, the D must have knowledge of the facts giving rise to the obligation but need not know that they are under a civil legal obligation.[160] However, if a D genuinely believes that they are legally justified in doing what they do with the money, it will be difficult to establish dishonesty.

(d) The obligation must be a legal one

It is not enough that the D is under a social or moral obligation to deal with the property in a particular way. They must be under a legal obligation. This means that the party imposing the obligation must be able to commence legal proceedings against D at civil law for a failure to perform their obligation. One must be careful here to distinguish a legal obligation to do something (for example, pay one's rent)[161] from a legal obligation to use particular property or its proceeds in the performance of that obligation (for example, using the housing benefit to pay one's rent). It is only when there is a legal obligation of the latter kind that property is deemed to belong to another for the purposes of the law of theft. **8–061**

In *Mainwaring*,[162] it was held that there must be a legal obligation at civil law for the purposes of s.5(3). This was confirmed in *Dubar*, where it was stated that it is:

> ". . . the trial judge's function to direct the jury as to matters of law, including the existence of an obligation within s.5(3) if, but only if, he fully and fairly leaves it to the jury to decide the facts which give rise to such an obligation."[163]

While this means, yet again, that criminal liability can depend on highly complex points of civil law,[164] nevertheless such an approach can be supported on the basis that:

> "Parliament is not in the habit of legislating about moral obligations as such; and that Parliament should do so without making its meaning plain is inconceivable."[165]

---

159 *Wain* [1995] 2 Cr. App. R. 660 at 666.
160 See also *R. v Dubar (David Nicholas)* [1994] 1 W.L.R. 1484; [1995] 1 Cr. App. R. 280 at 2.
161 See *Huskinson* [1988] Crim. L.R. 620 QBD.
162 *R. v Mainwaring (Paul Rex)* (1982) 74 Cr. App. R. 99 CA.
163 *Dubar* [1995] 1 Cr. App. R. 280 at 287. Approved in *Arnold* [1997] 4 All E.R. 1 at 10 and *R. v Breaks (Peter)* [1998] Crim. L.R. 349 CA.
164 See, e.g. *R. v Williams and Lamb* [1995] Crim. L.R. 77. In *R. v Hallam* [1995] Crim. L.R. 323 CA, the Court of Appeal was highly critical of the civil law technicalities that have been grafted on to s.5.
165 Williams, *Textbook of Criminal Law*, 2nd edn (1983), p.752.

(e) Section 5(3) and fair labelling

8–062 A large proportion of reported cases involving s.5(3) involve dishonest business operations by travel agents, estate agents, investment companies and so on. Assuming criminalisation is justified in such cases (as opposed to using civil remedies or administrative disabilities such as disqualification of directors), the question becomes: is s.5(3) so defined as to criminalise behaviour that ought to be subject to criminal sanctions and, if so, is theft the correct label to describe such wrongdoing?

In *Hall*, D was dishonest (the jury at first instance convicted him) and Edmund-Davies LJ described his conduct as scandalous.[166] Yet he escaped liability. Is it justifiable to draw a moral line between his conduct and that of the applicant in *Re Kumar* purely because there was an agreed trustee relationship in the latter case? Part of the problem is that s.5(3) is embracing conduct too far removed from the paradigm of theft. In *Klineberg and Marsden,* the essence of the prosecution case was that the appellants "were involved in a timeshare fraud".[167] Indeed, in many of the above cases, the real wrongdoing constituted fraud and not theft. Many of the above Ds would now fall within the provisions of the Fraud Act 2006. It is thus doubtful whether s.5(3) any longer performs a useful role.

(f) Criminalising breach of contract

8–063 In many of the above cases, the D was in breach of contract. In some of these cases (for example, *Re Kumar*) there was liability; in others (for example, *Hall*[168]) there was no liability. Whether a dishonest breach of contract should be criminalised has also arisen in cases not turning on s.5(3). For example, in *Clowes (No.2)*,[169] a central point on appeal was whether signed agreements were contracts or trust documents. Criminal liability could only be imposed in the latter situation as only then would the property "belong to another".

Quite apart from the above point concerning the appropriateness of "theft" as the offence label, this raises the broader question whether *all* dishonest breaches of contract should be criminalised. A breach of contract can have as disastrous an impact upon the innocent party as stealing from them. If accompanied by dishonesty, why should it not be criminalised?

It could be asserted that there is the entire structure of the civil law to provide remedies for breach of contract. Criminalisation is unnecessary. This argument, however, collapses when one recalls that there are similar civil remedies provided for those who "lose" their property wrongfully. The existence of civil remedies is no argument for the decriminalisation of theft.

8–064 With the typical breach of contract, one is dealing with two parties, both "free" and "equal" who have both chosen to enter into a contractual nexus. The risk of one party breaching their contract is always there and, in a free market economy, a factor to be assessed at the time of entering into the

---

166 *Hall* [1973] Q.B. 126 at 131. cf. *Lewis v Lethbridge* [1987] Crim. L.R. 59 Div Ct where the court commented that that the defendant was a "civil debtor and a naughty one without question, but not a thief".

167 *Klineberg* [1999] 1 Cr. App. R. 427 at 428.

168 *Hall* [1973] Q.B. 126.

169 *R. v Clowes (Peter) (No.2)* [1994] 2 All E.R. 316 CA.

contract—taking account of the civil remedies available. Bearing in mind the basic proposition that conduct should not be made criminal merely because it is immoral, but that, additionally, criminalisation should be "necessary" and "proportionate"[170] one should only expand the reaches of the criminal law with the utmost caution. Certain instances of dishonest breach of contract have already been made criminal, particularly where the contract is breached by a false representation, or the D is attempting unilaterally to avoid their liability in circumstances where it would be difficult to trace them.[171] The criminal law should not go beyond such cases. Section 5(3) does extend the tentacles of the law of theft beyond the paradigmatic instances. Great caution must be exercised to keep some rein over the subsection so that it does not stray too far from ordinary understandings of criminality. In this regard, the CPS has advised that: "Prosecutors should guard against the criminal law being used as a debt collection agency or to protect the commercial interests of companies and organisations."[172]

(iv) Obligation to make restoration

THEFT ACT 1968 S.5(4)

"Where a person gets property by another's mistake, and is under an obligation to make restoration (in whole or in part) of the property or its proceeds or of the value thereof, then to the extent of that obligation the property or proceeds shall be regarded (as against him) as belonging to the person entitled to restoration, and an intention not to make restoration shall be regarded accordingly as an intention to deprive that person of the property or proceeds." **8–065**

This subsection was specifically enacted to combat the mischief revealed in the case of *Moynes v Coopper*[173] where an employee was given a pay packet which, owing to a mistake, contained too much money. When he opened the packet and saw the excess, he dishonestly kept the whole. He was acquitted of larceny. If these facts were to reoccur, the case could be brought within s.5(4) and, therefore, even though property in the excess money might have passed to the employee when their salary was paid, they could be liable:[174] on discovering and keeping the excess money there is an appropriation of property (the money) which is deemed to belong to the employer by virtue of s.5(4) because he has got the money by mistake and is under an obligation to make restoration of the excess—or its proceeds or value. **8–066**

Section 5(4) is in fact of limited use. Where a person receives property by another's mistake, the mistake may be fundamental, in which case property does not pass at all and the property will still belong to the other by virtue of s.5(1) (proprietary right or interest). Section 5(4) is not needed in such cases. On the other hand, where the mistake is not sufficiently fundamental as to prevent property passing, the receiver of the property will not necessarily be under an obligation to make restoration of the property.

---

170 See paras 1–034–1–045.

171 Making off without payment contrary to the Theft Act 1978 s.3.

172 CPS, *The Fraud Act 2006: Legal Guidance, Fraud and economic crime* (2024).

173 *Moynes v Coopper* [1956] 1 Q.B. 439; [1956] 2 W.L.R. 562 Div Ct.

174 *Att-Gen's Refence (No.1 of 1983)* [1985] Q.B. 182; [1984] 3 W.L.R. 686 CA.

Whether there is an obligation to make restoration is a complex matter governed by the law of restitution.

Accordingly, the following points can be made about s.5(4):

1. The obligation must be a legal one—i.e. under the civil law of restitution.[175]
2. The obligation must be to return *the* property or *its* proceeds or the *value* thereof. (Under s.5(3) only the property or its proceeds is specified.)
3. The subsection says "is" under an obligation. The use of the present tense is significant here. If in a supermarket a cashier makes a mistake as a result of which the contract is *voidable*, property does pass, but the recipient of the property *is* not *there and then* under an obligation to make restitution. The obligation to make restitution only comes into existence when the person who made the mistake "avoids" the contract. At that point, the recipient will become under an obligation to make restitution and only then does the present tense "is" become applicable. However, as Heaton[176] points out, upon rescission ownership in the property will revert to the person who made the mistake and any subsequent "keeping or dealing with it as owner" will be an appropriation of property that belongs to another by virtue of s.5(1).

It ought to be pointed out, however, that courts have not been rigorous in their application of these civil law principles and, while insisting with one breath that the obligation be a legal one, they have at the same time tended to adopt a more cavalier approach.

Attorney General's Reference (No.1 of 1983) [1985] Q.B. 182 (Court of Appeal, Criminal Division):

8-067 The D, a police officer was overpaid her wages. The money was paid by Direct Debit straight into her bank account. When she realised the mistake, she decided to keep the excess. The judge directed an acquittal and the Attorney General referred a question on a point of law for the court's opinion under the Criminal Justice Act 1972 s.36.

LORD LANE CJ:

> "In order to determine the effect of that subsection upon this case one has to take it piece by piece to see what the result is read against the circumstances of this particular prosecution. First of all: 'Did the respondent get property?' The word 'get' is about as wide a word as could possibly have been adopted by the draftsman of the Act. The answer is 'Yes', the respondent in this case did get her chose in action, that is, her right to sue the bank for the debt which they owed her—money which they held in their hands to which she was entitled by virtue of the contract between bank and customer.

175 *Gilks* [1972] 1 W.L.R. 1341.
176 Heaton, "Deceiving without Thieving" [2001] Crim. L.R. 712, 723.

Secondly: 'Did she get it by another's mistake?' The answer to that is plainly 'Yes'. The Receiver of the Metropolitan Police made the mistake of thinking she was entitled to £74.74 when she was not entitled to that at all.

'Was she under an obligation to make restoration of either the property or its proceeds or its value?' We take each of those in turn. 'Was she under an obligation to make restoration of the property?'—the chose in action. The answer to that is 'No'. It was something which could not be restored in the ordinary meaning of the word. 'Was she under an obligation to make restoration of its proceeds?' The answer to that is 'No'. There were no proceeds of the chose in action to restore. 'Was she under an obligation to make restoration of the value thereof?'—the value of the chose in action. The answer to that seems to us to be 'Yes'.

I should say here, in parenthesis, that a question was raised during the argument this morning as to whether 'restoration' is the same as 'making restitution'. We think that on the wording of section 5(4) as a whole, the answer to that question is 'Yes'. One therefore turns to see whether, under the general principles of restitution, this respondent was obliged to restore or pay for the benefit which she received. Generally speaking, the respondent, in these circumstances, is obliged to pay for a benefit received when the benefit has been given under a mistake on the part of the giver as to a material fact. The mistake must be as to a fundamental or essential fact and the payment must have been due to that fundamental or essential fact. The mistake here was that this police officer had been working on a day when she had been at home and not working at all . . .

As a result of the provisions of section 5(4) the debt of £74.74 due from the respondent's bank to the respondent notionally belonged to the Receiver of the Metropolitan Police; therefore the prosecution, up to this point, have succeeded in proving—remarkable though it may seem—that the 'property' in this case belonged to another within the meaning of section 1 in the Theft Act 1968 from the moment when the respondent became aware that this mistake had been made and that her account had been credited with the £74.74 and she consequently became obliged to restore the value . . .

Before parting with the case we would like to say that it should often be possible to resolve this type of situation without resorting to the criminal law. We do, however, accept that there may be occasions—of which this may have been one—where a prosecution is necessary."

Opinion accordingly

The D here owed a debt and dishonestly tried to avoid paying that debt. This is yet another instance of the grey area of criminality discussed above: when, if ever, should not paying one's debts or breaching one's contract be a crime? In one sense the D in this case was even more blameless than most debtors because they did not choose to incur the debt. It was thrust upon them by the mistake of another. And again, there were civil remedies available. The money could have been recovered. The court rightly stressed that such cases could usually be dealt with without resort to the criminal law. In *Att-Gen's* **8-068**

Reference (No.1 of 1983) the amount of the overpayment was some £74. In *Shadrokh-Cigari*,[177] a bank account was credited $286,000 instead of $286. English law does not formally take account of the value of property in assessing criminality, or level thereof. Yet this is surely an instance where the sums involved are so huge that perhaps criminal liability is appropriate. Or is it that the value of the property affects our assessment as to dishonesty? We can conceive of perhaps "turning a blind eye" to a relatively small sum being credited to our bank account, but when the excess amount is some $286,000, an assessment of dishonesty becomes inevitable.[178]

It was noted earlier that there have been considerable changes in the civil law since the coming into force of the Theft Act 1968. Some of these changes have rendered s.5(4) largely superfluous. In *Chase Manhattan Bank v Israel British Bank*,[179] it was held that a person who pays money to another under a mistake of fact retains an equitable interest in the money. Accordingly, in such cases the money "belongs" to that person by virtue of s.5(1) and s.5(4) is unnecessary. This point was recognised in *Shadrokh-Cigari*, discussed above, although s.5(4) was used as an alternative basis to establish liability. *Shadrokh-Cigari* was applied by the Court Martial Appeal Court in *Webster*.[180] In that case, a duplicate medal had been sent in error to an army captain, who handed it over to the defendant, his staff support assistant. Instead of returning it, the defendant sold it on eBay. The court, upholding Webster's conviction for theft of the medal, held that, although usually a medal gifts from the Sovereign to the person to whom it is presented, where the medal is sent in error, the Crown retains a proprietary interest in the medal, which may therefore be regarded as "belonging to another".[181]

B. MENS REA

1. Dishonesty

8–069 The mens rea of theft is twofold: dishonesty and intention of permanent deprivation. Mens rea is normally taken to refer to a state of mind in relation to consequences or circumstances of a defendant's actions—for example, did they intend, foresee or know of something happening? But, apart from the requirement of intending permanent deprivation, this traditional concept of mens rea fits ill with property offences where, in essence, a judgement is being made about behaviour and the general state of mind of the defendant in relation to their actions. As was said in one of the leading cases, *Feely*,[182] the taking of property must be one to which "moral obloquy can reasonably" be attached.

The interference with property rights must be such that we can blame the defendant for disregarding the value system inherent in the law of theft. The requirement of "dishonesty" is introduced as a

---

177 *R. v Shadrokh-Cigari (Hamid)* [1988] Crim. L.R. 465 CA.

178 In 2017, Sandeep Singh pleaded guilty to theft at Leicester Crown Court and was imprisoned for a year for failing to return £766,098 accidentally transferred into his bank account: M. Molloy, "Man jailed for theft after £766k was accidentally transferred into his bank account" *The Telegraph*, 10 October 2017.

179 *Chase Manhattan Bank v Israel British Bank* [1981] Ch. 105.

180 *R. v Webster (Craig Alexander)* [2006] EWCA Crim 2894.

181 *Webster* [2006] EWCA Crim 2894 at [29]–[34].

182 *R. v Feely* [1973] Q.B. 530; [1973] 2 W.L.R. 201 CA.

mechanism by which moral judgements can be made and blame attributed: the term "connotes a lack of honesty, probity of integrity; a thievishness".[183]

Dishonesty is only partially defined by the Theft Act 1968. Where defined, the meaning of dishonesty is a question of law. Where undefined, it is a question of fact.

(i) Question of law

THEFT ACT 1968 S.2:

"(1) A person's appropriation of property belonging to another is not to be regarded as dishonest— **8–070**

(a) if he appropriates the property in the belief that he has in law the right to deprive the other of it, on behalf of himself or of a third person; or
(b) if he appropriates the property in the belief that he would have the other's consent if the other knew of the appropriation and the circumstances of it; or
(c) (except where the property came to him as trustee or personal representative) if he appropriates the property in the belief that the person to whom the property belongs cannot be discovered by taking reasonable steps.

(2) A person's appropriation of property belonging to another may be dishonest notwithstanding that he is willing to pay for the property."

THEFT ACT 1968 S.1(2):

"It is immaterial whether the appropriation is made with a view to gain, or is made for the thief's own benefit." **8–071**

(a) Belief in legal right

Section 2(1)(a) provides that a person who genuinely believes that they have a legal right to the property is not to be regarded as dishonest—irrespective of the reasonableness or otherwise of the belief.[184] There is a well-known maxim that "ignorance of the law is no defence". This, however, relates to ignorance of the criminal law, for instance, to a D who claims that they did not know theft was a crime. Section 2(1)(a) only applies to persons who have made a mistake as to the *civil law*—believing they have legal rights to property when, perhaps, they have no such rights. **8–072**

Where D claims that they honestly believed that they were legally entitled to the property appropriated, it is suggested that the jury should be given a tailored direction in the precise terms of s.2(1)(a), rather

183 Green, *13 Ways to Steal a Bicycle: Theft Law in the Information Age* (2012) p.113.
184 *R. v Small (Adrian Anthony)* (1988) 86 Cr. App. R. 170; [1988] R.T.R. 32 CA; *R. v Holden* [1991] Crim. L.R. 478 CA.

than leaving the jury to decide the issue under the general dishonesty test.[185] However, the Court of Appeal did not find a failure to give a tailored direction problematic in *Barton*[186] or *Matthews-Williams*,[187] and it has indicated that a specific s.2 direction is only required "where it would add materially to what else is being included in a direction on dishonesty".[188]

(b) Belief in consent

8–073 It will be recalled that, under *Gomez*, a D can appropriate property even though the other has consented to such appropriation. However, if D genuinely believes that she has the other's real consent to deal with the property she cannot be condemned as dishonest. Again, the reasonableness of her belief is irrelevant except in evidential terms.

(c) Belief that property is lost

8–074 Lost property continues to belong to the owner and so the finder of lost property is appropriating property belonging to another. However, if they genuinely (again, a subjective test) believe that the owner "*cannot* be discovered by taking reasonable steps", they are not to be condemned for deciding to keep the property. Obviously, factors such as the type and value of the property and the location where it was found will be important evidence in assessing D's belief. For example, in 2017, it was reported that a woman had been convicted of stealing a £20 note which she had found on the floor of a convenience store, put in her purse, and kept. Her actions were recorded on CCTV and she presumably pleaded guilty because that showed that she had taken no steps to find the owner.[189]

It should be noted that s.2(1)(c) relates to lost property which does still belong to someone else. It does not concern property which the D believes is abandoned. Of course, if property actually is abandoned, it does not belong to another and so the actus reus of theft will not be made out. However, what is the position if property is not abandoned but the D believes that it has been abandoned? As a matter of strict interpretation, because this situation is not covered by the exclusions in s.2, whether there is dishonesty should be determined as a matter of fact under the rules about to be examined.[190] However, in *Wood*,[191] it was held as a *matter of law* that if the D genuinely believed that the property was abandoned there would be no dishonesty.

(d) Willingness to pay

8–075 Section 2(2) makes it clear that a willingness to pay will not necessarily exempt one from a finding of dishonesty. The owner might not wish to sell at whatever price, and it would be unthinkable to allow

---

185 Judicial College, *The Crown Court Compendium: Part I: Jury and Trial Management and Summing Up* (2023), 8-21: ". . . the jury must be reminded of the s.2 provisions whenever they are raised by the evidence". cf. *R. v Falconer Atlee (Joan Olive)* [1973] 58 Cr. App. R. 348 CA; *R. v Wootton and Peake* [1990] Crim. L.R. 201 CA and *R. v Mahmud (Muhammed Abdi)* [2024] EWCA Crim 130 at [25]–[27]; [2024] Crim. L.R. 414. See below, para.8–084 re the general test for dishonesty.

186 *Barton* [2020] EWCA Crim 575; [2021] Q.B. 685 at [127]–[129].

187 *R. v Matthews-Williams (Richard Simon)* [2023] EWCA Crim 1486 at [16].

188 *Matthews-Williams* [2023] EWCA Crim 1486 at [16].

189 L. Bannerman, "Finders weepers: woman who took £20 note guilty of theft" *The Times*, 1 March 2017.

190 Also, there could hardly be an intention permanently to deprive another of the property if D believes it has been abandoned.

191 *R. v Wood (Peter)* [2002] EWCA Crim 832.

the unscrupulous to help themselves to other people's property and escape liability simply by being able to pay. In *Wheatley*,[192] it was held that the fact that no loss was suffered was not determinative of dishonesty.

(e) Not for the thief's benefit

Despite dishonesty being a moral concept, s.1(2) makes it clear that, even though the theft is for the good of others, with the thief gaining nothing, they can still be found dishonest.[193] **8–076**

(ii) Question of fact: the test for dishonesty

Apart from the above specific instances, the concept of dishonesty was left undefined in the Theft Act 1968. In *Feely*,[194] the Court of Appeal made it clear that the issue of whether D was dishonest was a matter of fact for the jury (or magistrate) to determine. **8–077**

> "In section 1(1) of the Theft Act 1968 the word 'dishonesty' can only relate to the state of mind of the person who does the act which amounts to appropriation. Whether an accused person has a particular state of mind is a question of fact which has to be decided by the jury . . . We do not agree that judges should define what 'dishonesty' means."

As dishonesty is not defined in the Theft Act 1968, the courts have had to decide how judges should direct juries to approach the question of whether a defendant is, or is not, dishonest. In *Feely*,[195] the Court of Appeal held that the test for dishonesty was objective, and that jurors, when deciding whether an appropriation was dishonest, should "apply the current standards of ordinary decent people". However, in 1982, the Court of Appeal in *Ghosh*[196] established a two-stage test for the tribunal of fact to apply:

(i) Was the D's conduct dishonest according to the ordinary standards of reasonable and honest people?
(ii) If it was dishonest by those standards, then did the D realise that what he was doing was by those standards dishonest?

If a jury were sure that the answer to both of these questions was "yes", then they should find that the D was dishonest.

The hybrid test created by the Court of Appeal in *Ghosh* was intended to militate against the possible injustice which might arise in some cases from a purely objective test: **8–078**

---

192 *Wheatley v Commissioner of Police of the British Virgin Islands* [2006] UKPC 24; [2006] 2 Cr. App. R. 21 PC.
193 The Criminal Law Revision Committee gave two more limited instances that s.1(2) was designed to meet, *viz.*, taking property that is either useless to the taker or which they intend to destroy (8th Report, *Theft and Related Offences* (1966) Cmnd.2977, p.125).
194 *Feely* [1973] Q.B. 530.
195 *Feely* [1973] Q.B. 530 at 538.
196 *R. v Ghosh (Deb Baran)* [1982] Q.B. 1053; [1982] 3 W.L.R. 110 CA.

> "Take for example a man who comes from a country where public transport is free. On his first day here he travels on a bus. He gets off without paying. He never had any intention of paying. His mind is clearly honest; but his conduct, judged objectively by what he has done, is dishonest. It seems to us that in using the word "dishonestly" in the Theft Act 1968, Parliament cannot have intended to catch dishonest conduct in that sense, that is to say conduct to which no moral obloquy could possibly attach."[197]

But, on the other hand, to avoid the problems of a purely subjective test, which would "abandon all standards but that of the accused himself, and . . . bring about a state of affairs in which Robin Hood would be no robber".[198] The second limb of the *Ghosh* test was not purely subjective, the D had to believe that their conduct was honest "according to the ordinary standards of reasonable and honest people".[199]

Although the *Ghosh* test was the subject of much academic criticism,[200] it remained the test for dishonesty for 30 years and appears to have been unproblematic in most cases. Indeed, because the second limb of the *Ghosh* direction need only be put to the jury in those cases where the D raised the special plea that they did not think that they were being dishonest by their own standards,[201] the full direction was rarely given.[202] However, in some cases, concern about the test appears to have inhibited prosecutions. For example, in 2007, the ship,[203] MSC Napoli, was grounded off the South Devon coast and 37 of its cargo containers were washed up on a nearby beach Large crowds came to the beach to "salvage" property that that had come ashore (including BMW motorbikes), yet no arrests were made and there were no prosecutions for theft. It has been suggested that at least part of the reason for this was that, because the local West country culture appeared to be tolerant of the looting of wrecks, "the police were not satisfied that a court would regard the 'salvors' as dishonest because of the uncertainty surrounding the concept of dishonesty in the offence of theft". Following press revelations in relation to the inappropriate and excessive claiming of expenses by MPs and peers,[204] over 100 were found to have wrongfully claimed expenses, yet few of these were prosecuted, apparently because it was anticipated that there might be difficulties in proving dishonesty save in the most blatant cases, in circumstances where it was argued that there was a culture amongst MPs and peers of claiming the maximum level of expenses, to compensate for the low salary paid to MPs and the fact that peers were not paid a salary.[205]

---

197 *Ghosh* [1982] Q.B. 1053 per Lord Lane CJ at 1063.

198 *Ghosh* [1982] Q.B. 1053 per Lord Lane CJ at 1064. cf. *Gilks* [1972] 1 W.L.R. 1353; *Boggeln v Williams* [1978] 1 W.L.R. 873; (1978) 67 Cr. App. R. 50 QBD.

199 *Ghosh* [1982] Q.B. 1053 per Lord Lane CJ at 1064.

200 See, e.g. D.W. Elliott, "Dishonesty in Theft: A Dispensable Concept" [1982] Crim. L.R. 395; K. Campbell, "The Test of Dishonesty in *R. v Ghosh*" (1984) 43 C.L.J. 349; E. Griew, "Dishonesty: The Objections to Feely and Ghosh" [1985] Crim. L.R. 341; M. Wasik, "Mens Rea, Motive and the Problem of 'Dishonestly' in the Law of Theft" [1979] Crim. L.R. 543.

201 *R. v Roberts (William)* (1987) 84 Cr. App. R. 117; [1986] Crim. L.R. 188 CA; *Wood* [2002] EWCA Crim 832; *R. v Jouman (Bibi Shameera)* [2012] EWCA Crim 1850 at [22].

202 *R. v Balogun (Olaleken Tijani Oluranti)* [2016] EWCA Crim 174 at [31].

203 R. Glover, "Can Dishonesty be Salvaged? Theft and the Grounding of the MCS Napoli" (2010) 74 J.C.L. 53–76, 55.

204 See, e.g. M. Wright, "MP's expenses: how much can you claim? One rule for them, a very different set of rules and restrictions for the rest of us" *The Sunday Telegraph*, 10 May 2009, p.8.

205 J. Roberts, "Case comment: Dishonesty in the first LIBOR trial" [2016] 3 *Archbold Review* 7, 9. See, e.g. D. Brown, "Lords regarded expenses as salary" *The Times*, 21 January 2011, p.22; C. Gammell, "Peer 'thought expenses lie acceptable'" *The Daily Telegraph*, 18 January 2011, pp.1 and 4.

It had been well known amongst criminal law practitioners that, for some time, the Court of Appeal had been keen to re-visit the *Ghosh* test. In the case of *Cornelius*,[206] a five-judge Court of Appeal was assembled with a view to tackling this issue, but the issue did not arise, and the appeal was determined on other grounds. In the civil case of *Ivey v Genting Casinos*[207] the Supreme Court seized the opportunity to overrule *Ghosh*.

IVEY V GENTING CASINOS (UK) LTD (TRADING AS CROCKFORDS CLUB) [2017] UKSC 67; [2018] A.C. 391

Ivey, a professional gambler, had used a technique called "edge sorting" (which involved noting tiny physical irregularities on the edges of playing cards), whilst playing a game of chance at the respondent casino. He won £7.7 million by using this technique, but the casino refused to pay, on the grounds that he had cheated. Ivey brought an action for the recovery of his winnings, claiming, inter alia, that the test for cheating involved dishonesty, which had not been proven. The first instance judge found that, although Ivey was genuinely convinced that what he had done was not cheating, he had, as a matter of fact and law cheated, and had therefore breached the implied term against cheating in his contract with the casino. The Court of Appeal dismissed Ivey's appeal. **8–079**

LORD HUGHES JSC (with whom BARONESS HALE OF RICHMOND PSC, LORD KERR OF TONAGHMORE JSC, LORD NEUBERGER OF ABBOTSBURY and LORD THOMAS OF CWMGIEDD agreed):

> "[57] Thirty years on, however, it can be seen that there are a number of serious problems about the second leg of the rule adopted in *R v Ghosh*.
>
> (1) It has the unintended effect that the more warped the defendant's standards of honesty are, the less likely it is that he will be convicted of dishonest behaviour.
> (2) It was based on the premise that it was necessary in order to give proper effect to the principle that dishonesty, and especially criminal responsibility for it, must depend on the actual state of mind of the defendant, whereas the rule is not necessary to preserve this principle.
> (3) It sets a test which jurors and others often find puzzling and difficult to apply.
> (4) It has led to an unprincipled divergence between the test for dishonesty in criminal proceedings and the test of the same concept when it arises in the context of a civil action.
> (5) It represented a significant departure from the pre- Theft Act 1968 law, when there is no indication that such a change had been intended.
> (6) Moreover, it was not compelled by authority. Although the pre- *Ghosh* cases were in a state of some entanglement, the better view is that the preponderance of authority favoured the simpler rule that, once the defendant's state of knowledge and belief has

---

206 *R. v Cornelius (Benjamin Jason)* [2012] EWCA Crim 500 at [1]; [2012] Lloyd's Rep. F.C. 435 . The case is considered in para.8–130.

207 *Ivey v Genting Casinos (UK) Ltd (trading as Crockfords Club)* [2017] UKSC 67; [2018] A.C. 391. For a fuller account of this case see Baroness Hale of Richmond, "Dishonesty" (2019) 48 *Common Law World Review* 5.

> been established, whether that state of mind was dishonest or not is to be determined by the application of the standards of the ordinary honest person, represented in a criminal case by the collective judgement of jurors or justices.

[58] The principal objection to the second leg of the *Ghosh* test is that the less the defendant's standards conform to what society in general expects, the less likely he is to be held criminally responsible for his behaviour. It is true that *R v Ghosh* attempted to reconcile what it regarded as the dichotomy between a 'subjective' and an 'objective' approach by a mixed test. The court addressed the present objection in this way, [1982] QB 1053, 1064:

> 'There remains the objection that to adopt a subjective test is to abandon all standards but that of the accused himself, and to bring about a state of affairs in which "Robin Hood would be no robber": R v Greenstein [1975] 1 WLR 1353. This objection misunderstands the nature of the subjective test. It is no defence for a man to say "I knew that what I was doing is generally regarded as dishonest; but I do not regard it as dishonest myself. Therefore I am not guilty". What he is however entitled to say is "I did not know that anybody would regard what I was doing as dishonest". He may not be believed; just as he may not be believed if he sets up "a claim of right" under section 2(1) of the Theft Act 1968, or asserts that he believed in the truth of a misrepresentation under section 15 of the 1968 Act. But if he is believed, or raises a real doubt about the matter, the jury cannot be sure that he was dishonest.'

And a little later the court added that upon the test which it was setting:

> 'In most cases, where the actions are obviously dishonest by ordinary standards, there will be no doubt about it. It will be obvious that the defendant himself knew that he was acting dishonestly. It is dishonest for a defendant to act in a way which he knows ordinary people consider to be dishonest, even if he asserts or genuinely believes that he is morally justified in acting as he did. For example, Robin Hood or those ardent anti-vivisectionists who remove animals from vivisection laboratories are acting dishonestly, even though they may consider themselves to be morally justified in doing what they do, because they know that ordinary people would consider these actions to be dishonest.'

8–080 [59] Even if this were correct, it would still mean that the defendant who thinks that stealing from a bookmaker is not dishonest (as in *R v Gilks* [1972] 1 WLR 1341 . . .) is entitled to be acquitted. It is no answer to say that he will be convicted if he realised that ordinary honest people would think that stealing from a bookmaker is dishonest, for by definition he does not realise this. Moreover, the court's proposition was not correct, because it is not in the least unusual for the accused not to share the standards which ordinary honest people set for society as a whole . . . It cannot by any means be assumed that the appropriators of animals from laboratories, to whom the court referred in *R v Ghosh* [1982] QB 1053, know that ordinary people would consider their actions to be dishonest; it is just as likely that they are so convinced, however perversely, of the justification for what they do that they persuade themselves that no one could call it dishonest. There is no reason why the law should excuse those who make a mistake about what contemporary standards of honesty are, whether in the context of insurance claims, high finance, market manipulation or tax evasion. The law does not, in principle, excuse those whose standards are criminal by the benchmarks set by society, nor ought it to do so. On the contrary, it is an important, even crucial, function of the criminal law to determine what is criminal and what is not; its purpose is to set the standards of behaviour which are acceptable. As it was put in Smith's Law of Theft, 9th ed (2007), para.2.296:

> 'the second limb allows the accused to escape liability where he has made a mistake of fact as to the contemporary standards of honesty. But why should that be an excuse?'

[60] It is plain that in *R v Ghosh* [1982] QB 1053 the court concluded that its compromise second leg test was necessary in order to preserve the principle that criminal responsibility for dishonesty must depend on the actual state of mind of the defendant . . .

[Lord Hughes then quoted the "man on a bus" example provided By Lord Lane CJ in *Ghosh*, set out at para.9–086].

But the man in this example would inevitably escape conviction by the application of the (objective) first leg of the *Ghosh* test. That is because, in order to determine the honesty or otherwise of a person's conduct, one must ask what he knew or believed about the facts affecting the area of activity in which he was engaging. In order to decide whether this visitor was dishonest by the standards of ordinary people, it would be necessary to establish his own actual state of knowledge of how public transport works. Because he genuinely believes that public transport is free, there is nothing objectively dishonest about his not paying on the bus. The same would be true of a child who did not know the rules, or of a person who had innocently misread the bus pass sent to him and did not realise that it did not operate until after 10.00 in the morning. The answer to the court's question is that 'dishonestly', where it appears, is indeed intended to characterise what the defendant did, but in characterising it one must first ascertain his actual state of mind as to the facts in which he did it. It was not correct to postulate that the conventional objective test of dishonesty involves judging only the actions and not the state of knowledge or belief as to the facts in which they were performed. What is objectively judged is the standard of behaviour, given any known actual state of mind of the actor as to the facts.

[61] Although there have been relatively few appeals based upon *R v Ghosh*, that is because **8–081**
judges have dutifully given the two-leg direction where there has been any occasion for it. But the existence of the second leg has frequently led to trials being conducted on the basis that even if the defendant's actions, in his actual state of knowledge or belief about the relevant facts, would be characterised by most people as dishonest, the defendant himself thought that what he was doing was not wrong, and it was for that reason honest. Juries are

then required first to ask the so-called objective question, that is to say to apply their own standards of honesty, but then to depart from them in order to ask what the defendant himself thought. The idea that something which is dishonest by ordinary standards can become honest just because the defendant thinks it is may often not be an easy one for jurors to grasp.

[62] Dishonesty is by no means confined to the criminal law. Civil actions may also frequently raise the question whether an action was honest or dishonest. The liability of an accessory to a breach of trust is, for example, not strict, as the liability of the trustee is . . . fault-based . . . Nothing less than dishonest assistance will suffice. Successive cases at the highest level have decided that the test of dishonesty is objective.

[63] . . . there can be no logical or principled basis for the meaning of dishonesty (as distinct from the standards of proof by which it must be established) to differ according to whether it arises in a civil action or a criminal prosecution. Dishonesty is a simple, if occasionally imprecise, English word. It would be an affront to the law if its meaning differed according to the kind of proceedings in which it arose . . .

[64] Prior to the Theft Act 1968, the expression 'dishonestly' had not appeared in the legal definition of acquisitive offences. The mental element was usually marked by the expression 'fraudulently'. There is no doubt that that latter expression involved an objective evaluation of the defendant's conduct, given his actual state of knowledge and belief as to the facts. The Criminal Law Revision Committee, in its Eighth Report, advised the substitution of the word 'dishonestly', on the grounds that "fraudulently" had become technical and its meaning had departed somewhat from the ordinary understanding of lay people. It recommended that 'dishonestly' would be more easily understood by lay fact-finders and the public generally. At para.39 the Committee advised that

> '"Dishonestly" seems to us a better word than "fraudulently". The question "Was this dishonest?' is easier for a jury to answer than the question "Was this fraudulent?". "Dishonesty" is something which laymen can easily recognise when they see it, whereas "fraud" may seem to involve technicalities which have to be explained by a lawyer.'

It was in accordance with this substitution that in *R v Feely* [1973] QB 530 a five-judge Court of Appeal, Criminal Division, held that the question whether a defendant had behaved dishonestly was to be left to the jury and should not, as had been the case with 'fraudulently', be the subject of judicial ruling. But there is no hint in the Committee's report of any contemplation that whether a man was or was not dishonest should henceforth depend on his own view of his behaviour. On the contrary, the report clearly assumed that the prior objective approach would continue, save that the question would be a jury matter rather than one of law . . .

[The Supreme Court then examined the pre-*Ghosh* authorities on the issue of dishonesty.][208]

[74] These several considerations provide convincing grounds for holding that the second leg of the test propounded in *R v Ghosh* [1982] QB 1053 does not correctly represent the law and that directions based upon it ought no longer to be given . . . When dishonesty is in question the fact-finding tribunal must first ascertain (subjectively) the actual state of the individual's knowledge or belief as to the facts. The reasonableness or otherwise of his belief is a matter of evidence (often in practice determinative) going to whether he held the belief, but it is not an additional requirement that his belief must be reasonable; the question is whether it is genuinely held. When once his actual state of mind as to knowledge or belief as to facts is established, the question whether his conduct was honest or dishonest is to be determined by the fact-finder by applying the (objective) standards of ordinary decent people. There is no requirement that the defendant must appreciate that what he has done is, by those standards, dishonest."

Appeal dismissed

The Supreme Court's pronouncements in *Ivey* in relation to the criminal law test for dishonesty were strictly obiter, but it was a unanimous decision of the court, and a five-judge bench of the Court of Appeal has firmly indicated that *Ivey* represents the law in relation to the test for dishonesty.[209] **8–082**

R. v Barton (David) and Booth (Rosemary) [2020] EWCA Crim 575; [2021] Q.B. 685

"[102] The undoubted reality is that in *Ivey* the Supreme Court altered the established common law approach to precedent in the criminal courts by stating that the test for dishonesty they identified, albeit strictly contained in obiter dicta, should be followed in preference to an otherwise binding authority of the Court of Appeal . . . we do not consider that it is for this court to conclude that it was beyond their powers to act in this way . . . **8–083**

[104] We conclude that where the Supreme Court itself directs that an otherwise binding decision of the Court of Appeal should no longer be followed and proposes an alternative test that it says must be adopted, the Court of Appeal is bound to follow what amounts to a direction from the Supreme Court even though it is strictly obiter. To that limited extent the ordinary rules of precedent (or stare decisis) have been modified. We emphasise that this limited modification is confined to cases in which all the judges in the appeal in question in the Supreme Court agree that to be the effect of the decision. Such was a necessary condition before adjusting the rules of

208 See C. Griffiths, "The honest cheat: a timely history of cheating and fraud following *Ivey v Genting Casinos (UK) Ltd. t/a Crockfords* [2017] UKSC 67" (2020) 40 Leg. Stud. 252, for a critical discussion of this historical analysis, described as "a remarkable example of judicial cherry-picking, the Justices selecting precedent from past centuries in a manner which supports a particular conclusion" (at 268).

209 *Barton* [2020] EWCA Crim 575; [2021] Q.B. 685. See also *DPP v Patterson* [2017] EWHC 2820 (Admin); [2018] 1 Cr. App. R. 28; *R. v B* [2018] EWCA Crim 73; *R. v Pabon (Alex Julian)* [2018] EWCA Crim 420; [2018] Lloyd's Rep. F.C. 258. For further discussion on this issue, see: Laird, "Dishonesty: *Ivey v Genting Casinos UK Ltd (t/a Crockfords Club)*" [2018] Crim. L.R. 395.

precedent accepted by this court in James in relation to the Privy Council. Had the minority of the Privy Council in Holley not agreed that the effect of the judgment was to state definitively the law in England, it would not have been accepted as such by this court. The same approach is necessary here because it forms the foundation for the conclusion that the result is considered by the Supreme Court to be definitive, with the consequence that a further appeal would be a foregone conclusion, and binding on lower courts.

[105] In the result, the test for dishonesty in all criminal cases is that established in *Ivey*.

[106] We would not wish it to be thought that we are following Ivey reluctantly. The concerns about *Ghosh* have resonated through academic debate for decades. Lord Hughes's reasoning is compelling.

[107] That said, we wish to endorse the respondent's submission that the test of dishonesty formulated in *Ivey* remains a test of the defendant's state of mind—his or her knowledge or belief—to which the standards of ordinary decent people are applied. This results in dishonesty being assessed by reference to society's standards rather than the defendant's understanding of those standards. Lord Nicholls of Birkenhead, . . . observed in Royal Brunei Airlines at page 389:

> '. . . acting dishonestly, or with a lack of probity, which is synonymous, means simply not acting as an honest person would in the circumstances. This is an objective standard. At first sight this may seem surprising. Honesty has a connotation of subjectivity, as distinct from the objectivity of negligence. Honesty, indeed, does have a strong subjective element in that it is a description of a type of conduct assessed in the light of what a person actually knew at the time, as distinct from what a reasonable person would have known or appreciated. . . . However, these subjective characteristics of honesty do not mean that individuals are free to set their own standard of honesty in particular circumstances. The standard of what constitutes honest conduct is not subjective. Honesty is not an optional scale, with higher or lower values accordingly to the moral standards of each individual. If a person knowingly appropriates another's property, he will not escape a finding of dishonesty simply because he sees nothing wrong in such behaviour.'

And at page 391:

> '. . . when called upon to decide whether a person was acting honestly a court will look at all the circumstances known to the third party at the time. The court will also have regard to personal attributes of the third party, such as his experience and intelligence, and the reason why he acted as he did.'

[108] This approach, which was the approach of the Supreme Court in *Ivey*, makes clear that when Lord Hughes talked in [74] of the 'actual state of mind as to knowledge or belief *as to the facts*' [emphasis added] he was referring to all the circumstances known to the accused and not limiting consideration to past facts. All matters that lead an accused to act as he or she did will form part of the subjective mental state, thereby forming a part of the fact-finding exercise before applying

> the objective standard. That will include consideration, where relevant, of the experience and intelligence of an accused. In an example much used in debate on this issue, the visitor to London who fails to pay for a bus journey believing it to be free (as it is, for example, in Luxembourg) would be no more dishonest that the diner or shopper who genuinely forgets to pay before leaving a restaurant or shop. The Magistrates or jury in such cases would first establish the facts and then apply an objective standard of dishonesty to those facts, with those facts being judged by reference to the usual burden and standard of proof."

Following *Ivey* and *Barton*, the test is a two-stage one, with the jury considering the following two questions: **8–084**

(1) what was the defendant's actual state of knowledge or belief as to the facts? And
(2) was his conduct dishonest by the standards of ordinary decent people?[210]

The first question is a subjective enquiry, to establish "what D knew or believed to be the factual circumstances in which that conduct occurred". [211] This fact-finding exercise will involve consideration of all matters that led a D to act as they did, including "consideration, where relevant, of the experience and intelligence of an accused".[212] In both *Ivey* and *Barton*, the court gave the example of a foreign visitor travelling on public transport without a ticket, having just arrived from a country where such transport was always free, who would not be dishonest.[213] Whether D's belief in relation to the facts is reasonable is a matter of evidence which is relevant to the issue of whether they actually held the belief, but it is not an additional requirement that the belief be reasonable- the question is whether the belief is genuinely held.[214] Once the jury has decided what D's state of mind was, they must then consider the second question: whether D's conduct was honest or dishonest according to the (objective) standards of ordinary decent people.[215]

The Crown Court Compendium expressly directs judges that the *Ghosh* test no longer represents the law and that "Directions based on *Ghosh* should no longer be given".[216] It advises that, in most cases, the jury will need no further direction than the short, two-limbed direction set out above, but that:

> ". . . In cases in which D has adduced evidence to support a claim that he/she did not consider his/her conduct would be regarded as dishonest by ordinary decent people, it may be necessary to elaborate in two ways:
>
> By making clear that in assessing whether the conduct was dishonest by the standards of ordinary decent people, the jury is to have regard to D's beliefs [and explain those in the context of the case].

---

210 *Barton* [2020] EWCA Crim 575; [2021] Q.B. 685 at [84].
211 Judicial College, *The Crown Court Compendium: Part I: Jury and Trial Management and Summing Up* (2023), 8–19. The Compendium provides guidance to judges presiding over criminal cases in the Crown Court.
212 *Barton* [2020] EWCA Crim 575; [2021] Q.B. 685 at [108].
213 *Ivey* [2017] UKSC 67; [2018] A.C. 391 at [60]; *Barton* [2020] EWCA Crim 575; [2021] Q.B. 685 at [108].
214 Judicial College, *The Crown Court Compendium: Part I: Jury and Trial Management and Summing Up* (2023), 8–20.
215 Judicial College, *The Crown Court Compendium: Part I: Jury and Trial Management and Summing Up* (2023), 8–20.
216 Judicial College, The Crown Court Compendium: Part I: Jury and Trial Management and Summing Up (2023), 8–19.

To emphasise that D's beliefs as to whether the conduct would be seen as dishonest by the others is not determinative. The question whether it is dishonest conduct is for the jury to decide applying the standards of ordinary decent people."[217]

8–085 However, Ormerod and Laird have suggested that the "safest course" would be for the two limb *Barton* direction to be given in all cases to "maximise consistency" and avoid the "risk that jurors would simply apply an objective assessment without having proper regard to the defendant's knowledge or belief as to the facts".[218]

Whilst it has been praised in some quarters,[219] the reasoning of the Supreme Court in overturning *Ghosh* and reverting to an objective test has been subject to criticism.[220]

Graham Virgo, "Case Comment: Cheating and dishonesty" (2018) 77(1) Cambridge Law Journal 18, 20–21:

8–086 "But can the rejection of the second limb of the *Ghosh* test be justified? That limb was rejected for five reasons. First, because it meant that the more warped the defendant's standard of honesty the less likely they would be convicted. Secondly, because *Ghosh* was premised on the assumption that criminal responsibility depends on the actual state of the defendant's mind. Thirdly, because the test was considered to be difficult for juries to apply. Fourthly, because it involved an unprincipled divergence between the tests of dishonesty in criminal and civil law. Fifthly, because its recognition departed from the law before the enactment of the Theft Act 1968 and was not compelled by later authority.

Although certain of these reasons are correct, especially the last one, others are less convincing. For example, as regards the first reason, the second limb of the *Ghosh* test was specifically formulated with reference to the defendant's perception of the reasonable person's standard of honesty rather their own, although it is certainly true that a defendant who considered their own conduct to be honest would be more likely to believe that reasonable people would share that belief. Further, there is no evidence from the cases that juries found the Ghosh direction difficult to apply, although it did require the jury to consider what the defendant thought they (as

217 Judicial College, *The Crown Court Compendium: Part I: Jury and Trial Management and Summing Up* (2023), 8–20.

218 D. Ormerod and K. Laird, "The future of dishonesty- some practical considerations" [2020] 6 Arch. Rev. 8, 10.

219 J. Clough, "Giving up the *Ghosh*: *Ivey (Appellant) v Genting Casinos (UK) Ltd trading as Crockfords (Respondent)*" [2018] 236 *Criminal Lawyer* 2; M. Galli, "Oh my Ghosh: Supreme Court Redefines Test for Dishonesty in *Ivey v Genting*" (2018) 29 Ent. L.R. 55; B. Wang, "Mistaking theft: Dishonesty 'turns over a new leaf'" (2022) 86(1) J. Criminal Law 3.

220 Spencer, "Two cases on the law of theft: a concertina movement?" (2018) 8 *Archbold Review* 4; G. Virgo, "Case Comment: Cheating and dishonesty" (2018) 77(1) *Cambridge Law Journal* 18; Laird, "Dishonesty: *Ivey v Genting Casinos UK Ltd (t/a Crockfords Club)*" [2018] Crim. L.R. 395; M. Dyson and P. Jarvis, "Poison *Ivey* or herbal tea leaf?" (2018) 134 L.Q.R. 198; D. Ormerod and K. Laird, "*Ivey v Genting Casinos—Much Ado About Nothing?*" [2017–2018] 9 *The UK Supreme Court Yearbook* 380; Sullivan and Simester, "Judging Dishonesty" (2020) 136 L.Q.R. 523; Z. Leggett, "The New Test for Dishonesty in Criminal Law—Lessons from the Courts of Equity?" (2020) 84 J. Crim. L. 37; M. Thomas and S. Pegg, "Clarifying the applicable test for dishonesty and modifying stare decisis, but otherwise a missed opportunity" (2020) 84 J. Crim. L. 385; M. Bohlander, "Abandoning dishonesty—a brief German comment on the state of the law after *Ivey*" (2022) 86 J. Crim. L. 170.

> reasonable people) thought about defendant's conduct, which is not conceptually and evidentially straightforward. The fourth reason relating to divergence between criminal and civil law is not convincing, at least in the broad terms identified by Lord Hughes. There are many examples of situations where the criminal and civil law use the same concepts which are defined differently, and such divergence may be justified by virtue of the different functions of the criminal and civil law. Different tests of dishonesty could be justified because in the civil law dishonesty determines unacceptable conduct in order to impose liability, whereas dishonesty in the criminal law is concerned with identifying culpability, which requires consideration of the defendant's mental state. The effect of *Ivey* is to treat dishonesty in the criminal law as a mechanism for assessing conduct rather than culpability, albeit that the defendant's knowledge or belief about the facts is relevant to this objective assessment . . ."

In spite of the Supreme Court's expressed desire to remove inconsistency between the civil and criminal law, concern has been expressed that, in the light of the very broad approach to the test for appropriation adopted in *Gomez*[221] and *Hinks*,[222] inconsistency between the jurisdictions remains, resulting in an unacceptable expansion of the offence of theft. **8-087**

Graham Virgo, "Case Comment: Cheating and dishonesty" (2018) 77(1) Cambridge Law Journal 18, 21:

> "*Ivey* will impact other offences, notably theft for which it is dishonesty alone which renders conduct criminal, since, following *Hinks* [2001] 2 A.C. 241, appropriation does not require adverse interference with property rights contrary to the owner's wishes. When the *Ghosh* test of dishonesty applied, the defendant's belief that reasonable people would consider their conduct to be honest provided some protection against criminalising an otherwise legitimate interference with property rights. That safeguard has now gone, meaning that conviction for interference with property rights even though the owner of the property consents depends only on whether reasonable people would consider the conduct to be dishonest. Theft is now a crime which requires neither proof of harm nor subjective fault. Together with *Hinks*, *Ivey* has resulted in an unacceptable expansion of the criminal jurisdiction, one which is inconsistent with the civil jurisdiction and so constitutes an unprincipled divergence between criminal and civil law." **8-088**

---

221 *DPP v Gomez (Edwin)* [1993] A.C. 442; [1992] 3 W.L.R. 1067 HL.

222 *R. v Hinks (Karen Maria)* [2001] 2 A.C. 241; [2000] 3 W.L.R. 1590 HL. See above, paras 8-020–8-022.

M. Thomas and S. Pegg, "Clarifying the applicable test for dishonesty and modifying stare decisis, but otherwise a missed opportunity" (2020) 84 J. Crim. L. 385, 391:

8-089 "The emasculation of appropriation means that despite the approval of '*Ivey* dishonesty' in *Barton*, there is still divergence between the civil and criminal law in the protection of property rights. This causes practical difficulties throughout the offence of theft, particularly in regard to dishonesty,. . .

As a valid gift amounts to an appropriation, a defendant may rightfully seek to rely on s 2(1)(a) Theft Act 1968 that he has appropriated that property with the honest 'belief that he has in law the right to deprive the other of it'. In *Barton*, the Court considered that this matter had been adequately dealt with in the written directions given to the jury concerning whether the gifts had been given 'freely' by individuals with 'capacity' and that a direction on s 2(1)(a) was not then required (at [129]). Indeed, Lord Burnett CJ accepted that '[i]f his case on the "gifts" was or might have been true, [DB] was not dishonest and would have been acquitted' (at [129]). It appears that the Court were satisfied that the Ivey direction on dishonesty could be left to do the heavy lifting here. The question of how a valid gift can amount, for the purposes of the Theft Act 1968, to property 'belonging to another' has, once again, gone unanswered. That is a simple fact of *Barton*; the issue was simply not considered."

8-090 Questions also remain as to how the first limb of the *Ivey/Barton* test will apply in practice and the relationship between the two limbs.

D. Ormerod and K. Laird, "The future of dishonesty—some practical considerations" [2020] 6 Arch. Rev. 8, 9–10.

8-091 "*Barton*—**Limb 1**

The preliminary task, uncontroversially, is for the jury to establish the facts. Having done so the jury must then consider the first limb of the new test. That involves ascertaining the defendant's state of mind. In *Ivey* Lord Hughes was clear it is a subjective assessment—what was in this defendant's mind. This first limb is designed to address the well-worn example of the foreign tourist who does not realise that people must pay to use public transport in the UK. Whereas previously the second limb of *Ghosh* would come to the 'rescue' to ensure acquittal; now it is intended for the first limb to fulfil this purpose. What *Ivey* did not make clear was the scope of the jury's inquiry: what facts or beliefs which the defendant might have held are the jury to consider? Did the Supreme Court in *Ivey*, by removing the second limb of *Ghosh* but retaining subjectivity in this first limb, mean to (a) render totally irrelevant D's belief as to the perceptions of others about the honesty of the conduct? Or (b) remove the binding nature of that belief—so that if D did not believe others would see it as dishonest this could still result in his acquittal, as under *Ghosh*?

The court in *Barton* seems to have provided the answer at [108]: the reference in Ivey to the 'actual state of mind as to knowledge of belief as to the facts' was to all the circumstances known to the accused and not limited to consideration of past facts. Lord Burnett CJ explained that [*all*] *matters that lead an accused to act as he or she did will form part of the subjective mental state*, thereby forming a part of the fact-finding exercise before applying the objective standard. That will include consideration, where relevant, of the experience and intelligence of an accused [emphasis added].

We therefore suggest that in limb 1 the jury are to have regard not only to D's state of mind as to the facts, but also as to his beliefs about whether the conduct would be seen as dishonest (a matter which led him to act as he did).

Barton—**Limb 2** **8-092**

The second limb of the test requires the jury to decide whether the defendant's conduct (having regard to his beliefs about the conduct/facts), was dishonest according to the standards of ordinary decent people. As noted above, *Ghosh* also included an objective limb, but under *Ivey/Barton* the objective limb takes on primary significance. Academics' 'almost universal dissatisfaction' with *Ghosh* had largely focussed on the objective limb. Although the Supreme Court and the Court of Appeal acknowledged the existence of this academic commentary, neither judgment engages with the challenges raised. Perhaps the most problematic aspect of the test for dishonesty—that it assumes the existence of a community norm on dishonesty—has become its most prominent feature.

The relationship between the two limbs

The Supreme Court did not expand on the relationship between the subjective and objective limbs of the reformulated test for dishonesty and nor did the Court of Appeal in *Barton* other than explaining limb 1 as above.

Considering the way the test is expressed . . . it cannot have been intended that the two limbs of *Ghosh* were simply to be inverted. That would require the jury to ask what the defendant thought others would think was dishonest and then apply an objective assessment of dishonesty constrained by what the defendant thought others would consider was dishonest. Accepting that approach to be untenable, what is the correct interpretation?

We suggest that the answer lies in appreciating the nature of the assessment required by the first limb. As we have noted, the jury is required to assess the defendant's conduct and state of mind as broadly construed in [108] above. It would, in practice, be wrong for the judge to limit that assessment by restricting what the defendant can adduce in evidence about either what he thought was dishonest or what he thought others thought was dishonest. It follows from [108] that it cannot be right to direct a jury that such evidence is to be ignored as irrelevant. Such an interpretation would contradict [108] and would, in effect, overturn *Hayes*, but there is no suggestion this was the intention of either the Supreme Court or the Court of Appeal and it seems contrary to the language of both judgments.

Accepting that limb 1 requires the jury to consider D's beliefs about all the circumstances, we must consider how the jury is permitted to use that in applying the second (objective) limb. When it eventually confronts the issue, we suggest that there are at least two ways in which the Court of Appeal might answer that question. First, it could hold that evidence of what the defendant believed about the honesty of his actions was evidence relevant only to his credibility. This is, we suggest, an undesirable approach . . . to say in this context that the defendant's perception of the honesty of his conduct affects only his likely honesty as a witness seems particularly unhelpful. The second approach is more pragmatic: to recognise that defendants are entitled to adduce evidence of their perceptions of the honesty of their conduct; to tell the jury they can have regard to that evidence but also, crucially, to direct the jury that what the defendant believed is not determinative of whether that conduct was dishonest by objective standards. The relationship between the limbs and the way the jury is to be directed has real practical significance in cases such as *Hayes*. A defendant should be entitled to adduce evidence about industry practises (as they were entitled to do under the subjective limb of the *Ghosh* test), but the jury is no longer bound to acquit if the defendant held a belief that ordinary decent people would not regard his conduct as dishonest."

8–093 In a case where evidence is given as to the market ethos of a particular profession or group,[223] this is relevant to the subjective first limb of the *Ivey/Barton* test, but the standard of honesty remains objective, that of ordinary decent people. The jury must be sure that D's conduct was dishonest by the standards of ordinary decent people, the prosecution does not have to prove D recognised that their conduct was dishonest by those standards.[224]

The reliance upon the (objective) standards of ordinary decent people to determine whether conduct is dishonest has long been criticised, on the basis that it assumes that a community norm exists in relation to the issue of dishonesty which may not exist.[225] These views are supported by research which revealed huge variations in ordinary people's ideas of what constitutes dishonesty. Women are more likely than men, and older people are more likely than younger people, to categorise certain behaviour as dishonest. But, interestingly, men are more likely to convict someone of a dishonesty offence in court.[226] The result is that it becomes a lottery—dependent, inter alia, on the sex and age profile of the jury (or, perhaps of the magistrate)—whether someone will be convicted of an offence of dishonesty.

---

223 As was the case in *R. v Hayes (Tom Alexander William)* [2015] EWCA Crim 1944; [2018] 1 Cr. App. R. 10 and *R. v Bermingham (Colin)* [2020] EWCA Crim 1662; [2021] 1 Cr. App. R. 24.

224 *Bermingham* [2020] EWCA Crim 1662; [2021] 1 Cr. App. R. 24; Judicial College, *The Crown Court Compendium: Part I: Jury and Trial Management and Summing Up* (2023), paras 8-20–8-21, 8-23.

225 See e.g. E. Griew, "Dishonesty: The Objections to *Feeley* and *Ghosh*" [1985] Crim. L.R. 341. See also E. Finch, "The Elephant in the (Jury) Room: exploring mock jurors' understanding of different approaches to dishonesty" [2021] Crim. L.R. 513, 519. Finch's research with mock jury deliberations found this criticism to be borne out.

226 The "Honesty Lab" study conducted by Fafinski and Finch: Connor, "Sexes Differ Over Dishonesty Says New Study" *The Independent*, 7 September 2009; M. Henderson, "Many Potential Jurors Find it Hard to Tell Right from Wrong" *The Times*, 7 September 2009.

If has been argued that because large numbers of employees "fiddle" from their employers, such employees have lost all standards of knowing right from wrong and therefore, being in a moral vacuum, would be unable to assess "dishonesty" if sitting in a jury box.[227] But a plausible explanation is that most such employees know perfectly well that their conduct is dishonest, but have chosen nevertheless to go ahead and do it. Such persons remain capable of sitting on a jury and judging standards of dishonesty. Research has revealed that people are less likely to regard conduct as dishonest if they have done similar things themselves but are still capable of making a judgement of dishonesty. For example, nearly two-thirds of people have taken stationery home from work but 82% thought it was dishonest.[228] Charges of hypocrisy will not do, otherwise any juror who had ever committed a (relevant) offence would have to be disqualified—an impossible task given the vast unknown figure of unrecorded property crime.[229]

One of the reasons given by Lord Hughes in *Ivey* for reforming the test for dishonesty was that jurors often found the *Ghosh* test "puzzling and difficult to apply".[230] But Finch's research into the deliberations of mock juries found that none of the juries that were given a test for dishonesty (whether it be objective, the *Ghosh* test, or a purely subjective test) applied it correctly: "either due to misunderstanding or disapproval of the test or a combination of both".[231] She concluded that: "giving the jury no direction on dishonesty confuses them less and creates less conflict than giving them a test, irrespective of its wording and whether it is objective or subjective in nature".[232] However, the difficulty with giving no direction, is that the jury would be left to make the decision as to whether D is dishonest "using whatever approach they think is appropriate", which would lead to concern about "consistency and certainty" of their decision-making.[233] **8-094**

In spite of concerns that the *Ivey/Barton* test may lead to inconsistent jury decisions, the Court of Appeal in *Bermingham* declined to depart from the test and held that it was consistent with the European Convention of Human Rights (ECHR) art.7.[234]

2. Intention of permanent deprivation

The second mens rea requirement of theft is that D must intend to permanently deprive the other of the property. If they intend to return the goods, this is not theft. Dishonest borrowings are not theft. **8-095**

227 Williams, *Textbook of Criminal Law*, 2nd edn (1983), pp.726–730.

228 Connor, "Sexes Differ Over Dishonesty Says New Study" *The Independent*, 7 September 2009. cf. Law Commission Report No.276, *Fraud* (2002), para.5.9.

229 See, e.g. S. Karstedt and S. Farrall, "Law-abiding majority? The everyday crimes of the middle classes" (Centre for Crime and Justice Studies, 2007).

230 *Ivey* [2017] UKSC 67; [2018] A.C. 391 at [57].

231 E. Finch, "The Elephant in the (Jury) Room: exploring mock jurors' understanding of different approaches to dishonesty" [2021] Crim. L.R. 513, 530.

232 Finch, "The Elephant in the (Jury) Room: exploring mock jurors' understanding of different approaches to dishonesty" [2021] Crim. L.R. 513, 531.

233 Finch, "The Elephant in the (Jury) Room: exploring mock jurors' understanding of different approaches to dishonesty" [2021] Crim. L.R. 513, 531.

234 *Bermingham* [2020] EWCA Crim 1662; [2021] 1 Cr. App. R. 24 at [102]–[103]. *Bermingham* was followed in *Hayes* [2024] EWCA Crim 304 at [156]–[157]. See also *Barton* [2020] EWCA Crim 575 at [124]. All of these cases involved the offence of conspiracy to defraud.

What is required is an *intention* of permanent deprivation. Whether V is actually deprived of the property is irrelevant. This demonstrates again the inchoate nature of the offence of theft.

"Intention of permanently depriving the other of it" (s.1) is not defined by the Theft Act. However, s.6 *extends* the natural meaning of the phrase and provides that in certain circumstances even though D did not "mean" the other to lose the thing permanently they are "to be regarded" as having an intention of permanent deprivation.

THEFT ACT 1968 S.6:

8-096 "(1) A person appropriating property belonging to another without meaning the other permanently to lose the thing itself is nevertheless to be regarded as having the intention of permanently depriving the other of it if his intention is to treat the thing as his own to dispose of regardless of the other's rights; and a borrowing or lending of it may amount to so treating it if, but only if, the borrowing or lending is for a period and in circumstances making it equivalent to an outright taking or disposal.

(2) Without prejudice to the generality of subsection (1) above, where a person, having possession or control (lawfully or not) of property belonging to another, parts with the property under a condition as to its return which he may not be able to perform, this (if done for purposes of his own and without the other's authority) amounts to treating the property as his own to dispose of regardless of the other's rights."

8-097 In *Lloyd*,[235] it was made clear that s.6 should only be referred to in exceptional cases; for most purposes, it would be unnecessary to go beyond s.1(1).[236]

(i) Section 6(1)

8-098 Section 6(1) contains two limbs. The first refers to a D whose "intention is to treat the thing as his own to dispose of regardless of the other's rights". The second limb is a specific illustration of this in that certain borrowings "may amount to so treating it" as his own. Section 6(2) provides that the situation covered therein "amounts to treating the property as his own to dispose of regardless of the other's rights". This is thus just another specific illustration of the principle contained in the first limb of s.6(1).[237] Nevertheless, it is useful to look at the three situations separately.

---

235 *R. v Lloyd (Sidney Douglas)* [1985] Q.B. 829; [1985] 3 W.L.R. 30 CA.

236 *R. v Warner* (1970) 55 Cr. App. R. 93; *R. v Cocks (Eugene George)* (1976) 63 Cr. App. R. 79 CA; *R. v Mitchell (Walter Joby)* [2008] EWCA Crim 850.

237 *R. v Fernandes (Roland Anthony)* [1996] 1 Cr. App. R. 175 at 188 CA.

(a) If his intention is to treat the thing as his own to dispose of regardless of the other's rights

R. v Raphael [2008] EWCA Crim 1014 (Court of Appeal, Criminal Division):

D drove off in a car belonging to Adeosun and then demanded money for its return. **8-099**

PRESIDENT OF THE QUEEN'S BENCH DIVISION:

"[T]he section itself demonstrates that the necessary intention may sometimes be established when the person appropriating property belonging to another does not in fact intend that its true owner should be deprived of it permanently. It is properly described as a deeming provision. As Lord Lane LJ . . . observed in *Lloyd*:

> 'It must mean, if nothing else, that there are circumstances in which a defendant may be deemed to have the intention permanently to deprive, even though he may intend the owner eventually to get back the object which has been taken . . . The first part of section 6(1) seems to us to be aimed at the sort of case where a defendant takes things and then offers them back to the owner for the owner to buy if he wishes. If the taker intends to return them to the owner only upon such payment, then, on the wording of section 6(1) that is deemed to amount to the necessary intention permanently to deprive . . .'

He continued that there were other cases of 'similar intent': for instance, 'I have taken your valuable painting. You can have it back on payment to me of £X000. If you are not prepared to make that payment, then you are not going to get your painting back.'

The express language of section 6 specifies that the subjective element necessary to establish the mens rea for theft includes an intention on the part of the taker 'to treat the thing as his own to dispose of regardless of the other's rights'. In our judgment it is hard to find a better example of such an intention than an offer, not to return Adeosun's car to him in exactly the same condition it was when it was removed from his possession and control, but to sell his own property back to him, and to make its return subject to a condition or conditions inconsistent with his right to possession of his own property."

Appeal dismissed

In *Lavender*,[238] D removed doors from one council property undergoing repairs and used them to replace damaged doors at another council property. It was held that this was a "disposal" under s.6(1) because D "intended to treat the doors as his own, regardless of the council's rights". The problem with this interpretation is that it renders s.6 redundant in that an intention to treat property as one's own is already a necessary requirement for an appropriation. **8-100**

238 *DPP v Lavender (Melvyn)* [1994] Crim. L.R. 297 Div Ct.

In *Marshall*,[239] ticket touts obtained unexpired London Underground tickets and sold them to other potential customers. It was argued that there was no intention of permanent deprivation because the tickets would, in due course, be returned to the possession of London Underground. It was held, however, that the ticket touts had, under s.6(1), an intention to treat the tickets as their own to dispose of regardless of London Underground's rights.

The issue of intention of permanent deprivation needs to be approached with care by a trial judge in cases where goods are taken and abandoned shortly thereafter. Appropriation and intention of permanent deprivation are separate elements of the offence of theft, and it would be wrong for a trial judge in such a case to give the impression that a taking, even if violent, was sufficient in itself to establish an intention permanently to deprive the owner of the property. In *Mitchell*,[240] D, being pursued by police officers and needing a getaway car, pulled a woman out of her car, drove off in it and abandoned it shortly afterwards. The trial judge ruled that this taking, using and abandoning of the vehicle was sufficient evidence capable of amounting to an intention to dispose of property regardless of the owner's rights. On appeal, this was declared to be wrong. Section 6 was not meant to widen greatly the basic s.1 requirement of an intention of permanent deprivation. It was simply dealing with "a small number of difficult cases". Such a brief use of the car before abandoning it did not come within s.1. The relevance of abandonment must also be properly explained to the jury. In *Vinall*,[241] two cyclists riding along a cycling path were approached by the two Ds and another man. One of the cyclists was punched from his bicycle and chased off, and the three men walked off with his bicycle. The bicycle was found abandoned by a bus stop on a main road 50 yards from where the owner had left it. The trial judge invited the jury to consider whether the fact of the abandonment of the bicycle at the bus stop itself demonstrated: (1) an intention to assume the rights of an owner and, therefore, an appropriation of the bicycle; and (2) a deemed intention permanently to deprive the owner of it. The Court of Appeal held that the judge had allowed the "separate concepts of appropriation and intention permanently to deprive" to become "fatally confused".[242] The taking of the bicycle was a sufficient assumption of the rights of the owner to amount to an appropriation, and the abandonment of the bicycle was capable of being additional evidence that by taking the bicycle the appellants were assuming the rights of the owner over it. But the jury had also to be directed that they had to be sure that at the time of taking the bicycle either the appellants had an intention permanently to deprive (s.1) or they intended to treat the bicycle as their own to dispose of regardless of the other's rights (s.6).[243]

8–101 In *Raphael*,[244] it was held that D's demand that money be paid before the car was returned amounted to an intention of permanent deprivation, but what of the case where other, non-monetary conditions are attached to the return of property? In *R. v Waters (Sian)*,[245] D, who was convicted of robbery, had been involved in a confrontation with a group of young people and had taken a mobile phone from the

---

239 *R. v Marshall (Adrian John)* [1998] 2 Cr. App. R. 282; (1998) 162 J.P. 489 CA. See J.C. Smith, "Stealing Tickets" [1998] Crim. L.R. 723. See also *DPP v SJ (A Juvenile)* [2002] EWHC 291 (Admin) where it was held that an intention to render something useless demonstrated an intention of treating an article as one's own to dispose of.

240 *Mitchell* [2008] EWCA Crim 850.

241 *R. v Vinall (George Alfred)* [2011] EWCA Crim 2652; [2012] 1 Cr. App. R. 29. L.H. Leigh, "Robbery, Contemporaneity and intent Permanently to Deprive" (2012) 176 J.P.N. 201–202.

242 *Vinall* [2011] EWCA Crim 2652 at [10].

243 This case is further discussed in para.9–209, in relation to the offence of robbery. See also *R. v Zerei (Samuel Michael)* [2012] EWCA Crim 1114.

244 *R. v Raphael (Jermaine)* [2008] EWCA Crim 1014; [2008] Crim. L.R. 995.

245 *R. v Waters (Sian)* [2015] EWCA Crim 402.

V. There was evidence that D had informed V that the phone would be returned if another individual, H, was persuaded to come and talk to him. The trial judge directed the jury that, even if D made It plain that the phone would be returned if he was able to talk to H, that would still amount to an Intention permanently to deprive. The Court of Appeal, allowing the appeal, held that this was not a legally correct direction:

> ". . . if the condition attached to the return of the item is one which would not be fulfilled or not be fulfilled in the foreseeable future, then the circumstances may well amount to an intention permanently to deprive. On the other hand if the condition can readily be fulfilled and may be fulfilled in the near future, the jury may well conclude that intention to deprive has not been made out."[246]

(b) Borrowing or lending for a period and in circumstances making it equivalent to an outright taking or disposal

This makes it clear that certain borrowings are to be treated the same as outright takings. The classic example here is borrowing another's football season ticket and then returning the piece of paper at the end of the season after watching all the matches. At that stage, the ticket has no value and is useless; the "virtue" has gone out of the thing. **8–102**

R. v Lloyd [1985] Q.B. 829 (Court of Appeal, Criminal Division):

Film reels were removed from a cinema for a few hours and "pirate" copies made of them; the originals were then returned. D appealed against his conviction for conspiracy to steal. **8–103**

LORD LANE CJ:

> "[T]he intention of the appellants could more accurately be described as an intention temporarily to deprive the owner of the film and was indeed the opposite of an intention permanently to deprive . . .
>
> Borrowing is *ex hypothesi* not something which is done with an intention permanently to deprive. This half of the subsection, we believe, is intended to make it clear that a mere borrowing is never enough to constitute the necessary guilty mind unless the intention is to return the 'thing' in such a changed state that it can truly be said that all its goodness or virtue has gone: for example *R. v Beecham* (1851) 5 Cox C.C. 181, where the defendant stole railway tickets intending that they should be returned to the railway company in the usual way only after the journeys had been completed. He was convicted of larceny . . .

246 *Waters* [2015] EWCA Crim 402 at [18]. cf. *R. v Coffey* [1987] Crim. L.R. 498 CA.

> That being the case, we turn to inquire whether the feature films in this case can fall within that category. Our view is that they cannot. The goodness, the virtue, the practical value of the films to the owners has not gone out of the article. The film could still be projected to paying audiences . . .
>
> Our view is that those particular films which were the subject of this alleged conspiracy had not themselves diminished in value at all. What had happened was that the borrowed film had been used or was going to be used to perpetrate a copyright swindle on the owners whereby their commercial interests were grossly and adversely affected in the way that we have endeavoured to describe at the outset of this judgment. That borrowing, it seems to us, was not for a period, or in such circumstances, as made it equivalent to an outright taking or disposal. There was still virtue in the film."
>
> *Appeals allowed*

8–104 Difficult questions of fact will, of course, remain. In *Lloyd,* Lord Lane spoke of "all" the virtue or goodness being gone. This raises the problem of the football season ticket which is returned after it has been used for 19 matches, but is still valid for one final match. The ticket clearly has *some* value or virtue left. Presumably, questions such as these, were they to arise, would be left to the jury as questions of fact.

(ii) Section 6(2)

8–105 This deals with the situation of a person who takes unacceptable risks with the property of another. For example, they may pawn such property realising that they may be unable to redeem it. In *Fernandes,* a solicitor dishonestly made an insecure investment of a client's money. It was held that:

> ". . . section 6 may apply to a person in possession or control of another's property who, dishonestly and for his own purpose, deals with that property in such a manner that he knows he is risking its loss."[247]

It is uncertain whether D must realise that they may be unable to redeem the property or whether it suffices that they "may" objectively be so unable. Griew says: "The former view is doctrinally the purer; the latter is more readily suggested by the terms of the poorly-drafted section."[248] However, in *Fernandes* it was stated that D must *know* that they are risking the loss of the property.[249]

(a) Dishonest borrowings

8–106 Apart from these specific situations where s.6 has deemed dishonest borrowings to be the equivalent of an intention to permanently deprive, the Theft Act 1968 has generally chosen not to punish dishonest borrowings. There are two well-known exceptions to the intention of permanent deprivation rule (apart

247 *Fernandes* [1996] 1 Cr. App. R. 175 at 188.
248 E. Griew, *The Theft Acts*, 7th edn (London: Sweet & Maxwell, 1995), p.66.
249 This view is supported by D. Ormerod and D. Williams, *Smith's The Law of Theft*, 9th edn (Oxford: OUP, 2007), pp.123–124.

from the exceptions within s.6 itself). Section 11 creates the offence of removing articles from places open to the public, for example, removing works of art from museums or galleries albeit intending to return them at some time. The Theft Act 1968 s.12 creates the second exceptional offence of taking a motor vehicle or other conveyance without authority. This is designed to prevent "joyriding", where a car is taken and, after being driven around, abandoned. In such cases an intention of permanent deprivation would be difficult to establish.[250]

It is interesting to contrast this last activity of joyriding with the conduct of a person who walks into a bookshop and dishonestly removes a book which they take home and read before returning it to the shop. It appears that the only reasons for the criminalisation of the former but not the latter activity are, first, the prevalence of joyriding[251] and secondly, the difficulty of proving the necessary intent with taking cars (with the book example, a finding of intention of permanent deprivation would be almost irresistible and thus a conviction for theft would result in fact).

It is worth pausing at this point to reflect whether some insight can be gleaned into the real harm that is sought to be prevented by the crime of theft. When the book is dishonestly taken from the store, the store clearly suffers a harm. First, there is economic harm. The book is removed from their shelves, meaning it cannot be sold to another. The used book that is returned is not the same thing that was taken, which was a new book. The store sustains an economic loss of the difference in value between the new book and the second-hand book.[252] Secondly, there is all the non-economic harm associated with most thefts. The shop has had its rights of ownership assaulted. It has lost control of its property, lost the power to make choices and decisions about it. The identity of the borrower is probably unknown and, therefore, there can be no certainty as to when and if the property will be returned.[253]

It should be repeated at this stage that it is not necessary for V to lose their property permanently. **8-107**
What matters is that D, at the time of the appropriation, *intends* that they shall lose it permanently. Thus, the result may be the same as with cases of borrowing. In our example, the book is ultimately returned. It is the intention of the taker that distinguishes the cases. Is this approach justifiable?

The real harm in theft is that when D intends permanent deprivation there is a greater risk to V that they will lose their property permanently. (In most cases they will, in fact, have already lost the property.) As with the law of attempt, the threat to the property amounts to a "second order harm". This, however, only explains why the actual loss of property need not occur—but still does not explain why there must be an intention of permanent deprivation as opposed to an intention to borrow dishonestly.

What is being punished is disapproved of behaviour which poses an unacceptable risk to the property of another. It is fairly obvious that where there is an intention of permanent deprivation there is a greater

---

250 Section 12A provides for an offence of aggravated vehicle taking to cover instances where a vehicle is taken by D contrary to s.12 and, after it is taken but before it is recovered, damage is caused, or injury inflicted in the circumstances specified in s.12A(2). See D. Ormerod and K. Laird, *Smith and Hogan's Criminal Law*, 16th edn (2021), pp.953–955. For further exceptions see, e.g. the Postal Services Act 2000 s.84, and G. Williams, "Temporary Appropriation should be Theft" [1981] Crim. L.R. 129, 130.

251 CLRC, 8th Report, *Theft and Related Offences* (1966), Cmnd.2977, p.788. The offence was first created by the Road Traffic Act 1930 s.28 "to deal with a mischief which had even then become common" (para.82).

252 Fletcher, *Rethinking Criminal Law* (Brown, 1978), p.48.

253 e.g. Goya's portrait of the Duke of Wellington was "borrowed" from the National Gallery for four years: CLRC, 8th Report, *Theft and Related Offences* (1966), Cmnd.2977, p.788.

risk of actual permanent deprivation occurring (for much the same reason that there is greater danger when D is intending a consequence than when they are being reckless as to it: they are trying to achieve the objective and must, in general, stand more chance of success than if not so trying). So, the question reduces itself to whether permanent deprivation is sufficiently "worse" than temporary deprivation to justify criminalisation of the former but not the latter. Most people would surely agree that, in general, a permanent loss is qualitatively worse than a temporary loss.[254] The owner has been deprived completely and irrevocably of their property. Insurance, if obtainable, will not compensate for such loss of power and control over the property. Whether it is *so much* worse as to justify the criminalisation line being drawn between the two is uncertain. Perhaps, it is best at this stage to conclude that while a temporary loss caused by dishonest conduct is unfortunate and deserves moral condemnation, one should refrain from expanding the role of the criminal law without clear and strong reasons.

(b) Particular property

8–108 There must be an intention permanently to deprive the other of the *particular* property alleged to be appropriated. It is no defence that similar property was to be returned. This rule is most often applied to coins and banknotes. It is clear law that if one "borrows" money, intending to repay it the next day, one is not intending to return the same notes or coins; one therefore does have an intention of permanently depriving the other of the particular property alleged to be stolen.[255] Of course, actual liability still depends on a finding of dishonesty which, in such cases, may be difficult to establish.

(iii) Conditional intention

R. v Easom [1971] 2 Q.B. 315:

8–109 D picked up a woman's handbag in a cinema, rummaged through it and, having taken nothing, put it back near to the owner, who repossessed it. On appeal, Easom's conviction for stealing the handbag and specified contents (tissues, cosmetics etc) was quashed: D never had intention of permanently depriving the owner of the handbag of any of those specific items.

EDMUND DAVIES LJ

> "In every case of theft the appropriation must be accompanied by the intention of permanently depriving the owner of his property. What may be loosely described as a 'conditional' appropriation will not do. If the appropriator has it in mind merely to deprive the owner of such of his property as, on examination, proves worth taking and then, finding that the booty is valueless to the appropriator, leaves it ready to hand to be repossessed by the owner, the appropriator has not stolen. If a dishonest postal sorter picks up a pile of letters, intending to steal any which are registered, but, on finding that none of them are, replaces them, he has stolen nothing, and this is so notwithstanding the provisions of section 6 (1) of the Theft Act 1968."

---

254 cf. Tamblyn, "Reforming theft: taking without consent" [2020] Crim. L.R. 597, 602–603.

255 *R. v Williams (Hywell Rhys)* [1953] 1 Q.B. 660; [1953] 2 W.L.R. 937 CA; *R. v Velumyl* [1989] Crim. L.R. 299 CA.

Easom could not be convicted of the theft of the handbag, tissues etc, because he did not intend to keep any of these items. His intention was to steal anything that he found that was worth stealing, and "it cannot be said that one who has it in mind to steal only if what he finds is worth stealing has a present intention to steal".[256] Nor, since he replaced the bag near to the position from which it had been removed, could it be established that he had exercised such dominion over the property that it could be inferred that, at the time of the taking, he intended to treat the bag as his own to dispose of regardless of the owner's rights.[257] The D in such circumstances might be convicted of attempted theft if the charge were suitably worded as "attempting to steal from a handbag".[258] **8–110**

III. Fraud

A. BACKGROUND

The Theft Acts 1968 and 1978 created eight offences of dishonestly obtaining something by deception: **8–111**

(1) obtaining property;[259]
(2) obtaining a money transfer;[260]
(3) obtaining a pecuniary advantage;[261]
(4) procuring the execution of a valuable security;[262]
(5) obtaining services;[263]
(6) securing the remission of liability;[264]
(7) inducing a creditor to wait for or to forgo payment;[265] and
(8) obtaining an exemption from, or an abatement of, a liability.[266]

However, major problems emerged in relation to these deception offences.

256 *R. v Husseyn (Ulus)* (1978) 67 Cr. App. R. 131; [1978] Crim. L.R. 219 CA. But cf. the position in relation to s.9(1)(a) burglary: *Att-Gen's References (Nos 1 and 2 of 1979)* [1980] Q.B. 180; [1979] 3 W.L.R. 577, Ormerod and Williams, *Smith's The Law of Theft*, 9th edn (2007) p.253.

257 *Vinall* [2011] EWCA Crim 2652; [2012] 1 Cr. App. R. 29 at [19].

258 Ormerod and Laird, *Smith, Hogan and Ormerod's Criminal Law*, 16th edn (2021), pp.929–930. cf. Child, Simester, Spencer, Stark and Virgo, *Simester and Sullivan's Criminal Law: Theory and Doctrine*, 8th edn (2022), pp.632–634.

259 Theft Act 1968 s.15.

260 Theft Act 1968 s.15A, inserted by Theft (Amendment) Act 1996.

261 Theft Act 1968 s.16.

262 Theft Act 1968 s.20(2).

263 Theft Act 1978 s.1.

264 Theft Act 1978 s.2(1)(a).

265 Theft Act 1978 s.2(1)(b).

266 Theft Act 1978 s.2(1)(c).

8-112 First, it was necessary to prove that the deception *caused* the obtaining of the specified commodity. This caused immense difficulties. For instance, in one of the leading House of Lords' decisions, *Lambie*,[267] D, who had exceeded her credit limit and knew the bank was trying to recover the credit card, used the card to purchase goods. It was tolerably clear that the shop assistant who accepted the credit card had little interest in D's relationship with her bank. She knew the transaction would be honoured by the bank. That is the point of credit cards. Accordingly, it was difficult to see that the deception (the representation that D has actual authority to use the card) caused the shop assistant to hand over the property. To prevent such credit card frauds the House of Lords was forced to adopt the tortuous reasoning that the shop assistant was deceived and for that reason handed over the property:

> ". . . if she had been asked whether, had she known the respondent was acting dishonestly and, in truth, had no authority whatever from the bank to use the credit card in this way, she would have completed the transaction, only one answer is possible—no."

Secondly, the requirement that the deception be operative, that is, deceive someone, meant that machines could not be "deceived".[268] While this might not have been a particular problem in 1968 (other than in cases relating to vending machines etc), technological advances in a commercial world now dominated by credit and debit cards, electronic transfers of money and the provision of goods or services through the internet and call centres meant that there were significant gaps in the law in relation to deceiving machines. Accordingly, the Law Commission proposed replacing the concept of deception with the requirement of a misrepresentation.

Under this approach, the focus is on the D's wrongdoing rather than on whether the other person was induced to act in reliance on the misrepresentation. This approach also has the advantage that it makes no difference whether the misrepresentation was directed at a person or a machine.

8-113 Thirdly, the various deception offences were over-specific with the result that specific offences were often wrongly charged. There was an enormous overlap between the offences—quite apart from the overlap, already discussed, with theft. Such blurring of offences was morally confusing in fair labelling terms and made it difficult for prosecutors to know which charge to select.

Fourthly, some of the offences were unduly complex: a lawyer's dream or nightmare, depending on one's point of view.

Accordingly, the Law Commission proposed abolition of all the deception offences and their replacement by a general offence of fraud along with one separate offence of obtaining services dishonestly.

---

267 *R. v Lambie (Shiralee Ann)* [1982] A.C. 449; [1981] 3 W.L.R. 88 HL. *Lambie* and subsequent cases generated much academic debate. See, e.g. A.T.H. Smith, "The Idea of Criminal Deception" [1982] Crim. L.R. 721.

268 *Holmes v Governor of Brixton Prison* [2004] EWHC 2020 (Admin); [2005] 1 W.L.R. 1857; *Poland v Ulatowski* [2010] EWHC 2673 (Admin) at [30]–[32]; [2011] Lloyd's Rep. F.C. 18 QBD.

Law Commission Report No.276, Fraud (2002), paras 1.6–1.9:

> "1.6 [The issue is] whether the introduction of a general fraud offence would improve the criminal law. We have come to the conclusion that it would . . . 8–114
>
> (1) It should make the law more comprehensible to juries, especially in serious fraud trials. The charges which are currently employed in such trials are numerous, and none of them adequately describe or encapsulate the meaning of 'fraud'. The statutory offences are too specific to offer a general description of fraud; while the common law offence of conspiracy to defraud is so wide that it offers little guidance on the difference between fraudulent and lawful conduct . . .
>
> (2) A general offence of fraud would be a useful tool in effective prosecutions. Specific offences are sometimes wrongly charged, in circumstances when another offence would have been more suitable. This can result in unjustified acquittals and costly appeals . . .
>
> (3) Introducing a single crime of fraud would dramatically simplify the law of fraud. Clear, simple law is fairer than complicated, inaccessible law. If a citizen is contemplating activities which could amount to a crime, a clear, simple law gives better guidance on whether the conduct is criminal . . .
>
> (4) A general offence of fraud would be aimed at encompassing fraud in all its forms. It would not focus on particular ways or means of committing frauds. Thus it should be better able to keep pace with developing technology.
>
> 1.7 In line with these recommendations, we recommend that the eight offences of deception created by the Theft Acts 1968–96 should be repealed and that the common law offence of conspiracy to defraud should be abolished. In their place we recommend the creation of two new statutory offences—one of fraud, and one of obtaining services dishonestly."

Of course, more radical options were possible. The Law Commission's proposed offences (enacted in the Fraud Act 2006) pre-suppose the existence of the remaining property offences such as theft, handling stolen goods and so on. Reform could have gone further and have introduced an even broader offence, such as a general offence of dishonesty. Such ideas are considered later in this chapter. 8–115

B. The Fraud Act 2006

Following the above recommendations by the Law Commission, the various deception offences cited above were all abolished by the Fraud Act 2006. In their place, there is a single broad fraud offence, supported by ancillary offences. There is also an independent offence of obtaining services dishonestly. 8–116

1. Fraud

8–117 Section 1 creates an offence of fraud, punishable on conviction on indictment by a maximum of 10 years' imprisonment.[269] Sentencing guidelines have been issued in respect of this offence.[270] Section 1 identifies that there are three ways of committing the offence, as set out in the subsequent sections: fraud by false representation (s.2); fraud by failing to disclose information (s.3); and fraud by abuse of position (s.4).

Each of these three ways of committing the offence of fraud will be discussed in turn. As fraud by false representation is the broadest of these forms of committing the offence and is the one likely to be most frequently charged, those elements that are common to all three (dishonesty and intent to make a gain or cause loss) will be discussed in relation to this form of the offence.

(i) Fraud by false representation

FRAUD ACT 2006 S.2:

8–118 "(1) A person is in breach of this section if he—

(a) dishonestly makes a false representation, and
(b) intends, by making the representation—

(i) to make a gain for himself or another, or
(ii) to cause loss to another or to expose another to a risk of loss.

(2) A representation is false if—

(a) it is untrue or misleading, and
(b) the person making it knows that it is, or might be, untrue or misleading.

(3) 'Representation' means any representation as to fact or law, including a representation as to the state of mind of—

(a) the person making the representation, or
(b) any other person.

(4) A representation may be express or implied.

(5) For the purposes of this section a representation may be regarded as made if it (or anything implying it) is submitted in any form to any system or device designed to receive, convey or respond to communications (with or without human intervention)."

---

269 Fraud Act 2006 s.1(3).
270 Sentencing Council, *Fraud* (2014, revised 2016).

Under s.5 (discussed later) "gain" and "loss" extend only to gain and loss in money or other property. 8–119

The essence of this offence is telling lies for economic purposes. With the abolition of the requirement that there be a deception, there is no need to establish that anyone believed the lies or was induced to act in a certain way because of the lies. There is no need for D to obtain any advantage (economic or otherwise). All that is required is that there is a dishonest intention to secure a gain or cause a loss. The offence thus adopts an inchoate model of liability. The emphasis is on D's wrongdoing.

David Ormerod, "The Fraud Act 2006—Criminalising Lying?" [2007] Crim. L.R. 193, 196–197:

"This wholly inchoate offence appears to criminalise lying. 8–120

Should lying be a sufficient basis for criminal liability? What is the wrong which D performs which warrants the criminal sanction? It is not one derived from intentionally harming V's interests directly—there need be no such harm. Similarly, it is not one of potentially damaging V's interests. The wrong seems to be the act of lying or misleading with intent to gain or cause loss; the harm might be construed as one of destabilising society's processes of property and financial transfers. Even if this is sufficient to warrant criminalisation, is it properly called fraud?"

(a) Actus reus

The actus reus of this form of the offence requires that there be a representation which is false. 8–121

(1) Express or implied representations

Section 2(4) provides that a representation may be express or implied. Express representations are an obvious way of lying: for example, telling a purchaser that one is selling a diamond when it is, in fact, glass. The representation may be written, spoken, posted on a phishing website or sent by email.[271] In *McDermott*,[272] D was convicted of fraud when, having stolen clothing from a department store, he then returned the clothes and, representing that he had bought them, sought to recover a refund. In *Wenman*,[273] D told a complainant that his roof was in a poor state of repair and quoted him a total of £25,600 for repair works, in circumstances in which there was nothing basically wrong with the roof. In *Formhals*,[274] D sold items representing that they were signed by Winston Churchill, when in fact he had forged the signatures. In *Ali*,[275] D pretended to be a police officer in order to dupe an elderly lady into 8–122

---

271 CPS, *The Fraud Act 2006; Legal Guidance Fraud and Economic Crime (2024)*.

272 *R. v McDermott (Joseph Mark)* [2008] EWCA Crim 1713.

273 *R. v Wenman (Joseph William)* [2013] EWCA Crim 340. cf. *R. v Davies (Tudor)* [2008] EWCA Crim 980, where contracts for building work were solicited and cash deposits obtained, but the work was not done.

274 *R. v Formhals (Allen)* [2013] EWCA Crim 2624; [2014] 1 W.L.R. 2219. cf. *R. v Wiseman (Climate)* [2023] EWCA Crim 1363, where the false representation related to the marketing and sale of a "plague protection oil", which D claimed could cure, prevent or treat coronavirus.

275 *R. v Ali (Hamza)* [2018] EWCA Crim 3026. cf. *R. v Azhar (Muhammed)* [2019] EWCA Crim 326 (voice phishing fraud).

parting with money and valuables. In *Andrewes*,[276] D lied about his qualifications and experience in a job application form. In all of these cases there was a clear false representation.

No definition of an implied representation is provided in the Act. In *United Arab Emirates v Allen*,[277] it was suggested that "implied representations are legal constructs intended to give effect to that which honest parties involved in a transaction would reasonably read into the conduct of the other". Under the law before the Fraud Act 2006, proof of a deception involved, inter alia, establishing that there was an untrue representation. The courts, after the Fraud Act 2006, have drawn on this established body of law as to the meaning of an implied representation.[278] There are many established instances where the conduct of D will be regarded as amounting to an implied representation:[279]

(1) *hotels:* if one books into a hotel one is taken to be representing that one intends to pay the bill at the end of one's stay.[280]
(2) *restaurants:* ordering and eating a meal in a restaurant is a representation that one intends to pay for that meal. If during or after the meal one decides not to pay, then remaining at the table thereafter is a false representation that one still intends to pay.[281]

(b) Quotations

R. v Silverman (1988) 86 Cr. App. R. 213 (Court of Appeal, Criminal Division):

8–123 D charged two elderly sisters grossly excessive prices for work done to the central heating and wiring of their flat. They had trusted him to charge a fair price because of previous work done by him for their family. D placed no pressure on them to accept his quotation and there was nothing wrong with the work done. He was charged and convicted under s.15 (the now abolished offence of obtaining property by deception). He appealed on the grounds, inter alia, that an excessively high quotation did not amount to a false representation and that the trial judge had erred in not putting his defence (that the sisters seemed happy with his work) to the jury in express terms.

WATKINS LJ:

"Mr Hopmeier, who appears here for the appellant, has argued, first, that the appellant made no representations to the complainants. He has not shrunk from conceding that the appellant was dishonest. He has submitted that the appellant quoted the sisters for the work to be done but that it was open to them either to accept or reject the quotation upon such advice as they might seek and perhaps in the light of tenders by others, and that the appellant was in much

276 *R. v Andrewes (Jon)* [2022] UKSC 24; [2022] 1 W.L.R. 3878.
277 *United Arab Emirates v Allen* [2012] EWHC 1712 (Admin); [2012] 1 W.L.R. 3419 at [56].
278 e.g. in *Allen* [2012] EWHC 1712 (Admin); [2012] 1 W.L.R. 3419, the court referred to *Commissioner of Police of the Metropolis v Charles* [1977] A.C. 177; [1976] 3 W.L.R. 431; *R. v Gilmartin (Anthony)* [1983] Q.B. 953; [1983] 2 W.L.R. 547 CA and *DPP v Ray* [1974] A.C. 370 at [20] and [54]; [1973] 3 W.L.R. 359 HL.
279 See further, Smith, *Property Offences* (London: Sweet & Maxwell, 1994), pp.472–480.
280 *R. v Harris* (1975) 62 Cr. App. R. 28.
281 *Ray* [1974] A.C. 370.

the same position as anyone else who is asked to quote for work to be done. He has argued that it is a dangerous concept to introduce into the criminal law that an excessively high quotation amounts to a false representation under section 15(1) of the Theft Act 1968. In certain circumstances that submission may we think be well founded. But whether a quotation amounts to false representation must depend upon the circumstances.

It seems clear to us that the complainants, far from being worldly wise, were unquestionably gullible. Having left their former home, they relied implicitly upon the word of the appellant about their requirements in their maisonette. In such circumstances of mutual trust, one party depending upon the other for fair and reasonable conduct, the criminal law may apply if one party takes dishonest advantage of the other by representing as a fair charge that which he but not the other knows is dishonestly excessive . . .

There was material for a finding that there had been a false representation although it is true that the appellant had said nothing at the time he made his representations to encourage the sisters to accept the quotations. He applied no pressure upon them, and apart from mentioning the actual prices to be charged was silent as to other matters that may have arisen for question in their minds . . .

Here the situation has been built up over a long period of time. It was a situation of mutual trust and the appellant's silence on any matter other than the sums to be charged were, we think, as eloquent as if he had said: 'What is more, I can say to you that we are going to get no more than a modest profit out of this.'

There is, we think, no foundation for the criticism of the judge in the first ground of appeal nor any substance in this ground in law . . . ' [However, it was decided that the judge should have included D's defence 'worthless though it might have been in the minds of the jury' in the summing up]."

Appeal allowed

More recently, in *Greig*,[282] D did £300 worth of gardening work for a 77-year-old man with mental health problems. Two cheques for a total of £5,000 signed by the man were paid into the D's bank account. A further cheque for £1,850 made payable to a co-D was returned unpaid by the bank. The Court of Appeal upheld the D's conviction for an offence of fraud by false representation under s.2. The amounts charged by Greig were so far removed from a reasonable charge that the jury were entitled to infer that a dishonest false representation had been made. **8–124**

In a free-market economy it is usually regarded as acceptable to maximise one's profits—in short, to make as big a profit as possible. Prior to *Silverman*, those making grossly inflated quotations only to contend with the risk of their quotation being rejected, but following that case, the risk of criminal

282 *R. v Greig (Thomas Andrew)* [2010] EWCA Crim 1183.

prosecution is a possibility. Again, we are dealing with dubious business practice being criminalised. Rather than continually extending the reaches of the criminal law, it would surely be better here for the V to resort to civil remedies. Of course, "there may be different prices for the same type of work", and the Fraud Act does not criminalise all bad bargains.[283] It is important to stress that it is necessary to prove dishonesty before an inflated quotation could give rise to liability. It is highly unlikely that any jury would convict in cases of excessive quotations unless there were special circumstances as in *Silverman* (the taking advantage of a relationship of mutual trust) or *Greig* (the taking advantage of a vulnerable client).

(c) Credit and debit cards

8–125 Acceptance of a credit card gives rise to a contract between the acceptor and the card-issuing company under which the latter must honour the relevant voucher on presentation. Use of a credit card is thus an implied representation that one has actual authority from the card-issuing company:

(1) to use the card to make contracts on behalf of that company; and
(2) to bind the card-issuing company to honour the relevant voucher on presentation.

So, if D uses a credit or debit card to purchase goods knowing that they lack the authority to do so—because, for example, they have exceeded her credit limit or because the card is not theirs—there is a false representation. It is irrelevant that the trader will in fact be paid.[284]

(d) Insurance

8–126 "It is elementary law that a person applying for insurance is obliged to disclose all facts material to be known by the insurer."[285] An omission to disclose material facts on an application for insurance cover may amount to a false representation. For example, in *Martin*,[286] it was held that D's failure to inform motor insurers that he was a disqualified driver, when he was applying for car insurance, amounted to a false representation.

(e) Change of circumstances

8–127 If a representation, which was true when made, becomes untrue, the failure to reveal the change of circumstances may amount to a false representation. In *Rai*,[287] D applied for a council grant for a bathroom for his elderly mother. Before the work was done, his mother died. It was held that his failure to inform the council of the change of circumstances amounted to a deception and would now be a false representation. In these cases, involving a change of circumstances, it could well be that there is a legal duty to disclose the change of circumstances. The D in *Rai* would have been under such a duty.

---

283 This was recognised by the trial judge in *Greig* [2010] EWCA Crim 1183 at [14].

284 In *R. v Awosika (Oluwabunmi)* [2009] EWCA Crim 625, D was convicted of fraud when she tried to purchase a Rolex watch with an unauthorised Amex card. cf. *R. v Augunas (Darius)* [2013] EWCA Crim 2046; [2014] 1 Cr. App. R. 17, considered in para.8–134.

285 *R. v Martin (Derek Paul)* [2013] EWCA Crim 1986 at [8].

286 *Martin* [2013] EWCA Crim 1986 at [8].

287 *R. v Rai (Thomas)* [2000] 1 Cr. App. R. 242; (2000) 164 J.P. 121.

In such cases, the prosecution has a choice whether to charge fraud by false representation or fraud by failing to disclose information (s.3).[288]

It is interesting to compare the behaviour in all these cases with that required for theft. We saw earlier that the paradigmatic case of theft involves actions which are objectively inconsistent with the rights of the owner and thus accords with Fletcher's theory of manifest criminality.[289] Fraud by false representation, on the other hand, is more indicative of a theory of subjective liability: the actions of D will tend to look innocent, but their state of mind renders them criminal.[290] However, as a result of the case of *Gomez*, this distinction is all but lost in cases where the false representation leads to the obtaining of property. Such cases, that have all the hallmarks of fraud, may be charged as theft under s.1.[291]

The decision in *Rai* may be contrasted with the decision in *Allen*.[292] Here the Administrative Court rejected an argument that, after a mortgage advance had been made to D, she was under a continuing obligation to provide information about any later change in her financial circumstances, or that, by remaining silent about such a change, there was an implied continuing representation that she would be able to meet the mortgage repayments when they fell due.[293] It has been suggested that the outcome of this case might have been different if the loan had been payable by instalments and the D had, "like the defendant in *Rai*", allowed the bank "to confer a benefit on her after she knew that the situation had changed".[294]

Of course, the offence of fraud is much broader than the old offence of obtaining property by deception. There will be instances where nothing is obtained—and nothing appropriated—but the fraud offence is committed by an *intention* to make a gain or cause a loss.[295]

(1) Fact or law including state of mind

Section 2(3) provides that a representation means: **8–128**

> ". . . any representation as to fact or law, including a representation as to the state of mind of—(a) the person making the representation, or (b) any other person."

The inclusion of a representation as to a state of mind is appropriate: the implied representation of the restaurant customer that they intend to pay is just as much a representation as the fact that they have sufficient money to pay. Under the old law, a deception was defined to include "the present intentions"

---

288 cf. *R. v Waas (Jay)* [2015] EWCA Crim 1259 (failure to disclose work pension when claiming pension credit and housing and council tax benefits); *R. v Foxley (Caroline Ann)* [2016] EWCA Crim 798 (failing to disclose change of circumstances when claiming benefits).

289 See para.8–014.

290 Fletcher, *Rethinking Criminal Law* (1978), p.118.

291 This is recognised by the CPS in their guidance, *The Fraud Act 2006: Legal Guidance Fraud and economic crime* (2024).

292 *Allen* [2012] EWHC 1712 (Admin); [2012] 1 W.L.R. 3419. cf. *R. v Forrest (Nathan)* [2014] EWCA Crim 308.

293 *Allen* [2012] EWHC 1712 (Admin) at [56].

294 Child, Simester, Spencer, Stark and Virgo, *Simester and Sullivan's Criminal Law: Theory and Doctrine*, 7th edn (2022), p.716.

295 e.g. in *Idrees v DPP* [2011] EWHC 624 (Admin), D, who had failed his driving theory test 15 times, procured another person to impersonate him to take the test. That person presented himself at the driving test centre on the relevant day, but was not allowed to take the test because he was identified as an imposter. Mr Idrees was convicted of fraud by false representation and his conviction was upheld by the Administrative Court.

of the person making the representation. This gave rise to some controversy as to whether this included statements of opinion. This problem is solved by the broader formulation in s.2(3) that what is required is a representation as to "the state of mind" of the representor or another person. Whether an opinion is held is a "state of mind". As a matter of logic:

> ". . . any representation by a person about their state of mind can only be about their present (or past) state of mind. Their state of mind as to the future can only be a current perception."[296]

What is the position with advertising "puffs"? Some of these will be representations as to fact, for example, "our make-up will last longer than any others". Others will be representations as to opinion, for example "as good as a Rolex". Under the old law of deception, it was widely accepted that advertising "puffs" would not count as deceptions because potential victims would not be fooled by them. However, under the present law, such exaggerated advertising amounts to a representation either as to fact or as to the state of mind of the advertiser. It must be doubted whether such an expansion of the law is warranted. The CPS has stated:

> "Prosecutors should bear in mind that the principle of *caveat emptor* applies and should consider whether civil proceedings or the regulatory regime that applies to advertising and other commercial activities might be more appropriate. Not every advertising puff should lead to criminal conviction but it is also the case that fraudsters prey on the vulnerable."[297]

(2) Representations to machines

8–129 A major problem with the old law was that because a machine has no mind, it cannot be deceived.[298] Section 2(5) makes it clear that a representation is made if it is "submitted in any form to any system or device designed to receive, convey or respond to communications (with or without human intervention)". Thus representations can be made to cash machines, internet service providers, automated call centres and so on.[299] For example, in *United States v Sarao*,[300] D had used modified computer software to manipulate the price for "E-minis" (futures contracts) on the Chicago Mercantile Exchange, by placing multiple, large-volume sale orders (to drive the price down) and then modifying and cancelling these orders before they were executed. It was held that a representation was made by making these online orders.

This provision is not unproblematic. It is not entirely clear when a representation is "submitted". Ormerod and Laird suggest that a document could be regarded as submitted when the D saves typing

---

296 *Allen* [2012] EWHC 1712 (Admin); [2012] 1 W.L.R. 3419 at [49]. cf. *Voros v Hungary* [2012] EWHC 518 (Admin): in concluding a hire-purchase agreement in respect of a car, D was making a false (and dishonest) representation about his current intentions when he stated that he would pay the instalments as they fell due, when he knew that the car was shortly to be seized to satisfy a debt owed to a third party.

297 CPS, *The Fraud Act 2006: Legal Guidance, Fraud and economic crime* (2024).

298 cf. para.9–133; *Holmes* [2004] EWHC 2020 (Admin).

299 e.g. *R. v Saunders (Gabrielle Yinka)* [2012] EWCA Crim 1380; [2012] 2 Cr. App. R. 26: use of a laptop to make fraudulent online applications for credit card accounts.

300 *United States v Sarao* [2016] Lloyd's Rep. FC 339 Magistrates' Court. This case was an extradition case: Under the Extradition Act 2003 D could only be extradited if the conduct amounted to an offence under UK law punishable by 12 months or more detention of imprisonment.

on to the hard drive of a computer, or it might be regarded as being submitted when it is sent (for example, via email).[301] The alternative view, however (as they concede),[302] is that, drawing an analogy with business contracts in e-commerce where the communications only have operative effect when received, "the time of acceptance is when the electronic message was received by the ISP's network". However, as only "submission" (and not receipt) is required, it would most likely be regarded as submitted as soon as it is sent.[303]

In many of these cases, the false representation made to a machine will result in the provision of a service and the Law Commission envisaged that such cases would usually be prosecuted as obtaining services dishonestly.[304] This offence is discussed below.

(3) False

Section 2(2) provides that a representation is false if it is untrue or misleading. **8–130**

Whether a representation is true or not is a matter of fact. In many situations, however, a person may make a representation that is largely, but not wholly, true. If I say that my car, which I have driven for five years, has "never given me any trouble" when, in fact, I once had to replace a rear brake light, my representation is literally untrue. There is no requirement that the untrue representation be material or significant. However, in some cases, a court may need to consider complex issues of civil law in order to determine whether a representation is true or false. In *Cornelius*,[305] a solicitor had acted in eight property sale transactions and had provided bridging loans to the purchasers, which had been repaid out of the mortgage advances. As security for the bridging loans, D required each purchaser to execute a declaration of trust in his favour. The issue was whether D had made a false representation when he had provided a Certificate of Title stating that the property was free from "onerous encumbrances" and that he had no interest in the property as mortgagor. The Court of Appeal held that both of these representations were true. First, the trust deeds executed by the purchasers were not expressed to be by way of security or registered with HM Land Registry, and D was not in actual possession of the property. In these circumstances, the mortgages took priority over the interests created by the trust deeds[306] and the mortgagee therefore:

> ". . . acquired a good and marketable title free from the interest created by the trust. Even if it could be described as an encumbrance (which is itself doubtful) it could not be described as an 'onerous' encumbrance."[307]

---

301 Ormerod and Laird, *Smith, Hogan and Ormerod's Criminal Law*, 16th edn (2021), p.978.

302 Ormerod and Laird, *Smith, Hogan and Ormerod's Criminal Law*, 16th edn (2021), p.978.

303 cf. CPS, *The Fraud Act 2006: Legal Guidance, Fraud and economic crime: Legal Guidance* (2024).

304 Law Commission Paper No.276, *Fraud* (2002), para.8.2 fn.5.

305 *Cornelius* [2012] EWCA Crim 500. cf. *R. v Whattcott (Christopher)* [2019] EWCA Crim 1889; [2020] Lloyd's Rep. F.C. 65: Defendant's representations that late fees were due were false because the feeds were an unlawful penalty and unenforceable (see K. Laird [2020] Crim. L.R. 618).

306 *Cornelius* [2012] EWCA Crim 500 at [28]–[29]. This is by virtue of the Land Registration Act 2002 s.29 and Sch.3: *Halifax Plc v Curry Popeck (A Firm)* [2008] EWHC 1692 (Ch); (2008) 152(37) S.J.L.B. 31.

307 *Cornelius* [2012] EWCA Crim 500 at [30].

Second, the statement that D had no interest in the property as mortgagor was also true. The word mortgagor was a technical legal term, meaning "the person who grants the mortgage".[308] In this case, the mortgage had been granted not by D, but by the registered proprietor. The Court of Appeal took the view that it would be wrong to interpret this technical term more widely, given that it was included in a standard form of certificate.[309] As there was no false representation, D could not be convicted of the s.2 offences.

It is important to stress that there must be a causative link between the false representation and D's intention: D must intend "by making the representation" to make a gain or cause loss.[310] So, if the untrue part of the representation relates to a peripheral matter which D thinks will be of no importance to the other, they will not be liable. Also, of course, in cases where the untruth is trivial, dishonesty is unlikely to be established.

8–131 Whether a misrepresentation is "misleading" is more difficult. The Government, in enacting this legislation, stated that "misleading" meant "less than wholly true and capable of an interpretation to the detriment of the victim".[311] If I have just had my unreliable car serviced so that, for the moment, it is performing well and, on trying to sell it, I say: "This car is a really good runner", this is not an untrue statement: at the moment, the car is running well. Whether, however, this statement represents that it has always (or usually) performed well or whether my statement is misleading is more difficult. It is unclear whether the representation must be misleading to the person to whom it is made or misleading to reasonable people. With the emphasis in fraud having shifted away from deception and the effect of the representation on the mind of the victim, it seems that what is required is that the representation be objectively misleading.

The fact that misrepresentations need only be misleading, coupled with the fact that the intention need only be to make a gain for another, can potentially lead to extraordinary results. If I write a reference for a student to obtain a job (a gain for them) and I gloss over their weaknesses and exaggerate their strengths thus creating a misleading picture as to their overall abilities, this is (subject to dishonesty) fraud. It is questionable whether it is appropriate that misleading statements should suffice to make a representation false. Arguably there is a moral distinction between the actions of a person who tells a clear lie and one who is "merely economical with the truth, allowing the hearer to infer facts for which he must take some responsibility".[312]

---

308 *Cornelius* [2012] EWCA Crim 500 at [33].

309 *Cornelius* [2012] EWCA Crim 500 at [25], relying on *Barclays Bank Plc v Weeks Legg and Dean* [1999] Q.B. 309; [1998] 3 W.L.R. 656 CA and *Midland Bank v Cox McQueen (A Firm)* [1999] Lloyd's Rep. Bank. 78; [1999] P.N.L.R. 593 CA. The court refused to substitute a conviction for attempted fraud on the basis that he had dishonestly made a representation which, contrary to his belief, was in fact true.

310 *R. v Gilbert (Stephanie Rae)* [2012] EWCA Crim 2392 at [29]; [2013] Lloyd's Rep. F.C. 109.

311 Home Office, *Fraud Law Reform: Government Response to Consultations* (2004), para.19.

312 Ormerod and Laird, *Smith, Hogan and Ormerod's Criminal Law*, 16th edn (2021), p.990. cf. Green, *Lying, Cheating and Stealing: A Moral Theory of White-Collar Crime* (2006) pp.78–80.

(ii) Mens rea

The mens rea required for this form of the offence is threefold. 8–132

(a) Knowledge that the representation is, or might be, untrue or misleading

The offence is committed not only where D knows that they are making a representation that is untrue but also where they know it might be untrue or misleading. Knowledge includes "wilful blindness".[313] The case of *Augunas*[314] makes it clear that it is not sufficient for the prosecution to prove that D ought to have appreciated that his representation was, or may have been, untrue or misleading. 8–133

R. v Augunas [2013] EWCA Crim 2046 at [9]:

McCOMBE LJ: 8–134

"What is required is that the accused person knows that the representation is, or might be, misleading. It is not enough that a reasonable person might have known this; what matters is the accused person's actual knowledge. In our judgment, it is not good enough for the prosecutor to satisfy the jury that the accused ought to have appreciated that the representation made by him was or might be untrue or misleading, nor is it enough that the circumstances must have given rise to a reasonable suspicion that the representation was, or might be, untrue or misleading. Of course, if an accused person wilfully shuts his eyes to the obvious doubts as to the genuineness of the misrepresentation that he is making, then he knows that it might be untrue or misleading and he would be guilty of the offence."

Given that "misleading" is a vague and imprecise term, the potential net of criminal liability is being cast wide by requiring only that a defendant know that a representation might be misleading.

(b) Dishonesty

As with theft, where the concept of appropriation is broad and colourless, the requirement of dishonesty plays a crucial role in this offence. The slightest lie for economic purposes satisfies the actus reus of the offence. It is left to the concept of dishonesty to determine which lies are criminal. The test for dishonesty in relation to fraud is now the *Ivey/Barton*[315] test. However, it is suggested that, in relation to the offence of fraud, this is problematic for a number of reasons. 8–135

First, one of the reasons given by the Supreme Court for overruling *Ghosh*, was that it was contrary to the intention of Parliament, who had intended that the previous objective test would continue.[316] However,

---

313 cf. *Taylor's Central Garages (Exeter) v Roper* [1951] 2 T.L.R. 284; (1951) 115 J.P. 445.

314 *Augunas* [2013] EWCA Crim 2046.

315 *Ivey* [2017] UKSC 67; [2018] A.C. 391 and *Barton* [2020] EWCA Crim 575, discussed above: paras 8–079–8–094.

316 *Ivey* [2017] UKSC 67; [2018] A.C. 391 at [64].

this was not the case in relation to the Fraud Act 2006. Both the Law Commission and the Government[317] clearly intended that the two-stage *Ghosh* test would apply to the offence of fraud.[318] In relation to fraud, the rejection of the *Ghosh* test may be seen as being contrary to the intention of Parliament.

Second, the partial definition of dishonesty contained in the Theft Act 1968 s.2 does not apply to the offence of fraud. The Law Commission in its Consultation Paper[319] suggested that there should be a defence along the lines of the Theft Act 1968 s.2(1)(a) where D has, or believes that they have, a legal right to do what they do. But in its final Report this recommendation was abandoned.[320] Following *Ivey*, the absence of a s.2-type defence in the Fraud Act has become even more significant. Unfortunately, the possible ramifications of this were not considered by the Supreme Court.

M. Dyson and P. Jarvis, "Poison Ivey or herbal tea leaf?" (2018) 134 L.Q.R. 198, 201:

8–136 "... whereas the Theft Act 1968 s.2 declares when an appropriation will not be dishonest (such as where a defendant believes that he has a claim of right over the property in question) the Fraud Act 2006 does not; that may be because Parliament did not feel the need to enact them in the new legislation because it intended the subjective limb of the Ghosh test to do the same work. Now that the subjective limb is gone, an unfortunate chasm opens up between theft on the one hand and fraud on the other. It would not be theft for person A to take person B's coat if person A believed they had a claim of right over it, but it could be fraud if person A misled person C into fetching the coat with that same state of mind. One response to this would be that it is better to have clear statutory definitions of honest or dishonest conduct for at least some situations: for theft that means letting s.2 do the work that the second Ghosh limb was probably doing, but that does not solve the problem for fraud and any offences without s.2 analogues."

8–137 Suppose that D honestly believes that he has a claim of right to property and deliberately tells a lie in order to get (what he believes is) his property back. The fact that a false representation has been made might lead a jury to conclude that D is dishonest according to the (objective) standards of ordinary decent people. As Ormerod and Laird have observed:

"The fact that D can now be guilty even though he is genuinely unaware that his conduct would be considered dishonest by the standards of ordinary decent people makes the absence of an equivalent to s.2 of the Theft Act 1968 more keenly felt . . . In cases where D genuinely believes he

---

317 Law Commission Report No.276, *Fraud* (2002) para.7.11; Hansard, Fraud Bill, Standing Committee B, 20 June 2006, col.8 (Mike O'Brien, S-G); HL committee debates, 19 July 2006, col.1424 (Lord Goldsmith, A-G).

318 Dyson and Jarvis, "Poison Ivey or herbal tea leaf?" (2018) 134 L.Q.R. 198, 201; Laird, "Dishonesty: *Ivey v Genting Casinos UK Ltd (t/a Crockfords Club)*" [2018] Crim. L.R. 395, 399; Ormerod and Laird, "*Ivey v Genting Casinos*—Much Ado About Nothing?" [2017–2018] 9 *The UK Supreme Court Yearbook* 380, 398–399; M. Thomas and S. Pegg, "Clarifying the applicable test for dishonesty and modifying stare decisis, but otherwise a missed opportunity" (2020) 84 J. Crim L. 385, 388-389.

319 Law Commission Consultation Paper No.155, *Fraud and Deception* (1999).

320 Law Commission Report No.276, *Fraud* (2002) paras 7.66–7.67, 7.69.

> has a claim of right, it will be crucial for the trial judge to direct the jury to consider the facts and circumstances as D believe them to be, before directing the jury to consider whether D's conduct was objectively dishonest."[321]

Third, the concept of dishonesty plays a particularly important role in relation to the offence of fraud, because of the extremely wide nature of the offence. Nothing need be obtained for the offence of fraud by false representation to be committed. All that is required is an intention to make a gain (or cause a loss) and, as we shall see, "gain" includes "keeping what one has". So, for example, if one tells a charity collector with a tin on the street, "Sorry, but I have no loose change" (when one does have loose change), this satisfies all the other elements of the offence. It is a false representation made with a view to gain. In such cases, all the real work will be left to the concept of dishonesty to distinguish between harmless lies and the serious offence of fraud. The removal of the subjective element of the *Ghosh* test from the test for dishonesty may be seen as broadening what is already an arguably over-broad offence of fraud.[322]

(c) Intention to make gain or cause loss

For the repealed deception offences, causation had to be established. The deception had to cause the other to part with property etc. One of the reasons for the enactment of the new offence of fraud was to dispense with this requirement and all its associated problems. Accordingly, it is not necessary that the victim believe the false representation. However, s.2(1)(b) requires that D "intends, *by making the representation*" to make a gain for themselves or another, to cause a loss to another, or to expose another to a risk of loss.[323] So, if a street trader advertises a T-shirt "As worn by Beyoncé" they would not expect anyone actually to believe such a claim which is probably being made simply to attract attention. They would not intend that *by making that representation* they would make a gain. This provision is the distinguishing feature of the offence of fraud and is what transforms a lie into a criminal offence. **8–138**

FRAUD ACT 2006 S.5:

"(1) The references to gain and loss in sections 2 to 4 are to be read in accordance with this section. **8–139**

(2) 'Gain' and 'loss'—

(a) extend only to gain or loss in money or other property;
(b) include any such gain or loss whether temporary or permanent;

and 'property' means any property whether real or personal (including things in action and other intangible property).

---

321 Ormerod and Laird, *Smith, Hogan and Ormerod's Criminal Law*, 16th edn (2021), p.969.

322 Laird, "Dishonesty: *Ivey v Genting Casinos UK Ltd (t/a Crockfords Club)*" [2018] Crim. L.R. 395, 399.

323 *Gilbert* [2012] EWCA Crim 2392. It is a matter for the jury to decide whether, on the facts of the case, this causative link between the intention and the making of the false representation is proved: Roderick Evans J at [29]. Following the case of *R. v Ames (David)* [2023] EWCA Crim 1463 at [53]; [2024] 1 W.L.R. 1860 it appears that s.2(1)(b) creates a single legal ingredient of the offence: see below para.8–156.

> (3) 'Gain' includes a gain by keeping what one has, as well as a gain by getting what one does not have.
>
> (4) 'Loss' includes a loss by not getting what one might get, as well as a loss by parting with what one has."

8–140 This is extremely broad.[324] If D makes a false representation so that a rich person will take them to an expensive restaurant, they intend to make a gain for themselves of the food. It is clear mislabelling to describe such conduct as fraud—and highly dubious whether such actions should be criminalised at all.

In 2009, a D was prosecuted for fraud when she used a false address to apply for a place for her son at a popular primary school. The prosecution was abandoned because she had not intended to make a gain or cause a loss in money or other property. A school place is not "money or other property".[325]

It is not necessary that D intend any gain for themselves. It is enough that they intend a gain for another, intend to cause a loss to another, or to expose another to a risk of loss. For example, if D spreads malicious rumours that their enemy's company is in dire straits hoping that the value of its shares will fall, they have acted with intent to cause loss—even though they have no intention to buy the shares at the reduced price.

Unlike theft, it is not necessary that D intends to make a permanent gain. So, if a student falsely tells me that a book is currently out of stock and not available in the library and asks to borrow the book from me for a few hours, the elements of the offence (subject to dishonesty) are made out. Again, it must be questioned whether such "white lies" deserve criminalisation.

Law Commission Report No.276, Fraud (2002), paras 7.54–7.55:

8–141

> "7.54 Arguably the full offence should not be committed unless the defendant has succeeded in *actually* causing a loss or making a gain: where the defendant has acted with *intent* to cause loss or make a gain, but that intent has been frustrated, a conviction of attempt would adequately reflect the criminality of the defendant's conduct. It may sometimes be debatable, however, whether a loss has actually been caused or a gain made, whilst it is clear beyond doubt that

---

324 See, e.g. *Martin* [2013] EWCA Crim 1986 (granting of contract of insurance a gain for the purposes of s.5 because it conferred valuable rights which were of monetary value).

325 *The Guardian*, 4 July 2009; C. Monaghan, "To Prosecute or Not to Prosecute? A Reconsideration of the Over-zealous Prosecution of Parents under the Fraud Act 2006" (2010) 74 J.C.L. 259–278. The forging of documents (e.g. tenancy agreements) to support school applications may amount to an offence under the Forgery and Counterfeiting Act 1981 s.4: C. Monaghan, "School application forms and the criminal law" [2015] Crim. L.R. 270. Similar difficulties arose in relation to the use of the Fraud Act 2006 s.2 to prosecute students who use contract cheating services: M.J. Draper, V. Ibezim and P.M. Newton, "Are essay mills committing fraud? An analysis of their behaviours vs. the Fraud Act 2006" [2017] 13 *International Journal for Educational Integrity*. Advertising or offering to provide such services is now criminalised by the Skills and Post-16 Education Act 2022 ss.26–28.

> the defendant *intended* to bring about one or both of these outcomes. We think it would be unfortunate if, in such a case, it had to be determined whether there had in fact been gain or loss within the meaning of the Act, when that question had little bearing on the gravity of the defendant's conduct or the appropriate sentence . . . [I]t should be sufficient if the defendant acts *with intent* to make a gain or to cause a loss.
>
> 7.55 In the light of this conclusion we have considered whether it should be possible to prosecute for an *attempt* to commit the new offence . . . Under our recommendations there would be no need to charge an attempt in these cases, because the defendant would be guilty of the full offence."

The approach shifts the focus away from the "victim" and effectively adopts an inchoate model of liability with the emphasis on the "anti-social" conduct of D. One way of rationalising this approach is that liability should not depend on whether the so-called victims suffer harm to their "net wealth" but on whether their autonomy to direct their assets, without being influenced by another's fraud, has been infringed.[326] The interest the law is seeking to protect is commercial freedom and D is seen as threatening this interest. **8–142**

(iii) Fraud by failing to disclose information

Fraud Act 2006 s.3:

> "A person is in breach of this section if he— **8–143**
>
> (a) dishonestly fails to disclose to another person information which he is under a legal duty to disclose, and
> (b) intends, by failing to disclose the information—
>
> (i) to make a gain for himself or another, or
> (ii) to cause loss to another or to expose another to a risk of loss."

There is a significant overlap between this method of committing fraud and that under s.2. In many cases where D breaches a legal duty to disclose information, they can be regarded as making a false implied representation. **8–144**

326 cf. Fletcher, *Rethinking Criminal Law* (1978), pp.51–57.

(a) Actus reus

8–145 D must fail to disclose to another person information which they are under a legal duty to disclose.

The legal duty may arise from statute,[327] from the express or implied terms of a contract,[328] from the custom of a particular trade or market,[329] or from the existence of a fiduciary relationship between the parties.[330]

In *Rasoq*,[331] a hospital doctor had been excluded and suspended from work pending disciplinary proceedings. He then signed up with a number of locum agencies to obtain work as a physician, but did not disclose his exclusion. The Court of Appeal held that the evidence was "overwhelming" that the defendant was legally bound to inform these agencies of his exclusion.[332] Section 3 could also have been charged in the case of *Twaite*,[333] where an RAF officer obtained service family accommodation by falsely stating on a form that he was married, and lived there for almost a year, in breach of service regulations and without saying anything to the RAF, before he finally did get married. Whether there is a legal duty to disclose is not always a clear-cut matter and it is likely that the criminal courts will have to grapple with intricate questions of civil law. For example, in *R v D*,[334] the Court of Appeal, held that the Local Government Finance Act 1992 and subordinate legislation made under the Act did not impose a legal duty on residents liable to pay council to notify the local authority of their continuing residence in the property.

As with theft, the relationship between the civil and criminal law can be problematic.

(b) Mens rea

8–146 D must act dishonestly and intend to make a gain for themselves or another, or to cause loss to another or to expose another to a risk of loss.[335] These requirements are discussed above.[336]

---

327 See, e.g. *R. v Blight (John Simon)* [2019] EWCA Crim 280: duty to disclose to the Receiver of Wreck the fact that possession has been taken of item of wreck from ships lost at sea imposed by Merchant Shipping Act 1995 s.236(1); *R. v Williams (Monica)* [2023] EWCA Crim 1236: failure to disclose that D was no longer resident at home that she was purchasing from council under "Right to Buy" legislation (Housing Act 1985).

328 e.g. contracts of insurance are contracts of "utmost good faith" and those taking out insurance must disclose material facts to the insurer (*Martin* [2013] EWCA Crim 1986); an employee may be contractually required to disclose criminal convictions, or to give an undertaking that they are not working elsewhere (*R. v Daley (Patricia Rose)* [2010] EWCA Crim 2193).

329 cf. *Forrest* [2014] EWCA Crim 308, where the CA rejected an assertion that it was the usage or custom of the mortgage lending market that applicants for mortgages make full disclosure of matters relevant to the bargain beyond the information sought in the mortgage application form itself. In *R. v White (Anthony Alan)* [2014] EWCA Crim 714 at [14]; [2014] 2 Cr. App. R. 14 CA, it was held that D was not under a duty, for the purposes of s.3, to inform his mortgage lender that he was unemployed when making a mortgage application.

330 Home Office, *Fraud Law Reform: Consultation on Proposals for Legislation* (2004), para.20. For examples of cases in which it was held that, on the facts, no legal duty to disclose information arose, see *Allen* [2012] EWHC 1712 (Admin); [2012] 1 W.L.R. 3419 at [58]; *Forrest* [2014] EWCA Crim 308; *R. v D* [2019] EWCA Crim 209; [2019] 2 Cr. App. R. 15.

331 *R. v Razoq (Adil)* [2012] EWCA Crim 674. cf. *R. v Quinn (Phillip)* [2015] EWCA Crim 428 (D failed to disclose to the Pensions Administrator that his mother had died, and continued to receive her widow's pension).

332 *Razoq* [2012] EWCA Crim 674 at [83]. D was also convicted of s.2 offences in respect of lies made on application forms.

333 *R. v Twaite (Timothy)* [2010] EWCA Crim 2973; [2011] 1 W.L.R. 1125. D's conviction for fraud by false representation was quashed because he had been convicted on the wrong basis.

334 *R. v D* [2019] EWCA Crim 209.

335 Following the case of *Ames* [2023] EWCA Crim 1463 at [53] it appears that s.3(b) creates a single legal ingredient of the offence: see below para.8–156.

336 See paras 8–079–8–094, 8–135–8–137.

The section is silent as to whether D must know (or believe or suspect) that they are under a legal duty to disclose. Presumably, if D has no idea that they are under a legal duty to disclose, dishonesty would be unlikely to be established.

(iv) Fraud by abuse of position

FRAUD ACT 2006 S.4:

"(1) A person is in breach of this section if he— **8–147**

(a) occupies a position in which he is expected to safeguard, or not to act against, the financial interests of another person,
(b) dishonestly abuses that position, and
(c) intends, by means of the abuse of that position—

(i) to make a gain for himself or another, or
(ii) to cause loss to another or to expose another to a risk of loss.

(2) A person may be regarded as having abused his position even though his conduct consisted of an omission rather than an act."

(a) Actus reus

There must be an abuse of a position of trust. **8–148**

(1) Abuse

No definition of "abuse" is provided other than that the conduct may consist of an omission rather than an act. In *Pennock and Pennock,* the Court of Appeal stated that: **8–149**

"A good working meaning might be: 'uses incorrectly' or 'puts to improper use' the position held in a manner that is contrary to the expectation that arises because of that position."[337]

In that case, the Ds had removed £100,000 from a joint bank account in the names of Mr Pennock and the complainant, without the permission of the complainant. On appeal, the convictions were quashed because Mr Pennock, as one of the joint account holders, had authority to withdraw money from the account. No further permission was required from the other account holder. There had therefore been no abuse of position. There could be an abuse where, for example, an employee passes confidential information about the business of their employer to a commercial rival,[338] or omits to take up a chance

337 *R. v Pennock (Angela)* [2014] EWCA Crim 598; [2014] 2 Cr. App. R. 10.
338 *Theedom v Nourish Trading Ltd (t/a CSP Recruitment)* [2016] EWHC 1364 (QB); [2016] I.R.L.R. 866.

of a crucial contract, intending to enable an associate to pick up the contract instead.[339] This section has been used to prosecute employees who steal from their employers by writing out company cheques in their own favour,[340] or divert money held in client accounts,[341] or which is due to their employer[342] into their own bank accounts. It may also be used to prosecute company directors or employees who take secret profits at the expense of a company or employer.[343] Obviously, the mens rea requirement that the abuse be dishonest and with the intention of making a gain or causing a loss will limit what can count as an abuse. So, the lazy or incompetent employee who abuses their position (in ordinary language terms) by not bothering to make required phone calls to secure customers will not fall within this provision unless the failure to make the calls is considered dishonest and there was the requisite intent to make a gain or cause a loss. It is likely that all the real work here will be done by the mens rea requirement and so, like appropriation, "abuse" will become a neutral or colourless concept always satisfied if the requisite mens rea is present.

(2) Position

8–150 The statute does not use the phrase "position of trust". Instead, the requisite position is defined as existing when a person "occupies a position in which he is expected to safeguard, or not to act against, the financial interests of another person".

Law Commission Report No.276, Fraud (2002), paras 7.37, 7.38:

8–151 "7.37 The essence of the kind of relationship which in our view should be a prerequisite of this form of the offence is that the victim has voluntarily put the defendant in a privileged position, by virtue of which the defendant is expected to safeguard the victim's financial interests or given power to damage those interests. Such an expectation to safeguard or power to damage may arise, for example, because the defendant is given authority to exercise a discretion on the victim's behalf, or is given access to the victim's assets, premises, equipment or customers. In these cases the defendant does not need to enlist the victim's *further* co-operation in order to secure the desired result, because the necessary co-operation has been given in advance.

7.38 The necessary relationship will be present between trustee and beneficiary, director and company, professional person and client, agent and principal, employee and employer, or between partners. It may arise otherwise, for example within a family, or in the context of voluntary work, or in any context where the parties are not at arm's length. In nearly all cases where it arises, it will be recognised by the civil law as importing fiduciary duties, and any relationship that is so recognised will suffice. We see no reason, however, why the existence of such duties should be essential. This does not of course mean that it would be entirely a matter

---

339 Law Commission Paper No.276, *Fraud* (2002), para.7.39.

340 *R. v Moss (Pamela Jane)* [2013] EWCA Crim 1554.

341 *R. v Turner (Ruth Louise)* [2013] EWCA Crim 1206. cf. *R. v Woods (Natalie Frances)* [2011] EWCA Crim 1305.

342 cf. *Knowles* [2013] EWCA Crim 646.

343 *Evans v Serious Fraud Office* [2015] EWHC 263 (QB); [2015] 1 W.L.R. 3595. cf. *Att-Gen's Reference (No.1 of 1985)* [1986] Q.B. 491. Or who act against the interests of investors: *Ames* [2023] EWCA Crim 1463.

> for the fact-finders whether the necessary relationship exists. The question whether the particular facts alleged can properly be described as giving rise to that relationship will be an issue capable of being ruled upon by the judge and, if the case goes to the jury, of being the subject of directions."

Section 4 extends beyond fiduciary duties[344] and, as stated in the above extract, may potentially be used in relation to relationships which arise in family and other voluntary arrangements. To expand the ambit of fraud into such matters, extending beyond the ambit of the civil law, has the potential to create immense difficulties for judges and juries and to "elevate all sorts of trivial contractual and familial disputes into criminal matters".[345] Much therefore depends on the sensible exercise of prosecutorial discretion in relation to the decision to prosecute under this section, and the CPS has Issued guidance as to how this discretion is to be exercised. **8–152**

THE CROWN PROSECUTION SERVICE, THE FRAUD ACT 2006: LEGAL GUIDANCE, FRAUD AND ECONOMIC CRIME (2024):

> "Examples of the type of conduct that would give rise to a charge under Section 4 are: **8–153**
>
> - an employee of a software company who uses his position to clone software products with the intention of selling the products on his own behalf;
> - where a person is employed to care for an elderly or disabled person and has access to that person's bank account but abuses that position by removing funds for his own personal use.[346] (This may also be theft . . .)
> - an attorney who removes money from the grantor's accounts for his own use. The Power of Attorney allows him to do so but when excessive this will be capable of being an offence under Section 4;
> - an employee who fails to take up the chance of a crucial contract in order that an associate or rival company can take it up instead;
> - a trustee who dishonestly acts outside the terms of a trust deed in order to produce a gain or loss for himself or others;
> - a director of a company who dishonestly makes use of knowledge gained as a director to make a personal gain;
> - an employee who abuses his position in order to grant contracts or discounts to friends, relatives and associates;
> - a waiter who sells his own bottles of wine passing them off as belonging to the restaurant *R. v Doukas* [1978] 1 All E.R. 1071;

---

344 For further discussion of the circumstances in which a fiduciary relationship arises, see J. Fisher, A. Milne, J. Bewsey and A. Herd, *Arlidge and Parry on Fraud*, 6th edn (London: Sweet & Maxwell, 2020), paras 6–009–6–043.

345 Ormerod and Laird, *Smith, Hogan and Ormerod's Criminal Law*, 16th edn (2021), p.1001. For discussion re the rationale of the s.4 offence, see J. Collins, "Fraud by Abuse of Position: Theorising Section 4 of the Fraud Act 2006" [2011] Crim. L.R. 513–523.

346 *Marshall* [2009] EWCA Crim 2076; *R. v Dhupar (Amy)* [2015] EWCA Crim 2519; *R. v Douglas (Carly)* [2019] EWCA Crim 835.

> - a tradesman who helps an elderly person with odd jobs, gains influence over that person and removes money from their account. (This may also be theft . . .)[347]
> - the person entrusted to purchase lottery tickets on behalf of others . . . this will probably be theft as well.
>
> . . . prosecutors must be particularly mindful that the criminal law is not invoked by complainants for purely commercial purposes."

8–154 The position must be one in which D is *expected* to safeguard, etc the financial interests of another person. Expected by whom? The particular victim? The D? The reasonable person? In *Valujevs,*[348] it was alleged that the Ds had abused their position as unlicensed gang-masters by making unwarranted fines and deductions from workers' legitimate earnings, and by charging grossly excessive rental payments. On appeal, the issue was whether the Ds had a position of trust sufficient to bring their relationship with their workers within s.4. The Court of Appeal took the view that s.4 was not restricted to cases in which a fiduciary duty was owed to the victim:

> "It is clear from the wording that Parliament did not intend to restrict the operation of the section to those situations in which the defendant owes a fiduciary duty to the alleged victim, not least because this result could readily have been secured by appropriate drafting."[349]

The Court of Appeal ruled that the "expectation" in s.4 of the 2006 Act is an objective one, based on the position of a reasonable person:

> "It is for the judge to assess whether the position held by the individual is capable of being one 'in which he is expected to safeguard, or not to act against, the financial interests of another person'. If it is so capable, it will be for the jury thereafter to determine whether or not they are sure that was the case. It would be untenable to suggest that the expectation should be that of either the potential victim (the test would, in all likelihood, be too low) or the defendant (the test is likely to be set too high). Therefore, this is an objective test based on the position of the reasonable person."[350]

8–155 In relation to the type of duty that has to be shown by the prosecution, the Court of Appeal stated that they had to:

---

347 cf. *R. v Silverman (Michael John)* (1988) 86 Cr. App. R. 213; (1987) 151 J.P. 657.

348 *R. v Valujevs (Juris)* [2014] EWCA Crim 2888; [2015] Q.B. 745. See also *R. v Pennock (Angela)* [2014] EWCA Crim 598; [2014] 2 Cr. App. R. 10 at [6] and *R. (on the application of Col) v DPP* [2022] EWHC 601 (Admin); [2022] 2 Cr. App. R. 14.

349 *Valujevs* [2014] EWCA Crim 2888; [2015] Q.B. 745 at [34]. See Collins, "Fraud by abuse of position and unlicensed gangmasters" [2016] 79 M.L.R. 354.

350 *Valujevs* [2014] EWCA Crim 2888; [2015] Q.B. 745 at [41].

> "... demonstrate a breach of a fiduciary duty, or a breach of an obligation that is akin to a fiduciary duty. This can conveniently be described, for instance, as a breach of trust or a breach of a privileged position in relation to the financial interests of another person."[351]

However, they made it clear that s.4 should not apply in:

> "... the general commercial area where individuals and businesses compete in markets of one kind or another, including labour markets, and are entitled to and expected to look after their own interests ..."[352]

expressing the view that the section does not apply "to those who simply supply accommodation, goods, services or labour, whether on favourable or unfavourable terms and whether or not they have a stronger bargaining position".[353]

(b) Mens rea

D must dishonestly abuse the position and must intend, through that abuse, to make a gain for herself or another or to cause a loss to another, or to expose another to a risk of loss. These matters were discussed earlier.[354] In *Ames*, the Court of Appeal held that s.4(1)(c) creates a single ingredient of intention for the purpose of the s.4 offence: **8–156**

> "The ingredient is intention by means of the abuse of position to make a gain (for himself or another) or to cause loss to another (or to expose another to a risk of loss)—in other words, to have a financial impact, whether by way of gain or loss (actual or potential)."[355]

There is no express requirement that D must know that they occupy a position of trust whereby they are expected to safeguard, etc the financial interests of another person. Liability on this issue would appear to be strict. However, it will be very difficult to establish dishonesty without such knowledge.

2. Offences ancillary to fraud

The Fraud Act 2006 creates two ancillary offences to fraud. First, there is the offence of possession of articles for use in frauds[356] (punishable with a maximum of five years' imprisonment). Secondly, there **8–157**

---

351 *Valujevs* [2014] EWCA Crim 2888; [2015] Q.B. 745 at [43].

352 *Valujevs* [2014] EWCA Crim 2888; [2015] Q.B. 745 at [44].

353 *Valujevs* [2014] EWCA Crim 2888; [2015] Q.B. 745 at [43].

354 See paras 9–152–9–163.

355 *Ames* [2023] EWCA Crim 1463 at [53]. There is therefore no need to direct the jury that they must be satisfied that there is either intention under s.4(1)(c)(i) or under s.4(1)(c)(ii) before they can convict of the s.4 offence, [57]. See P. Hungerford-Welch, "Case Comment: Fraud: *Serious Fraud Office v Ames*" [2024] Crim. L.R. 254.

356 Fraud Act 2006 s.6. See, e.g. *R. v Sakalauskas (Gytis)* [2013] EWCA Crim 2278; [2014] 1 W.L.R. 1204; *R. v Smith (Andrew)* [2020] EWCA Crim 38; [2020] 1 W.L.R. 4921.

is the offence of making or supplying articles for use in frauds[357] (punishable with a maximum of 10 years' imprisonment).

3. Obtaining services dishonestly

8–158 Under the Theft Act 1978 s.1 it was an offence to obtain services by deception. This covered situations where someone was deceived into providing a service rather than parting with property. For example, someone could be induced to mow a lawn or provide a ride in a taxi by being falsely told they would be paid. Owing to the problems involved with the concept of "deception", particularly in relation to machines, this offence is now replaced by a new offence of obtaining services dishonestly.

FRAUD ACT 2006 S.11:

8–159 "(1) A person is guilty of an offence under this section if he obtains services for himself or another—

(a) by a dishonest act, and
(b) in breach of subsection (2).

(2) A person obtains services in breach of this subsection if—

(a) they are made available on the basis that payment has been, is being or will be made for or in respect of them,
(b) he obtains them without any payment having been made for or in respect of them or without payment having been made in full, and
(c) when he obtains them, he knows—

(i) that they are being made available on the basis described in paragraph (a), or
(ii) that they might be,

but intends that payment will not be made, or will not be made in full."

8–160 The offence is punishable by a maximum of 10 years' imprisonment.[358]

(i) Actus reus

(a) Act

8–161 The requirement that there be an "act" is designed to ensure that the offence cannot be committed by omission alone. So, if services were not requested there is no offence to refuse payment.[359]

357 Fraud Act 2006 s.7. See, e.g. *R. v Akpon (Azu)* [2013] EWCA Crim 2662.
358 Fraud Act 2006 s.11(3).
359 CPS, *The Fraud Act 2006: Legal Guidance, Fraud and economic crime* (2024).

The Law Commission give the example of a person who innocently happened to be on a boat and, despite hearing an announcement that anyone who had not paid for the next trip should disembark, remained on the boat and received a free ride. Such a person would not come within the ambit of the offence.[360]

(b) Obtains

Unlike the general offence of fraud, this offence is a result crime and is not inchoate in character. An actual obtaining of the service is required. Causation must be established. **8–162**

(c) Services

"Services" is undefined other than that it must be something that is made available on the basis that it has been, is being, or will be, paid for.[361] Any act done on the understanding that it will be paid for amounts to a service. For example, in *Widdowson*,[362] it was held that obtaining a van on hire-purchase was obtaining services. **8–163**

The Crown Prosecution Service, The Fraud Act 2006: Legal Guidance, Fraud and Economic Crime (2024):

"Section 11 will cover circumstances where the Defendant: **8–164**

- obtains chargeable data or software over the internet without paying;
- orders a meal in a restaurant knowing he has no means to pay;
- attaches a decoder to his TV to enable him to access chargeable satellite services without paying;
- uses the services of a members' club without paying and without being a member."

It is irrelevant that the service is obtained pursuant to an illegal or otherwise unenforceable contract. So, for example, a person who, without intending to pay, induces a prostitute to provide sexual services is liable even though the contract is illegal and unenforceable.[363] **8–165**

(d) Without payment

The section only applies to those services induced on the understanding that they will be paid for. Thus, the more effective one's lies, the less the chance of liability here. If one's dishonesty is so convincing that a service is provided free, there is no liability. **8–166**

360 Law Commission Paper No.276, *Fraud* (2002), para.8.11. It could, however, be argued that deliberately remaining on someone else's boat after hearing the announcement and thus knowingly choosing to receive a free ride constitutes an "act".

361 So, in the case of an application for a credit card or bank account, this section will only apply if the "service" is to be paid for: *R. v Sofroniou (Leon Florenzous)* [2003] EWCA Crim 3681; [2004] Q.B. 1218; CPS, *The Fraud Act 2006: Legal Guidance, Fraud and Economic Crime* (2024).

362 *R. v Widdowson (Stanley)* (1986) 82 Cr. App. R. 314; [1986] R.T.R. 124 CA.

363 Law Commission Paper No.276, *Fraud* (2002), para.7.53.

What is meant by "paid for" here? Does it extend to recompense in forms other than money? The better view is that the criminal law should not extend its reach into non-commercial, perhaps purely social, transactions, such as where a person induces another into fixing a broken tap by falsely stating that, in return, dinner will be cooked for the tap-mender.[364]

One of the examples given by the Law Commission of when this offence will apply is where false credit card details are given to an automated booking system.[365] It would appear, however, that the offence will not actually cover such conduct. Provided the card details (PIN and security number, etc) are correct, payment *will* be made by the bank or issuing company.[366] Such conduct will, however, be covered by the fraud offence under s.2.

(ii) Mens rea

8–167 The mens rea requirements of s.11 are as follows.

(a) Dishonesty

8–168 The act leading to the obtaining of the services must be dishonest. Again, the partial definition of dishonesty in the Theft Act 1978 s.2 does not apply and whether the act is dishonest will be governed by the *Ivey/Barton* test.[367]

(b) Knowing payment required

8–169 At the time when the services are obtained, D must know that the services are made available on the basis that payment has been, is being or will be made for or in respect of them or that they might only be available on that basis.

(c) Intention not to pay

8–170 The defendant must intend that payment will not be made, or that it will not be made in full. So, if the defendant is uncertain whether the services have been paid for (say, because they think another person *might* have already paid for them), there will be no liability. Recklessness will not suffice.

4. Conspiracy to defraud

8–171 The Law Commission proposed abolition of this offence as did the Home Office Consultation Paper on Fraud. This proposal was not, however, implemented on the basis that changing the law could lead to unforeseen circumstances with the developing technologies enabling fraudsters to exploit gaps in the law. Accordingly, to provide a "safety net",[368] the rather broad and unsatisfactory offence of conspiracy

364 cf. Ormerod and Laird, *Smith, Hogan and Ormerod's Criminal Law*, 15th edn (2018), p.968.
365 Law Commission Report No.276, *Fraud* (2002), para.8.1.
366 Ormerod and Laird, *Smith, Hogan and Ormerod's Criminal Law*, 15th edn (2018), p.968.
367 *Ivey* [2017] UKSC 67; [2018] A.C. 391 and; *Barton* [2020] EWCA Crim 575, discussed above: paras 8–079–8–094, 8–135–8–137.
368 Home Office, *Regulatory Impact Assessment: Fraud Bill* (2006).

to defraud still remains. The Government stated that it was committed to a review of the operation of the Fraud Act 2006 three years after its implementation and that it might at that point abolish the offence of conspiracy to defraud.[369] However, in its 2012 post-legislative assessment of the Fraud Act 2006, the Ministry of Justice concluded that the offence should be retained because it:

> ". . . continues to be an effective and essential tool in combating fraud. This is particularly pertinent where there are various levels of criminal activity involved and the court would not otherwise be aware of the full extent of criminality involved."[370]

This offence is discussed in Ch.10.

IV. Other Property Offences

There are a large number of other property offences, some serious like blackmail, robbery, burglary, criminal damage and handling stolen goods and some not so serious, like taking a conveyance. Whilst it is beyond the scope of this book to deal with all these offences in detail, the chief provisions of some of these offences will be sketched. **8–172**

A. ROBBERY

1. The law

THEFT ACT 1968 s.8:

> "(1) A person is guilty of robbery if he steals, and immediately before or at the time of doing so, and in order to do so, he uses force on any person or puts or seeks to put any person in fear of being then and there subjected to force. **8–173**
>
> (2) A person guilty of robbery, or of an assault with intent to rob, shall on conviction on indictment be liable to imprisonment for life."[371]

369 Hansard (HC), 13 March 2006, col.1110.

370 Ministry of Justice, *Post-legislative Assessment of the Fraud Act 2006*, Cm.8372 (2012), para.42.

371 Sentencing guidelines have been published for this offence: Sentencing Council: *Robbery—Dwelling* (2016); *Robbery—Professionally planned commercial* (2016); *Robbery—Street and less sophisticated commercial* (2016).

(i) Actus reus

(a) Theft

8–174 Robbery is theft aggravated by the threat or use of force. The elements of theft must be established if a conviction for robbery is to be obtained. Therefore the actus reus of theft must be proved.[372] If the defendant believes that they have a legal right to the property they take (even if not to the way they take it) then there can be no theft and, therefore, no robbery.[373]

(b) Use or threat of force against a person

8–175 The defendant must either:

(i) use force on any person. What amounts to "force" is a question of fact to be determined by a jury, although it would seem that very little force is actually required.[374] Wrenching a shopping basket,[375] handbag[376] or grabbing keys and an Iphone,[377] from the owner can suffice, although the mere opportunistic snatching of a banknote being passed from one person to another,[378] or a cigarette from between the victim's fingers will not;[379]
(ii) put any person in fear of being there and then subjected to force; or
(iii) seek to put any person in fear of being there and then subjected to force. The fact that the victim was not put in fear is irrelevant; the issue is whether the defendant sought to put the victim in fear of force.[380]

(c) Immediately before or at the time of the theft

8–176 The force or threat of force must take place immediately before or at the time of the theft.[381]

(ii) Mens rea

8–177 While the mens rea of the offence of robbery is not spelt out in s.8, it is clear that there must be:

(1) the mens rea of theft;[382] and
(2) the force or threatened force must be *in order to steal*; an accidental, negligent or even reckless use of force will not suffice.

---

372 Namely: (i) appropriation; (ii) of property; (iii) belonging to another. See paras 8–006–8–068.
373 *R. v Robinson* [1977] Crim. L.R. 173.
374 *R. v Dawson and James* (1976) 64 Cr. App. R. 170; *R. v Clouden* [1987] Crim. L.R. 56 CA.
375 *Clouden* [1987] Crim. L.R. 56.
376 *Corcoran v Anderton* (1980) 71 Cr. App. R. 104.
377 *R. v Martins (Joseph)* [2021] EWCA Crim 223; [1980] Crim. L.R. 385 Div Ct. See: M. Thomas and JJ. Bell, "'Snatch, grab, and jury speculation': reviewing the use of force in robbery" [2021] 85 J. Crim. L. 320.
378 *Martins* [2021] EWCA Crim 223.
379 *P v DPP* [2012] EWHC 1657 (Admin); [2013] 1 W.L.R. 2335, discussed by D. Ormerod in the case commentary at [2013] Crim. L.R. 151–152.
380 *R. v DPP* [2007] EWHC 739 (Admin); (2007) 171 J.P. 404.
381 In *R. v Atakpu (Austin)* [1994] Q.B. 69; [1993] 3 W.L.R. 812 CA, the court was of the view that it should be left to the common sense of the jury to decide at what point the theft finished. This will determine whether the force was used at the time of the theft. See paras 8–030–8–031.
382 Namely dishonesty (considered above at paras 8–079–8–094,and intention permanently to deprive the owner at the moment of taking the property: *Vinall* [2011] EWCA Crim 6252; [2012] 1 Cr. App. R. 29 at [12]; *R. v Zerei (Samuel Michael)* [2012] EWCA Crim 1114; *R. v Waters (Sian)*

B. BURGLARY AND AGGRAVATED BURGLARY

1. The law

THEFT ACT 1968 SS.9 AND 10:

"9.—(1) A person is guilty of burglary if— **8–178**

(a) he enters any building or part of a building as a trespasser and with intent to commit any such offence as is mentioned in subsection (2) below; or
(b) having entered any building or part of a building as a trespasser he steals or attempts to steal anything in the building or that part of it or inflicts or attempts to inflict on any person therein any grievous bodily harm.

(2) The offences referred to in subsection (1)(a) above are offences of stealing anything in the building or part of a building in question, of inflicting on any person therein any grievous bodily harm therein, and of doing unlawful damage to the building or anything therein . . .

(3) A person guilty of burglary shall on conviction on indictment be liable to imprisonment for a term not exceeding—

(a) where the offence was committed in respect of a building or part of a building which is a dwelling, fourteen years;
(b) in any other case, ten years.[383]

(4) References in subsections (1) and (2) above to a building, and the reference in subsection (3) above to a building which is a dwelling, shall apply also to an inhabited vehicle or vessel, and shall apply to any such vehicle or vessel at times when the person having a habitation in it is not there as well as at times when he is.

10.—(1) A person is guilty of aggravated burglary if he commits any burglary and at the time has with him any firearm or imitation firearm, any weapon of offence, or any explosive; and for this purpose—

(a) 'firearm' includes an airgun or air pistol, and 'imitation firearm' means anything which has the appearance of being a firearm, whether capable of being discharged or not; and
(b) 'weapon of offence' means any article made or adapted for use for causing injury to or incapacitating a person, or intended by the person having it with him for such use; and

---

[2015] EWCA Crim 402. See para.8-100. Theft Act 1968 s.2 applies to the offence of robbery, if D honestly believes that they are legally entitled to the property taken, they would not be dishonest: *Mahmud* [2024] EWCA Crim 130.

383 Sentencing Guidelines have been published for this offence: Sentencing Council, *Domestic Burglary* (2022); *Non-domestic Burglary* (2022).

> (c) 'explosive' means any article manufactured for the purpose of producing a practical effect by explosion, or intended by the person having it with him for that purpose.
>
> (2) A person guilty of aggravated burglary shall on conviction on indictment be liable to imprisonment for life."

8–179 The original s.9(2) also included the ulterior offence of rape. As can be seen in the case of *Collins* below, it would be burglary under the old law if a person entered a building as a trespasser with the intention of raping anyone therein. The Sexual Offences Act 2003 removed rape as an ulterior offence in s.9(2)[384] and created a new offence of trespass with intention to commit a sexual offence.[385] This additional offence is much wider than the old provision on burglary in that the person must be a trespasser "on any premises" (which is wider than "building or part of a building") and there must be an intention to commit "a relevant sexual offence" on the premises (which covers many sexual offences in addition to rape).

There are now four offences of burglary within s.9. Under s.9(1)(a), there are two offences of entering a building as a trespasser with the intention of stealing, inflicting grievous bodily harm or doing unlawful damage—one committed where the building is a "dwelling" and one where it is not. The former offence is known as "domestic burglary".[386] Similarly, under s.9(1)(b) having entered a "dwelling" as a trespasser and then stealing, etc is distinguished from other buildings or parts thereof. Section 10 creates a more serious offence: burglary aggravated by the presence of weapons.

(i) Actus reus: s.9(1)(a)

8–180 The offence of burglary contrary to s.9(1)(a) is essentially an inchoate offence, which involves the following elements.[387]

(a) Enters

8–181 Whether there has been an entry is a question of fact for the jury. The court in *Collins*[388] held that there had been to be an "effective and substantial" entry. In *Brown*,[389] the court qualified this approach requiring only an "effective" entry. Thus, it is unnecessary for the entire body of the defendant to be inside the building but minimal intrusions such as a few fingers would be generally insufficient. In *Ryan*,[390] it was held that the jury was entitled to consider whether there was an entry in a case where D's head and arm were inside a window when he became trapped. It is difficult to see how this could amount to an "effective" entry.

---

384 Sexual Offences Act 2003 Sch.6 para.17.
385 Sexual Offences Act 2003 s.63.
386 This is the terminology employed by the Powers of Criminal Courts (Sentencing) Act 2000 s.111.
387 The same elements are required under s.9(1)(b) subject to the necessary modifications.
388 *R. v Collins (Stephen William George)* [1973] Q.B. 100; [1972] 3 W.L.R. 243 CA.
389 *R. v Brown (Vincent)* [1985] Crim. L.R. 212 CA.
390 *R. v Ryan (Lee Bernard)* (1996) 160 J.P. 610; [1996] Crim. L.R. 320 CA.

(b) As a trespasser

Reference must be made to the civil law in order to understand the term "trespass". Under civil law, trespass is entry without the consent of the lawful possessor. No conviction for burglary can be obtained without a finding of civil trespass but, in *Collins* it was made clear that more than this is required: the defendant must enter "knowing that he is a trespasser . . . or, at the very least, is reckless whether or not he is entering the premises of another without the other party's consent".[391] In *Collins*, D, who was naked save for his socks, had climbed up a ladder to a bedroom window, with the intention of raping the woman inside that room. The woman saw a male crouched in the window with an erect penis and, believing him to be her boyfriend, invited him into the room. The issue was whether D had entered the building prior to being invited. If so, he was a trespasser.[392] **8–182**

Even if there is consent, if D acts in a way that goes beyond what the possessor would have consented to, they may be deemed to enter as a trespasser. Thus, in *Jones*,[393] D had left his parents' home but was a frequent, welcome visitor. One night he entered their home and stole two television sets. Despite the father's loyal statement that his son was welcome at any time, the court held that an inference could be drawn that he would not have consented to entry for the purposes of theft. The son was thus held to have entered as a trespasser.

(c) Any building or part of a building

Two issues are raised here. First, what constitutes a "building"? Section 9(4) gives an extended meaning to the term by including within it inhabited vehicles and vessels such as caravans and houseboats.[394] The occupant does not have to be present at the time in order to render it "inhabited" but it would seem that it would have to be lived in. **8–183**

Little other statutory guidance is given as to the ambit of "building"; generally, it would seem appropriate to take a common sense view of it. It would be too restrictive to think in terms of just houses, flats, offices and the like. Outbuildings such as garages and sheds must also be included. The courts have tended to regard both a degree of permanence and considerable size as appropriate criteria to determine whether something constitutes a "building".[395] So, tents and telephone kiosks are, therefore, probably not buildings for the purposes of burglary.[396]

The second issue relates to "part of a building". This does not necessarily mean a separate room. It includes areas such as those behind counters in shops from which the defendant is excluded.[397]

---

391 *Collins* [1973] Q.B. 100 at 105. Section 9(1)(a) burglary included trespass with intent to rape at this time.

392 *Collins* [1973] Q.B. 100 at 105; *Brown* [1985] Crim. L.R. 212. cf. *R. v McEneff (Karen)* [2014] EWCA Crim 1633, where the Court of Appeal held that the judge was wrong to direct the jury that, if, once Ds had entered the premises, they had stolen, they would by definition have become trespassers because nobody would have given them permission to steal.

393 *R. v Jones (John)* [1976] 1 W.L.R. 672; (1976) 63 Cr. App. R. 47 CA.

394 *R. v Coleman (Kenneth)* [2013] EWCA Crim 544; [2013] 2 Cr. App. R. (S.) 79: an inhabited narrow boat was held to be a building for the purposes of s.9(4).

395 *Stevens v Gorley* (1859) 7 C.B.(N.S.) 99.

396 Ormerod and Williams, *Smith's The Law of Theft*, 9th edn (2007), pp.257–258.

397 Either expressly or impliedly: *R. v Walkington (Terence John)* [1979] 1 W.L.R. 1169; (1979) 68 Cr. App. R. 427 CA.

(d) Dwelling

8–184 The Criminal Justice Act 1991 created a new and more serious offence of domestic burglary in respect of s.9(1)(a) and (b) where the building is a "dwelling".[398] As was observed In *Sticklen*:[399]

> "... the justification for treating a dwelling as being different from other properties ... is the very fact that it is someone's home, occupied, and with personal and sentimental property within it. It is for that reason that higher sentences are required."

Where it is alleged that a burglary was a domestic burglary, it must be proved that the burglary was of a dwelling. Dwelling is a somewhat old-fashioned word, and was not defined in the legislation, but has been described as referring "to the place where one lives and makes one's home".[400] In *Chipunza*, the Court of Appeal observed that:

> "In most cases, it is obvious whether or not a building is a dwelling. Houses and flats are generally built to be lived in, to be used as dwellings. The fact that no one is living in it at the time of a burglary does not necessarily render a building other than a dwelling[401] ... We can envisage a situation where, for example, a newly built house may not yet be a dwelling. It may well be possible for a building built and previously used as a dwelling to become derelict, or to become a building site. Whether the newly built house has become a dwelling, or the latter remains a dwelling would be a question of fact for a jury ..."[402]

A vessel or vehicle in which someone lives as their home is a dwelling.[403] Hotel rooms are generally not dwellings because "their commercial function is to provide a temporary place to stay".[404] However, a hotel or part of a hotel may be a dwelling where "someone lives in a hotel long term and uses it as their home",[405] depending on the facts of the case.

---

398 The indictment must specify that the property is a dwelling, and where this is disputed there should be alternative counts on the indictment, one specifying that the property is a dwelling and one charging non-domestic burglary, and the jury should determine the issue: *R. v Flack (Perry)* [2013] EWCA Crim 115; [2013] 2 Cr. App. R. (S.) 56. In *Flack*, the Court of Appeal declined to provide guidance as to how the issue of whether property was a dwelling was to be determined (at [8]).

399 *R. v Sticklen (Daniel John Lee)* [2013] EWCA Crim 615 at [10].

400 *Uratemp Ventures Ltd v Collins* [2001] UKHL 43; [2002] 1 A.C. 30 at [30]. Cited in *R. v Chipunza (Bruce)* [2021] EWCA Crim 597 at [13]; [2021] 4 W.L.R. 81.

401 See *Hudson v Crown Prosecution Service* [2017] EWHC 841 (Admin); [2017] 4 W.L.R. 108.

402 *Chipunza* [2021] EWCA Crim 597 at [14]. See G. Betts, "*R. v Chipunza (Bruce)*: criminal law—burglary- dwelling—hotel room (2022) 27 Cov. L.J. 131.

403 An inhabited houseboat or caravan is a "dwelling": *Coleman* [2013] EWCA Crim 544; [2013] 2 Cr. App. R. (S.) 79. See the case commentary by D. Thomas, [2013] Crim. L.R. 694–696. See Ormerod and Williams, *Smith's The Law of Theft*, 9th edn (2007), p.266; K. Laird, "Conceptualising the Interpretation of 'Dwelling' in Section 9 of the Theft Act 1968" [2013] Crim. L.R. 656–673.

404 *Chipunza* [2021] EWCA Crim 597 at [15].

405 *Chipunza* [2021] EWCA Crim 597 at [15].

(ii) Mens rea: s.9(1)(a)

The mens rea requirement for burglary under s.9(1)(a) is: **8–185**

(a) intention or recklessness as to trespass,
(b) intention to commit one of the offences in s.9(2):[406]
- stealing;[407]
- Inflicting grievous bodily harm to a person in the building;[408] or
- unlawful damage to the building or anything in the building.[409]

and
(c) with regard to domestic burglary, it has been argued that because this is an aggravating element it should import a requirement of mens rea; D should only be guilty if they know or foresee that somebody might be living there.[410]

(iii) Actus reus: s.9(1)(b)

The actus reus requirements of s.9(1)(b) are that D enters as a trespasser a building or part of a building, and whilst in the building: **8–186**

- steals,[411] or
- attempts to steal; or
- inflicts grievous bodily harm;[412] or
- attempts to inflict grievous bodily harm.

Dwelling: if it is alleged that the burglary is a domestic burglary, it must be proved that the burglary is of a dwelling. See para.8–184.

---

406 The prosecution must prove that, at the time of entry, D had the intention to commit the relevant offence, recklessness does not suffice: *A v DPP* [2003] EWHC 1676 (QB). The s.9(1)(a) offence is one of specific intent: *R. v Durante (Reginald William)* [1972] 1 W.L.R. 1612; (1972) 56 Cr. App. R. 708 CA. A defendant who enters a building as a trespasser intending to steal only if he finds items worth stealing has sufficient mens rea for the purposes of s.9(1)(a) burglary: *Att-Gen's References (Nos 1 and 2 of 1979)* [1980] Q.B. 180; Ormerod and Williams, *Smith's The Law of Theft*, 9th edn (2007), p.263. cf. the position in relation to conditional intention and theft, see para.8–109.

407 Theft, contrary to the Theft Act 1968 s.1. See paras 8–004–8–005.

408 Contrary to the Offences against the Person Act 1861 s.18.

409 Contrary to the Criminal Damage Act 1971.

410 Ormerod and Williams, *Smith's The Law of Theft*, 9th edn (2007), p.266. cf. *Collins* [1973] Q.B. 100 at 107, where it was held that the defendant must either know or be recklessness as to whether his entry on to the premises was with permission.

411 See Theft, contrary to the Theft Act 1968, s.1. See paras 8–004–8–005. The offence of theft will be complete when, with the relevant mens rea, D appropriates property and, following *Gomez* [1993] A.C. 242 (see paras 8–020–8–021), there may be an appropriation even if D does not succeed in removing the goods from the premises. e.g. if D enters a building as a trespasser and rolls up an antique rug, intending to steal it. D is then surprised by the occupier returning home and runs off without taking the rug. D will have appropriated the rug as soon as he rolled it up, and the offence of theft will be complete at this stage.

412 Unlike s.9(1)(a), s.9(1)(b) does not include the word "offence". This appears to have been omitted by accident: J.C. Smith, "Burglary under the Theft Bill" [1968] Crim. L.R. 367. In *R. v Jenkins (Edward John)* [1983] 76 Cr. App. R. 313 CA, Purchas LJ at 318, the Court of Appeal held that the "infliction" need not be an offence. The House of Lords allowed the appeal in *Jenkins* (*R. v Wilson (Clarence George)* [1994] A.C. 242; [1983] 3 W.L.R. 686 HL) but not on this point. It is suggested that *Jenkins* is wrong on this point and that the infliction of grievous bodily harm must be an offence under the OAPA 1861 ss.18, 20 or 23.

(iv) Mens rea: s.9(1)(b)

8–187 The mens rea requirement for s.9(1)(b) is:

(a) intention or recklessness with regard to the trespass; and
(b) the mens rea for the ulterior offence (theft, inflicting grievous bodily harm, or attempt to commit theft or to inflict grievous bodily harm.

See para.8–185, re mens rea as to whether the property is a dwelling.

(v) Aggravated burglary

8–188 If a person "commits any burglary and at the time has with him any firearm or imitation firearm, any weapon of offence, or any explosive", the offence becomes aggravated burglary.[413] For the purposes of this offence, it does not matter whether the burglary is of a dwelling or not.

For the purposes of s.9(1)(a) (entry with intent), D must have the article of aggravation with them at the time of entry. For the purposes of s.9(1)(b) (having entered), the relevant time is when the specified offence is committed. So, if a D, having entered as a trespasser, picks up a kitchen knife and uses it to force the householder to hand over the property, aggravated burglary is committed. In *Klass*,[414] it was held that:

> "... the gravamen of this offence is entry into the building with a weapon. The purpose of the section is to deter people from taking weapons into buildings whilst committing burglary. The fact that a getaway driver has a weapon with him in the car would not, in our judgment, be sufficient to turn an offence of burglary into one of aggravated burglary."[415]

So the offence is not committed if another party outside the building (e.g. a getaway driver in a car) is in sole possession of a weapon.[416] In *Chevannes*, a case involving a s.9(1)(b) burglary, the alleged weapon of offence (a bottle containing ammonia and water) had been left downstairs whilst two of the burglars stole items upstairs. The Court of Appeal stated that what mattered in such cases was:

> "... not whether the accused, or one of those with whom he was engaged in a joint enterprise, was actually holding the weapon at the time the theft took place, but whether the weapon was within his control so that it could be taken up and used if necessary."[417]

---

413 Theft Act 1968 s.10. A weapon that satisfies the definition of "offensive weapon" under the Prevention of Crime Act 1953 s.1 will also satisfy the definition of "weapons of offence": *R. v Cina (Carl)* [2021] EWCA Crim 140 at [13] (Double-bladed 6 inch "throwing knife" was a "weapon of offence"). The maximum sentence is life imprisonment, Theft Act 1968 s.10(2). Sentencing guidelines have been published for aggravated burglary: Sentencing Council, Aggravated Burglary (2022).

414 *R. v Klass (Kennedy Francis)* [1998] 1 Cr. App. R. 453; (1998) 162 J.P. 105 CA. Followed in *R. v Wiggins (Zaro Pierre)* [2012] EWCA Crim 885; (2012) 176 J.P. 305.

415 *Klass* [1998] 1 Cr. App. R. 453 at 456.

416 *Klass* [1998] 1 Cr. App. R. 453 at 456.

417 *R. v Chevannes (Justin Lee)* [2009] EWCA Crim 2725 per Moore-Bick J at [20]. This is a matter of fact for the jury.

C. HANDLING STOLEN GOODS

1. The law

THEFT ACT 1968 S.22:

"(1) A person handles stolen goods if (otherwise than in the course of the stealing) knowing or believing them to be stolen goods he dishonestly receives the goods, or dishonestly undertakes or assists in their retention, removal, disposal or realisation by or for the benefit of another person, or if he arranges to do so. **8–189**

(2) A person guilty of handling stolen goods shall on conviction on indictment be liable to imprisonment for a term not exceeding 14 years."

It should be noted that s.22 creates only *one* offence, although there are a large number of ways in which this offence can be committed. In fact, it renders culpable almost any way of dealing with stolen goods as long as there is mens rea. So, for example, the person who arranges to handle stolen goods commits the offence under s.22 despite the fact that, but for the provision, they would not even have done enough to be liable for an attempt. **8–190**

(i) Actus reus

The elements of the actus reus are as follows. **8–191**

(a) The goods must be stolen at the time of handling

Section 34(2)(b) defines "goods" as including money and every other description of property, except land. In addition, s.24 defines stolen goods as goods obtained by theft under s.1, by fraud under the Fraud Act 2006, by blackmail under s.21 and money dishonestly withdrawn from a wrongful credit under s.24A(8). Importantly, the goods must remain stolen at the time the handling occurs; so, for example, where the goods have been reduced to police custody and used to bait a trap to catch handlers there can be no conviction under s.22.[418] **8–192**

The handling must be "otherwise than in the course of the stealing". This provision is necessary to prevent thieves being simultaneously guilty of both theft and handling. This raises the problem of when theft ends which depends upon whether an appropriation can be regarded as a continuing act.[419] This matter was discussed earlier in relation to the meaning of an appropriation.[420]

418 See Theft Act 1968 s.24(2) and (3) and *Att-Gen's Reference (No.1 of 1974)* [1974] Q.B. 744; [1974] 2 W.L.R. 891. The exception will be where it is possible to establish arranging to handle at some earlier time. Alternatively, a charge of attempting to handle stolen goods may be possible.

419 See *R. v Hale (Robert Angus)* (1979) 68 Cr. App. R. 415; [1979] Crim. L.R. 596 CA; *R. v Lockley* [1995] Crim. L.R. 656.

420 At paras 8–029–8–031.

(b) There must be a handling of the goods

8–193 Although the preferred view, as indicated above, is that there is only one offence, there are 18 ways in which the property may be handled.[421] The stereotypical case of handling will involve receiving the goods but it will also encompass disposal (even by way of destruction) and assisting another to deal with the stolen goods. A brief look at the interpretation of this latter form of handling reinforces how very wide this offence is. In *Kanwar*,[422] the Court of Appeal held that "assistance" requires that something be done to aid the retention, removal, disposal or realisation of the goods but that this was not limited to physical acts. On the facts of the case, lying to protect one's husband who had brought stolen goods into the house was held to be sufficient.

(ii) Mens rea

8–194 The mens rea requirement for handling under s.22 is:

(1) D must know or believe the goods to be stolen. There seems to be hardly any difference in the meaning of these words in this context. Belief, if anything, falls only just short of knowledge: where no other reasonable conclusion can be drawn by the defendant but that the goods were stolen.[423] Mere suspicion that the goods could be stolen is, however, not sufficient;
(2) there must be dishonesty. Dishonesty here bears the same meaning as for theft, so the *Ivey/Barton* test[424] now applies. It is possible that a person could receive stolen goods knowing that they are stolen but intending to return them to the owner. In such a case, the Theft Act 1968 s.2 does not apply to the s.22 offence, and it would be a matter for the jury whether they regard the D's claim as being honest.

2. Punishment

8–195 The maximum penalty for handling stolen goods is 14 years' imprisonment.[425]

D. CRIMINAL DAMAGE

1. The Law

8–196 The Criminal Damage Act 1971 codified the law relating to criminal damage and arson.

421 *R. v Nicklin (David John)* [1977] 1 W.L.R. 403 at 407; (1977) 64 Cr. App. R. 205 CA.
422 *R. v Kanwar (Rena Louise)* [1982] 1 W.L.R. 845; (1982) 75 Cr. App. R. 87 CA.
423 In directing the jury, the judge should avoid trying to distinguish the two terms: *R. v Forsyth (Elizabeth)* [1997] 2 Cr. App. R. 299 at 321; [1997] Crim. L.R. 581 CA.
424 *Ivey* [2017] UKSC 67; *Barton* [2020] EWCA Crim 575. See paras 8–079–8–094.
425 Sentencing guidelines have been published for this offence: Sentencing Council, *Handling Stolen Goods* (2016).

Criminal Damage Act 1971 s.1(1) and (3)

"1.— Destroying or damaging property. **8–197**

(1) A person who without lawful excuse destroys or damages any property belonging to another intending to destroy or damage any such property or being reckless as to whether any such property would be destroyed or damaged shall be guilty of an offence.

(3) An offence committed under this section by destroying or damaging property by fire shall be charged as arson."

(i) Actus reus

The elements of the actus reus are as follows. **8–198**

(a) D destroys or damages

What amounts to criminal damage is a matter of fact and degree for the jury (or magistrate) to decide.[426] **8–199** There is no requirement that the damage be permanent or severe. For, example, grass (or other vegetation) may be damaged by walking across it and trampling it down,[427] and the "temporary functional derangement" of a policeman's hat, caused by jumping on it,[428] and the smearing of mud on the wall of a police cell, which costs £7 to clean, have been held to amount to damage.[429] Criminal damage committed by fire is charged as the offence of arson.[430]

Damage has been widely interpreted to include permanent or temporary impairment of value or usefulness of the property.[431]

(1) Reduction in value

Property may be damaged if it is rendered less valuable. For instance, a car would be damaged if its **8–200** paintwork were scratched, and milk (or any food) would be damaged if it was adulterated and spoiled.[432] In some cases, rather than focusing upon the diminution in value of the property damaged, the courts have found that damage has been caused based upon the expense incurred by the owner in restoring property to its pre-damaged state. In *Hardman v Chief Constable of Avon and Somerset Constabulary*,[433] it was held that human silhouettes painted in water soluble paint upon the pavement amounted to

---

426 *Roe v Kingerlee* [1986] Crim. L.R. 735 Div Ct.

427 *Gayford v Chouler* [1898] 1 Q.B. 316.

428 *Samuels v Stubbs* [1972] 4 S.A.S.R. 200.

429 *Kingerlee* [1986] Crim. L.R. 735. cf. *Grajewski v DPP (NSW)* [2019] HCA 8 (HC (Aus)), where the High Court of Australia held that simply impairing the functionality of property does not amount to criminal damage. See K. Grevling, "Damaging Property" [2020] Crim. L.R. 497.

430 Criminal Damage Act 1971 s.1(3).

431 *Morphitis v Salmon* (1990) 154 J.P. 365; [1990] Crim. L.R. 48 Div Ct; *R. v Whiteley (Nicholas Alan)* [1991] 93 Cr. App. R. 25; (1991) 155 J.P. 917 CA.

432 *Roper v Knott* [1898] 1 Q.B. 868 (watering down milk).

433 *Hardman v Chief Constable of Avon and Somerset* [1986] Crim. L.R. 330 Bristol Crown Court.

damage, in spite of the fact that they could be washed away by the rain, because expense and inconvenience had been caused to the local authority in removing them. In *Henderson v Battley*,[434] it was held that the dumping of rubbish upon land amounted to criminal damage because money had to be spent to clear the rubbish away. By contrast, in *A (A Juvenile) v R*,[435] a Crown Court held that there was no damage where D had allegedly spat upon a police officer's raincoat: no attempt had been made to clean the coat and the mark left on the coat could be removed by a damp cloth. Since human spittle is considered to be a biohazard, it is suggested that it would be reasonable for the officer to have the coat dry-cleaned and that the expense of such cleaning ought to be regarded as damage.[436]

(2) Impairment of usefulness

8–201 Property may be damaged if its usefulness is impaired. In *Fiak*,[437] D, whilst in police custody, had flooded his cell by putting a blanket down the toilet in his cell, which he then repeatedly flushed. The water was clean, and the cell floor was waterproof, but the court had no difficulty in finding that property had been damaged:

> "[20]. Applying these principles to the present case, while it is true that the effect of the appellant's actions in relation to the blanket and the cell were both remediable, the simple reality is that the blanket could not be used as a blanket by any other prisoner until it had been dried out (and, we believe, also cleaned) and the flooded cells remained out of action until the water was cleared. In our judgment it is clear that both sustained damage for the purposes of the 1971 Act."

By contrast, it has been held that wheel clamping a car does not amount to damage to the car.[438] A clamp may impair the usefulness of the car, to the extent that it cannot be driven away, but it does not cause any intrusion Into the "integrity of the object in question".[439] In *Morphitis v Salmon*,[440] D was convicted of the criminal damage of a scaffolding bar and clip removed from a barrier. Although the bar was scratched, on appeal, it was held that there was no criminal damage, since neither the value nor the usefulness of the bar or clip had been impaired. However, the Divisional Court indicated, obiter, that had D been charged with criminal damage to the barrier as a whole, the removal of the bar and clip would have amounted to damage of the whole structure. Without the bar and the clip, the usefulness of the barrier as a barrier was impaired. Damage may also be caused by removing or interfering with part of a machine, so that the machine as a whole will not work.[441]

---

434 *R. v Henderson and Batley* unreported, 27 November 1984 CA. The case is extensively quoted in *Cox v Riley* (1986) 83 Cr. App. R. 54 at 47; [1986] Crim. L.R. 460 QBD.

435 *A (A Juvenile) v Queen, The* [1978] Crim. L.R. 689 Kent Crown Court.

436 D might also have been charged with battery, see para.5–021.

437 *R. v Fiak (Engin)* [2005] EWCA Crim 2381; [2005] Po. L.R. 211.

438 *Drake v DPP* (1994) 158 J.P. 828; [1994] R.T.R. 411 QBD at 417–418.

439 *Drake* [1994] R.T.R. 411 per Laws J at 418. cf. *Lloyd v DPP* (1992) 156 J.P. 342; [1992] R.T.R. 215 Div Ct. It has been argued that these cases are wrongly decided, on the basis that the clamp physically interferes with the car, affecting its integrity: Simester, Spencer, Stark, Sullivan and Virgo, *Simester and Sullivan's Criminal Law*, 7th edn (2019), p.633.

440 *Morphitis v Salmon* [1990] Crim. L.R. 48 Div Ct.

441 *R. v Fisher (William)* (1865–72) L.R. 1 C.C.R. 7.

The Criminal Damage Act 1971 s.10(5)[442] provides that, for the purposes of this Act:

> ". . . modification of the contents of a computer shall not be regarded as damaging any computer or computer storage medium unless its effect on that computer or computer storage medium impairs its physical condition."

(b) Property

Criminal Damage Act 1971 s.10(1)

> "10.—Interpretation. **8-202**
>
> (1) In this Act 'property' means of a tangible nature, whether real or personal, including money and—
>
> (a) including wild creatures which have been tamed or are ordinarily kept in captivity, and any other wild creatures or their carcasses if, but only if, they have been reduced into possession which has not been lost or abandoned or are in the course of being reduced into possession; but
> (b) not including mushrooms growing wild on any land or flowers, fruit or foliage of a plant growing wild on any land.
>
> For the purposes of this subsection 'mushroom' includes any fungus and 'plant' includes any shrub or tree."

Whilst land generally cannot be stolen, it may be criminally damaged. On the other hand, whilst intangible property may be stolen, the offence of criminal damage only applies to tangible property.[443] **8-203**

(c) Belonging to another

The offence under s.1(1) is only committed where D destroys or damages property "belonging to another". Section 10 sets out a number of circumstances in which property is treated as belonging to another. **8-204**

442 Inserted into the Act by the Police and Justice Act 2006 Sch.14 para.2.
443 *R. v Whiteley (Nicholas Allen)* (1991) 93 Cr. App. R. 25; (1991) 155 J.P. 917 CA.

Criminal Damage Act 1971 s.10(2)

8-205 "(2) Property shall be treated for the purposes of this Act as belonging to any person—

(a) having the custody or control of it;
(b) having in it any proprietary right or interest (not being an equitable interest arising only from an agreement to transfer or grant an interest); or
(c) having a charge on it.

(3) Where property is subject to a trust, the persons to whom it belongs shall be so treated as including any person having a right to enforce the trust.

(4) Property of a corporation sole shall be so treated as belonging to the corporation notwithstanding a vacancy in the corporation."

(ii) Mens rea

(a) Intention or recklessness as to consequences

8-206 D must either intend to damage or destroy property, or be subjectively reckless as to property being damaged or destroyed). The leading authority on the test for recklessness in criminal damage and arson is *R. v G*,[444] discussed at paras 3-064–3-066. This requires that D foresee that property belonging to another may be destroyed or damaged, and nevertheless goes on to take the risk where it is unreasonable to do so.

(b) Intention or recklessness as to circumstances

8-207 D does not commit an offence if he damages or destroys property in the honest (but mistaken) belief that the property is his. In *Smith*,[445] D had installed some electrical wiring, which he had boarded over. When the tenancy ended, he had caused £130 worth of damage to the boards when he removed the wiring. He was actually not legally entitled to do this, because the wiring and boards had become fixtures in the property, and the trial judge withdrew Smith's claim that he believed that he had a lawful excuse to damage the property. The Court of Appeal held that the judge was wrong to do so, and allowed the appeal:

> "Applying the ordinary principles of *mens rea*, the intention and recklessness and the absence of lawful excuse required to constitute the offence have reference to property belonging to another. It follows that in our judgment no offence is committed under this section if a person destroys or causes damage to property belonging to another if he does so in the honest though mistaken belief that the property is his own, and provided that the belief is honestly held it is irrelevant to consider whether or not it is a justifiable belief."[446]

---

444 *R. v G* [2003] UKHL 50; [2004] 1 A.C. 1034.
445 *R. v Smith (David Raymond)* [1974] Q.B. 354; [1974] 2 W.L.R. 20.
446 *Smith* [1974] Q.B. 354 at 360.

(iii) Lawful excuse

CRIMINAL DAMAGE ACT 1971 s.5 (2)–(3)

"(2) A person charged with an offence to which this section applies, shall, whether or not he would be treated for the purposes of this Act as having a lawful excuse apart from this subsection, be treated for those purposes as having a lawful excuse— 8–208

(a) if at the time of the act or acts alleged to constitute the offence he believed that the person or persons whom he believed to be entitled to consent to the destruction of or damage to the property in question had so consented, or would have so consented to it if he or they had known of the destruction or damage and its circumstances; or
(b) if he destroyed or damaged or threatened to destroy or damage the property in question or, . . . in order to protect property belonging to himself or another or a right or interest in property which was or which he believed to be vested in himself or another, and at the time of the act or acts alleged to constitute the offence he believed—

   (i) that the property, right or interest was in immediate need of protection; and
   (ii) that the means of protection adopted or proposed to be adopted were or would be reasonable having regard to all the circumstances.

(3) For the purposes of this section it is immaterial whether a belief is justified or not if it is honestly held."

(a) Belief in consent

ATTORNEY-GENERAL'S REFERENCE ON A POINT OF LAW (NO.1 OF 2023) [2024] EWCA CRIM 243.

An "Extinction Rebellion" protester sought to rely on the statutory defence during her trial for criminal damage, the Court of Appeal explained the meaning and effect of the s.5(2)(a) defence. 8–209

"[40]. First, it is clear from the words 'at the time of the act or acts alleged to constitute the offence' that the belief on which a defendant relies to establish the defence must be one held by the defendant at the time of the commission of the offence. It cannot be one formed to explain the conduct after the event. Nor can it be a belief founded on the actual or potential effect of efforts that might be deployed after the event to persuade the owner to consent. As the Judge directed the jury in this case, the damage cannot be an instrument of persuasion.

[41]. Secondly, the belief required must be a genuine belief, otherwise it is not a belief at all. Section 5(3) provides that the belief does not need to be justified but it must be honestly held. It follows that this element of the defence involves a subjective test.

> [42.] Thirdly, the defendant's belief must be as to the consent of the person whom the defendant believed to be entitled to consent to the damage to the property in question (for convenience, described as the owner). The defendant must believe that the owner either had consented . . . or would have consented to the damage if they had known of the damage 'and its circumstances'. The inclusion of the phrase 'would have' involves a certainty in the belief in the owner's consent, not merely that the owner might (or should) have consented. There is therefore a requirement that the defendant's honest belief must be that she was sure that that the owner would have consented.
>
> [43]. Fourthly, in any case where the defence under section 5(2)(a) is raised there must be evidence that the defendant believed that the owner would have consented to the damage had they known of the damage and its circumstances.
>
> [44]. The possessive pronoun 'its' is central. It delimits the 'circumstances'. It is only the circumstances of the damage which are relevant. The circumstances must relate to the destruction of, or damage to, the property. Thus, the relevant circumstances may include matters such as the time, place and the extent of the damage caused. These factors would be linked to the damage and directly relevant to the owner's hypothetical decision as to consent. They do not include the political or philosophical beliefs of the person causing the damage.
>
> [45]. One commonly postulated circumstance where the defence in section 5(2)(a) is likely to arise is the case of the stranger discovering a child locked alone in a car on a hot day. The child is at risk of harm unless freed. If the stranger damages the car window in order to free the child, the defence of lawful excuse under section 5(2)(a) may be available to them: they believed at the time that the owner of the car would have consented to the damaging of the window because the circumstances of the damage included the need for speedy action, the importance of rescuing the child, and the relative unimportance of the damage to the vehicle. There would be a direct connection between the damage (the broken window) and the circumstances (the freeing of the child).
>
> 46. The need for a direct nexus between the circumstances of the damage and the anticipated giving of consent is implicit in the statutory language. The circumstances must belong to the damage, not to the defendant. To this extent there is an objective element to the defence. To draw the parallel with what was said in Hill and Hall in relation to the defence pursuant to section 5(2)(b), the circumstances cannot be so remote from the damage as no longer to be part of the damage. There must be a sufficient connection between the damage and its circumstances."

8–210 In *Denton*,[447] D set fire to some machinery in his employer's mill because he had been asked to do so by his employer, so that a fraudulent insurance claim could be made. On appeal, the Court of Appeal held

447 *R. v Denton (John Thomas)* [1981] 1 W.L.R. 1446; (1982) 74 Cr. App. R. 81 CA.

that he was not guilty of arson. In *Jaggard v Dickinson*,[448] D had been given permission to use the house of a friend as if it were her own. In a state of intoxication, she mistakenly entered a stranger's house. Mistakenly believing it to be her friend's property, she forced her way into the house, breaking two windowpanes and damaging a net curtain. The Divisional Court allowed her appeal. Since D had honestly believed that she would have had permission to cause the damage, she had a defence to the charge, even though her belief was founded on self-induced intoxication.

(b) Defence of property

For the defence to apply, the following conditions must be satisfied: **8–211**

(1) D must believe that the property (or interest in property) belongs to themself or another;[449]

(2) at the time of the criminal damage, D must believe that the property is in immediate need of protection. The issue of whether there is an "immediate" need for protection is to be assessed objectively, in the light of the facts as D believed them to be.[450] In *DPP v Ditchfield*,[451] another case involving an "Extinction Rebellion" protester, the court emphasised the importance of the use of the word "immediate" here, suggesting that, for an act to have been done "in order to protect property" it must be:

> "of a kind capable of conferring immediate protection on the property concerned. An act whose purpose is to put pressure on a public authority to take protective action is, on any natural reading of the word, not capable of conferring immediate protection in the sense required by the statute."

(3) D must believe that the means used to protect the property was a reasonable means of protecting the property. This is a subjective test, there is no requirement that it was reasonable for him to damage property. However, the more unreasonable the D's conduct is, the more likely it is that the jury will decide that he honestly believed that his conduct was reasonable;[452]

(4) the damage must be done in order to protect the property. From the wording of s.5(2) it might be presumed that D's purpose in damaging the property is a subjective matter, but the Court of Appeal has indicated that this is an objective test:

> "The question whether or not a particular act of destruction or damage or threat of destruction or damage was done or made in order to protect property belonging to another must be, on the true construction of the statute, an objective test. Therefore we have to ask ourselves whether, whatever the state of this man's mind and assuming an honest belief, that which he admittedly did was done in order to protect this particular property . . ."[453]

---

448 *Jaggard v Dickinson* [1981] Q.B. 527; [1981] 2 W.L.R. 118.

449 *Cresswell* [2006] EWHC 3379 (Admin) at [10]. A D charged with the simple offence of criminal damage or arson under s.1(1) would not have mens rea if they honestly but mistakenly believed that the property was their own: *Smith* [1974] Q.B. 354. However, the aggravated s.1(2) offence does not require that the property belong to another.

450 *R. v Hill (Valerie Mary)* (1989) 89 Cr. App. R. 74; [1989] Crim. L.R. 136 CA; *R. v Jones (Iowerth)* [2003] EWCA Crim 894 at [14].

451 *DPP v Ditchfield* [2021] EWHC 1090 (Admin) at [19].

452 *Unsworth v DPP* [2010] EWHC 3037 (Admin) at [42].

453 *R. v Hunt (Anthony Gerald)* (1978) 66 Cr. App. R. 105 CA at 108. This objective test was affirmed in *R. v Kelleher (Paul)* [2003] EWCA Crim 3525; (2003) 147 S.J.L.B. 1395. cf. *Hill* (1989) 89 Cr. App. R. 74; *Johnson v DPP* [1994] Crim. L.R. 673 QBD.

2. Aggravated criminal damage

Criminal Damage Act 1971 s.1(2)–(3)

8–212 "(2) A person who without lawful excuse destroys or damages any property, whether belonging to himself or another—

(a) intending to destroy or damage any property or being reckless as to whether any property would be destroyed or damaged; and
(b) intending by the destruction or damage to endanger the life of another or being reckless as to whether the life of another would be thereby endangered;

shall be guilty of an offence.

(3) An offence committed under this section by destroying or damaging property by fire shall be charged as arson."

8–213 The elements of this aggravated offence are as follows.

(i) Actus reus

8–214 D must destroy or damage property belonging either to himself, or to someone else. The s.5(2) defence of lawful excuse does not apply to this offence.

(ii) Mens rea

8–215 (1) D must intend to damage the property or be subjectively reckless as to whether the property would be damaged. This is discussed in paras 3–064–3–066.
(2) D must either:

(a) intend by the damage or destruction to endanger the life of another,[454] or
(b) be subjectively reckless as to whether the life of another will be endangered by the damage or destruction.

454 The endangerment must be by the damage or destruction: *R. v Steer (Dennis)* [1986] 1 W.L.R. 1286; (1987) 84 Cr. App. R. 25 CA.

V. Conclusion

What do all the different property offences have in common? Clearly, the common denominator in such offences is that they all involve an interference with the property interests of the victim. But what degree of interference is necessary? **8–216**

We have already seen that the emphasis is *not* on the actual loss of property. Indeed, there need not be any loss of property. In theft, for example, there need only be an *intention* of permanent deprivation; there need be no actual deprivation. In burglary, there need only be an entry to a building with one of the specified intents. No property need be taken. It was noted earlier in this chapter when dealing with the non-criminalisation of breach of contract that losses from such a breach can be significant while losses from theft can be minimal, or non-existent and many losses from theft and other property offences can be made good—either by actions for recovery of the goods or by insurance. In criminal damage, although in some cases property will be destroyed and completely lost, we have seen that the offence may be committed where quite minor temporary damage is caused.

It is thus clear that the emphasis is not on the loss of the property (which could be described as the direct or "first order" harm), but on the quality of the D's actions. The focus is on *wrongdoing*. The requirement of dishonesty for most property offences underlines this. The D's actions must be such that the community as a whole can reject them as "wrong". The D's actions pose a threat to the value system inherent in our whole concept of property; it involves an "indirect undermining of the proprietary regime".[455] This threat, which raises the risk that there will be actual loss to property, can be seen as the real harm in the property offences. It is not the only harm. Many of the offences have their own special and distinctive harms, but this threat is the harm common to all of them and can be seen as a "second-order" harm analogous to the "second-order" harms encountered in the law of attempt.

Although criminal damage involves interference with the rights of a property owner, much vandalism may also be regarded as an act of violence, albeit to property. The harms involved in criminal damage may be regarded as extending beyond mere interference with property rights, involving public order and safety. Public vandalism may cause alarm and distress to those living in the locality, or to those witnessing an attack. Damage caused to the whole, or part of an industrial machine or vehicle may pose a risk to the life and limb of others. Certain means of causing damage, in particular fire, may easily spread, posing considerable danger to those in the vicinity, and to firefighters. **8–217**

Many of the property offences are so similar that perhaps one ought to consider abolishing most of them and introducing a single broad offence of dishonesty or wrongful interference with property rights. The Law Commission[456] considered this option and rejected it on the grounds that it could extend the reach of the criminal law too far, would place too much reliance on the elusive concept of "dishonesty" and would probably be incompatible with the ECHR arts 5 and 7 which have been

---

455 Simester and Sullivan, "On the Nature and Rationale of Property Offences" in Duff and Green (eds), *Defining Crimes* (Oxford: OUP, 2005). See also, Green, *13 Ways to Steal a Bicycle: Theft Law in the Information Age* (2012), p.141.

456 Law Commission Consultation Paper No.155, *Fraud and Deception* (1999).

interpreted to require that offences be formulated with sufficient precision to enable people to regulate their conduct. Such a broad offence would clearly breach the principle of fair labelling whereby different offences should encapsulate different wrongs in a morally informative manner. It would be unthinkable to conflate all the existing property offences into a single new crime. For example, burglary and robbery involve wrongs quite separate from mere interference with property rights. The same is equally true of other offences such as handling and blackmail. Green argues that the:

> ". . . reactive emotions [that the different crimes are] likely to evoke . . . will differ depending on which wrong has been committed. That is, such wrongs generally feel different from each other—a significant psychological phenomenon since differences in reactive emotions, though not conclusive, are usually a reliable indicator of differences in moral content."[457]

An alternative solution could be the introduction of a smaller (than at present) number of more broadly drawn offences. A step in this direction has been taken by the abolition of all the deception offences and their replacement by a single offence of fraud and the new offence of obtaining services dishonestly. Other possibilities remain. For example, the offence of theft could be expanded to encompass the present offence of handling stolen goods. In most cases a person who handles stolen goods is "assuming the rights of owner" over property and is thereby appropriating it, becoming guilty of theft.[458]

It is submitted, however, that such an approach would be misguided. While there is much to be said for the introduction of the new broad offence of fraud, most of the core central property offences should be retained in something like their present form. Criminal offences should describe as accurately as possible the conduct which is prohibited. The moral messages sought to be communicated by the criminal law and by the punishment of offenders become confused if offence categorisations are not clearly understood by the public. There are important moral distinctions between these offences which the public, albeit only intuitively, recognise and which need protecting.

---

457 S.P. Green, *Lying, Cheating and Stealing: A Moral Theory of White-Collar Crime* (Oxford: OUP, 2006), p.128.
458 cf. Green, *13 Ways to Steal a Bicycle: Theft Law in the Information Age* (2012), pp.187–189.

Chapter 9

General Defences

I. Justification and Excuse

A. INTRODUCTION

D may commit the actus reus of an offence with the requisite mens rea and yet escape liability because they have a "general defence".[1] For example, D may have intentionally killed V but have been acting in self-defence because V had been trying to kill them. In such a case, assuming the requirements of self-defence are met, D is afforded an unequivocal acquittal and escapes all liability. **9–001**

It was seen in Ch.2 that there are different ways of analysing criminal liability. It could be, continuing the above example, that D is regarded as having committed the actus reus with an appropriate mens rea but is afforded a supervening defence. This mode of analysis could be useful in describing the shifting burdens of proof in a criminal trial in those jurisdictions[2] where it is for the prosecution to prove beyond reasonable doubt that D committed the actus reus with appropriate mens rea, but the burden then shifts to D to establish on a balance of probabilities that they have a defence. This "procedural analysis" is employed in England and Wales with the defences of insanity[3] and diminished responsibility.[4] Such an approach is, however, not accurate in describing the burden of proof in other cases in England and Wales where, in relation to common law defences, the burden remains on the prosecution throughout.[5] Nor is this "procedural analysis" helpful in understanding the true bases of criminal liability: who, why, and when persons should be adjudged blameworthy and held criminally responsible for their actions. Accordingly, a "substantive interpretation" tends to focus on the requirement of blameworthiness. Criminal liability is imposed on a blameworthy actor who causes a prohibited harm

---

1 W. Wilson, "How Criminal Defences Work" in A. Reed and M. Bohlander (eds), *General Defences in Criminal Law* (London: Routledge 2014).

2 e.g. Singapore and Malaysia: see K.L. Koh, C.M.V. Clarkson and N.A. Morgan, *Criminal Law in Singapore and Malaysia: Text and Materials* (Singapore: Malayan Law Journal 1989), p.103.

3 *Bratty v Att-Gen of Northern Ireland* [1963] A.C. 386; [1961] 3 W.L.R. 965 HL.

4 Homicide Act 1957 s.2(2).

5 It is typically the role of the defence to raise potential defences. However, in such cases, this does not equate to a reversal of the burden of proof. Rather, to raise a defence, D has an *evidential* burden, whereby D must simply adduce some evidence of the relevant matter. Having done so, it is then for the prosecution to disprove one or more of the elements of the defence beyond a reasonable doubt. Exceptions to this rule include the defences of insanity and diminished responsibility. To raise these defences, the legal burden of proof is placed on D to establish the elements of the defence, but only to the civil standard. *Woolmington v DPP* [1935] A.C. 462; (1935) 51 T.L.R. 446 HL; see D. Ormerod and K. Laird, *Smith and Hogan's Criminal Law*, 16th edn (Oxford: OUP, 2020), pp.23–25.

or completes a prohibited act or omission. If D has a "general defence", they are not blameworthy and deserve to escape criminal liability. Accordingly, as Horder states, the way in which defences are defined and restricted "represents criminal law's contribution to society's commitment to the common good of upholding respect for the individual and general interests of persons" just as much as the definition and scope of offences.[6]

The term "general defences" is used to convey that such defences are available to all crimes. There are some defences that are not "general" but specific to particular offences: for example, loss of control and diminished responsibility are partial defences to murder.[7] Furthermore, it must be stressed that the title "general defences" is adopted purely for expository convenience. It is patently untrue that all these defences are available to all offences. For example, duress is not available for murder. Another problematic area is the extent to which the "general defences" are available to offences of strict liability.

9–002 General defences used to be listed as isolated sets of identifiable conditions or circumstances which prevented D from being convicted. However, throughout the years, several attempts have been made to bring defences within an overall theoretical framework. The chief advantage of this is that it enables a more rational analysis of the ways in which the law has developed or been restricted.[8] Defences have been broadly classified into two groups: those that provide a *justification* for D's conduct and those that *excuse* D's conduct.[9] However, commentators have reworked the category of excusatory defences and increasingly exclude from it those which amount to denials of responsibility. This latter group may be called *exemptions*.[10]

It must be stressed, however, that the classification of defences into groups is not watertight. This is true in a number of respects. First, the majority of general defences are without statutory basis. This means that the judiciary has great flexibility in determining their boundaries, and it appears that judges have less regard for the classifications than many academic commentators.[11] Second, the categories themselves are still being refined. As we shall see, it has become commonplace to distinguish between the categories on the basis that excuses focus upon the *actor* and justifications upon *actions*. But it can be argued that, in reality, the focus has to be upon both actors *and* actions for both justifications and excuses. Thus, the distinction between the categories is often blurred.[12] Finally, it may be difficult to locate a particular defence within just one category:

---

6 J. Horder, *Excusing Crime* (Oxford: OUP, 2004), p.2.

7 The partial defences to murder were discussed in Ch.7.

8 cf. W. Wilson, "The Structure of Defences" [2005] Crim. L.R. 108, where he argues that the best way of improving the doctrinal stability, coherence and consistency of defences is to focus upon a common template for the structure of defences rather than searching for an underlying unifying rationale for them.

9 The distinction was important before 1828 as, under the common law, a killer's goods were forfeited if the killing was excusable but not if it was justifiable. In 1828, forfeiture was abolished. See further, J.C. Smith, *Justification and Excuse in the Criminal Law* (Oxford: OUP, 1989), p.7. The revived interest in the distinction can largely be traced back to the publication in 1978 of G.P. Fletcher, *Rethinking Criminal Law* (Boston: Little, Brown, 1978).

10 Duff, discussed below, has suggested reworking defences to introduce a fourth category of "warranted" actions. R.A. Duff, *Answering for Crime: Responsibility and Liability in the Criminal Law* (Oxford: Hart Publishing, 2007).

11 See, e.g. Robert Walker LJ in *A (Children) (Conjoined Twins: Medical Treatment) (No.1), Re* [2001] Fam. 147; [2000] 4 All E.R. 961 at 1064 CA.

12 See further, C.M.V. Clarkson, "Necessary Action: A New Defence" [2004] Crim. L.R. 81 and contra W.M. Chan and A.P. Simester, "Duress, Necessity: How Many Defences?" (2005) 16 K.C.L.J. 121. Some commentators have found the classification so flawed that they have almost entirely abandoned it: see J.J. Child, A.P. Simester, J.R. Spencer, F. Stark and G.J. Virgo, *Simester and Sullivan's Criminal Law: Theory and Doctrine*, 8th edn (Oxford: Hart Publishing, 2022), pp.773–779.

> "In English law this is compounded by the law's cautious insistence on having a belt as well as braces: in general no excuse is accepted into the criminal law which is not also a partial justification, and no justification is accepted which is not also a partial excuse."[13]

PAUL ROBINSON, "CRIMINAL LAW DEFENSES: A SYSTEMATIC ANALYSIS" (1982) 82 COL. L. R. 199, 213, 221, 229:

> "[J]ustification defences are not alterations of the statutory definition of the harm sought to be prevented or punished by an offense. The harm caused by the justified behaviour remains a legally recognised harm which is to be avoided whenever possible. Under the special justifying circumstances, however, that harm is outweighed by the need to avoid an even greater harm or to further a great societal interest . . . **9-003**
>
> Excuses admit that the deed may be wrong, but excuse the actor . . .
>
> Justifications and excuses may seem similar in that both are general defenses which exculpate an actor because of his blamelessness . . . The conceptual distinction remains an important one, however. Justified conduct is correct behaviour which is encouraged or at least tolerated. In determining whether conduct is justified, the focus is on the *act*, not the actor. An excuse represents a legal conclusion that the conduct is wrong, undesirable, but that criminal liability is inappropriate because some characteristic of the actor vitiates society's desire to punish him. Excuses do not destroy blame . . . rather, they shift it from the actor to the excusing condition. The focus in excuses is on the *actor*. Acts are justified; actors are excused."

Robinson's analysis has been very influential, but, as we shall see, both his description of justifications and excuses has come under fire. At times, it is far from clear-cut whether a particular defence is justificatory or excusatory in nature. **9-004**

B. JUSTIFICATIONS

It is often stated that a defence is justificatory whenever it denies the objective wrongness of the act, and that: **9-005**

> ". . . a justification is a defence, affirming that the act, state of affairs or consequences are on balance, to be socially approved, or are matters about which society is neutral."[14]

---

13 J. Gardner, "Justifications and Reasons" in A.P. Simester and A.T.H. Smith (eds), *Harm and Culpability* (Oxford: Clarendon Press, 1996), p.122. See further, A. Simester, "On Justifications and Excuses" in L. Zedner and J. Roberts (eds), *Principles and Values in the Criminal Law and Criminal Justice: Essays in Honour of Andrew Ashworth* (Oxford: OUP, 2012).

14 G. Williams, "The Theory of Excuses" [1982] Crim. L.R. 732, 735.

However, other commentators decline to go this far.

John Gardner, "Justifications and Reasons" in A.P. Simester and A.T.H. Smith (eds), Harm and Culpability (1996), pp.107–108:

9–006 "In classifying some action as criminal, the law asserts that there are *prima facie* reasons against its performance—indeed reasons sufficient to make its performance *prima facie* wrongful. In providing a justificatory defence the law nevertheless concedes that one may sometimes have sufficient reason to perform the unlawful act, all things considered . . .

The reasons against the action, which are the reasons for its criminalisation, may all have been defeated in the final analysis. It may have been alright for the defendant to act against them, all things considered. But it does not mean that they dropped out of the picture. That a reason is defeated does not mean that it is undermined or cancelled. It still continues to exert its rational appeal. It may indeed be a matter of bitter regret or disappointment that, thanks to the reasons which justified one's action, one nevertheless acted against the *prima facie* reasons for avoiding that action. It may even be a matter of regret or disappointment to the criminal law. The law certainly need not welcome it. But by granting a defence the law concedes that any regret or disappointment must be tolerated . . . By granting a *justificatory* defence the law concedes that this is true by virtue of the fact that the defendant had, at the time of her *prima facie* wrongful action, sufficient reason to perform it."

9–007 According to this view, it is not enough that the action may be justified on a utilitarian, balancing of interests basis (as favoured, for example, by Robinson). It is necessary to explore the *reasons* D had for acting. In order to have a justificatory defence, D's (explanatory) reasons for acting must correspond to the (guiding) reasons that exist for such actions.[15] In other words, D's actual reasons for acting must be one of the accepted reasons for acting. As Tadros explains, justifications "operate where the defendant has acted for good reason".[16]

Bringing the reasons for acting into the concept of justification creates a dilemma for theorists. How should we respond to the person who acts for what they believe to be a good reason when, in fact, that reason does not exist? Duff gives the example of the person who deliberately breaks a window of a house in order to obtain entry so that she can help a person she believes (wrongly) to be unconscious (the person being simply asleep). Gardner would, at most, treat this as an excuse (if the mistake had been a reasonable one to make). Tadros would regard this still as a justification.[17] Duff has suggested that this should be described as "warranted" and, in so doing, proposes a fourth category of defences:

---

15 Gardner, "Justifications and Reasons" in Simester and Smith (eds), *Harm and Culpability* (1996), p.111.

16 V. Tadros, *Criminal Responsibility* (Oxford: OUP, 2005), p.265. Excuses, on the other hand, operate where D has not acted for good reason. Tadros agrees with Gardner that D must have not just been aware of the good reasons for acting but also must have been *motivated by them* in order for the reasons that the criminal prohibition should not be breached to be counterbalanced (pp.273–280).

17 Tadros, *Criminal Responsibility* (2005), pp.280–290.

> "[By] calling her action warranted we can do justice both to the ways in which it unlike straightforwardly 'justified' actions (because it is not right) and to the ways in which it is unlike excused actions (because it is warranted)."[18]

Whether one confines one's analysis to a balancing of interests or looks for underlying guiding reasons for permitting action, the following defences can be classified as justificatory in nature.

1. Self-defence

Under any of the above theories, self-defence provides a justification. The interests of the person attacked (D) are greater than those of the attacker (V). V's culpability in starting the fight 'tips the scales' in favour of D.[19] Furthermore: **9–008**

> ". . . a rule allowing defensive action tends to inhibit aggression, or at least to restrain its continuance, as a rule forbidding defensive action would tend to promote it."[20]

2. Necessity (where the harm threatened is greater than the harm caused)

Where a lesser evil is committed to prevent a greater evil (for example, criminal damage is caused to save the lives of 20 people), the interests of the latter outweigh the interests of the owner of the property. In the US, necessity is widely regarded as a paradigmatic example of justification.[21] **9–009**

3. Public authority

The use of force by the police, for example, in effecting an arrest, is justified, the superior interest being the enforcement of the law. The same applies to acts "to prevent or terminate crime" or "to prevent or terminate a breach of the peace".[22] **9–010**

4. Discipline/chastisement

Parents are, controversially, regarded as justified in using force not amounting to actual bodily harm against their children, the superior interest being to "promote the welfare of the minor" and to prevent or punish misconduct.[23] **9–011**

---

18 Duff, *Answering for Crime: Responsibility and Liability in the Criminal Law* (2007), p.276. Warrants are "close relatives" of justifications (p.266).

19 Fletcher, *Rethinking Criminal Law* (1978), p.858.

20 Williams, "The Theory of Excuses" [1982] Crim. L.R. 732, 739.

21 The American Law Institute, Model Penal Code s.3.02; N.Y. Penal Law s.35.05. The relationship between necessity and duress (by circumstances) is discussed below at paras 9–164–9–165.

22 Draft Criminal Code Bill 1989 cl.44(1) (Law Com. No.177).

23 The American Law Institute, Model Penal Code, Proposed Official Draft (1962) s.308(1)(a). That this is a "superior interest" has become deeply contested (*Tyrer v United Kingdom* (1978) Eur.Ct. Series A. Vol.26; *Campbell v United Kingdom* (7511/76) (1981) 3 E.H.R.R. 531).

5. Consent

9–012 Force against a person who has consented is justified, the superior interest being the value of human autonomy. Individuals are free and responsible agents, and respect must be given to their right to consent to the infliction of force against them. However, in certain cases, the interests of society prevail over any value attached to human autonomy, and thus consent may not be given to certain types of force (mainly force causing death or serious bodily harm).

C. EXCUSES

9–013 Duff suggests that "to offer an excuse is to admit that I got it wrong: I acted as I should not have acted".[24] A defence is thus excusatory when a wrongful, unjustified act has been committed, but because of the excusing circumstances, the wrongdoer is not morally to blame for committing that act.

Sanford H. Kadish, "Excusing Crime" (1987) 75 Cal. L. Rev. 257, 264:

9–014 "To blame a person is to express a moral criticism, and if the person's action does not deserve criticism, blaming him is a kind of falsehood and is, to the extent the person is injured by being blamed, unjust to him. It is this feature of our everyday moral practices that lies behind the law's excuses. Excuses, then, . . . represent no sentimental compromise with the demands of a moral code; they are, on the contrary, of the essence of a moral code."

9–015 According to this view, an excuse destroys blame. However, the theoretical basis upon which this is done is far from agreed. Tadros writes:

> "Two theories of excuses are currently popular in criminal law theory: the character theory and the capacity theory. In the former, the claim that the defendant makes is 'although I did it, I wasn't really myself'. In the latter, the claim is 'I did it but I couldn't have done otherwise. I had no real choice.'"[25]

While the capacity-based approach, centred on notions of voluntariness,[26] was influential during the latter part of the 20th century, it has become subject to criticism.[27] The debate has been divided as to whether a character-based analysis or a modified capacity-based analysis[28] offers the best

24 Duff, *Answering for Crime: Responsibility and Liability in the Criminal Law* (2007), p.287.

25 Tadros, *Criminal Responsibility* (2005), p.293.

26 See H.L.A. Hart, *Punishment and Responsibility* (Oxford: OUP, 1968).

27 See, e.g. N. Lacey, "Partial Defences to Homicide" in A. Ashworth and B. Mitchell (eds), *Rethinking Homicide Law* (New York: OUP, 2000), pp.115–117; G. Mousourakis, *Criminal Responsibility and Partial Excuses* (Aldershot: Ashgate, 1998), pp.48–58.

28 Horder, *Excusing Crime* (2004), p.108 acknowledges that no theory is free from difficulty but defends capacity theory as the most important (pp.123–137). He comments that the courts have veered between two capacity theories—subjective and objective versions (p.131). His preference is for an objective version of the capacity theory.

way of understanding the role excuses play in the criminal law. Gardner, for example, prefers the character theory.

John Gardner, "The Gist of Excuses" (1998) 1 Buffalo Criminal Law Review 575, 575–579:

"[T]he gist of an excuse is not that the action was 'out of character', in the sense of being a departure from what we have come to expect from the person whose action it is. Quite the contrary, in fact. The gist of an excuse . . . is precisely that the person with the excuse lived up to our expectations . . . [T]he question, for excusatory purposes, is obviously not whether the person claiming the excuse lived up to expectations in the predictive sense of being true to form . . . The question is whether that person lived up to expectations in the *normative* sense. Did she manifest as much resilience, or loyalty, or thoroughness, or presence of mind as a person in her situation should have manifested? In the face of terrible threats, for example, did this person show as much fortitude as someone in his situation could properly be asked to show? . . . The character standards which are relevant to these and other excuses are not the standards of our own characters, not even the standards of most people's characters, but rather the standards to which our characters should, minimally, conform."[29] **9–016**

This assessment does not involve making broad or sweeping judgements about D's character as a person. Instead, the judgement, based in practice upon reasonableness, involves a specific assessment of whether the reasons upon which the action was taken correspond to the character standards to which we should conform.[30] Central to Gardner's argument is the point that those who claim excuses are not denying "responsibility" for their actions. This needs clarification because the word "responsibility" is ambiguous. Those who plead excusatory defences are obviously hoping to avoid responsibility in the sense of liability. However, they are not denying that they were their actions, for which there is an intelligible, rational explanation.[31] Indeed, Gardner argues it is part of being a self-respecting person: **9–017**

". . . to be able to give an intelligible rational account of herself, to be able to show that her actions were the actions of someone who aspired to live up to the proper standards . . . She wants it to be the case that her actions were not truly wrongful, or if they were wrongful, that they were at any rate justified, or if they were not justified, that they were at any rate excused."[32]

---

29 Gardner further argues (Gardner, "Justifications and Reasons" in Simester and Smith (eds), *Harm and Culpability* (1996), pp.580–587) that one cannot distinguish the capacity to act, say with the character trait of courage, from acting courageously. One either acts courageously or not; there is no underlying capacity to act courageously that does or does not kick into operation. This view has been challenged by Tadros, *Criminal Responsibility* (2005), pp.294–297.

30 See also Duff, *Answering for Crime: Responsibility and Liability in the Criminal Law* (2007) (who favours a capacity based account of responsibility), where he argues that a person "offering an excuse does not claim that her action was itself reasonable; she admits that it was unreasonable: but she claims this was a reasonable unreasonableness . . . even a reasonable person . . . might have acted in that unreasonable way in that situation" (p.289).

31 See further, J. Gardner, "The Mark of Responsibility" (2003) 23 O.J.L.S. 157, 161 where he argues that responsibility in "the basic sense is none other than an ability to offer justifications and excuses . . . It is exactly what it sounds like: response-ability, an ability to respond".

32 J. Gardner, "The Gist of Excuses" (1998) 1 *Buffalo Criminal Law Review* 575, 590. This idea that there is a normative priority to defences has been criticised but has also been answered by Gardner in "Reply to Critics" in *Offences and Defences: Selected Essays in the Philosophy of the*

It has been suggested that Gardner's explanation either leaves the category of excuses extremely limited or, indeed, that he is mistaken about the gist of excuses.[33] Other "defences", such as involuntary intoxication, fall outside this analysis, but some commentators have argued that they ought to provide an excuse.[34]

VICTOR TADROS, "THE CHARACTERS OF EXCUSE" (2001) 21 O.J.L.S. 495, 498:

9–018 "In fact, I would suggest that there is no single gist of excuses. The criminal law is supervised by a multitude of principles. In arguing that one has an excuse, one attempts to show that whilst one's action was wrongful, the principles of the criminal law would not be served by imposing criminal liability. Excuses, then, mop up where exemptions, offence definitions and justifications would lead to convictions in inappropriate cases . . . [It] may be because the defendant underwent a fundamental, and reasonable, shift in character before committing the wrongful act. Or it may be because the defendant only exhibited a vice that is an inappropriate target for criminal liability. Or it may be for some other reason, say because the defendant was, beyond her control, placed in a situation in which she was deprived of a fair opportunity to make her behaviour conform to the criminal law. In my view, that is as much as can be said for the gist of excuses."

9–019 Despite the continued debate surrounding the underlying rationale of excuses, it is possible to identify those defences which, broadly speaking, can be classified as excuses.

1. Mistake

9–020 Mistakes are typically classified as an excuse. Generally, the rules relating to mistake are simply an application of the principle that the prosecution must prove that D possessed the relevant mens rea. As such, this "defence" is simply a denial of the offence elements. Therefore, mistakes are only relevant if they relate to an issue that the prosecution must prove to establish D's liability.

There is an oft-cited saying that "ignorance of the law is no excuse". This, for the most part, is true. Traditionally, mistakes as to criminal law have been regarded as generally irrelevant. This is because if D mistakenly believes their conduct to be lawful when it is, in fact, unlawful, D will have no defence where D has committed the actus reus with the requisite mens rea; there is no requirement in English criminal law that D has knowledge of the relevant criminal law that renders their conduct unlawful.[35] Thus, if D (a tourist) commits an offence in England that is not an offence in their homeland, their mistake as to the lawfulness of the conduct provides no defence.[36] For the most serious criminal offences, the harshness of this rule is lessened since they are also widely recognised as moral "wrongs".

Criminal Law (2007), pp.269–276. See also, C. Bennett, "Excuses, Justifications and the Normativity of Expressive Behaviour" (2012) 32 O.J.L.S. 563.

33 Tadros, *Criminal Responsibility* (2005), p.293. This is a revision of the views Tadros expressed in "The Characters of Excuse" (2001) 21 O.J.L.S. 495 due to the fact that Tadros now characterises D who acts under a reasonable mistake as justified. This leaves very little scope for the category of excuses as developed by Gardner.

34 G.R. Sullivan, "Making Excuses" in Simester and Smith (eds), *Harm and Culpability* (1996).

35 *Churchill v Walton* [1967] 2 A.C. 224; [1967] 2 W.L.R. 682 HL.

36 *R. v Esop* 173 E.R. 203; (1836) 7 Car. & P. 456.

However, this does mean that D might fall foul of a regulatory offence of which they had no knowledge. There is a limited exception to this rule provided by the Statutory Instruments Act 1946 s.3(2). This provides that it is a defence to a crime created by a statutory instrument if the instrument has not been published and reasonable steps have not been taken to bring its contents to the notice of the public or the D.[37]

This approach has been criticised. Ashworth, for example, argues that the Government should make the criminal law clearer and more accessible as to enable citizens to guide their conduct.[38] That this is a fundamental constitutional principle was echoed in *Rimmington*,[39] where Lord Bingham held that under European Convention on Human Rights (ECHR) art.7, "the law must be adequately accessible—and an individual must have an indication of the legal rules applicable in a given case". Similarly, in *Christian*,[40] Lord Woolf stated that it was a "requirement of the rule of law" that persons must "be given actual or at least constructive notice of what the law requires". He added, however, that the onus is on citizens to ascertain the law rather than on the State to bring the law to every citizen's attention.

With the vast array of regulatory offences, many of which apply strict liability, the constantly changing and varying standards of permissible conduct, and the law often being unclear and uncertain even to lawyers, do we necessarily blame D if they make a mistake as to the criminal law? The paradigmatic blameworthy D is one who has culpably brought about the prohibited result or state of affairs and has acted in open defiance of the law. With mistake of law, there is no such flouting of the rules. Bearing in mind that one is not justifying the wrong done but merely excusing the actor, an excuse should only be available if the mistake was a *reasonable* one. In such circumstances, there must surely be a strong case for exempting such an actor from criminal liability.[41]

2. Duress

Duress is generally treated as an excuse rather than a justification. Some cases have identified the defence as hinging upon the morally involuntary response of the actor; in other words, D lacked a fair opportunity to conform to the law. It may also be explained by reference to Gardner's gist of excuses. It is not currently open to a D charged with murder or attempted murder to plead duress—although there have been proposals to reform the law in this respect.[42] **9–021**

3. Loss of control

The partial defence of loss of control, although having some features of a justificatory defence, provides D with a partial excuse for the killing of another. To satisfy the defence, the current law requires that D lost control, which can be categorised as an excusatory element.[43] One of the attractions of pleading **9–022**

37 cf. A. Ashworth, "Excusable Mistake of Law" [1974] Crim. L.R. 652.

38 A. Ashworth, "Ignorance of the criminal law, and duties to avoid it" (2011) 74 M.L.R. 1, 24–26.

39 *R. v Rimmington (Anthony)* [2005] UKHL 63; [2006] 1 A.C. 459.

40 *Christian v Queen, The* [2006] UKPC 47; [2007] 2 A.C. 400 PC.

41 Ashworth, "Ignorance of the criminal law, and duties to avoid it" (2011) 74 M.L.R. 1.

42 Law Com. No.304, *Murder, Manslaughter and Infanticide* (2006), para.6.21.

43 For a complete discussion of this partial defence, see Ch.7 paras 7–071–7–099. Additionally, the extent to which this defence is an excuse or justification is more fully discussed in those sections.

loss of control, as opposed to diminished responsibility, is that it gives self-respecting Ds the opportunity to give an intelligible rational account of their actions rather than denying responsibility.

4. Intoxication

9-023 Whether intoxication should be regarded as a "defence" at all is a problematic issue that was considered in Ch.3. The courts very frequently refer to it in such terms. Where D lacks mens rea because of voluntary intoxication, they will be acquitted of crimes requiring specific intent but will be convicted of lesser crimes of basic intent. Looked at in this way, intoxication appears to constitute a partial excuse.[44]

5. Necessity (where the harm threatened is equal to the harm caused)

9-024 As shall be seen, it is unlikely that English law affords a defence in such situations. Necessity or "duress of circumstances", as it has become known, is only available as a defence when D acts "proportionately in order to avoid a threat of death or serious injury"[45] and, as "duress of circumstances", is not a defence to a charge of murder. Accordingly, the only situations where the defence could conceivably be available in English law are where the harm threatened is equal to the harm caused. For example, where D causes serious injury to avoid a threat of serious harm. In such cases, the defence cannot be regarded as justificatory as the harm being caused is not less than the harm being threatened, but such a defence might be regarded as an excuse. We can understand the predicament of an actor who claims to have had no real choice.

D. EXEMPTIONS

9-025 While the gist of excuses may remain contested, there has been a growing acceptance of the view that excuses are not denials of responsibility. There must be a basic responsibility for one's actions for them to be amenable to excuse. However, there are other situations where the actor bears no basic responsibility for his actions. This occurs where D lacks practical reasoning skills and where the actions are not amenable to intelligible rational explanation. Defences in such situations (previously categorised as excuses) are now increasingly being regarded as *exemptions*:

> "[T]he focus on making sense of people's actions in the light of their reasons rightly brings to the surface the important point that those whose reasoning can't be made sense of in this way, whether because of profound mental illness or infancy or sleepwalking . . . are not responsible for their actions and therefore need no excuses for what they do."[46]

---

44 Some commentators have focused upon the particular problem of "involuntary" intoxication where D still has mens rea to construct a variety of arguments concerning the role of defences. While such Ds would currently be found guilty, Sullivan has argued that a defence of blamelessness ought to be available, conjoining a lapse from previous good character with circumstances of destabilisation: Sullivan, "Making Excuses" in Simester and Smith (eds), *Harm and Culpability* (1996), p.131. See further, Tadros, *Criminal Responsibility* (2005), pp.297–302; and A.P. Simester, "Intoxication is Never a Defence" [2009] Crim. L.R. 3, where the author argues that intoxication should be conceived of as a completely different doctrine that imposes constructive liability upon offenders.

45 *R. v Martin (Colin)* (1989) 88 Cr. App. R. 343 at 346; (1989) 153 J.P. 231 CA.

46 Gardner, "The Gist of Excuses" (1998) 1 *Buffalo Criminal Law Review* 575, 589. See also Duff, *Answering for Crime: Responsibility and Liability in the Criminal Law* (2007), pp.284–292.

A number of defences operate as exemptions.

1. Insanity

D who, because of a disease of the mind, cannot appreciate the nature and quality of their act, or cannot appreciate that it is wrong, lacks the practical reasoning skills to be found responsible for what they have done. On this basis, insanity ought to act as an exemption. However, as we shall see, the wording of the *M'Naghten* Rules tends to suggest otherwise.[47] **9–026**

2. Diminished responsibility

> "Diminished responsibility occupies the peculiar position of a 'partial exemption'—a position which is closely related to the specific context of the mandatory life sentence for murder."[48] **9–027**

It is, however, based on the notion that the actions were unreasonable:

> "The whole point of the diminished responsibility defence is that it depends on the unreasonableness of the defendant's reactions, i.e. their unamenability to intelligible rational explanation."[49]

3. Automatism

There is some dispute as to whether automatism is a defence or whether the need for voluntariness is part of the actus reus requirement.[50] What is clear is that automatism shares the same rationale as other conditions which give rise to exemption from criminal liability. **9–028**

4. Lack of age

Very young children are not regarded as sufficiently responsible to engage in practical reasoning and, accordingly, are exempt from criminal liability when they commit a wrong.[51] **9–029**

E. SIGNIFICANCE OF DISTINCTIONS

What is the point of the theoretical distinctions discussed above? For Wilson, the varying rationales that have been proffered for different general defences tend to hinder our comprehension of how they should **9–030**

47 See para.9–188.

48 Lacey, "Partial Defences to Homicide" in Ashworth and Mitchell (eds), *Rethinking Homicide Law* (2000), pp.119–120.

49 Gardner, "The Gist of Excuses" (1998) 1 *Buffalo Criminal Law Review* 575, 591. This view is challenged by Horder, *Excusing Crime* (2004), pp.153 onwards.

50 See also K.J.M. Smith and W. Wilson, "Impaired Voluntariness and Criminal Responsibility: Reworking Hart's Theory of Excuses—the English Judicial Response" (1993) 13 O.J.L.S. 69, 70–74; J. Child and A. Reed, "Automatism is never a defence" (2014) 65 (2) N.I.L.Q. 167.

51 See further, Tadros, *Criminal Responsibility* (2005), p.372.

operate in criminal law; thereby inhibiting the delivery of criminal justice.[52] However, for other commentators, the distinction between justification, excuse and exemption is regarded as the key to defining the parameters of each of the general defences and, in turn, the reach of the criminal law. Tadros has described these distinctions as "central to the moral architecture of the criminal law".[53] For example, approaching duress as an excuse and not as a justification informs one as to how its rules should be framed. Its importance as a theoretical guide, therefore, cannot be overestimated. However, there is a practical utility as well. The distinction between defences has the following important consequences:

(a) Whether one is entitled to resist conduct for which the aggressor has a defence or entitled to assist the aggressor depends upon whether the aggressor's defence is justificatory or excusatory in nature.[54]

Paul Robinson, "Criminal Law Defenses: A Systematic Analysis" (1982) 82 Col. L. R. 199, 274–275:

9-031 "Where an aggressor has a justification defence, the proper rule is clear: justified aggression should never be lawfully subject to resistance or interference. When conduct is deemed justified, it creates, by definition, a net benefit to society. The owner of a field should not be allowed to resist one who would burn it to stop a spreading fire, and others should be encouraged to assist, and not permitted to interfere.

An excused [or exempted] aggressor, on the other hand, should be subject to lawful resistance. That is, the victim of the psychotic attacker should be able lawfully to defend himself and to have others lawfully assist him in such defense. While the aggressor may be ultimately blameless, the conduct is clearly harmful. All required elements of the offense are satisfied and no justification exists."

9-032 Similar principles apply to accessories to crime. Thus, in *Quick and Paddison,*[55] the principal offender had a defence of automatism—an "exemption" under the above analysis. Paddison assisted him in his aggression and was held liable as an accessory. Had Quick's defence been justificatory in nature, say, acting reasonably to defend himself, then Paddison would have been entitled to assist him.

(b) When conduct is justified, some commentators argue that it is, in effect, "approved" of or, at least tolerated, and there is, arguably, no need to try to prevent such conduct from re-occurring. Where conduct is merely excused or exempted, however, society might wish to protect itself from the repetition of such conduct and might wish to resort to coercive remedies against D despite their acquittal. Thus, a successful defence of insanity can lead to commitment in a secure mental hospital. Lack of age is a defence to a criminal charge, but separate care proceedings may follow under the Children Act 1989. Diminished responsibility exempts the actor from liability for murder but not for manslaughter,

52 Wilson, "How Criminal Defences Work" in Reed and Bohlander (eds), *General Defences in Criminal Law* (2014), p.22.

53 Tadros, *Criminal Responsibility* (2005), p.266.

54 But see Tadros who argues "that there is no clear relationship between the fact that D has a justification defence and the rights of third parties to assist D. Where D reasonably believes that a jogger is a mugger, in order for D2 to be justified in assisting D, D2 must also reasonably believe that the jogger is a mugger". (See Tadros, *Criminal Responsibility* (2005), p.291.)

55 *R. v Quick (William George); R. v Paddison (William)* [1973] Q.B. 910; [1973] 3 W.L.R. 26 CA.

enabling the court to take appropriate steps in relation to D. Non-insane automatism, on the other hand, enables D to escape all coercive measures, but even here, there are suggestions that some new form of special verdict should be returned in such cases, enabling a court to exercise some supervision over such a person to prevent recurrence of the involuntary action. The remaining excuses, such as duress, present little threat of repetition of the conduct, and therefore, there is no need to resort to coercive measures, but, in general, a finding of an exemption (as opposed to a justification) does alert one to the possibility of considering some form of restriction, whether criminal or civil, over the D.

(c) Whether a defence is justificatory or excusatory may affect the law's response to Ds who claim to have made a mistake. Thus, the law's response at present seems to be that those who make a mistake in relation to a *justification*, for example, self-defence, need only have made a genuine mistake. On the other hand, those who make a mistake in relation to an *excuse*, for example, duress, must have made a reasonable mistake to escape liability.[56]

(d) Where conduct is justified, some commentators suggest that the law, for conduct in those circumstances, is effectively amended.[57] A precedent is generated that others, in similar circumstances, may act in the same manner. Excuses and exemptions, on the other hand, do not constitute exceptions or modifications to the law. They simply involve an assessment that, in the particular circumstances, it would be unjust to hold a particular actor accountable for their actions.

The moral message sent by an excuse, or an exemption, is different from that sent by justifications. This difference may be made clearer by the development of "special" verdicts. The case for this is, obviously, at its strongest in relation to exemptions. If, however, one takes the view that excuses, such as duress, are borderline justifications, the argument for a "special" verdict is very weak. Somebody who, according to Gardner's analysis, has lived up to the character standards of their role has done all that could reasonably be expected in the circumstances and should be entitled to a full and unqualified acquittal. **9–033**

We are now in a position to examine the various defences.

II. Consent

A. INTRODUCTION

"Consent" is a core concept in legal and moral philosophy. It is sometimes claimed as possessing "moral magic" which can transform prima facie unlawful conduct into entirely legitimate (and even condoned) conduct; "trespass into dinner parties . . . and rape into lovemaking".[58] Feinberg offers a **9–034**

56 See para.9–020.

57 As we have seen, other commentators, such as Gardner, would not subscribe to this view.

58 H. Hurd, "Was the frog prince sexually molested?: A review of Peter Westen's 'The logic of consent'" (2005) 103 *University of Michigan Law Review* 1329.

similar, but comparatively modest, account of consent expressed through his *volenti* maxim: *volenti non fit injuria* ("to one who consents, no wrong is done").[59] One interpretation of this maxim is that once V consents to D's harming of them, V forfeits their right after the fact to complain that D's conduct wronged them. Thus, if V asks D to punch them, V cannot complain once they have been punched. Although V may not have *moral* standing to complain against D, this does not mean that D has done nothing *legally* wrong.

English criminal law recognises the normative and legal force of consent to harm in two ways. First, some offences are defined in such a manner that they can only be committed without V's consent. Rape is the paradigmatic example of this; the actus reus of the offence requires penile penetration of the vagina, anus, or mouth of a person *who does not consent to it*.[60] Therefore, if D engages in *consensual* penetration, they do not plead consent as a defence but claim a denial of proof—that the actus reus of the offence has not been committed.[61] Secondly, because most offences are not defined with an "absence of defence" criterion within their actus reus, V's consent may, in some circumstances, provide D with a defence, absolving them from liability. In such cases, D admits that they have committed the full actus reus of the offence but that V's consent justifies the wrong they would otherwise be committing.

9–035 In the circumstances where consent operates as a defence, as opposed to a denial of proof, it has the effect of *justifying* D's conduct. A justificatory defence can be explained in terms of a superior interest being upheld; in relation to consent, that superior interest is human autonomy. The foundation of criminal law is the concept of responsibility, and here, it finds expression in the freedom of people to consent to what would otherwise be a criminal offence. English criminal law, however, does not always take this liberal stance.[62] In fact, the law frequently disregards V's sovereignty of choice and offers relatively little space for autonomous decision-making.

Throughout this chapter, we will evaluate the limits that are placed on this freedom to consent and whether the current position pays sufficient regard to individualistic notions of personal autonomy. This analysis will focus predominantly on consent to non-fatal injury; consent to sexual conduct was discussed in Ch.6.

B. THE RATIONALE OF CONSENT AS A DEFENCE

9–036 An attempt to understand the basis upon which, and the extent to which, consent currently operates as a defence involves consideration of the theories of liberalism, paternalism, and legal moralism. Those theories were considered in Ch.1 and will not be explored again here. However, two final insights may be presented.

59 J. Feinberg, *Harm to others* (Oxford: OUP, 1984), p.115.
60 Sexual Offences Act 2003 s.1.
61 *DPP v Morgan* [1976] A.C. 182; [1975] 2 W.L.R. 913 HL.
62 See Ch.1 paras 1–016–1–028.

George P. Fletcher, Rethinking Criminal Law (1978), pp.770–771:

"The principle that individuals are free and responsible agents informs the analysis of consent . . . Once accepted, the value of autonomy does not lend itself to being offset by competing social interests. So far as the rationale of consent is that individuals should be free to waive their rights, this capacity of waiver is not a contingent value, subject to repeated balancing against the opposing array of interests. **9–037**

There is some evidence that at the fringes, however, the principle of autonomy gives way to competing social values. The prevailing view in Western legal systems is that the individual has the right to take his own life or to torture himself, but he does not have the right to authorise others to do the killing or to perform a sado-masochistic beating. That there is a personal right to suffer in these cases indicates that the rationale for limiting personal autonomy is not a paternalistic governmental posture toward the victim's injuring himself. If the issue were paternalism, the government should employ sanctions as well against suicide and other forms of self-destruction.

A more convincing account of the distinction between self-injury and consenting to injury by others derives from the danger of implicating other persons in dangerous forms of conduct. The individual who kills or mutilates himself might affect the well-being of family and friends, but this result depends upon the actor's relationships with other people. In contrast, the self-destructive individual who induces another person to kill or to mutilate him implicates the latter in the violation of a significant social taboo. The person carrying out the killing or the mutilation crosses the threshold into a realm of conduct that, the second time, might be more easily carried out. And the second time, it might not be particularly significant whether the victim consents or not. Similarly, if someone is encouraged to inflict a sado-masochistic beating on a consenting victim, the experience of inflicting the beating might loosen the actor's inhibitions against sadism in general."

David Feldman, Civil Liberties and Human Rights in England and Wales, 2nd edn (2002), pp.715–716:

"[T]o imply . . . that carefully controlled, planned, and consensual violence as part of a sexual encounter has no redeeming social value, but to accept that boxing or rough and undisciplined play have social value which justifies the infliction of bodily harm, turns reality on its head. The object of respecting consent to the rough and tumble of sport (like consent to medical treatment) is primarily to protect the individual interests of the participants as they perceive them, rather than to advance any public interest. It is a recognition of individual autonomy, the right of individuals of sufficient understanding to make their own decisions about what is good for them. In principle, this should apply equally to people's sexual preferences. Indeed, it is hard to see how the interest (whether public or private) in allowing people to express their sexuality, which forms a fundamental part of people's personality, could be less important than the interest in allowing people to pursue sports. Sport is fun, but sex, for many people, is more than fun: it is a form of self-expression." **9–038**

9–039 Even if one concedes that, in certain cases, consent ought not to provide a complete defence, do we blame such Ds *as much* as those who commit similar harms against their Vs who are *not* consenting? Even if consent does not provide a complete justification, ought it not to provide a partial defence so as to reduce D's level of criminal liability and/or punishment?

These theoretical matters aside, we must now turn to the posited legal doctrine. As such, the remainder of this section on consent addresses three distinct issues: capacity to consent, the nature and level of harm that can be legally consented to, and law reform.

C. VALIDITY OF CONSENT

9–040 Before we consider the circumstances and harms for which consent is available as a defence, it is first necessary to consider whether V has provided *effective* consent to bodily injury. The principal issues to address in this context are V's mental capacity to consent, the degree of knowledge required for V to be capable of issuing effective consent, the effect D's fraud has on the effectiveness of V's apparent consent, and whether duress or improper pressure from D or another vitiates V's consent. We will consider each in turn.

1. Capacity

9–041 In order to provide consent, V must have sufficient capacity to give consent. This requires that V must possess a sufficiently mature capacity to understand the nature of the interaction and degree of harm that D (and or V) proposes.

Capacity may be lacking because of V's infancy, physical or mental condition or acute intoxication. In determining whether V has the capacity to consent, the courts are encouraged by legislation to evaluate V's capacity in an individualistic and decision-specific manner,[63] thus avoiding generalised status-based tests of the kind historically employed in *Burrell v Harmer*.[64] The Mental Capacity Act 2005, although not binding on criminal courts, cautions that capacity should not be inferred from "(a) a person's age or appearance, or (b) a condition of his, or an aspect of his behaviour, which might lead others to make unjustified assumptions about his capacity".

To illustrate this individualistic approach, let us consider the relationship between V's age and capacity to consent. All things equal, V can consent to medical treatment at the age of 16.[65] However, this does not mean that a younger person is unable to consent to medical treatment (or the causation of bodily harm). In *Gillick*, the House of Lords held that a person under 16 may consent to treatment "when the child achieves a sufficient understanding and intelligence to enable him or her to understand fully what is proposed".[66]

---

63 Mental Capacity Act 2005 s.1.

64 *Burrell v Harmer* [1967] Crim. L.R. 169; (1966) 116 N.L.J. 1658 Div Ct.

65 Family Law Reform Act 1969 s.8.

66 *Gillick v West Norfolk and Wisbech AHA* [1986] A.C. 112 per Lord Scarman at 189; [1985] 3 W.L.R. 830 HL. This test is approved by the Law Commission in Consultation Paper No.139, *Consent in the Criminal Law* (1995), para.5.21. See also *R. (on the application of Axon) v Secretary of State for Health* [2006] EWHC 37 (Admin); [2006] Q.B. 539.

However, the application of this principle has not been straightforward. There has been an asymmetry between consent to medical treatment and refusal of treatment cases. A number of family law cases have undermined this "*Gillick*-competence" test by holding that, although a *Gillick*-competent child may consent to medical treatment, the courts have the power to override a treatment refusal, particularly in cases where treatment is life-sustaining.[67] Thus, in *Re W*, a 16-year-old child suffering from anorexia nervosa refused medical treatment that would save her life. It was held that the court had the power to override her wishes even though she was "*Gillick*-competent".[68] Arguably, this conflict is reconcilable. In *Gillick*, the overriding interest was ensuring that sexually active girls under the age of 16 were able to obtain contraception, even if the parents or guardians were not involved in the decision-making process. However, in *Re W*, the overriding interest was ensuring that a patient with depression and anorexia nervosa received treatment, despite her refusal, in circumstances where one of the clinical manifestations of her illness was a desire not to be treated. As such, while the consequences of accepting treatment are (typically) good, the consequences of refusing treatment can be fatal.

2. Informed consent

In addition to the requirement that V has the requisite capacity to consent, V must also be *informed* as to the nature of the interaction and degree of harm. As a general proposition, the more serious the harm, the more knowledge is required for consent to be effective. The leading authority on this matter is *Konzani*, which involved D transmitting HIV to three uninformed sexual partners; the court held that: **9–042**

> "If an individual who knows that he is suffering from the HIV virus conceals this stark fact from his sexual partner, the principle of her personal autonomy is not enhanced if he is exculpated when he recklessly transmits the HIV virus to her through consensual sexual intercourse. On any view, the concealment of this fact from her almost inevitably means that she is deceived. Her consent is not properly informed, and she cannot give an informed consent to something of which she is ignorant . . ."[69]

Following *Konzani*, where V has consented to the central activity (e.g. sexual conduct), and the question becomes whether V has consented to the associated risks (e.g. transmission of HIV), three categories of case can be distinguished to inform whether D's conduct is lawful. First, where D has no knowledge of the associated risk of engaging in the central activity, D is not liable should the associated risk manifest in harm. For example, in circumstances where D does not know they are HIV-positive, yet inadvertently transmits it to V. Secondly, where D is aware of the associated risk and informs V of the necessary facts before engaging in the central activity, V's informed consent as to the associated risk is legally effective, and no liability will result if the risk manifests in harm. Finally, where D is aware of the

67 *R (A Minor) (Wardship: Consent to Treatment), Re* [1992] Fam. 11; [1991] 3 W.L.R. 592 CA.

68 *W (A Minor) (Medical Treatment: Court's Jurisdiction), Re* [1993] Fam. 64; [1992] 3 W.L.R. 758 CA. See further, *R (A Minor) (Wardship: Consent to Treatment), Re* [1992] Fam. 11; *J, Re* [1992] 3 W.L.R. 521. Once minors reach the age of 16, the Family Law Reform Act 1969 s.8 provides that their consent to medical treatment "shall be as effective" as if they were an adult. However, s.8(3) provides that this does not render ineffective "any consent which would have been effective if this section had not been enacted". The section is also silent in relation to treatment *refusals*.

69 *R. v Konzani (Reston)* [2005] EWCA Crim 706 at [23] (Judge LJ); [2005] 2 Cr. App. R. 14.

associated risk and fails to inform V of the necessary facts before engaging in the central activity, D may be liable if the risk manifests in harm.

3. Consent procured by fraud

9–043 In order for V's consent to be legally effective, it must not be procured by fraud. This can manifest in one of two ways.

First, fraud may arise when D deceives V as to their identity. If D obtains V's consent by impersonating another, V's consent is ineffective. As a general rule, this is straightforward. However, things become more complicated when D deceives V as to their qualifications or characteristics. To illustrate this, consider the facts of *Melin*.[70] D administered Botox injections to two women, having falsely told them he had medical qualifications. Both women subsequently suffered serious consequential injuries. The Court of Appeal held that D was impersonating a doctor and, therefore, deceiving them as to his identity, which vitiated their conduct. This can be distinguished from the earlier case of *Richardson*.[71] In this case, D (a registered dentist) performed surgery despite being suspended. D did not inform her patients that she was suspended. The patients said that they would not have consented to the surgery had they known this information. Despite this, the Court of Appeal held that as there had been no active deception as to either D's identity or the nature of the act, only a deception as to D's entitlement to perform the act, the patients' consent was not vitiated. Unfortunately, the outcome in *Richardson* is problematic; D was surely under a duty to inform her patients as to her qualification and certification status. If so, it would have been preferable for the court to find that when D lacks the entitlement to carry out a medical procedure, there is both a deception as to the nature or quality of the act *and* as to D's identity.[72] While *Melin* does not reject the approach in *Richardson*, it does clarify that if D's deception is passive and or does not play a causal role in V's consent, V's consent remains legally effective. However, if D's deception is active and brings about V's consent, V's consent is ineffectual.

Secondly, fraud may arise when D deceives V as to the nature of the act that is consented to. Here, V's consent may be ineffectual if D deceives V as to the core nature of the act. However, the courts have construed the remit of this deception very narrowly.[73] For example, in *Dica*,[74] where D infected two sexual partners with HIV, the Court of Appeal held that D's non-disclosure as to his sexual health status had not deceived V as to the nature of the sexual act, and thus D had not committed rape.[75]

---

70 *R. v Melin (Ozan)* [2019] EWCA Crim 557; [2019] Q.B. 1063.

71 *R. v Richardson (Diane)* [1999] Q.B. 444; [1998] 2 Cr. App. R. 200 CA.

72 This approach was adopted in *R. v Tabassum (Naveed)* [2000] 2 Cr. App. R. 328; [2000] Lloyd's Rep. Med. 404 CA.

73 e.g. see the facts of the Australian case of *R. v Mobilio* [1991] 1 V.R. 339. However, it is important to note that this decision has been reversed following the Crimes Act 1958 s.36(g), which provides that there is no consent where a person "mistakenly believes that the act is for medical or hygienic purposes".

74 *R. v Dica (Mohammed)* [2004] EWCA Crim 1103; [2004] Q.B. 1257 CA.

75 However, the court held that D had deceived V as to the nature of the associated risk of infection and was therefore guilty of inflicting GBH contrary OAPA 1861 s.20. See para.5–048.

4. Duress

Finally, V's consent will not be legally effective if it is gained by duress (e.g. by threats from D). For example, if V consents to a beating by D in order to avoid greater harm, the threat of greater harm may vitiate V's consent. This might also arise where D's threats are non-criminal (e.g. a threat to be dismissed from employment[76] or to bring a prosecution[77]). Similarly, duress may be implied from the relationship between the parties, for example between a teacher and a young pupil.[78] As was seen in Ch.6 on sexual offences, submission does not equate to consent.[79] **9–044**

Unlike the common law defence of duress (discussed below), the precise requirements for duress to vitiate consent are unclear. While it must be demonstrated that D's threats *caused* V to consent to the activity in question, it is unclear whether the threats must be such that they would have caused a person of reasonable firmness to succumb to the violence (objective test) or whether it is infused with an element of subjectivity if (say) D knew that V was particularly vulnerable due to their age, pregnancy, or physical or mental conditions.

D. CONSENT TO BODILY HARM: A CATEGORY-BASED APPROACH

In what circumstances does V's factual consent to D's conduct, which causes V bodily harm, provide D with a defence? The answer to this question is not simple. Broadly speaking, the appellate courts have considered both the seriousness of the harm caused to V and the circumstances in which the harm was caused to determine whether consent should be available as a defence. In this context, "harm" can be defined as any setback to V's interests, and the greater the harm caused, the more D must have some justification (in terms of social utility). Stephen J in *Coney* held: **9–045**

> "The principle as to consent seems to me to be this: When one person is indicted for inflicting personal injury upon another, the consent of the person who sustains the injury is no defence to the person who inflicts the injury, if the injury is of such a nature, or is inflicted under such circumstances, that its infliction is injurious to the public as well as to the person injured."[80]

Thus, if D kills a person at that other's request, it will still be murder;[81] to intentionally cause death is considered to be the gravest of all public wrongs. This is the case even where V's request to be killed by

76 *R. v McCoy* 1953 (2) S.A. 4. In this South African case, V (a member of cabin crew) was threatened by D (a manager of an airways corporation) that she could accept either a caning or loss of pay for failing to fasten her safety belt during landing. Rather than forfeit her pay, she reluctantly agreed to be caned. The court held that D's threat vitiated her consent.

77 *State v Volschenk* 1968 (2) PH. H. 283 (D). In another South African case, the court held that the threat by D (a policeman) of malicious prosecution for an imprisonable offence would vitiate V's consent to sexual intercourse so that D could be guilty of rape.

78 *R. v Nichol* 168 E.R. 720; (1807) Russ. & Ry. 130.

79 *R. v Ali (Yasir Ifran)* [2015] EWCA Crim 1279; [2015] 2 Cr. App. R. 33.

80 *R. v Coney* (1882) 8 Q.B.D. 534.

81 Or, possibly, manslaughter if D is able to plead diminished responsibility. See also *R. (on the application of Nicklinson) v Ministry of Justice* [2013] EWCA Civ 961 at [25]; [2014] 1 F.C.R. 316; *R. v Gnango (Armel)* [2011] UKSC 59; [2012] 1 A.C. 827 at [53] at [59] and [69]–[71]; *Airedale NHS Trust v Bland* [1993] A.C. 789 per Lord Mustill at 892–893; [1993] 2 W.L.R. 316 HL. In *Nicklinson*, the Court of Appeal rejected an argument based on necessity. In Stark's view, *Nicklinson* should have been argued on the ground that the defence of consent would be

D is both voluntary and forthcoming. One such infamous example of this is Armin Meiwes, dubbed the "Rotenburg Hannibal", who killed and ate Bernd Brandes for sexual gratification. Brandes' consent and desire for Meiwes to "dine from my live body" failed to provide Meiwes with a defence to a charge of murder.[82]

9–046 Consent may, however, be available as a defence to a non-fatal offence against the person. At the bottom of the non-fatal offences hierarchy, V's consent is relevant to a charge of common assault or battery, which involves only minimal or no injury.[83] For these offences, the "absence of consent" is an essential criterion that must be proven to establish D's liability. As such, D may adduce evidence of V's consent as a denial of proof of the offence elements. This analysis ensures that those who engage in behaviour that is not intended to be criminalised (e.g. a handshake or sex) do not require a defence for their conduct to be considered lawful.

However, what if D intends only to cause V minor harm (battery), with V's consent to that level of harm, but in fact causes actual or serious harm? On one view, D is liable where the greater harm is caused; Lord Lane, in *Att-Gen's Reference (No.6 of 1980)*, held that it was not in the public interest that people should try to or should cause each other bodily harm (for no good reason) and that it was an assault if actual bodily harm was intended and/or caused.[84] However, following *Meachen*,[85] this no longer represents the current position. In this case, the Court of Appeal held that where D causes V actual or serious injury but does not intend or foresee the risk of injury, V's consent to the underlying battery provides D with a defence. V's consent operates as a denial of proof for the actus reus of battery, and, consequently, there is no unlawful battery to construct liability for an assault occasioning actual bodily harm contrary to OAPA s.47. For more serious offences that do not require an underlying battery, such as s.20 OAPA, D's 'defence' is again a denial of proof, but this time that they lacked the necessary mens rea.

If D intentionally or recklessly causes V actual bodily harm or worse, the relevance of V's consent is more problematic. In such cases, D can only escape criminal liability if the restrictive "defence of consent" is satisfied.[86] Therefore, for ss.47, 20, and 18,[87] consent is only relevant as a supervening defence, to be considered once the offence elements have been proven. For example, in *Leach*,[88] V organised his own crucifixion on Hampstead Heath. The Ds nailed him to a wooden cross, his hands

---

available to a doctor assisting him to die, conceding, however, that such an argument would have been "doomed to fail": F. Stark, "Case Comment: Necessity and *Nicklinson*" [2013] Crim. L.R. 949–965, 949, 964. Consent would appear to be the more appropriate defence, since the essential plank of the case made by *Nicklinson* (and *R. (on the application of Pretty) v DPP [2001] UKHL 61;* [2002] 1 A.C. 800 and *R. (on the application of Purdy) v DPP [2009] UKHL 45;* [2010] 1 A.C. 345) was that their autonomous wish to end their lives should be respected. The Supreme Court has since made it clear that any changes to the law in this area are for Parliament to determine: *R. (on the application of Nicklinson) v Ministry of Justice* [2014] UKSC 38; [2015] A.C. 657.

82 For a discussion of this German case, see V. Bergelson, "The Right to be Hurt; Testing the Boundaries of Consent" (2007) 75 George Washington L.R. 165, 167.

83 *R. v Barnes (Mark)* [2004] EWCA Crim 3246 at [16]; [2005] 1 W.L.R. 910.

84 *Att-Gen's Reference (No.6 of 1980)* [1981] Q.B. 715 at 719; [1981] 3 W.L.R. 125 CA.

85 *R. v Meachen (David Nigel)* [2006] EWCA Crim 2414.

86 If V factually consents to common assault or battery, but D causes greater harm, the relevance of V's consent will depend on whether D intended or was reckless as to causing further harm. If D did not intend or was not reckless as to causing further harm, D will escape liability. See *Meachen* [2006] EWCA Crim 2414. This is discussed below, para.9–063.

87 Offences Against the Person Act 1861.

88 *R.v Leach, The Times*, 15 January 1969.

pierced by six-inch nails. The Ds were liable for unlawful wounding; V's consent was disregarded. The reason for this is that V's factual consent will only be relevant if the circumstances in which the harm was caused fall within one of the recognised "exceptional categories"; in *Leach*, it was not. The leading authority on this matter remains the House of Lords decision in *Brown*.

R. v Brown (and other appeals) [1994] 1 A.C. 212 (House of Lords):

The Ds belonged to a group of men who, over a 10-year period, participated in the commission of sadomasochistic acts of violence against each other, including genital torture, for the sexual pleasure engendered in the giving and receiving of pain. The partner in each case factually consented to the acts being committed and sustained no permanent injury. The participants had code words that enabled them to indicate when the pain became excessive. The Ds were charged with OAPA ss.47 and 20. The Ds changed their pleas to guilty when the trial judge ruled that consent was no defence to such charges and subsequently appealed. **9–047**

LORD TEMPLEMAN:

"The Court of Appeal upheld the convictions and certified the following point of law of general public importance:

> 'Where A wounds or assaults B occasioning him actual bodily harm in the course of a sado-masochistic encounter, does the prosecution have to prove lack of consent on the part of B before they can establish A's guilt under section 20 or section 47 of the Offences against the Person Act 1861?'

. . . In the present case each of the appellants intentionally inflicted violence upon another (to whom I refer as 'the victim') with the consent of the victim and thereby occasioned actual bodily harm or in some cases wounding or grievous bodily harm. Each appellant was therefore guilty of an offence under section 47 or section 20 of the Act of 1861 unless the consent of the victim was effective to prevent the commission of the offence or effective to constitute a defence to the charge.

In some circumstances violence is not punishable under the criminal law. When no actual bodily harm is caused, the consent of the person affected precludes him from complaining. There can be no conviction for the summary offence of common assault if the victim has consented to the assault. Even when violence is intentionally inflicted and results in actual bodily harm, wounding or serious bodily harm the accused is entitled to be acquitted if the injury was a foreseeable incident of a lawful activity in which the person injured was participating. Surgery involves intentional violence resulting in actual or sometimes serious bodily harm but surgery is a lawful activity. Other activities carried on with consent by or on behalf of the injured person have been accepted as lawful notwithstanding that they involve actual bodily harm or may cause serious bodily harm. Ritual circumcision, tattooing, ear-piercing and violent sports including boxing are lawful activities . . .

My Lords, the authorities dealing with the intentional infliction of bodily harm do not establish that consent is a defence to a charge under the Act of 1861. They establish that the courts have accepted that consent is a defence to the infliction of bodily harm in the course of some lawful activities. The question is whether the defence should be extended to the infliction of bodily harm in the course of sado-masochistic encounters . . . [This question] can only be decided by consideration of policy and public interest . . .

Counsel for some of the appellants argued that the defence of consent should be extended to the offence of occasioning actual bodily harm under section 47 of the Act of 1861 but should not be available to charges of serious wounding and the infliction of serious bodily harm under s.20. I do not consider that this solution is practicable. Sado-masochistic participants have no way of foretelling the degree of bodily harm which will result from their encounters . . .

Counsel for the appellants argued that consent should provide a defence to charges under both section 20 and section 47 because, it was said, every person has a right to deal with his body as he pleases. I do not consider that this slogan provides a sufficient guide to the policy decision which must now be made. It is an offence for a person to abuse his own body and mind by taking drugs. Although the law is often broken, the criminal law restrains a practice which is regarded as dangerous and injurious to individuals and which if allowed and extended is harmful to society generally. In any event the appellants in this case did not mutilate their own bodies. They inflicted bodily harm on willing victims. Suicide is no longer an offence but a person who assists another to commit suicide is guilty of murder or manslaughter.[89]

The assertion was made on behalf of the appellants that the sexual appetites of sadists and masochists can only be satisfied by the infliction of bodily harm and that the law should not punish the consensual achievement of sexual satisfaction. There was no evidence to support the assertion that sado-masochist activities are essential to the happiness of the appellants or any other participants but the argument would be acceptable if sado-masochism were only concerned with sex, as the appellants contend. In my opinion sado-masochism is not only concerned with sex. Sado-masochism is also concerned with violence. The evidence discloses that the practices of the appellants were unpredictably dangerous and degrading to body and mind and were developed with increasing barbarity and taught to persons whose consents were dubious or worthless . . .

In principle there is a difference between violence which is incidental and violence which is inflicted for the indulgence of cruelty. The violence of sado-masochistic encounters involves the indulgence of cruelty by sadists and the degradation of victims . . . I am not prepared to invent a defence of consent for sado-masochistic encounters which breed and glorify cruelty and result in offences under sections 47 and 20 of the Act of 1861."

89 With respect to His Lordship, it is only murder if D intentionally *causes* the death of "V". It is manslaughter if both had intended to die and D unexpectedly survives. In other circumstances, the crime involved is aiding and abetting suicide, contrary to the Suicide Act 1961 s.2.

LORD MUSTILL (DISSENTING): 9–048

"Throughout the argument of the appeal I was attracted by an analysis on the following lines. First, one would construct a continuous spectrum of the infliction of bodily harm, with killing at one end and a trifling touch at the other. Next, with the help of reported cases one would identify the point on this spectrum at which consent ordinarily ceases to be an answer to a prosecution for inflicting harm. This could be called 'the critical level.' It would soon become plain however that this analysis is too simple and that there are certain types of special situation to which the general rule does not apply. Thus, for example, surgical treatment which requires a degree of bodily invasion well on the upper side of the critical level will nevertheless be legitimate if performed in accordance with good medical practice and the consent of the patient. Conversely, there will be cases in which even a moderate degree of harm cannot be legitimated by consent . . .

For all the intellectual neatness of this method I must recognise that it will not do, for it imposes on the reported cases and on the diversities of human life an order which they do not possess. Thus, when one comes to map out the spectrum of ordinary consensual physical harm, to which the special situations form exceptions, it is found that the task is almost impossible, since people do not ordinarily consent to the infliction of harm. In effect, either all or almost all the instances of the consensual infliction of violence are special . . .

Furthermore, when one examines the situations which are said to found such a theory it is seen that the idea of consent as the foundation of a defence has in many cases been forced on to the theory, whereas in reality the reason why the perpetrator of the harm is not liable is not because of the recipient's consent, but because the perpetrator has acted in a situation where the consent of the recipient forms one, but only one, of the elements which make the act legitimate . . .

I thus see no alternative but to adopt a much narrower and more empirical approach, by looking at the situations in which the recipient consents or is deemed to consent to the infliction of violence upon him, to see whether the decided cases teach us how to react to this new challenge . . .

[Lord Mustill concluded that the case law left the way open for the House to determine the issue completely anew.]

As I have ventured to formulate the crucial question, it asks whether there is good reason to impress upon section 47 an interpretation which penalises the relevant level of harm irrespective of consent, i.e., to recognise sado-masochistic activities as falling into a special category of acts, such as duelling and prize-fighting, which 'the law says shall not be done.' This is very important, for if the question were differently stated it might well yield a different answer. In particular, if it were held that as a matter of law all infliction of bodily harm above the level of common assault is incapable of being legitimated by consent, except in special circumstances, then we would have to consider whether the public interest required the recognition of private sexual activities as being in a specially exempt category. This would be an altogether more difficult question and one which . . . [should be answered by Parliament] . . . I ask myself . . . whether the Act of 1861 (a statute which . . . was clearly intended to penalise conduct of a quite different nature) should in this new situation be interpreted so as to make it criminal?"

[His Lordship concluded that there were insufficient grounds to do so and allowed the appeals.]

9–049 LORD SLYNN (DISSENTING):

"[T]here exist areas where the law disregards the victim's consent even where that consent is freely and fully given. These areas may relate to the person (*e.g.* a child); they may relate to the place (*e.g.* in public); they may relate to the nature of the harm done. It is the latter which is in issue in the present case.

I accept that consent cannot be said simply to be a defence to any act which one person does to another. A line has to be drawn as to what can and as to what cannot be the subject of consent . . .

[T]o be workable, it cannot be allowed to fluctuate within particular charges and in the interests of legal certainty it has to be accepted that consent can be given to acts which are said to constitute actual bodily harm and wounding. Grievous bodily harm I accept to be different by analogy with and as an extension of the old cases on maiming. Accordingly, I accept that other than for cases of grievous bodily harm or death, consent can be a defence. This in no way means that the acts done are approved of or encouraged."

Appeal dismissed

9–050 By a bare majority, the House of Lords held that V's factual consent to the causation of actual or serious harm for sexual gratification is irrelevant to D's liability for serious non-fatal offences. While this decision can only be profoundly regretted as legal moralism prevailing over human autonomy and the right of persons to express their sexuality as they see fit,[90] it did, in some respects, help to clarify the law. The court reaffirmed the restrictive category-based approach to consent to bodily injury; persons should not be permitted to cause actual or serious bodily harm unless it is done in circumstances where there is a "policy and public interest". This, the court argued, is to protect social order, advance the public interest, and protect people from themselves.[91]

---

90 See L. Bibbings and P. Alldridge, "Sexual Expression, Body Alteration, and the Defence of Consent" (1993) 20 J. Law and Society 356. The appellants attempted to rely (unsuccessfully) upon the ECHR (most importantly, upon art.8 which guarantees respect for private and family life) during the course of their defence. Subsequently, the European Court of Human Rights unanimously held that there had been no violation of art.8 (*Laskey v United Kingdom* (1997) 24 E.H.R.R. 39). cf. D. Baker, "The Moral Limits of Consent as a Defence in the Criminal Law" (2009) 12 New Crim. L. Rev. 93; E. Craig, "Capacity to Consent to Sexual Risk" (2014) 17 New Crim. L. Rev. 103; and S. Cowan, "Criminalizing SM: Disavowing the Erotic, Instantiating Violence" in R.A. Duff, L. Farmer, S.E. Marshall, M. Renzo and V. Tadros, *The Structures of the Criminal Law* (Oxford: OUP, 2011).

91 *R. v Brown (Anthony Joseph)* [1994] 1 A.C. 212 at 235 (Lord Templeman) and 246 (Lord Jauncey); [1993] 2 W.L.R. 556 HL.

The six categories of exception that have been recognised are (1) proper medical treatment and reasonable surgical interference; (2) regulated sports; (3) tattooing, piercing and body modification; (4) harms related to religious or cultural practices; (5) bravado and horseplay; and (6) sexual pleasure and transmission of diseases. These categories are ad hoc, and their parameters are far from clear.[92]

1. Proper medical treatment and reasonable surgical interference

The most straightforward case where D can rely upon V's consent to provide a defence to the causation of serious injury is in the case of proper medical treatment and reasonable surgical interference. This is true for both therapeutic and non-therapeutic (e.g. plastic) surgery.[93] However, the limits of this exception remain uncertain because the courts have not defined what amounts to "proper medical treatment" or "reasonable surgery",[94] apart from indicating that treatment "in accordance with good medical practice"[95] is lawful. Since "Good Medical Practice" is the term used by the General Medical Council (GMC) to denote acceptable standards for medical practice,[96] this suggests that professional standards concerning qualification and practice are key to determining what is in the public interest. **9–051**

Whether it is the consent of the patient that renders the actions lawful or whether surgery itself forms a special category of its own is an issue which has yet to be fully resolved in the courts.[97] We know that at least one surgeon has performed amputation operations on two patients suffering from the rare medical disorder of apotemnophilia, which induces in its sufferers the desire to have a (healthy) limb amputated.[98] The legality of this (and its rationale) was not tested by a prosecution, but a similar scenario would provide a "limit" case for the courts on the issue of consent to surgery.

2. Regulated sports

It has long been held that V can consent to the risk of bodily harm in the course of "properly organised sports". One argument to support this position is that regulated sports offer a plethora of benefits, including health benefits, the instilling of discipline, and the opportunity for self-advancement. However, there is often a high risk of bodily injury in the course of sporting activities, and the parameters of this category of exception are far from clear. The legal doctrine on regulated sports and consent distinguishes between fighting and non-fighting sports. **9–052**

---

92 For criticisms of this category-based approach, see J. Tolmie, "Consent to Harmful Assaults: The Case for Moving Away from Category Based Decision Making" [2012] Crim. L.R. 656; D. Kell, "Social Disutility and Consent" (1994) 14 O.J.L.S. 121.

93 *Att-Gen's Reference (No.6 of 1980)* [1981] Q.B. 715; (1981) 73 Cr. App. R. 63 CA at 66 (Lord Lane); *Airedale NHS Trust v Bland* [1993] A.C. 789 at 891 (Lord Mustill); *Brown* [1994] 1 A.C. 212 at 266 (Lord Mustill).

94 M. Brazier and S. Fovargue, "Transforming wrong into right: What is 'proper medical treatment'?" in S. Fovargue and A. Mullock (eds), *The Legitimacy of Medical Treatment: What Role for the Medical Exception?* (Oxford: Routledge, 2016), p.14.

95 *Brown* [1994] 1 A.C. 212 at 258–259.

96 GMC, *Good Medical Practice* (2019). The GMC is the public body responsible for the registration and regulation of medical practitioners.

97 This latter view is taken by Lord Mustill in *Brown* [1994] 1 A.C. 212 at 266.

98 "News: Surgeon Amputated Healthy Legs" (2000) *British Medical Journal* 320. The surgeon, Robert Smith, effectively barred from performing any more such operations in the UK because no hospital will permit this surgery to take place on their premises, has argued that the condition (now usually known as Body Integrity Identity Disorder) is analogous to Gender Identity Disorder and, thus, may be appropriately treated by surgery: G.M. Furth and R. Smith, *Amputee Identity Disorder: Information, Questions, Answers and Recommendations about Self-Demand Amputation* (First Books Library, 2002); C. Fracassini, "Call for NHS Amputation of Healthy Limbs" *The Times*, 23 November 2003. The legality of gender reassignment surgery is well established, see, e.g. *Corbett v Corbett (otherwise Ashley) (No.1)* [1971] P. 83; [1970] 2 W.L.R. 1306; *Bellinger v Bellinger* [2003] UKHL 21; [2003] 2 A.C. 467; Law Consultation Paper No.139, paras 8.28–8.29 fn.97. See further, Elliott, "Body Dysmorphic Disorder, Radical Surgery and the Limits of Consent" (2009) 17 *Medical Law Review* 149.

For those sports where fighting is *not* the defining activity, if D intentionally injures V, criminal liability may arise even if the incident falls within the rules of the game.[99] Where the injury is non-intentional and a foreseeable consequence of participating in the sport, the rules of the game are likely to be relied upon to ascertain what risks are consented to by the players. For example, in *Billinghurst*, the jury was directed that rugby players consent to such force as can reasonably be expected during the game.[100]

However, in competitive sports, conduct outside the rules of the game can occur in the heat of the moment and not reach the threshold required to be criminal. In *Barnes*, D made a "crushing tackle, which was late, unnecessary, reckless, and high up the legs" on V (an opposing player) during an amateur football game; V suffered serious injuries to the ankle and calf bone.[101] On appeal, D's conviction for unlawfully and maliciously inflicting grievous bodily harm, contrary to the OAPA s.20, was quashed. D had impliedly consented to the *risk* of injury occurring outside the rules of the game. Determining whether such risks have been impliedly consented to requires an objective assessment, independent of the individual players, that considers the type of sport, the safety rules and level and conditions under which the game is played, the nature of the injuring act, the extent of the force employed, the degree of risk of injury, and the state of mind of the offending player.[102]

9–053 For those sports that involve rule-governed fighting, all injuries, up to and including death,[103] seem to be within the purview of the defence of consent, provided that the injury is caused within the rules of the game. It is likely that this only applies to well-established fighting sports, like boxing, and the position is uncomfortably uncertain with regard to newer fighting sports like cage fighting. The legality of boxing does not rest on any significant appellate decision but rather on the generally held assumption that it is lawful and to be tolerated. Lord Mustill, in *Brown*, held that:

> "For money, not recreation or personal improvement, each boxer tries to hurt the opponent more than he is hurt himself, and aims to end the contest prematurely by inflicting a brain injury serious enough to make the defendant unconscious . . . It is in my judgment best to regard this as another special situation which for the time being stands outside the ordinary law of violence because society chooses to tolerate it."[104]

For all sports, irrespective of whether they involve fighting as the defining activity, all instances of intentionally caused injuries falling outside the rules of any game, including the zone of tolerance, should lead to criminal liability. Similarly, where D injures V in the course of an unregulated sport, V's

---

99 *R. v Bradshaw* (1878) Cox C.C. 83.

100 *R. v Billinghurst* [1978] Crim. L.R. 553 CC. See further, J. Anderson, "No Licence for Thuggery: Violence, Sport and the Criminal Law" [2008] Crim. L.R. 751.

101 *R. v Barnes (Mark)* [2004] EWCA Crim 3246; [2005] 1 W.L.R. 910.

102 This follows the Canadian position espoused in *R. v Cicarelli* (1989) 54 C.C.C. (3d) 121.

103 In the circumstances where serious bodily injury is intended, and death is caused.

104 per Lord Mustill in *Brown* [1994] 1 A.C. 212 at 265. See further, M. Gunn and D. Ormerod, "The Legality of Boxing" (1995) 15 *Legal Studies* 181; J. Anderson, *The Legality of Boxing: A Punch Drunk Love?* (Abingdon: Birkbeck Law Press, 2007) and J. Anderson, "The right to a fair fight: sporting lessons on consensual harm" (2014) 17 New Crim. L. Rev 103. There are a number of martial arts activities which expose the participants to just as much potential risk as boxing, often without the same strict regulatory control (Law Commission Consultation Paper No.139, para.1.6 fn.97).

consent is ineffectual, and D may be criminally liable. In those cases where criminal liability does result, the courts will ordinarily respond to such offending by imposing a custodial sentence.[105]

3. Tattooing, piercing and body modification

This category of exception includes a range of routine procedures, from haircutting to piercing and tattooing. It will often be the case that these procedures are carried out by a professional, but that need not always be the case (like in *Wilson*). **9–054**

R. v Wilson [1996] 2 Cr. App. R. 241 (Court of Appeal, Criminal Division):

D was convicted of assaulting V (his wife) contrary to OAPA s.47. He admitted to the police (who had been informed by the wife's doctor) that he had used a hot knife to brand his initials on her buttocks. The judge ruled that he was bound by the decision in *Brown*. On appeal: **9–055**

RUSSELL LJ:

> "We are abundantly satisfied that there is no factual comparison to be made between the instant case and . . . and *Brown*: Mrs Wilson not only consented to that which the appellant did, she instigated it. There was no aggressive intent on the part of the appellant. On the contrary, far from wishing to cause injury to his wife, the appellant's desire was to assist her in what she regarded as the acquisition of a desirable piece of personal adornment, perhaps in this day and age no less understandable than the piercing of nostrils or even tongues for the purposes of inserting decorative jewellery.
>
> In our judgment *Brown* is not authority for the proposition that consent is no defence to a charge under section 47 of the 1861 Act, in all circumstances where actual bodily harm is deliberately inflicted. It is to be observed that the question certified for their Lordships in *Brown* related only to a 'sadomasochistic encounter'. However, their Lordships recognised in the course of their speeches, that it was necessary that there be exceptions to what is no more than a general proposition. The speeches of [several of their Lordships] . . . all refer to tattooing as being an activity which, if carried out with the consent of an adult, does not involve an offence under section 47, albeit that actual bodily harm is deliberately inflicted.
>
> For our part, we cannot detect any logical difference between what the appellant did and what he might have done in the way of tattooing. The latter activity apparently requires no state authorisation, and the appellant was as free to engage in it as anyone else.

---

105 See, e.g. *R. v Birkin (Paul Abbey)* (1988) 10 Cr. App. R. (S.) 303; [1988] Crim. L.R. 854 CA; *R. v Bowyer (David James)* [2001] EWCA Crim 1853; [2002] 1 Cr. App. R. (S.) 101; *R. v Cotterill (James Michael)* [2007] EWCA Crim 526; [2007] 2 Cr. App. R. (S.) 64; *R. v Lawrence (Jerome)* [2011] EWCA Crim 3129; [2012] 2 Cr. App. R. (S.) 42; *R. v Brown (Paul Brian)* [2011] EWCA Crim 786; [2011] 2 Cr. App. R. (S.) 88.

We do not think that we are entitled to assume that the method adopted by the appellant and his wife was any more dangerous or painful than tattooing . . . [W]e are firmly of the opinion that it is not in the public interest that activities such as the appellant's in this appeal should amount to criminal behaviour. Consensual activity between husband and wife, in the privacy of the matrimonial home, is not, in our judgment, a proper matter for criminal investigation, let alone criminal prosecution . . . In this field, in our judgment, the law should develop upon a case by case basis rather than upon general propositions to which, in the changing times we live, exceptions may arise from time to time not expressly covered by authority."

Appeal allowed

9–056 The Court of Appeal found that V's consent should have been accepted, making clear that this kind of activity, performed in private, was not deserving of criminal liability. While this decision can be welcomed, the judgment is non-committal about the precise point at which the state may intervene in one's private sexual life. Moreover, the reliance on the fact that the branding had been done as an act of affection rather than aggression is unhelpful.

The courts have also considered the lawfulness of extreme bodily modifications.

R. v BM [2019] Q.B. 1 (Court of Appeal, Criminal Division):

9–057 D was a registered tattooist and body piercer who also performed body modifications. The counts against D involved procedures carried out without anaesthetic, including: the removal of a customer's ear; the removal of a customer's nipple; and the splitting a customer's tongue to resemble that of a reptile. The judge, in deciding that consent could not provide a defence, relied on *Brown*, which held that consent was no defence to causing actual bodily harm or wounding, unless the conduct fell into a special exception to the general rule. The question for the court was whether body modification fell within a special exception.

LORD BURNETT OF MALDON CJ:

"40. Whilst the exceptions are incapable of being accommodated within any universally stated test, there are two features which may be thought to underpin almost all of them. First, they may produce discernible social benefit. That is true of the sporting exceptions and may even be true of boxing or 'dangerous exhibitions' as entertainment. It is possible that those with a religious hue might also be considered as conferring a social benefit, at least at the time they were recognised. But the second is that it would simply be regarded as unreasonable for the common law to criminalise the activity if engaged in with consent by (or on behalf of) the injured party. That would apply to tattooing and piercing and, again, perhaps to those with a religious hue, including ritual male circumcision.

41. New exceptions should not be recognised on a case-by-case basis, save perhaps where there is a close analogy with an existing exception to the general rule established in *R v Brown*

> *(Anthony)*. The recognition of an entirely new exception would involve a value judgment which is policy laden, and on which there may be powerful conflicting views in society. The criminal trial process is inapt to enable a wide ranging inquiry into the underlying policy issues, which are much better explored in the political environment."
>
> *Appeal dismissed*

In *BM*, these extreme body modifications, which involved the removal of body parts or mutilation, were held not to be analogous to tattooing and piercing. The Court of Appeal emphasised that the risk of infection and the severity of what were considered unlicensed surgical procedures with long-term consequences could not be classified as a lawful activity justified by personal autonomy. Unfortunately, the judgment offered little by way of guidance with regard to other less extreme, yet still controversial, body modifications, such as scarification, skin peels, branding and beading.[106] **9–058**

The court went on to assert that any new exceptions were a matter for Parliament. Whether other types of conduct not currently included within the lawful activities as set out in *Brown* and other case law will fall within an exception may well change over time. Indeed, in *Brown*, Lord Mustill recognised that societal attitudes and behaviour change and that the line between acceptable and unlawful behaviour might need to be revisited in the future:

> "It also seems plain that as the general social appreciation of what is tolerable and of the proper role of the state in regulating the lives of individuals changes with the passage of time, so we shall expect to find that the assumption of the criminal justice system about what types of conduct are properly excluded from its scope, and about what is meant by going 'too far' will not remain constant."[107]

4. Harms related to religious or cultural practices

This category encapsulates a broad range of activities where the deliberate infliction of bodily harm may be legitimated by consent. One example is the ritual circumcision of males.[108] The cultural acceptance this form of invasive action enjoys is very different to the position of female genital mutilation (FGM). FGM is a global practice that occurs for a complex range of reasons, including to protect virginity. It has been asserted that "its purpose lies in the control and oppression of women and the suppression of female sexuality".[109] Such circumcisions can cause very severe injuries and have **9–059**

---

106 For a discussion of this case and its implications, see S. Pegg, "Not so clear cut: the lawfulness of body modifications" (2019) Crim. L.R. 579; D. Bansal, "Bodily Modifications and the Criminal Law" (2018) J. Crim. Law 496. For a recent illustration of the courts' reluctance to permit extreme bodily modifications despite V's factual consent, see R v Gustavson and others, 09 May 2024 (Central Criminal Court).

107 *Brown* [1994] 1 A.C. 212 at 267.

108 Law Commission Consultation Paper No.139, para.3.25 fn.97. cf. M. Fox and M. Thompson, "A Covenant with the Status Quo? Male Circumcision and the New BMA Guidance to Doctors" (2005) 31 *Journal of Medical Ethics* 463. Feldman has argued that nontherapeutic circumcision conducted without the consent of the patient may violate the ECHR art.3: D. Feldman, *Civil Liberties and Human Rights in England and Wales*, 2nd edn (Oxford: OUP, 2002), p.272. cf. H. Gilbert, "Time to Reconsider the Lawfulness of Ritual Male Circumcision" [2007] E.H.R.L.R. 279.

109 L. Bibbings and P. Alldridge, "Sexual Expression, Body Alteration, and the Defence of Consent" (1993) 20 J. Law and Society 356.

been made criminal.[110] The legal status of other religious and cultural practices has developed ad hoc with scant appellate authority; for instance, religious flagellation is likely to be permitted, but customary and tribal scarification, especially regarding minors, is not.[111]

5. Bravado and horseplay

9-060 If D causes V actual or serious injury in the course of "rough, undisciplined horseplay", V's actual or implied consent will afford D a defence. In *Jones*,[112] the court held that this activity which occurs "in the school playground, in the barrack-room and on the factory floor"[113] was something that a person could consent to as long as there is no intention to cause injury. In *Jones*, a group of Ds (schoolboys) threw V into the air, causing a ruptured spleen that required surgical operation for its removal; their convictions for causing grievous bodily harm were quashed on the basis that the jury should have been entitled to consider the defence of consent.[114]

Lord Mustill, in *Brown*, stated that the criminal law could not concern itself with such activities "provided that they do not go too far".[115] This public policy approach was adopted in *P*, where it was held that in the context of horseplay, consent might be highly material in negating what would otherwise be an unlawful act.[116] In this case, two teenage Ds, after a post-exam celebration, threw V over a bridge to his death. Their convictions for manslaughter were upheld—not on the basis that consent was irrelevant in such circumstances—but on the basis that no consent had been given, and it was abundantly clear that V had been actively resisting the Ds.

These cases have the potential to be a bully's charter.[117] It is farfetched to suggest that the boys in *Jones* who were being held by several others to *prevent them from running away* were genuinely consenting to being thrown into the air. To suggest that boys can consent to grievous bodily harm or a risk of death but that sadomasochists, who are genuinely consenting, cannot consent to actual bodily harm provides an interesting insight into the way some of our judiciary view the world. Violence in the playground or barrack room is what is expected and normal in the male world; it is a "manly diversion". Two men wishing to express their sexuality together and in private are not doing the sort of thing "real men" do. It is an "evil thing" and "uncivilised"[118] and cannot be the subject of valid consent.

---

110 Female Genital Mutilation Act 2003 s.1. The offence carries a maximum sentence of 14 years' imprisonment. However, cosmetic genital surgery (e.g. labiaplasty) is lawful and apparently increasingly popular: C. Smyth, "Porn fuels rise in girls having risky genital cosmetic surgery" *The Times*, 15 November 2013. See T. Elliott, "Body Dysmorphic Disorder, Radical Surgery and the Limits of Consent" (2009) 17 *Medical Law Review* 149, 178–181.

111 In *Adesanya*, D (a mother) was convicted of assault occasioning actual bodily harm contrary to OAPA s.47 for performing an act of culturally motivated scarification on the faces of her two sons. *R. v Adesanya, The Times*, 16 July 1974.

112 *R. v Jones (Terance)* (1986) 83 Cr. App. R. 375; [1987] Crim. L.R. 123 CA. See also *R. v Aitken (Thomas Adam)* [1992] 1 W.L.R. 1006; (1992) 95 Cr. App. R. 304 CA and Law Commission Consultation Paper No.139, paras 14.1–14.21 fn.97.

113 per Lord Mustill in *Brown* [1994] 1 A.C. 212 at 267.

114 It should be noted that the appeal was allowed because the possibility of a defence of genuine belief by D that consent was present was not laid before the jury. As McCowan J observes, "[i]t may well be that if this jury had been given the opportunity of considering this defence, they would have had little difficulty in rejecting it": *Jones* (1986) 83 Cr. App. R. 375 at 379.

115 *Brown* [1994] 1 A.C. 212 at 267.

116 *R. v P* [2005] EWCA Crim 1960.

117 The defence *may* even operate where D makes a drunken mistake as to the consent of V: see *R. v Richardson (Nigel John)* [1999] 1 Cr. App. R. 392; [1999] Crim. L.R. 494 CA.

118 per Lord Templeman in *Brown* [1994] 1 A.C. 212 at 237.

6. Sexual pleasure and transmission of diseases

This category of exception is arguably the most controversial of all. This is because sexual conduct involves the causation and risk of harm at all levels. At its very core, it involves physical contact between two or more persons. However, since such contact would amount to no more than a technical battery, D and V's consent prevents the actus reus of battery from being completed. However, once this level of harm is exceeded, and D causes V actual or serious harm, there is a distinct lack of certainty as to whether V's factual consent will afford D a defence. The law has developed two avenues of analysis: (a) where D risks the sexual transmission of a disease or infection; and (b) where D risks or causes bodily injury *in the course of* sexual activity or *for* sexual gratification. We will consider both in turn. **9–061**

If V *knowingly* consents to the risk of (a potentially fatal) disease or infection from unprotected sexual intercourse with D, D is able to raise the defence of consent to avoid criminal liability. This has been confirmed by the Court of Appeal in *Dica* and *Konzani* and has been codified by the Domestic Abuse Act 2021 s.71(4).

R. v Dica [2004] Q.B. 1257 (Court of Appeal, Criminal Division):

D, who was HIV positive, had unprotected consensual sexual intercourse with two women on a number of occasions in the course of relationships with them. Both women subsequently contracted HIV. D was charged with inflicting grievous bodily harm contrary to the Offences Against the Person Act 1861 s.20. The prosecution alleged that he had been reckless as to whether the women might become infected and that they would never have agreed to sexual intercourse had they known of his condition. D was convicted and appealed, inter alia, on the issue of consent which the trial judge had withdrawn from the jury. **9–062**

JUDGE LJ:

> "The present case is concerned with and confined to s.20 offences alone . . . The question for decision is whether the victims' consent to sexual intercourse, which as a result of his alleged concealment was given in ignorance of the facts of the appellant's condition, necessarily amounted to consent to the risk of being infected by him. If that question must be answered 'Yes', the concept of consent in relation to s.20 is devoid of real meaning . . .
>
> In our view, on the assumed fact now being considered [that they had not known of his condition], the answer is entirely straightforward. These victims consented to sexual intercourse. Accordingly the appellant is not guilty of rape. Given the long-term nature of the relationships, if the appellant concealed the truth about his condition from them, and therefore kept them in ignorance of it, there was no reason for them to think that they were running any risk of infection, and they were not consenting to it. On this basis, there would be no consent sufficient in law to provide the appellant with a defence to the charge under s.20 . . .

In our judgment the impact of the authorities dealing with sexual gratification can too readily be misunderstood. It does not follow from them, and they do not suggest, that consensual acts of sexual intercourse are unlawful merely because there may be a known risk to the health of one or other participant. These participants are not intent on spreading or becoming infected with disease through sexual gratification. They are not indulging in serious violence for the purpose of sexual gratification. They are simply prepared, knowingly, to run the risk—not the certainty—of infection, as well as all the other risks inherent in and possible consequences of sexual intercourse, such as, and despite the most careful precautions, an unintended pregnancy . . .

These, and similar risks, have always been taken by adults consenting to sexual intercourse . . . Modern society has not thought to criminalise those who have willingly accepted the risks . . .

The problems of criminalizing the consensual taking of risks like these include the sheer impracticability of enforcement and the haphazard nature of its impact. The process would undermine the general understanding of the community that sexual relationships are pre-eminently private and essentially personal to the individuals involved in them . . .

In our judgment, interference of this kind with personal autonomy, and its level and extent, may only be made by Parliament."

[The court concluded that D would have had a defence had the women known of his condition and agreed to sexual intercourse because they were still prepared to run the risks involved. Accordingly, the trial judge had been wrong to withdraw the issue of consent from the jury.]

Appeal allowed. Retrial ordered[119]

9–063 In the subsequent decision of *Konzani*,[120] the Court of Appeal stressed the need for *informed* consent—which would almost invariably have to result from disclosure by the person with HIV.[121] The argument that by consenting to unprotected sex, the person is also impliedly consenting to the risk of infection was rejected.[122] Convictions have also been obtained under s.20 where Ds have failed to disclose infection with hepatitis B and genital herpes to their sexual partners.[123]

---

119 D was convicted and sentenced to four-and-a-half years' imprisonment.

120 *Konzani* [2005] EWCA Crim 706. See also *Barnes* [2004] EWCA Crim 3246 and *R. v Cort (Peter Laurence)* [2003] EWCA Crim 2149; [2004] Q.B. 388.

121 *Konzani* [2005] EWCA Crim 706 at [41]. Exceptionally, informed consent might result, even where there had been non-disclosure by D, if D develops a sexual relationship with V, who knew them while they were in the hospital, receiving treatment for the condition [44].

122 *Konzani* [2005] EWCA Crim 706 at [41]. See further, M. Weait, "Knowledge, Autonomy and Consent: *R. v Konzani*" [2005] Crim. L.R. 763 and A. Pedain, "HIV and Responsible Sexual Behaviour" [2005] 64 C.L.J. 540 for contrasting critiques of the decisions in *Dica* [2004] Q.B. 1257 and *Konzani*. cf. G.R. Mawhinney, "To be ill or to kill: the criminality of contagion" (2013) 77 J. Crim. L. 202–214 and M. Brazier, "Do no harm—do patients have responsibilities too?" [2006] 43 C.L.J. 397–422, 408–409, who suggest that legal responsibility for the reckless transmission of disease might be extended.

123 In 2008, Ercan Yasar was sentenced to two years' imprisonment for reckless transmission of hepatitis: "Man jailed for passing on hepatitis B" *The Times*, 19 November 2008. In 2011, David Golding was sentenced to custody for giving his girlfriend genital herpes: reduced on appeal to three months' imprisonment: *R. v Golding (David)* [2014] EWCA Crim 889; [2014] Crim. L.R. 686.

The key difference between the general rule as set out in *Brown* and the case law as it pertains to sexually transmitted infections is that the latter involves consenting to a risk of harm and not necessarily to the infliction of it. Yet based on these judgments, the applicability of consent still remains unclear in a number of scenarios involving sexual activity. It is not certain, for example, whether V can consent to a risk of harm where D thinks they may have an infection but is unsure. It is also unclear whether D must inform V that they have an infection such as HIV where they are on medication and where their viral load is very low or undetectable, making it *almost* impossible to contract the virus.[124] Such clarification is much needed for those who must manage lifelong viruses.[125]

Let us now turn to cases where D risks or causes bodily injury *in the course of* sexual activity or *for* sexual gratification. The case law that has developed on this matter is confused and requires us to distinguish between harms *incidental* to the pursuit of mutual sexual gratification from injuries caused *for* sexual gratification. If D causes V actual or serious injury but does not intend or foresee the risk of injury, V's consent to the underlying battery provides D with a defence (technically, a denial of proof).[126] In such circumstances, the injury sustained by V is *incidental* to the primary objective of mutual sexual gratification. In *Slingsby*, D fisted V's vagina and anus and caused serious injuries as a result of a signet ring he was wearing. V died of septicaemia. His defence, accepted by the Court of Appeal, was that he was not aware of the risk of harm and believed he was engaging in a battery (vigorous sexual activity) to which V consented. The injury was incidental to the pursuit of mutual sexual gratification; consent was an effective defence.

However, as was seen in *Brown* (extracted and discussed above), the criminal law does *not* recognise V's factual consent to the risk or causation of actual or serious bodily injury by D as legally effective when done for the purpose of obtaining sexual gratification.

R. v Emmett, Case No.9901191 ZR, The Times, 15 October 1999 (Court of Appeal, Criminal Division):

D and V (his partner) engaged in consensual sexual activity that on one occasion involved partial asphyxiation and, on another occasion, setting light to lighter fuel on her breast. As a result, V suffered subconjunctival haemorrhages in both eyes, some bruising around her neck, and a burn that at first was thought to be so serious as to require a skin graft. The offence came to light because the doctor treating V reported it to the police. D was convicted of assault occasioning actual bodily harm. The trial judge distinguished *Wilson* and followed *Brown* in ruling that consent was no defence where the parties foresaw the risk of injuries. On appeal: **9–064**

124 See e.g. who argued for a defence of "reasonable precautions", K. Harker and E. Wright, "The HIV stigma: duty or defence?" (2015) 4 UCL J.L. and J. 55–75.

125 For a critical discussion of this area of law, see M. Weait, *Intimacy and Responsibility: The Criminalisation of HIV Transmission* (Oxford: Routledge, 2007) and M. Weait, "Limit Cases: How and Why We Can and Should Decriminalise HIV Transmission, Exposure, And Non-Disclosure" (2019) 27(4) Med. L.R. 576.

126 *Meachen* [2006] EWCA Crim 2414.

WRIGHT J:

"[W]e have come to the clear conclusion that the evidence in the instant case, in striking contrast to that in *Wilson*, made it plain that the actual or potential damage to which the appellant's partner was exposed in this case, plainly went far beyond that which was established by the evidence in *Wilson*. The lady suffered a serious, and what must have been, an excruciating painful burn . . . As to the process of partial asphyxiation . . . while it may now be fairly well known that the restriction of oxygen to the brain is capable of heightening sexual sensation, it is also, or should be, equally well-known that such a practice contains within itself a grave danger of brain damage or even death . . . The appellant was plainly aware of that danger . . . Accordingly, whether the line beyond which consent becomes immaterial is drawn at the point . . . at which common assault becomes assault occasioning actual bodily harm, or at some higher level, where the evidence looked at objectively reveals a realistic risk of more than a transient or trivial injury, it is plain, in our judgment, that the activities involved in by this appellant and his partner went well beyond that line . . .

[The appellant argues that] the involvement of the processes of the criminal law, in the consensual activities that were carried on in this couple's bedroom, amount to a breach of Article 8 of the European Convention on Human Rights [right to respect for private and family life] . . . It seems clear to us that once the conduct of the accused person has gone beyond the permitted limit, however that is defined, in inflicting injury upon or exposing to potential risk his or her partner, in the course of sado-masochistic games whether homo- or heterosexual, so that he or she *prima facie* at least has committed an offence of a sufficient degree of seriousness, the institution of a criminal investigation and, if appropriate, criminal proceedings cannot amount to a breach of Article 8."

Appeal dismissed

9–065 The position in *Brown* has been codified by the Domestic Abuse Act 2021 s.71, which provides that:

"It is not a defence that V consented to the infliction of the serious harm for the purposes of obtaining sexual gratification."

The codification of *Brown* was principally in response to political pressures stemming from widespread criticism and calls for reform, in particular, the vociferous campaign by the group "We Can't Consent To This". The group sought a "change" in the law for several reasons: the increased normalisation of violence against women in sex, the volume of cases in which male Ds sought to advance the so-called "rough-sex" defence, and that vulnerable people are pressured into "consenting" in the context of abusive relationships. Unfortunately, while the statute carries some intrinsic weight, it does no more than codify the existing position at common law, including its many problems. As such, several issues remain: the law continues to fail to articulate what distinguishes sadomasochism from abuse, the current framework requires us to determine whether injuries sustained during sexual conduct are incidental to or for sexual gratification, and represents a departure from liberal legal method.

That the current position is unsatisfactory and confusing is overtly visible in *Broadhurst*.[127] D inflicted more than 40 injuries on V, including a blow-out fracture to the left eye socket and lacerations of the vagina, which resulted in arterial haemorrhage. V died as a result of these injuries. The latter injury was caused by the insertion of a bottle of carpet cleaner with protruding trigger head into her vagina, which D says was conducted during consensual rough sex. We can see how unclear and confusing the law is here. The trial judge accepted that the consent of V to the beating that caused injuries to her bottom and breasts was not a defence as the injuries involved the causation of actual harm *for* sexual gratification (*Brown*). However, the insertion of the bottle of carpet cleaner and its trigger mechanism was not unlawful as it was *incidental* to sexual gratification (*Slingsby*). However, it is difficult to believe that D did not foresee a *risk* of causing V actual harm or worse by engaging in these acts, which if proven, would have formed the basis of a constructive manslaughter charge.[128] More generally, the following problems remain:

Daniel Bansal and Tracey Elliott, "Consent to Bodily Harm and the 'Public Interest'" in M. Bone, J. Child and J. Rogers (eds) *Criminal Law Reform Now (Volume II)* (2024), pp.205–206

"Unfortunately, the current position implies that many common sex injuries are *de jure* unlawful. For instance, 'injuries' such as 'love bites', scratches, and teeth marks from affectionate biting may give rise to section 47 liability. These are deliberately inflicted injuries, meaning they fall within the scope of the general rule espoused in *Brown* and section 71, and render any consent by B ineffective. It is hard to describe such injuries as incidental to sexual conduct and lawful, given how they are caused; they are part of the sexual interaction. **9–066**

Whether injuries sustained during sexual conduct are incidental or for sexual gratification is not binary. Many sexual acts traverse the boundary between pain and pleasure. Indeed, a wide array of sexual acts are commonly performed between consenting adults where the risks of injury are well known, with anogenital injury from penile, digital, or object penetration commonly reported. If A and B take precautions (e.g. lubrication) before engaging in sexual activity, that is potent evidence they are aware of the risks of such conduct, even if the risk is slight. If A is aware of such risk, A's only 'defence' is that the conduct was justified to preclude a finding of recklessness. However, the courts have not analysed these cases in this way, and a court would likely think it inconsistent with *Brown* and section 71 to recognise the satisfaction of BDSM desires as a justified reason for risk-taking."

E. REFORM PROPOSALS

The topic of consent to bodily harm in criminal law has been subject to significant academic commentary **9–067**
and criticism. Most influentially, 30 years ago, prompted by *Brown*, the Law Commission reviewed the

127 *R. v Broadhurst (John Anthony)* [2019] EWCA Crim 2026.

128 Although D was not liable for the constructive manslaughter of V, he was convicted of gross negligence manslaughter and sentenced to three years and eight months' imprisonment.

law relating to consent to bodily harm. Following a detailed exposition of the history and development of the legal doctrine, they recommended law reform and offered the following framework as a suggestion as to how reform might be achieved.

Law Commission (Consultation Paper No.139), Consent in the Criminal Law (1995), paras 4.47–4.51:

9-068 "4.47 We provisionally propose that the intentional causing of seriously disabling injury to another person should continue to be criminal, even if the person injured consents to such injury or to the risk of such injury.

4.48 We provisionally propose that—

(1) the reckless causing of seriously disabling injury should continue to be criminal, even if the injured person consents to such injury or to the risk of such injury; but
(2) a person causing seriously disabling injury to another person should not be regarded as having caused it recklessly unless—

 (a) he or she was, at the time of the act or omission causing it, aware of a risk that such injury would result, and
 (b) it was at that time contrary to the best interests of the other person, having regard to the circumstances known to the person causing the injury (including, if known to him or her, the fact that the other person consented to such injury or to the risk of it), to take that risk.

4.49 We provisionally propose that the intentional [and reckless (4.50)] causing of any injury to another person other than seriously disabling injury . . . should not be criminal if, at the time of the act or omission causing the injury, the other person consented to injury of the type caused.

4.51 . . . 'seriously disabling injury' should be taken to refer to an injury or injuries which

(1) cause serious distress, and
(2) involve the loss of a bodily member or organ or permanent bodily injury or permanent functional impairment, or serious or permanent disfigurement, or severe and prolonged pain, or serious impairment of mental health, or prolonged unconsciousness; and in determining whether an effect is permanent, no account should be taken of the fact that it may be remediable by surgery."

[The Law Commission then goes on to identify a number of exceptions. Persons may give consent to a higher level of harm for medical treatment and surgery. There are a number of activities (such as tattooing, sport and horseplay) where the level of harm is to stay at that permitted by the present law. Those under the age of 18 would not be able to consent to injuries intentionally caused for sexual, religious, or spiritual purposes.]

The principal suggestion of the Law Commission's proposal was that V's factual consent should be legally effective in all spheres of activity, provided that the harm consented to falls short of serious disabling injury. It was their view that it would not be in V's best interests for consent to be effective for harms at or above the level of serious disabling injury, save for a few isolated exceptions (e.g. proper medical treatment). If implemented, these proposals would produce a law which would give greater scope for the availability of the defence of consent. **9–069**

However, this reform proposal has been subject to academic criticism. For example, Ormerod and Gunn criticised the use of "serious disabling injury" as the threshold to which consent is typically effective.[129] This was on the grounds that the definition of serious disabling injury, adopted from Glanville Williams' work,[130] included "permanent disfigurement" and therefore contradicted the Law Commission's position regarding tattooing and piercings. Similarly, they argued that, if implemented, there would be an offence-defence mismatch; there is no offence of causing serious disabling injury. Thus, if D were charged with causing grievous bodily harm contrary to ss.20 or 18, and relied on V's consent as a defence, defence counsel would have to prove that the injuries fell short of serious disabling injury, which would add confusion and complexity to proceedings.

These technical matters aside, other academic commentators have criticised the proposal more fundamentally. Roberts, for example, argued that the proposal is "unprincipled". In Roberts' view, the only principled approach to the matter of consent to bodily harm is through liberalism; that the law should respect *any* self-regarding choice made by V.[131] While such an approach would give full effect to Feinberg's *volenti* maxim mentioned at the start of this section, it would also mean that the choice made by Brandes to be eaten and killed by Miewes would fall outside the purview of the criminal law—an outcome which most liberalists would likely disagree.

Given the continued importance of needing maximum legal certainty in an area that affects all citizens' lives, Parliamentary reform is long overdue.[132]

III. Self-defence

A. INTRODUCTION

Almost as long as the criminal law has been in existence, it has consistently restricted the right of the individual to self-help; it is the function of the law to preserve law and order and protect the weak. **9–070**

---

129 D. Ormerod and M. Gunn, "Consent—A Second Bash" (1996) Crim. L.R. 694, 700–701.

130 G. Williams, "Force, Injury and Serious Injury" (1990) 140 N.L.J. 1227, 1229.

131 P. Roberts, "The Philosophical Foundations of Consent in the Criminal Law" (1997) 17 O.J.L.S. 389.

132 For a recent proposal for reform, see D. Bansal and T. Elliott, "Consent to Bodily Harm and the 'Public Interest', and the response by M.M. Dempsey, in M. Bone, J. Child, and J. Rogers, *Criminal Law Reform Now (Volume II)* (Oxford: Hart, 2024), pp.189–220.

There are, however, inevitably going to be occasions when relying upon the arrival of official help would result in disaster, and it would be extremely unjust if the remedy of self-help were altogether denied. The law recognises this and, in certain situations, deems the use of force to be lawful. It has been argued that:

> "The source of [this] right is a comparison of the competing interests of the aggressor and the defender, as modified by the important fact that the aggressor is the one party responsible for the fight . . . As the party morally at fault for threatening the defender's interests, the aggressor is entitled to lesser consideration in the balancing process."[133]

The underlying rationale of defensive force may also be understood in terms of Gardner's analysis:

> "By granting a *justificatory* defence the law concedes that . . . the defendant had, at the time of her *prima facie* wrongful action, sufficient reason to perform it."[134]

While most of the rules on self-defence were developed to cater for situations where an individual (D) is acting against an aggressor (V), Gardner's analysis provides a more complete explanation that covers cases where self-defensive action is taken against a non-culpable person, such as a small child who is inadvertently threatening D's interests.

9–071 Again, as with consent, it is possible to assert that necessary defence is not truly a "defence". D, acting in self-defence, is acting lawfully—an element of the actus reus is thus not established.[135] This method of characterisation has important implications in cases where D has made a mistake, i.e. mistakenly thinking that they need to defend themselves or others. But apart from such cases, the parameters of self-defence are constant, irrespective of whether it is regarded as a defence or a denial of a definitional element.

There are several defences that permit defensive action to be taken against an aggressor: the common law defence of self-defence (private defence),[136] the prevention of crime defence (public defence),[137] and the defence of property.[138] Although there are nuanced differences between these defences, there is considerable overlap in both scope and substance: they each permit D to use *reasonable* force to either protect themselves and their property or prevent crime. It is because of this common ground that things are now much simpler.[139]

---

133 Fletcher, *Rethinking Criminal Law* (1978), pp.857–858. See also, S. Uniacke, *Permissible Killings: The Self-Defence Justification for Homicide* (Cambridge: CUP, 1994), Chs 4 and 5 where she rejects the argument that killings in self-defence are morally permissible because they are unintended (but merely foreseen) and argues that they are permissible because of "the moral asymmetry between the parties" (p.229)—a development of the theory of forfeiture. cf. J. Dressler, *Understanding Criminal Law* (1987), pp.180–183.

134 Gardner, "Justifications and Reasons" in Simester and Smith (eds), *Harm and Culpability* (1996), p.108.

135 *R. v Abraham (Alan)* [1973] 1 W.L.R. 1270; (1973) 57 Cr. App. R. 799 CA; *R. v Williams (Gladstone)* (1984) 78 Cr. App. R. 276; [1984] Crim. L.R. 163 CA.

136 *R. v Duffy* [1949] 1 All E.R. 932.

137 Criminal Law Act s.3.

138 *Green v Goddard* 91 E.R. 540; (1704) 2 Salk 641. This defence was more recently discussed in *R. v Williams (Demario)* [2020] EWCA Crim 193.

139 Throughout this section, we will often refer to "self-defence" to describe both the public and private defences. However, the term "self-defence" is potentially misleading since these defences are not limited to the use of force to protect oneself.

The Criminal Justice and Immigration Act 2008 (CJIA) s.76 (as amended), brings these defences together.[140] This section does not repeal the earlier defences, but rather seeks to clarify the operation of self-defence by providing criteria for determining whether the force used by D is to be considered "reasonable". For this reason, this codification of common law has been criticised as "pointless"[141] and for ignoring the fact that the common law "urgently needs to be reformed".[142] What, then, is the importance of this section? Well, it offers guidance on several matters, including D's beliefs as regards the existence of any circumstances that require the use of defensive force and "householder" cases. More generally, if the language used in this section clearly covers the factual dispute, this must prevail. If, however, the language used in this section does not provide clear guidance, then the parties must argue the correct interpretation of the public or private defence, subject to the jurisprudence of the ECHR.

B. ELEMENTS OF SELF-DEFENCE

A number of circumstances must exist in order for an actor to be justified in acting in self-defence. **9–072**
These can be summarised as follows:

1. a threat of unjustified harm;
2. a protected interest;
3. an honest belief that defensive action was necessary; and
4. defensive force that is reasonable in the circumstances.

In determining whether these elements are satisfied, two additional questions may also be asked:

1. Was there an opportunity for the defender to retreat?
2. How imminent was the threatened attack?

1. Threat of unjustified harm

In the paradigmatic self-defence scenario, an unjustified aggressor (V) attacks an innocent person (D), **9–073**
and this triggers the right to self-defensive action. From this, it is clear that self-defence is not a defence against *justified* action. For example, against a police officer using reasonable force to make a lawful arrest. On the other hand, as seen earlier when the significance of the distinction between justifications, excuses and exemptions was explored, self-defence is permitted against an exempted actor. One is entitled to defend oneself against a small child firing a gun or an insane person wielding an axe. Such a person, while non-culpable, is still threatening unjustified harm.

140 CJIAs.76 has been extracted below, see paras 9–082–9–083.
141 I. Dennis, "Editorial: A Pointless Exercise" [2008] Crim. L.R. 507.
142 J. Rogers, "Have-a-go heroes" [2008] 158 N.L.J. 318, 318.

The force used in response to a threat will typically be directed towards the person who is posing the threat, whether innocent or not. Only in exceptional circumstances may D use force against an innocent third party to either resist personal violence and/or prevent a crime from being committed by another.

R. v HICHENS [2011] 2 CR. APP. R. 26:

9-074 D was convicted of assaulting V (his girlfriend); D slapped V to stop her from allowing O (her ex-boyfriend) to enter their apartment. D did so with good reason, anticipating violence from O. The trial judge withdrew the public and private defences from the jury on the basis that they did not extend to situations where force is used against an innocent third party.

GROSS LJ:

"[30] It is next convenient to focus on two separate strands. The first is whether self-defence at common law and the use of force in the prevention of crime under s.3 of the Criminal Law Act 1967 are capable of extending to the use of force, against an innocent third party, to prevent a crime being committed by someone else. If and in so far as the judge thought that these defences were not capable of extending to the use of force against an innocent third party, we respectfully disagree, and indeed [counsel for the Crown] did not seek to contend otherwise. Although we suspect that the facts capable realistically of giving rise to such a defence will only rarely be encountered, examples can be adduced and two will suffice:

1. A police constable bundles a passerby out of the way to get at a man he believes about to shoot with a firearm or detonate an explosive device;
2. Y seeks to give Z car keys with Z about to drive X, believing Z to be unfit to drive through drink, knocks the keys out of Y's hands and retains them.

As ever the fact that the defence is capable of being advanced is of course a very different question from whether it would succeed."

Appeal dismissed

9-075 Reluctantly, the court found that the judge was wrong to withdraw the public defence from the jury. However, the conviction was nevertheless safe; the court concluded that the remoteness of the threat posed by O meant that no reasonable jury, even if properly directed, would have acquitted D.

2. Protected interest

9-076 The "protected interests" currently recognised by the common law are protection of self, protection of others and property.[143] Overlapping these interests to a considerable extent is the further protected interest of acting in the prevention of crime.[144]

143 Criminal Justice and Immigration Act 2008 s.76(10)(b) makes it clear that references to self-defence also includes the defence of other people.
144 The overlap is not complete, e.g. if one defends oneself against an infant's attack, one is not preventing a "crime".

It seems only just that innocent persons who are attacked ought to be able to defend themselves and should also be able to go to the aid of their immediate family. But what if friends or even strangers are in need of help; should someone be blamed or protected if they choose to step in? Some authorities, including *Devlin v Armstrong,* suggest that there must be "some special nexus or relationship between the person relying on the doctrine to justify what he did in aid of another, and that other".[145] However, it is now clear that no such limitation exists; it makes no difference whether D is defending themselves or a complete stranger.[146] This has important implications for pub and street brawls; a fight between two people can soon escalate with persons who join in claiming that they are acting in defence of others. D may also use physical force to protect their property.[147] As we shall see, however, one of the real dilemmas here is in defining how much defensive physical force D may use to protect their property.

3. The necessity for any defensive action

In order for D to rely upon self-defence, it must be proven that it was *necessary* for D to use any defensive force against V on the facts that they believed to exist. If D is, in reality, the aggressor seeking to disguise their status behind a smoke screen of self-defence, the defence will not apply to them.[148] In such circumstances, D is the true aggressor. **9-077**

However, it will not always follow that D will be unable to use self-defence if they are the first to provoke or initiate violence. There are several cases where D was the first to initiate violence and was able to rely upon the defence.[149] This does, however, raise an interesting theoretical issue: when does D turn from aggressor to defender? In *Keane*, Hughes LJ said that just because V "turns the tables" on D does not necessarily mean that D becomes the defender at that turning point.[150] The key question is whether V's response to D's attack takes a disproportionate form. If it does, D will become the defender and the defence becomes available.

(i) Honest belief that force is necessary

The requirement that it be necessary for D to use any force against V is to be judged subjectively. Consequently, we are not concerned with whether a reasonable person in D's position would have believed that force was necessary. We only ask whether it was necessary on the facts that D *believes them to be*. Therefore, if D mistakenly believes that they are about to be attacked, they are permitted to use reasonable defensive force. It used to be thought that in such circumstances, D would only escape **9-078**

145 *Devlin v Armstrong* [1971] N.I. 13 at 35–36. Bernadette Devlin MP's relationship with her Londonderry constituents was held not to be sufficient.

146 *Williams* (1984) 78 Cr. App. R. 276; *R. v Tooley* 88 E.R. 1015 at 1020; (1709) 11 Mod. 242 at 250; *R. v Prince (Henry)* (1872–75) 2 C.C.R. 154 at 178; *People v Keatley* [1954] I.R. 12.

147 *R. v Hussey (Israel James)* (1925) 18 Cr. App. R. 160; (1925) 89 J.P. 28 CA. See further, Smith, *Justification and Excuse in the Criminal Law* (1989), pp.109–112.

148 *R. v Mason* (1756) 1 East P.C. 239; *R. v Browne* [1973] N.I. 96. See also, *R. v Rashford (Nicholas)* [2005] EWCA Crim 3377; [2006] Crim. L.R. 547. It is clear, however, that the defence will not succeed where D uses force which, *unknown to him*, is justified by the circumstances: *Dadson* (1850) 4 Cox C.C. 358. See B. Hogan, "The *Dadson* Principle" [1989] Crim. L.R. 679; and R.L. Christopher, "Unknowing Justification and the Logical Necessity of the *Dadson* Principle in Self-Defence" (1995) 15 O.J.L.S. 229.

149 *Rashford* [2006] Crim. L.R. 547; *Burns (Craig John) v HM Advocate (Self Defence)* 1995 J.C. 154; (1995) S.L.T. 1090; *R. v Harvey (Nadia Anne)* [2009] EWCA Crim 469.

150 *R. v Keane (Daniel)* [2010] EWCA Crim 2514; [2011] Crim. L.R. 393.

liability if the mistake was a reasonable one.[151] However, this is not the case; the necessity for force is judged almost entirely subjectively. This has been confirmed at common law, in *Williams (Gladstone)*,[152] which has been subsequently codified by the CJIA 2008.[153]

It was noted at the start of this chapter that self-defence is regarded as a *justificatory* defence. However, the claim that D is *justified* in using defensive force against V is predicated on the basis that such force was needed. If D made a mistake as to the need for defensive force and, therefore, be said to be attacking the interests of an innocent party, D's actions cannot be justified. This is because V has not wronged D. However, in these cases, the law has decided that such a mistake negates blameworthiness and *excuses* D from blame.[154] This approach of excusing all honest mistakes, even if unreasonable, is highly questionable.

Suppose two police officers see a man in a car (V). They think V is a dangerous, wanted criminal. They stop the car to arrest him. Genuinely believing V to be a violent criminal who would shoot them to escape, they remove him from the car, push him to the floor and hold him down so that he cannot run off. In doing so, they cause V actual bodily harm. It transpires that V is completely innocent. According to common law and statute, the actions of the police officers must be judged according to their subjective view of the facts.[155] On that basis, assuming their response was not excessive, they will escape all liability.[156] Now, if their mistake was a reasonable one—i.e. if the facts were such that all reasonable police officers would similarly have thought that V was the wanted criminal and that it was necessary to use force against him—we have sympathy with the police officers' actions and would wish to exempt them from blame and criminal liability (provided their response was not excessive). However, if their mistake was an unreasonable one—if there were no reasonable grounds for thinking that V was the wanted criminal or that V would attack them—then, surely, our response is entirely different. We are now appalled at the enormity of their error. We blame the police officers for making such an unreasonable mistake—and blame them to an extent that we feel they should be made criminally accountable for their actions. In other words, the previously held requirement that D's mistake had to be based on reasonable grounds not only mitigated the practical difficulty of proving whether D actually held the belief or not, but it also reflected a more fundamental attitude towards the determination of culpability.

---

151 e.g. *R. v Rose* (1884) 15 Cox C.C. 540, where D shot and killed V (his father), whom he mistakenly thought was killing his mother by cutting her throat; *Albert v Lavin* [1982] A.C. 546; [1981] 3 W.L.R. 955 HL.

152 *Williams* (1984) 78 Cr. App. R. 276.

153 Criminal Justice and Immigration Act 2008 s.76(4)(b). See paras 9-082–9-083. As Rogers comments, "neither in principle nor on policy grounds can one defend treating the drunkard more harshly" than, e.g. the incorrigible racist who wrongly believes himself to be under attack for that reason: J. Rogers, "Have-a-go heroes" [2008] 158 N.L.J. 318.

154 See further, Uniacke, *Permissible Killings: The Self-Defence Justification for Homicide* (1994), Ch.2 where she offers a more complex analysis of justification and excuse, based in part on a distinction between objective and agent-perspectival viewpoints.

155 See *Davis v Commissioner of the Police of the Metropolis* [2016] EWHC 38 (QB). In this case, D (a police officer), believing V had a pistol, shot and seriously injured V. D had been told (erroneously) that V was carrying a gun and that he had already fired at the police while committing another offence. V sued the Metropolitan Police Service, arguing that they had been negligent in shooting him and that they had breached his right to life under Article 2. The court held that despite the erroneous information, the officer had honestly and reasonably believed that he was about to be shot, and therefore the shooting did not amount to a breach of V's right to life. Although negligence on the part of the officer could be relevant to a claim under art.2, the court determined that there had been no material negligence either in the actual shooting or in the planning of the operation. See paras 9-104–9-106 (on art.2).

156 This is broadly what occurred in *Finch and Jardine* unreported, 12–19 October 1982 (Central Criminal Court). See also *Davis v Commissioner of the Police of the Metropolis* [2016] EWHC 38 (QB).

However, arguing that the subjective approach to determining the necessity of the force is misconceived does not necessarily mean that the old reasonableness test should simply be resurrected. If the assessment of reasonableness is based upon typical male responses to violence, then change is necessary. What is needed is a test that is capable of taking into account the characteristics of D, including, for example, prior history. The question ought to be whether it was reasonable for *that* person to have used such force in *that* situation. This will be considered further in the context of the next issue. In the meantime, as a result of *Williams (Gladstone)* as codified, we are unable to distinguish between those who, when every consideration has been taken of the anguish of the situation, are still blameworthy and those whom we would wish to excuse. In other words, as long as the belief that force is needed is an honest one, it matters not that other reasonable people would not have considered force necessary.[157] **9–079**

This rule needs one final caveat. Although D can rely on an honest but unreasonable mistake regarding the need for defensive force against V, this will not be permissible where such beliefs arise from voluntary intoxication. If D is voluntarily intoxicated, they can only raise self-defence if a reasonable sober person would have made the same mistake as D. This was the position at common law,[158] and has been codified by the CJIA s.76(5). Despite criticisms from academic commentators,[159] the approach is grounded in public policy considerations, which have been consistently endorsed by both the appellate courts[160] and the Law Commission.[161] The scope of this rule is significant and even applies, exceptionally, where drink or drugs is not active in D's system at the time of the commission of the offence. In *Taj*,[162] D came across V's broken down car and stopped to help. In a paranoid state (from drug-induced psychosis), D became convinced that V (who was entirely innocent) was a terrorist intending to detonate a bomb. D called the police, who arrived and reassured D and asked him to move on. D returned after the police left and attacked V, causing serious injury. D raised self-defence in response to a charge of attempted murder. The Court of Appeal held that a mistake may be attributable to voluntary intoxication even where D does not have drugs (or alcohol) in their system; in this case, D's paranoia causing the mistaken belief in the need for defensive force, was connected to D's drug-induced paranoia that was caused by previous drug taking. This approach significantly expands the application of the intoxication rules in relation to self-defence, and further legal clarification by the appellate courts is much needed.[163]

4. The responsive force must be reasonable in the circumstances

Once it has been established that it was necessary for D to use defensive action, the next question to consider is the degree of force used by D. It has long been accepted that D may only use such force as is *reasonable* in the circumstances. Whether the response is "reasonable" is a judgement to be made by the jury with reference to the circumstances as D believed them to be.[164] The general rule is that the **9–080**

157 Although, of course, this may provide evidence that D did not in fact honestly believe force was required.

158 *R. v Hatton (Jonathan)* [2005] EWCA Crim 2951; [2006] 1 Cr. App. R. 16.

159 G. Dingwall, "Intoxicated Mistakes About the Need for Self-Defence" (2007) 70 M.L.R. 127; J.R. Spencer, "Drunken Defence" (2006) 65 C.L.J. 267.

160 *R. v O'Grady (Patrick Gerald)* [1987] Q.B. 995; [1987] 3 W.L.R. 321 CA; *R. v O'Conner* [1991] Crim. L.R. 135 CA.

161 Law Commission, *Intoxication and Criminal Liability* (No.314, 2009), para.3.53.

162 *R. v Taj (Simon)* [2018] EWCA Crim 1743; [2019] Q.B. 655.

163 For a critical discussion of *Taj* [2018] EWCA Crim 1743 and the implications of the judgment for intoxication and self-defence, see M. Dsouza, "Intoxication, Psychoses, and Self-Defence: Evaluating *Taj*" [2018] 9 Arch. Rev. 6.

164 *R. v Press (William)* [2013] EWCA Crim 1849.

jury must consider whether D's response is *proportionate* to V's attack. This is the case for both the common law defence of self-defence (private defence) and the prevention of crime defence (public defence). The overlap and commonality between the public and private defence have been discussed above, and with regards to determining the degree of defensive force that can be used by D, both share the sentiment expressed by Justice Oliver Wendell Holmes that "detached reflection cannot be demanded in the presence of an uplifted knife".[165]

That D's defensive force needs to be reasonable in the circumstances is required by both the Criminal Law Act 1967 s.3 and the CJIA 2008 s.76.

Criminal Law Act 1967 s.3

9-081 "3.—(1) A person may use such force as is reasonable in the circumstances in the prevention of crime, or in effecting or assisting in the lawful arrest of offenders or suspected offenders or of persons unlawfully at large.

(2) Subsection (1) above shall replace the rules of the common law on the question when force used for a purpose mentioned in the subsection is justified by that purpose."

Criminal Justice and Immigration Act 2008 s.76

9-082 "76 Reasonable force for purposes of self-defence etc.

(1) This section applies where in proceedings for an offence—

(a) an issue arises as to whether a person charged with the offence ('D') is entitled to rely on a defence within subsection (2), and
(b) the question arises whether the degree of force used by D against a person ('V') was reasonable in the circumstances.

(2) The defences are—

(a) the common law defence of self-defence;
(aa) the common law defence of defence of property; and
(b) the defences provided by section 3(1) of the Criminal Law Act 1967 (c. 58) or section 3(1) of the Criminal Law Act (Northern Ireland) 1967 (c. 18 (N.I.)) (use of force in prevention of crime or making arrest).

(3) The question whether the degree of force used by D was reasonable in the circumstances is to be decided by reference to the circumstances as D believed them to be, and subsections (4) to (8) also apply in connection with deciding that question.

165 *Brown v United States* (1921) 256 U.S. 335.

(4) If D claims to have held a particular belief as regards the existence of any circumstances—

(a) the reasonableness or otherwise of that belief is relevant to the question whether D genuinely held it; but
(b) if it is determined that D did genuinely hold it, D is entitled to rely on it for the purposes of subsection (3), whether or not—
(i) it was mistaken, or
(ii) (if it was mistaken) the mistake was a reasonable one to have made.

(5) But subsection (4)(b) does not enable D to rely on any mistaken belief attributable to intoxication that was voluntarily induced.
(5A) In a householder case, the degree of force used by D is not to be regarded as having been reasonable in the circumstances as D believed them to be if it was grossly disproportionate in those circumstances.
(6) In a case other than a householder case, the degree of force used by D is not to be regarded as having been reasonable in the circumstances as D believed them to be if it was disproportionate in those circumstances.
(6A) In deciding the question mentioned in subsection (3), a possibility that D could have retreated is to be considered (so far as relevant) as a factor to be taken into account, rather than as giving rise to a duty to retreat.
(7) In deciding the question mentioned in subsection (3) the following considerations are to be taken into account (so far as relevant in the circumstances of the case)—

(a) that a person acting for a legitimate purpose may not be able to weigh to a nicety the exact measure of any necessary action; and
(b) that evidence of a person's having only done what the person honestly and instinctively thought was necessary for a legitimate purpose constitutes strong evidence that only reasonable action was taken by that person for that purpose.

(8) Subsections (6A) and (7) are not to be read as preventing other matters from being taken into account where they are relevant to deciding the question mentioned in subsection (3).
(8A) For the purposes of this section "a householder case" is a case where—

(a) the defence concerned is the common law defence of self-defence,
(b) the force concerned is force used by D while in or partly in a building, or part of a building, that is a dwelling or is forces accommodation (or is both),
(c) D is not a trespasser at the time the force is used, and
(d) at that time D believed V to be in, or entering, the building or part as a trespasser.

(8B) Where— 9–083

(a) a part of a building is a dwelling where D dwells,
(b) another part of the building is a place of work for D or another person who dwells in the first part, and

(c) that other part is internally accessible from the first part, that other part, and any internal means of access between the two parts, are each treated for the purposes of subsection (8A) as a part of a building that is a dwelling.

(8C) Where—

(a) a part of a building is forces accommodation that is living or sleeping accommodation for D,
(b) another part of the building is a place of work for D or another person for whom the first part is living or sleeping accommodation, and
(c) that other part is internally accessible from the first part, that other part, and any internal means of access between the two parts, are each treated for the purposes of subsection (8A) as a part of a building that is forces accommodation.

(8D) Subsections (4) and (5) apply for the purposes of subsection (8A)(d) as they apply for the purposes of subsection (3).
(8E) The fact that a person derives title from a trespasser, or has the permission of a trespasser, does not prevent the person from being a trespasser for the purposes of subsection (8A).
(8F) In subsections (8A) to (8C)—
'building' includes a vehicle or vessel, and
'forces accommodation' means service living accommodation for the purposes of Part 3 of the Armed Forces Act 2006 by virtue of section 96(1)(a) or (b) of that Act.
(9) This section, except so far as making different provision for householder cases, is intended to clarify the operation of the existing defences mentioned in subsection (2).
(10) In this section—

(a) 'legitimate purpose' means—
(i) the purpose of self-defence under the common law,
(ia) the purpose of defence of property under the common law, or
(ii) the prevention of crime or effecting or assisting in the lawful arrest of persons mentioned in the provisions referred to in subsection (2)(b);
(b) references to self-defence include acting in defence of another person; and
(c) references to the degree of force used are to the type and amount of force used."[166]

(i) Non-householder cases

9-084 In non-householder cases, D must use reasonable defensive force for the defence to succeed. If D uses unreasonable or disproportionate force, the defence will fail completely. How are we to interpret the requirement of "reasonable force"? In *Reed v Wastie*, the court held "reasonableness" should be judged on broad and liberal grounds; jewellers' scales are not required.[167] Therefore, if the trial judge comes to

166 As amended by the Legal Aid, Sentencing and Punishment of Offenders Act 2012 s.148 and the Crime and Courts Act 2013 s.43.
167 *Reed v Wastie* [1972] Crim. L.R. 221. This is also emphasised by the CJIA 2008 s.75(7)(a).

the view that, even on the most favourable view of the evidence, no reasonable jury could find that the force employed by D was necessary or reasonable, they should withdraw the defence from the jury. It is important to note, at this stage, that the focus is on D's degree of *force* and not the *harm* caused. Suppose that V attempts to steal D's mobile phone or purse, and D pushes V away. It is very likely that the degree of force used here is both necessary and reasonable. However, what if V falls to the ground and hits their head on the kerb and dies? In such a case, D can still rely upon self-defence; our focus is on the reasonableness of the force (push) and not the resulting harm (death).

However, what is "reasonable" in the circumstances depends upon the viewpoint from which it is assessed. For this reason, the courts have now adopted a middle ground between objective and subjective reasonableness, which we will review shortly. However, this was not always the case. English criminal law *used* to insist on a fairly rigorous and objective test of reasonableness. Such an approach can be supported when one recalls that self-defence amounts to a *justification*:

> "[C]haracterizing self-defence as justification . . . involves finding that the attacker's life has become of less value *to society* than the life of the person attacked. To reach this difficult conclusion, the law must make the self-defence elements strict enough to ensure that the attacker was really the more culpable party and that there was really no reasonable alternative to killing him."[168]

A wholly objective test would require an assessment of what degree of force a reasonable person would have used in D's circumstances. However, the appellate courts moved away from this approach and increasingly favoured D's interests. In *Palmer*,[169] D, who carried a gun, went with other men to buy cannabis. During a dispute, they left with the cannabis without paying. During the following chase, one of the pursuers was shot by D. D was charged and convicted of murder, although he had claimed self-defence. D's appeal against conviction was dismissed, but more generally, Lord Morris held: **9–085**

> "[A] person defending himself cannot weigh to a nicety the exact measure of his necessary defensive action. If a jury thought that in a moment of unexpected anguish a person attacked had only done what he honestly and instinctively thought was necessary that would be most potent evidence that only reasonable defensive action had been taken."

Building on dicta in *Palmer*, subsequent cases such as *Shannon*,[170] *Whyte*[171] and *Scarlett*[172] appeared increasingly to be abandoning the objective requirement. Provided that D believed that they were using an appropriate amount of force, it seemed there could be no conviction. This dramatic change of approach was untenable, and could have led to the result that the more habituated D was to violence,

168 D.L. Creach, "Partially Determined Imperfect Self-Defense: The Battered Wife Kills and Tells Why" (1982) 34 Stan. L.R. 616, 632.

169 *Palmer (Sigismund) v Queen, The* [1971] A.C. 814; [1971] 2 W.L.R. 831 PC.

170 *R. v Shannon (James Russell)* (1980) 71 Cr. App. R. 192; [1980] Crim. L.R. 438 CA.

171 *R. v Whyte (Ese Etenyin)* (1987) 85 Cr. App. R. 283 CA.

172 *R. v Scarlett (John)* (1994) 98 Cr. App. R. 290; [1994] Crim. L.R. 288 CA. See also *Att-Gen's Reference (No.2 of 1983)* [1984] Q.B. 456; [1984] 2 W.L.R. 465.

the more retaliatory force they were allowed to use. The Court of Appeal finally halted the trend towards a completely subjective test in *Owino*.

R. v OWINO [1996] 2 CR. APP. R. 128 (COURT OF APPEAL, CRIMINAL DIVISION):

9–086 D was charged with assault occasioning actual bodily harm upon V (his wife). D claimed that the injuries had been caused when he had acted defensively to stop her assaulting him. He was convicted and appealed on the ground, inter alia, that the jury had not been properly directed on the issue of self-defence.

COLLINS J:

> "The essential elements of self-defence are clear enough. The jury have to decide whether a defendant honestly believed that the circumstances were such as required him to use force to defend himself from an attack or threatened attack. In this respect a defendant must be judged in accordance with his honest belief, even though that belief may have been mistaken. But the jury must then decide whether the force used was reasonable in the circumstances as he believed them to be . . .
>
> What . . . [Beldam LJ in *Scarlett*] was not saying, in our view (and indeed if he had said it, it would be contrary to authority) was that the belief, however ill-founded, of the defendant that the degree of force he was using was reasonable, will enable him to do what he did . . . [I]f that argument was correct, then it would justify, for example, the shooting of someone who was merely threatening to throw a punch, on the basis that the defendant honestly believed, although unreasonably and mistakenly, that it was justifiable for him to use that degree of force. That clearly is not, and cannot be, the law."

Appeal dismissed

9–087 This was an important clarification of the law, which quite properly discarded any suggestion of an entirely subjective test.[173] The initial aggressor, in making the attack, is culpable and deserves to forfeit some of their rights, but they do not sacrifice every right. Allowing unreasonable retaliatory force to constitute a justification would be, in effect, to endorse it. As such, the current position adopts a middle ground between these two approaches. To determine whether D's defensive force was reasonable in the circumstances, the jury is to consider whether the degree of force used by D was objectively reasonable based on the subjective facts that D believed them to be. This has been codified by the CJIA s.76(3)–(4).

The requirement that the degree of force used by D must be reasonable is an important element of self-defence, and English criminal law appears to have done enough to avoid problems with the ECHR art.2. Article 2, which secures the right to life, states that fatal force may be used only if "absolutely

173 See also *R. v Yaman (Tolga)* [2012] EWCA Crim 1075; [2012] Crim. L.R. 896 where the court held that the Criminal Justice and Immigration Act 2008 s.76 makes it clear that the trigger for using force is assessed subjectively while D's response to it must be assessed objectively.

necessary".[174] In practice, the ECHR has looked for a "strictly proportionate" response, although there has been a degree of flexibility in interpreting this requirement.[175] In *R. (Bennett) v HM Coroner for Inner South London*, it was held that the English reasonableness test is compatible with art.2:

> "If any police officer reasonably decides that he must use lethal force, it will inevitably be because it is absolutely necessary to do so. To kill when it is not absolutely necessary to do so is surely to act unreasonably."[176]

It was accepted in this case that allowances must be made for the fact that decisions to use defensive force may be made in the heat of the moment under extraordinary pressure. The CJIA s.76 provides several times that the defensive force must be "reasonable in the circumstances" (s.76(1)(b), (3), (6)). This is defined in s.76(6) as "not to be regarded as having been reasonable in the circumstances as D believed them to be if it was disproportionate in those circumstances". Drawing on the precise wording in *Palmer*, s.76(7) states that account should be taken of the fact that D may not be able "to weigh to a nicety" the amount of defensive force to use and that "the evidence of a person's having only done what the person honestly and instinctively thought was necessary for a legitimate purpose constitutes strong evidence[177] that only reasonable action was taken by that person for that purpose".[178] This second formulation is problematic. As Dennis has commented: **9–088**

> "What is the significance of 'strong evidence'? Does it create some kind of presumption of reasonableness? And suppose the defendant's action was not instinctive, but a considered response to a situation justifying the use of force, as it might be in some cases of military or police operations—is this no longer a case of being strong evidence of reasonableness?"[179]

Rather than clarifying the operation of the common law, therefore, s.76 creates potential problems. However, one thing seems clear. Despite the insistence in s.76 that the defensive action be "reasonable in the circumstances", that action need not *actually* be objectively reasonable. Whether it is "reasonable" will be influenced by D's *perception* of the situation. The more one moves away from an objective standard of proportionality, the more self-defence ceases to have features of a justificatory defence and takes on attributes of an excusatory defence.[180]

---

174 See paras 9–104–9–106 (on art.2 below).

175 *Andronicou v Cyprus* (25052/94) (1998) 25 E.H.R.R. 491; [1998] Crim. L.R. 823. See commentary by A. Ashworth [1998] Crim. L.R. 823.

176 *R. (on the application of Bennett) v HM Coroner for Inner South London* [2006] EWHC 196 (Admin) at [25]; (2006) 170 J.P. 109, upheld on appeal at [2007] EWCA Civ 617; [2007] Inquest L.R. 163. See also *Bubbins v United Kingdom* (50196/99) 2005) 41 E.H.R.R. 24; [2005] Inquest L.R. 24.

177 In *Palmer v Queen, The* [1971] A.C. 814 PC, the phrase "most potent evidence" was used.

178 The courts have noted that the jury, in particular, should be directed as to this principle, *R. v Yaman (Tolga)* [2012] EWCA Crim 1075.

179 Dennis, "Editorial: A Pointless Exercise" [2008] Crim. L.R. 507, 507–508.

180 For a theoretical exploration of objective, subjective and "hybrid" tests for self-defence, see H. Frowe, "A Practical Account of Self-Defence" (2010) 29 Law & Phil. 245. See also *Taj* [2019] Q.B. 655 at [42]–[43].

(ii) Householder cases

9–089 In some cases, it will be necessary for a householder (D) to use defensive force against a trespasser (V) who enters their home.[181] If D uses defensive force, they will (likely) be acting in self-defence, the prevention of crime, and the protection of property. Following *Martin*,[182] there was concern from the public that householders were not adequately protected by these defences where force was used against V. In this case, D was convicted of murder, having shot a teenage burglar who broke into his isolated Norfolk farmhouse. This case attracted considerable (often inaccurate) publicity, much of it sympathetic to D.[183]

The difficulty is that, for many persons, such a degree of force is often the only method by which they can protect themselves and their property. If they are not permitted to use such force, they are, in effect, condemned to forfeiting their property and having to rely on subsequent legal remedies for redress—remedies that will often be useless. However, one might consider that the alternative is even worse. Are we to allow persons to cause death or serious personal injury to others merely in defence of property? This seems to be the view upheld by the ECHR art.2. Fatal force may be used if "absolutely necessary", but only in response to "unlawful violence". In *Faraj*, it was held that if D believes that the only threat is to his property rather than the person, reasonable force may be used to detain the intruder, but no aggressive force is permitted.[184]

However, this can no longer be said to be true for householder cases. The amendments made to the CJIA s.76 by the Crime and Courts Act 2013 s.43 mean that cases involving trespassers in the home should now be treated differently to other cases of self-defence.[185] Section 76(5A) states:

> "In a householder case, the degree of force used by D is not to be regarded as having been reasonable in the circumstances as D believed them to be if it was grossly disproportionate in those circumstances."

---

181 D must genuinely believe that V is a trespasser for the householder provision to apply, and D's belief needs to be supported by evidence. For an example of when V was *not* a trespasser and, therefore, the householder provision was not applicable, see *R. v Magson (Emma-Jayne)* [2022] EWCA Crim 1064; [2023] Crim. L.R. 81. Nor does the householder provision apply if D pursues V out of the property before inflicting violence, per *R. v Williams (Demario)* [2020] EWCA Crim 193; [2020] Crim. L.R. 637. However, it has recently been held that a householder does not lose the benefit of the defence just because they have admitted to unlawful acts, per *R. v Gill (Kuran)* [2023] EWCA Crim 259 at [33]; [2024] Crim. L.R. 114.

182 *R. v Martin (Anthony Edward)* [2001] EWCA Crim 2245; [2002] 2 W.L.R. 1.

183 S. Yeo, "Killing in Defence of Property" (2000) N.L.J. 730 cites a poll indicating that fewer than 4% of people were in favour of Martin's conviction and sentence. The Government responded to the publicity by issuing "reassurance" to the public about the law (HO Press Release No.004/2005, 12 January 2005) and the CPS has issued new guidance.

184 *R. v Faraj (Shwan)* [2007] EWCA Crim 1033; [2007] 2 Cr. App. R. 25.

185 This includes cases where V enters lawfully and, on D's belief, later becomes a trespasser; *R. v Cheeseman (Steven)* [2019] EWCA Crim 149; [2019] 1 W.L.R. 3621.

This is to be contrasted with s.76(6) which states: **9–090**

> "In a case other than a householder case, the degree of force used by D is not to be regarded as having been reasonable in the circumstances as D believed them to be if it was disproportionate in those circumstances."

This now means that there are two separate tests for what is "reasonable" and "proportionate" in cases involving self-defence and defence of property. It is difficult to justify such a stark divergence in approach to these discrete forms of self-defence. As the court noted in *Bennett*, "[t]o kill when it is not absolutely necessary to do so is surely to act unreasonably".[186] How, then, can killing in the protection of one's property, in circumstances when the force used is disproportionate, ever be justified on the basis of reasonableness? During the second reading speech for the Crime and Courts Bill, the Secretary of State for the Home Department explained the reasoning for new provisions:

> "The Bill . . . delivers on our coalition commitment to ensure that the law is on the side of people who defend themselves when confronted by an intruder in their home. Few situations can be more frightening than when someone's own home is violated. Faced with that scenario, a person will do what it takes to protect themselves and their loved ones. They cannot be expected dispassionately to weigh up the niceties of whether the level of force they are using is proportionate in the circumstances. If the intruder is injured, perhaps seriously, in such an encounter, the householder should not automatically be treated as the perpetrator where, with hindsight, the force used is considered to have been disproportionate. Clause 30 will ensure that, in such a context, the use of disproportionate force can be regarded as reasonable, while continuing to rule out the use of grossly disproportionate force."[187]

R. (Collins) v Secretary of State for Justice [2016] Q.B. 862 (Divisional Court):

V, a trespasser in a house in the early hours of the morning, was restrained by D (the householder), who held him in a headlock for six minutes, causing V serious personal injury. Following a police investigation, the Crown Prosecution Service (CPS) decided not to prosecute D based on a determination made by a specialist prosecutor that the force used must have been *grossly* disproportionate for it to be considered unreasonable under the CJIA s.76(5A). V sought judicial review by way of a declaration that s.76(5A) was incompatible with the right to life guaranteed by the ECHR art.2. **9–091**

186 *R. (on the application of Bennett) v HM Coroner for Inner South London* [2006] EWHC 196 (Admin).

187 *Hansard*, HC, Vol.449 col.641 (14 January 2013).

SIR BRIAN LEVESON:

> "19 The operation of section 76(5A) automatically excludes a degree of force which is grossly disproportionate from being reasonable in householder cases. If the degree of force was not grossly disproportionate, section 76(5A) does not prevent that degree of force from being considered reasonable within the meaning of the second self-defence limb. On the other hand, it does not direct that any degree of force less than grossly disproportionate is reasonable. Whether it was or was not reasonable will depend on the particular facts and circumstances of the case.
>
> 20 Thus, section 76(5A), read together with section 76(3) and the common law on self-defence, requires two separate questions to be put to the jury in a householder case. Presuming that D genuinely believed that it was necessary to use force to defend himself, these are:
>
> (i) Was the degree of force the defendant used grossly disproportionate in the circumstances as he believed them to be? If the answer is 'yes', he cannot avail himself of self-defence. If 'no', then;
> (ii) Was the degree of force the defendant used nevertheless reasonable in the circumstances he believed them to be? If it was reasonable, he has a defence. If it was unreasonable, he does not.
>
> 22 On the plain words of section 76, a jury should consider these two questions disjunctively. The answer to the first question does not provide the answer to the second question . . .
>
> 23 The effect, and no doubt purpose, of section 76(5A) is to allow for a discretionary area of judgment in householder cases, with a different emphasis to that which applies in other cases. The obvious example concerns the extent to which it is appropriate to take into account the duty to retreat (which, by section 76(6A) remains a factor to be taken into account). In a householder case, the failure to do so and, thus, the use of force, may be disproportionate but still reasonable although in a non-householder case, that would be unreasonable by virtue of section 76(6) . . .
>
> 33 To summarise, on a proper construction of section 76(5A), its true meaning and effect is: (i) whether the degree of force used in any case is reasonable is to be considered by reference to the circumstances as the defendant believed them to be (the common law and section 76(3)); (ii) a householder is not regarded as having acted reasonably in the circumstances if the degree of force used was grossly disproportionate (section 76(5A)); (iii) a degree of force that went completely over the top prima facie would be grossly disproportionate; (iv) however, a householder may or may not be regarded as having acted reasonably in the circumstances if the degree of force used was disproportionate."

Application dismissed

9–092 Leveson LJ held that the CPS had fundamentally misunderstood the law. The householder provisions do not permit the use of disproportionate force without qualification. Force of the degree illustrated in this case might or *might not* be considered reasonable by a jury. The test to be applied is whether the force applied was reasonable in the circumstances as D believed them to be. Therefore, on this analysis, the householder provisions do not contravene the ECHR art.2.[188]

This matter was considered once again in *Ray*.[189] In this case, D had formed a relationship with a new partner (A). A's former partner (V) was unhappy about their relationship and threatened extreme violence against both D and A. One evening, V arrived at D's house, threatening violence once again. D tried to persuade V to leave the house, but a physical altercation ensued. D believing that V had a weapon, reached for a knife, and fatally stabbed V. D was convicted of murder and appealed on the grounds that *Collins* undermined Parliament's intention to permit householders to use *any* defensive force necessary, provided that it was not *grossly* disproportionate force.

The Court of Appeal, while confirming D's conviction for murder, held that the Divisional Court in *Collins* had correctly interpreted the law. Although householders are in a privileged position compared to non-householders, the jury must still evaluate, taking into account all the circumstances, whether the degree of force used by D was reasonable or unreasonable. Therefore, if D uses disproportionate force, this does not determine whether the force used was reasonable or unreasonable; it can be reasonable, but this will not necessarily be so in every instance. While this more nuanced approach to interpreting reasonable force is preferable to the CPS' original position, it is questionable whether this reflects the original intention of Parliament.[190] Furthermore, it is highly questionable whether a jury can fully comprehend and apply what is an extraordinarily convoluted distinction between conduct that is grossly disproportionate, and that which is disproportionate but still considered reasonable, taking into consideration the circumstances as D believed them.

R. v Ray [2018] Q.B. 948 (Court of Appeal, Criminal Division)

LORD THOMAS OF CWMGIEDD CJ: 9–093

"35 . . . It may be helpful to explain to the jury in general terms that Parliament has conferred a greater latitude in cases of a householder in his own home, for reasons they will doubtless readily understand. It can be pointed out that what might be an unreasonable degree of force used when confronting an aggressive individual in a club might not be so when used by a householder confronting an intruder in his own home. That is why it is particularly important that the jury assess the defendant's actions by reference to the circumstances in which he found himself and as he believed them to be—a point that can then be illustrated and expanded in the summing up with the detail appropriate to the case . . .

37. It would often be helpful, for that purpose, to spell out the kind of circumstances which the jury should consider in determining whether the degree of force used by a householder was reasonable. These might, for example, include the shock of coming upon an intruder, the time

188 See paras 9–104–9–106 (on art.2 below).

189 *R. v Ray (Steven Jason)* [2017] EWCA Crim 1391; [2018] Q.B. 948.

190 M.P. Thomas, "Defenceless castles: the use of grossly disproportionate force by householders in light of *R. (Collins) v Secretary of State for Justice*" (2016) 80(6) J. Crim. L. 407.

> of day, the presence of other help, the desire to protect the home and its occupants, the vulnerability of the occupants, particularly children, or the picking up of an object (such as a knife or stick that would lawfully be to hand in the home), the conduct of the intruder at the time (or on any relevant previous occasion if known to the defendant). Each of these might lead to the view that what was done, such as using a knife, which otherwise in a different context might be unreasonable, in the circumstances of a householder coming on an intruder might, in all the circumstances of such a case, be reasonable."

9–094 Despite the useful clarification in *Ray*, the householder provision remains complex and problematic.

(iii) D's characteristics and the perception of danger

9–095 While the CJIA s.76 offered some clarity with regard to the availability of self-defence, it failed to offer a solution to an issue that has beset the common law: how should the law respond when a mental characteristic distorts D's perception of the danger? *Martin*,[191] briefly discussed above, grappled with the question of which characteristics may be taken into account when assessing the reasonableness of D's response when the plea is one of self-defence. Recall that D shot and killed a burglar and was convicted of murder. On appeal, new medical evidence was accepted that he was suffering from a paranoid personality disorder that would have made him perceive a much greater danger to his physical safety than the average person. The Court of Appeal held that although the facts must be presumed to be as D believed them, the danger presented by those facts must be evaluated objectively. In Anthony Martin's case, his plea of mistaken self-defence failed because his response to the objectively assessed danger (based on the facts he believed to exist) was excessive. This approach is one that can be supported. Unlike duress, for example, which is an excuse, self-defence provides a justification and so there is good reason to insist that D's response be reasonable without account being taken of individual characteristics.

This forced distinction, and why we do not take a wholly subjective analysis based on D's beliefs, is based on the outcome that a successful self-defence plea generates. If D successfully pleads self-defence, they are afforded an unqualified acquittal. In cases where D mistakenly assesses the danger because of a recognised mental condition and kills another, it could be argued that the partial defence of diminished responsibility better secures the interests of the public.[192] There is also a strong argument, in the interests of public protection, that should D be insane at the time of the commission of the offence, the proper defence should be insanity; mistaken self-defence should be unavailable. In *Oye*,[193] D punched police officers believing they were evil spirits rushing him. There was psychiatric evidence before the jury at the Crown Court that D was insane at the applicable time. D appealed his conviction on the basis that the judge had failed adequately to address the issue of mistaken self-defence based on the fact that an insanely held delusion on D's part that he was being attacked, causing him to respond violently, had entitled him to be acquitted on the basis of reasonable self-defence. The court

---

191 *R. v Martin* [2001] EWCA Crim 2245.

192 For offences other than murder, D's reduced culpability due to a medical condition can be reflected by a reduced sentence.

193 *R. v Oye (Seun)* [2013] EWCA Crim 1725; [2014] 1 Cr. App. R. 11.

held that D could not rely on his delusional belief to support a claim that he had used reasonable force in self-defence because "[a]n insane person cannot set the standards of reasonableness as to the degree of force used by reference to his own insanity".[194] If such a claim were to succeed, it would have "most disconcerting" implications as:

> "... [i]t could mean that the more insanely deluded a person may be in using violence in purported self-defence the more likely that an entire acquittal may result."[195]

5. The duty to retreat

It should by now be clear that defensive force cannot be justified unless such force was necessary and reasonable in the circumstances. If D is aware of an alternative, they must take it. So, if D can prevent a burglary by locking the front door, they should do that rather than allowing a burglar to enter and then ejecting them. This raises the important question of whether there is a requirement to retreat. Should D always seek to take a safe avenue of retreat? The old common law defence of self-defence required this.[196] Ashworth is a firm advocate of this rule, stating that self-defence should be unavailable to a D who has to use lethal force to stand their ground.[197] The rationale for this view is that if D is obliged to retreat, then there is full compliance with the right to life. In such circumstances, both D and V live. **9–096**

However, the Court of Appeal in *Julien* took a different view.[198] The court held that the question is now whether D's use of force was reasonable in the circumstances and whether D could have retreated is merely a consideration to be considered when determining reasonableness. This approach (save for householders) focuses on the autonomy of D. If D is behaving in a non-threatening way, in a place where they have a right to be, they should be under no duty to remove themselves at the (unlawful) request of V. This is true even if D enters into a known place of danger, say on the basis of sexist, racist, or other disreputable grounds.[199] Similarly, if D maintains a voluntary lawful presence, they will not lose the right to defend themselves.

This approach has now been adopted within the CJIA s.76(6A), which states:

> "... [i]n deciding the question mentioned in subsection (3), a possibility that D could have retreated is to be considered (so far as relevant) as a factor to be taken into account, rather than as giving rise to a duty to retreat."

---

194 *Oye* [2014] 1 Cr. App. R. 11 at [47].

195 *Oye* [2014] 1 Cr. App. R. 11 at [45]. D could, however, rely on the defence of insanity. Note that the physical characteristics of D can be considered. e.g. if D is physically disabled or is a pregnant woman (to borrow examples from duress) and less able to escape or use lesser force, this can be taken into account in assessing whether the actions were reasonable. This approach opens up the possibility of (weaker) women being permitted a wider range of defensive action against (stronger) men.

196 J.W. Cecil Turner, *Kenney's Outlines of Criminal Law*, 16th edn (Cambridge: CUP, 1952), pp.113–114.

197 A. Ashworth, *Principles of Criminal Law*, 6th edn (Oxford: OUP, 2009), pp.120–124.

198 *R. v Julien (Thomas)* [1969] 1 W.L.R. 839; (1969) 53 Cr. App. R. 407 CA.

199 *R. v Field* [1972] Crim. L.R. 435 CA.

This may militate against a woman who fails to leave a repeatedly violent partner being able to plead self-defence.

KATHERINE O'DONOVAN, "DEFENCES FOR BATTERED WOMEN WHO KILL" (1991) 18 J. LAW AND SOCIETY 219, 222, 235:

9-097 "Despite the abolition of the duty to retreat, retreat might be considered an appropriate response. In the context of killing following prolonged domestic violence the questions look rather different. There may be a history of previous retreat which, as it were, has not worked. How relevant is the previous relationship of those involved, the lack of a safe place to go, the ideology of family privacy, the presence of children? . . . leaving without one's children may seem a frightening prospect. But women's own accounts reveal emotional ties to the abuser which increase the difficulty of leaving. If the legal process is to come to terms with this it will have to accept that for many women connection to others is important. In other words, women's ways of looking at relationships will have to be valued equally with those of men."

6. The imminence of the threatened attack

9-098 The imminence of the threatened attack by V is essential to determining whether it was necessary for D to use defensive force. However, the precise parameters of the imminence requirement are unclear. To illustrate this issue, consider a typical Western film. Two protagonists stand at opposite ends of a dusty street, each with their fingers hovering near their holster, ready to draw and fire. The "baddie" draws first; the "goodie" follows suit; who is inevitably quicker on the draw, and the "baddie" is killed. The film then ends with the "goodie" looking brave and honourable. The "baddie" drew first. The "goodie" was thus fully justified in acting in self-defence.

In such an example, the threat is clearly imminent. But what is the case where the time between the threat and defensive action is drawn out? The CJIA s.76 is silent on the meaning of "imminence". In *Hichens,* Lord Gross simply notes:

"Plainly both the common law and statutory defences have greater scope for operation where it is certain or nearly certain that a crime will be committed immediately if action is not taken. Conversely, the lower the degree of likelihood of a crime being committed and the greater the time between awareness of the risk and the time when the crime might be committed, so the scope for any defence to have any realistic prospect of success will be correspondingly reduced, even recognising, as we of course do, the subjective element in these defences."[200]

Furthermore, what if the "goodie" in our example above is the person to draw first in *anticipation* that violence will ensue? A plea of anticipatory self-defence would be meaningless in a Hollywood Western.

200 *R. v Hichens (Peter Craig)* [2011] EWCA Crim 1626; [2011] 2 Cr. App. R. 26 at [31]. See also, *R. v Keane (Daniel)* [2010] EWCA Crim 2514; [2011] Crim. L.R. 393, discussed in para.4-077.

By reaching for their gun first, they would have become the aggressor. Life, however, is not lived on a Hollywood film set. Restricting self-defence to purely defensive retaliation could effectively condemn innocent persons to death or other injury. The problem may be particularly acute where a substantial difference in size and strength exists, as may well be the case when a man attacks a woman. In certain limited circumstances, the law must permit the right to pre-emptively strike. As Lord Griffiths said in *Beckford*:

> "A man about to be attacked does not have to wait for his assailant to strike the first blow or fire the first shot; circumstances may justify a pre-emptive strike."[201]

The problem, however, is in defining the parameters of such a right. Allowing too much anticipatory defensive action could become a charter for vigilantism.

DEVLIN V ARMSTRONG [1971] N.I. 13 (COURT OF APPEAL FOR NORTHERN IRELAND)

D, during a riot in Londonderry, urged others to build barricades and throw petrol bombs at the police. She was convicted of riotous behaviour and incitement to riotous behaviour. She appealed on the basis that she thought her action necessary to prevent people from being assaulted and property damaged by the police. **9–099**

MACDERMOTT LJ:

> "The plea of self-defence may afford a defence where the party raising it uses force, not merely to counter an actual attack, but to ward off or prevent an attack which he has honestly and reasonably anticipated. In that case, however, the anticipated attack must be imminent: see *R. v Chisam* (1963) 47 Cr. App. R. 130 . . . and the excerpt from Lord Normand's judgment in *Owens v H.M. Advocate* (1946) S.C.(J.) 119 which is there quoted and which runs:
>
> > 'In our opinion self-defence is made out when it is established to the satisfaction of the jury that the panel believed that he was in imminent danger and that he held that belief on reasonable grounds. Grounds for such belief may exist though they are founded on a genuine mistake of fact'
>
> However reasonable and convinced the appellant's apprehensions may have been, I find it impossible to hold that the danger she anticipated was sufficiently specific or imminent to justify the actions she took as measures of self-defence."

Appeal dismissed

201 *Beckford v Queen, The* [1988] A.C. 130 at 144; [1987] 3 W.L.R. 611 PC. In *R. v Murphy (Michael Anthony)* [2007] EWCA Crim 2810, the Court of Appeal held that the jury does not necessarily have to be explicitly informed that pre-emptive force may be used in self-defence.

The appellate courts have subsequently interpreted the imminence requirement very narrowly.[202] For example, in cases where D argues self-defence to justify their possession of a firearm with intent to endanger life, the risk of harm must be imminent.[203] This interpretation ensures that the defence does not cover aggressive behaviour guised as defensive behaviour. Unfortunately, this approach has the effect of limiting the availability of the defence for those abused women who kill their abusers in circumstances where they pre-empt violent attacks that are not imminent.[204] For those abused women who kill, they have often been subjected to years of violence, inadequate help from the police, an inability to leave and killed in circumstances where they anticipated further violence or followed it. However, they do not comply with the imminence requirement to successfully raise self-defence.[205] This may be because they have waited for their abuser to fall asleep before killing them,[206] or because they have gone to another room to fetch a weapon.[207] It seems that the time scale within which pre-emptive defensive action is often taken is unlikely to be stretched for the purposes of self-defence. Yet, as Glanville Williams has pointed out:

> "[T]here is a distinction between the immediacy of the necessity for acting and the immediacy of the threatened violence. The use of force may be immediately necessary to prevent an attack in the future."[208]

Moreover, as has been stated before; in determining the necessity for acting at all, one does not have to jettison the requirement of reasonableness (as *Williams (Gladstone)* has done) in order to do justice to the differing sizes and strengths of the attacker and defender.

9–100 The Criminal Law Revision Committee recommended the retention of the imminence rule:

> "it is desirable to make it clear that a man is not allowed to take the law into his own hands by striking before self-defence becomes necessary."[209]

This view was reflected in the Draft Criminal Code Bill 1989.[210] However, the Law Commission subsequently concluded that the jury would be able to decide whether the use of pre-emptive force was reasonable without any specific reference to a requirement of imminence.[211] Accordingly, no reference was made to it in the Draft Bill. This approach had much to commend because it raises the

202 *Malnik v DPP* [1989] Crim. L.R. 451 Div Ct.

203 See also *R. v Salih (Guner)* [2007] EWCA Crim 2750; [2008] 1 W.L.R. 2627. See also D. Ormerod, "Firearms: possessing a firearm with intent to endanger life" [2008] Crim. L.R. 386.

204 In recognition of these difficulties, the Domestic Abuse Bill proposed a defence equivalent to the householder provision to enable those experiencing domestic abuse a "margin of appreciation" in evaluating the reasonableness of their defensive force. However, this proposal was rejected in the final stages of the parliamentary process. See V. Bettinson, "Adding to the Domestic Abuse Criminal Law Framework: The Domestic Abuse Act 2021" [2022] Crim. L.R. 88.

205 C.P. Ewing, *Battered Woman Who Kill: Psychological Self-Defence as Legal Justification* (Lanham: Lexington Books, 1987).

206 *R. v Ahluwalia (Kiranjit)* (1993) 96 Cr. App. R. 133; [1993] Crim. L.R. 63 CA.

207 *R. v Thornton (Sara Elizabeth) (No.1)* (1993) 96 Cr. App. R. 112; [1992] Crim. L.R. 54 CA.

208 D.J. Baker, *Glanville Williams, Textbook of Criminal Law*, 2nd edn (London: Stevens & Sons, 1983), p.503.

209 Criminal Law Revision Committee, 14th Report, *Offences Against the Person* (Cmnd 7844, 1980), para.286.

210 Law Com. No.177 (1989), cl.44 fn.22.

211 Draft Criminal Law Bill 1993, Law Com. No.218 (1993), paras 39.6–39.7.

possibility, at least, of self-defence being available to domestically abused women who kill. However, the CJIA s.76 only codified the common law in this regard, thus upholding the requirement of imminence.

7. Excessive self-defence

The effect of a successful plea of self-defence is that it justifies D's conduct, resulting in an unqualified acquittal. Accordingly, the courts are likely to continue to regard it as a rigorous test to satisfy. One instance where the test will not be met is where D uses excessive force.[212] **9–101**

This leads to the question, should excessive or premature defensive actions outside the home be regarded as completely unjustified? In terms of assessing their moral culpability, such persons are clearly not on par with those who cold-bloodedly kill or injure others. Their reasons for acting are understandable. It is only the execution of those actions that is unacceptable. In short, there is a strong case for excusing, or at least partially excusing, such actors. Where the injuries inflicted are short of death, the fact that they were acting in self-defence can be considered as a mitigating factor in sentencing. But where they kill, the only verdict is murder with a mandatory sentence of life imprisonment.

If D's reasons for acting are self-defensive and not *because* of an abnormality of mind or loss of control, what is needed is a defence—or partial defence—that accurately explains why they are not guilty of murder. Such thinking has led to increasing calls for the introduction of a new partial defence to murder termed "excessive self-defence", which would result in a manslaughter verdict.[213] For example, Australia used to adopt an approach whereby those who killed using excessive self-defensive force were not guilty of murder but of manslaughter.[214] They were partially excused:

> "[T]he moral culpability of a person who kills another in defending himself but who fails in a plea of self-defence only because the force which he believed to be necessary exceeded that which was reasonably necessary falls short of moral culpability ordinarily associated with murder."[215]

This approach recognised excessive self-defence as a partial excuse. However, the Australian courts have since abandoned this "halfway house",[216] and the House of Lords has confirmed that such an approach is not part of English law.

---

212 This includes those who act in public and private. Consequently, the excessive self-defence doctrine will encapsulate D (a domestically abused woman) who kills V (their partner) during their sleep, being fearful of violence when they awaken and D knowing that their strength is inadequate to match V's. See further, S.S.M. Edwards, "Abolishing Provocation and Reframing Self-Defence—the Law Commission's Options for Reform" [2004] Crim. L.R. 181 where the law is condemned as "exorbitantly gendered".

213 See, e.g. Lacey, "Partial Defences to Homicide" in Ashworth and Mitchell (eds), *Rethinking Homicide Law* (2000), pp.124 and 129.

214 *R. v McKay* [1957] V.R. 560; *R. v Howe* [1958] 100 C.L.R. 448. The Report of the Select Committee on Murder and Life Imprisonment, HL Paper 78–1, 1989, para.89 expressed support for this approach. For a comparative analysis of householder's right to kill in England and Wales and Australia, see I. Dobinson and E. Elliott, "A householder's right to kill or injure an intruder under the Crime and Courts Act 2013: an Australian comparison" (2014) 78 J. Crim. L. 80.

215 *Viro v R.* (1976–78) 141 C.L.R. 88 at 139 per Mason J.

216 *Zecevic v DPP* (1987) 71 A.L.R. 641. See D. Lanham, "Death of a Qualified Defence?" (1988) 104 L.Q.R. 239.

R. v Clegg [1995] 1 A.C. 482 (House of Lords):

9–102 D, a soldier on duty in Northern Ireland, was on patrol when he shot and killed the driver of a stolen car and his passenger. He was charged with murder of the passenger and attempted murder of the driver. D claimed that he had fired four shots in self-defence. The judge accepted this defence in relation to the first three shots. However, since the fourth shot (which was a significant cause of the passenger's death) was fired after the car had passed and the soldier was thus in no further danger, the defence was rejected. D was convicted of murder and appealed.

LORD LLOYD OF BERWICK:

> "Strictly speaking, the [issue of self-defence] does not arise on the facts of the present case. Since the danger had already passed when Private Clegg fired his fourth shot, there could be no question of self-defence, and therefore no question of excessive force in self-defence. But it is convenient to deal with this issue all the same . . . [His Lordship then surveyed the authorities, including *Palmer*.] In other words, there is no half-way house. There is no rule that a defendant who has used a greater degree of force than was necessary in the circumstances should be found guilty of manslaughter rather than murder . . . [S]o far as self-defence is concerned, it is all or nothing. The defence either succeeds or fails. If it succeeds, the defendant is acquitted. If it fails, he is guilty of murder . . .
>
> [His Lordship acknowledged the weight to be given to the views of those who argued for reform and concluded] I am not averse to judges developing law, or indeed making new law, when they can see their way clearly, even when questions of social policy are involved . . . But in the present case I am in no doubt that your Lordships should abstain from law-making. The reduction of what would otherwise be murder to manslaughter in a particular class of case seems to me essentially a matter for decision by the legislature, and not by this House in its judicial capacity. For the point in issue is, in truth, part of the wider issue whether the mandatory life sentence for murder should still be retained."

Appeal dismissed

9–103 This matter was subsequently considered by the Law Commission as part of the review of the law of homicide.[217] The Law Commission recommended that D should be liable of second-degree murder, rather than first-degree murder, if D killed V because they were in fear of serious violence and a person of "ordinary stability" might have done the same or something similar in the same circumstances. This, as a matter of principle, is desirable: the right to use some force *should* diminish your culpability. Unfortunately, unless D loses self-control and kills due to a fear of serious violence, thus affording the defence of loss of control,[218] D is afforded no partial defence for using disproportionate self-defensive force.

217 Law Com. No. 304, *Murder, Manslaughter and Infanticide* (2006).
218 Coroners and Justice Act 2009 s.55(3).

Therefore, should a jury find that the force used was excessive, the defence of self-defence will fail completely. If there was an entitlement to use *some* force, this may lessen D's culpability. When the sentence is passed, if it is subject to the discretion of the judge, they can take this into account when passing sentence.[219] However, with the householder provision potentially leading to complete acquittals for those who use disproportionate (but reasonable) force to protect their homes, the contrast between these outcomes and the mandatory life sentence for those who use excessive force in public arenas will become starker than ever.

8. European Convention on Human Rights

As we have seen, the law recognises the right to protect both personal and proprietary interests.[220] It is because of this that D can use violence to repel an attack or to protect their property.[221] However, as has been illustrated above, there are stringent restrictions as to the circumstances in which D is justified in using such defensive force; D does not have *carte blanche* to defend themselves entirely as they choose. For instance, the law will simply not accept that it is justifiable to kill a human being in order to protect a much-loved pet guinea pig. For conduct to be justified, D must only use *such force as is necessary* to avert the attack. **9–104**

In many of the leading self-defence cases, the aggressor has been killed. The importance that is attached to the sanctity of life (and the corresponding need for any exception to it to be closely circumscribed) is enshrined in the ECHR art.2:

> "(1) Everyone's right to life shall be protected by law. No-one shall be deprived of his life intentionally save in execution of a sentence of a court following his conviction of a crime for which this penalty is provided by law.
> (2) Deprivation of life shall not be regarded as inflicted in contravention of this article when it results from the use of force which is no more than absolutely necessary:
>
> (a) in defence of any person from unlawful violence;
> (b) in order to effect a lawful arrest or prevent the escape of a person lawfully detained."[222]

Thus, art.2 provides that everyone's right to life shall be protected by law, and deprivation of life will not contravene this provision if death results from the use of force which is no more than "absolutely

219 Criminal Justice Act 2003 Sch.21 para.11(e). See *R. v Roe (Thomas Patrick)* [2008] EWCA Crim 2946.

220 It is clear that if self-defence arises on the facts, it should be put to the jury even though the defence has not been raised by D (*DPP (Jamaica) v Bailey* [1995] 1 Cr. App. R. 257; [1995] Crim. L.R. 313 PC). The judge should also explain that the prosecution has to prove beyond reasonable doubt that D was not acting in self-defence (*Anderson* [1995] Crim. L.R. 430).

221 However, it is not just offences of violence where the defence can be applied. For instance, in the case of *R. v Riddell (Tracey)* [2017] EWCA Crim 413; [2017] 1 W.L.R. 3593, the Court of Appeal stated, obiter, that self-defence could apply to dangerous or careless driving offences. While it was likely to be a rare case where the defence would arise, it was, in principle, capable, as a matter of law, of being available for such offences. However, if D does not use *force* in the commission of a driving offence, they will be unable to raise the defence, per *R. v Bailey (Marcus James)* [2013] EWCA Crim 378. For a discussion, see E. Freer, "Driving Force: Self-Defence and Dangerous Driving" (2018) 77 C.L.J. 9.

222 The final exception is: (c) in action lawfully taken for the purpose of quelling a riot or insurrection. Clearly, all three exceptions may be relevant when considering the defence of prevention of crime.

necessary". It is because of this that some academic commentators have argued that the current law on self-defence is incompatible with art.2.[223] The arguments of incompatibility highlight a number of points. Before outlining these, it should be noted that where D (a private individual) uses force against V (another individual), the state is not directly implicated in any wrong that may have arisen. However, the state *may* be in breach of art.2 if the domestic law provides inadequate protection for the lives of its citizens.

9–105 The first point to note is that, under English law, D may be acquitted of murder even though their lethal attack against V turns out to have been entirely unnecessary. This is on the grounds that, according to *Williams (Gladstone)*[224] and the CJIA s.76(4)(b), D is to be judged on the facts that they genuinely, though possibly unreasonably, believed them to be.[225] In such cases, D's use of defensive force is not "absolutely necessary".

Secondly, art.2 refers to the "intentional" taking of life only. It has been argued that this means that the action must be taken with the "purpose" of killing and "that a person acting in order to defend themselves or others is not acting for the purpose of killing".[226] However, this view was rejected in *R. (on the application of Bennett) v HM Coroner for Inner South London,* where it was held that the protection of art.2 is available in respect of unintentional as well as intentional deaths.[227]

Thirdly, despite art.2 referring to the protection and deprivation of life, it may also apply in cases where D intends to deprive life in self-defence but does not actually cause death. In *Davis*,[228] where a police officer shot V, seriously (but not fatally) injuring him, the court held that the shooting itself did not amount to a breach of art.2 because it had been carried out with the honest and reasonable belief that the police officer was about to be shot.[229]

Fourthly, it has also been argued that art.2 will be confined to cases involving agents of the state, but *Bennett* rejects the idea that a different test should be applied in the case of state officials, such as police officers, to that applicable in general to the issue of self-defence.[230] However, Foster and Leigh have noted that:

---

223 F. Leverick, "The Use of Force in Public or Private Defence and Article 2" [2002] Crim. L.R. 347; J.C. Smith, "The Use of Force in Public or Private Defence and Article 2" [2002] Crim. L.R. 958; and F. Leverick, "The Use of Force in Public or Private Defence and Article 2: A Reply to Professor Sir John Smith" [2002] Crim. L.R. 963.

224 *Williams* (1984) 78 Cr. App. R. 276.

225 cf. *McCann v United Kingdom* (19009/04) [2008] 2 F.L.R. 899; (1996) 21 E.H.R.R. 95; *Andronicou v Cyprus* (25052/94) (1998) 25 E.H.R.R. 491; [1998] Crim. L.R. 823; and *Bubbins v United Kingdom* (50196/99) 2005) 41 E.H.R.R. 24. where the court held that D must have had "good grounds" to use defensive force. This is an objective test and contrary to the current position in England and Wales. However, there has not yet been a case before the Strasbourg Court in which D used lethal force based on an unreasonable mistake; should such an eventuality occur, there is likely to be a conflict between English law and Strasbourg jurisprudence.

226 J.C. Smith, "The Use of Force in Public or Private Defence and Article 2" [2002] Crim. L.R. 956, 957 citing *Re A (Conjoined Twins: Surgical Separation)* [2001] Fam. 147 as the authority.

227 *R. (on the application of Bennett) v HM Coroner for Inner South London* [2006] EWHC 196 (Admin). The court added, however, that it was "not obvious that the absolute necessity requirement is appropriate where the death was neither intended nor foreseeable as an inevitable consequence of the force used" at [22]. See also F. Leverick, "Is English Law Incompatible with Article 2 of the ECHR" [2002] Crim. L.R. 347 and F. Leverick, "The Use of Force in Public or Private Defence and Article 2: A Reply to Professor Sir John Smith" [2002] Crim. L.R. 961.

228 *Davis v Commissioner of the Police of the Metropolis* [2016] EWHC 38 (QB).

229 See also *R. (on the application of Collins) v Secretary of State for Justice* [2016] EWHC 33 (Admin); [2016] Q.B. 862.

230 *R. (on the application of Bennett) v HM Coroner for Inner South London* [2006] EWHC 196 (Admin) at [27]. On appeal, the Court of Appeal upheld the decision without discussing these particular issues: [2007] EWCA Civ 617.

> "... in *Collins*, the court made it clear that in cases involving private individuals the duty of the state under art.2(1) is more circumscribed and that the framework obligation is limited by the reluctance of the Court to impose impossible burdens on the state."[231]

However, the *system* of English law has been found wanting in relation to protecting children against excessive physical punishment,[232] and one cannot always confidently predict, therefore, that the law of self-defence between citizens will be safe from challenge.[233] **9–106**

Finally, art.2 only permits a killing to protect oneself or others against "unlawful violence" and does not extend to the protection of property. However, the defence is available in householder cases. In *Collins*, involving serious injury to a trespasser who was held in a headlock by the homeowner, the Divisional Court confirmed that the householder provision (CJIA s.76(5A)) was compatible with and fulfilled the obligation under art.2.

IV. Chastisement

Parents in England are currently entitled to take reasonable disciplinary measures against their children, including the use of moderate physical punishment,[234] although this defence of "reasonable chastisement" was never meant to protect parents from criminal prosecution if the force used was excessive.[235] Deciding what is "moderate" (and lawful) on the one hand and "excessive" (and unlawful) on the other hand, has always been problematic. Indeed, the whole issue of the physical punishment of children is deeply controversial, especially in the light of the ECHR art.3, which prohibits inhuman or degrading treatment or punishment. In *A v United Kingdom*,[236] a boy was beaten with a cane by his stepfather-to-be. The man was subsequently acquitted of assault occasioning actual bodily harm contrary to the OAPA s.47, having pleaded reasonable chastisement. The boy's case was taken to the European Court of Human Rights, where it was held that the UK was in breach of the ECHR art.3 for failing to protect the child from such treatment.[237] **9–107**

231 S. Foster and G. Leigh, "Self-defence and the right to life; the use of lethal or potentially lethal force, UK domestic law, the common law and article 2 EHRC" (2016) E.H.R.L.R. 398, 9.

232 *A v United Kingdom* [1998] 2 F.L.R. 959; (1999) 27 E.H.R.R. 611; see para.4–122.

233 See Leverick, "Is English Law Incompatible with Article 2 of the ECHR" [2002] Crim. L.R. 347, 358–359.

234 Note that all corporal punishment in schools is banned by the Schools Standards and Framework Act 1998 s.131.

235 By nature, duration, degree or inflicted for the gratification of rage: *R. v Hopley* 175 E.R. 1024; (1860) 2 F.& F. 202.

236 *A v United Kingdom* (1999) 27 E.H.R.R. 611. See also *Campbell v United Kingdom* (7511/76) 1981) 3 E.H.R.R. 531 and *Costello-Roberts v United Kingdom* (13134/87) [1994] 1 F.C.R. 65; (1995) 19 E.H.R.R. 112.

237 The court did not go so far as to state that all physical punishment of children breached the ECHR art.3.

The Government accepted that the ruling required a change in the law to ensure that children would be protected from inhuman or degrading treatment. In 2000, it published a consultation paper in which it proposed to set out the defence of reasonable chastisement on a statutory basis.[238] These modest proposals, which would have required courts to have regard to the nature and context of the treatment, its duration, and its physical and mental effects[239] were subsequently abandoned.[240] However, international and domestic pressure to, at the very least, reform the defence continued.[241] In 2004, the defence was abolished by the Children Act 2004 s.58 in those instances when physical punishment results in actual bodily harm to the child. The defence is retained for "mild" smacks where only transient harm is caused. Unfortunately, the distinction between assault occasioning actual bodily harm and common assault is far from clear, and yet this is now the basis of the distinction between punishment which is unlawful and that which is permitted.

The Government chose to restrict rather than abolish the defence of reasonable chastisement, believing:

> ". . . that it would be quite unacceptable to outlaw physical punishment of a child by a parent. Nor, we believe, would the majority of parents support such a measure. It would be intrusive and incompatible with our aim of helping and encouraging parents in their role."[242]

9–108 The Government was influenced, in part, by the results of a survey conducted for them in 2000 in which 88% of respondents believed that it was sometimes necessary to smack a naughty child.[243] However, maintaining the current law cannot be based solely on public attitudes towards smacking. Indeed, in 2023, 68% of respondents believed that it was unacceptable for a parent to use physical punishment on a child, clearly evidencing a shift in societal norms and values.[244] We must also question whether the physical punishment of children can be justified in principle. The defence of reasonable chastisement is based largely on an archaic attitude that regards children as less entitled to the right to be free from physical violence than adults. Newell contests this proposition, stating that:

---

238 *Protecting Children, Supporting Parents: A Consultation Document on the Physical Punishment of Children* (London: Department of Health 2000).

239 In order to constitute a breach, the ill-treatment would have to reach a minimum level of severity depending on all the circumstances identified here: para.5.3.

240 On the basis that with the implementation of the Human Rights Act 1998 courts would, in any event, have to apply *A v United Kingdom*: Department of Health Press release, 8 November 2001. See *R. v H (Assault of Child: Reasonable Chastisement)* [2001] EWCA Crim 1024; [2002] 1 Cr. App. R. 7.

241 See further, H. Keating, "Protecting or Punishing Children: Physical Punishment, Human Rights and English Law Reform" [2006] 26 *Legal Studies* 394.

242 Protecting Children, Supporting Parents: A Consultation Document on the Physical Punishment of Children (London: Department of Health 2000), para.2.14.

243 *Protecting Children, Supporting Parents: A Consultation Document on the Physical Punishment of Children* (London: Department of Health 2000), para.2.9. Fewer than 1% of respondents thought punishment reasonable if it left marks and bruises which lasted for more than a few days.

244 Additionally, 58% of respondents to this recent survey believed that it was unlawful to use physical punishment on a child. See YouGov/NSPCC survey results (2023), *https://docs.cdn.yougov.com/r174szdh2m/NSPCC_PhysicalPunishment_230302_W.pdf*.

> "... [t]here is an injustice and illogicality in suggesting that it is acceptable to hit children, but that it is quite unacceptable to hit others, or for adults to hit anyone else. Hitting people is wrong—and children are people too."[245]

Such a position has led to the abolition of the reasonable chastisement of children in Scotland,[246] Jersey[247] and Wales.[248] The latter is of particular note as it creates a different legal standard for Wales, which remains within the single common law jurisdiction of England and Wales. Many other European countries have also acted to ban the physical punishment of children, and it is to be hoped that England can be persuaded to follow suit in the near future.[249]

V. Duress and Necessity

A. INTRODUCTION

The defence of *duress* arises where D is threatened by another with death, serious injury or rape if they do not commit a crime. For example, in *Hudson and Taylor*,[250] two girls gave false evidence in an unlawful wounding case in which they were the principal witnesses. When charged with perjury they claimed they had been threatened that they would be "cut up" unless they committed perjury; they had been so frightened that they had duly told the lies in court. It was held that the defence of duress should have been put to the jury.[251] The source of the threat must be another person. This species of duress is sometimes termed "duress by threats". **9–109**

The defence of *necessity* potentially arises where D claims that they "had" to commit the crime, not because someone was threatening them, but because something (in the shape of surrounding circumstances which may or may not have been caused by a human being) deprived her of any real alternative. In short, they are claiming that they committed a crime to prevent a greater evil. For

245 P. Newell, *Children are People Too: Case Against Physical Punishment* (London: Bedford Square, 1989), p.12.

246 Children (Equal Protection from Assault) (Scotland) Act 2019 s.1. For a critical discussion of the position in Scotland, see E. Sutherland, "Skelping away" (2020) 65 *Journal of the Law Society of Scotland* 22.

247 Children and Education (Amendment) (Jersey) Law 2020, which abolishes the customary law defence of "reasonable corporal punishment".

248 Children (Abolition of Defence of Reasonable Punishment) (Wales) Act 2020 s.1.

249 The Royal College of Paediatrics and Child Health (RCPCH) has described the law on reasonable chastisement in England and Northern Ireland as "unjust and dangerously vague" and recommended that the defence be abolished. See the Royal College of Paediatrics and Child Health, "Equal protection from assault in England and Northern Ireland" (Policy report, 17 April 2024), *https://www.rcpch.ac.uk/sites/default/files/2024-04/rcpch-equal-protection-from-assault-england-ni_policy-report-2024.pdf*. However, it is uncertain whether the position in England will change any time soon. In 2023, the Government rejected calls to abolish the defence. See "Government rejects call to ban smacking in England" BBC online, 12 April 2023, *https://www.bbc.co.uk/news/uk-politics-65243518*.

250 *R. v Hudson (Linda)* [1971] 2 Q.B. 202; [1971] 2 W.L.R. 1047 CA.

251 It should be noted that the decision in *R. v Hudson* [1971] 2 Q.B. 202 was disapproved in the case of *R. v Hasan (Aytach)* [2005] UKHL 22; [2005] 2 Cr. App. R. 22 at [27], because there were opportunities available to avoid complying with the threat.

example, 10 people are climbing a ladder to safety from a vessel that is sinking. One of them is so petrified that he "freezes" on the ladder and cannot be persuaded to move. Eventually, he is pushed from the ladder and dies.[252] If charged with murder, the survivors would claim that their actions were necessary and that it was better for one to die so that nine could live.

The defence of duress by threats has long been recognised by English law. However, until fairly recently it was commonly thought that the defence of necessity did not exist in English law. For example, in *Buckoke v Greater London Council*, it was stated (obiter) that the driver of a fire engine was compelled to stop at red traffic lights even though:

> ". . . he sees 200 yards down the road a blazing house with a man at an upstairs window in extreme peril . . . [and if he] waits for that time, the man's life will be lost."[253]

9–110 Since the 1980s, the courts have been actively extending the defence of duress to apply to a broader range of situations where the threat does not necessarily arise from other persons, but where D is faced with a crisis or emergency. This extended defence has been referred to as *duress of circumstances*. For example, in *Martin*, D drove his son to work (otherwise he would have been late and at risk of losing his job) because he feared his wife would kill herself if he did not. He was afforded a defence to a charge of driving while disqualified on grounds of "duress of circumstances":

> "English law does, in extreme circumstances, recognise a defence of necessity. Most commonly this defence arises as duress, that is pressure upon the accused's will from the wrongful threats or violence of another. Equally, however, it can arise from other objective dangers threatening the accused or others. Arising thus it is conveniently called 'duress of circumstances'."[254]

It would be tempting simply to regard duress, duress of circumstances and necessity as three prongs of a single broad defence. However, while such a development might be perceived to be desirable, it would be both misleading and premature to conclude that English law has fully embraced this approach. First, as we shall see, in developing the defence of duress of circumstances the courts have largely, but not universally, accepted that the conditions for its application are the same as for duress by threats. We shall see that the two defences are not completely identical. More significantly, however, the rationale for the application of each defence is still contested. Duress by threats is, classically, seen as an excusatory defence: we understand the plight of the hapless person whose "will is overborne" by terrible threats. Duress of circumstances, however, appears to have a more justificatory flavour. D has committed a crime to prevent something terrible befalling himself or others: they are driven to commit the crime by force of circumstances. Despite the fact that English law has cast this defence in an excusatory mould, duress of circumstances looks more like a synonym for necessity. Indeed, it has been

---

252 This seems to have happened during the sinking of the *Herald of Free Enterprise*, *The Times*, 13 June 1988. See *Re A (Conjoined Twins: Surgical Operation)* [2000] 4 All E.R. 961 at 1041.

253 *Buckoke v Greater London Council* [1971] Ch. 655 at 668; [1971] 2 W.L.R. 760 CA.

254 *Martin* (1989) 88 Cr. App. R. 343 at 344. cf. *R. v Shayler (David Michael)* [2001] EWCA Crim 1977; [2001] 1 W.L.R. 2206.

referred to as "necessity by circumstances".[255] Yet, for the courts, the operation of the defence as a justification is reserved for instances of "pure" necessity, such as, life-saving actions by doctors. Ds pleading that their actions (which involved conspiring to cause criminal damage at an RAF airbase) were necessary to prevent an illegal war in Iraq will be deemed to be pleading excusatory duress of circumstances, if anything, and not justificatory necessity.[256]

The approach taken by the Court of Appeal,[257] emphasising the context-specific nature of duress by threats, duress of circumstances and necessity, leads one to be cautious about the prospects of the emergence of a single defence. **9–111**

This brings us to the second reason for distinguishing the defences. A fully-fledged defence of necessity would be far broader than the present defence of duress of circumstances. As will be discussed later, it would involve a pure balancing of evils (whereas under the present law on duress of circumstances there has to be a threat of death or serious injury) and it would be a defence to all crimes (whereas duress of circumstances at present is not a defence to murder or attempted murder). As we shall see, it would be premature to regard such a broad necessity defence as having been accepted into English law.

The extent to which these are separate defences or are simply different labels for three prongs of a single defence will be explored in the following sections. As the three do not all share the same theoretical underpinnings and as they have developed differently and, to some extent, have different rules governing their applicability, they will be dealt with separately.

One final initial point should be made. In the past, claims that actions were done out of necessity or because of duress were frequently made late, once the trial had commenced, and not, say, at the point of arrest. The burden to disprove such a claim beyond reasonable doubt was then placed upon the prosecution, and it was argued that such defence "ambushes" could cause very considerable problems for the Crown: a claim of duress, it is said, is easily made and far from easily refuted.[258] This was one reason why, after a period of increasing relaxation of the law, the House of Lords made an effort to restrain the continued development of the defence of duress.[259] However, for some time now, the defence have been required to disclose the nature of their case well before the trial,[260] and the courts have made It clear on a number of occasions that the days of "trial by ambush" are effectively over.[261] **9–112**

---

255 *R. v Quayle (Barry)* [2005] EWCA Crim 1415; [2005] 2 Cr. App. R. 34 at [35].

256 *R. v Jones (Margaret)* [2004] EWCA Crim 1981; [2005] Q.B. 259. In fact, this defence was denied to the Ds; below, para.9–161. See further, J. Gardner, "Direct Action and the Defence of Necessity" [2005] Crim. L.R. 371.

257 *Quayle* [2005] 2 Cr. App. R. 527. See also Chan and Simester, "Duress, Necessity: How Many Defences?" (2005) 16 K.C.L.J. 121, where support is expressed for maintaining the distinctions between both justification and excuse and different defences.

258 It is partly because of this that the Law Commission has recommended that if duress becomes a defence to murder and attempted murder that the burden should be placed upon D to show, on balance of probabilities, that they acted under duress: Law Com. No.304 (2006), see para.6.101 fn.37.

259 *Hasan* [2005] 2 A.C. 467 at [20] and [22] per Lord Bingham. The Court of Appeal has followed this lead: see, e.g. *R. v van Dao (Vinh)* [2012] EWCA Crim 1717 at [44]–[49] per Goss LJ; [2013] Crim. L.R. 234.

260 See the Criminal Procedure and Investigations Act 1996 Pt 1, which requires D to serve upon the prosecution a defence statement setting out the nature of the defence, the matters on which issue is taken with the prosecution, and why, and any facts or points of law on which the defence intend to rely. Notice must also be given of any defence witnesses (s.6C): P.J. Richardson, *Archbold Criminal Pleading, Evidence and Procedure* (London: Sweet & Maxwell, 2024), paras 12–062–12–072.

261 See, e.g. *R. (on the application of DPP) v Chorley Magistrates Court* [2006] EWHC 1795 (Admin) at [28]; *Whittle v DPP* [2009] EWHC 236 (Admin) at [15]; (2009) 173 J.P. 224; *R. v Penner (Steven Henry)* [2010] EWCA Crim 1155 at [6]; [2010] Crim. L.R. 936 CA and *R. v Farooqi (Munir Ahmend)* [2013] EWCA Crim 1649 at [114]; [2014] 1 Cr. App. R. 8.

It may therefore be argued that this particular reason no longer provides a justification for restricting the defence.

B. DURESS BY THREATS

9–113 As seen, this is the well-established defence that is afforded to persons who are threatened with death or serious injury unless they commit a crime. It is subject to very stringent qualifying conditions.[262]

1. Rationale of duress by threats as a defence

Law Commission (Law Com. No.83), Report on Defences of General Application (1977), para.2.14:

9–114 "Those who favour the conclusion that duress should not afford a defence which absolves criminal liability contend that it can never be justifiable for a person to do wrong, in particular to do serious harm to another merely to avoid some harm to himself; that it is not for the individual to balance the doing of wrong against the avoidance of harm to himself. They argue that duress does not destroy the will or negative intention in the legal sense, but that it merely deflects the will so that intention conflicts with the wish; in short that it provides a motive for the wrongful act and that motive is, on general principle, irrelevant to whether a crime has been committed."

Abbott v The Queen [1977] A.C. 755 (Privy Council):

9–115 LORD SALMON:

"It seems incredible to their Lordships that in any civilised society, acts such as the appellant's whatever threats may have been made to him, could be regarded as excusable or within the law. We are not living in a dream world in which the mounting wave of violence and terrorism can be contained by strict logic and intellectual niceties alone. Common sense surely reveals the added dangers to which in this modern world the public would be exposed, if the change in the law proposed on behalf of the appellant were affected. It might well . . . prove to be a character for terrorists, gang leaders and kidnappers . . . [If the accused were allowed to go free he would now have] gained some real experience and expertise, he might again be approached by the terrorist who would make the same threats . . . [the accused] would then give a repeat performance, killing even more men, women and children. Is there any limit to the number of people you may kill to save your own life and that of your family?"[263]

---

262 Law Com. No.304 (2006), para.6.9 fn.37.

263 cf. N. Tamblyn, *The Law of Duress and Necessity: Crime, Tort, Contract* (London: Routledge, 2018), 5.11.

The arguments against a general defence of duress fall broadly into two groups: **9–116**

(i) the law would lose some of its deterrent effect if duress were allowed as a defence; and
(ii) D is morally blameworthy and, accordingly, deserves punishment. Because of the duress their blameworthiness might be *less* and so they can receive a mitigated sentence—but they are still, to some extent, morally blameworthy.

(i) Deterrence[264]

Are the law's threats likely to serve any useful purpose to a person placed in such a perilous situation? **9–117**

Ian Dennis, "Duress, Murder and Criminal Responsibility" (1980) 96 L.Q.R. 208, 234, 236:

"The deterrent argument is clear. If we assume that the accused acted as a reasonable man in not resisting the threat, and that both he and the reasonable man would act in the same way again whatever the attitude of the law, then the imposition of punishment cannot act as either an individual or a general deterrent. It will amount only to the useless infliction of a penalty and, on a utilitarian hypothesis, will therefore be unjustifiable . . . **9–118**

[A] man under pressure to kill or be killed may well reason correctly that he does, at least, gain time by ignoring the law's prohibition; the alternative of heeding the prohibition and resisting the threat simply leads more quickly to unpleasant consequences. Secondly, if duress is to be taken into account anyway when sentence is passed, then the law's sanction for ignoring its threat is uncertain and may well not be heavy . . . An appeal to the deterrent value of the law disallowing duress as a defence is thus an empty gesture; the deterrent is ineffective because it is not immediate and because it is subverted by admitting duress through the back door as evidence in mitigation."

On the other hand, **9–119**

". . . [t]here is an argument for saying that we should nourish the hope, however faint, that the threat of punishment may be enough to tip the balance of decision by those who have only doubtfully sufficient fortitude to undergo martyrdom for the sake of a moral principle."[265]

Furthermore, the "educative" function of deterrence that regards legal norms and sanctions as operating upon values and character is of relevance here. The denial of a defence of duress may be

264 The other utilitarian arguments hardly seem applicable here. A person who has committed a crime because of duress does not need rehabilitation. They are also not a danger to society needing incapacitation (unless, as Lord Salmon suggested in *Abbott v Queen, The* [1977] A.C. 755; [1976] 3 W.L.R. 462 PC, they were to be continually subjected to threats to induce them to commit crimes; this is highly unlikely—a terrorist or gang leader would be extremely foolish to use the same "agent", to whom the police were now alerted, more than once).
265 Baker, *Glanville Williams, Textbook of Criminal Law*, 4th edn (2015), para.28–015.

seen as strengthening values so that persons in situations of duress would be less likely to submit to the threats.

(ii) Moral blameworthiness

9–120 Is the actor who submits to duress morally blameworthy and responsible for their actions so that they deserve punishment for them?

We saw in Ch.3 that moral responsibility has been traditionally confined to those who choose to break the law and thus *choose* to become subject to criminal liability.[266] The question in duress is whether the actor had this "fair opportunity" to choose between conforming to the law or breaking it. Where the circumstances have overwhelmed their capacity for choice, where their freedom of choice is too restricted, we do not hold them to be blameworthy and responsible.[267] This is what was meant by Lord Widgery CJ in *Kray*,[268] when he spoke of the D being "so terrified that he ceased to be an independent actor" and what he meant in *Hudson and Taylor*,[269] when he required that the Ds' "will" must have been "overborne"; the threats had to "neutralise the will". This does not mean that the D lacked mens rea.[270] Hudson and Taylor both told their lies deliberately and intentionally. As Lord Hailsham emphasised in the leading case of Howe, *it is unacceptable to view duress as a defence that only affects the existence or absence of mens rea. The true view is that expressed in Lynch*:[271]

> "the decision of the threatened man whose constancy is overborne so that he yields to the threat, is a calculated decision to do what he knows to be wrong, and is therefore that of a man with, perhaps to some exceptionally limited extent, a 'guilty mind'. But he is at the same time a man whose mind is less guilty than is his who acts as he does but under no such constraint."[272]

9–121 The basis of the defence of duress is that D did not have an effective opportunity to make a choice as to whether to commit the crime. Of course, in one sense, D does make a choice, but it is only "Hobson's choice". Their dilemma is to choose between two "morally unacceptable courses of action".[273] As the external pressure is so great, in a moral sense, it "coerces" the actor into committing the crime. Fletcher describes such conduct as "morally involuntary".[274] Morally involuntary conduct is not blameworthy; D does not deserve punishment.

---

266 See Hart, *Punishment and Responsibility* (1968), pp.22–23.

267 Tamblyn, *The Law of Duress and Necessity: Crime, Tort, Contract* (2018), pp.202–203. cf. G. Williams, "Duress and Loss of Control: Fear and Anger in Excusatory Defences" (2020) 71 N.I.L.Q. 401, where it is argued that the defence should be reconstructed to take into account the emotional response of fear.

268 *R. v Kray (Ronald)* [1970] 1 Q.B. 125; [1969] 3 W.L.R. 831 CA.

269 *R. v Hudson* [1971] 2 Q.B. 202.

270 As was suggested by Lord Goddard CJ in *R. v Bourne (Sydney Joseph)* (1952) 36 Cr. App. R. 125 CA. *Fisher* [2004] Crim. L.R. 938 confirms that duress does not negate either the actus reus or the mens rea. cf. R.F. Schopp, *Justifications, Defenses and Just Convictions* (Cambridge: CUP, 1998), Ch.5.

271 *DPP for Northern Ireland v Lynch* [1975] A.C. 653 per Lord Kilbrandon at 703; [1975] 2 W.L.R. 641 HL.

272 *R. v Howe (Michael Anthony)* [1987] A.C. 417; see also Lord Bridge's similar comments in *Howe* at 436.

273 J. Horder, "Occupying the Moral High Ground? The Law Commission on Duress" [1994] Crim. L.R. 334, 340–341.

274 Fletcher, *Rethinking Criminal Law* (1978), p.803.

English, judges have made repeated reference to the notion of moral involuntariness in the acceptance of duress as a defence[275]—primarily on the ground that it would be unjust or unfair to punish in such circumstances.[276]

DPP v Lynch [1975] A.C. 653 (House of Lords):

LORD MORRIS: **9–122**

"[I]t is proper that any rational system of law should take fully into account the standards of honest and reasonable men. By those standards it is fair that actions and reactions may be tested. If then someone is really threatened with death or serious injury unless he does what he is told to do is the law to pay no heed to the miserable, agonising plight of such a person? For the law to understand not only how the timid but also the stalwart may in a moment of crisis behave is not to make the law weak but to make it just. In the calm of the court-room measures of fortitude or of heroic behaviour are surely not to be demanded when they could not in moments for decision reasonably have been expected even of the resolute and the well disposed . . .

The law must, I think, take a common sense view. If someone is forced at gun-point either to be inactive or to do something positive—must the law not remember that the instinct and perhaps the duty of self-preservation is powerful and natural? I think it must. A man who is attacked is allowed within reason to take necessary steps to defend himself. The law would be censorious and inhumane which did not recognise the appalling plight of a person who perhaps suddenly finds his life in jeopardy unless he submits and obeys."

Does recognising "the appalling plight" of D reduce itself to taking motive into account? Motive is **9–123** generally irrelevant under the criminal law—because the law seeks to set an objective standard of behaviour—yet there can be no doubt that motives other than the threat of death or serious harm may be compelling. Indeed, as we shall see, this was one of the factors involved in the resistance of English law to the defence of necessity. However, as far as duress is concerned it has to be recognised that it is a "concession to human frailty"[277] which is available only when the threats are extreme. If one adopts the terminology of excuse/justification it is thus best viewed as the former rather than the latter.[278] D has done wrong; they have violated the interests of an innocent person, but because of their appalling predicament, they are excused from blame.[279]

---

275 However, it is clear that moral involuntariness is not actually a requirement for the operation of the defence. If it were "the well-established requirements for duress as a defence (e.g. reasonable steadfastness) could have no place in a completely subjectively orientated defence where the only concern was whether the defendant's actions were 'morally involuntary'": Clarkson, "Necessary Action: A New Defence" [2004] Crim. L.R. 81, 83.

276 With the exception of murder, attempted murder and some forms of treason.

277 *Howe* [1987] A.C. 417; *R. v Shepherd (Martin Brian)* (1988) 86 Cr. App. R.47; [1987] Crim. L.R. 686 CA.

278 There are elements of a justificatory defence, however, which further illustrates the difficulties inherent in classification in relation to this area of law. In Lord Hailsham's speech in *Howe* [1987] A.C. 417, e.g. he spoke of the defendant possibly regarding their choice "as the lesser of two evils". In other words, D claims to have done the *right* thing (or, at least, the only reasonable thing) in the circumstances; this is a justificatory claim. The Law Commission rejected the notion of a balancing of harms approach; para.4–149. But see: J. Horder, "Autonomy, Provocation and Duress" [1992] Crim. L.R. 706.

279 *Hasan* [2005] 2 A.C. 467 at [19] per Lord Bingham. S. Kadish, "Excusing Crime" (1987) 75 Cal. L. Rev. 257; K.J.M. Smith, "Must Heroes Behave Heroically?" [1989] Crim. L.R. 622.

2. Parameters of the defence

9–124 In what circumstances may D break the law but escape liability because of duress? When will the circumstances be such that we will not account the defendant blameworthy for their actions?

The attribution of blame involves a moral judgement relating, inter alia, to our expectations of how people should act in certain situations. This inevitably involves a comparison between D's response and how we imagine *we*, or other "ordinary people", would respond in that situation. If we perceive that ordinary people would have responded as D did, then we do not blame D for their actions. But if we perceive that ordinary people would have withstood the threats, then we legitimately blame D for a failure to do so.

This test provides us with the key to answering the following questions concerning the parameters of the defence of duress.

(i) Threat of death or serious harm

9–125 In making our moral judgement as to whether to blame D, we would surely wish to compare the crime committed with the nature of the threats to which D was exposed. Suppose D had been threatened that his house would be burnt to the ground if he did not steal a tin of beans from the local supermarket. We would not blame the D who committed such a crime. Suppose a D who had access to the water supply of London was threatened with death or serious bodily harm if they did not place a deadly poison in the water supply. If they poisoned the water and 10,000 people died (as they knew would be the case), we would blame them for their actions because the harm that they caused was so much greater than the harm threatened. This "balancing of harms" approach ought not to operate in a rigid mechanistic manner, but it is a useful aid to our moral judgement as to whether to blame D.[280] In *Howe*, Lord Hailsham said he:

> ". . . believe[d] that some degree of proportionality between the threat and the offence must, at least to some extent, be a prerequisite of the defence under the existing law."[281]

English law, however, is committed to the view that only threats of death or serious harm will suffice for a defence of duress.[282] If the threats are less terrible they should be matters of mitigation only.[283]

What is meant be serious harm here? Must this be serious physical harm or will serious psychological harm suffice? For the purposes of offences against the person, the term "grievous bodily harm" has been interpreted to include serious psychiatric harm.[284] Such an approach was rejected in the context

---

280 Fletcher, *Rethinking Criminal Law* (1978), p.804.

281 *Howe* [1987] A.C. 417 at 432–433.

282 *R. v Hudson* [1971] 2 Q.B. 202; *DPP for Northern Ireland v Lynch* [1975] A.C. 653; *R. v Conway (Francis Gerald)* [1989] Q.B. 290; [1988] 3 W.L.R. 1238 CA; *Martin* (1989) 88 Cr. App. R. 343; *DPP v Davis; DPP v Pittaway* [1994] Crim. L.R. 600; (1995) 159 J.P.N. 194 QBD.

283 *Hasan* [2005] 2 A.C. 467 at [22] per Lord Bingham; Law Commission, *Report on Defences of General Application*, Law Com. No.83 (1977), para.2.18.

284 *R. v Ireland (Robert Matthew); R. v Burstow (Anthony Cristopher)* [1998] A.C. 147; [1997] 3 W.L.R. 534.

of the defence of duress in *Baker and Wilkins*[285] but *Shayler*[286] seems to support the view that a threat of serious psychological harm can suffice as it is stated that "protection of the physical and mental well-being of a person from serious harm is still being required". Of course, where the threat is one of serious psychological harm, it will be difficult (but not impossible) to satisfy the test, to be explored shortly, that the threat must be one of imminent harm.[287]

The Court of Appeal has stated that it had no doubt that rape would fall within the ambit of serious injury,[288] while in *van Dao*, it commented obiter that its provisional view was that it was "strongly disinclined" to allow a threat of false imprisonment (without any additional threat of serious harm) to suffice for a plea of duress on the basis that any widening of the defence would be ill-advised.[289] It is settled law that a threat of damage to property (however valuable) is not sufficient for the defence to apply.[290]

The threat must be extraneous to the offender. In *Rodger and Rose*,[291] it was held that the defence of duress of circumstances was not available to a charge of breaking prison where the Ds claimed that if they had not escaped, they would have committed suicide.[292] **9–126**

(ii) Threats indirectly relayed

It appears that there is no requirement that the threat of death or serious Injury be conveyed directly to D. For example, in *Hudson* and *Taylor*[293] the threat was made to Hudson, who then passed it on to Taylor, yet the Court of Appeal did not regard this as being fatal to the defence. This issue has been considered more recently in the case of *Brandford*. **9–127**

R. v Brandford (Olivia) [2016] EWCA Crim 1794 (Court of Appeal (Criminal Division)):

D was convicted of conspiracy to supply cocaine and heroin. She claimed that she had been told by Alford, a man with whom she was infatuated or in love with, that he had been told by a drug dealer that he had inherited a debt from a person who had been murdered, and that if he did not sell drugs for him, "it would not be nice for him". As a result of this, she was fearful that Alford's life was at risk and agreed to assist him by carrying drugs for him. The trial judge ruled that D was **9–128**

---

285 *R. v Baker (Janet); R. v Wilkins (Carl)* [1997] Crim. L.R. 497 CA.

286 *Shayler* [2001] 1 W.L.R. 2206.

287 See further, J. Loveless, "Domestic Violence, Coercion and Duress" [2010] Crim. L.R. 93 where it is argued that this reduces the possibility of female victims of domestic violence pleading duress. See also *R. v A* [2012] EWCA Crim 434; [2012] 2 Cr. App. R. 8 and *R. v GAC* [2013] EWCA Crim 1472.

288 *R. v A* [2012] EWCA Crim 434 per Lord Judge CJ at [63].

289 *van Dao* [2012] EWCA Crim 1717 at [33], followed in *R. v Brandford (Olivia)* [2016] EWCA Crim 1794 at [32]; [2017] 4 W.L.R. 17. In *R. v Joseph (Verna Sermanfure)* [2017] EWCA Crim 36; [2017] 1 W.L.R. 3153, the Court of Appeal agreed with this provisional view.

290 *Brandford* [2016] EWCA Crim 1794 at [32].

291 *R. v Rodger (Andrew); R. v Rose (Keith John)* [1998] 1 Cr. App. R.143 CA. cf. *R. v Hammond (Dean Paul)* [2013] EWCA Crim 2709 where it was held that the defence of duress was unavailable to D who claimed that he needed to escape from prison because otherwise he would not be able to resist attacking a man who has made sexual advances to him.

292 This requirement has been insisted upon in *Quayle* [2005] 2 Cr. App. R. 527 in which the "necessity" of using cannabis for pain relief was the basis of defences in a number of appeals heard together. The plea of necessity was rejected: see paras 9–161–9–162.

293 *Hudson and Taylor* (1972) 56 Cr. App. 1 at 2. cf. *R. v Safi (Ali Ahmed)* [2003] EWCA Crim 1809 at [28]; [2004] 1 Cr. App. R. 14. Both cases are considered in *Brandford* [2016] EWCA Crim 1794 at [39].

unable to rely on duress based on threats of which she had no first-hand knowledge and withdrew the defence from the jury. Whilst the Court of Appeal dismissed her appeal against conviction on the basis that the threats lacked immediacy, there was insufficient evidence of compulsion, and that she had voluntarily associated with known criminals,[294] they ruled that the judge had erred in ruling that first-hand knowledge of the threats was required.

LORD JUSTICE GROSS:

> "[39] . . . (ii) It is striking that amongst the limits on duress canvassed in the authorities to which we have referred, the indirect relaying of a threat is nowhere mentioned. For our part, we can envisage a situation where a threat is indeed very real, regardless of the fact that it is indirectly relayed. Take a threat made to a hypothetical D and her family by a messenger from an organised crime group, conveying a threat from a 'crime boss' or the equivalent passing on of a threat from an emissary of a terrorist group. In our judgment, the question is not whether the threat was directly or indirectly relayed which is of significance, so much as its immediacy, imminence, the possibility of taking evasive action, the question of whether D reasonably believed the threat, his/her response to that threat and questions as to the response of a sober person of reasonable firmness sharing D's characteristics. It is very likely that the more directly a threat is conveyed, the more it will be capable of founding a defence of duress: e.g., the telling example of the loaded pistol in the back, given by Lord Simon of Glaisdale in *Director of Public Prosecutions for Northern Ireland v Lynch* [1975] A.C. 653 at 687. Conversely, the more indirectly the threat is relayed the more, all other things being equal, a defendant will struggle to satisfy the requirements of the defence, or (put in burden of proof terms) the more readily the prosecution will disprove it. However, the mere fact that the threat was conveyed indirectly does not seem to us to constitute a fatal bar to the defence. All must depend on the circumstances, of which the manner in which the threat is conveyed is but one, however important it may be . . ."

Appeal dismissed

(iii) Multiple threats

9–129 In *Valderrama-Vega*,[295] D was threatened with the disclosure of his homosexuality, was under financial pressure and received threats of death or serious harm. The first two are incapable of amounting to duress but the court held that the jury was entitled to look at the cumulative effect of all of the threats. It was wrong to direct the jury that the threat of death or serious injury had to be the sole reason for him committing the crime. In *Ortiz*,[296] however, a direction that the threat to life be the sole threat was upheld, although the court also thought the use of the word "solely" should normally not be included. The special feature of *Ortiz* appears to have been the possibility of D's actions also being motivated by

294 *Brandford* [2016] EWCA Crim 1794 at [39].

295 *R. v Valderrama-Vega* [1985] Crim. L.R. 220 CA. For discussion of this case see: P. Alldridge, "Developing the defence of duress" [1986] Crim. L.R. 433.

296 *R. v Ortiz (Fernando)* (1986) 83 Cr. App. R. 173 CA.

the large amount of money he was making from dealing in cocaine and on that basis the authority of *Valderrama-Vega* is to be preferred.[297]

(iv) Threats to others

"Duress of circumstances" cases have indicated that the threat can be to D or "some other person".[298] **9–130**

R. v Shayler [2001] 1 W.L.R. 2206 (Court of Appeal, Criminal Division):

D, a former member of MI5, was charged with breaching the Official Secrets Act 1989 s.1(1) by disclosing deficiencies in MI5. He claimed that it was necessary to do so because if MI5 continued to operate in this manner, it would inevitably create a danger to the public. He was convicted and appealed. **9–131**

LORD WOOLF CJ:

> "It is also necessary to consider in greater detail the nature of the responsibility and the category of persons to whom the defendant must owe the responsibility for the purposes of the defence. Mr Shayler contends that, as a member of the government secret services, he owed a responsibility to the general public at large. His acts were necessary to protect a yet to be identified group from among the public for whose protection MI5 had responsibilities who would inevitably suffer because of MI5's incompetence . . .
>
> So in our judgment the way to reconcile the authorities to which we have referred is to regard the defence as being available when a defendant commits an otherwise criminal act to avoid an imminent peril of danger to life or serious injury to himself or towards somebody for whom he reasonably regards himself as being responsible. That person may not be ascertained and may not be identifiable. However, if it is not possible to name the individuals beforehand, it has at least to be possible to describe the individuals by reference to the action which is threatened would be taken which would make them victims absent avoiding action being taken by the defendant. The defendant has responsibility for them because he is placed in a position where he is required to make a choice whether to take or not to take the action which it is said will avoid them being injured. Thus if the threat is to explode a bomb in a building if the defendant does not accede to what is demanded the defendant owes responsibility to those who would be in the building if the bomb exploded."

Appeal dismissed[299]

---

297 See also *DPP v Bell (Derek)* [1992] R.T.R. 335; [1992] Crim. L.R. 176 Div Ct.

298 *Conway* [1988] 3 W.L.R. 1238; *Martin* (1989) 88 Cr. App. R. 343. cf. Law Commission, Legislating the Criminal Code: Offences Against the Person and General Principles, Law Com. No.218 (1993), cl.25(2)(a), where it was suggested that the threat must be to D "or another".

299 On appeal, the House of Lords declined to discuss these issues on the basis that the facts were "not within measurable distance of affording him a defence of necessity or duress of circumstances" (*Shayler* [2002] 2 All E.R. 477 at 491).

9–132 As this bomb example demonstrates, most endangered strangers can be brought within the test as being persons for whom D "reasonably regards himself as being responsible"[300] provided they can be identified in a general way: for example, persons in a building. On the facts of *Shayler* itself, it was stated that:

> "... if it is possible to identify the members of the public at risk this will only be by hindsight. This creates difficulty over the requirement of responsibility ..."

Where the threat is directed against the D, their family or others to whom a direct responsibility is owed, one can legitimately describe D's conduct as being "morally involuntary" and excusable. However, where strangers are involved, it is questionable whether D should be permitted to, say, cause grievous bodily harm to one stranger in order to save another stranger from grievous bodily harm (especially as there must always be a chance, however small, that the threat will not be carried out). This is in effect allowing such D to choose between the two strangers. How are they to assess their relative "worth"? Of course, in many cases the harm to be inflicted by D will be much less than that threatened against the stranger and in such situations, it ought certainly to be an excuse that D committed the crime to save the third party from, at least, serious injury.

(v) Stipulated crime

9–133 Duress by threats is a defence where D is threatened with death or serious injury unless they commit a particular, stipulated crime. What is the position if there is no link between the threat and the offence committed? In *Cole*,[301] D robbed two building societies and claimed that he had done so to pay off a debt to moneylenders who had hit him with a baseball bat and had threatened him and his family. The Court of Appeal held that the defence of duress is only available if the threats are directed at the offence committed. In this case, the moneylenders had not stipulated that D commit robbery in order to meet their demands and there was, therefore, an insufficient nexus between the threat and the offence.[302]

As we shall see, for the defence of "duress of circumstances" there is no requirement that D commit a stipulated crime. For example, in *Martin*,[303] the evil to be averted was his wife killing herself; the crime committed was driving while disqualified. There was no link between them. There are two views that can be adopted in relation to this. First, while duress and duress of circumstances are

300 This test was adopted by the House of Lords in *Hasan* [2005] 2 A.C. 467: see Lord Bingham's speech at para.4–181, and by the Court of Appeal in *Brandford* [2016] EWCA Crim 1794 at [32].

301 *R. v Cole* [1994] Crim. L.R. 582 CA.

302 This approach was followed in *Hasan* [2005] 2 A.C. 467, where it was stated that, for duress to apply, the criminal conduct sought to be excused must be "directly caused by the threats which are relied upon" [2005] 2 A.C. 467 at [3]. In *R. v Ryan* [2013] S.C.C. 3, D had been the V of abusive and controlling behaviour by her husband. Believing that her husband would kill or cause serious bodily harm to either her, or her daughter, she paid a "hitman" (who was, in fact, an undercover police officer) to kill her husband. The Canadian Supreme Court held that the defence of duress was only available where D commits an offence under compulsion of a threat made for the purpose of compelling her to commit a specific offence. See: J. Maclean, N. Verrelli and L. Chambers, "Battered women under duress: The Supreme Court of Canada's abandonment of context and purpose in *R. v Ryan*" [2017] 29 *Canadian Journal of Women and the Law* 60; Tamblyn, *The Law of Duress and Necessity: Crime, Tort, Contract* (2018), pp.191–192.

303 *Martin* (1989) 88 Cr. App. R. 343.

largely identical in the conditions for their application, there are differences and this is one of them. Secondly, if they are in reality, two "prongs" of the same defence, simply bearing different labels to describe the different situations involved, it may be argued that *Cole* should no longer be regarded as good law on this issue. If a person's will is so overborne by terrible threats that their actions become "morally involuntary", it hardly seems material that they commit a crime other than the one stipulated.[304]

(vi) Belief in threat; steadfastness: subjective or objective

There are two issues here. First, what is the position if D thinks that they have been threatened with death or serious injury but a reasonable person in their situation would not have interpreted the threat thus? Secondly, what is the position if D is terrified by the threats and duly commits a crime, but the reasonable person would have "stood his ground" and not committed the crime? These two questions are often dealt with jointly. However, as each raises rather different issues they will be dealt with separately after the following extract. **9–134**

R. v Graham (1982) 74 Cr. App. R. 235 (Court of Appeal, Criminal Division):

D, who was gay, lived in a flat with his wife and another gay man, K, in a *ménage à trois*. D was taking drugs for anxiety which made him more susceptible to bullying. K was a violent man and was jealous of D's wife. One night after D and K had been drinking heavily, K put a flex round the wife's neck, pulled it tight and then told D to take hold of the other end of the flex and pull on it. D did so for about a minute as a result of which the wife was killed. D was charged with murder, as was K, who pleaded guilty. D pleaded not guilty and in evidence said that he had complied with K's demand to pull on the flex because of his fear of K. The Crown conceded that it was open to D to raise the defence of duress and did not seek to contend that the defence was not available to a principal to murder. In his directions, the judge posed two questions for the jury: (i) the subjective question of whether D took part in the killing because he feared for his life or personal safety as a result of K's words or conduct; and (ii) if so, the objective question of whether, taking into account all the circumstances, including the appellant's age, sex, sexual propensities and other personal characteristics, and his state of mind and the drink and drugs he had taken, it was reasonable for D, because of fear of K, to take part in killing his wife. The judge further stated that the test of reasonableness in that context was whether, having regard to those circumstances, D's behaviour reflected the degree of self-control and firmness of purpose to be expected from a person in today's society. D was convicted of murder and appealed. **9–135**

LORD LANE CJ:

> "[T]he direction appropriate . . . [to the first question] should have been in these words: 'Was this man at the time of the killing taking part because he held a well-grounded fear of death [or serious physical injury] as a result of the words or conduct on the part of King?' The

---

304 Although in the light of the House of Lords decision in *Hasan* [2005] 2 A.C. 467 it is highly unlikely that this approach would be favoured by a court.

bracketed words may be too favourable to the defendant. The point was not argued before us. . . . [Counsel for the appellant] contends that no second question arises at all; the test is purely subjective. He argues that if the appellant's will was in fact overborne by threats of the requisite cogency, he is entitled to be acquitted and no question arises as to whether a reasonable man, with or without his characteristics, would have reacted similarly . . .

[Counsel for the Crown], on the other hand, submits that such dicta as can be found on the point are in favour of a second test; this time an objective test . . .

As a matter of public policy, it seems to us essential to limit the defence of duress by means of an objective criterion formulated in terms of reasonableness. Consistency of approach in defences to criminal liability is obviously desirable. Provocation and duress are analogous. In provocation the words or actions of one person break the self-control of another. In duress the words or actions of one person break the will of another. The law requires a defendant to have the self-control reasonably to be expected to the ordinary citizen in his situation. It should likewise require him to have the steadfastness reasonably to be expected of the ordinary citizen in his situation. So too with self-defence, in which the law permits the use of no more force than is reasonable in the circumstances. And, in general, if a mistake is to excuse what would otherwise be criminal, the mistake must be a reasonable one.

It follows that we accept [counsel for the Crown's] submission that the direction in this case was too favourable to the appellant. The Crown having conceded that the issue of duress was open to the appellant and was raised on the evidence, the correct approach on the facts of this case would have been as follows: (1) Was the defendant, or may he have been, impelled to act as he did because, as a result of what he reasonably believed King had said or done, he had good cause to fear that if he did not so act King would kill him or (if this is to be added) cause him serious physical injury? (2) If so, have the prosecution made the jury sure that a sober person of reasonable firmness, sharing the characteristics of the defendant, would not have responded to whatever he reasonably believed King said or did by taking part in the killing? The fact that a defendant's will to resist has been eroded by the voluntary consumption of drink or drugs or both is not relevant to this test.

We doubt whether the Crown were right to concede that the question of duress ever arose on the facts of this case. The words and deeds of King relied on by the defence were far short of those needed to raise a threat of the requisite gravity. However, the Crown having made the concession, the judge was right to pose the second objective question to the jury. His only error lay in putting it too favourably to the appellant."

Appeal dismissed

(a) Belief in threat

According to *Graham*, D must *reasonably* believe that they have been threatened with death or serious injury ("the first question").[305] It is interesting that Lord Lane asserts that "consistency of approach in defences to criminal liability is obviously desirable" yet in the self-defence case of *Williams (Gladstone)*,[306] he ruled that D had to be judged according to the facts as he believed them to be. *Graham* has been approved by the House of Lords in *Howe*[307] and has been followed in a number of subsequent cases.[308] Suggestions from the Court of Appeal that an entirely subjective approach should be taken in duress cases[309] have fallen on stony ground: in *Hasan*, Lord Bingham stated that "there is no warrant for relaxing the requirement that the belief must be reasonable as well as genuine".[310] **9–136**

This is the appropriate approach and the one recommended by the Law Commission.[311] While mistakes as to justifications (such as self-defence) need only be honest, mistakes as to excuses (such as duress) should have to be reasonable as well. While this argument could potentially be problematic when applied to duress of circumstances which contains elements of a justificatory nature, the fact remains that the English courts have treated duress of circumstances as being an excuse. If excuses are to exempt Ds from liability, they should be plausible—i.e. reasonable—excuses.[312]

(b) Steadfastness

It is clear from *Graham* ("the second question") that D must display reasonable steadfastness or bravery. This was also confirmed in *Howe*. The test is that the threats must be such that a person of reasonable firmness *sharing the characteristics of the D* would have given way to the threats. There have been a number of cases in which the courts have struggled to distinguish relevant characteristics from those which should be ignored.[313] In *Emery*, for example, the Court of Appeal held that medical evidence about "learned or dependent helplessness" was rightly admitted in determining whether the defendant, charged with cruelty to a child, could have withstood threats from the child's father.[314] The following case attempted to synthesise the principles which have emerged. **9–137**

305 The threat will usually be express but an implied threat can suffice: see *R. v N* [2007] EWCA Crim 3479.

306 *Williams* (1984) 78 Cr. App. R. 276.

307 *Howe* [1987] A.C. 417.

308 e.g. in *DPP v Davis; DPP v Pittaway* [1994] Crim. L.R. 600; *Brandford* [2016] EWCA Crim 1794.

309 *R. v Martin (David Paul)* [2000] 2 Cr. App. R. 42; (2000) 164 J.P. 174 CA and *Safi* [2004] 1 Cr. App. R. 14.

310 *Hasan* [2005] 2 A.C. 467 at [23].

311 In relation to duress as a defence to murder and attempted murder, Law Com. No.304 (2006), paras 6.77–6.82 fn.37. The Law Commission takes the view that this would not prevent the particular circumstances of the defendant being taken into account in determining whether the belief was reasonably held.

312 In *R. v Cairns (John)* [1999] 2 Cr. App. R. 137; [2000] R.T.R. 15 CA, a duress of circumstances case, it was emphasised that D must reasonably believe that there was a threat of death or serious injury.

313 *R. v Hegarty* [1994] Crim. L.R. 353 CA (evidence of emotional instability and a grossly elevated neurotic state inadmissible); *R. v Horne* [1994] Crim. L.R. 584 CA (evidence that unusually pliable and vulnerable to pressure inadmissible); *R. v Hurst (Marnie Michelle)* [1995] 1 Cr. App. R. 82 CA (evidence of possible effects upon D of child abuse as a child inadmissible); and *R. v Flatt (David Sean)* [1996] Crim. L.R. 576 CA (evidence of drug addiction excluded as a self-induced condition not a characteristic).

314 *R. v Emery (Sally Lorraine)* (1993) 14 Cr. App. R. (S.) 394 CA. The condition is also known as post-traumatic stress disorder. D was convicted but her sentence was reduced on appeal from four years to 30 months. See also *R. v Antar (Kayad Kevin)* [2004] EWCA Crim 2708.

R. v Bowen [1996] 2 Cr. App. R. 157 (Court of Appeal, Criminal Division):

9–138 D was charged with obtaining services by deception. He claimed that he had been forced to do so, having been accosted by two men who threatened him and his family with petrol-bombing if he did not obtain the goods. He was convicted and appealed on the ground that his abnormal suggestibility and vulnerability (low IQ was added at the appeal stage) were relevant characteristics not put to the jury as affecting his ability to withstand the threats.

STUART-SMITH LJ:

> "[T]he question remains, what are the relevant characteristics of the accused to which the jury should have regard in considering the second objective test? This question has given rise to considerable difficulty in recent cases. It seems clear that age and sex are, and physical health or disability may be, relevant characteristics. But beyond that it is not altogether easy to determine from the authorities what others may be relevant . . .

[His Lordship then surveyed the case law.]

What principles are to be derived from these authorities? We think they are as follows:

(1) The mere fact that the accused is more pliable, vulnerable, timid or susceptible to threats than a normal person are not characteristics with which it is legitimate to invest the reasonable/ordinary person for the purpose of considering the objective test.
(2) The defendant may be in a category of persons who the jury may think less able to resist pressure than people not within that category. Obvious examples are age, where a young person may well not be so robust as a mature one;[315] possibly sex, though many women would doubtless consider they had as much moral courage to resist pressure as men; pregnancy, where there is added fear for the unborn child; serious physical disability, which may inhibit self-protection; recognised mental illness or psychiatric condition, such as post-traumatic stress disorder leading to learned helplessness.
(3) Characteristics which may be relevant in considering provocation, because they relate to the nature of the provocation,[316] itself will not necessarily be relevant in cases of duress. Thus, homosexuality may be relevant to provocation if the provocative words or conduct are related to this characteristic; it cannot be relevant in duress, since there is no reason to think that homosexuals are less robust in resisting threats of the kind that are relevant in duress cases.
(4) Characteristics due to self-induced abuse, such as alcohol, drugs or glue-sniffing, cannot be relevant.

---

315 This relaxation of the standard could not, however, assist the 13-year-old D in *R. v W* [2007] EWCA Crim 1251; [2007] 2 Cr. App. R. 31 because he was charged with murder. See further A. Ashworth, "Murder: defence—young defendant—intention to kill—defendant's father instructing him to assist—murder" [2008] Crim. L.R. 138.

316 See Ch.7 paras 7–094–7–096. Similarly, characteristics relevant to relation to the loss of control defence under the Coroners and Justice Act 2009 s.54, because they relate to D's circumstances and have a relevance beyond the D's general capacity for tolerance or self-restraint (see para.7–098), are not necessarily relevant to the defence of duress.

(5) Psychiatric evidence may be admissible to show that the accused is suffering from some mental illness, mental impairment or recognised psychiatric condition provided persons generally suffering from such condition may be more susceptible to pressure and threats and thus to assist the jury in deciding whether a reasonable person suffering from such a condition might have been impelled to act as the defendant did. It is not admissible simply to show that in the doctor's opinion an accused, who is not suffering from such illness or condition, is especially timid, suggestible or vulnerable to pressure and threats. Nor is medical opinion admissible to bolster or support the credibility of the accused.

(6) Where counsel wishes to submit that the accused has some characteristic which falls within (2) above, this must be made plain to the judge. The question may arise in relation to the admissibility of medical evidence of the nature set out in (5). If so, the judge will have to rule at that stage. There may, however, be no medical evidence, or, as in this case, medical evidence may have been introduced for some other purpose, *e.g.* to challenge the admissibility or weight of a confession. In such a case counsel must raise the question before speeches in the absence of the jury, so that the judge can rule whether the alleged characteristic is capable of being relevant. If he rules that it is, then he must leave it to the jury.

(7) In the absence of some direction from the judge as to what characteristics are capable of being regarded as relevant, we think that the direction approved in *Graham* without more will not be as helpful as it might be, since the jury may be tempted, especially if there is evidence, as there was in this case, relating to suggestibility and vulnerability, to think that these are relevant. In most cases it is probably only the age and sex of the accused that is capable of being relevant. If so, the judge should, as he did in this case, confine the characteristics in question to these.

How are these principles to be applied in this case? [Counsel for the Crown] accepts, rightly in our opinion, that the evidence that the appellant was abnormally suggestible and a vulnerable individual is irrelevant. But she submits that the fact that he had, or may have had, a low IQ of 68 is relevant since it might inhibit his ability to seek the protection of the police. We do not agree. We do not see how low IQ, short of mental impairment or mental defectiveness, can be said to be a characteristic that makes those who have it less courageous and less able to withstand threats and pressure."

Appeal dismissed

In *GAC*,[317] it was argued on behalf of D, that she had been suffering from "learned helplessness", a feature of battered woman syndrome (BWS) at the time of her participation in an importation of cocaine, and was acting under duress because, by the time that the offence was committed, she was in such a state of passivity that she would have complied with anything that her co-D required her to do. It was also argued that this "learned helplessness" meant that she was unable to identify evasive **9–139**

317 *R. v GAC* [2013] EWCA Crim 1472. cf. *R. v A* [2012] EWCA Crim 434; [2012] 2 Cr. App. R. 8, where it was held that although D had suffered domestic abuse, there was no evidence of duress (D's appeal to the ECtHR was ruled inadmissible: *RA v United Kingdom (Admissibility)* (73521/12) (2016) 63 E.H.R.R. SE5). For further analysis of this case see: J. Loveless, "*R. v GAC*: Battered Woman 'Syndromization'" [2014] Crim. L.R. 655.

action and avoid committing the crime. The Court of Appeal considered that "learned helplessness would be of particular relevance to the defence of duress",[318] recognising that victims of this condition may suffer "traumatic bonding", which may lead to them remaining with their abuser,[319] and that courts should bear in mind that they may be inconsistent in their complaints of abuse.[320] Hallett LJ emphasised that "not every woman who suffers from BWS can claim the defence of duress",[321] suggesting that "an accused would need to be suffering from BWS in a severe form to claim that their will was overborne",[322] to the extent that she had "lost her free will".[323] On the facts, it was concluded that C did not exhibit BWS at the time of the offence, and that the violence perpetrated against her was not of a severity or degree that would afford a defence of duress. However, by focusing on the issue of whether C exhibited "learned helplessness", the Court of Appeal did not explore fully the questions that the court must answer when considering whether a D with this condition may avail themselves of the defence, in particular, whether a reasonable person suffering from learned helplessness might have reacted in the way that this D did.[324]

The Law Commission takes the view that, in so far as duress as a proposed defence to murder and attempted murder is concerned, the jury should be able to take into account all the circumstances of D, including their age but not those which bear upon D's capacity to withstand duress. This is controversial. It would mean that two different tests would exist. *Bowen* would continue to apply in non-homicide cases, but a more stringent test would be applied in instances where the crime charged was murder or attempted murder. The Law Commission justifies this in two ways. First, given the seriousness of the offence charged, a strict objective test should be maintained to limit the scope of the defence. Secondly, the defence of diminished responsibility is available for those Ds suffering from mental disorder who might be less able to withstand threats.[325]

One must ask whether this steadfastness rule—as under *Bowen* or as reformulated by the Law Commission for murder and attempted murder—serves any useful purpose? Bearing in mind that duress can only be pleaded if there has been a threat of death or serious injury and that it is not currently a defence to murder, when would it ever be unreasonable to give in to such grave threats?

K.J.M. Smith, "Duress and Steadfastness: In Pursuit of the Unintelligible" [1999] Crim. L.R. 363, 370, 375:

9–140 "Is it being maintained that, when faced with a belief in the threat of death or serious harm, the question is, *should* that defendant have capitulated bearing in mind their personal characteristics? In other words, does the reasonable steadfastness test envisage some defendants of strong

318 *GAC* [2013] EWCA Crim 1472 at [26].

319 *GAC* [2013] EWCA Crim 1472 at [27].

320 *GAC* [2013] EWCA Crim 1472 at [50].

321 *GAC* [2013] EWCA Crim 1472 at [49].

322 *GAC* [2013] EWCA Crim 1472 at [51].

323 *GAC* [2013] EWCA Crim 1472.

324 For further discussion see: Loveless, "*R. v GAC*: battered woman 'syndromization'" [2014] Crim. L.R. 655. cf. Ormerod and Laird, *Smith, Hogan and Ormerod's Criminal Law*, 16th edn (2021), pp.370-372.

325 Law Com. No.304 (2006), paras 6.83–6.86 fn.37.

emotional or physical disposition who will be denied a defence of duress and who must not choose self-preservation? . . . [N]o coherent function can be assigned to the steadfastness requirement . . .

[T]he presence of a steadfastness test deflects attention away from legitimate defence conditions relating to the neutralization or avoidance of threats . . . [T]he steadfastness requirement cannot coherently relate to anything other than the distinct conditions that defendants take all reasonable opportunities to escape from or neutralize an aggressor's threat."

(vii) Imminence of threat

It is generally stated that the defence of duress is only available if there is a threat of *immediate* harm. **9–141**
Thus, in *Gill*,[326] D was threatened with personal violence if he did not steal his employer's lorry. It was held obiter that he probably could not have pleaded duress because there had been a period of time during which he could have raised the alarm and wrecked the whole enterprise. As Lord Morris said in *Lynch*:

> "[The question is whether] a person the subject of duress could reasonably have extricated himself or could have sought protection or had what has been called a 'safe avenue of escape'."[327]

This approach can be supported. We would blame someone who had a reasonable opportunity to raise the alarm and wreck the criminal enterprise,[328] but we would not blame someone who had no such opportunity. What is the position if D has an opportunity to seek help but fears that police protection will be ineffective?

R. v Hudson and Taylor [1971] 2 Q.B. 202 (Court of Appeal, Criminal Division):

[The facts are set out above at para.9–109.] **9–142**

WIDGERY LJ:

"In the present case the threats . . . were likely to be no less compelling, because their execution could not be effected in the court room, if they could be carried out in the streets of Salford the same night . . .

[Counsel for the Crown] . . . submits on grounds of public policy that an accused should not be able to plead duress if he had the opportunity to ask for protection from the police before

---

326 *R. v Gill (Samuel James)* [1963] 1 W.L.R. 841; (1963) 47 Cr. App. R. 166 CA. See also *Cole* [1994] Crim. L.R. 582.
327 *DPP for Northern Ireland v Lynch* [1975] A.C. 653 at 668.
328 A. Ashworth, "Reason, Logic and Criminal Liability" (1975) 91 L.Q.R. 102, 104.

committing the offence and failed to do so. The argument does not distinguish cases in which the police would be able to provide effective protection, from those when they would not, and it would, in effect, restrict the defence of duress to cases where the person threatened had been kept in custody by the maker of the threats, or where the time interval between the making of the threats and the commission of the offence had made recourse to the police impossible . . .

In the opinion of this court it is always open to the Crown to prove that the accused failed to avail himself of some opportunity which was reasonably open to him to render the threat ineffective, and that upon this being established the threat in question can no longer be relied on by the defence. In deciding whether such an opportunity was reasonably open to the accused the jury should have regard to his age and circumstances, and to any risks to him which may be involved in the course of action relied upon."

9–143 In *Hudson and Taylor*, the threats could have been reported to the police, but the two young girls, aged 17 and 19, were convinced that the police protection would be ineffective. Are we to blame them for their failure to seek official protection? It would appear that their response was typical of the response of most ordinary girls of that age faced with such a predicament. It would be absurd to assert that the defence of duress would only be available to them if there had been a sniper sitting in court ready to execute his threats immediately. These views were echoed by Lord Griffiths in *Howe*:

"[I]f duress is introduced as a merciful concession to human frailty it seems hard to deny it to a man who knows full well that any official protection he may seek will not be effective to save him from the threat of death under which he has acted."[329]

However, *Hudson and Taylor* caused disquiet among some members of the judiciary and commentators: Glanville Williams, for example, described it as an "indulgent decision".[330]

R. v Hasan [2005] 2 A.C. 467 (House of Lords):

9–144 [The facts are set out below at para.9–147.]

LORD BINGHAM:

"27. . . [*Hudson*] had the unfortunate effect of weakening the requirement that execution of a threat must be reasonably believed to be imminent and immediate if it is to support a plea of

---

329 *Howe* [1987] A.C. 417 at 433.

330 Baker, *Glanville Williams, Textbook of Criminal Law*, 4th edn (2015), para.28–035. The Law Commission suggested that, where a D under duress failed to seek police protection, the full defence should not be available and it should be a matter of mitigation only: Law Com, Working Paper No.55, *Defences of General Application* (1974) para.20. In *R. v Heath (Patrick Nicholas)* [2000] Crim. L.R. 109 CA, the defence was denied to a D who had "more than one avenue of escape open to him" on the basis that he could have gone to the police or his parents. See also *R. v Baker (Tony) (No.1)* [1999] 2 Cr. App. R. 335 CA; *R. v Batchelor (William Lucas)* [2013] EWCA Crim 2638; *Brandford* [2016] EWCA Crim 1794 at [32] at para.9–128; and *R. v Khan (Danhyal Younis)* [2018] EWCA Crim 1913 at [24].

duress . . . I can understand that the Court of Appeal in *R v Hudson* had sympathy with the predicament of the young appellants but I cannot, consistently with principle, accept that a witness testifying in the Crown Court of Manchester has no opportunity to avoid complying with a threat incapable of execution then or there . . .

28. . . It should . . . be made clear to juries that if the retribution threatened against the defendant or his family or a person for whom he reasonably feels responsible is not such as he reasonably expects to follow on almost immediately on his failure to comply with the threat, there may be little if any room for doubt that he could take evasive action, whether by going to the police or in some other way, to avoid committing the offence with which he is charged."

The approach in *Hasan* was followed in *Moss v The King*.[331] D had been convicted of the offence of conspiracy to murder a man (V) who had been shot dead before he could give evidence for the prosecution in the trial of a gang leader for murder. There had been an appreciable period of time between an alleged co-conspirator approaching D and her driving V to the venue where the killers could implement their plan. The Privy Council rejected an argument that the trial judge had been wrong to withdraw the defence of duress from the jury, on the basis that she could have taken evasive action "either by way of going to the police or simply by not going through with the plan to pick up the deceased and drive him to the spot".[332] **9–145**

This more robust stance[333] means that the approach taken by the Court of Appeal in the pre-*Hasan* decision of *Abdul-Hussain*[334] in the context of duress of circumstances does not apply where the plea is one of duress by threats.[335] This latter case concerned an appeal by a group of Iraqis who had hijacked a Sudanese aeroplane. Their plea was they would be killed if returned to Iraq. Rose VP held that:

"the execution of the threat need not be immediately in prospect . . . [and that] the period of time which elapses between the inception of the peril and the defendant's act, and between that act and execution of the threat, are relevant but not determinative factors for a judge and jury in deciding whether duress operates . . . In our judgment, although the judge was right to look for a close nexus between the threat and the criminal act, he interpreted the law too strictly in seeking a virtually spontaneous reaction."[336]

This difference in approach adopted with regard to duress by threats (*Hasan, Moss*) and duress of circumstances (*Abdul-Hussain*) to the issue of imminence reinforces the point that these defences are context-sensitive: the more one slides along the continuum from duress to duress of circumstances

---

331 *The King (Bahamas)v Moss (Caryn)* [2023] UKPC 28; [2024] Crim. L.R. 250. See: U. Azmeh, "Case Comment: Duress: *Moss (Caryn) v The King* [2024] 4 Crim. L.R. 250.

332 *Moss* [2023] UKPC 28 at [68].

333 See also *R. v Aldridge (Jonathan)* [2006] EWCA Crim 1970; *R. v N* [2007] EWCA Crim 3479; and *Khan* [2018] EWCA Crim 78 at [22].

334 *R. v Abdul-Hussain (Mustafa Shakir)* [1999] Crim. L.R. 570 CA.

335 Alternatively, it is possible that *Abdul-Hussain* [1999] Crim. L.R. 570 has been impliedly overruled by *Hasan* [2005] 2 A.C. 467 at [27].

336 This passage was approved in *Shayler* [2001] 1 W.L.R. 2206.

and through to necessity, the less rigorous this requirement becomes. This is because in cases of duress by threats the rationale for the excuse is that the D's "will has been overborne" whereas at the other extreme (necessity) D is making a more rational choice. It was stressed in *Re A (Conjoined Twins)*,[337] a classic case of necessity, that the principle is "one of necessity, not emergency". In this case, the death of both twins was not an immediate or even imminent prospect; they could both well have lived for many months. However, as their deaths within that period were a certainty, a severance operation that would kill the weaker twin was a necessity.

(viii) Defendants placing themselves in a position where they might be open to threats

9–146 Ds who join a criminal association (whether terrorist, gangster or otherwise) which could force them to commit crimes can be blamed for their actions. In joining such an organisation, fault can be laid at their door and their subsequent actions described as blameworthy. This is the approach adopted by English law which denies the defence of duress to such persons.

R. v Hasan [2005] 2 A.C. 467 (House of Lords):

9–147 D worked as a driver and minder for a woman who ran an escort agency and was involved in prostitution. The woman's boyfriend, Sullivan, had a reputation for violence and was involved in drug dealing. D was charged with aggravated burglary and claimed that he had been forced to commit the offence by Sullivan. He was convicted and appealed. The Court of Appeal allowed the appeal.

LORD BINGHAM:

"22. For many years it was possible to regard the defence of duress as something of an antiquarian curiosity, with little practical application . . . This has changed . . . This is borne out by the steady flow of cases reaching the appellate courts over the last 30 years or so . . . I must acknowledge that the features of duress . . . incline me, where policy choices are to be made, towards tightening rather than relaxing the conditions to be met before duress may be successfully relied upon . . .

29. . . The Court of Appeal ruled that [the trial judge had misdirected the jury] . . . because the judge had not directed the jury to consider whether the defendant knew that he was likely to be subjected to threats to commit a crime of the type with which he was charged. It is this ruling which gave rise to the certified question on this part of the case, which is:

'Whether the defence of duress is excluded when as a result of the accused's voluntary association with others; (i) he foresaw (or possibly should have foreseen) the risk of being subjected to any compulsion by threats of violence, or (ii) only when he foresaw (or should have foreseen) the risk of being subjected to compulsion to commit

337 *Re A (Conjoined Twins: Surgical Separation)* [2001] Fam. 147.

> criminal offences, and if the latter, (iii) only if the offences foreseen (or which should have been foreseen) were of the same type (or possibly of the same type and gravity) as that ultimately committed.'

The Crown contend for answer (i) in its objective form. The defendant commends the third answer, omitting the first parenthesis . . .

37. The principal issue . . . is whether *R v Baker* correctly stated the law . . . The defendant is seeking to be wholly exonerated from the consequences of a crime deliberately committed. The prosecution must negative his defence of duress, if raised by the evidence, beyond reasonable doubt. The defendant is, ex hypothesi, a person who has voluntarily surrendered his will to the dominion of another. Nothing should turn on foresight of the manner in which, in the event, the dominant party chooses to exploit the defendant's subservience. There need not be foresight of coercion to commit crimes, although it is not easy to envisage circumstances in which a party might be coerced to act lawfully. In holding that there must be foresight of coercion to commit crimes of the kind with which the defendant is charged, *R. v Baker* misstated the law.

38. There remains the question, which the Court of Appeal left open . . . whether the defendant's foresight must be judged by a subjective or an objective test: i.e. does the defendant lose the benefit of the defence of duress only if he actually foresaw the risk of coercion or does he lose it if he ought reasonably to have foreseen the risk of coercion, whether he actually foresaw the risk or not? I do not think any decided case has addressed this question, and I am conscious that application of an objective reasonableness test to the other ingredients of duress has attracted criticism . . . The practical importance of the distinction in this context may not be very great, since if a jury concluded that a person voluntarily associating with known criminals ought reasonably to have foreseen the risk of future coercion they would not, I think, be very likely to accept that he did not in fact do so. But since there is a choice to be made, policy in my view points towards an objective test of what the defendant, placed as he was and knowing what he did, ought reasonably to have foreseen. I am not persuaded otherwise by analogies based on self-defence or provocation . . . The policy of the law must be to discourage association with known criminals, and it should be slow to excuse the criminal conduct of those who do so. If a person voluntarily becomes or remains associated with others engaged in criminal activity in a situation where he knows or ought reasonably to know that he may be the subject of compulsion by them or their associates, he cannot rely on the defence of duress to excuse any act which he is thereafter compelled to do by them . . .

39. I would answer this certified question by saying that the defence of duress is excluded when as a result of the accused's voluntary association with others engaged in criminal activity he foresaw or ought reasonably to have foreseen the risk of being subjected to any compulsion by threats of violence."

Appeal allowed

9–148 Duress is an excuse and, on principle, there ought to be a plausible—or reasonable—excuse for the actions. The basis of the rule here is that a D has no plausible excuse and is blameworthy if he associates with such criminal enterprises or organisations. If the risks of compulsion were obvious, even though he gave no thought to them, the case for denying the defence is compelling.[338] However, it is true that Lord Bingham's approach is very robust and goes further than the Court of Appeal in *Sharp*,[339] where it was held that:

> "...where a person has voluntarily, and with knowledge of its nature, joined a criminal organisation or gang which he knew might bring pressure on him to commit an offence and was an active member when he was put under such pressure, he cannot avail himself of the defence of duress."

All that is required is that there is a foreseeable risk of being subjected to any compulsion by threats of violence.[340] It is not necessary that D foresaw or ought reasonably to have foreseen that he might be the subject of compulsion to commit a particular type of crime or any criminal offence at all.[341] In *Hasan*, Lady Hale expressed concern about the majority's approach on this issue might mean that the defence was unavailable to victims of domestic abuse if they were compelled to commit crime:[342]

> "... The battered wife knows that she is exposing herself to a risk of unlawful violence if she stays, but she may have no reason to believe that her husband will eventually use her broken will to force her to commit crimes. For the same reason, I would say that it must be foreseeable that duress will be used to compel the person to commit crimes of some sort. I have no difficulty envisaging circumstances in which a person may be coerced to act lawfully. The battered wife knows very well that she may be compelled to cook the dinner, wash the dishes, iron the shirts and submit to sexual intercourse. That should not deprive her of the defence of duress if she is obliged by the same threats to herself or her children to commit perjury or shoplift for food."

However, although it has been argued that the defence should only be removed if there are foreseeable threats of serious violence to commit a crime,[343] *Hasan* is clearly the leading authority.[344]

(ix) Length of time after threats

9–149 D can only rely upon the defence as long as the threat is operative. In *DPP v Davis; DPP v Pittaway*,[345] both Ds were charged separately with driving with excess alcohol, contrary to the Road Traffic Act 1988

338 Under the Draft Criminal Law Bill 1993 cl.25(4), the defence is not available to a person who has knowingly and without reasonable excuse exposed themselves to the risk of a threat (Law Com. No.218 (1993), fn.352). In its report on homicide, the Law Commission commented that the narrower approach adopted in *Hasan* [2005] 2 A.C. 467 "will serve to exclude the most unmeritorious cases where the defence should simply not be available", Law Com. No.304 (2006), para.6.52 fn.37. cf. the case of *R. v Phair (Nathan)* [2022] NICA 66, in relation to the defence of duress of circumstances, below para.9–160.

339 *R. v Sharp (David Bruce)* [1987] Q.B. 853 per Lord Lane CJ at 861; [1987] 3 W.L.R. 1 CA.

340 In *Brandford* [2016] EWCA Crim 1794 at [34], it was observed that Lord Bingham had "cast the net of voluntary association deliberately wide".

341 Judicial College, *The Crown Court Compendium: Part 1, Jury and Trial Management and Summing* Up (2023), para.18–18.

342 *Hasan* [2005] 2 A.C. 467. [77].

343 D. Ibbetson, "Duress Revisited" [2004] 64 C.L.J. 530, 531.

344 It has been applied, e.g. in *R. v Ali (Israr)* [2008] EWCA Crim 716; *R. v Hussain (Mohammed)* [2008] EWCA Crim 1117; and *Brandford* [2016] EWCA Crim 1794. In *Phair* [2022] NICA 66, the Court of Appeal in Northern Ireland held that this limitation also applied to the defence of duress of circumstances, see para.9–160.

345 *DPP v Davis; DPP v Pittaway* [1994] Crim. L.R. 600.

s.5(1)(a). Both pleaded duress. However, on appeal by way of case stated, the Divisional Court held (on a number of grounds) that there was no evidence of duress. In particular, the fact that one of the Ds had driven for two miles without any suggestion that he was being pursued and that the other had decided to drive off after a five-minute pause in which no threat had materialised meant that duress could not apply.[346]

(x) Crimes to which duress is a defence

If D's conduct can be described as being "morally involuntary", and if we are satisfied that we do not blame D for their actions, because ordinary people would have responded in the same way, it follows that they ought to have a defence to any crime. However, English law adopts the view that duress is a defence to all crimes *except* murder, attempted murder[347] and treason.[348] In *Lynch*, the House of Lords decided that duress was a defence to an accessory to murder but in *Abbott*, the Privy Council ruled that it was not a defence to the principal offender (the one who actually does the killing) of murder. In *Howe*,[349] the House of Lords held that duress was not a defence to murder, irrespective of the degree of participation. **9–150**

R. v Howe [1987] A.C. 417 (House of Lords):

Two Ds, Howe and Bannister, participated with others in torturing, kicking, punching and sexually abusing a man. The man was then strangled to death by one of the others. These events were repeated on a second occasion but this time it was Howe and Bannister who themselves killed the victim by strangling him with a shoelace. The D claimed that they had acted under duress at the orders of and through fear of one, Murray. At their trial the judge, following *Lynch* and *Abbott*, directed the jury that duress could be a defence to the first killing where the Ds were only accessories, but not to the second killing where the Ds were the principal offenders. The Court of Appeal held this was correct. The Ds appealed to the House of Lords. **9–151**

LORD HAILSHAM LC:

> "In general, I must say that I do not at all accept in relation to the defence of murder it is either good morals, good policy or good law to suggest, as did the majority in *Lynch* and the minority in *Abbott* that the ordinary man of reasonable fortitude is not to be supposed to be capable of heroism if he is asked to take an innocent life rather than sacrifice his own. Doubtless in actual practice many will succumb to temptation, as they did in *Dudley and Stephens*. But many will

---

346 See *R. v Pommell (Fitzroy Derek)* [1995] 2 Cr. App. R. 607; (1995) 92(27) L.S.G. 32 CA; *Bell* [1992] Crim. L.R. 176; *DPP v Jones* [1990] R.T.R. 33 Div Ct; *DPP v Tomkinson* [2001] EWHC Admin 182; [2001] R.T.R. 38; *DPP v Mullally* [2006] EWHC 3448 (Admin); and *Crown Prosecution Service v Brown* [2007] EWHC 3274 (Admin) where similar reasoning was applied in duress of circumstances cases.

347 *R. v Gotts (Benjamin)* [1992] 2 A.C. 412; [1992] 2 W.L.R. 284 HL.

348 "Prosecutions for treason are virtually confined to the circumstances of war. Perhaps in war even the private citizen is expected to cast himself in a heroic mould" (Baker, *Glanville Williams, Textbook of Criminal Law*, 4th edn (2015), para.28–010). There are, however, dicta in *DPP for Northern Ireland v Lynch* [1975] A.C. 653 to the effect that duress could in some circumstances be a defence to treason. See, e.g. Lord Morris at 672.

349 *Howe* [1987] A.C. 417. For discussion of the historical development of this rule, see: A. Elkington, "The historical development of duress and the unfounded result of denying duress as a defence to murder" [2023] 87 J. Crim. L. 207.

not, and I do not believe that as a 'concession to human frailty' the former should be exempt from liability to criminal sanctions if they do. I have known in my own lifetime of too many acts of heroism by ordinary human beings of no more than ordinary fortitude to regard a law as either 'just or humane' which withdraws the protection of the criminal law from the innocent victim and casts the cloak of its protection upon the coward and the poltroon in the name of a 'concession to human frailty'.

I must not, however, underestimate the force of the arguments on the other side . . .

A long line of cases . . . establish duress as an available defence in a wide range of crimes, some at least, like wounding with intent to commit grievous bodily harm, carrying the heaviest penalties commensurate with their gravity. To cap this, it is pointed out that at least in theory, a defendant accused of this crime under section 18 of the Offences against the Person Act 1861, but acquitted on the grounds of duress, will still be liable to a charge of murder if the victim dies . . . I am not, perhaps, persuaded of this last point as much as I should. It is not simply an anomaly based on the defence of duress. It is a product of the peculiar *mens rea* allowed on a charge of murder which is not confined to an intent to kill . . .

I . . . believe that some degree of proportionality between the threat and the offence must, at least to some extent, be a prerequisite of the defence under existing law. Few would resist threats to the life of a loved one if the alternative were driving across the red lights or in excess of 70 mph on the motorway. But . . . it would take rather more than the threat of a slap on the wrist or even moderate pain or injury to discharge the evidential burden even in the case of a fairly serious assault. In such a case the 'concession to human frailty' is no more than to say that in such circumstances a reasonable man of average courage is entitled to embrace as a matter of choice the alternative which a reasonable man could regard as the lesser of two evils. Other considerations necessarily arise where the choice is between the threat of death or *a fortiori* of serious injury and deliberately taking an innocent life. In such a case a reasonable man might reflect that one innocent human life is at least as valuable as his own or that of his loved one. In such case a man cannot claim that he is choosing the lesser of two evils. Instead he is embracing the cognate but morally disreputable principle that the end justifies the means . . .

During the course of argument it was suggested that there was available to the House some sort of half-way house between allowing these appeals and dismissing them. The argument ran that we might treat duress in murder as analogous to provocation, or perhaps diminished responsibility, and say that, in indictments for murder, duress might reduce the crime to one of manslaughter. I find myself quite unable to accept this. The cases show that duress, if available and made out, entitles the accused to a clean acquittal, without, it has been said, the 'stigma' of a conviction . . . [The suggestion] is also contrary to principle. Unlike the doctrine of provocation, which is based on emotional loss of control, the defence of duress, as I have already shown, is put forward as a 'concession to human frailty' whereby a conscious decision, it may be coolly undertaken, to sacrifice an innocent human life is made as an evil lesser than a wrong which might otherwise be suffered by the accused or his loved ones at the hands of a wrong doer."

LORD GRIFFITHS: 9–152

"It is therefore neither rational nor fair to make the defence dependent upon whether the accused is the actual killer or took some other part in the murder . . .

As I can find no fair and certain basis upon which to differentiate between participants to a murder and as I am firmly convinced that the law should not be extended to the killer, I would depart from the decision of this House in . . . *Lynch* and declare the law to be that duress is not available as a defence to a charge of murder, or to attempted murder. I add attempted murder because it is to be remembered that the prosecution have to prove an even more evil intent to convict of attempted murder than in actual murder.

. . . This leaves, of course, the anomaly that duress is available for the offence of wounding with intent but not to murder if the victim dies subsequently. But this flows from the special regard that the law has for human life, it may not be logical but it is real and has to be accepted.

[Lords Bridge, Brandon and Mackay agreed that duress should never be a defence to murder irrespective of the defendant's degree of participation. In addition to the above concerns over the special value accorded human life and the difficulty in drawing moral and legal distinctions between perpetrators and accomplices, the House felt there were three further reasons justifying their approach:

(1) if duress were to be made a defence to the perpetrator of murder, that should be done by Parliament, not the courts; the Law Commission (Law Com. No. 83) recommended ten years previously that duress should be a defence to the principal offender of murder; Parliament's failure to enact this recommendation is an indication that they have rejected the proposal.
(2) The defence of duress is imprecisely defined and extending it to murder would cause too much uncertainty;
(3) administrative remedies such as not prosecuting, use of parole and the royal prerogative would ensure that no injustice was perpetrated.]"

Appeals dismissed

R. v GOTTS [1992] 2 A.C. 412 (HOUSE OF LORDS):

D, aged 16, seriously injured his mother with a knife. In his defence to a charge of attempted murder, he claimed that his father had threatened to shoot him unless he killed his mother. The judge ruled that such evidence was inadmissible since duress was not a defence to such a charge. D pleaded guilty but then appealed. 9–153

LORD JAUNCEY:

"My Lords, I share the view of Lord Griffiths [in *Howe*] that 'it would have been better had [the development of the defence of duress] not taken place and that duress had been regarded as a factor to be taken into account in mitigation' . . . At the time of the earlier writings on duress as a defence, offences against the person were much more likely to have involved only one or two victims. Weapons and substances capable of inflicting mass injury were not readily available to terrorists and other criminals as they are in the reputedly more civilised times in which we now live. While it is not now possible for this House to restrict the availability of the defence of duress in those cases where it has been recognised to exist, I feel constrained to express the personal view that given the climate of violence and terrorism which ordinary law-abiding citizens now have to face Parliament might do well to consider whether the defence should continue to be available in the case of all very serious crimes . . . The reason why duress has for so long been stated not to be available as a defence to a murder charge is that the law regards the sanctity of human life and the protection thereof as of paramount importance. Does that reason apply to attempted murder as well as to murder? As Lord Griffiths pointed out [in *Howe*] . . . an intent to kill must be proved in the case of attempted murder but not necessarily in the case of murder. Is there logic in affording the defence to one who intends to kill but fails and denying it to one who mistakenly kills intending only to injure? . . .

It is of course true that withholding the defence in any circumstances will create some anomalies but I would agree with Lord Griffiths . . . that nothing should be done to undermine in any way the highest duty of the law to protect the freedom and lives of those who live under it. I can therefore see no justification in logic, morality or law in affording to an attempted murderer the defence which is withheld from a murderer. The intent required of an attempted murderer is more evil than that required of the murderer and the line which divides the two is seldom, if ever, of the deliberate making of the criminal. A man shooting to kill but missing a vital organ by a hair's breadth can justify his action no more than can the man who hits the organ. It is pure chance that the attempted murderer is not a murderer . . .

I have no doubt that the Court of Appeal reached the correct decision and that the appeal should be dismissed."

Appeal dismissed

9–154 The fact that the D in *Gotts* was 16 years old made no difference to the outcome of the trial.[350] More starkly, in *W*, the fact that D was 13 years old was irrelevant: the Court of Appeal accepted that there might be grounds for criticising a principle of law that did not afford such a boy any defence but the law was that a 13-year-old boy was responsible for his actions and duress no defence to a charge of

350 D was sentenced to three years' probation, so clearly some recognition was taken of his plight.

murder.[351] As Ashworth has commented, the "decision was inevitable, but reflects badly on English criminal law".[352]

Is duress a defence to conspiracy and encouraging or assisting to murder? Authority on the point is very limited. In the Court of Appeal in *Gotts*, it was commented that there was "a legitimate distinction to be drawn" between these crimes and attempted murder because they are a "stage further away from the completed offence than is the attempt"[353] and this was the basis given for allowing duress to be pleaded in the unreported Crown Court decision of *Ness*.[354] In *Moss*,[355] the Privy Council declined to resolve the issue of whether duress could be a defence to the offence of conspiracy to murder.

Thus, while the defence is not available to murder or attempted murder (or treason), it is available to these other serious crimes as well as manslaughter, causing grievous bodily harm with intent contrary to the OAPA 1861 s.18 and arson intending to endanger life or being reckless as to whether life is endangered contrary to the Criminal Damage Act 1971 s.1(2).[356] As Lord Lowry stressed in his dissenting speech in *Gotts*, such anomalies are bound to result unless the defence is extended or denied to all crimes.[357] The view espoused by Lord Jauncey in *Gotts* that duress ought to be only a matter of mitigation in sentencing rather than a defence to serious crimes is one that needs to be resisted for the reasons explored at the beginning of this section.

What is disappointing about these decisions is the lack of attention paid to the theoretical basis of the defence. In *Gotts*, the House concentrated upon whether early writings established duress as a defence to attempted murder and then on its relationship to the crime of murder. At no time did they address fully why duress is a defence.[358] Prior to *Gotts, Howe* had already been roundly condemned as requiring unrealistic heroism.[359] Heroism might be a desirable quality, but it is unduly harsh to sentence someone to life imprisonment for failing to achieve such heights. The criminal law should rest content if its exhortations induce persons to act reasonably. It seems an odd and unjust law that can proclaim that D has acted perfectly reasonably but is guilty of murder. And it is simply no answer to assert that injustice will be avoided either by the use of prosecutorial discretion or by more lenient sentencing.[360] **9–155**

351 *R. v W* [2007] EWCA Crim 1251.

352 Ashworth, "Reason, Logic and Criminal Liability" (1975) 91 L.Q.R. 102, 139. The Law Commission considered whether there should be a special provision for duress affecting juveniles and young persons (although this received little support) (Law Com. No.304 (2006), para.6.142 fn.37). If duress were to become a defence to murder, the Law Commission's recommendation is that youth should continue to be a relevant characteristic.

353 *Gotts* (1991) 92 Cr. App. R. 269 at 276.

354 D. Ormerod, "Duress: conspiracy to murder" [2011] Crim. L.R. 645.

355 *Moss* [2023] UKPC 28 at [54].

356 *Gotts* (1991) 92 Cr. App. R. 269 at 273. cf. the position In Canada, where the defence of "acting under compulsion by threats of bodily harm" is inapplicable to a wide range of offences, including sexual assault, robbery and arson: Criminal Code, RSC 1985, cc-46 s.17. See Tamblyn, *The Law of Duress and Necessity: Crime, Tort, Contract* (2018), pp.190–192.

357 *Gotts* [1992] 2 A.C. 412 at 441.

358 See J. Gardner, "Duress in Attempted Murder" (1991) 107 L.Q.R. 389, 391; J. Gardner, "Duress in the House of Lords" (1992) 108 L.Q.R. 349.

359 cf. Ormerod and Laird, *Smith, Hogan and Ormerod's Criminal Law*, 16th edn (2021), pp.380–382; P. Alldridge, "Duress, Murder and the House of Lords" (1988) 52 Jo.C.L. 186; H.P. Milgate, "Duress and the Criminal Law: Another About Turn by the House of Lords" [1988] C.L.J. 61; L. Walters, "Murder under Duress and Judicial Decision-making in the House of Lords" (1988) 8 *Legal Studies* 61. See also A. Reed, "Duress and Normative Moral Excuse: Comparative Standardisations and the Ambit of Affirmative Defences" in A. Reed and M. Bohlander, *General Defences In Criminal Law: Domestic and Comparative Perspectives* (London: Routledge, 2014), Ch.7; K.J. Arenson, "The paradox of disallowing duress as a defence to murder" [2014] J. Crim. L. 65.

360 The sentencing guidelines for murder under the Criminal Justice Act 2003 s.269 and Sch.21 remove much of the discretion formerly permitted judges and do not even include duress as a mitigating factor. The sentencing guidelines for attempted murder specifically mention

Furthermore, these platitudes have been heard before in other areas of criminal law—and been blatantly ignored.[361] In an otherwise policy-driven attempt to restrict the defence of duress, Lord Bingham in *Hasan* acknowledged that the logic of the argument for extending the defence to murder is irresistible.[362] This call for reform was endorsed by the Law Commission.

Law Commission (Law Com. No.304), Murder, Manslaughter and Infanticide (2006), paras 6.36–6.53:

9–156 "A full defence to first degree murder

In the CP, we provisionally proposed a different approach in relation to first degree murder [and duress] . . . There were two main reasons:

(1) We thought it important that there should be consistency with the partial defences of provocation and diminished responsibility, both of which we were proposing should reduce first degree murder to second degree murder;
(2) It would not be right for a person who had intentionally killed to be completely exonerated . . .

We now believe that, in this context, we exaggerated the importance of treating duress in a manner that was consistent with the way provocation and diminished responsibility fitted into our proposed structure . . .

We also acknowledge that we exaggerated the strength of the case for duress being a partial defence to first degree murder merely because, under our proposals, there would be more categories of murder. We now accept that . . . the mere fact that there are more categories of murder does not assist in deciding whether or not as a matter of principle duress should be a full defence to first degree murder . . .

The argument that duress should be a full defence to first degree murder has a moral basis. It is that the law should not stigmatise a person who, on the basis of a genuine and reasonably held belief, intentionally killed in fear of death or life-threatening injury in circumstances where a jury is satisfied that an ordinary person of reasonable fortitude might have acted in the same way . . .

[W]e believe that there is . . . force in the views expressed by consultees who believe that duress should be a complete defence to first degree murder. For example, [one consultee] said that withholding duress as a complete defence implies that the criminal law should support the view

---

"the use of duress or threats against another person to facilitate the commission of the offence" as a specific aggravating factor, but do not mention duress as a mitigating factor: Sentencing Council, *Attempted Murder* (2021).

361 e.g. the prosecution that was brought in *Anderton v Ryan* [1985] A.C. 560; [1985] 2 W.L.R. 968 HL—exactly the sort of case in which the Law Commission (Law Com. Working Paper No.102) had predicted that a prosecution would never be brought.

362 *Hasan* [2005] 2 A.C. 467.

that 'people ought to act in an exceptionally moral and courageous way. They are being punished for giving way to what will often be enormous fear and wholly understandable human frailty.'

We also think it important to bear in mind the stringent qualifying conditions that attach to the defence. In particular, the majority in *Hasan* were firmly of the view that the defence ought not to be available to D if he or she saw or ought to have foreseen the risk of being subjected to any compulsion by threats of violence. We believe that this will serve to exclude the most unmeritorious cases where the defence should simply not be available. It is true that it will not itself exclude all undeserving cases but we believe that juries should be trusted not to accept the defence in undeserving cases.

Above all, we believe that it is essential to recognize and accord proper weight to the fact that for the defence to succeed, a jury must form a judgement that a reasonable person in D's position might have committed first degree murder. If a jury forms that judgment, we believe that D should be completely exonerated despite having intentionally killed."

The Law Commission's proposals in this respect are to be supported: duress should be a defence to all crimes.[363] What D has done remains wrong but we can understand his predicament and excuse him. Given the severe threats, his actions are in effect morally involuntary. Perhaps if the majority in *Abbott* had realised this they might have produced a different result. Instead, they seemed to think they were dealing with a justificatory defence when they spoke of duress bringing the D's act "within the law".[364] Lord Mackay in *Howe* spoke of a D subject to duress having a "right" to commit a crime.[365] This is simply not so. With excusatory defences, one has no "right" to commit crimes. One is simply excused from blame: "To acquit him on grounds of duress is merely to sympathise, understand, commiserate with what he did."[366] **9–157**

C. DURESS OF CIRCUMSTANCES

As seen earlier, until fairly recently it was clear that no general defence of necessity existed in English law. However, starting in the 1980s, the judiciary has actively developed this area of law in a way that "can be likened to the overnight growth of a mushroom".[367] Rather than simply introducing or developing a new full-blown defence of necessity, the courts have chosen to expand the defence of duress by threats to cover what is termed "duress of circumstances". While often describing the defence as "necessity or duress of circumstances" or even as "duress of necessity"[368] the courts have been **9–158**

363 However, the Law Commission proposes that the burden of proof would lie with D. This is controversial: see A. Ashworth, "Principles, Pragmatism and the Law Commission's Recommendations on Homicide Law Reform" [2007] Crim. L.R. 333, 340–342.

364 *Abbott v Queen, The* [1977] A.C. 755 at 766; see Fletcher, *Rethinking Criminal Law* (1978), p.832.

365 *Howe* [1987] A.C. 417 at 456; see Walters, "Murder under Duress and Judicial Decision-making in the House of Lords" (1988) 8 *Legal Studies* 61.

366 L. Katz, *Bad Acts and Guilty Minds* (Chicago: University of Chicago Press, 1987), p.65.

367 D.W. Elliott, "Necessity, Duress and Self-Defence" [1989] Crim. L.R. 611, 612.

368 *Abdul-Hussain* [1999] Crim. L.R. 570 and *Cairns* [1999] 2 Cr. App. R. 137; [2000] R.T.R. 15 CA, respectively.

careful to ensure that the new defence of "duress of circumstances" has largely followed the contours of the existing defence of duress by threats. By emphasising the similarities between the two defences and, importantly, imposing similar rigorous restraints upon the defence, judges have been able to overcome their reluctance to admit a defence of necessity into English law.

The emergence of this defence occurred "more or less by accident".[369] In *Willer*,[370] D was charged with reckless driving when he drove on a pavement to escape from a gang of youths. It was held that regardless of whether necessity had been established or was available, the defence of "duress of circumstances" was applicable.[371] "Duress of circumstances" was also considered in the case of *Conway*, another case of reckless driving.[372] D pleaded that he had to make off in his car when approached by two men (who were in fact police officers) because his passenger was fearful of an attack. In saying that the defence of duress of circumstances should have been put to the jury, the Court of Appeal indicated that it was immaterial whether the defence was called necessity or duress. In *Bell*,[373] the Queen's Bench Divisional Court referred to the defence that was available to the D who had driven with excess alcohol in his blood in order to escape attackers as "duress/necessity".

R. v MARTIN (1989) 88 CR. APP. R. 343 (COURT OF APPEAL, CRIMINAL DIVISION):

9–159 D was charged with driving whilst disqualified under the Road Traffic Act 1972 s.99(b). The facts appear from the judgment.

SIMON BROWN J:

> "The circumstances which the appellant desired to advance by way of defence of necessity were essentially these. His wife has suicidal tendencies. On a number of occasions before the day in question she had attempted to take her own life. On the day in question her son, the appellant's stepson, had overslept. He had done so to the extent that he was bound to be late for work and at risk of losing his job unless, so it was asserted, the appellant drove him to work. The appellant's wife was distraught. She was shouting, screaming, banging her head against a wall. More particularly, it is said she was threatening suicide unless the appellant drove the boy to work.
>
> The defence had a statement from a doctor which expressed the opinion that 'in view of her mental condition it is likely that Mrs Martin would have attempted suicide if her husband did not drive her son to work.'

369 Ormerod and Laird, *Smith, Hogan and Ormerod's Criminal Law*, 16th edn (2021), p.383.

370 *R. v Willer (Mark Edward)* (1986) 83 Cr. App. R. 225; [1987] R.T.R. 22.

371 See also *R. v Denton (Stanley Arthur)* (1987) 85 Cr. App. R. 246; (1987) 131 S.J. 476 CA.

372 *Conway* [1988] 3 W.L.R. 1238. See Alldridge, "Duress, Duress of Circumstances and Necessity" (1989) 139 N.L.J. 911. cf. *R. v Riddell (Tracey)* [2017] EWCA Crim 413; [2017] 1 W.L.R. 3593.

373 *Bell* [1992] Crim. L.R. 176. See also *DPP v Jones* [1990] R.T.R. 33 at 39. In *DPP v Tomkinson* [2001] EWHC Admin 182; [2001] R.T.R. 38 Div Ct, D's claim of duress of circumstances in relation to a charge of driving with excess alcohol in her breath was rejected on appeal because there was no basis for the justices to conclude that a sober woman of reasonable firmness would have driven the 72 miles driven by D having consumed alcohol above the legal limit.

The appellant's case . . . was that he genuinely, and he would suggest reasonably, believed that his wife would carry out that threat unless he did as she demanded. Despite his disqualification he therefore drove the boy. He was in fact apprehended by the police within about a quarter of a mile of the house.

Sceptically though one may regard that defence on the facts . . . the sole question before this court is whether those facts, had the jury accepted they were or might be true, amounted in law to a defence . . . As it was, such a defence was pre-empted by the ruling. Should it have been?

In our judgment the answer is plainly not. The authorities are now clear. Their effect is perhaps most conveniently to be found in the judgment of this court in *R. v Conway*. The decision reviews earlier relevant authorities.

The principles may be summarised thus. First, English law does, in extreme circumstances, recognise a defence of necessity. Most commonly this defence arises as duress, that is pressure on the accused's will from the wrongful threats or violence of another. Equally however it can arise from other objective dangers threatening the accused or others. Arising thus it is conveniently called 'duress of circumstances'.

Secondly, the defence is available only if, from an objective standpoint, the accused can be said to be acting reasonably and proportionately in order to avoid a threat of death or serious injury.

Thirdly, assuming the defence to be open to the accused on his account of the facts, the issue should be left to the jury, who should be directed to determine these two questions: first, was the accused, or may he have been, impelled to act as he did because as a result of what he reasonably believed to be the situation he had good cause to fear that otherwise death or serious physical injury would result? Second, if so, would a sober person of reasonable firmness, sharing the characteristics of the accused, have responded to that situation by acting as the accused acted? If the answer to both those questions was Yes, then the jury would acquit; the defence of necessity would have been established . . .

We see no material distinction between offences of reckless driving and driving whilst disqualified so far as the application and scope of this defence is concerned. Equally we can see no distinction in principle between various threats of death; it matters not whether the risk of death is by murder or by suicide or indeed by accident. One can illustrate the latter by considering a disqualified driver being driven by his wife, she suffering a heart attack in remote countryside and he needing instantly to get her to hospital.

It follows from this that the judge quite clearly did come to a wrong decision on the question of law, and the appellant should have been permitted to raise this defence for what it was worth before the jury."

Appeal allowed. Conviction quashed

9–160 This approach has been followed in numerous other decisions[374] where it has been emphasised that both species of duress are governed by the same principles, which were canvassed above. Importantly, this means that the defence is not available to murder, attempted murder and certain forms of treason.[375] In *Phair*,[376] D was charged with a number of driving and drugs offences following a fatal car chase which had taken place as a result of an altercation between D and a man called Toher over drugs that Toher had paid D for, but which were not supplied. D argued that he had acted under duress of circumstances as he was escaping from Toher who had arrived with a metal bar and inflicted damage to his car prior to the chase. The Court of Appeal in Northern Ireland held that the trial judge had been right to direct the jury that the defence of duress of circumstances was not available if D had voluntarily put himself in a position in which he knew or ought reasonably to have known that he might be compelled to commit a crime by threats of violence made by other people and that it would be "artificial and against public policy to make a distinction" between the two defences,[377] although they commented that a trial judge should take "particular care" to "relate the specific facts of a case to the law."[378]

> "As a matter of policy and principle we consider that the defendant who accepts money to supply illegal drugs but does not supply them puts himself in a position where he is likely to be subjected to threats requiring him to commit crimes at the behest of the duressor should also attract this limitation. In other words, this person cannot take advantage of his own criminal behaviour . . ."[379]

However, the rather different nature of the defences has involved some inevitable divergence in the application of the two defences. For example, as already seen, for duress by threats there must be a link between the threat and the crime whereas for duress of circumstances there is no such requirement. Furthermore, the courts have taken a more flexible approach to the requirement of imminence with duress of circumstances than that pertaining to duress by threats.

9–161 In reality, duress of circumstances covers situations that are termed "necessity" in other jurisdictions. However, necessity is widely regarded as a *justificatory* defence. On that basis, duress of circumstances could logically be regarded similarly as a justification. However, by building on the blocks of duress by threats, the courts have been able to develop duress of circumstances as an excusatory defence.[380] It is recognised that Ds have done wrong but we do not think it appropriate, because of their plight, to

---

374 e.g. *Cairns* [1999] 2 Cr. App. R. 137, and *Abdul-Hussain* [1999] Crim. L.R. 570. In *Hampshire CC v E* [2007] EWHC 2584 (Admin); [2008] E.L.R. 260, the court expressed some doubt about whether duress of circumstances could be pleaded in relation to an offence of strict liability (the crime in question being that of failing to secure the attendance of a child at school under Education Act 1996 s.444(1)), however, the better view is that it can be. In *R. v Gregory (Thomas Dennis)* [2011] EWCA Crim 1712, e.g. the court accepted that there might be circumstances when the defence might arise in answer to a charge of possession of a firearm without a certificate (the Firearms Act 1968 s.1).

375 In *R. v Petgrave (Pascoe)* [2018] EWCA Crim 1397 at [23]; [2019] R.T.R. 6, it was noted that the defence "may in principle be a defence to most crimes (with certain specific exceptions)" and accepted that it could be a defence to an offence of causing injury by dangerous driving, contrary to Road Traffic Act 1988 s.1A. For discussion of this case, see K. Laird, "Case Comment: Duress: *R. v Petgrave (Pascoe)*" [2019] Crim. L.R. 1397.

376 *Phair* [2022] NICA 66. J. Taggart, "'Duress of circumstances and voluntary association': *R. v Phair* [2022] NICA 66" (2023) 74 NILQ 388.

377 *Phair* [2022] NICA 66 at [84].

378 *Phair* [2022] NICA 66 at [84].

379 *Phair* [2022] NICA 66 at [89].

380 Padfield, "Duress, Necessity and the Law Commission" [1992] Crim. L.R. 778. cf. Z. Akhtar, "Duress, justification and the defence of necessity" (2021) 89 S.L.G. 27.

blame them. This means that Ds can only be excused if they are able to satisfy stringent requirements: their will must be overborne by threats of death or serious bodily harm.

Such an approach leaves no scope for a claim that actions were justified and that the D's will was not overborne. In *Jones (Margaret)*,[381] the Ds argued that their actions in conspiring to cause criminal damage to an air-force base (where preparations were being made for war) were necessary in order to prevent an illegal war.[382] Just as in *Shayler*,[383] the court regarded this as, if anything,[384] an excusatory plea of duress of circumstances. Yet this does not satisfactorily reflect the reality of the defendants' claim. A further illustration is the case of *Quayle* in which a number of appeals were heard together.[385] All involved the possession or supply of cannabis for relief from chronic and acute pain. The Court of Appeal described the defendants' pleas as "necessity by extraneous circumstances" and took the view that, following *Hasan*, a restrictive approach to the defence was applicable. It was not possible to plead it in circumstances where it would legitimise conduct that was contrary to the clear legislative policy and scheme relating to controlled drugs.[386] In dismissing the appeals the Court of Appeal concluded:

> "Where there is no imminent or immediate threat or peril, but only a general assertion of an internal motivation to engage in prohibited activities in order to prevent or alleviate pain, it is also difficult to identify any extraneous or objective factors by reference to which a jury could be expected to measure whether the motivation was such as to override the defendant's will or to force him to act as he did. If the response is that the defendant was not forced, but chose to act as he did, then [a continuous and deliberate course of otherwise unlawful self-help is unlikely to give rise to the defence."[387]

In *Thacker*,[388] "the Stansted 15" case, protestors entered the restricted area at London Stansted Airport in order to disrupt a Home Office flight which was due to deport a group of detainees to West Africa They erected scaffolding tripods, and chained themselves to one another around the base of the tripods and around the nose cone of the airplane. On appeal, an argument that the trial judge had been wrong to withdraw the defence of necessity and/or duress of circumstances from the jury was rejected by the

381 *R. v Jones (Margaret)* [2004] EWCA Crim 1981; [2005] Q.B. 259.

382 The case subsequently went to the House of Lords but did not deal with the issue of necessity of circumstances: *R. v Jones (Margaret)* [2006] UKHL 16; [2007] 1 A.C. 136. See also *R. v Thacker (Edward)* [2021] EWCA Crim 97; [2021] Q.B. 644.

383 *Shayler* [2001] 1 W.L.R. 2206.

384 In both *Shayler* [2001] 1 W.L.R. 2206 and *R. v Jones (Margaret)* [2004] EWCA Crim 1981, the defence failed. In *Jones*, the Court of Appeal held that the defence was limited to situations where the defendant was faced with a crime under domestic law. This has rightly been criticised. Ormerod and Laird, *Smith, Hogan and Ormerod's Criminal Law,* 16th edn (2021), points out that the defence "was available to *Martin* when his wife was threatening suicide (not a crime)" (p.386). See further, J. Gardner, "Direct Action and the Defence of Necessity" [2005] Crim. L.R. 371.

385 *Quayle* [2005] 2 Cr. App. R. 527.

386 This approach was followed in *R. v S* [2012] EWCA Crim 389; [2012] 1 W.L.R. 3081 where it was held that it was not possible to plead necessity/duress of circumstances (the court left open the question of whether there was a difference between them) in answer to a charge of child abduction under the Child Abduction Act 1984 s.1 as the purpose of the legislation was to prevent removal of a child from the jurisdiction so that he or she could remain under the protection of the court (at [13]). See further, D. Ormerod, "*R. v S*: removing a child from the jurisdiction" [2012] Crim. L.R. 624.

387 *Hasan* [2005] 2 A.C. 467 at [81].

388 *Thacker* [2021] EWCA Crim 97; [2021] Q.B. 644. For critical discussion of this case see: S. Cammis, G. Hayes and B. Doherty, "Necessity, Non-Violent Direct Activism and the Stansted 15: Reasserting 'Hoffman's Bargain'" (2022) 85 M.L.R. 1515. cf. Z. Akhter, "Duress, Justification and the Defence of Necessity" (2021) 89 *Scottish Law Gazette* 27.

Court of Appeal, who held that the case fell "four-square" with the decision in *Jones*.[389] Unfortunately, the court conflated the defences in its analysis of the case law, without examining with clarity the doctrinal distinction between these defences in the context of political protest.[390]

9–162 In *Quayle*, the court rejected the argument that denying a defence in these circumstances amounted to a breach of the ECHR art.8. Similarly, in *Altham*,[391] it was held that the denial of the defence did not breach art.3.

Recognition of the defence of excusatory necessity may, it seems, leave the development of justificatory necessity perpetually in the shadows. In the Draft Criminal Code Bill the Law Commission proposed statutory endorsement of the defence of duress of circumstances.[392] Since then, the Law Commission has considered the whole defence of duress as part of its review of the law of homicide. Prefacing its recommendations with the statement that there are two forms of duress: duress by threats and duress of circumstances, the Report acknowledges that the issue of whether duress should be a defence to murder has been discussed primarily in relation to duress by threats.[393] However, it takes the view that the general principles that govern duress of circumstances are substantially the same,[394] and thus, if the stringent requirements for the defence were met, a D would, if the recommendations became law, be able to plead duress of circumstances to a charge of murder.

D. NECESSITY

9–163 The defence of necessity is well-established in other jurisdictions and applies to situations where a defendant chooses to commit a crime in order to avert a greater evil.

1. Distinction between necessity and duress of circumstances

9–164 All the cases on duress of circumstances, considered above, concern situations of necessity and we have seen that many recent cases use the terms "duress of circumstances" and "necessity" interchangeably as simply being "different labels for essentially the same thing".[395]

There are, however, important differences between the two defences. Necessity is widely regarded in other jurisdictions as a justificatory defence whereas, as seen, the defence of duress of circumstances has been viewed as an excuse by English law. This difference in theoretical approach has important

389 *Thacker* [2021] EWCA Crim 97; [2021] Q.B. 644 at [102]. The appeal was allowed on the basis that there was no case to answer in respect of the offence charged.
390 *Thacker* [2021] EWCA Crim 97; [2021] Q.B. 644 at [91]–[103].
391 *R. v Altham (Lee)* [2006] EWCA Crim 7; [2006] 1 W.L.R. 3287.
392 Law Com. No.218 (1993), cl.26 fn.328. The defence would be available to all crimes—even murder—as with duress by threats (Law Commission Consultation Paper No.122, *Legislating the Criminal Code: Offences Against the Person and General Principles* (1992), para.19.9, confirmed in Law Com. No.218 (1993), para.35.10 fn.328).
393 Law Com. No.304 (2006), para.6.6 fn.37.
394 Law Com. No.304 (2006), para.6.8 fn.37.
395 *Shayler* [2001] 1 W.L.R. 2206, see para.9–131.

consequences for the rules that govern the developing defences,[396] although it has to be accepted that the courts are not always clear or consistent in their application of these rules.[397]

First, duress of circumstances is a defence only when there has been a threat of death or serious injury. With an excusatory defence, the essence of which involves the D's will being overborne and the actions being morally involuntary, one can perhaps understand the view that this will only be so if the threat is truly awesome as in the case of a threat of death or serious injury. With a justificatory defence, however, the emphasis is on the actor making a choice between two evils and pursuing the lesser of them. So, with necessity the threat need not be of death or serious injury. The essence of the defence is that it involves a balancing of evils. The threat can take any form but the crime committed by the defendant must involve a lesser evil.

Secondly, with duress of circumstances the threat must be "imminent" in the sense of being operative on the mind of D and overbearing their will. With necessity, the principle is one of "necessity, not emergency".[398] A rational choice is made to avert a greater evil that will necessarily occur even if it would be some time before it occurs. **9–165**

Thirdly, the cases on duress of circumstances have allowed certain aspects of the vulnerability of D to be taken into account; the test is whether the reasonable person, sharing the same characteristics as the D, would have given in to the threats. This is an appropriate test for determining whether a person should be excused because his will was overborne. With necessity, the focus is on the balancing of evils and not on the particular D's condition. There should be no scope for making allowance for the D's condition or vulnerability.

Finally, duress of circumstances is not a defence to murder, attempted murder or certain forms of treason. With necessity, the focus is on the balancing of evils and judging the choices of the defendant. In principle, necessity ought to be a defence when D kills one person in order to save the lives of more than one person.

2. The traditional approach of English law

Until the development of duress of circumstances in the 1980s, it was commonly thought that a defence of necessity did not exist in English law.[399] In *O'Toole*[400] and *Wood v Richards*,[401] an ambulance **9–166**

---

396 See Clarkson, "Necessary Action: A New Defence" [2004] Crim. L.R. 81, where it is argued that the defences of self-defence, duress, duress of circumstances and necessity should be combined as one defence of "necessary action". This would have the advantage of simplicity and allow the focus to be upon the issue that unites all the defences: whether the defendant's response was reasonable and proportionate. See the critique of this proposal by Chan and Simester, "Duress, Necessity: How Many Defences?" (2005) 16 K.C.L.J. 121. cf. S. Edwards, "The Claims of Necessity: Good and Hard, Excuse and Justification and the Moral Narratives of Necessity" in A. Reed and N. Wake (eds), *General Defences In Criminal Law: Domestic and Comparative Perspectives* (London: Routledge, 2014), Ch.6.

397 See, e.g. *R. v S Ltd* [2009] EWCA Crim 85; [2009] 2 Cr. App. R. 11 and the case comment by Ormerod [2009] Crim. L.R. 723.

398 *Re A (Conjoined Twins: Surgical Separation)* [2001] Fam. 147.

399 *R. v Dudley (Thomas)* (1884) 14 Q.B.D. 273 is usually cited to support this proposition. It has been argued that the facts of that case did not disclose a true case of necessity: Ormerod and Laird, *Smith, Hogan and Ormerod's Criminal Law*, 16th edn (2021), pp.392–393, but it is submitted that the overall tenor of the judgment indicates that Lord Coleridge was simply not prepared to accept necessity as a defence to murder. The House of Lords in *Howe* [1987] A.C. 417 (paras 9–151–9–152) interpreted the case in this way.

400 *R. v O'Toole (Robert John)* (1971) 55 Cr. App. R. 206; [1974] R.T.R. 88 CA.

401 *Wood v Richards* (1977) 65 Cr. App. R. 300; [1977] Crim. L.R. 295 Div Ct.

driver and a police officer, respectively, were involved in car crashes while rushing to answer emergency calls. Both were convicted of road traffic offences, necessity being no defence.[402] In *Kitson*,[403] a passenger woke up drunk in a car to find it running downhill; he steered the car on to a grass verge to avoid a possible collision; he was convicted of driving while under the influence of drink; the defence of necessity was not even raised. And in *Southwark LBC v Williams*, where Ds in dire need of housing accommodation entered empty houses owned by the local authority, it was held that the defence of necessity did not apply. Lord Denning MR stated:

> "If homelessness were once admitted as a defence to trespass, no one's house could be safe. Necessity would open a door which no man could shut. It would not only be those in extreme need who would enter. There would be others who would imagine that they were in need, or would invent a need, so as to gain entry."[404]

Edmund Davis LJ held:

> "[T]he law regards with the deepest suspicion any remedies of self-help, and permits those remedies to be resorted to only in very special circumstances. The reason for such circumspection is clear—necessity can very easily become simply a mask for anarchy."[405]

9–167 However, later in the same case Edmund-Davis LJ stated:

> "[I]t appears that all the cases where a plea of necessity has succeeded are cases which deal with an urgent situation of imminent peril; for example, the forcible feeding of an obdurate suffragette . . . or performing an abortion to avert a grave threat to the life, or . . . health of a pregnant young girl who had been ravished in circumstances of great brutality."[406]

This apparent recognition of the defence of necessity in extreme cases demonstrates that there has never been a blanket condemnation of it in all guises and in all situations. The following two situations require separate consideration.

(i) Medical treatment

9–168 Edmund-Davies LJ spoke of the forced feeding of suffragettes and emergency abortions being defended on the basis of necessity. More recently, one interpretation of the case of *Gillick*[407] is that it involved a "hidden" defence of necessity. The doctor who prescribes contraceptive advice or treatment

---

402 cf. *Johnson v Phillips* [1976] 1 W.L.R. 65; [1976] R.T.R. 170 QBD where necessity was accepted as a basis for *convicting* a defendant.
403 *R. v Kitson (Herbert)* (1955) 39 Cr. App. R. 66.
404 *Southwark LBC v Williams* [1971] Ch. 734 at 744; [1971] 2 W.L.R. 467 CA.
405 *Southwark LBC v Williams* [1971] Ch. 734 at 745–746.
406 *Southwark LBC v Williams* [1971] Ch. 734 at 746, referring to the cases of Leigh v Gladstone (1909) 26 TLR 139 and R v Bourne [1939] 1 KB 687 respectively.
407 *Gillick v West Norfolk and Wisbech AHA* [1986] A.C. 112; [1985] 3 W.L.R. 830 HL.

to a girl under the age of 16 does not commit the offence of aiding and abetting underage sexual intercourse if he does so (inter alia) in the belief that unless she receives it her physical or mental health would be likely to suffer.[408]

In *F v West Berkshire HA*,[409] it was held that doctors were justified in carrying out a sterilisation operation upon a woman who was incapable of giving informed consent because of her mental handicap. Lord Goff's argument was based upon necessity; there was a grave risk of her becoming pregnant if she was not sterilised and it was agreed that such a condition would have a very disturbing impact upon her.[410]

What is significant about this development is that necessity is not used to excuse wrongful conduct but to justify conduct as the *right* thing to do. "[T]here is no question of the defence depending on the actor's resistance being overcome."[411] An example given by Lord Goff during his speech makes this clear:

> ". . . a man who seizes another and forcibly drags him from the path of an oncoming vehicle, thereby saving him from injury or even death, commits no wrong."[412]

(ii) Statutory defences that are in substance necessity

Some statutes expressly provide defences that are in substance defences of necessity. For example, fire-engines, police and ambulances are exempted from observing the speed limit in certain circumstances,[413] and in specified circumstances they may treat a red traffic light as a warning to give way.[414] In such cases, it is not possible to plead a general defence of necessity. The only possible defence is under the regulation itself.[415] Another important statutory example is that in order to protect property that is in immediate need of protection, it is permissible to destroy the property of another person.[416] This provision is meant, of course, to provide a defence to, say, a fireman who breaks down a door in order to rescue the occupants of a burning building. Remarkably, however, in 2008, a jury acquitted six climate change protesters charged with criminal damage to a coal-fired power station, having heard defence arguments that the damage caused was lawfully excused by the need to prevent the even greater damage caused by climate change.[417] **9–169**

---

408 Smith, *Justification and Excuse in the Criminal Law* (1989), pp.64–68. Smith argues that there are many other "concealed defences" in the criminal law (pp.61–72).

409 *F v West Berkshire HA* [1990] 2 A.C. 1; [1989] 2 W.L.R. 1025 HL.

410 To similar effect, see *R. v Bournewood Community and Mental Health NHS Trust Ex p. L* [1999] 1 A.C. 458; [1998] 3 W.L.R. 107 HL. The common law in relation to the treatment and care of incapacitated adults has been superseded by the Mental Capacity Act 2005.

411 Law Commission Consultation Paper No.122 (1992), para.19.5 fn.412.

412 *F v West Berkshire HA* [1990] 2 A.C. 1 at 74. In *Pipe v DPP* [2012] EWHC 1821 (Admin), it was held that justices had been wrong to reject a defence of necessity to a charge of driving at an excessive speed in circumstance where D had broken the speed limit to get a young boy with a broken leg to hospital. The boy had sustained a serious Injury, was in severe pain and was in urgent need of treatment.

413 Road Traffic Regulation Act 1984 s.87.

414 Traffic Signs Regulations and General Directions 2016 (SI 2016/362) Sch.14 Pt 1 reg.5(3)–(6).

415 *DPP v Harris (Nigel)* [1995] 1 Cr. App. R. 170; (1994) 158 J.P. 896 QBD. In such cases, if there is a threat of death or serious injury, duress of circumstances can be pleaded (*R. v Backshall (David Anthony)* [1998] 1 W.L.R. 1506; [1999] 1 Cr. App. R. 35 CA).

416 Criminal Damage Act 1971 s.5(2)(b).

417 M. McCarthy, "Cleared: Jury decides that threat of global warming justifies breaking the law" *The Independent*, 11 September 2008.

Furthermore, many statutes contain phrases such as "unlawful", "without lawful excuse"[418] or "without reasonable excuse", which may be construed to cover situations in which a defence of necessity might be appropriate: for example, the old Forgery Act 1913 ss.8–10 prohibited the possession of forged bank notes "without lawful authority or excuse".[419] In *Wuyts*,[420] it was held that if the defendant's sole purpose in retaining possession of the notes was to hand them to the police, it would have been a "lawful excuse".[421]

(iii) Necessity and homicide

R. V DUDLEY AND STEPHENS (1884) 14 Q.B.D. 273 (QUEENS BENCH DIVISION):

9–170 The two Ds, with a third man and a 17-year-old boy, were cast away on the high seas in an open boat, 1,600 miles from land. They drifted in the boat for 20 days. When they had been eight days without food and six days without water, and fearing they would all die soon without some sustenance, the Ds killed the boy, who was likely to die first. The men ate his flesh and drank his blood for four days. They were then rescued by a passing vessel and were subsequently charged with murder. The jury found the facts of the case in a special verdict and the case was referred to the Queen's Bench Division for its decision.

LORD COLERIDGE CJ:

> "[T]he prisoners put to death a weak and unoffending boy upon the chance of preserving their own lives by feeding upon his flesh and blood after he was killed, and with a certainty of depriving *him* of any possible chance of survival. The verdict finds in terms that: 'if the men had not fed upon the body of the boy, they would *probably* have not survived . . .' and that 'the boy, being in a much weaker condition, was *likely* to have died before them'. They might possibly have been picked up next day by a passing ship; they might not have been picked up at all; in either case it is obvious that the killing of the boy would have been an unnecessary and profitless act. It is found by the verdict that the boy was incapable of resistance, and, in fact, made none . . .
>
> [I]t is admitted that the deliberate killing of this unoffending and unresisting boy was clearly murder, unless the killing can be justified by some well-recognised excuse admitted by the law. It is further admitted that there was in this case no such excuse, unless the killing was justified by what has been called 'necessity.' But the temptation to the act which existed here was not what the law has ever called necessity. Nor is this to be regretted. Though law and morality are not the same, and though many things may be immoral which are not necessarily illegal, yet the absolute divorce of law from morality would be of fatal consequence, and such divorce

418 See, e.g. Criminal Damage Act 1971 s. 5(2); *DPP v Ditchfield* [2021] EWHC 1090 (Admin); *Att-Gen's Ref on a Point of Law (No.1 of 2023)* [2024] EWCA Crim 243 and paras 8–208–8–211.

419 See now the Forgery and Counterfeiting Act 1981 s.16(2).

420 *R. v Wuyts (Nicholas Charles)* [1969] 2 Q.B. 474; [1969] 3 W.L.R. 1. See also *R. v Jones (Margaret)* [2005] Q.B. 259.

421 For a full discussion of the circumstances when a statute can be construed to cover situations of necessity, see P.R. Glazebrook, "The Necessity Plea in English Criminal Law" [1972] C.L.J. 87.

would follow if the temptation to murder in this case were to be held by law an absolute defence of it. It is not so. To preserve one's life is generally speaking, a duty, but it may be the plainest and the highest duty to sacrifice it. War is full of instances in which it is a man's duty not to live, but to die . . .

It is not needful to point out the awful danger of admitting the principle which has been contended for. Who is to be the judge of this sort of necessity? By what measure is the comparative value of lives to be measured? Is it to be strength, or intellect, or what? It is plain that the principle leaves to him who is to profit by it to determine the necessity which will justify him in deliberately taking another's life to save his own. In this case the weakest, the youngest, the most unresisting was chosen. Was it more necessary to kill *him* than one of the grown men? The answer be, No . . .

It must not be supposed that, in refusing to admit temptation to be an excuse for crime, it is forgotten how terrible the temptation was; how awful the suffering; how hard in such trials to keep the judgment straight and the conduct pure. We are often compelled to set up standards we cannot reach ourselves, and to lay down rules which we could not ourselves satisfy. But a man has no right to declare temptation to be an excuse, though he might himself have yielded to it, nor allow compassion for the criminal to change or weaken in any manner the legal definition of the crime. It is therefore our duty to declare that the prisoners' act in this case was wilful murder."

Judgment for the Crown. Sentence of death, later commuted to six months' imprisonment

Dudley and Stephens *received judicial confirmation in* ***Howe****.*

R. v Howe [1987] A.C. 417 (House of Lords):

[For the facts, see para.9–151.] **9–171**

LORD HAILSHAM LC:

"[I]f we were to allow this appeal [against a conviction for murder on the basis of duress], we should, I think, also have to say that *Dudley and Stephens* was bad law. There is, of course, an obvious distinction between duress and necessity as potential defences; duress arises from the wrongful threats of violence of another human being and necessity arises from any other objective dangers threatening the accused. This, however, is in my view a distinction without a relevant difference, since on this view duress is only that species of the genus of necessity which is caused by wrongful threats. I cannot see that there is any way in which a person of ordinary fortitude can be excused from the one type of pressure on his will rather than the other."

Lord Hailsham's view is that because the defences of duress and necessity are so similar, neither is **9–172**
available to the person who kills. This could be regarded as an implicit acknowledgement of the

existence of a defence of necessity to crimes other than murder, attempted murder, and certain forms of treason. Perhaps it was dicta such as these that permitted the rapid development of the defence of duress of circumstances.

All the above extracts rightly treat necessity as a justificatory defence. In *Dudley and Stephens*, Lord Coleridge expressed the view that a defence of necessity would alter "the legal definition of the crime" which would only be the case if it acted as justificatory defence. This approach raises the intractable problem discussed in *Dudley and Stephens* and in *Holmes* of having to decide whose lives should be sacrificed. Perhaps the law might have developed in a different direction if the defendants in *Dudley and Stephens* had been viewed as pleading an excuse. It was not a case of the lives of the three men being superior to that of the cabin boy. However, given that their lives were of equal value, due consideration should have been given to the awfulness of the situation they were in. The fact that their sentences were so rapidly commuted gives further strength to this argument. Indeed, it has been said that the pardon had been arranged well in advance of the sentences being passed.[422] To the extent that the Ds were arguing that their killing of the boy were driven by the threat of death from starvation and/or dehydration, they may be seen as raising a defence which would today be recognised as duress of circumstances, although as *Howe* makes clear, this is not a defence to murder.[423]

9–173 The shadow of *Dudley and Stephens* has long hung over English law. In 1974, the Law Commission proposed that a general defence of necessity be introduced into English law.[424] However, three years later it rejected the idea, going so far as to say that if a defence of necessity already existed at common law, it should be abolished. It felt that allowing such a defence to a charge of murder could effectively legalise euthanasia in England. For "human rights" reasons it would not be prepared to see necessity covering a situation where:

> ". . . an immediate blood transfusion must be made in order to save an injured person: the only one who has the same blood type as the injured refuses to give blood. Can he be overpowered and the blood taken from him?"[425]

Instead, the Draft Criminal Code Bill 1993 proposed a statutory formulation of duress of circumstances, cast as an excuse, but applying to all offences.

3. Emergence of a new defence?

9–174 By the turn of the century, English law thus appeared fairly settled. Whatever the nomenclature, necessity had been let in the back door under the guise of duress of circumstances and was viewed as an excuse with the implications discussed earlier, including the fact that it was not a defence to murder,

---

422 Katz, *Bad Acts and Guilty Minds* (1987), p.27.

423 *Howe* [1987] A.C. 417; Law Commission, L.Com No.304, para.6.8; Child, Simester, Spencer, Stark and Virgo, *Simester and Sullivan's Criminal Law: Theory and Doctrine*, 8th edn (2022), p.919.

424 Law Com. No.55, *Defences of General Application* (1955), para.57.

425 Law Com. No.83 (1977), para.4.27 fn.307.

attempted murder and certain forms of treason. This tranquillity was shattered by the following decision.

Re A (Conjoined Twins: Surgical Separation) [2001] Fam.147 (Court of Appeal, Civil Division):

"Jodie" and "Mary" were conjoined twins. Leaving them joined would result in the death of both of them within six months. A separation operation would certainly result in the death of Mary who was not capable of separate survival but would give Jodie a good prospect of a normal life. The parents objected to the operation and an application was made to the High Court and then to the Court of Appeal for a declaration, inter alia, that the operation would be lawful despite the fact that it would result in the death of Mary under circumstances making the surgeons prima facie liable for murder. **9–175**

WARD LJ:

"The first important feature is that the doctors cannot be denied a right of choice if they are under a duty to choose. They are under a duty to Mary not to operate because it will kill Mary, but they are under a duty to Jodie to operate because not to do so will kill her . . . What then is the position where there is a conflict of duty? . . . Wilson J . . . in *Perka v The Queen* (1984) 13 DLR (4th) 1, 36 [stated]:

> 'the ethical considerations of the "charitable and the good" must be kept analytically distinct from duties imposed by law. Accordingly, where necessity is invoked as a justification for violation of the law, the justification must, in my view, be restricted to situations where the accused's act constitutes the discharge of a duty recognised by law. The justification is not, however, established simply by showing a conflict of legal duties. The rule of proportionality is central to the evaluation of a justification premised on two conflicting duties since the defence rests on the rightfulness of the accused's choice of one over the other.'

So far I agree . . . In [these] circumstances it seems to me that the law must allow an escape through choosing the lesser of the two evils. The law cannot say, 'Heads I win, tails you lose.' Faced as they are with an apparently irreconcilable conflict, the doctors should be in no different position from that in which the court itself was placed in the performance of its duty to give paramount consideration to the welfare of each child. The doctors must be given the same freedom of choice as the court has given itself and the doctors must make that choice along the same lines as the court has done, giving the sanctity of life principle its place in the balancing exercise that has to be undertaken. The respect the law must have for the right to life of each must go in the scales and weigh equally but other factors have to go in the scales as well. For the same reasons that led to my concluding that consent should be given to operate, so the conclusion has to be that the carrying out of the operation will be justified as the lesser evil and no unlawful act would be committed."

9–176 BROOKE LJ:

"I have described how in modern times Parliament has sometimes provided 'necessity' defences in statutes and how the courts in developing the defence of duress of circumstances have sometimes equated it with the defence of necessity. They do not, however, cover exactly the same ground. In cases of pure necessity the actor's mind is not irresistibly overborne by external pressures. The claim is that his or her conduct was not harmful because on a choice of two evils the choice of avoiding the greater harm was justified . . .

I have considered very carefully the policy reasons for the decision in *R. v Dudley and Stephens* supported as it was by the House of Lords in *R. v Howe*. These are, in short, that there were two insuperable objections to the proposition that necessity might be available as a defence for the *Mignonette* sailors. The first objection was evident in the court's questions: who is to be the judge of this sort of necessity? By what measure is the comparative value of lives to be measured? The second objection was that to permit such a defence would mark an absolute divorce of law from morality. In my judgment, neither of these objections are dispositive of the present case. Mary is, sadly, self-designated for a very early death. Nobody can extend her life beyond a very short span . . . [With regard to the second objection] all that a court can say is that it is not at all obvious that this is the sort of clear-cut case, marking an absolute divorce from law and morality, which was of such concern to Lord Coleridge CJ and his fellow judges.

There are sound reasons for holding that the existence of an emergency in the normal sense of the word is not an essential prerequisite for the application of the doctrine of necessity. The principle is one of necessity, not emergency . . .

If a sacrificial separation operation on conjoined twins were to be permitted in circumstances like these, there need be no room for the concern felt by Sir James Stephen that people would be too ready to avail themselves of exceptions to the law which they might suppose to apply to their cases, at the risk of other people's lives. Such an operation is, and is always likely to be, an exceptionally rare event . . .

According to Sir James Stephen there are three necessary requirements for the application of the doctrine of necessity: (i) the act is needed to avoid inevitable and irreparable evil; (ii) no more should be done than is reasonably necessary for the purpose to be achieved; (iii) the evil inflicted must not be disproportionate to the evil avoided. Given that the principles of modern family law point irresistibly to the conclusion that the interests of Jodie must be preferred to the conflicting interests of Mary, I consider that all three of these requirements are satisfied in this case."

9–177 ROBERT WALKER LJ:

"Duress of circumstances can therefore be seen as a third or residual category of necessity, along with self-defence and duress by threats. I do not think it matters whether these defences are regarded as justifications or excuses. Whatever label is used, the moral merits of the defence will vary with the circumstances . . .

> In the absence of parliamentary intervention the law as to the defence of necessity is going to have to develop on a case by case basis . . . I would extend it, if it needs to be extended, to cover this case. It is a case of doctors owing conflicting legal, and not merely social or moral, duties. It is a case where the test of proportionality is met, since it is a matter of life and death, and on the evidence Mary is bound to die soon in any event. It is not a case of evaluating the relative worth of two human lives, but of undertaking surgery without which neither life will have the bodily integrity, or wholeness, which is its due. It should not be regarded as a further step down a slippery slope because the case of conjoined twins presents an unique problem."

The full implications of this decision have not yet been considered by the courts. A narrower **9–178**
interpretation is that this is an extension of the "medical necessity" principle discussed above. Ward LJ limited his judgment to cases where there was a conflict between a doctor's duties. A doctor is under a legal duty to do what is best for a patient. Here, there were conflicting duties owed to the twins and, in exercising their duty, the doctors had to make a choice of the lesser of two evils. Although this narrower interpretation involves a significant extension of the law in that it allows doctors to kill their patients in these tightly-defined circumstances it does provide one of the many reasons why arguments in the courts that doctors should be able to plead necessity to a charge of assisting suicide (or even euthanasia) have been unsuccessful: in *Re A*, the conflict was resolved in favour of taking action to *preserve* at least one life. As Stark comments, this is what makes *Re A* distinguishable from cases such as *Nicklinson, where the applicant sought to argue that it would not be unlawful for a doctor, to assist the termination of his life, on the basis that the defence of necessity would be available to such a person.*[426] In the words of the Court of Appeal in *Nicklinson*:

> "[T]here is a world of difference between taking a life to save a life and taking a life because the deceased wishes it to end . . . [*Re A*] is too slender a thread on which to hang such a far-reaching development of the common law."[427]

A bolder interpretation of *Re A* is one which has the potential to lead to the development of a true defence of necessity, cut free from its theoretical links to duress. Many of the examples of necessity Brooke LJ cites and discusses extend beyond medical necessity and suggest a wider role for the defence.

---

426 Stark, "Case Comment: Necessity and *Nicklinson*" [2013] Crim. L.R. 949–965, 960. See also S. Ost, "Euthanasia and the Defence of Necessity: Advocating a More Appropriate Legal Response" [2005] Crim. L.R. 355. cf. Tamblyn, *The Law of Duress and Necessity* (2018), pp.159–161.

427 *R. (on the application of Nicklinson) v Ministry of Justice* [2013] EWCA Civ 961 at [63]. The court further states that "it is simply not appropriate for the court to fashion a defence of necessity in such a complex and controversial field; this is a matter for Parliament" (at [56]). See para.7–124. The necessity argument was not pursued when the case was appealed to the Supreme Court: see *Nicklinson v United Kingdom (Admissibility)* (2478/15) (2015) 61 E.H.R.R. SE7 at [24], although Lord Neuberger expressed approval of the Court of Appeal's approach to this issue: ". . . to extend the defence of necessity to a charge of assisted suicide would be a revolutionary step, which would be wholly inconsistent with both recent judicial data of high authority, and the legislature's intentions", *R. (on the application of Nicklinson) v Ministry of Justice* [2014] UKSC 38 at [130]. For further discussion, see: J. Rogers, "Assisted Suicide Saga—The *Nicklinson* Episode" (2014) 7 *Archbold Review* 7.

IAN DENNIS, "ON NECESSITY AS A DEFENCE TO CRIME: POSSIBILITIES, PROBLEMS AND THE LIMITS OF JUSTIFICATION AND EXCUSE" (2009) CRIM. LAW AND PHILOS. 29, 44–45:

9–179 "It would seem, although this is not completely clear, that he [Brooke LJ] regarded this form of necessity defence as an act-utilitarian principle. It is not a statement of the classic 'lesser evils' form of necessity because it allows for harm to be done equal to that which is threatened, as long as the harm done is not disproportionate . . .

However, there are problems with an unqualified act-utilitarian principle. One of them is the potential devaluing of personal autonomy. Suppose P, a hospital patient, urgently needs a blood transfusion to survive, but she has a very rare blood group. As it happens, Q, the patient in the next bed, has the same rare blood group, but refuses to make a donation of blood even though she could do so without risk to herself. May, D, the doctor treating P, take the blood from Q without her consent? The blood is needed to avoid 'inevitable and irreparable evil', and the physical harm done in the form of assault on Q to obtain the blood is not disproportionate to the harm threatened of P's death. Is the assault on Q 'no more than reasonably necessary to achieve the purpose of preventing P's death?' Everything then turns on the one word 'reasonably'. A test of reasonableness is a flexible standard that inevitably requires an accommodation of competing values. But in states that subscribe to liberal democratic values personal autonomy is not something that can be traded against other values. Persons have rights to be treated as ends in themselves and not as means to the achievement of other social goals. Accordingly, if Q chose to assert her autonomy by refusing her consent to give blood that would normally be the end of the matter, but the principle adopted by Brooke LJ, applied without qualification, would leave the matter in doubt."

9–180 Brooke LJ, when dealing with necessity as a defence to murder, was careful to limit his judgment to the killing of those already "designated for death". This means that D cannot choose (by whatever criterion) to throw four people off a boat to their death in order to save 10 others: those four people have not been designated for death. Similarly, on the facts of *Dudley and Stephens* there would still not be a defence of necessity. While the cabin boy was the weakest and most likely to die first, they could all have been rescued. He was not designated for death.[428]

However, that still leaves situations, as the example from Dennis illustrates, where a defence of necessity could be pleaded to avoid "an inevitable and irreparable evil". Brooke LJ's interpretation could allow necessity as a defence to murder. For example, if after a car crash a driver and passenger were seriously injured but it was clear that the driver was dying with no prospect of recovery but the passenger's life could be saved, it could be open to paramedics or other emergency services personnel to kill the driver in cutting them loose if that was the only means by which they could get to the passenger in time to save his or her life. Smith used an even more telling example:

428 If the Law Commission's recommendations were followed, this would be duress of circumstances as a partial defence to murder—on the basis not of lesser evils but Ds' will being overborne: See L.Com No.304. para.6.8, at paras 7–151–7–155.

> "Following the destruction of the World Trade Centre in New York by hijacked aircraft it now appears to be recognised that it would be lawful to shoot down the plane, killing all the innocent passengers and crew if this were the only way to prevent a much greater impending disaster . . . Even if duress cannot be a defence to murder,[429] it seems quite clear that necessity can."[430]

What has yet to be determined is how far this will extend.

VI. Involuntary Conduct

A. INTRODUCTION

The need for voluntary conduct, and some of the philosophical problems associated with the meaning of terms such as "voluntary" and "involuntary", were discussed in Ch.2. A claim of involuntariness is a "denial of authorship"[431] and "it is only where defendants are agents and not mere causers of harm that they are to be regarded as responsible for causing that harm".[432] The object of this section is to examine the implications and consequences of a finding that conduct is involuntary. It is worth noting at the outset that the relationship between automatism, insanity and the law relating to defendants who commit offences whilst intoxicated is complex and that this area of law has been reviewed by the Law Commission.[433] **9–181**

If conduct is involuntary there is no actus reus (and certainly no mens rea). This indicates that D should be exempted completely from criminal liability. For example, in the Australian case of *Cogden*,[434] a woman, in a somnambulistic state, dreaming that her daughter was being attacked by ghosts, spiders and North Korean soldiers, axed her to death. She was acquitted on the ground that her actions were

---

429 Of course, if the recommendations of the Law Commission become law, duress (including duress of circumstances) would be a defence to murder. In fact, one of the illustrations given by the Law Commission is a classic illustration of necessity: Law Com. No.304 (2006), para.6.61 fn.37.

430 See Ormerod and Laird, *Smith, Hogan and Ormerod's Criminal Law*, 16th edn (2021), pp.395–396. See further, M. Bohlander, "In extremis—Hijacked Airplanes, 'Collateral Damage' and the Limits of the Criminal Law" [2006] Crim. L.R. 579 and D. Ormerod, "Letter to the Editor" [2006] Crim. L.R. 786 (responding to Bohlander's article); T. Hörnle, "Hijacked Planes: May They Be Shot Down?" (2007) 10 New Crim. L.R. 582. In Germany, the Act that allowed the Minister of Defence to order the shooting down of a plane in such circumstances (Aviation Security Act s.14(3)) has been held to be unconstitutional: K. Moler, "On Treating People as Means: The German Aviation Security Act, Human Dignity, and the German Federal Constitutional Court" [2006] P.L. 457. See further, P. Gaeta, "May Necessity be Available as a Defence for Torture in the Interrogation of Suspected Terrorists?" [2004] 2 J. Int'l Crim. Just. 785; N. Tamblyn, "Necessity and Murder" (2015) J. Crim. L. 46; U. Neumann, "Necessity/Duress" in M.D. Dubber and T. Hörnle (eds), *The Oxford Handbook of Criminal Law* (Oxford: OUP, 2014), Ch.26.

431 Ashworth and Horder, *Principles of Criminal Law*, 7th edn (2013), p.86; A. Loughnan, *Manifest Madness: Mental Incapacity in Criminal Law* (Oxford: OUP, 2012), p.128.

432 J. Horder, "Pleading Involuntary Lack of Capacity" (1993) 52 C.L.J. 298 at 300. See also: J.J. Childs and A. Reed, "Automatism is never defence" (2014) 65 N.I.L.Q. 167.

433 Law Commission, *Criminal Liability: Insanity and Automatism, A Discussion Paper* (2013), p.416.

434 *Cogden*, unreported, December 1950, Supreme Court of Victoria, King J. See N. Morris, "Somnambulistic Homicide: Ghosts, Spiders and North Koreans" (1951) V *Res Judicatae* 29.

not voluntary. Because a finding of involuntariness can potentially lead to a complete acquittal (with the danger that the conduct could be repeated), English courts have approached the problem of involuntariness with great circumspection and have adopted a restrictive approach as to when there should be a complete exemption from liability. This caution has manifested itself in three ways.

1. Narrow definition of involuntariness

9–182 The criminal law has adopted a narrow interpretation of "involuntary conduct". Not only is this because of the possibility of a complete acquittal, but also because of the difficulty of distinguishing a genuine claim from a fraudulent one. In *Bratty v Att-Gen for Northern Ireland*,[435] it was acknowledged that pleading a blackout is one of the first refuges of a guilty conscience and is a popular excuse.[436] Accordingly, the law has tended to take the view that there is a continuum of involuntariness ranging from complete absence of consciousness, through persons acting in a confused or semi-conscious manner, to those who actually know what they are doing but claim that their actions were morally involuntary because their will was overborne and they were forced to act as they did. The courts, in determining where to draw the line on this continuum, have been strongly influenced by the context, nature and dangerousness of the behaviour. In cases where D is engaged in a particularly dangerous activity, such as driving a car, the law has adopted a strict stance that only a complete absence of consciousness will exempt from liability. In *Broome v Perkins*,[437] D, when charged with driving without due care and attention, claimed to be in a hypoglycaemic condition. He was acquitted at first instance on the basis that his conduct was involuntary. However, an appeal by case stated resulted in a direction to the magistrates to convict. It was held that, because from time to time he appeared to be exercising control over his car to avoid a collision, his actions were only automatic at intervals; at times "the respondent's mind must have been controlling his limbs (from the evidence) and thus he was driving". This decision has been criticised for its severity:

> "This is a very harsh decision, resulting in the conviction of a person who appears to have suffered a misfortune, not to have been at fault in any real sense and to have behaved most responsibly by going to the police and saying that he believed he must have been involved in a road accident."[438]

Despite this view, the same approach was adopted in *Att-Gen's Reference (No.2 of 1992)* where it was held that conduct was only involuntary if there was a total loss of voluntary control. In this case, D, a lorry driver, crashed into a broken-down vehicle parked on the hard shoulder of a motorway and killed two people. Experts described the defendant's condition as "driving without awareness".[439] Whilst not asleep, "the driver's capacity to avoid a collision ceased to exist because of repetitive stimuli experienced on straight flat featureless motorways could induce a trance-like state". However, the expert

---

435 *Bratty v Att-Gen of Northern Ireland* [1963] A.C. 386; [1961] 3 W.L.R. 965 HL.

436 Citing Stable J in *Cooper v McKenna* [1960] Q.L.R. 406 at 419.

437 *Broome v Perkins* (1987) 85 Cr. App. R. 321; [1987] Crim. L.R. 271 Div Ct.

438 J.C. Smith, "Commentary to *Broome v Perkins*" [1987] Crim. L.R. 373.

439 *Att-Gen's Reference (No.2 of 1992)* (1993) 97 Cr. App. R. 429 at 431; [1993] 3 W.L.R. 982 CA.

acknowledged that this amounted to reduced or imperfect awareness and, accordingly, the Court of Appeal ruled that this could not amount to involuntary conduct.

This very robust approach, requiring that there be a complete loss of voluntary control, was confirmed in *Coley* in which Hughes LJ stated that:

> "The essence of . . . [the defence of automatism] is that the movements or actions of the defendant at the material time were wholly involuntary. The better expression is complete destruction of voluntary control."[440]

As *Coley* concerned a D charged with attempted murder, the Law Commission is right to conclude that "the overwhelming weight of authority supports" the view that the requirement of total loss of control is not restricted to widely practiced dangerous activities, such as driving, only.[441]

2. Prior fault

The rationale for requiring voluntary conduct is that there can be no authorship or responsibility for involuntary conduct and, accordingly, blame is inappropriate. It is not a person's fault if she is attacked and, in a state of concussion, causes harm to another. Punishment is not deserved, and no deterrent goals can be achieved by holding such a person criminally liable. In some situations, however, it might be the D's own fault that the state of involuntariness was brought about. In such cases, the courts, conscious of the fact that D is not only blameworthy in precipitating the involuntariness but could do it again, have been careful to ensure that criminal liability is not evaded.[442] **9–183**

In *Quick and Paddison*, D, a diabetic, was charged with an assault that occurred during a hypoglycaemic episode. This arose from eating too little and drinking too much alcohol after having taken insulin. It led to an aggressive outburst and an impairment of consciousness. Lawton LJ stated that:

> ". . . a self-induced incapacity will not excuse . . . nor will one which could have been reasonably foreseen as a result of either doing, or omitting to do something, as, for example, taking alcohol against medical advice after using certain prescribed drugs, or failing to have regular meals while taking insulin."[443]

---

440 *R. v Coley (Scott)* [2013] EWCA Crim 223 at [22]; [2013] M.H.L.R. 171. Hughes LJ drew a distinction between the involuntary conduct required for a plea of automatism and the irrational conduct of D (brought on by self-induced intoxication at [22]–[23]. In *McGhee (Colin) v The Queen* (an appeal heard at the same time as *Coley*, Hughes LJ also distinguished automatism from disinhibited behaviour brought on by intoxication: at [46]. See further, R. Mackay, "*R. v Coley; R. v McGhee; R. v Harris*: insanity—distinction between voluntary intoxication and disease of the mind caused by voluntary intoxication" [2013] Crim. L.R. 923. cf. *Taj* [2018] EWCA Crim 1743; [2018] EWCA Crim 1743, in relation to the defence of self-defence, discussed at para.9–079.

441 Law Commission, *Criminal Liability: Insanity and Automatism, A Discussion Paper* (2013), para.5.29 fn.453.

442 See the discussion above at paras 3–109–3–112.

443 *R. v Quick (William George); R. v Paddison (William)* [1973] 1 Q.B. 910 at 922; [1973] 3 W.L.R. 26. For further discussion of the use of the defence in cases of hypoglycaemia, see: V. Marks, "Hypoglycaemia and automatism" (2015) 55 *Medicine, Science and the Law* 186.

So, while "accidental" hypoglycaemia could have secured an acquittal, Quick's abuse of his body meant that he could be blamed for the ensuing hypoglycaemic episode. Although the conviction was actually reversed on appeal (on the basis that the issue of involuntariness should have been left to the jury), it was made clear that self-induced involuntariness will not provide a defence to crimes of basic intent.[444]

9–184 What, however, is meant by "preceding fault" in this context? Must D know that his conduct will cause the involuntary conduct or is it sufficient that the reasonable person would know this? In *Quick and Paddison*, the question was whether the incapacity could reasonably have been foreseen. In *Bailey*,[445] D was a diabetic who had not taken sufficient food after a dose of insulin to combat its effects. It was held (somewhat controversially) that it was not common knowledge amongst diabetics that such failure could lead to aggressive, dangerous or unpredictable behaviour. Accordingly, it could not be inferred that D knew of the risks and he should not be penalised for his lack of knowledge.[446] One way of reconciling these cases would be to restrict the operation of the rule in *Quick and Paddison* to cases involving alcohol and drugs because it is so widely known that intoxicants can have such an effect[447] and, because of the statistical correlation between intoxication and crime, policy demands that no relief from criminal liability be afforded to intoxicated persons. Such an approach is arguably supported by *Hardie*,[448] where it was held that a D who took Valium could escape liability for subsequent involuntary conduct because it was not known to the defendant, nor generally known, that Valium could cause unpredictability and aggressiveness.[449] The essence of the *Quick and Paddison* principle is that one can legitimately blame persons who, through their own fault, cause their own involuntary conduct. When such fault is established, the requirement of voluntariness is dispensed with—largely because that requirement is only there to protect the faultless.[450] The question of whether one can only blame those who knew of the risks they were running or whether blame is appropriate because the risks were obvious and they ought to have appreciated them raises broadly the same issues as were canvassed in relation to the concepts of recklessness and negligence in Ch.3

It is important that there be precision in locating the act alleged to be involuntary.[451] The rule that preceding fault negates automatism could be employed in driving cases where the driver falls asleep or suffers some form of attack that could have been predicted.[452] However, where the driver has

---

444 For the meaning of this term, see paras 3–096–3–109.

445 *R. v Bailey (John Graham)* [1983] 1 W.L.R. 760.

446 The appeal was in fact dismissed because of insufficient evidence that D's actions had been involuntary. cf. *R. v de Boise (Anthony Peter)* [2014] EWCA Crim 1121, where the Court of Appeal stated that it was not sufficient to show a mere "possibility" that D was suffering from hypoglycaemia at the time that he committed a number of Indecent assaults.

447 *R. v Allen (Kevin)* [1988] Crim. L.R. 698 CA. cf. *Coley* [2013] EWCA Crim 223 at [24]: ". . . the voluntary consumption of intoxicants leading to an acute condition is the prime example of self-induced behaviour." D had repeatedly stabbed his neighbour's partner with a knife after smoking "a good deal of cannabis".

448 *R. v Hardie (Paul Deverall)* [1985] 1 W.L.R. 64; (1985) 80 Cr. App. R. 157 CA. But cf. *R. v McKay (Peter)* [2015] EWCA Crim 2098; [2016] 2 Cr. App. R. 1 where D had claimed to be in a state of automatism following the Ingestion of alcohol and a prescribed sedative.

449 See the discussion on intoxication in Ch.3 paras 3–089–3–091.

450 See further, Smith and Wilson, "Impaired Voluntariness and Criminal Responsibility: Reworking Hart's Theory of Excuses—the English Judicial Response" (1993) 13 O.J.L.S. 69. cf. F. Stark, "Prior fault" (2014) 73 C.L.J. 8; N. Wake and A. Loughnan, "Of Blurred Boundaries and Prior Fault: Insanity, Automatism and Intoxication" in Reed and Wake (eds), *General Defences in Criminal Law: Domestic and Comparative Perspectives* (2014), Ch.8.

451 cf. J.J. Child, H.S. Cromberg and G.R. Sullivan, "Defending the delusional, the irrational and the dangerous" [2020] Crim. L.R. 306, 308–310.

452 See *Kay v Butterworth* (1947) 173 L.T. 191; *Hill v Baxter* [1958] 1 Q.B. 277; [1958] 2 W.L.R. 76 QBD. In *Alexander v Dunn* [2016] HCJAC 3; 2016 J.C. 125, the Scottish High Court of Justiciary stated that: "a driver who knows of his medical condition, and can foresee that he may fall asleep, will be precluded from relying on that condition" at [5]. cf. *R. v Lusher (Stuart Thomas)* [2016] EWCA Crim 2055; *Jones v Crown Prosecution Service* [2019] EWHC 2826 (Admin); [2020] 1 W.L.R. 99.

previously had similar attacks, the act of driving can in itself amount to dangerous driving. In *Marison*,[453] D suffered a hypoglycaemic episode while driving; he lost control of the car and caused the death of another driver.[454] It was held that even though D had become an automaton at the moment of the collision this was not a case of automatism. Being aware that he might have a hypoglycaemic attack while driving meant that the driver was "in a dangerously defective state due to diabetes". The offence of dangerous driving had already been committed before the attack occurred.

3. Cause of involuntariness

Bearing in mind the central point that a finding of involuntariness can lead to a complete acquittal, the courts have been anxious to investigate the cause of the involuntary conduct. If the cause of the involuntary conduct is something internal to D—a disease of the mind—then clearly there is the potential danger that the involuntary conduct could be repeated. Society could need protection from such persons. Accordingly, where D is suffering from a disease of the mind, the involuntary conduct is described as **insane automatism**. Such an insane D, while escaping formal criminal liability, nevertheless receives a special verdict of "not guilty by reason of insanity" whereupon the courts have power to restrain the person. On the other hand, if the cause of the involuntary conduct is something external to D—such as a blow on the head—there is little chance of repetition; D is not dangerous. Such cases are described as **non-insane automatism**—or simply **automatism**—and D is afforded a complete acquittal. Given this critical distinction between insanity and automatism, one way in which the courts can reduce the number of Ds escaping all liability is to expand the category of insanity thereby reducing the scope of the defence of automatism. **9–185**

The distinction between insanity and automatism is thus one of fundamental importance and each will be considered in turn.

B. INSANITY

1. Introduction

The defence of insanity brings into sharp focus many of the issues discussed in previous chapters and has been the source of much debate.[455] Requiring a jury to decide whether a person accused of a crime is to be punished as criminal or "treated" as insane forces two major questions to the surface. The first addresses itself to the premise upon which the sane individual is punished. We have seen in Ch.3 that inherent in the criminal justice system is a view of people as responsible agents. Individuals possess freedom of will and can choose one course of action rather than another. If they step outside the limits of legal action we are, therefore, justified in imposing blame and punishment. By the same argument, we cannot blame people who do not have this ability to choose or control their actions.[456] The insanity **9–186**

453 *R. v Marison (Lee John)* [1997] R.T.R. 457; [1996] Crim. L.R. 909 CA.

454 See further, J. Rumbold and M. Wasik, "Diabetic drivers, hypoglycaemic unawareness, and automatism" [2011] Crim. L.R. 863.

455 This is despite the fact that there are only approximately 20–30 findings of insanity per year (R.D. Mackay, "Ten more years of the Insanity Defence" [2012] Crim. L.R. 946); Mackay, "The Insanity Defence in Operation" [2014] 65 N.I.L.Q. 155.

456 H. Gross, *A Theory of Criminal Justice* (New York: OUP, 1979), pp.361–362, points out that three contentions may be involved. It may, first, be

defence thus seeks to distinguish the responsible from those lacking responsibility. The difficulty lies in determining where the line between sanity and responsibility on the one hand, and insanity and irresponsibility on the other hand, is to be drawn. It has been increasingly argued that absolute states of sanity and insanity rarely (if ever) exist; instead there are shades of sanity. This attitude towards sanity and responsibility has expressed itself in a number of forms.[457] For some commentators, it has necessitated a more rigorous approach to the search for the crucial dividing line. For them the question of ascertaining who is responsible has been made more important, not less. The same doubt has, however, led others to demand that the insanity defence (or the concept of responsibility itself) be abolished.

Secondly, how are the traditional objectives of punishment, which largely assume responsibility, affected when it comes to the punishment of a D who satisfies the legal test to be regarded as "insane"? Such a D is regarded as being mentally disordered, so on the one hand not blameworthy for their actions, yet those who have suffered as a result of the D's conduct are likely to feel anger and that some retributive action is needed, and there may be fears about the risk that D poses to the public. D also lacks the necessary knowledge or foresight to be able to choose the lawful course or to control their actions, so the individual or general deterrent functions of the criminal law are ineffective. In such circumstances, it is not surprising that it was felt necessary to have special rules to satisfy these concerns.[458]

9–187 Is the insanity defence really a "defence" at all? The issue of insanity is invariably included in discussions of defences to crime, yet this classification is not without its difficulties. To assert that a defendant has a defence to crime has connotations that may or may not prove to be applicable to the case of insanity. Three matters, in particular, require consideration.

(a) Is insanity regarded as a general exempting condition or as a specific excuse to a particular wrongful act? According to the analysis of defences at the start of this chapter, insanity should be perceived as akin to the general defence of infancy and act as an exemption. As the Law Commission has stated,[459] D lacks *capacity/responsibility* for his "wrongful" actions—and thus requires no excuse. This incapacity may well be demonstrated in many ways other than the particular act. However, this analogy does not sit well with the current wording of the legal test for insanity. As we shall see, the *M'Naghten* Rules link the mental condition of the accused causally to the prohibited *act*. In other words, it appears to focus upon *attribution-responsibility*. Our inclusion of insanity as an exemption, therefore, is, in part, based upon the way it ought to operate and serves to highlight in advance one of the many flaws of the current test.[460]

---

thought that it is wrong in these situations to punish the accused *for being sick*, or, secondly, that it is wrong to punish someone for what they do *as a result of being sick*, or, lastly, that it is cruel to add to the suffering of someone who is sick: in other words, that it is wrong to punish someone *when* they are *sick*.

457 See e.g. A.V. Horwitz, *Between Sanity and Madness: Mental Illness from Ancient Greece to the Neuroscientific Era* (Oxford: OUP, 2020).

458 A.S. Goldstein, *The Insanity Defense* (Yale University Press, 1967), pp.11–15.

459 Law Commission, *Criminal Liability: Insanity and Automatism, A Discussion Paper* (2013), para.1.52 fn.453, taking the view that this is the true rationale of the defence rather than simply a denial of mens rea.

460 See V. Tadros, "Insanity and the Capacity for Criminal Responsibility" (2000) 5 *Edinburgh Law Review* 325 for an analysis of the significance of the difference between capacity and attribution responsibility.

(b) Is insanity a true defence or does it negate a definitional element? Support for the view that it performs this latter function comes from the argument that prior to the statutory creation of the special verdict, a finding of insanity would lead to a complete acquittal at common law.[461] Indeed, it has been argued further that this is still true today of defendants pleading insanity in the magistrates' courts.[462] However, it may be that conclusions about whether insanity negates mens rea are best drawn once the *M'Naghten* Rules have been explored.

(c) In view of the consequences of a finding of insanity, can it really be said that it is a "defence"? The result of a successful plea of insanity is the special verdict of not guilty by reason of insanity.[463] Yet, as we will see, this verdict does not necessarily mean that D will be released into the community, since they may be indefinitely detained in a mental hospital.[464]

As a result of the Criminal Procedure (Insanity and Unfitness to Plead) Act 1991 (as amended by the Domestic Violence, Crimes and Victims Act 2004), the State may not hold D responsible for their actions but it still retains the right to dispose of them as it thinks fit.

2. The law

(i) The *M'Naghten* Rules

M'NAGHTEN'S CASE (1843) 10 C. & F. 200, 8 ENG. REP. 718:

D was indicted for the murder of Edward Drummond, Secretary to the Prime Minister, Sir Robert Peel. The defence introduced evidence of D's insanity, particularly his obsession with certain morbid delusions. The presiding judge, Lord Tindal CJ, directed the jury in the following terms: **9–188**

> "The question to be asked is whether . . . the prisoner had or had not the use of his understanding, so as to know that he was doing a wrong and wicked act."

The jury returned a verdict of not guilty by reason of insanity. The furore occasioned by the verdict led to the whole issue of insanity being debated in the House of Lords. As a result, five questions were put to the judges of the day; the answers to questions two and three form the basis of the "*M'Naghten* Rules" by which lack of criminal responsibility is tested.

LORD TINDAL CJ:

> "Your lordships are pleased to inquire of us, secondly, 'What are the proper questions to be submitted to the jury, where a person alleged to be afflicted with insane delusion respecting

---

461 Criminal Lunatics Act 1800; S. White, "Insanity Defences and the Magistrates' Courts" [1991] Crim. L.R. 501, 502.

462 White, "Insanity Defences and the Magistrates' Courts" [1991] Crim. L.R. 501: S. White and P. Bowen, "Insanity Defences in Summary Trials" [1997] 61 J. Crim. L. 198; Law Commission, *Criminal Liability: Insanity and Automatism, A Discussion Paper* (2013), paras 7.7–7.10. See, e.g. *R. (on the application of Singh) v Stratford Magistrates' Court* [2007] EWCA 1582 (Admin); [2007] 1 W.L.R. 3119; *Loake v Crown Prosecution Service* [2017] EWHC 2855 (Admin) at [29]; [2018] Q.B. 998.

463 Criminal Procedure (Insanity) Act 1964 s.1. On the origins of the special verdict, see A. Loughnan, "'Manifest madness': towards a new understanding of the insanity defence" (2007) 70 M.L.R. 379.

464 See below, para.9–209. Goldstein, *The Insanity Defense* (1967), p.19.

> one or more particular subjects or persons, is charged with the commission of a crime (murder, for example), and insanity is set up as a defence?' And, thirdly, 'In what terms ought the question to be left to the jury as to the prisoner's state of mind at the time when the act was committed?' And as these two questions appear to us to be more conveniently answered together, we have to submit our opinion to be, that the jurors ought to be told in all cases that every man is to be presumed to be sane, and to possess a sufficient degree of reason to be responsible for his crimes, until the contrary be proved to their satisfaction; and that to establish a defence on the ground of insanity, *it must be clearly proved that, at the time of the committing of the act, the party accused was labouring under such a defect of reason, from disease of the mind, as not to know the nature and quality of the act he was doing; or, if he did know it, that he did not know he was doing what was wrong.* The mode of putting the latter part of the question to the jury on these occasions has generally been, whether the accused at the time of doing the act knew the difference between right and wrong: which mode, though rarely, if ever, leading to any mistake with the jury, is not, as we conceive, so accurate when put generally and in the abstract, as when put with reference to the party's knowledge of right and wrong in respect to the very act with which he is charged. If the question were to be put as to the knowledge of the accused solely and exclusively with reference to the law of the land, it might tend to confound the jury, by inducing them to believe that an actual knowledge of the law of the land was essential in order to lead to a conviction; whereas the law is administered upon the principle that everyone must be taken conclusively to know it, without proof that he does know it. If the accused was conscious that the act was one which he ought not to do, and if the act was at the same time contrary to the law of the land, he is punishable; and the usual course therefore has been to leave the question to the jury, whether the party accused had a sufficient degree of reason to know that he was doing an act that was wrong: and this course we think is correct, accompanied with such observations and explanations as the circumstances of each particular case may require." (Emphasis added)

9–189 Before examining the test for insanity, it should be noted that, exceptionally, the burden of proof rests with defendants to show on a balance of probabilities that they were insane at the time of the act[465] and that it is for the judge to determine whether a defence raised by defendants is, in fact, one of insanity. The question of reverse burden of proof has become deeply problematic with the implementation of the ECHR. The issue is whether placing the burden of proof upon the defendant contravenes the presumption of innocence protected by the ECHR art.6(2). While the point has yet to be tested in relation to insanity, an indication of the way in which courts might approach this issue in relation to the defence of insanity is provided by the cases of *Foye*[466] and *Wilcocks*,[467] in which the Court

465 *Woolmington v DPP* [1935] A.C. 462 at 475–476; (1935) 51 T.L.R. 446 HL. The same is true for diminished responsibility: the Homicide Act 1957 s.2(2). There are difficulties with this exception. e.g. if D pleads (simple) lack of mens rea the burden of proof rests with the prosecution to prove beyond reasonable doubt that he did have mens rea; however, if D adds that the absence of mens rea was due to a disease of the mind the burden then shifts to D. If D pleads automatism the burden will only shift in cases of insane automatism. See further, T. Jones, "Insanity, Automatism and the Burden of Proof on the Accused" [1995] 111 L.Q.R. 475.

466 *R. v Foye (Lee Robert)* [2013] EWCA Crim 475; (2013) 177 J.P. 449.

467 *R. v Wilcocks (Callum Paul)* [2016] EWCA Crim 2043; [2017] 4 W.L.R. 39.

of Appeal decided that placing the onus upon D to establish the defence of diminished responsibility did not contravene art.6(2).

Although the essence of the *M'Naghten* Rules may be simply stated—it asks whether D knew what they were doing at the time the crime was committed—certain of the phrases used in the formulation of the rules have been subject to much judicial (and academic) interpretation.

One can envisage the *M'Naghten* Rules as a series of hurdles over which the defendant must jump in order to be excused liability.

(a) Disease of the mind

D must be suffering from a "*disease of the mind*". This phrase: **9–190**

> "... initially seems to have attracted no judicial scrutiny ... However, the development of the automatism defence changed this. For suddenly the courts were confronted by the fact that a successful defence based on 'unconscious involuntary action' could result in an unqualified acquittal. For obvious social defence reasons this fact began to worry the courts and in order to restrict the availability of such acquittals the judiciary began to develop a complex body of law built upon the phrase 'disease of the mind'."[468]

The case of *Kemp*[469] (where D suffered from arteriosclerosis which induced a state of unconsciousness during which he attacked his wife with a hammer) makes it clear that the condition of the brain is irrelevant. The test is not necessarily whether there is some damage to that physical entity (although the mental disease may have a physical origin) but, more widely, whether the mental faculties of reason, understanding and memory are impaired or absent. This approach has been affirmed by the House of Lords.

R. v Sullivan [1984] A.C. 156 (House of Lords):

D was charged with inflicting grievous bodily harm, contrary to the OAPA 1861 s.20, after he had attacked Payne, his friend, during the postictal stage of an epileptic seizure. The trial judge ruled that this amounted to insanity rather than automatism; consequently, D changed his plea to guilty to the lesser offence of assault occasioning actual bodily harm. He then appealed against conviction on the basis that he should have been allowed to raise the issue of automatism.[470] **9–191**

468 Mackay, *Mental Condition Defences in the Criminal Law* (1995), p.97.

469 *R. v Kemp (Albert)* [1957] 1 Q.B. 399; [1956] 3 W.L.R. 724.

470 For a discussion of the medical background to this case, see N. Eastman, "Defending the Mentally Ill" in R.D. Mackay and K. Russell (eds), *Psychiatry and the Criminal Process* (Leicester: Milttak Ltd, 1986).

LORD DIPLOCK:

"The M'Naghten Rules have been used as a comprehensive definition for this purpose by the courts for the last 140 years. Most importantly, they were so used by this House in *Bratty v Attorney-General for Northern Ireland* [1963] A.C. 386. That case was in some respects the converse of the instant case. Bratty was charged with murdering a girl by strangulation. He claimed to have been unconscious of what he was doing at the time he strangled the girl and he sought to run as alternative defences non-insane automatism and insanity. The only evidential foundation that he laid for either of these pleas was medical evidence that he might have been suffering from psychomotor epilepsy which, if he were, would account for his having been unconscious of what he was doing. No other pathological explanation of his actions having been carried out in a state of automatism was supported by evidence. The trial judge first put the defence of insanity to the jury. The jury rejected it; they declined to bring in the special verdict. Thereupon, the judge refused to put to the jury the alternative defence of automatism. His refusal was upheld by the Court of Criminal Appeal of Northern Ireland and subsequently by this House.

The question before this House was whether, the jury having rejected the plea of insanity, there was any evidence on non-insane automatism fit to be left to the jury. The ratio decidendi of its dismissal of the appeal was that the jury having negatived the explanation that Bratty might have been acting unconsciously in the course of an attack of psychomotor epilepsy, there was no evidential foundation for the suggestion that he was acting unconsciously from any other cause.

In the instant case, as in *Bratty*, the only evidential foundation that was laid for any finding by the jury that Mr Sullivan was acting unconsciously and involuntarily when he was kicking Mr Payne, was that when he did so he was in the postictal stage of a seizure of psychomotor epilepsy. The evidential foundation in the case of Bratty, that he was suffering from psychomotor epilepsy at the time he did the act with which he was charged, was very weak and was rejected by the jury; the evidence in Mr Sullivan's case, that he was so suffering when he was kicking Mr Payne, was very strong and would almost inevitably be accepted by a properly directed jury. It would be the duty of the judge to direct the jury that if they did accept that evidence the law required them to bring in a special verdict and none other. The governing statutory provision is to be found in section 2 of the Trial of Lunatics Act 1883. This says 'the jury *shall* return a special verdict . . .'

My Lords, I can deal briefly with the various grounds on which it has been submitted that the instant case can be distinguished from what constituted the *ratio decidendi* in *Bratty v Attorney-General for Northern Ireland*, and that it falls outside the ambit of the M'Naghten Rules.

First, it is submitted the medical evidence in the instant case shows that psychomotor epilepsy is not a disease of the mind, whereas in *Bratty* it was accepted by all the doctors that it was. The only evidential basis for this submission is that Dr Fenwick said that in medical terms to constitute a 'disease of the mind' or 'mental illness,' which he appeared to regard as interchangeable descriptions, a disorder of brain functions (which undoubtedly occurs during a seizure in psychomotor epilepsy) must be prolonged for a period of time usually more than a day; while Dr Taylor would have it that the disorder must continue for a minimum of a month to qualify for the description 'a disease of the mind'.

The nomenclature adopted by the medical profession may change from time to time; Bratty was tried in 1961. But the meaning of the expression 'disease of the mind' as the cause of 'a defect of reason' remains unchanged for the purposes of the application of the M'Naghten Rules. I agree with what was said by Devlin J in *R. v Kemp* that 'mind' in the M'Naghten Rules is used in the ordinary sense of the mental faculties of reason, memory and understanding. If the effect of a disease is to impair these faculties so severely as to have either of the consequences referred to in the latter part of the rules, it matters not whether the aetiology of the impairment is organic, as in epilepsy, or functional, or whether the impairment itself is permanent or is transient and intermittent, provided that it subsisted at the time of commission of the act. The purpose of the legislation relating to the defence of insanity, ever since its origin in 1800, has been to protect society against recurrence of the dangerous conduct. The duration of a temporary suspension of the mental faculties, of reason, memory and understanding, particularly if, as in Mr Sullivan's case, it is recurrent, cannot on any rational ground be relevant to the application by the courts of the M'Naghten Rules, though it may be relevant to the course adopted by the Secretary of State, to whom the responsibility for how the defendant is to be dealt with passes after the return of the special verdict 'not guilty by reason of insanity.' **9–192**

To avoid misunderstanding I ought perhaps to add that in expressing my agreement with what was said by Devlin J in *Kemp*, where the disease that caused the temporary and intermittent impairment of the mental faculties was arteriosclerosis, I do not regard that learned judge as excluding the possibility of non-insane automatism (for which the proper verdict would be a verdict of 'not guilty') in cases where temporary impairment (not being self-induced by consuming drink or drugs) results from some external physical factor such as a blow on the head causing concussion or the administration of an anaesthetic for therapeutic purposes . . . The instant case, however, does not in my view afford an appropriate occasion for exploring possible causes of non-insane automatism . . .

My Lords, it is natural to feel reluctant to attach the label of insanity to a sufferer from psychomotor epilepsy of the kind to which Mr Sullivan was subject, even though the expression in the context of a special verdict of 'not guilty by reason of insanity' is a technical one which includes a purely temporary and intermittent suspension of the mental faculties of reason, memory and understanding resulting from the occurrence of an epileptic fit. But the label is contained in the current statute, it has appeared in this statute's predecessors ever since 1800. It does not lie within the power of the courts to alter it. Only Parliament can do that. It has done so twice; it could do so once again.

Sympathise though I do with Mr Sullivan, I see no other course open to your Lordships than to dismiss this appeal."

Appeal dismissed

R. v BURGESS [1991] 2 W.L.R. 1206 (COURT OF APPEAL, CRIMINAL DIVISION):

9–193 D attacked his friend, Miss Curtis, with a bottle and then a video-recorder, finally putting a hand round her throat. D claimed that he was acting unconsciously in that he had been sleepwalking and was entitled to be acquitted as a non-insane automaton. The trial judge ruled that the jury had to decide whether D was acting consciously or whether he was not guilty by reason of insanity. The jury returned the latter verdict against which the defendant appealed.

LORD LANE CJ:

"Where the defence of automatism is raised by the defendant, two questions fall to be decided by the judge before the defence can be left to the jury. The first is whether a proper evidential foundation for the defence of automatism has been laid. The second is whether the evidence shows the case to be one of insane automatism, that is to say, a case which falls within the M'Naghten Rules, or one of non-insane automatism . . . There can be no doubt but that the appellant on the basis of the jury's verdict, was labouring under . . . such a defect of reason as not to know what he was doing when he wounded Miss Curtis. The question is whether that was from 'disease of the mind' . . .

The appellant plainly suffered from a defect of reason from some sort of failure (for lack of a better term) of the mind causing him to act as he did without conscious motivation. His mind was to some extent controlling his actions which were purposive rather than the result of muscular spasm, but without his being consciously aware of what he was doing. Can it be said that that 'failure' was a *disease* of the mind rather than a defect or failure of the mind not due to disease? That is the distinction, by no means easy to draw, upon which this case depends, as others have depended in the past.

One can perhaps narrow the field of enquiry still further by eliminating what are sometimes called the 'external factors' such as concussion caused by a blow on the head. There were no such factors here. Whatever the cause may have been, it was an internal cause.

[His Lordship then cited the case of *Sullivan*]

What help does one derive from the authorities as to the meaning of 'disease' in this context? Lord Denning in *Bratty v Attorney-General for Northern Ireland* [1963] A.C. 236 at 412 said:

> . . . 'It seems to me that any mental disorder which has manifested itself in violence and is prone to recur is a disease of the mind. At any rate it is the sort of disease for which a person should be detained in hospital rather than be given an unqualified acquittal.'

9–194 It seems to us that if there is a danger of recurrence that may be an added reason for categorising the condition as a disease of the mind. On the other hand, the absence of the danger of recurrence is not a reason for saying that it cannot be a disease of the mind. Subject to that possible qualification, we respectfully adopt Lord Denning's suggested definition.

There have been several occasions when during the course of judgments in the Court of Appeal and the House of Lords observations have been made, obiter, about the criminal responsibility of sleep-walkers, where sleep-walking has been used as a -self-evident illustration of non-insane automatism. For example in the speech of Lord Denning, from which we have already cited an extract, appears this passage, at 409:

> 'No act is punishable if it is done involuntarily: and an involuntary act in this context—some people nowadays prefer to speak of it as "automatism"—means an act which is done by the muscles without any control by the mind, such as a spasm, a reflex action or a convulsion; or an act done by a person who is not conscious of what he is doing, such as an act done whilst suffering from concussion or whilst sleep-walking. The point was well put by Stephen J in 1889:
>
> "Can anyone doubt that a man who, though he might be perfectly sane, committed what would otherwise be a crime in a state of somnambulism, would be entitled to be acquitted? And why is this? Simply because he would not know what he was doing."'. . .

We accept of course that sleep is a normal condition, but the evidence in the instant case indicates that sleep-walking, and particularly violence in sleep, is not normal . . . [I]n none of the other cases where sleep walking has been mentioned, so far as we can discover, has the court had the advantage of the sort of expert medical evidence which was available to the judge here.

One turns then to examine the evidence upon which the judge had to base his decision . . . Dr d'Orban in examination-in-chief said . . . [that]:

> 'Burgess's actions had occurred during the course of a sleep disorder.'

He was asked, 'Assuming this is a sleep associated automatism, is it an internal or external factor?' Answer: 'In this particular case, I think that one would have to see it as an internal factor'.

Then in cross-examination: Question: 'Would you go so far as to say that it was liable to recur?' Answer: 'It is possible for it to recur, yes'. Finally, in answer to a question from the judge, namely, 'Is this a case of automatism associated with a pathological condition or not?' Answer: 'I think the answer would have to be yes, because it is an abnormality of the brain function, so it would be regarded as a pathological condition'.

Dr Eames in cross-examination agreed with Dr d'Orban as to the internal rather than the external factor. He accepted that there is a liability to recurrence of sleep-walking. He could not go so far as to say that there is no liability of recurrence of serious violence but he agreed with the other medical witnesses that there is no recorded case of violence of this sort recurring.

> It seems to us that on this evidence the judge was right to conclude that this was an abnormality or disorder, albeit transitory, due to an internal factor, whether functional or organic, which had manifested itself in criminality. It was a disorder or abnormality which might recur, though the possibility of it recurring in the form of serious violence was unlikely. Therefore since this was a legal problem to be answered on legal principles, it seems to us that on those principles the answer was as the judge found it to be."
>
> *Appeal dismissed*

9–195 These two cases are highly significant. They bear witness to the continued development of the distinction between internal and external causes as a basis for determining whether a particular condition is a *"disease of the mind"*. It has long been recognised that psychomotor epilepsy is a disease of the mind but dicta, at least, had placed sleepwalking into the category of non-insane automatism. However, the medical evidence relied on in *Burgess*—that sleepwalking is a "near cousin" of epilepsy—gave the court little choice but to decide that sleepwalking should be perceived as arising from some internal factor. The logic in *Burgess* in this respect can be supported. Nevertheless, its categorisation of sleepwalking as insane automatism has divided the medico-legal community: not all experts agree that it is caused by an internal factor. In Canada, for example, it is held to be sane automatism: what causes the defendant's suspension of mental faculties is falling asleep (a perfectly normal occurrence).[471] Moreover, there have been instances in England where Ds have been acquitted of offences on the basis that they were sleepwalking at the time: for example, in *Thomas*, "a decent man and devoted husband" who strangled his wife during a nightmare in which he believed he was attacking an intruder was acquitted after the prosecution withdrew the case.[472]

However, the problem with the (increasingly contested) categorisation of sleepwalking is illustrative of a much more fundamental problem. The distinction between internal and external causes is fundamentally flawed. "It makes illogical, hair-splitting distinctions inevitable."[473] We are forced to conclude that epileptics (0.5% of the population) will be regarded as insane if they commit offences during epileptic fits.[474] The same is true of some diabetics. Diabetics can experience hyperglycaemic episodes (triggered by too much blood sugar and caused by the diabetic condition itself) or hypoglycaemic episodes (too little blood sugar, arising from the combination of diabetes, insulin, food

---

471 *R. v Parks* [1992] 2 S.C.R. 871; *Canada v Campbell*, 16 June 2000, Ontario Superior Court of Justice; D. Ebrahim, P.B. Fenwick, R.L. Marks and K.W. Peacock, "Violence, Sleepwalking and the Criminal Law: Part 1: The Medical Aspects" [2005] Crim. L.R. 601, 603. See also R.D. Mackay, "Sleepwalkers are Not Insane" (1992) 55 M.L.R. 71, cf. I. Ebrahim and J. Rumbold, "Medico-legal evaluation of sleep-related automatism" (2015) 55 *Medicine, Science and the Law* 168.

472 *R. v Thomas, The Independent,* 21 November 2009. In *Bilton, The Independent,* 20 December 2005, D was acquitted of rape; in *Davies, The Times,* 11 February 2006, D was acquitted of sexual assault but in *Lowe, The Times,* 19 March 2005, a plea of insane automatism was accepted. A number of additional cases have been reported in the tabloid press, see, e.g. T. Payne, "Gulf war veteran cleared of rape because he suffered sexsomnia" *Daily Mail,* 10 February 2017; T. Palmer, "'Sleepwalking' transsexual Met worker cleared of murder bid" *Evening Standard,* 11 August 2015; "Sleepwalker cleared of sexual assault given sexual harm order" BBC News, 4 October 2019. See further, R.D. Mackay and B.J. Mitchell, "Sleepwalking, Automatism and Insanity" [2006] Crim. L.R. 901; J. De Silva, "The curious case of the homicidal somnambulist" (2014) 178 *C.L. & J. Weekly* 9; A. Jackson, G. Rees and N. Wortley, "Sleep or/sexsomnia: the role of the expert and the external/internal factor dichotomy" in B. Livings, A. Redd and N. Wake (eds), *Mental Condition Defences and the Criminal Justice System: Perspectives from Law and Medicine* (Newcastle upon Tyne: Cambridge Scholars Publishing, 2015), Ch.9.

473 W. Wilson, "Violence, Sleepwalking and the Criminal Law: Part 2: The Legal Aspects" [2005] Crim. L.R. 614, 617.

474 See further, R.D. Mackay and M. Reuber, "Epilepsy and the Defence of Insanity: Time for Change?" [2007] Crim. L.R. 782. cf. *R. v Norman (Benjamin)* [2023] EWCA Crim 1112; [2024] R.T.R. 17.

(or lack of it) and possibly alcohol). In *Quick and Paddison*,[475] the court distinguished these two conditions, holding that a transitory malfunctioning of the mind caused by hypoglycaemia due to external factors (for example, the taking of insulin) is non-insane automatism, entitling D to an acquittal.[476] On the other hand, in *Hennessy*,[477] it was held that hyperglycaemia gave rise to insane automatism. In this case, D was charged with taking a conveyance and with driving while disqualified. His defence was that at the relevant time he had failed to take his proper dose of insulin due to stress, anxiety and depression and this caused the ensuing state of hyperglycaemia. The Court of Appeal accepted the *Quick and Paddison* distinction between hyper- and hypoglycaemia and rejected the defence argument that stress, anxiety and depression were factors that could count as external for the purposes of non-insane automatism. The court added that they constituted a state of mind that was prone to recur and lacked the feature of novelty or accident traditionally associated with non-insane automatism.

The result of these decisions is that we are left with a law under which some diabetics will be able to secure a complete acquittal while others will be regarded as insane. In *Coley*,[478] the Court of Appeal observed that: **9–196**

> "It is well known that the distinction drawn in Quick between external factors inducing a condition of the mind and internal factors which can properly be described as a disease can give rise to apparently strange results at the margin."

With respect, the current position is not merely strange, but absurd. Moreover, the harshness of these categorisations is hardly tempered by telling defendants (and their families), as Lord Diplock does in *Sullivan* and Lord Lane echoes in *Burgess*, that the label "insanity" is merely a technical one.

The key to evaluating these cases depends upon whether the concept "disease of the mind" requires anything more than a finding that the cause is an internal one. In particular, we need to know whether there is any requirement that the internal cause be associated with violence. Lord Denning in *Bratty* stated that "any mental disorder which has manifested itself in violence and is prone to recur is a disease of the mind".[479] This was cited with approval in *Sullivan* but in *Burgess* Lord Lane said that "the absence of the danger of recurrence is not a reason for saying that it cannot be a disease of the mind". It was this that enabled his Lordship to state that the D could be said to have a disease of the mind despite the fact that the experts could point to no reported incident of a sleep-walker being repeatedly violent. This modification of *Bratty* flies in the face of Lord Diplock's statement in *Sullivan* that "the purpose of the legislation relating to the defence of insanity, ever since its origin, has been to protect society against dangerous conduct". However, this social defence argument could not withstand rigorous scrutiny even before *Burgess*. For example, how can one say that epileptics are more dangerous than diabetics having a hypoglycaemic episode? Can mental disorders that do not manifest themselves **9–197**

475 *R. v Quick (William George); R. v Paddison (William)* [1973] Q.B. 910. See also *Bailey* [1983] 1 W.L.R. 760.

476 Marks, "Hypoglycaemia and automatism" (2015) 55 *Medicine, Science and the Law* 186.

477 *R. v Hennessy (Andrew Michael)* [1989] 1 W.L.R. 287; (1989) 89 Cr. App. R. 10 CA.

478 *Coley* [2013] EWCA Crim 223 at [20]. cf. *Loake v Crown Prosecution Service* [2017] EWHC 2855 (Admin) at [33].

479 *Bratty v Attorney General of Northern Ireland* [1963] A.C. 386 at 412.

in violence, for example, kleptomania, never be diseases of the mind? Nevertheless, despite such weaknesses, the social defence argument did have a valuable limiting function. As a result of *Burgess*, all that "*disease of the mind*" seems to mean is any internal factor that has, on one occasion at least, manifested itself in criminality.

The interaction between mental disorder and the voluntary consumption of intoxicants has posed particular difficulties for the courts. Where the taking of intoxicants causes an episode of mental disorder, it appears that the courts will not regard this as amounting to a "disease of the mind" for the purpose of the *M'Naghten* rules, but will instead regard the case as being one of voluntary intoxication.[480] For instance, in *Coley*,[481] the psychiatric evidence was that D had attacked his neighbour's partner during a brief psychotic episode, triggered by smoking cannabis. The Court of Appeal ruled that the defence of insanity did not arise:

> "The precise line between the law of voluntary intoxication and the law of insanity may, we do not doubt, be difficult to identify in some borderline cases. But the present case falls comfortably on the side of the line covered by voluntary intoxication . . . In order to engage the law of insanity, it is not enough that there is an effect on the mind, or, in the language of the M'Naghten rules, a 'defect of reason'. There must also be what the law classifies as a disease of the mind. Direct acute effects on the mind of intoxicants, voluntarily taken, are not so classified."

9–198 However, the abuse of alcohol and drugs may cause or exacerbate mental disorder, and "Substance Use Disorder" is recognised as a mental disorder in the American Psychiatric Association's Diagnostic and Statistical Manual of Mental Disorders (DSM-5-TR).[482] In *DPP v Beard*,[483] Lord Birkenhead made it clear that, where intoxication led to a defendant suffering from a mental disorder, he was not disentitled from relying upon that condition to relieve him from liability:

> "But drunkenness is one thing and the diseases to which drunkenness leads are different things; and if a man by drunkenness brings on a state of disease which causes such a degree of madness, even for a time, which would have relieved him from responsibility if it had been caused in any other way, then he would not be criminally responsible."

In the case of a D suffering from alcohol dependency, suddenly stopping drinking may also cause mental illness. In *Harris*,[484] D had set fire to his house whilst suffering from mental disorder, with psychotic symptoms which included hallucinations and the hearing of voices. These had been brought on by D suddenly stopping drinking alcohol. At his trial for arson, being reckless as to whether the life

---

480 See para.9–079.

481 *Coley* [2013] EWCA Crim 223. For further discussion of this case see: R. Mackay, "*R. v Coley, R. v McGhee, R. v Harris*: insanity- distinction between involuntary intoxication and disease of mind caused by voluntary intoxication" [2013] Crim. L.R. 923; J.J. Childs and G.R. Sullivan, "When does the insanity defence apply? Some recent cases" [2014] Crim. L.R. 788. cf. *Taj* [2018] EWCA Crim 1743; [2019] Q.B. 655, discussed at para.9–079.

482 "*Substance-Related and Addictive Disorders*" (American Psychiatric Association, 2022).

483 [1920] A.C. 479 at 501.

484 *R. v Harris (Darren)* [2013] EWCA Crim 223.

of another would be endangered, the trial judge ruled that, because D's mental disorder was a direct case of voluntary intoxication, the defence of insanity was unavailable.[485] The Court of Appeal declined to follow this approach:

> "[59] The argument for the Crown in this case is that the mental illness from which the defendant was suffering was brought on by his past voluntary drinking. Therefore, it is contended, it should be treated in the same way as if he were still drunk. We agree that there is scope for the argument that an illness caused by his own fault ought as a matter of policy to be treated in the same way as is drunkenness at the time of the offence. This would, however, represent a significant extension of *DPP v Majewski* and of the similar principle expounded in *Quick*, which likewise concerned a case where what was asserted was an acute condition (there of automatism) induced arguably by the defendant's fault. A great many mental illnesses have their roots in culpable past misconduct of the sufferer: those attributable to many years of past drug or alcohol abuse are perhaps the most obvious, but there could be many other examples, such as perhaps a culpable failure to follow a recommended medical regime, or maybe the consequences of traumatic brain injury caused by one's own drunken driving . . . This defendant was, it is clear, suffering from a condition of mental illness when he set fire to his own house. That it was not long-lasting does not mean that it was not a true illness. In our view he was entitled to have tried the question of whether, in the condition in which he was, he was actually aware of the risk which he created for his neighbours."[486]

Where the misuse of intoxicants causes D to suffer from a drug-induced delusion, this is not regarded as a "disease of the mind" for the purposes of the M'Naghten rules.[487] Nor, if D is in a state of automatism, will they be able to rely upon the defence of non-insane automatism.[488] Such cases are "governed by the law of voluntary intoxication".[489] **9–199**

The above discussion demonstrates that the internal/external factor distinction is unable to bear the weight of distinguishing insanity from non-insane automatism. It highlights the failure of the insanity test (and perhaps, any insanity test) to come to terms with the issue of the responsibility of the individual D on the one hand, and the protection of the public (and the defendant himself) against harm on the other. We shall return to this question later, once the remaining elements of the test of insanity, and the proposals for reform thereof, have been considered.

(b) Defect of reason

Assuming that D is suffering from a disease of the mind, the next hurdle to be overcome is that this **9–200**
disease of the mind must induce a *"defect of reason"*. The reasoning ability of the D must be affected; it

---

485 As a result of this ruling, the defendant pleaded guilty *Harris* [2013] EWCA Crim 223 at [55].

486 The Court of Appeal took the view that the defence of insanity did not apply because, although the defendant was affected by a mental disorder, "he knew what he was doing and he knew that it was wrong", at [56].

487 *Coley* [2013] EWCA Crim 223.

488 *R. v Lipman (Robert)* [1970] 1 Q.B. 152; [1969] 3 W.L.R. 819 CA.

489 *Coley* [2013] EWCA Crim 223 at [19].

is not enough that he or she simply failed to use powers of reasoning which they had.[490] This aspect of the insanity test is classically illustrative of one of the basic premises of responsibility in law: guilt cannot be adduced in the absence of the *capacity* to reason.

(c) Nature and quality of the act

9–201 Having passed over the initial hurdles, D may be brought within the ambit of the special verdict if either of two further conditions are satisfied.

First, D must not know *"the nature and quality of his acts"*. This in narrowly construed, and the Administrative Court in *Loake* cited three vivid examples of this:[491]

> "Three examples often given where it could be said that the defendant did not know the nature and quality of his act are: (a) where A kills B under an insane delusion that he is breaking a jar (Stephen, *A Digest of the Criminal Law*, 8th Edn, p8); (b) where a madman cuts a woman's throat under the delusion that he is cutting a loaf of bread (CS Kenny, *Outlines of the Criminal Law* (19th Edn, 1966, by JWC Turner, p76); (c) where a drunken nurse puts a baby on the fire thinking it is a log: *Attorney-General for Northern Ireland v Gallagher* [1963] AC 349, 381, citing an 18th century case."

D will also not know the "nature and quality of his acts" where, because of his "disease of the mind", at the time of his act, "he did not know what he was doing"[492] at all, and was acting unconsciously and involuntarily. In the case of crimes requiring subjective mens rea, a D who does not know the nature and quality of their act will lack the mens rea for that offence and be liable to acquittal on that basis. This was recognised in *Loake*:[493]

> "In virtually every case where the defendant proves that he did not know the nature and quality of his act at the time he performed it, then he will not be criminally responsible irrespective of the first limb of the M'Naghten test, because he will lack the mens rea for the alleged offence. The woman who squeezes her husband's throat believing she is strangling a deadly snake does not have the mens rea for murder, because she lacks the necessary intention to kill or cause really serious harm . . ."

---

490 *R. v Clarke (May)* (1972) 56 Cr. App. R. 225; (1971) 116 S.J. 56 CA.

491 *Loake v Crown Prosecution Service* [2017] EWHC 2855 (Admin) at [38].

492 *R. v Sullivan (Patrick Joseph)* [1984] A.C. 156 at 173; [1983] 3 W.L.R. 123.

493 *Loake v Crown Prosecution Service* [2017] EWHC 2855 (Admin) at [39].

(d) Knowledge of wrong

Alternatively, it must be established that D does not know that his actions are *"wrong"*.[494] The case of *Windle*[495] decided that this means knowledge that the acts are legally (and not merely morally)[496] wrong. It is often thought that this limb adds very little to the insanity test, yet research has shown that it is this part of the test that is most commonly used to secure a special verdict.[497] For example, in one case: **9–202**

> "A 22 year old male attempted to kill his parents because he believed that they were to be tortured and that he must kill them in order that they would die in a humane way. Two psychiatrists stated that while he knew the nature and quality of the act of stabbing his parents, he did not know that what he was doing was wrong . . . His mind was plagued with delusional perceptions which confused his rational thinking to the extent that the wrongness of his act would not have been a consideration."[498]

Research also shows that commonly a broad-brush approach is taken to this requirement. Little effort is made to distinguish between cases where D does not know that her actions are legally wrong and those where there is a lack of knowledge that the actions are morally wrong.[499]

> "In so doing, it may be argued that psychiatrists in many respects are adopting a common sense approach and that the courts by accepting this interpretation are, in reality, expanding the scope of the M'Naghten Rules."[500]

In *Keal*, the Court of Appeal, having reviewed the authorities, effectively narrowed the scope of this limb by making it clear that, to satisfy this element of the M'Naghten test, D must establish both: **9–203**

"(a) he did not know that his act was unlawful (i.e. contrary to law) and (b) he did not know that his act was "morally" wrong (also expressed as wrong "by the standards of ordinary people"). In our judgment, "wrong" means both against the law and wrong by the standards of ordinary reasonable people. Strictly a jury must be satisfied that the defendant did not know that what he was doing was against the law nor wrong by the standards of reasonable ordinary people . . ."[501]

---

494 In *Harris* [2013] EWCA Crim 223, D was convicted of arson. His conviction was quashed on the basis that although he was affected by a mental disorder he knew what he was doing and that it was wrong, so insanity did not arise, nevertheless, his claim that he did not foresee the risk because of mental disorder (i.e. a claim of lack of mens rea) should have been put to the jury (at [56]).

495 *R. v Windle (Francis Wilfred)* [1952] 2 Q.B. 826; [1952] 1 T.L.R. 1344.

496 cf. *R. v Codere (Georges)* (1917) 12 Cr. App. R. 21 CA.

497 R.D. Mackay and G. Kearns, "More Fact(s) about the Insanity Defence" [1999] Crim. L.R. 714.

498 Mackay, *Mental Condition Defences in the Criminal Law* (1995), p.104.

499 Mackay and Kearns, "More Fact(s) about the Insanity Defence" [1999] Crim. L.R. 714.

500 Mackay and Kearns, "More Fact(s) about the Insanity Defence" [1999] Crim. L.R. 714 at 723.

501 *R v Keal (Jonathan Robert)* [2022] EWCA Crim 341 at [41]; [2022] 4 W.L.R. 41.

Mackay has suggested that this "has sent out a message that the Rules are now even more difficult to satisfy".[502]

It is not a prerequisite that D lack mens rea for this limb of the M'Naghten test to be established.[503] In *Loake*,[504] the Administrative Court observed that:

> "It is possible for someone to have the full mens rea for a criminal offence whilst at the same time, because of a defect of reason arising from a disease of the mind, not know what he is doing is wrong. If a man intentionally kills his wife because of his deluded belief that he is under threat from a representative of Satan and has received a divine order to slay, and that it is lawful to comply with divine orders, then he possesses the mens rea for murder but is not guilty of murder because he does not know that what he is doing is unlawful."

(e) Delusions, compulsion and the M'Naghten Rules

9–204 In *M'Naghten's Case*,[505] the court considered a fourth question, which has attracted considerably less judicial scrutiny:

> "If a person under an insane delusion as to existing facts, commits an offence in consequence thereof, is he thereby excused?"[506]

Tindal LCJ answered this question as follows:

> "... the answer must of course depend on the nature of the delusion: but, making the same assumption as we did before, namely that he labours under such partial delusion only, and is not in other respects insane, we think he must be considered in the same situation as to responsibility as if the facts with respect to which the delusion exists were real. For example, if under the influence of his delusion he supposes another man to be in the act of attempting to take away his life, and he kills that man, as he supposes, in self-defence, he would be exempt from punishment. If his delusion was that the deceased had inflicted a serious injury to his character and fortune, and he killed him in revenge for such supposed injury, he would be liable to punishment."[507]

This passage was considered in *Oye*,[508] where D had assaulted police officers whilst suffering from an insane delusion that they were evil spirits intent on harming him. The Court of Appeal substituted D's conviction for a verdict of not guilty by reason of insanity. Following *Oye*, it has been suggested that this

---

502 R. Mackay, "*M'Naghten* Rules (Letter to the Editor)" [2022] EWCA Crim 341.
503 *Moore v Trinidad and Tobago* [2001] UKPC 4 at [13]; *R. v Antoine (Pierre Harrison)* [2001] 1 A.C. 340 at 374; [2000] 2 W.L.R. 703 HL.
504 *Loake v Crown Prosecution Service* [2017] EWHC 2855 (Admin) at [41]. For further discussion of this case, see para.9–201.
505 *R. v M'Naghten* 3 E.R. 718; (1843) 10 Cl. & F. 200.
506 *M'Naghten's Case* 8 E.R. 718 at 723.
507 *M'Naghten's Case* 8 E.R. 718 at 723.
508 *R. v Oye (Seun)* [2013] EWCA Crim 1725; [2014] 1 W.L.R. 3354 at [35].

limb of the *M'Naghten* rules "may become more prominent".[509] However, any hope that this limb might be used to expand the *M'Naghten* test was crushed in *Keal*.

R v Keal (Jonathan) [2022] EWCA Crim 341[510]

D, who had a long history of severe mental disorder, ferociously attacked his parents and grandmother with an array of weapons. During the attack, he apologised for his actions and indicated that he was unable to stop himself, saying to his mother, "I'm sorry this isn't me, it's the devil". At trial, the expert psychiatrists agreed that D met the first two requirements of the M'Naghten test, namely that he was suffering from a disease of the mind leading to a defect of reasons, and that D understood the nature and quality of his actions. However, they disagreed on the issue of whether D knew that what he was doing was wrong, and D was convicted of attempted murder. On appeal, an argument that a broad interpretation of the M'Naghten rules should be favoured, which would supplement the current cognitive limbs with a "loss of capacity to control" limb was rejected by the Court of Appeal. **9–205**

Lord Burnett of Maldon CJ:

"[48] . . . we conclude that under the M'Naghten Rules, the defence of insanity is not available to a defendant who, although he knew what he was doing was wrong, he believed that he had no choice but to commit the act in question.

(3) Should the current law on insanity be interpreted as involving an element of 'choice'?

[49] This is the question posed by . . . [Counsel for the appellant's] broader approach It invites us substantially to develop the law of insanity as it has been understood in the criminal law of England and Wales for over a century and a half. We are doubtful whether sitting in the Court of Appeal we could do so properly in the light of the authorities that bind us. Such was the view of Latham LJ in *Johnson*. Nothing has changed. But there are more profound reasons why this matter is not suitable for judicial rewriting.

[50]. First, we are dealing with the facts of a single appeal without the wide-ranging exploration of the issues which should underpin significant law reform of the sort which informed the Law Commission work to which we have referred. An individual case does not provide an apt vehicle for the reconsideration of the 'wrongdoing' elements of the *M'Naghten* rules.

[51] Secondly, this is an area of criminal law in which Parliament has been active. It has legislated in the past recognising that insanity is a defence to a criminal charge on the basis that the M'Naghten rules govern the underlying question: e.g. Criminal Procedure (Insanity) Act 1964. In the context of murder Parliament has introduced the partial defence of diminished responsibility:

509 Child, Simester, Spencer, Stark and Virgo, *Simester and Sullivan's Criminal Law: Theory and Doctrine*, 8th edn (2022) pp.838.

510 For discussion of this case, see N. Wortley, "Case Comment: M'Naghten Rules: *R v Keal*" [2022] EWCA Crim 341; M. Grainger, "Insanity and Command Delusions" (2022) 81 C.L.J. 467.

section 2 of the Homicide Act 1957 as amended by section 52(1) of the Coroners and Justice Act 2009 which at the least has some overlap with reform of the law of insanity in crime. In our judgment significant changes to an aspect of our criminal law that has remained undisturbed for so long, laden with policy choices as they would be, are more properly for Parliament."

Appeal dismissed.

9–206 Given that the M'Naghten rules "are in desperate need of reform",[511] it is a great pity that the Court of Appeal has taken such a stance.

(f) Role of medical evidence

9–207 The courts have made it plain from *M'Naghten* onwards that they regard all these questions as legal ones for their determination. Medical evidence is, in theory, just that—evidence from which decisions can be made. However, there can be little doubt that a large part of the decision-making can rest with the medical expert. Under the Criminal Procedure (Insanity and Unfitness to Plead) Act 1991 s.1 no verdict of not guilty by reason of insanity can be returned except on the written or oral evidence of two or more registered medical practitioners (at least one of whom has to be approved under the Mental Health Act 1983 s.12). The reasons advanced for the introduction of this requirement are of interest. In some cases, insanity verdicts had been returned without any medical evidence to support the plea.[512] Clearly, giving so little weight to the role of experts was unsatisfactory.[513] The position now, however, is that experts are called upon to do too much *if* the issue is a legal one. Medical experts may not be asked baldly: "Do you think this person is insane?" (The word would be of no medical significance in any event.) But they may well be asked: "Do you think this defendant has a disease of the mind?" This intermingling of medical and legal concepts is fraught with danger,[514] and the situation is not improved by the decision in *Burgess* where, despite stating that the issues involved were legal ones, considerable reliance was placed upon the expert's statement that the defendant's condition was pathological. Furthermore, not only may medical experts fundamentally disagree amongst themselves about a particular diagnosis but they may, if their sympathies are engaged with their "patient", distort the evidence to fit the "manifest absurdity of the M'Naghten test".[515] One possibility is that it was because neither the judiciary nor the medical experts seemed wholly convinced about their role in the adjudication process that s.1 was passed. It has been argued that it is an "effort to ensure greater congruence between the evidence necessary for a person to be found not guilty by reason of insanity and that necessary for long-term detention under the Mental Health Act 1983 on grounds of mental disorder".[516] If this argument is correct then it would help to rebut a challenge that the *M'Naghten* Rules contravene the ECHR.[517] It is by no means clear, however, that s.1 was meant to be anything more

511 R. Mackay, "*M'Naghten* Rules (Letter to the Editor)" [2022] EWCA Crim 341.

512 R.D. Mackay, "Fact and Fiction about the Insanity Defence" [1990] Crim. L.R. 247, 251; E. Baker, "Human Rights, M'Naghten and the 1991 Act" [1994] Crim. L.R. 84, 86.

513 Although see Loughnan, "Between fairness and 'dangerousness': reforming the law on unfitness to plead" (2016) Crim. L.R. 451 for a discussion of the role that collective, lay knowledge of madness has in understandings of insanity in the criminal trial.

514 cf. D. Brahams and H. Zeitlin, "Communication between doctors and lawyers" (2018) 86 Med. Leg. J. 61.

515 Royal Commission on Capital Punishment, Cmnd.8932 (1953), p.104.

516 P. Fennell, "The Criminal Procedure (Insanity and Unfitness to Plead) Act 1991" (1992) 55 M.L.R. 547, 549.

517 See para.9–210. See further, Baker, "Human Rights, M'Naghten and the 1991 Act" [1994] Crim. L.R. 84.

than a procedural change and the Draft Criminal Code expressly rejects the assimilation of the two concepts on the basis that the definition of mental disorder under the Mental Health Act 1983 is too wide and was designed for different purposes.[518]

As matters stand, even if medical experts and judges are clear in their own minds about their respective roles, juries appear to have little role to play in most cases. Research has revealed that in 86% of cases there was agreed expert evidence and the jury was simply directed (with both prosecution and defence agreement) to return a verdict of not guilty by reason of insanity.[519]

(ii) Applicability of the defence

In *DPP v Harper*,[520] it was held that insanity could be a defence in the magistrates' court, but only if the offence charged was one in which mens rea was an element. However, this was held to be wrong in *Loake*.[521] D had been charged with harassment, contrary to the Protection from Harassment Act 1997 s.2, by sending a very large amount of text messages to her husband, from whom she was separated. At her trial in the magistrates' court, she sought to rely upon the defence of insanity, but both the magistrates' court, and the Crown Court on appeal, ruled that the defence was not available, because the s.2 offence did not require subjective mens rea. On appeal, the Administrative Court held that the defence of insanity was of general application and applied to the s.2 offence and all other offences. **9–208**

(iii) Criminal Procedure (Insanity and Unfitness to Plead) Act 1991

Before the 1991 Act, the result of a finding of "not guilty by reason of insanity" was mandatory commitment to such hospital as directed by the Home Secretary (commonly a special hospital such as Broadmoor) without limitation of time. Not unnaturally, Ds faced with this possibility, when their plea had originally been not guilty (because of non-insane automatism), often decided to change their pleas to guilty; indeed, Sullivan did precisely this. Whilst research reveals that Ds did not spend as long in hospital as they feared,[522] this forced change of plea was clearly unacceptable. Furthermore, given the diversity of cases brought within the concept of "disease of the mind" by the development of the internal/external distinction, there was a pressing need for this to be reflected in the methods of disposal available to the court. It was profoundly unsatisfactory that judges could not make an order that distinguished between the treatment appropriate for an epileptic, a diabetic or a schizophrenic. **9–209**

518 Law Com. No.177 (1989), paras 11.26–11.28 fn.22.

519 Mackay and Kearns, "More Fact(s) about the Insanity Defence" [1999] Crim. L.R. 714. A follow-up study, examining the use of the insanity plea in the years 1997–2001, confirmed the finding that juries "have little real deliberative role to play" in such cases: R.D. Mackay, B.J. Mitchell and L. Howe, "Yet More Facts About the Insanity Defence" [2006] Crim. L.R. 399, 404.

520 *DPP v Harper* [1997] 1 W.L.R. 1406, McCowan LJ at 1409; (1997) 161 J.P. 697, following *R. v Horseferry Road Magistrates' Court Ex p. K* [1977] Q.B. 23; [1996] 3 W.L.R. 68 QBD.

521 *Loake v Crown Prosecution Service* [2017] EWHC 2855 (Admin); [2018] Q.B. 998. For further discussion of this case, see: R. Mackay, "Case Comment: Insanity defence: *Loake v Crown Prosecution Service*" [2018] Crim. L.R. 336; Stuart-Cole, "Insane harassment: is the defence of insanity available for a defendant charged with an offence of harassment, contrary to section 2(1) PFHA?" [2018] 82 J. Crim. L. 7.

522 Mackay, "Fact and Fiction about the Insanity Defence" [1990] Crim. L.R. 247, 251–255 and Mackay, *Mental Condition Defences in the Criminal Law* (1995), pp.104–105.

The Criminal Procedure (Insanity and Unfitness to Plead) Act 1991 (as amended) enables the Crown Court to do this. Until 2004, mandatory commitment followed a finding of insanity in cases of murder. However, in all cases the Crown Court may now make a hospital order (with or without restriction order), a supervision order or an order for absolute discharge.[523] This provision does not apply to the magistrates' courts. There is no statutory provision for the special verdict of not guilty by reason of insanity in the magistrates' court.[524] Where an accused establishes the defence of insanity in the magistrates' court, the court may either acquit him, or make a hospital or guardianship order under the Mental Health Act 1983 s.37(3).[525]

It should be stressed that this section does nothing to alter the *M'Naghten* Rules themselves.[526] Indeed, it is possible that by removing mandatory commitment reform may now be less likely than ever, although both the insanity defence and unfitness to plead were considered by the Law Commission as part of its programme of law reform. Despite their limited nature, however, these reforms are welcome and it seems that the judiciary have embraced the new flexibility[527] and that, although still very rare, an increase in the use of the insanity plea has occurred.[528]

(iv) Compatibility with the ECHR

9-210 In addition to the issues with the M'Naghten Rules discussed above, there is still a possibility that they could be found to be incompatible with the ECHR art.5. This provision protects the right of individuals to "liberty and security of person" and deprivation of this right has to be "in accordance with a procedure prescribed by law". Furthermore, "persons of unsound mind" can only be detained where proper account of objective medical expertise has been taken. This has been interpreted to mean that there must be a strong relationship between legal and medical criteria used to assess those who are insane.[529] Because of these concerns the forms of disposal following a finding of not guilty by reason of insanity (or a finding of unfitness) were changed, as we have seen, in 2004. However, while in this respect the law is now compatible with art.5, it is not entirely safe from further challenge. Whilst s.1 states that the evidence of two doctors is needed before a finding of not guilty by reason of insanity can be made, the weight to be given to this evidence remains unspecified. Certainly, it is not binding because, as we have seen, the test of insanity is regarded as a legal one. The result may be that *M'Naghten* contravenes the Convention.[530]

---

523 Criminal Procedure (Insanity) Act 1964 s.5 as amended by the Criminal Procedure (Insanity and Unfitness to Plead) Act 1991 and the Domestic Violence, Crimes and Victims Act 2004. If the charge is one of murder *and* the court has the power to make a hospital order (broadly, because of the nature of the condition of the defendant) a hospital order with a restriction order must be made (s.5(3)).

524 *R. (on the application of Singh) v Stratford Magistrates' Court* [2007] EWHC 1582 (Admin); [2008] 1 Cr. App. R. 2 at [25].

525 *R. (on the application of Singh) v Stratford Magistrates' Court* [2007] EWHC 1582 (Admin); [2008] 1 Cr. App. R. 2; Mackay, "Case Comment: Insanity defence: *Loake v Crown Prosecution Service*" [2018] Crim. L.R. 336, 339.

526 There is an argument, canvassed earlier, that s.1 of the Act does effect a change. See para.9-207.

527 Mackay's research (over a 10-year period between 1991–2001) revealed that in over 50% of cases a community-based order was made: Mackay, Mitchell and Howe, "Yet More Facts About the Insanity Defence" [2006] Crim. L.R. 399, 407.

528 In the first five years of Mackay's research there was an average of 8.8 findings per year of not guilty by reason of insanity; by 1997–2001 this had risen to an average of 14.4 per year: Mackay, Mitchell and Howe, "Yet More Facts About the Insanity Defence" [2006] Crim. L.R. 399, 400. The average is now approximately 20–30 per year: Mackay, *Mental Condition Defences in the Criminal Law* (1995); Mackay, "The Insanity Defence in Operation" [2014] 65 N.I.L.Q. 155.

529 *Winterwerp v The Netherlands* (A/33) (1979–80) 2 E.H.R.R. 387. See further, *R. v Grant (Heather)* [2001] EWCA Crim 2611; [2002] Q.B. 1030; *R. (on the application of Juncal) v Secretary of State for the Home Department* [2008] EWCA Civ 869; [2008] M.H.L.R. 193 and P.J. Sutherland and C.A. Gearty, "Insanity and the European Court of Human Rights" [1992] Crim. L.R. 418.

530 Indeed, this view was accepted in Jersey at first instance (R.D. Mackay and C.A. Gearty, "On Being Insane in Jersey—the case of *Att-Gen v Jason Prior*" [2001] Crim. L.R. 560). However, the appeal court disagreed (Mackay, "On Being Insane in Jersey Part Two—the Appeal in *Jason*

(v) Proposals for reform

As far back as 1975, the Butler Committee on Mentally Abnormal Offenders[531] reported that major reform was necessary, but this Report has been ignored by successive governments. The Law Commission has also recommended reform.[532] Responses to the Law Commission's Scoping Paper[533] revealed that while criticisms of the law are regarded as justified, both legal and medical practitioners work around the problems and that reform to the fitness to plead test was more urgent.[534] The Law Commission thus prioritised that work but, nonetheless, regards reform of the law on automatism and insanity as necessary as it is "outmoded, inappropriate and complicated".[535] Its provisional proposals would constitute a radical change.[536] The verdict of not guilty by reason of insanity would be replaced by one of "not criminally responsible by reason of a recognised medical condition" (or "RMC") (reflecting the view, noted earlier, that the true rationale of the defence is a lack of capacity). The phrase "recognised medical condition" is deliberately wide so as to encompass physical as well as mental conditions.[537] A number of implications flow from this: for example, the stigmatising label "insanity" would become even more inappropriate than under the existing law and would be jettisoned. The concept would encompass a wide range of conditions, which might now lead to a finding of automatism; thus, the boundary between the two defences would shift. However, in addition to establishing that D was suffering from a recognised medical condition, it would also be necessary to establish that: **9–211**

> ". . . the defendant wholly lacked the capacity
> (i) rationally to form a judgment about the relevant conduct or circumstances;
> (ii) to understand the wrongfulness of what he or she is charged with having done;[538] or
> (iii) to control his or her physical acts in relation to the relevant conduct or circumstances."[539]

There was much to commend in the discussion paper, including the proposal that the defence would apply in the magistrates' court as well as the Crown Court and that D would bear only an "elevated evidential burden" rather than have to prove the defence, but there are also justifiable concerns about the proposed defences. As Ashworth has commented: **9–212**

Prior v Att-Gen" [2002] Crim. L.R. 728). cf. *Nawrot v Poland* (77850/12) [2020] M.H.L.R. 236 ECtHR, and the case commentary by J. Dute at [2018] 25 E.J.H.L. By negating the criminal responsibility of an individual based on his mental disability or lack of capacity, the current defence of insanity also fails to comply with the requirements of the Convention on the Rights of Persons with Disabilities: see, e.g. T. Minkowitz, "Rethinking criminal responsibility from a critical disability perspective: The abolition of insanity/incapacity acquittals and unfitness to plead, and beyond" (2014) 23 G.L.R. 434.

531 Cmnd.6244 (1975).

532 Law Com. No.177 (1989), cll.35–36 fn.22, largely drawing upon the Butler recommendations.

533 Law Commission, *Insanity and Automatism, A Scoping Paper* (2012). See further, J. Peay, "Insanity and Automatism: questions from and about the Law Commission's Scoping Paper" [2012] Crim. L.R. 927.

534 Law Commission Discussion Paper (2013), para.1.10 fn.453.

535 Law Commission Discussion Paper (2013), para.1.84 fn.453.

536 Law Commission Discussion Paper (2013), para.1.85 fn.453.

537 It would, however, exclude "acute intoxication". See paras 9–197–9–199.

538 "Wrongfulness" would not be limited to illegality as under the existing law: Law Commission Discussion Paper (2013), para.4.33 fn.453.

539 Law Commission Discussion Paper (2013), para.1.93 fn.453.

> "How often the new defences would be used is unclear, since the RMC defence will require two expert reports and if successful, may lead to a medical disposal. As now, some defendants may prefer to take their chances with ordinary sentencing powers. Both new defences are narrowly drawn, requiring a total lack of capacity or control, and that may ensure that few cases end in a special verdict or an acquittal on grounds of automatism."[540]

(vi) Criminal Law v Mental Health Powers

9–213 Commentators have increasingly voiced doubts about the uneasy mixture of the criminal law and its objectives with the power of courts under mental health legislation to confine dangerous people to hospitals. Some critics of the insanity defence have argued that discussion of mental disorder should be limited to the issue of mens rea. If the mental condition of the defendant negated the mens rea required for the offence, then no further criminal questions could arise—the defendant would be entitled to an acquittal. There would, however, remain the separate issue of civil commitment.[541] A contrasting approach has been taken by, Morris, who concludes that the mentally disordered are entitled to be held responsible for their actions, but that their condition may be relevant in sentencing and might result in mitigation on grounds of less moral blameworthiness, or aggravation because of constituting a danger to the public.[542]

Moore has argued that the prevailing viewpoint in relation to the insanity defence is misguided, and has instead suggested the adoption of a "status" approach, which regards the irrationality of mental illness as being in itself excusing:

> "One who is mentally ill is not morally blameworthy for harm he incurs while he is ill. Not being morally blameworthy, he cannot be held liable to the sanctions of the criminal law. Some form of insanity defence is a proper reflection of our moral sentiments in this regard. Further, not only should the defence be retained, but it should be phrased so as to correspond to the moral issue being adjudicated by juries. The question put to juries should not be phrased in terms of the knowledge or compulsion of the accused, and certainly not in terms of speculative hypotheses about physical causation of the accused's behaviour. We can also dispense with the fiction that a mentally ill person's criminal action could not have been intentional. Rather, the question put to juries should be the moral question framed in terms of the actual criterion by which such moral judgements are made, that is, in terms of the irrationality of the accused: was the accused so irrational that he cannot justly be held responsible?"[543]

---

540 A. Ashworth, "Editorial, Insanity and automatism: a discussion paper" [2013] Crim. L.R. 787, 788. For further critical discussion of the Law Commission's paper, see J. Stanton-Ife, "Total Incapacity" and R.A. Duff, "Incapacity and Insanity: Do we Need the Insanity Defence?" in Livings, Reed and Wake (eds), *Mental Condition Defences and the Criminal Justice System: Perspectives from Law and Medicine* (2015), Chs 5 and 6.

541 See, e.g. J. Goldstein and J. Katz, "Abolish the 'Insanity Defense'—Why Not?" (1963) 72 Yale L.J. 853, 854–855, 862–865.

542 N. Morris, *Madness and the Criminal Law* (1982), pp.31–32, 61–64. See also M.S. Moore, "The Quest for a Responsible Responsibility Test: Norwegian Insanity Law After Breivik" (2015) 9 Crim. Law and Philos. 645. cf. J. Bijlsma, "A new interpretation of the modern two-pronged tests for insanity: Why legal insanity should not be a 'status defense'" (2018) 27 *Netherlands Journal of Legal Philosophy* 29; L. Gröning, "Has Norway abandoned its medical model? Thoughts about the criminal insanity law reform post 22 July" [2021] Crim. L.R. 191.

543 M.S. Moore, *Placing Blame: A Theory of the Criminal Law* (2010), pp.608–609.

(vii) Abolition of the insanity defence

Some commentators have gone so far as to recommend abolition of the offence. Slobogin has suggested the insanity defence be abolished, and that the most appropriate way of recognising the impact of mental disorder upon a defendant's blameworthiness is by regarding it as a factor which is relevant to the general defences.[544] Whilst Szasz, a psychiatrist, goes even further and argues that the insanity defence is nothing more than a tactical construct employed in cases where law and psychiatry do not wish to treat an individual as a moral agent, and that mental illness is merely a myth, with those regarded by psychiatrists as being "mentally ill" remaining responsible for their actions.[545] 9–214

How are we to respond to arguments such as these? Do they constitute a persuasive case for abolition that "trumps" the arguments addressed in the introductory discussion of this defence? Fletcher, for example, remains unconvinced.

George P. Fletcher, "Rethinking Criminal Law" (1978), p.846:

"The criminal law expresses respect for the autonomy of the sane as much as it shows compassion for the insane. The line between the two may shift over time. Our theories of sanity may change. But the line remains. If the criminal law is to be an institution expressing respect as well as compassion, its institutions must be able both to punish the guilty and excuse the weak. These two sentiments depend on each other. Compassion is possible only so far as punishment is the norm. Punishing wrongdoing is possible only so far as we have a concept of accountability for wrongdoing. Respect for autonomy and compassion for the weak are too important to our culture to be easily shaken by the skeptics." 9–215

C. AUTOMATISM

1. Evaluation

In the two preceding sections we have seen that non-insane automatism (commonly termed simply "automatism") entitles D to a complete acquittal and that, fearful of allowing too many such acquittals, the law has rigorously circumscribed the parameters of the defence of automatism. This has been achieved in three ways. First, by insisting that D be blameless in causing the state of automatism: "the defence of automatism is not available to D who has induced an acute state of involuntary behaviour by his own fault".[546] Second, by adopting a broad definition of "disease of the mind" to ensure that in many cases, where there is the slightest risk of repetition of the conduct, D is adjudged insane giving the courts power to make orders in relation to that person. Third, by requiring that there be "a total 9–216

544 C. Slogbogin, "Abolition of the Insanity Defense" in P.H. Robinson, S. Garvey and K. Kessler Ferzan (eds), *Criminal Law Conversations* (2011), p.474.

545 T. Szasz, "Mental Illness: Psychiatry's Phlogiston" (2001) 27 *Journal of Medical Ethics* 297, 298–299.

546 *Coley* [2013] EWCA Crim 223 at [24].

destruction of voluntary control on the defendant's part".[547] This does not require that D be unconscious, in the sense of being comatose, but that there is an absence of conscious control over his physical actions.[548] It is not sufficient that D's behaviour be merely disinhibited or irrational, or that he have impaired, reduced or partial control.[549]

There have been two main consequences of this restrictive approach. First, the number of situations in which automatism can be successfully pleaded are few and far between. Apart from hypoglycaemia and the (possibly anomalous) decisions involving sleep-walking, already discussed, it would appear that it is only in cases involving isolated incidents of an external cause prompting the involuntary behaviour that the defence will be available. Examples would include physical compulsion (for example, being pushed over so as to injure another) and reflex actions of external origin (for example, reflexive movements while being attacked by a swarm of bees[550]). More problematic is involuntary action caused by a blow. Clearly, a physical blow which causes concussion will qualify here.[551] But, in some cases, there might be a less immediate connection between the "blow" and the automatic behaviour. In *T*,[552] D, on a charge of robbery and assault causing actual bodily harm, claimed that she had been raped three days previously and that this caused her to suffer from post-traumatic stress disorder with the result that she was in a state of psychogenic fugue rendering her actions automatic. At her trial, it was ruled that she was entitled to have this defence put to the jury as one of non-insane automatism.[553] It is, however, doubtful whether the law would extend this to purely non-physical psychological "blows" such as receiving a shock or distressing news. In such a situation, it has been held that the ensuing behaviour has its source in the internal psychological or emotional condition of the defendant thus rendering the case one of insanity.[554] Such distinctions are, however, difficult to sustain. It is unrealistic to conclude that the post-traumatic stress disorder in *T* was purely the product of the physical impact of the rape; presumably it was the psychological shock thereof that produced this state. Yet given the law's reluctance to expand the category of automatism, it seems unlikely that the approach adopted in *T* would be approved if directly tested in the appellate courts.[555]

9–217 Another problematic cause of "involuntary" behaviour is hypnotism. There are dicta in *Quick*[556] and *Coley*,[557] to the effect that this could give rise to automatism. On the other hand, it seems unlikely that the courts would go so far as to hold that "brainwashing" can lead to automatic behaviour. Such a holding would be dangerously close to concluding that a person's unfortunate upbringing should exempt him from criminal liability.

---

547 *Att-Gen's Reference (No.2 of 1992)* [1994] Q.B. 91 at 105; [1993] 3 W.L.R. 982 CA; *Coley* [2015] EWCA Crim 223 at [22].
548 *Coley* 2013] EWCA Crim 223 at [23].
549 *Att-Gen's Reference (No.2 of 1992)* [1994] Q.B. 91 at 105; *R. v McGhee (Colin)* [2015] EWCA Crim 223 at [43], [46].
550 *Hill v Baxter* [1958] 1 Q.B. 277; [1958] 2 W.L.R. 76 QBD. For discussion in relation to volition and hypnotised Ds see, e.g. B. Williams, "The Actus Reus of Dr. Caligari" (1994) 142 U. Pa. L. Rev. 1661; J. Mason, "The Willed Trance: volition, voluntariness and hypnotised defendants! (2021) 85 .J Crim. L. 26.b.
551 *Att-Gen's Reference (No.2 of 1992)* [1994] Q.B. 91 at 104.
552 *R. v T* [1990] Crim. L.R. 256 CC.
553 She was convicted.
554 *R. v Rabey* [1980] S.C.R. 513 (Canada). cf. A. Reed, "Quasi-Involuntary Actions and Moral Capacity: The Narrative of Emotional Excuse and Psychological-Blow Automatism" in Livings, Reed and Wake (eds), *Mental Condition Defences and the Criminal Justice System: Perspectives from Law and Medicine* (Newcastle: Cambridge Scholars Publishing, 2015), Ch.7.
555 In *R. v Huckerby (Graham)* [2004] EWCA Crim 3251, the issue was not one of automatism but the Court of Appeal did conclude that a conviction for robbery was unsafe because the trial court had not heard evidence about the full impact (including post-traumatic stress) an earlier robbery upon the defendant might have had upon him.
556 *R. v Quick (William George); R. v Paddison (William)* [1973] 1 Q.B. 910.
557 *Coley* [2015] EWCA Crim 223 at [22].

There is a great deal of dissatisfaction with the present response of the law to the problem of automatism. Along with proposals to modify the insanity defence, reforms have been suggested to the law of non-insane automatism.[558] As noted in the discussion of insanity, the Law Commission has made provisional recommendations for reform of the law to both insanity and automatism. Automatism would only be a defence, as now, if there was no prior fault,[559] and:

> ". . . if the jury or magistrates find that the accused raises evidence that at the time of the alleged offence he or she wholly lacked the capacity to control his or her conduct and the loss of capacity was not the result of a recognised medical condition . . . he or she shall be acquitted unless the prosecution disprove this to the criminal standard."[560]

While this would not lead to a different outcome for an epileptic who commits offences during a seizure (because under the current law the condition is regarded as internally caused and thus raising the plea of insanity) it would do so for a diabetic who, to use an example given by the Law Commission, causes death by dangerous driving during a hypoglycaemic episode where there was no warning of the onset of the episode.[561] Without prior fault and with a complete absence of control, such a D would currently secure an acquittal. Under the proposed reform, the result would be the new special verdict of "not criminally responsible by reason of a recognised medical condition". While the removal of the hair-splitting internal/external distinction is wholly to be commended, there must be doubt as to whether Ds will wish to risk a special verdict—even one which does not have the negative connotations associated with the label "insanity". **9–218**

Finally, we need to examine whether this whole approach is sound. Should automatism provide a complete defence? The result may be open to doubt at two levels.

Coles has suggested that scientific evidence supports the thesis that many of the crimes which the courts have decided were committed in a state of automatism may actually have been committed whilst D was in a disinhibited state, where their consciousness was diminished rather than absent:

> "The behaviours with which the courts are confronted involve an individual with a novel goal, objective, or reason for his/her behaviour, and carrying it out in the face of a changing interpersonal environment. Being neither reflexive nor habitual, these behaviours require some degree of conscious awareness and volitional control . . ."[562]

---

558 Law Com. No.177 (1989), fn.22 cl.33. See further, R.D. Mackay, "Craziness and Codification—Revising the Automatism and Insanity Defences" in I. Dennis (ed), *Criminal Law and Justice* (London: Sweet & Maxwell, 1987), pp.112–118; and Wilson, "Violence, Sleepwalking and the Criminal Law: Part 2: The Legal Aspects" [2005] Crim. L.R. 614.

559 Law Commission Discussion Paper (2013), para.5.111 fn.453. For an overview of the provisions, see D. Ormerod, "The Law Commission's proposals for the reform of the defences of insanity and automatism" (2015) 55 *Medicine, Science and the Law* 156. See R. Mackay and D. Hughes, "Insanity and blaming the mentally ill—a critique of the prior fault principle in the Law Commission's discussion paper" [2021] Crim. L.R. 191, for criticism of this proposal.

560 Law Commission Scoping Paper, para.5.124 fn.582.

561 Law Commission Discussion Paper (2013), para.1.113 fn.453.

562 E. Michael Coles, "Scientific Support for the Legal Conception of Automatism" (2000) 7 *Psychiatry, Psychology and Law* 33, 45–46.

If one accepts Coles' view that the evidence indicates that those acting in a so-called state of automatism are disinhibited, rather than lacking voluntary control, then this raises a number of questions about the law's response to such conduct. Should the defence of automatism be broadened to recognise semi-voluntariness through disinhibition?[563] Should Ds have a complete defence? Or should the defence abolished entirely?

Even those who would not go so far as to accept the above view of autonomic acts have sometimes expressed concern that certain automatons have been given absolute acquittals.

R. Cross, "Reflections on Bratty's Case" (1962) 78 L.Q.R. 236, 238–239:

9–219 "Although they are still comparatively rare, pleas of non-insane automatism are becoming increasingly frequent, and questions may be legitimately raised concerning the sufficiency of the courts' powers. Is it right that someone who has been acquitted on the ground of non-insane automatism should inevitably go free? In *R. v Charlson* (1955) 29 Cr.App.R.37 the accused was acquitted on various charges of causing grievous bodily harm to his son because he acted in a state of automatism which may have been due to a cerebral tumour. It is only natural to feel the deepest sympathy for the accused in such a case, but it is equally natural to question the propriety of an unqualified acquittal. One way of dealing with such problems would be to give the judge powers in all cases of a successful plea of automatism, insane or non-insane, to order the detention of the accused pending a medical inquiry, after which the appropriate order could be made."

9–220 We have seen that as a result of *Sullivan*, epileptics, sleepwalkers, those suffering from arteriosclerosis and diabetics during hyperglycaemic episodes, may all now be regarded as insane. It has been argued that this is inappropriate. Although mandatory commitment no longer follows a finding of insanity, there is an undeniable stigma attached to such a finding.

2. Proposals for reform

9–221 The concern about the risk potentially posed to members of the public by certain types of automatons would largely be addressed if the Law Commission's provisional proposals in respect of the defence of automatism were to be enacted. The Law Commission has proposed ending the stigma of labelling certain automatons as insane, and that the defence of automatism should be de-medicalised, by abolishing the common law rules and replacing it with a new statutory defence of automatism:

". . . where at the time of the alleged offence the accused suffered a total loss of capacity to control his or her actions which was not caused by a recognised medical condition."[564]

---

563 cf. Reed, "Quasi-Involuntary Actions and Moral Capacity: The Narrative of Emotional Excuse and Psychological-Blow Automatism" in Livings, Reed and Wake (eds), *Mental Condition Defences and the Criminal Justice System: Perspectives from Law and Medicine* (2015), Ch.7; S. Yeo, "Clarifying Automatism" (2002) 7 *Psychiatry, Psychology and the Law* 445.

564 Law Commission Discussion Paper (2013), Ch.5 fn.453.

This defence would still lead to a complete acquittal, but would be much narrower, and would be likely to apply only in very limited "one-off" circumstances, such as where a defendant acted whilst in an hypnotic trance, or where a driver lost voluntary control of a vehicle because he was being stung by bees, or because he had been temporarily stunned by a stone flying through the window.[565] Ds who committed an alleged offence in a state of automatism caused by a recognised medical condition (such as diabetes and epilepsy) would fall within the proposed new defence of "not criminally responsible by reason of recognised medical condition", which if successful, would result, not in an acquittal, but in the special verdict of "not criminally responsible by reason of a recognised medical condition".[566]

VII. Lack of Age

A. INTRODUCTION

Crime (particularly less serious forms of crime) is predominantly a youthful phenomenon. Both official statistics and self-report studies confirm that the peak age of offending is in mid-teens and that most such offenders (particularly females) will "grow out of crime".[567] The response of the criminal justice system to crime by children has fluctuated sharply and has been fundamentally affected by political considerations. The pendulum has swung between a punitive approach (which holds a child responsible as if an adult) and one based upon considerations of welfare. As part of an ever-changing uneasy balance between the two, the law does take some account of the different stages of childhood. Of course, in reality, the process of maturation is a gradual one.[568] The criminal law is rather less subtle than this: it recognises that very young children should not be held responsible for their actions and so there is a fixed age limit below which they will be excused liability. **9–222**

The age of criminal responsibility is currently set at 10.[569] This is considerably lower than many other European countries, where the average age at which responsibility is imposed is 14 years old.[570] There

565 Law Commission Discussion Paper (2013), paras 5–104, 5–106 fn.453. The Law Commission suggest that, if D acted whilst in a state of concussion following a blow to the head, that would amount to a recognised medical condition, which would not be covered by the defence: para.5–106.

566 Law Commission Discussion Paper (2013), Ch.4 fn.453. See: M.D. Kopelman, "Automatism: are we throwing the baby out with the bathwater?" (2022) 62 Med. Sci. Law 245.

567 J. Fionda, *Devils and Angels* (London: Blackwell, 2005), pp.59–69; A. Rutherford, *Growing out of Crime: The New Era* (Winchester: Waterside Press, 2002).

568 Civil law reflects this by reference to the test of "*Gillick*-competence": *Gillick v West Norfolk and Wisbech AHA* [1986] A.C. 112. See further, H. Keating, "The Responsibility of Children in the Criminal Law" (2007) 19 C.F.L.Q. 183. The Law Commission favours consideration being given to a defence of "developmental immaturity": Law Commission Discussion Paper (2013), paras 9.1–9.24 fn.453, cf. Law Com. No.364, *Unfitness to Plead, Volume I: Report* HC 714-1 (2016), para.7.54.

569 The Children and Young Persons Act 1933 s.50 as amended by the Children and Young Persons Act 1963 s.16. At common law, the age of criminal responsibility was seven. The Children and Young Persons Act 1969 s.4 raised the age of responsibility to 14, but this was never implemented and was repealed by the Criminal Justice Act 1991 s.72. See further H. Keating, "Children's Rights and Children's Criminal Responsibility" in A. Diduck and H. Reece, *Essays in Honour of Michael Freeman* (Cambridge: CUP, 2014).

570 Child Rights International Network, *Minimum Ages of Criminal Responsibility in Europe*. The Age of Criminal Responsibility (Scotland) Act 2019 s.1, which came fully into effect on 17 December 2021, raised the age of criminal responsibility in Scotland to 12. Ireland increased the

was formerly a transitional phase between the ages of 10 and 14, during which time the child used to be presumed to be "*doli incapax*". Only if the prosecution could rebut the presumption by proof that the child knew what he/she was doing was seriously or gravely wrong and not merely naughty or mischievous could the child be held criminally responsible for her actions.[571] Although entirely sound in relation to the underlying principles of the criminal law, the presumption increasingly came under fire as illogical, lacking in common-sense, out-dated, a serious disservice to the law and unnecessary.[572] In *C v DPP*, the House of Lords urged that the presumption be subject to "parliamentary investigation, deliberation and legislation".[573] With less deliberation than was warranted by the significance of the reform, the Crime and Disorder Act 1998 s.34 was passed. This states that "[t]he rebuttable presumption of criminal law that a child aged ten or over is incapable of committing an offence is hereby abolished".[574] On a strict reading, this section abolished the *presumption* only and it was thus argued that it was still open to a child between the ages of 10 and 14 to show that he/she did not understand that what he/she had done was seriously wrong.[575] In *CPS v P*, Smith LJ expressed the view (obiter) that the defence remained in existence but also flagged up the issue for another court to consider fully.[576] In *R. v JTB*,[577] the House of Lords, whilst acknowledging the ambiguity of the provision, ruled that s.34 abolished both the presumption and the defence of *doli incapax* entirely for children aged 10 and over. It is regrettable that such an important change in the law's approach to the criminal responsibility of children should have been achieved in such an ambiguous manner.

This reform was a very significant part of a policy which sought to make children—even very young children—increasingly liable for their actions.[578] Despite the fact that only a small number of very young children are brought before the courts,[579] and that the 1980s saw considerable success in diverting children away from custody and from the courts by use of formal cautioning etc,[580] the perception has grown that children are out of control. Concerns about the use of multiple cautions[581] and the perceived

---

age of criminal responsibility to 12 in 2006 (the Criminal Justice Act 2006 s.129, amending the Children Act 2001 s.52) although it remains at 10 for murder, manslaughter, rape or aggravated sexual assault.

571 *C (A Minor) v DPP* [1996] A.C. 1; [1995] 2 W.L.R. 383 HL. For a discussion of the historical development of the age of criminal responsibility, see A.W.G. Kean, "The Age of Criminal Responsibility" (1937) 53 L.Q.R. 364; T. Clinton Jaja, "The Modern Legal History of Criminal Liability of Children in the United Kingdom 1938–2008" (2011) 2 *New Journal of European Criminal Law* 301.

572 These views were not shared by all commentators: see, e.g. P. Cavadino, "Goodbye *doli*, Must We Leave You?" (1997) 9 C.F.L.Q. 165; S. Bandalli, "Abolition of the Presumption of *doli incapax* and the Criminalisation of Children" (1998) 37 *Howard Journal* 114 and D. Hamer and T. Crofts, "The logic and value of the presumption of doli incapax (failing that an incapacity defence" (2023) 43 O.J.L.S. 546.

573 *C (A Minor) v DPP* [1996] A.C. 1 at 40.

574 The Act was not retrospective, so the presumption and defence still apply to crimes committed before s.34 came into effect: *R. v PF* [2017] EWCA Crim 983. See also N. Wortley, "Merely naughty or seriously wrong? 'Childish sexual experimentation' and the presumption of *doli incapax*" (2017) 81 J. Crim. L. 346.

575 N. Walker, "The End of an Old Song" (1999) 149 N.L.J. 64.

576 *Crown Prosecution Service v P* [2007] EWHC 946 (Admin); [2008] 1 W.L.R. 1005. See also D. Ormerod, "Young person: young person having low IQ" [2008] Crim. L.R. 165.

577 *R. v T* [2009] UKHL 20; [2009] 1 A.C. 1310. See F.A.R. Bennion, "Mens rea and defendants below the age of discretion" [2009] Crim. L.R. 757 and A. Ashworth, "*R. v T*: Children and Young Persons—doli incapax—Crime and Disorder Act 1998 s.34" [2009] Crim. L.R. 581.

578 Without a corresponding increase in emphasis upon the rights of natural justice such as those pertaining to the trial of adults (M.D.A. Freeman, "The Rights of Children When They Do Wrong" (1981) 21 Brit. J. Criminol. 210).

579 In 2012, 262 children aged 10 and 11 were proceeded against at court (*Hansard*, HL Deb, Vol.749, col.488 (8 November 2013)). A 2019 investigative study by the *Guardian* newspaper indicated that, in 2018, 123 offences were committed by 10 year olds: H. Pidd, J. Halliday, M. Wolfe-Robinson and N. Parveen, "Children In the dock: Age of criminal responsibility must be raised, say experts" 4 November 2019.

580 Fionda, *Devils and Angels* (2005), pp.88–97.

581 Crime and Disorder Act 1998 ss.61 and 62 replaced cautioning with a statutory scheme of reprimands and warnings. This scheme was abolished by the Legal Aid, Sentencing and Punishment of Offenders Act 2012, which has introduced a scheme of youth cautions (s.135, inserting s.66ZA into the Crime and Disorder Act 1998).

growth in both the prevalence and gravity of young children's crime, fed, in part, by the highly-publicised killing of James Bulger by two 10 year olds[582] led to a flurry of punitive initiatives.

The measures adopted have led to intense criticism both domestically and internationally.[583] In particular, the UN Committee on the Rights of the Child has recommended that the UK "raise the minimum age of criminal responsibility in accordance with International standards", as one of a number of recommended measures to bring its juvenile justice system Into line with standards required by the Convention on the Rights of the Child.[584] Given that reform has already taken place in Scotland and Ireland, with legislation being passed to increase the age of criminal responsibility to 12,[585] and the 2019 recommendation of the Commission on Justice in Wales, chaired by former Lord Chief Justice Thomas, that the Welsh age of criminal responsibility be "raised to at least 12 years old",[586] it is hoped that the Government will feel able to change its previous stance and raise the age of criminal responsibility in England and Wales to 12.[587] **9-223**

B. BELOW THE AGE OF 10

Children below this age are irrebuttably presumed to be incapable of committing crime. Care proceedings may be brought if it is thought that the child: **9-224**

> ". . . is suffering or is likely to suffer significant harm and that the care given to him is not what it would be reasonable to expect a parent to give, or the child is beyond parental control."[588]

---

582 *R. v Secretary of State for the Home Department Ex p. Venables; Secretary of State for the Home Department Ex p. Thompson* [1998] A.C. 407; [1997] 3 W.L.R. 23 HL. On the issue of child homicides (and their scarcity) see Justice, *Children and Homicide* (London: Justice, 1996); P. Cavadino, *Children Who Kill: an examination of the treatment of Juveniles* (Winchester: Waterside Press, 1996); and C. McDiarmid, "Children who Murder" [2000] Crim. L.R. 547. See also the debate engendered by the trial of two boys, aged 10 and 11, who were convicted of causing grievous bodily harm with intent contrary to the Offences Against the Person Act 1861 s.18 to two other young children: *The Independent*, 23 January 2010 and *The Telegraph*, 23 January 2010.

583 See, e.g. UN Committee on the Rights of the Child, *Concluding Observations: United Kingdom of Great Britain and Northern Ireland* (49th session) (2008), paras 77–80 and Keating, "The Responsibility of Children in the Criminal Law" (2007) 19 C.F.L.Q. 183; B. Goldson, "'Unsafe, Unjust and Harmful to Wider Society': Grounds for Raising the Minimum Age of Criminal Responsibility in England and Wales" (2013) 13 *Youth Justice* 111; H. Wishart, "Young minds, old legal problems: can neuroscience fill the void? Young offenders & the Age of Criminal Responsibility Bill—promise and perils" (2018) 82 J. Crim. L. 311 and H. Keating, "How should the Criminal Law Respond to the 'Special Status' of Children?" and G. Yaffe's comment, in J.J. Child and R.A. Duff, *Criminal Law Reform Now* (Oxford: Hart, 2018), Ch.6 and p.184.

584 UN Committee on the Rights of the Child, *Concluding observations on the fifth periodic report of the United Kingdom of Great Britain and Northern Ireland* (CRC/C/GBR/CO/5) (2016), para.79(a). The Law Commission has expressed the view that there "may be sound policy reasons for looking afresh at the age of criminal responsibility": Law Com. No.364, *Unfitness to Plead, Volume I: Report*, HC 714-1 (2016), para.7.54.

585 Age of Criminal Responsibility (Scotland) 2019, s.1. The relevant Irish legislation is the Children Act 2001, s.52.

586 Commission on Justice in Wales, *Justice in Wales for the People of Wales* (2019), para.4.195; Lord Thomas of Cwmgiedd, "Justice in Wales for the People of Wales" [2020] Crim LR 1.

587 Lord Dholakia has, on a number of occasions, introduced private member's Bills (Age of Criminal Responsibility Bills 2013–2014, 2015–2016 and 2016–2017, 2017–2019 and 2019–2021) in the House of Lords with the aim of raising the age of criminal responsibility to 12. None of these Bills managed to complete their passage through Parliament. The Government's response in relation to the previous Bills has been that been to maintain that "having the age of criminal responsibility set at ten years allows flexibility to deal with young offenders" and that "children aged ten and above are, for the most part, able to *differentiate* between bad behaviour and serious wrongdoing and should therefore be held accountable for their actions": House of Lords, Library Briefing, *Age of Criminal Responsibility Bill [HL] (HL Bill 3 of 2017–19)* (2017).

588 Children Act 1989 s.31(2).

These proceedings are entirely civil and decisions are based upon the welfare of the child.[589] However, over the last three decades, an increasing number of other measures have been introduced with the aim of controlling the anti-social behaviour of children under the age of 10 (and their parents).[590] Although these measures are said to be to "protect young children from being drawn into crime" and to "help them change their bad behaviour",[591] there can be little doubt that they are experienced as punishment, and are part of a deeply unsatisfactory trend which could render the concept of the age of criminal responsibility meaningless.

C. ABOVE THE AGE OF 10

9-225 Between the ages of 10 and 13, offenders are categorised as children, and between 14 and 17 years old as young persons.[592] The sentencing options available to the youth court[593] depend upon this categorisation. A further, transitional category, referred to in the preceding White Paper[594] as "near adults" has been included in the young person category. The courts are given additional sentencing powers for 16–17 year olds whose maturity warrants such treatment. Courts must "have regard to the welfare of the child or young person"[595] but as this is not the only consideration, the court may find persuasive, for example, the need to protect the public.

VIII. Sundry Defences

9-226 In addition to the general defences discussed in this chapter, there are defences of entrapment,[596] superior orders[597] and the statutory defence provided in the Modern Slavery Act 2015 s.45,[598] besides numerous other specific defences which are beyond the scope of this book. It is, for example, a defence

589 Care orders in criminal proceedings were abolished by Children Act 1989 Sch.12(I) para.1, repealing the Children and Young Persons Act 1969 s.12AA.

590 Under the Crime and Disorder Act 1998 ss.8–15, e.g. child safety orders, curfews, and parenting orders may be imposed.

591 Home Office, *Tackling Youth Crime: A Consultation Paper* (1997), paras 98–99.

592 Criminal Justice Act 1991 s.68, Sch.8.

593 Criminal Justice Act 1991 s.70(1). The youth court hears all cases involving young offenders except where the offence is homicide or a "grave crime" or where the child is charged jointly with an adult or there is other adult involvement in the crime (see the Powers of Criminal Courts Act (Sentencing) Act 2000 ss.90, 91).

594 *Crime, Justice and Protecting the Public* (Cmnd.965, 1990), para.8.16.

595 Children and Young Persons Act 1933 s.44(1), as amended. This must be read subject to the Crime and Disorder Act 1998 s.37, which states that the principal aim of the youth justice system is to prevent offending by children and young persons.

596 Currently there is no substantive defence of entrapment in English law. Where the conduct of law enforcement officers may be regarded as having incited or instigated crime, or lured a person into committing a crime, the House of Lords has indicated that the most appropriate remedy is a stay of the proceedings as an abuse of the court's process: *Att-Gen's Reference (No.3 of 2000)* [2001] UKHL 53; [2001] 1 W.L.R. 2060. See Child, Simester, Spencer, Stark and Virgo, *Simester and Sullivan's Criminal Law: Theory and Doctrine*, 8th edn (2022), pp.712–716.

597 This is not a defence known to English law: see *R. v Clegg (Lee William)* [1995] 1 A.C. 482 at 498; [1995] 2 W.L.R. 80. cf. Ormerod and Laird, *Smith, Hogan and Ormerod's Criminal Law*, 16th edn (2021) pp.399.

598 See, e.g. Laird, "Evaluating the relationship between section 45 of the Modern Slavery Act 2015 and the defence of duress: an opportunity missed? [2016] Crim. L.R. 395.

to a charge of use of a firearm to resist arrest to show possession of the firearm for a lawful object.[599] Likewise, it is a defence to the offence of failing to provide a specimen of breath or blood or urine (for the purposes of the offence of driving or being in charge of a vehicle with a blood/alcohol concentration above the prescribed limit) to show a reasonable excuse.[600] Another example of a specific defence is that a police officer may use such force as is reasonable in effecting a lawful arrest.[601]

---

599 Firearms Act 1968 s.17(2).

600 Road Traffic Act 1988 s.7(6).

601 Criminal Law Act 1967 s.3(1).

Chapter 10

Inchoate Offences

I. Introduction

An inchoate crime is one that is "committed by doing an act with the purpose of effecting some other offence".[1] It is committed when the defendant takes certain steps towards the commission of a crime. There are three main inchoate offences in English law—attempt, conspiracy and encouraging or assisting crime (formerly incitement)—and the nature of the requisite steps that need be taken varies with each. With attempt, the defendant must have tried to commit the offence and have got relatively close to achieving the objective. With conspiracy, at least two people must have agreed to commit a crime. With encouraging or assisting crime, the defendant must have encouraged or assisted another to commit a crime. **10–001**

An inchoate offence is one that is "relative to the offence-in-chief".[2] It consists of actions falling short of the consummated crime. It is thus not a crime existing in the abstract. One cannot be charged with "conspiracy" or "attempt". The indictment must be drafted with reference to the complete offence, for example, conspiracy to murder or attempt to steal.

There are many other offences in English law that might be thought of as inchoate in the sense that they penalise conduct that might be preparatory to the commission of other offences. For example, under the Terrorism Act 2006 s.5, there is an offence of preparation of terrorist acts. These offences are, however, "crimes in themselves" and are charged as such without reference to any further offence. Such offences are commonly described as endangerment offences.

Both inchoate and endangerment offences share a common element. No harm is caused, in the ordinary sense of the word; no person need be injured; no proprietary interest is damaged. A crucial question, therefore, running through the analysis of such offences will be: how can one justify the existence of these offences and how should they be punished in comparison with the complete offence? **10–002**

1 D.J. Baker, *Glanville Williams, Textbook of Criminal Law*, 4th edn (London: Sweet & Maxwell, 2015), para.18–001.
2 G.P. Fletcher, *Rethinking Criminal Law* (New York: OUP, 1978), p.132.

II. Attempt

A. SHOULD THERE BE A LAW OF ATTEMPT?

10-003 Generally, criminal liability is imposed upon a *blameworthy* actor who causes a prohibited *harm*. With attempts, the blameworthiness element is clearly satisfied. The person who attempts to commit an offence clearly has the mens rea of that full offence.[3] But no harm has been caused in the usual sense of the word: for instance, the V has not died or has not lost any property. Are we justified in imposing criminal liability upon an actor who has caused no such harm?

There are two distinct ways of answering this question—both leading to the conclusion that criminal liability should be imposed for attempts:

1. In terms of desert, an attempter's "moral culpability is (broadly) comparable to that of a successful offender".[4] As Horder puts it:

> "A person who tries to cause a prohibited harm and fails is, in terms of moral culpability, not materially different from the person who tries and succeeds: the difference in outcome is determined by chance rather than choice, and a censuring institution like the criminal law should not subordinate itself to the vagaries of fortune by focusing on results rather than culpability."[5]

Furthermore, where a crime is attempted, there *is* a harm, namely, a threat to security. We all have rights to bodily and proprietary security. An attempt to commit a crime represents a danger to these rights. Our right to security has been infringed. This infringement of our rights constitutes, in itself, a harm that the criminal law seeks to punish. Gross expresses the point well:

> "Where there is only attempt liability, the conduct itself may usefully be regarded as a second order harm: in itself it is the sort of conduct that normally presents a threat of harm; and that, by itself, is a violation of an interest that concerns the law. The interest is one in security from harm and merely presenting a threat of harm violates that security interest."[6]

10-004 2. In utilitarian terms, criminal liability for attempts may be justified in the absence of any harm. A person who attempts to commit a crime is dangerous and needs restraining. Such a person is also in need of rehabilitation and punishment for individual deterrence, otherwise they might try to commit the crime again being more careful the next time. There is a final important instrumental justification here: the police should be given every encouragement to prevent crime, not simply to detect it. On this

---

3 Indeed, as shall be seen, this mens rea will often have to be of a *greater* degree than that required for the completed offence.

4 Law Commission Consultation Paper No.183, *Conspiracy and Attempts: A Consultation Paper* (2007), para.15.7.

5 J. Horder, *Ashworth's Principles of Criminal Law*, 10th edn (Oxford: OUP, 2022), p.514.

6 H. Gross, *A Theory of Criminal Justice* (New York: OUP, 1979), p.125.

basis, the police should be empowered to arrest and the Crown Prosecution Service to prosecute, for attempts to commit crimes.

Of course, whenever arguments such as these are raised, we find ourselves faced with the same central question: while utilitarian considerations might explain the *purpose* of punishment, are we ever justified in punishing exclusively for such reasons? Or may we only punish offenders who *deserve* punishment? If the latter, then we are back to our starting point that, generally, punishment is only deserved where there is a combination of blame and harm. However, this is not a cast-iron rule. With crimes of strict liability, the law is prepared to dispense with the element of blame in imposing liability. It could be that with crimes of attempt, the utilitarian arguments for punishment are so strong that we are prepared to dispense with the element of harm, and assert that punishment is justified (i.e. deserved) on the basis of the blame element alone.

Thus, under either of these explanations, it is possible to justify the existence of a law of attempt. The contours of such a law will vary, however, depending on which of the two views is accepted. This is because the first view focuses on attempts as threats to people's interests in security from interference. Thus, unless the attempter gets near to completing the crime (and, generally, unless the crime is possible), no interests are threatened and criminal liability is not justified. But the emphasis in the second view is on the mens rea of the attempter: if they have the requisite mens rea, they need not get near to committing the complete offence (and, generally, it will be irrelevant whether the crime is possible). The tensions between these two approaches and their impact upon the law will be explored further when we examine the actus reus of attempt.

Can there be an attempt to commit all crimes? The Criminal Attempts Act 1981 s.1(4) provides that there can only be criminal liability for attempts to commit "any offence which, if it were completed, would be triable . . . as an indictable offence". This includes offences "triable either way".[7] **10–005**

Criminal liability for attempts to commit summary offences was excluded because there is:

> ". . . no social need to extend the punishment of attempt outside the class of serious crime. The amount of time spent considering complicated questions would be out of all proportion to the advantage accruing from allowing the law to intervene at an early stage."[8]

It is submitted that such an approach is justifiable. With attempts, criminal liability is imposed in the absence of any direct harm (other than a threat to security). When dealing with serious offences we are arguably justified in dispensing with the requirement of harm. However, when dealing with the lesser

---

7 An indictable offence is an offence "which, if committed by an adult, is triable on indictment, whether it is exclusively so triable, or triable either way": Interpretation Act 1978 Sch.1 para.1. An offence is an "indictable offence" even if it is one, such as low value criminal damage, that has to be proceeded with as if it were triable only summarily (*R. v Bristol Magistrates' Court Ex p. E* [1999] 1 W.L.R. 390; [1999] Crim. L.R. 161; Interpretation Act 1978 Sch.1 para.1). In *R. v Nelson (Gary)* [2013] EWCA Crim 30; [2013] 1 W.L.R. 2861 the offence of attempted battery was recognised, despite battery being a summary offence; the unconvincing reason being that it is possible to try battery (and common assault) on indictment where it forms part of a series of offences of the same or similar character as an indictable offence. For further discussion of this case, see: P. Hungerford-Welch, "Case Comment, *R. v Nelson (Gary)*; trial-Indictment" [2013] Crim. L.R. 689.

8 HC Deb., Vol.2, ser.6, col.214 (1981).

summary offences which pose less of a threat to security, we should insist on harm actually occurring as a prerequisite to any criminal liability.[9] The Law Commission proposed that there should be liability for attempts to commit a summary offence because some summary offences are relatively serious and the demarcation line between indictable and summary offences is somewhat arbitrary.[10] However, after consultation, this proposal was abandoned. It would have involved an increase in the reach of the substantive criminal law and there was no broad consensus amongst consultees for such an extension of the law.[11]

10-006 Section 1(4) of the Act also excludes liability for attempted: (a) conspiracy; (b) aiding, abetting, counselling, procuring or suborning an offence;[12] and (c) offences under s.4(1) (assisting offenders) or s.5(1) (accepting or agreeing to accept consideration for not disclosing information about an arrestable offence) of the Criminal Law Act 1967. However, there probably can be liability for attempting the offences of encouraging or assisting crime.[13] The worrying development of double inchoate liability is considered at the end of this chapter.

B. THE LAW

1. Actus reus

(i) Act must be more than merely preparatory

CRIMINAL ATTEMPTS ACT 1981 s.1(1):

10-007 "If, with intent to commit an offence to which this section applies, a person does an act which is more than merely preparatory to the commission of the offence, he is guilty of attempting to commit the offence."

10-008 Suppose D wakes up one morning and decides to kill his wife by poisoning her. He walks to a shop where he purchases some rat poison. He returns home and adds the poison to the whisky in his whisky decanter. That evening he offers his wife a drink of whisky; she accepts. He pours the poisoned whisky into a glass and hands it to her. She starts drinking the whisky. At what point in this chain of actions could he be said to have done an act which was "more than merely preparatory to the commission of the offence"? When he handed her the whisky? When he put the poison in the decanter? When he purchased the poison?

---

9 See paras 1-016–1-028.

10 Law Commission Consultation Paper No.183, *Conspiracy and Attempts* (2007), paras 16.99–16.100.

11 Law Commission Paper No.318, *Conspiracy and Attempts* (2009), paras 8.159–8.160.

12 See further, M. Bohlander, "The Conflict between the Serious Crime Act 2009 and Section 1(4)(b) Criminal Attempts Act 1981—A Missed Repeal" [2010] Crim. L.R. 483 and J. Child, "The Differences between Attempted Complicity and Inchoate Assisting and Encouraging—A Reply to Professor Bohlander" [2010] Crim. L.R. 924.

13 Law Commission Paper No.300, *Inchoate Liability for Assisting and Encouraging Crime* (2006), para.5.28 fn.29. See para.10-120.

Questions such as these cannot be answered in a theoretical vacuum; they, and all the contours of the law of attempt, can only be determined by reference to the underlying justification (and policy) of the law of attempt. Thus, if attempts are viewed as being threats to people's interests in security from interference (the "second order harm" discussed earlier), one ought to insist on the attempter getting near to completing the crime. Until he has got near to committing the complete crime, the wife's interests in security from interference are not threatened. On the other hand, if the law of attempt is justified on the utilitarian bases canvassed above, then the emphasis is on the mens rea of the attempter and liability can be imposed at a much earlier stage in the chain of actions. Of course, such an approach still does not tell us exactly when the husband has done enough to threaten the wife's interests; or when his mens rea is sufficiently manifested to justify the imposition of criminal liability for attempt, but adoption of one or other of these views does provide an important indication of *how* to try to answer the question.

Fletcher and Duff suggest another approach, not dissimilar in its effect.

George P. Fletcher, Rethinking Criminal Law (1978), pp.138–139:

"The critical question . . . is the elementary issue whether the act of attempting is a distinct and discernible element of the crime of attempting. To say that the act is a distinct element is to require that the act conform to objective criteria defined in advance. The act must evidence attributes subject to determination independently of the actor's intent. In short, there must be features of the attempt as palpable as the death of the victim in homicide or a trespassory taking in larceny. We shall refer to the set of arguments favoring this approach as the 'objectivist' theory of attempts. Though the term 'objective' may have a different connotation in some contexts, we shall use the term to mean a legal standard for assessing conduct that does not presuppose a prior determination of the actor's intent. 10–009

The opposing school is appropriately called 'subjectivist', for it dispenses with the objective criteria of attempting. The act of execution is important so far as it verifies the firmness of the intent. No act of specific contours is necessary to constitute the attempt, for any act will suffice to demonstrate the actor's commitment to carry out his criminal plan.

As we delve more deeply into objectivist and subjectivist theories of liability for criminal attempts, we shall discover that objectivists tend to favor a minimalist approach, subjectivists, a maximalist approach to liability . . . [T]his means that objectivists tend to draw the line of liability as close as possible to consummation of the offense and tend, further, to be sympathetic to claims of impossibility as a bar to liability. This combination of views generates a minimalist approach to liability. Subjectivists, in contrast, tend to push back the threshold of attempting and reject the relevance of impossibility—a stance that yields a maximalist net of liability. In turning to a more detailed study of objectivist and subjectivist theories, we should keep in mind that the watershed between them is the question whether the act of attempting is a distinct element of liability."

10-010 There are two competing theories underlying the law of attempt. First, the "objectivist" theory requires D to have come sufficiently close to committing the crime for their conduct to generate apprehension and thus amount to a "second order harm". Duff supports this objectivist approach because, by insisting that conduct comes close to the actual commission of the offence, one is affording intending criminals an opportunity to abandon their criminal enterprise. By doing this, even if we think it unlikely they will desist, we are according to the person respect as a responsible agent "who is in principle susceptible to rational persuasion".[14] Secondly, there is the "subjectivist" theory which stresses the mental element of the D: if they have mens rea they are dangerous and need restraining. Liability can accordingly be imposed at a much earlier stage (which will facilitate the task of the police and other law enforcement agencies). The only conduct required would be some action that would be corroborative of this intention: "If a defendant sets out to bring about a criminal end and in doing so performs an equivalent intentional action; that . . . ought to suffice for liability".[15] The tensions between these two theories is demonstrated by a consideration of the various "tests" employed by English law in its effort to demarcate how much action is required for the actus reus of attempt.

(a) The common law

10-011 Until 1981, the common law flirted with various tests. One such test was Stephen's "series of acts" test under which it was necessary to determine whether D had committed an act which was one of a series of acts that would lead to the crime if it were not interrupted. This test was also of little utility: it was too imprecise and could have led to the imposition of liability at an intolerably early state. The test finally adopted by the common law[16] was the "proximity test". D's actions had to be proximate to the completed offence in the sense of being "immediately and not merely remotely, connected"[17] with the completed offence. In *Robinson*, a jeweller, who had insured his stock against burglary, hid the jewellery, tied himself up, called for help and represented to the police that his premises had been burgled. His object was to obtain policy money from his insurance company. It was held that his actions were still merely preparatory; they were "only remotely connected with the commission of the full offence, and not immediately connected with it".[18] He would have needed to have communicated with the insurance company before an attempt could be committed. In *Stonehouse*, Lord Diplock stated that in order to have passed the threshold of proximity, D must have "crossed the Rubicon and burnt his boats".[19] All the cases confirming this test emphasised that D had to get very close to committing the offence; in some cases, such as *Robinson*, it appeared that D would only be liable if he had committed the last act dependent upon himself—although from other cases it is clear that the proximity test did not demand as a matter of law that D go so far.[20] This proximity test was very much in tune with Fletcher's objectivist theory of attempts: the emphasis was on the objective acts and not on the intentions of the D.

---

14 R.A. Duff, *Criminal Attempts* (Oxford: Clarendon Press, 1996), p.388.

15 Donnelly-Lazarov, *A Philosophy of Criminal Attempts: The Subjective Approach* (2015), pp.129–130.

16 History is in the process of being rewritten with cases since the 1981 Act suggesting that it is not clear which test was applied at common law. However, two House of Lords' decisions, *Haughton v Smith* [1975] A.C. 476; [1974] 2 W.L.R. 1 HL and *DPP v Stonehouse* [1978] A.C. 55; [1977] 3 W.L.R. 143 HL made it plain that the proximity test was the favoured one.

17 *Jones v Brooks* (1968) 52 Cr. App. R. 614 at 616; [1968] Crim. L.R. 498 Div Ct; *Davey v Lee* [1968] 1 Q.B. 366 at 371; [1967] 3 W.L.R. 105, approved in *Haughton v Smith* [1975] A.C. 476. cf. *R. v Eagleton* 169 E.R. 766; (1855) 6 Cox C.C. 559.

18 *R. v Robinson (Harry)* [1915] 2 K.B. 342 at 349; (1916) 11 Cr. App. R. 124.

19 *Stonehouse* [1978] A.C. 55.

20 Again, post-1981 Act cases are rewriting history by suggesting that the proximity test was synonymous with a last act test. It was not. See, e.g. *R. v Harris (Paul Andrew)* (1976) 62 Cr. App. R. 28; [1976] Crim. L.R. 514 CA.

(b) Criminal Attempts Act 1981

Section 1(1) states that D must do "an act which is more than merely preparatory to the commission of the offence". Is this different in any way from the proximity test developed by the common law? **10–012**

One view is that no real change in the law was intended by the enactment of s.1(1). The Government, in the course of the parliamentary proceedings, took the view that the law on this matter was not being altered.[21] The Law Commission, whose Report led to the legislation, felt that it was "undesirable to recommend anything more complex than a rationalisation of the present law".[22] Under *Eagleton*,[23] the common law always distinguished between preparatory and non-preparatory acts and non-preparatory acts were simply called "proximate" acts.

The Law Commission was concerned that the terminology used in s.1(1) could open the door to conviction in cases such as *Robinson*. However, unlike the position at common law, not all preparatory acts are excluded; only *merely* preparatory acts do not suffice.[24] Indeed, in *Tosti*[25] it was stated that the Ds "had committed acts which were preparatory, but not merely so".

Before examining the cases, it is important to stress that the ultimate decision here is one for the jury. The Criminal Attempts Act 1981 s.4(3) provides: **10–013**

> "Where . . . there is evidence sufficient in law to support a finding that he did an act falling within [s.1(1)] . . ., the question whether or not his act fell within that subsection is a question of fact."

So the judge, using the law about to be outlined, must decide whether there is sufficient evidence that D *could* come within the law of attempt, and then, if so, it must be left to the jury to decide whether the acts did or did not come within the definition of the actus reus provided in s.1(1). There Is the danger that this might lead to inconsistency of jury verdicts,[26] although no empirical studies have been conducted on this. It also involves the jury having to decide what is essentially a matter of law. Whether certain acts satisfy certain legislative criteria ("more than merely preparatory") so as to amount in law to a crime, is a question of law which ought to be left to the judges to develop.[27] The Law Commission in 2007, recommended that s.4(3) be repealed and that the test become a legal one for the judge to determine.[28] This proposal was not supported strongly enough and the Law Commission abandoned it.[29]

The following is the leading case which has been cited in most subsequent decisions.

---

21 I. Dennis, "The Criminal Attempts Act 1981" [1982] Crim. L.R. 379.

22 Law Commission Paper No.102 (1980), para.2.47.

23 *Eagleton* (1855) 6 Cox C.C. 559.

24 D. Ormerod and K. Laird, *Smith, Hogan and Ormerod's Criminal Law*, 16th edn (Oxford: OUP, 2021), p.445.

25 *R. v Tosti* [1997] Crim. L.R. 746.

26 Law Commission Paper No.318, *Conspiracy and Attempts* (2009), paras 8-9–8-10.

27 See further, Williams, "Wrong Turnings in the Law of Attempt" [1991] Crim. L.R. 416.

28 Law Commission Consultation Paper No.183, *Conspiracy and Attempts* (2007), paras 16.89–16.95.

29 Law Commission Paper No.318, *Conspiracy and Attempts* (2009), para.8.184.

R. v GULLEFER (1990) 91 CR. APP. R. 356 (COURT OF APPEAL, CRIMINAL DIVISION):

10–014 During a race at a greyhound racing stadium, D climbed on to the track in front of the dogs and attempted to distract them by waving his arms. His efforts were only marginally successful and the stewards decided it was unnecessary to declare "no race". D told the police he had attempted to stop the race because the dog on which he had staked £18 was losing. He had hoped for a no-race declaration and the recovery of his stake. He was convicted of attempted theft and appealed on the ground that his acts were not "sufficiently proximate to the completed offence of theft to be capable of comprising an attempt to commit theft".

LANE LCJ:

"The first task of the court is to apply the words of the Act of 1981 to the facts of the case. Was the appellant still in the stage of preparation to commit the substantive offence, or was there a basis of fact which would entitle the jury to say that he had embarked on the theft itself? Might it properly be said that when he jumped on to the track he was trying to steal £18 from the bookmaker?

Our view is that it could not properly be said that at that stage he was in the process of committing theft. What he was doing was jumping on to the track in an effort to distract the dogs, which in its turn, he hoped would have the effect of forcing the stewards to declare 'no race', which would in turn give him the opportunity to go back to the bookmaker and demand the £18 he had staked. In our view there was insufficient evidence for it to be said that he had, when he jumped on to the track, gone beyond mere preparation . . .

[His Lordship considered the common law proximity test and Stephen's "series of acts" test.]

It seems to us that the words of the Act of 1981 seek to steer a midway course. They do not provide, as they might have done, that the *Eagleton* test is to be followed, or that, as Lord Diplock suggested, the defendant must have reached a point from which it was impossible for him to retreat before the actus reus of an attempt is proved. On the other hand the words give perhaps as clear a guidance as is possible in the circumstances on the point of time at which *Stephen's* 'series of acts' begin. It begins when the merely preparatory acts come to an end and the defendant embarks upon the crime proper. When that is will depend of course upon the facts in any particular case."

Appeal allowed

10–015 Lord Lane clearly thought he was pushing back the point at which liability could be imposed. In adopting his "midway course" he rejected the "Rubicon test". But what else was there left for D to do? Assuming his efforts had been successful and the race declared void, all that remained for him to do was to claim his refund which would have been his last act, comparable to Robinson filing a claim with his insurance company. Accordingly, the approach adopted in *Gullefer* looks indistinguishable from that adopted in the much-criticised common law decision of *Robinson*.

The test laid down in *Gullefer* is that D must have "embarked on the crime proper". Ds must have started committing the crime. They must be "on the job".[30] Such a test works well when applied to some cases. In *Boyle and Boyle*,[31] the Ds had broken down a door in their effort to commit burglary. Burglary requires an entry as a trespasser. To break down a door means that you have embarked on the process of securing entry to the building and can clearly amount to embarking on committing the crime. This approach was extended in *Tosti*[32] where it was held that a D who was merely examining a padlock (having hidden oxyacetylene equipment behind a hedge) was liable for attempted burglary. Similarly, in *Toothill*,[33] it was held that a D who knocked at the proposed victim's door was in the "executory stage of his plan" and liable for attempted burglary. In *Litholetovs*,[34] the D was liable for attempted arson when he poured petrol over the door of a house—even though he had not produced or lit the cigarette lighter that he had on him.

In other cases, the application of the test of embarking on the crime proper has not been so straightforward. In *Rowley*,[35] D left notes in public places offering money and presents to boys. These notes, which were not indecent in themselves and did not contain any propositions, were designed to lure boys for immoral purposes. On appeal, he was found not liable for attempted incitement of a child under the age of 14 years to commit an act of gross indecency. His actions were merely preparatory as they "went no further than to seek to engineer a preliminary meeting". He was "at most preparing the ground for an attempt". It was stated that an attempted incitement would require, for example, a posted letter inviting a boy to commit gross indecency which did not reach the boy.[36] **10–016**

The problem with this decision is that had he met the boys and said anything suggestive, he would have committed the full offence of incitement. The example of the non-arriving letter is a classic instance of a D having performed the last act there was for him to do. Again, it appears that the 1981 Act has not effected any change to the law.

R. v Jones (1990) 91 Cr. App. R. 351 (Court of Appeal, Criminal Division):

D, a married man, had an affair with a woman who then started a relationship with another man, Foreman. When she refused to resume their association, D applied for a shotgun certificate and three days later bought some guns. He shortened the barrel of one of them and test fired it twice. Three days later he told his wife he was going to Spain to work on their chalet and left home dressed normally for work. He then changed into a disguise of overalls and a crash helmet with the visor down. He waited outside a school where Foreman dropped his daughter off and then jumped into the rear seat and asked Foreman to drive on. They drove to a grass verge where D took the **10–017**

---

30 Ormerod and Laird, *Smith, Hogan and Ormerod's Criminal Law*, 16th edn (2021), p.446, citing Rowlatt J in *R. v Osborn* (1919) 84 J.P. 63. cf. *Moore v DPP* [2010] EWHC 1822 (Admin); [2010] R.T.R. 36 at [27], where Toulson LJ indicated that he found this phrase "unhelpful" because it "raised other questions as to when the job begins" and doubted if it was correct if it was meant to suggest that the actus reus of the full offence must have commenced.

31 *R. v Boyle (George)* (1987) 84 Cr. App. R. 270; [1987] Crim. L.R. 111 CA.

32 *Tosti* [1997] Crim. L.R. 746.

33 *R. v Toothill (Peter Kendall)* [1998] Crim. L.R. 876 CA.

34 *R. v Litholetovs (Mihails)* [2002] EWCA Crim 1154.

35 *R. v Rowley (Michael)* [1991] 1 W.L.R. 1020; (1992) 94 Cr. App. R. 95 CA.

36 Citing *R. v Ransford* (1874) 31 L.T. 488. For a similar decision to *Rowley* (1992) 94 Cr. App. R. 95, see *Nash* [1999] Crim. L.R. 308. cf. *R. v R* [2008] EWCA Crim 619; [2009] 1 W.L.R. 713.

loaded sawn-off shotgun from a bag and pointed it at Foreman at a range of some 10–12 inches and said: "You are not going to like this". The safety catch of the shotgun was in the on position. Foreman grabbed the end of the gun and after a struggle managed to throw it out of the window and escape. D was convicted of attempted murder and appealed on the ground that he had not yet committed the actus reus of this offence.

TAYLOR LJ:

"[At his trial the defence had argued] that since the appellant would have had to perform at least three more acts before the full offence could have been completed, i.e. remove the safety catch, put his finger on the trigger and pull it, the evidence was insufficient to support the charge . . .

The 1981 Act is a codifying statute. It amends and sets out completely the law relating to attempts and conspiracies. In those circumstances the correct approach is to look first at the natural meaning of the statutory words, not to turn back to earlier case law and seek to fit some previous test to the words of the section . . . [He then cited *Gullefer* with approval.] We respectfully adopt those words. We do not accept . . . [the] contention that section 1(1) of the 1981 Act in effect embodies the 'last act' test derived from *Eagleton*

[T]he 1981 Act followed a report from the Law Commission [No. 102] [which] states:

> '. . . the definition must cover those instances where a person has to take some further step to complete the crime, assuming that there is evidence of the necessary mental element on his part to commit it; for example, when the defendant has raised the gun to take aim at another but has not yet squeezed the trigger.'

Clearly, the draftsman of section 1(1) must be taken to have been aware of . . . the Law Commission's report. The words 'an act which is more than merely preparatory to the commission of the offence' would be inapt if they were intended to mean 'the last act which lay in his power towards the commission of the offence.' . . . Clearly his actions in obtaining the gun, in shortening it, in loading it, in putting on his disguise, and in going to the school could only be regarded as preparatory acts. But, in our judgment, once he had got into the car, taken out the loaded gun and pointed it at the victim with the intention of killing him, there was sufficient evidence for the consideration of the jury on the charge of attempted murder."

Appeal dismissed

R. v Campbell (1991) 93 Cr. App. R. 350 (Court of Appeal, Criminal Division):

10–018 D planned to rob a sub-post office. He drove a motorbike near to the post office, parked it and approached, wearing a disguise of sun glasses and a crash helmet, although he later placed the sunglasses in his pocket. He was carrying an imitation gun and a threatening note which he planned to pass to the cashier in the sub-post office. He was walking down the street and when one yard from the post office door, police, who had been tipped off, grabbed the appellant and arrested him. He was convicted of attempted robbery and appealed.

WATKINS LJ:

"[His Lordship repeated the *Gullefer* test that the 1981 Act was steering a 'midway course' and that preparatory acts ended when the defendant 'embarks on the crime proper'. He endorsed the stance in *Jones* that judges 'should stick to the definition of an attempt in the Act itself' and that it was 'wholly unnecessary' to refer to the common law.]

Looking at the circumstances here it was beyond dispute that the appellant, at the material time, was carrying an imitation firearm which he made no attempt to remove from his clothing. He was not, as he had done previously that day, wearing, as a form of disguise, sunglasses. It was not suggested that he had, in the course of making his way down the road . . ., moved towards the door of the post office so as to indicate that he intended to enter that place.

In order to effect the robbery it is equally beyond dispute it would have been quite impossible unless obviously he had entered the post office, gone to the counter and made some kind of hostile act—directed, of course, at whoever was behind the counter and in a position to hand him money. A number of acts remained undone and the series of acts which he had already performed—namely, making his way from his home . . ., dismounting from the cycle and walking towards the post office door—were clearly acts which were, in the judgment of this court, indicative of mere preparation . . . If a person, in circumstances such as this, has not even gained the place where he could be in a position to carry out the offence, it is extremely unlikely that it could ever be said that he had performed an act which could be properly said to be an attempt."

Appeal allowed

There can only be an attempt when D has "embarked on the crime proper" and in this case, it is suggested that D could have embarked on the crime of robbery when he entered the sub-post office. Robbery involves the use of force or threatened force.[37] It is difficult to see how someone who has entered a post office, but has not yet reached the counter or issued any threats can be said to have embarked on the crime of robbery. Clearly, the court in *Campbell* was adopting a more flexible approach to the notion of "embarking on the crime proper". This flexibility was reinforced in the following case. **10–019**

Attorney General's Reference (No.1 of 1992) (1993) 96 Cr. App. R. 298 (Court of Appeal, Criminal Division):

D, who was walking a girl home (both of them drunk), pulled her behind a hedge, forced her to the ground and lay on top of her. She lost consciousness. He then dragged her up some nearby steps **10–020**

37 Theft Act 1968 s.8.

to a shed. The girl, who had regained consciousness, was crying and trying to scream. D had lowered his trousers and interfered with her private parts but had not actually attempted penetration because his penis was flaccid. He claimed he was unable to have intercourse "cause I was drunk, so I couldn't, could I?" The trial judge directed an acquittal because there was no evidence of an actual physical attempt at penetration. The Attorney-General referred the following point of law for the opinion of the Court of Appeal:

> "Whether, on a charge of attempted rape, it is incumbent upon the prosecution, as a matter of law, to prove that the defendant physically attempted to penetrate the woman's vagina with his penis."

TAYLOR LCJ:

> "The words [in the 1981 Act] are not to be interpreted so as to re-introduce either of the earlier common law tests. Indeed one of the objects of the Act was to resolve the uncertainty those tests created . . .
>
> It is not, in our judgment, necessary, in order to raise a prima facie case of attempted rape, to prove that the defendant with the requisite intent had necessarily gone as far as to attempt physical penetration of the vagina. It is sufficient if there is evidence from which the intent can be inferred and there are proved acts which a jury could properly regard as more than merely preparatory to the commission of the offence. For example, and merely as an example, in the present case the evidence of the young woman's distress, of the state of her clothing, and the position in which she was seen, together with the respondent's acts of dragging her up the steps, lowering his trousers and interfering with her private parts, and his answers to the police, left it open to a jury to conclude that the respondent had the necessary intent and had done acts which were more than merely preparatory. In short that he had embarked on committing the offence itself."

Opinion accordingly

10–021 Clearly, when D is trying to commit the offence (trying to penetrate the woman), he can be said to have embarked on the crime. However, in this case it is stated that even prior to that, D can be held to have "embarked on the crime proper". This decision is understandable in both common sense and policy terms in that D had progressed relatively far in the series of acts that might have culminated in penetration: in particular, he had lowered his trousers and interfered with her private parts. However, in *Patnaik*,[38] it was held that it was unnecessary for D to have removed any clothing or to have done "some unequivocal sexual act". In this case, D had not undone any of his clothing and had not indecently disarranged the woman's clothing or intimately touched her. It was held that pushing her over a wall, straddling her legs and attempting to kiss her amounted to sufficient evidence to go to the jury that his acts were more than merely preparatory to the crime of rape: "the threshold was essentially a matter

38 *Patnaik* unreported 1 February 2000.

for the judge's judgment of the facts of the case". Similarly, in *Dagnall*,[39] it was held that by telling a woman that he wanted to "fuck her", pulling her hair and pushing her against a fence and causing her to feel that rape was inevitable, D's acts were capable of being more than merely preparatory despite the fact that the girl's clothing had not been disarranged and D might not have touched her in a sexual way.

Such an approach renders the test of "embarking on the crime" useless. The D in *Patnaik* had clearly embarked on the crime of sexual assault in trying to kiss the woman and, in his other actions, had committed several complete offences. Similarly, the D in *Dagnall* had committed a common assault (and possibly a sexual assault) on the woman. Such Ds would now clearly be liable for the offence under the Sexual Offences Act 2003 s.62 of committing an offence with intent to commit a sexual offence. It is not easy to see, however, that these men had embarked on the crime of rape.

The difficulty of applying this test is revealed by a consideration of reported decisions involving attempted false imprisonment and attempted child abduction. In *Geddes*,[40] D, with no legitimate purpose for being there, was seen on school premises, equipped with a knife, lengths of rope and masking tape. In quashing D's conviction for attempted false imprisonment, Lord Bingham CJ stated:

> "[T]here is not much room for doubt about the appellant's intention. Furthermore, the evidence is clearly capable of showing that he made preparations, that he equipped himself, that he got ready, that he put himself in a position to commit the offence charged . . . But was the evidence sufficient in law to support a finding that the appellant had actually tried to or attempted to commit the offence of imprisoning someone? Had he moved from the realm of intention, preparation and planning into the area of execution or implementation? . . . [I]t is true that the appellant had entered the school but he had never had any contact or communication with any pupil; he had never confronted any pupil at the school in any way . . . The whole story is one which fills the court with the gravest unease. Nonetheless, . . . we feel bound to conclude that the evidence in law was not sufficient to support a finding that the appellant did an act which was more than merely preparatory . . ."[41]

In *Griffin*,[42] a mother planning to abduct her children and take them out of the country, bought ferry tickets to Ireland and went to the children's school and told the teacher she had come to take them to the dentist. These actions were held to constitute an attempt to abduct children. The full offence here, under the Child Abduction Act 1984 s.1(1), is only committed if the child is taken or sent out of the UK. The court rejected an argument that the mother would at least have had the children in her custody **10–022**

---

39 *R. v Dagnall (Chris)* [2003] EWCA Crim 2441; (2003) 147 S.J.L.B. 995 CA (Crim Div). See also: *R v MH* [2004] EWCA Crim 1468; *R. v Bryan (Delroy)* [2015] EWCA Crim 548. cf. *R. v Ferriter (Maurice)* [2012] EWCA Crim 2211: D struggled with barmaid, trying to get her trousers down. His actions were held to have gone beyond mere preparation, but the conviction for attempted rape was substituted with a conviction for sexual assault, on the basis that there was an absence of evidence to prove that D had intent to commit the specific offence of rape.

40 *R. v Geddes (Gary William)* (1996) 160 J.P. 697; [1996] Crim. L.R. 894. cf. the approach taken by the New Zealand Supreme Court in *Johnstone (Justin Ames) v The Queen* [2016] N.Z.S.C. 83, where the relevant New Zealand legislation (Crimes Act 1961 s.72) requires the act or omission to be "immediately or proximately connected with the intended offence".

41 As J.C. Smith points out in his commentary [1996] Crim. L.R. 894 at 896, there was no endangerment or ulterior intent crime (such as going equipped with intent to kidnap) with which the defendant could be charged.

42 *R. v Griffin* [1993] Crim. L.R. 515 CA.

and have embarked on the journey. Similarly, in *MS*,[43] D, who was forbidden by court order from removing her daughter from the jurisdiction, had left her home with the intention of leaving the country with her children and her new boyfriend. She was in possession of passports and one-way ferry tickets from Dover to Calais, had booked accommodation through France to Italy, and had forged a permission document from her daughter's father. Her car was stopped by the police some 85 miles from Dover. An argument that there had to be "geographical proximity", suggesting that D had to be at the ferry port, attempting to board the ferry for her actions to have become more than merely preparatory was, unsurprisingly, rejected by the Court of Appeal:

> "[34] It is important in our judgment not to lose sight of the considerable differences that exist between the various offences which may be attempted . . . Depending always on the facts, the proximity of the accused to an intended murder victim may be critical in determining whether the steps taken by the accused were more than preparatory. In many cases when a sole offender contemplates murder (or an assault) by way of a direct physical attack, an attempt to commit the crime will only occur when the perpetrator and victim are in close proximity, when the action necessary (the actus reus) for attempting to kill or harm takes place (although we stress there will be undoubted exceptions to this sweeping generalisation). Similarly, in an attempted armed robbery, of the kind contemplated in *Campbell*, proximity to the target premises, along with an evinced intention to enter, may be critical. Distance, or rather proximity, therefore, may be an important factor for attempted crimes of that kind. But no single factor, including proximity, constitutes a uniform test that applies to all species of offences. Child abduction by a person connected with the child is an entirely different offence from murder, assault and robbery. The action necessary for an attempted parental abduction, as in the instant case, may have been 'embarked upon' at a considerable distance from the port or airport. For child abduction, geographical proximity does not have the same relevance as with other alleged crimes. Whether, prima facie, steps had been taken as part of the execution of the plan which were sufficiently close to the final act will always depend, therefore, on the ingredients of the offence and the facts of the case."

Given the multiple steps that D had taken, which were part of her plan to abduct her daughter, she had embarked "upon the crime proper".[44]

It is, of course, inevitable that fine distinctions have to be drawn in determining liability for attempt but as a result of these cases it is virtually impossible to predict at what stage D will have passed beyond the point of mere preparation and have "embarked on the crime proper".

---

43 *R. v MS* [2021] EWCA Crim 600; [2021] 1 W.L.R. 5019.

44 *MS* [2021] EWCA Crim 600; [2021] 1 W.L.R. 5019 at [36]. cf. *Perry v Government of the United States of America* [2021] EWHC 1956 (Admin), an extradition case, where D had removed his daughter from the mother's care and control and was concealing her from the authorities, but had not obtained passport documentation, booked travel tickets and was not near a transport hub. It was held that there was insufficient evidence that D had taken sufficient steps to satisfy the Criminal Attempts Act 1981 s.1.

Most of the above cases concerned attempts to commit offences against the person. In *Qadir and Khan*,[45] it was stated that because attempted killing or wounding concentrates on a particular moment, acts earlier in time are more likely to be merely preparatory. On the other hand, with attempts to commit offences involving deception or evasion then there is more likely to be a "stratagem carried on over a period of time" and thus the moment of embarkation on the crime "may be quite remote in time from its final outcome".

(c) Conclusion

It is almost impossible to extract any clear principles from the cases interpreting s.1(1). Three points can be stated with confidence, although quite where they lead and what they mean in real cases is another matter. **10–023**

First, the courts are striving at some sort of half-way house between the old proximity test and Stephen's "series of acts" tests. The problem with this is that it is impossible to find a "midway" point between proximity (which meant different things to different judges) and something completely unascertainable (which is all that can be said for Stephen's test). In short, talk about a "midway" point is rhetoric disguising the judges' desire to give themselves maximum flexibility.

Secondly, the "Rubicon test" has been abandoned.[46] D need not have reached the point of no return. Similarly, the fact that he has reached such a point will not necessarily indicate that his actions are more than merely preparatory. When a D climbs on to a racetrack in front of racing dogs and waves his arms at the animals it would surely be permissible to assert that he has "crossed the Rubicon and burnt his boats". This is what the D did in *Gullefer* and yet it was insufficient for liability.

Thirdly, the test now appears to be whether D has "embarked on the crime proper". As seen from the above cases, however, there is no clear view as to what "embarking on the crime proper" means. **10–024**

A theme uniting many of the cases where there has been liability for attempt is that there has been a "confrontation" with the victim or the property, whereas in the cases where acts have been held to be merely preparatory there has been no such confrontation. For example, in *Geddes* and *Rowley* the D had not met any of the children; in *Gullefer*, D, who was charged with attempted theft, had not confronted the bookmakers. In *Campbell*, there had been no confrontation with the cashier. On the other hand, in *Jones* and the attempted rape cases, there had been such a confrontation and in *Boyle and Boyle*, and the other attempted burglary cases there had been a "confrontation" with the building.

However, confrontation can be no more than evidence that acts are more than merely preparatory. In an attempted rape scenario, a man might confront a woman and pull her arm. Even under the broadest approach adopted above, this could never amount to acts more than merely preparatory to the crime of rape.

45 *Qadir and Khan*, *Archbold News*, 17 November 1997.

46 It was never a "test" in the sense that the proximity test was. It was one method for establishing whether the proximity test had been satisfied. Had it ever been a "test" gunman would not have been guilty of attempted murder until they had pulled the trigger.

As the above cases demonstrate, in many instances this test of "embarking on the crime proper" is problematic and appears to be little more than yet another smokescreen behind which policy can dictate when liability should be imposed.

(ii) Reform

10-025 The Law Commission in 2007[47] argued that there are two main defects to the present law of attempt. First, the "more than merely preparatory" test of proximity has proved to be too vague and uncertain.[48] Secondly, many leading decisions such as *Geddes* and *Campbell* have rendered the offence unduly narrow.[49] Too much emphasis has "been placed on the offence's label ('attempt')—and therefore on the notion of 'trying' to commit an offence".[50] Accordingly, the Law Commission proposed that the present law of attempt should be repealed and replaced by two separate inchoate offences:

(1) an offence of criminal attempt which would be limited to last acts needed to commit the intended offence; and
(2) an offence of criminal preparation, limited to acts of preparation which are "properly to be regarded as part of the execution of the plan to commit the intended offence".[51]

With regard to the proposed restricted offence of attempt, the Law Commission emphasised that "'last acts' should not be understood to extend only to the very last act that was required".[52] It argued that this new offence would accord with society's understanding of the word and would not involve any narrowing of the offence as "in practice, most cases charged as attempts will have involved a last act or acts needing to be done".[53] The new offence of criminal preparation would not cover mere preparation. D would only be liable if they were "in the process of executing his or her plan to commit an intended offence";[54] there had to be "on the job"[55] preparation. The Law Commission proposed that both these new offences should carry the same maximum penalty.[56]

There were many objections to this proposal to subdivide the present law of attempt into two separate offences.[57] For example, separate offences should capture different wrongs but both the proposed new offences are aimed at the same wrongdoing; the offence of attempt, being restricted to last acts, would become very narrow; there would be immense difficulty in distinguishing attempts from criminal preparation; the new crime of preparation would be too broad and could lead to the risk of over-criminalisation; there is the danger of introducing confusing labels and so on. Accordingly, in its final

47 Law Commission Consultation Paper No.183, *Conspiracy and Attempts* (2007).
48 Law Commission Consultation Paper No.183, *Conspiracy and Attempts* (2007), para.12.14.
49 Law Commission Consultation Paper No.183, *Conspiracy and Attempts* (2007), paras 12.17–12.22.
50 Law Commission Consultation Paper No.183, *Conspiracy and Attempts* (2007), para.12.15.
51 Law Commission Consultation Paper No.183, *Conspiracy and Attempts* (2007), Proposal 15.
52 Law Commission Consultation Paper No.183, *Conspiracy and Attempts* (2007), para.16.17.
53 Law Commission Consultation Paper No.183, *Conspiracy and Attempts* (2007), para.16.11.
54 Law Commission Consultation Paper No.183, *Conspiracy and Attempts* (2007), para.16.41.
55 Law Commission Consultation Paper No.183, *Conspiracy and Attempts* (2007), para.16.19.
56 Law Commission Consultation Paper No.183, *Conspiracy and Attempts* (2007), paras 16.18–16.22.
57 C.M.V. Clarkson, "Attempt: The Conduct Requirement" (2009) 29 O.J.L.S. 25. See also J. Rogers, "The Codification of Attempts and the Case for 'Preparation'" [2008] Crim. L.R. 937.

Report, the Law Commission abandoned this proposal and, with one exception,[58] did not recommend any reform of the conduct element of attempts.[59]

(iii) Abandonment

What is the position if D, with intention to commit the complete offence, does an act which is more than merely preparatory, but then decides to abandon the criminal enterprise? For example, in one US case, a man who was about to rape a woman discovered that she was pregnant and, in response to her pleas that he would hurt her baby, abandoned the plan.[60] Should such a D be guilty of attempted rape? Would it make any difference if, instead of discovering the woman was pregnant, the D had simply been struck by remorse and had desisted saying: "I won't do it; God has stayed my hand"?[61] **10–026**

It is clear that there is no "defence" of abandonment in English law.

HAUGHTON V SMITH [1975] A.C. 476 (HOUSE OF LORDS):

LORD HAILSHAM: **10–027**

"First [the defendant] may simply change his mind before committing any act sufficiently overt to amount to an attempt. Second, he may change his mind, but too late to deny that he had got so far as an attempt in the first case no criminal attempt is committed. At the relevant time there was no *mens rea* since there had been a change of intention, and the only overt acts relied upon would be preparatory and not immediately connected with the completed offence. In the second case there is both *mens rea* and an act immediately connected with the completed offence . . . It follows that there is a criminal attempt."

Should English law allow a defence of voluntary abandonment?[62] **10–028**

---

58 As there is doubt over the existing law, the Commission proposed clarification to ensure that persons can be convicted of attempted murder by omission (assuming they are under a legal duty to act) (Law Commission Paper No.318, *Conspiracy and Attempts* (2009), para.8.151). The Law Commission's proposals were accepted by the Government but will not be implemented.

59 Law Commission Paper No.318, *Conspiracy and Attempts* (2009), para.8.79.

60 *Le Barron v State* 32 Wis.2d 294; 145 N.W.2d 79 (1966).

61 *People v Graham* 176 App. Div. 38; 162 N.Y.S. 334 (1916).

62 Some jurisdictions do recognise such a defence: e.g. in the US, the Model Penal Code (s.5.01(4)) recognises a defence of voluntary renunciation of criminal purpose, and both the Dutch and German Criminal Codes (art.46(b) and s.24, respectively) allow Ds to escape liability if they voluntarily abandon the execution of the offence. See: Duff, *Criminal Attempts* (Oxford: OUP, 1996) pp.68–71; J. Keiler and D. Roef, "Inchoate Offences: Attempt and Preparation" in J. Keiler and D. Roef (eds), *Comparative Concepts of Criminal Law*, 3rd edn (Cambridge: Intersentia, 2019), Ch.IX pp.278–283. cf. S. Bock and F. Stark, "Preparatory Offences" in K. Ambos, A. Duff, J. Roberts, T. Weigend and A. Heinze (eds), *Core Concepts in Criminal law and Criminal Justice*, Vol.I (Cambridge: CUP, 2019), pp.81–84.

Martin Wasik, "Abandoning Criminal Intent" [1980] Crim. L.R. 785, 787–788, 790–794:

10-029 "It is clear that the *voluntary* nature of the abandonment is an essential requirement for the success of any excuse in this area . . . [T]wo reasons [are put forward] for the central importance of the requirement of voluntariness. Sometimes it is argued that voluntary desistance provides clear evidence that the actor lacked the resolve to carry out the crime, and hence was not truly dangerous, and sometimes it is said that voluntary desistance is a 'good act' which somehow compensates for or erases the initial criminal act, thus making an acquittal appropriate.[63]

> . . . One argument in favour of excusing the defendant who renounces a criminal purpose is in terms of negation of *mens rea*. According to Glanville Williams (*Criminal Law: The General Part* (1961), pp.620–621) 'where the accused has changed his mind, it would only be just to interpret his previous intention where possible as only half-formed or provisional, and hold it to be an insufficient *mens rea*' . . . Any [such] suggestion . . . would greatly undermine the law of attempt. There must be few cases where the defendant would not accept the need to give up the attempt in certain circumstances . . . [Also] the problems of proof would be considerable . . .
>
> [W]hat other reasons exist for allowing [the excuse] to relieve the defendant of responsibility? First, it is argued that any dangerousness of character is negatived by clear evidence of abandonment. An acceptance of abandonment as an excuse would . . . show that the psychological barrier had not been crossed. Under English law, as we have seen, such late abandonment could not amount to an excuse because a proximate act has already been committed. On the other hand such questions of individual psychology and relative dangerousness are the very stuff of mitigation and sentencing policy . . .
>
> The second reason often advanced for allowing a defence of withdrawal is one of legal policy. It is claimed that since it is a prime purpose of the criminal law to prevent the occurrence of harm, it makes sense to provide a reasonable inducement for the attempter to desist before any real harm is done . . . The importance of the argument turns upon how realistic it is. How likely is it that a man who is sufficiently far along the path towards committing a criminal offence, that he would be guilty of an attempt if stopped, and who then decides not to commit it, would change his mind again and decide to carry on, since he realises he is guilty of the attempt anyway? The argument is far-fetched[64] . . .
>
> It has been strongly argued, then, that mitigation is not enough in cases of voluntary abandonment and that 'No argument of deterrence, reformation or prevention seems to require the punishment of one who is truly repentant and has done no harm.'

[Wasik, nevertheless, concludes that abandonment should only be relevant in mitigation of sentence.]"

---

63 If this latter view is adopted, must the abandonment be prompted by a commendable motive? cf. Fletcher, *Rethinking Criminal Law* (1978), pp.193–194.

64 cf. H. Wechsler, "The Treatment in Inchoate Crimes in the Model Penal Code" (1961) 61 Col. L.R. 571, 617–618.

R.A. Duff, Criminal Attempts (1996), pp.395–396:

"The intending rapist, murderer, or wounder who voluntarily abandons his attempt at the last moment has already attacked his victim, even if he aborted the attack himself . . . Surely he should not be able to escape all criminal liability by his abandonment? . . . [W]e should retain a narrow general law of attempts, supplemented (when necessary) by more specific offences capturing particularly wrongful kinds of conduct which fall outside its scope." 10–030

Duff's objectivist account would not necessarily lead to the complete acquittal of those who abandon their attempts (as they would be guilty of other offences) but would restrict the crime of attempt itself. Is such an approach preferable to that of the current law's reliance upon judicial discretion at the sentencing stage? 10–031

2. Mens rea

The Criminal Attempts Act 1981 s.1(1) provides that the defendant must act "with intent to commit an offence". 10–032

In *Whybrow*,[65] D constructed a device and administered an electric shock to his wife while she was taking a bath. The Court of Appeal held that while an intention to kill or to cause grievous bodily harm would suffice for the completed crime of murder, for attempted murder an intention to kill was necessary. This was because for attempted murder "the intent becomes the principal ingredient of the crime". In *O'Toole*,[66] D was charged with attempted arson (causing criminal damage by fire). It was held that while recklessness would suffice for the completed offence,[67] there had to be intention for the attempted offence.

If the complete crime can be committed recklessly or negligently, why does this same mens rea not suffice for an attempt to commit the crime?

R. v Mohan [1976] Q.B. 1 (Court of Appeal, Criminal Division):

JAMES LJ: 10–033

"In our judgment it is well established law that intent (*mens rea*) is an essential ingredient of the offence of attempt . . .

An attempt to commit crime is itself an offence. Often it is a grave offence. Often it is as morally culpable as the completed offence which is attempted but not in fact committed. Nevertheless it falls within the class of conduct which is preparatory to the commission of a

65 *R. v Whybrow (Arthur George)* (1951) 35 Cr. App. R. 141; (1951) 95 S.J. 745 CA. See also *R. v Pond* [1984] Crim. L.R. 164 CA.

66 *R. v O'Toole (Michael)* [1987] Crim. L.R. 759 CA.

67 Criminal Damage Act 1971 s.1(2).

> crime and is one step removed from the offence which is attempted. The court must not strain to bring within the offence of attempt, conduct which does not fall within the well-established bounds of the offence. On the contrary, the court must safeguard against extension of those bounds save by the authority of Parliament."

10–034 In the case of attempted crime, we are punishing in the absence of any harm (or "first order harm"). While such an approach can be justified, it is surely only permissible when dealing with the highest degree of blame. Exceptions to the paradigm of criminal liability involve extensions of liability and should be rigidly controlled. As attempt is essentially a crime of mens rea, with the actus reus performing only a secondary or subsidiary role, only the clearest form of mens rea should suffice, namely, intention.

This reasoning was given statutory force by the Criminal Attempts Act 1981 s.1(1). It is now clear that even for attempting a crime of strict liability, D must intend to produce the prohibited consequence.[68]

10–035 What meaning is to be attributed to the word "intention" in s.1(1)? In *Mohan*,[69] it was held that this involved "proof of specific intent, a decision to bring about, in so far as it lies within the accused's power, the commission of the offence which it is alleged the D attempted to commit, no matter whether the D desired that consequence of his act or not". This was approved, after the coming into force of the Criminal Attempts Act 1981, in *Millard and Vernon*,[70] where it was stated that a direct or purposive intention was required. Intention had to bear its "ordinary meaning", namely, that D must have "decided, so far as in him lay, to bring about" the result. It would, of course, be possible (albeit messy) for intention to bear different meanings in different contexts and for direct intent to be required here as the concept of an "attempt" connotes trying or meaning to achieve a result. However, the courts have rejected such an approach holding that "intention" bears the same meaning, whether for a completed crime or an attempt.

R. v Pearman (1984) 80 Cr. App. R. 259 (Court of Appeal, Criminal Division):

10–036 STUART-SMITH J:

> "We see no reason why the passing of the 1981 Act should have altered the law as to what is meant by the word 'intent'. The purpose of the Act was to deal with other matters rather than the content of the word 'intent'. We can see no reason why the judgment of the court in that case [*Mohan*] should not still be binding upon this court.

68 This was probably the position at common law: *Gardner v Akeroyd* [1952] 2 Q.B. 743; [1952] 2 T.L.R. 169 Div Ct; cf. *R. v Collier* [1960] Crim. L.R. 204. It should, however, be borne in mind that most strict liability offences are summary offences which cannot be attempted. For further discussion, see: Duff, *Criminal Attempts* (1996), pp.17–22; G. Yaffe, *Attempts* (Oxford: OUP, 2010), Ch.4.

69 *R. v Mohan (John Patrick)* [1976] Q.B. 1; [1975] 2 W.L.R. 859 CA.

70 *R. v Millard and Vernon* [1987] Crim. L.R. 393 CA.

> The words of James LJ [in *Mohan*] which he used at the end of that passage, namely 'no matter whether the accused desired that consequence of his act or not', are probably designed to deal with a case where the accused has, as a primary purpose, some other object, for example, a man who plants a bomb in an aeroplane, which he knows is going to take off, it being his primary intention that he should claim the insurance on the aeroplane when the freight goes down into the sea. The jury would not be put off from saying that he intended to murder the crew simply by saying that he did not want or desire to kill the crew, but that was something that he inevitably intended to do. Similarly, for example, a man who is cornered by the police when he is in a car may have the primary purpose of simply escaping from that situation. If he drives straight at the police officers at high speed, a jury is likely to conclude that he intended to injure a police officer and maybe cause him serious grievous bodily harm."

In *Hales*,[71] it was accepted that the *Woollin* test of intention applied to attempted murder but that, on the facts, a *Woollin* direction was not necessary. Accordingly, it seems clear now that the concept of "intention" bears the same meaning here as elsewhere in the criminal law. The Law Commission has endorsed this approach, stating that it would be inappropriate to have a special test for "intent" that differed from that applied to all other criminal offences. Intention "should not be limited to purpose but should encompass '*Woollin*' intent".[72] **10–037**

What mens rea is required with regard to relevant surrounding circumstances? The position at common law appears to have been that while the consequence had to be intended, recklessness with regard to circumstances would suffice for attempt, provided such recklessness would suffice for the completed offence.[73] Thus if D, being reckless as to whether his first wife was alive, were about to go through a second marriage ceremony, he could be convicted of attempted bigamy. The 1981 Act draws no distinction between consequences and circumstances, but simply states that the D must act "with intent to commit an offence". Despite the wording of this statute, the common law approach was confirmed in the case of *Khan*.

In *Khan*,[74] D attempted to have sexual intercourse with a non-consenting girl, but failed. The trial judge directed the jury that recklessness as to whether the girl consented was sufficient for attempted rape.[75] On appeal, the Court of Appeal held that, for the offence of attempted rape, D had the requisite intention if they had an intention to have intercourse plus a knowledge of or recklessness as to the circumstances of the woman's absence of consent.[76]

---

71 *R. v Hales (Ricky)* [2005] EWCA Crim 1118.

72 Law Commission Paper No.318, *Conspiracy and Attempts* (2009), para.8.91.

73 *R. v Pigg (Stephen)* [1982] 1 W.L.R. 762; (1982) 74 Cr. App. R. 352 CA; R. Buxton, "Inchoate Offences: Incitement and Attempt" [1973] Crim. L.R. 656, 661–664.

74 *R. v Khan (Mohammed Iqbal)* [1990] 1 W.L.R. 813; (1990) 91 Cr. App. R. 29 CA. See R.A. Duff, "The Circumstances of an Attempt" (1991) 50 C.L.J. 100; G.R. Sullivan, "Intent, Subjective Recklessness and Culpability" (1992) 12 O.J.L.S. 381; D. Yang, "Recklessness and Circumstances in Criminal Attempts" (2023) 17 Crim. Law and Philosophy 359.

75 It should be noted that this case pre-dates the Sexual Offences Act 2003. At the time of the offence, the mens rea of the offence of rape required that D intended penile penetration with a woman and that, at the time, he either knew or was reckless as to whether she consented: Sexual Offences (Amendment) Act 1976 s.1(1). Recklessness is no longer part of the mens rea for rape: see paras 6-035-6-040.

76 *R. v Khan* (1990) 91 Cr. App. R. 29 at 34.

10–038 It is possible to support such an approach. If recklessness as to surrounding circumstances suffices for the complete offence it should also suffice for an attempt, as "the mens rea of the complete crime should be modified only in so far as it is necessary in order to accommodate the concept of attempt".[77]

The approach adopted in *Khan* was followed in *Att-Gen's Reference (No.3 of 1992)*[78] where it was held that on a charge of attempted arson contrary to the Criminal Damage Act 1971 s.1(2) it was sufficient to prove an intention to cause damage by fire and that D was reckless as to whether life would thereby be endangered. It was stated that for an attempt "it must be shown that the defendant intended to achieve that which was missing from the full offence". In *Khan*, what was missing was sexual intercourse. In *Att-Gen's Reference (No.3 of 1992)* what was missing was damage to property. Intention must be proved in relation to these missing elements but beyond that only the same mens rea as for the full crime need be proved.

However, *Khan* and *Att-Gen's Reference (No.3 of 1992)* are distinguishable from each other. *Khan* was clearly dealing with a surrounding circumstance: whether the woman was consenting. In *Att-Gen's Reference (No.3 of 1992)* the offence element of "whether the life of another would be thereby endangered" can be viewed as a consequence. Under s.1(2), two consequences need to be achieved: damage to property and a state of affairs perceived to be life-threatening by an ordinary prudent person. While intention is required for the first consequence (damage to property) because that was what was "missing", recklessness with regard to the second consequence (creating a life-threatening situation) suffices. If this reading of the case is adopted:

> ". . . [t]he cases decided prior to *Attorney-General's Reference (No.3 of 1992)* are reconcilable on the basis that, in the earlier decisions, the relevant consequences had always been a 'missing element', i.e. something that had not materialised."

But this nevertheless represents a significant extension of the law.[79]

10–039 What mens rea is required for surrounding circumstances in offences of negligence (for example, rape) or strict liability (for example, rape of a child under 13)? On a "simplistic"[80] reading of *Att-Gen's Reference (No.3 of 1992)* there only need be intent with regard to "what is missing" and, beyond that, only that mens rea (or lack of it) required for the full offence need be established. So, for attempted rape D would need to intend penetration but negligence as to consent would suffice. For attempted rape of a child under 13, D would need to intend penetration but his honest and reasonable belief that the child was 16 would not exculpate. The Law Commission proposed that for crimes that require recklessness or

---

77 Ormerod and Laird, *Smith, Hogan and Ormerod's Criminal Law*, 16th edn (2021), p.439. cf. J.J. Child, A.P. Simester, J.R. Spencer, F. Stark, and G.J. Virgo, *Simester and Sullivan's Criminal Law: Theory and Doctrine*, 8th edn (Oxford: Hart, 2022) p.380, and Yang, "Recklessness and Circumstances in Criminal Attempts" (2023) 17 Crim. Law and Philosophy 359, who argues that recklessness about circumstances amounts to an act of endangerment which should be dealt with by a new inchoate endangerment offence.

78 *Att-Gen's Reference (No.3 of 1992)* [1994] 1 W.L.R. 409; (1994) 98 Cr. App. R. 383 CA.

79 Child, Simester, Spencer, Stark, and Virgo, *Simester and Sullivan's Criminal Law: Theory and Doctrine*, 8th edn (Oxford: Hart, 2022), pp.383-384. cf. J.J. Child, "The Structure, Coherence and Limits of Inchoate Liability: The New Ulterior Element" (2014) 34 L.S. 537.

80 Law Commission Consultation Paper No.183, *Conspiracy and Attempts* (2007), para.14.48.

negligence or strict liability a D should only be liable for an attempt to commit that crime if he was subjectively reckless as to the circumstances:

> "[T]here may be very good reasons for defining a substantive offence with a requirement of objective fault, or with no fault at all, but the justification may be substantially weaker when applied to an inchoate offence of attempt."[81]

On the other hand, it can be argued that recklessness should not suffice even for clear circumstances such as those in *Khan*. The 1981 Act specifies very clearly that the defendant must act "with intent to commit an offence" and thus for surrounding circumstances, knowledge (the general equivalent to intention when dealing with surrounding circumstances).[82] This is the approach which has been taken in the case of *Pace*,[83] which is inconsistent with the earlier decisions in *Khan* and *Att-Gen's Reference (No.3 of 1992)*.

R. v Pace [2014] EWCA Crim 186 (Court of Appeal, Criminal Division):

The Ds, who were scrap metal dealers, received a series of visits from undercover police officers in pursuance of a police operation to test whether scrap metal yards would accept purportedly stolen items. The Ds bought metal items such as earthing tape and power cables described to them by the officers as "having been stolen from the back of a van". It was an agreed fact that the property was not stolen but belonged to the police. The Ds were charged with attempting to convert criminal property contrary to s.327 of Pt 7 (Money Laundering) of the Proceeds of Crime Act 2002, the state of mind applicable to the substantive offence being knowledge or suspicion (s.340(3)). They were convicted and appealed. **10–040**

DAVIS LJ:

"1. The principal issue raised on these two appeals relates to the mental element required for criminal attempt. It is one that, albeit in the context of differing underlying substantive criminal offences, has caused difficulties over the years. Various decisions of the courts in those years do not always reveal a consistency in approach and sometimes, it has to be said, reveal a possible inconsistency in approach. It is also an area which has attracted much academic debate; and there too considerable divergences in approach have been manifested.

81 Law Commission Paper No.318, *Conspiracy and Attempts* (2009), para.8.128.

82 An earlier Law Commission Paper (No.102, 1980) stated that an intention as to every element of the offence was required (although in practice knowledge of surrounding circumstances would suffice to establish the necessary intent) (para.2.15).

83 *R. v Pace (Martin Edward)* [2014] EWCA Crim 186; [2014] 1 W.L.R. 2867. Following *Pace*, the Crown conceded that the convictions had to be quashed in *R. v Smith (Joseph)* [2014] EWCA Crim 1941 (a case which arose out of the same undercover operation that involved *Pace*), and in *R. v Wheeler (Stephen)* [2014] EWCA Crim 2706 (a case which arose out of a similar operation).

2. This issue requires consideration of the meaning and effect of s.1 of the Criminal Attempts Act 1981 ('the 1981 Act'): a section which in the past has been judicially described as 'winning no prize for lucidity' . . .

3. The trial judge decided that in this case the applicable mens rea for the offences of [attempting to conceal, disguise or convert criminal property] . . . was capable of being suspicion . . .

21. . . . [The trial judge told the jury]

'The law is clear: the prosecution must prove against each defendant on each count in which they are allegedly involved that at the time of accepting, checking, weighing or paying for the goods he either knew or suspected that they were stolen or had otherwise been obtained dishonestly' . . .

He went on to explain to the jury, among other things, that 'suspicion . . . falls below knowledge or belief'. He further instructed them that the suspicion did not need to be firmly grounded or even based on reasonable grounds.

22. Complaint is made by the appellants with regard to these directions . . .

35. That, then, leads to what is at the heart of these appeals: the mens rea which the prosecution was, in law, required to prove if it could make out its case of attempting to conceal, disguise or convert criminal property. (For shorthand, we will hereafter describe it as attempting to convert criminal property) . . .

46. A convenient starting point is this. Where the substantive criminal offence specifically requires the consequence of an act, it is well established that an attempt to commit that offence ordinarily requires proof of intent as to that consequence. To take a familiar example, the required intent for murder is either an intent to kill or an intent to cause really serious injury. The required consequence of the act is, of course, death. Accordingly, for a charge of attempted murder to be made out the intent which must be proved is an intent to kill: see *Whybrow* (1951) 35 Cr App R 141. That remains the case since the 1981 Act. Of course, that is an offence different from the present case. But . . . [counsel for the appellants] is at least entitled to make the point that that case is an illustration of the proposition that the mental element required to make a person guilty of an attempted offence may well be different from, and at a higher level than, that applicable to the substantive offence itself . . .

61. The starting point has to be section 1(1) of the 1981 . . . Mr Farrell [leading counsel for the prosecution] did at one stage . . . suggest that section 1(3) of the 1981 Act of itself provided a complete answer in favour of the Crown. But this cannot be right. That subsection only applies where 'the facts of the case' had been as the accused had believed them to be. But in the present proceedings the Crown's case had been put not on the basis of belief but on the basis of suspicion. Accordingly, one has to revert to section 1(1). That said, we would at least agree

with Mr Farrell's acceptance that the 'intention' referred to in section 1(3) must be the same as the intention referred to in section 1(1): that is to say, an intent to commit the offence.

62. Turning, then, to s.1(1) [of the 1981 Act] we consider that, as a matter of ordinary language and in accordance with principle, an 'intent to commit an offence' connotes an intent to commit all the elements of the offence. We can see no sufficient basis, whether linguistic or purposive, for construing it otherwise.

63. Once that is appreciated, the fault line in the Crown's argument is revealed. A constituent element of the offence of converting criminal property is, as we have said, that the property in question *is* criminal property. That is an essential part of the offence. Accordingly, an intent to commit the offence involves, in the present case, an intent to convert criminal property: and that connotes an intent that the property should *be* criminal property. But the Crown's argument glosses over that. Its argument connotes that the property in question which it is intended to be converted is *property* known or suspected to constitute or represent benefit from criminal conduct. It ignores the requirement for the substantive offence that the property concerned must be *criminal property* (as defined). The Crown, in effect, thus seeks to make it a criminal offence to intend to convert property suspecting, if not knowing, that it is stolen. But that is not what s.327, read with s.340(3), provides.

64. Reflecting this difficulty in the Crown's argument, there is this further point to be made. **10–041**
For the purpose of the substantive offence, a person may in point of fact convert property intending and believing that it is criminal property: yet he will not be guilty of the substantive offence if, in fact, it is not criminal property (*Montila* [2004] UKHL 50). It is most odd that, on the Crown's case, such a person who cannot on such a scenario be liable for the substantive offence can nevertheless be made liable, where his state of mind is one of suspicion only, if what is charged is, instead, an attempt to commit the offence. We have the greatest difficulty in seeing that the provisions of s.1 of the 1981 Act were designed to bring about such a result.

65. We further consider . . . that such a conclusion is supported by the approach of Parliament taken to conspiracy cases as enunciated in s.1 of the 1977 Act, as amended, and as interpreted by the courts . . .

66. We say that for the following reasons.

i) First, the provisions of s.1 of the 1977 Act, as amended, were introduced by the 1981 Act itself. One would therefore be predisposed to anticipate a coherence of approach in the relevant provisions of the two statutes in this regard.

ii) Second, offences of criminal attempt and offences of criminal conspiracy are both inchoate offences. Both have in common that they are looking to what is planned for the future. That remains so even if counts formulated as conspiracy counts are commonly sought to be proved by proof of the commission of substantive offences.

iii) Third, it is not difficult to envisage scenarios—not least, as it happens, in money laundering cases—where what may be charged as an attempt would be capable of being charged as conspiracy, and vice versa.

67. In this regard, we think that the approach taken by the courts to s.1 of the 1977 Act is most revealing. [His lordship then reviewed the case-law, including *Saik*, discussed above at 512] . . .

74. [T]his authority establishes that a conspiracy to commit an offence under s.327 of the 2002 Act . . . can require a higher level of mens rea than that applicable to the actual commission of the substantive offence itself. True it is that the language of s.1 of the 1977 Act is not precisely the same as s.1 of the 1981 Act. Even so . . . s.1 of the 1977 Act can properly be read so as to take account of the 1981 Act, and vice versa. Accordingly it makes it, in our view, all the more principled to conclude that likewise in the case of attempt a higher level of mens rea may be required under s.1(1) than is applicable to the substantive offence itself: and thus that, in the present case, proof of suspicion will not suffice on a count of attempted money laundering . . .

78. For the reasons we have given, we conclude that the appeals must be allowed. For the purposes of a count of attempted money laundering proof of a mental element of suspicion (only) does not suffice . . .

79. We do appreciate the anxieties of the Crown in the context of money laundering. Such cases are not always easy of proof . . . But, . . . the policy behind the substantive offences of money laundering cannot be allowed to distort the meaning of s.1 of the 1981 Act . . .

81. That may or may not create problems for prosecutors. However, we observe that there in any event may well be . . . other charges potentially available . . . [Further] the margin between knowledge and suspicion is perhaps not all that great, at all events where the person has reasonable grounds for suspicion. Where a defendant can be shown deliberately to have turned a blind eye to the provenance of goods and deliberately to have failed to ask obvious questions, that can be capable, depending on the circumstances, of providing evidence going to prove knowledge or belief . . ."

Appeal allowed

10–042 Attempt is essentially a crime of mens rea. Given this, there is a strong argument that it ought to be restricted to those who act with intent (or its equivalent, knowledge or, it seems, according to *Pace*, belief)) in relation to all the elements of the offence: "the *mens rea* elements of criminal attempts do significant work in preventing over-criminalisation, and ought not to be narrowed without statutory authority."[84] Such an approach may be seen as being compatible with the wording of the Criminal Attempts Act and as achieving "a coherent model of attempts liability".[85]

84 D. Bruneau and A. Taylor, "In defence of Pace and Rogers" [2015] *Archbold Review* 6, 7.

85 J.J. Child and A. Hunt, "*Pace* and *Rogers* and the *mens rea* of criminal attempt: *Khan* on the scrapheap?" (2014) J. Crim. L. 220, 225. cf. P. Mirfield, "Intention and criminal attempts" [2015] Crim. L.R. 142 and A.P. Simester, "The Mens Rea of Criminal Attempts" (2015) 131

> "The Criminal Attempts Act locates the wrong of attempt as acting with the 'intent' to commit an offence. This approach isolates that wrong."[86]

It also has the merit of observing the rule of statutory interpretation that "where there is uncertainty, criminal statutes should be interpreted in the way least favourable to the prosecution".[87] Thus, the decision in *Pace*, that a conviction for attempt cannot be based upon suspicion is to be supported. However, although the Court of Appeal was critical of aspects of the decision in *Khan* it did not overrule it.[88] Instead, it was distinguished on the questionable basis that, unlike *Khan*, in which the full offence of rape would have been committed if the defendants had succeeded in penetrating the victim, the case before it concerned an impossible attempt, since the "scrap" metal involved belonged to the police and was not criminal property.[89] The Court of Appeal certified a point of general public importance, but refused leave to appeal. Although commentators have highlighted the desirability of the Supreme Court considering the case, in order to clarify the mens rea of attempt,[90] an appeal to the Supreme Court was not pursued.[91] In the meantime, we are in the difficult position of having "a trio of appeal cases, in *Khan, Att-Gen's Reference (No.3 of 1992)* and *Pace*, that sound wholly conflicting notes",[92] with *Khan* apparently dealing with possible attempts and *Pace* with those which are impossible.[93] Furthermore, as *Att-Gen's Reference (No.3 of 1992)* demonstrates, it is difficult to draw a clear distinction between consequences and circumstances. For example, it could be argued that s.1(2) requires the causing of criminal damage to be committed in the circumstances of it being life-endangering. It is highly inappropriate to make criminal liability hinge on such fine distinctions that have no bearing on culpability.

A final problem remains: will a so-called "conditional intention" suffice for attempt? If D opens a suitcase, intending to steal its contents "on condition they are of some value", can they be convicted of attempted theft?[94]

L.Q.R. 169. By contrast, Virgo suggests that *Pace* has "destabilised" the offence of attempt "by holding that the relevant mental element is intention" and that the court should have relied upon the Criminal Attempts Act 1981 s.1(3), holding that "the defendants . . . were properly acquitted of the attempt if they only suspected rather than believed that the metal had been stolen": G. Virgo, "Criminal attempts: the law of unintended circumstances" (2014) 73 C.L.J. 244, 244–246. See also Stark, "The Mens Rea of Criminal Attempt" [2014] *Archbold Review* 7, 9.

86 Child and Hunt, "*Pace* and *Rogers* and the *mens rea* of criminal attempt: *Khan* on the scrapheap?" (2014) J. Crim. L. 220, 225.

87 Mirfield, "Intention and criminal attempts" [2015] Crim. L.R. 142, 147.

88 cf. Child, Simester, Spencer, Stark and Virgo, *Simester and Sullivan's Criminal Law: Theory and Doctrine*, 8th edn (2022), pp.380-381 and 384, who suggest that the preferable approach Is to treat both *Khan* and *Att-Gen's Reference (No.3 of 1992)* [1994] 1 W.L.R. 409; (1994) 98 Cr. App. R. 383 as having been overruled by *Pace*.

89 *Pace* [2014] EWCA Crim 186; [2014] 1 W.L.R. 2867 at [52]. For further discussion, see Stark, "The Mens Rea of Criminal Attempt" [2014] *Archbold Review* 7, 9; Bruneau and Taylor, "In defence of Pace and Rogers" [2015] *Archbold Review* 6, 8; Child and Hunt, "*Pace* and *Rogers* and the *mens rea* of criminal attempt: *Khan* on the scrapheap?" (2014) J. Crim. L. 220, 222–223; Mirfield, "Intention and criminal attempts" [2015] Crim. L.R. 142, 145, A.P. Simester, "The law of criminal attempts" (2015) 131 L.Q.R. 169, 170.

90 Mirfield, "Intention and criminal attempts" [2015] Crim. L.R. 142, 148; Simester, "The law of criminal attempts" (2015) 131 L.Q.R. 169, 170; Bruneau and Taylor, "In defence of Pace and Rogers" [2015] *Archbold Review* 6, 8; Child and Hunt, "*Pace* and *Rogers* and the *mens rea* of criminal attempt: *Khan* on the scrapheap?" (2014) J. Crim. L. 220, 222–223.

91 Ormerod and Laird, *Smith, Hogan and Ormerod's Criminal Law*, 16th edn (2022), p.437 fn.36.

92 Mirfield, "Intention and criminal attempts" [2015] Crim. L.R. 142, 148.

93 See further, Stark, "The Mens Rea of Criminal Attempt" [2014] *Archbold Review* 7, 9, who argues that the Court of Appeal reached the right decision but for the wrong reasons and, in particular, that the criticism of *Khan* was misplaced. cf. Bruneau and Taylor, "In defence of Pace and Rogers" [2015] *Archbold Review* 6, 9.

94 In relation to conditional intention and the law of theft, see para.8–109.

The Law Commission has proposed that an "intention to commit an offence includes a conditional intent to commit it".[95] As they state:

> "If D breaks into a car intending to steal if he or she finds something worth stealing, that is intention to steal. Such an intention is functionally equivalent to the intention of someone who drops a stone off a tall building, saying, 'I intend this stone to hit anyone who happens to be passing below'. Such a person intends to strike someone with the stone."[96]

3. Impossibility

10–043 Can there be criminal liability for attempting the impossible? If D shoots at V trying to kill them, but unknown to D, V has had a heart attack and is already dead, can D be liable for attempted murder?

Before the enactment of the Criminal Attempts Act 1981, the common law recognised three types of impossible attempts. First, an attempt will be legally impossible where D performs all the physical actions he intends to perform, but, unknown to him, what he has done does not amount to a crime. For example, he intends to steal an umbrella but unknown to him, the umbrella turns out to be his own. In *Haughton v Smith*,[97] D was charged with attempting to handle stolen goods contrary to the Theft Act 1968 s.22. D had actually handled the goods but, unknown to them, they were not stolen goods.[98] The House of Lords unanimously held that there could be no liability for attempt in such circumstances. Second, an attempt may be physically impossible. For example, where D intends to pick a pocket and places their hand in V's pocket, but it is empty; there is nothing to steal. In *Partington v Williams*, it was held that there could be no liability in such cases because the commission of the substantive offence was, in the circumstances, impossible.[99] In *DPP v Nock*,[100] the House of Lords held that liability depended on the manner in which the particular indictment was framed. If, in an attempted theft case, the indictment was limited to an attempt to steal specific property or property from a specific place, then if the property was not there, the actus reus of the complete crime, namely, the appropriation of the *specific* property belonging to another, would be incapable of proof and D would escape liability. On the other hand, if the indictment alleged an attempt to steal from the person generally, then the pickpocket who puts their hand in an empty pocket could be liable for attempted theft. Third, a crime may be impossible in the circumstances because of D's ineptitude, inefficiency or the adoption of insufficient means. For example, where D tries to force open a door with an iron bar, but the iron bar is too weak ever to do so. Here the common law took a different approach from that adopted in relation to the above two categories of impossibility and held that there could be criminal liability for attempt. The reasoning was that such crimes were not really "impossible"

95 Law Commission Paper No.318, *Conspiracy and Attempts* (2009), para.8.106.
96 Law Commission Consultation Paper No.183, *Conspiracy and Attempts* (2007), para.16.74.
97 *Haughton v Smith* [1975] A.C. 476.
98 The goods had been stolen, but when the police commandeered the van in which the goods were travelling, the goods ceased to be "stolen" by virtue of the Theft Act 1968 s.24(3) as they had been "restored to lawful custody".
99 *Partington v Williams* (1976) 62 Cr. App. R. 220; [1977] Crim. L.R. 609 Div Ct.
100 *DPP v Nock* [1978] A.C. 979; [1978] 3 W.L.R. 57 HL.

because the crime *was* possible with different means. D could open the door; they simply needed to fetch and use a stronger iron bar.[101]

CRIMINAL ATTEMPTS ACT 1981 S.1:

"(2) A person may be guilty of attempting to commit an offence to which this section applies even though the facts are such that the commission of the offence is impossible. **10–044**

(3) In any case where—

(a) apart from this subsection a person's intention would not be regarded as having amounted to an intent to commit an offence; but
(b) if the facts of the case had been as he believed them to be, his intention would be so regarded,

then, for the purposes of subsection (1) above, he shall be regarded as having had an intent to commit that offence.

(4) This section applies to any offence which, if it were completed, would be triable in England and Wales as an indictable offence . . ."

Section 1(2) provides that there can be liability for attempting the impossible, irrespective of the category of impossibility. Section 1(3) purports to confirm the self-evident proposition that where a person believes the facts to be such that they would be committing a crime, they are to be regarded as having the necessary intention to commit the offence. This means that a D who intends to handle a particular mobile phone believing it to be stolen, when in fact it is not stolen, cannot argue that they intended to handle a "non-stolen mobile phone". Section 1(3) makes it plain that if they believed the mobile phone was stolen, they intended to handle a "stolen mobile phone". This provision is actually completely redundant. Intention relates purely to a D's subjective state of mind. An intention to handle a stolen mobile phone is just that: an intention to handle a mobile phone believed to be stolen. The objective status of the goods (stolen or not stolen) has no bearing upon the defendant's intention. **10–045**

These provisions represent a clear and emphatic victory for the "subjectivist" theory of attempts where emphasis is placed on the intention of the defendant and the firmness of that intention. However, in *Anderton v Ryan*,[102] the House of Lords was not prepared to accept such blatant subjectivism and, declaring that the statute would lead to "asinine"[103] results, proceeded to subvert the legislation from its original purpose. In this case, D had purchased a video recorder, believing it to be stolen, and had made a confession to this effect to the police. However, since there was no evidence that the recorder had been stolen, the prosecution had to treat it as if it was not stolen. D was convicted of dishonestly

101 *Haughton* [1975] A.C. 476 at 500.
102 *Anderton v Ryan* [1985] A.C. 560; (1985) 81 Cr. App. R. 166 HL.
103 *Anderton v Ryan* (1985) 81 Cr. App. R. 166 at 175.

attempting to handle the stolen video recorder. The House of Lords quashed D's conviction, adopting the objectivist approach that, where a person with a guilty mind "embarks on and completes a course of conduct which is objectively innocent",[104] they did not commit an offence under the Criminal Attempts Act 1981 s.1.

10-046 In a dramatic about-turn, the House of Lords within months overruled itself and held that there could be criminal liability in all cases of attempting the impossible.

R. v Shivpuri [1987] A.C. 1 (House of Lords):

10-047 D thought he was dealing in prohibited drugs but it transpired that the substance in his possession was only snuff or similarly harmless vegetable matter. He was convicted of attempting to be knowingly concerned in dealing with prohibited drugs, contrary to the Criminal Attempts Act 1981 s.1(1) and the Customs and Excise Management Act 1979 s.170(1)(b). He appealed against his conviction.

LORD BRIDGE:

"[T]he first question to be asked is whether the appellant intended to commit the offences of being knowingly concerned in dealing with and harbouring drugs of Class A or Class B with intent to evade the prohibition on their importation. Translated into more homely language the question may be rephrased, without in any way altering its legal significance, in the following terms: did the appellant intend to receive and store (harbour) and in due course pass on to third parties (deal with) packages of heroin or cannabis which he knew had been smuggled into England from India? The answer is plainly yes, he did. Next, did he in relation to each offence, do an act which was more than merely preparatory to the commission of the offence? The act relied on in relation to harbouring was the receipt and retention of the packages found in the lining of the suitcase. The act relied on in relation to dealing was the meeting at Southall station with the intended recipient of one of the packages. In each case the act was clearly more than preparatory to the commission of the *intended* offence; it was not and could not be more than merely preparatory to the commission of the *actual* offence, because the facts were such that the commission of the actual offence was impossible. Here then is the nub of the matter. Does the 'act which is more than merely preparatory to the commission of the offence' in section 1(1) of the Act of 1981 (the *actus reus* of the statutory offence of attempt) require any more than an act which is more than merely preparatory to the commission of the offence which the defendant intended to commit? Section 1(2) must surely indicate a negative answer; if it were otherwise, whenever the facts were such that the commission of the actual offence was impossible, it would be impossible to prove an act more than merely preparatory to the commission of that offence and subsections (1) and (2) would contradict each other.

---

104 *Anderton v Ryan* (1985) 81 Cr. App. R. 166 per Lord Bridge at 180.

This very simple, perhaps over simple, analysis leads me to the provisional conclusion that the appellant was rightly convicted of the two offences of attempt with which he was charged. But can this conclusion stand with *Anderton v Ryan*? . . .

Running through Lord Roskill's speech and my own in *Anderton v Ryan* is the concept of 'objectively innocent' acts which, in my speech certainly, are contrasted with 'guilty acts'.

I am satisfied on further consideration that the concept of 'objective innocence' is incapable of sensible application in relation to the law of criminal attempts. The reason for this is that any attempt to commit an offence which involves 'an act which is more than merely preparatory to the commission of the offence' but for any reason fails, so that in the event no offence is committed, must ex hypothesi, from the point of view of the criminal law, be 'objectively innocent'. What turns what would otherwise, from the point of view of the criminal law, be an innocent act into a crime is the intent of the actor to commit an offence . . . A puts his hand into B's pocket. Whether or not there is anything in the pocket capable of being stolen, if A intends to steal, his act is a criminal attempt; if he does not so intend, his act is innocent. A plunges a knife into a bolster in a bed. To avoid the complication of an offence of criminal damage, assume it to be A's bolster. If A believes the bolster to be his enemy, B, and intends to kill him, his act is an attempt to murder B; if he knows the bolster is only a bolster, his act is innocent. These considerations lead me to the conclusion that the distinction sought to be drawn in *Anderton v Ryan* between innocent and guilty acts considered 'objectively' and independently of the state of mind of the actor cannot be sensibly maintained.

Another conceivable ground of distinction which was to some extent canvassed in argument, **10–048**
both in *Anderton v Ryan* and in the instant case, though no trace of it appears in the speeches in *Anderton v Ryan*, is a distinction which would make guilt or innocence of the crime of attempt in a case of mistaken belief dependent on what, for want of a better phrase, I will call the defendant's dominant intention. According to the theory necessary to sustain this distinction, the appellant's dominant intention in *Anderton v Ryan* was to buy a cheap video recorder; her belief that it was stolen was merely incidental. Likewise in the hypothetical case of attempted unlawful sexual intercourse, the young man's dominant intention was to have intercourse with the particular girl; his mistaken belief that she was under 16 was merely incidental. By contrast, in the instant case, the appellant's dominant intention was to receive and distribute illegally imported heroin or cannabis.

Whilst I see the superficial attraction of this suggested ground of distinction, I also see formidable practical difficulties in its application. By what test is a jury to be told that a defendant's dominant intention is to be recognised and distinguished from his incidental but mistaken belief? But there is perhaps a more formidable theoretical difficulty. If this ground of distinction is relied on to support the acquittal of the appellant in *Anderton v Ryan*, it can only do so on the basis that her mistaken belief that the video recorder was stolen played no significant part in her decision to buy it and therefore she may be acquitted of the intent to handle stolen goods. But this line of reasoning runs into head-on collision with section 1(3) of the Act of 1981. The theory produces a situation where, apart from the subsection, her intention would not be regarded as having amounted to any intent to commit an offence. Section 1(3) (b) then requires one to ask whether, if the video recorder had in fact been stolen, her intention would have been regarded as an intent to handle stolen goods. The answer must clearly be yes, it would. If she had bought the video recorder knowing it to be stolen, when in fact it was, it would have availed her nothing to say that her dominant intention was to buy a video recorder because it was cheap and that her knowledge that it was stolen was merely incidental. This seems to me fatal to the dominant intention theory.[105]

. . . there is no valid ground on which *Anderton v Ryan* can be distinguished. I have made clear my own conviction . . . that the decision was wrong."

Appeal dismissed

10-049 The law is now clear. There can be liability in all cases of attempting the impossible. In *Att-Gen's Reference (Nos 3 and 4 of 2005)*,[106] D was convicted of attempting to cause grievous bodily harm when he kicked a man who was already dead. In *Jones*,[107] D was convicted of attempting to incite (by text message) a child under the age of 13 to engage in sexual activity contrary to the Sexual Offences Act 2003 s.8. On the facts, the crime was impossible as the recipient of the message was an adult policewoman pretending to be a child under the age of 13.

Is such an approach justifiable?

LAW COMMISSION (LAW COM. NO.102), ATTEMPT (1980), PARAS 2.96–2.98:

10-050 "2.96. We think it would be generally accepted that if a man possesses the appropriate *mens rea* and commits acts which are sufficiently proximate to the *actus reus* of a criminal offence, he is guilty of attempting to commit that offence. Where, with that intention, he commits acts which, if the facts were as he believed them to be, would have amounted to the *actus reus* of the full crime or would have been sufficiently proximate to amount to an attempt, we cannot see why his failure to appreciate the true facts should, in principle, relieve him of liability for the attempt. We stress that this solution to the problem does not punish people simply for their intentions. The necessity for proof of proximate acts remains. The fact that the impossibility of committing the full crime reduces the social danger is adequately reflected in the generally milder penalty which an attempt attracts instead of that for the full offence. And even if it is conceded that there may be some reduction in the social danger in cases of impossibility, it has to be borne in mind that a certain social danger undoubtedly remains. Defendants in cases such as *Haughton v Smith* and *Nock and Alsford* are prepared to do all they can to break the criminal law even though in the circumstances their attempts are

105 For a discussion of this dominant intention theory, see para.10-053.
106 *Att-Gen's Reference (Nos.3 and 4 of 2005)* [2005] EWCA Crim 574; [2005] 2 Cr. App. R. (S.) 98.
107 *R. v Jones (Ian Anthony)* [2007] EWCA Crim 1118; [2008] Q.B. 460.

> doomed to failure; and if they go unpunished, they may be encouraged to do better at the next opportunity. Finally, if the solution under consideration is accepted, it makes it possible to dispense with the doctrine of 'inadequate means' and with stained efforts to catch those who might otherwise escape by resort to broadly drawn indictments and an 'inferred general intention'.
>
> 2.97. If it is right in principle that an attempt should be chargeable even though the crime which it is sought to commit could not possibly be committed, we do not think that we should be deterred by the consideration that such a change in our law would also cover some extreme and exceptional cases in which a prosecution would be theoretically possible. An example would be where a person is offered goods at such a low price that he believes that they are stolen, when in fact they are not; if he actually purchases them, upon the principles which we have discussed he would be liable for an attempt to handle stolen goods. Another case which has been much debated is that raised in argument by Bramwell B in *R. v Collins* (1864) 9 Cox C.C. 497. If A takes his own umbrella, mistaking it for one belonging to B and intending to steal B's umbrella, is he guilty of attempted theft? Again, on the principles which we have discussed he would in theory be guilty but in neither case would it be realistic to suppose that a complaint would be made or that a prosecution would ensue. On the other hand, if our recommendations were formulated so as to exclude such cases, then it might well be impossible to obtain convictions in cases such as *Haughton v Smith*, where a defendant handles goods which were originally stolen, intending to handle stolen goods, but where, unknown to him, the goods had meanwhile been restored to lawful custody. Another example of possible difficulty which has been suggested is where a person in the erroneous belief that he can kill by witchcraft or magic takes action such as sticking pins into a model of his enemy—intending thereby to bring about his enemy's death. Could that person be charged with attempted murder? It may be that such conduct could be more than an act of mere preparation on the facts as the defendant believes them to be; and in theory, therefore, it is possible that such a defendant could be found guilty. In the ordinary course, we think that discretion in bringing a prosecution will be sufficient answer to any problems raised by such unusual cases; but even if a prosecution ensued, it may be doubted whether a jury would regard the acts in question as sufficient to amount to an attempt."

Supporters of the objective theory of attempts tend to reject such reasoning and assert that such "subjectivism" amounts to little more than punishing people for their guilty intentions. The Law Commission conceded the absurdity of there being liability in situations where a person buys legitimate goods but at such a low price that she thinks (wrongly) that they are stolen. It concluded that prosecutions would never be brought in such cases. Yet it was on broadly similar facts that a prosecution was brought in *Anderton v Ryan* leading the House of Lords to adopt some highly innovative techniques to ensure an acquittal. **10–051**

However, even the hardened "objectivist" concedes the necessity for liability in certain obvious cases. The problem is in isolating such situations.

George P. Fletcher, "Rethinking Criminal Law" (1978), pp.149–150, 152–154, 161–163, 165–166:

10–052 "It is agreed by all supporters of an objectivist approach to attempts that there should be no liability in the case of shooting at a tree stump with the intent to kill. Yet the courts have found liability in closely related situations . . . [A] Missouri court convicted on a charge of attempted murder for shooting at the bed where the intended victim usually slept (*State v Mitchell* 170 Mo. 633, 71 S.W. 175 (1902)) . . . Shooting at the intended victim's bed and aiming a gun manifest the intent to kill. In shooting at a tree stump, in contrast, there is nothing in the facts to indicate that an attempt is under way. According to objectivist theory, attempting is not just an event of inner experience. It is an effort in the real world to accomplish one's objective. Therefore, when the act is aptly related to that actor's objective, the courts perceive a manifest attempt to commit an offense. Yet when the act is objectively unrelated to the intent, as in the case of shooting at a tree stump, judges and theorists properly balk at positing an act of attempting. The notion of aptness here is obviously closely related to the principle of manifest criminality . . .

[T]he problem of aptness is one of assessing whether in the long run the type of conduct involved is likely to produce harm. If the type of conduct would produce harm in the long run, then the defendant's act is apt and a punishable attempt, even though it is impossible under the circumstances . . .

The principle that inapt efforts should be exempt from liability readily explains why the courts do not discern an act of attempting in the giving of an innocuous substance as an intended poison or abortifacient.

The difficult problem in these cases is drawing the distinction between giving the intended victim an innocuous substance and giving him too small a dosage of a noxious poison. It is the distinction between trying to kill by putting sugar in his coffee and trying to kill by administering a harmless dosage of cyanide. In the latter cases, the courts have been willing to convict, and as a result we are put to the challenge to explain why sugar makes the attempt inapt but a harmless dosage of cyanide makes it apt. As we discovered in our analysis of the shooting cases, the standard of aptness does not apply to isolated events, but rather to types or classes of acts. Apt attempts belong to a class of acts that are likely to generate harm. If the class is defined as administering a dosage of cyanide or other deadly poison, there is no doubt that the class of acts is likely to generate harm, and therefore we can regard every instance of the class as an apt attempt . . .

. . . The thesis is this: mistaken beliefs are relevant to what the actor is trying to do if they affect his incentive in acting. They affect his incentive if knowing of the mistake would give him a good reason for changing his course of conduct . . . Suppose the accused engages in sexual intercourse with a girl he takes to be under the age of consent; in fact, she is over age. Is he guilty of attempted statutory rape? In the normal case it would not be part of the actor's incentive that the girl be underage (again, one could imagine a variation in which the youth of the girl did bear upon the actor's motivation). If he is just as happy to have intercourse with a girl over age, then his mistake would not bear on his incentive and it would be incorrect to describe his act as trying to have intercourse with a girl under the age of consent . . . The thesis is that there should be liability in a case of impossibility only if the actor fails in his purpose. The only way to determine whether the actor is attempting an act that includes a particular circumstance, X, is to inquire: what would the actor do if he knew that X was not so? If he would behave in precisely the same way, we cannot say that his mistaken belief in X bears on his motivation; and if it does not, we cannot say that he is attempting to act with reference to X . . .

If applied to the cases of shooting at stumps and 'poisoning' with sugar, the test of rational motivation leads to convictions where the standard of aptness would favour an acquittal. It is obviously part of the actor's system of incentives that he believes the stump to be a person, or the dosage to be sufficient to kill. If told of the truth, he would presumably change his plans. So far as the standard of incentive is controlling, the person shooting at the stump is undoubtedly attempting to kill. The problem is whether the test of aptness should prevail over the theory of rational motivation in cases involving assaults on the core interests protected by the criminal law . . .

One reason to believe that the principle of aptness is indispensable in a comprehensive theory of attempt liability is that there is no other way to solve one case in which virtually everyone agrees that there should be no liability. That is the case of nominal efforts to inflict harm by superstitious means, say by black magic or witchcraft. The consensus of Western legal systems is that there should be no liability, regardless of the wickedness of intent, for sticking pins in a doll or chanting an incantation to banish one's enemy to the nether world. Against the background of the fears and taboos prevailing in modern Western society, objectivist theorists take these cases to be inapt attempts, therefore exempt from punishment. Yet the theory of rational motivation points in the direction of liability. If the intending party knows the truth about black magic (namely, that it does not work), he would have a good reason to change his plan of attack. To account for the consensus favouring an exemption in this type of case, we need the principle of aptness to offset the implications of the competing theory of rational motivation.

The problem that remains to be resolved is determining the relative scope of these two competing theories."

Duff supports an approach broadly similar to Fletcher's theory of rational motivation. Under his view, Mrs Ryan did not intend to handle a stolen video recorder as that played no motivational part in her conduct; her actions were not directed towards handling stolen goods; the fact that the goods were stolen was merely a side effect.[108] Both of these approaches are similar to the "dominant intention" theory rejected in *Shivpuri*. The problem with these theories is that they boil down to making liability dependent on motive. This is problematic in evidential terms and questionable in moral terms. Furthermore, as Fletcher points out, it leads to liability in the shooting at the tree-stump case. **10–053**

108 Duff, *Criminal Attempts* (1996), pp.378–379.

Duff rejects liability in such cases on the ground that the attack "fails so radically to engage with the world that it does not even amount to a failed attack". Fletcher's theory of aptness would similarly resolve some of these issues, but the real problem with his analysis is the failure to spell out the exact circumstances in which the theory of aptness is applicable and those in which it is appropriate to apply the theory of rational motivation.

English law has rejected the dominant intention (rational motivation) theory. The theory of aptness is broadly similar to the "objectively innocent" v "guilty acts" approach approved in *Anderton v Ryan*, which was rejected in *Shivpuri*. It is, of course, extremely difficult to capture these notions in a practicable statutory formulation.[109] However, it must remain questionable whether English law has adopted the right solution in ignoring these important considerations of principle and imposing liability in all these situations and then relying on prosecutorial discretion to avoid injustice.

C. PUNISHMENT OF ATTEMPTS

CRIMINAL ATTEMPTS ACT 1981 s.4(1):

10-054 "A person guilty . . . of attempting to commit an offence shall—

(a) if the offence attempted is murder or any other offence the sentence for which is fixed by law, be liable on conviction on indictment to imprisonment for life; and
(b) if the offence attempted is indictable but does not fall within paragraph (a) above, be liable on conviction on indictment to any penalty to which he would have been liable on conviction on indictment of that offence; and
(c) if the offence attempted is triable either way, be liable on summary conviction to any penalty to which he would have been liable on summary conviction of that offence."

10-055 The completed crime of theft carries a maximum sentence of seven years' imprisonment in England and Wales and attempted theft is punishable on conviction on indictment, up to the same maximum term of imprisonment. But this is not the approach taken in all jurisdictions. For example, in California, if theft there carried a presumptive penalty of seven years' imprisonment in the state prison, attempted theft would carry a presumptive penalty of three-and-a-half years' imprisonment, half the prescribed term of imprisonment.[110] This divergence of approach raises the fundamental question: should attempts be punished to the same, or to a lesser, extent as the completed crime? On what basis can either of these approaches be rationalised?

---

109 Duff, *Criminal Attempts* (1996), p.384. cf. B. Donnelly-Lazarov, *A Philosophy of Criminal Attempts* (Cambridge: CUP, 2015), Ch.6; S. Bock and F. Stark, "Preparatory Offences" in Ambos, Duff, Roberts, Weigend and Heinze (eds), *Core Concepts in Criminal law and Criminal Justice*, Vol.I (2019), pp.75–78. For a detailed alternative analysis to the subjectivist/objectivist approaches, see: G. Jaffe, "Criminal Attempts" (2014) 124 Yale L.J. 92.

110 California Penal Code (2020) s.664.

ANDREW ASHWORTH, "BELIEF, INTENT AND CRIMINAL LIABILITY" IN J. EEKELAAR AND J. BELL (EDS), OXFORD ESSAYS IN JURISPRUDENCE (1987), PP.16–17:

"Is A, who shoots at X intending to kill him but misses because X unexpectedly moves, any less culpable than B, who shoots at Y intending to kill him and does so? An external description of both sets of events would probably not suggest that they have 'done' the same thing, whereas an account which paid more attention to the actor's point of view and to matters which lay within the actor's control would suggest that they both intended and tried, to the same extent, to do the same thing. The argument here is that, because of the element of uncertainty in the outcome of things which we try to do, it would be wrong for assessments of culpability to depend on the occurrence or non-occurrence of the intended consequences. **10–056**

> 'Success or failure . . . makes no difference at all to [an agent's] moral status in relation to his original act. His original act, strictly considered, was simply his trying and *that* is what moral assessment must concern itself with.' (Winch, *Ethics and Action*, 1972, p.139)

. . . Moral blame and criminal liability should be based so far as possible on choice and control, on the trying and not on what actually happened thereafter.

What are the reasons for wishing to reduce the influence of chance upon criminal liability? It cannot be doubted that luck plays a considerable part in everyday events. Actual results also play a considerable part in judgements of others, and tend to dominate assessments in such fields as business, sport, and education. Those who try hard but are unsuccessful often receive less recognition than those who achieve goals (no matter how little effort they put into it). But these are not moral assessments of the individuals or their characters. If one turns to moral and social judgements, it is doubtful whether outcomes should be proper criteria. It may be desirable overall to have fewer bad outcomes and more good outcomes in society, but that does not lead to the conclusion that moral praise and blame should be allocated solely according to result. Indeed, a bad outcome stemming from a good intent may be a better predictor of good outcomes than a good outcome born of a bad intent. From time to time we may praise someone for producing a good result, even though it was not what he was trying to do, but this is more a reflection of our pleasure at the outcome than an assessment of his conduct and character. If we turn to blaming, is it not unacceptable to blame people for causing results irrespective of whether they were caused intentionally, negligently, or purely accidentally? Blaming is a moral activity which is surely only appropriate where the individual had some choice or control over the matter. For this reason the criminal law should seek to minimize the effect of luck upon the incidence and scale of criminal liability."[111]

---

111 See also A. Ashworth, "Criminal Attempts and the Role of Resulting Harm under the Code and in the Common Law" (1988) 19 *Rutgers Law Journal* 74, cf. B. Donnelly-Lazarov, *A Philosophy of Criminal Attempts: The Subjective Approach* (Cambridge: CUP, 2015) Ch.7; Duff, *Criminal Attempts* (1996), Ch.12.

10-057 A relatively common view is that punishment for attempts should depend upon the dangerousness of the defendant's actions; this is measured by determining how imminent the threatened harm is and by examining the reason for failure.

Sir Rupert Cross and Andrew Ashworth: The English Sentencing System, 3rd edn (1981), pp.154–155:

10-058 "[T]he question whether an attempt should be punished less severely than the completed crime is largely dependent on the reason why the attempt failed. If it failed because the attempter voluntarily abandoned the attempt, he should be punished less because he is less wicked or needs less deterring. If it failed because of his incompetence, either in executing his design clumsily or in choosing a method which, owing to his failure to appreciate the true facts, proved to be impossible, he may be punished less on the ground that he represents less of a social danger than successful criminals. If it failed because of someone's intervention before he had done all he set out to do, he may be treated more leniently than the successful criminal: his wickedness may be less, since (as Blackstone said) it takes more wickedness to carry through a plan than to conceive it, and it may be desirable (on a utilitarian view) to mark each stage of an attempt by a portion of punishment in order to deter the attempter from pursuing his criminal design to its conclusion. There remain difficulties, however, with cases . . . where the attempter has done all the acts he intended and has failed to produce the planned result . . . On principle . . . there is no distinction in point of either wickedness or social danger between the successful criminal and the unsuccessful attempter in this last class. Chance may well be the only explanation of why one attempt succeeded and the other failed, and a sound sentencing policy should take little notice of a factor which lies outside the offender's control. He should be judged on the basis of what he intended to do, believed he was doing or knowingly risked."

10-059 Gross pushes the argument to its logical conclusion by asserting:

> "In some cases, then, attempt liability will be as extensive as liability for the completed crime, and may even be greater, for sometimes, even though harm does not occur, the conduct of the accused was more dangerous than in a case in which harm does occur. In other cases of attempt the conduct is less dangerous and so liability is less extensive."[112]

It is our submission that it can *never* be justifiable to impose greater punishment for an attempt than for the completed crime. Indeed, it is our submission that attempts should *always* be punished to a lesser extent than the completed crime. This is because the paradigm of criminal liability is the combination of blame and harm and the absence of one of these should be reflected by, at least, less punishment. In relation to the law of attempt there is no harm (or, at most, there

112 See Gross, *A Theory of Criminal Justice* (1979), p.460. For a criticism of Gross's views, see J.B. Brady, "Punishing Attempts" (1980) 63 *The Monist* 246, 251–255.

is only a second-order harm) so punishment should be lower than for the completed crime.[113] The reasons for this view need to be explored. Why should the causing of harm be regarded as so significant?

III. Conspiracy

A. INTRODUCTION

Conspiracy is an inchoate crime because it penalises steps towards the commission of a crime. In the case of conspiracy, an *agreement* is the essence of the offence. The agreement may be to commit murder as part of a terrorist plot, to launder money derived from drug trafficking, to cause damage as part of an animal rights campaign or to publish names and information about prostitutes. The law on conspiracy has been described as "the least systematic, the most irrational branch of English penal law".[114] Whilst some reform has taken place since that statement was made, it is still the case that in terms of its rationale, its content and its use, the crime of conspiracy is highly suspect. In 2006, in the light of concerns about the offence, the Government asked the Law Commission to review the law. Its report[115] recommended some important changes to conspiracy but although they have been accepted, they will not be implemented. **10–060**

B. SHOULD THERE BE A LAW OF CONSPIRACY?

The arguments for retaining a crime of conspiracy may be grouped into three main strands. **10–061**

(1) The prevention of crime including, increasingly, the assistance of intelligence-led policing: if these are now regarded as key objectives (the view taken by the Law Commission[116]) then it would seem to follow that the agreement should be to do something that would be *criminal* if completed. As we shall see, the Criminal Law Act 1977 only partially succeeded in reducing conspiracy to this formula. But these justifications depend to a significant degree on the ambit of other inchoate offences. If English law had adopted the substantial step test[117] for determining the extent of action required for an attempt, this justification for conspiracy would have been undermined: in most cases the only evidence of the agreement will be overt

113 C.M.V. Clarkson, "Aggravated Endangerment Offences" (2007) 60 C.L.P. 278, 282.

114 *R. v Bhagwan (Dharam Singh)* [1972] A.C. 60 at 79; [1970] 3 W.L.R. 501 HL.

115 Law Commission Paper No.318, *Conspiracy and Attempts* (2009).

116 Law Commission Consultation Paper No.183, *Conspiracy and Attempts* (2007), paras 2.4–2.10. See also Law Commission Paper No.76, *Conspiracy and Criminal Law Reform* (1976), para.1.5.

117 Law Commission Working Paper No.50, *Inchoate Offences* (1973), para.75. Under this test the focus was on whether D had taken a substantial step towards the commission of the crime, e.g. reconnoitering the building contemplated for a burglary. It was not adopted because it would have cast the net of liability too wide in the sequence of actions: Law Commission Paper No.102 (1980) para.2.32.

acts that could have satisfied the substantial step test. However, this test has not been adopted by English law (instead requiring the defendant to have done acts that are more than merely preparatory to the commission of the offence) and until very recently, therefore, it was possible, in crime prevention terms, to justify a crime of conspiracy. With the introduction of three new inchoate offences dealing with encouraging or assisting crime in the Serious Crime Act 2007,[118] the crime prevention rationale has again come under scrutiny, although the Law Commission has rejected the argument that these offences are so broad that conspiracy, as a preventative tool, has become redundant on the ground that it facilitates "the effective use of intelligence-led policing".[119] Despite this, the fact that large numbers of conspiracy charges are brought *after* the crime has been completed[120] does support the view that other justifications are increasingly important in responding to serious crime.[121]

(2) The "full story" rationale: a conspiracy charge enables a number of crimes, which may or may not be serious in themselves, to be brought before the court in their "true" light.[122] It enables larger numbers of those involved to be held responsible. However, this largely ignores the role of the law relating to complicity and may lead to the conspiracy charge being abused.[123]

(3) The "general danger" rationale: that people working in concert with one another are more dangerous than lone actors. Not only are they able to commit more complex crimes but they will be more likely to carry out their intentions. It is this argument which enabled conspiracy to develop so as to embrace an agreement with others to do an act, such as trespass, which was not in itself criminal and while this is no longer the law, this claim remains problematic. However, it is notable that the Law Commission's recent defence of conspiracy is influenced by research which lends some support to this justification: conspiracy may be justified on an economic basis (it permits a specialisation of labour) and a psychological basis (where a group loyalty and solidarity develops), both of which advance the criminal purpose.[124]

10–062 One has to conclude that conspiracy is used as more than an inchoate crime.[125] The reality is that its use, when the crime has been completed, brings substantial advantages for the prosecution. Not only does it provide the prosecution with another chance of securing a conviction where the evidence relating to the completed crime is doubtful, but there are evidential benefits as well.[126] As we shall see,

---

118 Replacing the common-law offence of incitement, paras 10–088–10–119.

119 Law Commission Consultation Paper No.183, *Conspiracy and Attempts* (2007), para.2.9.

120 There is no bar under English law to including both conspiracy and substantive offence charges on an indictment when the offence has been completed (they do not "merge"), but the prosecution has to justify to the judge the inclusion of the conspiracy count and if the judge is not satisfied then the prosecution has to elect to proceed with either the conspiracy or the substantive count: Criminal Practice Direction II (Preliminary Proceedings) 10A, para.4; P.J. Richardson, *Archbold Criminal Pleading, Evidence and Practice* (London: Sweet & Maxwell, 2024), para.33–59.

121 This extends beyond organised or terrorist crimes. In *Skidmore* [2009] Crim. L.R. 42, a conviction for conspiracy was upheld when the substantive offence of preventing a lawful and decent burial of a child had occurred.

122 See, e.g. *R. v Dove (Matthew Jonathon)* [2005] EWCA Crim 1982 where 12 robberies were committed by the defendants within a short space of time.

123 In *R. v Barratt (Paul Henry)* [1996] Crim. L.R. 495 CA, e.g. the court felt that the evidence fell far short of establishing a single conspiracy extending over two years to burgle houses. As Smith comments [1996] Crim. L.R. 495, at 497 the idea was "utterly far-fetched".

124 Law Commission Consultation Paper No.183, *Conspiracy and Attempts* (2007), paras 2.11–2.20.

125 The Government's White Paper, *One Step Ahead: A 21st Century Strategy to Defeat Organised Crime* (Cmnd.6167, 2004) even contemplated changing the link between conspiracy and certain predicate (underlying) crimes as part of its strategy to respond to organised crime (para.6.1).

126 The normal rule of evidence, e.g. that prevents the statements of one co-defendant being used against another does not apply in conspiracy trials. See further, Law Commission Consultation Paper No.183, *Conspiracy and Attempts* (2007), paras 2.20–2.21.

some doubt over the continued attractiveness to prosecutors of conspiracy charges, where the crime has occurred, has been cast by the House of Lords' decision in *Saik*.[127] In this case, Lord Hope refers to the device of bringing conspiracy charges where the crime has been completed as "trying to fit a square peg into a round hole":[128] the crime was not designed to be used in this way.

As with attempts, a conspiracy, if charged when the offence has not been completed, causes no actual harm. Bearing in mind the discussion of the rationale of the law of attempt, two questions need to be considered. Do conspiracies pose a "second order" harm—in the sense of posing a threat to security? Alternatively, is the blameworthiness of a conspirator so great as to justify dispensing with the requirement of harm which is normally required for the imposition of criminal liability? Or are there (and can there ever be) sufficient utilitarian arguments to justify dispensing with the requirement of harm?

C. THE LAW

1. Types of conspiracy

At common law, a conspiracy was an agreement between two or more persons "to do an unlawful act, or to do a lawful act by unlawful means".[129] Thus it was not necessary to prove that there was an agreement to commit a crime; agreements to commit other "unlawful acts", such as some torts or corruption of public morals, clearly sufficed. For instance, in *Kamara v DPP*,[130] an agreement to commit the tort of trespass to land, if accompanied by an intention to inflict more than merely nominal damage, was held to be a criminal conspiracy. Of course, it was virtually impossible to justify making it a crime to agree to do something that if actually done by one person acting alone would not have been criminal. Accordingly, the Criminal Law Act 1977 sought to limit conspiracy primarily to agreements to commit crimes. However, fearing that gaps might be created, and pending a comprehensive review of the law of fraud, obscenity and indecency, s.5 preserved certain common law conspiracies. We are thus left with the following rather unsatisfactory situation. **10–063**

(1) There are agreements to commit a crime. These are termed statutory conspiracies and are governed by the provisions of the Criminal Law Act 1977 s.1.
(2) There are common law conspiracies governed by the old common law rules. Under the Criminal Law Act 1977 s.5, two species of common law conspiracy have been preserved. These are conspiracy to defraud and conspiracy to corrupt public morals or outrage public decency. Commentators have been saying since 1977 that these retentions were designed to be temporary. In 2002, the Law Commission proposed the abolition of the crime of conspiracy to defraud.[131] However, the Fraud Act 2006 did not give effect to this recommendation. Moreover, a 2012 report by the Ministry of Justice concludes that conspiracy to defraud works well

127 *R. v Saik (Abdulrahman)* [2006] UKHL 18; [2007] 1 A.C. 18. Note that the Law Commission's recommendations are designed to remove the barrier erected by *Saik*: paras 10–069–10–070.
128 *Saik* [2007] 1 A.C. 18 at [41].
129 *Mulcahy v R.* (1868) L.R. 3 H.L. 306.
130 *Kamara v DPP* [1974] A.C. 104; [1973] 3 W.L.R. 198 HL.
131 Law Commission Paper No.276, *Fraud* (2002).

alongside the Fraud Act and is an essential tool in combatting fraud.[132] It is considered to be far too useful a charge to prosecutors where there are multiple offences[133] (especially if more than one jurisdiction is involved) to abolish it. It is now clear that outraging public decency is a substantive common law offence,[134] so now charges of conspiracy to outrage public decency have to be brought as statutory conspiracies under the Criminal Law Act 1977. It is not clear whether there is a substantive offence of conspiracy to corrupt public morals. The Court of Appeal in *Shaw*[135] took the view that there was a substantive offence of corrupting public morals, but the House of Lords did not resolve this issue, although it affirmed the existence of the offence of conspiracy to corrupt public morals.[136]

2. Statutory conspiracy

(i) Definition

CRIMINAL LAW ACT 1977 S.1:

10–064 "(1) Subject to the following provisions of this Part of this Act, if a person agrees with any other person or persons that a course of conduct shall be pursued which, if the agreement is carried out in accordance with their intentions, either—

(a) will necessarily amount to or involve the commission of any offence or offences by one or more of the parties to the agreement, or
(b) would do so but for the existence of facts which render the commission of the offence or any of the offences impossible,

he is guilty of conspiracy to commit the offence or offences in question.

(2) Where liability for any offence may be incurred without knowledge on the part of the person committing it of any particular fact or circumstance necessary for the commission of the offence, a person shall nevertheless not be guilty of conspiracy to commit that offence by virtue of subsection (1) above unless he and at least one other party to the agreement intend or know that that fact or circumstances shall or will exist at the time when the conduct constituting the offence is to take place."

---

132 Ministry of Justice, *Post-Legislative Assessment of the Fraud Act 2006, Memorandum to the Justice Select Committee* (2012, Cm.8372), paras 36–38.

133 See, e.g. *Mba* [2006] All E.R. (D) 73. In this case, Ds were convicted on a single charge of conspiracy to defraud which involved many transactions, using false identities to obtain loans, withdraw cash or transfer money. It Is commonly used in cases of large-scale fraud, e.g. *R. v Moyoussef (Philippe)* [2020] EWCA Crim 455 and *R. v Bermingham (Colin)* [2020] EWCA Crim 1662; [2021] 1 Cr. App. R. 24, both cases involving manipulation of the Euro Interbank Offered Rate benchmark interest rate (Euribor).

134 *R. v Gibson (Richard Norman)* [1990] 2 Q.B. 619; [1990] 3 W.L.R. 595 CACD, *R. v Walker (Steven)* [1996] 1 Cr. App. R. 111; [1995] Crim. L.R. 826 CACD; *R. v Hamilton (Simon Austin)* [2007] EWCA Crim 2062; [2008] Q.B. 224; Criminal Justice Act 2003 s.320. The Law Commission has recommended that the substantive common law offence of outraging public decency be replaced by a statutory offence and that the offence of conspiracy to outrage public decency be abolished: Law Commission No.358, *Simplification of Criminal Law: Public Nuisance and Outraging Public Decency* (2015), para.2.68.

135 *Shaw v DPP* [1962] A.C. 220 at 223; [1961] 2 W.L.R. 897 HL.

136 *Shaw v DPP* [1962] A.C. 220.

(ii) Agreement

There must be an agreement between at least two persons. There must have been a meeting of minds; decisions must have been communicated between the parties[137] although it is not necessary that each conspirator is aware of all the details of the conspiracy as long as there is a shared common purpose.[138] However, s.2(2)(a) provides that a husband and wife cannot be liable for conspiracy, if they are the only parties to the agreement.[139] This provision was extended to civil partners by the Civil Partnership Act 2004,[140] but does not apply to unmarried couples who live together in a relationship akin to marriage.[141] The Law Commission has proposed abolishing the archaic marital exception.[142] The Act also provides that a person cannot be liable if the only other party to the "agreement" is a person under the age of criminal responsibility (s.2(2)(b)) or is the intended victim of the offence (s.2(2)(c)). "Victim" is not defined in the Act but its meaning has now been considered by the Supreme Court in *Gnango*[143] where Lord Phillips argued that a narrow interpretation should be given to the word whereby 'victim' is confined to persons of a class the law intends to protect, otherwise: **10–065**

> "If . . . [victim] is given the wide meaning it would seem to produce the surprising result that a conspiracy by two persons that one will commit a terrorist atrocity as a suicide bomber, or set fire to a house owned by one of them in furtherance of some ulterior motive, would appear not to subject either to criminal liability."[144]

Although obiter, it would seem likely that this approach would be followed if the issue were to come before a court. It also accords with the recommendation of the Law Commission that the exemption should be abolished for the non-victim conspirator but be retained for the V where the conspiracy is to commit an offence which exists for the protection of a class of persons to which the V belongs.[145] This would bring the law in line with the provisions in the Serious Crime Act 2007 and complicity.[146] **10–066**

137 *R. v Scott (Valerie)* (1979) 68 Cr. App. R. 164; [1979] Crim. L.R. 456 CA. Parties does not include someone who is the intended victim of the offence (s.2(1)).

138 *R. v Fritzl (Jaqueline)* [2011] EWCA Crim 1220; *R. v Griffiths* (1969) 49 Cr. App. R. 279. Even if there is sufficient evidence to point to an agreement having been made, if there is no credible evidence that it is anything other than a "fantasy", there can be no conspiracy: in *R. v G* [2012] EWCA Crim 1756; [2013] Crim. L.R. 678 it stated that an "executory intent" is needed.

139 This confirms the common law decision of *Mawji v The Queen* [1957] A.C. 126; [1957] 2 W.L.R. 277. See *R. v Chrastny (Charlotte Barbara) (No.1)* [1991] 1 W.L.R. 1381; (1992) 94 Cr. App. R. 283 CA and *R. v Singh (Harbans)* [2011] EWCA Crim 2992. This exception extends to the wife in a polygamous marriage which is valid in the place in which it is celebrated, and which is not void under English law: *R. v Bala (Yilkyes Finok)* [2016] EWCA Crim 560; [2017] Q.B. 430.

140 Civil Partnership Act 2004 Sch.27. The Marriage (Same Sex Couples) Act 2013 s.11 and Sch.3 Pt 1 extend this provision to parties to a same-sex marriage.

141 *R. v Suski (Dariusz Tomas)* [2016] EWCA Crim 24; [2016] 2 Cr. App. R. 3 at [23]: "There are very good grounds why a court trying a charge of conspiracy should not have to inquire closely into the nature of personal relationships of alleged conspirators, infinitely variable as they are likely to be from case to case."

142 Law Commission Paper No.318, *Conspiracy and Attempts* (2009), paras 5.7–5.16.

143 *R. v Gnango (Armel)* [2011] UKSC 59; [2012] 1 A.C. 827.

144 *Gnango* [2011] UKSC 59 at [49].

145 Law Commission Paper No.318, *Conspiracy and Attempts* (2009), paras 5.7–5.16.d, paras 5.17–5.35. The Law Commission also recommends retention of the exemption for a child conspirator under the age of 10 (paras 5.36–5.45). However, the other adult co-conspirator could be prosecuted for encouraging the formation of a conspiracy under the Serious Crime Act 2007 s.44. cf. J. Herring, "Victims as Defendants: When Victims Participate in Crimes Against Themselves" in A. Reed and M. Bohlander (eds), *Participation in Crime: Domestic and Comparative Perspectives* (London: Routledge, 2013), Ch.5.

146 Serious Crime Act 2007 s.51. See paras 5–143–5–144. cf. C. de Than and J. Elvin, "Towards a Rational Reconstruction of the Law on Secondary Participation and Inchoate Offences: Conspiracy" in Reed and Bohlander (eds), *Participation in Crime: Domestic and Comparative Perspectives* (2013), Ch.9.

As the law stands, it would thus appear that there *can* be liability if D conspires with any other person having a defence (say insanity) other than the above, provided that such person is capable of reaching an *agreement* with D.[147] Where D and others are charged with conspiracy and those others are acquitted, s.5(8) provides that D may nevertheless be convicted "unless under all the circumstances of the case his conviction is inconsistent with the acquittal of the other person or persons in question".[148] This is sensible. There may be evidence admissible against D that he conspired with A and B, but that evidence might not be admissible against A or B. Alternatively, it might be clear that he conspired with either A or B, but it is not certain which one it was. A and B must be given the benefit of the doubt and acquitted, but there is no reason why D, whose guilt is beyond doubt, should be offered the same indulgence.[149]

(iii) Object of agreement

10–067 There must be an agreement that:

(a) a course of conduct be pursued;
(b) which if carried out in accordance with their intentions;
(c) will necessarily amount to (or involve) a crime.

Each of the phrases will now be examined in turn.

(a) Course of conduct be pursued

10–068 The phrase "course of conduct" here does not refer purely to physical actions, but must be taken to include intended consequences—in short, the plan. This point is best illustrated with an example. Suppose two persons agree to place a bomb under another's car and detonate the bomb so as to kill the owner. The physical course of conduct agreed to, namely, the physical actions of planting the bomb, will not necessarily amount to the crime because the bomb may never go off. However, if the *plan* is carried out according to their intentions, the bomb will explode and the owner of the car will be killed. This necessarily amounts to a crime; killing someone in such circumstances is murder. The Law Commission has confirmed that this is the correct interpretation of the current law.[150]

To say that the agreed course of conduct includes the planned consequences is also a limiting qualification. Only planned consequences can be included within the agreed course of conduct. Thus, as stated in *Siracusa*,[151] an agreement to cause grievous bodily harm is not sufficient to support a charge of conspiracy to murder even though an intention to cause grievous bodily harm is sufficient to support

---

147 This confirms the common law decision of *Duguid* (1906) 75 L.J. K.B. 470.

148 This was already the position at common law in relation to separate trials (*DPP v Shannon (David Charles)* [1975] A.C. 717; [1974] 3 W.L.R. 155 HL), but reverses the common law position in relation to joint trials (*R. v Thompson, Tillotson and Maddock* 117 E.R. 1100; (1851) 16 Q.B. 832; *R. v Coughlan (Joseph John)* (1977) 64 Cr. App. R. 11 CA).

149 See, e.g. *R. v Testouri (Adel Ben)* [2003] EWCA Crim 3735; [2004] 2 Cr. App. R. 4 and *R. v Austin (Alan Brian)* [2011] EWCA Crim 345; [2012] 1 Cr. App. R. 24. See further, *R. v Mehta (Subhash)* [2012] EWCA Crim 2824 and *R. v Shillam (Wayne Lee)* [2013] EWCA Crim 160; [2013] Crim. L.R. 592. cf. *Serious Fraud Office v Papachristos (Miltiades)* [2014] EWCA Crim 1863; [2015] Lloyd's Rep. F.C. 88.

150 Law Commission Paper No.318, *Conspiracy and Attempts* (2009), para.2.13.

151 *R. v Siracusa (Francesco)* (1990) 90 Cr. App. R. 340; [1989] Crim. L.R. 712 CA.

a charge of murder itself. In *Siracusa*, it was held that although a person smuggling heroin could be convicted of a substantive offence if she thought that they were smuggling cannabis, the same was not true on a conspiracy charge:

> ". . . the essence of the crime of conspiracy was the agreement and, in simple terms, one did not prove an agreement to import heroin by proving an agreement to import cannabis."[152]

The basis of this decision is that heroin and cannabis are different class drugs, involving separate offences. In *Broad*,[153] it was held to be immaterial that one conspirator thought heroin was to be produced while the other thought it would be cocaine. Both are Class A drugs; they had agreed to commit the same offence. It is further submitted that planned consequences mean intended consequences. If arson is planned between conspirators who are reckless as to whether anyone is killed during their fire, the death of those persons is not part of their plan. One does not plan for and intend an event possibly happening. Intention here, of course, should bear the same meaning as in other areas of law—bearing in mind that such intention may be inferred or established from foresight of a consequence as virtually certain.

The planned course of conduct also includes (and only includes) *intended* or *known* surrounding circumstances.[154] This phrase came under intense scrutiny in relation to conspiracies to traffic drugs[155] or to launder money. Under the Criminal Justice Act 1988 s.93C(2), Ds could be convicted of money laundering if they knew or *had reasonable grounds to suspect* that the property was the proceeds of crime.[156] Controversially, the Court of Appeal held that where Ds were charged with conspiracy to launder money, the prosecution need only establish that D suspected (rather than knew) that the money was the proceeds of crime in order to convict.[157] This approach was ended by the following important decision.

R. v Saik [2007] 1 A.C. 18 (House of Lords):

The facts appear from the judgment. **10–069**

LORD NICHOLLS:

"[1] This appeal raises questions about the ingredients of the statutory offence of conspiracy and their application in the circumstances of this case. Shorn of its complexities the context is a charge of conspiracy to launder money brought against the Appellant, Mr Abdulrahman Saik.

---

152 This was confirmed in *R. v Taylor (Robert John)* [2001] EWCA Crim 1044; [2002] Crim. L.R. 205.

153 *R. v Broad (Christopher)* [1997] Crim. L.R. 666 CA.

154 Criminal Damage Act 1971 s.1(2). On its actual wording s.1(2) appears to be limited to crimes of strict liability but, as *Saik* [2007] A.C. 18 makes clear, it cannot mean this.

155 Drug Trafficking Act 1994 s.49(2).

156 Both this provision and the Drug Trafficking Act 1994 s.49(2) have now been repealed and replaced by the Proceeds of Crime Act 2002. The issue of suspicion does not arise with the new offences under the Act.

157 See *R. v Sakavickas (Rolandas)* [2004] EWCA Crim 2686; [2005] 1 Cr. App. R. 36; *R. v Singh (Gulbir Rana)* [2003] EWCA Crim 3712; *R. v Rizvi (Zafar)* [2003] EWCA Crim 3575.

He operated a bureau de change in London, near Marble Arch. At his trial he pleaded guilty, subject to the qualification that he did not know the money was the proceeds of crime. He only suspected this was so. This qualified plea was accepted. The issue before your Lordships is whether the offence to which the Appellant pleaded guilty is an offence known to law. Reasonable grounds for suspicion are enough for the substantive offence of laundering money. But are they enough for a conspiracy to commit that offence?

[2] The mental ingredient in the statutory offence of conspiracy has given rise to difficulty. Some of the case law is confusing, and the academic commentators do not always speak with one voice . . .

[4] . . . [T]he mental element of the offence, apart from the mental element involved in making an agreement, comprises the intention to pursue a course of conduct which will necessarily involve commission of the crime in question by one or more of the conspirators. The conspirators must intend to do the act prohibited by the substantive offence. The conspirators' state of mind must also satisfy the mental ingredients of the substantive offence. If one of the ingredients of the substantive offence is that the act is done with a specific intent, the conspirators must intend to do the prohibited act and must intend to do the prohibited act with the prescribed intent . . .

[6] Section 1(2) qualifies the scope of the offence created by section 1(1). This subsection is more difficult. Its essential purpose is to ensure that strict liability and recklessness have no place in the offence of conspiracy . . .

[7] Under this subsection conspiracy involves a third mental element: intention or knowledge that a fact or circumstances necessary for the commission of the substantive offence will exist . . .

[8] It follows from this requirement of intention or knowledge that proof of the mental element needed for the commission of the substantive offence will not always suffice on a charge of conspiracy to commit that offence. In respect of a material fact or circumstance conspiracy has its own mental element. In conspiracy this mental element is set as high as 'intend or know' . . . In this respect the mental element of conspiracy is distinct from and supersedes the mental element in the substantive offence . . .

[13] The rationale underlying this approach is that conspiracy imposes criminal liability on the basis of a person's intention. This is a different harm from the commission of the substantive offence. So it is right that the intention which is being criminalized in the offence of conspiracy should itself be blameworthy. This should be so, irrespective of the provisions of the substantive offence.

10-070 [14] Against this background I turn to some issues concerning the scope and effect of section 1(2). The starting point is to note that this relieving provision is not confined to substantive offences attracting strict liability. The subsection does not so provide. Nor would such an interpretation of the subsection make sense. It would make no sense for section 1(2) to apply, and only require proof of intention or knowledge, where liability for the substantive offence is absolute but not where the substantive offence has built into it a mental ingredient less than knowledge, such as suspicion.

[15] So much is clear. A more difficult question arises where an ingredient of the substantive offence is that the defendant must know of a material fact or circumstance. On its face section 1(2) does not apply in this case. The opening words of section 1(2), on their face, limit the scope of the subsection to cases where a person may commit an offence without knowledge of a material fact or circumstance.

[16] Plainly Parliament did not intend that a person would be liable for conspiracy where he lacks the knowledge required to commit the substantive offence. That could not be right. Parliament could not have intended such an absurd result. Rather, the assumption underlying section 1(2) is that, where knowledge of a material fact is an ingredient of a substantive offence, knowledge of that fact is also an ingredient of the crime of conspiring to commit the substantive offence.

[17] There are two ways this result might be achieved. One is simply to treat section 1(2) as inapplicable in this type of case . . .

[18] The other route is to adopt the interpretation of section 1(2) suggested by Sir John Smith. The suggestion is that section 1(2) applies despite the opening words of the subsection . . .

[19] The first route accords more easily with the language of section 1(2), but I prefer the second route for the following reason. A conspiracy is looking to the future. It is an agreement about future conduct. When the agreement is made the 'particular fact or circumstance necessary for the commission' of the substantive offence may not have happened. So the conspirator cannot be said to know of the fact or circumstance at that time. Nor, if the happening of the fact or circumstance is beyond his control, can it be said that the conspirator will know of that fact or circumstance.

[20] Section 1(2) expressly caters for this situation. The conspirator must 'intend or know' that this fact or circumstance 'shall or will exist' when the conspiracy is carried into effect. Although not the happiest choice of language, 'intend' is descriptive of a state of mind which is looking to the future . . . Thus on a charge of conspiracy to handle stolen property where the property has not been identified when the agreement is made, the prosecution must prove that the conspirator intended that the property which was the subject of the conspiracy would be stolen property . . .

[23] . . . [In relation to conspiracy to launder money his Lordship continued] Hence, where the property has not been identified when the conspiracy agreement is reached, the prosecution must prove that the defendant intended that the property would be the proceeds of criminal conduct . . .

> [25] What, however, if the property to which the conspiracy relates was specifically identified when the conspirators made their agreement? In that event the prosecution must prove the conspirators 'knew' the property was the proceeds of crime. This is the next point of difficulty with the interpretation of section 1(2). [D]oes 'know' in this context mean 'believe'? . . .
>
> [26] I do not think . . . [this] approach can be accepted. The phrase under consideration ('intend or know') in section 1(2) is a provision of general application to all conspiracies. In this context the word 'know' should be interpreted strictly and not watered down. In this context knowledge means true belief . . .
>
> [30] From what has been said above, it is evident that this conviction cannot stand. Suspicion is not sufficient in respect of a fact to which section 1(2) applies. Knowledge or intention regarding the provenance of the property must be proved or admitted."
>
> *Appeal allowed*

10–071 This decision settles, for now at least, a number of the interpretative difficulties which had plagued s.1(2). We now know that s.1(2) applies to conspiracies to commit all offences. This is clearly right. We also know that mere suspicion will not suffice and that intention or knowledge must be proved. As Ormerod has commented:

> "In this respect the offence of conspiracy is stricter than that of attempt where the courts have accepted that recklessness as to circumstances is a sufficient *mens rea* where that would suffice for the substantive crime attempted. This is not objectionable or illogical, it is submitted, since conspiracy is a distinct crime reflecting a different wrong from that involved in attempt."[158]

So much is clear from *Saik*. Beyond this, however, as the Law Commission has commented, their Lordships held different views as to what would constitute "knowledge".[159] Furthermore, although Lord Nicholls distinguished between agreements relating to identified and as yet unidentified property (when in the latter case, the appropriate word for prosecutors to use would be "intend" and not "knowledge"), this distinction could give rise to difficulties.[160]

---

158 D. Ormerod, "Conspiracy: Conspiracy to Launder Money" [2006] Crim. L.R. 998, 1001. See more generally, D. Ormerod, "Making Sense of Statutory Conspiracies" (2006) C.L.P. 277.

159 Law Commission Paper No.318, *Conspiracy and Attempts* (2009), para.2.64. One issue is whether knowledge here can include wilful blindness. For an application of *Saik* [2006] UKHL 18; [2007] 1 A.C. 18, see *R. v Ahmed* [2013] EWCA Crim 1755.

160 e.g. whether a property's status is to be established objectively or whether the particular conspirators need to have identified the property is unclear. Ormerod and Laird have suggested that, post *Ivey v Genting Casinos (UK) Ltd (t/a Crockfords)* [2017] UKSC 67; [2018] A.C. 319 and *R. v Barton (David) and Booth (Rosemary)* [2020] EWCA Crim 575, it might be argued, in the case of a statutory conspiracy to commit an offence of dishonesty, that it is now necessary to prove that D knew/intended that the agreed course of conduct would be considered dishonest by ordinary decent people: Ormerod and Laird, *Smith, Hogan and Ormerod's Criminal Law*, 16th edn (2021), p.478. cf. K. Laird, "Case Comment: Fraud: *R. v Nyonyintono (Winifred)*" [2021] Crim. L.R. 135.

This more rigorous interpretation of the elements of conspiracy has the potential of reducing its usefulness to prosecutors where the completed crime has taken place.[161] It was to be anticipated, therefore, that in light of *Saik* the Government would ask the Law Commission to review the law of conspiracy.

Law Commission (Consultation Paper No. 183), Conspiracy and Attempts (2007), paras 4.107–4.108:

"4.107 As a matter of statutory interpretation, on the facts the correct conclusion was reached by the majority of the House of Lords in *Saik*. As Lord Nicholls noted, '[a] decision to deal with money suspected to be the proceeds of crime is not the same as a conscious decision to deal with the proceeds of crime.' Only the latter behaviour is prohibited on the correct construction of section 1(2). **10–072**

4.108 However, in our view, this reading of section 1(2) renders the offence unacceptably narrow. If the prosecution have to prove in every case that, at the time of the agreement, the parties knew or intended that the relevant facts or circumstance existed, then the law is too generous to those who plan to engage in conduct that may well be criminal. It does not extend to highly blameworthy behaviour that we believe should be encompassed within the offence of conspiracy."

[The Law Commission recommends that the law should be changed so that] "An alleged conspirator must be shown at the time of the agreement to be reckless whether a circumstance element of a substantive offence (or other relevant circumstance) would be present at the relevant time, when the substantive offence requires no proof of fault, or has a requirement for proof only of negligence (or its equivalent), in relation to that circumstance."[162]

[This would] "ensure that defendants such as Mr Saik, those who agree to commit rape believing that the victim 'might not' consent and those who agree to handle stolen goods believing that, should they do so, the goods will be stolen, would all be guilty of statutory conspiracy."[163]

This change would also bring the law in this respect into line with the offences of encouraging or assisting crime and would accord with an interpretation of mens rea that has in the past been adopted in relation to attempt, although it is not consistent with the approach adopted in *Pace*.[164]

---

161 There was also concern that *Saik* [2006] UKHL 18; [2007] 1 A.C. 18 would lead to a large number of appeals by defendants convicted under the old law. However, in *R. v R (Amer)* [2006] EWCA Crim 1974 (where the Court of Appeal heard seven appeals together) it was held that, although such convictions were unsafe in the light of *Saik*, leave to appeal out of time would not be granted as no injustice had been done to any of those convicted. In all cases there was evidence that would have convicted them of the substantive offences. See further, D. Ormerod, "Proceeds of Crime: Conspiracy—Mens Rea" [2007] Crim. L.R. 79 and *R. v Suchedina (Hasnain)* [2006] EWCA Crim 2543; [2007] Crim. L.R. 301 (and commentary thereto).

162 Law Commission Paper No.318, *Conspiracy and Attempts* (2009), para.2.137. Where the substantive offence has a fault requirement not involving mere negligence (or its equivalent) this fault requirement must also be proved for conspiracy (para.2.146).

163 Law Commission Consultation Paper No.183, *Conspiracy and Attempts* (2007), para.1.33.

164 *Pace* 2014] EWCA Crim 186; [2014] 1 W.L.R. 2867; Child, Simester, Spencer, Stark and Virgo, *Simester and Sullivan's Criminal Law: Theory and Doctrine*, 8th edn (2022), p.362. See paras 10–040–10–041.

(b) If carried out in accordance with their intentions

10-073 What is the position if the parties' intentions are equivocal? For example, they might agree to burgle a house if a window has been left open. The better view here is that the "plan" is a plan to burgle a house (albeit subject to a condition) and if that plan is carried out it will necessarily amount to a crime. As Lord Nicholls comments in *Saik*:

> "An intention to do a prohibited act is within the scope of section 1(1) even if the intention is expressed to be conditional on the happening, or non-happening, of some particular event. The question always is whether the agreed course of conduct, if carried out in accordance with the parties' intentions, would necessarily involve an offence. A conspiracy to rob a bank tomorrow if the coast is clear when the conspirators reach the bank is not, by reason of this qualification, any less a conspiracy to rob. In the nature of things, every agreement to do something in the future is hedged about with conditions, implicit if not explicit."[165]

R. v Jackson [1985] Crim. L.R. 442 (Court of Appeal, Criminal Division):

10-074 The Ds agreed to shoot their friend, W, in the leg if he was convicted of a burglary for which he was being tried. They thought this would provide mitigation. W was shot and permanently disabled. The Ds appealed against their conviction for conspiracy to pervert the course of justice on the ground that their agreement did not necessarily involve the commission of a crime, as everything depended on a contingency (W's conviction for burglary) which might not have taken place.

> Held, "[P]lanning was taking place for a contingency and if that contingency occurred the conspiracy would necessarily involve the commission of an offence. 'Necessarily' is not to be held to mean that there must inevitably be the carrying out of an offence. It means, if the agreement is carried out in accordance with the plan, there must be the commission of the offence referred to in the conspiracy count."

Appeal dismissed

10-075 In *O'Hadhmaill*,[166] the defendant, a member of the IRA, agreed to a bombing campaign if the cease-fire in Northern Ireland ended. This was held to be sufficient intention for the crime of conspiracy.

The approach adopted in all these cases is defensible. Virtually all agreements are conditional. It is implicit in most agreements to commit a crime that the actions will only be carried out if there is not the metaphoric "policeman at one's elbow" at the scene of the crime. However, there is still some uncertainty about the precise scope of conditional intention in relation to s.1(2) that has been exposed by the decision in *Saik*. What if two Ds agree that they will have sex with a woman and they suspect that she may not consent? Although the issue of conditional intention did not fall to be determined in *Saik*

---

165 *Saik* [2007] A.C. 18 at [5].

166 *R. v O'Hadhmaill* [1996] Crim. L.R. 509 CA. See also *R. v Reed* [1982] Crim. L.R. 818.

it would appear that this state of mind will not now suffice for liability for conspiracy to rape. However, as Baroness Hale in her dissenting speech argues, the Ds have an intent to rape—they have agreed that they will go ahead even if at the time when they go ahead they know she is not consenting—and this ought to be a conspiracy to commit rape. If recklessness rather than intention or knowledge were required in relation to facts or circumstances, as proposed by the Law Commission, the liability of such defendants would be clear.[167]

The plan must also be carried out "in accordance with their intentions". What does this mean? What is the position of a person who agrees to the commission of a crime and agrees to supply tools for the crime but who thereafter has no interest in what happens and indeed thinks the planned crime is over-ambitious and will never be committed? Or what is the position of a plain-clothes police officer who, with a view to entrapping the others, "agrees" to a plan to commit a crime, but actually intends to prevent the crime at the last moment? In short, must each conspirator intend that the crime actually be carried out?

R. v Anderson [1986] A.C. 27 (House of Lords):

D agreed for a fee to supply diamond wire to cut through bars in order to enable another person, Andaloussi, to escape from prison. He claimed that he only intended to supply the wire and then go abroad. He believed the plan could never succeed. He appealed against his conviction for conspiring with others to effect the release of one of them from prison claiming that as he did not intend or expect the plan to be carried out, he lacked the necessary mens rea for the offence of conspiracy. **10-076**

LORD BRIDGE:

"[I]t is not necessary that more than one of the participants in the agreed course of conduct shall commit a substantive offence. It is, of course, necessary that any party to the agreement shall have assented to play his part in the agreed course of conduct, however innocent in itself, knowing that the part to be played by one or more of the others will amount to or involve the commission of an offence.

. . . The heart of the submission for the appellant is that in order to be convicted of conspiracy to commit a given offence . . . the party charged should not only have agreed that a course of conduct shall be pursued which will necessarily amount to or involve the commission of that offence by himself or one or more other parties to the agreement, but must also be proved himself to have intended that that offence should be committed. Thus, it is submitted here that the appellant's case that he never intended that Andaloussi should be enabled to escape from prison raised an issue to be left to the jury, who should have been directed to convict him only if satisfied that he did so intend . . .

---

167 See further, Law Commission Paper No.318, *Conspiracy and Attempts* (2009), paras 2.99–2.128. cf. J. Child, "Understanding ulterior mens rea: future conduct intention is conditional intention" (2017) 76 C.L.J. 311.

I am clearly driven by consideration of the diversity of roles which parties may agree to play in criminal conspiracies to reject any construction of the statutory language which would require the prosecution to prove an intention on the part of each conspirator that the criminal offence or offences which will necessarily be committed by one or more of the conspirators if the agreed course of conduct is fully carried out should in fact be committed . . . In these days of highly organised crime the most serious statutory conspiracies will frequently involve an elaborate and complex agreed course of conduct in which many will consent to play necessary but subordinate roles, not involving them in any direct participation in the commission of the offence or offences at the centre of the conspiracy. Parliament cannot have intended that such parties should escape conviction of conspiracy on the basis that it cannot be proved against them that they intended that the relevant offence or offences should be committed.

10-077 There remains the important question whether a person who has agreed that a course of conduct will be pursued which, if pursued as agreed, will necessarily amount to or involve the commission of an offence is guilty of statutory conspiracy irrespective of his intention, and, if not, what is the *mens rea* of the offence. I have no hesitation in answering the first part of the question in the negative. There may be many situations in which perfectly respectable citizens, more particularly those concerned with law enforcement, may enter into agreements that a course of conduct shall be pursued which will involve commission of a crime without the least intention of playing any part in furtherance of the ostensibly agreed criminal objective, but rather with the purpose of exposing and frustrating the criminal purpose of the other parties to the agreement. To say this is in no way to encourage schemes by which the police act, directly or through the agency of informers, as agents provocateurs for the purpose of entrapment. That is conduct of which the courts have always strongly disapproved. But it may sometimes happen, as most of us with experience in criminal trials well know, that a criminal enterprise is well advanced in the course of preparation when it comes to the notice either of the police or of some honest citizen in such circumstances that the only prospect of exposing and frustrating the criminals is that some innocent person should play the part of an intending collaborator in the course of criminal conduct proposed to be pursued. The *mens rea* implicit in the offence of statutory conspiracy must clearly be such as to recognise the innocence of such a person, notwithstanding that he will, in literal terms, be obliged to agree that a course of conduct be pursued involving the commission of an offence . . .

[B]eyond the mere fact of agreement, the necessary *mens rea* of the crime is, in my opinion, established if, and only if, it is shown that the accused, when he entered into the agreement, intended to play some part in the agreed course of conduct in furtherance of the criminal purpose which the agreed course of conduct was intended to achieve. Nothing less will suffice; nothing more is required.

Applying this test to the facts which, for the purposes of the appeal, we must assume, the appellant, in agreeing that a course of conduct be pursued that would, if successful, necessarily involve the offence of effecting Andaloussi's escape from lawful custody, clearly intended, by

> providing diamond wire to be smuggled into the prison, to play a part in the agreed course of conduct in furtherance of that criminal objective. Neither the fact that he intended to play no further part in attempting to effect the escape, nor that he believed the escape to be impossible, would, if the jury had supposed they might be true, have afforded him any defence."
>
> *Appeal dismissed*

One of the major reservations underlying all the inchoate offences is that no (first order) harm has been caused. How do we justify the invocation of the criminal law? We saw that (apart from arguments of there being a second order harm) the main case for criminalisation was on grounds of blameworthiness. With attempted crime the absence of harm is compensated by a requirement that the defendant intended to commit the complete offence; the highest degree of blame is required. An examination of the Criminal Law Act 1977 s.1 should lead one to a similar conclusion in relation to conspiracy—as, indeed, it has done in relation to s.1(2). One would have thought that no one could be convicted of an offence if they did not intend the consequences comprising the offence. *Anderson* refutes this view with the result that a defendant can be guilty of a serious criminal offence when there has been no conduct beyond a bare agreement and where the defendant never intended that the offence be carried out. **10–078**

Subsequent decisions have appeared to share this concern and have not all followed *Anderson*. In *McPhillips*,[168] a defendant was acquitted of conspiracy to murder because he intended to give a warning before a bomb was exploded. It was held that he could only be liable if he had intended that the plan be carried out. *Anderson* was distinguished on the unconvincing ground that in that case there had been no intention of frustrating the plan. In *Edwards*,[169] the Court of Appeal stated that the trial judge had been right to direct the jury that the defendant could only be guilty of conspiring to supply amphetamine if he had intended to supply amphetamine. *Anderson* was again distinguished in the Privy Council decision of *Yip Chiu-Cheung*. In *Yip Chiu-Cheung*,[170] D was convicted of conspiracy to traffic in heroin. He appealed on the basis that his co-conspirator, Needham (who had not been prosecuted), was an undercover drugs enforcement agent who had had no intention that the crime would be committed. The Privy Council held that D was rightly convicted of conspiracy because Needham had intended to commit that offence by carrying the heroin through customs at the airport, and on to an aeroplane bound for Australia. The fact that in the circumstances the authorities would not prosecute Needham because this was part of an undercover scheme to combat drug dealing did not mean that he did not commit the crime.[171] In *Saik*, Lord Nicholls, without referring to *Anderson*, commented that the conspirators must intend to do the act prohibited by the substantive offence.[172]

---

168 *McPhillips* (1990) 6 B.N.I.L. (Northern Ireland).

169 *R. v Edwards* [1991] Crim. L.R. 45 CA.

170 *Yip Chiu-Cheung v The Queen* [1995] 1 A.C. 111; [1994] 3 W.L.R. 514 PC.

171 To respond to the problems raised by law enforcement agents working under cover and in furtherance of the justification of conspiracy in assisting intelligence-led policing, the Law Commission has recommended that the defence of acting reasonably under the Serious Crime Act 2007 s.50 be extended to conspiracy: Law Commission Paper No.318, *Conspiracy and Attempts* (2009), para.6.56. See paras 10–112–10–113.

172 *Saik* [2007] A.C. 18 at [4].

The D in *Anderson* was not truly a conspirator. In such circumstances, it is now possible to use the inchoate offences of encouraging or assisting crime under the Serious Crimes Act 2007.[173]

(c) Necessarily amount to (or involve) a crime

10-079 We have already examined the meaning of "necessarily". It does not matter whether the actual conduct will in fact amount to a crime. What matters is whether the plan, if successfully carried out, will do so. It therefore follows that it is irrelevant whether the crime is even possible. As shall be seen, this is confirmed by the Criminal Law Act 1977 s.1(1)(b).

What is meant by "amount to or involve the commission of any offence or offences by one or more of the parties to the agreement"? In *Hollinshead,*[174] the Court of Appeal held that this meant that one of the parties had to intend to commit the offence as a principal offender. This means that there cannot be a conspiracy to aid and abet an offence.[175]

(iv) Impossibility

10-080 At common law, the House of Lords in *Nock*[176] followed *Haughton v Smith*[177] and held there could be no liability for a conspiracy to commit the impossible. This decision has now been reversed by the amendment to s.1(1) which states that there can be liability even though there exist facts which render the commission of the offence impossible. Thus, if two defendants agree to kill X, but unknown to them X is already dead, they can nevertheless still be liable for conspiracy to murder. This provision is, however, limited to statutory conspiracies. The result is somewhat anomalous: there can be liability for a statutory conspiracy to commit the impossible, but no liability for similar common law conspiracies. In relation to statutory conspiracies, the question must be asked again: when defendants have done no more than agree to commit a crime, and when it is quite impossible in any event for that crime to be committed, are we justified in imposing criminal liability?

(v) Repentance

10-081 If a conspirator repents and withdraws immediately after the agreement has been reached, it would appear that he is still guilty of conspiracy.[178] In the light of the material on repentance in the law of attempt,[179] should not a defendant who never gets further than agreeing to commit a crime, and who never does anything in pursuance of that agreement—indeed, who positively disassociates himself from it—be entitled to a defence? Unless one attaches very considerable significance to the

---

173 See paras 10-093–10-109 below.

174 *R. v Hollinshead (Peter Gordon)* [1985] 2 W.L.R. 761; (1985) 80 Cr. App. R. 285 CA.

175 This was confirmed in *R. v Kenning (David Matthew)* [2008] EWCA Crim 1534; [2009] Q.B. 221. However, Ds who agree to assist others commit crimes may now be charged under the Serious Crime Act 2007 ss.44–46: see paras 10-095–10-109.

176 *Nock* [1978] A.C. 979.

177 *Haughton* [1975] A.C. 476.

178 "Abandoning Criminal Intent" [1980] Crim. L.R. 785, 788; *R. v Barnard (Philip Charles)* (1980) 70 Cr. App. R. 28; [1980] Crim. L.R. 235 CA. See also J.R. Spencer, "Is the present offence of conspiracy too broad?" [2022] 8 Arch. Rev. 7, 7–8; Bock and Stark, "Preparatory Offences" in Ambos, Duff, Roberts, Weigend and Heinze (eds), *Core Concepts in Criminal law and Criminal Justice*, Vol.I (2019), pp.77–78.

179 See paras 10-026–10-031.

"dangerousness of collaboration" argument, liability cannot be justified in such cases. It is disappointing, therefore, that the Law Commission has rejected the idea of withdrawal amounting to a defence.[180]

3. Conspiracy to defraud

The Criminal Law Act 1977 s.5(2) provides that common law rules continue to apply "so far as relates to conspiracy to defraud". Two issues need to be addressed: the relationship between this common law conspiracy and statutory conspiracy and the width of this offence.[181] **10–082**

(i) Relationship to statutory conspiracy

Common law conspiracies to defraud will usually involve agreements to commit crimes. At one stage, the House of Lords took the view that any conspiracy which involved an agreement to commit a crime had to be dealt with under the Criminal Law Act 1977 rather than the common law.[182] This caused the prosecution considerable difficulties with both indictments and convictions for common law conspiracy being quashed when belatedly it was realised that the agreement was to commit an offence. The position now is that Ds may be charged with either offence in such cases.[183] **10–083**

(ii) Width of the offence

In *Scott v Metropolitan Police Commissioner*, the leading case on conspiracy to defraud, the House of Lords stated: **10–084**

> "[I]t is clearly the law that an agreement by two or more by dishonesty to deprive a person of something which is his or to which he is or would be or might be entitled and an agreement by two or more by dishonesty to injure some proprietary right of his, suffices to constitute the offence of conspiracy to defraud."[184]

In 2002, the Law Commission provided an extensive list of conduct that could be prosecuted only as conspiracy to defraud.[185] Since then, however, the Fraud Act 2006 has expanded the reach of the law

---

180 Law Commission Consultation Paper No.183, *Conspiracy and Attempts* (2007), paras 2.32–2.44. For criticism of the Law Commission's conclusions, see Spencer, "Is the present offence of conspiracy too broad?" [2022] 8 Arch Rev 7. cf. Bock and Stark, "Preparatory Offences", in Ambos, Duff, Roberts, Weigend and Heinze (eds), *Core Concepts in Criminal law and Criminal Justice*, Vol.I (2019), pp.81–84.

181 For further details of conspiracy to defraud, see A.T.H. Smith, *Property Offences* (Oxford: OUP, 1994), Ch.19.

182 *R. v Ayres (David Edward)* [1984] A.C. 447; [1984] 2 W.L.R. 257 HL.

183 Criminal Justice Act 1987 s.12. For guidelines on when to charge conspiracy to defraud, see: CPS, *Inchoate Offences: Legal* Guidance (2021) and the *Attorney General's guidelines for prosecutors on the use of the common law offence of conspiracy to defraud* (revised 2012). In *R. v Dady (Marc)* [2013] EWHC 475 (QB); [2013] Lloyd's Rep. F.C. 300, the court indicated that, following *R. v Rimmington (Anthony)* [2005] UKHL 63; [2006] 1 A.C. 459, where an agreement could be charged as a statutory conspiracy or a conspiracy to defraud, it should usually be charged as a statutory conspiracy unless there are good reasons to charge conspiracy to defraud.

184 *Scott v Commissioner of Police of the Metropolis* [1975] A.C. 819 at 840; [1974] 3 W.L.R. 741 HL. In *R. v Barton (David) and Booth (Rosemary)* [2020] EWCA Crim 575; [2021] Q.B. 685, a five-judge Court of Appeal stated that: ". . . there must be a dishonest agreement which includes unlawfulness, either as to the object of the agreement or the means by which it will be carried out. It is not necessary to prove an intent to deceive or an intent to cause economic or financial loss to the victim or victims, but instead either a proprietary right or interest of the potential victim must be injured (or potentially injured)".

185 Law Commission Paper No.276, *Fraud* (2002), paras 4.5–4.59.

of completed offences. From the original list it would appear that only the following forms of conduct will not amount to the offence of fraud and so can only be prosecuted as conspiracy to defraud:

(i) dishonestly obtaining a benefit which does not amount to property or services (as defined in the Fraud Act 2006) for example, obtaining confidential information;
(ii) deception without an intention to obtain a gain, or cause a loss, but which prejudices another's financial interests;
(iii) deception for a non-financial purpose; and
(iv) "fixing" an event on which bets have been placed.

10–085 In general, there need be no deception or false representation in order for the offence to be committed. In *Scott*, for example, D agreed with employees of cinema owners temporarily to remove films so that he could make pirate copies which could be distributed commercially.[186] There was no deception played on the owners who were unaware of what was happening. The House of Lords rejected the idea that deception was a necessary ingredient of the offence. There must, of course, be dishonesty.[187] However, the offence is so broad that many activities that would otherwise be legitimate can become fraudulent if the conduct is regarded as dishonest.[188]

Despite the width of the offence, there are some limits. In *GG (Plc)*,[189] for example, in relation to a prosecution brought by the Serious Fraud Office, the House of Lords refused to accept that a large-scale price-fixing agreement amounted to a conspiracy to defraud even though it had been conducted secretly and, arguably, dishonestly. As a price-fixing agreement (prior to introduction of the cartel offence in the Enterprise Act 2002 s.188[190]) was not criminal, aggravating factors such as misrepresentation needed to be proved upon which a conspiracy to defraud charge could be based.

There is no requirement that actual economic loss be involved as long as the victim's economic interests are put at risk.[191] There also need be no intent to defraud in the sense of intending to cause another economic loss. The Privy Council has held that it is sufficient if the conspirators have dishonestly agreed to do something:

---

186 For a more recent example of the use of conspiracy to defraud to prosecute internet users who produced and distributed unlawful "pirate" copies of recently released films, see: *R. v Baker (Reece)* [2016] EWCA Crim 1637.

187 The test for dishonesty is now the test in *Ivey v Genting Casinos (UK) Ltd (t/a Crockfords)* [2017] UKSC 67; [2018] A.C. 319, and *R. v Barton (David) and Booth (Rosemary)* [2020] EWCA Crim 575, discussed at paras 8–079–8–094.

188 Law Commission Paper No.276, *Fraud* (2002), para.3.6.

189 *R. v Goldshield Group Plc* [2008] UKHL 17; [2009] 1 W.L.R. 458. cf. *R. v Evans (Eric)* [2014] 1 W.L.R. 2817 CC and the comment by P. Jarvis, "Conspiracy to defraud: a siren to lure unwary prosecutors" [2014] Crim. L.R. 738. The Queen's Bench Division subsequently refused the Crown's application for a voluntary bill of indictment (*Serious Fraud Office v Evans* [2014] EWHC 3803 (QB); [2015] 1 W.L.R. 3526), although *Evans* was doubted by the Court of Appeal in *R. v H* [2015] EWCA Crim 46, a case in which it was held that it was appropriate for the Crown to charge conspiracy to defraud in respect of the alleged dishonest manipulation of the LIBOR rate to increase the profits of his employers and his own bonuses. See also *Norris v United States* [2008] UKHL 16; [2008] 1 A.C. 920. cf. J.R. Spencer, "The criminal liability of directors whose companies collapse" [2016] *Archbold Review* 5, 9.

190 This section was amended to remove "dishonesty" as a mens rea element: Enterprise and Regulatory Reform Act 2013 s.47(2).

191 *R. v Allsop (Anthony Adward)* (1977) 64 Cr. App. R. 29; [1976] Crim. L.R. 738 CA; *Wai Yu-Tsang v The Queen* [1992] 1 A.C. 269; [1991] 3 W.L.R. 1006 (trial judge's direction approved on appeal by the Privy Council). See also *Adams v The Queen* [1995] 1 W.L.R. 52; [1995] 2 Cr. App. R. 295 PC.

> ". . . which they realise will or may deceive the victim into so acting, or failing to act, that he will suffer economic loss or his economic interests will be put at risk."[192]

The Ds may not wish to harm V (they may even think they are acting with the best of motives)[193] but if they intend to bring about the state of affairs realising that V's interests could be put at risk, they will be guilty.

In *Barton and Booth*,[194] and *Bermingham*,[195] the Court of Appeal rejected arguments that the offence lacked certainty and was in breach of the European Convention on Human Rights art.7, on the basis that "the offence of conspiracy to defraud was properly described in the indictment, revealing in each instance an offence on which the jury were entitled to convict", and that the defendants would therefore have been "readily able to identify the case they had to meet".[196] **10–086**

D. PUNISHMENT OF CONSPIRACIES

At common law, the punishment of those convicted of conspiracy was at the discretion of the court.[197] In *Verrier v DPP*, the House of Lords stated that a sentence higher than that for the substantive offence could be justified "only in very exceptional cases".[198] In the case of those conspiracies which now fall within the Criminal Law Act 1977 s.1, punishment is limited to the maximum sentence for the complete crime which the defendants conspired to commit.[199] In the case of common law conspiracies to defraud, the maximum sentence has been reduced to 10 years.[200] **10–087**

---

192 *Wai Yu-Tsang* [1992] 1 A.C. 269 at 280.

193 As in the case of *Wai Yu-Tsang* [1992] 1 A.C. 269 where one of the conspirators thought he was acting in the defrauded bank's best interests by trying to prevent a run on it.

194 *R. v Barton (David) and Booth (Rosemary)* [2020] EWCA Crim 575 at [124].

195 *Bermingham* [2020] EWCA Crim 1662; [2021] 1 Cr. App. R. 24.

196 *R. v Barton (David) and Booth (Rosemary)* [2020] EWCA Crim 575 at [124], approved in *Bermingham* [2020] EWCA Crim 1662; [2021] 1 Cr. App. R. 24 at [101]. In *R. v Hayes (Tom)* [2024] EWCA Crim 304 at [157]–[158], the Court of Appeal held that it was bound by *Barton* and *Bermingham* on this issue. See also J. Collins, "Testing conspiracy to defraud's resilience" [2021] Crim. L.R. 902.

197 *Verrier v DPP* [1967] 2 A.C. 195; [1966] 3 W.L.R. 924.

198 *Verrier* [1967] 2 A.C. 195 at 223–223.

199 Criminal Law Act 1977 s.3(3).

200 Criminal Justice Act 1987 s.12. For sentencing guidelines in relation to common law conspiracy to defraud, see Sentencing Council, *Fraud*, (2014) 2024.

IV. Encouraging or Assisting Crime

A. INTRODUCTION

10-088 At common law there was an inchoate offence of incitement[201] if D persuaded or encouraged another to commit a crime. It could be used, for example, against Ds who encouraged others to view pornographic images of children, to grow cannabis or to attack unbelievers. However, the Law Commission formed the view that the offence of incitement was in need of clarification and reform[202] and in 2007, the common law offence was abolished and replaced with three new inchoate offences dealing with encouraging or assisting crime. These offences, contained within the Serious Crime Act 2007 Pt 2, were designed as part of the response to serious and organised crime, although they are not limited to such offences. They have been subject to sustained criticism from the beginning by academic commentators and by the House of Commons Justice Committee[203] and the Court of Appeal.[204] The provisions are undeniably complex[205] and raise profound concerns about the breadth of the law.

B. RATIONALE FOR LIABILITY

10-089 Consider again our earlier discussion of the rationale and punishment of attempts and conspiracies. In relation to conduct that now falls within the description of "encouraging", bear in mind that if the person encouraged agrees to commit the crime there will be a criminal conspiracy. Thus, the offence amounts to no more than an attempted conspiracy (an offence abolished by the Criminal Attempts Act 1981 s.1(4)), and this raises the question of whether the existence of this form of inchoate liability is justified. Such persons clearly have indicated some degree of dangerousness and it is obviously desirable to deter people from encouraging others to commit crime, but, unlike attempt, such actors are far removed from the complete crime. It can be argued that their actions are not *manifestly* dangerous; they constitute no "second order" harm and, unlike conspiracy, there is not necessarily the "dangerousness of combination" argument that can justify the existence of the offence. In short, given the reasons why the law does not punish guilty intentions alone but insists upon a manifestation of those intentions, does the law push back the threshold of criminal liability too far? Or have we reached the point where serious and organised crime represents such a threat to society that liability is justified? Even if the crime could now be justified, surely for the same reasons, it could *never* be justifiable to impose the same sentence (let alone a greater one, as was possible under the common law) as for the completed crime.

---

201 Statute sometimes prohibits certain specific incitements—e.g. incitement to racial hatred contrary to the Public Order Act 1986 s.18(1). These are generally not true inchoate offences in the sense of being steps on the way to the commission of a crime: there is no substantive crime of "racial hatred". See also incitement to sedition contrary to the Aliens Restriction (Amendment) Act 1919 s.3. These offences are unaffected by the abolition of common law incitement.

202 Law Commission Paper No.300, *Inchoate Liability for Assisting and Encouraging Crime* (2006), para.1.5.

203 *Post-legislative Scrutiny of Part 2 (Encouraging or Assisting Crime) of the Serious Crime Act 2007, Sixth Report of the Justice Committee* (HC 639, 2013).

204 *R. v Sadique (Omar)* [2013] EWCA Crim 1150; [2014] 1 W.L.R. 986.

205 Described by Ormerod and Laird as "one of the most complex pieces of criminal legislation to have been drafted in recent times": Ormerod and Laird, *Smith, Hogan and Ormerod's Criminal Law*, 16th edn (2021), p.493. cf. *DPP v Scott* [2022] EWHC 91 (Admin); [2022] 1 W.L.R. 2231 at [31].

That does not, however, conclude the discussion. Unlike the common law offence of incitement, the replacement statutory offences criminalise the doing of acts which "assist" as well as encourage the commission of offences. Indeed, one of the main catalysts for reform was the absence of an offence of facilitating crime.

LAW COMMISSION (LAW COM. NO.300), INCHOATE LIABILITY FOR ASSISTING AND ENCOURAGING CRIME (2006), PARAS 1.3–1.5:

"1.3 [W]e consider [this] to be a major defect of the common law. At common law if D *encourages* P to commit an offence that subsequently P does not commit or attempt to commit, D may nevertheless be criminally liable. By contrast, if D *assists* P to commit an offence, D incurs no criminal liability at common law if subsequently P, for whatever reason, does not commit or attempt to commit the offence: 10–090

Example 1A

D, in return for payment, lends a van to P believing that P will use the van in order to commit a robbery. The police arrest P in connection with another matter before P can even attempt to commit the robbery. D is not criminally liable despite the fact that he or she intended to bring about harm and, by lending the van to P, has manifested that intention. If, however, in addition to giving P the van, D had uttered words encouraging P to rob V, D would be guilty of incitement to commit robbery. The common law appears to treat words more seriously than deeds. Yet, it might be thought that seeking to bring about harm by assisting a person to commit an offence is as culpable as seeking to do so by means of encouragement.

1.4 Increasingly, the police, through the gathering of intelligence, are able to identify preliminary acts of assistance by D before P commits or attempts to commit the principal offence. Yet, the common law only partially reflects this significant development. As a result, if D assists but does not encourage P to commit an offence, the police may have to forego at least some of the advantages of more sophisticated and effective methods of investigation by having to wait until P commits or attempts to commit the offence before they can proceed against D."

Thus, the legislation attempts to remedy the defects of the common law and plug the gaps caused by the lack of a crime of facilitation (the absence of which, in the view of the Law Commission, had led to an unacceptable extension of the law of conspiracy[206]). In relation to the flaws with incitement, it has been commented that even the Law Commission acknowledged that they "rarely troubled the courts"[207] and that although some statutory clarification might have been desirable, none of the reasons above provided "a compelling case for outright abolition of incitement".[208] Furthermore, despite the Law 10–091

206 Law Commission Paper No.300, *Inchoate Liability for Assisting and Encouraging Crime* (2006), para.3.9.

207 Law Commission Paper No.305, *Participating in Crime* (2007), para.3.17.

208 D. Ormerod and R. Fortson, "Serious Crime Act 2007: the Part 2 Offences" [2009] Crim. L.R. 389, 395–396.

Commission's arguments, views are divided as to whether there was a need to criminalise acts of assistance at all or in the way adopted. While some commentators argue that the broad approach is an understandable response to serious, organised and terrorist crime,[209] others remain sceptical and believe that even if criminalisation might be justified, it could have been achieved in a much more straightforward way[210] by simply creating a new inchoate offence of facilitation.[211]

Finally, it should be noted that the proposals of the Law Commission in relation to incitement went hand in hand with their proposals in relation to complicity. Whilst the Government has taken up the first proposals it has failed to do so in relation to parties to crime. The Law Commission's original proposals were an attempt to introduce a coherent range of measures where the width of the new encouraging and assisting offences was balanced by a narrowing of the law on complicity. It is most unfortunate that as a result of the Government's response we are left with laws which significantly extend the net of liability.

C. THE LAW

10–092 The Serious Crime Act 2007 Pt 2 creates three offences of encouraging and assisting crime.[212] Despite the legislation having been in force since 2008, there has been relatively little case law on the provisions, and most to date has related to sentencing,[213] although the difficulties inherent in s.46 have, as will be seen below, been subject to judicial scrutiny. These provisions have been used, for example, to prosecute cases arising from the 2011 riots,[214] and for those involved in the supply of drugs.[215]

1. Common elements

10–093 The three offences share certain key words and phrases; notably "encouraging", "assisting" and "capable of". In a piece of legislation in which so much is spelt out one might have anticipated that

---

209 G. Sullivan, "Inchoate Liability for Assisting and Encouraging Crime" [2006] Crim. L.R. 1047; J.R. Spencer, "Helping Another Person to Commit a Crime" in P. Smith (ed), *Essays in Honour of J.C. Smith* (London: Butterworths, 1987); and W. Wilson, "A Rational Scheme of Liability for Participating in Crime" [2008] Crim. L.R. 3.

210 Ormerod and Fortson, "Serious Crime Act 2007: the Part 2 Offences" [2009] Crim. L.R. 389, 397.

211 J.R. Spencer and G. Virgo, "Encouraging and Assisting Crime: Legislate in Haste, Repent at Leisure" (2008) *Archbold News* 7.

212 Section 59 abolishes the common law of incitement.

213 See e.g. *R. v Garner-Harris (Jonathan Leslie)* [2012] EWCA Crim 2996; *R. v Lanphier (Tyler Phoenix)* [2012] EWCA Crim 731; *R. v Watling (Mark)* [2012] EWCA Crim 2894; *R. v Bell* [2014] EWCA Crim 1660; *R. v McCaffery* [2014] EWCA Crim 2550; *R. v Hutchinson* [2016] EWCA Crim 2145; *R. v Loonat (Farhan Ismail)* [2018] EWCA Crim 1835; [2013] 2 Cr. App. R. (S.) 37, *R. v Wood (Kayleigh)* [2019] EWCA Crim 1633; [2020] 1 Cr. App. R. (S.) 34, *R. v Simpson (Craig)* [2023] EWCA Crim 734 and *R. v Arcari (Richard Taylor)* [2020] EWCA Crim 1489. For a non-exhaustive list of the crimes in respect of which the Pt II offences have been successfully used, see T. Storey, "Encouraging the continuation of a pre-existing offence under the Serious Crimes Act 2007" (2022) 86 J. Crim. L. 495, 497.

214 *R. v Blackshaw (Jordan Philip)* [2011] EWCA Crim 2312; [2012] 1 W.L.R. 1126: the case involved 10 appeals against sentence. cf. C. Lightowlers and H. Quirk, "The 2011 English 'riots': prosecutorial zeal and judicial abandon" (2015) 55 Brit. J. Criminol. 165. The provisions may also be increasingly used to deal with organised crime: see *Sadique* [2013] EWCA Crim 1150, see paras 10–107–10–110.

215 See e.g. *Watling* [2012] EWCA Crim 2894; *R. v King (Gregory)* [2019] EWCA Crim 2434; *Broad* [2019] EWCA Crim 2477; *R. v Fradley (Andrew)* [2021] EWCA Crim 950 and *R. v Jones (Christopher)* [2021] EWCA Crim 1054. In relation to the use of the Act, see T. Storey, "Encouraging the continuation of a pre-existing offence under the Serious Crimes Act 2007" (2022) 86 J. Crim. L. 495 and Ministry of Justice, Post-legislative Scrutiny of the Serious Crime Act 2007, Memorandum to the Home Affairs Committee and Justice Committee (2012, Cm.8502), para.52. In 2009, there were 13 prosecutions under Pt 2 of the Act; by 2012, the number had risen to 1962, Justice Committee, Post-legislative scrutiny of Part 2 (Encouraging or assisting crime) of the Serious Crime Act 2007: Appendix B – Correspondence with the Lord Chancellor and Secretary of State for Justice and Additional Memorandum (2013).

these terms would have been defined. However, the Act does not define what acts[216] are capable of being encouragement or assistance. In so far as "encouragement" is concerned, the Law Commission's view was that "encouragement" should carry the same broad meaning that incitement had had at common law,[217]and that it included persuading, suggesting, requesting, commanding or goading another person (P) to commit a crime.[218] But it should be noted that in *Scott v DPP*, the Administrative Court stated that the Law Commission's views "cannot be conclusive on the question of what the Act means or how it is to be applied".[219] Section 65(1) does make clear that, just as with the common law, encouragement includes threatening another or otherwise putting pressure on P to commit the offence. Beyond this, the concept is one for the courts to develop. In relation to "assistance" the term is also undefined although the Law Commission's view was that it "extends to any conduct on the part of D that, as a matter of fact, makes it easier for P to commit the principal offence".[220] It is also of concern that any act of assistance, however trivial, appears to suffice for liability if it is capable of assisting another.[221]

The third common element is that D's acts must be "capable of" encouraging or assisting another to commit an offence. As the focus is upon D's conduct it is unnecessary for it, in fact to encourage or assist P to commit an offence.[222] Indeed, it is unnecessary for P to be aware of D's conduct as long as the act "is capable" of assisting or encouraging the commission of a crime.[223] This means that these offences are wider than the old law of incitement where the acts constituting the incitement had to be communicated to the incitee.[224] Under s.65(2), acts that are capable of encouraging or assisting can include "taking steps to reduce the possibility of criminal proceedings being brought in respect of that offence". While the mischief aimed at by inchoate offences is acts done prior to the commission of the substantive offence, it was made clear in *Scott* that the word "capable" in this context has a prospective meaning and is not restricted to assistance or encouragement before the commencement of the principal's offending:[225]

> "The question is whether the act may at some future point encourage or assist the commission of an offence, rather than whether the act is already providing encouragement or assistance."[226]

For example, in *Scott*, it was held that exchanging calls and texts with a prisoner (P) in possession of an unauthorised mobile phone was capable of encouraging or assisting an offence under the

216 Care is needed here. Serious Crime Act 2007 Pt 2 uses the term "act" throughout the provisions. But sometimes it refers to the defendant's act and sometimes to that of P. One notable potential cause for confusion is s.47(8) where it states that reference in s.47 to the "doing of an act" includes a failure to act; the continuation of an act that has already begun; and an attempt to do an act. The phrase "doing of an act" refers to the act of P and not to that of the defendant. See *Scott* [2022] EWHC 91 (Admin); [2022] 1 W.L.R. 2231 at [36].

217 Law Commission Paper No.300, *Inchoate Liability for Assisting and Encouraging Crime* (2006), para.5.37.

218 *R. v Goldman (Terence)* [2001] EWCA Crim 1684; [2001] Crim. L.R. 822.

219 *Scott* [2022] EWHC 91 (Admin); [2022] 1 W.L.R. 2231 at [32].

220 Law Commission Consultation Paper No.131, *Assisting and Encouraging Crime* (1993), para.4.48.

221 Law Commission Paper No.300, *Inchoate Liability for Assisting and Encouraging Crime* (2006), para.5.5.

222 *Scott* [2022] EWHC 91 (Admin); [2022] 1 W.L.R. 2231 at [33].

223 Law Commission Paper No.300, *Inchoate Liability for Assisting and Encouraging Crime* (2006), para.5.29.

224 *R. v Banks* (1873) 12 Cox C.C. 393. Although where communication failed it was possible to prosecute for an attempt to incite: *R. v Chelmsford Justices Ex p. Amos (JJ)* [1973] Crim. L.R. 437 Div Ct.

225 *Scott* [2022] EWHC 91 (Admin); [2022] 1 W.L.R. 2231 at [33]–[34].

226 *Scott* [2022] EWHC 91 (Admin); [2022] 1 W.L.R. 2231 at [33].

Prison Act 1952 s.40D(3A) even though P had had possession of the phone before D made any contact with him.[227]

10-094 Section 65(2)(b) states that Ds are liable if they fail to take reasonable steps to discharge a duty—but only if the failure is a deliberate one rather than mere forgetfulness.[228] The Law Commission gave, as an example, a security guard who omits to turn on the burglar alarm with the intention of assisting another to burgle the premises.[229] Furthermore, under s.66, D may be liable where their encouragement or assistance is indirect, for example, a gang leader who instructs a member of the gang to encourage another person to kill the victim would be liable under s.44.[230]

Given these common elements the key difference between the three new offences is in relation to the mens rea requirements.

2. Intentionally encouraging or assisting an offence

Serious Crime Act 2007 s.44:

10-095 "(1) A person commits an offence if—

(a) he does an act capable of encouraging or assisting the commission of an offence; and
(b) he intends to encourage or assist its commission.

(2) But he is not to be taken to have intended to encourage or assist the commission of an offence merely because such encouragement or assistance was a foreseeable consequence of his act."

By virtue of s.55 the offence is triable in the same way as the "anticipated offence" (the offence which D is encouraging or assisting another to commit).

(i) Actus reus

10-096 D's acts must be capable of encouraging or assisting the commission of an offence and may include a "course of conduct".[231] As noted above, the focus is very much upon the acts of D and not upon the impact it has upon P. Unlike ss.45 and 46 below, the offence encouraged or assisted can be the other inchoate offences of conspiracy or attempt; thus, D could be found liable for encouraging P to enter into a conspiracy if they possess the necessary mens rea. The existence of this double inchoate liability is a worrying illustration of the width of this offence.

---

227 *Scott* [2022] EWHC 91 (Admin); [2022] 1 W.L.R. 2231.
228 R. Fortson, *Blackstone's Guide to the Serious Crime Act 2007* (London: Blackstone, 2008), p.81; s.65(3) excludes from this provision a failure to respond to a constable's request for assistance.
229 Law Commission Paper No.300, *Inchoate Liability for Assisting and Encouraging Crime* (2006), para.3.34.
230 Home Office, *Explanatory Notes to the Serious Crime Act 2007* (2007), para.232.
231 Serious Crime Act 2007 s.67.

(ii) Mens rea

At first sight, the mens rea requirement under s.44 appears straightforward: D must intend by their act to assist or encourage the commission of the offence. Section 44(2) states that such a D cannot be taken to have intended to encourage or assist merely because such encouragement or assistance was a foreseeable consequence of his conduct. Thus, only intention suffices.[232] However, beyond this the provisions become much more complex. **10–097**

SERIOUS CRIME ACT 2007 S.47:

"47 Proving an offence under this Part **10–098**

(1) Sections 44, 45, and 46 are to be read in accordance with this section.

(5) In proving for the purposes of this section whether an act is one which, if done, would amount to the commission of an offence—

(a) if the offence is one requiring proof of fault, it must be proved that—

(i) D believed that, were the act to be done, it would be done with that fault;
(ii) D was reckless as to whether or not it would be done with that fault; or
(iii) D's state of mind was such that, were he to do it, it would be done with that fault; and

(b) if the offence is one requiring proof of particular circumstances or consequences (or both), it must be proved that—

(i) D believed that, were the act to be done, it would be done in those circumstances or with those consequences; or
(ii) D was reckless as to whether or not it would be done in those circumstances or with those consequences."

Section 44 penalises the encouragement or assistance of *an offence*; thus, where that offence requires proof of fault D must also have mens rea in relation to it. By virtue of s.47(5)(a), for offences requiring proof of fault, it must be proved that: (i) D intended[233] or believed that the act would be done with the necessary fault; (ii) was reckless whether it would be done with that fault; or (iii) that D's state of mind was such that, were they to do it, it would be done with that fault.[234] **10–099**

---

232 It is not clear whether oblique intention suffices here. The *Woollin* test requiring foresight of virtual certainty could well be applicable as this involves a far greater degree of foresight than merely being a "foreseeable consequence", but Ormerod and Laird suggest that the effect of s.44(2) is that D must have direct intention: Ormerod and Laird, *Smith, Hogan and Ormerod's Criminal Law*, 16th edn (2021), p.500.

233 Serious Crime Act 2007 s.47(7)(a).

234 The Supreme Court in *R. v Jogee (Ameen Hassan)* [2016] UKSC 8; [2016] 2 W.L.R. 651, Lords Hughes and Toulson at [86], appear to have failed to appreciate that, by virtue of s.47(5)(a), recklessness might be sufficient mens rea for the s.44 offence: ". . . Parliament has provided that foresight is not sufficient mens rea for the offence of intentionally encouraging or assisting another to commit an offence." See G. Virgo, "The relationship between inchoate and accessorial liability after *Jogee*" [2016] 9 *Archbold Review* 6.

Furthermore, if the offence is one that requires proof of consequences or circumstances or both, s.47(5)(b) requires that D believed or was reckless as to whether P's conduct would have those consequences or be done in those circumstances. The relationship between these two provisions is important. Suppose D provides P with a baseball bat, intending that P use it to cause grievous bodily harm to V but P uses it intentionally to kill V. Under s.47(5)(a), D has the requisite mens rea for encouraging murder but under s.47(5)(b), D does not believe and is not reckless as to the consequence (death) and so cannot be liable for encouraging murder. Equally, they cannot be liable for encouraging manslaughter. While P (if he had a lesser mens rea) can be liable for constructive manslaughter if they perform a dangerous unlawful act which causes death, D must foresee the consequence (death). There is no room for constructive liability here. In the baseball bat example, it is possible, however, that D could be liable for encouraging grievous bodily harm, contrary to the Offences Against the Person Act 1861 s.18—provided this offence was specified in the indictment. According to the Explanatory Notes to the Act, it would be unfair to hold D liable for encouraging and assisting murder, unless they also believed or were reckless as to whether V was killed.[235] While this is a useful safeguard (and in the context of strict liability offences means rightly that D cannot be liable without belief or recklessness as to circumstances), it does demonstrate how much overlap there now is between these inchoate offences and participatory liability: this example clearly suggests that the fact that the crime has been committed is no bar to bringing a prosecution for an inchoate offence.[236]

Finally, if D's act is capable of encouraging or assisting the commission of more than one offence, under s.49(2) they can be charged with s.44 in relation to each of the offences they intend to encourage or assist to be committed.

3. Encouraging or assisting an offence believing it will be committed

Serious Crime Act 2007 s.45:

10–100 "A person commits an offence if—

(a) he does an act capable of encouraging or assisting the commission of an offence; and
(b) he believes—

    (i) that the offence will be committed; and
    (ii) that his act will encourage or assist its commission."

10–101 As with s.44, by virtue of s.55, the offence is triable in the same way as the "anticipated offence" (the offence which D is encouraging or assisting another to commit).

---

235 Home Office, *Explanatory Notes to the Serious Crime Act 2007* (2007), para.157.

236 See further, Child, "The Differences Between Attempted Complicity and Inchoate Assisting and Encouraging—A Reply to Professor Bohlander" [2010] Crim. L.R. 924; J. Child, "Exploring the Mens Rea Requirements of the Serious Crime Act 2007 Assisting and Encouraging Offences" [2012] 76 Jo. Cr. L. 220; and D. Baker, "Lesser included offences, alternative offences and accessorial liability" (2016) Jo. Crim. L. 446, 451.

(i) Actus reus

As with s.44, D must do an act capable of encouraging or assisting the commission of an offence. The "commission of an offence" in s.45(a) includes "not only the doing of an act but also the continuation of an act by the principal".[237] Reference should be made to the discussion above of common elements.[238] **10–102**

If D's act is capable of encouraging or assisting the commission of more than one offence, by virtue of s.49(2) they can be charged with s.45 in relation to each of the offences they believe will be encouraged or assisted.

Finally, while it is possible for Ds to be charged under s.44 when they *intend* to encourage or assist in the commission of an inchoate offence, liability does not extend under s.45 to acts which a D merely *believes* will encourage or assist another inchoate offence.[239]

(ii) Mens rea

Two main features distinguish this offence from the offence in s.44. First, s.44 requires D to have acted with the purpose of encouraging or assisting the commission of an offence. Whether they believe that their endeavours will be successful is irrelevant. Under s.45, on the other hand, D must believe that the offence that they are encouraging or assisting will be committed. If a person sells a gun to another (purely because they need the money and hope that the gun will not be used) they cannot be liable under s.44, but will be liable under s.45 if they believe the offence will be committed.[240] **10–103**

The second distinguishing feature is that, for an offence under s.45, D must believe that their act will encourage or assist P to commit the offence. Under s.44, in contrast, as long as D intends to encourage or assist the commission of the offence, it is irrelevant whether they believe that their acts will actually be successful in encouraging or assisting the commission of the crime.

The term "believes" is not defined by the Act and, as commentators have said, "its boundaries remain ambiguous, lying as it does between the equally vague concepts of suspicion and knowledge".[241] However, it is much closer to knowledge than mere suspicion and when coupled with the word *will*, "indicates a high level of confidence in D's mind that P is going to commit the anticipated offence".[242] Where the offence is one involving fault, s.47(5) applies just as it does in relation to s.44.

---

237 *Scott* [2022] EWHC 91 (Admin); [2022] 1 W.L.R. 2231 at [37].

238 Above, paras 10–093–10–094. See *Scott* [2022] EWHC 91 (Admin); [2022] 1 W.L.R. 2231.

239 Serious Crime Act 2007 s.49(4); Sch.3.

240 cf. Child, "Exploring the Mens Rea Requirements of the Serious Crime Act 2007: Assisting and Encouraging Offences" (2012) 76 J. Crim. L. 220; R. Fortson, "Inchoate Liability and the Part 2 Offences under the Serious Crime Act 2007" in Reed and Bohlander (eds), *Participation in Crime: Domestic and Comparative Perspectives* (London: Routledge, 2013), Ch.10.

241 Ormerod and Fortson, "Serious Crime Act 2007: the Part 2 Offences" [2009] Crim. L.R. 389, 405.

242 Horder, *Ashworth's Principles of Criminal Law*, 10th edn (Oxford: OUP, 2022), p.543.

4. Encouraging or assisting offences believing one or more will be committed

10–104 This offence is the:

> ". . . broadest, most complex and most controversial of the new offences. It is introduced to deal with the problem encountered in secondary liability where D gives assistance and D is aware that P is likely to commit one of a number of offences, but is unsure which. For example, D drives P to a public house, being unsure whether P is likely to commit robbery, murder, explosives offences or offences against the person."[243]

SERIOUS CRIME ACT 2007 S.46:

10–105 "(1) A person commits an offence if—

(a) he does an act capable of encouraging or assisting the commission of one or more of a number of offences; and
(b) he believes—

(i) that one or more of those offences will be committed (but has no belief as to which); and
(ii) that his act will encourage or assist the commission of one or more of them.

It is immaterial for the purposes of subsection (1)(b)(ii) whether the person has any belief as to which offence will be encouraged or assisted."

Under s.55(5), this offence is triable only on indictment.

(i) Actus reus

10–106 D must do an act capable of encouraging or assisting the commission of one or more offences. The only difference between this and the earlier sections is the need to establish that the act was capable of encouraging or assisting more than one offence (which the prosecution must specify in the indictment[244]). Other than this, reference should be had to the discussion above of common elements.[245]

As with s.45, under Sch.3 D cannot be found liable for acts which they believe will encourage or assist another inchoate offence such a conspiracy or attempt.

---

243 Ormerod and Fortson, "Serious Crime Act 2007: the Part 2 Offences" [2009] Crim. L.R. 389 referring to *DPP of Northern Ireland v Maxwell* [1978] 1 W.L.R. 1350; (1979) 68 Cr. App. R. 128 HL (paras 11–023–11–024).
244 Serious Crime Act 2007 s.48(3).
245 Above, paras 10–093–10–094.

(ii) Mens rea

As with s.45, the mens rea is two-fold: D must both believe that one or more offences will be committed (including reference to s.47(5)) and that their act will encourage or assist the commission of one or more of them. However, they need not have any belief as to which of the offences will be committed in fact. In *Blackshaw,* D was convicted of this offence, having posted messages on Facebook encouraging both associates and the public to meet at a particular place and time. He believed that a number of different offences, including burglary, criminal damage and riot might be committed and that at least one would be committed.[246] **10–107**

The offence has twice come under close scrutiny by the Court of Appeal in the case of *Sadique*. D was alleged to have been involved in a national distribution business supplying chemical cutting agents (such as benzocaine) both to regional distributors of chemical cutting agents and to drug dealers. This supply was alleged to have been capable of encouraging or assisting one or more offences of supplying or being concerned in the supply of Class A or Class B drugs; that Sadique believed that one or more of these offences would be committed and that his act would assist the commission of one or more of the offences. He was charged with one count under s.46: that he assisted in the supply of Class A or Class B drugs. In an interlocutory appeal before the Court of Appeal, Sadique claimed that the offence was so vague as to be incompatible with the ECHR art.7. This argument was rejected. However, the reasoning which the court then adopted, interpreting the elements of the s.46 offence and providing guidance on the framing of indictments, divided some academic commentators.[247] It has now been found to have been flawed by a differently constituted Court of Appeal which heard Sadique's appeal against conviction.

R. v Sadique (Omar) (No.2) [2013] EWCA Crim 1150 (Court of Appeal):

JUDGE CJ: **10–108**

"**[18]** . . . [In the first case of *Sadique*] the court observed that s 46 'should only be used when the prosecution allege that D's act is capable of encouraging or assisting more than one offence', and continued that '. . . the indictment need only specify two offences and could specify any number greater than two'. The court then explained s 46 in the context of a case in which it was alleged that the count in the indictment specified offence X, punishable by life imprisonment, Y, punishable by 14 years imprisonment, and Z, punishable by ten years imprisonment. In that context the court observed that:

> "section 46 should only be used, and needs only to be used, when it may be that D, at the time of doing the act, believes that one or more of either offence X, or offence Y or offence Z will be committed, but has no belief as to which of one or ones of the three will be committed.'

246 *Blackshaw* [2011] EWCA Crim 2312.

247 See, e.g. R. Fortson, "*R. v S and H*: Assisting and Encouraging—Trial—Indictment" [2012] Crim. L.R. 449 (supporting the decision); G. Virgo, "Encouraging or Assisting More than One Offence" *Archbold Review,* 13 March 2012; and G. Virgo, "Enough is Enough", *Archbold News,* 12 April 2013 (criticising the decision).

In the case of a trial involving these issues, the court agreed with the prosecution that it would be better practice to have a separate s 46 count for X, Y and Z, and indeed went on to say 'that there should always be separate counts if D pleads not guilty' adding, however, that the failure to do so (that is to produce separate counts) 'would not of itself affect the safety of the conviction'. On this basis the observations of the court were directed not to issues of substantive law, but to process.

[19] According to Professor Virgo, *Encouraging or Assisting More Than One Offence* (Archbold Review, 13 March 2012) the effect of the judgment, which was addressing the issue of vagueness and uncertainty has, 'if anything made the offence vague, uncertain and effectively redundant'. The offence in s 46 was rendered 'practically obsolete'. In issue 3 dated 12 April 2013 of Archbold News—*Enough is Enough'* Professor Virgo returned to the impact of the decision which, he suggests:

'. . . drives a coach and horses through the s 46 offence, bears out my concerns about the drafting and comprehensibility of the legislation, which has made the task of the senior judiciary very difficult in making sense of the law . . . The effect of their (the judges') decision is to render that offence otiose. Since each contemplated offence must now be charged as a separate count, the Defendant can only be convicted if he or she believed that a specific offence would be committed; that is the same as the conditions for conviction under s 45. It follows that a Defendant who contemplates a number of offences being committed but does not believe any specific crime would be committed, cannot be guilty of assisting or encouraging an offence. That is an unfortunate restriction on the ambit of liability and will cause problems in future . . .'

10–109 **[20]** The problem, if we may say so, rightly identified by Professor Virgo arises, as it seems to us, from the starting point in the reasoning of the court, found at para 49 of the judgment:

'D cannot be convicted of count 1 (the other ingredients being satisfied) unless at the time of doing the act:

(a) Either

 (i) D believes that X will be committed; or
 (ii) D believes that one or more of the offences specified in the indictment (X, Y and Z) will be committed but has no belief as to which; and

(b) D believes that his act will encourage or assist the commission of X; and
(c) D believes that X will be committed with the necessary fault for X.'

[21] We are concerned that in this analysis it appears that a reference to the offence created by s 45 of the Act has been included as an ingredient of the offence created by s 46. In this paragraph of the judgment (a)(i) 'D believes that X will be committed'; repeats the precise language in s 45(b)(i) that D believes that the offence will be committed. Section 45, of course, is directed to 'an offence' or 'the offence'. However the entire thrust of s 46 is directed to the encouragement or assistance of offences in the belief that one or more of a number of offences will be committed. As the offences created by ss, 44, 45 and 46 are distinct offences, we have concluded that the foundation for the analysis was flawed, and that we are not bound by obiter observations of the court directed to procedural matters relating to the indictment rather than the full ambit of the offence . . .

[30] As we have already explained, the 2007 Act created three distinct offences. It is not open to the court to set one or other of them aside and the legislation must be interpreted to give effect to the creation by statute of the three offences. It may well be that the common law offence of inciting someone else to commit an offence was less complex. It may equally be that the purpose of the legislation could have been achieved in less tortuous fashion. Nevertheless these three distinct offences were created by the 2007 Act, with none taking priority over the other two. Section 46 creates the offence of encouraging or assisting the commission of one or more offences. Its specific ingredients and the subsequent legislative provisions underline that an indictment charging a s 46 offence of encouraging one or more offences is permissible.

[31] This has the advantage of reflecting practical reality. A Defendant may very well believe that his conduct will assist in the commission of one or more of a variety of different offences by another individual without knowing or being able to identify the precise offence or offences which the person to whom he offers encouragement or assistance intends to commit, or will actually commit. As Professor Virgo explains in his most recent article, the purpose of the s 46 was 'to provide for the relatively common case where a Defendant contemplates that one of a variety of offences might be committed as a result of his or her encouragement'. We entirely agree . . .

[34] In our judgment the ingredients of the s 46 offence, and the ancillary provisions, and s 58(4)–(7) in particular, underline that an indictment charging a s 46 offence by reference to one or more offences is permissible, and covers the precise situation for which the legislation provides. Before the Appellant in the present case could be convicted, the jury had to be satisfied that:

(a) he was involved in the supply of the relevant chemicals and
(b) that, if misused criminally, the chemicals were capable of misuse by others to commit offences of supplying or being concerned in the supply of, or being in possession with intent to supply class A and/or class B drugs. None of this would be criminal unless it was also proved
(c) that at the time when the relevant chemicals were being supplied, the Appellant believed that what he was doing would encourage or assist the commission of one or more of these drug related offences and
(d) that he also believed that this was the purpose, or one of the purposes, for which the chemicals would be used by those to whom he supplied them. If those ingredients were

> established, as the chemicals could be used for cutting agents for class A drugs or class B drugs, or both, it was not necessary for the Crown to prove that he had a specific belief about the particular drug related offence which those he was encouraging or assisting would or did commit . . .
>
> **[36]** In our judgment count 1 of the indictment was appropriately charged and fell within the proper ambit of the s 46 offence created by the 2007 Act . . .
>
> **[40]** The Appellant was properly convicted of this offence. The appeal against conviction will therefore be dismissed . . ."
>
> *Appeal dismissed*

10–110 As has been commented, the fact that two differently constituted Court of Appeals could come to different interpretations of s.46 is not the fault of the judiciary.[248] It illustrates the profound difficulties inherent with this provision. Whilst the second appeal restores purpose to the provision, not only are we left with a very wide offence, but also the interpretative difficulties have not been fully resolved: prosecutors are still likely to encounter difficulties in framing appropriate indictments.

5. Defences

10–111 As the three offences are inchoate it is, of course, no defence to put forward a defence that P did not actually commit an offence.[249] But the Serious Crime Act 2007 Pt 2 does create two special defences to the three offences.

(i) The defence of acting reasonably

SERIOUS CRIME ACT 2007 S.50:

10–112

> "(1) A person is not guilty of an offence under this Part if he proves—
>
> a. that he knew certain circumstances existed; and
> b. that it was reasonable for him to act as he did in those circumstances.
>
> (2) A person is not guilty of an offence under this Part if he proves—
>
> a. that he believed certain circumstances to exist;
> b. that his belief was reasonable; and
> c. that it was reasonable for him to act as he did in the circumstances as he believed them to be.

248 R. Fortson, "*R. v Sadique (Omar)*: Assisting and Encouraging—Trial—Indictment' [2014] Crim. L.R. 61, 66. See also F. Stark, "Encouraging or assisting clarity?" [2013] 72 C.L.J. 497; G. Virgo, "Making sense of section 46 of the Serious Crime Act 2007" (2013) 7 *Archbold Review* 4.

249 Serious Crime Act 2007 s.49(1). By virtue of s.47(2) it is also no defence for the defendant to claim that he did not know that the conduct that he was encouraging or assisting P to commit was a criminal offence. Ignorance of the law is no defence.

(3) Factors to be considered in determining whether it was reasonable for a person to act as he did include—

a. the seriousness of the anticipated offence (or, in the case of an offence under section 46, the offences specified in the indictment);
b. any purpose for which he claims to have been acting;
c. any authority by which he claims to have been acting."

Two points must be noted. First, the question of whether D's belief is reasonable is one to be determined by a jury; it is not enough that D believes their acts to be reasonable. Secondly, the burden of proof rests with D to prove reasonableness. **10–113**

This defence applies to all three of the offences despite the Law Commission's view that it should not be available to s.44. However, given that s.44 requires intention it is most unlikely that the defence will be available in any event. The Law Commission provided illustrations of when the defence might operate: for example, D, a motorist, who moves into an inside lane to allow P, another motorist to overtake, even though D is aware that P is exceeding the speed limit, could use the defence of acting reasonably in answer to a charge under s.45.[250] Bock and Stark have described this defence as "a shameful definitional cop-out":

"Rather than identify properly the preparatory conduct that merits criminalisation, when balanced against citizens' interests in liberty etc., the legislature has left it to D to prove that his conduct did not unjustifiably threaten some legal good. "[251]

(ii) Defence for the victim assister

Serious Crime Act 2007 s.51:

"(1) In the case of protective offences, a person does not commit an offence under this Part by reference to such an offence if— **10–114**

a. he falls within the protected category; and
b. he is the person in respect of whom the protective offence was committed or would have been if it had been committed.

(2) 'Protective offence' means an offence that exists (wholly or in part) for the protection of a particular category of persons ('the protected category')."

---

250 Law Commission Paper No.300, *Inchoate Liability for Assisting and Encouraging Crime* (2006), para.A.63.
251 Bock and Stark, 'Preparatory Offences', in Ambos, Duff, Roberts, Weigend and Heinze (eds), *Core Concepts in Criminal law and Criminal Justice*, Vol.I (2019), p.71.

10–115 This section codifies the principle established in the case of *Tyrrell*.[252] The effect of the section is to make it clear that Ds cannot be liable for encouraging or assisting offences which are designed to protect them.[253] For example, if a 12-year-old girl intentionally encourages P, a man of 21, to have sex with her and he declines, s.51 prevents her being liable for the offence of encouraging child rape because the offence of child rape was created to protect children under 13 years old.

6. Impossibility

10–116 Originally, under the common law of incitement it had been held in *McDonough*[254] that there could be liability for an incitement to commit the impossible. This was approved obiter by the House of Lords in *Nock*.[255] However, in *Fitzmaurice*,[256] it was held that in many cases there could be no liability for incitement to commit the impossible.[257]

In proposing the new offences, the Law Commission stated:

> "We believe that impossibility should not be a defence to the new offences that we are recommending. D's state of mind and, therefore, his or her culpability, is unaffected by the unknown impossibility of the principal offence being committed. Further, if D can be liable notwithstanding that, contrary to D's belief, P never intends to commit the principal offence, it would be illogical if D was able to plead that it would have been impossible to commit the principal offence."[258]

The Serious Crime Act 2007 has not addressed this point directly. However, for all three offences D's acts must be capable of encouraging or assisting the commission of an offence. So, if D encourages or does an act to assist P to kill X, but X is already dead (one of the classic examples of impossibility), D has not done an act capable of encouraging or assisting the murder of X. Because of the impossibility of the crime, there can be no liability.[259]

10–117 Such an approach would, however, place the law here at odds with the law on attempting the impossible and statutory conspiracies to commit the impossible. One can, therefore, predict that the courts will follow the approach in these other areas of law and simply require that the acts be capable of encouraging or assisting the commission of the *anticipated* offence (the murder of X). For oblique support, the courts could draw on s.49(7) which provides that for the purposes of

---

252 *R. v Tyrrell* [1894] 1 Q.B. 710 CC.

253 In *Gnango* [2011] UKSC 59; [2012] 1 A.C. 827 at [50], Lord Phillips and Lord Judge CJ described this section as providing a "limited exemption" from liability.

254 *R. v McDonough (Bernard Joseph Gerrard)* (1963) 47 Cr. App. R. 37 CA.

255 *Nock* [1978] A.C. 979.

256 *R. v Fitzmaurice (Robert)* [1983] Q.B. 1083; [1983] 2 W.L.R. 227 CA.

257 See the 6th edition of this book, pp.538–539.

258 Law Commission Paper No.300, *Inchoate Liability for Assisting and Encouraging Crime* (2006), para.6.61.

259 In *R. (on the application of the United States) v Nirvana* [2018] EWHC 706 (Admin) at [15]–[16]; [2018] A.C.D. 49, the Administrative Court rejected an argument that the sale of cannabis seeds to the US amounted to an offence under the Serious Crime Act 2007 s.44 (encouraging or assisting the cultivation of cannabis). Exporting cannabis seeds was not an offence in the UK, so the dual criminality test was not satisfied.

s.45(b)(i) and s.46(1)(b)(i) (believing that the offence will be committed), it is sufficient for the defendant to believe that the offence will be committed if certain conditions are met. One of these conditions could be that X is alive.

It is unfortunate, given the length and complexities of the Serious Crime Act 2007 Pt 2, that nothing explicit has been stated about the issue of impossibility.[260]

7. Punishment

Section 58 provides the penalties that apply to the three new offences. Where the offence encouraged or assisted is murder, s.58(2) states that the maximum penalty is imprisonment for life. Section 58(3) provides that, other than for murder, the maximum penalty available for an offence under s.44 or s.45 is the same as the maximum available on conviction for the full offence. This rule also applies to s.46 but is restricted to where D is found guilty in relation to one offence only: **10–118**

> "For example D lends P a van, false number plates and a gun. The prosecution argue that he believed that either burglary or murder would be committed. The jury find D guilty in relation to burglary but not guilty in relation to murder. The maximum sentence available for the conviction under section 46 will be the maximum sentence available for the offence of burglary (14 years)."[261]

The situation where a D is convicted of more than one offence under s.46 is provided for under s.58(5) and (7). Where one of the offences is murder, the maximum available penalty is imprisonment for life. Where none of the full offences is murder, but one or more of them is punishable by imprisonment, the maximum sentence is limited to the offence that carries the highest penalty. If none of the offences is punishable by imprisonment the maximum penalty is a fine.[262]

8. Conclusion

The offences contained within the Serious Crime Act 2007 Pt 2 were created to remedy defects in the old common law of incitement despite the fact that the case for abolition was far from overwhelming and to remove the gap caused by the lack of a crime of facilitation—and doubts still exist as to whether this was a real lacuna. Even if a lacuna existed, reform could have been much more straightforward. Instead, the legislation is "overdetailed, convoluted and unreadable"[263] amply demonstrated by the differing interpretations of s.46 in *Sadique*. Reform is much needed.[264] **10–119**

---

260 For one instance where impossibility has been provided for, see Serious Crime Act 2007 s.47(6) (where the defendant is *assumed* to be able to do the relevant act) and Home Office, *Explanatory Notes to the Serious Crime Act 2007* (2007), para.159.

261 Ministry of Justice, *Serious Crime Act 2007: Implementation of Part 2* (2008), para.70.

262 Serious Crime Act 2007 s.58(7).

263 Spencer and Virgo, "Encouraging and Assisting Crime: Legislate in Haste, Repent at Leisure" (2008) *Archbold News* 7, 8.

264 See, e.g. the comments by Stark, "Encouraging or Assisting Clarity" [2013] 72 C.L.J. 497, 501.

V. Double Inchoate Liability

10–120 Double inchoate liability arises when D is convicted of committing an inchoate offence that relates to another inchoate offence. Under the old common law of incitement, for example, it was an offence to incite someone to incite a crime.[265] In view of the issues considered at the beginning of this chapter, any such liability should be viewed with considerable caution. It is far from clear that there is a need for criminal liability in circumstances where the defendant's actions are so far removed from a substantive offence. However, the trend in recent years has been to expand the reach of the criminal law to cover such cases.

As the law stands, the following double inchoate crimes may be prosecuted:

- it is an offence to intentionally encourage or assist an act of encouragement or assistance in relation to an offence;[266]
- it is an offence to intentionally encourage or assist a conspiracy;[267]
- it is an offence to intentionally encourage or assist an attempt.[268]

In none of the above three situations is it an offence to encourage or assist the commission of an inchoate offence if D merely believes that his acts will encourage or assist the commission of an offence:[269]

- it is an offence to attempt to encourage or assist the commission of an offence;[270]
- furthermore, as already seen, it is possible to attempt any indictable offence (other than those excluded by the Criminal Attempts Act 1981 s.1(4)) even if that offence is one that only punishes acts of preparation.[271]

The Law Commission had favoured making it an offence to attempt to conspire[272] in the interests of consistency in this area of law, but the strength of opposition to the proposal resulted in it being abandoned.[273] The argument that the "ultimate harm would be too remote and that [it] would therefore result in an unjustified expansion of the law"[274] is persuasive and it is to be hoped that this will act as a brake upon further development of double inchoate liability.

---

265 *Sirat* (1985) 83 Cr. App. R. 41. See Law Commission Paper No.300, *Inchoate Liability for Assisting and Encouraging Crime* (2006), para.3.36.

266 Serious Crime Act 2007 s.49(4). This applies to intentional encouragement or assistance only, i.e. the s.44 offence.

267 By virtue of the repeal of the Criminal Law Act 1977 s.5(7) (which stated that it is not an offence to incite a conspiracy) by the Serious Crime Act 2007 Sch.14.

268 By virtue of the Serious Crime Act 2007 ss.44, 49(4) and Sch.3.

269 i.e. Offences under the Serious Crime Act 2007 ss.45 and 46 are excluded by s.49(4) and Sch.3.

270 Criminal Attempts Act 1981 s.1(4) (see para.5–072) excludes certain forms of liability, such as attempted conspiracy and attempts to aid and abet a crime, from its ambit, but does not exclude the possibility of an attempt to encourage or assist a crime. As it was technically possible to conspire to incite under the common law it is possibly unlawful to conspire to encourage or assist. See Horder, *Ashworth's Principles of Criminal Law*, 8th edn (Oxford: OUP, 2016), p.486.

271 *R. v R* [2008] 2 Cr. App. R. 38. See para.10–006.

272 By repealing the Criminal Attempts Act 1981 s.1(4)(a).

273 Law Commission Paper No.318, *Conspiracy and Attempts* (2009), paras 3.1–3.23.

274 Law Commission Paper No.318, *Conspiracy and Attempts* (2009), para.3.16.

VI. Endangerment Offences

R.A. Duff, "Intentions Legal and Philosophical" (1989) 9 O.J.L.S. 76, 86:

"What harms should the criminal law aim to prevent? Death, bodily injury and the loss of property may seem to be three obvious 'primary harms' (each primary harm will generate a range of 'secondary harms', which take their character as harms from their relation to a primary harm; if death is a primary harm, then being subjected to the threat, risk or fear of death is a secondary and derivative harm); 10-121

Though these harms are initially identified without reference to human actions as their causes, the criminal law, as a set of sanction-backed prohibitions, can help to prevent them by prohibiting and thus preventing actions which cause them. It can do this in various ways: by directly prohibiting actions which cause such harms ('killing', 'wounding and causing grievous bodily harm', 'damaging or destroying property' or 'depriving another of his property'); by prohibiting actions which are likely to cause such harms, under descriptions which refer directly to those harms ('attempting to kill'; 'reckless driving', defined in terms of the creation of an 'obvious and serious risk of causing physical injury'; or 'causing danger to the lieges by culpable recklessness'); by prohibiting conduct which is likely to cause such harms, but under descriptions which make no *direct* reference to those harms ('driving with excess alcohol in the blood,' or offences under s.19 and s.20 of the Firearms Act 1968)."

The term "endangerment offences" is used here to describe those offences that are complete in themselves and not dependent upon proof that any further offence was intended.[275] Some of these offences have the same rationale as inchoate offences; they are conceived of as being steps to the commission of further offences. For example, people who carry offensive weapons in public places could well use those weapons. More commonly, however, conduct is criminalised simply because of its potential to cause harm. For example, dangerous driving is conduct that is likely to cause harm and is criminalised, again, for reasons similar to the criminalisation of inchoate offences, namely, in the hope of preventing the materialisation of the harm. The seriousness of endangerment offences is loosely linked to the likelihood (and potential gravity) of the harm materialising. For example, dangerous driving is more likely to cause harm than careless driving and accordingly carries a heavier penalty. 10-122

English law abounds with a wide variety of such offences and the number of them continues to increase. There are many offences of possessing prohibited articles, such as possessing explosives,[276] firearms[277] or counterfeiting tools.[278] A recent example may be found in the offences created by the Coronavirus

275 See generally, R.A. Duff, "Criminalizing Endangerment" in R.A. Duff and S. Green (eds), *Defining Crimes* (Oxford: OUP, 2005). cf. A. Ashworth, "A new generation of omissions offences?" [2018] Crim. L.R. 354.

276 Explosive Substances Act 1883 s.4(1).

277 Firearms Act 1968 ss.16–22.

278 Forgery and Counterfeiting Act 1981 s.17.

Regulations.[279] The object of the legislation prohibiting such possession is "frequently to prevent the articles being used for criminal purposes".[280] The Road Traffic Act 1988 penalises various forms of bad driving: for example, dangerous driving, careless driving and driving when under the influence of drink or drugs.[281] The Criminal Attempts Act 1981 s.9, creates the offence of interfering with vehicles; such conduct is regarded as being indicative that theft or a similar offence is likely to be committed. Under the Criminal Damage Act 1971 it is an offence to cause criminal damage "intending . . . or being reckless as to whether the life of another would be thereby endangered".[282] The Sexual Offences Act 2003 creates an offence of meeting following grooming to try to deal with the dangers posed by adults using internet chat-rooms to seduce children.[283] Finally, by way of example, new terrorism offences have also been created: the Terrorism Act 2000 s.58(1)(b) creates an offence of possessing information likely to be useful to a person committing or preparing an act of terrorism.[284]

There are numerous endangerment driving offences which do not require that any damage or injury occur as a result of the prohibited conduct.[285] The rationale for these offences has been examined by Kyd and Cammiss.

S. Kyd and S. Cammiss, "Driving offences: promoting consistency for victims in "victimless" crimes of endangerment" [2020] Crim. L.R. 223, 225–226:

10–123 **"The theoretical underpinnings of endangerment offences**

. . . What [the offences of careless driving, dangerous driving, and using a mobile phone whilst driving] have in common is that they do not require any result to have been caused by the offending behaviour of the defendant. In relation to both careless and dangerous driving the test is objective, insofar as D's driving is assessed against the standard of a competent and careful driver. Where the driving falls below that standard, the driving is careless; where it falls *far* below that standard, it is dangerous. Neither offence requires any particular result to have occurred, although dangerous driving does require that a competent and careful driver would realise that the driving was dangerous, in the sense that it created a *risk* of injury or of serious damage to property.

---

279 e.g. the Health Protection (Coronavirus, Restrictions) (All Tiers)(England) Regulations 2020 (SI 2020/1374). cf. *R. (on the application of Michli) v Westminster Magistrates' Court* [2024] EWHC 559 (Admin); [2024] Crim. L.R. 405.

280 Baker, *Glanville Williams, Textbook of Criminal Law*, 4th edn (London: Sweet & Maxwell, 2016), p.636.

281 Road Traffic Act 1988 ss.1, 3 and 4, respectively.

282 Criminal Damage Act 1971 s.1(2).

283 Sexual Offences Act 2003 s.15. See further, B. Gallagher, *International and Internet Child Sexual Abuse and Exploitation* (Huddersfield: Huddersfield University, 2006).

284 See also the offence of preparing terrorist acts, contrary to the Terrorism Act 2006 s.5(1)(a); R. Kelly, "Sentencing Terrorism Offences: No Harm Intended?" (2019) Crim. L.R. 764. For a list of offences under the Offences Against the Person Act 1861 involving danger to life or bodily harm, see Criminal Law Revision Committee, 14th Report, *Offences Against the Person*, Cmnd.7844 (1980), paras 192–214. See generally, K.J.M. Smith, "Liability for Endangerment: English *Ad Hoc* Pragmatism and American Innovation" [1983] Crim. L.R. 127.

285 e.g. dangerous driving (Road Traffic Act 1988 s.2), careless driving (Road Traffic Act 1988 s.3), using a mobile phone whilst driving (Road Vehicles (Construction and Use) Regulations 1986 (SI 1986/1078) reg.110. Kyd and Cammiss have shown that prosecutions for careless and dangerous driving do take place in the absence of direct harm having been caused: S. Kyd and S. Cammiss, "Driving offences: promoting consistency for victims in "victimless" crimes of endangerment" [2020] Crim. L.R. 223. In cases where a death has resulted, English law has several aggravated endangerment offences such as causing death by dangerous driving: Road Traffic Act 1988 s.1. See, generally, Clarkson, "Aggravated Endangerment Offences" (2007) 60 C.L.P. 278.

In one sense they are 'victimless' crimes, in that it is not necessary for a complainant to have suffered any identifiable harm as a result of the offence. On the other hand, they are offences that have the potential to cause considerable harm and result in death, depending on circumstances and factors that may be outside the control of the offender. Given that these offences may result in 'near misses' or even collisions resulting in anything from minor damage to property to injuries to the person, in reality they are often not 'victimless'. In short, the current offences exist as endangerment offences to punish causing the second-order harm of risking harm to others. At a theoretical level, Finkelstien [C. Finkelstein, "Is Risk Harm?" (2003) 151 University of Pennsylvania Law Review 963] has defended the criminalisation of endangerment offences through her Risk Harm Thesis, arguing that: 'a person who inflicts a risk of harm on another damages that interest, thus lowering the victim's baseline welfare'. It is worth noting that Finkelstein does not conceive of such offences as 'victimless':

> 'if the risk of harm is itself a harm, then we can punish risky behavior without having to regard such behavior as an instance of the controversial category of 'victimless crimes.' And, . . . there are already legal doctrines that might be best explained in terms of exposure to risk, such as attempts and reckless driving.'

It is not clear from Finkelstein's thesis how remote a risk could be and yet remain a second-order harm. This, it is argued, is the difficulty in measuring an appropriate response to endangerment offences such as careless driving. Where a cyclist experiences a near-miss as the result of a 'close-pass' they are clearly the victim, their baseline welfare having been lowered. But careless driving does not require an individual to have been affected by driving that falls below the required standard. If D drives on an empty road at a standard below that of a competent and careful driver, the offence of careless driving is nevertheless committed; the question will be whether it is in the public interest to prosecute."

In cases other than driving offences where the harm has materialised, D is simply convicted of the endangerment offence but is given an increased punishment to reflect the causing of the harm. For example, under the Dangerous Dogs Act 1991 s.3(1), a person is liable for a basic endangerment offence if his dog is dangerously out of control in a public place; this offence is punishable with a maximum of six months' imprisonment. If that dog injures any person, an aggravated offence is committed which is punishable by a maximum of two years' imprisonment on conviction on indictment. This has been the usual way of dealing with cases where a death has resulted at work as a result of a breach of the endangerment offences contained in the Health and Safety at Work etc. Act 1974 ss.2–4. Greater punishment is imposed to reflect that death or other serious injury has occurred.[286] **10–124**

286 See para.4–097.

In evaluating these endangerment offences, it is important to remember that, unlike the inchoate offences, they are all complete crimes in themselves and each carries its own penalty. Indeed, if they are indictable offences, there may be liability for attempting to commit them,[287] or for conspiracy or for encouraging or assisting someone to commit them. Can one ever justify liability for an inchoate offence when the offence-in-chief is itself only an endangerment offence?

With these offences there is a harm, albeit a second-order harm. For example, the harm involved in unauthorised possession of a firearm or other offensive weapons is the violation of society's interests in security and freedom from alarm. Firearms are inherently dangerous and their widespread, unlicensed possession could lead to an increase in their usage. Whether conduct that has the potential for causing harm is criminalised depends on balancing the seriousness of the possible harm and the likelihood of its occurrence against the social value of the conduct. So, possession of firearms is prohibited while possession of other dangerous weapons with greater social value, such as kitchen knives, is not criminalised.[288]

10–125 Following this reasoning, it is possible to justify the existence of these offences on the basis of there being a secondary harm.[289] However, it is disturbing that many of these offences are ones of strict liability. For example, in *Hussain*,[290] D was convicted of possessing a firearm which he believed was his son's toy. With attempts, the second-order harm has to be backed up by "first degree blameworthiness" in the form of intention. With endangerment offences, such as possession of a firearm, the second-order harm need be accompanied by no blameworthiness at all. This hardly seems justifiable. In such cases, there ought to be a "due-diligence defence" to enable defendants such as Hussain to escape liability.

In the US, many states have general offences of "reckless endangerment". For example, the Model Penal Code s.211.2 provides that:

> "A person commits a misdemeanour if he recklessly engages in conduct which places or may place another person in danger of death or serious bodily injury. Recklessness and danger shall be presumed where a person knowingly points a firearm at or in the direction of another, whether or not the actor believed the firearm to be loaded."[291]

English law has no such general counterpart, preferring to focus instead on specific areas of risk-creation as instanced above. Is this ad hoc approach justifiable?

---

287 e.g. *R. v R* [2008] EWCA Crim 619; [2009] 1 W.L.R. 713.

288 See, generally, A. von Hirsch, "Extending the Harm Principle: 'Remote' Harm and Fair Imputation" in Simester and Smith (eds), *Harm and Culpability* (Oxford: Clarendon Press, 1996); A. Ashworth, "The Unfairness of Risk-Based Possession Offences" in *Positive Obligations in Criminal Law*" (Oxford: Hart Publishing, 2015), Ch.6.

289 cf. R.A. Duff and S.E. Marshall, "'Abstract Endangerment', Two Harm Principles and Two Routes to Criminalization" (2015) *Minnesota Legal Studies Research Paper* No.15–19.

290 *R. v Hussain* (1981) 47 Cr. App. R. 143. See also *R. v Bradish (Liam Christopher)* [1990] 1 Q.B. 981; [1990] Crim. L.R. 723 CA; *R. v Waller* [1991] Crim. L.R. 381 CA; *R. v Steele* [1993] Crim. L.R. 298.

291 In Australia, many states have separate endangerment offences relating to death and to serious injury. See D. Lanham, "Danger Down Under" [1999] Crim. L.R. 960. cf. the comparison between German and English endangerment laws in R.A. Duff and T. Hörnle, "Crimes of Endangerment" in K. Ambos (ed), *Core Concepts in Criminal Law and Criminal Justice*, vol.II (2022).

C.M.V. Clarkson, "General Endangerment Offences: The Way Forward?" (2005) 32(2) University of Western Australia Law Review 131, 135–137, 141–143:

"**CASE FOR A GENERAL ENDANGERMENT OFFENCE** 10–126

. . . One of the main reasons for having a general endangerment offence is to ensure that there are no gaps, which might exist if there were only specific endangerment offences . . . While specific endangerment offences can be tailored to certain dangerous activities such as driving motor vehicles or running factories, there are a host of other everyday activities where we depend on others to perform their actions safely (e.g., electricians and builders working in our houses, or child carers looking after our children, or doctors caring for our health). It is almost impossible to cater in advance, through specific offences, for all such persons who might act in a manner dangerous to our lives or safety. Only a general offence is capable of covering all such cases.

CASE AGAINST A GENERAL ENDANGERMENT OFFENCE

When the general endangerment offence was introduced in Western Australia . . . many specific offences [were retained] . . . The result is too many overlapping offences. This is undesirable. One of the main functions of the criminal law is to communicate clearly with citizens exactly what conduct is prohibited and the consequences of a violation of that law. If any individual action can give rise to a myriad of offences, that communication will necessarily be obscured. A further and very significant objection to having too many overlapping offences is that this confers too much discretion on the prosecution as to which charge(s) to bring . . . [T]the result is that defendants may feel pressured into pleading guilty to lesser offences rather than face the more serious charges . . .

[Another] . . . objection to the introduction of a general endangerment offence is that it could lead to over-criminalisation and offend the minimalism principle (i.e., the last resort principle) . . . A potential problem with a general endangerment offence is that it can be so broad as to sweep conduct within its ambit that would not warrant criminalisation under these strict criteria. Controversial examples that have been cited include the following: the solo yachtsman sailing around the world, or the mountain climber who causes someone to undertake a dangerous rescue, or firemen going on strike. Given the much publicised dangers of passive smoking it could well be argued that smoking in public threatens the life, health and safety of those around the smoker. Such conduct could presumably be swept within the ambit of a general endangerment offence . . .

Decisions to make it an offence to be drunk in the street or to smoke in the presence of others or to engage in sexual activity while HIV positive (bearing in mind that in Australia the general endangerment offences are relatively serious offences) require careful debate before being swept within the ambit of a broad new offence. The existence of a general endangerment offence means that full discussion of whether such conduct should be criminalised is avoided. One of the fundamental principles underpinning the criminal law is that of fair warning. People should know in advance what conduct is impermissible. In all these above scenarios this principle is violated."

Chapter 11

Participation in Crime

I. Introduction

So far in our analysis of the criminal law, we have assumed that only one defendant is involved, and we have considered that person's liability for acting alone. This may well be the case but it is also likely that at some stage either in the planning or commission of the crime other persons have become involved.[1] They may have supplied tools, information, advice, kept a look-out or even instigated the crime. In many cases, however, the crime may have been unplanned and spontaneous, brought about on the spur of the moment when a suggestion from one member of a group is taken up by others and acted upon. Where crime is a group activity it is arguable that a distinct set of problems arise in relation to using punishment to deter criminal activity. 11–001

Paul H. Robinson and John M. Darley, "Does Criminal Law Deter? A Behavioural Science Investigation" (2004) 24 O.J.L.S. 173–205, 180–181:

"[B]oth the ability and the motivation to make the calculations required for deterrence can be influenced by a variety of contextual effects, . . . Perhaps the most important of these stems from the fact that crimes are often committed by groups. When offenders commit crimes in street gangs, for instance, several effects can temporarily reduce the possible impact of a threatened future prison term on current law-breaking activities: an 'arousal effect' leads to sprees and reduced sensitivity to risk, and an increase in the immediate rewards can arise from an increase in esteem in which the group holds the member who boldly breaks the law. 11–002

Of exacerbating effect is the fact of differential association . . . Interviews with criminals consistently show that the individual feels 'led to' the commission of the crime by the confidence that other

1 Between 1990 and 2000, 22% of murders and 15% of involuntary manslaughters involved multiple parties (S. Weston, "Criminal Complicity: A Comparative Analysis of Homicide Liability" (Swansea: University of Wales, PhD thesis, 2002). Although only looking at joint enterprise, a report revealing that between 2005 and 2020 there were 10,696 prosecutions for homicide involving two or more defendants also gives an indication of the extent to which multiple suspects are prosecuted for the worst types of cases: H.H. Mills, M. Ford and R. Grimshaw, *The usual suspects: Joint enterprise prosecutions before and after the Supreme Court ruling*, 2nd edn (London: Centre for Crime and Justice Studies, 2022), p.10, *https://www.crimeandjustice.org.uk/publications/usual-suspects-second-edition*.

> gang members give them that 'they will not get caught' . . . Behavioural scientists will recognize this as an instance of the well-known 'risky shift' phenomenon, in which a group that comes to a collective decision after discussion comes to a decision that is often more risky than the average of the decisions that individuals held prior to the discussion. This means that the group tends to badly underestimate the risk of being caught.
>
> Yet another process likely to lead groups toward crime commission is the phenomenon called 'deindividuation' in which the individual is 'lost in a crowd'; he perceives a loss of accountability for his individual actions when those actions are taken in a crowd or mob and thus engages in many more anti-social acts. The effect is illustrated most dramatically by gangs of teenagers or soccer crowds who sweep through neighbourhoods, breaking windows, assaulting those unlucky enough to be in their paths, but is at work in most groups of potential offenders.
>
> Available data suggests that a significant proportion of offences are committed by offenders in groups. Except in cases of murders and rapes without theft, which are crimes in which offenders usually know their victim, 'the majority of offenders commit their offences with accomplices'. To sum up, . . . individual pathologies are likely to be extended and amplified by the fact that the decision to commit a crime is often a group rather than an individual decision, and the group processes shift its members toward taking more risky actions, and deindividuates them, facilitating the commission of destructive behaviours. It is difficult to fit this to the image of a person who is affected by complex rational deterrence considerations."[2]

11–003 In addition to questions of deterrence there is also the issue of desert requiring separate consideration in relation to group criminality. If several group members encouraged the offence, but only one individual actually carried out the actus reus, the need arises to find some way of measuring the blameworthiness of the other group members and the degree to which the end result can be attributed to them. How does the law respond to such group criminality? The approach taken by the English law of complicity is to make those individuals who help in the commission of offences liable for the full crime. Such secondary parties[3] are "liable to be tried, indicted and punished"[4] as if they had committed the crime themselves. This means, for example, that a defendant who assisted another to rape a woman (say, by blocking any entrance to the room) is guilty of rape, even though he never touched the woman. Unlike the inchoate offences, there is no crime of "aiding and abetting rape" or any other offence. References to "aiding and abetting rape" or other offences are simply a short-hand way of describing *how* the secondary party (D2) came to be liable for the offence. Another consequence of this approach is that an accessory can plead common law defences such as duress or self-defence. Also, it means accessories are sentenced as if they were principals in cases where fixed or automatic

---

2 See also, B. Livings and E. Smith, "Locating Complicity: Choice, Character, Participation, Dangerousness and the Liberal Subjectivist" in A. Reed and M. Bohlander (eds), *Participation in Crime: Domestic and Comparative Perspectives* (Farnham: Ashgate, 2013).

3 Whilst the terms "secondary offenders", "accomplices" and "accessories" are often used interchangeably, the Court of Appeal has expressed the view that the term "secondary parties" is preferable because it emphasises that secondary liability is derivative from the liability of the principal offender: *R. v Bryce (Craig Brian)* [2004] EWCA Crim 1231; [2004] 2 Cr. App. R. 35 at [38]. In this chapter, D2 denotes a secondary party or accessory (although those terms are also sometimes used for clarity).

4 Accessories and Abettors Act 1861 s.8. It is also possible to aid and abet a summary offence: the Magistrates' Courts Act 1980 s.44.

sentences apply.[5] Whether it is appropriate to regard all of those involved in crimes as equally blameworthy is a question which can only be considered once the law has been examined. But what needs to be explored now is *how* the law is able to come to a conclusion that such parties are guilty of the same offence as the principal offender.

There are two stumbling-blocks to the imposition of full liability. The first is that it may be difficult to say that the secondary offender's conduct *caused* the crime, particularly where they were not even present at the scene. The second is that D2 may lack the mens rea of the offence. Thus, whatever links D2 with the crime, it cannot be the same actus reus and mens rea as that required for the principal offender. The question then becomes one of ascertaining what the different requirements are.

Present English law on participation is committed to the principle of *derivative liability*. The liability of the secondary party derives from, and is dependent on, the commission of an offence by the principal offender. Unlike the law of attempt where the focus is forward-looking on D's actions and endeavours towards the commission of a crime, accessorial liability is backwards-looking. A crime must have been committed.[6] The issue is one of determining which persons participated sufficiently in that crime to be held liable for it. How is one to determine whether there has been "sufficient participation"?

As D2 is fully liable for the offence committed, logic dictates that there should be a high degree of mens rea as well as a substantial contribution (actus reus) towards the offence. However, because the accessory's liability is based not only on their own acts, but also on their involvement or participation in the offence committed by another, the actus reus and mens rea required for secondary liability have to be assessed, not in isolation, but also in relation to the actus reus and mens rea of the principal offender. **11–004**

II. The Law

A. PRINCIPAL OFFENDERS

Despite the fact that all parties to a crime may, by virtue of the Accessories and Abettors Act 1861 s.8, be tried, indicted and punished in the same way,[7] it is common[8] to distinguish between the principal **11–005**

5 *Att-Gen's Reference (No.71 of 1998)* [1999] 2 Cr. App. R. (S.) 369; [1999] Crim. L.R. 587 CA. The mandatory life sentence for murder applies to secondary parties in the same way as it applies to principal offenders. In *R. v Height (John)* [2008] EWCA Crim 2500; [2009] 1 Cr. App. R. (S.) 117, it was held that although no reference was made to secondary parties in the Criminal Justice Act 2003 Sch.21 paras (4) and (5), those guidelines could be applied to secondary parties in the same way as they applied to principal offenders, and it would be wrong in the present case for the starting point for the secondary party's minimum term of imprisonment for murder to be lower than that of the principal offender, given that the former had arranged for his wife to be killed.

6 This is the key to distinguishing secondary liability from the offences of encouraging or assisting crime under the Serious Crime Act 2007 ss.44, 45 and 46, which do not require that the offence that is encouraged or assisted actually be committed. See Ch.10, paras 10–092–10–110.

7 Until 1967, principals were known as principals in the first degree and secondary parties as principals in the second degree if they were present at the crime and accessories if they were not. The Criminal Law Act 1967 effectively abolished the need for that distinction to be drawn.

8 There is no legal obligation to draw this distinction in an indictment. Indeed, it is possible for D2 to be charged with committing the crime without any reference to the terms in s.8: *R. v Forman and Ford* [1988] Crim. L.R. 677.

offender and secondary parties.[9] The principal offender is usually described as the one who played a part in the commission of the actus reus of the offence.[10] It is the principal offender (D1) who shoots and kills the victim (V) in a crime of murder or who snatches the bag in the crime of theft or robbery. Clearly, there may be more than one principal offender: two or more Ds may fatally stab V.

R. v Jogee [2016] UKSC 8 (Supreme Court):

11-006 LORD HUGHES AND LORD TOULSON . . .

"[1] In the language of the criminal law a person who assists or encourages another to commit a crime is known as an accessory or secondary party. The actual perpetrator is known as a principal, even if his role may be subordinate to that of others. It is a fundamental principle of the criminal law that the accessory is guilty of the same offence as the principal. The reason is not difficult to see. He shares the physical act because even if it was not his hand which struck the blow, ransacked the house, smuggled the drugs or forged the cheque, he has encouraged or assisted those physical acts. Similarly he shares the culpability precisely because he encouraged or assisted the offence. No one doubts that if the principal and the accessory are together engaged on, for example, an armed robbery of a bank, the accessory who keeps guard outside is as guilty of the robbery as the principal who enters with a shotgun and extracts the money from the staff by threat of violence. Nor does anyone doubt that the same principle can apply where, as sometimes happens, the accessory is nowhere near the scene of the crime. The accessory who funded the bank robbery or provided the gun for the purpose is as guilty as those who are at the scene. Sometimes it may be impossible for the prosecution to prove whether a defendant was a principal or an accessory, but that does not matter so long as it can prove that he participated in the crime either as one or as the other. These basic principles are long established and uncontroversial."

11-007 There is one exception to the rule that the principal offender is the one whose act is the most immediate cause of the actus reus. Where D2 acts through an intermediary who is an "innocent agent" because, for example, they are below the age of criminal responsibility, it will be the instigator who will be regarded as the principal offender. The same result will apply if D2 acts through someone who has no mens rea, as in the situation where the agent is instructed to put what is described as a harmless substance into someone's food, which D2 knows will kill.[11]

---

9 Not least because strict liability does not extend to accessories (*Callow v Tillstone* (1900) 8 L.T. 411). Even if a principal can be convicted without proof of mens rea, secondary parties must act with the requisite mental element.

10 D. Ormerod and K. Laird, *Smith, Hogan and Ormerod's Criminal Law*, 15th edn (Oxford: OUP, 2018), p.174.

11 See *R. v Stringer (Neil Bancroft)* (1992) 94 Cr. App. R. 13; [1991] Crim. L.R. 639 CA where D, a business manager of a company, signed false invoices with the intention that innocent company employees would pass them for payment. When the company's bank account was duly debited, D was convicted of theft of the money involved, through innocent agents.

B. SECONDARY PARTIES

1. Distinct modes of participation?

The liability of secondary parties is governed by the Accessories and Abettors Act 1861 s.8: **11–008**

> ". . . whosoever shall **aid**, **abet**, **counsel** or **procure** the commission of any indictable offence shall be liable to be tried, indicted and punished as a principal offender."

What is the significance of the four different words in bold? The Court of Appeal has stated that:

> "We approach s.8 of the 1861 Act on the basis that the words should be given their ordinary meaning, if possible. We approach the section on the basis also that if four words are employed here 'aid, abet, counsel or procure', the probability is that there is a difference between each of those four words and the other three, because, if there were no difference, then Parliament would be wasting time in using four words where two or three would do."[12]

It is, however, extremely difficult to give these archaic words their "ordinary meaning". At a simplistic level, "aid" means help or assistance. While "abet" is generally regarded as largely synonymous with "aid", there have been suggestions that while "aid" is a neutral term, "abet" suggests wrongdoing: "'abet' clearly imports mens rea, which 'aid' may not".[13] "Counsel" normally (although not invariably) refers to help given before the commission of the crime. It may take a wide variety of forms but includes advice, encouragement or the supply of information or equipment. "Procure" means to "produce by endeavour".[14] This terminology was, perhaps, apt before 1967 when a distinction had been drawn between those present at the crime (aiders and abetters) and those not present (counsellors and procurers).[15] However, this distinction is no longer part of the law[16] and in more recent years it has become clear that, with the possible exception of "procure", these words are mere synonyms for **assisting or encouraging**.[17] Given that no real conceptual distinctions can be drawn between most of the terms, the following analysis of the law will not focus on its antiquated terminology but will concentrate on the different ways in which persons can be said to participate in the commission of a crime. However, as there might still be some justification for regarding procuring as distinct, this form of complicity is discussed later in the chapter. **11–009**

---

12 *Att-Gen's Reference (No.1 of 1975)* [1975] Q.B. 773 at 779; [1975] 3 W.L.R. 11 CA.
13 *DPP for Northern Ireland v Lynch* [1975] A.C. 653 at 698; [1975] 2 W.L.R. 641 HL.
14 *Att-Gen's Reference (No.1 of 1975)* [1975] Q.B. 773.
15 This distinction is no longer drawn as a result of the Criminal Law Act 1967.
16 In *Stringer* [2011] EWCA Crim 1396, the Court of Appeal reaffirmed this, rejecting an argument that in order to aid and abet, D had to be present at the time of the commission of the crime.
17 e.g. in *Att-Gen v Able* [1984] Q.B. 795; [1983] 3 W.L.R. 845 QBD, all the words were regarded as synonyms for "helping".

2. Causation

11–010 English law on participation in crime is theoretically underpinned by the doctrine of derivative liability.[18] As seen, this means accessories are held responsible for the result (the crime) that occurs. Unlike an inchoate model of liability, the focus is not simply on their contribution. If they are being blamed for the end result, it would follow logically that their actions should have had a role in *causing* that result. This view has support. K.J.M. Smith argues that a "it has always been implied in the concept of complicity that an accessory's involvement (whether as an 'assister' or 'encourager') did make some difference to the outcome".[19] In the 2010 decision of *Mendez,*[20] Toulson LJ was also of this view.

However, causation is difficult to establish here because of the central principle that a causal chain is generally broken by voluntary, willed human action. In participation cases this means that the voluntary, willed actions of D1 would normally be regarded as breaking the causal chain. As Kadish says:

> "Causation applies where results of a person's actions happen in the physical world. Complicity applies where results take the form of another person's voluntary action. Complicity emerges as a separate ground of liability because causation doctrine cannot satisfactorily deal with results that take the form of another's voluntary action."[21]

English law has accepted this second view.

R. v Calhaem [1985] Q.B. 808 (Court of Appeal, Criminal Division):

11–011 The defendant, Mrs Calhaem, was infatuated with her solicitor. She was charged with the murder of a woman who was having an affair with her solicitor. She had instructed one Zajac to commit the murder. He pleaded guilty to the murder but said in evidence that up to the point when he went berserk and killed the woman, he had come to a decision not to go through with the plan. The defendant appealed against her conviction for murder on the basis that counselling required a substantial causal connection between the acts of the counsellor and the commission of the offence and that none existed on the facts.

PARKER LJ:

> "We must therefore approach the question raised on the basis that we should give to the word 'counsel' its ordinary meaning, which is as the judge said, 'advise', 'solicit', or something of that sort. There is no implication in the word itself that there should be any causal connection

---

18 The exception being procurement.

19 K.J.M. Smith, *A Modern Treatise on the Law of Complicity* (Oxford: Clarendon Press, 1991), p.246.

20 *R. v Mendez (Reece)* [2010] EWCA Crim 516; [2011] Q.B. 876.

21 S.H. Kadish, "Complicity, Cause and Blame: A Study in the Interpretation of Doctrine" (1985) 73 Cal. L. Rev. 324, 327. See also, G. Williams, "Complicity, Purpose and the Draft Code—I" [1990] Crim. L.R. 4, 6.

> between the counselling and the offence. It is true that, unlike the offence of incitement at common law, the actual offence must have been committed and by the person counselled. To this extent there must clearly be, first, contact between the parties, and secondly, a connection between the counselling and the murder. Equally, the act done must, we think, be done within the scope of the authority or advice, and not, for example, accidentally when the mind of the final murderer did not go with his actions. For example, if the principal offender happened to be involved in a football riot in the course of which he laid about him with a weapon of some sort and killed someone, who, unknown to him, was the person whom he had been counselled to kill, he would not, in our view, have been acting within the scope of his authority; he would have been acting entirely outside it, albeit what he had done was what he had been counselled to do.
>
> We see, however, no need to import anything further into the meaning of the word."
>
> *Appeal dismissed*

Subsequently, the Court of Appeal has followed this decision. In *Luffman*,[22] the D1, who had been paid to kill V and been given a sawn-off shotgun for that purpose by the secondary parties, claimed that he never intended to go through with the plan but met with V with the intention of robbing him, and shot him when the robbery went wrong. The secondary parties argued that there was no causal connection between their encouragement and the murder and so they should not be liable. The Court of Appeal, whilst resisting the invitation to provide more guidance as to how strong a connection was needed for aiding, abetting or counselling an offence,[23] was content that sufficient connection was proved in the present case and that D1 had not acted outside the scope of his authority, given that he did exactly what he had been contracted to do. Some further guidance as to what constitutes a "connecting link" is provided by Toulson LJ in *Stringer*:[24] **11–012**

> "[E]ncouragement by its nature involves some form of transmission by words or conduct, whether directly or via an intermediary. An un-posted letter of encouragement would not be encouragement unless [D1] chanced to discover it and read it. Similarly, it would be unreal to regard [D1] as acting with the . . . encouragement of [D2] if the only encouragement took the form of words spoken by [D2] out of [D1]'s earshot."[25]

22 *R. v Luffman* [2008] EWCA Crim 1739.

23 The court accepted that causation would be important in a case of procuring (see *Att-Gen's Reference (No.1 of 1975)* [1975] Q.B. 773) but treated the present case as one that involved aiding, abetting or counselling, but not procuring.

24 *Stringer* [2011] EWCA Crim 1396.

25 *Stringer* [2011] EWCA Crim 1396 at [49].

As long as the encouragement has "the capacity to act on [D1]'s mind"[26] it seems clear that liability is not restricted to situations where there is a causal relationship between the accessory's acts and the principal's acts. This was underlined in *Giannetto*[27] where the court was of the view that liability would follow if a husband merely said "Oh goody" to a plan already in existence to kill his wife.[28] In such a case, it cannot be asserted that D2's acts made any causal contribution to the end result. The Supreme Court confirmed this approach in *Jogee*, stating:

> "[o]nce encouragement or assistance is proved to have been given, the prosecution does not have to go so far as to prove that it had a positive effect on D1's conduct or on the outcome . . . Ultimately it is a question of fact and degree whether D2's conduct was so distanced in time, place or circumstance's form the conduct of D1 that it would not be realistic to regard D1's offence as encouraged or assisted by it."[29]

In so far as assistance, rather than encouragement, is concerned, far from a causal connection being required,[30] it is possible that one could aid a crime without the principal even being aware that assistance is being provided.[31] However, with regard to "procuring", it has been held that causation is necessary[32] although consensus is not required. This, again, underlines the need for procuring to be dealt with separately.

3. Assistance and encouragement

11–013 Whether conduct amounts to assistance or encouragement is a question of fact.[33] Although the following are not distinct legal categories, it is useful, for purposes of exposition, to group the types of assistance and encouragement that may be provided as follows:

(i) Unplanned presence at the crime

11–014 Generally, being present when a crime is committed does not, necessarily, implicate one in the crime. But, what if a fight starts in a pub and those present start to "egg on" the participants? The following is the leading decision on this point.

---

26 *Stringer* [2011] EWCA Crim 1396 per Toulson LJ, citing the words of the Law Commission: Law Com. No.300, *Inchoate Liability for Assisting and Encouraging Crime* (2006), para.2.36.

27 *R. v Giannetto (Robert Vincent)* [1997] 1 Cr. App. R. 1; [1996] Crim. L.R. 722 CA.

28 See further, J.C. Smith, "Criminal Liability of Accessories: Law and Law Reform" (1997) 113 L.Q.R. 453, 458. See also *Att-Gen v Able* [1984] 1 Q.B. 795 where it was stated that it "does not make any difference" whether the person counselled would have acted anyway.

29 *R. v Jogee (Ameen Hassan)* [2016] UKSC 8 at [12]; [2017] A.C. 387.

30 In *Bryce* [2004] 2 Cr. App. R. 35 at [75], the court concluded that as long as there is no "overwhelming supervening event" between D2's act of assistance and the commission of the offence then liability will be established. The position is different with regard to procuring.

31 Ormerod and Laird, *Smith and Hogan's Criminal Law*, 16th edn (2021), p.188. One may certainly procure an offence without the principal's knowledge.

32 *Att-Gen's Reference (No.1 of 1975)* [1975] Q.B. 773.

33 *Stringer* [2011] EWCA Crim 1396 at [51].

R. v Clarkson (1971) 55 Cr. App. R. 445 (Courts-Martial Appeal Court):

The defendant was convicted of aiding and abetting the rape of a woman in an army barracks. He and another defendant, Carroll, appealed. **11–015**

MEGAW LJ:

"[T]he presence of those two appellants in the room where the offence was taking place was not accidental in any sense and it was not by chance, unconnected with the crime, that they were there. Let it be accepted that they entered the room when the crime was committed because of what they had heard, which indicated that a woman was being raped, and they remained there.

Coney (1882) 8 Q.B.D. 534 decides that non-accidental presence at the scene of the crime is not conclusive of aiding and abetting . . .

What has to be proved is stated by Hawkins J in a well-known passage in his judgment in *Coney* at 557 of the report. What he said was this:

> '. . . In my opinion, to constitute an aider and abettor some active steps must be taken by word, or action, with the intent to instigate the principal, or principals. Encouragement does not of necessity amount to aiding and abetting, it may be intentional or unintentional, a man may unwittingly encourage another in fact by his presence, by misinterpreted words, or gestures, or by his silence, or non-interference, or he may encourage intentionally by expressions, gestures, or actions intended to signify approval. In the latter case he aids and abets, in the former he does not. It is no criminal offence to stand by, a mere passive spectator of a crime, even of a murder. Non-interference to prevent a crime is not itself a crime. But the fact that a person was voluntarily and purposely present witnessing the commission of a crime, and offered no opposition to it, though he might reasonably be expected to prevent and had the power so to do, or at least to express his dissent, might, under some circumstances, afford cogent evidence upon which a jury would be justified in finding that he wilfully encouraged and so aided and abetted. But it would be purely a question for the jury whether he did so or not.'

It is not enough, then, that the presence of the accused person has, in fact, given encouragement. It must be proved that he intended to give encouragement; that he *wilfully* encouraged. In a case such as the present, more than in many other cases where aiding and abetting is alleged, it was essential that that element should be stressed; for there was here at least the possibility that a drunken man with his self-discipline loosened by drink, being aware that a woman was being raped, might be attracted to the scene and might stay on the scene in the capacity of what is known as a voyeur; and, while his presence and the presence of others might in fact encourage the rapers or discourage the victim, he himself, enjoying the scene or at least standing by assenting, might not intend that his presence should offer encouragement to rapers and would-be rapers or discouragement to the victim; he might not realise that he was giving encouragement; so that, while encouragement there might be, it would not be a case in which, to use the words of Hawkins J., the accused person 'wilfully encouraged'. . .

From that it follows that mere intention is not in itself enough. There must be an intention to encourage; and there must also be encouragement in fact in cases such as the present case."

Appeal allowed[34]

11-016 In *Tait*,[35] the Court of Appeal confirmed that both an intention to encourage and encouragement in fact must be established. Fletcher, however, has questioned the necessity for such a psychological effect on the principal:

> "After all, whether the aid is actually rendered is fortuitous; the actor is equally culpable and his dangerousness is equally great if the perpetrator never receives the aid."[36]

Such an argument provides a justification for the inchoate offences of encouraging or assisting crime under the Serious Crime Act 2007, leaving the law on complicity to punish those who in fact encourage a completed offence. While causal explanations of complicity have been generally rejected by English law (except in relation to procuring), it would seem that in these cases of unplanned presence at the scene of the crime, the law's insistence upon actual encouragement does manifest vestiges of a causal theory of complicity. This can best be explained by looking at the problem from another perspective. If, in these cases, liability were imposed in the absence of actual encouragement, this would be tantamount to punishing persons for an omission to act in situations where there was no pre-existing duty to act.[37]

(ii) Failure to exercise control

11-017 Exceptionally, presence without intended and actual encouragement may give rise to liability if D2 has a right to control the actions of D1. If, for instance, the owner of a vehicle sits in the passenger seat and does nothing whilst D1 behind the wheel drives dangerously, their omission may inculpate them.[38] Perhaps because visions of owners grabbing the steering wheel from the dangerous driver (and exacerbating the situation) arose before the judges' eyes, the rule of control being the legal equivalent of actual encouragement is now regarded as *evidence* only that the owner may have encouraged the commission of the crime.[39] If a prosecution for dangerous driving is to be based on the car owner's omission to intervene upon D1's commission of the offence, it must be shown that the owner had the

---

34 See also *Wilcox v Jeffrey* [1951] 1 T.L.R. 706; (1951) 115 J.P. 151 Div Ct and *R. v Bland* (1987) 151 J.P. 857; [1988] Crim. L.R. 41 CA.

35 *R. v Tait* [1993] Crim. L.R. 538 CA. See also the Privy Council decision in *Robinson v The Queen* [2011] UKPC 3.

36 G.P. Fletcher, *Rethinking Criminal Law* (New York: OUP, 1978), p.679.

37 Such persons could be liable for encouraging crime under the Serious Crime Act 2007, provided that they either intended to encourage the commission of an offence or believed that their act would encourage its commission.

38 *Du Cros v Lambourne* [1907] 1 K.B. 40.

39 *Cassady v Morris (Reg) (Transport) Ltd* [1975] R.T.R. 470; [1975] Crim. L.R. 398 Div Ct; *R. v Forman and Ford* [1988] Crim. L.R. 677 CC.

opportunity to do so.[40] In *Alford Transport Ltd,*[41] it was held that actual presence at the scene of the crime was not necessary. Where a transport manager or the managing director of a company who had a right to control the actions of its employees deliberately refrained from exercising control, it could be inferred that there was positive encouragement.

(iii) Joint enterprise

Where two or more people embark on a joint unlawful enterprise, for example a burglary or an attack on someone, the law has long adopted the view that all the parties should be liable for the direct and agreed consequences of that joint enterprise. Where the co-defendants merely commit the planned offence—the type of joint enterprise that Lord Hoffmann described as a "plain vanilla" version of joint enterprise[42]—the finding of guilt for each co-defendant involved in the plan is straightforward. However, problems arise in cases other than the "plain vanilla" variety (cases which could perhaps be termed the "tutti frutti" variety), where D1 goes beyond what was agreed and commits a second offence, often referred to as the "collateral" offence.[43] Following a line of authorities culminating in the decisions of the Privy Council in *Chan-Wing Siu*[44] and the House of Lords in *Powell; English,*[45] such cases resulted in liability for the secondary offender under what became known as the doctrine of "parasitic accessorial liability". **11–018**

An example of the parasitic accessorial liability rule operating in practice can be found in *Slack*.[46] Here, D2 handed a knife to D1 during a burglary so that he could threaten the occupier if she started screaming. While D2 was out of the room, D1 stabbed and killed the occupier. The question of when D2 will be guilty of the collateral offence of murder in such a case has plagued the English courts for decades. This issue was addressed by the Supreme Court in the case of *Jogee*, which is now the leading case on joint enterprise liability. *Jogee* abolishes any doctrine of parasitic accessorial liability applying in cases of joint unlawful enterprise. The key issue addressed by the Supreme Court in *Jogee*, discussed below, is the question of what mens rea is required on the part of a secondary party to a joint enterprise.

4. Mens rea of accessories

Accessorial liability involves a "two-fold structure",[47] and mens rea must exist in relation to both of these structural elements: **11–019**

(i) Mens rea relating to D2's own act of assisting or encouraging D1.
(ii) Mens rea relating to the offence committed by D1.

It is the second of these requirements that has caused more controversy. We will deal with each in turn.

---

40 *R. v Webster (Peter David)* [2006] EWCA Crim 415; [2006] 2 Cr. App. R. 6.
41 *R. v JF Alford Transport Ltd* [1997] 2 Cr. App. R. 326; [1999] R.T.R. 51 CA.
42 *Brown and Isaac v The State* [2003] UKPC 10 at [13].
43 See, e.g. Law Commission Paper No.300, *Inchoate Liability for Assisting and Encouraging Crime* (2006), para.2.3; R. Buxton, "Joint Enterprise" [2009] Crim. L.R. 233.
44 *Chan Wing Siu v R.* [1985] A.C. 168; [1984] 3 W.L.R. 677 PC.
45 *R. v Powell (Anthony Glassford)* [1999] 1 A.C. 1; [1997] 3 W.L.R. 959 HL.
46 *R. v Slack (Martin Andrew)* [1989] Q.B. 775; [1989] 3 W.L.R. 513 CA.
47 Law Commission Consultation Paper No.131, *Assisting and Encouraging Crime* (1993), para.2.49.

(i) Mens rea relating to D's own act of assisting or encouraging the principal offender

11–020 The accessory who is assisting or encouraging the crime must have mens rea in relation to their own conduct. For example, in *Clarkson* it was said there must be an "intention to encourage". It is implicit in the notion of counselling that one can only encourage or influence another to do something if it is one's intention to encourage. This was confirmed in *Bryce* where Potter LJ stated:

> "[I]t is necessary to show firstly that the act which constitutes the aiding, abetting [counselling] etc was done intentionally in the sense of deliberately and not accidentally and secondly that the accused knew it to be an act capable of assisting or encouraging the crime."[48]

(ii) Mens rea relating to the offence committed by the principal offender

11–021 In addition to D2 having to form mens rea in relation to their own act of assistance or encouragement, they must also have mens rea in relation to the offence committed by the D1. However, D2 need not form the mens rea of the offence itself. What exactly is required has been in doubt relating to cases of joint enterprise, at least until *Jogee*, but in relation to other cases a fairly clear test has been applied, with *NCB v Gamble*[49] being the leading and much cited authority. According to that case, it is simply necessary to prove that D2 knew that the offence was to be committed. The facts were that a weigh-bridge operator, in the course of his job, issued a ticket to a driver leaving the colliery premises, knowing that the lorry was over-loaded. The Coal Board (as the weigh-bridge operator's employer) was convicted of being an accessory to the offence of using a lorry on the road with a load weighing more than that permitted.[50] It was held that the only mens rea required was knowledge of the circumstances rendering the act criminal. Devlin J concluded that:

> ". . . an indifference to the result of crime does not of itself negative abetting. If one man deliberately sells to another a gun to be used for murdering a third, he may be indifferent about whether the third man lives or dies and interested only in the cash profit to be made out of the sale, but he can still be an aider and abettor."[51]

This approach has been criticised by Williams:

> "It seems a strong thing to hold that a man who is simply pursuing his ordinary and lawful vocation, and takes no special steps to assist illegalities, becomes involved as a party to crime committed by the customer merely because he realises that his customer will be enabled by what he himself does to commit such a crime."[52]

---

48 *Bryce* [2004] 2 Cr. App. R. 35 at [42].

49 *National Coal Board v Gamble* [1959] 1 Q.B. 11; [1958] 3 W.L.R. 434 Div Ct. See also *DPP v Lynch* [1975] A.C. 653.

50 Contrary to the Motor Vehicles (Construction and Use) Regulations 1955 (SI 1955/990) regs 68 and 104.

51 *Gamble* [1959] 1 Q.B. 11 at 23.

52 D.J. Baker, *Glanville Williams, Textbook of Criminal Law*, 4th edn (London: Sweet & Maxwell, 2015), para.17–031.

On the other hand, it is possible to defend the approach adopted in *Gamble*. If D2 knows that a crime is to be committed, why should he be allowed to shelter behind a shield that he was "just doing his job"? Legitimate business enterprise should not be permitted to extend to the knowing provision of tools for the commission of crime.

In *Gamble,* the offence which was being aided, abetted or counselled was clear, and depended on the circumstances in which D2 acted, rather than a particular harm resulting. The test there does not help to determine what ought to be required in a case of counselling in which D2 provides assistance in advance of the commission of the crime, perhaps by providing a weapon, knowing that the weapon will be used to commit a crime, but not knowing more. To what extent must the counsellor know the details of the principal's intended offence? Is it enough that he knows that some sort of offence of violence is being planned or does he need to have a fair idea of when or how or where? In *Bainbridge*,[53] it was held that as long as D2 was aware of the type of offence to be committed, that would be enough to incriminate him. The "type of offence" formula was not without difficulties (establishing, for example, whether one offence was of a similar type to another) and so the issue was re-examined by the House of Lords in the following case. **11–022**

MAXWELL V DPP FOR NORTHERN IRELAND (1979) 68 CR. APP. R. 128 (HOUSE OF LORDS):

The appellant was a member of the UVF, then a proscribed organisation in Northern Ireland, which organisation had been responsible for sectarian killings and bombings in the Province. One night he was told by another member of the UVF to drive his car to a remote country area where there was an inn run by Roman Catholics. The appellant had local knowledge of the area in question, and the object was that he should guide another car containing three or four men, also members of the UVF, who were strangers to the area. Having reached the inn, the appellant drove off and one of the men in the following car placed a bomb with a burning fuse in the hallway of the inn and drove off. The attack failed because the son of the landlord detached the fuse and threw the bomb into the road where the detonator exploded. Only afterwards did the appellant know that the "job" he was on for the UVF was an attempt to bomb the inn. He was charged and convicted of doing an act with intent to cause an explosion by a bomb, contrary to the Explosive Substances Act 1883 s.3(a) and with possession of a bomb contrary to s.3(b) of that Act. He appealed against conviction to the Court of Appeal of Northern Ireland, who dismissed the appeal but certified under the Criminal Appeal (Northern Ireland) Act 1968 s.36(2) that a point of law of general public importance was involved, i.e. if the crime committed by the principal, and actually assisted by the accused, was one of a number of offences, one of which the accused knew the principal would probably commit, was the guilty mind which must be proved against an accomplice thereby proved against the accused? The appellant appealed to the House of Lords. **11–023**

53 *R. v Bainbridge (Alan)* [1960] 1 Q.B. 129; [1959] 3 W.L.R. 656 CA.

11-024 LORD SCARMAN:

"I think *Bainbridge* . . . was correctly decided. But I agree with counsel for the appellant that in the instant case the Court of Criminal Appeal in Northern Ireland has gone further than the Court of Criminal Appeal for England and Wales found it necessary to go in *Bainbridge*. It is not possible in the present case to declare that it is proved, beyond reasonable doubt, that the appellant knew a bomb attack upon the Inn was intended by those whom he was assisting. It is not established, therefore, that he knew the particular type of crime intended. The Court, however, refused to limit criminal responsibility by reference to knowledge by the accused of the type or class of crime intended by those whom he assisted. Instead, the Court has formulated a principle which avoids the uncertainties and ambiguities of classification. The guilt of an accessory springs, according to the Court's formulation, 'from the fact that he contemplates the commission of one (or more) of a number of crimes by the principal and he intentionally lends his assistance in order that such a crime will be committed': *per* Sir Robert Lowry CJ 'The relevant crime', the Lord Chief Justice continues:

> 'must be within the contemplation of the accomplice and only exceptionally would evidence be found to support the allegation that the accomplice had given the principal a completely blank cheque.'

The principle thus formulated has great merit. It directs attention to the state of mind of the accused—not what he ought to have in contemplation, but what he did have: it avoids definition and classification, while ensuring that a man will not be convicted of aiding and abetting any offence his principal may commit, but only one which is within his contemplation. He may have in contemplation only one offence, or several: and the several which he contemplates he may see as alternatives. An accessory who leaves it to his principal to choose is liable, provided always the choice is made from the range of offences from which the accessory contemplates the choice will be made. Although the court's formulation of the principle goes further than the earlier cases, it is a sound development of the law and in no way inconsistent with them. I accept it as good judge-made law in a field where there is no statute to offer guidance."

11-025 It should be noted, first, that *Maxwell* is the kind of case which the Law Commission had in mind when drafting the new inchoate offences of assisting and encouraging crime. A D such as *Maxwell* would now be liable for one of the inchoate offences under the Serious Crime Act 2007,[54] although they could also remain liable for the substantive offences as an accomplice.

A crucial question, however, is whether these rules apply in the same way in cases of joint enterprise. With joint enterprise cases, participation in the enterprise is deemed to be intentional assistance. However, because D2 is liable for the crime committed by D1 (as opposed to being simply liable for

54 See Ch.10 above.

their own acts of encouragement etc), D2 also needs some form of mens rea in relation to that crime. For some time, there was a dispute over whether joint enterprise liability formed a separate doctrine with its own special rules for establishing accessorial liability, or whether taking part in a joint enterprise was just one way in which it could be shown that D had aided, abetted or counselled the principal's offence. As a result of this dispute, it was unclear as to whether the mens rea for accessories in cases of joint enterprise was something distinct from other forms of participation. Virgo,[55] Smith[56] and Buxton[57] all expressed the opinion that joint enterprise is not distinct from other modes of accessorial liability. Simester and Sullivan, on the other hand, thought that "joint enterprise is a special case of secondary participation and not merely a sub-species of assistance and encouragement".[58] The Law Commission favoured Simester's views, arguing that a secondary party to a joint enterprise is different to an aider or abettor because they need not have contributed to the commission of the principal's offence, but have condoned it by changing their normative position in choosing to take part in the joint enterprise.[59] Given that joint enterprise is rejected by many as being a separate doctrine of accessorial liability, the cases that apply should be interchangeable as between different modes of participation. A practical reason why the same rules should apply is that it is impossible in practice, and pointless in principle, to draw sharp distinctions between counsellors and parties to joint unlawful enterprises. In an area of law renowned for its complexity, there would be much to be gained from the development of a single rule applicable to most cases of complicity. This was recognised by the Supreme Court in its judgment in *Jogee*.

This area of law is, and has been, extremely complex, and the way in which the mens rea requirement applies in cases of joint enterprise murder has been particularly controversial. In essence, until the recent Supreme Court decision in *Jogee* the position was that D2 could be liable for murder where they foresaw that D1 might kill with intent to do so or with intent to cause grievous bodily harm, provided that the D1's lethal act was not "fundamentally different" to that foreseen by D2.[60] As is explained elsewhere in this book, for a principal offender to be liable for murder they must intend to kill or cause grievous bodily harm (GBH); nothing short of foresight of death or GBH as a virtual certainty will suffice. The position of the law towards secondary parties has therefore been extremely harsh. In *Jogee*, however, the Supreme Court decided that the law took a "wrong turn" 30 years before in the case of *Chan Wing-Siu*,[61] and that the law had subsequently been wrongly applied. In that case, the three Ds appealed against their convictions for murder and wounding with intent to cause grievous bodily harm. They had each been armed with a knife when they went to a flat used by a prostitute, where it was alleged they planned to rob the prostitute's husband. The husband was stabbed to death and his wife was slashed across the head. The trial judge directed the jury that an accused was guilty on each count if he was proved to have had in his contemplation that a knife might be used by one of his co-adventurers with intent to inflict serious bodily injury. The appeals against conviction were dismissed.

---

55 G. Virgo, "Clarifying Accessorial Liability" (1998) 57 C.L.J. 13, 15: "It is to be hoped that in future joint enterprise liability can be treated simply as a historical footnote and not as a distinct part of accessorial liability."

56 Commentary to *Marks* [1998] Crim. L.R. 676: "it is unfortunate that the phrase 'joint enterprise' has been given a special status for which there is no proper foundation" (677).

57 Buxton, "Joint Enterprise" [2009] Crim. L.R. 233, 238.

58 A.P. Simester, *Simester and Sullivan's Criminal Law: Theory and Doctrine*, 5th edn (Oxford: Hart, 2013), p.245. See also A.P. Simester, "The Mental Element in Complicity" (2006) 122 L.Q.R. 578–601; and B. Kreb, "Joint Criminal Enterprise" [2010] 73 M.L.R. 578.

59 Law Commission Report No.305, *Participating in Crime* (2007), para.3.52.

60 *Powell* [1999] 1 A.C. 1.

61 *Chan Wing-Siu* [1985] A.C. 168.

The Supreme Court identified that the essence of the wrong turn was that in *Chan Wing-Siu* Sir Robin Cooke, giving the judgment of the Privy Council, concluded that there was no doubt that there existed a principle whereby a secondary party was criminally liable for acts by the primary offender of a type which the former foresaw but did not necessarily intend.[62] This principle was further applied and elucidated in subsequent cases, the most important being *Powell; English*,[63] all of which were based on an error of law. It had thus allowed secondary parties to be convicted of murder on the basis of recklessness rather than intention, through the doctrine of parasitic accessorial liability.

11-026 The Supreme Court's judgment in *Jogee* is extraordinary, not only for the fact that it seeks to correct this wrong turn, but also in the way in which the case came to be decided. Members of the Supreme Court, having become increasingly frustrated by the lack of clarity in the law of joint enterprise, identified the case as a vehicle through which to inject some clarity into the law. This included the opportunity for "interveners" to make representations as to the state of the law,[64] and allowed the court to engage in a detailed examination of the case law on joint enterprise.

R. v Jogee [2016] UKSC 8 (Supreme Court):

11-027 H and J spent the evening taking drink and drugs and, as they became more intoxicated, their behaviour became more and more aggressive. They went to Miss Reid's house where, according to Miss Reid, J picked up a knife from a kitchen bock and waved it about, saying he was going to "shank" V, with whom Miss Reid was having a relationship. Miss Reid wanted them to leave and told them that V would be back shortly. J and H replied that they were not scared of V and would sort him out. After some coming and going, with V having returned home, J and H came back, and had an angry exchange with V. V went upstairs to put his jeans on while H took the knife from the kitchen. V came down and tried to get H and J to leave. V was in the hallway with H inside the front door, and J was out in the street striking a car with a bottle and shouting encouragement to H to do something to V. At some stage, J came to the doorway, with the bottle raised, and leaned forward past H towards V saying he wanted to smash it over V's head, but he was too far away. Miss Reid threatened to call the police and H pointed the knife at her chest and grabbed her by the throat. She backed away but saw H make a stabbing motion towards V's chest and H and J ran off. V died of stab wounds to the chest. Both H and J were convicted of murder. J appealed.

LORD HUGHES AND LORD TOULSON:

11-028 **"Restatement of the principles**

[89] In cases of alleged secondary participation there are likely to be two issues. The first is whether the defendant was in fact a participant, that is, whether he assisted or encouraged the commission of the crime. Such participation may take many forms. It may include providing support by contributing to the force of numbers in a hostile confrontation.

---

62 *Chan Wing-Siu* [1985] AC 168 at 175.

63 See summary of the case in [52]–[58] of the extract from *R. v Jogee* [2016] UKSC 8, at para.6-030.

64 Lawyers were instructed by two campaign groups: Just for Kids Law and Joint Enterprise Not Guilty by Association (JENGbA).

[90] The second issue is likely to be whether the accessory intended to encourage or assist D1 to commit the crime, acting with whatever mental element the offence requires of D1 (as stated in [10] above). If the crime requires a particular intent, D2 must intend (it may be conditionally) to assist D1 to act with such intent. To take a homely example, if D2 encourages D1 to take another's bicycle without permission of the owner and return it after use, but D1 takes it and keeps it, D1 will be guilty of theft but D2 of the lesser offence of unauthorised taking, since he will not have encouraged D1 to act with intent permanently to deprive. In cases of concerted physical attack there may often be no practical distinction to draw between an intention by D2 to assist D1 to act with the intention of causing grievous bodily harm at least and D2 having the intention himself that such harm be caused. In such cases it may be simpler, and will generally be perfectly safe, to direct the jury (as suggested in *Wesley Smith* and *Reid*) that the Crown must prove that D2 intended that the victim should suffer grievous bodily harm at least. However, as a matter of law, it is enough that D2 intended to assist D1 to act with the requisite intent. That may well be the situation if the assistance or encouragement is rendered some time before the crime is committed and at a time when it is not clear what D1 may or may not decide to do. Another example might be where D2 supplies a weapon to D1, who has no lawful purpose in having it, intending to help D1 by giving him the means to commit a crime (or one of a range of crimes), but having no further interest in what he does, or indeed whether he uses it at all.

[91] It will therefore in some cases be important when directing juries to remind them of the difference between intention and desire.

[92] In cases of secondary liability arising out of a prior joint criminal venture, it will also often be necessary to draw the jury's attention to the fact that the intention to assist, and indeed the intention that the crime should be committed, may be conditional. The bank robbers who attack the bank when one or more of them is armed no doubt hope that it will not be necessary to use the guns, but it may be a perfectly proper inference that all were intending that if they met resistance the weapons should be used with the intent to do grievous bodily harm at least. The group of young men which faces down a rival group may hope that the rivals will slink quietly away, but it may well be a perfectly proper inference that all were intending that if resistance were to be met, grievous bodily harm at least should be done.

[93] Juries frequently have to decide questions of intent (including conditional intent) by a process of inference from the facts and circumstances proved. The same applies when the question is whether D2, who joined with others in a venture to commit crime A, shared a common purpose or common intent (the two are the same) which included, if things came to it, the commission of crime B, the offence or type of offence with which he is charged, and which was physically committed by D1. A time honoured way of inviting a jury to consider such a question is to ask the jury whether they are sure that D1's act was within the scope of the joint venture, that is, whether D2 expressly or tacitly agreed to a plan which included D1 going as far as he did, and committing crime B, if the occasion arose.

[94] If the jury is satisfied that there was an agreed common purpose to commit crime A, and if it is satisfied also that D2 must have foreseen that, in the course of committing crime A, D1 might well commit crime B, it may in appropriate cases be justified in drawing the conclusion that D2 had the necessary conditional intent that crime B should be committed, if the occasion arose; or in other words that it was within the scope of the plan to which D2 gave his assent and intentional support. But that will be a question of fact for the jury in all the circumstances.

[95] In cases where there is a more or less spontaneous outbreak of multi-handed violence, the evidence may be too nebulous for the jury to find that there was some form of agreement, express or tacit. But, as we have said, liability as an aider or abettor does not necessarily depend on there being some form of agreement between the defendants; it depends on proof of intentional assistance or encouragement, conditional or otherwise. If D2 joins with a group which he realises is out to cause serious injury, the jury may well infer that he intended to encourage or assist the deliberate infliction of serious bodily injury and/or intended that that should happen if necessary. In that case, if D1 acts with intent to cause serious bodily injury and death results, D1 and D2 will each be guilty of murder.

11–029 [96] If a person is a party to a violent attack on another, without an intent to assist in the causing of death or really serious harm, but the violence escalates and results in death, he will be not guilty of murder but guilty of manslaughter. So also if he participates by encouragement or assistance in any other unlawful act which all sober and reasonable people would realise carried the risk of some harm (not necessarily serious) to another, and death in fact results: *R. v Church* [1965] 1 Q.B. 59, approved in *Director of Public Prosecutions v Newbury* [1977] A.C. 500 and very recently re-affirmed in *R. v F (J) & E (N)* [2015] EWCA Crim 351; [2015] 2 Cr. App. R. 5. The test is objective. As the Court of Appeal held in *Reid*, if a person goes out with armed companions to cause harm to another, any reasonable person would recognise that there is not only a risk of harm, but a risk of the violence escalating to the point at which serious harm or death may result. Cases in which D2 intends some harm falling short of grievous bodily harm are a fortiori, but manslaughter is not limited to these.

[97] The qualification to this (recognised in *Wesley Smith, Anderson and Morris* and *Reid*) is that it is possible for death to be caused by some overwhelming supervening act by the perpetrator which nobody in the defendant's shoes could have contemplated might happen and is of such a character as to relegate his acts to history; in that case the defendant will bear no criminal responsibility for the death.

[98] This type of case apart, there will normally be no occasion to consider the concept of 'fundamental departure' as derived from *English*. What matters is whether D2 encouraged or assisted the crime, whether it be murder or some other offence. He need not encourage or assist a particular way of committing it, although he may sometimes do so. In particular, his intention to assist in a crime of violence is not determined only by whether he knows what

> kind of weapon D1 has in his possession. The tendency which has developed in the application of the rule in *Chan Wing-Siu* to focus on what D2 knew of what weapon D1 was carrying can and should give way to an examination of whether D2 intended to assist in the crime charged. If that crime is murder, then the question is whether he intended to assist the intentional infliction of grievous bodily harm at least, which question will often, as set out above, be answered by asking simply whether he himself intended grievous bodily harm at least. Very often he may intend to assist in violence using whatever weapon may come to hand. In other cases he may think that D1 has an iron bar whereas he turns out to have a knife, but the difference may not at all affect his intention to assist, if necessary, in the causing of grievous bodily harm at least. Knowledge or ignorance that weapons generally, or a particular weapon, is carried by D1 will be evidence going to what the intention of D2 was, and may be irresistible evidence one way or the other, but it is evidence and no more.
>
> [99] Where the offence charged does not require mens rea, the only mens rea required of the secondary party is that he intended to encourage or assist the perpetrator to do the prohibited act, with knowledge of any facts and circumstances necessary for it to be a prohibited act: *National Coal Board v Gamble* . . .
>
> . . .
>
> [106] Ms Felicity Gerry QC submitted on behalf of the appellant that he could not properly have been convicted either of murder or of manslaughter.
>
> [107] We regard that submission as hopeless. The jury's verdict means that it was sure, at the very least, that the appellant knew that Hirsi had the knife and appreciated that he might use it to cause really serious harm . . . There was a case fit to go to the jury that [the appellant] had the mens rea for murder. At a minimum, he was party to a violent adventure carrying the plain objective risk of some harm to a person and which resulted in death; he was therefore guilty of manslaughter at least. The choice of disposal is whether to quash the appellant's conviction for murder and order a re-trial or whether to quash his conviction for murder and substitute a conviction for manslaughter. We invite the parties' written submissions on that question."
>
> *Appeal allowed*

The outcome of the case was that the Supreme Court ordered that Jogee be retried on murder and manslaughter charges. He was acquitted of murder and convicted of manslaughter, being sentenced to 12 years' imprisonment.[65] **11–030**

---

65 O. Bowcott, "Ameen Jogee jailed for manslaughter in joint enterprise test case" *The Guardian*, 21 September 2016, *https://www.theguardian.com/law/2016/sep/12/ameen-jogee-jailed-manslaughter-police-officer-joint-enterprise-test-case*.

Whether the Supreme Court achieved what it set out to achieve in *Jogee* has been hotly debated. The lengthy judgment is valuable in reviewing the existing case law, but there are those who take issue with some of the court's conclusions. The essence of the decision can be found in [90]–[96] in providing the mens rea requirement for D2 in a murder case, and clarifying that manslaughter is the appropriate offence where D has encouraged and assisted violence but does not have such mens rea.

It Is true to say that the mens rea requirement for accessories in murder cases has been tightened, although providing clear directions to a jury that can be easily followed remains a difficult task.[66] D2 will not be liable if they only foresaw a risk that the principal might kill or cause GBH; they must intend to assist the principal to act with intent to kill or cause serious injury.[67] However, the Supreme Court acknowledged that foresight of such a result would provide strong evidence of intent. Yet this stops short of requiring that D2 foresee the result as virtually certain, as required in relation to principal offenders according to *Woollin*. As noted by Ormerod and Laird:

> ". . . [c]rucially . . . there is no explicit statement as to what threshold of foresight the defendant must possess before the jury will be entitled to infer the requisite intent—will the defendant's foresight of even the slightest possibility of the principal intentionally acting in the proscribed way be sufficient for a jury to be entitled to infer that he possessed the requisite intention?"[68]

11–031 At [92] of the judgment, the Supreme Court makes it clear that intention to assist or encourage D1 may be conditional. In *Anwar*,[69] the Court of Appeal considered the application of the concept of conditional intent in a case of attempted murder. As has been noted by commentators,[70] *Jogee* was not the most suitable case for the Supreme Court to use as a case for re-examining the law of parasitic accessorial liability, in that it was not a case where D2 had encouraged one offence leading to an additional collateral offence being committed. It seems clear that Jogee and Hirsi were both in agreement that V should suffer some degree of injury, and that is what occurred, albeit that Hirsi's actions went beyond those intended by Jogee. *Anwar*, on the other hand, is a far better example of a classic case to illustrate a collateral offence committed as a result of a joint enterprise. All participants were involved in a conspiracy to rob the V, and it was argued by the prosecution that it was common knowledge that one of the participants was in possession of a loaded gun which would be used to kill V *if* the need arose (suggesting conditional intent). In that case, the Crown appealed against the judge's decision that there was no case to answer on the charge of attempted murder. The Court of Appeal ruled in favour of the Crown and held that there was sufficient evidence to go to the jury that an inference could be made that all the participants had the relevant intent due to the level of advanced planning evidenced.

---

66 As illustrated in the case of *R. v N* [2019] EWCA Crim 2280; [2020] 4 W.L.R. 64, in which the Court of Appeal expressed the view that judges should provide written directions to the jury, although it was held that a conviction was not necessarily unsafe in the absence of written directions. Suggested routes to verdict are provided to judges in the Crown Court Compendium, Pt 1 paras 7-15–7-21, *https://www.judiciary.uk/wp-content/uploads/2023/06/Crown-Court-Compendium-Part-I-June-2023-updated-Feb-2024.pdf*.

67 The need for D to have such intention, not just to have foreseen that the principal might kill or cause GBH, was highlighted by the Court of Appeal quashing a conviction for murder in *R. v Dreszer (Kamil)* [2018] EWCA Crim 454; [2019] Crim. L.R. 624.

68 D. Ormerod and K. Laird, "*Jogee*—Not the End of a Legal Saga but the Start of a New One?" [2016] Crim. L.R. 539, 546.

69 *R. v Anwar (Umar)* [2016] EWCA Crim 551; [2016] 4 W.L.R. 127.

70 See, e.g. R. Buxton, "*Jogee*: Upheaval in Secondary Liability for Murder" [2016] Crim. L.R. 324, 227.

Sir Brian Leveson P was of the opinion that the evidential requirements justifying that there is a case to answer are likely to be the same now as before *Jogee*.[71]

What does amount to a change to the law as previously set out in *English* is that there is no longer an "all or nothing" element to homicide liability in joint enterprise cases. It is not the case that D2 will necessarily escape all criminal liability for the death caused by D1 if D2 does not meet the mens rea requirements to be liable for murder. Those who do not intend to encourage D1 to commit murder as part of the joint enterprise, but who do intend that some degree of injury be inflicted, will now be liable for manslaughter.[72] That was in fact Jogee's fate after retrial at the Crown Court in Nottingham. Although this result appears to be in accordance with the constructive nature of liability for manslaughter based on an unlawful and dangerous act, its correctness has not been beyond doubt. Baker argues that it is "conceptually impossible" for D2 to be liable for a different offence to D1, since if D1 has not committed manslaughter it cannot be said that D2 has aided and abetted manslaughter.[73]

This misunderstands the basis upon which liability is to be established in such a case, however. The better way to conceive of these cases is that D2 is liable for manslaughter because they have assisted or encouraged an unlawful and dangerous act (often an assault or battery) which has caused death. It might be thought that the principal's voluntary act of intentionally inflicting death or serious injury breaks the chain of causation between D2's encouragement and the death, but it should be remembered that causation in the strict sense is not needed.[74] This leads to some perceived injustices, discussed further below.

5. Procuring

Whilst aiding, abetting and counselling are all forms of "assistance and encouragement" which does not involve proof of causation in the strict sense, procuring has been interpreted to require something quite different. **11–032**

Attorney General's Reference (No.1 of 1975) [1975] Q.B. 773 (Court of Appeal, Criminal Division):

The defendant surreptitiously laced a friend's drinks with double measures of spirits when he knew his friend would be driving home. He was charged with aiding, abetting, counselling and procuring the offence of driving with an excess quantity of alcohol in the blood under the Road Traffic Act 1972 s.6(1). The reference concerned the question of whether there had to be a shared intention between the parties or encouragement of the offence. **11–033**

71 *Anwar* [2016] EWCA Crim 551 at [22].

72 *Jogee* [2016] UKSC 8 at [96].

73 D. Baker, "Letter: *Jogee*: jury directions and the manslaughter alternative" [2017] Crim. L.R. 51–56, 52.

74 *Jogee* [2016] UKSC 8 at [12].

LORD WIDGERY CJ:

"Of course it is the fact that in the great majority of instances where a secondary party is sought to be convicted of an offence there has been a contact between the principal offender and the secondary party. Aiding and abetting almost inevitably involves a situation in which the secondary party and the main offender are together at some stage discussing the plans which they may be making in respect of the alleged offence, and are in contact so that each knows what is passing through the mind of the other.

In the same way it seems to us that a person, who counsels the commission of a crime by another, almost inevitably comes to a moment when he is in contact with the other, when he is discussing the offence with that other and when, to use the words of the statute, he counsels the other to commit the offence.

The fact that so often the relationship between the secondary party and the principal will be such that there is a meeting of minds between them caused the trial judge in the case from which this reference is derived to think that this was really an essential feature of proving or establishing the guilt of the secondary party and, as we understand his judgment, he took the view that in the absence of some sort of meeting of minds, some sort of mental link between the secondary party and the principal, there could be no aiding, abetting or counselling of the offence within the meaning of the section.

So far as aiding, abetting and counselling is concerned we would go a long way with that conclusion. It may very well be, as I said a moment ago, difficult to think of a case of aiding, abetting or counselling when the parties have not met and have not discussed in some respects the terms of the offence which they have in mind. But we do not see why a similar principle should apply to procuring. We approach section 8 of the Act of 1861 on the basis that the words should be given their ordinary meaning, if possible. We approach the section on the basis also that if four words are employed here, 'aid, abet, counsel or procure', the probability is that there is a difference between each of those four words and the other three, because, if there were no such difference, then Parliament would be wasting time in using four words where two or three would do. Thus, in deciding whether that which is assumed to be done under our reference was a criminal offence we approach the section on the footing that each word must be given its ordinary meaning.

To procure means to produce by endeavour. You procure a thing by setting out to see that it happens and taking the appropriate steps to produce that happening. We think that there are plenty of instances in which a person may be said to procure the commission of a crime by another even though there is no sort of conspiracy between the two, even though there is no attempt at agreement or discussion as to the form which the offence should take. In our judgment the offence described in this reference is such a case.

If one looks back at the facts of the reference: the accused surreptitiously laced his friend's drink. This is an important element and, although we are not going to decide today anything other than the problem posed to us, it may well be that, in similar cases where the lacing of the drink or the introduction of the extra alcohol is known to the driver, quite different considerations may apply. We say that because, where the driver has no knowledge of what is happening, in most instances he would have no means of preventing the offence from being committed. If the driver is unaware of what has happened, he will not be taking precautions. He will get into his car seat, switch on the ignition and drive home and, consequently, the conception of another procuring the commission of the offence by the driver is very much stronger where the driver is innocent of all knowledge of what is happening, as in the present case where the lacing of the drink was surreptitious.

The second thing which is important in the facts set out in our reference is that, following and in consequence of the introduction of the extra alcohol, the friend drove with an excess quantity of alcohol in his blood. Causation here is important. You cannot procure an offence unless there is a causal link between what you do and the commission of the offence, and here we are told that in consequence of the addition of this alcohol the driver, when he drove home, drove with an excess quantity of alcohol in his body.

Giving the words their ordinary meaning in English, and asking oneself whether in those circumstances the offence has been procured, we are in no doubt that the answer is that it has. It has been procured because, unknown to the driver and without his collaboration, he has been put in a position in which in fact he has committed an offence which he never would have committed otherwise." (Emphasis added)

Opinion accordingly

Following this case, if one accepts that to procure is "to produce by endeavour" then it is impossible to avoid the conclusion that intention is required and that there is some merit in continuing to regard procuring in this way. If this is the case, there is also an argument that "procuring" an offence ought to be treated in law as a more serious form of participation than others such as counselling, which only require foresight of the offence. Take the example of the generous host who makes drink available for their guests but leaves them to decide whether they will drink, walk home or drive. If charged with procuring the principal's offence of drink-driving, then, following *Att-Gen's Reference (No.1 of 1975)*, they should be acquitted. But, if the case is argued on the basis of counselling which can be satisfied by mere contemplation and does not require D2 to "cause" the offence, then generous hosts (and publicans) would be convicted, so long as it could also be proved that the accomplice intended to assist or encourage the principal.[75] The offence for which they would be convicted is that of drink-driving, whether or not the case succeeds on the basis of procuring (requiring intention) or counselling (where foresight suffices). Does this satisfactorily identify those who are truly deserving of blame? **11-034**

75 The Law Commission states that a generous host is liable for drink-driving even if they are indifferent to whether the principal commits the offence, and that it is enough that they believe that they will commit the offence as a result of the alcohol they supply. In a footnote, the Law Commission further admits that, following *Blakely v DPP* [1991] R.T.R. 405; [1991] Crim. L.R. 763 Div Ct; and *Webster* [2006] EWCA Crim 415, it is enough that they foresee that the principal might, or was likely to, commit the offence: Law Commission Paper No.300, *Inchoate Liability for Assisting and Encouraging Crime* (2006), para.4.17.

6. Reform proposals

11–035 The Law Commission in 1993 proposed a radical rethink of the law relating to complicity.[76] Under these proposals, the terms "aid, abet, counsel or procure" would be jettisoned, as would the derivative principle of liability for the full offence. Instead, two new inchoate offences would be created: assisting crime and encouraging crime. Whilst the Law Commission's analysis of complicity as consisting of either encouraging or assisting was generally welcomed, there was much less support for the radical proposal to abandon derivative liability.[77]

The Law Commission later abandoned the proposal to abolish secondary liability, although its proposals concerning inchoate liability were eventually enacted, with some amendment, under the Serious Crime Act 2007 (see Ch.10). The most recent report on participation in crime recommends further offences of assisting or encouraging crime, which would follow the current law in enabling D2 to be convicted of the same offence as D1. The Law Commission produced this report a year after the report on inchoate liability and clearly had in mind that together the two reports should make a package of reform,[78] but this has not transpired.

As the law currently stands, there is considerable overlap between the inchoate offences of assisting or encouraging crime and secondary liability. Arguably, this overlap raises questions of fair labelling, given that where D2 has assisted in the commission of an offence which has actually been committed by D1, there is nothing to stop the Crown charging one of the inchoate offences rather than trying to prove liability under the 1861 Act. This is problematic because, as noted by Ormerod and Fortson, "criminal liability Imposed for secondary participation reflects a distinctive type of wrong from that of inchoate liability".[79]

11–036 The Law Commission's proposals in 2007 were for two separate statutory provisions to replace the law of aiding, abetting, and counselling. The first of these would create an offence of "intentional encouraging or assisting" crime, whilst the second provides a separate route to liability for participants of joint enterprises (or "joint criminal ventures"). Assisting or encouraging an offence would require D2 to do an act with the intention that one or more of a number of other acts would be done by another person.[80] Participation in a joint criminal venture would provide liability both in cases of the "plain vanilla" variety of joint enterprises (where D1 commits the agreed offence) and the "tutti frutti" variety (where D2 commits a collateral offence). It was an attempt to codify the law applicable to joint

---

76 Law Commission Consultation Paper No.131, *Assisting and Encouraging Crime* (1993). For an argument that complicity ought to be abolished, see G. Sullivan, "Doing without Complicity" [2012] J. of Commonwealth Crim. Law 199.

77 Smith, "Criminal Liability of Accessories: Law and Law Reform" (1997) 113 L.Q.R. 453, 463 and K.J.M. Smith, "The Law Commission Consultation Paper on Complicity: (1) A Blueprint for Rationalisation" [1994] Crim. L.R. 239, 250.

78 See Law Commission Report No.305, *Participating in Crime* (2007), para.1.4. Before the Law Commission completed its report on secondary liability it had already, however, made recommendations relating to secondary liability in cases of homicide (Law Commission Paper No.304, *Murder, Manslaughter and Infanticide* (2006)). These recommendations were originally adopted in part by the Government in drafting the Coroners and Justice Bill. However, following the consultation process they were dropped from the Bill on the basis that secondary liability needs to be reformed as a whole rather than in parts: Ministry of Justice, *Murder, Manslaughter and Infanticide: Proposals for Reform of the Law: Summary of Responses and Government Position*, CP(R) 19 August 2009, paras 105–106.

79 D. Ormerod and R. Fortson, "Serious Crime Act 2007: The Part 2 Offences" [2009] Crim. L.R. 389, 393.

80 Law Commission Report No.305, *Participating in Crime* (2007).

enterprise liability at the time the proposals were made.[81] Given the changes made in *Jogee*, it is not necessary to delve deeper into such codification here.

Beyond these replacements for aiding, abetting and counselling, the Law Commission decided against an additional offence of "procurement", and thought that most cases of procuring would be covered by "assisting or encouraging". However, it was deemed that a separate offence of some kind was needed to cater for those defendants whose conduct causes another person to commit a no-fault offence.[82] This offence of "causing a no-fault offence", requiring intention that the offence be committed, would cover the kind of situation which arose in *Att-Gen's Reference (No.1 of 1975)*.[83] **11–037**

III. The Limits of Accessorial Liability

A. NO PRINCIPAL OFFENDER

As we have seen, complicity is a form of derivative liability. It presupposes the existence of a crime. "There is one crime and that it has been committed must be established before there can be any question of criminal guilt or participation in it".[84] This simple proposition requires qualification. **11–038**

(a) D1 may be acquitted through lack of evidence or because of some procedural defect that applies to them. D2 may nevertheless be convicted if the evidence shows clearly that there was a crime.
(b) D1 may be acquitted for a reason such as lacking essential knowledge or being under the age of criminal responsibility,[85] and the court can apply the doctrine of innocent agency to justify the conviction of D2. In such a case, D2 in fact deemed to be the principal offender.
(c) In situations where the doctrine of innocent agency is inapplicable but where the actus reus has been committed, D2 may be convicted even though D1 is acquitted because of lack of mens rea or the existence of a defence.

The relationship between the last two propositions needs to be examined.

81 G.R. Sullivan, "Participating in Crime: Law Com No.305—Joint Criminal Ventures" [2008] Crim. L.R. 19.
82 Law Commission Report No.305, *Participating in Crime* (2007).
83 The Law Commission propose one further offence, considered at para.6–056.
84 J.W.C. Turner, *Russell on Crime*, 12th edn (London: Stevens & Sons, 1964), p.128; affirmed in *Surujpaul v The Queen* [1958] 1 W.L.R. 1050; 3 All E.R. 300 at 301 PC.
85 See above para.9–222.

R. v Bourne (1952) 36 Cr. App. R. 125 (Court of Criminal Appeal):

11–039 The defendant terrorised his wife into committing buggery with a dog. He was convicted of aiding and abetting his wife to commit buggery with a dog. He appealed.

LORD GODDARD CJ:

> "I am willing to assume for the purpose of this case . . . that if this woman had been charged herself with committing the offence, she could have set up the plea of duress, not as showing that no offence had been committed, but as showing that she had no *mens rea* because her will was overborne by threats of imprisonment or violence so that she would be excused from punishment . . . [T]he offence of buggery . . . depends on the act, and if an act of buggery is committed, the felony is committed . . .
>
> The evidence was . . . that he caused his wife to have connection with a dog, and . . . he is guilty, whether you call him an aider and abettor or an accessory, as a principal in the second degree."

Appeal dismissed

R. v Cogan and Leak [1976] Q.B. 217 (Court of Appeal, Criminal Division):

11–040 Leak compelled his wife to have sexual intercourse with Cogan, who believed that she consented. As Cogan's conviction was quashed on the strength of his belief,[86] it became necessary to decide whether Leak's conviction as aider and abettor could stand.

LAWTON LJ:

> "Leak's appeal against conviction was based on the proposition that he could not be found guilty of aiding and abetting Cogan to rape his wife if Cogan was acquitted of that offence as he was deemed in law to have been when his conviction was quashed . . .
>
> Cogan had had sexual intercourse with her without her consent. The fact that Cogan was innocent of rape because he believed that she was consenting does not affect the position that she was raped.
>
> Her ravishment had come about because Leak had wanted it to happen and had taken action to see that it did by persuading Cogan to use his body as the instrument for the necessary physical act. In the language of the law the act of sexual intercourse without the wife's consent was the *actus reus*; it had been procured by Leak who had the appropriate *mens rea*, namely his intention that Cogan should have sexual intercourse with her without her consent. In our

---

86 This case was decided well before the Sexual Offences Act 2003 became law. At the time, a defendant's belief in consent only needed to be honest, and did not need to be reasonable, in order for him to escape liability.

judgment it is irrelevant that the man whom Leak had procured to do the physical act himself did not intend to have sexual intercourse with the wife without her consent. Leak was using him as a means to procure a criminal purpose . . .

Had Leak been indicted as a principal offender, the case against him would have been clear beyond argument. Should he be allowed to go free because he was charged with 'being aider and abettor to the same offence'? If we are right in our opinion that the wife had been raped (and no one outside a court of law would say that she had not been), then the particulars of offence accurately stated what Leak had done, namely he had procured Cogan to commit the offence. This would suffice to uphold the conviction. We would prefer, however, to uphold it on a wider basis. In our judgment convictions should not be upset because of mere technicalities of pleading in an indictment. Leak knew what the case against him was and the facts in support of that case were proved. But for the fact that the jury thought that Cogan in his intoxicated condition might have mistaken the wife's sobs and distress for expressions of her consent, no question of any kind would have arisen about the form of pleading. By his written statement Leak virtually admitted what he had done. As Judge Chapman said in *R. v Humphreys* [1965] 3 All E.R. 689 at 692:

> 'It would be anomalous if a person who admitted to a substantial part in the perpetration of a misdemeanour as aider and abettor could not be convicted on his own admission merely because the person alleged to have been aided and abetted was not or could not be convicted.'

In the circumstances of this case it would be more than anomalous: it would be an affront to justice and to the common sense of ordinary folk. It was for these reasons that we dismissed the appeal against conviction."

Appeal dismissed

We see in this case from the assertion by Lawton LJ that it was clear that "the wife had been raped" and that Leak had procured the rape (a similar view is implicit in *Bourne*). However, a finding of rape could only follow if both actus reus and mens rea were established and the argument is, thus, of doubtful validity. However, it has been refined and developed in subsequent cases. In *Millward,*[87] it was held that D2 could be liable for procuring a driving offence provided there is an actus reus even though D1 is acquitted.[88] There are doubts about whether there was an actus reus on the facts of *Millward*[89] but the principle itself appears to have gained momentum. **11–041**

87 *R. v Millward (Sidney Booth)* (1994) 158 J.P. 1091; [1994] Crim. L.R. 527 CA.

88 *Wheelhouse* [1994] Crim. L.R. 756 followed *Millward* [1994] Crim. L.R. 527, although it was unnecessary to do so on the facts since the doctrine of innocent agency applied.

89 In this case, D2 was the owner of a tractor who had failed to maintain it, resulting in the two-bar deteriorating, and told D1 to use it to tow a trailer. The trailer had come detached whilst D1 was driving, and had hit a car, causing a passenger's death. The court identified the actus reus of the offence (causing death by reckless driving) as being taking a tractor in a defective condition on the road so as to cause the death. Later cases cast doubt on this analysis of the offence: see, e.g. commentary to *R. v Loukes (Noel Martyn)* [1996] Crim. L.R. 341 at 343; [1996] R.T.R. 164 CA; and R. Taylor, "Complicity, Legal Scholarship and the Law of Unintended Consequences" (2009) 29 L.S. 1, 7.

DPP v K and B [1997] 1 Cr. App. R. 36 (Court of Appeal, Criminal Division):

11–042 Two girls, aged 14 and 11, were alleged to have procured the rape of another girl by the D1, a boy (never traced) aged between 10 and 14. The magistrates acquitted the girls on the basis (inter alia) that the prosecution had failed to rebut the presumption of *doli incapax* in relation to the boy. The prosecution appealed by way of case stated.

RUSSELL LJ:

> "In my judgment, the decision of the magistrate in this appeal cannot be supported. There is no doubt whatever that 'W' was the victim of unlawful sexual intercourse without her consent; such was not disputed. The *actus reus* was proved. The respondents procured the situation which included the sexual intercourse. It would, in my view, be singularly unattractive to find that because of the absence of a mental element on the part of the principal, the procurers could thereby escape conviction when, as the magistrate found, K and B had the requisite *mens rea* namely, the desire that rape should take place and the procuring of it.
>
> In my judgment, neither authority nor common sense nor justice compels this Court to support the finding of the magistrates."

Appeal allowed

11–043 A point to stress is that the principle that D2 can be liable despite there being no D1 has only been applied in cases of procuring, and only if the actus reus of the offence has been committed. This does, at first sight, seem anomalous. There appears to be one rule for procuring and another for other forms of complicity. This is compounded when one considers that the prosecution does not even have to specify the form of complicity in the charge. However, the problem may not, in fact, be as significant as it seems. If D2 does have the appropriate mens rea and the crime is committed by a principal offender who lacks mens rea or who has a defence such as duress, the situation would almost certainly be regarded as one of procuring or innocent agency. Liability could then be imposed under the above principles.

B. ACCESSORY CAN BE GUILTY OF GRAVER OFFENCE THAN THE ONE COMMITTED

11–044 Until the following decision in *Howe*, the law was that if D1 had the mens rea of one offence, such as manslaughter, it was not possible for D2, who was not present at the scene of the crime, to be guilty of the graver offence of murder.[90]

90 *R. v Richards (Isabelle Christina)* [1974] Q.B. 776; [1973] 3 W.L.R. 888 CA.

R. v Howe [1987] 1 A.C. 417 (House of Lords):

[The facts and a fuller extract appear above at para.9–151.] **11–045**

LORD MACKAY OF CLASHFERN:

> "I turn now to the second certified question [whether a secondary party can be convicted of murder despite the conviction of the principal for manslaughter] . . . I am of the opinion that the Court of Appeal reached the correct conclusion upon it as a matter of principle.
>
> Giving the judgment of the Court of Appeal Lord Lane CJ said [1986] Q.B. 626 at 641–642:
>
>> 'The judge based himself on a decision of this court in *R. v Richards*. The facts in that case were that Mrs Richards paid two men to inflict injuries on her husband which she intended should "put him in hospital for a month". The two men wounded the husband but not seriously. They were acquitted of wounding with intent but convicted of unlawful wounding. Mrs Richards herself was convicted of wounding with intent, the jury plainly, and not surprisingly, believing that she had the necessary intent, though the two men had not. She appealed against her conviction on the ground that she could not properly be convicted as accessory before the fact to a crime more serious than that committed by the principals in the first degree. The appeal was allowed and the conviction for unlawful wounding was substituted. The court followed a passage from Hawkins' Pleas of the Crown, vol.2. c.29 para.15: "I take it to be an uncontroverted rule that [the offence of the accessory can never rise higher than that of the principal]; it seeming incongruous and absurd that he who is punished only as a partaker of the guilt of another, should be adjudged guilty of a higher crime than the other."'
>
> James LJ delivering the judgment in *R. v Richards* said:
>
>> 'If there is only one offence committed, and that is the offence of unlawful wounding, then the person who has requested that offence to be committed, or advised that that offence be committed, cannot be guilty of a graver offence than that in fact which was committed.'
>
> The decision in *R. v Richards* has been the subject of some criticism . . . Counsel before us posed the situation where A hands a gun to D informing him that it is loaded with blank ammunition only and telling him to go and scare X by discharging it. The ammunition is in fact live, as A knows, and X is killed. D is convicted only of manslaughter, as he might be on those facts. It would seem absurd that A should thereby escape conviction for murder. We take the view that *R. v Richards* was incorrectly decided, but it seems to us that it cannot properly be distinguished from the instant case.

I consider that the reasoning of Lord Lane C.J. is entirely correct and I would affirm his view that where a person has been killed and that result is the result intended by another participant, the mere fact that the actual killer may be convicted only of the reduced charge of manslaughter for some reason special to himself does not, in my opinion in any way, result in a compulsory reduction for the other participant."

Appeal dismissed

11–046 It has been pointed out that in neither *Howe* nor *Richards* was any real attempt made to understand the theoretical underpinnings of the two positions.[91] Since it has long been possible to convict those present at the scene of the crime of a more serious offence than the principal, at one level, *Howe* merely reflects the increasing trend of regarding presence as not determinative of anything. However, it is a departure "from orthodox complicity theory that insists on the parties' sharing in liability for *one* offence".[92] In other words, this may be a departure from derivative liability similar to that in cases such as *Cogan*. Furthermore, despite all the criticism of *Richards* there may have been a sound principle underlying it: that of control. Mrs Richards lacked control over D1 and should not have been guilty of a more serious offence despite her greater mens rea.

C. WITHDRAWAL OF ACCESSORIES

11–047 A withdrawal from a criminal enterprise may amount to a claim that there is no actus reus or mens rea of complicity. For example, a person may lend a gun to D1 to commit murder, but later take the gun back. If D1 shoots V with a different gun, the original provider of the gun will not be liable as there will be no actus reus of complicity.[93] However, in other cases D2's involvement might clearly satisfy the actus reus and mens rea requirements of complicity but there might be a "withdrawal" before the commission of the offence.[94] This latter scenario is exemplified by the following leading case.

R. v Becerra and Cooper (1975) 62 Cr. App. R. 212 (Court of Appeal, Criminal Division):

11–048 Becerra broke into a house with Cooper and another. They intended to steal but Becerra gave a knife to Cooper which he was to use if anyone interrupted them. Lewis, an upstairs tenant, came to investigate the noise, at which Becerra said, "There's a bloke coming. Let's go", and jumped out of a window. As he ran away Cooper stabbed and killed Lewis with the knife. Becerra was convicted with Cooper of murder, and appealed.

---

91 Smith, *A Modern Treatise on the Law of Complicity* (1991), p.130.

92 Law Commission Consultation Paper No.131, *Assisting and Encouraging Crime* (1993), para.2.38. See also Smith, *A Modern Treatise on the Law of Complicity* (1991), pp.127–133.

93 K.J.M. Smith, "Withdrawal in Complicity: A Restatement of Principles" [2001] Crim. L.R. 769.

94 Smith (K.J.M. Smith, "Withdrawal in Complicity: A Restatement of Principles" [2001] Crim. L.R. 769) argues that the nature and scope of a withdrawal defence should depend on the rationale for having such a defence: whether it is an incentive for the accessory to desist or whether it is evidence of the accessory's lack of (or diminished) culpability or future dangerousness.

ROSKILL LJ:

"It was argued in the alternative on behalf of Becerra, that even if there were this common design, nonetheless Becerra had open to him a second line of defence, namely that . . . whatever Cooper did immediately before and at the time of the killing of Lewis, Becerra had by then withdrawn from that common design and so should not be convicted of the murder of Lewis, even though the common design had previously been that which I have stated . . .

It is necessary, before dealing with that argument in more detail, to say a word or two about the relevant law. [Roskill L.J. then cited a decision of the Court of Appeal of British Columbia in *Whitehouse (alias Savage)* (1941) 1 W.W.R. 112 at 115 and 116.]

> 'Can it be said on the facts of this case that a mere change of mental intention and a quitting of the scene of the crime just immediately prior to the striking of the fatal blow will absolve those who participate in the commission of the crime by overt acts up to that moment from all the consequences of its accomplishment by the one who strikes in ignorance of his companion's change of heart? I think not. After a crime has been committed and before a prior abandonment of the common enterprise may be found by a jury there must be, in my view, in the absence of exceptional circumstances, something more than a mere mental change of intention and physical change of place by those associates who wish to dissociate themselves from the consequences attendant upon their willing assistance up to the moment of the actual commission of that crime. I would not attempt to define too closely what must be done in criminal matters involving participation in a common unlawful purpose to break the chain of causation and responsibility. That must depend upon the circumstances of each case but it seems to me that one essential element ought to be established in a case of this kind. Where practicable and reasonable there must be timely communication of the intention to abandon the common purpose from those who wish to dissociate themselves from the contemplated crime to those who desire to continue in it. What is "timely communication" must be determined by the facts of each case but where practicable and reasonable it ought to be such communication, verbal or otherwise, that will serve unequivocal notice upon the other party to the common unlawful cause that if he proceeds upon it he does so without the further aid and assistance of those who withdraw. The unlawful purpose of him who continues alone is then his own and not one in common with those who are no longer parties to it nor liable to its full and final consequences.' . . .

In the view of each member of this Court, that passage, if we may respectfully say so, could not be improved upon and we venture to adopt it in its entirety as a correct statement of the law which is to be applied in this case . . .

We therefore turn back to consider the direction which the learned judge gave in the present case to the jury and what was the suggested evidence that Becerra had withdrawn from the

> common agreement. The suggested evidence is the use by Becerra of the words 'Come on let's go', coupled with his act in going out through the window. The evidence, as the judge pointed out, was that Cooper never heard that nor did the third man. But let it be supposed that that was said and the jury took the view that it was said.
>
> On the facts of this case, in the circumstances then prevailing, the knife having already been used and being contemplated for further use when it was handed over by Becerra to Cooper for the purpose of avoiding (if necessary) by violent means the hazards of identification, if Becerra wanted to withdraw at that stage, he would have to 'countermand,' to use the word that is used in some of the cases or 'repent' to use another word so used, in some manner vastly different and vastly more effective than merely to say 'Come on, let's go' and go out through the window.
>
> . . . It is enough for the purposes of deciding this application to say that under the law of this country as it stands, and on the facts (taking them at their highest in favour of Becerra), that which was urged as amounting to withdrawal from the common design was not capable of amounting to such withdrawal. Accordingly Becerra remains responsible, in the eyes of the law, for everything that Cooper did and continued to do after Becerra's disappearance through the window as much as if he had done them himself."
>
> *Appeal dismissed*

11–049 Accordingly, there must be, at least, a "timely communication" of the decision to withdraw. This was confirmed in ***Rook***[95] where D2 tried to disassociate himself from the planned murder by simply not being around when the others came to collect him on the way to the crime:

> "[T]he appellant never told the others that he was not going ahead with the crime. His absence on the day could not possibly amount to 'unequivocal communication' of his withdrawal . . . he had made it quite clear to himself that he did not want to be there on the day. But he did not make it clear to the others."

However, in *Mitchell*,[96] it was held that the requirement of communication of withdrawal only applies in cases of pre-planned violence and not to cases of spontaneous violence, although in these latter cases it would be more difficult evidentially to establish withdrawal if there had been no communication. This was followed in *O'Flaherty*,[97] where it was held that the question of whether or not D2 had withdrawn is no more than a consideration of whether D1 had departed from the joint enterprise.[98] This was

---

95 *R. v Rook (Adrian)* [1993] 1 W.L.R. 1005; (1993) 97 Cr. App. R. 327 CA. See also *R. v Grundy* [1977] Crim. L.R. 543 CA, where the party also sought (successfully) to withdraw before the commission of the crime (some two weeks hence); see also *R. v Croft (William James)* [1944] K.B. 295; (1944) 29 Cr. App. R. 169 CA; *R. v Whitefield (Arthur Armour)* (1984) 79 Cr. App. R. 36; [1984] Crim. L.R. 97 CA; and *R. v Baker* [1994] Crim. L.R. 444 CA.

96 *R. v Mitchell (Frank)* (1999) 163 J.P. 75; [1999] Crim. L.R. 496 CA.

97 *R. v O'Flaherty (Errol Carlton)* [2004] EWCA Crim 526; [2004] 2 Cr. App. R. 20.

98 This was also the approach taken in *R. v D* [2005] EWCA Crim 1981.

another case of spontaneous violence in which, as pointed out by Ashworth,[99] the principals may have been as unaware of Ds' participation in the joint enterprise as they were of their withdrawal. Three appellants, O'F, R and T, joined in an attack on V with various weapons. Subsequently, V was chased by a group of individuals, including O'F, but R and T did not join the group and instead chose to leave. The victim sustained fatal injuries during a second attack. O'F did not take part in the second attack but was present at the scene, and looked on whilst holding a cricket bat. R and T had not communicated their withdrawal from the attack but it was held that they did not need to do so as the second attack could not be said to be part of the joint enterprise to which they were party, and their appeal against conviction for murder was allowed. O'F's presence at the scene of the second attack was, however, enough to show that he had aided and abetted the crime of murder. *O'Flaherty* has been followed in another case of *Mitchell*,[100] where D2's argument that there were two distinct joint enterprises and that her presence at the second was only to look for her shoes and not to encourage further violence was rejected by the Court of Appeal. In its judgment (pre-*Jogee*), the court stated that there was ample evidence that D2 had not withdrawn from the joint enterprise.

In some cases, depending on the circumstances,[101] it may be that timely communication alone is not enough and that some further action is required. In *Rook*, for example, the Court of Appeal stated that a suggestion that "a declared intent to withdraw from a conspiracy to dynamite a building is not enough, if the fuse has been set; he must step on the fuse" went too far. "It may be enough that he should have done his best to step on the fuse". Presumably in such cases:

> "... some form of correlation [should] exist between the nature or form of the defendant's—complicitous behaviour and the nature or form of his required exculpatory action. In crude terms: the greater the extent of inculpatory behaviour the more demanding will be the price of exculpation."[102]

The Supreme Court in *Jogee* did not expressly deal with the issue of withdrawal, although what is said at [12] of the judgment is relevant: **11–050**

> "Ultimately it is a question of fact and degree whether D2's conduct was so distanced in time, place or circumstances from the conduct of D1 that it would not be realistic to regard D1's offence as encouraged or assisted by it."[103]

The Law Commission has recommended that in certain circumstances D2 ought to have a specific defence where they made efforts to undo some of the work of D1. This would apply where D2 was able

99 *R. v O'Flaherty (Errol Carlton)* [2004] EWCA Crim 526; [2004] Crim. L.R. 751 at 752.

100 *R. v Mitchell (Laura)* [2008] EWCA Crim 2552; [2009] Crim L.R. 287. A second appeal following a reference from the Criminal Cases Review Commission post-*Jogee* was similarly dismissed: *Mitchell* [2018] EWCA Crim 2687.

101 In a case of spontaneous violence it is clear that it is not necessary for the accessory to take reasonable steps to prevent crime: *O'Flaherty* [2004] 2 Cr. App. R. 20 at [61].

102 Smith "Withdrawal in Complicity: A Restatement of Principles" [2001] Crim. L.R. 769, 776.

103 *Jogee* [2016] UKSC 8 at [12].

to prove, on the balance of probabilities, that they acted for the purposes of preventing the commission of an offence or the occurrence of harm.[104]

D. OVERWHELMING SPUPERVENING ACT

11–051 In joint enterprise homicide cases, the effect of the combination of constructive liability for murder (through the GBH rule) manslaughter (through unlawful and dangerous act manslaughter), and lack of a need for causation for secondary parties to be liable, has the potential to draw the arc of liability for death unacceptably wide, leading the Supreme Court in *Jogee* to resurrect a mechanism by which D2 can escape all liability for death in the event of:

> ". . . some **overwhelming supervening act** by the perpetrator which nobody in the defendant's shoes could have contemplated might happen and is of such a character as to relegate his acts to history . . ."[105]

The role of this "overwhelming supervening act" (OSA) rule is to replace the previous "fundamentally different" rule applied in *Powell; English*,[106] which had the result of exempting D2 of all liability, including liability for manslaughter, where D1 in a murder case had acted in a way which was judged to be "fundamentally different" to the act foreseen by D2. An example of this can be seen in *English* itself, where the principal's use of a knife to wound and kill V was an act of a fundamentally different nature to the agreed enterprise of attacking V with wooden fence posts, leading to D2's conviction for murder being quashed, and D2 also escaping liability for manslaughter. The "all or nothing" aspect of this rule has been removed by *Jogee*,[107] meaning that the harshness of the law on constructive manslaughter now extends to incorporate accomplice liability. A D2 who intends to encourage or assist D1 to commit an assault of some kind, but does not intend D1 to act with intent to kill or cause GBH, will not be liable for murder but will be liable for manslaughter. Only an OSA will lead to D2 escaping all liability for the death.

Shortly after *Jogee*, the issue of OSA and liability for manslaughter was considered by the Court of Appeal in *Tas*, in which D2 became involved in a fight during which his friend stabbed V. The friend, D1, was convicted of murder, along with a third defendant, and D2 was convicted of manslaughter rather

---

104 Law Commission Report No.305, *Participating in Crime* (2007).

105 *Jogee* [2016] UKSC 8 at [97]. Emphasis added.

106 *Powell* [1999] 1 A.C. 1.

107 However, as noted by Krebs, it will often be advantageous for the prosecution to argue for a broad description of the incident as in R. v *Bristow (Terrance)* [2013] EWCA Crim 1540; [2014] Crim. L.R. 457 (see para.7–040). Where the prosecution characterises an incident in a narrow sense, they risk a secondary party avoiding liability altogether. This was the outcome in *R. v Rowe (Talib)* [2022] EWCA Crim 27, where the joint venture was described as a shooting rather than an attack. D2 argued on appeal against conviction for manslaughter that he either intended to assist or encourage a shooting, which would imply that he intended V to suffer death or GBH and the jury would have convicted him for murder, or he did not, in which case he should have been acquitted. It would not be logically possible for someone to intend to shoot V at close range and not intend to cause them anything less than serious bodily harm. The characterisation of the prosecution case in *Rowe* led to an all-or-nothing route to liability, resulting in what was ruled to be an unsafe conviction, and D2's conviction for manslaughter was quashed: B. Krebs, "Charactering Joint Criminal Enterprises: Case Note on *R. v Rowe* [2022] EWCA Crim 27" (2023) 87 (3) *Journal of Criminal Law* 223–226.

than murder because it was accepted that he had not foreseen the stabbing. He appealed against his conviction on the basis that D1's use of a knife constituted an overwhelming supervening event which, according to the Supreme Court in *Jogee*, relieved him of any liability for the homicide, and the judge should have directed the jury to this effect.

R. v Tas [2018] EWCA Crim 2603 (Court of Appeal):

"37 . . . [I]n underlining the requirement for proof of intention, one of the effects of *Jogee* is to reduce the significance of knowledge of the weapon so that it impacts as evidence (albeit very important if not potentially irresistible) going to proof of intention, rather than being a pre-requisite of liability for murder . . . **11–052**

38. The argument can be tested in this way. The joint enterprise is to participate in the attack on another and events proceed as happened in this case with Tas punching one of the victims (otherwise than in self-defence), then providing backup (and an escape vehicle) to the others as they chased after them. One of the principals kicks the deceased to death (or, as articulated in [96] of *Jogee*, the violence has escalated). Alternatively, a bottle is used or a weapon found on the ground. Both based on principle and the correct application of *Church* (participation by encouragement or assistance in any other unlawful act which all sober and reasonable people would realise carried the risk of some, not necessarily serious, harm to another, with death resulting), a conviction for manslaughter would result: the unlawful act is the intentional use of force otherwise than in self defence.

39. On the facts which must have been found by the jury in this case, Tas took the risk that the others involved in the joint enterprise with him would go further than to inflict 'some harm'. Consistent with the principles identified in the authorities and the modern approach to knowledge of a specific weapon, there is no reason to distinguish the case where the victim is kicked to death or killed with a weapon either that is picked up off the ground or brought by the principal to the scene.

40. What then is left of overwhelming supervening act? It is important not to abbreviate the test articulated above which postulates an act that 'nobody in the defendant's shoes could have contemplated might happen and is of such a character as to relegate his acts to history'. In the context of this case, the question can be asked whether the judge was entitled to conclude that there was insufficient evidence to leave to the jury that if they concluded (as they must have) that, in the course of a confrontation sought by Tas and his friends leading to an ongoing and moving street fight (which had Tas driving his car following the chase to ensure that his friends could be taken from the scene), the production of a knife is a wholly supervening event rather than a simple escalation."

Appeal dismissed

The Court of Appeal has similarly upheld convictions in subsequent homicide cases, suggesting that the bar for an OSA is set very high. This is true for accomplices convicted of both murder and **11–053** manslaughter. So, in *Grant*,[108] where D2 had an intention to cause at least serious harm in a face-to-face encounter, the fact that D1 used his car as a weapon did not amount to an OSA relieving D2 of liability for murder. The Court of Appeal stated:

> "On a charge of murder, if the accessory intentionally assisted or encouraged the perpetrator and intended that the perpetrator should cause grievous bodily harm with intent, he or she will have satisfied the elements of the offence of murder. The precise manner in which the victim happens to be killed and whether the perpetrator intended to kill as opposed to inflict really serious harm are by the way, so long as the encouragement or assistance of the accessory has not been 'relegated to history' as set out above. Save perhaps for exceptional circumstances which are not readily easy to envisage, there will be no need to direct the jury on the concept of OSA simply because the fatal injuries were inflicted using an entirely different kind of weapon or method of killing than that originally contemplated and/or the perpetrator intended to kill rather than to inflict really serious harm."[109]

In the more commonplace example of a group attack where D1 produces a knife and stabs V, D2 is now extremely unlikely to avoid liability for manslaughter, as seen in cases such as *Lanning and Camille*.[110] In a spontaneous altercation at an underground station, V was stabbed and killed by D1, whilst D1's accomplice (who was a friend of a friend), D2, was fighting with V's friend. D1 was convicted of murder and D2 of manslaughter. On appeal, D2 argued that the judge should have directed the jury on the issue of OSA on the basis that D2 was unaware that D1 had a knife and did not see it being used. Describing the event as "a paradigm of rapidly escalating violence which was part of a joint enterprise attack"[111] the Court of Appeal dismissed the appeal against conviction, with the opinion that:

> "bearing in mind that knives are produced in situations of this kind with a high degree of frequency leading to serious injury or death, the judge was entitled to conclude that there was insufficient factual basis for a jur y to conclude (adopting the language from *Jogee* at [97]), that '*nobody in the defendant's shoes could have contemplated*' that the production and use of a knife in the joint attack might happen."[112]

Cases such as this suggest that, following *Jogee*, the defendant in *English* would similarly not now escape liability for manslaughter,[113] due to what the Crown in *Lanning and Camille* described as expected in terms of knife crime in "today's social climate". Krebs notes that the case of *Lanning and Camille* clarifies that:

108 *R. v Grant (Tony Lee)* [2021] EWCA Crim 1243; [2022] Q.B. 857.

109 *Grant* [2021] EWCA Crim 1243 at [38].

110 *R. v Lanning (Alex Christopher)* [2021] EWCA Crim 450.

111 *Lanning* [2021] EWCA Crim 450 at [71].

112 *Lanning* [2021] EWCA Crim 450 at [69].

113 Krebs argues that this is "defensible": B. Krebs, "Overwhelming Supervening Acts, Fundamental Differences, and Back Again?" (2022) 86(6) *Journal of Criminal Law* 420–440, 437.

> "OSA looks to the wholly unexpected, not from the defendant's point of view, but ultimately from the perspective of general life experience (which is then attributed to someone in the defendant's position). And even then, the wholly unexpected needs to be so momentous as to consign the accessory's deeds to history—a taxing two-limbed test."[114]

The prevalence of knife crime in modern England has led the law to arguably take a step backwards here in effectively barring a defence to accomplices in a case of joint enterprise, even if they genuinely did not realise that there was a risk that D1 might use a knife. As such, whilst *Jogee* may be seen as narrowing the net of liability for murder accomplices by tightening the test for mens rea, the way that OSA has now been interpreted by the courts means it at the same time widened the net for manslaughter liability. Given the Court of Appeal was unable to envisage an example of what might amount to an OSA,[115] it seems that despite the Supreme Court's apparent intentions in this regard, it does not provide much of a limit to accessorial liability at all.

E. VICTIMS CANNOT BE ACCESSORIES

The case of *Tyrell*[116] established a general principle that where a statutory offence exists in order to protect a particular class of victim, such a victim cannot be held liable for participating in the offence as an accessory. This, and subsequent cases,[117] concerned sexual offences such as incest and underage sexual intercourse. If D1 has sexual intercourse in a situation where to do so is an offence by virtue of the identity of the other party (because of their age or relationship), that V cannot be said to have aided, abetted, counselled or procured the offence.[118] **11–054**

While the *Tyrell* principle has, to date, only been applied to sexual offences, there is no reason why it should not be applied to other offences.[119] However, the principle is uncertain and interpretative difficulty surrounds the notion of "victim". For example, the notion of "victim" appeared to take on different meanings in *Brown*.[120] Prior to the prosecution, 26 people were cautioned for aiding and abetting offences against themselves.[121] It thus seems that the passive participants in the sado-masochistic activities in *Brown* were not "victims" for the purpose of the protection afforded by the rules on accessorial liability but, of course, were regarded as "victims" for the purpose of assessing the

---

114 B. Krebs, "Underwhelming supervening acts: Case Comment" (2021) 85(5) *Journal of Criminal Law* 405-405, 405.

115 *Grant* [2021] EWCA Crim 1243 at [38].

116 *R. v Tyrell* [1894] 1 Q.B. 710 CC.

117 e.g. *R. v Whitehouse (Arthur)* [1977] Q.B. 868; [1977] 2 W.L.R. 925 CA.

118 Although this principle has not been repealed by legislation, it has been argued that certain provisions under the Sexual Offences Act 2003 manage to circumvent its application, thereby criminalising victims one would expect to see protected by the law (M. Bohlander, "The Sexual Offences Act 2003 and the *Tyrell* Principle—Criminalising the Victims?" [2005] Crim. L.R. 701). The Law Commission considered the point at some length in its most recent report on secondary liability: Law Commission Report No.305, *Participating in Crime* (2007), paras 5.24–5.38.

119 Serious Crime Act 2007 s.51 codifies *Tyrell* [1894] 1 Q.B. 710, and excludes liability for encouraging or assisting crime for victims in cases of any "protective offence". See Ch.5. A similar draft provision is included in cl.6 of the draft Participating in Crime Bill, appended to Law Commission Report No.305, *Participating in Crime* (2007).

120 *R. v Brown (Anthony Joseph)* [1994] 1 A.C. 212; [1993] 2 W.L.R. 556 HL.

121 Prior to the prosecution in *Brown*, the sadomasochistic activities uncovered by the police investigation led to 26 people being cautioned for aiding and abetting offences against themselves. *The Guardian*, 8 February 1992.

criminal liability of the principal offender.[122] The following decision drew upon *Brown* (even though, as Herring points out, the "victims" were not actually prosecuted but only those who inflicted harm[123]) in reaching its conclusion that a narrow interpretation should be given to the victim rule.

R. v GNANGO [2011] UKSC 59 (SUPREME COURT):

11–055 D2 voluntarily exchanged gunfire with an opponent, D1, referred to as "Bandana Man", in a public car park. A shot by D1 killed an innocent passer-by. A man thought to be D1 was arrested but there was insufficient evidence to charge him. D2 was charged with V's murder. At trial, the judge held that it was not relevant that D2 and D1 had reciprocally opposing intentions to shoot each other. He rejected the Crown's argument that D2 could be liable for aiding and abetting the killing, directing the jury that D2 would be guilty of murder if they were sure that he and D1 had been in a joint enterprise (whether planned or spontaneous) to use unlawful violence against each other, and that in the course of that joint enterprise fight, the victim had been murdered by D1 on the basis of transferred malice. D2 was convicted and appealed. The Court of Appeal allowed the appeal, holding that there was no evidence of a shared common purpose. The Crown appealed to the Supreme Court, contending, inter alia, that D2's conviction could be justified on the basis that 2D had aided and abetted the commission of the murder by actively encouraging D1 to shoot at him.

LORD PHILLIPS P and LORD JUDGE CJ:

"[1] Permission to appeal was granted in this case in order to enable this court to consider the following point of law, certified by the Court of Appeal as being of general public importance:

> 'If (1) D1 and D2 voluntarily engage in fighting each other, each intending to kill or cause grievous bodily harm to the other and each foreseeing that the other has the reciprocal intention, and if (2) D1 mistakenly kills V in the course of the fight, in what circumstances, if any, is D2 guilty of the offence of murdering V?'

The facts of this case are unusual, but the importance of the point of law lies in the implications that it may have in respect of the scope of potential liability of those who permit themselves to become involved in public order offences.

[2] No previous decision in this jurisdiction provides a clear indication of how the point of law should be resolved . . . In resolving the point of law it will be appropriate to have regard to policy . . .

[29] Before this court . . . the Crown has sought to revive the case . . . that the respondent had been an accessory to Bandana Man's attempt to kill him and thus shared Bandana Man's

---

122 L. Bibbings and P. Alldridge, "Sexual Expression, Body Alteration, and the Defence of Consent" (1993) 20 J.L. and Soc. 356, 364.

123 J. Herring, "Victims as Defendants: When Victims Participate in Crimes Against Themselves" in Reed and Bohlander (eds), *Participation in Crime: Domestic and Comparative Perspectives* (2013), p.83.

liability, as a result of the doctrine of transferred malice, for the murder . . . [relying upon parasitic accessory liability in the alternative] . . .

[44] Why was the Crown so keen to establish liability under the doctrine of parasitic accessory liability? The answer is, we believe, that the Crown believed that this route would enable it to by-pass what was perceived to be a barrier to the direct route to the respondent's liability for murder. The direct route was as follows: (i) Bandana Man attempted to kill the respondent; (ii) by agreeing to the shoot-out, the respondent aided and abetted Bandana Man in this attempted murder; (iii) Bandana Man accidentally killed Ms Pniewska instead of the respondent. Under the doctrine of transferred malice he was guilty of her murder; (iv) the doctrine of transferred malice applied equally to the respondent as aider and abetter of Bandana Man's attempted murder. He also was guilty of Ms Pniewska's murder.

[45] The Crown believed that there was a barrier to this direct route to the respondent's liability for murder. This was the application of the victim rule . . . the respondent could not aid and abet his own attempted murder. If this proposition correctly represents the law, we do not see how the Crown can avoid its effect by invoking the doctrine of parasitic accessory liability. Parasitic accessory liability does not differ in principle from the more common basis for finding someone guilty of aiding, abetting, counselling or procuring the commission of a crime. In so far as the law precludes conviction for aiding and abetting a crime in respect of which the defendant is the victim, it must surely do so whatever the route by which the defendant would otherwise be held to have been an accomplice.

[46] We turn then to consider the Crown's new case, which is that the conviction of the defendant can be justified on the basis that the defendant aided and abetted the commission of the murder by actively encouraging Bandana Man to shoot at him. In relation to this case it seems to us that the issues for the court are as follows: (i) Does the victim rule preclude the conviction of a defendant for aiding and abetting a crime in respect of which he is the victim, even where the crime is not designed to protect a particular class of which the victim is a member? If yes, (ii) does the victim rule preclude the conviction of a defendant for aiding and abetting a crime in respect of which he was the intended victim, but where the actual victim is a third party? . . .

[51] [T]here is no applicable statutory victim rule that precludes conviction of the respondent on the basis that he aided and abetted Bandana Man's attempt to kill him or cause him serious injury. Is there, or should there be, a common law rule that does so?

[52] The fact that Parliament found it necessary to enact s 2(1) of the [Criminal Law Act] 1977[124] Act and s 51 of the [Serious Crime Act] 2007 Act[125] is cogent indication that there is no common law rule that precludes conviction of a defendant of being party to a crime of which he was the actual or intended victim. We are satisfied that there is no such rule. This is evident from the fact that, under common law, attempted suicide was a crime, as was aiding and abetting suicide . . .

---

124 See para.10–065.
125 See para.10–114.

> [53] We can see no reason why this court should consider extending the common law so as to protect from conviction any defendant who is, or is intended to be, harmed by the crime that he commits, or attempts to commit. Such an extension would defeat the intention of Parliament in circumscribing the victim rule in s 51 of the 2007 Act. In *R. v Brown* [1993] 2 All ER 75, [1994] 1 AC 212 sado-masochists were held to have been rightly convicted of causing injury to others who willingly consented to the injuries that they received. There would have been no bar to conviction of the latter of having aided and abetted the infliction of those injuries upon themselves. It is no doubt appropriate for prosecuting authorities to consider carefully whether there is justification for prosecuting anyone as party to a crime where he is the victim, or intended victim of that crime, but that is not to say that the actual or intended victim of a crime should on that ground alone be absolved from criminal responsibility in relation to it . . .
>
> [54] In the light of the conclusion that we have just reached, no question arises as to the application of the victim rule where, although the intended victim of the crime to which the defendant is party is the defendant himself, the actual victim proves to be a third party."
>
> *Appeal allowed*

11–056 By a majority of six to one, the Supreme Court restored D2's conviction for murder. Beyond this, however, there are fundamental differences of view among the majority which make it difficult to assess the impact of this controversial decision. Lords Phillips and Judge (with whom Lord Wilson agrees) and Lord Dyson adopt one approach:

1. that D2 was guilty of murder;
2. not on the basis of joint enterprise or "parasitical accessorial liability", because, put simply, there was no collateral crime (NB this was before *Jogee*); but
3. on the basis that he had aided and abetted the murder by encouraging "Bandana Man" to shoot back at him, foreseeing that he might do so; and
4. applying the doctrine of transferred malice so that D2's intention towards "Bandana Man" was transferred to V.

They come to this conclusion despite the fact that the trial judge had rejected this mode of analysis, meaning that the jury never considered the prosecution case on this basis, and some profound difficulties with this approach exposed by Lord Kerr in his persuasive dissent. Two of the remaining Supreme Court judges in the majority, Lords Brown and Clarke, on the other hand, find D2 guilty of murder as a principal, despite the difficulties in establishing causation given the voluntary actions of "Bandana Man" which would ordinarily break the chain of causation between D2's actions and the death of the passer-by.[126] The decision is controversial for several reasons, not least the fact that the judges could not agree on *why* D2 was liable.

---

126 See para.2–067.

In trying to make sense of the decision in *Gnango*, one fact stands out as significant: "Bandana Man" was arrested but not charged and subsequently disappeared. Had he been charged it seems unlikely that the convoluted prosecution of Gnango for murder (as opposed to the appropriate charge of attempted murder of "Bandana Man") would have been pursued. Policy or the desire that someone should be brought to justice for the death of the innocent passer-by[127] are important considerations in this Supreme Court decision, as is evident from Lord Brown's comment: **11–057**

> "[T]o my mind the all-important consideration here is that both A and B were intentionally engaged in a potentially lethal unlawful gunfight (a 'shoot-out' as it has also been described) in the course of which an innocent passer-by was killed. The general public would in my opinion be astonished and appalled if in those circumstances the law attached liability for the death only to the gunman who actually fired the fatal shot (which, indeed, it would not always be possible to determine). Is he alone to be regarded as guilty of the victim's murder? Is the other gunman really to be regarded as blameless and exonerated from all criminal liability for that killing? Does the decision of the Court of Appeal here, allowing A's appeal against his conviction for murder, really represent the law of the land? . . .
>
> To my mind the answer to these questions is a plain 'No'."[128]

F. ACCOMPLICES AND TRANSFERRED MALICE

DAVID LANHAM, "ACCOMPLICES AND TRANSFERRED MALICE" (1980) 96 L.Q.R. 110, 110–111:

> "An accomplice (A) instigates a principal offender (PO) to commit a specific crime. PO commits a crime of the same description but against a different victim or subject-matter or in a different manner. In what circumstances is A criminally liable for the crime committed by PO? . . . **11–058**
>
> . . . While the problem is basically one of transferred malice, the situations requiring the transfer can arise in various different ways. First, PO may attempt to harm the right victim (X) but harm another (V) by accident. Secondly, he may believe that V is X and so harm the wrong victim by mistake. Thirdly, he may do more harm than A ordered, e.g. injuring V (an unintended victim) as well as X (the intended victim). Fourthly, he may deliberately depart from A's orders and injure V even though he knows that V is not X. Fifthly, he may commit the crime ordered by A against the correct victim but at a different time, place or in a different manner from that ordered or advised by A. Finally, he may commit the crime ordered but against the wrong subject-matter."

Authority on this problem is scarce with most of the controversy revolving around the following case. **11–059**

---

127 E. Freer, "*R. v Gnango*: The Curious Case of Bandana Man" (2012) 176 Crim. Law and Justice Weekly 218.

128 *R. v Gnango (Armel)* [2011] UKSC 59 at [68]–[69]; [2012] 1 A.C. 827. See further D. Ormerod, "Worth the Wait?" [2012] Crim. L.R. 79, 80.

R. v Saunders and Archer (1573) 2 Plowden 473; 75 E.R. 706 (Warwick Assizes):

11-060 Saunders wished to kill his wife so that he could marry another woman. He explained his plans to Archer who advised him to kill her by poison. Archer bought the poison and gave it to Saunders to give to his wife. Saunders mixed the poison with two pieces of roasted apple and gave it to his wife. After tasting it the wife handed the rest of the apple to Eleanor, their three-year-old daughter. Saunders, on seeing this, merely said that "apples were not good for such infants" but when his wife persisted he simply watched his daughter eat the apple and did nothing "lest he be suspected". The daughter died of the poison. Saunders was found guilty of murder but the question remained as to the liability of Archer.

LORD DYER CJ:

> "But the most difficult point in this case . . . was whether or not Archer should be adjudged accessory to the murder. For the offence which Archer committed was the aid and advice which he gave to Saunders, and that was only to kill his wife, and no other, for there was no . . . communication between them concerning the daughter, and although by the consequences which followed from the giving of the poison by Saunders the principal, it so happened that the daughter was killed, yet Archer did not precisely procure her death, nor advise him to kill her, and therefore whether or not he should be accessory to this murder which happened by a thing consequential to the first act, seemed to them to be doubtful. For which reason they thought proper to advise and consider of it until the next gaol delivery, and in the meantime to consult with the justices in the term . . . [It was finally agreed] that they ought not to give judgment against the said Alexander Archer, because they took the law to be that he could not be adjudged accessory to the said offence of murder, for that he did not assent that the daughter should be poisoned, but only that the wife should be poisoned, which assent cannot be drawn further than he gave it, for the poisoning of the daughter is a distinct thing from that to which he was privy, and therefore he shall not be adjudged accessory to it; and so they were resolved before this time."

11-061 A broad interpretation of this case is that the accomplice will only be liable if they expressly authorise or foresee the harm which occurs. A narrower interpretation of *Saunders and Archer* suggests that secondary parties will not be liable if D1 *deliberately* chooses another victim; effectively this is what Saunders did. He chose to let a different victim die, rather than step in to prevent it. On the other hand, if Saunders had not been present when his daughter ate the apple, he would not have deliberately changed the plan and the doctrine of transferred malice could apply and Archer would have been liable. The first case to arise on similar facts in more recent times is *Leahy*.[129] In this case, where a deliberate wounding of a different victim took place, D2 was held not to have aided and abetted the principal's offence.

129 *R. v Leahy* [1985] Crim. L.R. 99 CC.

In the decision of *Gnango*, where, very unusually, the mens rea of D1 *towards* D2 (with whom he was engaged in a shoot-out) was transferred to the killing of an innocent passer-by, leaving the D2 liable for murder as an accessory, Lords Phillips and Judge stated that:

> "The doctrine applies to secondary parties as it does to principal offenders. Thus if D2 attempts to aid, abet, counsel or procure D1 to murder V1 but D1, intending to kill V1, accidentally kills V2 instead, D2 will be guilty of the murder of V2."[130]

The Draft Criminal Code Bill 1989 proposed that the accessory be liable where the intended offence takes place on an unintended victim or property, but not liable, as in *Leahy*, for "an offence intentionally committed by the principal in respect of some other person or thing".[131] The Law Commission's more recent recommendations take a similar approach when looking at the "scope of the venture" test for joint criminal ventures.[132] The following example is provided to illustrate how a secondary party would escape liability for murder, although they would be liable for the inchoate offence of assisting or encouraging crime:

> "[D2] agrees with [D1], a professional assassin, to provide [D1] with a gun to murder [D2]'s wife. [D1] is then paid a large sum of money by X to murder X's wife, V. [D1] murders V with [D2]'s gun. [D1] does not shoot [D2]'s wife."[133]

However, the transferred malice doctrine would apply to enable the conviction of the secondary party in this second example: **11–062**

> "[D2] encourages [D1] to hit X and gives [D1] a stick with which to do it. [D1] takes a swing at X but X ducks and the blow strikes and injures V."[134]

IV. Evaluation

We have seen that underpinning the present law are two assumptions. The first is that complicity is a form of derivative liability—there is only one offence, that of D1—and the second is that accessories are **11–063**

130 *Gnango* [2011] UKSC 59 at [16].

131 Law Commission No.177 (1989), cl.27(5).

132 The Law Commission is of the opinion that the issue would not arise in cases of complicity other than those involving a joint criminal venture: Law Commission Report No.305, *Participating in Crime* (2007), para.3.165.

133 Law Commission Report No.305, *Participating in Crime* (2007), para.3.163.

134 Law Commission Report No.305, *Participating in Crime* (2007), para.3.164.

as blameworthy as principal offenders. They are liable to the same extent and deserve comparable punishment.

Despite commitment to the first assumption, it is necessary to question the second assumption that accessories are as blameworthy as principal offenders and deserve comparable punishment. At a superficial level, of course, the rationale for this is obvious: D2's role may have greatly facilitated the commission of the crime; they "may sometimes be more guilty than the perpetrator. Lady Macbeth was worse than Macbeth".[135]

It should now be apparent (particularly from the chapter on inchoate offences) that a basic theme of this book is that criminal liability ought generally to be imposed only when a blameworthy actor has caused a specified harm. This is only a general proposition, not a necessary rule. Thus, as we have seen, one *might* be justified in imposing criminal liability in the absence of blameworthiness (as in crimes of strict liability) or in the absence of obvious harm, or "first order harm" (as with inchoate offences). However, where one of these elements is missing and liability is nevertheless justified, the equation ought only to be balanced by imposing *less* criminal liability. This model provides the key for the structuring of all criminal offences and ascertaining appropriate levels of punishment. Thus, there can be degrees of blameworthiness (for instance, intentionally causing harm being regarded as worse than recklessly causing harm), and, of course, there are degrees of harm (for instance, killing V is worse than injuring them). The correlation of the degree of blameworthiness with the degree of harm ought to provide a fairly precise level of criminal liability with appropriate level(s) of punishment.

11-064 How does accessorial liability fit into such a model of criminal liability and punishment? The answer is clear. If D2 is less blameworthy or causes less harm than D1, then they deserve less criminal liability. If they are *both* less blameworthy *and* cause less harm, then they deserve *even less* criminal liability and punishment. So the central questions become:

(1) are accessories less blameworthy; and/or
(2) do they cause less harm than the principal offender?

A. BLAMEWORTHINESS

11-065 The liability of the accessory is derivative; it stems from the offence committed by the principal:

> "Since the source of culpability as an accessory is not the offence definition, there is no logical imperative that the mental element for an accessory should be the same as that required for a principal."[136]

---

135 G. Williams, *Textbook of Criminal Law*, 1st edn (London: Stevens & Sons, 1978), p.287; see also J.C. Smith, "A Note on Duress" [1974] Crim. L.R. 349, 351, cited with approval by Lord Edmund-Davies in *Lynch v DPP* [1975] A.C. 653 at 709. Lord Simon in *Lynch* and Lords Wilberforce and Edmund-Davies in *Abbott v The Queen* [1977] A.C. 755; [1976] 3 W.L.R. 462 PC, all opined that no distinction could be based on the degree of participation in a crime.

136 I. Dennis, "The Mental Element for Accessories" in P. Smith (ed), *Essays in Honour of J.C. Smith* (London: Butterworths, 1987), p.40.

As we have seen, the courts appear now to have accepted this proposition, up to a point. *Jogee* can be seen as improving the position regarding the mens rea requirement to be liable as a secondary party to murder, and also allows D2 to be liable for manslaughter where D2 intended to assist and encourage D1 to harm V, but did not intend that D1 do so with the necessary intent for murder. We see this in *Crilly*,[137] *the first case following Jogee in which the Court of Appeal granted leave to appeal to a secondary party who had been convicted before the judgment in Jogee was passed down.* In that case, D2 participated in what he thought would be a burglary, without any foresight or intention that violence would be used. However, the burglary had "gone wrong" and became a robbery when the occupant had failed to hear knocks on the door and the parties to the burglary had entered and found themselves face to face with the 71-year-old victim. V was killed as the result of what might only have been "a push and a punch", involving no weapons or severe violence. D2's conviction for murder was quashed on the basis that, following *Jogee*, mere foresight that D1 might cause GBH is insufficient to prove murder.

Although this avoids accomplices being liable for murder through mere foresight, as was previously the case, it does not go far in mitigating the harshness of being convicted of a constructive homicide offence where D2 has no control over the behaviour of D1. As we have seen, the doctrine of overwhelming supervening act does little, if anything, to address this problem.

If it were accepted that the concept of mens rea presupposes a capacity to control one's actions and to choose between alternative courses of conduct, then the implications become clear. D2 lacks control over D1; D2 cannot make choices for D1. (If they could we should classify them as a principal acting through an innocent agent, or as a co-principal.) The principal is:

> ". . . always the dominant party in the transaction. In criminal schemes, the principal is the actor-on-stage, who makes the final determination whether to commit the discrete criminal act."[138]

D1 can have the mens rea of the actual offence because of their hegemony and control. D2, at most, has choice and control over *their own actions, namely, their acts of assistance or encouragement*. Once it is realised that this mens rea of D2 is not the mens rea of the offence itself, that it is, in a sense, a step removed from the offence, we can then focus on the real question: is this mens rea of assisting as reprehensible as the mens rea of D1 who actually commits the offence? The answer to this question must be delayed until we have considered the next problem.

B. CAUSING HARM

Except in cases of procuring, an accessory, by definition, does not cause the ultimate harm. They **11–066**
contribute to the crime by their assistance or encouragement, but they do not actually cause the ultimate harm if it is inflicted by a responsible principal. So, in *Lynch v DPP*,[139] for example, Lynch drove

137 *R. v Crilly (John Anthony)* [2018] EWCA Crim 168; [2018] 4 W.L.R. 114 CA.
138 Fletcher, *Rethinking Criminal Law* (1978), p.656.
139 *Lynch* [1975] A.C. 653.

some IRA gunmen to a place where they killed a policeman. By his driving, Lynch assisted in the commission of the crime, but his actions clearly did not "cause" the death of the policeman. Indeed, the rules of accessorial liability only exist because such an accessory does not cause the prohibited harm; if they did, they would be a principal offender (or co-principal) and such rules would be unnecessary.[140] A different rule is needed for accessories, given that they cannot be liable as principals due to the free, deliberate and informed actions of D1 breaking the chain of causation between D2's assistance or encouragement, and the end result. The exception here is cases of innocent agency, where a characteristic of D1 (age, the fact that they are acting under duress, or without relevant knowledge) means that their act is not "free, deliberate and informed" and so does not break the causal chain, allowing D2 (the instigator) to be seen as the principal offender.

In cases where D2 has assisted or encouraged D1 as part of a joint unlawful enterprise, we have seen that D2 will be liable for the end result so long as they have the necessary mens rea of intending to assist or encourage D1 to act with the mens rea of the relevant offence. Whilst Jogee can be seen as improving the law in relation to the mens rea of secondary parties, the way that the law applies to accomplices in homicide cases remains harsh, given that D2 will be liable whether or not they exerted any influence over the end result of death. Dyson has argued that the law ought to be developed to require that D2's assistance or encouragement must make a "significant contribution" to D1's crime, falling short of a "but-for" cause.[141] This idea has recently been presented to Parliament through a Private Members Bill. In January 2024, Kim Johnson, a Labour MP from Liverpool, put before Parliament the Joint Enterprise (Significant Contribution) Bill. This Bill would insert into the Accessories and Abettors Act 1861 s.8 a requirement that D2 only be liable for an offence where their assistance or encouragement made "a significant contribution to its commission".

Under current law, even though D2s do not cause the ultimate harm, it is clear that they do cause a "harm", namely, the harm of assisting or encouraging D1. The harm involved in assisting or encouraging other criminals, like the "harm" in endangerment offences, is quite different from the ultimate harm actually inflicted and does not necessarily deserve the same level of criminal liability and punishment.

C. LESSER LIABILITY AND PUNISHMENT

11-067 A secondary party causes a different harm from the principal (the harm of assisting or encouraging a criminal act); D2 has a different mens rea from D1 (the mens rea of assisting or encouraging). If this is a lesser (as well as different) degree of blameworthiness and harm, this should result in a lesser level of criminal liability and punishment.

D2 who provides assistance or encouragement is clearly blameworthy, but not as blameworthy as D1 who actually pulls the trigger, stabs with the knife or takes the property. It is D1 who is the dominant party who has to make the final decision to commit the crime. It is D1 who is in control and has the

140 But see Smith, *A Modern Treatise on the Law of Complicity* (1991), pp.54–93 where he explores causation's role in complicity and concludes that "narrowing complicity's coverage to cases of provable causal contribution would offer a basis of liability which was more intuitively appealing and morally consistent (with that of a principal)" (p.90).

141 M. Dyson, "The Contribution of Complicity" (2022) 86(6) Journal of Criminal Law 389–419.

power to choose whether to commit the crime or not. In moral terms, this makes their actions "worse" than those of D2. D1 is "tainted",[142] contaminated by being the direct instrument of the crime; they are the one with the "blood on their hands". D2 is likewise tainted or contaminated—but for what they have done, namely their lesser role of assistance or encouragement. German law, for example, recognises the different levels of culpability between principal and accessory by providing that, in cases where D2 is to be sentenced to a fixed term, they be sentenced to no more than three-quarters of the statutory maximum.[143]

However, it does not follow that all secondary parties should be treated the same. One might wish to distinguish between different classes of accessories in terms of their liability and punishment. The actions of the instigator or mastermind behind the crime are generally more reprehensible than those of an accessory simply assisting the principal at the scene of the crime; the causal contribution of such an instigator towards the ultimate crime is certainly greater; they may thus deserve greater punishment.

D. CONCLUSION

In recent history, the joint enterprise doctrine has made the law on accomplice liability excessively complicated. Despite the honourable intentions of the Supreme Court, and the hopes raised for campaign groups such as JENGbA[144] that *Jogee* would prevent prosecutions based on "guilt by association", Dyson identified early on that "in practice not a vast amount will change" following the judgment in *Jogee,* and that: **11-068**

> "... the majority of prosecutions ... will still be put before the courts on the basis that all the parties were 'in it together', an allegation which if proven, would show that every party intended each crime within the common purpose to take place."[145]

As well as *Jogee* being lamented by some as a failed opportunity to bring true clarity to the law on joint enterprise, it has also been criticised at a more fundamental level for misapplying pre-existing law. Simester is of the opinion that the court in *Chan Wing-Siu* did not make a "wrong turn"[146] and maintains the position he held prior to *Jogee* that joint criminal enterprises are a "distinct moral phenomenon".[147] Similarly, after conducting his own in-depth historical review of case law since the 16th century, Stark argues that *Chan Wing-Siu* was not an anomaly but simply confirmed that a "wider principle" of parasitic accessorial liability existed beyond standard aiding and abetting.[148] Consequently, "*Jogee* was thus not mere common law housekeeping. It was substantive and significant law reform".[149] Whether

---

142 Fletcher, *Rethinking Criminal Law* (1978), pp.345–347.

143 StGB art.49, *https://www.gesetze-im-internet.de/englisch_stgb/englisch_stgb.html*. See Fletcher, *Rethinking Criminal Law* (1978), p.650.

144 Joint Enterprise Not Guilty by Association, *https://jengba.co.uk/*.

145 M. Dyson, "*Letter to the Editor*" [2016] Crim. L.R. 638–643, 642.

146 A. Simester, "Accessory liability and common unlawful purposes" (2017) 133 L.Q.R. 73–90, 81.

147 Simester, "Accessory liability and common unlawful purposes" (2017) 133 L.Q.R. 73–90, 90.

148 F. Stark, "The Demise of "Parasitic Accessorial Liability": Substantive Judicial Law Reform, Not Common Law Housekeeping" (2016) 75(3) *Cambridge Law Journal* 550–579, 577.

149 Stark, "The Demise of "Parasitic Accessorial Liability": Substantive Judicial Law Reform, Not Common Law Housekeeping" (2016) 75(3) *Cambridge Law Journal* 550–579, 551.

one agrees with Simester and Stark or not, all the signs are there that far from putting this controversial issue to bed, the Supreme Court has perpetuated confusion and complexity in this area of the law. Criminologists who have conducted empirical research into the experience of accomplices convicted under the joint enterprise doctrine question the "legal legitimacy" of a law that leads to a disproportionate number of minority ethnic men being convicted of murder:

Susie Hulley, Ben Crewe and Serena Wright, "Making sense of 'joint enterprise' for murder: legal legitimacy or instrumental acquiescence?" (2019) 59 Brit. J. Criminol. 1328–1346, 1343:

11-069 "Despite the recent reinterpretation of the doctrine, there is little evidence of a drastic change in the application of joint enterprise or of joint enterprise prisoners being released on appeal. Consequently, what is estimated to be hundreds of individuals continue to serve extraordinarily long sentences for murders that they may have neither intended to occur nor, in some cases, witnessed. In this context, we believe that there is a moral and practical imperative on those in power to change the law, not merely by 'tweaking' the joint enterprise doctrine—as seems to be the reality of the post-*Jogee* legal landscape—but by fundamentally reviewing the law of murder and the formulation of the offence of being a secondary party, to offer a label and a resulting sentence that better represent the actions and intentions of each individual."

11-070 The fact that the law has a disproportionate impact on minority ethnic defendants has recently been confirmed by the Crown Prosecution Service, which in September 2023 reported on a pilot project that monitored data on secondary offenders in homicide prosecutions. This data shows that 30% of defendants prosecuted as accomplices are recorded as "black" ethnicity, despite only 4% of the general population being of black ethnicity.[150] Delving into the reasons why this might be the case goes beyond the scope of this textbook on Criminal Law, but it is clear that the statistics tell a story that should not be ignored in reflecting on whether the law ought to be reformed.[151]

150 Crown Prosecution Service, *Joint Enterprise Pilot 2023: Data Analysis, https://www.cps.gov.uk/publication/crown-prosecution-service-joint-enterprise-pilot-2023-data-analysis*.

151 Hulley and Young argue that it is not just the substantive law that requires reform to solve the problems here. They advocate for a change in the law on the right to silence (under the Criminal Justice and Public Order Act 1994, s.34) in order to avoid over-charging of young people on the periphery of violence. They found that the current law on joint enterprise means that talking to the police about being present at the scene of a violent incident or being associated with a key suspect poses particular legal risks of being charged with the principal offence, and that the "legal risks of talking" persuade young suspects drawn in into the joint enterprise "net" to remain silent, becoming "ensnared in a legal trap" as their silence is used to infer guilt: S. Hulley and T. Young, "Silence, joint enterprise and the legal trap" (2022) 22(5) Criminology and Criminal Justice 714–732.

INDEX

LEGAL TAXONOMY

FROM SWEET & MAXWELL

This index has been prepared using Sweet and Maxwell's Legal Taxonomy. Main index entries conform to keywords provided by the Legal Taxonomy except where references to specific documents or non-standard terms (denoted by quotation marks) have been included. These keywords provide a means of identifying similar concepts in other Sweet & Maxwell publications and online services to which keywords from the Legal Taxonomy have been applied. Readers may find some minor differences between terms used in the text and those which appear in the index.
Suggestions to *sweetandmaxwell.taxonomy@tr.com*.

(All references are to paragraph number)

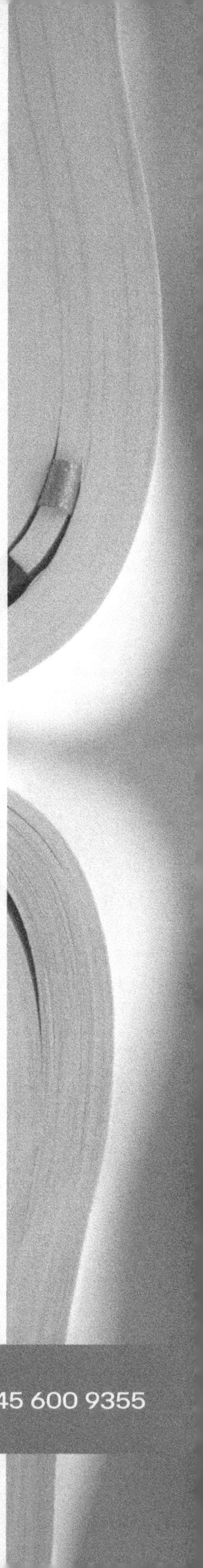